Patient Protection and Affordable Care Act Health Care and Education Reconciliation Act of 2010

Text of P.L. 111-148, as signed by the President on March 23, 2010

Text of P.L. 111-152, as signed by the President on March 30, 2010

JCT Technical Explanation of P.L. 111-148 and P.L. 111-152

CCH
a Wolters Kluwer business

ISBN 978-0-8080-2415-6

4025 W. Peterson Ave.
Chicago, IL 60646-6085
1 800 248 3248
www.CCHGroup.com

Printed in the United States of America

About This Publication

This CCH publication reproduces the text of the Patient Protection and Affordable Care Act (the Patient Protection Act) (P.L. 111-148), and the Health Care and Education Reconciliation Act of 2010 (2010 Reconciliation Act) (P.L. 111-152). It also includes the Joint Committee on Taxation (JCT) Technical Explanation of the Revenue Provisions of the "Reconciliation Act of 2010," as amended, in combination with the "Patient Protection and Affordable Care Act" (JCX-18-10), which explains the intent of Congress regarding the provisions of these two Acts, but cannot be cited as the official House, Senate or Conference Committee Report.

The Patient Protection Act, as amended by the 2010 Reconciliation Act, is designed to effectuate fundamental reforms to the United States health care system. Almost all individuals not covered by Medicaid or Medicare would be required to obtain health care coverage or pay penalties. Employer-provided coverage would generally satisfy the universal coverage requirement. Lower-income individuals, as well as some middle-class families, would receive a credit or voucher to help pay for health insurance, which can be used at one of the American Health Benefits Exchanges that are required to be established by every state. Employers electing not to offer qualifying coverage would be subject to an additional tax to help finance the health care coverage for their employees. Exceptions would be made for small businesses.

The new law includes over $400 billion in revenue raisers and new taxes on employers and individuals, including a 40-percent surtax on high-end employer-sponsored health plans, an increase in the employee portion of the Medicare tax to 2.35 percent for couples with adjusted gross incomes (AGI) over $250,000 a year and individuals with AGI over $200,000, new fees on certain health-related industries, an increase in the threshold for the deduction of eligible unreimbursed medical expenses from 7.5% to 10% of AGI starting in 2013, and more.

Pursuant to the Patient Protection Act, the IRS is responsible for overseeing a significant part of health care reform, such as the administration of additional taxes on individuals and employers, determinations of various exemptions from those taxes, and oversight of new information reporting requirements. Many of the new requirements have phased-in and delayed effective dates, giving the IRS and taxpayers a window of time to prepare.

The road to enact this comprehensive health care reform legislation required an unprecedented series of compromises by Congress and intervention by President Obama. On November 7, 2009, the House passed the Affordable Health Care for America Act of 2009 (H.R. 3962). The 2,000+ page bill proposed an overhaul of the health insurance industry, included a public option, and broadly expanded the number of Americans who would be covered under some kind of insurance. The proposal also included a new surtax on higher-income individuals at a cost of more than $400 billion over 10 years to help pay for nearly universal coverage.

Health care reform took another major step forward on November 18, 2009, when Senate Democratic leaders unveiled the Patient Protection and Affordable Care Act (H.R. 3590). The bill blended proposals passed earlier by the Senate Finance Committee (SFC) and the Senate Health, Education, Labor, and Pensions (HELP) Committee. The $849 billion package, with $370 billion in revenue raisers, was drafted not only with an eye toward garnering the 60 votes necessary for full Senate approval but also in preparation for conference committee negotiations. Although the Senate bill was similar in scope to the House-passed Affordable Health Care for America Act (H.R. 3962), there were significant differences between the two bills. Most notably, the Senate bill lacked a public option. The Senate passed the Patient Protection and Affordable Care Act (H.R. 3590), on

December 24, 2009, by a vote of 60 to 39. The Senate vote paved the way for a conference between the House and Senate in early 2010.

The hopes of President Obama and Democratic leaders for a quick conference to reconcile the differences between the House and Senate passed health care reform bills were dashed on January 19, 2010, when Republican Scott Brown won the special election in Massachusetts for the Senate seat formerly held by the late Ted Kennedy. As a result, Senate democrats lost the 60-seat super majority required to defeat a filibuster in the Senate. With near unanimous Republican opposition in the Senate to a public option and the House-passed bill, and significant opposition from House Representatives who argued that the Senate-passed bill did not go far enough, a compromise seemed unlikely.

Faced with the realization that a compromise was improbable, House leaders agreed to bring the Senate passed Patient Protection Act to the floor. In effort to address those objectionable portions of the legislation, House leaders unveiled the 2010 Reconciliation Act. The 2010 Reconciliation Act served as a "sidecar" bill, allowing the House to move changes to the Patient Protection Act using the budget reconciliation rules. The budget reconciliation process allows the Senate to pass the package with only 51 votes, rather than a 60-vote super-majority.

The House passed the Patient Protection Act, along with the 2010 Reconciliation Act, on March 21, 2010. President Obama signed the Patient Protection Act into law on March 23, 2010. The Senate subsequently began debate on the 2010 Reconciliation Act on March 23, 2010. After defeating numerous amendments and points of order, the Senate passed the 2010 Reconciliation Act on March 25, 2010. However, prior to passage, the Senate parliamentarian sustained objections to two sections of the bill related to student loans. As a result, the House was required to take a second vote. The House passed the amended, Senate-passed version on March 25, 2010. On March 30, 2010, President Obama signed the 2010 Reconciliation Act into law.

March 2010

H. R. 3590

One Hundred Eleventh Congress of the United States of America

AT THE SECOND SESSION

Begun and held at the City of Washington on Tuesday, the fifth day of January, two thousand and ten

An Act

Entitled The Patient Protection and Affordable Care Act.

Be it enacted by the Senate and House of Representatives of the United States of America in Congress assembled,

SECTION 1. SHORT TITLE; TABLE OF CONTENTS.

(a) SHORT TITLE.—This Act may be cited as the "Patient Protection and Affordable Care Act".

(b) TABLE OF CONTENTS.—The table of contents of this Act is as follows:

TITLE I—QUALITY, AFFORDABLE HEALTH CARE FOR ALL AMERICANS

Subtitle A—Immediate Improvements in Health Care Coverage for All Americans

SEC. 1001. AMENDMENTS TO THE PUBLIC HEALTH SERVICE ACT.

Part A of title XXVII of the Public Health Service Act (42 U.S.C. 300gg et seq.) is amended—

(1) by striking the part heading and inserting the following:

"PART A—INDIVIDUAL AND GROUP MARKET REFORMS";

(2) by redesignating sections 2704 through 2707 as sections 2725 through 2728, respectively;

(3) by redesignating sections 2711 through 2713 as sections 2731 through 2733, respectively;

(4) by redesignating sections 2721 through 2723 as sections 2735 through 2737, respectively; and

(5) by inserting after section 2702, the following:

"Subpart II—Improving Coverage

"SEC. 2711. NO LIFETIME OR ANNUAL LIMITS.

"(a) IN GENERAL.—A group health plan and a health insurance issuer offering group or individual health insurance coverage may not establish—

"(1) lifetime limits on the dollar value of benefits for any participant or beneficiary; or

"(2) unreasonable annual limits (within the meaning of section 223 of the Internal Revenue Code of 1986) on the dollar value of benefits for any participant or beneficiary.

"(b) PER BENEFICIARY LIMITS.—Subsection (a) shall not be construed to prevent a group health plan or health insurance coverage that is not required to provide essential health benefits under section 1302(b) of the Patient Protection and Affordable Care Act from placing annual or lifetime per beneficiary limits on specific covered benefits to the extent that such limits are otherwise permitted under Federal or State law.

"SEC. 2712. PROHIBITION ON RESCISSIONS.

"A group health plan and a health insurance issuer offering group or individual health insurance coverage shall not rescind such plan or coverage with respect to an enrollee once the enrollee is covered under such plan or coverage involved, except that this section shall not apply to a covered individual who has performed an act or practice that constitutes fraud or makes an intentional misrepresentation of material fact as prohibited by the terms of the plan or coverage. Such plan or coverage may not be cancelled except with prior notice to the enrollee, and only as permitted under section 2702(c) or 2742(b).

"SEC. 2713. COVERAGE OF PREVENTIVE HEALTH SERVICES.

"(a) IN GENERAL.—A group health plan and a health insurance issuer offering group or individual health insurance coverage shall, at a minimum provide coverage for and shall not impose any cost sharing requirements for—

"(1) evidence-based items or services that have in effect a rating of 'A' or 'B' in the current recommendations of the United States Preventive Services Task Force;

"(2) immunizations that have in effect a recommendation from the Advisory Committee on Immunization Practices of the Centers for Disease Control and Prevention with respect to the individual involved; and

"(3) with respect to infants, children, and adolescents, evidence-informed preventive care and screenings provided for in the comprehensive guidelines supported by the Health Resources and Services Administration.

"(4) with respect to women, such additional preventive care and screenings not described in paragraph (1) as provided for in comprehensive guidelines supported by the Health Resources and Services Administration for purposes of this paragraph.

"(5) for the purposes of this Act, and for the purposes of any other provision of law, the current recommendations of the United States Preventive Service Task Force regarding breast cancer screening, mammography, and prevention shall be considered the most current other than those issued in or around November 2009.

Nothing in this subsection shall be construed to prohibit a plan or issuer from providing coverage for services in addition to those recommended by United States Preventive Services Task Force or to deny coverage for services that are not recommended by such Task Force.

"(b) INTERVAL.—

"(1) IN GENERAL.—The Secretary shall establish a minimum interval between the date on which a recommendation described in subsection (a)(1) or (a)(2) or a guideline under subsection (a)(3) is issued and the plan year with respect to which the requirement described in subsection (a) is effective with respect to the service described in such recommendation or guideline.

"(2) MINIMUM.—The interval described in paragraph (1) shall not be less than 1 year.

"(c) VALUE-BASED INSURANCE DESIGN.—The Secretary may develop guidelines to permit a group health plan and a health insurance issuer offering group or individual health insurance coverage to utilize value-based insurance designs.

"SEC. 2714. EXTENSION OF DEPENDENT COVERAGE.

"(a) IN GENERAL.—A group health plan and a health insurance issuer offering group or individual health insurance coverage that provides dependent coverage of children shall continue to make such coverage available for an adult child (who is not married) until the child turns 26 years of age. Nothing in this section shall require a health plan or a health insurance issuer described in the preceding sentence to make coverage available for a child of a child receiving dependent coverage.

"(b) REGULATIONS.—The Secretary shall promulgate regulations to define the dependents to which coverage shall be made available under subsection (a).

"(c) RULE OF CONSTRUCTION.—Nothing in this section shall be construed to modify the definition of 'dependent' as used in the Internal Revenue Code of 1986 with respect to the tax treatment of the cost of coverage.

"SEC. 2715. DEVELOPMENT AND UTILIZATION OF UNIFORM EXPLANATION OF COVERAGE DOCUMENTS AND STANDARDIZED DEFINITIONS.

"(a) IN GENERAL.—Not later than 12 months after the date of enactment of the Patient Protection and Affordable Care Act, the Secretary shall develop standards for use by a group health plan and a health insurance issuer offering group or individual health insurance coverage, in compiling and providing to enrollees a summary of benefits and coverage explanation that accurately describes the benefits and coverage under the applicable plan or coverage. In developing such standards, the Secretary shall consult with the National Association of Insurance Commissioners (referred to in this section as the 'NAIC'), a working group composed of representatives of health insurance-related consumer advocacy organizations, health insurance issuers, health care professionals, patient advocates including those representing individuals with limited English proficiency, and other qualified individuals.

"(b) REQUIREMENTS.—The standards for the summary of benefits and coverage developed under subsection (a) shall provide for the following:

"(1) APPEARANCE.—The standards shall ensure that the summary of benefits and coverage is presented in a uniform format that does not exceed 4 pages in length and does not include print smaller than 12-point font.

"(2) LANGUAGE.—The standards shall ensure that the summary is presented in a culturally and linguistically appropriate manner and utilizes terminology understandable by the average plan enrollee.

"(3) CONTENTS.—The standards shall ensure that the summary of benefits and coverage includes—

"(A) uniform definitions of standard insurance terms and medical terms (consistent with subsection (g)) so that consumers may compare health insurance coverage and understand the terms of coverage (or exception to such coverage);

"(B) a description of the coverage, including cost sharing for—

"(i) each of the categories of the essential health benefits described in subparagraphs (A) through (J) of section 1302(b)(1) of the Patient Protection and Affordable Care Act; and

"(ii) other benefits, as identified by the Secretary;

"(C) the exceptions, reductions, and limitations on coverage;

"(D) the cost-sharing provisions, including deductible, coinsurance, and co-payment obligations;

"(E) the renewability and continuation of coverage provisions;

"(F) a coverage facts label that includes examples to illustrate common benefits scenarios, including pregnancy and serious or chronic medical conditions and related cost sharing, such scenarios to be based on recognized clinical practice guidelines;

"(G) a statement of whether the plan or coverage—

"(i) provides minimum essential coverage (as defined under section 5000A(f) of the Internal Revenue Code 1986); and

"(ii) ensures that the plan or coverage share of the total allowed costs of benefits provided under the plan or coverage is not less than 60 percent of such costs;

"(H) a statement that the outline is a summary of the policy or certificate and that the coverage document itself should be consulted to determine the governing contractual provisions; and

"(I) a contact number for the consumer to call with additional questions and an Internet web address where a copy of the actual individual coverage policy or group certificate of coverage can be reviewed and obtained.

"(c) PERIODIC REVIEW AND UPDATING.—The Secretary shall periodically review and update, as appropriate, the standards developed under this section.

"(d) REQUIREMENT TO PROVIDE.—

"(1) IN GENERAL.—Not later than 24 months after the date of enactment of the Patient Protection and Affordable Care Act, each entity described in paragraph (3) shall provide, prior to any enrollment restriction, a summary of benefits and coverage explanation pursuant to the standards developed by the Secretary under subsection (a) to—

"(A) an applicant at the time of application;

"(B) an enrollee prior to the time of enrollment or reenrollment, as applicable; and

"(C) a policyholder or certificate holder at the time of issuance of the policy or delivery of the certificate.

"(2) COMPLIANCE.—An entity described in paragraph (3) is deemed to be in compliance with this section if the summary of benefits and coverage described in subsection (a) is provided in paper or electronic form.

"(3) ENTITIES IN GENERAL.—An entity described in this paragraph is—

"(A) a health insurance issuer (including a group health plan that is not a self-insured plan) offering health insurance coverage within the United States; or

"(B) in the case of a self-insured group health plan, the plan sponsor or designated administrator of the plan (as such terms are defined in section 3(16) of the Employee Retirement Income Security Act of 1974).

"(4) NOTICE OF MODIFICATIONS.—If a group health plan or health insurance issuer makes any material modification in any of the terms of the plan or coverage involved (as defined for purposes of section 102 of the Employee Retirement Income Security Act of 1974) that is not reflected in the most recently provided summary of benefits and coverage, the plan or issuer shall provide notice of such modification to enrollees not later than 60 days prior to the date on which such modification will become effective.

"(e) PREEMPTION.—The standards developed under subsection (a) shall preempt any related State standards that require a summary of benefits and coverage that provides less information to consumers than that required to be provided under this section, as determined by the Secretary.

"(f) FAILURE TO PROVIDE.—An entity described in subsection (d)(3) that willfully fails to provide the information required under this section shall be subject to a fine of not more than $1,000 for each such failure. Such failure with respect to each enrollee shall constitute a separate offense for purposes of this subsection.

"(g) DEVELOPMENT OF STANDARD DEFINITIONS.—

"(1) IN GENERAL.—The Secretary shall, by regulation, provide for the development of standards for the definitions of terms used in health insurance coverage, including the insurance-related terms described in paragraph (2) and the medical terms described in paragraph (3).

"(2) INSURANCE-RELATED TERMS.—The insurance-related terms described in this paragraph are premium, deductible, co-insurance, co-payment, out-of-pocket limit, preferred provider, non-preferred provider, out-of-network co-payments, UCR (usual, customary and reasonable) fees, excluded services, grievance and appeals, and such other terms as the Secretary determines are important to define so that consumers may compare health insurance coverage and understand the terms of their coverage.

"(3) MEDICAL TERMS.—The medical terms described in this paragraph are hospitalization, hospital outpatient care, emergency room care, physician services, prescription drug coverage, durable medical equipment, home health care, skilled nursing care, rehabilitation services, hospice services, emergency medical transportation, and such other terms as the Secretary determines are important to define so that consumers may compare the medical benefits offered by health insurance and understand the extent of those medical benefits (or exceptions to those benefits).

"SEC. 2716. PROHIBITION OF DISCRIMINATION BASED ON SALARY.

"(a) IN GENERAL.—The plan sponsor of a group health plan (other than a self-insured plan) may not establish rules relating to the health insurance coverage eligibility (including continued eligibility) of any full-time employee under the terms of the plan that are based on the total hourly or annual salary of the employee or otherwise establish eligibility rules that have the effect of discriminating in favor of higher wage employees.

"(b) LIMITATION.—Subsection (a) shall not be construed to prohibit a plan sponsor from establishing contribution requirements for enrollment in the plan or coverage that provide for the payment by employees with lower hourly or annual compensation of a lower dollar or percentage contribution than the payment required of similarly situated employees with a higher hourly or annual compensation.

"SEC. 2717. ENSURING THE QUALITY OF CARE.

"(a) QUALITY REPORTING.—

"(1) IN GENERAL.—Not later than 2 years after the date of enactment of the Patient Protection and Affordable Care Act, the Secretary, in consultation with experts in health care quality and stakeholders, shall develop reporting requirements for use by a group health plan, and a health insurance issuer offering group or individual health insurance coverage, with respect to plan or coverage benefits and health care provider reimbursement structures that—

"(A) improve health outcomes through the implementation of activities such as quality reporting, effective case management, care coordination, chronic disease management, and medication and care compliance initiatives, including through the use of the medical homes model as defined for purposes of section 3602 of the Patient Protection and Affordable Care Act, for treatment or services under the plan or coverage;

"(B) implement activities to prevent hospital readmissions through a comprehensive program for hospital discharge that includes patient-centered education and counseling, comprehensive discharge planning, and post discharge reinforcement by an appropriate health care professional;

"(C) implement activities to improve patient safety and reduce medical errors through the appropriate use of best clinical practices, evidence based medicine, and health information technology under the plan or coverage; and

"(D) implement wellness and health promotion activities.

"(2) REPORTING REQUIREMENTS.—

"(A) IN GENERAL.—A group health plan and a health insurance issuer offering group or individual health insurance coverage shall annually submit to the Secretary, and to enrollees under the plan or coverage, a report on whether the benefits under the plan or coverage satisfy the elements described in subparagraphs (A) through (D) of paragraph (1).

"(B) TIMING OF REPORTS.—A report under subparagraph (A) shall be made available to an enrollee under the plan or coverage during each open enrollment period.

"(C) AVAILABILITY OF REPORTS.—The Secretary shall make reports submitted under subparagraph (A) available to the public through an Internet website.

"(D) PENALTIES.—In developing the reporting requirements under paragraph (1), the Secretary may develop and impose appropriate penalties for non-compliance with such requirements.

"(E) EXCEPTIONS.—In developing the reporting requirements under paragraph (1), the Secretary may provide for exceptions to such requirements for group health plans and health insurance issuers that substantially meet the goals of this section.

"(b) WELLNESS AND PREVENTION PROGRAMS.—For purposes of subsection (a)(1)(D), wellness and health promotion activities may include personalized wellness and prevention services, which are coordinated, maintained or delivered by a health care provider, a wellness and prevention plan manager, or a health, wellness or prevention services organization that conducts health risk assessments or offers ongoing face-to-face, telephonic or web-based intervention efforts for each of the program's participants, and which may include the following wellness and prevention efforts:

"(1) Smoking cessation.

"(2) Weight management.

"(3) Stress management.

"(4) Physical fitness.

"(5) Nutrition.

"(6) Heart disease prevention.

"(7) Healthy lifestyle support.

"(8) Diabetes prevention.

"(c) REGULATIONS.—Not later than 2 years after the date of enactment of the Patient Protection and Affordable Care Act, the Secretary shall promulgate regulations that provide criteria for determining whether a reimbursement structure is described in subsection (a).

"(d) STUDY AND REPORT.—Not later than 180 days after the date on which regulations are promulgated under subsection (c), the Government Accountability Office shall review such regulations and conduct a study and submit to the Committee on Health, Education, Labor, and Pensions of the Senate and the Committee on Energy and Commerce of the House of Representatives a report regarding the impact the activities under this section have had on the quality and cost of health care.

"SEC. 2718. BRINGING DOWN THE COST OF HEALTH CARE COVERAGE.

"(a) CLEAR ACCOUNTING FOR COSTS.—A health insurance issuer offering group or individual health insurance coverage shall, with respect to each plan year, submit to the Secretary a report concerning the percentage of total premium revenue that such coverage expends—

"(1) on reimbursement for clinical services provided to enrollees under such coverage;

"(2) for activities that improve health care quality; and

"(3) on all other non-claims costs, including an explanation of the nature of such costs, and excluding State taxes and licensing or regulatory fees.

The Secretary shall make reports received under this section available to the public on the Internet website of the Department of Health and Human Services.

"(b) ENSURING THAT CONSUMERS RECEIVE VALUE FOR THEIR PREMIUM PAYMENTS.—

"(1) REQUIREMENT TO PROVIDE VALUE FOR PREMIUM PAYMENTS.—A health insurance issuer offering group or individual health insurance coverage shall, with respect to each plan year, provide an annual rebate to each enrollee under such coverage, on a pro rata basis, in an amount that is equal to the amount by which premium revenue expended by the issuer on activities described in subsection (a)(3) exceeds—

"(A) with respect to a health insurance issuer offering coverage in the group market, 20 percent, or such lower percentage as a State may by regulation determine; or

"(B) with respect to a health insurance issuer offering coverage in the individual market, 25 percent, or such lower percentage as a State may by regulation determine, except that such percentage shall be adjusted to the extent the Secretary determines that the application of such percentage with a State may destabilize the existing individual market in such State.

"(2) CONSIDERATION IN SETTING PERCENTAGES.—In determining the percentages under paragraph (1), a State shall seek to ensure adequate participation by health insurance issuers, competition in the health insurance market in the State, and value for consumers so that premiums are used for clinical services and quality improvements.

"(3) TERMINATION.—The provisions of this subsection shall have no force or effect after December 31, 2013.

"(c) STANDARD HOSPITAL CHARGES.—Each hospital operating within the United States shall for each year establish (and update) and make public (in accordance with guidelines developed by the Secretary) a list of the hospital's standard charges for items and services provided by the hospital, including for diagnosis-related groups established under section 1886(d)(4) of the Social Security Act.

"(d) DEFINITIONS.—The Secretary, in consultation with the National Association of Insurance Commissions, shall establish uniform definitions for the activities reported under subsection (a).

"SEC. 2719. APPEALS PROCESS.

"A group health plan and a health insurance issuer offering group or individual health insurance coverage shall implement an effective appeals process for appeals of coverage determinations and claims, under which the plan or issuer shall, at a minimum—

"(1) have in effect an internal claims appeal process;

"(2) provide notice to enrollees, in a culturally and linguistically appropriate manner, of available internal and external appeals processes, and the availability of any applicable office of health insurance consumer assistance or ombudsman established under section 2793 to assist such enrollees with the appeals processes;

"(3) allow an enrollee to review their file, to present evidence and testimony as part of the appeals process, and to receive continued coverage pending the outcome of the appeals process; and

"(4) provide an external review process for such plans and issuers that, at a minimum, includes the consumer protections set forth in the Uniform External Review Model Act promulgated by the National Association of Insurance Commissioners and is binding on such plans.".

SEC. 1002. HEALTH INSURANCE CONSUMER INFORMATION.

Part C of title XXVII of the Public Health Service Act (42 U.S.C. 300gg–91 et seq.) is amended by adding at the end the following:

"SEC. 2793. HEALTH INSURANCE CONSUMER INFORMATION.

"(a) IN GENERAL.—The Secretary shall award grants to States to enable such States (or the Exchanges operating in such States) to establish, expand, or provide support for—

"(1) offices of health insurance consumer assistance; or

"(2) health insurance ombudsman programs.

"(b) ELIGIBILITY.—

"(1) IN GENERAL.—To be eligible to receive a grant, a State shall designate an independent office of health insurance consumer assistance, or an ombudsman, that, directly or in coordination with State health insurance regulators and consumer assistance organizations, receives and responds to inquiries and complaints concerning health insurance coverage with respect to Federal health insurance requirements and under State law.

"(2) CRITERIA.—A State that receives a grant under this section shall comply with criteria established by the Secretary for carrying out activities under such grant.

"(c) DUTIES.—The office of health insurance consumer assistance or health insurance ombudsman shall—

"(1) assist with the filing of complaints and appeals, including filing appeals with the internal appeal or grievance process of the group health plan or health insurance issuer involved and providing information about the external appeal process;

"(2) collect, track, and quantify problems and inquiries encountered by consumers;

"(3) educate consumers on their rights and responsibilities with respect to group health plans and health insurance coverage;

"(4) assist consumers with enrollment in a group health plan or health insurance coverage by providing information, referral, and assistance; and

"(5) resolve problems with obtaining premium tax credits under section 36B of the Internal Revenue Code of 1986.

"(d) DATA COLLECTION.—As a condition of receiving a grant under subsection (a), an office of health insurance consumer assistance or ombudsman program shall be required to collect and report data to the Secretary on the types of problems and inquiries encountered by consumers. The Secretary shall utilize such data to identify areas where more enforcement action is necessary and shall share such information with State insurance regulators, the Secretary of Labor, and the Secretary of the Treasury for use in the enforcement activities of such agencies.

"(e) FUNDING.—

"(1) INITIAL FUNDING.—There is hereby appropriated to the Secretary, out of any funds in the Treasury not otherwise appropriated, $30,000,000 for the first fiscal year for which this section applies to carry out this section. Such amount shall remain available without fiscal year limitation.

"(2) AUTHORIZATION FOR SUBSEQUENT YEARS.—There is authorized to be appropriated to the Secretary for each fiscal year following the fiscal year described in paragraph (1), such sums as may be necessary to carry out this section.".

SEC. 1003. ENSURING THAT CONSUMERS GET VALUE FOR THEIR DOLLARS.

Part C of title XXVII of the Public Health Service Act (42 U.S.C. 300gg–91 et seq.), as amended by section 1002, is further amended by adding at the end the following:

"SEC. 2794. ENSURING THAT CONSUMERS GET VALUE FOR THEIR DOLLARS.

"(a) INITIAL PREMIUM REVIEW PROCESS.—

"(1) IN GENERAL.—The Secretary, in conjunction with States, shall establish a process for the annual review, beginning with the 2010 plan year and subject to subsection (b)(2)(A), of unreasonable increases in premiums for health insurance coverage.

"(2) JUSTIFICATION AND DISCLOSURE.—The process established under paragraph (1) shall require health insurance issuers to submit to the Secretary and the relevant State a justification for an unreasonable premium increase prior to the implementation of the increase. Such issuers shall prominently post such information on their Internet websites. The Secretary shall ensure the public disclosure of information on such increases and justifications for all health insurance issuers.

"(b) CONTINUING PREMIUM REVIEW PROCESS.—

"(1) INFORMING SECRETARY OF PREMIUM INCREASE PATTERNS.—As a condition of receiving a grant under subsection (c)(1), a State, through its Commissioner of Insurance, shall—

"(A) provide the Secretary with information about trends in premium increases in health insurance coverage in premium rating areas in the State; and

"(B) make recommendations, as appropriate, to the State Exchange about whether particular health insurance issuers should be excluded from participation in the Exchange based on a pattern or practice of excessive or unjustified premium increases.

"(2) MONITORING BY SECRETARY OF PREMIUM INCREASES.—

"(A) IN GENERAL.—Beginning with plan years beginning in 2014, the Secretary, in conjunction with the States and consistent with the provisions of subsection (a)(2), shall monitor premium increases of health insurance coverage offered through an Exchange and outside of an Exchange.

"(B) CONSIDERATION IN OPENING EXCHANGE.—In determining under section 1312(f)(2)(B) of the Patient Protection and Affordable Care Act whether to offer qualified health plans in the large group market through an Exchange, the State shall take into account any excess of premium growth outside of the Exchange as compared to the rate of such growth inside the Exchange.

"(c) GRANTS IN SUPPORT OF PROCESS.—

"(1) PREMIUM REVIEW GRANTS DURING 2010 THROUGH 2014.—The Secretary shall carry out a program to award grants to States during the 5-year period beginning with fiscal year 2010 to assist such States in carrying out subsection (a), including—

"(A) in reviewing and, if appropriate under State law, approving premium increases for health insurance coverage; and

"(B) in providing information and recommendations to the Secretary under subsection (b)(1).

"(2) FUNDING.—

"(A) IN GENERAL.—Out of all funds in the Treasury not otherwise appropriated, there are appropriated to the Secretary $250,000,000, to be available for expenditure for grants under paragraph (1) and subparagraph (B).

"(B) FURTHER AVAILABILITY FOR INSURANCE REFORM AND CONSUMER PROTECTION.—If the amounts appropriated under subparagraph (A) are not fully obligated under grants under paragraph (1) by the end of fiscal year 2014, any remaining funds shall remain available to the Secretary for grants to States for planning and implementing the insurance reforms and consumer protections under part A.

"(C) ALLOCATION.—The Secretary shall establish a formula for determining the amount of any grant to a State under this subsection. Under such formula—

"(i) the Secretary shall consider the number of plans of health insurance coverage offered in each State and the population of the State; and

"(ii) no State qualifying for a grant under paragraph (1) shall receive less than $1,000,000, or more than $5,000,000 for a grant year.".

SEC. 1004. EFFECTIVE DATES.

(a) IN GENERAL.—Except as provided for in subsection (b), this subtitle (and the amendments made by this subtitle) shall become effective for plan years beginning on or after the date that is 6 months after the date of enactment of this Act, except that the amendments made by sections 1002 and 1003 shall become effective for fiscal years beginning with fiscal year 2010.

(b) SPECIAL RULE.—The amendments made by sections 1002 and 1003 shall take effect on the date of enactment of this Act.

Subtitle B—Immediate Actions to Preserve and Expand Coverage

SEC. 1101. IMMEDIATE ACCESS TO INSURANCE FOR UNINSURED INDIVIDUALS WITH A PREEXISTING CONDITION.

(a) IN GENERAL.—Not later than 90 days after the date of enactment of this Act, the Secretary shall establish a temporary high risk health insurance pool program to provide health insurance coverage for eligible individuals during the period beginning on the date on which such program is established and ending on January 1, 2014.

(b) ADMINISTRATION.—

(1) IN GENERAL.—The Secretary may carry out the program under this section directly or through contracts to eligible entities.

(2) ELIGIBLE ENTITIES.—To be eligible for a contract under paragraph (1), an entity shall—

(A) be a State or nonprofit private entity;

(B) submit to the Secretary an application at such time, in such manner, and containing such information as the Secretary may require; and

(C) agree to utilize contract funding to establish and administer a qualified high risk pool for eligible individuals.

(3) MAINTENANCE OF EFFORT.—To be eligible to enter into a contract with the Secretary under this subsection, a State shall agree not to reduce the annual amount the State expended for the operation of one or more State high risk pools during the year preceding the year in which such contract is entered into.

(c) QUALIFIED HIGH RISK POOL.—

(1) IN GENERAL.—Amounts made available under this section shall be used to establish a qualified high risk pool that meets the requirements of paragraph (2).

(2) REQUIREMENTS.—A qualified high risk pool meets the requirements of this paragraph if such pool—

(A) provides to all eligible individuals health insurance coverage that does not impose any preexisting condition exclusion with respect to such coverage;

(B) provides health insurance coverage—

(i) in which the issuer's share of the total allowed costs of benefits provided under such coverage is not less than 65 percent of such costs; and

(ii) that has an out of pocket limit not greater than the applicable amount described in section 223(c)(2) of the Internal Revenue Code of 1986 for the year involved, except that the Secretary may modify such limit if necessary to ensure the pool meets the actuarial value limit under clause (i);

(C) ensures that with respect to the premium rate charged for health insurance coverage offered to eligible individuals through the high risk pool, such rate shall—

(i) except as provided in clause (ii), vary only as provided for under section 2701 of the Public Health Service Act (as amended by this Act and notwithstanding the date on which such amendments take effect);

(ii) vary on the basis of age by a factor of not greater than 4 to 1; and

(iii) be established at a standard rate for a standard population; and

(D) meets any other requirements determined appropriate by the Secretary.

(d) ELIGIBLE INDIVIDUAL.—An individual shall be deemed to be an eligible individual for purposes of this section if such individual—

(1) is a citizen or national of the United States or is lawfully present in the United States (as determined in accordance with section 1411);

(2) has not been covered under creditable coverage (as defined in section 2701(c)(1) of the Public Health Service Act as in effect on the date of enactment of this Act) during the 6-month period prior to the date on which such individual is applying for coverage through the high risk pool; and

(3) has a pre-existing condition, as determined in a manner consistent with guidance issued by the Secretary.

(e) PROTECTION AGAINST DUMPING RISK BY INSURERS.—

(1) IN GENERAL.—The Secretary shall establish criteria for determining whether health insurance issuers and employment-based health plans have discouraged an individual from remaining enrolled in prior coverage based on that individual's health status.

(2) SANCTIONS.—An issuer or employment-based health plan shall be responsible for reimbursing the program under this section for the medical expenses incurred by the program for an individual who, based on criteria established by the Secretary, the Secretary finds was encouraged by the issuer to disenroll from health benefits coverage prior to enrolling in coverage through the program. The criteria shall include at least the following circumstances:

(A) In the case of prior coverage obtained through an employer, the provision by the employer, group health plan, or the issuer of money or other financial consideration for disenrolling from the coverage.

(B) In the case of prior coverage obtained directly from an issuer or under an employment-based health plan—

(i) the provision by the issuer or plan of money or other financial consideration for disenrolling from the coverage; or

(ii) in the case of an individual whose premium for the prior coverage exceeded the premium required by the program (adjusted based on the age factors applied to the prior coverage)—

(I) the prior coverage is a policy that is no longer being actively marketed (as defined by the Secretary) by the issuer; or

(II) the prior coverage is a policy for which duration of coverage form issue or health status are factors that can be considered in determining premiums at renewal.

(3) CONSTRUCTION.—Nothing in this subsection shall be construed as constituting exclusive remedies for violations of criteria established under paragraph (1) or as preventing States

from applying or enforcing such paragraph or other provisions under law with respect to health insurance issuers.

(f) OVERSIGHT.—The Secretary shall establish—

(1) an appeals process to enable individuals to appeal a determination under this section; and

(2) procedures to protect against waste, fraud, and abuse.

(g) FUNDING; TERMINATION OF AUTHORITY.—

(1) IN GENERAL.—There is appropriated to the Secretary, out of any moneys in the Treasury not otherwise appropriated, $5,000,000,000 to pay claims against (and the administrative costs of) the high risk pool under this section that are in excess of the amount of premiums collected from eligible individuals enrolled in the high risk pool. Such funds shall be available without fiscal year limitation.

(2) INSUFFICIENT FUNDS.—If the Secretary estimates for any fiscal year that the aggregate amounts available for the payment of the expenses of the high risk pool will be less than the actual amount of such expenses, the Secretary shall make such adjustments as are necessary to eliminate such deficit.

(3) TERMINATION OF AUTHORITY.—

(A) IN GENERAL.—Except as provided in subparagraph (B), coverage of eligible individuals under a high risk pool in a State shall terminate on January 1, 2014.

(B) TRANSITION TO EXCHANGE.—The Secretary shall develop procedures to provide for the transition of eligible individuals enrolled in health insurance coverage offered through a high risk pool established under this section into qualified health plans offered through an Exchange. Such procedures shall ensure that there is no lapse in coverage with respect to the individual and may extend coverage after the termination of the risk pool involved, if the Secretary determines necessary to avoid such a lapse.

(4) LIMITATIONS.—The Secretary has the authority to stop taking applications for participation in the program under this section to comply with the funding limitation provided for in paragraph (1).

(5) RELATION TO STATE LAWS.—The standards established under this section shall supersede any State law or regulation (other than State licensing laws or State laws relating to plan solvency) with respect to qualified high risk pools which are established in accordance with this section.

SEC. 1102. REINSURANCE FOR EARLY RETIREES.

(a) ADMINISTRATION.—

(1) IN GENERAL.—Not later than 90 days after the date of enactment of this Act, the Secretary shall establish a temporary reinsurance program to provide reimbursement to participating employment-based plans for a portion of the cost of providing health insurance coverage to early retirees (and to the eligible spouses, surviving spouses, and dependents of such retirees) during the period beginning on the date on which such program is established and ending on January 1, 2014.

(2) REFERENCE.—In this section:

(A) HEALTH BENEFITS.—The term “health benefits” means medical, surgical, hospital, prescription drug, and such other benefits as shall be determined by the Secretary, whether self-funded, or delivered through the purchase of insurance or otherwise.

(B) EMPLOYMENT-BASED PLAN.—The term "employment-based plan" means a group health benefits plan that—

(i) is—

(I) maintained by one or more current or former employers (including without limitation any State or local government or political subdivision thereof), employee organization, a voluntary employees' beneficiary association, or a committee or board of individuals appointed to administer such plan; or

(II) a multiemployer plan (as defined in section 3(37) of the Employee Retirement Income Security Act of 1974); and

(ii) provides health benefits to early retirees.

(C) EARLY RETIREES.—The term "early retirees" means individuals who are age 55 and older but are not eligible for coverage under title XVIII of the Social Security Act, and who are not active employees of an employer maintaining, or currently contributing to, the employment-based plan or of any employer that has made substantial contributions to fund such plan.

(b) PARTICIPATION.—

(1) EMPLOYMENT-BASED PLAN ELIGIBILITY.—A participating employment-based plan is an employment-based plan that—

(A) meets the requirements of paragraph (2) with respect to health benefits provided under the plan; and

(B) submits to the Secretary an application for participation in the program, at such time, in such manner, and containing such information as the Secretary shall require.

(2) EMPLOYMENT-BASED HEALTH BENEFITS.—An employment-based plan meets the requirements of this paragraph if the plan—

(A) implements programs and procedures to generate cost-savings with respect to participants with chronic and high-cost conditions;

(B) provides documentation of the actual cost of medical claims involved; and

(C) is certified by the Secretary.

(c) PAYMENTS.—

(1) SUBMISSION OF CLAIMS.—

(A) IN GENERAL.—A participating employment-based plan shall submit claims for reimbursement to the Secretary which shall contain documentation of the actual costs of the items and services for which each claim is being submitted.

(B) BASIS FOR CLAIMS.—Claims submitted under subparagraph (A) shall be based on the actual amount expended by the participating employment-based plan involved within the plan year for the health benefits provided to an early retiree or the spouse, surviving spouse, or dependent of such retiree. In determining the amount of a claim for purposes of this subsection, the participating employment-based plan shall take into account any negotiated price concessions (such as discounts, direct or indirect subsidies, rebates, and direct or indirect remunerations) obtained by such plan with respect to such health benefit. For purposes of determining the amount of any such claim, the costs paid by the early retiree or the retiree's spouse, surviving spouse, or dependent in the form of deductibles, co-payments, or co-insurance shall be included in the amounts paid by the participating employment-based plan.

(2) PROGRAM PAYMENTS.—If the Secretary determines that a participating employment-based plan has submitted a valid claim under paragraph (1), the Secretary shall reimburse such plan for 80 percent of that portion of the costs attributable to such claim that exceed $15,000, subject to the limits contained in paragraph (3).

(3) LIMIT.—To be eligible for reimbursement under the program, a claim submitted by a participating employment-based plan shall not be less than $15,000 nor greater than $90,000. Such amounts shall be adjusted each fiscal year based on the percentage increase in the Medical Care Component of the Consumer Price Index for all urban consumers (rounded to the nearest multiple of $1,000) for the year involved.

(4) USE OF PAYMENTS.—Amounts paid to a participating employment-based plan under this subsection shall be used to lower costs for the plan. Such payments may be used to reduce premium costs for an entity described in subsection (a)(2)(B)(i) or to reduce premium contributions, co-payments, deductibles, co-insurance, or other out-of-pocket costs for plan participants. Such payments shall not be used as general revenues for an entity described in subsection (a)(2)(B)(i). The Secretary shall develop a mechanism to monitor the appropriate use of such payments by such entities.

(5) PAYMENTS NOT TREATED AS INCOME.—Payments received under this subsection shall not be included in determining the gross income of an entity described in subsection (a)(2)(B)(i) that is maintaining or currently contributing to a participating employment-based plan.

(6) APPEALS.—The Secretary shall establish—

(A) an appeals process to permit participating employment-based plans to appeal a determination of the Secretary with respect to claims submitted under this section; and

(B) procedures to protect against fraud, waste, and abuse under the program.

(d) AUDITS.—The Secretary shall conduct annual audits of claims data submitted by participating employment-based plans under this section to ensure that such plans are in compliance with the requirements of this section.

(e) FUNDING.—There is appropriated to the Secretary, out of any moneys in the Treasury not otherwise appropriated, $5,000,000,000 to carry out the program under this section. Such funds shall be available without fiscal year limitation.

(f) LIMITATION.—The Secretary has the authority to stop taking applications for participation in the program based on the availability of funding under subsection (e).

SEC. 1103. IMMEDIATE INFORMATION THAT ALLOWS CONSUMERS TO IDENTIFY AFFORDABLE COVERAGE OPTIONS.

(a) INTERNET PORTAL TO AFFORDABLE COVERAGE OPTIONS.—

(1) IMMEDIATE ESTABLISHMENT.—Not later than July 1, 2010, the Secretary, in consultation with the States, shall establish a mechanism, including an Internet website, through which a resident of any State may identify affordable health insurance coverage options in that State.

(2) CONNECTING TO AFFORDABLE COVERAGE.—An Internet website established under paragraph (1) shall, to the extent practicable, provide ways for residents of any State to receive information on at least the following coverage options:

(A) Health insurance coverage offered by health insurance issuers, other than coverage that provides reimbursement only for the treatment or mitigation of—

(i) a single disease or condition; or

(ii) an unreasonably limited set of diseases or conditions (as determined by the Secretary);

(B) Medicaid coverage under title XIX of the Social Security Act.

(C) Coverage under title XXI of the Social Security Act.

(D) A State health benefits high risk pool, to the extent that such high risk pool is offered in such State; and

(E) Coverage under a high risk pool under section 1101.

(b) ENHANCING COMPARATIVE PURCHASING OPTIONS.—

(1) IN GENERAL.—Not later than 60 days after the date of enactment of this Act, the Secretary shall develop a standardized format to be used for the presentation of information relating to the coverage options described in subsection (a)(2). Such format shall, at a minimum, require the inclusion of information on the percentage of total premium revenue expended on nonclinical costs (as reported under section 2718(a) of the Public Health Service Act), eligibility, availability, premium rates, and cost sharing with respect to such coverage options and be consistent with the standards adopted for the uniform explanation of coverage as provided for in section 2715 of the Public Health Service Act.

(2) USE OF FORMAT.—The Secretary shall utilize the format developed under paragraph (1) in compiling information concerning coverage options on the Internet website established under subsection (a).

(c) AUTHORITY TO CONTRACT.—The Secretary may carry out this section through contracts entered into with qualified entities.

SEC. 1104. ADMINISTRATIVE SIMPLIFICATION.

(a) PURPOSE OF ADMINISTRATIVE SIMPLIFICATION.—Section 261 of the Health Insurance Portability and Accountability Act of 1996 (42 U.S.C. 1320d note) is amended—

(1) by inserting "uniform" before "standards"; and

(2) by inserting "and to reduce the clerical burden on patients, health care providers, and health plans" before the period at the end.

(b) OPERATING RULES FOR HEALTH INFORMATION TRANSACTIONS.—

(1) DEFINITION OF OPERATING RULES.—Section 1171 of the Social Security Act (42 U.S.C. 1320d) is amended by adding at the end the following:

"(9) OPERATING RULES.—The term 'operating rules' means the necessary business rules and guidelines for the electronic exchange of information that are not defined by a standard or its implementation specifications as adopted for purposes of this part.".

(2) TRANSACTION STANDARDS; OPERATING RULES AND COMPLIANCE.—Section 1173 of the Social Security Act (42 U.S.C. 1320d–2) is amended—

(A) in subsection (a)(2), by adding at the end the following new subparagraph:

"(J) Electronic funds transfers.";

(B) in subsection (a), by adding at the end the following new paragraph:

"(4) REQUIREMENTS FOR FINANCIAL AND ADMINISTRATIVE TRANSACTIONS.—

"(A) IN GENERAL.—The standards and associated operating rules adopted by the Secretary shall—

"(i) to the extent feasible and appropriate, enable determination of an individual's eligibility and financial responsibility for specific services prior to or at the point of care;

"(ii) be comprehensive, requiring minimal augmentation by paper or other communications;

"(iii) provide for timely acknowledgment, response, and status reporting that supports a transparent claims and denial management process (including adjudication and appeals); and

"(iv) describe all data elements (including reason and remark codes) in unambiguous terms, require that such data elements be required or conditioned upon set values in other fields, and prohibit additional conditions (except where necessary to implement State or Federal law, or to protect against fraud and abuse).

"(B) REDUCTION OF CLERICAL BURDEN.—In adopting standards and operating rules for the transactions referred to under paragraph (1), the Secretary shall seek to reduce the number and complexity of forms (including paper and electronic forms) and data entry required by patients and providers."; and

(C) by adding at the end the following new subsections:

"(g) OPERATING RULES.—

"(1) IN GENERAL.—The Secretary shall adopt a single set of operating rules for each transaction referred to under subsection (a)(1) with the goal of creating as much uniformity in the implementation of the electronic standards as possible. Such operating rules shall be consensus-based and reflect the necessary business rules affecting health plans and health care providers and the manner in which they operate pursuant to standards issued under Health Insurance Portability and Accountability Act of 1996.

"(2) OPERATING RULES DEVELOPMENT.—In adopting operating rules under this subsection, the Secretary shall consider recommendations for operating rules developed by a qualified nonprofit entity that meets the following requirements:

"(A) The entity focuses its mission on administrative simplification.

"(B) The entity demonstrates a multi-stakeholder and consensus-based process for development of operating rules, including representation by or participation from health plans, health care providers, vendors, relevant Federal agencies, and other standard development organizations.

"(C) The entity has a public set of guiding principles that ensure the operating rules and process are open and transparent, and supports nondiscrimination and conflict of interest policies that demonstrate a commitment to open, fair, and nondiscriminatory practices.

"(D) The entity builds on the transaction standards issued under Health Insurance Portability and Accountability Act of 1996.

"(E) The entity allows for public review and updates of the operating rules.

"(3) REVIEW AND RECOMMENDATIONS.—The National Committee on Vital and Health Statistics shall—

"(A) advise the Secretary as to whether a nonprofit entity meets the requirements under paragraph (2);

"(B) review the operating rules developed and recommended by such nonprofit entity;

"(C) determine whether such operating rules represent a consensus view of the health care stakeholders and are consistent with and do not conflict with other existing standards;

"(D) evaluate whether such operating rules are consistent with electronic standards adopted for health information technology; and

"(E) submit to the Secretary a recommendation as to whether the Secretary should adopt such operating rules.

"(4) IMPLEMENTATION.—

"(A) IN GENERAL.—The Secretary shall adopt operating rules under this subsection, by regulation in accordance with subparagraph (C), following consideration of the operating rules developed by the non-profit entity described in paragraph (2) and the recommendation submitted by the National Committee on Vital and Health Statistics under paragraph (3)(E) and having ensured consultation with providers.

"(B) ADOPTION REQUIREMENTS; EFFECTIVE DATES.—

"(i) ELIGIBILITY FOR A HEALTH PLAN AND HEALTH CLAIM STATUS.—The set of operating rules for eligibility for a health plan and health claim status transactions shall be adopted not later than July 1, 2011, in a manner ensuring that such operating rules are effective not later than January 1, 2013, and may allow for the use of a machine readable identification card.

"(ii) ELECTRONIC FUNDS TRANSFERS AND HEALTH CARE PAYMENT AND REMITTANCE ADVICE.—The set of operating rules for electronic funds transfers and health care payment and remittance advice transactions shall—

"(I) allow for automated reconciliation of the electronic payment with the remittance advice; and

“(II) be adopted not later than July 1, 2012, in a manner ensuring that such operating rules are effective not later than January 1, 2014.

“(iii) HEALTH CLAIMS OR EQUIVALENT ENCOUNTER INFORMATION, ENROLLMENT AND DISENROLLMENT IN A HEALTH PLAN, HEALTH PLAN PREMIUM PAYMENTS, REFERRAL CERTIFICATION AND AUTHORIZATION.—The set of operating rules for health claims or equivalent encounter information, enrollment and disenrollment in a health plan, health plan premium payments, and referral certification and authorization transactions shall be adopted not later than July 1, 2014, in a manner ensuring that such operating rules are effective not later than January 1, 2016.

“(C) EXPEDITED RULEMAKING.—The Secretary shall promulgate an interim final rule applying any standard or operating rule recommended by the National Committee on Vital and Health Statistics pursuant to paragraph (3). The Secretary shall accept and consider public comments on any interim final rule published under this subparagraph for 60 days after the date of such publication.

“(h) COMPLIANCE.—

“(1) HEALTH PLAN CERTIFICATION.—

“(A) ELIGIBILITY FOR A HEALTH PLAN, HEALTH CLAIM STATUS, ELECTRONIC FUNDS TRANSFERS, HEALTH CARE PAYMENT AND REMITTANCE ADVICE.—Not later than December 31, 2013, a health plan shall file a statement with the Secretary, in such form as the Secretary may require, certifying that the data and information systems for such plan are in compliance with any applicable standards (as described under paragraph (7) of section 1171) and associated operating rules (as described under paragraph (9) of such section) for electronic funds transfers, eligibility for a health plan, health claim status, and health care payment and remittance advice, respectively.

“(B) HEALTH CLAIMS OR EQUIVALENT ENCOUNTER INFORMATION, ENROLLMENT AND DISENROLLMENT IN A HEALTH PLAN, HEALTH PLAN PREMIUM PAYMENTS, HEALTH CLAIMS ATTACHMENTS, REFERRAL CERTIFICATION AND AUTHORIZATION.—Not later than December 31, 2015, a health plan shall file a statement with the Secretary, in such form as the Secretary may require, certifying that the data and information systems for such plan are in compliance with any applicable standards and associated operating rules for health claims or equivalent encounter information, enrollment and disenrollment in a health plan, health plan premium payments, health claims attachments, and referral certification and authorization, respectively. A health plan shall provide the same level of documentation to certify compliance with such transactions as is required to certify compliance with the transactions specified in subparagraph (A).

“(2) DOCUMENTATION OF COMPLIANCE.—A health plan shall provide the Secretary, in such form as the Secretary may require, with adequate documentation of compliance with the standards and operating rules described under paragraph (1). A health plan shall not be considered to have provided adequate documentation and shall not be certified as being in compliance with such standards, unless the health plan—

"(A) demonstrates to the Secretary that the plan conducts the electronic transactions specified in paragraph (1) in a manner that fully complies with the regulations of the Secretary; and

"(B) provides documentation showing that the plan has completed end-to-end testing for such transactions with their partners, such as hospitals and physicians.

"(3) SERVICE CONTRACTS.—A health plan shall be required to ensure that any entities that provide services pursuant to a contract with such health plan shall comply with any applicable certification and compliance requirements (and provide the Secretary with adequate documentation of such compliance) under this subsection.

"(4) CERTIFICATION BY OUTSIDE ENTITY.—The Secretary may designate independent, outside entities to certify that a health plan has complied with the requirements under this subsection, provided that the certification standards employed by such entities are in accordance with any standards or operating rules issued by the Secretary.

"(5) COMPLIANCE WITH REVISED STANDARDS AND OPERATING RULES.—

"(A) IN GENERAL.—A health plan (including entities described under paragraph (3)) shall file a statement with the Secretary, in such form as the Secretary may require, certifying that the data and information systems for such plan are in compliance with any applicable revised standards and associated operating rules under this subsection for any interim final rule promulgated by the Secretary under subsection (i) that—

"(i) amends any standard or operating rule described under paragraph (1) of this subsection; or

"(ii) establishes a standard (as described under subsection (a)(1)(B)) or associated operating rules (as described under subsection (i)(5)) for any other financial and administrative transactions.

"(B) DATE OF COMPLIANCE.—A health plan shall comply with such requirements not later than the effective date of the applicable standard or operating rule.

"(6) AUDITS OF HEALTH PLANS.—The Secretary shall conduct periodic audits to ensure that health plans (including entities described under paragraph (3)) are in compliance with any standards and operating rules that are described under paragraph (1) or subsection (i)(5).

"(i) REVIEW AND AMENDMENT OF STANDARDS AND OPERATING RULES.—

"(1) ESTABLISHMENT.—Not later than January 1, 2014, the Secretary shall establish a review committee (as described under paragraph (4)).

"(2) EVALUATIONS AND REPORTS.—

"(A) HEARINGS.—Not later than April 1, 2014, and not less than biennially thereafter, the Secretary, acting through the review committee, shall conduct hearings to evaluate and review the adopted standards and operating rules established under this section.

"(B) REPORT.—Not later than July 1, 2014, and not less than biennially thereafter, the review committee shall provide recommendations for updating and improving such standards and operating rules. The review committee shall recommend a single set of operating rules per transaction standard and maintain the goal of creating as much uniformity as possible in the implementation of the electronic standards.

"(3) INTERIM FINAL RULEMAKING.—

"(A) IN GENERAL.—Any recommendations to amend adopted standards and operating rules that have been approved by the review committee and reported to the Secretary under paragraph (2)(B) shall be adopted by the Secretary through promulgation of an interim final rule not later than 90 days after receipt of the committee's report.

"(B) PUBLIC COMMENT.—

"(i) PUBLIC COMMENT PERIOD.—The Secretary shall accept and consider public comments on any interim final rule published under this paragraph for 60 days after the date of such publication.

"(ii) EFFECTIVE DATE.—The effective date of any amendment to existing standards or operating rules that is adopted through an interim final rule published under this paragraph shall be 25 months following the close of such public comment period.

"(4) REVIEW COMMITTEE.—

"(A) DEFINITION.—For the purposes of this subsection, the term 'review committee' means a committee chartered by or within the Department of Health and Human services that has been designated by the Secretary to carry out this subsection, including—

"(i) the National Committee on Vital and Health Statistics; or

"(ii) any appropriate committee as determined by the Secretary.

"(B) COORDINATION OF HIT STANDARDS.—In developing recommendations under this subsection, the review committee shall ensure coordination, as appropriate, with the standards that support the certified electronic health record technology approved by the Office of the National Coordinator for Health Information Technology.

"(5) OPERATING RULES FOR OTHER STANDARDS ADOPTED BY THE SECRETARY.—The Secretary shall adopt a single set of operating rules (pursuant to the process described under subsection (g)) for any transaction for which a standard had been adopted pursuant to subsection (a)(1)(B).

"(j) PENALTIES.—

"(1) PENALTY FEE.—

"(A) IN GENERAL.—Not later than April 1, 2014, and annually thereafter, the Secretary shall assess a penalty fee (as determined under subparagraph (B)) against a health plan that has failed to meet the requirements under subsection (h) with respect to certification and documentation of compliance with—

"(i) the standards and associated operating rules described under paragraph (1) of such subsection; and "(ii) a standard (as described under subsection (a)(1)(B)) and associated operating rules (as described under subsection (i)(5)) for any other financial and administrative transactions.

"(B) FEE AMOUNT.—Subject to subparagraphs (C), (D), and (E), the Secretary shall assess a penalty fee against a health plan in the amount of $1 per covered life until certification is complete. The penalty shall be assessed per person covered by the plan for which its data systems for major medical policies are not in compliance and shall be imposed against the health plan for each day that the plan is not in compliance with the requirements under subsection (h).

"(C) ADDITIONAL PENALTY FOR MISREPRESENTATION.—A health plan that knowingly provides inaccurate or incomplete information in a statement of certification or documentation of compliance under subsection (h) shall be subject to a penalty fee that is double the amount that would otherwise be imposed under this subsection.

"(D) ANNUAL FEE INCREASE.—The amount of the penalty fee imposed under this subsection shall be increased on an annual basis by the annual percentage increase in total national health care expenditures, as determined by the Secretary.

"(E) PENALTY LIMIT.—A penalty fee assessed against a health plan under this subsection shall not exceed, on an annual basis—

"(i) an amount equal to $20 per covered life under such plan; or

"(ii) an amount equal to $40 per covered life under the plan if such plan has knowingly provided inaccurate or incomplete information (as described under subparagraph (C)).

"(F) DETERMINATION OF COVERED INDIVIDUALS.—The Secretary shall determine the number of covered lives under a health plan based upon the most recent statements and filings that have been submitted by such plan to the Securities and Exchange Commission.

"(2) NOTICE AND DISPUTE PROCEDURE.—The Secretary shall establish a procedure for assessment of penalty fees under this subsection that provides a health plan with reasonable notice and a dispute resolution procedure prior to provision of a notice of assessment by the Secretary of the Treasury (as described under paragraph (4)(B)).

"(3) PENALTY FEE REPORT.—Not later than May 1, 2014, and annually thereafter, the Secretary shall provide the Secretary of the Treasury with a report identifying those health plans that have been assessed a penalty fee under this subsection.

"(4) COLLECTION OF PENALTY FEE.—

"(A) IN GENERAL.—The Secretary of the Treasury, acting through the Financial Management Service, shall administer the collection of penalty fees from health plans that have been identified by the Secretary in the penalty fee report provided under paragraph (3).

"(B) NOTICE.—Not later than August 1, 2014, and annually thereafter, the Secretary of the Treasury shall provide notice to each health plan that has been assessed a penalty fee by the Secretary under this subsection. Such notice shall include the amount of the penalty fee assessed by the Secretary and the due date for payment of such fee to the Secretary of the Treasury (as described in subparagraph (C)).

"(C) PAYMENT DUE DATE.—Payment by a health plan for a penalty fee assessed under this subsection shall be made to the Secretary of the Treasury not later than November 1, 2014, and annually thereafter.

"(D) UNPAID PENALTY FEES.—Any amount of a penalty fee assessed against a health plan under this subsection for which payment has not been made by the due date provided under subparagraph (C) shall be—

"(i) increased by the interest accrued on such amount, as determined pursuant to the underpayment rate established under section 6621 of the Internal Revenue Code of 1986; and

"(ii) treated as a past-due, legally enforceable debt owed to a Federal agency for purposes of section 6402(d) of the Internal Revenue Code of 1986.

"(E) ADMINISTRATIVE FEES.—Any fee charged or allocated for collection activities conducted by the Financial Management Service will be passed on to a health plan on a pro-rata basis and added to any penalty fee collected from the plan.".

(c) PROMULGATION OF RULES.—

(1) UNIQUE HEALTH PLAN IDENTIFIER.—The Secretary shall promulgate a final rule to establish a unique health plan identifier (as described in section 1173(b) of the Social Security Act (42 U.S.C. 1320d–2(b))) based on the input of the National Committee on Vital and Health Statistics. The Secretary may do so on an interim final basis and such rule shall be effective not later than October 1, 2012.

(2) ELECTRONIC FUNDS TRANSFER.—The Secretary shall promulgate a final rule to establish a standard for electronic funds transfers (as described in section 1173(a)(2)(J) of the Social Security Act, as added by subsection (b)(2)(A)). The Secretary may do so on an interim final basis and shall adopt such standard not later than January 1, 2012, in a manner ensuring that such standard is effective not later than January 1, 2014.

(3) HEALTH CLAIMS ATTACHMENTS.—The Secretary shall promulgate a final rule to establish a transaction standard and a single set of associated operating rules for health claims attachments (as described in section 1173(a)(2)(B) of the Social Security Act (42 U.S.C. 1320d–2(a)(2)(B))) that is consistent with the X12 Version 5010 transaction standards. The Secretary may do so on an interim final basis and shall adopt a transaction standard and a single set of associated operating rules not later than January 1, 2014, in a manner ensuring that such standard is effective not later than January 1, 2016.

(d) EXPANSION OF ELECTRONIC TRANSACTIONS IN MEDICARE.—Section 1862(a) of the Social Security Act (42 U.S.C. 1395y(a)) is amended—

(1) in paragraph (23), by striking the "or" at the end;

(2) in paragraph (24), by striking the period and inserting "; or"; and

(3) by inserting after paragraph (24) the following new paragraph:

"(25) not later than January 1, 2014, for which the payment is other than by electronic funds transfer (EFT) or an electronic remittance in a form as specified in ASC X12 835 Health Care Payment and Remittance Advice or subsequent standard.".

SEC. 1105. EFFECTIVE DATE.

This subtitle shall take effect on the date of enactment of this Act.

Subtitle C—Quality Health Insurance Coverage for All Americans

PART I—HEALTH INSURANCE MARKET REFORMS

SEC. 1201. AMENDMENT TO THE PUBLIC HEALTH SERVICE ACT.

Part A of title XXVII of the Public Health Service Act (42 U.S.C. 300gg et seq.), as amended by section 1001, is further amended—

(1) by striking the heading for subpart 1 and inserting the following:

"Subpart I—General Reform";

(2)(A) in section 2701 (42 U.S.C. 300gg), by striking the section heading and subsection (a) and inserting the following:

"SEC. 2704. PROHIBITION OF PREEXISTING CONDITION EXCLUSIONS OR OTHER DISCRIMINATION BASED ON HEALTH STATUS.

"(a) IN GENERAL.—A group health plan and a health insurance issuer offering group or individual health insurance coverage may not impose any preexisting condition exclusion with respect to such plan or coverage."; and

(B) by transferring such section (as amended by subparagraph (A)) so as to appear after the section 2703 added by paragraph (4);

(3)(A) in section 2702 (42 U.S.C. 300gg–1)—

(i) by striking the section heading and all that follows through subsection (a);

(ii) in subsection (b)—

(I) by striking "health insurance issuer offering health insurance coverage in connection with a group health plan" each place that such appears and inserting "health insurance issuer offering group or individual health insurance coverage"; and

(II) in paragraph (2)(A)—

(aa) by inserting "or individual" after "employer"; and

(bb) by inserting "or individual health coverage, as the case may be" before the semicolon; and

(iii) in subsection (e)—

(I) by striking "(a)(1)(F)" and inserting "(a)(6)";

(II) by striking "2701" and inserting "2704"; and

(III) by striking "2721(a)" and inserting "2735(a)"; and

(B) by transferring such section (as amended by subparagraph (A)) to appear after section 2705(a) as added by paragraph (4); and

(4) by inserting after the subpart heading (as added by paragraph (1)) the following:

"SEC. 2701. FAIR HEALTH INSURANCE PREMIUMS.

"(a) PROHIBITING DISCRIMINATORY PREMIUM RATES.—

"(1) IN GENERAL.—With respect to the premium rate charged by a health insurance issuer for health insurance coverage offered in the individual or small group market—

"(A) such rate shall vary with respect to the particular plan or coverage involved only by—

"(i) whether such plan or coverage covers an individual or family;

"(ii) rating area, as established in accordance with paragraph (2);

"(iii) age, except that such rate shall not vary by more than 3 to 1 for adults (consistent with section 2707(c)); and

"(iv) tobacco use, except that such rate shall not vary by more than 1.5 to 1; and

"(B) such rate shall not vary with respect to the particular plan or coverage involved by any other factor not described in subparagraph (A).

"(2) RATING AREA.—

"(A) IN GENERAL.—Each State shall establish 1 or more rating areas within that State for purposes of applying the requirements of this title.

"(B) SECRETARIAL REVIEW.—The Secretary shall review the rating areas established by each State under subparagraph (A) to ensure the adequacy of such areas for purposes of carrying out the requirements of this title. If the Secretary determines a State's rating areas are not adequate, or that a State does not establish such areas, the Secretary may establish rating areas for that State.

"(3) PERMISSIBLE AGE BANDS.—The Secretary, in consultation with the National Association of Insurance Commissioners, shall define the permissible age bands for rating purposes under paragraph (1)(A)(iii).

"(4) APPLICATION OF VARIATIONS BASED ON AGE OR TOBACCO USE.—With respect to family coverage under a group health plan or health insurance coverage, the rating variations permitted under clauses (iii) and (iv) of paragraph (1)(A) shall be applied based on the portion of the premium that is attributable to each family member covered under the plan or coverage.

"(5) SPECIAL RULE FOR LARGE GROUP MARKET.—If a State permits health insurance issuers that offer coverage in the large group market in the State to offer such coverage through the State Exchange (as provided for under section 1312(f)(2)(B)

of the Patient Protection and Affordable Care Act), the provisions of this subsection shall apply to all coverage offered in such market in the State.

"SEC. 2702. GUARANTEED AVAILABILITY OF COVERAGE.

"(a) GUARANTEED ISSUANCE OF COVERAGE IN THE INDIVIDUAL AND GROUP MARKET.—Subject to subsections (b) through (e), each health insurance issuer that offers health insurance coverage in the individual or group market in a State must accept every employer and individual in the State that applies for such coverage.

"(b) ENROLLMENT.—

"(1) RESTRICTION.—A health insurance issuer described in subsection (a) may restrict enrollment in coverage described in such subsection to open or special enrollment periods.

"(2) ESTABLISHMENT.—A health insurance issuer described in subsection (a) shall, in accordance with the regulations promulgated under paragraph (3), establish special enrollment periods for qualifying events (under section 603 of the Employee Retirement Income Security Act of 1974).

"(3) REGULATIONS.—The Secretary shall promulgate regulations with respect to enrollment periods under paragraphs (1) and (2).

"SEC. 2703. GUARANTEED RENEWABILITY OF COVERAGE.

"(a) IN GENERAL.—Except as provided in this section, if a health insurance issuer offers health insurance coverage in the individual or group market, the issuer must renew or continue in force such coverage at the option of the plan sponsor or the individual, as applicable.

"SEC. 2705. PROHIBITING DISCRIMINATION AGAINST INDIVIDUAL PARTICIPANTS AND BENEFICIARIES BASED ON HEALTH STATUS.

"(a) IN GENERAL.—A group health plan and a health insurance issuer offering group or individual health insurance coverage may not establish rules for eligibility (including continued eligibility) of any individual to enroll under the terms of the plan or coverage based on any of the following health status-related factors in relation to the individual or a dependent of the individual:

"(1) Health status.

"(2) Medical condition (including both physical and mental illnesses).

"(3) Claims experience.

"(4) Receipt of health care.

"(5) Medical history.

"(6) Genetic information.

"(7) Evidence of insurability (including conditions arising out of acts of domestic violence).

"(8) Disability.

"(9) Any other health status-related factor determined appropriate by the Secretary.

"(j) PROGRAMS OF HEALTH PROMOTION OR DISEASE PREVENTION.—

"(1) GENERAL PROVISIONS.—

"(A) GENERAL RULE.—For purposes of subsection (b)(2)(B), a program of health promotion or disease prevention (referred to in this subsection as a 'wellness program') shall be a program offered by an employer that is designed to promote health or prevent disease that meets the applicable requirements of this subsection.

"(B) NO CONDITIONS BASED ON HEALTH STATUS FACTOR.—If none of the conditions for obtaining a premium discount or rebate or other reward for participation in a wellness program is based on an individual satisfying a standard that is related to a health status factor, such wellness program shall not violate this section if participation in the program is made available to all similarly situated individuals and the requirements of paragraph (2) are complied with.

"(C) CONDITIONS BASED ON HEALTH STATUS FACTOR.—If any of the conditions for obtaining a premium discount or rebate or other reward for participation in a wellness program is based on an individual satisfying a standard that is related to a health status factor, such wellness program shall not violate this section if the requirements of paragraph (3) are complied with.

"(2) WELLNESS PROGRAMS NOT SUBJECT TO REQUIREMENTS.—If none of the conditions for obtaining a premium discount or rebate or other reward under a wellness program as described in paragraph (1)(B) are based on an individual satisfying a standard that is related to a health status factor (or if such a wellness program does not provide such a reward), the wellness program shall not violate this section if participation in the program is made available to all similarly situated individuals. The following programs shall not have to comply with the requirements of paragraph (3) if participation in the program is made available to all similarly situated individuals:

"(A) A program that reimburses all or part of the cost for memberships in a fitness center.

"(B) A diagnostic testing program that provides a reward for participation and does not base any part of the reward on outcomes.

"(C) A program that encourages preventive care related to a health condition through the waiver of the copayment or deductible requirement under group health plan for the costs of certain items or services related to a health condition (such as prenatal care or well-baby visits).

"(D) A program that reimburses individuals for the costs of smoking cessation programs without regard to whether the individual quits smoking.

"(E) A program that provides a reward to individuals for attending a periodic health education seminar.

"(3) WELLNESS PROGRAMS SUBJECT TO REQUIREMENTS.—If any of the conditions for obtaining a premium discount, rebate, or reward under a wellness program as described in paragraph (1)(C) is based on an individual satisfying a standard that is related to a health status factor, the wellness program shall not violate this section if the following requirements are complied with:

"(A) The reward for the wellness program, together with the reward for other wellness programs with respect to the plan that requires satisfaction of a standard related to a health status factor, shall not exceed 30 percent of the cost of employee-only coverage under the plan. If, in addition to employees or individuals, any class of dependents (such as spouses or spouses and dependent children) may participate fully in the wellness program, such reward shall not exceed 30 percent of the cost of the coverage in which an employee or individual and any dependents are enrolled. For purposes of this paragraph, the cost of coverage shall be determined based on the total amount of employer and employee contributions for the benefit package under which the employee is (or the employee and any dependents are) receiving coverage. A reward may be in the form of a discount or rebate of a premium or contribution, a waiver of all or part of a cost-sharing mechanism (such as deductibles, copayments, or coinsurance), the absence of a surcharge, or the value of a benefit that would otherwise not be provided under the plan. The Secretaries of Labor, Health and Human Services, and the Treasury may increase the reward available under this subparagraph to up to 50 percent of the cost of coverage if the Secretaries determine that such an increase is appropriate.

"(B) The wellness program shall be reasonably designed to promote health or prevent disease. A program complies with the preceding sentence if the program has a reasonable chance of improving the health of, or preventing disease in, participating individuals and it is not overly burdensome, is not a subterfuge for discriminating based on a health status factor, and is not highly suspect in the method chosen to promote health or prevent disease.

"(C) The plan shall give individuals eligible for the program the opportunity to qualify for the reward under the program at least once each year.

"(D) The full reward under the wellness program shall be made available to all similarly situated individuals. For such purpose, among other things:

"(i) The reward is not available to all similarly situated individuals for a period unless the wellness program allows—

"(I) for a reasonable alternative standard (or waiver of the otherwise applicable standard) for obtaining the reward for any individual for whom, for that period, it is unreasonably difficult due to a medical condition to satisfy the otherwise applicable standard; and

"(II) for a reasonable alternative standard (or waiver of the otherwise applicable standard) for obtaining the reward for any individual for whom, for that period, it is medically inadvisable to attempt to satisfy the otherwise applicable standard.

"(ii) If reasonable under the circumstances, the plan or issuer may seek verification, such as a statement from an individual's physician, that a health status factor makes it unreasonably difficult or medically inadvisable for the individual to satisfy or attempt to satisfy the otherwise applicable standard.

"(E) The plan or issuer involved shall disclose in all plan materials describing the terms of the wellness program the availability of a reasonable alternative standard (or the possibility of waiver of the otherwise applicable standard) required under subparagraph (D). If plan materials disclose that such a program is available, without describing its terms, the disclosure under this subparagraph shall not be required.

"(k) EXISTING PROGRAMS.—Nothing in this section shall prohibit a program of health promotion or disease prevention that was established prior to the date of enactment of this section and applied with all applicable regulations, and that is operating on such date, from continuing to be carried out for as long as such regulations remain in effect.

"(l) WELLNESS PROGRAM DEMONSTRATION PROJECT.—

"(1) IN GENERAL.—Not later than July 1, 2014, the Secretary, in consultation with the Secretary of the Treasury and the Secretary of Labor, shall establish a 10-State demonstration project under which participating States shall apply the provisions of subsection (j) to programs of health promotion offered by a health insurance issuer that offers health insurance coverage in the individual market in such State.

"(2) EXPANSION OF DEMONSTRATION PROJECT.—If the Secretary, in consultation with the Secretary of the Treasury and the Secretary of Labor, determines that the demonstration project described in paragraph (1) is effective, such Secretaries may, beginning on July 1, 2017 expand such demonstration project to include additional participating States.

"(3) REQUIREMENTS.—

"(A) MAINTENANCE OF COVERAGE.—The Secretary, in consultation with the Secretary of the Treasury and the Secretary of Labor, shall not approve the participation of a State in the demonstration project under this section unless the Secretaries determine that the State's project is designed in a manner that—

"(i) will not result in any decrease in coverage; and

"(ii) will not increase the cost to the Federal Government in providing credits under section 36B of the Internal Revenue Code of 1986 or cost-sharing assistance under section 1402 of the Patient Protection and Affordable Care Act.

"(B) OTHER REQUIREMENTS.—States that participate in the demonstration project under this subsection—

"(i) may permit premium discounts or rebates or the modification of otherwise applicable copayments or deductibles for adherence to, or participation in, a reasonably designed program of health promotion and disease prevention;

"(ii) shall ensure that requirements of consumer protection are met in programs of health promotion in the individual market;

"(iii) shall require verification from health insurance issuers that offer health insurance coverage in the individual market of such State that premium discounts—

"(I) do not create undue burdens for individuals insured in the individual market;

"(II) do not lead to cost shifting; and

"(III) are not a subterfuge for discrimination;

"(iv) shall ensure that consumer data is protected in accordance with the requirements of section 264(c) of the Health Insurance Portability and Accountability Act of 1996 (42 U.S.C. 1320d–2 note); and

"(v) shall ensure and demonstrate to the satisfaction of the Secretary that the discounts or other rewards provided under the project reflect the expected level of participation in the wellness program involved and the anticipated effect the program will have on utilization or medical claim costs.

"(m) REPORT.—

"(1) IN GENERAL.—Not later than 3 years after the date of enactment of the Patient Protection and Affordable Care Act, the Secretary, in consultation with the Secretary of the Treasury and the Secretary of Labor, shall submit a report to the appropriate committees of Congress concerning—

"(A) the effectiveness of wellness programs (as defined in subsection (j)) in promoting health and preventing disease;

"(B) the impact of such wellness programs on the access to care and affordability of coverage for participants and non-participants of such programs;

"(C) the impact of premium-based and cost-sharing incentives on participant behavior and the role of such programs in changing behavior; and

"(D) the effectiveness of different types of rewards.

"(2) DATA COLLECTION.—In preparing the report described in paragraph (1), the Secretaries shall gather relevant information from employers who provide employees with access to wellness programs, including State and Federal agencies.

"(n) REGULATIONS.—Nothing in this section shall be construed as prohibiting the Secretaries of Labor, Health and Human Services, or the Treasury from promulgating regulations in connection with this section.

"SEC. 2706. NON-DISCRIMINATION IN HEALTH CARE.

"(a) PROVIDERS.—A group health plan and a health insurance issuer offering group or individual health insurance coverage shall not discriminate with respect to participation under the plan or coverage against any health care provider who is acting within the scope of that provider's license or certification under applicable State law. This section shall not require that a group health plan or health insurance issuer contract with any health care provider willing to abide by the terms and conditions for participation established by the plan or issuer. Nothing in this section shall be construed as preventing a group health plan, a health insurance issuer, or the Secretary from establishing varying reimbursement rates based on quality or performance measures.

"(b) INDIVIDUALS.—The provisions of section 1558 of the Patient Protection and Affordable Care Act (relating to non-discrimination) shall apply with respect to a group health plan or health insurance issuer offering group or individual health insurance coverage.

"SEC. 2707. COMPREHENSIVE HEALTH INSURANCE COVERAGE.

"(a) COVERAGE FOR ESSENTIAL HEALTH BENEFITS PACKAGE.—A health insurance issuer that offers health insurance coverage in the individual or small group market shall ensure that such coverage includes the essential health benefits package required under section 1302(a) of the Patient Protection and Affordable Care Act.

"(b) COST-SHARING UNDER GROUP HEALTH PLANS.—A group health plan shall ensure that any annual cost-sharing imposed under the plan does not exceed the limitations provided for under paragraphs (1) and (2) of section 1302(c).

"(c) CHILD-ONLY PLANS.—If a health insurance issuer offers health insurance coverage in any level of coverage specified under section 1302(d) of the Patient Protection and Affordable Care Act, the issuer shall also offer such coverage in that level as a plan in which the only enrollees are individuals who, as of the beginning of a plan year, have not attained the age of 21.

"(d) DENTAL ONLY.—This section shall not apply to a plan described in section 1302(d)(2)(B)(ii)(I).

"SEC. 2708. PROHIBITION ON EXCESSIVE WAITING PERIODS.

"A group health plan and a health insurance issuer offering group or individual health insurance coverage shall not apply any waiting period (as defined in section 2704(b)(4)) that exceeds 90 days.".

PART II—OTHER PROVISIONS

SEC. 1251. PRESERVATION OF RIGHT TO MAINTAIN EXISTING COVERAGE.

(a) NO CHANGES TO EXISTING COVERAGE.—

(1) IN GENERAL.—Nothing in this Act (or an amendment made by this Act) shall be construed to require that an individual terminate coverage under a group health plan or health insurance coverage in which such individual was enrolled on the date of enactment of this Act.

(2) CONTINUATION OF COVERAGE.—With respect to a group health plan or health insurance coverage in which an individual was enrolled on the date of enactment of this Act, this subtitle and subtitle A (and the amendments made by such subtitles) shall not apply to such plan or coverage, regardless of whether the individual renews such coverage after such date of enactment.

(b) ALLOWANCE FOR FAMILY MEMBERS TO JOIN CURRENT COVERAGE.—With respect to a group health plan or health insurance coverage in which an individual was enrolled on the date of enactment of this Act and which is renewed after such date, family members of such individual shall be permitted to enroll in such plan or coverage if such enrollment is permitted under the terms of the plan in effect as of such date of enactment.

(c) ALLOWANCE FOR NEW EMPLOYEES TO JOIN CURRENT PLAN.—A group health plan that provides coverage on the date of enactment of this Act may provide for the enrolling of new employees (and their families) in such plan, and this subtitle and subtitle A (and the amendments made by such subtitles) shall not apply with respect to such plan and such new employees (and their families).

(d) EFFECT ON COLLECTIVE BARGAINING AGREEMENTS.—In the case of health insurance coverage maintained pursuant to one or more collective bargaining agreements between employee representatives and one or more employers that was ratified before the date of enactment of this Act, the provisions of this subtitle and subtitle A (and the amendments made by such subtitles) shall not apply until the date on which the last of the collective bargaining agreements relating to the coverage terminates. Any coverage amendment made pursuant to a collective bargaining agreement relating to the coverage which amends the coverage solely to conform to any requirement added by this subtitle or subtitle A (or amendments) shall not be treated as a termination of such collective bargaining agreement.

(e) DEFINITION.—In this title, the term "grandfathered health plan" means any group health plan or health insurance coverage to which this section applies.

SEC. 1252. RATING REFORMS MUST APPLY UNIFORMLY TO ALL HEALTH INSURANCE ISSUERS AND GROUP HEALTH PLANS.

Any standard or requirement adopted by a State pursuant to this title, or any amendment made by this title, shall be applied uniformly to all health plans in each insurance market to which the standard and requirements apply. The preceding sentence shall also apply to a State standard or requirement relating to the standard or requirement required by this title (or any such amendment) that is not the same as the standard or requirement but that is not preempted under section 1321(d).

SEC. 1253. EFFECTIVE DATES.

This subtitle (and the amendments made by this subtitle) shall become effective for plan years beginning on or after January 1, 2014.

Subtitle D—Available Coverage Choices for All Americans

PART I—ESTABLISHMENT OF QUALIFIED HEALTH PLANS

SEC. 1301. QUALIFIED HEALTH PLAN DEFINED.

(a) QUALIFIED HEALTH PLAN.—In this title:

(1) IN GENERAL.—The term "qualified health plan" means a health plan that—

(A) has in effect a certification (which may include a seal or other indication of approval) that such plan meets the criteria for certification described in section 1311(c) issued or recognized by each Exchange through which such plan is offered;

(B) provides the essential health benefits package described in section 1302(a); and

(C) is offered by a health insurance issuer that—

(i) is licensed and in good standing to offer health insurance coverage in each State in which such issuer offers health insurance coverage under this title;

(ii) agrees to offer at least one qualified health plan in the silver level and at least one plan in the gold level in each such Exchange;

(iii) agrees to charge the same premium rate for each qualified health plan of the issuer without regard to whether the plan is offered through an Exchange or whether the plan is offered directly from the issuer or through an agent; and

(iv) complies with the regulations developed by the Secretary under section 1311(d) and such other requirements as an applicable Exchange may establish.

(2) INCLUSION OF CO-OP PLANS AND COMMUNITY HEALTH INSURANCE OPTION.—Any reference in this title to a qualified health plan shall be deemed to include a qualified health plan offered through the CO-OP program under section 1322 or a community health insurance option under section 1323, unless specifically provided for otherwise.

(b) TERMS RELATING TO HEALTH PLANS.—In this title:

(1) HEALTH PLAN.—

(A) IN GENERAL.—The term "health plan" means health insurance coverage and a group health plan.

(B) EXCEPTION FOR SELF-INSURED PLANS AND MEWAS.—Except to the extent specifically provided by this title, the term "health plan" shall not include a group health plan or multiple employer welfare arrangement to the extent the plan or arrangement is not subject to State insurance regulation under section 514 of the Employee Retirement Income Security Act of 1974.

(2) HEALTH INSURANCE COVERAGE AND ISSUER.—The terms "health insurance coverage" and "health insurance issuer" have the meanings given such terms by section 2791(b) of the Public Health Service Act.

(3) GROUP HEALTH PLAN.—The term "group health plan" has the meaning given such term by section 2791(a) of the Public Health Service Act.

SEC. 1302. ESSENTIAL HEALTH BENEFITS REQUIREMENTS.

(a) ESSENTIAL HEALTH BENEFITS PACKAGE.—In this title, the term "essential health benefits package" means, with respect to any health plan, coverage that—

(1) provides for the essential health benefits defined by the Secretary under subsection (b);

(2) limits cost-sharing for such coverage in accordance with subsection (c); and

(3) subject to subsection (e), provides either the bronze, silver, gold, or platinum level of coverage described in subsection (d).

(b) ESSENTIAL HEALTH BENEFITS.—

(1) IN GENERAL.—Subject to paragraph (2), the Secretary shall define the essential health benefits, except that such benefits shall include at least the following general categories and the items and services covered within the categories:

(A) Ambulatory patient services.

(B) Emergency services.

(C) Hospitalization.

(D) Maternity and newborn care.

(E) Mental health and substance use disorder services, including behavioral health treatment.

(F) Prescription drugs.

(G) Rehabilitative and habilitative services and devices.

(H) Laboratory services.

(I) Preventive and wellness services and chronic disease management.

(J) Pediatric services, including oral and vision care.

(2) LIMITATION.—

(A) IN GENERAL.—The Secretary shall ensure that the scope of the essential health benefits under paragraph (1) is equal to the scope of benefits provided under a typical employer plan, as determined by the Secretary. To inform this determination, the Secretary of Labor shall conduct a survey of employer-sponsored coverage to determine the benefits typically covered by employers, including multiemployer plans, and provide a report on such survey to the Secretary.

(B) CERTIFICATION.—In defining the essential health benefits described in paragraph (1), and in revising the benefits under paragraph (4)(H), the Secretary shall submit a report to the appropriate committees of Congress containing a certification from the Chief Actuary of the Centers for Medicare & Medicaid Services that such essential health benefits meet the limitation described in paragraph (2).

(3) NOTICE AND HEARING.—In defining the essential health benefits described in paragraph (1), and in revising the benefits under paragraph (4)(H), the Secretary shall provide notice and an opportunity for public comment.

(4) REQUIRED ELEMENTS FOR CONSIDERATION.—In defining the essential health benefits under paragraph (1), the Secretary shall—

(A) ensure that such essential health benefits reflect an appropriate balance among the categories described in such subsection, so that benefits are not unduly weighted toward any category;

(B) not make coverage decisions, determine reimbursement rates, establish incentive programs, or design benefits in ways that discriminate against individuals because of their age, disability, or expected length of life;

(C) take into account the health care needs of diverse segments of the population, including women, children, persons with disabilities, and other groups;

(D) ensure that health benefits established as essential not be subject to denial to individuals against their wishes on the basis of the individuals' age or expected length of life or of the individuals' present or predicted disability, degree of medical dependency, or quality of life;

(E) provide that a qualified health plan shall not be treated as providing coverage for the essential health benefits described in paragraph (1) unless the plan provides that—

(i) coverage for emergency department services will be provided without imposing any requirement under the plan for prior authorization of services or any limitation on coverage where the provider of services does not have a contractual relationship with the plan for the providing of services that is more restrictive than the requirements or limitations that apply to emergency department services received from providers who do have such a contractual relationship with the plan; and

(ii) if such services are provided out-of-network, the cost-sharing requirement (expressed as a copayment amount or coinsurance rate) is the same requirement that would apply if such services were provided in-network;

(F) provide that if a plan described in section 1311(b)(2)(B)(ii) (relating to stand-alone dental benefits plans) is offered through an Exchange, another health plan offered through such Exchange shall not fail to be treated as a qualified health plan solely because the plan does not offer coverage of benefits offered through the stand-alone plan that are otherwise required under paragraph (1)(J); and

(G) periodically review the essential health benefits under paragraph (1), and provide a report to Congress and the public that contains—

(i) an assessment of whether enrollees are facing any difficulty accessing needed services for reasons of coverage or cost;

(ii) an assessment of whether the essential health benefits needs to be modified or updated to account for changes in medical evidence or scientific advancement;

(iii) information on how the essential health benefits will be modified to address any such gaps in access or changes in the evidence base;

(iv) an assessment of the potential of additional or expanded benefits to increase costs and the interactions between the addition or expansion of benefits and reductions in existing benefits to meet actuarial limitations described in paragraph (2); and

(H) periodically update the essential health benefits under paragraph (1) to address any gaps in access to coverage or changes in the evidence base the Secretary identifies in the review conducted under subparagraph (G).

(5) RULE OF CONSTRUCTION.—Nothing in this title shall be construed to prohibit a health plan from providing benefits in excess of the essential health benefits described in this subsection.

(c) REQUIREMENTS RELATING TO COST-SHARING.—

(1) ANNUAL LIMITATION ON COST-SHARING.—

(A) 2014.—The cost-sharing incurred under a health plan with respect to self-only coverage or coverage other than self-only coverage for a plan year beginning in 2014 shall not exceed the dollar amounts in effect under section 223(c)(2)(A)(ii) of the Internal Revenue Code of 1986 for self-only and family coverage, respectively, for taxable years beginning in 2014.

(B) 2015 AND LATER.—In the case of any plan year beginning in a calendar year after 2014, the limitation under this paragraph shall—

(i) in the case of self-only coverage, be equal to the dollar amount under subparagraph (A) for self-only coverage for plan years beginning in 2014, increased by an amount equal to the product of that amount and the premium adjustment percentage under paragraph (4) for the calendar year; and

(ii) in the case of other coverage, twice the amount in effect under clause (i).

If the amount of any increase under clause (i) is not a multiple of $50, such increase shall be rounded to the next lowest multiple of $50.

(2) ANNUAL LIMITATION ON DEDUCTIBLES FOR EMPLOYER-SPONSORED PLANS.—

(A) IN GENERAL.—In the case of a health plan offered in the small group market, the deductible under the plan shall not exceed—

(i) $2,000 in the case of a plan covering a single individual; and

(ii) $4,000 in the case of any other plan.

The amounts under clauses (i) and (ii) may be increased by the maximum amount of reimbursement which is reasonably available to a participant under a flexible spending arrangement described in section 106(c)(2) of the Internal Revenue Code of 1986 (determined without regard to any salary reduction arrangement).

(B) INDEXING OF LIMITS.—In the case of any plan year beginning in a calendar year after 2014—

(i) the dollar amount under subparagraph (A)(i) shall be increased by an amount equal to the product of that amount and the premium adjustment percentage under paragraph (4) for the calendar year; and

(ii) the dollar amount under subparagraph (A)(ii) shall be increased to an amount equal to twice the amount in effect under subparagraph (A)(i) for plan years beginning in the calendar year, determined after application of clause (i).

If the amount of any increase under clause (i) is not a multiple of $50, such increase shall be rounded to the next lowest multiple of $50.

(C) ACTUARIAL VALUE.—The limitation under this paragraph shall be applied in such a manner so as to not affect the actuarial value of any health plan, including a plan in the bronze level.

(D) COORDINATION WITH PREVENTIVE LIMITS.—Nothing in this paragraph shall be construed to allow a plan to have a deductible under the plan apply to benefits described in section 2713 of the Public Health Service Act.

(3) COST-SHARING.—In this title—

(A) IN GENERAL.—The term "cost-sharing" includes—

(i) deductibles, coinsurance, copayments, or similar charges; and

(ii) any other expenditure required of an insured individual which is a qualified medical expense (within the meaning of section 223(d)(2) of the Internal Revenue Code of 1986) with respect to essential health benefits covered under the plan.

(B) EXCEPTIONS.—Such term does not include premiums, balance billing amounts for non-network providers, or spending for non-covered services.

(4) PREMIUM ADJUSTMENT PERCENTAGE.—For purposes of paragraphs (1)(B)(i) and (2)(B)(i), the premium adjustment percentage for any calendar year is the percentage (if any) by which the average per capita premium for health insurance coverage in the United States for the preceding calendar year (as estimated by the Secretary no later than October 1 of such preceding calendar year) exceeds such average per capita premium for 2013 (as determined by the Secretary).

(d) LEVELS OF COVERAGE.—

(1) LEVELS OF COVERAGE DEFINED.—The levels of coverage described in this subsection are as follows:

(A) BRONZE LEVEL.—A plan in the bronze level shall provide a level of coverage that is designed to provide benefits that are actuarially equivalent to 60 percent of the full actuarial value of the benefits provided under the plan.

(B) SILVER LEVEL.—A plan in the silver level shall provide a level of coverage that is designed to provide benefits that are actuarially equivalent to 70 percent of the full actuarial value of the benefits provided under the plan.

(C) GOLD LEVEL.—A plan in the gold level shall provide a level of coverage that is designed to provide benefits that are actuarially equivalent to 80 percent of the full actuarial value of the benefits provided under the plan.

(D) PLATINUM LEVEL.—A plan in the platinum level shall provide a level of coverage that is designed to provide benefits that are actuarially equivalent to 90 percent of the full actuarial value of the benefits provided under the plan.

(2) ACTUARIAL VALUE.—

(A) IN GENERAL.—Under regulations issued by the Secretary, the level of coverage of a plan shall be determined on the basis that the essential health benefits described in subsection (b) shall be provided to a standard population (and without regard to the population the plan may actually provide benefits to).

(B) EMPLOYER CONTRIBUTIONS.—The Secretary may issue regulations under which employer contributions to a health savings account (within the meaning of section 223 of the Internal Revenue Code of 1986) may be taken into account in determining the level of coverage for a plan of the employer.

(C) APPLICATION.—In determining under this title, the Public Health Service Act, or the Internal Revenue Code of 1986 the percentage of the total allowed costs of benefits provided under a group health plan or health insurance coverage that are provided by such plan or coverage, the rules contained in the regulations under this paragraph shall apply.

(3) ALLOWABLE VARIANCE.—The Secretary shall develop guidelines to provide for a de minimis variation in the actuarial valuations used in determining the level of coverage of a plan to account for differences in actuarial estimates.

(4) PLAN REFERENCE.—In this title, any reference to a bronze, silver, gold, or platinum plan shall be treated as a reference to a qualified health plan providing a bronze, silver, gold, or platinum level of coverage, as the case may be.

(e) CATASTROPHIC PLAN.—

(1) IN GENERAL.—A health plan not providing a bronze, silver, gold, or platinum level of coverage shall be treated as meeting the requirements of subsection (d) with respect to any plan year if—

(A) the only individuals who are eligible to enroll in the plan are individuals described in paragraph (2); and

(B) the plan provides—

(i) except as provided in clause (ii), the essential health benefits determined under subsection (b), except that the plan provides no benefits for any plan year until the individual has incurred cost-sharing expenses in an amount equal to the annual limitation in effect under subsection (c)(1) for the plan year (except as provided for in section 2713); and

(ii) coverage for at least three primary care visits.

(2) INDIVIDUALS ELIGIBLE FOR ENROLLMENT.—An individual is described in this paragraph for any plan year if the individual—

(A) has not attained the age of 30 before the beginning of the plan year; or

(B) has a certification in effect for any plan year under this title that the individual is exempt from the requirement under section 5000A of the Internal Revenue Code of 1986 by reason of—

(i) section 5000A(e)(1) of such Code (relating to individuals without affordable coverage); or

(ii) section 5000A(e)(5) of such Code (relating to individuals with hardships).

(3) RESTRICTION TO INDIVIDUAL MARKET.—If a health insurance issuer offers a health plan described in this subsection, the issuer may only offer the plan in the individual market.

(f) CHILD-ONLY PLANS.—If a qualified health plan is offered through the Exchange in any level of coverage specified under subsection (d), the issuer shall also offer that plan through the Exchange in that level as a plan in which the only enrollees are individuals who, as of the beginning of a plan year, have not attained the age of 21, and such plan shall be treated as a qualified health plan.

SEC. 1303. SPECIAL RULES.

(a) SPECIAL RULES RELATING TO COVERAGE OF ABORTION SERVICES.—

(1) VOLUNTARY CHOICE OF COVERAGE OF ABORTION SERVICES.—

(A) IN GENERAL.—Notwithstanding any other provision of this title (or any amendment made by this title), and subject to subparagraphs (C) and (D)—

(i) nothing in this title (or any amendment made by this title), shall be construed to require a qualified health plan to provide coverage of services described in subparagraph (B)(i) or (B)(ii) as part of its essential health benefits for any plan year; and

(ii) the issuer of a qualified health plan shall determine whether or not the plan provides coverage of services described in subparagraph (B)(i) or (B)(ii) as part of such benefits for the plan year.

(B) ABORTION SERVICES.—

(i) ABORTIONS FOR WHICH PUBLIC FUNDING IS PROHIBITED.—The services described in this clause are abortions for which the expenditure of Federal funds appropriated for the Department of Health and Human Services is not permitted, based on the law as in effect as of the date that is 6 months before the beginning of the plan year involved.

(ii) ABORTIONS FOR WHICH PUBLIC FUNDING IS ALLOWED.—The services described in this clause are abortions for which the expenditure of Federal funds appropriated for the Department of Health and Human Services is permitted, based on the law as in effect as of the date that is 6 months before the beginning of the plan year involved.

(C) PROHIBITION ON FEDERAL FUNDS FOR ABORTION SERVICES IN COMMUNITY HEALTH INSURANCE OPTION.—

(i) DETERMINATION BY SECRETARY.—The Secretary may not determine, in accordance with subparagraph (A)(ii), that the community health insurance option established under section 1323 shall provide coverage of services described in subparagraph (B)(i) as part of benefits for the plan year unless the Secretary—

(I) assures compliance with the requirements of paragraph (2);

(II) assures, in accordance with applicable provisions of generally accepted accounting requirements, circulars on funds management of the Office of Management and Budget, and guidance on accounting of the Government Accountability Office, that no Federal funds are used for such coverage; and

(III) notwithstanding section 1323(e)(1)(C) or any other provision of this title, takes all necessary steps to assure that the United States does not bear the insurance risk for a community health insurance option's coverage of services described in subparagraph (B)(i).

(ii) STATE REQUIREMENT.—If a State requires, in addition to the essential health benefits required under section 1323(b)(3) (A), coverage of services described in subparagraph (B)(i) for enrollees of a community health insurance option offered in such State, the State shall assure that no funds flowing through or from the community health insurance option, and no other Federal funds, pay or defray the cost of providing coverage of services described in subparagraph (B)(i). The United States shall not bear the insurance risk for a State's required coverage of services described in subparagraph (B)(i).

(iii) EXCEPTIONS.—Nothing in this subparagraph shall apply to coverage of services described in subparagraph (B)(ii) by the community health insurance option. Services described in subparagraph (B)(ii) shall be covered to the same extent as such services are covered under title XIX of the Social Security Act.

(D) ASSURED AVAILABILITY OF VARIED COVERAGE THROUGH EXCHANGES.—

(i) IN GENERAL.—The Secretary shall assure that with respect to qualified health plans offered in any Exchange established pursuant to this title—

(I) there is at least one such plan that provides coverage of services described in clauses (i) and (ii) of subparagraph (B); and

(II) there is at least one such plan that does not provide coverage of services described in subparagraph (B)(i).

(ii) SPECIAL RULES.—For purposes of clause (i)—

(I) a plan shall be treated as described in clause (i)(II) if the plan does not provide coverage of services described in either subparagraph (B)(i) or (B)(ii); and

(II) if a State has one Exchange covering more than 1 insurance market, the Secretary shall meet the requirements of clause (i) separately with respect to each such market.

(2) PROHIBITION ON THE USE OF FEDERAL FUNDS.—

(A) IN GENERAL.—If a qualified health plan provides coverage of services described in paragraph (1)(B)(i), the issuer of the plan shall not use any amount attributable to any of the following for purposes of paying for such services:

(i) The credit under section 36B of the Internal Revenue Code of 1986 (and the amount (if any) of the advance payment of the credit under section 1412 of the Patient Protection and Affordable Care Act).

(ii) Any cost-sharing reduction under section 1402 of thePatient Protection and Affordable Care Act (and the amount (if any) of the advance payment of the reduction under section 1412 of the Patient Protection and Affordable Care Act).

(B) SEGREGATION OF FUNDS.—In the case of a plan to which subparagraph (A) applies, the issuer of the plan shall, out of amounts not described in subparagraph (A), segregate an amount equal to the actuarial amounts determined under subparagraph (C) for all enrollees from the amounts described in subparagraph (A).

(C) ACTUARIAL VALUE OF OPTIONAL SERVICE COVERAGE.—

(i) IN GENERAL.—The Secretary shall estimate the basic per enrollee, per month cost, determined on an average actuarial basis, for including coverage under a qualified health plan of the services described in paragraph (1)(B)(i).

(ii) CONSIDERATIONS.—In making such estimate, the Secretary—

(I) may take into account the impact on overall costs of the inclusion of such coverage, but may not take into account any cost reduction estimated to result from such services, including prenatal care, delivery, or postnatal care;

(II) shall estimate such costs as if such coverage were included for the entire population covered; and

(III) may not estimate such a cost at less than $1 per enrollee, per month.

(3) PROVIDER CONSCIENCE PROTECTIONS.—No individual health care provider or health care facility may be discriminated against because of a willingness or an unwillingness, if doing so is contrary to the religious or moral beliefs of the provider or facility, to provide, pay for, provide coverage of, or refer for abortions.

(b) APPLICATION OF STATE AND FEDERAL LAWS REGARDING ABORTION.—

(1) NO PREEMPTION OF STATE LAWS REGARDING ABORTION.—Nothing in this Act shall be construed to preempt or otherwise have any effect on State laws regarding the prohibition of (or requirement of) coverage, funding, or procedural requirements on abortions, including parental notification or consent for the performance of an abortion on a minor.

(2) NO EFFECT ON FEDERAL LAWS REGARDING ABORTION.—

(A) IN GENERAL.—Nothing in this Act shall be construed to have any effect on Federal laws regarding—

(i) conscience protection;

(ii) willingness or refusal to provide abortion; and

(iii) discrimination on the basis of the willingness or refusal to provide, pay for, cover, or refer for abortion or to provide or participate in training to provide abortion.

(3) NO EFFECT ON FEDERAL CIVIL RIGHTS LAW.—Nothing in this subsection shall alter the rights and obligations of employees and employers under title VII of the Civil Rights Act of 1964.

(c) APPLICATION OF EMERGENCY SERVICES LAWS.—Nothing in this Act shall be construed to relieve any health care provider from providing emergency services as required by State or Federal law, including section 1867 of the Social Security Act (popularly known as "EMTALA").

SEC. 1304. RELATED DEFINITIONS.

(a) DEFINITIONS RELATING TO MARKETS.—In this title:

(1) GROUP MARKET.—The term "group market" means the health insurance market under which individuals obtain health insurance coverage (directly or through any arrangement) on behalf of themselves (and their dependents) through a group health plan maintained by an employer.

(2) INDIVIDUAL MARKET.—The term "individual market" means the market for health insurance coverage offered to individuals other than in connection with a group health plan.

(3) LARGE AND SMALL GROUP MARKETS.—The terms "large group market" and "small group market" mean the health insurance market under which individuals obtain health insurance coverage (directly or through any arrangement) on behalf of themselves (and their dependents) through a group health plan maintained by a large employer (as defined in subsection

(b)(1)) or by a small employer (as defined in subsection (b)(2)), respectively.

(b) EMPLOYERS.—In this title:

(1) LARGE EMPLOYER.—The term "large employer" means, in connection with a group health plan with respect to a calendar year and a plan year, an employer who employed an average of at least 101 employees on business days during the preceding calendar year and who employs at least 1 employee on the first day of the plan year.

(2) SMALL EMPLOYER.—The term "small employer" means, in connection with a group health plan with respect to a calendar year and a plan year, an employer who employed an average of at least 1 but not more than 100 employees on business days during the preceding calendar year and who employs at least 1 employee on the first day of the plan year.

(3) STATE OPTION TO TREAT 50 EMPLOYEES AS SMALL.—In the case of plan years beginning before January 1, 2016, a State may elect to apply this subsection by substituting "51 employees" for "101 employees" in paragraph (1) and by substituting "50 employees" for "100 employees" in paragraph (2).

(4) RULES FOR DETERMINING EMPLOYER SIZE.—For purposes of this subsection—

(A) APPLICATION OF AGGREGATION RULE FOR EMPLOYERS.—All persons treated as a single employer under subsection (b), (c), (m), or (o) of section 414 of the Internal Revenue Code of 1986 shall be treated as 1 employer.

(B) EMPLOYERS NOT IN EXISTENCE IN PRECEDING YEAR.—In the case of an employer which was not in existence throughout the preceding calendar year, the determination of whether such employer is a small or large employer shall be based on the average number of employees that it is reasonably expected such employer will employ on business days in the current calendar year.

(C) PREDECESSORS.—Any reference in this subsection to an employer shall include a reference to any predecessor of such employer.

(D) CONTINUATION OF PARTICIPATION FOR GROWING SMALL EMPLOYERS.—If—

(i) a qualified employer that is a small employer makes enrollment in qualified health plans offered in the small group market available to its employees through an Exchange; and

(ii) the employer ceases to be a small employer by reason of an increase in the number of employees of such employer;

the employer shall continue to be treated as a small employer for purposes of this subtitle for the period beginning with the increase and ending with the first day on which the employer does not make such enrollment available to its employees.

(c) SECRETARY.—In this title, the term "Secretary" means the Secretary of Health and Human Services.

(d) STATE.—In this title, the term "State" means each of the 50 States and the District of Columbia.

PART II—CONSUMER CHOICES AND INSURANCE COMPETITION THROUGH HEALTH BENEFIT EXCHANGES

SEC. 1311. AFFORDABLE CHOICES OF HEALTH BENEFIT PLANS.

(a) ASSISTANCE TO STATES TO ESTABLISH AMERICAN HEALTH BENEFIT EXCHANGES.—

(1) PLANNING AND ESTABLISHMENT GRANTS.—There shall be appropriated to the Secretary, out of any moneys in the Treasury not otherwise appropriated, an amount necessary to enable the Secretary to make awards, not later than 1 year after the date of enactment of this Act, to States in the amount specified in paragraph (2) for the uses described in paragraph (3).

(2) AMOUNT SPECIFIED.—For each fiscal year, the Secretary shall determine the total amount that the Secretary will make available to each State for grants under this subsection.

(3) USE OF FUNDS.—A State shall use amounts awarded under this subsection for activities (including planning activities) related to establishing an American Health Benefit Exchange, as described in subsection (b).

(4) RENEWABILITY OF GRANT.—

(A) IN GENERAL.—Subject to subsection (d)(4), the Secretary may renew a grant awarded under paragraph (1) if the State recipient of such grant—

(i) is making progress, as determined by the Secretary, toward—

(I) establishing an Exchange; and

(II) implementing the reforms described in subtitles A and C (and the amendments made by such subtitles); and

(ii) is meeting such other benchmarks as the Secretary may establish.

(B) LIMITATION.—No grant shall be awarded under this subsection after January 1, 2015.

(5) TECHNICAL ASSISTANCE TO FACILITATE PARTICIPATION IN SHOP EXCHANGES.—The Secretary shall provide technical assistance to States to facilitate the participation of qualified small businesses in such States in SHOP Exchanges.

(b) AMERICAN HEALTH BENEFIT EXCHANGES.—

(1) IN GENERAL.—Each State shall, not later than January 1, 2014, establish an American Health Benefit Exchange (referred to in this title as an "Exchange") for the State that—

(A) facilitates the purchase of qualified health plans;

(B) provides for the establishment of a Small Business Health Options Program (in this title referred to as a "SHOP Exchange") that is designed to assist qualified employers in the State who are small employers in facilitating the enrollment of their employees in qualified health plans offered in the small group market in the State; and

(C) meets the requirements of subsection (d).

(2) MERGER OF INDIVIDUAL AND SHOP EXCHANGES.—A State may elect to provide only one Exchange in the State for providing both Exchange and SHOP Exchange services to both qualified individuals and qualified small employers, but only

if the Exchange has adequate resources to assist such individuals and employers.

(c) RESPONSIBILITIES OF THE SECRETARY.—

(1) IN GENERAL.—The Secretary shall, by regulation, establish criteria for the certification of health plans as qualified health plans. Such criteria shall require that, to be certified, a plan shall, at a minimum—

(A) meet marketing requirements, and not employ marketing practices or benefit designs that have the effect of discouraging the enrollment in such plan by individuals with significant health needs;

(B) ensure a sufficient choice of providers (in a manner consistent with applicable network adequacy provisions under section 2702(c) of the Public Health Service Act), and provide information to enrollees and prospective enrollees on the availability of in-network and out-of-network providers;

(C) include within health insurance plan networks those essential community providers, where available, that serve predominately low-income, medically-underserved individuals, such as health care providers defined in section 340B(a)(4) of the Public Health Service Act and providers described in section 1927(c)(1)(D)(i)(IV) of the Social Security Act as set forth by section 221 of Public Law 111–8, except that nothing in this subparagraph shall be construed to require any health plan to provide coverage for any specific medical procedure;

(D)(i) be accredited with respect to local performance on clinical quality measures such as the Healthcare Effectiveness Data and Information Set, patient experience ratings on a standardized Consumer Assessment of Healthcare Providers and Systems survey, as well as consumer access, utilization management, quality assurance, provider credentialing, complaints and appeals, network adequacy and access, and patient information programs by any entity recognized by the Secretary for the accreditation of health insurance issuers or plans (so long as any such entity has transparent and rigorous methodological and scoring criteria); or

(ii) receive such accreditation within a period established by an Exchange for such accreditation that is applicable to all qualified health plans;

(E) implement a quality improvement strategy described in subsection (g)(1);

(F) utilize a uniform enrollment form that qualified individuals and qualified employers may use (either electronically or on paper) in enrolling in qualified health plans offered through such Exchange, and that takes into account criteria that the National Association of Insurance Commissioners develops and submits to the Secretary;

(G) utilize the standard format established for presenting health benefits plan options; and

(H) provide information to enrollees and prospective enrollees, and to each Exchange in which the plan is offered, on any quality measures for health plan performance endorsed under section 399JJ of the Public Health Service Act, as applicable.

(2) RULE OF CONSTRUCTION.—Nothing in paragraph (1)(C) shall be construed to require a qualified health plan to contract with a provider described in such paragraph if such provider refuses to accept the generally applicable payment rates of such plan.

(3) RATING SYSTEM.—The Secretary shall develop a rating system that would rate qualified health plans offered through an Exchange in each benefits level on the basis of the relative quality and price. The Exchange shall include the quality rating in the information provided to individuals and employers through the Internet portal established under paragraph (4).

(4) ENROLLEE SATISFACTION SYSTEM.—The Secretary shall develop an enrollee satisfaction survey system that would evaluate the level of enrollee satisfaction with qualified health plans offered through an Exchange, for each such qualified health plan that had more than 500 enrollees in the previous year. The Exchange shall include enrollee satisfaction information in the information provided to individuals and employers through the Internet portal established under paragraph (5) in a manner that allows individuals to easily compare enrollee satisfaction levels between comparable plans.

(5) INTERNET PORTALS.—The Secretary shall—

(A) continue to operate, maintain, and update the Internet portal developed under section 1103(a) and to assist States in developing and maintaining their own such portal; and

(B) make available for use by Exchanges a model template for an Internet portal that may be used to direct qualified individuals and qualified employers to qualified health plans, to assist such individuals and employers in determining whether they are eligible to participate in an Exchange or eligible for a premium tax credit or cost-sharing reduction, and to present standardized information (including quality ratings) regarding qualified health plans offered through an Exchange to assist consumers in making easy health insurance choices.

Such template shall include, with respect to each qualified health plan offered through the Exchange in each rating area, access to the uniform outline of coverage the plan is required to provide under section 2716 of the Public Health Service Act and to a copy of the plan's written policy.

(6) ENROLLMENT PERIODS.—The Secretary shall require an Exchange to provide for—

(A) an initial open enrollment, as determined by the Secretary (such determination to be made not later than July 1, 2012);

(B) annual open enrollment periods, as determined by the Secretary for calendar years after the initial enrollment period;

(C) special enrollment periods specified in section 9801 of the Internal Revenue Code of 1986 and other special enrollment periods under circumstances similar to such periods under part D of title XVIII of the Social Security Act; and

(D) special monthly enrollment periods for Indians (as defined in section 4 of the Indian Health Care Improvement Act).

(d) REQUIREMENTS.—

(1) IN GENERAL.—An Exchange shall be a governmental agency or nonprofit entity that is established by a State.

(2) OFFERING OF COVERAGE.—

(A) IN GENERAL.—An Exchange shall make available qualified health plans to qualified individuals and qualified employers.

(B) LIMITATION.—

(i) IN GENERAL.—An Exchange may not make available any health plan that is not a qualified health plan.

(ii) OFFERING OF STAND-ALONE DENTAL BENEFITS.— Each Exchange within a State shall allow an issuer of a plan that only provides limited scope dental benefits meeting the requirements of section 9832(c)(2)(A) of the Internal Revenue Code of 1986 to offer the plan through the Exchange (either separately or in conjunction with a qualified health plan) if the plan provides pediatric dental benefits meeting the requirements of section 1302(b)(1)(J)).

(3) RULES RELATING TO ADDITIONAL REQUIRED BENEFITS.—

(A) IN GENERAL.—Except as provided in subparagraph (B), an Exchange may make available a qualified health plan notwithstanding any provision of law that may require benefits other than the essential health benefits specified under section 1302(b).

(B) STATES MAY REQUIRE ADDITIONAL BENEFITS.—

(i) IN GENERAL.—Subject to the requirements of clause (ii), a State may require that a qualified health plan offered in such State offer benefits in addition to the essential health benefits specified under section 1302(b).

(ii) STATE MUST ASSUME COST.—A State shall make payments to or on behalf of an individual eligible for the premium tax credit under section 36B of the Internal Revenue Code of 1986 and any cost-sharing reduction under section 1402 to defray the cost to the individual of any additional benefits described in clause (i) which are not eligible for such credit or reduction under section 36B(b)(3)(D) of such Code and section 1402(c)(4).

(4) FUNCTIONS.—An Exchange shall, at a minimum—

(A) implement procedures for the certification, recertification, and decertification, consistent with guidelines developed by the Secretary under subsection (c), of health plans as qualified health plans;

(B) provide for the operation of a toll-free telephone hotline to respond to requests for assistance;

(C) maintain an Internet website through which enrollees and prospective enrollees of qualified health plans may obtain standardized comparative information on such plans;

(D) assign a rating to each qualified health plan offered through such Exchange in accordance with the criteria developed by the Secretary under subsection (c)(3);

(E) utilize a standardized format for presenting health benefits plan options in the Exchange, including the use of the uniform outline of coverage established under section 2715 of the Public Health Service Act;

(F) in accordance with section 1413, inform individuals of eligibility requirements for the medicaid program under title XIX of the Social Security Act, the CHIP program under title XXI of such Act, or any applicable State or local public program and if through screening of the application by the Exchange, the Exchange determines that such individuals are eligible for any such program, enroll such individuals in such program;

(G) establish and make available by electronic means a calculator to determine the actual cost of coverage after the application of any premium tax credit under section 36B of the Internal Revenue Code of 1986 and any cost-sharing reduction under section 1402;

(H) subject to section 1411, grant a certification attesting that, for purposes of the individual responsibility penalty under section 5000A of the Internal Revenue Code of 1986, an individual is exempt from the individual requirement or from the penalty imposed by such section because—

(i) there is no affordable qualified health plan available through the Exchange, or the individual's employer, covering the individual; or

(ii) the individual meets the requirements for any other such exemption from the individual responsibility requirement or penalty;

(I) transfer to the Secretary of the Treasury—

(i) a list of the individuals who are issued a certification under subparagraph (H), including the name and taxpayer identification number of each individual;

(ii) the name and taxpayer identification number of each individual who was an employee of an employer but who was determined to be eligible for the premium tax credit under section 36B of the Internal Revenue Code of 1986 because—

(I) the employer did not provide minimum essential coverage; or

(II) the employer provided such minimum essential coverage but it was determined under section 36B(c)(2)(C) of such Code to either be unaffordable to the employee or not provide the required minimum actuarial value; and

(iii) the name and taxpayer identification number of each individual who notifies the Exchange under section 1411(b)(4) that they have changed employers and of each individual who ceases coverage under a qualified health plan during a plan year (and the effective date of such cessation);

(J) provide to each employer the name of each employee of the employer described in subparagraph (I)(ii) who ceases coverage under a qualified health plan during a plan year (and the effective date of such cessation); and

(K) establish the Navigator program described in subsection (i).

(5) FUNDING LIMITATIONS.—

(A) NO FEDERAL FUNDS FOR CONTINUED OPERATIONS.—In establishing an Exchange under this section, the State shall ensure that such Exchange is self-sustaining beginning on January 1, 2015, including allowing the Exchange to charge assessments or user fees to participating health insurance issuers, or to otherwise generate funding, to support its operations.

(B) PROHIBITING WASTEFUL USE OF FUNDS.—In carrying out activities under this subsection, an Exchange shall not utilize any funds intended for the administrative and operational expenses of the Exchange for staff retreats, promotional giveaways, excessive executive compensation, or promotion of Federal or State legislative and regulatory modifications.

(6) CONSULTATION.—An Exchange shall consult with stakeholders relevant to carrying out the activities under this section, including—

(A) health care consumers who are enrollees in qualified health plans;

(B) individuals and entities with experience in facilitating enrollment in qualified health plans;

(C) representatives of small businesses and self-employed individuals;

(D) State Medicaid offices; and

(E) advocates for enrolling hard to reach populations.

(7) PUBLICATION OF COSTS.—An Exchange shall publish the average costs of licensing, regulatory fees, and any other payments required by the Exchange, and the administrative costs of such Exchange, on an Internet website to educate consumers on such costs. Such information shall also include monies lost to waste, fraud, and abuse.

(e) CERTIFICATION.—

(1) IN GENERAL.—An Exchange may certify a health plan as a qualified health plan if—

(A) such health plan meets the requirements for certification as promulgated by the Secretary under subsection (c)(1); and

(B) the Exchange determines that making available such health plan through such Exchange is in the interests of qualified individuals and qualified employers in the State or States in which such Exchange operates, except that the Exchange may not exclude a health plan—

(i) on the basis that such plan is a fee-for-service plan;

(ii) through the imposition of premium price controls; or

(iii) on the basis that the plan provides treatments necessary to prevent patients' deaths in circumstances the Exchange determines are inappropriate or too costly.

(2) PREMIUM CONSIDERATIONS.—The Exchange shall require health plans seeking certification as qualified health plans to submit a justification for any premium increase prior to implementation of the increase. Such plans shall prominently post such information on their websites. The Exchange may take this information, and the information and the recommendations provided to the Exchange by the State under

section 2794(b)(1) of the Public Health Service Act (relating to patterns or practices of excessive or unjustified premium increases), into consideration when determining whether to make such health plan available through the Exchange. The Exchange shall take into account any excess of premium growth outside the Exchange as compared to the rate of such growth inside the Exchange, including information reported by the States.

(f) FLEXIBILITY.—

(1) REGIONAL OR OTHER INTERSTATE EXCHANGES.—An Exchange may operate in more than one State if—

(A) each State in which such Exchange operates permits such operation; and

(B) the Secretary approves such regional or interstate Exchange.

(2) SUBSIDIARY EXCHANGES.—A State may establish one or more subsidiary Exchanges if—

(A) each such Exchange serves a geographically distinct area; and

(B) the area served by each such Exchange is at least as large as a rating area described in section 2701(a) of the Public Health Service Act.

(3) AUTHORITY TO CONTRACT.—

(A) IN GENERAL.—A State may elect to authorize an Exchange established by the State under this section to enter into an agreement with an eligible entity to carry out 1 or more responsibilities of the Exchange.

(B) ELIGIBLE ENTITY.—In this paragraph, the term "eligible entity" means—

(i) a person—

(I) incorporated under, and subject to the laws of, 1 or more States;

(II) that has demonstrated experience on a State or regional basis in the individual and small group health insurance markets and in benefits coverage; and

(III) that is not a health insurance issuer or that is treated under subsection (a) or (b) of section 52 of the Internal Revenue Code of 1986 as a member of the same controlled group of corporations (or under common control with) as a health insurance issuer; or

(ii) the State medicaid agency under title XIX of the Social Security Act.

(g) REWARDING QUALITY THROUGH MARKET-BASED INCENTIVES.—

(1) STRATEGY DESCRIBED.—A strategy described in this paragraph is a payment structure that provides increased reimbursement or other incentives for—

(A) improving health outcomes through the implementation of activities that shall include quality reporting, effective case management, care coordination, chronic disease management, medication and care compliance initiatives, including through the use of the medical home model, for treatment or services under the plan or coverage;

(B) the implementation of activities to prevent hospital readmissions through a comprehensive program for hospital discharge that includes patient-centered education and counseling, comprehensive discharge planning, and post discharge reinforcement by an appropriate health care professional;

(C) the implementation of activities to improve patient safety and reduce medical errors through the appropriate use of best clinical practices, evidence based medicine, and health information technology under the plan or coverage; and

(D) the implementation of wellness and health promotion activities.

(2) GUIDELINES.—The Secretary, in consultation with experts in health care quality and stakeholders, shall develop guidelines concerning the matters described in paragraph (1).

(3) REQUIREMENTS.—The guidelines developed under paragraph (2) shall require the periodic reporting to the applicable Exchange of the activities that a qualified health plan has conducted to implement a strategy described in paragraph (1).

(h) QUALITY IMPROVEMENT.—

(1) ENHANCING PATIENT SAFETY.—Beginning on January 1, 2015, a qualified health plan may contract with—

(A) a hospital with greater than 50 beds only if such hospital—

(i) utilizes a patient safety evaluation system as described in part C of title IX of the Public Health Service Act; and

(ii) implements a mechanism to ensure that each patient receives a comprehensive program for hospital discharge that includes patient-centered education and counseling, comprehensive discharge planning, and post discharge reinforcement by an appropriate health care professional; or

(B) a health care provider only if such provider implements such mechanisms to improve health care quality as the Secretary may by regulation require.

(2) EXCEPTIONS.—The Secretary may establish reasonable exceptions to the requirements described in paragraph (1).

(3) ADJUSTMENT.—The Secretary may by regulation adjust the number of beds described in paragraph (1)(A).

(i) NAVIGATORS.—

(1) IN GENERAL.—An Exchange shall establish a program under which it awards grants to entities described in paragraph (2) to carry out the duties described in paragraph (3).

(2) ELIGIBILITY.—

(A) IN GENERAL.—To be eligible to receive a grant under paragraph (1), an entity shall demonstrate to the Exchange involved that the entity has existing relationships, or could readily establish relationships, with employers and employees, consumers (including uninsured and underinsured consumers), or self-employed individuals likely to be qualified to enroll in a qualified health plan.

(B) TYPES.—Entities described in subparagraph (A) may include trade, industry, and professional associations, commercial fishing industry organizations, ranching and farming organizations, community and consumer-focused nonprofit groups, chambers of commerce, unions, small business development centers, other licensed insurance agents and brokers, and other entities that—

(i) are capable of carrying out the duties described in paragraph (3);

(ii) meet the standards described in paragraph (4); and

(iii) provide information consistent with the standards developed under paragraph (5).

(3) DUTIES.—An entity that serves as a navigator under a grant under this subsection shall—

(A) conduct public education activities to raise awareness of the availability of qualified health plans;

(B) distribute fair and impartial information concerning enrollment in qualified health plans, and the availability of premium tax credits under section 36B of the Internal Revenue Code of 1986 and cost-sharing reductions under section 1402;

(C) facilitate enrollment in qualified health plans;

(D) provide referrals to any applicable office of health insurance consumer assistance or health insurance ombudsman established under section 2793 of the Public Health Service Act, or any other appropriate State agency or agencies, for any enrollee with a grievance, complaint, or question regarding their health plan, coverage, or a determination under such plan or coverage; and

(E) provide information in a manner that is culturally and linguistically appropriate to the needs of the population being served by the Exchange or Exchanges.

(4) STANDARDS.—

(A) IN GENERAL.—The Secretary shall establish standards for navigators under this subsection, including provisions to ensure that any private or public entity that is selected as a navigator is qualified, and licensed if appropriate, to engage in the navigator activities described in this subsection and to avoid conflicts of interest. Under such standards, a navigator shall not—

(i) be a health insurance issuer; or

(ii) receive any consideration directly or indirectly from any health insurance issuer in connection with the enrollment of any qualified individuals or employees of a qualified employer in a qualified health plan.

(5) FAIR AND IMPARTIAL INFORMATION AND SERVICES.—The Secretary, in collaboration with States, shall develop standards to ensure that information made available by navigators is fair, accurate, and impartial.

(6) FUNDING.—Grants under this subsection shall be made from the operational funds of the Exchange and not Federal funds received by the State to establish the Exchange.

(j) APPLICABILITY OF MENTAL HEALTH PARITY.—Section 2726 of the Public Health Service Act shall apply to qualified health plans in the same manner and to the same extent as such section applies to health insurance issuers and group health plans.

(k) CONFLICT.—An Exchange may not establish rules that conflict with or prevent the application of regulations promulgated by the Secretary under this subtitle.

SEC. 1312. CONSUMER CHOICE.

(a) CHOICE.—

(1) QUALIFIED INDIVIDUALS.—A qualified individual may enroll in any qualified health plan available to such individual.

(2) QUALIFIED EMPLOYERS.—

(A) EMPLOYER MAY SPECIFY LEVEL.—A qualified employer may provide support for coverage of employees under a qualified health plan by selecting any level of coverage under section 1302(d) to be made available to employees through an Exchange.

(B) EMPLOYEE MAY CHOOSE PLANS WITHIN A LEVEL.—Each employee of a qualified employer that elects a level of coverage under subparagraph (A) may choose to enroll in a qualified health plan that offers coverage at that level.

(b) PAYMENT OF PREMIUMS BY QUALIFIED INDIVIDUALS.—A qualified individual enrolled in any qualified health plan may pay any applicable premium owed by such individual to the health insurance issuer issuing such qualified health plan.

(c) SINGLE RISK POOL.—

(1) INDIVIDUAL MARKET.—A health insurance issuer shall consider all enrollees in all health plans (other than grandfathered health plans) offered by such issuer in the individual market, including those enrollees who do not enroll in such plans through the Exchange, to be members of a single risk pool.

(2) SMALL GROUP MARKET.—A health insurance issuer shall consider all enrollees in all health plans (other than grandfathered health plans) offered by such issuer in the small group market, including those enrollees who do not enroll in such plans through the Exchange, to be members of a single risk pool.

(3) MERGER OF MARKETS.—A State may require the individual and small group insurance markets within a State to be merged if the State determines appropriate.

(4) STATE LAW.—A State law requiring grandfathered health plans to be included in a pool described in paragraph (1) or (2) shall not apply.

(d) EMPOWERING CONSUMER CHOICE.—

(1) CONTINUED OPERATION OF MARKET OUTSIDE EXCHANGES.—Nothing in this title shall be construed to prohibit—

(A) a health insurance issuer from offering outside of an Exchange a health plan to a qualified individual or qualified employer; and

(B) a qualified individual from enrolling in, or a qualified employer from selecting for its employees, a health plan offered outside of an Exchange.

(2) CONTINUED OPERATION OF STATE BENEFIT REQUIREMENTS.—Nothing in this title shall be construed to terminate, abridge, or limit the operation of any requirement under State law with respect to any policy or plan that is offered outside of an Exchange to offer benefits.

(3) VOLUNTARY NATURE OF AN EXCHANGE.—

(A) CHOICE TO ENROLL OR NOT TO ENROLL.—Nothing in this title shall be construed to restrict the choice of a qualified individual to enroll or not to enroll in a qualified health plan or to participate in an Exchange.

(B) PROHIBITION AGAINST COMPELLED ENROLLMENT.— Nothing in this title shall be construed to compel an individual to enroll in a qualified health plan or to participate in an Exchange.

(C) INDIVIDUALS ALLOWED TO ENROLL IN ANY PLAN.— A qualified individual may enroll in any qualified health plan, except that in the case of a catastrophic plan described in section 1302(e), a qualified individual may enroll in the plan only if the individual is eligible to enroll in the plan under section 1302(e)(2).

(D) MEMBERS OF CONGRESS IN THE EXCHANGE.—

(i) REQUIREMENT.—Notwithstanding any other provision of law, after the effective date of this subtitle, the only health plans that the Federal Government may make available to Members of Congress and congressional staff with respect to their service as a Member of Congress or congressional staff shall be health plans that are—

(I) created under this Act (or an amendment made by this Act); or

(II) offered through an Exchange established under this Act (or an amendment made by this Act).

(ii) DEFINITIONS.—In this section:

(I) MEMBER OF CONGRESS.—The term "Member of Congress" means any member of the House of Representatives or the Senate.

(II) CONGRESSIONAL STAFF.—The term "congressional staff" means all full-time and part-time employees employed by the official office of a Member of Congress, whether in Washington, DC or outside of Washington, DC.

(4) NO PENALTY FOR TRANSFERRING TO MINIMUM ESSENTIAL COVERAGE OUTSIDE EXCHANGE.—An Exchange, or a qualified health plan offered through an Exchange, shall not impose any penalty or other fee on an individual who cancels enrollment in a plan because the individual becomes eligible for minimum essential coverage (as defined in section 5000A(f) of the Internal Revenue Code of 1986 without regard to paragraph (1)(C) or (D) thereof) or such coverage becomes affordable (within the meaning of section 36B(c)(2)(C) of such Code).

(e) ENROLLMENT THROUGH AGENTS OR BROKERS.—The Secretary shall establish procedures under which a State may allow agents or brokers—

(1) to enroll individuals in any qualified health plans in the individual or small group market as soon as the plan is offered through an Exchange in the State; and

(2) to assist individuals in applying for premium tax credits and cost-sharing reductions for plans sold through an Exchange.

Such procedures may include the establishment of rate schedules for broker commissions paid by health benefits plans offered through an exchange.

(f) QUALIFIED INDIVIDUALS AND EMPLOYERS; ACCESS LIMITED TO CITIZENS AND LAWFUL RESIDENTS.—

(1) QUALIFIED INDIVIDUALS.—In this title:

(A) IN GENERAL.—The term “qualified individual” means, with respect to an Exchange, an individual who—

(i) is seeking to enroll in a qualified health plan in the individual market offered through the Exchange; and

(ii) resides in the State that established the Exchange (except with respect to territorial agreements under section 1312(f)).

(B) INCARCERATED INDIVIDUALS EXCLUDED.—An individual shall not be treated as a qualified individual if, at the time of enrollment, the individual is incarcerated, other than incarceration pending the disposition of charges.

(2) QUALIFIED EMPLOYER.—In this title:

(A) IN GENERAL.—The term “qualified employer” means a small employer that elects to make all full-time employees of such employer eligible for 1 or more qualified health plans offered in the small group market through an Exchange that offers qualified health plans.

(B) EXTENSION TO LARGE GROUPS.—

(i) IN GENERAL.—Beginning in 2017, each State may allow issuers of health insurance coverage in the large group market in the State to offer qualified health plans in such market through an Exchange. Nothing in this subparagraph shall be construed as requiring the issuer to offer such plans through an Exchange.

(ii) LARGE EMPLOYERS ELIGIBLE.—If a State under clause (i) allows issuers to offer qualified health plans in the large group market through an Exchange, the term “qualified employer” shall include a large employer that elects to make all full-time employees of such employer eligible for 1 or more qualified health plans offered in the large group market through the Exchange.

(3) ACCESS LIMITED TO LAWFUL RESIDENTS.—If an individual is not, or is not reasonably expected to be for the entire period for which enrollment is sought, a citizen or national of the United States or an alien lawfully present in the United States, the individual shall not be treated as a qualified individual and may not be covered under a qualified health plan in the individual market that is offered through an Exchange.

SEC. 1313. FINANCIAL INTEGRITY.

(a) ACCOUNTING FOR EXPENDITURES.—

(1) IN GENERAL.—An Exchange shall keep an accurate accounting of all activities, receipts, and expenditures and shall annually submit to the Secretary a report concerning such accountings.

(2) INVESTIGATIONS.—The Secretary, in coordination with the Inspector General of the Department of Health and Human Services, may investigate the affairs of an Exchange, may examine the properties and records of an Exchange, and may require periodic reports in relation to activities undertaken by an Exchange. An Exchange shall fully cooperate in any investigation conducted under this paragraph.

(3) AUDITS.—An Exchange shall be subject to annual audits by the Secretary.

(4) PATTERN OF ABUSE.—If the Secretary determines that an Exchange or a State has engaged in serious misconduct with respect to compliance with the requirements of, or carrying out of activities required under, this title, the Secretary may rescind from payments otherwise due to such State involved under this or any other Act administered by the Secretary an amount not to exceed 1 percent of such payments per year until corrective actions are taken by the State that are determined to be adequate by the Secretary.

(5) PROTECTIONS AGAINST FRAUD AND ABUSE.—With respect to activities carried out under this title, the Secretary shall provide for the efficient and non-discriminatory administration of Exchange activities and implement any measure or procedure that—

(A) the Secretary determines is appropriate to reduce fraud and abuse in the administration of this title; and

(B) the Secretary has authority to implement under this title or any other Act.

(6) APPLICATION OF THE FALSE CLAIMS ACT.—

(A) IN GENERAL.—Payments made by, through, or in connection with an Exchange are subject to the False Claims Act (31 U.S.C. 3729 et seq.) if those payments include any Federal funds. Compliance with the requirements of this Act concerning eligibility for a health insurance issuer to participate in the Exchange shall be a material condition of an issuer's entitlement to receive payments, including payments of premium tax credits and cost-sharing reductions, through the Exchange.

(B) DAMAGES.—Notwithstanding paragraph (1) of section 3729(a) of title 31, United States Code, and subject to paragraph (2) of such section, the civil penalty assessed under the False Claims Act on any person found liable under such Act as described in subparagraph (A) shall be increased by not less than 3 times and not more than 6 times the amount of damages which the Government sustains because of the act of that person.

(b) GAO OVERSIGHT.—Not later than 5 years after the first date on which Exchanges are required to be operational under this title, the Comptroller General shall conduct an ongoing study of Exchange activities and the enrollees in qualified health plans offered through Exchanges. Such study shall review—

(1) the operations and administration of Exchanges, including surveys and reports of qualified health plans offered through Exchanges and on the experience of such plans (including data on enrollees in Exchanges and individuals purchasing health insurance coverage outside of Exchanges), the expenses of Exchanges, claims statistics relating to qualified health plans, complaints data relating to such plans, and the manner in which Exchanges meet their goals;

(2) any significant observations regarding the utilization and adoption of Exchanges;

(3) where appropriate, recommendations for improvements in the operations or policies of Exchanges; and

(4) how many physicians, by area and specialty, are not taking or accepting new patients enrolled in Federal Government health care programs, and the adequacy of provider networks of Federal Government health care programs.

PART III—STATE FLEXIBILITY RELATING TO EXCHANGES

SEC. 1321. STATE FLEXIBILITY IN OPERATION AND ENFORCEMENT OF EXCHANGES AND RELATED REQUIREMENTS.

(a) ESTABLISHMENT OF STANDARDS.—

(1) IN GENERAL.—The Secretary shall, as soon as practicable after the date of enactment of this Act, issue regulations setting standards for meeting the requirements under this title, and the amendments made by this title, with respect to—

(A) the establishment and operation of Exchanges (including SHOP Exchanges);

(B) the offering of qualified health plans through such Exchanges;

(C) the establishment of the reinsurance and risk adjustment programs under part V; and

(D) such other requirements as the Secretary determines appropriate.

The preceding sentence shall not apply to standards for requirements under subtitles A and C (and the amendments made by such subtitles) for which the Secretary issues regulations under the Public Health Service Act.

(2) CONSULTATION.—In issuing the regulations under paragraph (1), the Secretary shall consult with the National Association of Insurance Commissioners and its members and with health insurance issuers, consumer organizations, and such other individuals as the Secretary selects in a manner designed to ensure balanced representation among interested parties.

(b) STATE ACTION.—Each State that elects, at such time and in such manner as the Secretary may prescribe, to apply the requirements described in subsection (a) shall, not later than January 1, 2014, adopt and have in effect—

(1) the Federal standards established under subsection (a); or

(2) a State law or regulation that the Secretary determines implements the standards within the State.

(c) FAILURE TO ESTABLISH EXCHANGE OR IMPLEMENT REQUIREMENTS.—

(1) IN GENERAL.—If—

(A) a State is not an electing State under subsection (b); or

(B) the Secretary determines, on or before January 1, 2013, that an electing State—

(i) will not have any required Exchange operational by January 1, 2014; or

(ii) has not taken the actions the Secretary determines necessary to implement—

(I) the other requirements set forth in the standards under subsection (a); or

(II) the requirements set forth in subtitles A and C and the amendments made by such subtitles;

the Secretary shall (directly or through agreement with a not-for-profit entity) establish and operate such Exchange within the State and the Secretary shall take such actions as are necessary to implement such other requirements.

(2) ENFORCEMENT AUTHORITY.—The provisions of section 2736(b) of the Public Health Services Act shall apply to the enforcement under paragraph (1) of requirements of subsection (a)(1) (without regard to any limitation on the application of those provisions to group health plans).

(d) NO INTERFERENCE WITH STATE REGULATORY AUTHORITY.—Nothing in this title shall be construed to preempt any State law that does not prevent the application of the provisions of this title.

(e) PRESUMPTION FOR CERTAIN STATE-OPERATED EXCHANGES.—

(1) IN GENERAL.—In the case of a State operating an Exchange before January 1, 2010, and which has insured a percentage of its population not less than the percentage of the population projected to be covered nationally after the implementation of this Act, that seeks to operate an Exchange under this section, the Secretary shall presume that such Exchange meets the standards under this section unless the Secretary determines, after completion of the process established under paragraph (2), that the Exchange does not comply with such standards.

(2) PROCESS.—The Secretary shall establish a process to work with a State described in paragraph (1) to provide assistance necessary to assist the State's Exchange in coming into compliance with the standards for approval under this section.

SEC. 1322. FEDERAL PROGRAM TO ASSIST ESTABLISHMENT AND OPERATION OF NONPROFIT, MEMBER-RUN HEALTH INSURANCE ISSUERS.

(a) ESTABLISHMENT OF PROGRAM.—

(1) IN GENERAL.—The Secretary shall establish a program to carry out the purposes of this section to be known as the Consumer Operated and Oriented Plan (CO–OP) program.

(2) PURPOSE.—It is the purpose of the CO–OP program to foster the creation of qualified nonprofit health insurance issuers to offer qualified health plans in the individual and small group markets in the States in which the issuers are licensed to offer such plans.

(b) LOANS AND GRANTS UNDER THE CO–OP PROGRAM.—

(1) IN GENERAL.—The Secretary shall provide through the CO–OP program for the awarding to persons applying to become qualified nonprofit health insurance issuers of—

(A) loans to provide assistance to such person in meeting its start-up costs; and

(B) grants to provide assistance to such person in meeting any solvency requirements of States in which the person seeks to be licensed to issue qualified health plans.

(2) REQUIREMENTS FOR AWARDING LOANS AND GRANTS.—

(A) IN GENERAL.—In awarding loans and grants under the CO–OP program, the Secretary shall—

(i) take into account the recommendations of the advisory board established under paragraph (3);

(ii) give priority to applicants that will offer qualified health plans on a Statewide basis, will utilize integrated care models, and have significant private support; and

(iii) ensure that there is sufficient funding to establish at least 1 qualified nonprofit health insurance issuer in each State, except that nothing in this clause shall prohibit the Secretary from funding the establishment of multiple qualified nonprofit health insurance issuers in any State if the funding is sufficient to do so.

(B) STATES WITHOUT ISSUERS IN PROGRAM.—If no health insurance issuer applies to be a qualified nonprofit health insurance issuer within a State, the Secretary may use amounts appropriated under this section for the awarding of grants to encourage the establishment of a qualified nonprofit health insurance issuer within the State or the expansion of a qualified nonprofit health insurance issuer from another State to the State.

(C) AGREEMENT.—

(i) IN GENERAL.—The Secretary shall require any person receiving a loan or grant under the CO–OP program to enter into an agreement with the Secretary which requires such person to meet (and to continue to meet)—

(I) any requirement under this section for such person to be treated as a qualified nonprofit health insurance issuer; and

(II) any requirements contained in the agreement for such person to receive such loan or grant.

(ii) RESTRICTIONS ON USE OF FEDERAL FUNDS.—The agreement shall include a requirement that no portion of the funds made available by any loan or grant under this section may be used—

(I) for carrying on propaganda, or otherwise attempting, to influence legislation; or

(II) for marketing.

Nothing in this clause shall be construed to allow a person to take any action prohibited by section 501(c)(29) of the Internal Revenue Code of 1986.

(iii) FAILURE TO MEET REQUIREMENTS.—If the Secretary determines that a person has failed to meet any requirement described in clause (i) or (ii) and has failed to correct such failure within a reasonable period of time of when the person first knows (or reasonably should have known) of such failure, such person shall repay to the Secretary an amount equal to the sum of—

(I) 110 percent of the aggregate amount of loans and grants received under this section; plus

(II) interest on the aggregate amount of loans and grants received under this section for the period the loans or grants were outstanding.

The Secretary shall notify the Secretary of the Treasury of any determination under this section of a failure that results in the termination of an issuer's tax-exempt status under section 501(c)(29) of such Code.

(D) TIME FOR AWARDING LOANS AND GRANTS.—The Secretary shall not later than July 1, 2013, award the loans and grants under the CO–OP program and begin the distribution of amounts awarded under such loans and grants.

(3) ADVISORY BOARD.—

(A) IN GENERAL.—The advisory board under this paragraph shall consist of 15 members appointed by the Comptroller General of the United States from among individuals with qualifications described in section 1805(c)(2) of the Social Security Act.

(B) RULES RELATING TO APPOINTMENTS.—

(i) STANDARDS.—Any individual appointed under subparagraph (A) shall meet ethics and conflict of interest standards protecting against insurance industry involvement and interference.

(ii) ORIGINAL APPOINTMENTS.—The original appointment of board members under subparagraph (A)(ii) shall be made no later than 3 months after the date of enactment of this Act.

(C) VACANCY.—Any vacancy on the advisory board shall be filled in the same manner as the original appointment.

(D) PAY AND REIMBURSEMENT.—

(i) NO COMPENSATION FOR MEMBERS OF ADVISORY BOARD.—Except as provided in clause (ii), a member of the advisory board may not receive pay, allowances, or benefits by reason of their service on the board.

(ii) TRAVEL EXPENSES.—Each member shall receive travel expenses, including per diem in lieu of subsistence under subchapter I of chapter 57 of title 5, United States Code.

(E) APPLICATION OF FACA.—The Federal Advisory Committee Act (5 U.S.C. App.) shall apply to the advisory board, except that section 14 of such Act shall not apply.

(F) TERMINATION.—The advisory board shall terminate on the earlier of the date that it completes its duties under this section or December 31, 2015.

(c) QUALIFIED NONPROFIT HEALTH INSURANCE ISSUER.—For purposes of this section—

(1) IN GENERAL.—The term "qualified nonprofit health insurance issuer" means a health insurance issuer that is an organization—

(A) that is organized under State law as a nonprofit, member corporation;

(B) substantially all of the activities of which consist of the issuance of qualified health plans in the individual and small group markets in each State in which it is licensed to issue such plans; and

(C) that meets the other requirements of this subsection.

(2) CERTAIN ORGANIZATIONS PROHIBITED.—An organization shall not be treated as a qualified nonprofit health insurance issuer if—

(A) the organization or a related entity (or any predecessor of either) was a health insurance issuer on July 16, 2009; or

(B) the organization is sponsored by a State or local government, any political subdivision thereof, or any instrumentality of such government or political subdivision.

(3) GOVERNANCE REQUIREMENTS.—An organization shall not be treated as a qualified nonprofit health insurance issuer unless—

(A) the governance of the organization is subject to a majority vote of its members;

(B) its governing documents incorporate ethics and conflict of interest standards protecting against insurance industry involvement and interference; and

(C) as provided in regulations promulgated by the Secretary, the organization is required to operate with a strong consumer focus, including timeliness, responsiveness, and accountability to members.

(4) PROFITS INURE TO BENEFIT OF MEMBERS.—An organization shall not be treated as a qualified nonprofit health insurance issuer unless any profits made by the organization are required to be used to lower premiums, to improve benefits, or for other programs intended to improve the quality of health care delivered to its members.

(5) COMPLIANCE WITH STATE INSURANCE LAWS.—An organization shall not be treated as a qualified nonprofit health insurance issuer unless the organization meets all the requirements that other issuers of qualified health plans are required to meet in any State where the issuer offers a qualified health plan, including solvency and licensure requirements, rules on payments to providers, and compliance with network adequacy rules, rate and form filing rules, any applicable State premium assessments and any other State law described in section 1324(b).

(6) COORDINATION WITH STATE INSURANCE REFORMS.—An organization shall not be treated as a qualified nonprofit health insurance issuer unless the organization does not offer a health plan in a State until that State has in effect (or the Secretary has implemented for the State) the market reforms required by part A of title XXVII of the Public Health Service Act (as amended by subtitles A and C of this Act).

(d) ESTABLISHMENT OF PRIVATE PURCHASING COUNCIL.—

(1) IN GENERAL.—Qualified nonprofit health insurance issuers participating in the CO–OP program under this section may establish a private purchasing council to enter into collective purchasing arrangements for items and services that increase administrative and other cost efficiencies, including claims administration, administrative services, health information technology, and actuarial services.

(2) COUNCIL MAY NOT SET PAYMENT RATES.—The private purchasing council established under paragraph (1) shall not set payment rates for health care facilities or providers participating in health insurance coverage provided by qualified nonprofit health insurance issuers.

(3) CONTINUED APPLICATION OF ANTITRUST LAWS.—

(A) IN GENERAL.—Nothing in this section shall be construed to limit the application of the antitrust laws to any private purchasing council (whether or not established under this subsection) or to any qualified nonprofit health insurance issuer participating in such a council.

(B) ANTITRUST LAWS.—For purposes of this subparagraph, the term "antitrust laws" has the meaning given the term in subsection (a) of the first section of the Clayton Act (15 U.S.C. 12(a)). Such term also includes section 5 of the Federal Trade Commission Act (15 U.S.C. 45) to the extent that such section 5 applies to unfair methods of competition.

(e) LIMITATION ON PARTICIPATION.—No representative of any Federal, State, or local government (or of any political subdivision or instrumentality thereof), and no representative of a person described in subsection (c)(2)(A), may serve on the board of directors of a qualified nonprofit health insurance issuer or with a private purchasing council established under subsection (d).

(f) LIMITATIONS ON SECRETARY.—

(1) IN GENERAL.—The Secretary shall not—

(A) participate in any negotiations between 1 or more qualified nonprofit health insurance issuers (or a private purchasing council established under subsection (d)) and any health care facilities or providers, including any drug manufacturer, pharmacy, or hospital; and

(B) establish or maintain a price structure for reimbursement of any health benefits covered by such issuers.

(2) COMPETITION.—Nothing in this section shall be construed as authorizing the Secretary to interfere with the competitive nature of providing health benefits through qualified nonprofit health insurance issuers.

(g) APPROPRIATIONS.—There are hereby appropriated, out of any funds in the Treasury not otherwise appropriated, $6,000,000,000 to carry out this section.

(h) TAX EXEMPTION FOR QUALIFIED NONPROFIT HEALTH INSURANCE ISSUER.—

(1) IN GENERAL.—Section 501(c) of the Internal Revenue Code of 1986 (relating to list of exempt organizations) is amended by adding at the end the following:

"(29) CO–OP HEALTH INSURANCE ISSUERS.—

"(A) IN GENERAL.—A qualified nonprofit health insurance issuer (within the meaning of section 1322 of the Patient Protection and Affordable Care Act) which has received a loan or grant under the CO–OP program under such section, but only with respect to periods for which the issuer is in compliance with the requirements of such section and any agreement with respect to the loan or grant.

"(B) CONDITIONS FOR EXEMPTION.—Subparagraph (A) shall apply to an organization only if—

"(i) the organization has given notice to the Secretary, in such manner as the Secretary may by regulations prescribe, that it is applying for recognition of its status under this paragraph,

"(ii) except as provided in section 1322(c)(4) of the Patient Protection and Affordable Care Act, no part of the net earnings of which inures to the benefit of any private shareholder or individual,

"(iii) no substantial part of the activities of which is carrying on propaganda, or otherwise attempting, to influence legislation, and

"(iv) the organization does not participate in, or intervene in (including the publishing or distributing of statements), any political campaign on behalf of (or in opposition to) any candidate for public office.".

(2) ADDITIONAL REPORTING REQUIREMENT.—Section 6033 of such Code (relating to returns by exempt organizations) is amended by redesignating subsection (m) as subsection (n) and by inserting after subsection (l) the following:

"(m) ADDITIONAL INFORMATION REQUIRED FROM CO–OP INSURERS.—An organization described in section 501(c)(29) shall include on the return required under subsection (a) the following information:

"(1) The amount of the reserves required by each State in which the organization is licensed to issue qualified health plans.

"(2) The amount of reserves on hand.".

(3) APPLICATION OF TAX ON EXCESS BENEFIT TRANSACTIONS.—Section 4958(e)(1) of such Code (defining applicable tax-exempt organization) is amended by striking "paragraph (3) or (4)" and inserting "paragraph (3), (4), or (29)".

(i) GAO STUDY AND REPORT.—

(1) STUDY.—The Comptroller General of the General Accountability Office shall conduct an ongoing study on competition and market concentration in the health insurance market in the United States after the implementation of the reforms in such market under the provisions of, and the amendments made by, this Act. Such study shall include an analysis of new issuers of health insurance in such market.

(2) REPORT.—The Comptroller General shall, not later than December 31 of each even-numbered year (beginning with 2014), report to the appropriate committees of the Congress the results of the study conducted under paragraph (1), including any recommendations for administrative or legislative changes the Comptroller General determines necessary or appropriate to increase competition in the health insurance market.

SEC. 1323. COMMUNITY HEALTH INSURANCE OPTION.

(a) VOLUNTARY NATURE.—

(1) NO REQUIREMENT FOR HEALTH CARE PROVIDERS TO PARTICIPATE.—Nothing in this section shall be construed to require a health care provider to participate in a community health insurance option, or to impose any penalty for non-participation.

(2) NO REQUIREMENT FOR INDIVIDUALS TO JOIN.—Nothing in this section shall be construed to require an individual to participate in a community health insurance option, or to impose any penalty for non-participation.

(3) STATE OPT OUT.—

(A) IN GENERAL.—A State may elect to prohibit Exchanges in such State from offering a community health insurance option if such State enacts a law to provide for such prohibition.

(B) TERMINATION OF OPT OUT.—A State may repeal a law described in subparagraph (A) and provide for the offering of such an option through the Exchange.

(b) ESTABLISHMENT OF COMMUNITY HEALTH INSURANCE OPTION.—

(1) ESTABLISHMENT.—The Secretary shall establish a community health insurance option to offer, through the Exchanges established under this title (other than Exchanges

in States that elect to opt out as provided for in subsection (a)(3)), health care coverage that provides value, choice, competition, and stability of affordable, high quality coverage throughout the United States.

(2) COMMUNITY HEALTH INSURANCE OPTION.—In this section, the term "community health insurance option" means health insurance coverage that—

(A) except as specifically provided for in this section, complies with the requirements for being a qualified health plan;

(B) provides high value for the premium charged;

(C) reduces administrative costs and promotes administrative simplification for beneficiaries;

(D) promotes high quality clinical care;

(E) provides high quality customer service to beneficiaries;

(F) offers a sufficient choice of providers; and

(G) complies with State laws (if any), except as otherwise provided for in this title, relating to the laws described in section 1324(b).

(3) ESSENTIAL HEALTH BENEFITS.—

(A) GENERAL RULE.—Except as provided in subparagraph (B), a community health insurance option offered under this section shall provide coverage only for the essential health benefits described in section 1302(b).

(B) STATES MAY OFFER ADDITIONAL BENEFITS.—Nothing in this section shall preclude a State from requiring that benefits in addition to the essential health benefits required under subparagraph (A) be provided to enrollees of a community health insurance option offered in such State.

(C) CREDITS.—

(i) IN GENERAL.—An individual enrolled in a community health insurance option under this section shall be eligible for credits under section 36B of the Internal Revenue Code of 1986 in the same manner as an individual who is enrolled in a qualified health plan.

(ii) NO ADDITIONAL FEDERAL COST.—A requirement by a State under subparagraph (B) that benefits in addition to the essential health benefits required under subparagraph (A) be provided to enrollees of a community health insurance option shall not affect the amount of a premium tax credit provided under section 36B of the Internal Revenue Code of 1986 with respect to such plan.

(D) STATE MUST ASSUME COST.—A State shall make payments to or on behalf of an eligible individual to defray the cost of any additional benefits described in subparagraph (B).

(E) ENSURING ACCESS TO ALL SERVICES.—Nothing in this Act shall prohibit an individual enrolled in a community health insurance option from paying out-of-pocket the full cost of any item or service not included as an essential health benefit or otherwise covered as a benefit by a health plan. Nothing in subparagraph (B) shall prohibit any type of medical provider from accepting an out-of-pocket payment from an individual enrolled in a community health insurance option for a service otherwise not included as an essential health benefit.

(F) PROTECTING ACCESS TO END OF LIFE CARE.—A community health insurance option offered under this section shall be prohibited from limiting access to end of life care.

(4) COST SHARING.—A community health insurance option shall offer coverage at each of the levels of coverage described in section 1302(d).

(5) PREMIUMS.—

(A) PREMIUMS SUFFICIENT TO COVER COSTS.—The Secretary shall establish geographically adjusted premium rates in an amount sufficient to cover expected costs (including claims and administrative costs) using methods in general use by qualified health plans.

(B) APPLICABLE RULES.—The provisions of title XXVII of the Public Health Service Act relating to premiums shall apply to community health insurance options under this section, including modified community rating provisions under section 2701 of such Act.

(C) COLLECTION OF DATA.—The Secretary shall collect data as necessary to set premium rates under subparagraph (A).

(D) NATIONAL POOLING.—Notwithstanding any other provision of law, the Secretary may treat all enrollees in community health insurance options as members of a single pool.

(E) CONTINGENCY MARGIN.—In establishing premium rates under subparagraph (A), the Secretary shall include an appropriate amount for a contingency margin.

(6) REIMBURSEMENT RATES.—

(A) NEGOTIATED RATES.—The Secretary shall negotiate rates for the reimbursement of health care providers for benefits covered under a community health insurance option.

(B) LIMITATION.—The rates described in subparagraph (A) shall not be higher, in aggregate, than the average reimbursement rates paid by health insurance issuers offering qualified health plans through the Exchange.

(C) INNOVATION.—Subject to the limits contained in subparagraph (A), a State Advisory Council established or designated under subsection (d) may develop or encourage the use of innovative payment policies that promote quality, efficiency and savings to consumers.

(7) SOLVENCY AND CONSUMER PROTECTION.—

(A) SOLVENCY.—The Secretary shall establish a Federal solvency standard to be applied with respect to a community health insurance option. A community health insurance option shall also be subject to the solvency standard of each State in which such community health insurance option is offered.

(B) MINIMUM REQUIRED.—In establishing the standard described under subparagraph (A), the Secretary shall require a reserve fund that shall be equal to at least the dollar value of the incurred but not reported claims of a community health insurance option.

(C) CONSUMER PROTECTIONS.—The consumer protection laws of a State shall apply to a community health insurance option.

(8) REQUIREMENTS ESTABLISHED IN PARTNERSHIP WITH INSURANCE COMMISSIONERS.—

(A) IN GENERAL.—The Secretary, in collaboration with the National Association of Insurance Commissioners (in this paragraph referred to as the "NAIC"), may promulgate regulations to establish additional requirements for a community health insurance option.

(B) APPLICABILITY.—Any requirement promulgated under subparagraph (A) shall be applicable to such option beginning 90 days after the date on which the regulation involved becomes final.

(c) START-UP FUND.—

(1) ESTABLISHMENT OF FUND.—

(A) IN GENERAL.—There is established in the Treasury of the United States a trust fund to be known as the "Health Benefit Plan Start-Up Fund" (referred to in this section as the "Start-Up Fund"), that shall consist of such amounts as may be appropriated or credited to the Start-Up Fund as provided for in this subsection to provide loans for the initial operations of a community health insurance option. Such amounts shall remain available until expended.

(B) FUNDING.—There is hereby appropriated to the Start-Up Fund, out of any moneys in the Treasury not otherwise appropriated an amount requested by the Secretary of Health and Human Services as necessary to—

(i) pay the start-up costs associated with the initial operations of a community health insurance option; and

(ii) pay the costs of making payments on claims submitted during the period that is not more than 90 days from the date on which such option is offered.

(2) USE OF START-UP FUND.—The Secretary shall use amounts contained in the Start-Up Fund to make payments (subject to the repayment requirements in paragraph (4)) for the purposes described in paragraph (1)(B).

(3) PASS THROUGH OF REBATES.—The Secretary may establish procedures for reducing the amount of payments to a contracting administrator to take into account any rebates or price concessions.

(4) REPAYMENT.—

(A) IN GENERAL.—A community health insurance option shall be required to repay the Secretary of the Treasury (on such terms as the Secretary may require) for any payments made under paragraph (1)(B) by the date that is not later than 9 years after the date on which the payment is made. The Secretary may require the payment of interest with respect to such repayments at rates that do not exceed the market interest rate (as determined by the Secretary).

(B) SANCTIONS IN CASE OF FOR-PROFIT CONVERSION.—In any case in which the Secretary enters into a contract with a qualified entity for the offering of a community health insurance option and such entity is determined to be a for-profit entity by the Secretary, such entity shall be—

(i) immediately liable to the Secretary for any payments received by such entity from the Start-Up Fund; and

(ii) permanently ineligible to offer a qualified health plan.

(d) STATE ADVISORY COUNCIL.—

(1) ESTABLISHMENT.—A State (other than a State that elects to opt out as provided for in subsection (a)(3)) shall establish or designate a public or non-profit private entity to serve as the State Advisory Council to provide recommendations to the Secretary on the operations and policies of a community health insurance option in the State. Such Council shall provide recommendations on at least the following:

(A) policies and procedures to integrate quality improvement and cost containment mechanisms into the health care delivery system;

(B) mechanisms to facilitate public awareness of the availability of a community health insurance option; and

(C) alternative payment structures under a community health insurance option for health care providers that encourage quality improvement and cost control.

(2) MEMBERS.—The members of the State Advisory Council shall be representatives of the public and shall include health care consumers and providers.

(3) APPLICABILITY OF RECOMMENDATIONS.—The Secretary may apply the recommendations of a State Advisory Council to a community health insurance option in that State, in any other State, or in all States.

(e) AUTHORITY TO CONTRACT; TERMS OF CONTRACT.—

(1) AUTHORITY.—

(A) IN GENERAL.—The Secretary may enter into a contract or contracts with one or more qualified entities for the purpose of performing administrative functions (including functions described in subsection (a)(4) of section 1874A of the Social Security Act) with respect to a community health insurance option in the same manner as the Secretary may enter into contracts under subsection (a)(1) of such section. The Secretary shall have the same authority with respect to a community health insurance option under this section as the Secretary has under subsections (a)(1) and (b) of section 1874A of the Social Security Act with respect to title XVIII of such Act.

(B) REQUIREMENTS APPLY.—If the Secretary enters into a contract with a qualified entity to offer a community health insurance option, under such contract such entity—

(i) shall meet the criteria established under paragraph (2); and

(ii) shall receive an administrative fee under paragraph (7).

(C) LIMITATION.—Contracts under this subsection shall not involve the transfer of insurance risk to the contracting administrator.

(D) REFERENCE.—An entity with which the Secretary has entered into a contract under this paragraph shall be referred to as a "contracting administrator".

(2) QUALIFIED ENTITY.—To be qualified to be selected by the Secretary to offer a community health insurance option, an entity shall—

(A) meet the criteria established under section 1874A(a)(2) of the Social Security Act;

(B) be a nonprofit entity for purposes of offering such option;

(C) meet the solvency standards applicable under subsection (b)(7);

(D) be eligible to offer health insurance or health benefits coverage;

(E) meet quality standards specified by the Secretary;

(F) have in place effective procedures to control fraud, abuse, and waste; and

(G) meet such other requirements as the Secretary may impose.

Procedures described under subparagraph (F) shall include the implementation of procedures to use beneficiary identifiers to identify individuals entitled to benefits so that such an individual's social security account number is not used, and shall also include procedures for the use of technology (including front-end, prepayment intelligent data-matching technology similar to that used by hedge funds, investment funds, and banks) to provide real-time data analysis of claims for payment under this title to identify and investigate unusual billing or order practices under this title that could indicate fraud or abuse.

(3) TERM.—A contract provided for under paragraph (1) shall be for a term of at least 5 years but not more than 10 years, as determined by the Secretary. At the end of each such term, the Secretary shall conduct a competitive bidding process for the purposes of renewing existing contracts or selecting new qualified entities with which to enter into contracts under such paragraph.

(4) LIMITATION.—A contract may not be renewed under this subsection unless the Secretary determines that the contracting administrator has met performance requirements established by the Secretary in the areas described in paragraph (7)(B).

(5) AUDITS.—The Inspector General shall conduct periodic audits with respect to contracting administrators under this subsection to ensure that the administrator involved is in compliance with this section.

(6) REVOCATION.—A contract awarded under this subsection shall be revoked by the Secretary, upon the recommendation of the Inspector General, only after notice to the contracting administrator involved and an opportunity for a hearing. The Secretary may revoke such contract if the Secretary determines that such administrator has engaged in fraud, deception, waste, abuse of power, negligence, mismanagement of taxpayer dollars, or gross mismanagement. An entity that has had a contract revoked under this paragraph shall not be qualified to enter into a subsequent contract under this subsection.

(7) FEE FOR ADMINISTRATION.—

(A) IN GENERAL.—The Secretary shall pay the contracting administrator a fee for the management, administration, and delivery of the benefits under this section.

(B) REQUIREMENT FOR HIGH QUALITY ADMINISTRATION.—The Secretary may increase the fee described in subparagraph (A) by not more than 10 percent, or reduce the fee described in subparagraph (A) by not more than 50 percent, based on the extent to which the contracting administrator, in the determination of the Secretary, meets performance requirements established by the Secretary, in at least the following areas:

(i) Maintaining low premium costs and low cost sharing requirements, provided that such requirements are consistent with section 1302.

(ii) Reducing administrative costs and promoting administrative simplification for beneficiaries.

(iii) Promoting high quality clinical care.

(iv) Providing high quality customer service to beneficiaries.

(C) NON-RENEWAL.—The Secretary may not renew a contract to offer a community health insurance option under this section with any contracting entity that has been assessed more than one reduction under subparagraph (B) during the contract period.

(8) LIMITATION.—Notwithstanding the terms of a contract under this subsection, the Secretary shall negotiate the reimbursement rates for purposes of subsection (b)(6).

(f) REPORT BY HHS AND INSOLVENCY WARNINGS.—

(1) IN GENERAL.—On an annual basis, the Secretary shall conduct a study on the solvency of a community health insurance option and submit to Congress a report describing the results of such study.

(2) RESULT.—If, in any year, the result of the study under paragraph (1) is that a community health insurance option is insolvent, such result shall be treated as a community health insurance option solvency warning.

(3) SUBMISSION OF PLAN AND PROCEDURE.—

(A) IN GENERAL.—If there is a community health insurance option solvency warning under paragraph (2) made in a year, the President shall submit to Congress, within the 15-day period beginning on the date of the budget submission to Congress under section 1105(a) of title 31, United States Code, for the succeeding year, proposed legislation to respond to such warning.

(B) PROCEDURE.—In the case of a legislative proposal submitted by the President pursuant to subparagraph (A), such proposal shall be considered by Congress using the same procedures described under sections 803 and 804 of the Medicare Prescription Drug, Improvement, and Modernization Act of 2003 that shall be used for a medicare funding warning.

(g) MARKETING PARITY.—In a facility controlled by the Federal Government, or by a State, where marketing or promotional materials related to a community health insurance option are made available to the public, making available marketing or promotional materials relating to private health insurance plans shall not be prohibited. Such materials include informational pamphlets, guidebooks, enrollment forms, or other materials determined reasonable for display.

(h) AUTHORIZATION OF APPROPRIATIONS.—There is authorized to be appropriated such sums as may be necessary to carry out this section.

SEC. 1324. LEVEL PLAYING FIELD.

(a) IN GENERAL.—Notwithstanding any other provision of law, any health insurance coverage offered by a private health insurance issuer shall not be subject to any Federal or State law described in subsection (b) if a qualified health plan offered under the Consumer Operated and Oriented Plan program under section 1322, a community health insurance option under section 1323, or a nationwide qualified health plan under section 1333(b), is not subject to such law.

(b) LAWS DESCRIBED.—The Federal and State laws described in this subsection are those Federal and State laws relating to—

(1) guaranteed renewal;
(2) rating;
(3) preexisting conditions;
(4) non-discrimination;
(5) quality improvement and reporting;
(6) fraud and abuse;
(7) solvency and financial requirements;
(8) market conduct;
(9) prompt payment;
(10) appeals and grievances;
(11) privacy and confidentiality;
(12) licensure; and
(13) benefit plan material or information.

PART IV—STATE FLEXIBILITY TO ESTABLISH ALTERNATIVE PROGRAMS

SEC. 1331. STATE FLEXIBILITY TO ESTABLISH BASIC HEALTH PROGRAMS FOR LOW-INCOME INDIVIDUALS NOT ELIGIBLE FOR MEDICAID.

(a) ESTABLISHMENT OF PROGRAM.—

(1) IN GENERAL.—The Secretary shall establish a basic health program meeting the requirements of this section under which a State may enter into contracts to offer 1 or more standard health plans providing at least the essential health benefits described in section 1302(b) to eligible individuals in lieu of offering such individuals coverage through an Exchange.

(2) CERTIFICATIONS AS TO BENEFIT COVERAGE AND COSTS.—Such program shall provide that a State may not establish a basic health program under this section unless the State establishes to the satisfaction of the Secretary, and the Secretary certifies, that—

(A) in the case of an eligible individual enrolled in a standard health plan offered through the program, the State provides—

(i) that the amount of the monthly premium an eligible individual is required to pay for coverage under the standard health plan for the individual and the individual's dependents does not exceed the amount of the monthly premium that the eligible individual would have been required to pay (in the rating area in which the individual resides) if the individual had enrolled in the applicable second lowest cost silver plan (as defined in section 36B(b)(3)(B) of the Internal Revenue Code of 1986) offered to the individual through an Exchange; and

(ii) that the cost-sharing an eligible individual is required to pay under the standard health plan does not exceed—

(I) the cost-sharing required under a platinum plan in the case of an eligible individual with household income not in excess of 150 percent of the poverty line for the size of the family involved; and

(II) the cost-sharing required under a gold plan in the case of an eligible individual not described in subclause (I); and

(B) the benefits provided under the standard health plans offered through the program cover at least the essential health benefits described in section 1302(b).

For purposes of subparagraph (A)(i), the amount of the monthly premium an individual is required to pay under either the standard health plan or the applicable second lowest cost silver plan shall be determined after reduction for any premium tax credits and cost-sharing reductions allowable with respect to either plan.

(b) STANDARD HEALTH PLAN.—In this section, the term "standard heath plan" means a health benefits plan that the State contracts with under this section—

(1) under which the only individuals eligible to enroll are eligible individuals;

(2) that provides at least the essential health benefits described in section 1302(b); and

(3) in the case of a plan that provides health insurance coverage offered by a health insurance issuer, that has a medical loss ratio of at least 85 percent.

(c) CONTRACTING PROCESS.—

(1) IN GENERAL.—A State basic health program shall establish a competitive process for entering into contracts with standard health plans under subsection (a), including negotiation of premiums and cost-sharing and negotiation of benefits in addition to the essential health benefits described in section 1302(b).

(2) SPECIFIC ITEMS TO BE CONSIDERED.—A State shall, as part of its competitive process under paragraph (1), include at least the following:

(A) INNOVATION.—Negotiation with offerors of a standard health plan for the inclusion of innovative features in the plan, including—

(i) care coordination and care management for enrollees, especially for those with chronic health conditions;

(ii) incentives for use of preventive services; and

(iii) the establishment of relationships between providers and patients that maximize patient involvement in health care decision-making, including providing incentives for appropriate utilization under the plan.

(B) HEALTH AND RESOURCE DIFFERENCES.—Consideration of, and the making of suitable allowances for, differences in health care needs of enrollees and differences in local availability of, and access to, health care providers. Nothing in this subparagraph shall be construed as allowing discrimination on the basis of pre-existing conditions or other health status-related factors.

(C) MANAGED CARE.—Contracting with managed care systems, or with systems that offer as many of the attributes of managed care as are feasible in the local health care market.

(D) PERFORMANCE MEASURES.—Establishing specific performance measures and standards for issuers of standard health plans that focus on quality of care and improved health outcomes, requiring such plans to report to the State with respect to the measures and standards, and making the performance and quality information available to enrollees in a useful form.

(3) ENHANCED AVAILABILITY.—

(A) MULTIPLE PLANS.—A State shall, to the maximum extent feasible, seek to make multiple standard health plans available to eligible individuals within a State to ensure individuals have a choice of such plans.

(B) REGIONAL COMPACTS.—A State may negotiate a regional compact with other States to include coverage of eligible individuals in all such States in agreements with issuers of standard health plans.

(4) COORDINATION WITH OTHER STATE PROGRAMS.—A State shall seek to coordinate the administration of, and provision of benefits under, its program under this section with the State medicaid program under title XIX of the Social Security Act, the State child health plan under title XXI of such Act, and other State-administered health programs to maximize the efficiency of such programs and to improve the continuity of care.

(d) TRANSFER OF FUNDS TO STATES.—

(1) IN GENERAL.—If the Secretary determines that a State electing the application of this section meets the requirements of the program established under subsection (a), the Secretary shall transfer to the State for each fiscal year for which 1 or more standard health plans are operating within the State the amount determined under paragraph (3).

(2) USE OF FUNDS.—A State shall establish a trust for the deposit of the amounts received under paragraph (1) and amounts in the trust fund shall only be used to reduce the premiums and cost-sharing of, or to provide additional benefits for, eligible individuals enrolled in standard health plans within the State. Amounts in the trust fund, and expenditures of such amounts, shall not be included in determining the amount of any non-Federal funds for purposes of meeting any matching or expenditure requirement of any federally-funded program.

(3) AMOUNT OF PAYMENT.—

(A) SECRETARIAL DETERMINATION.—

(i) IN GENERAL.—The amount determined under this paragraph for any fiscal year is the amount the Secretary determines is equal to 85 percent of the premium tax credits under section 36B of the Internal

Revenue Code of 1986, and the cost-sharing reductions under section 1402, that would have been provided for the fiscal year to eligible individuals enrolled in standard health plans in the State if such eligible individuals were allowed to enroll in qualified health plans through an Exchange established under this subtitle.

(ii) SPECIFIC REQUIREMENTS.—The Secretary shall make the determination under clause (i) on a per enrollee basis and shall take into account all relevant factors necessary to determine the value of the premium tax credits and cost-sharing reductions that would have been provided to eligible individuals described in clause (i), including the age and income of the enrollee, whether the enrollment is for self-only or family coverage, geographic differences in average spending for health care across rating areas, the health status of the enrollee for purposes of determining risk adjustment payments and reinsurance payments that would have been made if the enrollee had enrolled in a qualified health plan through an Exchange, and whether any reconciliation of the credit or cost-sharing reductions would have occurred if the enrollee had been so enrolled. This determination shall take into consideration the experience of other States with respect to participation in an Exchange and such credits and reductions provided to residents of the other States, with a special focus on enrollees with income below 200 percent of poverty.

(iii) CERTIFICATION.—The Chief Actuary of the Centers for Medicare & Medicaid Services, in consultation with the Office of Tax Analysis of the Department of the Treasury, shall certify whether the methodology used to make determinations under this subparagraph, and such determinations, meet the requirements of clause (ii). Such certifications shall be based on sufficient data from the State and from comparable States about their experience with programs created by this Act.

(B) CORRECTIONS.—The Secretary shall adjust the payment for any fiscal year to reflect any error in the determinations under subparagraph (A) for any preceding fiscal year.

(4) APPLICATION OF SPECIAL RULES.—The provisions of section 1303 shall apply to a State basic health program, and to standard health plans offered through such program, in the same manner as such rules apply to qualified health plans.

(e) ELIGIBLE INDIVIDUAL.—

(1) IN GENERAL.—In this section, the term "eligible individual" means, with respect to any State, an individual—

(A) who a resident of the State who is not eligible to enroll in the State's medicaid program under title XIX of the Social Security Act for benefits that at a minimum consist of the essential health benefits described in section 1302(b);

(B) whose household income exceeds 133 percent but does not exceed 200 percent of the poverty line for the size of the family involved;

(C) who is not eligible for minimum essential coverage (as defined in section 5000A(f) of the Internal Revenue Code of 1986) or is eligible for an employer-sponsored plan that is not affordable coverage (as determined under section 5000A(e)(2) of such Code); and

(D) who has not attained age 65 as of the beginning of the plan year.

Such term shall not include any individual who is not a qualified individual under section 1312 who is eligible to be covered by a qualified health plan offered through an Exchange.

(2) ELIGIBLE INDIVIDUALS MAY NOT USE EXCHANGE.—An eligible individual shall not be treated as a qualified individual under section 1312 eligible for enrollment in a qualified health plan offered through an Exchange established under section 1311.

(f) SECRETARIAL OVERSIGHT.—The Secretary shall each year conduct a review of each State program to ensure compliance with the requirements of this section, including ensuring that the State program meets—

(1) eligibility verification requirements for participation in the program;

(2) the requirements for use of Federal funds received by the program; and

(3) the quality and performance standards under this section.

(g) STANDARD HEALTH PLAN OFFERORS.—A State may provide that persons eligible to offer standard health plans under a basic health program established under this section may include a licensed health maintenance organization, a licensed health insurance insurer, or a network of health care providers established to offer services under the program.

(h) DEFINITIONS.—Any term used in this section which is also used in section 36B of the Internal Revenue Code of 1986 shall have the meaning given such term by such section.

SEC. 1332. WAIVER FOR STATE INNOVATION.

(a) APPLICATION.—

(1) IN GENERAL.—A State may apply to the Secretary for the waiver of all or any requirements described in paragraph (2) with respect to health insurance coverage within that State for plan years beginning on or after January 1, 2017. Such application shall—

(A) be filed at such time and in such manner as the Secretary may require;

(B) contain such information as the Secretary may require, including—

(i) a comprehensive description of the State legislation and program to implement a plan meeting the requirements for a waiver under this section; and

(ii) a 10-year budget plan for such plan that is budget neutral for the Federal Government; and

(C) provide an assurance that the State has enacted the law described in subsection (b)(2).

(2) REQUIREMENTS.—The requirements described in this paragraph with respect to health insurance coverage within the State for plan years beginning on or after January 1, 2014, are as follows:

(A) Part I of subtitle D.

(B) Part II of subtitle D.

(C) Section 1402.

(D) Sections 36B, 4980H, and 5000A of the Internal Revenue Code of 1986.

(3) PASS THROUGH OF FUNDING.—With respect to a State waiver under paragraph (1), under which, due to the structure of the State plan, individuals and small employers in the State would not qualify for the premium tax credits, cost-sharing reductions, or small business credits under sections 36B of the Internal Revenue Code of 1986 or under part I of subtitle E for which they would otherwise be eligible, the Secretary shall provide for an alternative means by which the aggregate amount of such credits or reductions that would have been paid on behalf of participants in the Exchanges established under this title had the State not received such waiver, shall be paid to the State for purposes of implementing the State plan under the waiver. Such amount shall be determined annually by the Secretary, taking into consideration the experience of other States with respect to participation in an Exchange and credits and reductions provided under such provisions to residents of the other States.

(4) WAIVER CONSIDERATION AND TRANSPARENCY.—

(A) IN GENERAL.—An application for a waiver under this section shall be considered by the Secretary in accordance with the regulations described in subparagraph (B).

(B) REGULATIONS.—Not later than 180 days after the date of enactment of this Act, the Secretary shall promulgate regulations relating to waivers under this section that provide—

(i) a process for public notice and comment at the State level, including public hearings, sufficient to ensure a meaningful level of public input;

(ii) a process for the submission of an application that ensures the disclosure of—

(I) the provisions of law that the State involved seeks to waive; and

(II) the specific plans of the State to ensure that the waiver will be in compliance with subsection (b);

(iii) a process for providing public notice and comment after the application is received by the Secretary, that is sufficient to ensure a meaningful level of public input and that does not impose requirements that are in addition to, or duplicative of, requirements imposed under the Administrative Procedures Act, or requirements that are unreasonable or unnecessarily burdensome with respect to State compliance;

(iv) a process for the submission to the Secretary of periodic reports by the State concerning the implementation of the program under the waiver; and

(v) a process for the periodic evaluation by the Secretary of the program under the waiver.

(C) REPORT.—The Secretary shall annually report to Congress concerning actions taken by the Secretary with respect to applications for waivers under this section.

(5) COORDINATED WAIVER PROCESS.—The Secretary shall develop a process for coordinating and consolidating the State waiver processes applicable under the provisions of this section, and the existing waiver processes applicable under titles XVIII, XIX, and XXI of the Social Security Act, and any other Federal law relating to the provision of health care items or services. Such process shall permit a State to submit a single application for a waiver under any or all of such provisions.

(6) DEFINITION.—In this section, the term "Secretary" means—

(A) the Secretary of Health and Human Services with respect to waivers relating to the provisions described in subparagraph (A) through (C) of paragraph (2); and

(B) the Secretary of the Treasury with respect to waivers relating to the provisions described in paragraph (2)(D).

(b) GRANTING OF WAIVERS.—

(1) IN GENERAL.—The Secretary may grant a request for a waiver under subsection (a)(1) only if the Secretary determines that the State plan—

(A) will provide coverage that is at least as comprehensive as the coverage defined in section 1302(b) and offered through Exchanges established under this title as certified by Office of the Actuary of the Centers for Medicare & Medicaid Services based on sufficient data from the State and from comparable States about their experience with programs created by this Act and the provisions of this Act that would be waived;

(B) will provide coverage and cost sharing protections against excessive out-of-pocket spending that are at least as affordable as the provisions of this title would provide;

(C) will provide coverage to at least a comparable number of its residents as the provisions of this title would provide; and

(D) will not increase the Federal deficit.

(2) REQUIREMENT TO ENACT A LAW.—

(A) IN GENERAL.—A law described in this paragraph is a State law that provides for State actions under a waiver under this section, including the implementation of the State plan under subsection (a)(1)(B).

(B) TERMINATION OF OPT OUT.—A State may repeal a law described in subparagraph (A) and terminate the authority provided under the waiver with respect to the State.

(c) SCOPE OF WAIVER.—

(1) IN GENERAL.—The Secretary shall determine the scope of a waiver of a requirement described in subsection (a)(2) granted to a State under subsection (a)(1).

(2) LIMITATION.—The Secretary may not waive under this section any Federal law or requirement that is not within the authority of the Secretary.

(d) DETERMINATIONS BY SECRETARY.—

(1) TIME FOR DETERMINATION.—The Secretary shall make a determination under subsection (a)(1) not later than 180

days after the receipt of an application from a State under such subsection.

(2) EFFECT OF DETERMINATION.—

(A) GRANTING OF WAIVERS.—If the Secretary determines to grant a waiver under subsection (a)(1), the Secretary shall notify the State involved of such determination and the terms and effectiveness of such waiver.

(B) DENIAL OF WAIVER.—If the Secretary determines a waiver should not be granted under subsection (a)(1), the Secretary shall notify the State involved, and the appropriate committees of Congress of such determination and the reasons therefore.

(e) TERM OF WAIVER.—No waiver under this section may extend over a period of longer than 5 years unless the State requests continuation of such waiver, and such request shall be deemed granted unless the Secretary, within 90 days after the date of its submission to the Secretary, either denies such request in writing or informs the State in writing with respect to any additional information which is needed in order to make a final determination with respect to the request.

SEC. 1333. PROVISIONS RELATING TO OFFERING OF PLANS IN MORE THAN ONE STATE.

(a) HEALTH CARE CHOICE COMPACTS.—

(1) IN GENERAL.—Not later than July 1, 2013, the Secretary shall, in consultation with the National Association of Insurance Commissioners, issue regulations for the creation of health care choice compacts under which 2 or more States may enter into an agreement under which—

(A) 1 or more qualified health plans could be offered in the individual markets in all such States but, except as provided in subparagraph (B), only be subject to the laws and regulations of the State in which the plan was written or issued;

(B) the issuer of any qualified health plan to which the compact applies—

(i) would continue to be subject to market conduct, unfair trade practices, network adequacy, and consumer protection standards (including standards relating to rating), including addressing disputes as to the performance of the contract, of the State in which the purchaser resides;

(ii) would be required to be licensed in each State in which it offers the plan under the compact or to submit to the jurisdiction of each such State with regard to the standards described in clause (i) (including allowing access to records as if the insurer were licensed in the State); and

(iii) must clearly notify consumers that the policy may not be subject to all the laws and regulations of the State in which the purchaser resides.

(2) STATE AUTHORITY.—A State may not enter into an agreement under this subsection unless the State enacts a law after the date of the enactment of this title that specifically authorizes the State to enter into such agreements.

(3) APPROVAL OF COMPACTS.—The Secretary may approve interstate health care choice compacts under paragraph (1)

only if the Secretary determines that such health care choice compact—

(A) will provide coverage that is at least as comprehensive as the coverage defined in section 1302(b) and offered through Exchanges established under this title;

(B) will provide coverage and cost sharing protections against excessive out-of-pocket spending that are at least as affordable as the provisions of this title would provide;

(C) will provide coverage to at least a comparable number of its residents as the provisions of this title would provide;

(D) will not increase the Federal deficit; and

(E) will not weaken enforcement of laws and regulations described in paragraph (1)(B)(i) in any State that is included in such compact.

(4) EFFECTIVE DATE.—A health care choice compact described in paragraph (1) shall not take effect before January 1, 2016.

(b) AUTHORITY FOR NATIONWIDE PLANS.—

(1) IN GENERAL.—Except as provided in paragraph (2), if an issuer (including a group of health insurance issuers affiliated either by common ownership and control or by the common use of a nationally licensed service mark) of a qualified health plan in the individual or small group market meets the requirements of this subsection (in this subsection a "nationwide qualified health plan")—

(A) the issuer of the plan may offer the nationwide qualified health plan in the individual or small group market in more than 1 State; and

(B) with respect to State laws mandating benefit coverage by a health plan, only the State laws of the State in which such plan is written or issued shall apply to the nationwide qualified health plan.

(2) STATE OPT-OUT.—A State may, by specific reference in a law enacted after the date of enactment of this title, provide that this subsection shall not apply to that State. Such opt-out shall be effective until such time as the State by law revokes it.

(3) PLAN REQUIREMENTS.—An issuer meets the requirements of this subsection with respect to a nationwide qualified health plan if, in the determination of the Secretary—

(A) the plan offers a benefits package that is uniform in each State in which the plan is offered and meets the requirements set forth in paragraphs (4) through (6);

(B) the issuer is licensed in each State in which it offers the plan and is subject to all requirements of State law not inconsistent with this section, including but not limited to, the standards and requirements that a State imposes that do not prevent the application of a requirement of part A of title XXVII of the Public Health Service Act or a requirement of this title;

(C) the issuer meets all requirements of this title with respect to a qualified health plan, including the requirement to offer the silver and gold levels of the plan in each Exchange in the State for the market in which the plan is offered;

(D) the issuer determines the premiums for the plan in any State on the basis of the rating rules in effect in that State for the rating areas in which it is offered;

(E) the issuer offers the nationwide qualified health plan in at least 60 percent of the participating States in the first year in which the plan is offered, 65 percent of such States in the second year, 70 percent of such States in the third year, 75 percent of such States in the fourth year, and 80 percent of such States in the fifth and subsequent years;

(F) the issuer shall offer the plan in participating States across the country, in all geographic regions, and in all States that have adopted adjusted community rating before the date of enactment of this Act; and

(G) the issuer clearly notifies consumers that the policy may not contain some benefits otherwise mandated for plans in the State in which the purchaser resides and provides a detailed statement of the benefits offered and the benefit differences in that State, in accordance with rules promulgated by the Secretary.

(4) FORM REVIEW FOR NATIONWIDE PLANS.—Notwithstanding any contrary provision of State law, at least 3 months before any nationwide qualified health plan is offered, the issuer shall file all nationwide qualified health plan forms with the regulator in each participating State in which the plan will be offered. An issuer may appeal the disapproval of a nationwide qualified health plan form to the Secretary.

(5) APPLICABLE RULES.—The Secretary shall, in consultation with the National Association of Insurance Commissioners, issue rules for the offering of nationwide qualified health plans under this subsection. Nationwide qualified health plans may be offered only after such rules have taken effect.

(6) COVERAGE.—The Secretary shall provide that the health benefits coverage provided to an individual through a nationwide qualified health plan under this subsection shall include at least the essential benefits package described in section 1302.

(7) STATE LAW MANDATING BENEFIT COVERAGE BY A HEALTH BENEFITS PLAN.—For the purposes of this subsection, a State law mandating benefit coverage by a health plan is a law that mandates health insurance coverage or the offer of health insurance coverage for specific health services or specific diseases. A law that mandates health insurance coverage or reimbursement for services provided by certain classes of providers of health care services, or a law that mandates that certain classes of individuals must be covered as a group or as dependents, is not a State law mandating benefit coverage by a health benefits plan.

PART V—REINSURANCE AND RISK ADJUSTMENT

SEC. 1341. TRANSITIONAL REINSURANCE PROGRAM FOR INDIVIDUAL AND SMALL GROUP MARKETS IN EACH STATE.

(a) IN GENERAL.—Each State shall, not later than January 1, 2014—

(1) include in the Federal standards or State law or regulation the State adopts and has in effect under section 1321(b) the provisions described in subsection (b); and

(2) establish (or enter into a contract with) 1 or more applicable reinsurance entities to carry out the reinsurance program under this section.

(b) MODEL REGULATION.—

(1) IN GENERAL.—In establishing the Federal standards under section 1321(a), the Secretary, in consultation with the National Association of Insurance Commissioners (the "NAIC"), shall include provisions that enable States to establish and maintain a program under which—

(A) health insurance issuers, and third party administrators on behalf of group health plans, are required to make payments to an applicable reinsurance entity for any plan year beginning in the 3-year period beginning January 1, 2014 (as specified in paragraph (3); and

(B) the applicable reinsurance entity collects payments under subparagraph (A) and uses amounts so collected to make reinsurance payments to health insurance issuers described in subparagraph (A) that cover high risk individuals in the individual market (excluding grandfathered health plans) for any plan year beginning in such 3-year period.

(2) HIGH-RISK INDIVIDUAL; PAYMENT AMOUNTS.—The Secretary shall include the following in the provisions under paragraph (1):

(A) DETERMINATION OF HIGH-RISK INDIVIDUALS.—The method by which individuals will be identified as high risk individuals for purposes of the reinsurance program established under this section. Such method shall provide for identification of individuals as high-risk individuals on the basis of—

(i) a list of at least 50 but not more than 100 medical conditions that are identified as high-risk conditions and that may be based on the identification of diagnostic and procedure codes that are indicative of individuals with pre-existing, high-risk conditions; or

(ii) any other comparable objective method of identification recommended by the American Academy of Actuaries.

(B) PAYMENT AMOUNT.—The formula for determining the amount of payments that will be paid to health insurance issuers described in paragraph (1)(A) that insure high-risk individuals. Such formula shall provide for the equitable allocation of available funds through reconciliation and may be designed—

(i) to provide a schedule of payments that specifies the amount that will be paid for each of the conditions identified under subparagraph (A); or

(ii) to use any other comparable method for determining payment amounts that is recommended by the American Academy of Actuaries and that encourages the use of care coordination and care management programs for high risk conditions.

(3) DETERMINATION OF REQUIRED CONTRIBUTIONS.—

(A) IN GENERAL.—The Secretary shall include in the provisions under paragraph (1) the method for determining the amount each health insurance issuer and group health plan described in paragraph (1)(A) contributing to the reinsurance program under this section is required to contribute under such paragraph for each plan year beginning in the 36-month period beginning January 1, 2014. The contribution amount for any plan year may be based on the percentage of revenue of each issuer and the total costs of providing benefits to enrollees in self-insured plans or on a specified amount per enrollee and may be required to be paid in advance or periodically throughout the plan year.

(B) SPECIFIC REQUIREMENTS.—The method under this paragraph shall be designed so that—

(i) the contribution amount for each issuer proportionally reflects each issuer's fully insured commercial book of business for all major medical products and the total value of all fees charged by the issuer and the costs of coverage administered by the issuer as a third party administrator;

(ii) the contribution amount can include an additional amount to fund the administrative expenses of the applicable reinsurance entity;

(iii) the aggregate contribution amounts for all States shall, based on the best estimates of the NAIC and without regard to amounts described in clause (ii), equal $10,000,000,000 for plan years beginning in 2014, $6,000,000,000 for plan years beginning 2015, and $4,000,000,000 for plan years beginning in 2016; and

(iv) in addition to the aggregate contribution amounts under clause (iii), each issuer's contribution amount for any calendar year under clause (iii) reflects its proportionate share of an additional $2,000,000,000 for 2014, an additional $2,000,000,000 for 2015, and an additional $1,000,000,000 for 2016.

Nothing in this subparagraph shall be construed to preclude a State from collecting additional amounts from issuers on a voluntary basis.

(4) EXPENDITURE OF FUNDS.—The provisions under paragraph (1) shall provide that—

(A) the contribution amounts collected for any calendar year may be allocated and used in any of the three calendar years for which amounts are collected based on the reinsurance needs of a particular period or to reflect experience in a prior period; and

(B) amounts remaining unexpended as of December, 2016, may be used to make payments under any reinsurance program of a State in the individual market in effect in the 2-year period beginning on January 1, 2017.

Notwithstanding the preceding sentence, any contribution amounts described in paragraph (3)(B)(iv) shall be deposited into the general fund of the Treasury of the United States and may not be used for the program established under this section.

(c) APPLICABLE REINSURANCE ENTITY.—For purposes of this section—

(1) IN GENERAL.—The term "applicable reinsurance entity" means a not-for-profit organization—

(A) the purpose of which is to help stabilize premiums for coverage in the individual and small group markets in a State during the first 3 years of operation of an Exchange for such markets within the State when the risk of adverse selection related to new rating rules and market changes is greatest; and

(B) the duties of which shall be to carry out the reinsurance program under this section by coordinating the funding and operation of the risk-spreading mechanisms designed to implement the reinsurance program.

(2) STATE DISCRETION.—A State may have more than 1 applicable reinsurance entity to carry out the reinsurance program under this section within the State and 2 or more States may enter into agreements to provide for an applicable reinsurance entity to carry out such program in all such States.

(3) ENTITIES ARE TAX-EXEMPT.—An applicable reinsurance entity established under this section shall be exempt from taxation under chapter 1 of the Internal Revenue Code of 1986. The preceding sentence shall not apply to the tax imposed by section 511 such Code (relating to tax on unrelated business taxable income of an exempt organization).

(d) COORDINATION WITH STATE HIGH-RISK POOLS.—The State shall eliminate or modify any State high-risk pool to the extent necessary to carry out the reinsurance program established under this section. The State may coordinate the State high-risk pool with such program to the extent not inconsistent with the provisions of this section.

SEC. 1342. ESTABLISHMENT OF RISK CORRIDORS FOR PLANS IN INDIVIDUAL AND SMALL GROUP MARKETS.

(a) IN GENERAL.—The Secretary shall establish and administer a program of risk corridors for calendar years 2014, 2015, and 2016 under which a qualified health plan offered in the individual or small group market shall participate in a payment adjustment system based on the ratio of the allowable costs of the plan to the plan's aggregate premiums. Such program shall be based on the program for regional participating provider organizations under part D of title XVIII of the Social Security Act.

(b) PAYMENT METHODOLOGY.—

(1) PAYMENTS OUT.—The Secretary shall provide under the program established under subsection (a) that if—

(A) a participating plan's allowable costs for any plan year are more than 103 percent but not more than 108 percent of the target amount, the Secretary shall pay to the plan an amount equal to 50 percent of the target amount in excess of 103 percent of the target amount; and

(B) a participating plan's allowable costs for any plan year are more than 108 percent of the target amount, the Secretary shall pay to the plan an amount equal to the sum of 2.5 percent of the target amount plus 80 percent of allowable costs in excess of 108 percent of the target amount.

(2) PAYMENTS IN.—The Secretary shall provide under the program established under subsection (a) that if—

(A) a participating plan's allowable costs for any plan year are less than 97 percent but not less than 92 percent of the target amount, the plan shall pay to the Secretary an amount equal to 50 percent of the excess of 97 percent of the target amount over the allowable costs; and

(B) a participating plan's allowable costs for any plan year are less than 92 percent of the target amount, the plan shall pay to the Secretary an amount equal to the sum of 2.5 percent of the target amount plus 80 percent of the excess of 92 percent of the target amount over the allowable costs.

(c) DEFINITIONS.—In this section:

(1) ALLOWABLE COSTS.—

(A) IN GENERAL.—The amount of allowable costs of a plan for any year is an amount equal to the total costs (other than administrative costs) of the plan in providing benefits covered by the plan.

(B) REDUCTION FOR RISK ADJUSTMENT AND REINSURANCE PAYMENTS.—Allowable costs shall reduced by any risk adjustment and reinsurance payments received under section 1341 and 1343.

(2) TARGET AMOUNT.—The target amount of a plan for any year is an amount equal to the total premiums (including any premium subsidies under any governmental program), reduced by the administrative costs of the plan.

SEC. 1343. RISK ADJUSTMENT.

(a) IN GENERAL.—

(1) LOW ACTUARIAL RISK PLANS.—Using the criteria and methods developed under subsection (b), each State shall assess a charge on health plans and health insurance issuers (with respect to health insurance coverage) described in subsection (c) if the actuarial risk of the enrollees of such plans or coverage for a year is less than the average actuarial risk of all enrollees in all plans or coverage in such State for such year that are not self-insured group health plans (which are subject to the provisions of the Employee Retirement Income Security Act of 1974).

(2) HIGH ACTUARIAL RISK PLANS.—Using the criteria and methods developed under subsection (b), each State shall provide a payment to health plans and health insurance issuers (with respect to health insurance coverage) described in subsection (c) if the actuarial risk of the enrollees of such plans or coverage for a year is greater than the average actuarial risk of all enrollees in all plans and coverage in such State for such year that are not self-insured group health plans (which are subject to the provisions of the Employee Retirement Income Security Act of 1974).

(b) CRITERIA AND METHODS.—The Secretary, in consultation with States, shall establish criteria and methods to be used in carrying out the risk adjustment activities under this section. The Secretary may utilize criteria and methods similar to the criteria and methods utilized under part C or D of title XVIII of the Social Security Act. Such criteria and methods shall be included in the standards and requirements the Secretary prescribes under section 1321.

(c) SCOPE.—A health plan or a health insurance issuer is described in this subsection if such health plan or health insurance issuer provides coverage in the individual or small group market within the State. This subsection shall not apply to a grandfathered health plan or the issuer of a grandfathered health plan with respect to that plan.

Subtitle E—Affordable Coverage Choices for All Americans

PART I—PREMIUM TAX CREDITS AND COST-SHARING REDUCTIONS

Subpart A—Premium Tax Credits and Cost-sharing Reductions

SEC. 1401. REFUNDABLE TAX CREDIT PROVIDING PREMIUM ASSISTANCE FOR COVERAGE UNDER A QUALIFIED HEALTH PLAN.

(a) IN GENERAL.—Subpart C of part IV of subchapter A of chapter 1 of the Internal Revenue Code of 1986 (relating to refundable credits) is amended by inserting after section 36A the following new section:

"SEC. 36B. REFUNDABLE CREDIT FOR COVERAGE UNDER A QUALIFIED HEALTH PLAN.

"(a) IN GENERAL.—In the case of an applicable taxpayer, there shall be allowed as a credit against the tax imposed by this subtitle for any taxable year an amount equal to the premium assistance credit amount of the taxpayer for the taxable year.

"(b) PREMIUM ASSISTANCE CREDIT AMOUNT.—For purposes of this section—

"(1) IN GENERAL.—The term 'premium assistance credit amount' means, with respect to any taxable year, the sum of the premium assistance amounts determined under paragraph (2) with respect to all coverage months of the taxpayer occurring during the taxable year.

"(2) PREMIUM ASSISTANCE AMOUNT.—The premium assistance amount determined under this subsection with respect to any coverage month is the amount equal to the lesser of—

"(A) the monthly premiums for such month for 1 or more qualified health plans offered in the individual market within a State which cover the taxpayer, the taxpayer's spouse, or any dependent (as defined in section 152) of the taxpayer and which were enrolled in through an Exchange established by the State under 1311 of the Patient Protection and Affordable Care Act, or

"(B) the excess (if any) of—

"(i) the adjusted monthly premium for such month for the applicable second lowest cost silver plan with respect to the taxpayer, over "(ii) an amount equal to 1/12 of the product of the applicable percentage and the taxpayer's household income for the taxable year.

"(3) OTHER TERMS AND RULES RELATING TO PREMIUM ASSISTANCE AMOUNTS.—For purposes of paragraph (2)—

"(A) APPLICABLE PERCENTAGE.—

"(i) IN GENERAL.—Except as provided in clause (ii), the applicable percentage with respect to any taxpayer for any taxable year is equal to 2.8 percent, increased by the number of percentage points (not greater than 7) which bears the same ratio to 7 percentage points as—

"(I) the taxpayer's household income for the taxable year in excess of 100 percent of the poverty line for a family of the size involved, bears to

"(II) an amount equal to 200 percent of the poverty line for a family of the size involved.

"(ii) SPECIAL RULE FOR TAXPAYERS UNDER 133 PERCENT OF POVERTY LINE.—If a taxpayer's household income for the taxable year is in excess of 100 percent, but not more than 133 percent, of the poverty line for a family of the size involved, the taxpayer's applicable percentage shall be 2 percent.

"(iii) INDEXING.—In the case of taxable years beginning in any calendar year after 2014, the Secretary shall adjust the initial and final applicable percentages under clause (i), and the 2 percent under clause (ii), for the calendar year to reflect the excess of the rate of premium growth between the preceding calendar year and 2013 over the rate of income growth for such period.

"(B) APPLICABLE SECOND LOWEST COST SILVER PLAN.—The applicable second lowest cost silver plan with respect to any applicable taxpayer is the second lowest cost silver plan of the individual market in the rating area in which the taxpayer resides which—

"(i) is offered through the same Exchange through which the qualified health plans taken into account under paragraph (2)(A) were offered, and

"(ii) provides—

"(I) self-only coverage in the case of an applicable taxpayer—

"(aa) whose tax for the taxable year is determined under section 1(c) (relating to unmarried individuals other than surviving spouses and heads of households) and who is not allowed a deduction under section 151 for the taxable year with respect to a dependent, or

"(bb) who is not described in item (aa) but who purchases only self-only coverage, and

"(II) family coverage in the case of any other applicable taxpayer.

If a taxpayer files a joint return and no credit is allowed under this section with respect to 1 of the spouses by reason of subsection (e), the taxpayer shall be treated as described in clause (ii)(I) unless a deduction is allowed under section 151 for the taxable year with respect to a dependent other than either spouse and subsection (e) does not apply to the dependent.

"(C) ADJUSTED MONTHLY PREMIUM.—The adjusted monthly premium for an applicable second lowest cost silver plan is the monthly premium which would have been charged (for the rating area with respect to which the premiums under paragraph (2)(A) were determined) for the plan if each individual covered under a qualified health plan taken into account under paragraph (2)(A) were covered by such silver plan and the premium was adjusted only for the age of each such individual in the manner allowed under section 2701 of the Public Health Service Act. In the case of a State participating in the wellness discount demonstration project under section 2705(d) of the Public Health Service Act, the adjusted monthly premium shall be determined without regard to any premium discount or rebate under such project.

"(D) ADDITIONAL BENEFITS.—If—

"(i) a qualified health plan under section 1302(b)(5) of the Patient Protection and Affordable Care Act offers benefits in addition to the essential health benefits required to be provided by the plan, or

"(ii) a State requires a qualified health plan under section 1311(d)(3)(B) of such Act to cover benefits in addition to the essential health benefits required to be provided by the plan,

the portion of the premium for the plan properly allocable (under rules prescribed by the Secretary of Health and Human Services) to such additional benefits shall not be taken into account in determining either the monthly premium or the adjusted monthly premium under paragraph (2).

"(E) SPECIAL RULE FOR PEDIATRIC DENTAL COVERAGE.—For purposes of determining the amount of any monthly premium, if an individual enrolls in both a qualified health plan and a plan described in section 1311(d)(2)(B)(ii)(I) of the Patient Protection and Affordable Care Act for any plan year, the portion of the premium for the plan described in such section that (under regulations prescribed by the Secretary) is properly allocable to pediatric dental benefits which are included in the essential health benefits required to be provided by a qualified health plan under section 1302(b)(1)(J) of such Act shall be treated as a premium payable for a qualified health plan.

"(c) DEFINITION AND RULES RELATING TO APPLICABLE TAXPAYERS, COVERAGE MONTHS, AND QUALIFIED HEALTH PLAN.—For purposes of this section—

"(1) APPLICABLE TAXPAYER.—

"(A) IN GENERAL.—The term 'applicable taxpayer' means, with respect to any taxable year, a taxpayer whose household income for the taxable year exceeds 100 percent but does not exceed 400 percent of an amount equal to the poverty line for a family of the size involved.

"(B) SPECIAL RULE FOR CERTAIN INDIVIDUALS LAWFULLY PRESENT IN THE UNITED STATES.—If—

"(i) a taxpayer has a household income which is not greater than 100 percent of an amount equal to the poverty line for a family of the size involved, and

"(ii) the taxpayer is an alien lawfully present in the United States, but is not eligible for the medicaid program under title XIX of the Social Security Act by reason of such alien status,

the taxpayer shall, for purposes of the credit under this section, be treated as an applicable taxpayer with a household income which is equal to 100 percent of the poverty line for a family of the size involved.

"(C) MARRIED COUPLES MUST FILE JOINT RETURN.—If the taxpayer is married (within the meaning of section 7703) at the close of the taxable year, the taxpayer shall be treated as an applicable taxpayer only if the taxpayer and the taxpayer's spouse file a joint return for the taxable year.

"(D) DENIAL OF CREDIT TO DEPENDENTS.—No credit shall be allowed under this section to any individual with respect to whom a deduction under section 151 is allowable to another taxpayer for a taxable year beginning in the calendar year in which such individual's taxable year begins.

"(2) COVERAGE MONTH.—For purposes of this subsection—

"(A) IN GENERAL.—The term 'coverage month' means, with respect to an applicable taxpayer, any month if—

"(i) as of the first day of such month the taxpayer, the taxpayer's spouse, or any dependent of the taxpayer is covered by a qualified health plan described in subsection (b)(2)(A) that was enrolled in through an Exchange established by the State under section 1311 of the Patient Protection and Affordable Care Act, and

"(ii) the premium for coverage under such plan for such month is paid by the taxpayer (or through advance payment of the credit under subsection (a) under section 1412 of the Patient Protection and Affordable Care Act).

"(B) EXCEPTION FOR MINIMUM ESSENTIAL COVERAGE.—

"(i) IN GENERAL.—The term 'coverage month' shall not include any month with respect to an individual if for such month the individual is eligible for minimum essential coverage other than eligibility for coverage described in section 5000A(f)(1)(C) (relating to coverage in the individual market).

"(ii) MINIMUM ESSENTIAL COVERAGE.—The term 'minimum essential coverage' has the meaning given such term by section 5000A(f).

"(C) SPECIAL RULE FOR EMPLOYER-SPONSORED MINIMUM ESSENTIAL COVERAGE.—For purposes of subparagraph (B)—

"(i) COVERAGE MUST BE AFFORDABLE.—Except as provided in clause (iii), an employee shall not be treated as eligible for minimum essential coverage if such coverage—

"(I) consists of an eligible employer-sponsored plan (as defined in section 5000A(f)(2)), and

"(II) the employee's required contribution (within the meaning of section 5000A(e)(1)(B)) with respect to the plan exceeds 9.8 percent of the applicable taxpayer's household income.

This clause shall also apply to an individual who is eligible to enroll in the plan by reason of a relationship the individual bears to the employee.

"(ii) COVERAGE MUST PROVIDE MINIMUM VALUE.—Except as provided in clause (iii), an employee shall not be treated as eligible for minimum essential coverage if such coverage consists of an eligible employer-sponsored plan (as defined in section 5000A(f)(2)) and the plan's share of the total allowed costs of benefits provided under the plan is less than 60 percent of such costs.

"(iii) EMPLOYEE OR FAMILY MUST NOT BE COVERED UNDER EMPLOYER PLAN.—Clauses (i) and (ii) shall not apply if the employee (or any individual described in the last sentence of clause (i)) is covered under the eligible employer-sponsored plan or the grandfathered health plan.

"(iv) INDEXING.—In the case of plan years beginning in any calendar year after 2014, the Secretary shall adjust the 9.8 percent under clause (i)(II) in the same manner as the percentages are adjusted under subsection (b)(3)(A)(ii).

"(3) DEFINITIONS AND OTHER RULES.—

"(A) QUALIFIED HEALTH PLAN.—The term 'qualified health plan' has the meaning given such term by section 1301(a) of the Patient Protection and Affordable Care Act, except that such term shall not include a qualified health plan which is a catastrophic plan described in section 1302(e) of such Act.

"(B) GRANDFATHERED HEALTH PLAN.—The term 'grandfathered health plan' has the meaning given such term by section 1251 of the Patient Protection and Affordable Care Act.

"(d) TERMS RELATING TO INCOME AND FAMILIES.—For purposes of this section—

"(1) FAMILY SIZE.—The family size involved with respect to any taxpayer shall be equal to the number of individuals for whom the taxpayer is allowed a deduction under section 151 (relating to allowance of deduction for personal exemptions) for the taxable year.

"(2) HOUSEHOLD INCOME.—

"(A) HOUSEHOLD INCOME.—The term 'household income' means, with respect to any taxpayer, an amount equal to the sum of—

"(i) the modified gross income of the taxpayer, plus

"(ii) the aggregate modified gross incomes of all other individuals who—

"(I) were taken into account in determining the taxpayer's family size under paragraph (1), and

"(II) were required to file a return of tax imposed by section 1 for the taxable year.

"(B) MODIFIED GROSS INCOME.—The term 'modified gross income' means gross income—

"(i) decreased by the amount of any deduction allowable under paragraph (1), (3), (4), or (10) of section 62(a),

"(ii) increased by the amount of interest received or accrued during the taxable year which is exempt from tax imposed by this chapter, and

"(iii) determined without regard to sections 911, 931, and 933.

"(3) POVERTY LINE.—

"(A) IN GENERAL.—The term 'poverty line' has the meaning given that term in section 2110(c)(5) of the Social Security Act (42 U.S.C. 1397jj(c)(5)).

"(B) POVERTY LINE USED.—In the case of any qualified health plan offered through an Exchange for coverage during a taxable year beginning in a calendar year, the poverty line used shall be the most recently published poverty line as of the 1st day of the regular enrollment period for coverage during such calendar year.

"(e) RULES FOR INDIVIDUALS NOT LAWFULLY PRESENT.—

"(1) IN GENERAL.—If 1 or more individuals for whom a taxpayer is allowed a deduction under section 151 (relating to allowance of deduction for personal exemptions) for the taxable year (including the taxpayer or his spouse) are individuals who are not lawfully present—

"(A) the aggregate amount of premiums otherwise taken into account under clauses (i) and (ii) of subsection (b)(2)(A) shall be reduced by the portion (if any) of such premiums which is attributable to such individuals, and

"(B) for purposes of applying this section, the determination as to what percentage a taxpayer's household income bears to the poverty level for a family of the size involved shall be made under one of the following methods:

"(i) A method under which—

"(I) the taxpayer's family size is determined by not taking such individuals into account, and

"(II) the taxpayer's household income is equal to the product of the taxpayer's household income (determined without regard to this subsection) and a fraction—

"(aa) the numerator of which is the poverty line for the taxpayer's family size determined after application of subclause (I), and

"(bb) the denominator of which is the poverty line for the taxpayer's family size determined without regard to subclause (I).

"(ii) A comparable method reaching the same result as the method under clause (i).

"(2) LAWFULLY PRESENT.—For purposes of this section, an individual shall be treated as lawfully present only if the individual is, and is reasonably expected to be for the entire period of enrollment for which the credit under this section is being claimed, a citizen or national of the United States or an alien lawfully present in the United States.

"(3) SECRETARIAL AUTHORITY.—The Secretary of Health and Human Services, in consultation with the Secretary, shall prescribe rules setting forth the methods by which calculations of family size and household income are made for purposes of this subsection. Such rules shall be designed to ensure that the least burden is placed on individuals enrolling in qualified health plans through an Exchange and taxpayers eligible for the credit allowable under this section.

"(f) RECONCILIATION OF CREDIT AND ADVANCE CREDIT.—

"(1) IN GENERAL.—The amount of the credit allowed under this section for any taxable year shall be reduced (but not below zero) by the amount of any advance payment of such credit under section 1412 of the Patient Protection and Affordable Care Act.

"(2) EXCESS ADVANCE PAYMENTS.—

"(A) IN GENERAL.—If the advance payments to a taxpayer under section 1412 of the Patient Protection and Affordable Care Act for a taxable year exceed the credit allowed by this section (determined without regard to paragraph (1)), the tax imposed by this chapter for the taxable year shall be increased by the amount of such excess.

"(B) LIMITATION ON INCREASE WHERE INCOME LESS THAN 400 PERCENT OF POVERTY LINE.—

"(i) IN GENERAL.—In the case of an applicable taxpayer whose household income is less than 400 percent of the poverty line for the size of the family involved for the taxable year, the amount of the increase under subparagraph (A) shall in no event exceed $400 ($250 in the case of a taxpayer whose tax is determined under section 1(c) for the taxable year).

"(ii) INDEXING OF AMOUNT.—In the case of any calendar year beginning after 2014, each of the dollar amounts under clause (i) shall be increased by an amount equal to—

"(I) such dollar amount, multiplied by

"(II) the cost-of-living adjustment determined under section 1(f)(3) for the calendar year, determined by substituting 'calendar year 2013' for 'calendar year 1992' in subparagraph (B) thereof.

If the amount of any increase under clause (i) is not a multiple of $50, such increase shall be rounded to the next lowest multiple of $50.

"(g) REGULATIONS.—The Secretary shall prescribe such regulations as may be necessary to carry out the provisions of this section, including regulations which provide for—

"(1) the coordination of the credit allowed under this section with the program for advance payment of the credit under section 1412 of the Patient Protection and Affordable Care Act, and

"(2) the application of subsection (f) where the filing status of the taxpayer for a taxable year is different from such status used for determining the advance payment of the credit.".

(b) DISALLOWANCE OF DEDUCTION.—Section 280C of the Internal Revenue Code of 1986 is amended by adding at the end the following new subsection:

"(g) CREDIT FOR HEALTH INSURANCE PREMIUMS.—No deduction shall be allowed for the portion of the premiums paid by the taxpayer for coverage of 1 or more individuals under a qualified health plan which is equal to the amount of the credit determined for the taxable year under section 36B(a) with respect to such premiums.".

(c) STUDY ON AFFORDABLE COVERAGE.—

(1) STUDY AND REPORT.—

(A) IN GENERAL.—Not later than 5 years after the date of the enactment of this Act, the Comptroller General shall conduct a study on the affordability of health insurance coverage, including—

(i) the impact of the tax credit for qualified health insurance coverage of individuals under section 36B of the Internal Revenue Code of 1986 and the tax credit for employee health insurance expenses of small employers under section 45R of such Code on maintaining and expanding the health insurance coverage of individuals;

(ii) the availability of affordable health benefits plans, including a study of whether the percentage of household income used for purposes of section 36B(c)(2)(C) of the Internal Revenue Code of 1986 (as added by this section) is the appropriate level for determining whether employer-provided coverage is affordable for an employee and whether such level may be lowered without significantly increasing the costs to the Federal Government and reducing employer-provided coverage; and

(iii) the ability of individuals to maintain essential health benefits coverage (as defined in section 5000A(f) of the Internal Revenue Code of 1986).

(B) REPORT.—The Comptroller General shall submit to the appropriate committees of Congress a report on the study conducted under subparagraph (A), together with legislative recommendations relating to the matters studied under such subparagraph.

(2) APPROPRIATE COMMITTEES OF CONGRESS.—In this subsection, the term "appropriate committees of Congress" means the Committee on Ways and Means, the Committee on Education and Labor, and the Committee on Energy and Commerce of the House of Representatives and the Committee on Finance and the Committee on Health, Education, Labor and Pensions of the Senate.

(d) CONFORMING AMENDMENTS.—

(1) Paragraph (2) of section 1324(b) of title 31, United States Code, is amended by inserting "36B," after "36A,".

(2) The table of sections for subpart C of part IV of subchapter A of chapter 1 of the Internal Revenue Code of 1986 is amended by inserting after the item relating to section 36A the following new item:

"Sec. 36B. Refundable credit for coverage under a qualified health plan.".

(e) EFFECTIVE DATE.—The amendments made by this section shall apply to taxable years ending after December 31, 2013.

SEC. 1402. REDUCED COST-SHARING FOR INDIVIDUALS ENROLLING IN QUALIFIED HEALTH PLANS.

(a) IN GENERAL.—In the case of an eligible insured enrolled in a qualified health plan—

(1) the Secretary shall notify the issuer of the plan of such eligibility; and

(2) the issuer shall reduce the cost-sharing under the plan at the level and in the manner specified in subsection (c).

(b) ELIGIBLE INSURED.—In this section, the term "eligible insured" means an individual—

(1) who enrolls in a qualified health plan in the silver level of coverage in the individual market offered through an Exchange; and

(2) whose household income exceeds 100 percent but does not exceed 400 percent of the poverty line for a family of the size involved.

In the case of an individual described in section 36B(c)(1)(B) of the Internal Revenue Code of 1986, the individual shall be treated as having household income equal to 100 percent for purposes of applying this section.

(c) DETERMINATION OF REDUCTION IN COST-SHARING.—

(1) REDUCTION IN OUT-OF-POCKET LIMIT.—

(A) IN GENERAL.—The reduction in cost-sharing under this subsection shall first be achieved by reducing the applicable out-of pocket limit under section 1302(c)(1) in the case of—

(i) an eligible insured whose household income is more than 100 percent but not more than 200 percent of the poverty line for a family of the size involved, by two-thirds;

(ii) an eligible insured whose household income is more than 200 percent but not more than 300 percent of the poverty line for a family of the size involved, by one-half; and

(iii) an eligible insured whose household income is more than 300 percent but not more than 400 percent of the poverty line for a family of the size involved, by one-third.

(B) COORDINATION WITH ACTUARIAL VALUE LIMITS.—

(i) IN GENERAL.—The Secretary shall ensure the reduction under this paragraph shall not result in an increase in the plan's share of the total allowed costs of benefits provided under the plan above—

(I) 90 percent in the case of an eligible insured described in paragraph (2)(A);

(II) 80 percent in the case of an eligible insured described in paragraph (2)(B); and

(III) 70 percent in the case of an eligible insured described in clause (ii) or (iii) of subparagraph (A).

(ii) ADJUSTMENT.—The Secretary shall adjust the out-of pocket limits under paragraph (1) if necessary to ensure that such limits do not cause the respective actuarial values to exceed the levels specified in clause (i).

(2) ADDITIONAL REDUCTION FOR LOWER INCOME INSUREDS.—The Secretary shall establish procedures under which the issuer of a qualified health plan to which this section applies shall further reduce cost-sharing under the plan in a manner sufficient to—

(A) in the case of an eligible insured whose household income is not less than 100 percent but not more than 150 percent of the poverty line for a family of the size involved, increase the plan's share of the total allowed costs of benefits provided under the plan to 90 percent of such costs; and

(B) in the case of an eligible insured whose household income is more than 150 percent but not more than 200 percent of the poverty line for a family of the size involved, increase the plan's share of the total allowed costs of benefits provided under the plan to 80 percent of such costs.

(3) METHODS FOR REDUCING COST-SHARING.—

(A) IN GENERAL.—An issuer of a qualified health plan making reductions under this subsection shall notify the Secretary of such reductions and the Secretary shall make periodic and timely payments to the issuer equal to the value of the reductions.

(B) CAPITATED PAYMENTS.—The Secretary may establish a capitated payment system to carry out the payment of cost-sharing reductions under this section. Any such system shall take into account the value of the reductions and make appropriate risk adjustments to such payments.

(4) ADDITIONAL BENEFITS.—If a qualified health plan under section 1302(b)(5) offers benefits in addition to the essential health benefits required to be provided by the plan, or a State requires a qualified health plan under section 1311(d)(3)(B) to cover benefits in addition to the essential health benefits required to be provided by the plan, the reductions in cost-sharing under this section shall not apply to such additional benefits.

(5) SPECIAL RULE FOR PEDIATRIC DENTAL PLANS.—If an individual enrolls in both a qualified health plan and a plan described in section 1311(d)(2)(B)(ii)(I) for any plan year, subsection (a) shall not apply to that portion of any reduction in cost-sharing under subsection (c) that (under regulations prescribed by the Secretary) is properly allocable to pediatric dental benefits which are included in the essential health benefits required to be provided by a qualified health plan under section 1302(b)(1)(J).

(d) SPECIAL RULES FOR INDIANS.—

(1) INDIANS UNDER 300 PERCENT OF POVERTY.—If an individual enrolled in any qualified health plan in the individual market through an Exchange is an Indian (as defined in section 4(d) of the Indian Self-Determination and Education Assistance Act (25 U.S.C. 450b(d))) whose household income is not more than 300 percent of the poverty line for a family of the size involved, then, for purposes of this section—

(A) such individual shall be treated as an eligible insured; and

(B) the issuer of the plan shall eliminate any cost-sharing under the plan.

(2) ITEMS OR SERVICES FURNISHED THROUGH INDIAN HEALTH PROVIDERS.—If an Indian (as so defined) enrolled in a qualified health plan is furnished an item or service directly by the Indian Health Service, an Indian Tribe, Tribal Organization, or Urban Indian Organization or through referral under contract health services—

(A) no cost-sharing under the plan shall be imposed under the plan for such item or service; and

(B) the issuer of the plan shall not reduce the payment to any such entity for such item or service by the amount of any cost-sharing that would be due from the Indian but for subparagraph (A).

(3) PAYMENT.—The Secretary shall pay to the issuer of a qualified health plan the amount necessary to reflect the increase in actuarial value of the plan required by reason of this subsection.

(e) RULES FOR INDIVIDUALS NOT LAWFULLY PRESENT.—

(1) IN GENERAL.—If an individual who is an eligible insured is not lawfully present—

(A) no cost-sharing reduction under this section shall apply with respect to the individual; and

(B) for purposes of applying this section, the determination as to what percentage a taxpayer's household income bears to the poverty level for a family of the size involved shall be made under one of the following methods:

(i) A method under which—

(I) the taxpayer's family size is determined by not taking such individuals into account, and

(II) the taxpayer's household income is equal to the product of the taxpayer's household income (determined without regard to this subsection) and a fraction—

(aa) the numerator of which is the poverty line for the taxpayer's family size determined after application of subclause (I), and

(bb) the denominator of which is the poverty line for the taxpayer's family size determined without regard to subclause (I).

(ii) A comparable method reaching the same result as the method under clause (i).

(2) LAWFULLY PRESENT.—For purposes of this section, an individual shall be treated as lawfully present only if the individual is, and is reasonably expected to be for the entire period of enrollment for which the cost-sharing reduction under this section is being claimed, a citizen or national of the United States or an alien lawfully present in the United States.

(3) SECRETARIAL AUTHORITY.—The Secretary, in consultation with the Secretary of the Treasury, shall prescribe rules setting forth the methods by which calculations of family size and household income are made for purposes of this subsection. Such rules shall be designed to ensure that the least burden is placed on individuals enrolling in qualified health plans through an Exchange and taxpayers eligible for the credit allowable under this section.

(f) DEFINITIONS AND SPECIAL RULES.—In this section:

(1) IN GENERAL.—Any term used in this section which is also used in section 36B of the Internal Revenue Code of 1986 shall have the meaning given such term by such section.

(2) LIMITATIONS ON REDUCTION.—No cost-sharing reduction shall be allowed under this section with respect to coverage for any month unless the month is a coverage month with respect to which a credit is allowed to the insured (or an applicable taxpayer on behalf of the insured) under section 36B of such Code.

(3) DATA USED FOR ELIGIBILITY.—Any determination under this section shall be made on the basis of the taxable year for which the advance determination is made under section

1412 and not the taxable year for which the credit under section 36B of such Code is allowed.

Subpart B—Eligibility Determinations

SEC. 1411. PROCEDURES FOR DETERMINING ELIGIBILITY FOR EXCHANGE PARTICIPATION, PREMIUM TAX CREDITS AND REDUCED COST-SHARING, AND INDIVIDUAL RESPONSIBILITY EXEMPTIONS.

(a) ESTABLISHMENT OF PROGRAM.—The Secretary shall establish a program meeting the requirements of this section for determining—

(1) whether an individual who is to be covered in the individual market by a qualified health plan offered through an Exchange, or who is claiming a premium tax credit or reduced cost-sharing, meets the requirements of sections 1312(f)(3), 1402(e), and 1412(d) of this title and section 36B(e) of the Internal Revenue Code of 1986 that the individual be a citizen or national of the United States or an alien lawfully present in the United States;

(2) in the case of an individual claiming a premium tax credit or reduced cost-sharing under section 36B of such Code or section 1402—

(A) whether the individual meets the income and coverage requirements of such sections; and

(B) the amount of the tax credit or reduced cost-sharing;

(3) whether an individual's coverage under an employer-sponsored health benefits plan is treated as unaffordable under sections 36B(c)(2)(C) and 5000A(e)(2); and

(4) whether to grant a certification under section 1311(d)(4)(H) attesting that, for purposes of the individual responsibility requirement under section 5000A of the Internal Revenue Code of 1986, an individual is entitled to an exemption from either the individual responsibility requirement or the penalty imposed by such section.

(b) INFORMATION REQUIRED TO BE PROVIDED BY APPLICANTS.—

(1) IN GENERAL.—An applicant for enrollment in a qualified health plan offered through an Exchange in the individual market shall provide—

(A) the name, address, and date of birth of each individual who is to be covered by the plan (in this subsection referred to as an "enrollee"); and

(B) the information required by any of the following paragraphs that is applicable to an enrollee.

(2) CITIZENSHIP OR IMMIGRATION STATUS.—The following information shall be provided with respect to every enrollee:

(A) In the case of an enrollee whose eligibility is based on an attestation of citizenship of the enrollee, the enrollee's social security number.

(B) In the case of an individual whose eligibility is based on an attestation of the enrollee's immigration status, the enrollee's social security number (if applicable) and such identifying information with respect to the enrollee's immigration status as the Secretary, after consultation with the Secretary of Homeland Security, determines appropriate.

(3) ELIGIBILITY AND AMOUNT OF TAX CREDIT OR REDUCED COST-SHARING.—In the case of an enrollee with respect to whom a premium tax credit or reduced cost-sharing under section 36B of such Code or section 1402 is being claimed, the following information:

(A) INFORMATION REGARDING INCOME AND FAMILY SIZE.—The information described in section 6103(l)(21) for the taxable year ending with or within the second calendar year preceding the calendar year in which the plan year begins.

(B) CHANGES IN CIRCUMSTANCES.—The information described in section 1412(b)(2), including information with respect to individuals who were not required to file an income tax return for the taxable year described in subparagraph (A) or individuals who experienced changes in marital status or family size or significant reductions in income.

(4) EMPLOYER-SPONSORED COVERAGE.—In the case of an enrollee with respect to whom eligibility for a premium tax credit under section 36B of such Code or cost-sharing reduction under section 1402 is being established on the basis that the enrollee's (or related individual's) employer is not treated under section 36B(c)(2)(C) of such Code as providing minimum essential coverage or affordable minimum essential coverage, the following information:

(A) The name, address, and employer identification number (if available) of the employer.

(B) Whether the enrollee or individual is a full-time employee and whether the employer provides such minimum essential coverage.

(C) If the employer provides such minimum essential coverage, the lowest cost option for the enrollee's or individual's enrollment status and the enrollee's or individual's required contribution (within the meaning of section 5000A(e)(1)(B) of such Code) under the employer-sponsored plan.

(D) If an enrollee claims an employer's minimum essential coverage is unaffordable, the information described in paragraph (3).

If an enrollee changes employment or obtains additional employment while enrolled in a qualified health plan for which such credit or reduction is allowed, the enrollee shall notify the Exchange of such change or additional employment and provide the information described in this paragraph with respect to the new employer.

(5) EXEMPTIONS FROM INDIVIDUAL RESPONSIBILITY REQUIREMENTS.—In the case of an individual who is seeking an exemption certificate under section 1311(d)(4)(H) from any requirement or penalty imposed by section 5000A, the following information:

(A) In the case of an individual seeking exemption based on the individual's status as a member of an exempt religious sect or division, as a member of a health care sharing ministry, as an Indian, or as an individual eligible for a hardship exemption, such information as the Secretary shall prescribe.

(B) In the case of an individual seeking exemption based on the lack of affordable coverage or the individual's status as a taxpayer with household income less than 100 percent of the poverty line, the information described in paragraphs (3) and (4), as applicable.

(c) VERIFICATION OF INFORMATION CONTAINED IN RECORDS OF SPECIFIC FEDERAL OFFICIALS.—

(1) INFORMATION TRANSFERRED TO SECRETARY.—An Exchange shall submit the information provided by an applicant under subsection (b) to the Secretary for verification in accordance with the requirements of this subsection and subsection (d).

(2) CITIZENSHIP OR IMMIGRATION STATUS.—

(A) COMMISSIONER OF SOCIAL SECURITY.—The Secretary shall submit to the Commissioner of Social Security the following information for a determination as to whether the information provided is consistent with the information in the records of the Commissioner:

(i) The name, date of birth, and social security number of each individual for whom such information was provided under subsection (b)(2).

(ii) The attestation of an individual that the individual is a citizen.

(B) SECRETARY OF HOMELAND SECURITY.—

(i) IN GENERAL.—In the case of an individual—

(I) who attests that the individual is an alien lawfully present in the United States; or

(II) who attests that the individual is a citizen but with respect to whom the Commissioner of Social Security has notified the Secretary under subsection (e)(3) that the attestation is inconsistent with information in the records maintained by the Commissioner;

the Secretary shall submit to the Secretary of Homeland Security the information described in clause (ii) for a determination as to whether the information provided is consistent with the information in the records of the Secretary of Homeland Security.

(ii) INFORMATION.—The information described in clause (ii) is the following:

(I) The name, date of birth, and any identifying information with respect to the individual's immigration status provided under subsection (b)(2).

(II) The attestation that the individual is an alien lawfully present in the United States or in the case of an individual described in clause (i)(II), the attestation that the individual is a citizen.

(3) ELIGIBILITY FOR TAX CREDIT AND COST-SHARING REDUCTION.—The Secretary shall submit the information described in subsection (b)(3)(A) provided under paragraph (3), (4), or (5) of subsection (b) to the Secretary of the Treasury for verification of household income and family size for purposes of eligibility.

(4) METHODS.—

(A) IN GENERAL.—The Secretary, in consultation with the Secretary of the Treasury, the Secretary of Homeland

Security, and the Commissioner of Social Security, shall provide that verifications and determinations under this subsection shall be done—

(i) through use of an on-line system or otherwise for the electronic submission of, and response to, the information submitted under this subsection with respect to an applicant; or

(ii) by determining the consistency of the information submitted with the information maintained in the records of the Secretary of the Treasury, the Secretary of Homeland Security, or the Commissioner of Social Security through such other method as is approved by the Secretary.

(B) FLEXIBILITY.—The Secretary may modify the methods used under the program established by this section for the Exchange and verification of information if the Secretary determines such modifications would reduce the administrative costs and burdens on the applicant, including allowing an applicant to request the Secretary of the Treasury to provide the information described in paragraph (3) directly to the Exchange or to the Secretary. The Secretary shall not make any such modification unless the Secretary determines that any applicable requirements under this section and section 6103 of the Internal Revenue Code of 1986 with respect to the confidentiality, disclosure, maintenance, or use of information will be met.

(d) VERIFICATION BY SECRETARY.—In the case of information provided under subsection (b) that is not required under subsection (c) to be submitted to another person for verification, the Secretary shall verify the accuracy of such information in such manner as the Secretary determines appropriate, including delegating responsibility for verification to the Exchange.

(e) ACTIONS RELATING TO VERIFICATION.—

(1) IN GENERAL.—Each person to whom the Secretary provided information under subsection (c) shall report to the Secretary under the method established under subsection (c)(4) the results of its verification and the Secretary shall notify the Exchange of such results. Each person to whom the Secretary provided information under subsection (d) shall report to the Secretary in such manner as the Secretary determines appropriate.

(2) VERIFICATION.—

(A) ELIGIBILITY FOR ENROLLMENT AND PREMIUM TAX CREDITS AND COST-SHARING REDUCTIONS.—If information provided by an applicant under paragraphs (1), (2), (3), and (4) of subsection (b) is verified under subsections (c) and (d)—

(i) the individual's eligibility to enroll through the Exchange and to apply for premium tax credits and cost-sharing reductions shall be satisfied; and

(ii) the Secretary shall, if applicable, notify the Secretary of the Treasury under section 1412(c) of the amount of any advance payment to be made.

(B) EXEMPTION FROM INDIVIDUAL RESPONSIBILITY.—If information provided by an applicant under subsection (b)(5) is verified under subsections (c) and (d), the Secretary shall issue the certification of exemption described in section 1311(d)(4)(H).

(3) INCONSISTENCIES INVOLVING ATTESTATION OF CITIZENSHIP OR LAWFUL PRESENCE.—If the information provided by any applicant under subsection (b)(2) is inconsistent with information in the records maintained by the Commissioner of Social Security or Secretary of Homeland Security, whichever is applicable, the applicant's eligibility will be determined in the same manner as an individual's eligibility under the medicaid program is determined under section 1902(ee) of the Social Security Act (as in effect on January 1, 2010).

(4) INCONSISTENCIES INVOLVING OTHER INFORMATION.—

(A) IN GENERAL.—If the information provided by an applicant under subsection (b) (other than subsection (b)(2)) is inconsistent with information in the records maintained by persons under subsection (c) or is not verified under subsection (d), the Secretary shall notify the Exchange and the Exchange shall take the following actions:

(i) REASONABLE EFFORT.—The Exchange shall make a reasonable effort to identify and address the causes of such inconsistency, including through typographical or other clerical errors, by contacting the applicant to confirm the accuracy of the information, and by taking such additional actions as the Secretary, through regulation or other guidance, may identify.

(ii) NOTICE AND OPPORTUNITY TO CORRECT.—In the case the inconsistency or inability to verify is not resolved under subparagraph (A), the Exchange shall—

(I) notify the applicant of such fact;

(II) provide the applicant an opportunity to either present satisfactory documentary evidence or resolve the inconsistency with the person verifying the information under subsection (c) or (d) during the 90-day period beginning the date on which the notice required under subclause (I) is sent to the applicant.

The Secretary may extend the 90-day period under subclause (II) for enrollments occurring during 2014.

(B) SPECIFIC ACTIONS NOT INVOLVING CITIZENSHIP OR LAWFUL PRESENCE.—

(i) IN GENERAL.—Except as provided in paragraph (3), the Exchange shall, during any period before the close of the period under subparagraph (A)(ii)(II), make any determination under paragraphs (2), (3), and (4) of subsection (a) on the basis of the information contained on the application.

(ii) ELIGIBILITY OR AMOUNT OF CREDIT OR REDUCTION.—If an inconsistency involving the eligibility for, or amount of, any premium tax credit or cost-sharing reduction is unresolved under this subsection as of the close of the period under subparagraph (A)(ii)(II), the Exchange shall notify the applicant of the amount (if any) of the credit or reduction that is determined on the basis of the records maintained by persons under subsection (c).

(iii) EMPLOYER AFFORDABILITY.—If the Secretary notifies an Exchange that an enrollee is eligible for a premium tax credit under section 36B of such Code or cost-sharing reduction under section 1402 because the enrollee's (or related individual's) employer does not provide minimum essential coverage through an employer-sponsored plan or that the employer does provide that coverage but it is not affordable coverage, the Exchange shall notify the employer of such fact and that the employer may be liable for the payment assessed under section 4980H of such Code.

(iv) EXEMPTION.—In any case where the inconsistency involving, or inability to verify, information provided under subsection (b)(5) is not resolved as of the close of the period under subparagraph (A)(ii)(II), the Exchange shall notify an applicant that no certification of exemption from any requirement or payment under section 5000A of such Code will be issued.

(C) APPEALS PROCESS.—The Exchange shall also notify each person receiving notice under this paragraph of the appeals processes established under subsection (f).

(f) APPEALS AND REDETERMINATIONS.—

(1) IN GENERAL.—The Secretary, in consultation with the Secretary of the Treasury, the Secretary of Homeland Security, and the Commissioner of Social Security, shall establish procedures by which the Secretary or one of such other Federal officers—

(A) hears and makes decisions with respect to appeals of any determination under subsection (e); and

(B) redetermines eligibility on a periodic basis in appropriate circumstances.

(2) EMPLOYER LIABILITY.—

(A) IN GENERAL.—The Secretary shall establish a separate appeals process for employers who are notified under subsection (e)(4)(C) that the employer may be liable for a tax imposed by section 4980H of the Internal Revenue Code of 1986 with respect to an employee because of a determination that the employer does not provide minimum essential coverage through an employer-sponsored plan or that the employer does provide that coverage but it is not affordable coverage with respect to an employee. Such process shall provide an employer the opportunity to—

(i) present information to the Exchange for review of the determination either by the Exchange or the person making the determination, including evidence of the employer-sponsored plan and employer contributions to the plan; and

(ii) have access to the data used to make the determination to the extent allowable by law.

Such process shall be in addition to any rights of appeal the employer may have under subtitle F of such Code.

(B) CONFIDENTIALITY.—Notwithstanding any provision of this title (or the amendments made by this title) or section 6103 of the Internal Revenue Code of 1986, an employer shall not be entitled to any taxpayer return information with respect to an employee for purposes of determining whether the employer is subject to the penalty under section 4980H of such Code with respect to the employee, except that—

(i) the employer may be notified as to the name of an employee and whether or not the employee's income is above or below the threshold by which the affordability of an employer's health insurance coverage is measured; and

(ii) this subparagraph shall not apply to an employee who provides a waiver (at such time and in such manner as the Secretary may prescribe) authorizing an employer to have access to the employee's taxpayer return information.

(g) CONFIDENTIALITY OF APPLICANT INFORMATION.—

(1) IN GENERAL.—An applicant for insurance coverage or for a premium tax credit or cost-sharing reduction shall be required to provide only the information strictly necessary to authenticate identity, determine eligibility, and determine the amount of the credit or reduction.

(2) RECEIPT OF INFORMATION.—Any person who receives information provided by an applicant under subsection (b) (whether directly or by another person at the request of the applicant), or receives information from a Federal agency under subsection (c), (d), or (e), shall—

(A) use the information only for the purposes of, and to the extent necessary in, ensuring the efficient operation of the Exchange, including verifying the eligibility of an individual to enroll through an Exchange or to claim a premium tax credit or cost-sharing reduction or the amount of the credit or reduction; and

(B) not disclose the information to any other person except as provided in this section.

(h) PENALTIES.—

(1) FALSE OR FRAUDULENT INFORMATION.—

(A) CIVIL PENALTY.—

(i) IN GENERAL.—If—

(I) any person fails to provides correct information under subsection (b); and

(II) such failure is attributable to negligence or disregard of any rules or regulations of the Secretary,

such person shall be subject, in addition to any other penalties that may be prescribed by law, to a civil penalty of not more than $25,000 with respect to any failures involving an application for a plan year. For purposes of this subparagraph, the terms "negligence" and "disregard" shall have the same meanings as when used in section 6662 of the Internal Revenue Code of 1986.

(ii) REASONABLE CAUSE EXCEPTION.—No penalty shall be imposed under clause (i) if the Secretary determines that there was a reasonable cause for the failure and that the person acted in good faith.

(B) KNOWING AND WILLFUL VIOLATIONS.—Any person who knowingly and willfully provides false or fraudulent information under subsection (b) shall be subject, in addition to any other penalties that may be prescribed by law, to a civil penalty of not more than $250,000.

(2) IMPROPER USE OR DISCLOSURE OF INFORMATION.—Any person who knowingly and willfully uses or discloses information in violation of subsection (g) shall be subject, in addition to any other penalties that may be prescribed by law, to a civil penalty of not more than $25,000.

(3) LIMITATIONS ON LIENS AND LEVIES.—The Secretary (or, if applicable, the Attorney General of the United States) shall not—

(A) file notice of lien with respect to any property of a person by reason of any failure to pay the penalty imposed by this subsection; or

(B) levy on any such property with respect to such failure.

(i) STUDY OF ADMINISTRATION OF EMPLOYER RESPONSIBILITY.—

(1) IN GENERAL.—The Secretary of Health and Human Services shall, in consultation with the Secretary of the Treasury, conduct a study of the procedures that are necessary to ensure that in the administration of this title and section 4980H of the Internal Revenue Code of 1986 (as added by section 1513) that the following rights are protected:

(A) The rights of employees to preserve their right to confidentiality of their taxpayer return information and their right to enroll in a qualified health plan through an Exchange if an employer does not provide affordable coverage.

(B) The rights of employers to adequate due process and access to information necessary to accurately determine any payment assessed on employers.

(2) REPORT.—Not later than January 1, 2013, the Secretary of Health and Human Services shall report the results of the study conducted under paragraph (1), including any recommendations for legislative changes, to the Committees on Finance and Health, Education, Labor and Pensions of the Senate and the Committees of Education and Labor and Ways and Means of the House of Representatives.

SEC. 1412. ADVANCE DETERMINATION AND PAYMENT OF PREMIUM TAX CREDITS AND COST-SHARING REDUCTIONS.

(a) IN GENERAL.—The Secretary, in consultation with the Secretary of the Treasury, shall establish a program under which—

(1) upon request of an Exchange, advance determinations are made under section 1411 with respect to the income eligibility of individuals enrolling in a qualified health plan in the individual market through the Exchange for the premium tax credit allowable under section 36B of the Internal Revenue Code of 1986 and the cost-sharing reductions under section 1402;

(2) the Secretary notifies—

(A) the Exchange and the Secretary of the Treasury of the advance determinations; and

(B) the Secretary of the Treasury of the name and employer identification number of each employer with respect to whom 1 or more employee of the employer were determined to be eligible for the premium tax credit under section 36B of the Internal Revenue Code of 1986 and the cost-sharing reductions under section 1402 because—

(i) the employer did not provide minimum essential coverage; or

(ii) the employer provided such minimum essential coverage but it was determined under section 36B(c)(2)(C) of such Code to either be unaffordable to the employee or not provide the required minimum actuarial value; and

(3) the Secretary of the Treasury makes advance payments of such credit or reductions to the issuers of the qualified health plans in order to reduce the premiums payable by individuals eligible for such credit.

(b) ADVANCE DETERMINATIONS.—

(1) IN GENERAL.—The Secretary shall provide under the program established under subsection (a) that advance determination of eligibility with respect to any individual shall be made—

(A) during the annual open enrollment period applicable to the individual (or such other enrollment period as may be specified by the Secretary); and

(B) on the basis of the individual's household income for the most recent taxable year for which the Secretary, after consultation with the Secretary of the Treasury, determines information is available.

(2) CHANGES IN CIRCUMSTANCES.—The Secretary shall provide procedures for making advance determinations on the basis of information other than that described in paragraph (1)(B) in cases where information included with an application form demonstrates substantial changes in income, changes in family size or other household circumstances, change in filing status, the filing of an application for unemployment benefits, or other significant changes affecting eligibility, including—

(A) allowing an individual claiming a decrease of 20 percent or more in income, or filing an application for unemployment benefits, to have eligibility for the credit determined on the basis of household income for a later period or on the basis of the individual's estimate of such income for the taxable year; and

(B) the determination of household income in cases where the taxpayer was not required to file a return of tax imposed by this chapter for the second preceding taxable year.

(c) PAYMENT OF PREMIUM TAX CREDITS AND COST-SHARING REDUCTIONS.—

(1) IN GENERAL.—The Secretary shall notify the Secretary of the Treasury and the Exchange through which the individual is enrolling of the advance determination under section 1411.

(2) PREMIUM TAX CREDIT.—

(A) IN GENERAL.—The Secretary of the Treasury shall make the advance payment under this section of any premium tax credit allowed under section 36B of the Internal Revenue Code of 1986 to the issuer of a qualified health plan on a monthly basis (or such other periodic basis as the Secretary may provide).

(B) ISSUER RESPONSIBILITIES.—An issuer of a qualified health plan receiving an advance payment with respect to an individual enrolled in the plan shall—

(i) reduce the premium charged the insured for any period by the amount of the advance payment for the period;

(ii) notify the Exchange and the Secretary of such reduction;

(iii) include with each billing statement the amount by which the premium for the plan has been reduced by reason of the advance payment; and

(iv) in the case of any nonpayment of premiums by the insured—

(I) notify the Secretary of such nonpayment; and

(II) allow a 3-month grace period for nonpayment of premiums before discontinuing coverage.

(3) COST-SHARING REDUCTIONS.—The Secretary shall also notify the Secretary of the Treasury and the Exchange under paragraph (1) if an advance payment of the cost-sharing reductions under section 1402 is to be made to the issuer of any qualified health plan with respect to any individual enrolled in the plan. The Secretary of the Treasury shall make such advance payment at such time and in such amount as the Secretary specifies in the notice.

(d) NO FEDERAL PAYMENTS FOR INDIVIDUALS NOT LAWFULLY PRESENT.—Nothing in this subtitle or the amendments made by this subtitle allows Federal payments, credits, or cost-sharing reductions for individuals who are not lawfully present in the United States.

(e) STATE FLEXIBILITY.—Nothing in this subtitle or the amendments made by this subtitle shall be construed to prohibit a State from making payments to or on behalf of an individual for coverage under a qualified health plan offered through an Exchange that are in addition to any credits or cost-sharing reductions allowable to the individual under this subtitle and such amendments.

SEC. 1413. STREAMLINING OF PROCEDURES FOR ENROLLMENT THROUGH AN EXCHANGE AND STATE MEDICAID, CHIP, AND HEALTH SUBSIDY PROGRAMS.

(a) IN GENERAL.—The Secretary shall establish a system meeting the requirements of this section under which residents of each State may apply for enrollment in, receive a determination of eligibility for participation in, and continue participation in, applicable State health subsidy programs. Such system shall ensure that if an individual applying to an Exchange is found through screening to be eligible for medical assistance under the State medicaid plan under title XIX, or eligible for enrollment under a State children's health insurance program (CHIP) under title XXI of such Act, the individual is enrolled for assistance under such plan or program.

(b) REQUIREMENTS RELATING TO FORMS AND NOTICE.—

(1) REQUIREMENTS RELATING TO FORMS.—

(A) IN GENERAL.—The Secretary shall develop and provide to each State a single, streamlined form that—

(i) may be used to apply for all applicable State health subsidy programs within the State;

(ii) may be filed online, in person, by mail, or by telephone;

(iii) may be filed with an Exchange or with State officials operating one of the other applicable State health subsidy programs; and

(iv) is structured to maximize an applicant's ability to complete the form satisfactorily, taking into account the characteristics of individuals who qualify for applicable State health subsidy programs.

(B) STATE AUTHORITY TO ESTABLISH FORM.—A State may develop and use its own single, streamlined form as an alternative to the form developed under subparagraph (A) if the alternative form is consistent with standards promulgated by the Secretary under this section.

(C) SUPPLEMENTAL ELIGIBILITY FORMS.—The Secretary may allow a State to use a supplemental or alternative form in the case of individuals who apply for eligibility that is not determined on the basis of the household income (as defined in section 36B of the Internal Revenue Code of 1986).

(2) NOTICE.—The Secretary shall provide that an applicant filing a form under paragraph (1) shall receive notice of eligibility for an applicable State health subsidy program without any need to provide additional information or paperwork unless such information or paperwork is specifically required by law when information provided on the form is inconsistent with data used for the electronic verification under paragraph (3) or is otherwise insufficient to determine eligibility.

(c) REQUIREMENTS RELATING TO ELIGIBILITY BASED ON DATA EXCHANGES.—

(1) DEVELOPMENT OF SECURE INTERFACES.—Each State shall develop for all applicable State health subsidy programs a secure, electronic interface allowing an exchange of data (including information contained in the application forms described in subsection (b)) that allows a determination of eligibility for all such programs based on a single application. Such interface shall be compatible with the method established for data verification under section 1411(c)(4).

(2) DATA MATCHING PROGRAM.—Each applicable State health subsidy program shall participate in a data matching arrangement for determining eligibility for participation in the program under paragraph (3) that—

(A) provides access to data described in paragraph (3);

(B) applies only to individuals who—

(i) receive assistance from an applicable State health subsidy program; or

(ii) apply for such assistance—

(I) by filing a form described in subsection (b); or

(II) by requesting a determination of eligibility and authorizing disclosure of the information described in paragraph (3) to applicable State health coverage subsidy programs for purposes of determining and establishing eligibility; and

(C) consistent with standards promulgated by the Secretary, including the privacy and data security safeguards described in section 1942 of the Social Security Act or that are otherwise applicable to such programs.

(3) DETERMINATION OF ELIGIBILITY.—

(A) IN GENERAL.—Each applicable State health subsidy program shall, to the maximum extent practicable—

(i) establish, verify, and update eligibility for participation in the program using the data matching arrangement under paragraph (2); and

(ii) determine such eligibility on the basis of reliable, third party data, including information described in sections 1137, 453(i), and 1942(a) of the Social Security Act, obtained through such arrangement.

(B) EXCEPTION.—This paragraph shall not apply in circumstances with respect to which the Secretary determines that the administrative and other costs of use of the data matching arrangement under paragraph (2) outweigh its expected gains in accuracy, efficiency, and program participation.

(4) SECRETARIAL STANDARDS.—The Secretary shall, after consultation with persons in possession of the data to be matched and representatives of applicable State health subsidy programs, promulgate standards governing the timing, contents, and procedures for data matching described in this subsection. Such standards shall take into account administrative and other costs and the value of data matching to the establishment, verification, and updating of eligibility for applicable State health subsidy programs.

(d) ADMINISTRATIVE AUTHORITY.—

(1) AGREEMENTS.—Subject to section 1411 and section 6103(l)(21) of the Internal Revenue Code of 1986 and any other requirement providing safeguards of privacy and data integrity, the Secretary may establish model agreements, and enter into agreements, for the sharing of data under this section.

(2) AUTHORITY OF EXCHANGE TO CONTRACT OUT.—Nothing in this section shall be construed to—

(A) prohibit contractual arrangements through which a State medicaid agency determines eligibility for all applicable State health subsidy programs, but only if such agency complies with the Secretary's requirements ensuring reduced administrative costs, eligibility errors, and disruptions in coverage; or

(B) change any requirement under title XIX that eligibility for participation in a State's medicaid program must be determined by a public agency.

(e) APPLICABLE STATE HEALTH SUBSIDY PROGRAM.—In this section, the term "applicable State health subsidy program" means—

(1) the program under this title for the enrollment in qualified health plans offered through an Exchange, including the premium tax credits under section 36B of the Internal Revenue Code of 1986 and cost-sharing reductions under section 1402;

(2) a State medicaid program under title XIX of the Social Security Act;

(3) a State children's health insurance program (CHIP) under title XXI of such Act; and

(4) a State program under section 1331 establishing qualified basic health plans.

SEC. 1414. DISCLOSURES TO CARRY OUT ELIGIBILITY REQUIREMENTS FOR CERTAIN PROGRAMS.

(a) DISCLOSURE OF TAXPAYER RETURN INFORMATION AND SOCIAL SECURITY NUMBERS.—

(1) TAXPAYER RETURN INFORMATION.—Subsection (l) of section 6103 of the Internal Revenue Code of 1986 is amended by adding at the end the following new paragraph:

"(21) DISCLOSURE OF RETURN INFORMATION TO CARRY OUT ELIGIBILITY REQUIREMENTS FOR CERTAIN PROGRAMS.—

"(A) IN GENERAL.—The Secretary, upon written request from the Secretary of Health and Human Services, shall disclose to officers, employees, and contractors of the Department of Health and Human Services return information of any taxpayer whose income is relevant in determining any premium tax credit under section 36B or any cost-sharing reduction under section 1402 of the Patient Protection and Affordable Care Act or eligibility for participation in a State medicaid program under title XIX of the Social Security Act, a State's children's health insurance program under title XXI of the Social Security Act, or a basic health program under section 1331 of Patient Protection and Affordable Care Act. Such return information shall be limited to—

"(i) taxpayer identity information with respect to such taxpayer,

"(ii) the filing status of such taxpayer,

"(iii) the number of individuals for whom a deduction is allowed under section 151 with respect to the taxpayer (including the taxpayer and the taxpayer's spouse),

"(iv) the modified gross income (as defined in section 36B) of such taxpayer and each of the other individuals included under clause (iii) who are required to file a return of tax imposed by chapter 1 for the taxable year,

"(v) such other information as is prescribed by the Secretary by regulation as might indicate whether the taxpayer is eligible for such credit or reduction (and the amount thereof), and

"(vi) the taxable year with respect to which the preceding information relates or, if applicable, the fact that such information is not available.

"(B) INFORMATION TO EXCHANGE AND STATE AGENCIES.—The Secretary of Health and Human Services may disclose to an Exchange established under the Patient Protection and Affordable Care Act or its contractors, or to a State agency administering a State program described in subparagraph (A) or its contractors, any inconsistency between the information provided by the Exchange or State agency to the Secretary and the information provided to the Secretary under subparagraph (A).

"(C) RESTRICTION ON USE OF DISCLOSED INFORMATION.—Return information disclosed under subparagraph (A) or (B) may be used by officers, employees, and contractors of the Department of Health and Human Services, an Exchange, or a State agency only for the purposes of, and to the extent necessary in—

"(i) establishing eligibility for participation in the Exchange, and verifying the appropriate amount of, any credit or reduction described in subparagraph (A),

"(ii) determining eligibility for participation in the State programs described in subparagraph (A).".

(2) SOCIAL SECURITY NUMBERS.—Section 205(c)(2)(C) of the Social Security Act is amended by adding at the end the following new clause:

"(x) The Secretary of Health and Human Services, and the Exchanges established under section 1311 of the Patient Protection and Affordable Care Act, are authorized to collect and use the names and social security account numbers of individuals as required to administer the provisions of, and the amendments made by, the such Act.".

(b) CONFIDENTIALITY AND DISCLOSURE.—Paragraph (3) of section 6103(a) of such Code is amended by striking "or (20)" and inserting "(20), or (21)".

(c) PROCEDURES AND RECORDKEEPING RELATED TO DISCLOSURES.—Paragraph (4) of section 6103(p) of such Code is amended—

(1) by inserting ", or any entity described in subsection (l)(21)," after "or (20)" in the matter preceding subparagraph (A),

(2) by inserting "or any entity described in subsection (l)(21)," after "or (o)(1)(A)" in subparagraph (F)(ii), and

(3) by inserting "or any entity described in subsection (l)(21)," after "or (20)" both places it appears in the matter after subparagraph (F).

(d) UNAUTHORIZED DISCLOSURE OR INSPECTION.—Paragraph (2) of section 7213(a) of such Code is amended by striking "or (20)" and inserting "(20), or (21)".

SEC. 1415. PREMIUM TAX CREDIT AND COST-SHARING REDUCTION PAYMENTS DISREGARDED FOR FEDERAL AND FEDERALLY-ASSISTED PROGRAMS.

For purposes of determining the eligibility of any individual for benefits or assistance, or the amount or extent of benefits or assistance, under any Federal program or under any State or local program financed in whole or in part with Federal funds—

(1) any credit or refund allowed or made to any individual by reason of section 36B of the Internal Revenue Code of 1986 (as added by section 1401) shall not be taken into account as income and shall not be taken into account as resources for the month of receipt and the following 2 months; and

(2) any cost-sharing reduction payment or advance payment of the credit allowed under such section 36B that is made under section 1402 or 1412 shall be treated as made to the qualified health plan in which an individual is enrolled and not to that individual.

PART II—SMALL BUSINESS TAX CREDIT

SEC. 1421. CREDIT FOR EMPLOYEE HEALTH INSURANCE EXPENSES OF SMALL BUSINESSES.

(a) IN GENERAL.—Subpart D of part IV of subchapter A of chapter 1 of the Internal Revenue Code of 1986 (relating to business-related credits) is amended by inserting after section 45Q the following:

"SEC. 45R. EMPLOYEE HEALTH INSURANCE EXPENSES OF SMALL EMPLOYERS.

"(a) GENERAL RULE.—For purposes of section 38, in the case of an eligible small employer, the small employer health insurance credit determined under this section for any taxable year in the credit period is the amount determined under subsection (b).

"(b) HEALTH INSURANCE CREDIT AMOUNT.—Subject to subsection (c), the amount determined under this subsection with respect to any eligible small employer is equal to 50 percent (35 percent in the case of a tax-exempt eligible small employer) of the lesser of—

"(1) the aggregate amount of nonelective contributions the employer made on behalf of its employees during the taxable year under the arrangement described in subsection (d)(4) for premiums for qualified health plans offered by the employer to its employees through an Exchange, or

"(2) the aggregate amount of nonelective contributions which the employer would have made during the taxable year under the arrangement if each employee taken into account under paragraph (1) had enrolled in a qualified health plan which had a premium equal to the average premium (as determined by the Secretary of Health and Human Services) for the small group market in the rating area in which the employee enrolls for coverage.

"(c) PHASEOUT OF CREDIT AMOUNT BASED ON NUMBER OF EMPLOYEES AND AVERAGE WAGES.—The amount of the credit determined under subsection (b) without regard to this subsection shall be reduced (but not below zero) by the sum of the following amounts:

"(1) Such amount multiplied by a fraction the numerator of which is the total number of full-time equivalent employees of the employer in excess of 10 and the denominator of which is 15.

"(2) Such amount multiplied by a fraction the numerator of which is the average annual wages of the employer in excess of the dollar amount in effect under subsection (d)(3)(B) and the denominator of which is such dollar amount.

"(d) ELIGIBLE SMALL EMPLOYER.—For purposes of this section—

"(1) IN GENERAL.—The term 'eligible small employer' means, with respect to any taxable year, an employer—

"(A) which has no more than 25 full-time equivalent employees for the taxable year,

"(B) the average annual wages of which do not exceed an amount equal to twice the dollar amount in effect under paragraph (3)(B) for the taxable year, and

"(C) which has in effect an arrangement described in paragraph (4).

"(2) FULL-TIME EQUIVALENT EMPLOYEES.—

"(A) IN GENERAL.—The term 'full-time equivalent employees' means a number of employees equal to the number determined by dividing—

"(i) the total number of hours of service for which wages were paid by the employer to employees during the taxable year, by

"(ii) 2,080.

Such number shall be rounded to the next lowest whole number if not otherwise a whole number.

"(B) EXCESS HOURS NOT COUNTED.—If an employee works in excess of 2,080 hours of service during any taxable year, such excess shall not be taken into account under subparagraph (A).

"(C) HOURS OF SERVICE.—The Secretary, in consultation with the Secretary of Labor, shall prescribe such regulations, rules, and guidance as may be necessary to determine the hours of service of an employee, including rules for the application of this paragraph to employees who are not compensated on an hourly basis.

"(3) AVERAGE ANNUAL WAGES.—

"(A) IN GENERAL.—The average annual wages of an eligible small employer for any taxable year is the amount determined by dividing—

"(i) the aggregate amount of wages which were paid by the employer to employees during the taxable year, by

"(ii) the number of full-time equivalent employees of the employee determined under paragraph (2) for the taxable year.

Such amount shall be rounded to the next lowest multiple of $1,000 if not otherwise such a multiple.

"(B) DOLLAR AMOUNT.—For purposes of paragraph (1)(B)—

"(i) 2011, 2012, AND 2013.—The dollar amount in effect under this paragraph for taxable years beginning in 2011, 2012, or 2013 is $20,000.

"(ii) SUBSEQUENT YEARS.—In the case of a taxable year beginning in a calendar year after 2013, the dollar amount in effect under this paragraph shall be equal to $20,000, multiplied by the cost-of-living adjustment determined under section 1(f)(3) for the calendar year, determined by substituting 'calendar year 2012' for 'calendar year 1992' in subparagraph (B) thereof.

"(4) CONTRIBUTION ARRANGEMENT.—An arrangement is described in this paragraph if it requires an eligible small employer to make a nonelective contribution on behalf of each employee who enrolls in a qualified health plan offered to employees by the employer through an exchange in an amount equal to a uniform percentage (not less than 50 percent) of the premium cost of the qualified health plan.

"(5) SEASONAL WORKER HOURS AND WAGES NOT COUNTED.—For purposes of this subsection—

"(A) IN GENERAL.—The number of hours of service worked by, and wages paid to, a seasonal worker of an employer shall not be taken into account in determining the full-time equivalent employees and average annual wages of the employer unless the worker works for the employer on more than 120 days during the taxable year.

"(B) DEFINITION OF SEASONAL WORKER.—The term 'seasonal worker' means a worker who performs labor or services on a seasonal basis as defined by the Secretary of Labor, including workers covered by section 500.20(s)(1) of title 29, Code of Federal Regulations and retail workers employed exclusively during holiday seasons.

"(e) OTHER RULES AND DEFINITIONS.—For purposes of this section—

"(1) EMPLOYEE.—

"(A) CERTAIN EMPLOYEES EXCLUDED.—The term 'employee' shall not include—

"(i) an employee within the meaning of section 401(c)(1),

"(ii) any 2-percent shareholder (as defined in section 1372(b)) of an eligible small business which is an S corporation,

"(iii) any 5-percent owner (as defined in section 416(i)(1)(B)(i)) of an eligible small business, or

"(iv) any individual who bears any of the relationships described in subparagraphs (A) through (G) of section 152(d)(2) to, or is a dependent described in section 152(d)(2)(H) of, an individual described in clause (i), (ii), or (iii).

"(B) LEASED EMPLOYEES.—The term 'employee' shall include a leased employee within the meaning of section 414(n).

"(2) CREDIT PERIOD.—The term 'credit period' means, with respect to any eligible small employer, the 2-consecutive-taxable year period beginning with the 1st taxable year in which the employer (or any predecessor) offers 1 or more qualified health plans to its employees through an Exchange.

"(3) NONELECTIVE CONTRIBUTION.—The term 'nonelective contribution' means an employer contribution other than an employer contribution pursuant to a salary reduction arrangement.

"(4) WAGES.—The term 'wages' has the meaning given such term by section 3121(a) (determined without regard to any dollar limitation contained in such section).

"(5) AGGREGATION AND OTHER RULES MADE APPLICABLE.—

"(A) AGGREGATION RULES.—All employers treated as a single employer under subsection (b), (c), (m), or (o) of section 414 shall be treated as a single employer for purposes of this section.

"(B) OTHER RULES.—Rules similar to the rules of subsections (c), (d), and (e) of section 52 shall apply.

"(f) CREDIT MADE AVAILABLE TO TAX-EXEMPT ELIGIBLE SMALL EMPLOYERS.—

"(1) IN GENERAL.—In the case of a tax-exempt eligible small employer, there shall be treated as a credit allowable under subpart C (and not allowable under this subpart) the lesser of—

"(A) the amount of the credit determined under this section with respect to such employer, or

"(B) the amount of the payroll taxes of the employer during the calendar year in which the taxable year begins.

"(2) TAX-EXEMPT ELIGIBLE SMALL EMPLOYER.—For purposes of this section, the term 'tax-exempt eligible small employer' means an eligible small employer which is any organization described in section 501(c) which is exempt from taxation under section 501(a).

"(3) PAYROLL TAXES.—For purposes of this subsection—

"(A) IN GENERAL.—The term 'payroll taxes' means—

"(i) amounts required to be withheld from the employees of the tax-exempt eligible small employer under section 3401(a),

"(ii) amounts required to be withheld from such employees under section 3101(b), and

"(iii) amounts of the taxes imposed on the tax-exempt eligible small employer under section 3111(b).

"(B) SPECIAL RULE.—A rule similar to the rule of section 24(d)(2)(C) shall apply for purposes of subparagraph (A).

"(g) APPLICATION OF SECTION FOR CALENDAR YEARS 2011, 2012, AND 2013.—In the case of any taxable year beginning in 2011, 2012, or 2013, the following modifications to this section shall apply in determining the amount of the credit under subsection (a):

"(1) NO CREDIT PERIOD REQUIRED.—The credit shall be determined without regard to whether the taxable year is in a credit period and for purposes of applying this section to taxable years beginning after 2013, no credit period shall be treated as beginning with a taxable year beginning before 2014.

"(2) AMOUNT OF CREDIT.—The amount of the credit determined under subsection (b) shall be determined—

"(A) by substituting '35 percent (25 percent in the case of a tax-exempt eligible small employer)' for '50 percent (35 percent in the case of a tax-exempt eligible small employer)',

"(B) by reference to an eligible small employer's nonelective contributions for premiums paid for health insurance coverage (within the meaning of section 9832(b)(1)) of an employee, and

"(C) by substituting for the average premium determined under subsection (b)(2) the amount the Secretary of Health and Human Services determines is the average premium for the small group market in the State in which the employer is offering health insurance coverage (or for such area within the State as is specified by the Secretary).

"(3) CONTRIBUTION ARRANGEMENT.—An arrangement shall not fail to meet the requirements of subsection (d)(4) solely because it provides for the offering of insurance outside of an Exchange.

"(h) INSURANCE DEFINITIONS.—Any term used in this section which is also used in the Public Health Service Act or subtitle A of title I of the Patient Protection and Affordable Care Act shall have the meaning given such term by such Act or subtitle.

"(i) REGULATIONS.—The Secretary shall prescribe such regulations as may be necessary to carry out the provisions of this section, including regulations to prevent the avoidance of the 2-year limit on the credit period through the use of successor entities and the avoidance of the limitations under subsection (c) through the use of multiple entities.".

(b) CREDIT TO BE PART OF GENERAL BUSINESS CREDIT.—Section 38(b) of the Internal Revenue Code of 1986 (relating to current year business credit) is amended by striking "plus" at the end of paragraph (34), by striking the period at the end of paragraph (35) and inserting ", plus", and by inserting after paragraph (35) the following:

"(36) the small employer health insurance credit determined under section 45R.".

(c) CREDIT ALLOWED AGAINST ALTERNATIVE MINIMUM TAX.—Section 38(c)(4)(B) of the Internal Revenue Code of 1986 (defining specified credits) is amended by redesignating clauses (vi), (vii), and (viii) as clauses (vii), (viii), and (ix), respectively, and by inserting after clause (v) the following new clause:

"(vi) the credit determined under section 45R,".

(d) DISALLOWANCE OF DEDUCTION FOR CERTAIN EXPENSES FOR WHICH CREDIT ALLOWED.—

(1) IN GENERAL.—Section 280C of the Internal Revenue Code of 1986 (relating to disallowance of deduction for certain expenses for which credit allowed), as amended by section 1401(b), is amended by adding at the end the following new subsection:

"(h) CREDIT FOR EMPLOYEE HEALTH INSURANCE EXPENSES OF SMALL EMPLOYERS.—No deduction shall be allowed for that portion of the premiums for qualified health plans (as defined in section 1301(a) of the Patient Protection and Affordable Care Act), or for health insurance coverage in the case of taxable years beginning in 2011, 2012, or 2013, paid by an employer which is equal to the amount of the credit determined under section 45R(a) with respect to the premiums.".

(2) DEDUCTION FOR EXPIRING CREDITS.—Section 196(c) of such Code is amended by striking "and" at the end of paragraph (12), by striking the period at the end of paragraph (13) and inserting ", and", and by adding at the end the following new paragraph:

"(14) the small employer health insurance credit determined under section 45R(a).".

(e) CLERICAL AMENDMENT.—The table of sections for subpart D of part IV of subchapter A of chapter 1 of the Internal Revenue Code of 1986 is amended by adding at the end the following:

"Sec. 45R. Employee health insurance expenses of small employers.".

(f) EFFECTIVE DATES.—

(1) IN GENERAL.—The amendments made by this section shall apply to amounts paid or incurred in taxable years beginning after December 31, 2010.

(2) MINIMUM TAX.—The amendments made by subsection (c) shall apply to credits determined under section 45R of the Internal Revenue Code of 1986 in taxable years beginning after December 31, 2010, and to carrybacks of such credits.

Subtitle F—Shared Responsibility for Health Care

PART I—INDIVIDUAL RESPONSIBILITY

SEC. 1501. REQUIREMENT TO MAINTAIN MINIMUM ESSENTIAL COVERAGE.

(a) FINDINGS.—Congress makes the following findings:

(1) IN GENERAL.—The individual responsibility requirement provided for in this section (in this subsection referred to as the "requirement") is commercial and economic in nature, and substantially affects interstate commerce, as a result of the effects described in paragraph (2).

(2) EFFECTS ON THE NATIONAL ECONOMY AND INTERSTATE COMMERCE.—The effects described in this paragraph are the following:

(A) The requirement regulates activity that is commercial and economic in nature: economic and financial decisions about how and when health care is paid for, and when health insurance is purchased.

(B) Health insurance and health care services are a significant part of the national economy. National health spending is projected to increase from $2,500,000,000,000, or 17.6 percent of the economy, in 2009 to $4,700,000,000,000 in 2019. Private health insurance spending is projected to be $854,000,000,000 in 2009, and pays for medical supplies, drugs, and equipment that are shipped in interstate commerce. Since most health insurance is sold by national or regional health insurance companies, health insurance is sold in interstate commerce and claims payments flow through interstate commerce.

(C) The requirement, together with the other provisions of this Act, will add millions of new consumers to the health insurance market, increasing the supply of, and demand for, health care services. According to the Congressional Budget Office, the requirement will increase the number and share of Americans who are insured.

(D) The requirement achieves near-universal coverage by building upon and strengthening the private employer-based health insurance system, which covers 176,000,000 Americans nationwide. In Massachusetts, a similar requirement has strengthened private employer-based coverage: despite the economic downturn, the number of workers offered employer-based coverage has actually increased.

(E) Half of all personal bankruptcies are caused in part by medical expenses. By significantly increasing health insurance coverage, the requirement, together with the other provisions of this Act, will improve financial security for families.

(F) Under the Employee Retirement Income Security Act of 1974 (29 U.S.C. 1001 et seq.), the Public Health Service Act (42 U.S.C. 201 et seq.), and this Act, the Federal Government has a significant role in regulating health insurance which is in interstate commerce.

(G) Under sections 2704 and 2705 of the Public Health Service Act (as added by section 1201 of this Act), if there were no requirement, many individuals would wait to purchase health insurance until they needed care. By significantly increasing health insurance coverage, the requirement, together with the other provisions of this Act, will minimize this adverse selection and broaden the health insurance risk pool to include healthy individuals, which will lower health insurance premiums. The requirement is essential to creating effective health insurance markets in which improved health insurance products that are guaranteed issue and do not exclude coverage of pre-existing conditions can be sold.

(H) Administrative costs for private health insurance, which were $90,000,000,000 in 2006, are 26 to 30 percent of premiums in the current individual and small group markets. By significantly increasing health insurance coverage and the size of purchasing pools, which will increase economies of scale, the requirement, together with the other provisions of this Act, will significantly reduce administrative costs and lower health insurance premiums. The requirement is essential to creating effective health insurance markets that do not require underwriting and eliminate its associated administrative costs.

(3) SUPREME COURT RULING.—In United States v. South-Eastern Underwriters Association (322 U.S. 533 (1944)), the Supreme Court of the United States ruled that insurance is interstate commerce subject to Federal regulation.

(b) IN GENERAL.—Subtitle D of the Internal Revenue Code of 1986 is amended by adding at the end the following new chapter:

"CHAPTER 48—MAINTENANCE OF MINIMUM ESSENTIAL COVERAGE

"SEC. 5000A. REQUIREMENT TO MAINTAIN MINIMUM ESSENTIAL COVERAGE.

"(a) REQUIREMENT TO MAINTAIN MINIMUM ESSENTIAL COVERAGE.—An applicable individual shall for each month beginning after 2013 ensure that the individual, and any dependent of the individual who is an applicable individual, is covered under minimum essential coverage for such month.

"(b) SHARED RESPONSIBILITY PAYMENT.—

"(1) IN GENERAL.—If an applicable individual fails to meet the requirement of subsection (a) for 1 or more months during any calendar year beginning after 2013, then, except as provided in subsection (d), there is hereby imposed a penalty with respect to the individual in the amount determined under subsection (c).

"(2) INCLUSION WITH RETURN.—Any penalty imposed by this section with respect to any month shall be included with a taxpayer's return under chapter 1 for the taxable year which includes such month.

"(3) PAYMENT OF PENALTY.—If an individual with respect to whom a penalty is imposed by this section for any month—

"(A) is a dependent (as defined in section 152) of another taxpayer for the other taxpayer's taxable year including such month, such other taxpayer shall be liable for such penalty, or

"(B) files a joint return for the taxable year including such month, such individual and the spouse of such individual shall be jointly liable for such penalty.

"(c) AMOUNT OF PENALTY.—

"(1) IN GENERAL.—The penalty determined under this subsection for any month with respect to any individual is an amount equal to 1⁄12 of the applicable dollar amount for the calendar year.

"(2) DOLLAR LIMITATION.—The amount of the penalty imposed by this section on any taxpayer for any taxable year with respect to all individuals for whom the taxpayer is liable under subsection (b)(3) shall not exceed an amount equal to 300 percent the applicable dollar amount (determined without regard to paragraph (3)(C)) for the calendar year with or within which the taxable year ends.

"(3) APPLICABLE DOLLAR AMOUNT.—For purposes of paragraph (1)—

"(A) IN GENERAL.—Except as provided in subparagraphs (B) and (C), the applicable dollar amount is $750.

"(B) PHASE IN.—The applicable dollar amount is $95 for 2014 and $350 for 2015.

"(C) SPECIAL RULE FOR INDIVIDUALS UNDER AGE 18.—If an applicable individual has not attained the age of 18 as of the beginning of a month, the applicable dollar amount with respect to such individual for the month shall be equal to one-half of the applicable dollar amount for the calendar year in which the month occurs.

"(D) INDEXING OF AMOUNT.—In the case of any calendar year beginning after 2016, the applicable dollar amount shall be equal to $750, increased by an amount equal to—

"(i) $750, multiplied by

"(ii) the cost-of-living adjustment determined under section 1(f)(3) for the calendar year, determined by substituting 'calendar year 2015' for 'calendar year 1992' in subparagraph (B) thereof.

If the amount of any increase under clause (i) is not a multiple of $50, such increase shall be rounded to the next lowest multiple of $50.

"(4) TERMS RELATING TO INCOME AND FAMILIES.—For purposes of this section—

"(A) FAMILY SIZE.—The family size involved with respect to any taxpayer shall be equal to the number of individuals for whom the taxpayer is allowed a deduction under section 151 (relating to allowance of deduction for personal exemptions) for the taxable year.

"(B) HOUSEHOLD INCOME.—The term 'household income' means, with respect to any taxpayer for any taxable year, an amount equal to the sum of—

"(i) the modified gross income of the taxpayer, plus

"(ii) the aggregate modified gross incomes of all other individuals who—

"(I) were taken into account in determining the taxpayer's family size under paragraph (1), and

"(II) were required to file a return of tax imposed by section 1 for the taxable year.

"(C) MODIFIED GROSS INCOME.—The term 'modified gross income' means gross income—

"(i) decreased by the amount of any deduction allowable under paragraph (1), (3), (4), or (10) of section 62(a),

"(ii) increased by the amount of interest received or accrued during the taxable year which is exempt from tax imposed by this chapter, and

"(iii) determined without regard to sections 911, 931, and 933.

"(D) POVERTY LINE.—

"(i) IN GENERAL.—The term 'poverty line' has the meaning given that term in section 2110(c)(5) of the Social Security Act (42 U.S.C. 1397jj(c)(5)).

"(ii) POVERTY LINE USED.—In the case of any taxable year ending with or within a calendar year, the poverty line used shall be the most recently published poverty line as of the 1st day of such calendar year.

"(d) APPLICABLE INDIVIDUAL.—For purposes of this section—

"(1) IN GENERAL.—The term 'applicable individual' means, with respect to any month, an individual other than an individual described in paragraph (2), (3), or (4).

"(2) RELIGIOUS EXEMPTIONS.—

"(A) RELIGIOUS CONSCIENCE EXEMPTION.—Such term shall not include any individual for any month if such individual has in effect an exemption under section 1311(d)(4)(H) of the Patient Protection and Affordable Care Act which certifies that such individual is a member of a recognized religious sect or division thereof described in section 1402(g)(1) and an adherent of established tenets or teachings of such sect or division as described in such section.

"(B) HEALTH CARE SHARING MINISTRY.—

"(i) IN GENERAL.—Such term shall not include any individual for any month if such individual is a member of a health care sharing ministry for the month.

"(ii) HEALTH CARE SHARING MINISTRY.—The term 'health care sharing ministry' means an organization—

"(I) which is described in section 501(c)(3) and is exempt from taxation under section 501(a),

"(II) members of which share a common set of ethical or religious beliefs and share medical expenses among members in accordance with those beliefs and without regard to the State in which a member resides or is employed,

"(III) members of which retain membership even after they develop a medical condition,

"(IV) which (or a predecessor of which) has been in existence at all times since December 31, 1999, and medical expenses of its members have been shared continuously and without interruption since at least December 31, 1999, and

"(V) which conducts an annual audit which is performed by an independent certified public accounting firm in accordance with generally accepted accounting principles and which is made available to the public upon request.

"(3) INDIVIDUALS NOT LAWFULLY PRESENT.—Such term shall not include an individual for any month if for the month the individual is not a citizen or national of the United States or an alien lawfully present in the United States.

"(4) INCARCERATED INDIVIDUALS.—Such term shall not include an individual for any month if for the month the individual is incarcerated, other than incarceration pending the disposition of charges.

"(e) EXEMPTIONS.—No penalty shall be imposed under subsection (a) with respect to—

"(1) INDIVIDUALS WHO CANNOT AFFORD COVERAGE.—

"(A) IN GENERAL.—Any applicable individual for any month if the applicable individual's required contribution (determined on an annual basis) for coverage for the month exceeds 8 percent of such individual's household income for the taxable year described in section 1412(b)(1)(B) of the Patient Protection and Affordable Care Act. For purposes of applying this subparagraph, the taxpayer's household income shall be increased by any exclusion from gross income for any portion of the required contribution made through a salary reduction arrangement.

"(B) REQUIRED CONTRIBUTION.—For purposes of this paragraph, the term 'required contribution' means—

"(i) in the case of an individual eligible to purchase minimum essential coverage consisting of coverage through an eligible-employer-sponsored plan, the portion of the annual premium which would be paid by the individual (without regard to whether paid through salary reduction or otherwise) for self-only coverage, or

"(ii) in the case of an individual eligible only to purchase minimum essential coverage described in subsection (f)(1)(C), the annual premium for the lowest cost bronze plan available in the individual market through the Exchange in the State in the rating area in which the individual resides (without regard to whether the individual purchased a qualified health plan through the Exchange), reduced by the amount of the credit allowable under section 36B for the taxable year (determined as if the individual was covered by a qualified health plan offered through the Exchange for the entire taxable year).

"(C) SPECIAL RULES FOR INDIVIDUALS RELATED TO EMPLOYEES.—For purposes of subparagraph (B)(i), if an applicable individual is eligible for minimum essential coverage through an employer by reason of a relationship to an employee, the determination shall be made by reference to the affordability of the coverage to the employee.

"(D) INDEXING.—In the case of plan years beginning in any calendar year after 2014, subparagraph (A) shall be applied by substituting for '8 percent' the percentage the Secretary of Health and Human Services determines reflects the excess of the rate of premium growth between the preceding calendar year and 2013 over the rate of income growth for such period.

"(2) TAXPAYERS WITH INCOME UNDER 100 PERCENT OF POVERTY LINE.—Any applicable individual for any month during a calendar year if the individual's household income for the taxable year described in section 1412(b)(1)(B) of the Patient Protection and Affordable Care Act is less than 100 percent of the poverty line for the size of the family involved (determined in the same manner as under subsection (b)(4)).

"(3) MEMBERS OF INDIAN TRIBES.—Any applicable individual for any month during which the individual is a member of an Indian tribe (as defined in section 45A(c)(6)).

"(4) MONTHS DURING SHORT COVERAGE GAPS.—

"(A) IN GENERAL.—Any month the last day of which occurred during a period in which the applicable individual was not covered by minimum essential coverage for a continuous period of less than 3 months.

"(B) SPECIAL RULES.—For purposes of applying this paragraph—

"(i) the length of a continuous period shall be determined without regard to the calendar years in which months in such period occur,

"(ii) if a continuous period is greater than the period allowed under subparagraph (A), no exception shall be provided under this paragraph for any month in the period, and

"(iii) if there is more than 1 continuous period described in subparagraph (A) covering months in a calendar year, the exception provided by this paragraph shall only apply to months in the first of such periods.

The Secretary shall prescribe rules for the collection of the penalty imposed by this section in cases where continuous periods include months in more than 1 taxable year.

"(5) HARDSHIPS.—Any applicable individual who for any month is determined by the Secretary of Health and Human Services under section 1311(d)(4)(H) to have suffered a hardship with respect to the capability to obtain coverage under a qualified health plan.

"(f) MINIMUM ESSENTIAL COVERAGE.—For purposes of this section—

"(1) IN GENERAL.—The term 'minimum essential coverage' means any of the following:

"(A) GOVERNMENT SPONSORED PROGRAMS.—Coverage under—

"(i) the Medicare program under part A of title XVIII of the Social Security Act,

"(ii) the Medicaid program under title XIX of the Social Security Act,

"(iii) the CHIP program under title XXI of the Social Security Act,

"(iv) the TRICARE for Life program,

"(v) the veteran's health care program under chapter 17 of title 38, United States Code, or

"(vi) a health plan under section 2504(e) of title 22, United States Code (relating to Peace Corps volunteers).

"(B) EMPLOYER-SPONSORED PLAN.—Coverage under an eligible employer-sponsored plan.

"(C) PLANS IN THE INDIVIDUAL MARKET.—Coverage under a health plan offered in the individual market within a State.

"(D) GRANDFATHERED HEALTH PLAN.—Coverage under a grandfathered health plan.

"(E) OTHER COVERAGE.—Such other health benefits coverage, such as a State health benefits risk pool, as the Secretary of Health and Human Services, in coordination with the Secretary, recognizes for purposes of this subsection.

"(2) ELIGIBLE EMPLOYER-SPONSORED PLAN.—The term 'eligible employer-sponsored plan' means, with respect to any employee, a group health plan or group health insurance coverage offered by an employer to the employee which is—

"(A) a governmental plan (within the meaning of section 2791(d)(8) of the Public Health Service Act), or

"(B) any other plan or coverage offered in the small or large group market within a State.

Such term shall include a grandfathered health plan described in paragraph (1)(D) offered in a group market.

"(3) EXCEPTED BENEFITS NOT TREATED AS MINIMUM ESSENTIAL COVERAGE.—The term 'minimum essential coverage' shall not include health insurance coverage which consists of coverage of excepted benefits—

"(A) described in paragraph (1) of subsection (c) of section 2791 of the Public Health Service Act; or

"(B) described in paragraph (2), (3), or (4) of such subsection if the benefits are provided under a separate policy, certificate, or contract of insurance.

"(4) INDIVIDUALS RESIDING OUTSIDE UNITED STATES OR RESIDENTS OF TERRITORIES.—Any applicable individual shall be treated as having minimum essential coverage for any month—

"(A) if such month occurs during any period described in subparagraph (A) or (B) of section 911(d)(1) which is applicable to the individual, or

"(B) if such individual is a bona fide resident of any possession of the United States (as determined under section 937(a)) for such month.

"(5) INSURANCE-RELATED TERMS.—Any term used in this section which is also used in title I of the Patient Protection and Affordable Care Act shall have the same meaning as when used in such title.

"(g) ADMINISTRATION AND PROCEDURE.—

"(1) IN GENERAL.—The penalty provided by this section shall be paid upon notice and demand by the Secretary, and except as provided in paragraph (2), shall be assessed and collected in the same manner as an assessable penalty under subchapter B of chapter 68.

"(2) SPECIAL RULES.—Notwithstanding any other provision of law—

"(A) WAIVER OF CRIMINAL PENALTIES.—In the case of any failure by a taxpayer to timely pay any penalty imposed by this section, such taxpayer shall not be subject to any criminal prosecution or penalty with respect to such failure.

"(B) LIMITATIONS ON LIENS AND LEVIES.—The Secretary shall not—

"(i) file notice of lien with respect to any property of a taxpayer by reason of any failure to pay the penalty imposed by this section, or

"(ii) levy on any such property with respect to such failure.".

(c) CLERICAL AMENDMENT.—The table of chapters for subtitle D of the Internal Revenue Code of 1986 is amended by inserting after the item relating to chapter 47 the following new item:

"CHAPTER 48—MAINTENANCE OF MINIMUM ESSENTIAL COVERAGE.".

(d) EFFECTIVE DATE.—The amendments made by this section shall apply to taxable years ending after December 31, 2013.

SEC. 1502. REPORTING OF HEALTH INSURANCE COVERAGE.

(a) IN GENERAL.—Part III of subchapter A of chapter 61 of the Internal Revenue Code of 1986 is amended by inserting after subpart C the following new subpart:

"Subpart D—Information Regarding Health Insurance Coverage

"SEC. 6055. REPORTING OF HEALTH INSURANCE COVERAGE.

"(a) IN GENERAL.—Every person who provides minimum essential coverage to an individual during a calendar year shall, at such time as the Secretary may prescribe, make a return described in subsection (b).

"(b) FORM AND MANNER OF RETURN.—

"(1) IN GENERAL.—A return is described in this subsection if such return—

"(A) is in such form as the Secretary may prescribe, and

"(B) contains—

"(i) the name, address and TIN of the primary insured and the name and TIN of each other individual obtaining coverage under the policy,

"(ii) the dates during which such individual was covered under minimum essential coverage during the calendar year,

"(iii) in the case of minimum essential coverage which consists of health insurance coverage, information concerning—

"(I) whether or not the coverage is a qualified health plan offered through an Exchange established under section 1311 of the Patient Protection and Affordable Care Act, and

"(II) in the case of a qualified health plan, the amount (if any) of any advance payment under section 1412 of the Patient Protection and Affordable Care Act of any cost-sharing reduction under section 1402 of such Act or of any premium tax credit under section 36B with respect to such coverage, and

"(iv) such other information as the Secretary may require.

"(2) INFORMATION RELATING TO EMPLOYER-PROVIDED COVERAGE.—If minimum essential coverage provided to an individual under subsection (a) consists of health insurance coverage of a health insurance issuer provided through a group health plan of an employer, a return described in this subsection shall include—

"(A) the name, address, and employer identification number of the employer maintaining the plan,

"(B) the portion of the premium (if any) required to be paid by the employer, and

"(C) if the health insurance coverage is a qualified health plan in the small group market offered through an Exchange, such other information as the Secretary may require for administration of the credit under section 45R (relating to credit for employee health insurance expenses of small employers).

"(c) STATEMENTS TO BE FURNISHED TO INDIVIDUALS WITH RESPECT TO WHOM INFORMATION IS REPORTED.—

"(1) IN GENERAL.—Every person required to make a return under subsection (a) shall furnish to each individual whose name is required to be set forth in such return a written statement showing—

"(A) the name and address of the person required to make such return and the phone number of the information contact for such person, and

"(B) the information required to be shown on the return with respect to such individual.

"(2) TIME FOR FURNISHING STATEMENTS.—The written statement required under paragraph (1) shall be furnished on or before January 31 of the year following the calendar year for which the return under subsection (a) was required to be made.

"(d) COVERAGE PROVIDED BY GOVERNMENTAL UNITS.—In the case of coverage provided by any governmental unit or any agency or instrumentality thereof, the officer or employee who enters into the agreement to provide such coverage (or the person appropriately designated for purposes of this section) shall make the returns and statements required by this section.

"(e) MINIMUM ESSENTIAL COVERAGE.—For purposes of this section, the term 'minimum essential coverage' has the meaning given such term by section 5000A(f).".

(b) ASSESSABLE PENALTIES.—

(1) Subparagraph (B) of section 6724(d)(1) of the Internal Revenue Code of 1986 (relating to definitions) is amended by striking "or" at the end of clause (xxii), by striking "and" at the end of clause (xxiii) and inserting "or", and by inserting after clause (xxiii) the following new clause:

"(xxiv) section 6055 (relating to returns relating to information regarding health insurance coverage), and".

(2) Paragraph (2) of section 6724(d) of such Code is amended by striking "or" at the end of subparagraph (EE), by striking the period at the end of subparagraph (FF) and inserting ", or" and by inserting after subparagraph (FF) the following new subparagraph:

"(GG) section 6055(c) (relating to statements relating to information regarding health insurance coverage).".

(c) NOTIFICATION OF NONENROLLMENT.—Not later than June 30 of each year, the Secretary of the Treasury, acting through the Internal Revenue Service and in consultation with the Secretary of Health and Human Services, shall send a notification to each individual who files an individual income tax return and who is not enrolled in minimum essential coverage (as defined in section 5000A of the Internal Revenue Code of 1986). Such notification shall contain information on the services available through the Exchange operating in the State in which such individual resides.

(d) CONFORMING AMENDMENT.—The table of subparts for part III of subchapter A of chapter 61 of such Code is amended by inserting after the item relating to subpart C the following new item:

"SUBPART D—INFORMATION REGARDING HEALTH INSURANCE COVERAGE".

(e) EFFECTIVE DATE.—The amendments made by this section shall apply to calendar years beginning after 2013.

PART II—EMPLOYER RESPONSIBILITIES

SEC. 1511. AUTOMATIC ENROLLMENT FOR EMPLOYEES OF LARGE EMPLOYERS.

The Fair Labor Standards Act of 1938 is amended by inserting after section 18 (29 U.S.C. 218) the following:

"SEC. 18A. AUTOMATIC ENROLLMENT FOR EMPLOYEES OF LARGE EMPLOYERS.

"In accordance with regulations promulgated by the Secretary, an employer to which this Act applies that has more than 200 full-time employees and that offers employees enrollment in 1 or more health benefits plans shall automatically enroll new full-time employees in one of the plans offered (subject to any waiting period authorized by law) and to continue the enrollment of current employees in a health benefits plan offered through the employer. Any automatic enrollment program shall include adequate notice and the opportunity for an employee to opt out of any coverage the individual or employee were automatically enrolled in. Nothing in this section shall be construed to supersede any State law which establishes, implements, or continues in effect any standard or requirement relating to employers in connection with payroll except to the extent that such standard or requirement prevents an employer from instituting the automatic enrollment program under this section.".

SEC. 1512. EMPLOYER REQUIREMENT TO INFORM EMPLOYEES OF COVERAGE OPTIONS.

The Fair Labor Standards Act of 1938 is amended by inserting after section 18A (as added by section 1513) the following:

"SEC. 18B. NOTICE TO EMPLOYEES.

"(a) IN GENERAL.—In accordance with regulations promulgated by the Secretary, an employer to which this Act applies, shall provide to each employee at the time of hiring (or with respect to current employees, not later than March 1, 2013), written notice—

"(1) informing the employee of the existence of an Exchange, including a description of the services provided by such Exchange, and the manner in which the employee may contact the Exchange to request assistance;

"(2) if the employer plan's share of the total allowed costs of benefits provided under the plan is less than 60 percent of such costs, that the employee may be eligible for a premium tax credit under section 36B of the Internal Revenue Code of 1986 and a cost sharing reduction under section 1402 of the Patient Protection and Affordable Care Act if the employee purchases a qualified health plan through the Exchange; and

"(3) if the employee purchases a qualified health plan through the Exchange, the employee will lose the employer contribution (if any) to any health benefits plan offered by the employer and that all or a portion of such contribution may be excludable from income for Federal income tax purposes.

"(b) EFFECTIVE DATE.—Subsection (a) shall take effect with respect to employers in a State beginning on March 1, 2013.".

SEC. 1513. SHARED RESPONSIBILITY FOR EMPLOYERS.

(a) IN GENERAL.—Chapter 43 of the Internal Revenue Code of 1986 is amended by adding at the end the following:

"SEC. 4980H. SHARED RESPONSIBILITY FOR EMPLOYERS REGARDING HEALTH COVERAGE.

"(a) LARGE EMPLOYERS NOT OFFERING HEALTH COVERAGE.—If—

"(1) any applicable large employer fails to offer to its full-time employees (and their dependents) the opportunity to enroll in minimum essential coverage under an eligible employer-sponsored plan (as defined in section 5000A(f)(2)) for any month, and

"(2) at least one full-time employee of the applicable large employer has been certified to the employer under section 1411 of the Patient Protection and Affordable Care Act as having enrolled for such month in a qualified health plan with respect to which an applicable premium tax credit or cost-sharing reduction is allowed or paid with respect to the employee,

then there is hereby imposed on the employer an assessable payment equal to the product of the applicable payment amount and the number of individuals employed by the employer as full-time employees during such month.

"(b) LARGE EMPLOYERS WITH WAITING PERIODS EXCEEDING 30 DAYS.—

"(1) IN GENERAL.—In the case of any applicable large employer which requires an extended waiting period to enroll in any minimum essential coverage under an employer-sponsored plan (as defined in section 5000A(f)(2)), there is hereby imposed on the employer an assessable payment, in the amount specified in paragraph (2), for each full-time employee of the employer to whom the extended waiting period applies.

"(2) AMOUNT.—For purposes of paragraph (1), the amount specified in this paragraph for a full-time employee is—

"(A) in the case of an extended waiting period which exceeds 30 days but does not exceed 60 days, $400, and

"(B) in the case of an extended waiting period which exceeds 60 days, $600.

"(3) EXTENDED WAITING PERIOD.—The term 'extended waiting period' means any waiting period (as defined in section 2701(b)(4) of the Public Health Service Act) which exceeds 30 days.

"(c) LARGE EMPLOYERS OFFERING COVERAGE WITH EMPLOYEES WHO QUALIFY FOR PREMIUM TAX CREDITS OR COST-SHARING REDUCTIONS.—

"(1) IN GENERAL.—If—

"(A) an applicable large employer offers to its full-time employees (and their dependents) the opportunity to enroll in minimum essential coverage under an eligible employer-sponsored plan (as defined in section 5000A(f)(2)) for any month, and

"(B) 1 or more full-time employees of the applicable large employer has been certified to the employer under section 1411 of the Patient Protection and Affordable Care Act as having enrolled for such month in a qualified health plan with respect to which an applicable premium tax credit or cost-sharing reduction is allowed or paid with respect to the employee,

then there is hereby imposed on the employer an assessable payment equal to the product of the number of full-time employees of the applicable large employer described in subparagraph (B) for such month and 400 percent of the applicable payment amount.

"(2) OVERALL LIMITATION.—The aggregate amount of tax determined under paragraph (1) with respect to all employees of an applicable large employer for any month shall not exceed the product of the applicable payment amount and the number of individuals employed by the employer as full-time employees during such month.

"(d) DEFINITIONS AND SPECIAL RULES.—For purposes of this section—

"(1) APPLICABLE PAYMENT AMOUNT.—The term 'applicable payment amount' means, with respect to any month, 1⁄12 of $750.

"(2) APPLICABLE LARGE EMPLOYER.—

"(A) IN GENERAL.—The term 'applicable large employer' means, with respect to a calendar year, an employer who employed an average of at least 50 full-time employees on business days during the preceding calendar year.

"(B) EXEMPTION FOR CERTAIN EMPLOYERS.—

"(i) IN GENERAL.—An employer shall not be considered to employ more than 50 full-time employees if—

"(I) the employer's workforce exceeds 50 full-time employees for 120 days or fewer during the calendar year, and

"(II) the employees in excess of 50 employed during such 120-day period were seasonal workers.

"(ii) DEFINITION OF SEASONAL WORKERS.—The term 'seasonal worker' means a worker who performs labor or services on a seasonal basis as defined by the Secretary of Labor, including workers covered by section 500.20(s)(1) of title 29, Code of Federal Regulations and retail workers employed exclusively during holiday seasons.

"(C) RULES FOR DETERMINING EMPLOYER SIZE.—For purposes of this paragraph—

"(i) APPLICATION OF AGGREGATION RULE FOR EMPLOYERS.—All persons treated as a single employer under subsection (b), (c), (m), or (o) of section 414 of the Internal Revenue Code of 1986 shall be treated as 1 employer.

"(ii) EMPLOYERS NOT IN EXISTENCE IN PRECEDING YEAR.—In the case of an employer which was not in existence throughout the preceding calendar year, the determination of whether such employer is an applicable large employer shall be based on the average number of employees that it is reasonably expected such employer will employ on business days in the current calendar year.

"(iii) PREDECESSORS.—Any reference in this subsection to an employer shall include a reference to any predecessor of such employer.

"(3) APPLICABLE PREMIUM TAX CREDIT AND COST-SHARING REDUCTION.—The term 'applicable premium tax credit and cost-sharing reduction' means—

"(A) any premium tax credit allowed under section 36B,

"(B) any cost-sharing reduction under section 1402 of the Patient Protection and Affordable Care Act, and

"(C) any advance payment of such credit or reduction under section 1412 of such Act.

"(4) FULL-TIME EMPLOYEE.—

"(A) IN GENERAL.—The term 'full-time employee' means an employee who is employed on average at least 30 hours of service per week.

"(B) HOURS OF SERVICE.—The Secretary, in consultation with the Secretary of Labor, shall prescribe such regulations, rules, and guidance as may be necessary to determine the hours of service of an employee, including rules for the application of this paragraph to employees who are not compensated on an hourly basis.

"(5) INFLATION ADJUSTMENT.—

"(A) IN GENERAL.—In the case of any calendar year after 2014, each of the dollar amounts in subsection (b)(2) and (d)(1) shall be increased by an amount equal to the product of—

"(i) such dollar amount, and

"(ii) the premium adjustment percentage (as defined in section 1302(c)(4) of the Patient Protection and Affordable Care Act) for the calendar year.

"(B) ROUNDING.—If the amount of any increase under subparagraph (A) is not a multiple of $10, such increase shall be rounded to the next lowest multiple of $10.

"(6) OTHER DEFINITIONS.—Any term used in this section which is also used in the Patient Protection and Affordable Care Act shall have the same meaning as when used in such Act.

"(7) TAX NONDEDUCTIBLE.—For denial of deduction for the tax imposed by this section, see section 275(a)(6).

"(e) ADMINISTRATION AND PROCEDURE.—

"(1) IN GENERAL.—Any assessable payment provided by this section shall be paid upon notice and demand by the Secretary, and shall be assessed and collected in the same manner as an assessable penalty under subchapter B of chapter 68.

"(2) TIME FOR PAYMENT.—The Secretary may provide for the payment of any assessable payment provided by this section on an annual, monthly, or other periodic basis as the Secretary may prescribe.

"(3) COORDINATION WITH CREDITS, ETC..—The Secretary shall prescribe rules, regulations, or guidance for the repayment of any assessable payment (including interest) if such payment is based on the allowance or payment of an applicable premium tax credit or cost-sharing reduction with respect to an employee, such allowance or payment is subsequently disallowed, and the assessable payment would not have been required to be made but for such allowance or payment.".

(b) CLERICAL AMENDMENT.—The table of sections for chapter 43 of such Code is amended by adding at the end the following new item:

"Sec. 4980H. Shared responsibility for employers regarding health coverage.".

(c) STUDY AND REPORT OF EFFECT OF TAX ON WORKERS' WAGES.—

(1) IN GENERAL.—The Secretary of Labor shall conduct a study to determine whether employees' wages are reduced by reason of the application of the assessable payments under section 4980H of the Internal Revenue Code of 1986 (as added by the amendments made by this section). The Secretary shall make such determination on the basis of the National Compensation Survey published by the Bureau of Labor Statistics.

(2) REPORT.—The Secretary shall report the results of the study under paragraph (1) to the Committee on Ways and Means of the House of Representatives and to the Committee on Finance of the Senate.

(d) EFFECTIVE DATE.—The amendments made by this section shall apply to months beginning after December 31, 2013.

SEC. 1514. REPORTING OF EMPLOYER HEALTH INSURANCE COVERAGE.

(a) IN GENERAL.—Subpart D of part III of subchapter A of chapter 61 of the Internal Revenue Code of 1986, as added by section 1502, is amended by inserting after section 6055 the following new section:

"SEC. 6056. LARGE EMPLOYERS REQUIRED TO REPORT ON HEALTH INSURANCE COVERAGE.

"(a) IN GENERAL.—Every applicable large employer required to meet the requirements of section 4980H with respect to its full-time employees during a calendar year shall, at such time as the Secretary may prescribe, make a return described in subsection (b).

"(b) FORM AND MANNER OF RETURN.—A return is described in this subsection if such return—

"(1) is in such form as the Secretary may prescribe, and

"(2) contains—

"(A) the name, date, and employer identification number of the employer,

"(B) a certification as to whether the employer offers to its full-time employees (and their dependents) the opportunity to enroll in minimum essential coverage under an eligible employer-sponsored plan (as defined in section 5000A(f)(2)),

"(C) if the employer certifies that the employer did offer to its full-time employees (and their dependents) the opportunity to so enroll—

"(i) the length of any waiting period (as defined in section 2701(b)(4) of the Public Health Service Act) with respect to such coverage,

"(ii) the months during the calendar year for which coverage under the plan was available,

"(iii) the monthly premium for the lowest cost option in each of the enrollment categories under the plan, and

"(iv) the applicable large employer's share of the total allowed costs of benefits provided under the plan,

"(D) the number of full-time employees for each month during the calendar year,

"(E) the name, address, and TIN of each full-time employee during the calendar year and the months (if any) during which such employee (and any dependents) were covered under any such health benefits plans, and

"(F) such other information as the Secretary may require.

"(c) STATEMENTS TO BE FURNISHED TO INDIVIDUALS WITH RESPECT TO WHOM INFORMATION IS REPORTED.—

"(1) IN GENERAL.—Every person required to make a return under subsection (a) shall furnish to each full-time employee whose name is required to be set forth in such return under subsection (b)(2)(E) a written statement showing—

"(A) the name and address of the person required to make such return and the phone number of the information contact for such person, and

"(B) the information required to be shown on the return with respect to such individual.

"(2) TIME FOR FURNISHING STATEMENTS.—The written statement required under paragraph (1) shall be furnished on or before January 31 of the year following the calendar year for which the return under subsection (a) was required to be made.

"(d) COORDINATION WITH OTHER REQUIREMENTS.—To the maximum extent feasible, the Secretary may provide that—

"(1) any return or statement required to be provided under this section may be provided as part of any return or statement required under section 6051 or 6055, and

"(2) in the case of an applicable large employer offering health insurance coverage of a health insurance issuer, the employer may enter into an agreement with the issuer to include information required under this section with the return and statement required to be provided by the issuer under section 6055.

"(e) COVERAGE PROVIDED BY GOVERNMENTAL UNITS.—In the case of any applicable large employer which is a governmental unit or any agency or instrumentality thereof, the person appropriately designated for purposes of this section shall make the returns and statements required by this section.

"(f) DEFINITIONS.—For purposes of this section, any term used in this section which is also used in section 4980H shall have the meaning given such term by section 4980H.".

(b) ASSESSABLE PENALTIES.—

(1) Subparagraph (B) of section 6724(d)(1) of the Internal Revenue Code of 1986 (relating to definitions), as amended by section 1502, is amended by striking "or" at the end of clause (xxiii), by striking "and" at the end of clause (xxiv) and inserting "or", and by inserting after clause (xxiv) the following new clause:

"(xxv) section 6056 (relating to returns relating to large employers required to report on health insurance coverage), and".

(2) Paragraph (2) of section 6724(d) of such Code, as so amended, is amended by striking "or" at the end of subparagraph (FF), by striking the period at the end of subparagraph

(GG) and inserting ", or" and by inserting after subparagraph (GG) the following new subparagraph:

"(HH) section 6056(c) (relating to statements relating to large employers required to report on health insurance coverage).".

(c) CONFORMING AMENDMENT.—The table of sections for subpart D of part III of subchapter A of chapter 61 of such Code, as added by section 1502, is amended by adding at the end the following new item:

"Sec. 6056. Large employers required to report on health insurance coverage.".

(d) EFFECTIVE DATE.—The amendments made by this section shall apply to periods beginning after December 31, 2013.

SEC. 1515. OFFERING OF EXCHANGE-PARTICIPATING QUALIFIED HEALTH PLANS THROUGH CAFETERIA PLANS.

(a) IN GENERAL.—Subsection (f) of section 125 of the Internal Revenue Code of 1986 is amended by adding at the end the following new paragraph:

"(3) CERTAIN EXCHANGE-PARTICIPATING QUALIFIED HEALTH PLANS NOT QUALIFIED.—

"(A) IN GENERAL.—The term 'qualified benefit' shall not include any qualified health plan (as defined in section 1301(a) of the Patient Protection and Affordable Care Act) offered through an Exchange established under section 1311 of such Act.

"(B) EXCEPTION FOR EXCHANGE-ELIGIBLE EMPLOYERS.—Subparagraph (A) shall not apply with respect to any employee if such employee's employer is a qualified employer (as defined in section 1312(f)(2) of the Patient Protection and Affordable Care Act) offering the employee the opportunity to enroll through such an Exchange in a qualified health plan in a group market.".

(b) CONFORMING AMENDMENTS.—Subsection (f) of section 125 of such Code is amended—

(1) by striking "For purposes of this section, the term" and inserting "For purposes of this section—

"(1) IN GENERAL.—The term", and

(2) by striking "Such term shall not include" and inserting the following:

"(2) LONG-TERM CARE INSURANCE NOT QUALIFIED.—The term 'qualified benefit' shall not include".

(c) EFFECTIVE DATE.—The amendments made by this section shall apply to taxable years beginning after December 31, 2013.

Subtitle G—Miscellaneous Provisions

SEC. 1551. DEFINITIONS.

Unless specifically provided for otherwise, the definitions contained in section 2791 of the Public Health Service Act (42 U.S.C. 300gg–91) shall apply with respect to this title.

SEC. 1552. TRANSPARENCY IN GOVERNMENT.

Not later than 30 days after the date of enactment of this Act, the Secretary of Health and Human Services shall publish on the Internet website of the Department of Health and Human Services, a list of all of the authorities provided to the Secretary under this Act (and the amendments made by this Act).

SEC. 1553. PROHIBITION AGAINST DISCRIMINATION ON ASSISTED SUICIDE.

(a) IN GENERAL.—The Federal Government, and any State or local government or health care provider that receives Federal financial assistance under this Act (or under an amendment made by this Act) or any health plan created under this Act (or under an amendment made by this Act), may not subject an individual or institutional health care entity to discrimination on the basis that the entity does not provide any health care item or service furnished for the purpose of causing, or for the purpose of assisting in causing, the death of any individual, such as by assisted suicide, euthanasia, or mercy killing.

(b) DEFINITION.—In this section, the term "health care entity" includes an individual physician or other health care professional, a hospital, a provider-sponsored organization, a health maintenance organization, a health insurance plan, or any other kind of health care facility, organization, or plan.

(c) CONSTRUCTION AND TREATMENT OF CERTAIN SERVICES.—Nothing in subsection (a) shall be construed to apply to, or to affect, any limitation relating to—

(1) the withholding or withdrawing of medical treatment or medical care;

(2) the withholding or withdrawing of nutrition or hydration;

(3) abortion; or

(4) the use of an item, good, benefit, or service furnished for the purpose of alleviating pain or discomfort, even if such use may increase the risk of death, so long as such item, good, benefit, or service is not also furnished for the purpose of causing, or the purpose of assisting in causing, death, for any reason.

(d) ADMINISTRATION.—The Office for Civil Rights of the Department of Health and Human Services is designated to receive complaints of discrimination based on this section.

SEC. 1554. ACCESS TO THERAPIES.

Notwithstanding any other provision of this Act, the Secretary of Health and Human Services shall not promulgate any regulation that—

(1) creates any unreasonable barriers to the ability of individuals to obtain appropriate medical care;

(2) impedes timely access to health care services;

(3) interferes with communications regarding a full range of treatment options between the patient and the provider;

(4) restricts the ability of health care providers to provide full disclosure of all relevant information to patients making health care decisions;

(5) violates the principles of informed consent and the ethical standards of health care professionals; or

(6) limits the availability of health care treatment for the full duration of a patient's medical needs.

SEC. 1555. FREEDOM NOT TO PARTICIPATE IN FEDERAL HEALTH INSURANCE PROGRAMS.

No individual, company, business, nonprofit entity, or health insurance issuer offering group or individual health insurance coverage shall be required to participate in any Federal health insurance program created under this Act (or any amendments made by this Act), or in any Federal health insurance program expanded by this Act (or any such amendments), and there shall be no penalty or fine imposed upon any such issuer for choosing not to participate in such programs.

SEC. 1556. EQUITY FOR CERTAIN ELIGIBLE SURVIVORS.

(a) REBUTTABLE PRESUMPTION.—Section 411(c)(4) of the Black Lung Benefits Act (30 U.S.C. 921(c)(4)) is amended by striking the last sentence.

(b) CONTINUATION OF BENEFITS.—Section 422(l) of the Black Lung Benefits Act (30 U.S.C. 932(l)) is amended by striking ", except with respect to a claim filed under this part on or after the effective date of the Black Lung Benefits Amendments of 1981".

(c) EFFECTIVE DATE.—The amendments made by this section shall apply with respect to claims filed under part B or part C of the Black Lung Benefits Act (30 U.S.C. 921 et seq., 931 et seq.) after January 1, 2005, that are pending on or after the date of enactment of this Act.

SEC. 1557. NONDISCRIMINATION.

(a) IN GENERAL.—Except as otherwise provided for in this title (or an amendment made by this title), an individual shall not, on the ground prohibited under title VI of the Civil Rights Act of 1964 (42 U.S.C. 2000d et seq.), title IX of the Education Amendments of 1972 (20 U.S.C. 1681 et seq.), the Age Discrimination Act of 1975 (42 U.S.C. 6101 et seq.), or section 504 of the Rehabilitation Act of 1973 (29 U.S.C. 794), be excluded from participation in, be denied the benefits of, or be subjected to discrimination under, any health program or activity, any part of which is receiving Federal financial assistance, including credits, subsidies, or contracts of insurance, or under any program or activity that is administered by an Executive Agency or any entity established under this title (or amendments). The enforcement mechanisms provided for and available under such title VI, title IX, section 504, or such Age Discrimination Act shall apply for purposes of violations of this subsection.

(b) CONTINUED APPLICATION OF LAWS.—Nothing in this title (or an amendment made by this title) shall be construed to invalidate or limit the rights, remedies, procedures, or legal standards available to individuals aggrieved under title VI of the Civil Rights Act of 1964 (42 U.S.C. 2000d et seq.), title VII of the Civil Rights Act of 1964 (42 U.S.C. 2000e et seq.), title IX of the Education Amendments of 1972 (20 U.S.C. 1681 et seq.), section 504 of the Rehabilitation Act of 1973 (29 U.S.C. 794), or the Age Discrimination Act of 1975 (42 U.S.C. 611 et seq.), or to supersede State laws that provide additional protections against discrimination on any basis described in subsection (a).

(c) REGULATIONS.—The Secretary may promulgate regulations to implement this section.

SEC. 1558. PROTECTIONS FOR EMPLOYEES.

The Fair Labor Standards Act of 1938 is amended by inserting after section 18B (as added by section 1512) the following:

"SEC. 18C. PROTECTIONS FOR EMPLOYEES.

"(a) PROHIBITION.—No employer shall discharge or in any manner discriminate against any employee with respect to his or her compensation, terms, conditions, or other privileges of employment because the employee (or an individual acting at the request of the employee) has—

"(1) received a credit under section 36B of the Internal Revenue Code of 1986 or a subsidy under section 1402 of this Act;

"(2) provided, caused to be provided, or is about to provide or cause to be provided to the employer, the Federal Government, or the attorney general of a State information relating to any violation of, or any act or omission the employee reasonably believes to be a violation of, any provision of this title (or an amendment made by this title);

"(3) testified or is about to testify in a proceeding concerning such violation;

"(4) assisted or participated, or is about to assist or participate, in such a proceeding; or

"(5) objected to, or refused to participate in, any activity, policy, practice, or assigned task that the employee (or other such person) reasonably believed to be in violation of any provision of this title (or amendment), or any order, rule, regulation, standard, or ban under this title (or amendment).

"(b) COMPLAINT PROCEDURE.—

"(1) IN GENERAL.—An employee who believes that he or she has been discharged or otherwise discriminated against by any employer in violation of this section may seek relief in accordance with the procedures, notifications, burdens of proof, remedies, and statutes of limitation set forth in section 2087(b) of title 15, United States Code.

"(2) NO LIMITATION ON RIGHTS.—Nothing in this section shall be deemed to diminish the rights, privileges, or remedies of any employee under any Federal or State law or under any collective bargaining agreement. The rights and remedies in this section may not be waived by any agreement, policy, form, or condition of employment.".

SEC. 1559. OVERSIGHT.

The Inspector General of the Department of Health and Human Services shall have oversight authority with respect to the administration and implementation of this title as it relates to such Department.

SEC. 1560. RULES OF CONSTRUCTION.

(a) NO EFFECT ON ANTITRUST LAWS.—Nothing in this title (or an amendment made by this title) shall be construed to modify, impair, or supersede the operation of any of the antitrust laws. For the purposes of this section, the term "antitrust laws" has the meaning given such term in subsection (a) of the first section of the Clayton Act, except that such term includes section 5 of the Federal Trade Commission Act to the extent that such section 5 applies to unfair methods of competition.

(b) RULE OF CONSTRUCTION REGARDING HAWAII'S PREPAID HEALTH CARE ACT.—Nothing in this title (or an amendment made by this title) shall be construed to modify or limit the application of the exemption for Hawaii's Prepaid Health Care Act (Haw. Rev. Stat. §§ 393–1 et seq.) as provided for under section 514(b)(5) of the Employee Retirement Income Security Act of 1974 (29 U.S.C. 1144(b)(5)).

(c) STUDENT HEALTH INSURANCE PLANS.—Nothing in this title (or an amendment made by this title) shall be construed to prohibit an institution of higher education (as such term is defined for purposes of the Higher Education Act of 1965) from offering a student health insurance plan, to the extent that such requirement is otherwise permitted under applicable Federal, State or local law.

(d) NO EFFECT ON EXISTING REQUIREMENTS.—Nothing in this title (or an amendment made by this title, unless specified by direct statutory reference) shall be construed to modify any existing Federal requirement concerning the State agency responsible for determining eligibility for programs identified in section 1413.

SEC. 1561. HEALTH INFORMATION TECHNOLOGY ENROLLMENT STANDARDS AND PROTOCOLS.

Title XXX of the Public Health Service Act (42 U.S.C. 300jj et seq.) is amended by adding at the end the following:

"Subtitle C—Other Provisions

"SEC. 3021. HEALTH INFORMATION TECHNOLOGY ENROLLMENT STANDARDS AND PROTOCOLS.

"(a) IN GENERAL.—

"(1) STANDARDS AND PROTOCOLS.—Not later than 180 days after the date of enactment of this title, the Secretary, in consultation with the HIT Policy Committee and the HIT Standards Committee, shall develop interoperable and secure standards and protocols that facilitate enrollment of individuals in Federal and State health and human services programs, as determined by the Secretary.

"(2) METHODS.—The Secretary shall facilitate enrollment in such programs through methods determined appropriate by the Secretary, which shall include providing individuals and third parties authorized by such individuals and their designees notification of eligibility and verification of eligibility required under such programs.

"(b) CONTENT.—The standards and protocols for electronic enrollment in the Federal and State programs described in subsection (a) shall allow for the following:

"(1) Electronic matching against existing Federal and State data, including vital records, employment history, enrollment systems, tax records, and other data determined appropriate by the Secretary to serve as evidence of eligibility and in lieu of paper-based documentation.

"(2) Simplification and submission of electronic documentation, digitization of documents, and systems verification of eligibility.

"(3) Reuse of stored eligibility information (including documentation) to assist with retention of eligible individuals.

"(4) Capability for individuals to apply, recertify and manage their eligibility information online, including at home, at points of service, and other community-based locations.

"(5) Ability to expand the enrollment system to integrate new programs, rules, and functionalities, to operate at increased volume, and to apply streamlined verification and eligibility processes to other Federal and State programs, as appropriate.

"(6) Notification of eligibility, recertification, and other needed communication regarding eligibility, which may include communication via email and cellular phones.

"(7) Other functionalities necessary to provide eligibles with streamlined enrollment process.

"(c) APPROVAL AND NOTIFICATION.—With respect to any standard or protocol developed under subsection (a) that has been approved by the HIT Policy Committee and the HIT Standards Committee, the Secretary—

"(1) shall notify States of such standards or protocols; and

"(2) may require, as a condition of receiving Federal funds for the health information technology investments, that States or other entities incorporate such standards and protocols into such investments.

"(d) GRANTS FOR IMPLEMENTATION OF APPROPRIATE ENROLLMENT HIT.—

"(1) IN GENERAL.—The Secretary shall award grant to eligible entities to develop new, and adapt existing, technology systems to implement the HIT enrollment standards and protocols developed under subsection (a) (referred to in this subsection as 'appropriate HIT technology').

"(2) ELIGIBLE ENTITIES.—To be eligible for a grant under this subsection, an entity shall—

"(A) be a State, political subdivision of a State, or a local governmental entity; and

"(B) submit to the Secretary an application at such time, in such manner, and containing—

"(i) a plan to adopt and implement appropriate enrollment technology that includes—

"(I) proposed reduction in maintenance costs of technology systems;

"(II) elimination or updating of legacy systems; and

"(III) demonstrated collaboration with other entities that may receive a grant under this section that are located in the same State, political subdivision, or locality;

"(ii) an assurance that the entity will share such appropriate enrollment technology in accordance with paragraph (4); and

"(iii) such other information as the Secretary may require.

"(3) SHARING.—

"(A) IN GENERAL.—The Secretary shall ensure that appropriate enrollment HIT adopted under grants under this subsection is made available to other qualified State, qualified political subdivisions of a State, or other appropriate qualified entities (as described in subparagraph (B)) at no cost.

"(B) QUALIFIED ENTITIES.—The Secretary shall determine what entities are qualified to receive enrollment HIT under subparagraph (A), taking into consideration the recommendations of the HIT Policy Committee and the HIT Standards Committee.".

SEC. 1562. CONFORMING AMENDMENTS.

(a) APPLICABILITY.—Section 2735 of the Public Health Service Act (42 U.S.C. 300gg–21), as so redesignated by section 1001(4), is amended—

(1) by striking subsection (a);

(2) in subsection (b)—

(A) in paragraph (1), by striking "1 through 3" and inserting "1 and 2"; and

(B) in paragraph (2)—

(i) in subparagraph (A), by striking "subparagraph (D)" and inserting "subparagraph (D) or (E)";

(ii) by striking "1 through 3" and inserting "1 and 2"; and

(iii) by adding at the end the following:

"(E) ELECTION NOT APPLICABLE.—The election described in subparagraph (A) shall not be available with respect to the provisions of subpart 1.";

(3) in subsection (c), by striking "1 through 3 shall not apply to any group" and inserting "1 and 2 shall not apply to any individual coverage or any group"; and

(4) in subsection (d)—

(A) in paragraph (1), by striking "1 through 3 shall not apply to any group" and inserting "1 and 2 shall not apply to any individual coverage or any group";

(B) in paragraph (2)—

(i) in the matter preceding subparagraph (A), by striking "1 through 3 shall not apply to any group" and inserting "1 and 2 shall not apply to any individual coverage or any group"; and

(ii) in subparagraph (C), by inserting "or, with respect to individual coverage, under any health insurance coverage maintained by the same health insurance issuer"; and

(C) in paragraph (3), by striking "any group" and inserting "any individual coverage or any group".

(b) DEFINITIONS.—Section 2791(d) of the Public Health Service Act (42 U.S.C. 300gg–91(d)) is amended by adding at the end the following:

"(20) QUALIFIED HEALTH PLAN.—The term 'qualified health plan' has the meaning given such term in section 1301(a) of the Patient Protection and Affordable Care Act.

"(21) EXCHANGE.—The term 'Exchange' means an American Health Benefit Exchange established under section 1311 of the Patient Protection and Affordable Care Act.".

(c) TECHNICAL AND CONFORMING AMENDMENTS.—Title XXVII of the Public Health Service Act (42 U.S.C. 300gg et seq.) is amended—

(1) in section 2704 (42 U.S.C. 300gg), as so redesignated by section 1201(2)—

(A) in subsection (c)—

(i) in paragraph (2), by striking "group health plan" each place that such term appears and inserting "group or individual health plan"; and

(ii) in paragraph (3)—

(I) by striking "group health insurance" each place that such term appears and inserting "group or individual health insurance"; and

(II) in subparagraph (D), by striking "small or large" and inserting "individual or group";

(B) in subsection (d), by striking "group health insurance" each place that such term appears and inserting "group or individual health insurance"; and

(C) in subsection (e)(1)(A), by striking "group health insurance" and inserting "group or individual health insurance";

(2) by striking the second heading for subpart 2 of part A (relating to other requirements);

(3) in section 2725 (42 U.S.C. 300gg–4), as so redesignated by section 1001(2)—

(A) in subsection (a), by striking "health insurance issuer offering group health insurance coverage" and inserting "health insurance issuer offering group or individual health insurance coverage";

(B) in subsection (b)—

(i) by striking "health insurance issuer offering group health insurance coverage in connection with a group health plan" in the matter preceding paragraph (1) and inserting "health insurance issuer offering group or individual health insurance coverage"; and

(ii) in paragraph (1), by striking "plan" and inserting "plan or coverage";

(C) in subsection (c)—

(i) in paragraph (2), by striking "group health insurance coverage offered by a health insurance issuer" and inserting "health insurance issuer offering group or individual health insurance coverage"; and

(ii) in paragraph (3), by striking "issuer" and inserting "health insurance issuer"; and

(D) in subsection (e), by striking "health insurance issuer offering group health insurance coverage" and inserting "health insurance issuer offering group or individual health insurance coverage";

(4) in section 2726 (42 U.S.C. 300gg–5), as so redesignated by section 1001(2)—

(A) in subsection (a), by striking "(or health insurance coverage offered in connection with such a plan)" each place that such term appears and inserting "or a health insurance issuer offering group or individual health insurance coverage";

(B) in subsection (b), by striking "(or health insurance coverage offered in connection with such a plan)" each place that such term appears and inserting "or a health insurance issuer offering group or individual health insurance coverage"; and

(C) in subsection (c)—

(i) in paragraph (1), by striking "(and group health insurance coverage offered in connection with a group health plan)" and inserting "and a health insurance issuer offering group or individual health insurance coverage";

(ii) in paragraph (2), by striking "(or health insurance coverage offered in connection with such a plan)" each place that such term appears and inserting "or a health insurance issuer offering group or individual health insurance coverage";

(5) in section 2727 (42 U.S.C. 300gg–6), as so redesignated by section 1001(2), by striking "health insurance issuers providing health insurance coverage in connection with group health plans" and inserting "and health insurance issuers offering group or individual health insurance coverage";

(6) in section 2728 (42 U.S.C. 300gg–7), as so redesignated by section 1001(2)—

(A) in subsection (a), by striking "health insurance coverage offered in connection with such plan" and inserting "individual health insurance coverage";

(B) in subsection (b)—

(i) in paragraph (1), by striking "or a health insurance issuer that provides health insurance coverage in connection with a group health plan" and inserting "or a health insurance issuer that offers group or individual health insurance coverage";

(ii) in paragraph (2), by striking "health insurance coverage offered in connection with the plan" and inserting "individual health insurance coverage"; and

(iii) in paragraph (3), by striking "health insurance coverage offered by an issuer in connection with such plan" and inserting "individual health insurance coverage";

(C) in subsection (c), by striking "health insurance issuer providing health insurance coverage in connection with a group health plan" and inserting "health insurance issuer that offers group or individual health insurance coverage"; and

(D) in subsection (e)(1), by striking "health insurance coverage offered in connection with such a plan" and inserting "individual health insurance coverage";

(7) by striking the heading for subpart 3;

(8) in section 2731 (42 U.S.C. 300gg–11), as so redesignated by section 1001(3)—

(A) by striking the section heading and all that follows through subsection (b);

(B) in subsection (c)—

(i) in paragraph (1)—

(I) in the matter preceding subparagraph (A), by striking "small group" and inserting "group and individual"; and

(II) in subparagraph (B)—

(aa) in the matter preceding clause (i), by inserting "and individuals" after "employers";

(bb) in clause (i), by inserting "or any additional individuals" after "additional groups"; and

(cc) in clause (ii), by striking "without regard to the claims experience of those employers and their employees (and their dependents) or any health status-related factor relating to such" and inserting "and individuals without regard to the claims experience of those individuals, employers and their employees (and their dependents) or any health status-related factor relating to such individuals"; and

(ii) in paragraph (2), by striking "small group" and inserting "group or individual";

(C) in subsection (d)—

(i) by striking "small group" each place that such appears and inserting "group or individual"; and

(ii) in paragraph (1)(B)—

(I) by striking "all employers" and inserting "all employers and individuals";

(II) by striking "those employers" and inserting "those individuals, employers"; and

(III) by striking "such employees" and inserting "such individuals, employees";

(D) by striking subsection (e);

(E) by striking subsection (f); and

(F) by transferring such section (as amended by this paragraph) to appear at the end of section 2702 (as added by section 1001(4));

(9) in section 2732 (42 U.S.C. 300gg–12), as so redesignated by section 1001(3)—

(A) by striking the section heading and all that follows through subsection (a);

(B) in subsection (b)—

(i) in the matter preceding paragraph (1), by striking "group health plan in the small or large group market" and inserting "health insurance coverage offered in the group or individual market";

(ii) in paragraph (1), by inserting ", or individual, as applicable," after "plan sponsor";

(iii) in paragraph (2), by inserting ", or individual, as applicable," after "plan sponsor"; and

(iv) by striking paragraph (3) and inserting the following:

"(3) VIOLATION OF PARTICIPATION OR CONTRIBUTION RATES.—In the case of a group health plan, the plan sponsor has failed to comply with a material plan provision relating to employer contribution or group participation rules, pursuant to applicable State law.";

(C) in subsection (c)—

(i) in paragraph (1)—

(I) in the matter preceding subparagraph (A), by striking "group health insurance coverage offered in the small or large group market" and inserting "group or individual health insurance coverage";

(II) in subparagraph (A), by inserting "or individual, as applicable," after "plan sponsor";

(III) in subparagraph (B)—

(aa) by inserting "or individual, as applicable," after "plan sponsor"; and

(bb) by inserting "or individual health insurance coverage"; and

(IV) in subparagraph (C), by inserting "or individuals, as applicable," after "those sponsors"; and

(ii) in paragraph (2)(A)—

(I) in the matter preceding clause (i), by striking "small group market or the large group market, or both markets," and inserting "individual or group market, or all markets,"; and

(II) in clause (i), by inserting "or individual, as applicable," after "plan sponsor"; and

(D) by transferring such section (as amended by this paragraph) to appear at the end of section 2703 (as added by section 1001(4));

(10) in section 2733 (42 U.S.C. 300gg–13), as so redesignated by section 1001(4)—

(A) in subsection (a)—

(i) in the matter preceding paragraph (1), by striking "small employer" and inserting "small employer or an individual";

(ii) in paragraph (1), by inserting ", or individual, as applicable," after "employer" each place that such appears; and

(iii) in paragraph (2), by striking "small employer" and inserting "employer, or individual, as applicable,";

(B) in subsection (b)—

(i) in paragraph (1)—

(I) in the matter preceding subparagraph (A), by striking "small employer" and inserting "employer, or individual, as applicable,";

(II) in subparagraph (A), by adding "and" at the end;

(III) by striking subparagraphs (B) and (C); and

(IV) in subparagraph (D)—

(aa) by inserting ", or individual, as applicable," after "employer"; and

(bb) by redesignating such subparagraph as subparagraph (B);

(ii) in paragraph (2)—

(I) by striking "small employers" each place that such term appears and inserting "employers, or individuals, as applicable,"; and

(II) by striking "small employer" and inserting "employer, or individual, as applicable,"; and

(C) by redesignating such section (as amended by this paragraph) as section 2709 and transferring such section to appear after section 2708 (as added by section 1001(5));

(11) by redesignating subpart 4 as subpart 2;

(12) in section 2735 (42 U.S.C. 300gg–21), as so redesignated by section 1001(4)—

(A) by striking subsection (a);

(B) by striking "subparts 1 through 3" each place that such appears and inserting "subpart 1";

(C) by redesignating subsections (b) through (e) as subsections (a) through (d), respectively; and

(D) by redesignating such section (as amended by this paragraph) as section 2722;

(13) in section 2736 (42 U.S.C. 300gg–22), as so redesignated by section 1001(4)—

(A) in subsection (a)—

(i) in paragraph (1), by striking "small or large group markets" and inserting "individual or group market"; and

(ii) in paragraph (2), by inserting "or individual health insurance coverage" after "group health plans";

(B) in subsection (b)(1)(B), by inserting "individual health insurance coverage or" after "respect to"; and

(C) by redesignating such section (as amended by this paragraph) as section 2723;

(14) in section 2737(a)(1) (42 U.S.C. 300gg–23), as so redesignated by section 1001(4)—

(A) by inserting "individual or" before "group health insurance"; and

(B) by redesignating such section(as amended by this paragraph) as section 2724;

(15) in section 2762 (42 U.S.C. 300gg–62)—

(A) in the section heading by inserting "**AND APPLICATION**" before the period; and

(B) by adding at the end the following:

"(c) APPLICATION OF PART A PROVISIONS.—

"(1) IN GENERAL.—The provisions of part A shall apply to health insurance issuers providing health insurance coverage in the individual market in a State as provided for in such part.

"(2) CLARIFICATION.—To the extent that any provision of this part conflicts with a provision of part A with respect to health insurance issuers providing health insurance coverage in the individual market in a State, the provisions of such part A shall apply."; and

(16) in section 2791(e) (42 U.S.C. 300gg–91(e))—

(A) in paragraph (2), by striking "51" and inserting "101"; and

(B) in paragraph (4)—

(i) by striking "at least 2" each place that such appears and inserting "at least 1"; and

(ii) by striking "50" and inserting "100".

(d) APPLICATION.—Notwithstanding any other provision of the Patient Protection and Affordable Care Act, nothing in such Act (or an amendment made by such Act) shall be construed to—

(1) prohibit (or authorize the Secretary of Health and Human Services to promulgate regulations that prohibit) a group health plan or health insurance issuer from carrying out utilization management techniques that are commonly used as of the date of enactment of this Act; or

(2) restrict the application of the amendments made by this subtitle.

(e) TECHNICAL AMENDMENT TO THE EMPLOYEE RETIREMENT INCOME SECURITY ACT OF 1974.—Subpart B of part 7 of subtitle A of title I of the Employee Retirement Income Security Act of 1974 (29 U.S.C. 1181 et. seq.) is amended, by adding at the end the following:

"SEC. 715. ADDITIONAL MARKET REFORMS.

"(a) GENERAL RULE.—Except as provided in subsection (b)—

"(1) the provisions of part A of title XXVII of the Public Health Service Act (as amended by the Patient Protection and Affordable Care Act) shall apply to group health plans, and health insurance issuers providing health insurance coverage in connection with group health plans, as if included in this subpart; and

"(2) to the extent that any provision of this part conflicts with a provision of such part A with respect to group health plans, or health insurance issuers providing health insurance coverage in connection with group health plans, the provisions of such part A shall apply.

"(b) EXCEPTION.—Notwithstanding subsection (a), the provisions of sections 2716 and 2718 of title XXVII of the Public Health Service Act (as amended by the Patient Protection and Affordable Care Act) shall not apply with respect to self-insured group health plans, and the provisions of this part shall continue to apply to such plans as if such sections of the Public Health Service Act (as so amended) had not been enacted.".

(f) TECHNICAL AMENDMENT TO THE INTERNAL REVENUE CODE OF 1986.—Subchapter B of chapter 100 of the Internal Revenue Code of 1986 is amended by adding at the end the following:

"SEC. 9815. ADDITIONAL MARKET REFORMS.

"(a) GENERAL RULE.—Except as provided in subsection (b)—

"(1) the provisions of part A of title XXVII of the Public Health Service Act (as amended by the Patient Protection and Affordable Care Act) shall apply to group health plans, and health insurance issuers providing health insurance coverage in connection with group health plans, as if included in this subchapter; and

"(2) to the extent that any provision of this subchapter conflicts with a provision of such part A with respect to group health plans, or health insurance issuers providing health insurance coverage in connection with group health plans, the provisions of such part A shall apply.

"(b) EXCEPTION.—Notwithstanding subsection (a), the provisions of sections 2716 and 2718 of title XXVII of the Public Health Service Act (as amended by the Patient Protection and Affordable Care Act) shall not apply with respect to self-insured group health plans, and the provisions of this subchapter shall continue to apply to such plans as if such sections of the Public Health Service Act (as so amended) had not been enacted.".

SEC. 1563. SENSE OF THE SENATE PROMOTING FISCAL RESPONSIBILITY.

(a) FINDINGS.—The Senate makes the following findings:

(1) Based on Congressional Budget Office (CBO) estimates, this Act will reduce the Federal deficit between 2010 and 2019.

(2) CBO projects this Act will continue to reduce budget deficits after 2019.

(3) Based on CBO estimates, this Act will extend the solvency of the Medicare HI Trust Fund.

(4) This Act will increase the surplus in the Social Security Trust Fund, which should be reserved to strengthen the finances of Social Security.

(5) The initial net savings generated by the Community Living Assistance Services and Supports (CLASS) program are necessary to ensure the long-term solvency of that program.

(b) SENSE OF THE SENATE.—It is the sense of the Senate that—

(1) the additional surplus in the Social Security Trust Fund generated by this Act should be reserved for Social Security and not spent in this Act for other purposes; and

(2) the net savings generated by the CLASS program should be reserved for the CLASS program and not spent in this Act for other purposes.

TITLE II—ROLE OF PUBLIC PROGRAMS

Subtitle A—Improved Access to Medicaid

SEC. 2001. MEDICAID COVERAGE FOR THE LOWEST INCOME POPULATIONS.

(a) COVERAGE FOR INDIVIDUALS WITH INCOME AT OR BELOW 133 PERCENT OF THE POVERTY LINE.—

(1) BEGINNING 2014.—Section 1902(a)(10)(A)(i) of the Social Security Act (42 U.S.C. 1396a) is amended—

(A) by striking "or" at the end of subclause (VI);

(B) by adding "or" at the end of subclause (VII); and

(C) by inserting after subclause (VII) the following:

"(VIII) beginning January 1, 2014, who are under 65 years of age, not pregnant, not entitled to, or enrolled for, benefits under part A of title XVIII, or enrolled for benefits under part B of title XVIII, and are not described in a previous subclause of this clause, and whose income (as determined under subsection (e)(14)) does not exceed 133 percent of the poverty line (as defined in section 2110(c)(5)) applicable to a family of the size involved, subject to subsection (k);".

(2) PROVISION OF AT LEAST MINIMUM ESSENTIAL COVERAGE.—

(A) IN GENERAL.—Section 1902 of such Act (42 U.S.C. 1396a) is amended by inserting after subsection (j) the following:

"(k)(1) The medical assistance provided to an individual described in subclause (VIII) of subsection (a)(10)(A)(i) shall consist of benchmark coverage described in section 1937(b)(1) or benchmark equivalent coverage described in section 1937(b)(2). Such medical assistance shall be provided subject to the requirements of section 1937, without regard to whether a State otherwise has elected the option to provide medical assistance through coverage under that section, unless an individual described in subclause (VIII) of subsection (a)(10)(A)(i) is also an individual for whom, under subparagraph (B) of section 1937(a)(2), the State may not require enrollment in benchmark coverage described in subsection (b)(1) of section 1937 or benchmark equivalent coverage described in subsection (b)(2) of that section.".

(B) CONFORMING AMENDMENT.—Section 1903(i) of the Social Security Act, as amended by section 6402(c), is amended—

(i) in paragraph (24), by striking "or" at the end;

(ii) in paragraph (25), by striking the period and inserting "; or"; and

(iii) by adding at the end the following:

"(26) with respect to any amounts expended for medical assistance for individuals described in subclause (VIII) of subsection (a)(10)(A)(i) other than medical assistance provided through benchmark coverage described in section 1937(b)(1) or benchmark equivalent coverage described in section 1937(b)(2).".

(3) FEDERAL FUNDING FOR COST OF COVERING NEWLY ELIGIBLE INDIVIDUALS.—Section 1905 of the Social Security Act (42 U.S.C. 1396d), is amended—

(A) in subsection (b), in the first sentence, by inserting "subsection (y) and" before "section 1933(d)"; and

(B) by adding at the end the following new subsection:

"(y) INCREASED FMAP FOR MEDICAL ASSISTANCE FOR NEWLY ELIGIBLE MANDATORY INDIVIDUALS.—

"(1) AMOUNT OF INCREASE.—

"(A) 100 PERCENT FMAP.—During the period that begins on January 1, 2014, and ends on December 31, 2016, notwithstanding subsection (b), the Federal medical assistance percentage determined for a State that is one of the 50 States or the District of Columbia for each fiscal year occurring during that period with respect to amounts expended for medical assistance for newly eligible individuals described in subclause (VIII) of section 1902(a)(10)(A)(i) shall be equal to 100 percent.

"(B) 2017 AND 2018.—

"(i) IN GENERAL.—During the period that begins on January 1, 2017, and ends on December 31, 2018, notwithstanding subsection (b) and subject to subparagraph (D), the Federal medical assistance percentage determined for a State that is one of the 50 States or the District of Columbia for each fiscal year occurring during that period with respect to amounts expended for medical assistance for newly eligible individuals described in subclause (VIII) of section 1902(a)(10)(A)(i), shall be increased by the applicable percentage point increase specified in clause (ii) for the quarter and the State.

"(ii) APPLICABLE PERCENTAGE POINT INCREASE.—

"(I) IN GENERAL.—For purposes of clause (i), the applicable percentage point increase for a quarter is the following:

"For any fiscal year quarter occurring in the calendar year:	If the State is an expansion State, the applicable percentage point increase is:	If the State is not an expansion State, the applicable percentage point increase is:
2017	30.3	34.3
2018	31.3	33.3

"(II) EXPANSION STATE DEFINED.—For purposes of the table in subclause (I), a State is an expansion State if, on the date of the enactment of the Patient Protection and Affordable Care Act, the State offers health benefits coverage statewide to parents and nonpregnant, childless adults whose income is at least 100 percent of the poverty line, that is not dependent on access to employer coverage, employer contribution, or employment and is not limited to premium assistance, hospital-only benefits, a high deductible health plan, or alternative benefits under a demonstration program authorized under section 1938. A State that offers health benefits coverage to only parents or only nonpregnant childless adults described in the preceding sentence shall not be considered to be an expansion State.

"(C) 2019 AND SUCCEEDING YEARS.—Beginning January 1, 2019, notwithstanding subsection (b) but subject to subparagraph (D), the Federal medical assistance percentage determined for a State that is one of the 50 States or the District of Columbia for each fiscal year quarter occurring during that period with respect to amounts expended for medical assistance for newly eligible individuals described in subclause (VIII) of section 1902(a)(10)(A)(i), shall be increased by 32.3 percentage points.

"(D) LIMITATION.—The Federal medical assistance percentage determined for a State under subparagraph (B) or (C) shall in no case be more than 95 percent.

"(2) DEFINITIONS.—In this subsection:

"(A) NEWLY ELIGIBLE.—The term 'newly eligible' means, with respect to an individual described in subclause (VIII) of section 1902(a)(10)(A)(i), an individual who is not under 19 years of age (or such higher age as the State may have elected) and who, on the date of enactment of the Patient Protection and Affordable Care Act, is not eligible under the State plan or under a waiver of the plan for full benefits or for benchmark coverage described in subparagraph (A), (B), or (C) of section 1937(b)(1) or benchmark equivalent coverage described in section 1937(b)(2) that has an aggregate actuarial value that is at least actuarially equivalent to benchmark coverage described in subparagraph (A), (B), or (C) of section 1937(b)(1), or is eligible but not enrolled (or is on a waiting list) for such benefits or coverage through a waiver under the plan that has a capped or limited enrollment that is full.

"(B) FULL BENEFITS.—The term 'full benefits' means, with respect to an individual, medical assistance for all services covered under the State plan under this title that is not less in amount, duration, or scope, or is determined by the Secretary to be substantially equivalent, to the medical assistance available for an individual described in section 1902(a)(10)(A)(i).".

(4) STATE OPTIONS TO OFFER COVERAGE EARLIER AND PRESUMPTIVE ELIGIBILITY; CHILDREN REQUIRED TO HAVE COVERAGE FOR PARENTS TO BE ELIGIBLE.—

(A) IN GENERAL.—Subsection (k) of section 1902 of the Social Security Act (as added by paragraph (2)), is amended by inserting after paragraph (1) the following:

"(2) Beginning with the first day of any fiscal year quarter that begins on or after January 1, 2011, and before January 1, 2014, a State may elect through a State plan amendment to provide medical assistance to individuals who would be described in subclause (VIII) of subsection (a)(10)(A)(i) if that subclause were effective before January 1, 2014. A State may elect to phase-in the extension of eligibility for medical assistance to such individuals based on income, so long as the State does not extend such eligibility to individuals described in such subclause with higher income before making individuals described in such subclause with lower income eligible for medical assistance.

"(3) If an individual described in subclause (VIII) of subsection (a)(10)(A)(i) is the parent of a child who is under 19 years of age (or such higher age as the State may have elected) who is eligible for medical assistance under the State plan or under a waiver of such plan (under that subclause or under a State plan amendment under paragraph (2), the individual may not be enrolled under the State plan unless the individual's child is enrolled under the State plan or under a waiver of the plan or is enrolled in other health insurance coverage. For purposes of the preceding sentence, the term 'parent' includes an individual treated as a caretaker relative for purposes of carrying out section 1931.".

(B) PRESUMPTIVE ELIGIBILITY.—Section 1920 of the Social Security Act (42 U.S.C. 1396r–1) is amended by adding at the end the following:

"(e) If the State has elected the option to provide a presumptive eligibility period under this section or section 1920A, the State may elect to provide a presumptive eligibility period (as defined in subsection (b)(1)) for individuals who are eligible for medical assistance under clause (i)(VIII) of subsection (a)(10)(A) or section 1931 in the same manner as the State provides for such a period under this section or section 1920A, subject to such guidance as the Secretary shall establish.".

(5) CONFORMING AMENDMENTS.—

(A) Section 1902(a)(10) of such Act (42 U.S.C. 1396a(a)(10)) is amended in the matter following subparagraph (G), by striking "and (XIV)" and inserting "(XIV)" and by inserting "and (XV) the medical assistance made available to an individual described in subparagraph (A)(i)(VIII) shall be limited to medical assistance described in subsection (k)(1)" before the semicolon.

(B) Section 1902(l)(2)(C) of such Act (42 U.S.C. 1396a(l)(2)(C)) is amended by striking "100" and inserting "133".

(C) Section 1905(a) of such Act (42 U.S.C. 1396d(a)) is amended in the matter preceding paragraph (1)—

(i) by striking "or" at the end of clause (xii);

(ii) by inserting "or" at the end of clause (xiii); and

(iii) by inserting after clause (xiii) the following: "(xiv) individuals described in section 1902(a)(10)(A)(i)(VIII),".

(D) Section 1903(f)(4) of such Act (42 U.S.C. 1396b(f)(4)) is amended by inserting "1902(a)(10)(A)(i)(VIII)," after "1902(a)(10)(A)(i)(VII),".

(E) Section 1937(a)(1)(B) of such Act (42 U.S.C. 1396u–7(a)(1)(B)) is amended by inserting "subclause (VIII) of section 1902(a)(10)(A)(i) or under" after "eligible under".

(b) MAINTENANCE OF MEDICAID INCOME ELIGIBILITY.—Section 1902 of the Social Security Act (42 U.S.C. 1396a) is amended—

(1) in subsection (a)—

(A) by striking "and" at the end of paragraph (72);

(B) by striking the period at the end of paragraph (73) and inserting "; and"; and

(C) by inserting after paragraph (73) the following new paragraph:

"(74) provide for maintenance of effort under the State plan or under any waiver of the plan in accordance with subsection (gg)."; and

(2) by adding at the end the following new subsection:

"(gg) MAINTENANCE OF EFFORT.—

"(1) GENERAL REQUIREMENT TO MAINTAIN ELIGIBILITY STANDARDS UNTIL STATE EXCHANGE IS FULLY OPERATIONAL.—Subject to the succeeding paragraphs of this subsection, during the period that begins on the date of enactment of the Patient Protection and Affordable Care Act and ends on the date on which the Secretary determines that an Exchange established by the State under section 1311 of the Patient Protection and Affordable Care Act is fully operational, as a condition for receiving any Federal payments under section 1903(a) for calendar quarters occurring during such period, a State shall not have in effect eligibility standards, methodologies, or procedures under the State plan under this title or under any waiver of such plan that is in effect during that period, that are more restrictive than the eligibility standards, methodologies, or procedures, respectively, under the plan or waiver that are in effect on the date of enactment of the Patient Protection and Affordable Care Act.

"(2) CONTINUATION OF ELIGIBILITY STANDARDS FOR CHILDREN UNTIL OCTOBER 1, 2019.—The requirement under paragraph (1) shall continue to apply to a State through September 30, 2019, with respect to the eligibility standards, methodologies, and procedures under the State plan under this title or under any waiver of such plan that are applicable to determining the eligibility for medical assistance of any child who is under 19 years of age (or such higher age as the State may have elected).

"(3) NONAPPLICATION.—During the period that begins on January 1, 2011, and ends on December 31, 2013, the requirement under paragraph (1) shall not apply to a State with respect to nonpregnant, nondisabled adults who are eligible for medical assistance under the State plan or under a waiver of the plan at the option of the State and whose income exceeds 133 percent of the poverty line (as defined in section 2110(c)(5)) applicable to a family of the size involved if, on or after December 31, 2010, the State certifies to the Secretary that, with respect to the State fiscal year during which the certification is made, the State has a budget deficit, or with respect to the succeeding State fiscal year, the State is projected to have a budget deficit. Upon submission of such a certification to the Secretary, the requirement under paragraph (1) shall not apply to the State with respect to any remaining portion of the period described in the preceding sentence.

"(4) DETERMINATION OF COMPLIANCE.—

"(A) STATES SHALL APPLY MODIFIED GROSS INCOME.— A State's determination of income in accordance with subsection (e)(14) shall not be considered to be eligibility standards, methodologies, or procedures that are more restrictive than the standards, methodologies, or procedures in effect under the State plan or under a waiver of the plan on the date of enactment of the Patient Protection and Affordable Care Act for purposes of determining compliance with the requirements of paragraph (1), (2), or (3).

"(B) STATES MAY EXPAND ELIGIBILITY OR MOVE WAIVERED POPULATIONS INTO COVERAGE UNDER THE STATE PLAN.—With respect to any period applicable under paragraph (1), (2), or (3), a State that applies eligibility standards, methodologies, or procedures under the State plan under this title or under any waiver of the plan that are less restrictive than the eligibility standards, methodologies, or procedures, applied under the State plan or under a waiver of the plan on the date of enactment of the Patient Protection and Affordable Care Act, or that makes individuals who, on such date of enactment, are eligible for medical assistance under a waiver of the State plan, after such date of enactment eligible for medical assistance through a State plan amendment with an income eligibility level that is not less than the income eligibility level that applied under the waiver, or as a result of the application of subclause (VIII) of section 1902(a)(10)(A)(i), shall not be considered to have in effect eligibility standards, methodologies, or procedures that are more restrictive than the standards, methodologies, or procedures in effect under the State plan or under a waiver of the plan on the date of enactment of the Patient Protection and Affordable Care Act for purposes of determining compliance with the requirements of paragraph (1), (2), or (3).".

(c) MEDICAID BENCHMARK BENEFITS MUST CONSIST OF AT LEAST MINIMUM ESSENTIAL COVERAGE.—Section 1937(b) of such Act (42 U.S.C. 1396u–7(b)) is amended—

(1) in paragraph (1), in the matter preceding subparagraph (A), by inserting "subject to paragraphs (5) and (6)," before "each";

(2) in paragraph (2)—

(A) in the matter preceding subparagraph (A), by inserting "subject to paragraphs (5) and (6)" after "subsection (a)(1),";

(B) in subparagraph (A)—

(i) by redesignating clauses (iv) and (v) as clauses (vi) and (vii), respectively; and

(ii) by inserting after clause (iii), the following:

"(iv) Coverage of prescription drugs.

"(v) Mental health services."; and

(C) in subparagraph (C)—

(i) by striking clauses (i) and (ii); and

(ii) by redesignating clauses (iii) and (iv) as clauses (i) and (ii), respectively; and

(3) by adding at the end the following new paragraphs:

"(5) MINIMUM STANDARDS.—Effective January 1, 2014, any benchmark benefit package under paragraph (1) or benchmark equivalent coverage under paragraph (2) must provide at least essential health benefits as described in section 1302(b) of the Patient Protection and Affordable Care Act.

"(6) MENTAL HEALTH SERVICES PARITY.—

"(A) IN GENERAL.—In the case of any benchmark benefit package under paragraph (1) or benchmark equivalent coverage under paragraph (2) that is offered by an entity that is not a medicaid managed care organization and that provides both medical and surgical benefits and mental health or substance use disorder benefits, the entity shall ensure that the financial requirements and treatment limitations applicable to such mental health or substance use disorder benefits comply with the requirements of section 2705(a) of the Public Health Service Act in the same manner as such requirements apply to a group health plan.

"(B) DEEMED COMPLIANCE.—Coverage provided with respect to an individual described in section 1905(a)(4)(B) and covered under the State plan under section 1902(a)(10)(A) of the services described in section 1905(a)(4)(B) (relating to early and periodic screening, diagnostic, and treatment services defined in section 1905(r)) and provided in accordance with section 1902(a)(43), shall be deemed to satisfy the requirements of subparagraph (A).".

(d) ANNUAL REPORTS ON MEDICAID ENROLLMENT.—

(1) STATE REPORTS.—Section 1902(a) of the Social Security Act (42 U.S.C. 1396a(a)), as amended by subsection (b), is amended—

(A) by striking "and" at the end of paragraph (73);

(B) by striking the period at the end of paragraph (74) and inserting "; and"; and

(C) by inserting after paragraph (74) the following new paragraph:

"(75) provide that, beginning January 2015, and annually thereafter, the State shall submit a report to the Secretary that contains—

"(A) the total number of enrolled and newly enrolled individuals in the State plan or under a waiver of the plan for the fiscal year ending on September 30 of the preceding calendar year, disaggregated by population, including children, parents, nonpregnant childless adults, disabled individuals, elderly individuals, and such other categories or sub-categories of individuals eligible for medical assistance under the State plan or under a waiver of the plan as the Secretary may require;

"(B) a description, which may be specified by population, of the outreach and enrollment processes used by the State during such fiscal year; and

"(C) any other data reporting determined necessary by the Secretary to monitor enrollment and retention of individuals eligible for medical assistance under the State plan or under a waiver of the plan.".

(2) REPORTS TO CONGRESS.—Beginning April 2015, and annually thereafter, the Secretary of Health and Human Services shall submit a report to the appropriate committees of Congress on the total enrollment and new enrollment in Medicaid for the fiscal year ending on September 30 of the preceding calendar year on a national and State-by-State basis, and shall include in each such report such recommendations for administrative or legislative changes to improve enrollment in the Medicaid program as the Secretary determines appropriate.

(e) STATE OPTION FOR COVERAGE FOR INDIVIDUALS WITH INCOME THAT EXCEEDS 133 PERCENT OF THE POVERTY LINE.—

(1) COVERAGE AS OPTIONAL CATEGORICALLY NEEDY GROUP.—Section 1902 of the Social Security Act (42 U.S.C. 1396a) is amended—

(A) in subsection (a)(10)(A)(ii)—

(i) in subclause (XVIII), by striking "or" at the end;

(ii) in subclause (XIX), by adding "or" at the end; and

(iii) by adding at the end the following new subclause:

"(XX) beginning January 1, 2014, who are under 65 years of age and are not described in or enrolled under a previous subclause of this clause, and whose income (as determined under subsection (e)(14)) exceeds 133 percent of the poverty line (as defined in section 2110(c)(5)) applicable to a family of the size involved but does not exceed the highest income eligibility level established under the State plan or under a waiver of the plan, subject to subsection (hh);" and

(B) by adding at the end the following new subsection:

"(hh)(1) A State may elect to phase-in the extension of eligibility for medical assistance to individuals described in subclause (XX) of subsection (a)(10)(A)(ii) based on the categorical group (including nonpregnant childless adults) or income, so long as the State does not extend such eligibility to individuals described in such subclause with higher income before making individuals described in such subclause with lower income eligible for medical assistance.

"(2) If an individual described in subclause (XX) of subsection (a)(10)(A)(ii) is the parent of a child who is under 19 years of age (or such higher age as the State may have elected) who is eligible for medical assistance under the State plan or under a waiver of such plan, the individual may not be enrolled under the State plan unless the individual's child is enrolled under the State plan or under a waiver of the plan or is enrolled in other health insurance coverage. For purposes of the preceding sentence, the term 'parent' includes an individual treated as a caretaker relative for purposes of carrying out section 1931.".

(2) CONFORMING AMENDMENTS.—

(A) Section 1905(a) of such Act (42 U.S.C. 1396d(a)), as amended by subsection (a)(5)(C), is amended in the matter preceding paragraph (1)—

(i) by striking "or" at the end of clause (xiii);

(ii) by inserting "or" at the end of clause (xiv); and

(iii) by inserting after clause (xiv) the following: "(xv) individuals described in section 1902(a)(10)(A)(ii)(XX),".

(B) Section 1903(f)(4) of such Act (42 U.S.C. 1396b(f)(4)) is amended by inserting "1902(a)(10)(A)(ii)(XX)," after "1902(a)(10)(A)(ii)(XIX),".

(C) Section 1920(e) of such Act (42 U.S.C. 1396r–1(e)), as added by subsection (a)(4)(B), is amended by inserting "or clause (ii)(XX)" after "clause (i)(VIII)".

SEC. 2002. INCOME ELIGIBILITY FOR NONELDERLY DETERMINED USING MODIFIED GROSS INCOME.

(a) IN GENERAL.—Section 1902(e) of the Social Security Act (42 U.S.C. 1396a(e)) is amended by adding at the end the following:

"(14) INCOME DETERMINED USING MODIFIED GROSS INCOME.—

"(A) IN GENERAL.—Notwithstanding subsection (r) or any other provision of this title, except as provided in subparagraph (D), for purposes of determining income eligibility for medical assistance under the State plan or under any waiver of such plan and for any other purpose applicable under the plan or waiver for which a determination of income is required, including with respect to the imposition of premiums and cost-sharing, a State shall use the modified gross income of an individual and, in the case of an individual in a family greater than 1, the household income of such family. A State shall establish income eligibility thresholds for populations to be eligible for medical assistance under the State plan or a waiver of the plan using modified gross income and household income that are not less than the effective income eligibility levels that applied under the State plan or waiver on the date of enactment of the Patient Protection and Affordable Care Act. For purposes of complying with the maintenance of effort requirements under subsection (gg) during the transition to modified gross income and household income, a State shall, working with the Secretary, establish an equivalent income test that ensures individuals eligible for medical assistance under the State plan or under a waiver of the plan on the date of enactment of the Patient Protection and Affordable Care Act, do not lose coverage under the State plan or under a waiver of the plan. The Secretary may waive such provisions of this title and title XXI as are necessary to ensure that States establish income and eligibility determination systems that protect beneficiaries.

"(B) NO INCOME OR EXPENSE DISREGARDS.—No type of expense, block, or other income disregard shall be applied by a State to determine income eligibility for medical assistance under the State plan or under any waiver of such plan or for any other purpose applicable under the plan or waiver for which a determination of income is required.

"(C) NO ASSETS TEST.—A State shall not apply any assets or resources test for purposes of determining eligibility for medical assistance under the State plan or under a waiver of the plan.

"(D) EXCEPTIONS.—

"(i) INDIVIDUALS ELIGIBLE BECAUSE OF OTHER AID OR ASSISTANCE, ELDERLY INDIVIDUALS, MEDICALLY NEEDY INDIVIDUALS, AND INDIVIDUALS ELIGIBLE FOR MEDICARE COST-SHARING.—Subparagraphs (A), (B), and (C) shall not apply to the determination of eligibility under the State plan or under a waiver for medical assistance for the following:

"(I) Individuals who are eligible for medical assistance under the State plan or under a waiver of the plan on a basis that does not require a determination of income by the State agency administering the State plan or waiver, including as a result of eligibility for, or receipt of, other Federal or State aid or assistance, individuals who are eligible on the basis of receiving (or being treated as if receiving) supplemental security income benefits under title XVI, and individuals who are eligible as a result of being or being deemed to be a child in foster care under the responsibility of the State.

"(II) Individuals who have attained age 65.

"(III) Individuals who qualify for medical assistance under the State plan or under any waiver of such plan on the basis of being blind or disabled (or being treated as being blind or disabled) without regard to whether the individual is eligible for supplemental security income benefits under title XVI on the basis of being blind or disabled and including an individual who is eligible for medical assistance on the basis of section 1902(e)(3).

"(IV) Individuals described in subsection (a)(10)(C).

"(V) Individuals described in any clause of subsection (a)(10)(E).

"(ii) EXPRESS LANE AGENCY FINDINGS.—In the case of a State that elects the Express Lane option under paragraph (13), notwithstanding subparagraphs (A), (B), and (C), the State may rely on a finding made by an Express Lane agency in accordance with that paragraph relating to the income of an individual for purposes of determining the individual's eligibility for medical assistance under the State plan or under a waiver of the plan.

"(iii) MEDICARE PRESCRIPTION DRUG SUBSIDIES DETERMINATIONS.—Subparagraphs (A), (B), and (C) shall not apply to any determinations of eligibility for premium and cost-sharing subsidies under and in accordance with section 1860D–14 made by the State pursuant to section 1935(a)(2).

"(iv) LONG-TERM CARE.—Subparagraphs (A), (B), and (C) shall not apply to any determinations of eligibility of individuals for purposes of medical assistance for nursing facility services, a level of care in any institution equivalent to that of nursing facility services, home or community-based services furnished under a waiver or State plan amendment under section 1915 or a waiver under section 1115, and services described in section 1917(c)(1)(C)(ii).

"(v) GRANDFATHER OF CURRENT ENROLLEES UNTIL DATE OF NEXT REGULAR REDETERMINATION.—An individual who, on January 1, 2014, is enrolled in the State plan or under a waiver of the plan and who would be determined ineligible for medical assistance solely because of the application of the modified gross income or household income standard described in subparagraph (A), shall remain eligible for medical assistance under the State plan or waiver (and subject to the same premiums and cost-sharing as applied to the individual on that date) through March 31, 2014, or the date on which the individual's next regularly scheduled redetermination of eligibility is to occur, whichever is later.

"(E) TRANSITION PLANNING AND OVERSIGHT.—Each State shall submit to the Secretary for the Secretary's approval the income eligibility thresholds proposed to be established using modified gross income and household income, the methodologies and procedures to be used to determine income eligibility using modified gross income and household income and, if applicable, a State plan amendment establishing an optional eligibility category under subsection (a)(10)(A)(ii)(XX). To the extent practicable, the State shall use the same methodologies and procedures for purposes of making such determinations as the State used on the date of enactment of the Patient Protection and Affordable Care Act. The Secretary shall ensure that the income eligibility thresholds proposed to be established using modified gross income and household income, including under the eligibility category established under subsection (a)(10)(A)(ii)(XX), and the methodologies and procedures proposed to be used to determine income eligibility, will not result in children who would have been eligible for medical assistance under the State plan or under a waiver of the plan on the date of enactment of the Patient Protection and Affordable Care Act no longer being eligible for such assistance.

"(F) LIMITATION ON SECRETARIAL AUTHORITY.—The Secretary shall not waive compliance with the requirements of this paragraph except to the extent necessary to permit a State to coordinate eligibility requirements for dual eligible individuals (as defined in section 1915(h)(2)(B)) under the State plan or under a waiver of the plan and under title XVIII and individuals who require the level of care provided in a hospital, a nursing facility, or an intermediate care facility for the mentally retarded.

"(G) DEFINITIONS OF MODIFIED GROSS INCOME AND HOUSEHOLD INCOME.—In this paragraph, the terms 'modified gross income' and 'household income' have the meanings given such terms in section 36B(d)(2) of the Internal Revenue Code of 1986.

"(H) CONTINUED APPLICATION OF MEDICAID RULES REGARDING POINT-IN-TIME INCOME AND SOURCES OF INCOME.—The requirement under this paragraph for States to use modified gross income and household income to determine income eligibility for medical assistance under the State plan or under any waiver of such plan and for any other purpose applicable under the plan or waiver for which a determination of income is required shall not be construed as affecting or limiting the application of—

"(i) the requirement under this title and under the State plan or a waiver of the plan to determine an individual's income as of the point in time at which an application for medical assistance under the State plan or a waiver of the plan is processed; or

"(ii) any rules established under this title or under the State plan or a waiver of the plan regarding sources of countable income.".

(b) CONFORMING AMENDMENT.—Section 1902(a)(17) of such Act (42 U.S.C. 1396a(a)(17)) is amended by inserting "(e)(14)," before "(l)(3)".

(c) EFFECTIVE DATE.—The amendments made by subsections (a) and (b) take effect on January 1, 2014.

SEC. 2003. REQUIREMENT TO OFFER PREMIUM ASSISTANCE FOR EMPLOYER-SPONSORED INSURANCE.

(a) IN GENERAL.—Section 1906A of such Act (42 U.S.C. 1396e–1) is amended—

(1) in subsection (a)—

(A) by striking "may elect to" and inserting "shall";

(B) by striking "under age 19"; and

(C) by inserting ", in the case of an individual under age 19," after "(and";

(2) in subsection (c), in the first sentence, by striking "under age 19"; and

(3) in subsection (d)—

(A) in paragraph (2)—

(i) in the first sentence, by striking "under age 19"; and

(ii) by striking the third sentence and inserting "A State may not require, as a condition of an individual (or the individual's parent) being or remaining eligible for medical assistance under this title, that the individual (or the individual's parent) apply for enrollment in qualified employer-sponsored coverage under this section."; and

(B) in paragraph (3), by striking "the parent of an individual under age 19" and inserting "an individual (or the parent of an individual)"; and

(4) in subsection (e), by striking "under age 19" each place it appears.

(b) CONFORMING AMENDMENT.—The heading for section 1906A of such Act (42 U.S.C. 1396e–1) is amended by striking "OPTION FOR CHILDREN".

(c) EFFECTIVE DATE.—The amendments made by this section take effect on January 1, 2014.

SEC. 2004. MEDICAID COVERAGE FOR FORMER FOSTER CARE CHILDREN.

(a) IN GENERAL.—Section 1902(a)(10)(A)(i) of the Social Security Act (42 U.S.C. 1396a), as amended by section 2001(a)(1), is amended—

(1) by striking "or" at the end of subclause (VII);

(2) by adding "or" at the end of subclause (VIII); and

(3) by inserting after subclause (VIII) the following:

"(IX) who were in foster care under the responsibility of a State for more than 6 months (whether or not consecutive) but are no longer in such care, who are not described in any of subclauses (I) through (VII) of this clause, and who are under 25 years of age;".

(b) OPTION TO PROVIDE PRESUMPTIVE ELIGIBILITY.—Section 1920(e) of such Act (42 U.S.C. 1396r–1(e)), as added by section 2001(a)(4)(B) and amended by section 2001(e)(2)(C), is amended by inserting ", clause (i)(IX)," after "clause (i)(VIII)".

(c) CONFORMING AMENDMENTS.—

(1) Section 1903(f)(4) of such Act (42 U.S.C. 1396b(f)(4)), as amended by section 2001(a)(5)(D), is amended by inserting "1902(a)(10)(A)(i)(IX)," after "1902(a)(10)(A)(i)(VIII),".

(2) Section 1937(a)(2)(B)(viii) of such Act (42 U.S.C. 1396u–7(a)(2)(B)(viii)) is amended by inserting ", or the individual qualifies for medical assistance on the basis of section 1902(a)(10)(A)(i)(IX)" before the period.

(d) EFFECTIVE DATE.—The amendments made by this section take effect on January 1, 2019.

SEC. 2005. PAYMENTS TO TERRITORIES.

(a) INCREASE IN LIMIT ON PAYMENTS.—Section 1108(g) of the Social Security Act (42 U.S.C. 1308(g)) is amended—

(1) in paragraph (2), in the matter preceding subparagraph (A), by striking "paragraph (3)" and inserting "paragraphs (3) and (5)";

(2) in paragraph (4), by striking "and (3)" and inserting "(3), and (4)"; and

(3) by adding at the end the following paragraph:

"(5) FISCAL YEAR 2011 AND THEREAFTER.—The amounts otherwise determined under this subsection for Puerto Rico, the Virgin Islands, Guam, the Northern Mariana Islands, and American Samoa for the second, third, and fourth quarters of fiscal year 2011, and for each fiscal year after fiscal year 2011 (after the application of subsection (f) and the preceding paragraphs of this subsection), shall be increased by 30 percent.".

(b) DISREGARD OF PAYMENTS FOR MANDATORY EXPANDED ENROLLMENT.—Section 1108(g)(4) of such Act (42 U.S.C. 1308(g)(4)) is amended—

(1) by striking "to fiscal years beginning" and inserting "to—

"(A) fiscal years beginning";

(2) by striking the period at the end and inserting "; and"; and

(3) by adding at the end the following:

"(B) fiscal years beginning with fiscal year 2014, payments made to Puerto Rico, the Virgin Islands, Guam, the Northern Mariana Islands, or American Samoa with respect to amounts expended for medical assistance for newly eligible (as defined in section 1905(y)(2)) nonpregnant childless adults who are eligible under subclause (VIII) of section 1902(a)(10)(A)(i) and whose income (as determined under section 1902(e)(14)) does not exceed (in the case of each such commonwealth and territory respectively) the income eligibility level in effect for that population under title XIX or under a waiver on the date of enactment of the Patient Protection and Affordable Care Act, shall not be taken into account in applying subsection (f) (as increased in accordance with paragraphs (1), (2), (3), and (5) of this subsection) to such commonwealth or territory for such fiscal year.".

(c) INCREASED FMAP.—

(1) IN GENERAL.—The first sentence of section 1905(b) of the Social Security Act (42 U.S.C. 1396d(b)) is amended by striking "shall be 50 per centum" and inserting "shall be 55 percent".

(2) EFFECTIVE DATE.—The amendment made by paragraph (1) takes effect on January 1, 2011.

SEC. 2006. SPECIAL ADJUSTMENT TO FMAP DETERMINATION FOR CERTAIN STATES RECOVERING FROM A MAJOR DISASTER.

Section 1905 of the Social Security Act (42 U.S.C. 1396d), as amended by sections 2001(a)(3) and 2001(b)(2), is amended—

(1) in subsection (b), in the first sentence, by striking "subsection (y)" and inserting "subsections (y) and (aa)"; and

(2) by adding at the end the following new subsection:

"(aa)(1) Notwithstanding subsection (b), beginning January 1, 2011, the Federal medical assistance percentage for a fiscal year for a disaster-recovery FMAP adjustment State shall be equal to the following:

"(A) In the case of the first fiscal year (or part of a fiscal year) for which this subsection applies to the State, the Federal medical assistance percentage determined for the fiscal year without regard to this subsection and subsection (y), increased by 50 percent of the number of percentage points by which the Federal medical assistance percentage determined for the State for the fiscal year without regard to this subsection and subsection (y), is less than the Federal medical assistance percentage determined for the State for the preceding fiscal year after the application of only subsection (a) of section 5001 of Public Law 111–5 (if applicable to the preceding fiscal year) and without regard to this subsection, subsection (y), and subsections (b) and (c) of section 5001 of Public Law 111–5.

"(B) In the case of the second or any succeeding fiscal year for which this subsection applies to the State, the Federal medical assistance percentage determined for the preceding fiscal year under this subsection for the State, increased by 25 percent of the number of percentage points by which the Federal medical assistance percentage determined for the State for the fiscal year without regard to this subsection and subsection (y), is less than the Federal medical assistance percentage determined for the State for the preceding fiscal year under this subsection.

"(2) In this subsection, the term 'disaster-recovery FMAP adjustment State' means a State that is one of the 50 States or the District of Columbia, for which, at any time during the preceding 7 fiscal years, the President has declared a major disaster under section 401 of the Robert T. Stafford Disaster Relief and Emergency Assistance Act and determined as a result of such disaster that every county or parish in the State warrant individual and public assistance or public assistance from the Federal Government under such Act and for which—

"(A) in the case of the first fiscal year (or part of a fiscal year) for which this subsection applies to the State, the Federal medical assistance percentage determined for the State for the fiscal year without regard to this subsection and subsection (y), is less than the Federal medical assistance percentage determined for the State for the preceding fiscal year after the application of only subsection (a) of section 5001 of Public Law 111–5 (if applicable to the preceding fiscal year) and without regard to this subsection, subsection (y), and subsections (b) and (c) of section 5001 of Public Law 111–5, by at least 3 percentage points; and

"(B) in the case of the second or any succeeding fiscal year for which this subsection applies to the State, the Federal medical assistance percentage determined for the State for the fiscal year without regard to this subsection and subsection (y), is less than the Federal medical assistance percentage determined for the State for the preceding fiscal year under this subsection by at least 3 percentage points.

"(3) The Federal medical assistance percentage determined for a disaster-recovery FMAP adjustment State under paragraph (1) shall apply for purposes of this title (other than with respect to disproportionate share hospital payments described in section 1923 and payments under this title that are based on the enhanced FMAP described in 2105(b)) and shall not apply with respect to payments under title IV (other than under part E of title IV) or payments under title XXI.".

SEC. 2007. MEDICAID IMPROVEMENT FUND RESCISSION.

(a) RESCISSION.—Any amounts available to the Medicaid Improvement Fund established under section 1941 of the Social Security Act (42 U.S.C. 1396w–1) for any of fiscal years 2014 through 2018 that are available for expenditure from the Fund and that are not so obligated as of the date of the enactment of this Act are rescinded.

(b) CONFORMING AMENDMENTS.—Section 1941(b)(1) of the Social Security Act (42 U.S.C. 1396w–1(b)(1)) is amended—

(1) in subparagraph (A), by striking "$100,000,000" and inserting "$0"; and

(2) in subparagraph (B), by striking "$150,000,000" and inserting "$0".

Subtitle B—Enhanced Support for the Children's Health Insurance Program

SEC. 2101. ADDITIONAL FEDERAL FINANCIAL PARTICIPATION FOR CHIP.

(a) IN GENERAL.—Section 2105(b) of the Social Security Act (42 U.S.C. 1397ee(b)) is amended by adding at the end the following: "Notwithstanding the preceding sentence, during the period that begins on October 1, 2013, and ends on September 30, 2019, the enhanced FMAP determined for a State for a fiscal year (or for any portion of a fiscal year occurring during such period) shall be increased by 23 percentage points, but in no case shall exceed 100 percent. The increase in the enhanced FMAP under the preceding sentence shall not apply with respect to determining the payment to a State under subsection (a)(1) for expenditures described in subparagraph (D)(iv), paragraphs (8), (9), (11) of subsection (c), or clause (4) of the first sentence of section 1905(b).".

(b) MAINTENANCE OF EFFORT.—

(1) IN GENERAL.—Section 2105(d) of the Social Security Act (42 U.S.C. 1397ee(d)) is amended by adding at the end the following:

"(3) CONTINUATION OF ELIGIBILITY STANDARDS FOR CHILDREN UNTIL OCTOBER 1, 2019.—

"(A) IN GENERAL.—During the period that begins on the date of enactment of the Patient Protection and Affordable Care Act and ends on September 30, 2019, a State shall not have in effect eligibility standards, methodologies, or procedures under its State child health plan (including any waiver under such plan) for children (including children provided medical assistance for which payment is made under section 2105(a)(1)(A)) that are more restrictive than the eligibility standards, methodologies, or procedures, respectively, under such plan (or waiver) as in effect on the date of enactment of that Act. The preceding sentence shall not be construed as preventing a State during such period from—

"(i) applying eligibility standards, methodologies, or procedures for children under the State child health plan or under any waiver of the plan that are less restrictive than the eligibility standards, methodologies, or procedures, respectively, for children under the plan or waiver that are in effect on the date of enactment of such Act; or

"(ii) imposing a limitation described in section 2112(b)(7) for a fiscal year in order to limit expenditures under the State child health plan to those for which Federal financial participation is available under this section for the fiscal year.

"(B) ASSURANCE OF EXCHANGE COVERAGE FOR TARGETED LOW-INCOME CHILDREN UNABLE TO BE PROVIDED CHILD HEALTH ASSISTANCE AS A RESULT OF FUNDING SHORTFALLS.—In the event that allotments provided under section 2104 are insufficient to provide coverage to all children who are eligible to be targeted low-income children under the State child health plan under this title, a State shall establish procedures to ensure that such children are provided coverage through an Exchange established by the State under section 1311 of the Patient Protection and Affordable Care Act.".

(2) CONFORMING AMENDMENT TO TITLE XXI MEDICAID MAINTENANCE OF EFFORT.—Section 2105(d)(1) of the Social Security Act (42 U.S.C. 1397ee(d)(1)) is amended by adding before the period ", except as required under section 1902(e)(14)".

(c) NO ENROLLMENT BONUS PAYMENTS FOR CHILDREN ENROLLED AFTER FISCAL YEAR 2013.—Section 2105(a)(3)(F)(iii) of the Social Security Act (42 U.S.C. 1397ee(a)(3)(F)(iii)) is amended by inserting "or any children enrolled on or after October 1, 2013" before the period.

(d) INCOME ELIGIBILITY DETERMINED USING MODIFIED GROSS INCOME.—

(1) STATE PLAN REQUIREMENT.—Section 2102(b)(1)(B) of the Social Security Act (42 U.S.C. 1397bb(b)(1)(B)) is amended—

(A) in clause (iii), by striking "and" after the semicolon;

(B) in clause (iv), by striking the period and inserting "; and"; and

(C) by adding at the end the following:

"(v) shall, beginning January 1, 2014, use modified gross income and household income (as defined in section 36B(d)(2) of the Internal Revenue Code of 1986) to determine eligibility for child health assistance under the State child health plan or under any waiver of such plan and for any other purpose applicable under the plan or waiver for which a determination of income is required, including with respect to the imposition of premiums and cost-sharing, consistent with section 1902(e)(14).".

(2) CONFORMING AMENDMENT.—Section 2107(e)(1) of the Social Security Act (42 U.S.C. 1397gg(e)(1)) is amended—

(A) by redesignating subparagraphs (E) through (L) as subparagraphs (F) through (M), respectively; and

(B) by inserting after subparagraph (D), the following:

"(E) Section 1902(e)(14) (relating to income determined using modified gross income and household income).".

(e) APPLICATION OF STREAMLINED ENROLLMENT SYSTEM.—Section 2107(e)(1) of the Social Security Act (42 U.S.C. 1397gg(e)(1)), as amended by subsection (d)(2), is amended by adding at the end the following:

"(N) Section 1943(b) (relating to coordination with State Exchanges and the State Medicaid agency).".

(f) CHIP ELIGIBILITY FOR CHILDREN INELIGIBLE FOR MEDICAID AS A RESULT OF ELIMINATION OF DISREGARDS.—Notwithstanding any other provision of law, a State shall treat any child who is determined to be ineligible for medical assistance under the State Medicaid plan or under a waiver of the plan as a result of the elimination of the application of an income disregard based on expense or type of income, as required under section 1902(e)(14) of the Social Security Act (as added by this Act), as a targeted low-income child under section 2110(b) (unless the child is excluded under paragraph (2) of that section) and shall provide child health assistance to the child under the State child health plan (whether implemented under title XIX or XXI, or both, of the Social Security Act).

SEC. 2102. TECHNICAL CORRECTIONS.

(a) CHIPRA.—Effective as if included in the enactment of the Children's Health Insurance Program Reauthorization Act of 2009 (Public Law 111–3) (in this section referred to as "CHIPRA"):

(1) Section 2104(m) of the Social Security Act, as added by section 102 of CHIPRA, is amended—

(A) by redesignating paragraph (7) as paragraph (8); and

(B) by inserting after paragraph (6), the following:

"(7) ADJUSTMENT OF FISCAL YEAR 2010 ALLOTMENTS TO ACCOUNT FOR CHANGES IN PROJECTED SPENDING FOR CERTAIN PREVIOUSLY APPROVED EXPANSION PROGRAMS.—For purposes of recalculating the fiscal year 2010 allotment, in the case of one of the 50 States or the District of Columbia that has an approved State plan amendment effective January 1, 2006, to provide child health assistance through the provision of benefits under the State plan under title XIX for children from birth through age 5 whose family income does not exceed 200 percent of the poverty line, the Secretary shall increase the allotment by an amount that would be equal to the Federal share of expenditures that would have been claimed at the enhanced FMAP rate rather than the Federal medical assistance percentage matching rate for such population.".

(2) Section 605 of CHIPRA is amended by striking "legal residents" and insert "lawfully residing in the United States".

(3) Subclauses (I) and (II) of paragraph (3)(C)(i) of section 2105(a) of the Social Security Act (42 U.S.C. 1397ee(a)(3)(ii)), as added by section 104 of CHIPRA, are each amended by striking ", respectively".

(4) Section 2105(a)(3)(E)(ii) of the Social Security Act (42 U.S.C. 1397ee(a)(3)(E)(ii)), as added by section 104 of CHIPRA, is amended by striking subclause (IV).

(5) Section 2105(c)(9)(B) of the Social Security Act (42 U.S.C. 1397e(c)(9)(B)), as added by section 211(c)(1) of CHIPRA, is amended by striking "section 1903(a)(3)(F)" and inserting "section 1903(a)(3)(G)".

(6) Section 2109(b)(2)(B) of the Social Security Act (42 U.S.C. 1397ii(b)(2)(B)), as added by section 602 of CHIPRA, is amended by striking "the child population growth factor under section 2104(m)(5)(B)" and inserting "a high-performing State under section 2111(b)(3)(B)".

(7) Section 2110(c)(9)(B)(v) of the Social Security Act (42 U.S.C. 1397jj(c)(9)(B)(v)), as added by section 505(b) of CHIPRA, is amended by striking "school or school system" and inserting "local educational agency (as defined under section 9101 of the Elementary and Secondary Education Act of 1965".

(8) Section 211(a)(1)(B) of CHIPRA is amended—

(A) by striking "is amended" and all that follows through "adding" and inserting "is amended by adding"; and

(B) by redesignating the new subparagraph to be added by such section to section 1903(a)(3) of the Social Security Act as a new subparagraph (H).

(b) ARRA.—Effective as if included in the enactment of section 5006(a) of division B of the American Recovery and Reinvestment Act of 2009 (Public Law 111–5), the second sentence of section 1916A(a)(1) of the Social Security Act (42 U.S.C. 1396o–1(a)(1)) is amended by striking "or (i)" and inserting ", (i), or (j)".

Subtitle C—Medicaid and CHIP Enrollment Simplification

SEC. 2201. ENROLLMENT SIMPLIFICATION AND COORDINATION WITH STATE HEALTH INSURANCE EXCHANGES.

Title XIX of the Social Security Act (42 U.S.C. 1397aa et seq.) is amended by adding at the end the following:

"SEC. 1943. ENROLLMENT SIMPLIFICATION AND COORDINATION WITH STATE HEALTH INSURANCE EXCHANGES.

"(a) CONDITION FOR PARTICIPATION IN MEDICAID.—As a condition of the State plan under this title and receipt of any Federal financial assistance under section 1903(a) for calendar quarters beginning after January 1, 2014, a State shall ensure that the requirements of subsection (b) is met.

"(b) ENROLLMENT SIMPLIFICATION AND COORDINATION WITH STATE HEALTH INSURANCE EXCHANGES AND CHIP.—

"(1) IN GENERAL.—A State shall establish procedures for—

"(A) enabling individuals, through an Internet website that meets the requirements of paragraph (4), to apply for medical assistance under the State plan or under a waiver of the plan, to be enrolled in the State plan or waiver, to renew their enrollment in the plan or waiver, and to consent to enrollment or reenrollment in the State plan through electronic signature;

"(B) enrolling, without any further determination by the State and through such website, individuals who are identified by an Exchange established by the State under section 1311 of the Patient Protection and Affordable Care Act as being eligible for—

"(i) medical assistance under the State plan or under a waiver of the plan; or

"(ii) child health assistance under the State child health plan under title XXI;

"(C) ensuring that individuals who apply for but are determined to be ineligible for medical assistance under the State plan or a waiver or ineligible for child health assistance under the State child health plan under title XXI, are screened for eligibility for enrollment in qualified health plans offered through such an Exchange and, if applicable, premium assistance for the purchase of a qualified health plan under section 36B of the Internal Revenue Code of 1986 (and, if applicable, advance payment of such assistance under section 1412 of the Patient Protection and Affordable Care Act), and, if eligible, enrolled in such a plan without having to submit an additional or separate application, and that such individuals receive information regarding reduced cost-sharing for eligible individuals under section 1402 of the Patient Protection and Affordable

Care Act, and any other assistance or subsidies available for coverage obtained through the Exchange;

"(D) ensuring that the State agency responsible for administering the State plan under this title (in this section referred to as the 'State Medicaid agency'), the State agency responsible for administering the State child health plan under title XXI (in this section referred to as the 'State CHIP agency') and an Exchange established by the State under section 1311 of the Patient Protection and Affordable Care Act utilize a secure electronic interface sufficient to allow for a determination of an individual's eligibility for such medical assistance, child health assistance, or premium assistance, and enrollment in the State plan under this title, title XXI, or a qualified health plan, as appropriate;

"(E) coordinating, for individuals who are enrolled in the State plan or under a waiver of the plan and who are also enrolled in a qualified health plan offered through such an Exchange, and for individuals who are enrolled in the State child health plan under title XXI and who are also enrolled in a qualified health plan, the provision of medical assistance or child health assistance to such individuals with the coverage provided under the qualified health plan in which they are enrolled, including services described in section 1905(a)(4)(B) (relating to early and periodic screening, diagnostic, and treatment services defined in section 1905(r)) and provided in accordance with the requirements of section 1902(a)(43); and

"(F) conducting outreach to and enrolling vulnerable and underserved populations eligible for medical assistance under this title XIX or for child health assistance under title XXI, including children, unaccompanied homeless youth, children and youth with special health care needs, pregnant women, racial and ethnic minorities, rural populations, victims of abuse or trauma, individuals with mental health or substance-related disorders, and individuals with HIV/AIDS.

"(2) AGREEMENTS WITH STATE HEALTH INSURANCE EXCHANGES.—The State Medicaid agency and the State CHIP agency may enter into an agreement with an Exchange established by the State under section 1311 of the Patient Protection and Affordable Care Act under which the State Medicaid agency or State CHIP agency may determine whether a State resident is eligible for premium assistance for the purchase of a qualified health plan under section 36B of the Internal Revenue Code of 1986 (and, if applicable, advance payment of such assistance under section 1412 of the Patient Protection and Affordable Care Act), so long as the agreement meets such conditions and requirements as the Secretary of the Treasury may prescribe to reduce administrative costs and the likelihood of eligibility errors and disruptions in coverage.

"(3) STREAMLINED ENROLLMENT SYSTEM.—The State Medicaid agency and State CHIP agency shall participate in and comply with the requirements for the system established under section 1413 of the Patient Protection and Affordable Care Act (relating to streamlined procedures for enrollment through an Exchange, Medicaid, and CHIP).

"(4) ENROLLMENT WEBSITE REQUIREMENTS.—The procedures established by State under paragraph (1) shall include establishing and having in operation, not later than January 1, 2014, an Internet website that is linked to any website of an Exchange established by the State under section 1311 of the Patient Protection and Affordable Care Act and to the State CHIP agency (if different from the State Medicaid agency) and allows an individual who is eligible for medical assistance under the State plan or under a waiver of the plan and who is eligible to receive premium credit assistance for the purchase of a qualified health plan under section 36B of the Internal Revenue Code of 1986 to compare the benefits, premiums, and cost-sharing applicable to the individual under the State plan or waiver with the benefits, premiums, and cost-sharing available to the individual under a qualified health plan offered through such an Exchange, including, in the case of a child, the coverage that would be provided for the child through the State plan or waiver with the coverage that would be provided to the child through enrollment in family coverage under that plan and as supplemental coverage by the State under the State plan or waiver.

"(5) CONTINUED NEED FOR ASSESSMENT FOR HOME AND COMMUNITY-BASED SERVICES.—Nothing in paragraph (1) shall limit or modify the requirement that the State assess an individual for purposes of providing home and community-based services under the State plan or under any waiver of such plan for individuals described in subsection (a)(10)(A)(ii)(VI).".

SEC. 2202. PERMITTING HOSPITALS TO MAKE PRESUMPTIVE ELIGIBILITY DETERMINATIONS FOR ALL MEDICAID ELIGIBLE POPULATIONS.

(a) IN GENERAL.—Section 1902(a)(47) of the Social Security Act (42 U.S.C. 1396a(a)(47)) is amended—

(1) by striking "at the option of the State, provide" and inserting "provide—

"(A) at the option of the State,";

(2) by inserting "and" after the semicolon; and

(3) by adding at the end the following:

"(B) that any hospital that is a participating provider under the State plan may elect to be a qualified entity for purposes of determining, on the basis of preliminary information, whether any individual is eligible for medical assistance under the State plan or under a waiver of the plan for purposes of providing the individual with medical assistance during a presumptive eligibility period, in the same manner, and subject to the same requirements, as apply to the State options with respect to populations described in section 1920, 1920A, or 1920B (but without regard to whether the State has elected to provide for a presumptive eligibility period under any such sections), subject to such guidance as the Secretary shall establish;".

(b) CONFORMING AMENDMENT.—Section 1903(u)(1)(D)(v) of such Act (42 U.S.C. 1396b(u)(1)(D)v)) is amended—

(1) by striking "or for" and inserting "for"; and

(2) by inserting before the period at the end the following: ", or for medical assistance provided to an individual during a presumptive eligibility period resulting from a determination

of presumptive eligibility made by a hospital that elects under section 1902(a)(47)(B) to be a qualified entity for such purpose".

(c) EFFECTIVE DATE.—The amendments made by this section take effect on January 1, 2014, and apply to services furnished on or after that date.

Subtitle D—Improvements to Medicaid Services

SEC. 2301. COVERAGE FOR FREESTANDING BIRTH CENTER SERVICES.

(a) IN GENERAL.—Section 1905 of the Social Security Act (42 U.S.C. 1396d), is amended—

(1) in subsection (a)—

(A) in paragraph (27), by striking "and" at the end;

(B) by redesignating paragraph (28) as paragraph (29); and

(C) by inserting after paragraph (27) the following new paragraph:

"(28) freestanding birth center services (as defined in subsection (l)(3)(A)) and other ambulatory services that are offered by a freestanding birth center (as defined in subsection (l)(3)(B)) and that are otherwise included in the plan; and"; and

(2) in subsection (l), by adding at the end the following new paragraph:

"(3)(A) The term 'freestanding birth center services' means services furnished to an individual at a freestanding birth center (as defined in subparagraph (B)) at such center.

"(B) The term 'freestanding birth center' means a health facility—

"(i) that is not a hospital;

"(ii) where childbirth is planned to occur away from the pregnant woman's residence;

"(iii) that is licensed or otherwise approved by the State to provide prenatal labor and delivery or postpartum care and other ambulatory services that are included in the plan; and

"(iv) that complies with such other requirements relating to the health and safety of individuals furnished services by the facility as the State shall establish.

"(C) A State shall provide separate payments to providers administering prenatal labor and delivery or postpartum care in a freestanding birth center (as defined in subparagraph (B)), such as nurse midwives and other providers of services such as birth attendants recognized under State law, as determined appropriate by the Secretary. For purposes of the preceding sentence, the term 'birth attendant' means an individual who is recognized or registered by the State involved to provide health care at childbirth and who provides such care within the scope of practice under which the individual is legally authorized to perform such care under State law (or the State regulatory mechanism provided by State law), regardless of whether the individual is under the supervision of, or associated with, a physician or other health care provider. Nothing in this subparagraph shall be construed as changing State law requirements applicable to a birth attendant.".

(b) CONFORMING AMENDMENT.—Section 1902(a)(10)(A) of the Social Security Act (42 U.S.C. 1396a(a)(10)(A)), is amended in the matter preceding clause (i) by striking "and (21)" and inserting ", (21), and (28)".

(c) EFFECTIVE DATE.—

(1) IN GENERAL.—Except as provided in paragraph (2), the amendments made by this section shall take effect on the date of the enactment of this Act and shall apply to services furnished on or after such date.

(2) EXCEPTION IF STATE LEGISLATION REQUIRED.—In the case of a State plan for medical assistance under title XIX of the Social Security Act which the Secretary of Health and Human Services determines requires State legislation (other than legislation appropriating funds) in order for the plan to meet the additional requirement imposed by the amendments made by this section, the State plan shall not be regarded as failing to comply with the requirements of such title solely on the basis of its failure to meet this additional requirement before the first day of the first calendar quarter beginning after the close of the first regular session of the State legislature that begins after the date of the enactment of this Act. For purposes of the previous sentence, in the case of a State that has a 2-year legislative session, each year of such session shall be deemed to be a separate regular session of the State legislature.

SEC. 2302. CONCURRENT CARE FOR CHILDREN.

(a) IN GENERAL.—Section 1905(o)(1) of the Social Security Act (42 U.S.C. 1396d(o)(1)) is amended—

(1) in subparagraph (A), by striking "subparagraph (B)" and inserting "subparagraphs (B) and (C)"; and

(2) by adding at the end the following new subparagraph:

"(C) A voluntary election to have payment made for hospice care for a child (as defined by the State) shall not constitute a waiver of any rights of the child to be provided with, or to have payment made under this title for, services that are related to the treatment of the child's condition for which a diagnosis of terminal illness has been made.".

(b) APPLICATION TO CHIP.—Section 2110(a)(23) of the Social Security Act (42 U.S.C. 1397jj(a)(23)) is amended by inserting "(concurrent, in the case of an individual who is a child, with care related to the treatment of the child's condition with respect to which a diagnosis of terminal illness has been made" after "hospice care".

SEC. 2303. STATE ELIGIBILITY OPTION FOR FAMILY PLANNING SERVICES.

(a) COVERAGE AS OPTIONAL CATEGORICALLY NEEDY GROUP.—

(1) IN GENERAL.—Section 1902(a)(10)(A)(ii) of the Social Security Act (42 U.S.C. 1396a(a)(10)(A)(ii)), as amended by section 2001(e), is amended—

(A) in subclause (XIX), by striking "or" at the end;

(B) in subclause (XX), by adding "or" at the end; and

(C) by adding at the end the following new subclause:

"(XXI) who are described in subsection (ii) (relating to individuals who meet certain income standards);".

(2) GROUP DESCRIBED.—Section 1902 of such Act (42 U.S.C. 1396a), as amended by section 2001(d), is amended by adding at the end the following new subsection:

"(ii)(1) Individuals described in this subsection are individuals—

"(A) whose income does not exceed an income eligibility level established by the State that does not exceed the highest income eligibility level established under the State plan under this title (or under its State child health plan under title XXI) for pregnant women; and

"(B) who are not pregnant.

"(2) At the option of a State, individuals described in this subsection may include individuals who, had individuals applied on or before January 1, 2007, would have been made eligible pursuant to the standards and processes imposed by that State for benefits described in clause (XV) of the matter following subparagraph (G) of section subsection (a)(10) pursuant to a waiver granted under section 1115.

"(3) At the option of a State, for purposes of subsection (a)(17)(B), in determining eligibility for services under this subsection, the State may consider only the income of the applicant or recipient.".

(3) LIMITATION ON BENEFITS.—Section 1902(a)(10) of the Social Security Act (42 U.S.C. 1396a(a)(10)), as amended by section 2001(a)(5)(A), is amended in the matter following subparagraph (G)—

(A) by striking "and (XV)" and inserting "(XV)"; and

(B) by inserting ", and (XVI) the medical assistance made available to an individual described in subsection (ii) shall be limited to family planning services and supplies described in section 1905(a)(4)(C) including medical diagnosis and treatment services that are provided pursuant to a family planning service in a family planning setting" before the semicolon.

(4) CONFORMING AMENDMENTS.—

(A) Section 1905(a) of the Social Security Act (42 U.S.C. 1396d(a)), as amended by section 2001(e)(2)(A), is amended in the matter preceding paragraph (1)—

(i) in clause (xiv), by striking "or" at the end;

(ii) in clause (xv), by adding "or" at the end; and

(iii) by inserting after clause (xv) the following: "(xvi) individuals described in section 1902(ii),".

(B) Section 1903(f)(4) of such Act (42 U.S.C. 1396b(f)(4)), as amended by section 2001(e)(2)(B), is amended by inserting "1902(a)(10)(A)(ii)(XXI)," after "1902(a)(10)(A)(ii)(XX),".

(b) PRESUMPTIVE ELIGIBILITY.—

(1) IN GENERAL.—Title XIX of the Social Security Act (42 U.S.C. 1396 et seq.) is amended by inserting after section 1920B the following:

"PRESUMPTIVE ELIGIBILITY FOR FAMILY PLANNING SERVICES

"SEC. 1920C. (a) STATE OPTION.—State plan approved under section 1902 may provide for making medical assistance available to an individual described in section 1902(ii) (relating to individuals who meet certain income eligibility standard) during a presumptive eligibility period. In the case of an individual described in section 1902(ii), such medical assistance shall be limited to family planning services and supplies described in 1905(a)(4)(C) and, at the State's option, medical diagnosis and treatment services that are provided in conjunction with a family planning service in a family planning setting.

"(b) DEFINITIONS.—For purposes of this section:

"(1) PRESUMPTIVE ELIGIBILITY PERIOD.—The term 'presumptive eligibility period' means, with respect to an individual described in subsection (a), the period that—

"(A) begins with the date on which a qualified entity determines, on the basis of preliminary information, that the individual is described in section 1902(ii); and

"(B) ends with (and includes) the earlier of—

"(i) the day on which a determination is made with respect to the eligibility of such individual for services under the State plan; or

"(ii) in the case of such an individual who does not file an application by the last day of the month following the month during which the entity makes the determination referred to in subparagraph (A), such last day.

"(2) QUALIFIED ENTITY.—

"(A) IN GENERAL.—Subject to subparagraph (B), the term 'qualified entity' means any entity that—

"(i) is eligible for payments under a State plan approved under this title; and

"(ii) is determined by the State agency to be capable of making determinations of the type described in paragraph (1)(A).

"(B) RULE OF CONSTRUCTION.—Nothing in this paragraph shall be construed as preventing a State from limiting the classes of entities that may become qualified entities in order to prevent fraud and abuse.

"(c) ADMINISTRATION.—

"(1) IN GENERAL.—The State agency shall provide qualified entities with—

"(A) such forms as are necessary for an application to be made by an individual described in subsection (a) for medical assistance under the State plan; and

"(B) information on how to assist such individuals in completing and filing such forms.

"(2) NOTIFICATION REQUIREMENTS.—A qualified entity that determines under subsection (b)(1)(A) that an individual described in subsection (a) is presumptively eligible for medical assistance under a State plan shall—

"(A) notify the State agency of the determination within 5 working days after the date on which determination is made; and

"(B) inform such individual at the time the determination is made that an application for medical assistance is required to be made by not later than the last day of the month following the month during which the determination is made.

"(3) APPLICATION FOR MEDICAL ASSISTANCE.—In the case of an individual described in subsection (a) who is determined by a qualified entity to be presumptively eligible for medical assistance under a State plan, the individual shall apply for medical assistance by not later than the last day of the month following the month during which the determination is made.

"(d) PAYMENT.—Notwithstanding any other provision of law, medical assistance that—

"(1) is furnished to an individual described in subsection (a)—

"(A) during a presumptive eligibility period; and

"(B) by a entity that is eligible for payments under the State plan; and

"(2) is included in the care and services covered by the State plan,

shall be treated as medical assistance provided by such plan for purposes of clause (4) of the first sentence of section 1905(b).".

(2) CONFORMING AMENDMENTS.—

(A) Section 1902(a)(47) of the Social Security Act (42 U.S.C. 1396a(a)(47)), as amended by section 2202(a), is amended—

(i) in subparagraph (A), by inserting before the semicolon at the end the following: "and provide for making medical assistance available to individuals described in subsection (a) of section 1920C during a presumptive eligibility period in accordance with such section"; and

(ii) in subparagraph (B), by striking "or 1920B" and inserting "1920B, or 1920C".

(B) Section 1903(u)(1)(D)(v) of such Act (42 U.S.C. 1396b(u)(1)(D)(v)), as amended by section 2202(b), is amended by inserting "or for medical assistance provided to an individual described in subsection (a) of section 1920C during a presumptive eligibility period under such section," after "1920B during a presumptive eligibility period under such section,".

(c) CLARIFICATION OF COVERAGE OF FAMILY PLANNING SERVICES AND SUPPLIES.—Section 1937(b) of the Social Security Act (42 U.S.C. 1396u–7(b)), as amended by section 2001(c), is amended by adding at the end the following:

"(7) COVERAGE OF FAMILY PLANNING SERVICES AND SUPPLIES.—Notwithstanding the previous provisions of this section, a State may not provide for medical assistance through enrollment of an individual with benchmark coverage or benchmark-equivalent coverage under this section unless such coverage includes for any individual described in section 1905(a)(4)(C), medical assistance for family planning services and supplies in accordance with such section.".

(d) EFFECTIVE DATE.—The amendments made by this section take effect on the date of the enactment of this Act and shall apply to items and services furnished on or after such date.

SEC. 2304. CLARIFICATION OF DEFINITION OF MEDICAL ASSISTANCE.

Section 1905(a) of the Social Security Act (42 U.S.C. 1396d(a)) is amended by inserting "or the care and services themselves, or both" before "(if provided in or after".

Subtitle E—New Options for States to Provide Long-Term Services and Supports

SEC. 2401. COMMUNITY FIRST CHOICE OPTION.

Section 1915 of the Social Security Act (42 U.S.C. 1396n) is amended by adding at the end the following:

"(k) STATE PLAN OPTION TO PROVIDE HOME AND COMMUNITY-BASED ATTENDANT SERVICES AND SUPPORTS.—

"(1) IN GENERAL.—Subject to the succeeding provisions of this subsection, beginning October 1, 2010, a State may provide through a State plan amendment for the provision of medical assistance for home and community-based attendant services and supports for individuals who are eligible for medical assistance under the State plan whose income does not exceed 150 percent of the poverty line (as defined in section 2110(c)(5)) or, if greater, the income level applicable for an individual who has been determined to require an institutional level of care to be eligible for nursing facility services under the State plan and with respect to whom there has been a determination that, but for the provision of such services, the individuals would require the level of care provided in a hospital, a nursing facility, an intermediate care facility for the mentally retarded, or an institution for mental diseases, the cost of which could be reimbursed under the State plan, but only if the individual chooses to receive such home and community-based attendant services and supports, and only if the State meets the following requirements:

"(A) AVAILABILITY.—The State shall make available home and community-based attendant services and supports to eligible individuals, as needed, to assist in accomplishing activities of daily living, instrumental activities of daily living, and health-related tasks through hands-on assistance, supervision, or cueing—

"(i) under a person-centered plan of services and supports that is based on an assessment of functional need and that is agreed to in writing by the individual or, as appropriate, the individual's representative;

"(ii) in a home or community setting, which does not include a nursing facility, institution for mental diseases, or an intermediate care facility for the mentally retarded;

"(iii) under an agency-provider model or other model (as defined in paragraph (6)(C)); and

"(iv) the furnishing of which—

"(I) is selected, managed, and dismissed by the individual, or, as appropriate, with assistance from the individual's representative;

"(II) is controlled, to the maximum extent possible, by the individual or where appropriate, the individual's representative, regardless of who may act as the employer of record; and

"(III) provided by an individual who is qualified to provide such services, including family members (as defined by the Secretary).

"(B) INCLUDED SERVICES AND SUPPORTS.—In addition to assistance in accomplishing activities of daily living, instrumental activities of daily living, and health related tasks, the home and community-based attendant services and supports made available include—

"(i) the acquisition, maintenance, and enhancement of skills necessary for the individual to accomplish activities of daily living, instrumental activities of daily living, and health related tasks;

"(ii) back-up systems or mechanisms (such as the use of beepers or other electronic devices) to ensure continuity of services and supports; and

"(iii) voluntary training on how to select, manage, and dismiss attendants.

"(C) EXCLUDED SERVICES AND SUPPORTS.—Subject to subparagraph (D), the home and community-based attendant services and supports made available do not include—

"(i) room and board costs for the individual;

"(ii) special education and related services provided under the Individuals with Disabilities Education Act and vocational rehabilitation services provided under the Rehabilitation Act of 1973;

"(iii) assistive technology devices and assistive technology services other than those under (1)(B)(ii);

"(iv) medical supplies and equipment; or

"(v) home modifications.

"(D) PERMISSIBLE SERVICES AND SUPPORTS.—The home and community-based attendant services and supports may include—

"(i) expenditures for transition costs such as rent and utility deposits, first month's rent and utilities, bedding, basic kitchen supplies, and other necessities required for an individual to make the transition from a nursing facility, institution for mental diseases, or intermediate care facility for the mentally retarded to a community-based home setting where the individual resides; and

"(ii) expenditures relating to a need identified in an individual's person-centered plan of services that increase independence or substitute for human assistance, to the extent that expenditures would otherwise be made for the human assistance.

"(2) INCREASED FEDERAL FINANCIAL PARTICIPATION.—For purposes of payments to a State under section 1903(a)(1), with respect to amounts expended by the State to provide medical assistance under the State plan for home and community-based attendant services and supports to eligible individuals in accordance with this subsection during a fiscal year quarter occurring during the period described in paragraph (1), the Federal medical assistance percentage applicable to the State (as determined under section 1905(b)) shall be increased by 6 percentage points.

"(3) STATE REQUIREMENTS.—In order for a State plan amendment to be approved under this subsection, the State shall—

"(A) develop and implement such amendment in collaboration with a Development and Implementation Council established by the State that includes a majority of members with disabilities, elderly individuals, and their representatives and consults and collaborates with such individuals;

"(B) provide consumer controlled home and community-based attendant services and supports to individuals on a statewide basis, in a manner that provides such services and supports in the most integrated setting appropriate to the individual's needs, and without regard to the individual's age, type or nature of disability, severity of disability, or the form of home and community-based attendant services and supports that the individual requires in order to lead an independent life;

"(C) with respect to expenditures during the first full fiscal year in which the State plan amendment is implemented, maintain or exceed the level of State expenditures for medical assistance that is provided under section 1905(a), section 1915, section 1115, or otherwise to individuals with disabilities or elderly individuals attributable to the preceding fiscal year;

"(D) establish and maintain a comprehensive, continuous quality assurance system with respect to community-based attendant services and supports that—

"(i) includes standards for agency-based and other delivery models with respect to training, appeals for denials and reconsideration procedures of an individual plan, and other factors as determined by the Secretary;

"(ii) incorporates feedback from consumers and their representatives, disability organizations, providers, families of disabled or elderly individuals, members of the community, and others and maximizes consumer independence and consumer control;

"(iii) monitors the health and well-being of each individual who receives home and community-based attendant services and supports, including a process for the mandatory reporting, investigation, and resolution of allegations of neglect, abuse, or exploitation in connection with the provision of such services and supports; and

"(iv) provides information about the provisions of the quality assurance required under clauses (i) through (iii) to each individual receiving such services; and

"(E) collect and report information, as determined necessary by the Secretary, for the purposes of approving the State plan amendment, providing Federal oversight, and conducting an evaluation under paragraph (5)(A), including data regarding how the State provides home and community-based attendant services and supports and other home and community-based services, the cost of such services and supports, and how the State provides individuals with disabilities who otherwise qualify for institutional care under the State plan or under a waiver the choice to instead receive home and community-based services in lieu of institutional care.

"(4) COMPLIANCE WITH CERTAIN LAWS.—A State shall ensure that, regardless of whether the State uses an agency-provider model or other models to provide home and community-based attendant services and supports under a State plan amendment under this subsection, such services and supports are provided in accordance with the requirements of the Fair Labor Standards Act of 1938 and applicable Federal and State laws regarding—

"(A) withholding and payment of Federal and State income and payroll taxes;

"(B) the provision of unemployment and workers compensation insurance;

"(C) maintenance of general liability insurance; and

"(D) occupational health and safety.

"(5) EVALUATION, DATA COLLECTION, AND REPORT TO CONGRESS.—

"(A) EVALUATION.—The Secretary shall conduct an evaluation of the provision of home and community-based attendant services and supports under this subsection in order to determine the effectiveness of the provision of such services and supports in allowing the individuals receiving such services and supports to lead an independent life to the maximum extent possible; the impact on the physical and emotional health of the individuals who receive such services; and an comparative analysis of the costs of services provided under the State plan amendment under this subsection and those provided under institutional care in a nursing facility, institution for mental diseases, or an intermediate care facility for the mentally retarded.

"(B) DATA COLLECTION.—The State shall provide the Secretary with the following information regarding the provision of home and community-based attendant services and supports under this subsection for each fiscal year for which such services and supports are provided:

"(i) The number of individuals who are estimated to receive home and community-based attendant services and supports under this subsection during the fiscal year.

"(ii) The number of individuals that received such services and supports during the preceding fiscal year.

"(iii) The specific number of individuals served by type of disability, age, gender, education level, and employment status.

"(iv) Whether the specific individuals have been previously served under any other home and community based services program under the State plan or under a waiver.

"(C) REPORTS.—Not later than—

"(i) December 31, 2013, the Secretary shall submit to Congress and make available to the public an interim report on the findings of the evaluation under subparagraph (A); and

"(ii) December 31, 2015, the Secretary shall submit to Congress and make available to the public a final report on the findings of the evaluation under subparagraph (A).

"(6) DEFINITIONS.—In this subsection:

"(A) ACTIVITIES OF DAILY LIVING.—The term 'activities of daily living' includes tasks such as eating, toileting, grooming, dressing, bathing, and transferring.

"(B) CONSUMER CONTROLLED.—The term 'consumer controlled' means a method of selecting and providing services and supports that allow the individual, or where appropriate, the individual's representative, maximum control of the home and community-based attendant services and supports, regardless of who acts as the employer of record.

"(C) DELIVERY MODELS.—

"(i) AGENCY-PROVIDER MODEL.—The term 'agency-provider model' means, with respect to the provision of home and community-based attendant services and supports for an individual, subject to paragraph (4), a method of providing consumer controlled services and supports under which entities contract for the provision of such services and supports.

"(ii) OTHER MODELS.—The term 'other models' means, subject to paragraph (4), methods, other than an agency-provider model, for the provision of consumer controlled services and supports. Such models may include the provision of vouchers, direct cash payments, or use of a fiscal agent to assist in obtaining services.

"(D) HEALTH-RELATED TASKS.—The term 'health-related tasks' means specific tasks related to the needs of an individual, which can be delegated or assigned by licensed health-care professionals under State law to be performed by an attendant.

"(E) INDIVIDUAL'S REPRESENTATIVE.—The term 'individual's representative' means a parent, family member, guardian, advocate, or other authorized representative of an individual

"(F) INSTRUMENTAL ACTIVITIES OF DAILY LIVING.—The term 'instrumental activities of daily living' includes (but is not limited to) meal planning and preparation, managing finances, shopping for food, clothing, and other essential items, performing essential household chores, communicating by phone or other media, and traveling around and participating in the community.".

SEC. 2402. REMOVAL OF BARRIERS TO PROVIDING HOME AND COMMUNITY-BASED SERVICES.

(a) OVERSIGHT AND ASSESSMENT OF THE ADMINISTRATION OF HOME AND COMMUNITY-BASED SERVICES.—The Secretary of Health and Human Services shall promulgate regulations to ensure that all States develop service systems that are designed to—

(1) allocate resources for services in a manner that is responsive to the changing needs and choices of beneficiaries receiving non-institutionally-based long-term services and supports (including such services and supports that are provided under programs other the State Medicaid program), and that provides strategies for beneficiaries receiving such services to maximize their independence, including through the use of client-employed providers;

(2) provide the support and coordination needed for a beneficiary in need of such services (and their family caregivers or representative, if applicable) to design an individualized, self-directed, community-supported life; and

(3) improve coordination among, and the regulation of, all providers of such services under federally and State-funded programs in order to—

(A) achieve a more consistent administration of policies and procedures across programs in relation to the provision of such services; and

(B) oversee and monitor all service system functions to assure—

(i) coordination of, and effectiveness of, eligibility determinations and individual assessments;

(ii) development and service monitoring of a complaint system, a management system, a system to qualify and monitor providers, and systems for role-setting and individual budget determinations; and

(iii) an adequate number of qualified direct care workers to provide self-directed personal assistance services.

(b) ADDITIONAL STATE OPTIONS.—Section 1915(i) of the Social Security Act (42 U.S.C. 1396n(i)) is amended by adding at the end the following new paragraphs:

"(6) STATE OPTION TO PROVIDE HOME AND COMMUNITY-BASED SERVICES TO INDIVIDUALS ELIGIBLE FOR SERVICES UNDER A WAIVER.—

"(A) IN GENERAL.—A State that provides home and community-based services in accordance with this subsection to individuals who satisfy the needs-based criteria for the receipt of such services established under paragraph (1)(A) may, in addition to continuing to provide such services to such individuals, elect to provide home and community-based services in accordance with the requirements of this paragraph to individuals who are eligible for home and community-based services under a waiver approved for the State under subsection (c), (d), or (e) or under section 1115 to provide such services, but only for those individuals whose income does not exceed 300 percent of the supplemental security income benefit rate established by section 1611(b)(1).

"(B) APPLICATION OF SAME REQUIREMENTS FOR INDIVIDUALS SATISFYING NEEDS-BASED CRITERIA.—Subject to subparagraph (C), a State shall provide home and community-based services to individuals under this paragraph in the same manner and subject to the same requirements as apply under the other paragraphs of this subsection to the provision of home and community-based services to individuals who satisfy the needs-based criteria established under paragraph (1)(A).

"(C) AUTHORITY TO OFFER DIFFERENT TYPE, AMOUNT, DURATION, OR SCOPE OF HOME AND COMMUNITY-BASED SERVICES.—A State may offer home and community-based services to individuals under this paragraph that differ in type, amount, duration, or scope from the home and community-based services offered for individuals who satisfy the needs-based criteria established under paragraph (1)(A), so long as such services are within the scope of services described in paragraph (4)(B) of subsection (c) for which the Secretary has the authority to approve a waiver and do not include room or board.

"(7) STATE OPTION TO OFFER HOME AND COMMUNITY-BASED SERVICES TO SPECIFIC, TARGETED POPULATIONS.—

"(A) IN GENERAL.—A State may elect in a State plan amendment under this subsection to target the provision of home and community-based services under this subsection to specific populations and to differ the type, amount, duration, or scope of such services to such specific populations.

"(B) 5-YEAR TERM.—

"(i) IN GENERAL.—An election by a State under this paragraph shall be for a period of 5 years.

"(ii) PHASE-IN OF SERVICES AND ELIGIBILITY PERMITTED DURING INITIAL 5-YEAR PERIOD.—A State making an election under this paragraph may, during the first 5-year period for which the election is made, phase-in the enrollment of eligible individuals, or the provision of services to such individuals, or both, so long as all eligible individuals in the State for such services are enrolled, and all such services are provided, before the end of the initial 5-year period.

"(C) RENEWAL.—An election by a State under this paragraph may be renewed for additional 5-year terms if the Secretary determines, prior to beginning of each such renewal period, that the State has—

"(i) adhered to the requirements of this subsection and paragraph in providing services under such an election; and

"(ii) met the State's objectives with respect to quality improvement and beneficiary outcomes.".

(c) REMOVAL OF LIMITATION ON SCOPE OF SERVICES.—Paragraph (1) of section 1915(i) of the Social Security Act (42 U.S.C. 1396n(i)), as amended by subsection (a), is amended by striking "or such other services requested by the State as the Secretary may approve".

(d) OPTIONAL ELIGIBILITY CATEGORY TO PROVIDE FULL MEDICAID BENEFITS TO INDIVIDUALS RECEIVING HOME AND COMMUNITY-BASED SERVICES UNDER A STATE PLAN AMENDMENT.—

(1) IN GENERAL.—Section 1902(a)(10)(A)(ii) of the Social Security Act (42 U.S.C. 1396a(a)(10)(A)(ii)), as amended by section 2304(a)(1), is amended—

(A) in subclause (XX), by striking "or" at the end;

(B) in subclause (XXI), by adding "or" at the end; and

(C) by inserting after subclause (XXI), the following new subclause:

"(XXII) who are eligible for home and community-based services under needs-based criteria established under paragraph (1)(A) of section 1915(i), or who are eligible for home and community-based services under paragraph (6) of such section, and who will receive home and community-based services pursuant to a State plan amendment under such subsection;".

(2) CONFORMING AMENDMENTS.—

(A) Section 1903(f)(4) of the Social Security Act (42 U.S.C. 1396b(f)(4)), as amended by section 2304(a)(4)(B), is amended in the matter preceding subparagraph (A), by inserting "1902(a)(10)(A)(ii)(XXII)," after "1902(a)(10)(A)(ii)(XXI),".

(B) Section 1905(a) of the Social Security Act (42 U.S.C. 1396d(a)), as so amended, is amended in the matter preceding paragraph (1)—

(i) in clause (xv), by striking "or" at the end;

(ii) in clause (xvi), by adding "or" at the end; and

(iii) by inserting after clause (xvi) the following new clause:

"(xvii) individuals who are eligible for home and community-based services under needs-based criteria established under paragraph (1)(A) of section 1915(i), or who are eligible for home and community-based services under paragraph (6) of such section, and who will receive home and community-based services pursuant to a State plan amendment under such subsection,".

(e) ELIMINATION OF OPTION TO LIMIT NUMBER OF ELIGIBLE INDIVIDUALS OR LENGTH OF PERIOD FOR GRANDFATHERED INDIVIDUALS IF ELIGIBILITY CRITERIA IS MODIFIED.—Paragraph (1) of section 1915(i) of such Act (42 U.S.C. 1396n(i)) is amended—

(1) by striking subparagraph (C) and inserting the following:

"(C) PROJECTION OF NUMBER OF INDIVIDUALS TO BE PROVIDED HOME AND COMMUNITY-BASED SERVICES.—The State submits to the Secretary, in such form and manner, and upon such frequency as the Secretary shall specify, the projected number of individuals to be provided home and community-based services."; and

(2) in subclause (II) of subparagraph (D)(ii), by striking "to be eligible for such services for a period of at least 12 months beginning on the date the individual first received medical assistance for such services" and inserting "to continue to be eligible for such services after the effective date of the modification and until such time as the individual no longer meets the standard for receipt of such services under such pre-modified criteria".

(f) ELIMINATION OF OPTION TO WAIVE STATEWIDENESS; ADDITION OF OPTION TO WAIVE COMPARABILITY.—Paragraph (3) of section 1915(i) of such Act (42 U.S.C. 1396n(3)) is amended by striking "1902(a)(1) (relating to statewideness)" and inserting "1902(a)(10)(B) (relating to comparability)".

(g) EFFECTIVE DATE.—The amendments made by subsections (b) through (f) take effect on the first day of the first fiscal year quarter that begins after the date of enactment of this Act.

SEC. 2403. MONEY FOLLOWS THE PERSON REBALANCING DEMONSTRATION.

(a) EXTENSION OF DEMONSTRATION.—

(1) IN GENERAL.—Section 6071(h) of the Deficit Reduction Act of 2005 (42 U.S.C. 1396a note) is amended—

(A) in paragraph (1)(E), by striking "fiscal year 2011" and inserting "each of fiscal years 2011 through 2016"; and

(B) in paragraph (2), by striking "2011" and inserting "2016".

(2) EVALUATION.—Paragraphs (2) and (3) of section 6071(g) of such Act is amended are each amended by striking "2011" and inserting "2016".

(b) REDUCTION OF INSTITUTIONAL RESIDENCY PERIOD.—

(1) IN GENERAL.—Section 6071(b)(2) of the Deficit Reduction Act of 2005 (42 U.S.C. 1396a note) is amended—

(A) in subparagraph (A)(i), by striking ", for a period of not less than 6 months or for such longer minimum period, not to exceed 2 years, as may be specified by the State" and inserting "for a period of not less than 90 consecutive days"; and

(B) by adding at the end the following:

"Any days that an individual resides in an institution on the basis of having been admitted solely for purposes of receiving short-term rehabilitative services for a period for which payment for such services is limited under title XVIII shall not be taken into account for purposes of determining the 90-day period required under subparagraph (A)(i).".

(2) EFFECTIVE DATE.—The amendments made by this subsection take effect 30 days after the date of enactment of this Act.

SEC. 2404. PROTECTION FOR RECIPIENTS OF HOME AND COMMUNITY-BASED SERVICES AGAINST SPOUSAL IMPOVERISHMENT.

During the 5-year period that begins on January 1, 2014, section 1924(h)(1)(A) of the Social Security Act (42 U.S.C. 1396r–5(h)(1)(A)) shall be applied as though "is eligible for medical assistance for home and community-based services provided under subsection (c), (d), or (i) of section 1915, under a waiver approved under section 1115, or who is eligible for such medical assistance by reason of being determined eligible under section 1902(a)(10)(C) or by reason of section 1902(f) or otherwise on the basis of a reduction of income based on costs incurred for medical or other remedial care, or who is eligible for medical assistance for home and community-based attendant services and supports under section 1915(k)" were substituted in such section for "(at the option of the State) is described in section 1902(a)(10)(A)(ii)(VI)".

SEC. 2405. FUNDING TO EXPAND STATE AGING AND DISABILITY RESOURCE CENTERS.

Out of any funds in the Treasury not otherwise appropriated, there is appropriated to the Secretary of Health and Human Services, acting through the Assistant Secretary for Aging, $10,000,000 for each of fiscal years 2010 through 2014, to carry out subsections (a)(20)(B)(iii) and (b)(8) of section 202 of the Older Americans Act of 1965 (42 U.S.C. 3012).

SEC. 2406. SENSE OF THE SENATE REGARDING LONG-TERM CARE.

(a) FINDINGS.—The Senate makes the following findings:

(1) Nearly 2 decades have passed since Congress seriously considered long-term care reform. The United States Bipartisan Commission on Comprehensive Health Care, also know as the "Pepper Commission", released its "Call for Action" blueprint for health reform in September 1990. In the 20 years since those recommendations were made, Congress has never acted on the report.

(2) In 1999, under the United States Supreme Court's decision in Olmstead v. L.C., 527 U.S. 581 (1999), individuals

with disabilities have the right to choose to receive their long-term services and supports in the community, rather than in an institutional setting.

(3) Despite the Pepper Commission and Olmstead decision, the long-term care provided to our Nation's elderly and disabled has not improved. In fact, for many, it has gotten far worse.

(4) In 2007, 69 percent of Medicaid long-term care spending for elderly individuals and adults with physical disabilities paid for institutional services. Only 6 states spent 50 percent or more of their Medicaid long-term care dollars on home and community-based services for elderly individuals and adults with physical disabilities while ½ of the States spent less than 25 percent. This disparity continues even though, on average, it is estimated that Medicaid dollars can support nearly 3 elderly individuals and adults with physical disabilities in home and community-based services for every individual in a nursing home. Although every State has chosen to provide certain services under home and community-based waivers, these services are unevenly available within and across States, and reach a small percentage of eligible individuals.

(b) SENSE OF THE SENATE.—It is the sense of the Senate that—

(1) during the 111th session of Congress, Congress should address long-term services and supports in a comprehensive way that guarantees elderly and disabled individuals the care they need; and

(2) long term services and supports should be made available in the community in addition to in institutions.

Subtitle F—Medicaid Prescription Drug Coverage

SEC. 2501. PRESCRIPTION DRUG REBATES.

(a) INCREASE IN MINIMUM REBATE PERCENTAGE FOR SINGLE SOURCE DRUGS AND INNOVATOR MULTIPLE SOURCE DRUGS.—

(1) IN GENERAL.—Section 1927(c)(1)(B) of the Social Security Act (42 U.S.C. 1396r–8(c)(1)(B)) is amended—

(A) in clause (i)—

(i) in subclause (IV), by striking "and" at the end;

(ii) in subclause (V)—

(I) by inserting "and before January 1, 2010" after "December 31, 1995,"; and

(II) by striking the period at the end and inserting "; and"; and

(iii) by adding at the end the following new subclause:

"(VI) except as provided in clause (iii), after December 31, 2009, 23.1 percent."; and

(B) by adding at the end the following new clause:

"(iii) MINIMUM REBATE PERCENTAGE FOR CERTAIN DRUGS.—

"(I) IN GENERAL.—In the case of a single source drug or an innovator multiple source drug described in subclause (II), the minimum rebate percentage for rebate periods specified in clause (i)(VI) is 17.1 percent.

"(II) DRUG DESCRIBED.—For purposes of subclause (I), a single source drug or an innovator multiple source drug described in this subclause is any of the following drugs:

"(aa) A clotting factor for which a separate furnishing payment is made under section 1842(o)(5) and which is included on a list of such factors specified and updated regularly by the Secretary.

"(bb) A drug approved by the Food and Drug Administration exclusively for pediatric indications.".

(2) RECAPTURE OF TOTAL SAVINGS DUE TO INCREASE.—Section 1927(b)(1) of such Act (42 U.S.C. 1396r–8(b)(1)) is amended by adding at the end the following new subparagraph:

"(C) SPECIAL RULE FOR INCREASED MINIMUM REBATE PERCENTAGE.—

"(i) IN GENERAL.—In addition to the amounts applied as a reduction under subparagraph (B), for rebate periods beginning on or after January 1, 2010, during a fiscal year, the Secretary shall reduce payments to a State under section 1903(a) in the manner specified in clause (ii), in an amount equal to the product of—

"(I) 100 percent minus the Federal medical assistance percentage applicable to the rebate period for the State; and

"(II) the amounts received by the State under such subparagraph that are attributable (as estimated by the Secretary based on utilization and other data) to the increase in the minimum rebate percentage effected by the amendments made by subsections (a)(1), (b), and (d) of section 2501 of the Patient Protection and Affordable Care Act, taking into account the additional drugs included under the amendments made by subsection (c) of section 2501 of such Act.

The Secretary shall adjust such payment reduction for a calendar quarter to the extent the Secretary determines, based upon subsequent utilization and other data, that the reduction for such quarter was greater or less than the amount of payment reduction that should have been made.

"(ii) MANNER OF PAYMENT REDUCTION.—The amount of the payment reduction under clause (i) for a State for a quarter shall be deemed an overpayment to the State under this title to be disallowed against the State's regular quarterly draw for all Medicaid spending under section 1903(d)(2). Such a disallowance is not subject to a reconsideration under section 1116(d).".

(b) INCREASE IN REBATE FOR OTHER DRUGS.—Section 1927(c)(3)(B) of such Act (42 U.S.C. 1396r–8(c)(3)(B)) is amended—

(1) in clause (i), by striking "and" at the end;

(2) in clause (ii)—

(A) by inserting "and before January 1, 2010," after "December 31, 1993,"; and

(B) by striking the period and inserting "; and"; and

(3) by adding at the end the following new clause:

"(iii) after December 31, 2009, is 13 percent.".

(c) EXTENSION OF PRESCRIPTION DRUG DISCOUNTS TO ENROLLEES OF MEDICAID MANAGED CARE ORGANIZATIONS.—

(1) IN GENERAL.—Section 1903(m)(2)(A) of such Act (42 U.S.C. 1396b(m)(2)(A)) is amended—

(A) in clause (xi), by striking "and" at the end;

(B) in clause (xii), by striking the period at the end and inserting "; and"; and

(C) by adding at the end the following:

"(xiii) such contract provides that (I) covered outpatient drugs dispensed to individuals eligible for medical assistance who are enrolled with the entity shall be subject to the same rebate required by the agreement entered into under section 1927 as the State is subject to and that the State shall collect such rebates from manufacturers, (II) capitation rates paid to the entity shall be based on actual cost experience related to rebates and subject to the Federal regulations requiring actuarially sound rates, and (III) the entity shall report to the State, on such timely and periodic basis as specified by the Secretary in order to include in the information submitted by the State to a manufacturer and the Secretary under section 1927(b)(2)(A), information on the total number of units of each dosage form and strength and package size by National Drug Code of each covered outpatient drug dispensed to individuals eligible for medical assistance who are enrolled with the entity and for which the entity is responsible for coverage of such drug under this subsection (other than covered outpatient drugs that under subsection (j)(1) of section 1927 are not subject to the requirements of that section) and such other data as the Secretary determines necessary to carry out this subsection.".

(2) CONFORMING AMENDMENTS.—Section 1927 (42 U.S.C. 1396r–8) is amended—

(A) in subsection (b)—

(i) in paragraph (1)(A), in the first sentence, by inserting ", including such drugs dispensed to individuals enrolled with a medicaid managed care organization if the organization is responsible for coverage of such drugs" before the period; and

(ii) in paragraph (2)(A), by inserting "including such information reported by each medicaid managed care organization," after "for which payment was made under the plan during the period,"; and

(B) in subsection (j), by striking paragraph (1) and inserting the following:

"(1) Covered outpatient drugs are not subject to the requirements of this section if such drugs are—

"(A) dispensed by health maintenance organizations, including Medicaid managed care organizations that contract under section 1903(m); and

"(B) subject to discounts under section 340B of the Public Health Service Act.".

(d) ADDITIONAL REBATE FOR NEW FORMULATIONS OF EXISTING DRUGS.—

(1) IN GENERAL.—Section 1927(c)(2) of the Social Security Act (42 U.S.C. 1396r–8(c)(2)) is amended by adding at the end the following new subparagraph:

"(C) TREATMENT OF NEW FORMULATIONS.—

"(i) IN GENERAL.—Except as provided in clause (ii), in the case of a drug that is a new formulation, such as an extended-release formulation, of a single source drug or an innovator multiple source drug, the rebate obligation with respect to the drug under this section shall be the amount computed under this section for the new formulation of the drug or, if greater, the product of—

"(I) the average manufacturer price for each dosage form and strength of the new formulation of the single source drug or innovator multiple source drug;

"(II) the highest additional rebate (calculated as a percentage of average manufacturer price) under this section for any strength of the original single source drug or innovator multiple source drug; and

"(III) the total number of units of each dosage form and strength of the new formulation paid for under the State plan in the rebate period (as reported by the State).

"(ii) NO APPLICATION TO NEW FORMULATIONS OF ORPHAN DRUGS.—Clause (i) shall not apply to a new formulation of a covered outpatient drug that is or has been designated under section 526 of the Federal Food, Drug, and Cosmetic Act (21 U.S.C. 360bb) for a rare disease or condition, without regard to whether the period of market exclusivity for the drug under section 527 of such Act has expired or the specific indication for use of the drug.".

(2) EFFECTIVE DATE.—The amendment made by paragraph (1) shall apply to drugs that are paid for by a State after December 31, 2009.

(e) MAXIMUM REBATE AMOUNT.—Section 1927(c)(2) of such Act (42 U.S.C. 1396r–8(c)(2)), as amended by subsection (d), is amended by adding at the end the following new subparagraph:

"(D) MAXIMUM REBATE AMOUNT.—In no case shall the sum of the amounts applied under paragraph (1)(A)(ii) and this paragraph with respect to each dosage form and strength of a single source drug or an innovator multiple source drug for a rebate period beginning after December 31, 2009, exceed 100 percent of the average manufacturer price of the drug.".

(f) CONFORMING AMENDMENTS.—

(1) IN GENERAL.—Section 340B of the Public Health Service Act (42 U.S.C. 256b) is amended—

(A) in subsection (a)(2)(B)(i), by striking "1927(c)(4)" and inserting "1927(c)(3)"; and

(B) by striking subsection (c); and

(C) redesignating subsection (d) as subsection (c).

(2) EFFECTIVE DATE.—The amendments made by this subsection take effect on January 1, 2010.

SEC. 2502. ELIMINATION OF EXCLUSION OF COVERAGE OF CERTAIN DRUGS.

(a) IN GENERAL.—Section 1927(d) of the Social Security Act (42 U.S.C. 1397r–8(d)) is amended—

(1) in paragraph (2)—

(A) by striking subparagraphs (E), (I), and (J), respectively; and

(B) by redesignating subparagraphs (F), (G), (H), and (K) as subparagraphs (E), (F), (G), and (H), respectively; and

(2) by adding at the end the following new paragraph:

"(7) NON-EXCLUDABLE DRUGS.—The following drugs or classes of drugs, or their medical uses, shall not be excluded from coverage:

"(A) Agents when used to promote smoking cessation, including agents approved by the Food and Drug Administration under the over-the-counter monograph process for purposes of promoting, and when used to promote, tobacco cessation.

"(B) Barbiturates.

"(C) Benzodiazepines.".

(b) EFFECTIVE DATE.—The amendments made by this section shall apply to services furnished on or after January 1, 2014.

SEC. 2503. PROVIDING ADEQUATE PHARMACY REIMBURSEMENT.

(a) PHARMACY REIMBURSEMENT LIMITS.—

(1) IN GENERAL.—Section 1927(e) of the Social Security Act (42 U.S.C. 1396r–8(e)) is amended—

(A) in paragraph (4), by striking "(or, effective January 1, 2007, two or more)"; and

(B) by striking paragraph (5) and inserting the following:

"(5) USE OF AMP IN UPPER PAYMENT LIMITS.—The Secretary shall calculate the Federal upper reimbursement limit established under paragraph (4) as no less than 175 percent of the weighted average (determined on the basis of utilization) of the most recently reported monthly average manufacturer prices for pharmaceutically and therapeutically equivalent multiple source drug products that are available for purchase by retail community pharmacies on a nationwide basis. The Secretary shall implement a smoothing process for average manufacturer prices. Such process shall be similar to the smoothing process used in determining the average sales price of a drug or biological under section 1847A.".

(2) DEFINITION OF AMP.—Section 1927(k)(1) of such Act (42 U.S.C. 1396r–8(k)(1)) is amended—

(A) in subparagraph (A), by striking "by" and all that follows through the period and inserting "by—

"(i) wholesalers for drugs distributed to retail community pharmacies; and

"(ii) retail community pharmacies that purchase drugs directly from the manufacturer."; and

(B) by striking subparagraph (B) and inserting the following:

"(B) EXCLUSION OF CUSTOMARY PROMPT PAY DISCOUNTS AND OTHER PAYMENTS.—

"(i) IN GENERAL.—The average manufacturer price for a covered outpatient drug shall exclude—

"(I) customary prompt pay discounts extended to wholesalers;

"(II) bona fide service fees paid by manufacturers to wholesalers or retail community pharmacies, including (but not limited to) distribution service fees, inventory management fees, product stocking allowances, and fees associated with administrative services agreements and patient care programs (such as medication compliance programs and patient education programs);

"(III) reimbursement by manufacturers for recalled, damaged, expired, or otherwise unsalable returned goods, including (but not limited to) reimbursement for the cost of the goods and any reimbursement of costs associated with return goods handling and processing, reverse logistics, and drug destruction; and

"(IV) payments received from, and rebates or discounts provided to, pharmacy benefit managers, managed care organizations, health maintenance organizations, insurers, hospitals, clinics, mail order pharmacies, long term care providers, manufacturers, or any other entity that does not conduct business as a wholesaler or a retail community pharmacy.

"(ii) INCLUSION OF OTHER DISCOUNTS AND PAYMENTS.—Notwithstanding clause (i), any other discounts, rebates, payments, or other financial transactions that are received by, paid by, or passed through to, retail community pharmacies shall be included in the average manufacturer price for a covered outpatient drug."; and

(C) in subparagraph (C), by striking "the retail pharmacy class of trade" and inserting "retail community pharmacies".

(3) DEFINITION OF MULTIPLE SOURCE DRUG.—Section 1927(k)(7) of such Act (42 U.S.C. 1396r–8(k)(7)) is amended—

(A) in subparagraph (A)(i)(III), by striking "the State" and inserting "the United States"; and

(B) in subparagraph (C)—

(i) in clause (i), by inserting "and" after the semicolon;

(ii) in clause (ii), by striking "; and" and inserting a period; and

(iii) by striking clause (iii).

(4) DEFINITIONS OF RETAIL COMMUNITY PHARMACY; WHOLESALER.—Section 1927(k) of such Act (42 U.S.C. 1396r–8(k)) is amended by adding at the end the following new paragraphs:

"(10) RETAIL COMMUNITY PHARMACY.—The term 'retail community pharmacy' means an independent pharmacy, a chain pharmacy, a supermarket pharmacy, or a mass merchandiser pharmacy that is licensed as a pharmacy by the State and that dispenses medications to the general public at retail prices. Such term does not include a pharmacy that dispenses prescription medications to patients primarily through the mail, nursing home pharmacies, long-term care facility pharmacies, hospital pharmacies, clinics, charitable or not-for-profit pharmacies, government pharmacies, or pharmacy benefit managers.

"(11) WHOLESALER.—The term 'wholesaler' means a drug wholesaler that is engaged in wholesale distribution of prescription drugs to retail community pharmacies, including (but not limited to) manufacturers, repackers, distributors, own-label distributors, private-label distributors, jobbers, brokers, warehouses (including manufacturer's and distributor's warehouses, chain drug warehouses, and wholesale drug warehouses) independent wholesale drug traders, and retail community pharmacies that conduct wholesale distributions.".

(b) DISCLOSURE OF PRICE INFORMATION TO THE PUBLIC.—Section 1927(b)(3) of such Act (42 U.S.C. 1396r–8(b)(3)) is amended—

(1) in subparagraph (A)—

(A) in the first sentence, by inserting after clause (iii) the following:

"(iv) not later than 30 days after the last day of each month of a rebate period under the agreement, on the manufacturer's total number of units that are used to calculate the monthly average manufacturer price for each covered outpatient drug;"; and

(B) in the second sentence, by inserting "(relating to the weighted average of the most recently reported monthly average manufacturer prices)" after "(D)(v)"; and

(2) in subparagraph (D)(v), by striking "average manufacturer prices" and inserting "the weighted average of the most recently reported monthly average manufacturer prices and the average retail survey price determined for each multiple source drug in accordance with subsection (f)".

(c) CLARIFICATION OF APPLICATION OF SURVEY OF RETAIL PRICES.—Section 1927(f)(1) of such Act (42 U.S.C. 1396r–8(b)(1)) is amended—

(1) in subparagraph (A)(i), by inserting "with respect to a retail community pharmacy," before "the determination"; and

(2) in subparagraph (C)(ii), by striking "retail pharmacies" and inserting "retail community pharmacies".

(d) EFFECTIVE DATE.—The amendments made by this section shall take effect on the first day of the first calendar year quarter that begins at least 180 days after the date of enactment of this Act, without regard to whether or not final regulations to carry out such amendments have been promulgated by such date.

Subtitle G—Medicaid Disproportionate Share Hospital (DSH) Payments

SEC. 2551. DISPROPORTIONATE SHARE HOSPITAL PAYMENTS.

(a) IN GENERAL.—Section 1923(f) of the Social Security Act (42 U.S.C. 1396r–4(f)) is amended—

(1) in paragraph (1), by striking "and (3)" and inserting ", (3), and (7)";

(2) in paragraph (3)(A), by striking "paragraph (6)" and inserting "paragraphs (6) and (7)";

(3) by redesignating paragraph (7) as paragraph (8); and

(4) by inserting after paragraph (6) the following new paragraph:

"(7) REDUCTION OF STATE DSH ALLOTMENTS ONCE REDUCTION IN UNINSURED THRESHOLD REACHED.—

"(A) IN GENERAL.—Subject to subparagraph (E), the DSH allotment for a State for fiscal years beginning with the fiscal year described in subparagraph (C) (with respect to the State), is equal to—

"(i) in the case of the first fiscal year described in subparagraph (C) with respect to a State, the DSH allotment that would be determined under this subsection for the State for the fiscal year without application of this paragraph (but after the application of subparagraph (D)), reduced by the applicable percentage determined for the State for the fiscal year under subparagraph (B)(i); and

"(ii) in the case of any subsequent fiscal year with respect to the State, the DSH allotment determined under this paragraph for the State for the preceding fiscal year, reduced by the applicable percentage determined for the State for the fiscal year under subparagraph (B)(ii).

"(B) APPLICABLE PERCENTAGE.—For purposes of subparagraph (A), the applicable percentage for a State for a fiscal year is the following:

"(i) UNINSURED REDUCTION THRESHOLD FISCAL YEAR.—In the case of the first fiscal year described in subparagraph (C) with respect to the State—

"(I) if the State is a low DSH State described in paragraph (5)(B), the applicable percentage is equal to 25 percent; and

"(II) if the State is any other State, the applicable percentage is 50 percent.

"(ii) SUBSEQUENT FISCAL YEARS IN WHICH THE PERCENTAGE OF UNINSURED DECREASES.—In the case of any fiscal year after the first fiscal year described in subparagraph (C) with respect to a State, if the Secretary determines on the basis of the most recent American Community Survey of the Bureau of the Census, that the percentage of uncovered individuals residing in the State is less than the percentage of such individuals determined for the State for the preceding fiscal year—

"(I) if the State is a low DSH State described in paragraph (5)(B), the applicable percentage is equal to the product of the percentage reduction in uncovered individuals for the fiscal year from the preceding fiscal year and 25 percent; and

"(II) if the State is any other State, the applicable percentage is equal to the product of the percentage reduction in uncovered individuals for the fiscal year from the preceding fiscal year and 50 percent.

"(C) FISCAL YEAR DESCRIBED.—For purposes of subparagraph (A), the fiscal year described in this subparagraph with respect to a State is the first fiscal year that occurs after fiscal year 2012 for which the Secretary determines, on the basis of the most recent American Community Survey of the Bureau of the Census, that the percentage of uncovered individuals residing in the State is at least 45 percent less than the percentage of such individuals determined for the State for fiscal year 2009.

"(D) EXCLUSION OF PORTIONS DIVERTED FOR COVERAGE EXPANSIONS.—For purposes of applying the applicable percentage reduction under subparagraph (A) to the DSH allotment for a State for a fiscal year, the DSH allotment for a State that would be determined under this subsection for the State for the fiscal year without the application of this paragraph (and prior to any such reduction) shall not include any portion of the allotment for which the Secretary has approved the State's diversion to the costs of providing medical assistance or other health benefits coverage under a waiver that is in effect on July 2009.

"(E) MINIMUM ALLOTMENT.—In no event shall the DSH allotment determined for a State in accordance with this paragraph for fiscal year 2013 or any succeeding fiscal year be less than the amount equal to 35 percent of the DSH allotment determined for the State for fiscal year 2012 under this subsection (and after the application of this paragraph, if applicable), increased by the percentage change in the consumer price index for all urban consumers (all items, U.S. city average) for each previous fiscal year occurring before the fiscal year.

"(F) UNCOVERED INDIVIDUALS.—In this paragraph, the term 'uncovered individuals' means individuals with no health insurance coverage at any time during a year (as determined by the Secretary based on the most recent data available).".

(b) EFFECTIVE DATE.—The amendments made by subsection (a) take effect on October 1, 2011.

Subtitle H—Improved Coordination for Dual Eligible Beneficiaries

SEC. 2601. 5-YEAR PERIOD FOR DEMONSTRATION PROJECTS.

(a) IN GENERAL.—Section 1915(h) of the Social Security Act (42 U.S.C. 1396n(h)) is amended—

(1) by inserting "(1)" after "(h)";

(2) by inserting ", or a waiver described in paragraph (2)" after "(e)"; and

(3) by adding at the end the following new paragraph:

"(2)(A) Notwithstanding subsections (c)(3) and (d) (3), any waiver under subsection (b), (c), or (d), or a waiver under section 1115, that provides medical assistance for dual eligible individuals (including any such waivers under which non dual eligible individuals may be enrolled in addition to dual eligible individuals) may be conducted for a period of 5 years and, upon the request of the State, may be extended for additional 5-year periods unless the Secretary determines that for the previous waiver period the conditions for the waiver have not been met or it would no longer be cost-effective and efficient, or consistent with the purposes of this title, to extend the waiver.

"(B) In this paragraph, the term 'dual eligible individual' means an individual who is entitled to, or enrolled for, benefits under part A of title XVIII, or enrolled for benefits under part B of title XVIII, and is eligible for medical assistance under the State plan under this title or under a waiver of such plan.".

(b) CONFORMING AMENDMENTS.—

(1) Section 1915 of such Act (42 U.S.C. 1396n) is amended—

(A) in subsection (b), by adding at the end the following new sentence: "Subsection (h)(2) shall apply to a waiver under this subsection.";

(B) in subsection (c)(3), in the second sentence, by inserting "(other than a waiver described in subsection (h)(2))" after "A waiver under this subsection";

(C) in subsection (d)(3), in the second sentence, by inserting "(other than a waiver described in subsection (h)(2))" after "A waiver under this subsection".

(2) Section 1115 of such Act (42 U.S.C. 1315) is amended—

(A) in subsection (e)(2), by inserting "(5 years, in the case of a waiver described in section 1915(h)(2))" after "3 years"; and

(B) in subsection (f)(6), by inserting "(5 years, in the case of a waiver described in section 1915(h)(2))" after "3 years".

SEC. 2602. PROVIDING FEDERAL COVERAGE AND PAYMENT COORDINATION FOR DUAL ELIGIBLE BENEFICIARIES.

(a) ESTABLISHMENT OF FEDERAL COORDINATED HEALTH CARE OFFICE.—

(1) IN GENERAL.—Not later than March 1, 2010, the Secretary of Health and Human Services (in this section referred to as the "Secretary") shall establish a Federal Coordinated Health Care Office.

(2) ESTABLISHMENT AND REPORTING TO CMS ADMINISTRATOR.—The Federal Coordinated Health Care Office—

(A) shall be established within the Centers for Medicare & Medicaid Services; and

(B) have as the Office a Director who shall be appointed by, and be in direct line of authority to, the Administrator of the Centers for Medicare & Medicaid Services.

(b) PURPOSE.—The purpose of the Federal Coordinated Health Care Office is to bring together officers and employees of the Medicare and Medicaid programs at the Centers for Medicare & Medicaid Services in order to—

(1) more effectively integrate benefits under the Medicare program under title XVIII of the Social Security Act and the Medicaid program under title XIX of such Act; and

(2) improve the coordination between the Federal Government and States for individuals eligible for benefits under both such programs in order to ensure that such individuals get full access to the items and services to which they are entitled under titles XVIII and XIX of the Social Security Act.

(c) GOALS.—The goals of the Federal Coordinated Health Care Office are as follows:

(1) Providing dual eligible individuals full access to the benefits to which such individuals are entitled under the Medicare and Medicaid programs.

(2) Simplifying the processes for dual eligible individuals to access the items and services they are entitled to under the Medicare and Medicaid programs.

(3) Improving the quality of health care and long-term services for dual eligible individuals.

(4) Increasing dual eligible individuals' understanding of and satisfaction with coverage under the Medicare and Medicaid programs.

(5) Eliminating regulatory conflicts between rules under the Medicare and Medicaid programs.

(6) Improving care continuity and ensuring safe and effective care transitions for dual eligible individuals.

(7) Eliminating cost-shifting between the Medicare and Medicaid program and among related health care providers.

(8) Improving the quality of performance of providers of services and suppliers under the Medicare and Medicaid programs.

(d) SPECIFIC RESPONSIBILITIES.—The specific responsibilities of the Federal Coordinated Health Care Office are as follows:

(1) Providing States, specialized MA plans for special needs individuals (as defined in section 1859(b)(6) of the Social Security Act (42 U.S.C. 1395w–28(b)(6))), physicians and other relevant entities or individuals with the education and tools necessary for developing programs that align benefits under the Medicare and Medicaid programs for dual eligible individuals.

(2) Supporting State efforts to coordinate and align acute care and long-term care services for dual eligible individuals with other items and services furnished under the Medicare program.

(3) Providing support for coordination of contracting and oversight by States and the Centers for Medicare & Medicaid Services with respect to the integration of the Medicare and Medicaid programs in a manner that is supportive of the goals described in paragraph (3).

(4) To consult and coordinate with the Medicare Payment Advisory Commission established under section 1805 of the Social Security Act (42 U.S.C. 1395b–6) and the Medicaid and CHIP Payment and Access Commission established under section 1900 of such Act (42 U.S.C. 1396) with respect to policies relating to the enrollment in, and provision of, benefits to dual eligible individuals under the Medicare program under title XVIII of the Social Security Act and the Medicaid program under title XIX of such Act.

(5) To study the provision of drug coverage for new full-benefit dual eligible individuals (as defined in section 1935(c)(6) of the Social Security Act (42 U.S.C. 1396u–5(c)(6)), as well as to monitor and report annual total expenditures, health outcomes, and access to benefits for all dual eligible individuals.

(e) REPORT.—The Secretary shall, as part of the budget transmitted under section 1105(a) of title 31, United States Code, submit to Congress an annual report containing recommendations for legislation that would improve care coordination and benefits for dual eligible individuals.

(f) DUAL ELIGIBLE DEFINED.—In this section, the term "dual eligible individual" means an individual who is entitled to, or enrolled for, benefits under part A of title XVIII of the Social Security Act, or enrolled for benefits under part B of title XVIII of such Act, and is eligible for medical assistance under a State plan under title XIX of such Act or under a waiver of such plan.

Subtitle I—Improving the Quality of Medicaid for Patients and Providers

SEC. 2701. ADULT HEALTH QUALITY MEASURES.

Title XI of the Social Security Act (42 U.S.C. 1301 et seq.), as amended by section 401 of the Children's Health Insurance Program Reauthorization Act of 2009 (Public Law 111–3), is amended by inserting after section 1139A the following new section:

"SEC. 1139B. ADULT HEALTH QUALITY MEASURES.

"(a) DEVELOPMENT OF CORE SET OF HEALTH CARE QUALITY MEASURES FOR ADULTS ELIGIBLE FOR BENEFITS UNDER MEDICAID.— The Secretary shall identify and publish a recommended core set of adult health quality measures for Medicaid eligible adults in the same manner as the Secretary identifies and publishes a core set of child health quality measures under section 1139A, including with respect to identifying and publishing existing adult health quality measures that are in use under public and privately sponsored health care coverage arrangements, or that are part of reporting systems that measure both the presence and duration of health insurance coverage over time, that may be applicable to Medicaid eligible adults.

"(b) DEADLINES.—

"(1) RECOMMENDED MEASURES.—Not later than January 1, 2011, the Secretary shall identify and publish for comment a recommended core set of adult health quality measures for Medicaid eligible adults.

"(2) DISSEMINATION.—Not later than January 1, 2012, the Secretary shall publish an initial core set of adult health quality measures that are applicable to Medicaid eligible adults.

"(3) STANDARDIZED REPORTING.—Not later than January 1, 2013, the Secretary, in consultation with States, shall develop a standardized format for reporting information based on the initial core set of adult health quality measures and create procedures to encourage States to use such measures to voluntarily report information regarding the quality of health care for Medicaid eligible adults.

"(4) REPORTS TO CONGRESS.—Not later than January 1, 2014, and every 3 years thereafter, the Secretary shall include in the report to Congress required under section 1139A(a)(6) information similar to the information required under that section with respect to the measures established under this section.

"(5) ESTABLISHMENT OF MEDICAID QUALITY MEASUREMENT PROGRAM.—

"(A) IN GENERAL.—Not later than 12 months after the release of the recommended core set of adult health quality measures under paragraph (1)), the Secretary shall establish a Medicaid Quality Measurement Program in the same manner as the Secretary establishes the pediatric quality measures program under section 1139A(b). The aggregate amount awarded by the Secretary for grants and contracts for the development, testing, and validation of emerging and innovative evidence-based measures under such program shall equal the aggregate amount awarded by the Secretary for grants under section 1139A(b)(4)(A)

"(B) REVISING, STRENGTHENING, AND IMPROVING INITIAL CORE MEASURES.—Beginning not later than 24 months after the establishment of the Medicaid Quality Measurement Program, and annually thereafter, the Secretary shall publish recommended changes to the initial core set of adult health quality measures that shall reflect the results of the testing, validation, and consensus process for the development of adult health quality measures.

"(c) CONSTRUCTION.—Nothing in this section shall be construed as supporting the restriction of coverage, under title XIX or XXI or otherwise, to only those services that are evidence-based, or in anyway limiting available services.

"(d) ANNUAL STATE REPORTS REGARDING STATE-SPECIFIC QUALITY OF CARE MEASURES APPLIED UNDER MEDICAID.—

"(1) ANNUAL STATE REPORTS.—Each State with a State plan or waiver approved under title XIX shall annually report (separately or as part of the annual report required under section 1139A(c)), to the Secretary on the—

"(A) State-specific adult health quality measures applied by the State under the such plan, including measures described in subsection (a)(5); and

"(B) State-specific information on the quality of health care furnished to Medicaid eligible adults under such plan, including information collected through external quality reviews of managed care organizations under section 1932 and benchmark plans under section 1937.

"(2) PUBLICATION.—Not later than September 30, 2014, and annually thereafter, the Secretary shall collect, analyze, and make publicly available the information reported by States under paragraph (1).

"(e) APPROPRIATION.—Out of any funds in the Treasury not otherwise appropriated, there is appropriated for each of fiscal years 2010 through 2014, $60,000,000 for the purpose of carrying out this section. Funds appropriated under this subsection shall remain available until expended.".

SEC. 2702. PAYMENT ADJUSTMENT FOR HEALTH CARE-ACQUIRED CONDITIONS.

(a) IN GENERAL.—The Secretary of Health and Human Services (in this subsection referred to as the "Secretary") shall identify current State practices that prohibit payment for health care-acquired conditions and shall incorporate the practices identified, or elements of such practices, which the Secretary determines appropriate for application to the Medicaid program in regulations. Such regulations shall be effective as of July 1, 2011, and shall prohibit payments to States under section 1903 of the Social Security Act for any amounts expended for providing medical assistance for health care-acquired conditions specified in the regulations. The regulations shall ensure that the prohibition on payment for health care-acquired conditions shall not result in a loss of access to care or services for Medicaid beneficiaries.

(b) HEALTH CARE-ACQUIRED CONDITION.—In this section. the term "health care-acquired condition" means a medical condition for which an individual was diagnosed that could be identified by a secondary diagnostic code described in section 1886(d)(4)(D)(iv) of the Social Security Act (42 U.S.C. 1395ww(d)(4)(D)(iv)).

(c) MEDICARE PROVISIONS.—In carrying out this section, the Secretary shall apply to State plans (or waivers) under title XIX of the Social Security Act the regulations promulgated pursuant to section 1886(d)(4)(D) of such Act (42 U.S.C. 1395ww(d)(4)(D)) relating to the prohibition of payments based on the presence of a secondary diagnosis code specified by the Secretary in such regulations, as appropriate for the Medicaid program. The Secretary may exclude certain conditions identified under title XVIII of the Social Security Act for non-payment under title XIX of such Act when the Secretary finds the inclusion of such conditions to be inapplicable to beneficiaries under title XIX.

SEC. 2703. STATE OPTION TO PROVIDE HEALTH HOMES FOR ENROLLEES WITH CHRONIC CONDITIONS.

(a) STATE PLAN AMENDMENT.—Title XIX of the Social Security Act (42 U.S.C. 1396a et seq.), as amended by sections 2201 and 2305, is amended by adding at the end the following new section:

"SEC. 1945. STATE OPTION TO PROVIDE COORDINATED CARE THROUGH A HEALTH HOME FOR INDIVIDUALS WITH CHRONIC CONDITIONS.—

"(a) IN GENERAL.—Notwithstanding section 1902(a)(1) (relating to statewideness), section 1902(a)(10)(B) (relating to comparability), and any other provision of this title for which the Secretary determines it is necessary to waive in order to implement this section, beginning January 1, 2011, a State, at its option as a State plan amendment, may provide for medical assistance under this title to eligible individuals with chronic conditions who select a designated provider (as described under subsection (h)(5)), a team of health care professionals (as described under subsection (h)(6)) operating with such a provider, or a health team (as described under subsection (h)(7)) as the individual's health home for purposes of providing the individual with health home services.

"(b) HEALTH HOME QUALIFICATION STANDARDS.—The Secretary shall establish standards for qualification as a designated provider for the purpose of being eligible to be a health home for purposes of this section.

"(c) PAYMENTS.—

"(1) IN GENERAL.—A State shall provide a designated provider, a team of health care professionals operating with such a provider, or a health team with payments for the provision of health home services to each eligible individual with chronic conditions that selects such provider, team of health care professionals, or health team as the individual's health home. Payments made to a designated provider, a team of health care professionals operating with such a provider, or a health team for such services shall be treated as medical assistance for purposes of section 1903(a), except that, during the first 8 fiscal year quarters that the State plan amendment is in effect, the Federal medical assistance percentage applicable to such payments shall be equal to 90 percent.

"(2) METHODOLOGY.—

"(A) IN GENERAL.—The State shall specify in the State plan amendment the methodology the State will use for determining payment for the provision of health home services. Such methodology for determining payment—

"(i) may be tiered to reflect, with respect to each eligible individual with chronic conditions provided such services by a designated provider, a team of health care professionals operating with such a provider, or a health team, as well as the severity or number of each such individual's chronic conditions or the specific capabilities of the provider, team of health care professionals, or health team; and

"(ii) shall be established consistent with section 1902(a)(30)(A).

"(B) ALTERNATE MODELS OF PAYMENT.—The methodology for determining payment for provision of health home services under this section shall not be limited to a per-member per-month basis and may provide (as proposed by the State and subject to approval by the Secretary) for alternate models of payment.

"(3) PLANNING GRANTS.—

"(A) IN GENERAL.—Beginning January 1, 2011, the Secretary may award planning grants to States for purposes of developing a State plan amendment under this section. A planning grant awarded to a State under this paragraph shall remain available until expended.

"(B) STATE CONTRIBUTION.—A State awarded a planning grant shall contribute an amount equal to the State percentage determined under section 1905(b) (without regard to section 5001 of Public Law 111–5) for each fiscal year for which the grant is awarded.

"(C) LIMITATION.—The total amount of payments made to States under this paragraph shall not exceed $25,000,000.

"(d) HOSPITAL REFERRALS.—A State shall include in the State plan amendment a requirement for hospitals that are participating providers under the State plan or a waiver of such plan to establish procedures for referring any eligible individuals with chronic conditions who seek or need treatment in a hospital emergency department to designated providers.

"(e) COORDINATION.—A State shall consult and coordinate, as appropriate, with the Substance Abuse and Mental Health Services Administration in addressing issues regarding the prevention and treatment of mental illness and substance abuse among eligible individuals with chronic conditions.

"(f) MONITORING.—A State shall include in the State plan amendment—

"(1) a methodology for tracking avoidable hospital readmissions and calculating savings that result from improved chronic care coordination and management under this section; and

"(2) a proposal for use of health information technology in providing health home services under this section and improving service delivery and coordination across the care continuum (including the use of wireless patient technology to improve coordination and management of care and patient adherence to recommendations made by their provider).

"(g) REPORT ON QUALITY MEASURES.—As a condition for receiving payment for health home services provided to an eligible individual with chronic conditions, a designated provider shall report to the State, in accordance with such requirements as the Secretary shall specify, on all applicable measures for determining the quality of such services. When appropriate and feasible, a designated provider shall use health information technology in providing the State with such information.

"(h) DEFINITIONS.—In this section:

"(1) ELIGIBLE INDIVIDUAL WITH CHRONIC CONDITIONS.—

"(A) IN GENERAL.—Subject to subparagraph (B), the term 'eligible individual with chronic conditions' means an individual who—

"(i) is eligible for medical assistance under the State plan or under a waiver of such plan; and

"(ii) has at least—

"(I) 2 chronic conditions;

"(II) 1 chronic condition and is at risk of having a second chronic condition; or

"(III) 1 serious and persistent mental health condition.

"(B) RULE OF CONSTRUCTION.—Nothing in this paragraph shall prevent the Secretary from establishing higher levels as to the number or severity of chronic or mental health conditions for purposes of determining eligibility for receipt of health home services under this section.

"(2) CHRONIC CONDITION.—The term 'chronic condition' has the meaning given that term by the Secretary and shall include, but is not limited to, the following:

"(A) A mental health condition.

"(B) Substance use disorder.

"(C) Asthma.

"(D) Diabetes.

"(E) Heart disease.

"(F) Being overweight, as evidenced by having a Body Mass Index (BMI) over 25.

"(3) HEALTH HOME.—The term 'health home' means a designated provider (including a provider that operates in coordination with a team of health care professionals) or a health team selected by an eligible individual with chronic conditions to provide health home services.

"(4) HEALTH HOME SERVICES.—

"(A) IN GENERAL.—The term 'health home services' means comprehensive and timely high-quality services described in subparagraph (B) that are provided by a designated provider, a team of health care professionals operating with such a provider, or a health team.

"(B) SERVICES DESCRIBED.—The services described in this subparagraph are—

"(i) comprehensive care management;

"(ii) care coordination and health promotion;

"(iii) comprehensive transitional care, including appropriate follow-up, from inpatient to other settings;

"(iv) patient and family support (including authorized representatives);

"(v) referral to community and social support services, if relevant; and

"(vi) use of health information technology to link services, as feasible and appropriate.

"(5) DESIGNATED PROVIDER.—The term 'designated provider' means a physician, clinical practice or clinical group practice, rural clinic, community health center, community mental health center, home health agency, or any other entity or provider (including pediatricians, gynecologists, and obstetricians) that is determined by the State and approved by the Secretary to be qualified to be a health home for eligible individuals with chronic conditions on the basis of documentation evidencing that the physician, practice, or clinic—

"(A) has the systems and infrastructure in place to provide health home services; and

"(B) satisfies the qualification standards established by the Secretary under subsection (b).

"(6) TEAM OF HEALTH CARE PROFESSIONALS.—The term 'team of health care professionals' means a team of health professionals (as described in the State plan amendment) that may—

"(A) include physicians and other professionals, such as a nurse care coordinator, nutritionist, social worker, behavioral health professional, or any professionals deemed appropriate by the State; and

"(B) be free standing, virtual, or based at a hospital, community health center, community mental health center, rural clinic, clinical practice or clinical group practice, academic health center, or any entity deemed appropriate by the State and approved by the Secretary.

"(7) HEALTH TEAM.—The term 'health team' has the meaning given such term for purposes of section 3502 of the Patient Protection and Affordable Care Act.".

(b) EVALUATION.—

(1) INDEPENDENT EVALUATION.—

(A) IN GENERAL.—The Secretary shall enter into a contract with an independent entity or organization to conduct an evaluation and assessment of the States that have elected the option to provide coordinated care through a health home for Medicaid beneficiaries with chronic conditions under section 1945 of the Social Security Act (as added by subsection (a)) for the purpose of determining the effect of such option on reducing hospital admissions, emergency room visits, and admissions to skilled nursing facilities.

(B) EVALUATION REPORT.—Not later than January 1, 2017, the Secretary shall report to Congress on the evaluation and assessment conducted under subparagraph (A).

(2) SURVEY AND INTERIM REPORT.—

(A) IN GENERAL.—Not later than January 1, 2014, the Secretary of Health and Human Services shall survey States that have elected the option under section 1945 of the Social Security Act (as added by subsection (a)) and report to Congress on the nature, extent, and use of such option, particularly as it pertains to—

(i) hospital admission rates;

(ii) chronic disease management;

(iii) coordination of care for individuals with chronic conditions;

(iv) assessment of program implementation;

(v) processes and lessons learned (as described in subparagraph (B));

(vi) assessment of quality improvements and clinical outcomes under such option; and

(vii) estimates of cost savings.

(B) IMPLEMENTATION REPORTING.—A State that has elected the option under section 1945 of the Social Security Act (as added by subsection (a)) shall report to the Secretary, as necessary, on processes that have been developed and lessons learned regarding provision of coordinated care through a health home for Medicaid beneficiaries with chronic conditions under such option.

SEC. 2704. DEMONSTRATION PROJECT TO EVALUATE INTEGRATED CARE AROUND A HOSPITALIZATION.

(a) AUTHORITY TO CONDUCT PROJECT.—

(1) IN GENERAL.—The Secretary of Health and Human Services (in this section referred to as the "Secretary") shall establish a demonstration project under title XIX of the Social Security Act to evaluate the use of bundled payments for the provision of integrated care for a Medicaid beneficiary—

(A) with respect to an episode of care that includes a hospitalization; and

(B) for concurrent physicians services provided during a hospitalization.

(2) DURATION.—The demonstration project shall begin on January 1, 2012, and shall end on December 31, 2016.

(b) REQUIREMENTS.—The demonstration project shall be conducted in accordance with the following:

(1) The demonstration project shall be conducted in up to 8 States, determined by the Secretary based on consideration of the potential to lower costs under the Medicaid program while improving care for Medicaid beneficiaries. A State selected to participate in the demonstration project may target the demonstration project to particular categories of beneficiaries, beneficiaries with particular diagnoses, or particular geographic regions of the State, but the Secretary shall insure that, as a whole, the demonstration project is, to the greatest extent possible, representative of the demographic and geographic composition of Medicaid beneficiaries nationally.

(2) The demonstration project shall focus on conditions where there is evidence of an opportunity for providers of services and suppliers to improve the quality of care furnished to Medicaid beneficiaries while reducing total expenditures under the State Medicaid programs selected to participate, as determined by the Secretary.

(3) A State selected to participate in the demonstration project shall specify the 1 or more episodes of care the State proposes to address in the project, the services to be included in the bundled payments, and the rationale for the selection of such episodes of care and services. The Secretary may modify the episodes of care as well as the services to be included in the bundled payments prior to or after approving the project. The Secretary may also vary such factors among the different States participating in the demonstration project.

(4) The Secretary shall ensure that payments made under the demonstration project are adjusted for severity of illness and other characteristics of Medicaid beneficiaries within a category or having a diagnosis targeted as part of the demonstration project. States shall ensure that Medicaid beneficiaries are not liable for any additional cost sharing than

if their care had not been subject to payment under the demonstration project.

(5) Hospitals participating in the demonstration project shall have or establish robust discharge planning programs to ensure that Medicaid beneficiaries requiring post-acute care are appropriately placed in, or have ready access to, post-acute care settings.

(6) The Secretary and each State selected to participate in the demonstration project shall ensure that the demonstration project does not result in the Medicaid beneficiaries whose care is subject to payment under the demonstration project being provided with less items and services for which medical assistance is provided under the State Medicaid program than the items and services for which medical assistance would have been provided to such beneficiaries under the State Medicaid program in the absence of the demonstration project.

(c) WAIVER OF PROVISIONS.—Notwithstanding section 1115(a) of the Social Security Act (42 U.S.C. 1315(a)), the Secretary may waive such provisions of titles XIX, XVIII, and XI of that Act as may be necessary to accomplish the goals of the demonstration, ensure beneficiary access to acute and post-acute care, and maintain quality of care.

(d) EVALUATION AND REPORT.—

(1) DATA.—Each State selected to participate in the demonstration project under this section shall provide to the Secretary, in such form and manner as the Secretary shall specify, relevant data necessary to monitor outcomes, costs, and quality, and evaluate the rationales for selection of the episodes of care and services specified by States under subsection (b)(3).

(2) REPORT.—Not later than 1 year after the conclusion of the demonstration project, the Secretary shall submit a report to Congress on the results of the demonstration project.

SEC. 2705. MEDICAID GLOBAL PAYMENT SYSTEM DEMONSTRATION PROJECT.

(a) IN GENERAL.—The Secretary of Health and Human Services (referred to in this section as the "Secretary") shall, in coordination with the Center for Medicare and Medicaid Innovation (as established under section 1115A of the Social Security Act, as added by section 3021 of this Act), establish the Medicaid Global Payment System Demonstration Project under which a participating State shall adjust the payments made to an eligible safety net hospital system or network from a fee-for-service payment structure to a global capitated payment model.

(b) DURATION AND SCOPE.—The demonstration project conducted under this section shall operate during a period of fiscal years 2010 through 2012. The Secretary shall select not more than 5 States to participate in the demonstration project.

(c) ELIGIBLE SAFETY NET HOSPITAL SYSTEM OR NETWORK.—For purposes of this section, the term "eligible safety net hospital system or network" means a large, safety net hospital system or network (as defined by the Secretary) that operates within a State selected by the Secretary under subsection (b).

(d) EVALUATION.—

(1) TESTING.—The Innovation Center shall test and evaluate the demonstration project conducted under this section

to examine any changes in health care quality outcomes and spending by the eligible safety net hospital systems or networks.

(2) BUDGET NEUTRALITY.—During the testing period under paragraph (1), any budget neutrality requirements under section 1115A(b)(3) of the Social Security Act (as so added) shall not be applicable.

(3) MODIFICATION.—During the testing period under paragraph (1), the Secretary may, in the Secretary's discretion, modify or terminate the demonstration project conducted under this section.

(e) REPORT.—Not later than 12 months after the date of completion of the demonstration project under this section, the Secretary shall submit to Congress a report containing the results of the evaluation and testing conducted under subsection (d), together with recommendations for such legislation and administrative action as the Secretary determines appropriate.

(f) AUTHORIZATION OF APPROPRIATIONS.—There are authorized to be appropriated such sums as are necessary to carry out this section.

SEC. 2706. PEDIATRIC ACCOUNTABLE CARE ORGANIZATION DEMONSTRATION PROJECT.

(a) AUTHORITY TO CONDUCT DEMONSTRATION.—

(1) IN GENERAL.—The Secretary of Health and Human Services (referred to in this section as the "Secretary") shall establish the Pediatric Accountable Care Organization Demonstration Project to authorize a participating State to allow pediatric medical providers that meet specified requirements to be recognized as an accountable care organization for purposes of receiving incentive payments (as described under subsection (d)), in the same manner as an accountable care organization is recognized and provided with incentive payments under section 1899 of the Social Security Act (as added by section 3022).

(2) DURATION.—The demonstration project shall begin on January 1, 2012, and shall end on December 31, 2016.

(b) APPLICATION.—A State that desires to participate in the demonstration project under this section shall submit to the Secretary an application at such time, in such manner, and containing such information as the Secretary may require.

(c) REQUIREMENTS.—

(1) PERFORMANCE GUIDELINES.—The Secretary, in consultation with the States and pediatric providers, shall establish guidelines to ensure that the quality of care delivered to individuals by a provider recognized as an accountable care organization under this section is not less than the quality of care that would have otherwise been provided to such individuals.

(2) SAVINGS REQUIREMENT.—A participating State, in consultation with the Secretary, shall establish an annual minimal level of savings in expenditures for items and services covered under the Medicaid program under title XIX of the Social Security Act and the CHIP program under title XXI of such Act that must be reached by an accountable care organization in order for such organization to receive an incentive payment under subsection (d).

(3) MINIMUM PARTICIPATION PERIOD.—A provider desiring to be recognized as an accountable care organization under

the demonstration project shall enter into an agreement with the State to participate in the project for not less than a 3-year period.

(d) INCENTIVE PAYMENT.—An accountable care organization that meets the performance guidelines established by the Secretary under subsection (c)(1) and achieves savings greater than the annual minimal savings level established by the State under subsection (c)(2) shall receive an incentive payment for such year equal to a portion (as determined appropriate by the Secretary) of the amount of such excess savings. The Secretary may establish an annual cap on incentive payments for an accountable care organization.

(e) AUTHORIZATION OF APPROPRIATIONS.—There are authorized to be appropriated such sums as are necessary to carry out this section.

SEC. 2707. MEDICAID EMERGENCY PSYCHIATRIC DEMONSTRATION PROJECT.

(a) AUTHORITY TO CONDUCT DEMONSTRATION PROJECT.—The Secretary of Health and Human Services (in this section referred to as the "Secretary") shall establish a demonstration project under which an eligible State (as described in subsection (c)) shall provide payment under the State Medicaid plan under title XIX of the Social Security Act to an institution for mental diseases that is not publicly owned or operated and that is subject to the requirements of section 1867 of the Social Security Act (42 U.S.C. 1395dd) for the provision of medical assistance available under such plan to individuals who—

(1) have attained age 21, but have not attained age 65;

(2) are eligible for medical assistance under such plan; and

(3) require such medical assistance to stabilize an emergency medical condition.

(b) STABILIZATION REVIEW.—A State shall specify in its application described in subsection (c)(1) establish a mechanism for how it will ensure that institutions participating in the demonstration will determine whether or not such individuals have been stabilized (as defined in subsection (h)(5)). This mechanism shall commence before the third day of the inpatient stay. States participating in the demonstration project may manage the provision of services for the stabilization of medical emergency conditions through utilization review, authorization, or management practices, or the application of medical necessity and appropriateness criteria applicable to behavioral health.

(c) ELIGIBLE STATE DEFINED.—

(1) IN GENERAL.—An eligible State is a State that has made an application and has been selected pursuant to paragraphs (2) and (3).

(2) APPLICATION.—A State seeking to participate in the demonstration project under this section shall submit to the Secretary, at such time and in such format as the Secretary requires, an application that includes such information, provisions, and assurances, as the Secretary may require.

(3) SELECTION.—A State shall be determined eligible for the demonstration by the Secretary on a competitive basis among States with applications meeting the requirements of

paragraph (1). In selecting State applications for the demonstration project, the Secretary shall seek to achieve an appropriate national balance in the geographic distribution of such projects.

(d) LENGTH OF DEMONSTRATION PROJECT.—The demonstration project established under this section shall be conducted for a period of 3 consecutive years.

(e) LIMITATIONS ON FEDERAL FUNDING.—

(1) APPROPRIATION.—

(A) IN GENERAL.—Out of any funds in the Treasury not otherwise appropriated, there is appropriated to carry out this section, $75,000,000 for fiscal year 2011.

(B) BUDGET AUTHORITY.—Subparagraph (A) constitutes budget authority in advance of appropriations Act and represents the obligation of the Federal Government to provide for the payment of the amounts appropriated under that subparagraph.

(2) 5-YEAR AVAILABILITY.—Funds appropriated under paragraph (1) shall remain available for obligation through December 31, 2015.

(3) LIMITATION ON PAYMENTS.—In no case may—

(A) the aggregate amount of payments made by the Secretary to eligible States under this section exceed $75,000,000; or

(B) payments be provided by the Secretary under this section after December 31, 2015.

(4) FUNDS ALLOCATED TO STATES.—Funds shall be allocated to eligible States on the basis of criteria, including a State's application and the availability of funds, as determined by the Secretary.

(5) PAYMENTS TO STATES.—The Secretary shall pay to each eligible State, from its allocation under paragraph (4), an amount each quarter equal to the Federal medical assistance percentage of expenditures in the quarter for medical assistance described in subsection (a). As a condition of receiving payment, a State shall collect and report information, as determined necessary by the Secretary, for the purposes of providing Federal oversight and conducting an evaluation under subsection (f)(1).

(f) EVALUATION AND REPORT TO CONGRESS.—

(1) EVALUATION.—The Secretary shall conduct an evaluation of the demonstration project in order to determine the impact on the functioning of the health and mental health service system and on individuals enrolled in the Medicaid program and shall include the following:

(A) An assessment of access to inpatient mental health services under the Medicaid program; average lengths of inpatient stays; and emergency room visits.

(B) An assessment of discharge planning by participating hospitals.

(C) An assessment of the impact of the demonstration project on the costs of the full range of mental health services (including inpatient, emergency and ambulatory care).

(D) An analysis of the percentage of consumers with Medicaid coverage who are admitted to inpatient facilities as a result of the demonstration project as compared to those admitted to these same facilities through other means.

(E) A recommendation regarding whether the demonstration project should be continued after December 31, 2013, and expanded on a national basis.

(2) REPORT.—Not later than December 31, 2013, the Secretary shall submit to Congress and make available to the public a report on the findings of the evaluation under paragraph (1).

(g) WAIVER AUTHORITY.—

(1) IN GENERAL.—The Secretary shall waive the limitation of subdivision (B) following paragraph (28) of section 1905(a) of the Social Security Act (42 U.S.C. 1396d(a)) (relating to limitations on payments for care or services for individuals under 65 years of age who are patients in an institution for mental diseases) for purposes of carrying out the demonstration project under this section.

(2) LIMITED OTHER WAIVER AUTHORITY.—The Secretary may waive other requirements of titles XI and XIX of the Social Security Act (including the requirements of sections 1902(a)(1) (relating to statewideness) and 1902(1)(10)(B) (relating to comparability)) only to extent necessary to carry out the demonstration project under this section.

(h) DEFINITIONS.—In this section:

(1) EMERGENCY MEDICAL CONDITION.—The term "emergency medical condition" means, with respect to an individual, an individual who expresses suicidal or homicidal thoughts or gestures, if determined dangerous to self or others.

(2) FEDERAL MEDICAL ASSISTANCE PERCENTAGE.—The term "Federal medical assistance percentage" has the meaning given that term with respect to a State under section 1905(b) of the Social Security Act (42 U.S.C. 1396d(b)).

(3) INSTITUTION FOR MENTAL DISEASES.—The term "institution for mental diseases" has the meaning given to that term in section 1905(i) of the Social Security Act (42 U.S.C. 1396d(i)).

(4) MEDICAL ASSISTANCE.—The term "medical assistance" has the meaning given that term in section 1905(a) of the Social Security Act (42 U.S.C. 1396d(a)).

(5) STABILIZED.—The term "stabilized" means, with respect to an individual, that the emergency medical condition no longer exists with respect to the individual and the individual is no longer dangerous to self or others.

(6) STATE.—The term "State" has the meaning given that term for purposes of title XIX of the Social Security Act (42 U.S.C. 1396 et seq.).

Subtitle J—Improvements to the Medicaid and CHIP Payment and Access Commission (MACPAC)

SEC. 2801. MACPAC ASSESSMENT OF POLICIES AFFECTING ALL MEDICAID BENEFICIARIES.

(a) IN GENERAL.—Section 1900 of the Social Security Act (42 U.S.C. 1396) is amended—

(1) in subsection (b)—

(A) in paragraph (1)—

(i) in the paragraph heading, by inserting "FOR ALL STATES" before "AND ANNUAL"; and

(ii) in subparagraph (A), by striking "children's";

(iii) in subparagraph (B), by inserting ", the Secretary, and States" after "Congress";

(iv) in subparagraph (C), by striking "March 1" and inserting "March 15"; and

(v) in subparagraph (D), by striking "June 1" and inserting "June 15";

(B) in paragraph (2)—

(i) in subparagraph (A)—

(I) in clause (i)—

(aa) by inserting "the efficient provision of" after "expenditures for"; and

(bb) by striking "hospital, skilled nursing facility, physician, Federally-qualified health center, rural health center, and other fees" and inserting "payments to medical, dental, and health professionals, hospitals, residential and long-term care providers, providers of home and community based services, Federally-qualified health centers and rural health clinics, managed care entities, and providers of other covered items and services"; and

(II) in clause (iii), by inserting "(including how such factors and methodologies enable such beneficiaries to obtain the services for which they are eligible, affect provider supply, and affect providers that serve a disproportionate share of low-income and other vulnerable populations)" after "beneficiaries";

(ii) by redesignating subparagraphs (B) and (C) as subparagraphs (F) and (H), respectively;

(iii) by inserting after subparagraph (A), the following:

"(B) ELIGIBILITY POLICIES.—Medicaid and CHIP eligibility policies, including a determination of the degree to which Federal and State policies provide health care coverage to needy populations.

"(C) ENROLLMENT AND RETENTION PROCESSES.—Medicaid and CHIP enrollment and retention processes, including a determination of the degree to which Federal and State policies encourage the enrollment of individuals who are eligible for such programs and screen out individuals who are ineligible, while minimizing the share of program expenses devoted to such processes.

"(D) COVERAGE POLICIES.—Medicaid and CHIP benefit and coverage policies, including a determination of the degree to which Federal and State policies provide access to the services enrollees require to improve and maintain their health and functional status.

"(E) QUALITY OF CARE.—Medicaid and CHIP policies as they relate to the quality of care provided under those programs, including a determination of the degree to which Federal and State policies achieve their stated goals and interact with similar goals established by other purchasers of health care services.";

(iv) by inserting after subparagraph (F) (as redesignated by clause (ii) of this subparagraph), the following:

"(G) INTERACTIONS WITH MEDICARE AND MEDICAID.—Consistent with paragraph (11), the interaction of policies under Medicaid and the Medicare program under title XVIII, including with respect to how such interactions affect access to services, payments, and dual eligible individuals." and

(v) in subparagraph (H) (as so redesignated), by inserting "and preventive, acute, and long-term services and supports" after "barriers";

(C) by redesignating paragraphs (3) through (9) as paragraphs (4) through (10), respectively;

(D) by inserting after paragraph (2), the following new paragraph:

"(3) RECOMMENDATIONS AND REPORTS OF STATE-SPECIFIC DATA.—MACPAC shall—

"(A) review national and State-specific Medicaid and CHIP data; and

"(B) submit reports and recommendations to Congress, the Secretary, and States based on such reviews.";

(E) in paragraph (4), as redesignated by subparagraph (C), by striking "or any other problems" and all that follows through the period and inserting ", as well as other factors that adversely affect, or have the potential to adversely affect, access to care by, or the health care status of, Medicaid and CHIP beneficiaries. MACPAC shall include in the annual report required under paragraph (1)(D) a description of all such areas or problems identified with respect to the period addressed in the report.";

(F) in paragraph (5), as so redesignated,—

(i) in the paragraph heading, by inserting "AND REGULATIONS" after "REPORTS"; and

(ii) by striking "If" and inserting the following: "(A) CERTAIN SECRETARIAL REPORTS.—If"; and

(iii) in the second sentence, by inserting "and the Secretary" after "appropriate committees of Congress"; and

(iv) by adding at the end the following:

"(B) REGULATIONS.—MACPAC shall review Medicaid and CHIP regulations and may comment through submission of a report to the appropriate committees of Congress and the Secretary, on any such regulations that affect access, quality, or efficiency of health care.";

(G) in paragraph (10), as so redesignated, by inserting ", and shall submit with any recommendations, a report on the Federal and State-specific budget consequences of the recommendations" before the period; and

(H) by adding at the end the following:

"(11) CONSULTATION AND COORDINATION WITH MEDPAC.—

"(A) IN GENERAL.—MACPAC shall consult with the Medicare Payment Advisory Commission (in this paragraph referred to as 'MedPAC') established under section 1805 in carrying out its duties under this section, as appropriate and particularly with respect to the issues specified in paragraph (2) as they relate to those Medicaid beneficiaries who are dually eligible for Medicaid and the Medicare program under title XVIII, adult Medicaid beneficiaries (who are not dually eligible for Medicare), and beneficiaries under Medicare. Responsibility for analysis of and recommendations to change Medicare policy regarding Medicare beneficiaries, including Medicare beneficiaries who are dually eligible for Medicare and Medicaid, shall rest with MedPAC.

"(B) INFORMATION SHARING.—MACPAC and MedPAC shall have access to deliberations and records of the other such entity, respectively, upon the request of the other such entity.

"(12) CONSULTATION WITH STATES.—MACPAC shall regularly consult with States in carrying out its duties under this section, including with respect to developing processes for carrying out such duties, and shall ensure that input from States is taken into account and represented in MACPAC's recommendations and reports.

"(13) COORDINATE AND CONSULT WITH THE FEDERAL COORDINATED HEALTH CARE OFFICE.—MACPAC shall coordinate and consult with the Federal Coordinated Health Care Office established under section 2081 of the Patient Protection and Affordable Care Act before making any recommendations regarding dual eligible individuals.

"(14) PROGRAMMATIC OVERSIGHT VESTED IN THE SECRETARY.—MACPAC's authority to make recommendations in accordance with this section shall not affect, or be considered to duplicate, the Secretary's authority to carry out Federal responsibilities with respect to Medicaid and CHIP.";

(2) in subsection (c)(2)—

(A) by striking subparagraphs (A) and (B) and inserting the following:

"(A) IN GENERAL.—The membership of MACPAC shall include individuals who have had direct experience as enrollees or parents or caregivers of enrollees in Medicaid or CHIP and individuals with national recognition for their expertise in Federal safety net health programs, health finance and economics, actuarial science, health plans and integrated delivery systems, reimbursement for health care, health information technology, and other providers of health services, public health, and other related fields, who provide a mix of different professions, broad geographic representation, and a balance between urban and rural representation.

"(B) INCLUSION.—The membership of MACPAC shall include (but not be limited to) physicians, dentists, and other health professionals, employers, third-party payers, and individuals with expertise in the delivery of health services. Such membership shall also include representatives of children, pregnant women, the elderly, individuals with disabilities, caregivers, and dual eligible individuals, current or former representatives of State agencies responsible for administering Medicaid, and current or former representatives of State agencies responsible for administering CHIP.".

(3) in subsection (d)(2), by inserting "and State" after "Federal";

(4) in subsection (e)(1), in the first sentence, by inserting "and, as a condition for receiving payments under sections 1903(a) and 2105(a), from any State agency responsible for administering Medicaid or CHIP," after "United States"; and

(5) in subsection (f)—

(A) in the subsection heading, by striking "AUTHORIZATION OF APPROPRIATIONS" and inserting "FUNDING";

(B) in paragraph (1), by inserting "(other than for fiscal year 2010)" before "in the same manner"; and

(C) by adding at the end the following:

"(3) FUNDING FOR FISCAL YEAR 2010.—

"(A) IN GENERAL.—Out of any funds in the Treasury not otherwise appropriated, there is appropriated to MACPAC to carry out the provisions of this section for fiscal year 2010, $9,000,000.

"(B) TRANSFER OF FUNDS.—Notwithstanding section 2104(a)(13), from the amounts appropriated in such section for fiscal year 2010, $2,000,000 is hereby transferred and made available in such fiscal year to MACPAC to carry out the provisions of this section.

"(4) AVAILABILITY.—Amounts made available under paragraphs (2) and (3) to MACPAC to carry out the provisions of this section shall remain available until expended.".

(b) CONFORMING MEDPAC AMENDMENTS.—Section 1805(b) of the Social Security Act (42 U.S.C. 1395b–6(b)), is amended—

(1) in paragraph (1)(C), by striking "March 1 of each year (beginning with 1998)" and inserting "March 15";

(2) in paragraph (1)(D), by inserting ", and (beginning with 2012) containing an examination of the topics described in paragraph (9), to the extent feasible" before the period; and

(3) by adding at the end the following:

"(9) REVIEW AND ANNUAL REPORT ON MEDICAID AND COMMERCIAL TRENDS.—The Commission shall review and report on aggregate trends in spending, utilization, and financial performance under the Medicaid program under title XIX and the private market for health care services with respect to providers for which, on an aggregate national basis, a significant portion of revenue or services is associated with the Medicaid program. Where appropriate, the Commission shall conduct such review in consultation with the Medicaid and CHIP Payment and Access Commission established under section 1900 (in this section referred to as 'MACPAC').

"(10) COORDINATE AND CONSULT WITH THE FEDERAL COORDINATED HEALTH CARE OFFICE.—The Commission shall coordinate and consult with the Federal Coordinated Health Care Office established under section 2081 of the Patient Protection and Affordable Care Act before making any recommendations regarding dual eligible individuals.

"(11) INTERACTION OF MEDICAID AND MEDICARE.—The Commission shall consult with MACPAC in carrying out its duties under this section, as appropriate. Responsibility for analysis of and recommendations to change Medicare policy regarding Medicare beneficiaries, including Medicare beneficiaries who are dually eligible for Medicare and Medicaid, shall rest with the Commission. Responsibility for analysis of and recommendations to change Medicaid policy regarding Medicaid beneficiaries, including Medicaid beneficiaries who are dually eligible for Medicare and Medicaid, shall rest with MACPAC.".

Subtitle K—Protections for American Indians and Alaska Natives

SEC. 2901. SPECIAL RULES RELATING TO INDIANS.

(a) NO COST-SHARING FOR INDIANS WITH INCOME AT OR BELOW 300 PERCENT OF POVERTY ENROLLED IN COVERAGE THROUGH A STATE EXCHANGE.—For provisions prohibiting cost sharing for Indians enrolled in any qualified health plan in the individual market through an Exchange, see section 1402(d) of the Patient Protection and Affordable Care Act.

(b) PAYER OF LAST RESORT.—Health programs operated by the Indian Health Service, Indian tribes, tribal organizations, and Urban Indian organizations (as those terms are defined in section 4 of the Indian Health Care Improvement Act (25 U.S.C. 1603)) shall be the payer of last resort for services provided by such Service, tribes, or organizations to individuals eligible for services through such programs, notwithstanding any Federal, State, or local law to the contrary.

(c) FACILITATING ENROLLMENT OF INDIANS UNDER THE EXPRESS LANE OPTION.—Section 1902(e)(13)(F)(ii) of the Social Security Act (42 U.S.C. 1396a(e)(13)(F)(ii)) is amended—

(1) in the clause heading, by inserting "AND INDIAN TRIBES AND TRIBAL ORGANIZATIONS" after "AGENCIES"; and

(2) by adding at the end the following:

"(IV) The Indian Health Service, an Indian Tribe, Tribal Organization, or Urban Indian Organization (as defined in section 1139(c)).".

(d) TECHNICAL CORRECTIONS.—Section 1139(c) of the Social Security Act (42 U.S.C. 1320b–9(c)) is amended by striking "In this section" and inserting "For purposes of this section, title XIX, and title XXI".

SEC. 2902. ELIMINATION OF SUNSET FOR REIMBURSEMENT FOR ALL MEDICARE PART B SERVICES FURNISHED BY CERTAIN INDIAN HOSPITALS AND CLINICS.

(a) REIMBURSEMENT FOR ALL MEDICARE PART B SERVICES FURNISHED BY CERTAIN INDIAN HOSPITALS AND CLINICS.—Section 1880(e)(1)(A) of the Social Security Act (42 U.S.C. 1395qq(e)(1)(A)) is amended by striking "during the 5-year period beginning on" and inserting "on or after".

(b) EFFECTIVE DATE.—The amendments made by this section shall apply to items or services furnished on or after January 1, 2010.

Subtitle L—Maternal and Child Health Services

SEC. 2951. MATERNAL, INFANT, AND EARLY CHILDHOOD HOME VISITING PROGRAMS.

Title V of the Social Security Act (42 U.S.C. 701 et seq.) is amended by adding at the end the following new section:

"SEC. 511. MATERNAL, INFANT, AND EARLY CHILDHOOD HOME VISITING PROGRAMS.

"(a) PURPOSES.—The purposes of this section are—

"(1) to strengthen and improve the programs and activities carried out under this title;

"(2) to improve coordination of services for at risk communities; and

"(3) to identify and provide comprehensive services to improve outcomes for families who reside in at risk communities.

"(b) REQUIREMENT FOR ALL STATES TO ASSESS STATEWIDE NEEDS AND IDENTIFY AT RISK COMMUNITIES.—

"(1) IN GENERAL.—Not later than 6 months after the date of enactment of this section, each State shall, as a condition of receiving payments from an allotment for the State under section 502 for fiscal year 2011, conduct a statewide needs assessment (which shall be separate from the statewide needs assessment required under section 505(a)) that identifies—

"(A) communities with concentrations of—

"(i) premature birth, low-birth weight infants, and infant mortality, including infant death due to neglect, or other indicators of at-risk prenatal, maternal, newborn, or child health;

"(ii) poverty;

"(iii) crime;

"(iv) domestic violence;

"(v) high rates of high-school drop-outs;

"(vi) substance abuse;

"(vii) unemployment; or

"(viii) child maltreatment;

"(B) the quality and capacity of existing programs or initiatives for early childhood home visitation in the State including—

"(i) the number and types of individuals and families who are receiving services under such programs or initiatives;

"(ii) the gaps in early childhood home visitation in the State; and

"(iii) the extent to which such programs or initiatives are meeting the needs of eligible families described in subsection (k)(2); and

"(C) the State's capacity for providing substance abuse treatment and counseling services to individuals and families in need of such treatment or services.

"(2) COORDINATION WITH OTHER ASSESSMENTS.—In conducting the statewide needs assessment required under paragraph (1), the State shall coordinate with, and take into account, other appropriate needs assessments conducted by the State, as determined by the Secretary, including the needs assessment required under section 505(a) (both the most recently completed assessment and any such assessment in progress), the communitywide strategic planning and needs assessments conducted in accordance with section 640(g)(1)(C) of the Head Start Act, and the inventory of current unmet needs and current community-based and prevention-focused programs and activities to prevent child abuse and neglect, and other family resource services operating in the State required under section 205(3) of the Child Abuse Prevention and Treatment Act.

"(3) SUBMISSION TO THE SECRETARY.—Each State shall submit to the Secretary, in such form and manner as the Secretary shall require—

"(A) the results of the statewide needs assessment required under paragraph (1); and

"(B) a description of how the State intends to address needs identified by the assessment, particularly with respect to communities identified under paragraph (1)(A), which may include applying for a grant to conduct an early childhood home visitation program in accordance with the requirements of this section.

"(c) GRANTS FOR EARLY CHILDHOOD HOME VISITATION PROGRAMS.—

"(1) AUTHORITY TO MAKE GRANTS.—In addition to any other payments made under this title to a State, the Secretary shall make grants to eligible entities to enable the entities to deliver services under early childhood home visitation programs that satisfy the requirements of subsection (d) to eligible families in order to promote improvements in maternal and prenatal health, infant health, child health and development, parenting related to child development outcomes, school readiness, and the socioeconomic status of such families, and reductions in child abuse, neglect, and injuries.

"(2) AUTHORITY TO USE INITIAL GRANT FUNDS FOR PLANNING OR IMPLEMENTATION.—An eligible entity that receives a grant under paragraph (1) may use a portion of the funds made available to the entity during the first 6 months of the period for which the grant is made for planning or implementation activities to assist with the establishment of early childhood home visitation programs that satisfy the requirements of subsection (d).

"(3) GRANT DURATION.—The Secretary shall determine the period of years for which a grant is made to an eligible entity under paragraph (1).

"(4) TECHNICAL ASSISTANCE.—The Secretary shall provide an eligible entity that receives a grant under paragraph (1) with technical assistance in administering programs or activities conducted in whole or in part with grant funds.

"(d) REQUIREMENTS.—The requirements of this subsection for an early childhood home visitation program conducted with a grant made under this section are as follows:

"(1) QUANTIFIABLE, MEASURABLE IMPROVEMENT IN BENCHMARK AREAS.—

"(A) IN GENERAL.—The eligible entity establishes, subject to the approval of the Secretary, quantifiable, measurable 3- and 5-year benchmarks for demonstrating that the program results in improvements for the eligible families participating in the program in each of the following areas:

"(i) Improved maternal and newborn health.

"(ii) Prevention of child injuries, child abuse, neglect, or maltreatment, and reduction of emergency department visits.

"(iii) Improvement in school readiness and achievement.

"(iv) Reduction in crime or domestic violence.

"(v) Improvements in family economic self-sufficiency.

"(vi) Improvements in the coordination and referrals for other community resources and supports.

"(B) DEMONSTRATION OF IMPROVEMENTS AFTER 3 YEARS.—

"(i) REPORT TO THE SECRETARY.—Not later than 30 days after the end of the 3rd year in which the eligible entity conducts the program, the entity submits to the Secretary a report demonstrating improvement in at least 4 of the areas specified in subparagraph (A).

"(ii) CORRECTIVE ACTION PLAN.—If the report submitted by the eligible entity under clause (i) fails to demonstrate improvement in at least 4 of the areas specified in subparagraph (A), the entity shall develop and implement a plan to improve outcomes in each of the areas specified in subparagraph (A), subject to approval by the Secretary. The plan shall include provisions for the Secretary to monitor implementation of the plan and conduct continued oversight of the program, including through submission by the entity of regular reports to the Secretary.

"(iii) TECHNICAL ASSISTANCE.—

"(I) IN GENERAL.—The Secretary shall provide an eligible entity required to develop and implement an improvement plan under clause (ii) with technical assistance to develop and implement the plan. The Secretary may provide the technical assistance directly or through grants, contracts, or cooperative agreements.

"(II) ADVISORY PANEL.—The Secretary shall establish an advisory panel for purposes of obtaining recommendations regarding the technical assistance provided to entities in accordance with subclause (I).

"(iv) NO IMPROVEMENT OR FAILURE TO SUBMIT REPORT.—If the Secretary determines after a period of time specified by the Secretary that an eligible entity implementing an improvement plan under clause (ii) has failed to demonstrate any improvement in the areas specified in subparagraph (A), or if the Secretary determines that an eligible entity has failed to submit the report required under clause (i), the Secretary shall terminate the entity's grant and may include any unexpended grant funds in grants made to nonprofit organizations under subsection (h)(2)(B).

"(C) FINAL REPORT.—Not later than December 31, 2015, the eligible entity shall submit a report to the Secretary demonstrating improvements (if any) in each of the areas specified in subparagraph (A).

"(2) IMPROVEMENTS IN OUTCOMES FOR INDIVIDUAL FAMILIES.—

"(A) IN GENERAL.—The program is designed, with respect to an eligible family participating in the program, to result in the participant outcomes described in subparagraph (B) that the eligible entity identifies on the basis of an individualized assessment of the family, are relevant for that family.

"(B) PARTICIPANT OUTCOMES.—The participant outcomes described in this subparagraph are the following:

"(i) Improvements in prenatal, maternal, and newborn health, including improved pregnancy outcomes

"(ii) Improvements in child health and development, including the prevention of child injuries and maltreatment and improvements in cognitive, language, social-emotional, and physical developmental indicators.

"(iii) Improvements in parenting skills.

"(iv) Improvements in school readiness and child academic achievement.

"(v) Reductions in crime or domestic violence.

"(vi) Improvements in family economic self-sufficiency.

"(vii) Improvements in the coordination of referrals for, and the provision of, other community resources and supports for eligible families, consistent with State child welfare agency training.

"(3) CORE COMPONENTS.—The program includes the following core components:

"(A) SERVICE DELIVERY MODEL OR MODELS.—

"(i) IN GENERAL.—Subject to clause (ii), the program is conducted using 1 or more of the service delivery models described in item (aa) or (bb) of subclause (I) or in subclause (II) selected by the eligible entity:

"(I) The model conforms to a clear consistent home visitation model that has been in existence for at least 3 years and is research-based, grounded in relevant empirically-based knowledge, linked to program determined outcomes, associated with a national organization or institution of higher education that has comprehensive home visitation program standards that ensure high quality service delivery and continuous program quality improvement, and has demonstrated significant, (and in the case of the service delivery model described in item (aa), sustained) positive outcomes, as described in the benchmark areas specified in paragraph (1)(A) and the participant outcomes described in paragraph (2)(B), when evaluated using well-designed and rigorous—

"(aa) randomized controlled research designs, and the evaluation results have been published in a peer-reviewed journal; or

"(bb) quasi-experimental research designs.

"(II) The model conforms to a promising and new approach to achieving the benchmark areas specified in paragraph (1)(A) and the participant outcomes described in paragraph (2)(B), has been developed or identified by a national organization or institution of higher education, and will be evaluated through well-designed and rigorous process.

"(ii) MAJORITY OF GRANT FUNDS USED FOR EVIDENCE-BASED MODELS.—An eligible entity shall use not more than 25 percent of the amount of the grant paid to the entity for a fiscal year for purposes of conducting a program using the service delivery model described in clause (i)(II).

"(iii) CRITERIA FOR EVIDENCE OF EFFECTIVENESS OF MODELS.—The Secretary shall establish criteria for evidence of effectiveness of the service delivery models and shall ensure that the process for establishing the criteria is transparent and provides the opportunity for public comment.

"(B) ADDITIONAL REQUIREMENTS.—

"(i) The program adheres to a clear, consistent model that satisfies the requirements of being grounded in empirically-based knowledge related to home visiting and linked to the benchmark areas specified in paragraph (1)(A) and the participant outcomes described in paragraph (2)(B) related to the purposes of the program.

"(ii) The program employs well-trained and competent staff, as demonstrated by education or training, such as nurses, social workers, educators, child development specialists, or other well-trained and competent staff, and provides ongoing and specific training on the model being delivered.

"(iii) The program maintains high quality supervision to establish home visitor competencies.

"(iv) The program demonstrates strong organizational capacity to implement the activities involved.

"(v) The program establishes appropriate linkages and referral networks to other community resources and supports for eligible families.

"(vi) The program monitors the fidelity of program implementation to ensure that services are delivered pursuant to the specified model.

"(4) PRIORITY FOR SERVING HIGH-RISK POPULATIONS.—The eligible entity gives priority to providing services under the program to the following:

"(A) Eligible families who reside in communities in need of such services, as identified in the statewide needs assessment required under subsection (b)(1)(A).

"(B) Low-income eligible families.

"(C) Eligible families who are pregnant women who have not attained age 21.

"(D) Eligible families that have a history of child abuse or neglect or have had interactions with child welfare services.

"(E) Eligible families that have a history of substance abuse or need substance abuse treatment.

"(F) Eligible families that have users of tobacco products in the home.

"(G) Eligible families that are or have children with low student achievement.

"(H) Eligible families with children with developmental delays or disabilities.

"(I) Eligible families who, or that include individuals who, are serving or formerly served in the Armed Forces, including such families that have members of the Armed Forces who have had multiple deployments outside of the United States.

"(e) APPLICATION REQUIREMENTS.—An eligible entity desiring a grant under this section shall submit an application to the Secretary for approval, in such manner as the Secretary may require, that includes the following:

"(1) A description of the populations to be served by the entity, including specific information regarding how the entity will serve high risk populations described in subsection (d)(4).

"(2) An assurance that the entity will give priority to serving low-income eligible families and eligible families who reside in at risk communities identified in the statewide needs assessment required under subsection (b)(1)(A).

"(3) The service delivery model or models described in subsection (d)(3)(A) that the entity will use under the program and the basis for the selection of the model or models.

"(4) A statement identifying how the selection of the populations to be served and the service delivery model or models that the entity will use under the program for such populations is consistent with the results of the statewide needs assessment conducted under subsection (b).

"(5) The quantifiable, measurable benchmarks established by the State to demonstrate that the program contributes to improvements in the areas specified in subsection (d)(1)(A).

"(6) An assurance that the entity will obtain and submit documentation or other appropriate evidence from the organization or entity that developed the service delivery model or models used under the program to verify that the program is implemented and services are delivered according to the model specifications.

"(7) Assurances that the entity will establish procedures to ensure that—

"(A) the participation of each eligible family in the program is voluntary; and

"(B) services are provided to an eligible family in accordance with the individual assessment for that family.

"(8) Assurances that the entity will—

"(A) submit annual reports to the Secretary regarding the program and activities carried out under the program that include such information and data as the Secretary shall require; and

"(B) participate in, and cooperate with, data and information collection necessary for the evaluation required under subsection (g)(2) and other research and evaluation activities carried out under subsection (h)(3).

"(9) A description of other State programs that include home visitation services, including, if applicable to the State, other programs carried out under this title with funds made available from allotments under section 502(c), programs funded under title IV, title II of the Child Abuse Prevention and Treatment Act (relating to community-based grants for the prevention of child abuse and neglect), and section 645A of the Head Start Act (relating to Early Head Start programs).

"(10) Other information as required by the Secretary.

"(f) MAINTENANCE OF EFFORT.—Funds provided to an eligible entity receiving a grant under this section shall supplement, and not supplant, funds from other sources for early childhood home visitation programs or initiatives.

"(g) EVALUATION.—

"(1) INDEPENDENT, EXPERT ADVISORY PANEL.—The Secretary, in accordance with subsection (h)(1)(A), shall appoint an independent advisory panel consisting of experts in program evaluation and research, education, and early childhood development—

"(A) to review, and make recommendations on, the design and plan for the evaluation required under paragraph (2) within 1 year after the date of enactment of this section;

"(B) to maintain and advise the Secretary regarding the progress of the evaluation; and

"(C) to comment, if the panel so desires, on the report submitted under paragraph (3).

"(2) AUTHORITY TO CONDUCT EVALUATION.—On the basis of the recommendations of the advisory panel under paragraph (1), the Secretary shall, by grant, contract, or interagency agreement, conduct an evaluation of the statewide needs assessments submitted under subsection (b) and the grants made under subsections (c) and (h)(3)(B). The evaluation shall include—

"(A) an analysis, on a State-by-State basis, of the results of such assessments, including indicators of maternal and prenatal health and infant health and mortality, and State actions in response to the assessments; and

"(B) an assessment of—

"(i) the effect of early childhood home visitation programs on child and parent outcomes, including with respect to each of the benchmark areas specified in subsection (d)(1)(A) and the participant outcomes described in subsection (d)(2)(B);

"(ii) the effectiveness of such programs on different populations, including the extent to which the ability of programs to improve participant outcomes varies across programs and populations; and

"(iii) the potential for the activities conducted under such programs, if scaled broadly, to improve health care practices, eliminate health disparities, and improve health care system quality, efficiencies, and reduce costs.

"(3) REPORT.—Not later than March 31, 2015, the Secretary shall submit a report to Congress on the results of the evaluation conducted under paragraph (2) and shall make the report publicly available.

"(h) OTHER PROVISIONS.—

"(1) INTRA-AGENCY COLLABORATION.—The Secretary shall ensure that the Maternal and Child Health Bureau and the Administration for Children and Families collaborate with respect to carrying out this section, including with respect to—

"(A) reviewing and analyzing the statewide needs assessments required under subsection (b), the awarding and oversight of grants awarded under this section, the establishment of the advisory panels required under subsections (d)(1)(B)(iii)(II) and (g)(1), and the evaluation and report required under subsection (g); and

"(B) consulting with other Federal agencies with responsibility for administering or evaluating programs that serve eligible families to coordinate and collaborate with respect to research related to such programs and families, including the Office of the Assistant Secretary for Planning and Evaluation of the Department of Health and Human Services, the Centers for Disease Control and Prevention, the National Institute of Child Health and Human Development of the National Institutes of Health, the Office of Juvenile Justice and Delinquency Prevention of the Department of Justice, and the Institute of Education Sciences of the Department of Education.

"(2) GRANTS TO ELIGIBLE ENTITIES THAT ARE NOT STATES.—

"(A) INDIAN TRIBES, TRIBAL ORGANIZATIONS, OR URBAN INDIAN ORGANIZATIONS.—The Secretary shall specify requirements for eligible entities that are Indian Tribes (or a consortium of Indian Tribes), Tribal Organizations, or Urban Indian Organizations to apply for and conduct an early childhood home visitation program with a grant under this section. Such requirements shall, to the greatest extent practicable, be consistent with the requirements applicable to eligible entities that are States and shall require an Indian Tribe (or consortium), Tribal Organization, or Urban Indian Organization to—

"(i) conduct a needs assessment similar to the assessment required for all States under subsection (b); and

"(ii) establish quantifiable, measurable 3- and 5-year benchmarks consistent with subsection (d)(1)(A).

"(B) NONPROFIT ORGANIZATIONS.—If, as of the beginning of fiscal year 2012, a State has not applied or been approved for a grant under this section, the Secretary may use amounts appropriated under paragraph (1) of subsection (j) that are available for expenditure under paragraph (3) of that subsection to make a grant to an eligible entity that is a nonprofit organization described in subsection (k)(1)(B) to conduct an early childhood home visitation program in the State. The Secretary shall specify the requirements for such an organization to apply for and conduct the program which shall, to the greatest extent practicable, be consistent with the requirements applicable to eligible entities that are States and shall require the organization to—

"(i) carry out the program based on the needs assessment conducted by the State under subsection (b); and

"(ii) establish quantifiable, measurable 3- and 5-year benchmarks consistent with subsection (d)(1)(A).

"(3) RESEARCH AND OTHER EVALUATION ACTIVITIES.—

"(A) IN GENERAL.—The Secretary shall carry out a continuous program of research and evaluation activities in order to increase knowledge about the implementation and effectiveness of home visiting programs, using random assignment designs to the maximum extent feasible. The Secretary may carry out such activities directly, or through grants, cooperative agreements, or contracts.

"(B) REQUIREMENTS.—The Secretary shall ensure that—

"(i) evaluation of a specific program or project is conducted by persons or individuals not directly involved in the operation of such program or project; and

"(ii) the conduct of research and evaluation activities includes consultation with independent researchers, State officials, and developers and providers of home visiting programs on topics including research design and administrative data matching.

"(4) REPORT AND RECOMMENDATION.—Not later than December 31, 2015, the Secretary shall submit a report to Congress regarding the programs conducted with grants under this section. The report required under this paragraph shall include—

"(A) information regarding the extent to which eligible entities receiving grants under this section demonstrated improvements in each of the areas specified in subsection (d)(1)(A);

"(B) information regarding any technical assistance provided under subsection (d)(1)(B)(iii)(I), including the type of any such assistance provided; and

"(C) recommendations for such legislative or administrative action as the Secretary determines appropriate.

"(i) APPLICATION OF OTHER PROVISIONS OF TITLE.—

"(1) IN GENERAL.—Except as provided in paragraph (2), the other provisions of this title shall not apply to a grant made under this section.

"(2) EXCEPTIONS.—The following provisions of this title shall apply to a grant made under this section to the same extent and in the same manner as such provisions apply to allotments made under section 502(c):

"(A) Section 504(b)(6) (relating to prohibition on payments to excluded individuals and entities).

"(B) Section 504(c) (relating to the use of funds for the purchase of technical assistance).

"(C) Section 504(d) (relating to a limitation on administrative expenditures).

"(D) Section 506 (relating to reports and audits), but only to the extent determined by the Secretary to be appropriate for grants made under this section.

"(E) Section 507 (relating to penalties for false statements).

"(F) Section 508 (relating to nondiscrimination).

"(G) Section 509(a) (relating to the administration of the grant program).

"(j) APPROPRIATIONS.—

"(1) IN GENERAL.—Out of any funds in the Treasury not otherwise appropriated, there are appropriated to the Secretary to carry out this section—

"(A) $100,000,000 for fiscal year 2010;

"(B) $250,000,000 for fiscal year 2011;

"(C) $350,000,000 for fiscal year 2012;

"(D) $400,000,000 for fiscal year 2013; and

"(E) $400,000,000 for fiscal year 2014.

"(2) RESERVATIONS.—Of the amount appropriated under this subsection for a fiscal year, the Secretary shall reserve—

"(A) 3 percent of such amount for purposes of making grants to eligible entities that are Indian Tribes (or a consortium of Indian Tribes), Tribal Organizations, or Urban Indian Organizations; and

"(B) 3 percent of such amount for purposes of carrying out subsections (d)(1)(B)(iii), (g), and (h)(3).

"(3) AVAILABILITY.—Funds made available to an eligible entity under this section for a fiscal year shall remain available for expenditure by the eligible entity through the end of the second succeeding fiscal year after award. Any funds that are not expended by the eligible entity during the period in which the funds are available under the preceding sentence may be used for grants to nonprofit organizations under subsection (h)(2)(B).

"(k) DEFINITIONS.—In this section:

"(1) ELIGIBLE ENTITY.—

"(A) IN GENERAL.—The term 'eligible entity' means a State, an Indian Tribe, Tribal Organization, or Urban Indian Organization, Puerto Rico, Guam, the Virgin Islands, the Northern Mariana Islands, and American Samoa.

"(B) NONPROFIT ORGANIZATIONS.—Only for purposes of awarding grants under subsection (h)(2)(B), such term shall include a nonprofit organization with an established record of providing early childhood home visitation programs or initiatives in a State or several States.

"(2) ELIGIBLE FAMILY.—The term 'eligible family' means—

"(A) a woman who is pregnant, and the father of the child if the father is available; or

"(B) a parent or primary caregiver of a child, including grandparents or other relatives of the child, and foster parents, who are serving as the child's primary caregiver from birth to kindergarten entry, and including a noncustodial parent who has an ongoing relationship with, and at times provides physical care for, the child.

"(3) INDIAN TRIBE; TRIBAL ORGANIZATION.—The terms 'Indian Tribe' and 'Tribal Organization', and 'Urban Indian Organization' have the meanings given such terms in section 4 of the Indian Health Care Improvement Act.".

SEC. 2952. SUPPORT, EDUCATION, AND RESEARCH FOR POSTPARTUM DEPRESSION.

(a) RESEARCH ON POSTPARTUM CONDITIONS.—

(1) EXPANSION AND INTENSIFICATION OF ACTIVITIES.—The Secretary of Health and Human Services (in this subsection and subsection (c) referred to as the "Secretary") is encouraged to continue activities on postpartum depression or postpartum psychosis (in this subsection and subsection (c) referred to as "postpartum conditions"), including research to expand the understanding of the causes of, and treatments for, postpartum conditions. Activities under this paragraph shall include conducting and supporting the following:

(A) Basic research concerning the etiology and causes of the conditions.

(B) Epidemiological studies to address the frequency and natural history of the conditions and the differences among racial and ethnic groups with respect to the conditions.

(C) The development of improved screening and diagnostic techniques.

(D) Clinical research for the development and evaluation of new treatments.

(E) Information and education programs for health care professionals and the public, which may include a coordinated national campaign to increase the awareness and knowledge of postpartum conditions. Activities under such a national campaign may—

(i) include public service announcements through television, radio, and other means; and

(ii) focus on—

(I) raising awareness about screening;

(II) educating new mothers and their families about postpartum conditions to promote earlier diagnosis and treatment; and

(III) ensuring that such education includes complete information concerning postpartum conditions, including its symptoms, methods of coping with the illness, and treatment resources.

(2) SENSE OF CONGRESS REGARDING LONGITUDINAL STUDY OF RELATIVE MENTAL HEALTH CONSEQUENCES FOR WOMEN OF RESOLVING A PREGNANCY.—

(A) SENSE OF CONGRESS.—It is the sense of Congress that the Director of the National Institute of Mental Health may conduct a nationally representative longitudinal study (during the period of fiscal years 2010 through 2019) of the relative mental health consequences for women of resolving a pregnancy (intended and unintended) in various ways, including carrying the pregnancy to term and parenting the child, carrying the pregnancy to term and placing the child for adoption, miscarriage, and having an abortion. This study may assess the incidence, timing, magnitude, and duration of the immediate and long-term mental health consequences (positive or negative) of these pregnancy outcomes.

(B) REPORT.—Subject to the completion of the study under subsection (a), beginning not later than 5 years after the date of the enactment of this Act, and periodically thereafter for the duration of the study, such Director may prepare and submit to the Congress reports on the findings of the study.

(b) GRANTS TO PROVIDE SERVICES TO INDIVIDUALS WITH A POSTPARTUM CONDITION AND THEIR FAMILIES.—Title V of the Social Security Act (42 U.S.C. 701 et seq.), as amended by section 2951, is amended by adding at the end the following new section:

"SEC. 512. SERVICES TO INDIVIDUALS WITH A POSTPARTUM CONDITION AND THEIR FAMILIES.

"(a) IN GENERAL.—In addition to any other payments made under this title to a State, the Secretary may make grants to eligible entities for projects for the establishment, operation, and coordination of effective and cost-efficient systems for the delivery of essential services to individuals with or at risk for postpartum conditions and their families.

"(b) CERTAIN ACTIVITIES.—To the extent practicable and appropriate, the Secretary shall ensure that projects funded under subsection (a) provide education and services with respect to the diagnosis and management of postpartum conditions for individuals with or at risk for postpartum conditions and their families. The Secretary may allow such projects to include the following:

"(1) Delivering or enhancing outpatient and home-based health and support services, including case management and comprehensive treatment services.

"(2) Delivering or enhancing inpatient care management services that ensure the well-being of the mother and family and the future development of the infant.

"(3) Improving the quality, availability, and organization of health care and support services (including transportation services, attendant care, homemaker services, day or respite care, and providing counseling on financial assistance and insurance).

"(4) Providing education about postpartum conditions to promote earlier diagnosis and treatment. Such education may include—

"(A) providing complete information on postpartum conditions, symptoms, methods of coping with the illness, and treatment resources; and

"(B) in the case of a grantee that is a State, hospital, or birthing facility—

"(i) providing education to new mothers and fathers, and other family members as appropriate, concerning postpartum conditions before new mothers leave the health facility; and

"(ii) ensuring that training programs regarding such education are carried out at the health facility.

"(c) INTEGRATION WITH OTHER PROGRAMS.—To the extent practicable and appropriate, the Secretary may integrate the grant program under this section with other grant programs carried out by the Secretary, including the program under section 330 of the Public Health Service Act.

"(d) REQUIREMENTS.—The Secretary shall establish requirements for grants made under this section that include a limit on the amount of grants funds that may be used for administration, accounting, reporting, or program oversight functions and a requirement for each eligible entity that receives a grant to submit, for each grant period, a report to the Secretary that describes how grant funds were used during such period.

"(e) TECHNICAL ASSISTANCE.—The Secretary may provide technical assistance to entities seeking a grant under this section in order to assist such entities in complying with the requirements of this section.

"(f) APPLICATION OF OTHER PROVISIONS OF TITLE.—

"(1) IN GENERAL.—Except as provided in paragraph (2), the other provisions of this title shall not apply to a grant made under this section.

"(2) EXCEPTIONS.—The following provisions of this title shall apply to a grant made under this section to the same extent and in the same manner as such provisions apply to allotments made under section 502(c):

"(A) Section 504(b)(6) (relating to prohibition on payments to excluded individuals and entities).

"(B) Section 504(c) (relating to the use of funds for the purchase of technical assistance).

"(C) Section 504(d) (relating to a limitation on administrative expenditures).

"(D) Section 506 (relating to reports and audits), but only to the extent determined by the Secretary to be appropriate for grants made under this section.

"(E) Section 507 (relating to penalties for false statements).

"(F) Section 508 (relating to nondiscrimination).

"(G) Section 509(a) (relating to the administration of the grant program).

"(g) DEFINITIONS.—In this section:

"(1) The term 'eligible entity'—

"(A) means a public or nonprofit private entity; and

"(B) includes a State or local government, public-private partnership, recipient of a grant under section 330H of the Public Health Service Act (relating to the Healthy Start Initiative), public or nonprofit private hospital, community-based organization, hospice, ambulatory care facility, community health center, migrant health center, public housing primary care center, or homeless health center.

"(2) The term 'postpartum condition' means postpartum depression or postpartum psychosis.".

(c) GENERAL PROVISIONS.—

(1) AUTHORIZATION OF APPROPRIATIONS.—To carry out this section and the amendment made by subsection (b), there are authorized to be appropriated, in addition to such other sums as may be available for such purpose—

(A) $3,000,000 for fiscal year 2010; and

(B) such sums as may be necessary for fiscal years 2011 and 2012.

(2) REPORT BY THE SECRETARY.—

(A) STUDY.—The Secretary shall conduct a study on the benefits of screening for postpartum conditions.

(B) REPORT.—Not later than 2 years after the date of the enactment of this Act, the Secretary shall complete the study required by subparagraph (A) and submit a report to the Congress on the results of such study.

SEC. 2953. PERSONAL RESPONSIBILITY EDUCATION.

Title V of the Social Security Act (42 U.S.C. 701 et seq.), as amended by sections 2951 and 2952(c), is amended by adding at the end the following:

"SEC. 513. PERSONAL RESPONSIBILITY EDUCATION.

"(a) ALLOTMENTS TO STATES.—

"(1) AMOUNT.—

"(A) IN GENERAL.—For the purpose described in subsection (b), subject to the succeeding provisions of this section, for each of fiscal years 2010 through 2014, the Secretary shall allot to each State an amount equal to the product of—

"(i) the amount appropriated under subsection (f) for the fiscal year and available for allotments to States after the application of subsection (c); and

"(ii) the State youth population percentage determined under paragraph (2).

"(B) MINIMUM ALLOTMENT.—

"(i) IN GENERAL.—Each State allotment under this paragraph for a fiscal year shall be at least $250,000.

"(ii) PRO RATA ADJUSTMENTS.—The Secretary shall adjust on a pro rata basis the amount of the State allotments determined under this paragraph for a fiscal year to the extent necessary to comply with clause (i).

"(C) APPLICATION REQUIRED TO ACCESS ALLOTMENTS.—

"(i) IN GENERAL.—A State shall not be paid from its allotment for a fiscal year unless the State submits an application to the Secretary for the fiscal year and the Secretary approves the application (or requires changes to the application that the State satisfies) and meets such additional requirements as the Secretary may specify.

"(ii) REQUIREMENTS.—The State application shall contain an assurance that the State has complied with the requirements of this section in preparing and submitting the application and shall include the following as well as such additional information as the Secretary may require:

"(I) Based on data from the Centers for Disease Control and Prevention National Center for Health Statistics, the most recent pregnancy rates for the State for youth ages 10 to 14 and youth ages 15 to 19 for which data are available, the most recent birth rates for such youth populations in the State for which data are available, and trends in those rates for the most recently preceding 5-year period for which such data are available.

"(II) State-established goals for reducing the pregnancy rates and birth rates for such youth populations.

"(III) A description of the State's plan for using the State allotments provided under this section to achieve such goals, especially among youth populations that are the most high-risk or vulnerable for pregnancies or otherwise have special circumstances, including youth in foster care, homeless youth, youth with HIV/AIDS, pregnant youth who are under 21 years of age, mothers who are under 21 years of age, and youth residing in areas with high birth rates for youth.

"(2) STATE YOUTH POPULATION PERCENTAGE.—

"(A) IN GENERAL.—For purposes of paragraph (1)(A)(ii), the State youth population percentage is, with respect to a State, the proportion (expressed as a percentage) of—

"(i) the number of individuals who have attained age 10 but not attained age 20 in the State; to

"(ii) the number of such individuals in all States.

"(B) DETERMINATION OF NUMBER OF YOUTH.—The number of individuals described in clauses (i) and (ii) of subparagraph (A) in a State shall be determined on the basis of the most recent Bureau of the Census data.

"(3) AVAILABILITY OF STATE ALLOTMENTS.—Subject to paragraph (4)(A), amounts allotted to a State pursuant to this subsection for a fiscal year shall remain available for expenditure by the State through the end of the second succeeding fiscal year.

"(4) AUTHORITY TO AWARD GRANTS FROM STATE ALLOTMENTS TO LOCAL ORGANIZATIONS AND ENTITIES IN NONPARTICIPATING STATES.—

"(A) GRANTS FROM UNEXPENDED ALLOTMENTS.—If a State does not submit an application under this section for fiscal year 2010 or 2011, the State shall no longer be eligible to submit an application to receive funds from the amounts allotted for the State for each of fiscal years 2010 through 2014 and such amounts shall be used by the Secretary to award grants under this paragraph for each of fiscal years 2012 through 2014. The Secretary also shall use any amounts from the allotments of States that submit applications under this section for a fiscal year that remain unexpended as of the end of the period in which the allotments are available for expenditure under paragraph (3) for awarding grants under this paragraph.

"(B) 3-YEAR GRANTS.—

"(i) IN GENERAL.—The Secretary shall solicit applications to award 3-year grants in each of fiscal years 2012, 2013, and 2014 to local organizations and entities to conduct, consistent with subsection (b), programs and activities in States that do not submit an application for an allotment under this section for fiscal year 2010 or 2011.

"(ii) FAITH-BASED ORGANIZATIONS OR CONSORTIA.—The Secretary may solicit and award grants under this paragraph to faith-based organizations or consortia.

"(C) EVALUATION.—An organization or entity awarded a grant under this paragraph shall agree to participate in a rigorous Federal evaluation.

"(5) MAINTENANCE OF EFFORT.—No payment shall be made to a State from the allotment determined for the State under this subsection or to a local organization or entity awarded a grant under paragraph (4), if the expenditure of non-federal funds by the State, organization, or entity for activities, programs, or initiatives for which amounts from allotments and grants under this subsection may be expended is less than the amount expended by the State, organization, or entity for such programs or initiatives for fiscal year 2009.

"(6) DATA COLLECTION AND REPORTING.—A State or local organization or entity receiving funds under this section shall cooperate with such requirements relating to the collection of data and information and reporting on outcomes regarding the programs and activities carried out with such funds, as the Secretary shall specify.

"(b) PURPOSE.—

"(1) IN GENERAL.—The purpose of an allotment under subsection (a)(1) to a State is to enable the State (or, in the case of grants made under subsection (a)(4)(B), to enable a local organization or entity) to carry out personal responsibility education programs consistent with this subsection.

"(2) PERSONAL RESPONSIBILITY EDUCATION PROGRAMS.—

"(A) IN GENERAL.—In this section, the term 'personal responsibility education program' means a program that is designed to educate adolescents on—

"(i) both abstinence and contraception for the prevention of pregnancy and sexually transmitted infections, including HIV/AIDS, consistent with the requirements of subparagraph (B); and

"(ii) at least 3 of the adulthood preparation subjects described in subparagraph (C).

"(B) REQUIREMENTS.—The requirements of this subparagraph are the following:

"(i) The program replicates evidence-based effective programs or substantially incorporates elements of effective programs that have been proven on the basis of rigorous scientific research to change behavior, which means delaying sexual activity, increasing condom or contraceptive use for sexually active youth, or reducing pregnancy among youth.

"(ii) The program is medically-accurate and complete.

"(iii) The program includes activities to educate youth who are sexually active regarding responsible sexual behavior with respect to both abstinence and the use of contraception.

"(iv) The program places substantial emphasis on both abstinence and contraception for the prevention of pregnancy among youth and sexually transmitted infections.

"(v) The program provides age-appropriate information and activities.

"(vi) The information and activities carried out under the program are provided in the cultural context that is most appropriate for individuals in the particular population group to which they are directed.

"(C) ADULTHOOD PREPARATION SUBJECTS.—The adulthood preparation subjects described in this subparagraph are the following:

"(i) Healthy relationships, such as positive self-esteem and relationship dynamics, friendships, dating, romantic involvement, marriage, and family interactions.

"(ii) Adolescent development, such as the development of healthy attitudes and values about adolescent growth and development, body image, racial and ethnic diversity, and other related subjects.

"(iii) Financial literacy.

"(iv) Parent-child communication.

"(v) Educational and career success, such as developing skills for employment preparation, job seeking, independent living, financial self-sufficiency, and workplace productivity.

"(vi) Healthy life skills, such as goal-setting, decision making, negotiation, communication and interpersonal skills, and stress management.

"(c) RESERVATIONS OF FUNDS.—

"(1) GRANTS TO IMPLEMENT INNOVATIVE STRATEGIES.—From the amount appropriated under subsection (f) for the fiscal year, the Secretary shall reserve $10,000,000 of such amount for purposes of awarding grants to entities to implement innovative youth pregnancy prevention strategies and target services to high-risk, vulnerable, and culturally under-represented youth populations, including youth in foster care, homeless youth, youth with HIV/AIDS, pregnant women who are under 21 years of age and their partners, mothers who are under 21 years of age and their partners, and youth residing in areas with high birth rates for youth. An entity awarded a grant under this paragraph shall agree to participate in a rigorous Federal evaluation of the activities carried out with grant funds.

"(2) OTHER RESERVATIONS.—From the amount appropriated under subsection (f) for the fiscal year that remains after the application of paragraph (1), the Secretary shall reserve the following amounts:

"(A) GRANTS FOR INDIAN TRIBES OR TRIBAL ORGANIZATIONS.—The Secretary shall reserve 5 percent of such remainder for purposes of awarding grants to Indian tribes and tribal organizations in such manner, and subject to such requirements, as the Secretary, in consultation with Indian tribes and tribal organizations, determines appropriate.

"(B) SECRETARIAL RESPONSIBILITIES.—

"(i) RESERVATION OF FUNDS.—The Secretary shall reserve 10 percent of such remainder for expenditures by the Secretary for the activities described in clauses (ii) and (iii).

"(ii) PROGRAM SUPPORT.—The Secretary shall provide, directly or through a competitive grant process, research, training and technical assistance, including dissemination of research and information regarding effective and promising practices, providing consultation and resources on a broad array of teen pregnancy prevention strategies, including abstinence and contraception, and developing resources and materials to support the activities of recipients of grants and other State, tribal, and community organizations working to reduce teen pregnancy. In carrying out such functions, the Secretary shall collaborate with a variety of entities that have expertise in the prevention of teen pregnancy, HIV and sexually transmitted infections, healthy relationships, financial literacy, and other topics addressed through the personal responsibility education programs.

"(iii) EVALUATION.—The Secretary shall evaluate the programs and activities carried out with funds made available through allotments or grants under this section.

"(d) ADMINISTRATION.—

"(1) IN GENERAL.—The Secretary shall administer this section through the Assistant Secretary for the Administration for Children and Families within the Department of Health and Human Services.

"(2) APPLICATION OF OTHER PROVISIONS OF TITLE.—

"(A) IN GENERAL.—Except as provided in subparagraph (B), the other provisions of this title shall not apply to allotments or grants made under this section.

"(B) EXCEPTIONS.—The following provisions of this title shall apply to allotments and grants made under this section to the same extent and in the same manner as such provisions apply to allotments made under section 502(c):

"(i) Section 504(b)(6) (relating to prohibition on payments to excluded individuals and entities).

"(ii) Section 504(c) (relating to the use of funds for the purchase of technical assistance).

"(iii) Section 504(d) (relating to a limitation on administrative expenditures).

"(iv) Section 506 (relating to reports and audits), but only to the extent determined by the Secretary to be appropriate for grants made under this section.

"(v) Section 507 (relating to penalties for false statements).

"(vi) Section 508 (relating to nondiscrimination).

"(e) DEFINITIONS.—In this section:

"(1) AGE-APPROPRIATE.—The term 'age-appropriate', with respect to the information in pregnancy prevention, means topics, messages, and teaching methods suitable to particular ages or age groups of children and adolescents, based on developing cognitive, emotional, and behavioral capacity typical for the age or age group.

"(2) MEDICALLY ACCURATE AND COMPLETE.—The term 'medically accurate and complete' means verified or supported by the weight of research conducted in compliance with accepted scientific methods and—

"(A) published in peer-reviewed journals, where applicable; or

"(B) comprising information that leading professional organizations and agencies with relevant expertise in the field recognize as accurate, objective, and complete.

"(3) INDIAN TRIBES; TRIBAL ORGANIZATIONS.—The terms 'Indian tribe' and 'Tribal organization' have the meanings given such terms in section 4 of the Indian Health Care Improvement Act (25 U.S.C. 1603)).

"(4) YOUTH.—The term 'youth' means an individual who has attained age 10 but has not attained age 20.

"(f) APPROPRIATION.—For the purpose of carrying out this section, there is appropriated, out of any money in the Treasury not otherwise appropriated, $75,000,000 for each of fiscal years 2010 through 2014. Amounts appropriated under this subsection shall remain available until expended.".

SEC. 2954. RESTORATION OF FUNDING FOR ABSTINENCE EDUCATION.

Section 510 of the Social Security Act (42 U.S.C. 710) is amended—

(1) in subsection (a), by striking "fiscal year 1998 and each subsequent fiscal year" and inserting "each of fiscal years 2010 through 2014"; and

(2) in subsection (d)—

(A) in the first sentence, by striking "1998 through 2003" and inserting "2010 through 2014"; and

(B) in the second sentence, by inserting "(except that such appropriation shall be made on the date of enactment of the Patient Protection and Affordable Care Act in the case of fiscal year 2010)" before the period.

SEC. 2955. INCLUSION OF INFORMATION ABOUT THE IMPORTANCE OF HAVING A HEALTH CARE POWER OF ATTORNEY IN TRANSITION PLANNING FOR CHILDREN AGING OUT OF FOSTER CARE AND INDEPENDENT LIVING PROGRAMS.

(a) TRANSITION PLANNING.—Section 475(5)(H) of the Social Security Act (42 U.S.C. 675(5)(H)) is amended by inserting "includes information about the importance of designating another individual to make health care treatment decisions on behalf of the child if the child becomes unable to participate in such decisions and the child does not have, or does not want, a relative who would otherwise be authorized under State law to make such decisions, and provides the child with the option to execute a health care power of attorney, health care proxy, or other similar document recognized under State law," after "employment services,".

(b) INDEPENDENT LIVING EDUCATION.—Section 477(b)(3) of such Act (42 U.S.C. 677(b)(3)) is amended by adding at the end the following:

"(K) A certification by the chief executive officer of the State that the State will ensure that an adolescent participating in the program under this section are provided with education about the importance of designating another individual to make health care treatment decisions on behalf of the adolescent if the adolescent becomes unable to participate in such decisions and the adolescent does not have, or does not want, a relative who would otherwise be authorized under State law to make such decisions, whether a health care power of attorney, health care proxy, or other similar document is recognized under State law, and how to execute such a document if the adolescent wants to do so.".

(c) HEALTH OVERSIGHT AND COORDINATION PLAN.—Section 422(b)(15)(A) of such Act (42 U.S.C. 622(b)(15)(A)) is amended—

(1) in clause (v), by striking "and" at the end; and

(2) by adding at the end the following:

"(vii) steps to ensure that the components of the transition plan development process required under section 475(5)(H) that relate to the health care needs of children aging out of foster care, including the requirements to include options for health insurance, information about a health care power of attorney, health care proxy, or other similar document recognized under State law, and to provide the child with the option to execute such a document, are met; and".

(d) EFFECTIVE DATE.—The amendments made by this section take effect on October 1, 2010.

TITLE III—IMPROVING THE QUALITY AND EFFICIENCY OF HEALTH CARE

Subtitle A—Transforming the Health Care Delivery System

PART I—LINKING PAYMENT TO QUALITY OUTCOMES UNDER THE MEDICARE PROGRAM

SEC. 3001. HOSPITAL VALUE-BASED PURCHASING PROGRAM.

(a) PROGRAM.—

(1) IN GENERAL.—Section 1886 of the Social Security Act (42 U.S.C. 1395ww), as amended by section 4102(a) of the HITECH Act (Public Law 111–5), is amended by adding at the end the following new subsection:

"(o) HOSPITAL VALUE-BASED PURCHASING PROGRAM.—

"(1) ESTABLISHMENT.—

"(A) IN GENERAL.—Subject to the succeeding provisions of this subsection, the Secretary shall establish a hospital value-based purchasing program (in this subsection referred to as the 'Program') under which value-based incentive payments are made in a fiscal year to hospitals that meet the performance standards under paragraph (3) for the performance period for such fiscal year (as established under paragraph (4)).

"(B) PROGRAM TO BEGIN IN FISCAL YEAR 2013.—The Program shall apply to payments for discharges occurring on or after October 1, 2012.

"(C) APPLICABILITY OF PROGRAM TO HOSPITALS.—

"(i) IN GENERAL.—For purposes of this subsection, subject to clause (ii), the term 'hospital' means a subsection (d) hospital (as defined in subsection (d)(1)(B)).

"(ii) EXCLUSIONS.—The term 'hospital' shall not include, with respect to a fiscal year, a hospital—

"(I) that is subject to the payment reduction under subsection (b)(3)(B)(viii)(I) for such fiscal year;

"(II) for which, during the performance period for such fiscal year, the Secretary has cited deficiencies that pose immediate jeopardy to the health or safety of patients;

"(III) for which there are not a minimum number (as determined by the Secretary) of measures that apply to the hospital for the performance period for such fiscal year; or

"(IV) for which there are not a minimum number (as determined by the Secretary) of cases for the measures that apply to the hospital for the performance period for such fiscal year.

"(iii) INDEPENDENT ANALYSIS.—For purposes of determining the minimum numbers under subclauses (III) and (IV) of clause (ii), the Secretary shall have conducted an independent analysis of what numbers are appropriate.

"(iv) EXEMPTION.—In the case of a hospital that is paid under section 1814(b)(3), the Secretary may exempt such hospital from the application of this subsection if the State which is paid under such section submits an annual report to the Secretary describing how a similar program in the State for a participating hospital or hospitals achieves or surpasses the measured results in terms of patient health outcomes and cost savings established under this subsection.

"(2) MEASURES.—

"(A) IN GENERAL.—The Secretary shall select measures for purposes of the Program. Such measures shall be selected from the measures specified under subsection (b)(3)(B)(viii).

"(B) REQUIREMENTS.—

"(i) FOR FISCAL YEAR 2013.—For value-based incentive payments made with respect to discharges occurring during fiscal year 2013, the Secretary shall ensure the following:

"(I) CONDITIONS OR PROCEDURES.—Measures are selected under subparagraph (A) that cover at least the following 5 specific conditions or procedures:

"(aa) Acute myocardial infarction (AMI).

"(bb) Heart failure.

"(cc) Pneumonia.

"(dd) Surgeries, as measured by the Surgical Care Improvement Project (formerly referred to as 'Surgical Infection Prevention' for discharges occurring before July 2006).

"(ee) Healthcare-associated infections, as measured by the prevention metrics and targets established in the HHS Action Plan to Prevent Healthcare-Associated Infections (or any successor plan) of the Department of Health and Human Services.

"(II) HCAHPS.—Measures selected under subparagraph (A) shall be related to the Hospital Consumer Assessment of Healthcare Providers and Systems survey (HCAHPS).

"(ii) INCLUSION OF EFFICIENCY MEASURES.—For value-based incentive payments made with respect to discharges occurring during fiscal year 2014 or a subsequent fiscal year, the Secretary shall ensure that measures selected under subparagraph (A) include efficiency measures, including measures of 'Medicare spending per beneficiary'. Such measures shall be adjusted for factors such as age, sex, race, severity of illness, and other factors that the Secretary determines appropriate.

"(C) LIMITATIONS.—

"(i) TIME REQUIREMENT FOR PRIOR REPORTING AND NOTICE.—The Secretary may not select a measure under subparagraph (A) for use under the Program with respect to a performance period for a fiscal year (as established under paragraph (4)) unless such measure has been specified under subsection (b)(3)(B)(viii) and included on the Hospital Compare Internet website for at least 1 year prior to the beginning of such performance period.

"(ii) MEASURE NOT APPLICABLE UNLESS HOSPITAL FURNISHES SERVICES APPROPRIATE TO THE MEASURE.—A measure selected under subparagraph (A) shall not apply to a hospital if such hospital does not furnish services appropriate to such measure.

"(D) REPLACING MEASURES.—Subclause (VI) of subsection (b)(3)(B)(viii) shall apply to measures selected under subparagraph (A) in the same manner as such subclause applies to measures selected under such subsection.

"(3) PERFORMANCE STANDARDS.—

"(A) ESTABLISHMENT.—The Secretary shall establish performance standards with respect to measures selected under paragraph (2) for a performance period for a fiscal year (as established under paragraph (4)).

"(B) ACHIEVEMENT AND IMPROVEMENT.—The performance standards established under subparagraph (A) shall include levels of achievement and improvement.

"(C) TIMING.—The Secretary shall establish and announce the performance standards under subparagraph (A) not later than 60 days prior to the beginning of the performance period for the fiscal year involved.

"(D) CONSIDERATIONS IN ESTABLISHING STANDARDS.—In establishing performance standards with respect to measures under this paragraph, the Secretary shall take into account appropriate factors, such as—

"(i) practical experience with the measures involved, including whether a significant proportion of hospitals failed to meet the performance standard during previous performance periods;

"(ii) historical performance standards;

"(iii) improvement rates; and

"(iv) the opportunity for continued improvement.

"(4) PERFORMANCE PERIOD.—For purposes of the Program, the Secretary shall establish the performance period for a fiscal year. Such performance period shall begin and end prior to the beginning of such fiscal year.

"(5) HOSPITAL PERFORMANCE SCORE.—

"(A) IN GENERAL.—Subject to subparagraph (B), the Secretary shall develop a methodology for assessing the total performance of each hospital based on performance standards with respect to the measures selected under paragraph (2) for a performance period (as established under paragraph (4)). Using such methodology, the Secretary shall provide for an assessment (in this subsection referred to as the 'hospital performance score') for each hospital for each performance period.

"(B) APPLICATION.—

"(i) APPROPRIATE DISTRIBUTION.—The Secretary shall ensure that the application of the methodology developed under subparagraph (A) results in an appropriate distribution of value-based incentive payments under paragraph (6) among hospitals achieving different levels of hospital performance scores, with hospitals achieving the highest hospital performance scores receiving the largest value-based incentive payments.

"(ii) HIGHER OF ACHIEVEMENT OR IMPROVEMENT.—The methodology developed under subparagraph (A) shall provide that the hospital performance score is determined using the higher of its achievement or improvement score for each measure.

"(iii) WEIGHTS.—The methodology developed under subparagraph (A) shall provide for the assignment of weights for categories of measures as the Secretary determines appropriate.

"(iv) NO MINIMUM PERFORMANCE STANDARD.—The Secretary shall not set a minimum performance standard in determining the hospital performance score for any hospital.

"(v) REFLECTION OF MEASURES APPLICABLE TO THE HOSPITAL.—The hospital performance score for a hospital shall reflect the measures that apply to the hospital.

"(6) CALCULATION OF VALUE-BASED INCENTIVE PAYMENTS.—

"(A) IN GENERAL.—In the case of a hospital that the Secretary determines meets (or exceeds) the performance standards under paragraph (3) for the performance period for a fiscal year (as established under paragraph (4)), the Secretary shall increase the base operating DRG payment amount (as defined in paragraph (7)(D)), as determined after application of paragraph (7)(B)(i), for a hospital for each discharge occurring in such fiscal year by the value-based incentive payment amount.

"(B) VALUE-BASED INCENTIVE PAYMENT AMOUNT.—The value-based incentive payment amount for each discharge of a hospital in a fiscal year shall be equal to the product of—

"(i) the base operating DRG payment amount (as defined in paragraph (7)(D)) for the discharge for the hospital for such fiscal year; and

"(ii) the value-based incentive payment percentage specified under subparagraph (C) for the hospital for such fiscal year.

"(C) VALUE-BASED INCENTIVE PAYMENT PERCENTAGE.—

"(i) IN GENERAL.—The Secretary shall specify a value-based incentive payment percentage for a hospital for a fiscal year.

"(ii) REQUIREMENTS.—In specifying the value-based incentive payment percentage for each hospital for a fiscal year under clause (i), the Secretary shall ensure that—

"(I) such percentage is based on the hospital performance score of the hospital under paragraph (5); and

"(II) the total amount of value-based incentive payments under this paragraph to all hospitals in such fiscal year is equal to the total amount available for value-based incentive payments for such fiscal year under paragraph (7)(A), as estimated by the Secretary.

"(7) FUNDING FOR VALUE-BASED INCENTIVE PAYMENTS.—

"(A) AMOUNT.—The total amount available for value-based incentive payments under paragraph (6) for all hospitals for a fiscal year shall be equal to the total amount of reduced payments for all hospitals under subparagraph (B) for such fiscal year, as estimated by the Secretary.

"(B) ADJUSTMENT TO PAYMENTS.—

"(i) IN GENERAL.—The Secretary shall reduce the base operating DRG payment amount (as defined in subparagraph (D)) for a hospital for each discharge in a fiscal year (beginning with fiscal year 2013) by an amount equal to the applicable percent (as defined in subparagraph (C)) of the base operating DRG payment amount for the discharge for the hospital for such fiscal year. The Secretary shall make such reductions for all hospitals in the fiscal year involved, regardless of whether or not the hospital has been determined by the Secretary to have earned a value-based incentive payment under paragraph (6) for such fiscal year.

"(ii) NO EFFECT ON OTHER PAYMENTS.—Payments described in items (aa) and (bb) of subparagraph (D)(i)(II) for a hospital shall be determined as if this subsection had not been enacted.

"(C) APPLICABLE PERCENT DEFINED.—For purposes of subparagraph (B), the term 'applicable percent' means—

"(i) with respect to fiscal year 2013, 1.0 percent;

"(ii) with respect to fiscal year 2014, 1.25 percent;

"(iii) with respect to fiscal year 2015, 1.5 percent;

"(iv) with respect to fiscal year 2016, 1.75 percent; and

"(v) with respect to fiscal year 2017 and succeeding fiscal years, 2 percent.

"(D) BASE OPERATING DRG PAYMENT AMOUNT DEFINED.—

"(i) IN GENERAL.—Except as provided in clause (ii), in this subsection, the term 'base operating DRG payment amount' means, with respect to a hospital for a fiscal year—

"(I) the payment amount that would otherwise be made under subsection (d) (determined without regard to subsection (q)) for a discharge if this subsection did not apply; reduced by

“(II) any portion of such payment amount that is attributable to—

“(aa) payments under paragraphs (5)(A), (5)(B), (5)(F), and (12) of subsection (d); and

“(bb) such other payments under subsection (d) determined appropriate by the Secretary.

“(ii) SPECIAL RULES FOR CERTAIN HOSPITALS.—

“(I) SOLE COMMUNITY HOSPITALS AND MEDICARE-DEPENDENT, SMALL RURAL HOSPITALS.—In the case of a medicare-dependent, small rural hospital (with respect to discharges occurring during fiscal year 2012 and 2013) or a sole community hospital, in applying subparagraph (A)(i), the payment amount that would otherwise be made under subsection (d) shall be determined without regard to subparagraphs (I) and (L) of subsection (b)(3) and subparagraphs (D) and (G) of subsection (d)(5).

“(II) HOSPITALS PAID UNDER SECTION 1814.—In the case of a hospital that is paid under section 1814(b)(3), the term ‘base operating DRG payment amount’ means the payment amount under such section.

“(8) ANNOUNCEMENT OF NET RESULT OF ADJUSTMENTS.—Under the Program, the Secretary shall, not later than 60 days prior to the fiscal year involved, inform each hospital of the adjustments to payments to the hospital for discharges occurring in such fiscal year under paragraphs (6) and (7)(B)(i).

“(9) NO EFFECT IN SUBSEQUENT FISCAL YEARS.—The value-based incentive payment under paragraph (6) and the payment reduction under paragraph (7)(B)(i) shall each apply only with respect to the fiscal year involved, and the Secretary shall not take into account such value-based incentive payment or payment reduction in making payments to a hospital under this section in a subsequent fiscal year.

“(10) PUBLIC REPORTING.—

“(A) HOSPITAL SPECIFIC INFORMATION.—

“(i) IN GENERAL.—The Secretary shall make information available to the public regarding the performance of individual hospitals under the Program, including—

“(I) the performance of the hospital with respect to each measure that applies to the hospital;

“(II) the performance of the hospital with respect to each condition or procedure; and

“(III) the hospital performance score assessing the total performance of the hospital.

“(ii) OPPORTUNITY TO REVIEW AND SUBMIT CORRECTIONS.—The Secretary shall ensure that a hospital has the opportunity to review, and submit corrections for, the information to be made public with respect to the hospital under clause (i) prior to such information being made public.

"(iii) WEBSITE.—Such information shall be posted on the Hospital Compare Internet website in an easily understandable format.

"(B) AGGREGATE INFORMATION.—The Secretary shall periodically post on the Hospital Compare Internet website aggregate information on the Program, including—

"(i) the number of hospitals receiving value-based incentive payments under paragraph (6) and the range and total amount of such value-based incentive payments; and

"(ii) the number of hospitals receiving less than the maximum value-based incentive payment available to the hospital for the fiscal year involved and the range and amount of such payments.

"(11) IMPLEMENTATION.—

"(A) APPEALS.—The Secretary shall establish a process by which hospitals may appeal the calculation of a hospital's performance assessment with respect to the performance standards established under paragraph (3)(A) and the hospital performance score under paragraph (5). The Secretary shall ensure that such process provides for resolution of such appeals in a timely manner.

"(B) LIMITATION ON REVIEW.—Except as provided in subparagraph (A), there shall be no administrative or judicial review under section 1869, section 1878, or otherwise of the following:

"(i) The methodology used to determine the amount of the value-based incentive payment under paragraph (6) and the determination of such amount.

"(ii) The determination of the amount of funding available for such value-based incentive payments under paragraph (7)(A) and the payment reduction under paragraph (7)(B)(i).

"(iii) The establishment of the performance standards under paragraph (3) and the performance period under paragraph (4).

"(iv) The measures specified under subsection (b)(3)(B)(viii) and the measures selected under paragraph (2).

"(v) The methodology developed under paragraph (5) that is used to calculate hospital performance scores and the calculation of such scores.

"(vi) The validation methodology specified in subsection (b)(3)(B)(viii)(XI).

"(C) CONSULTATION WITH SMALL HOSPITALS.—The Secretary shall consult with small rural and urban hospitals on the application of the Program to such hospitals.

"(12) PROMULGATION OF REGULATIONS.—The Secretary shall promulgate regulations to carry out the Program, including the selection of measures under paragraph (2), the methodology developed under paragraph (5) that is used to calculate hospital performance scores, and the methodology used to determine the amount of value-based incentive payments under paragraph (6).".

(2) AMENDMENTS FOR REPORTING OF HOSPITAL QUALITY INFORMATION.—Section 1886(b)(3)(B)(viii) of the Social Security Act (42 U.S.C. 1395ww(b)(3)(B)(viii)) is amended—

(A) in subclause (II), by adding at the end the following sentence: "The Secretary may require hospitals to submit data on measures that are not used for the determination of value-based incentive payments under subsection (o).";

(B) in subclause (V), by striking "beginning with fiscal year 2008" and inserting "for fiscal years 2008 through 2012";

(C) in subclause (VII), in the first sentence, by striking "data submitted" and inserting "information regarding measures submitted"; and

(D) by adding at the end the following new subclauses:

"(VIII) Effective for payments beginning with fiscal year 2013, with respect to quality measures for outcomes of care, the Secretary shall provide for such risk adjustment as the Secretary determines to be appropriate to maintain incentives for hospitals to treat patients with severe illnesses or conditions.

"(IX)(aa) Subject to item (bb), effective for payments beginning with fiscal year 2013, each measure specified by the Secretary under this clause shall be endorsed by the entity with a contract under section 1890(a).

"(bb) In the case of a specified area or medical topic determined appropriate by the Secretary for which a feasible and practical measure has not been endorsed by the entity with a contract under section 1890(a), the Secretary may specify a measure that is not so endorsed as long as due consideration is given to measures that have been endorsed or adopted by a consensus organization identified by the Secretary.

"(X) To the extent practicable, the Secretary shall, with input from consensus organizations and other stakeholders, take steps to ensure that the measures specified by the Secretary under this clause are coordinated and aligned with quality measures applicable to—

"(aa) physicians under section 1848(k); and

"(bb) other providers of services and suppliers under this title.

"(XI) The Secretary shall establish a process to validate measures specified under this clause as appropriate. Such process shall include the auditing of a number of randomly selected hospitals sufficient to ensure validity of the reporting program under this clause as a whole and shall provide a hospital with an opportunity to appeal the validation of measures reported by such hospital.".

(3) WEBSITE IMPROVEMENTS.—Section 1886(b)(3)(B) of the Social Security Act (42 U.S.C. 1395ww(b)(3)(B)), as amended by section 4102(b) of the HITECH Act (Public Law 111–5), is amended by adding at the end the following new clause:

"(x)(I) The Secretary shall develop standard Internet website reports tailored to meet the needs of various stakeholders such as hospitals, patients, researchers, and policymakers. The Secretary shall seek input from such stakeholders in determining the type of information that is useful and the formats that best facilitate the use of the information.

"(II) The Secretary shall modify the Hospital Compare Internet website to make the use and navigation of that website readily available to individuals accessing it.".

(4) GAO STUDY AND REPORT.—

(A) STUDY.—The Comptroller General of the United States shall conduct a study on the performance of the hospital value-based purchasing program established under section 1886(o) of the Social Security Act, as added by paragraph (1). Such study shall include an analysis of the impact of such program on—

(i) the quality of care furnished to Medicare beneficiaries, including diverse Medicare beneficiary populations (such as diverse in terms of race, ethnicity, and socioeconomic status);

(ii) expenditures under the Medicare program, including any reduced expenditures under Part A of title XVIII of such Act that are attributable to the improvement in the delivery of inpatient hospital services by reason of such hospital value-based purchasing program;

(iii) the quality performance among safety net hospitals and any barriers such hospitals face in meeting the performance standards applicable under such hospital value-based purchasing program; and

(iv) the quality performance among small rural and small urban hospitals and any barriers such hospitals face in meeting the performance standards applicable under such hospital value-based purchasing program.

(B) REPORTS.—

(i) INTERIM REPORT.—Not later than October 1, 2015, the Comptroller General of the United States shall submit to Congress an interim report containing the results of the study conducted under subparagraph (A), together with recommendations for such legislation and administrative action as the Comptroller General determines appropriate.

(ii) FINAL REPORT.—Not later than July 1, 2017, the Comptroller General of the United States shall submit to Congress a report containing the results of the study conducted under subparagraph (A), together with recommendations for such legislation and administrative action as the Comptroller General determines appropriate.

(5) HHS STUDY AND REPORT.—

(A) STUDY.—The Secretary of Health and Human Services shall conduct a study on the performance of the hospital value-based purchasing program established under section 1886(o) of the Social Security Act, as added by paragraph (1). Such study shall include an analysis—

(i) of ways to improve the hospital value-based purchasing program and ways to address any unintended consequences that may occur as a result of such program;

(ii) of whether the hospital value-based purchasing program resulted in lower spending under the Medicare program under title XVIII of such Act or other financial savings to hospitals;

(iii) the appropriateness of the Medicare program sharing in any savings generated through the hospital value-based purchasing program; and

(iv) any other area determined appropriate by the Secretary.

(B) REPORT.—Not later than January 1, 2016, the Secretary of Health and Human Services shall submit to Congress a report containing the results of the study conducted under subparagraph (A), together with recommendations for such legislation and administrative action as the Secretary determines appropriate.

(b) VALUE-BASED PURCHASING DEMONSTRATION PROGRAMS.—

(1) VALUE-BASED PURCHASING DEMONSTRATION PROGRAM FOR INPATIENT CRITICAL ACCESS HOSPITALS.—

(A) ESTABLISHMENT.—

(i) IN GENERAL.—Not later than 2 years after the date of enactment of this Act, the Secretary of Health and Human Services (in this subsection referred to as the "Secretary") shall establish a demonstration program under which the Secretary establishes a value-based purchasing program under the Medicare program under title XVIII of the Social Security Act for critical access hospitals (as defined in paragraph (1) of section 1861(mm) of such Act (42 U.S.C. 1395x(mm))) with respect to inpatient critical access hospital services (as defined in paragraph (2) of such section) in order to test innovative methods of measuring and rewarding quality and efficient health care furnished by such hospitals.

(ii) DURATION.—The demonstration program under this paragraph shall be conducted for a 3-year period.

(iii) SITES.—The Secretary shall conduct the demonstration program under this paragraph at an appropriate number (as determined by the Secretary) of critical access hospitals. The Secretary shall ensure that such hospitals are representative of the spectrum of such hospitals that participate in the Medicare program.

(B) WAIVER AUTHORITY.—The Secretary may waive such requirements of titles XI and XVIII of the Social Security Act as may be necessary to carry out the demonstration program under this paragraph.

(C) BUDGET NEUTRALITY REQUIREMENT.—In conducting the demonstration program under this section, the Secretary shall ensure that the aggregate payments made by the Secretary do not exceed the amount which the Secretary would have paid if the demonstration program under this section was not implemented.

(D) REPORT.—Not later than 18 months after the completion of the demonstration program under this paragraph, the Secretary shall submit to Congress a report on the demonstration program together with—

(i) recommendations on the establishment of a permanent value-based purchasing program under the Medicare program for critical access hospitals with respect to inpatient critical access hospital services; and

(ii) recommendations for such other legislation and administrative action as the Secretary determines appropriate.

(2) VALUE-BASED PURCHASING DEMONSTRATION PROGRAM FOR HOSPITALS EXCLUDED FROM HOSPITAL VALUE-BASED PURCHASING PROGRAM AS A RESULT OF INSUFFICIENT NUMBERS OF MEASURES AND CASES.—

(A) ESTABLISHMENT.—

(i) IN GENERAL.—Not later than 2 years after the date of enactment of this Act, the Secretary shall establish a demonstration program under which the Secretary establishes a value-based purchasing program under the Medicare program under title XVIII of the Social Security Act for applicable hospitals (as defined in clause (ii)) with respect to inpatient hospital services (as defined in section 1861(b) of the Social Security Act (42 U.S.C. 1395x(b))) in order to test innovative methods of measuring and rewarding quality and efficient health care furnished by such hospitals.

(ii) APPLICABLE HOSPITAL DEFINED.—For purposes of this paragraph, the term "applicable hospital" means a hospital described in subclause (III) or (IV) of section 1886(o)(1)(C)(ii) of the Social Security Act, as added by subsection (a)(1).

(iii) DURATION.—The demonstration program under this paragraph shall be conducted for a 3-year period.

(iv) SITES.—The Secretary shall conduct the demonstration program under this paragraph at an appropriate number (as determined by the Secretary) of applicable hospitals. The Secretary shall ensure that such hospitals are representative of the spectrum of such hospitals that participate in the Medicare program.

(B) WAIVER AUTHORITY.—The Secretary may waive such requirements of titles XI and XVIII of the Social Security Act as may be necessary to carry out the demonstration program under this paragraph.

(C) BUDGET NEUTRALITY REQUIREMENT.—In conducting the demonstration program under this section, the Secretary shall ensure that the aggregate payments made by the Secretary do not exceed the amount which the Secretary would have paid if the demonstration program under this section was not implemented.

(D) REPORT.—Not later than 18 months after the completion of the demonstration program under this paragraph, the Secretary shall submit to Congress a report on the demonstration program together with—

(i) recommendations on the establishment of a permanent value-based purchasing program under the Medicare program for applicable hospitals with respect to inpatient hospital services; and

(ii) recommendations for such other legislation and administrative action as the Secretary determines appropriate.

SEC. 3002. IMPROVEMENTS TO THE PHYSICIAN QUALITY REPORTING SYSTEM.

(a) EXTENSION.—Section 1848(m) of the Social Security Act (42 U.S.C. 1395w–4(m)) is amended—

(1) in paragraph (1)—

(A) in subparagraph (A), in the matter preceding clause (i), by striking "2010" and inserting "2014"; and

(B) in subparagraph (B)—

(i) in clause (i), by striking "and" at the end;

(ii) in clause (ii), by striking the period at the end and inserting a semicolon; and

(iii) by adding at the end the following new clauses:

"(iii) for 2011, 1.0 percent; and

"(iv) for 2012, 2013, and 2014, 0.5 percent.";

(2) in paragraph (3)—

(A) in subparagraph (A), in the matter preceding clause (i), by inserting "(or, for purposes of subsection (a)(8), for the quality reporting period for the year)" after "reporting period"; and

(B) in subparagraph (C)(i), by inserting ", or, for purposes of subsection (a)(8), for a quality reporting period for the year" after "(a)(5), for a reporting period for a year";

(3) in paragraph (5)(E)(iv), by striking "subsection (a)(5)(A)" and inserting "paragraphs (5)(A) and (8)(A) of subsection (a)"; and

(4) in paragraph (6)(C)—

(A) in clause (i)(II), by striking ", 2009, 2010, and 2011" and inserting "and subsequent years"; and

(B) in clause (iii)—

(i) by inserting "(a)(8)" after "(a)(5)"; and

(ii) by striking "under subparagraph (D)(iii) of such subsection" and inserting "under subsection (a)(5)(D)(iii) or the quality reporting period under subsection (a)(8)(D)(iii), respectively".

(b) INCENTIVE PAYMENT ADJUSTMENT FOR QUALITY REPORTING.—Section 1848(a) of the Social Security Act (42 U.S.C. 1395w–4(a)) is amended by adding at the end the following new paragraph:

"(8) INCENTIVES FOR QUALITY REPORTING.—

"(A) ADJUSTMENT.—

"(i) IN GENERAL.—With respect to covered professional services furnished by an eligible professional during 2015 or any subsequent year, if the eligible professional does not satisfactorily submit data on quality measures for covered professional services for the quality reporting period for the year (as determined under subsection (m)(3)(A)), the fee schedule amount for such services furnished by such professional during the year (including the fee schedule amount for purposes of determining a payment based on such amount) shall be equal to the applicable percent of the fee schedule amount that would otherwise apply to such services under this subsection (determined after application of paragraphs (3), (5), and (7), but without regard to this paragraph).

"(ii) APPLICABLE PERCENT.—For purposes of clause (i), the term 'applicable percent' means—

"(I) for 2015, 98.5 percent; and

"(II) for 2016 and each subsequent year, 98 percent.

"(B) APPLICATION.—

"(i) PHYSICIAN REPORTING SYSTEM RULES.—Paragraphs (5), (6), and (8) of subsection (k) shall apply for purposes of this paragraph in the same manner as they apply for purposes of such subsection.

"(ii) INCENTIVE PAYMENT VALIDATION RULES.—Clauses (ii) and (iii) of subsection (m)(5)(D) shall apply for purposes of this paragraph in a similar manner as they apply for purposes of such subsection.

"(C) DEFINITIONS.—For purposes of this paragraph:

"(i) ELIGIBLE PROFESSIONAL; COVERED PROFESSIONAL SERVICES.—The terms 'eligible professional' and 'covered professional services' have the meanings given such terms in subsection (k)(3).

"(ii) PHYSICIAN REPORTING SYSTEM.—The term 'physician reporting system' means the system established under subsection (k).

"(iii) QUALITY REPORTING PERIOD.—The term 'quality reporting period' means, with respect to a year, a period specified by the Secretary.".

(c) MAINTENANCE OF CERTIFICATION PROGRAMS.—

(1) IN GENERAL.—Section 1848(k)(4) of the Social Security Act (42 U.S.C. 1395w–4(k)(4)) is amended by inserting "or through a Maintenance of Certification program operated by a specialty body of the American Board of Medical Specialties that meets the criteria for such a registry" after "Database)".

(2) EFFECTIVE DATE.—The amendment made by paragraph (1) shall apply for years after 2010.

(d) INTEGRATION OF PHYSICIAN QUALITY REPORTING AND EHR REPORTING.—Section 1848(m) of the Social Security Act (42 U.S.C. 1395w–4(m)) is amended by adding at the end the following new paragraph:

"(7) INTEGRATION OF PHYSICIAN QUALITY REPORTING AND EHR REPORTING.—Not later than January 1, 2012, the Secretary shall develop a plan to integrate reporting on quality measures under this subsection with reporting requirements under subsection (o) relating to the meaningful use of electronic health records. Such integration shall consist of the following:

"(A) The selection of measures, the reporting of which would both demonstrate—

"(i) meaningful use of an electronic health record for purposes of subsection (o); and

"(ii) quality of care furnished to an individual.

"(B) Such other activities as specified by the Secretary.".

(e) FEEDBACK.—Section 1848(m)(5) of the Social Security Act (42 U.S.C. 1395w–4(m)(5)) is amended by adding at the end the following new subparagraph:

"(H) FEEDBACK.—The Secretary shall provide timely feedback to eligible professionals on the performance of the eligible professional with respect to satisfactorily submitting data on quality measures under this subsection.".

(f) APPEALS.—Such section is further amended—

(1) in subparagraph (E), by striking "There shall" and inserting "Except as provided in subparagraph (I), there shall"; and

(2) by adding at the end the following new subparagraph:

"(I) INFORMAL APPEALS PROCESS.—The Secretary shall, by not later than January 1, 2011, establish and have in place an informal process for eligible professionals to seek a review of the determination that an eligible professional did not satisfactorily submit data on quality measures under this subsection.".

SEC. 3003. IMPROVEMENTS TO THE PHYSICIAN FEEDBACK PROGRAM.

(a) IN GENERAL.—Section 1848(n) of the Social Security Act (42 U.S.C. 1395w–4(n)) is amended—

(1) in paragraph (1)—

(A) in subparagraph (A)—

(i) by striking "GENERAL.—The Secretary" and inserting "GENERAL.—

"(i) ESTABLISHMENT.—The Secretary";

(ii) in clause (i), as added by clause (i), by striking "the 'Program')" and all that follows through the period at the end of the second sentence and inserting "the 'Program')."; and

(iii) by adding at the end the following new clauses:

"(ii) REPORTS ON RESOURCES.—The Secretary shall use claims data under this title (and may use other data) to provide confidential reports to physicians (and, as determined appropriate by the Secretary, to groups of physicians) that measure the resources involved in furnishing care to individuals under this title.

"(iii) INCLUSION OF CERTAIN INFORMATION.—If determined appropriate by the Secretary, the Secretary may include information on the quality of care furnished to individuals under this title by the physician (or group of physicians) in such reports."; and

(B) in subparagraph (B), by striking "subparagraph (A)" and inserting "subparagraph (A)(ii)";

(2) in paragraph (4)—

(A) in the heading, by inserting "INITIAL" after "FOCUS"; and

(B) in the matter preceding subparagraph (A), by inserting "initial" after "focus the";

(3) in paragraph (6), by adding at the end the following new sentence: "For adjustments for reports on utilization under paragraph (9), see subparagraph (D) of such paragraph."; and

(4) by adding at the end the following new paragraphs:

"(9) REPORTS ON UTILIZATION.—

"(A) DEVELOPMENT OF EPISODE GROUPER.—

"(i) IN GENERAL.—The Secretary shall develop an episode grouper that combines separate but clinically related items and services into an episode of care for an individual, as appropriate.

"(ii) TIMELINE FOR DEVELOPMENT.—The episode grouper described in subparagraph (A) shall be developed by not later than January 1, 2012.

"(iii) PUBLIC AVAILABILITY.—The Secretary shall make the details of the episode grouper described in subparagraph (A) available to the public.

"(iv) ENDORSEMENT.—The Secretary shall seek endorsement of the episode grouper described in subparagraph (A) by the entity with a contract under section 1890(a).

"(B) REPORTS ON UTILIZATION.—Effective beginning with 2012, the Secretary shall provide reports to physicians that compare, as determined appropriate by the Secretary, patterns of resource use of the individual physician to such patterns of other physicians.

"(C) ANALYSIS OF DATA.—The Secretary shall, for purposes of preparing reports under this paragraph, establish methodologies as appropriate, such as to—

"(i) attribute episodes of care, in whole or in part, to physicians;

"(ii) identify appropriate physicians for purposes of comparison under subparagraph (B); and

"(iii) aggregate episodes of care attributed to a physician under clause (i) into a composite measure per individual.

"(D) DATA ADJUSTMENT.—In preparing reports under this paragraph, the Secretary shall make appropriate adjustments, including adjustments—

"(i) to account for differences in socioeconomic and demographic characteristics, ethnicity, and health status of individuals (such as to recognize that less healthy individuals may require more intensive interventions); and

"(ii) to eliminate the effect of geographic adjustments in payment rates (as described in subsection (e)).

"(E) PUBLIC AVAILABILITY OF METHODOLOGY.—The Secretary shall make available to the public—

"(i) the methodologies established under subparagraph (C);

"(ii) information regarding any adjustments made to data under subparagraph (D); and

"(iii) aggregate reports with respect to physicians.

"(F) DEFINITION OF PHYSICIAN.—In this paragraph:

"(i) IN GENERAL.—The term 'physician' has the meaning given that term in section 1861(r)(1).

"(ii) TREATMENT OF GROUPS.—Such term includes, as the Secretary determines appropriate, a group of physicians.

"(G) LIMITATIONS ON REVIEW.—There shall be no administrative or judicial review under section 1869, section 1878, or otherwise of the establishment of the methodology under subparagraph (C), including the determination of an episode of care under such methodology.

"(10) COORDINATION WITH OTHER VALUE-BASED PURCHASING REFORMS.—The Secretary shall coordinate the Program with the value-based payment modifier established under subsection (p) and, as the Secretary determines appropriate, other similar provisions of this title.".

(b) CONFORMING AMENDMENT.—Section 1890(b) of the Social Security Act (42 U.S.C. 1395aaa(b)) is amended by adding at the end the following new paragraph:

"(6) REVIEW AND ENDORSEMENT OF EPISODE GROUPER UNDER THE PHYSICIAN FEEDBACK PROGRAM.—The entity shall provide for the review and, as appropriate, the endorsement of the episode grouper developed by the Secretary under section 1848(n)(9)(A). Such review shall be conducted on an expedited basis.".

SEC. 3004. QUALITY REPORTING FOR LONG-TERM CARE HOSPITALS, INPATIENT REHABILITATION HOSPITALS, AND HOSPICE PROGRAMS.

(a) LONG-TERM CARE HOSPITALS.—Section 1886(m) of the Social Security Act (42 U.S.C. 1395ww(m)), as amended by section 3401(c), is amended by adding at the end the following new paragraph:

"(5) QUALITY REPORTING.—

"(A) REDUCTION IN UPDATE FOR FAILURE TO REPORT.—

"(i) IN GENERAL.—Under the system described in paragraph (1), for rate year 2014 and each subsequent rate year, in the case of a long-term care hospital that does not submit data to the Secretary in accordance with subparagraph (C) with respect to such a rate year, any annual update to a standard Federal rate for discharges for the hospital during the rate year, and after application of paragraph (3), shall be reduced by 2 percentage points.

"(ii) SPECIAL RULE.—The application of this subparagraph may result in such annual update being less than 0.0 for a rate year, and may result in payment rates under the system described in paragraph (1) for a rate year being less than such payment rates for the preceding rate year.

"(B) NONCUMULATIVE APPLICATION.—Any reduction under subparagraph (A) shall apply only with respect to the rate year involved and the Secretary shall not take into account such reduction in computing the payment amount under the system described in paragraph (1) for a subsequent rate year.

"(C) SUBMISSION OF QUALITY DATA.—For rate year 2014 and each subsequent rate year, each long-term care hospital shall submit to the Secretary data on quality measures specified under subparagraph (D). Such data shall be submitted in a form and manner, and at a time, specified by the Secretary for purposes of this subparagraph.

"(D) QUALITY MEASURES.—

"(i) IN GENERAL.—Subject to clause (ii), any measure specified by the Secretary under this subparagraph must have been endorsed by the entity with a contract under section 1890(a).

"(ii) EXCEPTION.—In the case of a specified area or medical topic determined appropriate by the Secretary for which a feasible and practical measure has not been endorsed by the entity with a contract under section 1890(a), the Secretary may specify a measure that is not so endorsed as long as due consideration is given to measures that have been endorsed or adopted by a consensus organization identified by the Secretary.

"(iii) TIME FRAME.—Not later than October 1, 2012, the Secretary shall publish the measures selected under this subparagraph that will be applicable with respect to rate year 2014.

"(E) PUBLIC AVAILABILITY OF DATA SUBMITTED.—The Secretary shall establish procedures for making data submitted under subparagraph (C) available to the public. Such procedures shall ensure that a long-term care hospital has the opportunity to review the data that is to be made public with respect to the hospital prior to such data being made public. The Secretary shall report quality measures that relate to services furnished in inpatient settings in long-term care hospitals on the Internet website of the Centers for Medicare & Medicaid Services.".

(b) INPATIENT REHABILITATION HOSPITALS.—Section 1886(j) of the Social Security Act (42 U.S.C. 1395ww(j)) is amended—

(1) by redesignating paragraph (7) as paragraph (8); and

(2) by inserting after paragraph (6) the following new paragraph:

"(7) QUALITY REPORTING.—

"(A) REDUCTION IN UPDATE FOR FAILURE TO REPORT.—

"(i) IN GENERAL.—For purposes of fiscal year 2014 and each subsequent fiscal year, in the case of a rehabilitation facility that does not submit data to the Secretary in accordance with subparagraph (C) with respect to such a fiscal year, after determining the increase factor described in paragraph (3)(C), and after application of paragraph (3)(D), the Secretary shall reduce such increase factor for payments for discharges occurring during such fiscal year by 2 percentage points.

"(ii) SPECIAL RULE.—The application of this subparagraph may result in the increase factor described in paragraph (3)(C) being less than 0.0 for a fiscal year, and may result in payment rates under this subsection for a fiscal year being less than such payment rates for the preceding fiscal year.

"(B) NONCUMULATIVE APPLICATION.—Any reduction under subparagraph (A) shall apply only with respect to the fiscal year involved and the Secretary shall not take into account such reduction in computing the payment amount under this subsection for a subsequent fiscal year.

"(C) SUBMISSION OF QUALITY DATA.—For fiscal year 2014 and each subsequent rate year, each rehabilitation facility shall submit to the Secretary data on quality measures specified under subparagraph (D). Such data shall be submitted in a form and manner, and at a time, specified by the Secretary for purposes of this subparagraph.

"(D) QUALITY MEASURES.—

"(i) IN GENERAL.—Subject to clause (ii), any measure specified by the Secretary under this subparagraph must have been endorsed by the entity with a contract under section 1890(a).

"(ii) EXCEPTION.—In the case of a specified area or medical topic determined appropriate by the Secretary for which a feasible and practical measure has not been endorsed by the entity with a contract under section 1890(a), the Secretary may specify a measure that is not so endorsed as long as due consideration is given to measures that have been endorsed or adopted by a consensus organization identified by the Secretary.

"(iii) TIME FRAME.—Not later than October 1, 2012, the Secretary shall publish the measures selected under this subparagraph that will be applicable with respect to fiscal year 2014.

"(E) PUBLIC AVAILABILITY OF DATA SUBMITTED.—The Secretary shall establish procedures for making data submitted under subparagraph (C) available to the public. Such procedures shall ensure that a rehabilitation facility has the opportunity to review the data that is to be made public with respect to the facility prior to such data being made public. The Secretary shall report quality measures that relate to services furnished in inpatient settings in rehabilitation facilities on the Internet website of the Centers for Medicare & Medicaid Services.".

(c) HOSPICE PROGRAMS.—Section 1814(i) of the Social Security Act (42 U.S.C. 1395f(i)) is amended—

(1) by redesignating paragraph (5) as paragraph (6); and

(2) by inserting after paragraph (4) the following new paragraph:

"(5) QUALITY REPORTING.—

"(A) REDUCTION IN UPDATE FOR FAILURE TO REPORT.—

"(i) IN GENERAL.—For purposes of fiscal year 2014 and each subsequent fiscal year, in the case of a hospice program that does not submit data to the Secretary in accordance with subparagraph (C) with respect to such a fiscal year, after determining the market basket percentage increase under paragraph (1)(C)(ii)(VII) or paragraph (1)(C)(iii), as applicable, and after application of paragraph (1)(C)(iv), with respect to the fiscal year, the Secretary shall reduce such market basket percentage increase by 2 percentage points.

"(ii) SPECIAL RULE.—The application of this subparagraph may result in the market basket percentage increase under paragraph (1)(C)(ii)(VII) or paragraph (1)(C)(iii), as applicable, being less than 0.0 for a fiscal year, and may result in payment rates under this subsection for a fiscal year being less than such payment rates for the preceding fiscal year.

"(B) NONCUMULATIVE APPLICATION.—Any reduction under subparagraph (A) shall apply only with respect to the fiscal year involved and the Secretary shall not take into account such reduction in computing the payment amount under this subsection for a subsequent fiscal year.

"(C) SUBMISSION OF QUALITY DATA.—For fiscal year 2014 and each subsequent fiscal year, each hospice program shall submit to the Secretary data on quality measures specified under subparagraph (D). Such data shall be submitted in a form and manner, and at a time, specified by the Secretary for purposes of this subparagraph.

"(D) QUALITY MEASURES.—

"(i) IN GENERAL.—Subject to clause (ii), any measure specified by the Secretary under this subparagraph must have been endorsed by the entity with a contract under section 1890(a).

"(ii) EXCEPTION.—In the case of a specified area or medical topic determined appropriate by the Secretary for which a feasible and practical measure has not been endorsed by the entity with a contract under section 1890(a), the Secretary may specify a measure that is not so endorsed as long as due consideration is given to measures that have been endorsed or adopted by a consensus organization identified by the Secretary.

"(iii) TIME FRAME.—Not later than October 1, 2012, the Secretary shall publish the measures selected under this subparagraph that will be applicable with respect to fiscal year 2014.

"(E) PUBLIC AVAILABILITY OF DATA SUBMITTED.—The Secretary shall establish procedures for making data submitted under subparagraph (C) available to the public. Such procedures shall ensure that a hospice program has the opportunity to review the data that is to be made public with respect to the hospice program prior to such data being made public. The Secretary shall report quality measures that relate to hospice care provided by hospice programs on the Internet website of the Centers for Medicare & Medicaid Services.".

SEC. 3005. QUALITY REPORTING FOR PPS-EXEMPT CANCER HOSPITALS.

Section 1866 of the Social Security Act (42 U.S.C. 1395cc) is amended—

(1) in subsection (a)(1)—

(A) in subparagraph (U), by striking "and" at the end;

(B) in subparagraph (V), by striking the period at the end and inserting ", and"; and

(C) by adding at the end the following new subparagraph:

"(W) in the case of a hospital described in section 1886(d)(1)(B)(v), to report quality data to the Secretary in accordance with subsection (k)."; and

(2) by adding at the end the following new subsection:

"(k) QUALITY REPORTING BY CANCER HOSPITALS.—

"(1) IN GENERAL.—For purposes of fiscal year 2014 and each subsequent fiscal year, a hospital described in section 1886(d)(1)(B)(v) shall submit data to the Secretary in accordance with paragraph (2) with respect to such a fiscal year.

"(2) SUBMISSION OF QUALITY DATA.—For fiscal year 2014 and each subsequent fiscal year, each hospital described in such section shall submit to the Secretary data on quality measures specified under paragraph (3). Such data shall be submitted in a form and manner, and at a time, specified by the Secretary for purposes of this subparagraph.

"(3) QUALITY MEASURES.—

"(A) IN GENERAL.—Subject to subparagraph (B), any measure specified by the Secretary under this paragraph must have been endorsed by the entity with a contract under section 1890(a).

"(B) EXCEPTION.—In the case of a specified area or medical topic determined appropriate by the Secretary for which a feasible and practical measure has not been endorsed by the entity with a contract under section 1890(a), the Secretary may specify a measure that is not so endorsed as long as due consideration is given to measures that have been endorsed or adopted by a consensus organization identified by the Secretary.

"(C) TIME FRAME.—Not later than October 1, 2012, the Secretary shall publish the measures selected under this paragraph that will be applicable with respect to fiscal year 2014.

"(4) PUBLIC AVAILABILITY OF DATA SUBMITTED.—The Secretary shall establish procedures for making data submitted under paragraph (4) available to the public. Such procedures shall ensure that a hospital described in section 1886(d)(1)(B)(v) has the opportunity to review the data that is to be made public with respect to the hospital prior to such data being made public. The Secretary shall report quality measures of process, structure, outcome, patients' perspective on care, efficiency, and costs of care that relate to services furnished in such hospitals on the Internet website of the Centers for Medicare & Medicaid Services.".

SEC. 3006. PLANS FOR A VALUE-BASED PURCHASING PROGRAM FOR SKILLED NURSING FACILITIES AND HOME HEALTH AGENCIES.

(a) SKILLED NURSING FACILITIES.—

(1) IN GENERAL.—The Secretary of Health and Human Services (in this section referred to as the "Secretary") shall develop a plan to implement a value-based purchasing program for payments under the Medicare program under title XVIII of the Social Security Act for skilled nursing facilities (as defined in section 1819(a) of such Act (42 U.S.C. 1395i–3(a))).

(2) DETAILS.—In developing the plan under paragraph (1), the Secretary shall consider the following issues:

(A) The ongoing development, selection, and modification process for measures (including under section 1890 of the Social Security Act (42 U.S.C. 1395aaa) and section 1890A such Act, as added by section 3014), to the extent feasible and practicable, of all dimensions of quality and efficiency in skilled nursing facilities.

(i) IN GENERAL.—Subject to clause (ii), any measure specified by the Secretary under subparagraph (A)(iii) must have been endorsed by the entity with a contract under section 1890(a).

(ii) EXCEPTION.—In the case of a specified area or medical topic determined appropriate by the Secretary for which a feasible and practical measure has not been endorsed by the entity with a contract under section 1890(a), the Secretary may specify a measure that is not so endorsed as long as due consideration is given to measures that have been endorsed or adopted by a consensus organization identified by the Secretary.

(B) The reporting, collection, and validation of quality data.

(C) The structure of value-based payment adjustments, including the determination of thresholds or improvements in quality that would substantiate a payment adjustment, the size of such payments, and the sources of funding for the value-based bonus payments.

(D) Methods for the public disclosure of information on the performance of skilled nursing facilities.

(E) Any other issues determined appropriate by the Secretary.

(3) CONSULTATION.—In developing the plan under paragraph (1), the Secretary shall—

(A) consult with relevant affected parties; and

(B) consider experience with such demonstrations that the Secretary determines are relevant to the value-based purchasing program described in paragraph (1).

(4) REPORT TO CONGRESS.—Not later than October 1, 2011, the Secretary shall submit to Congress a report containing the plan developed under paragraph (1).

(b) HOME HEALTH AGENCIES.—

(1) IN GENERAL.—The Secretary of Health and Human Services (in this section referred to as the "Secretary") shall develop a plan to implement a value-based purchasing program for payments under the Medicare program under title XVIII of the Social Security Act for home health agencies (as defined in section 1861(o) of such Act (42 U.S.C. 1395x(o))).

(2) DETAILS.—In developing the plan under paragraph (1), the Secretary shall consider the following issues:

(A) The ongoing development, selection, and modification process for measures (including under section 1890 of the Social Security Act (42 U.S.C. 1395aaa) and section 1890A such Act, as added by section 3014), to the extent feasible and practicable, of all dimensions of quality and efficiency in home health agencies.

(B) The reporting, collection, and validation of quality data.

(C) The structure of value-based payment adjustments, including the determination of thresholds or improvements in quality that would substantiate a payment adjustment, the size of such payments, and the sources of funding for the value-based bonus payments.

(D) Methods for the public disclosure of information on the performance of home health agencies.

(E) Any other issues determined appropriate by the Secretary.

(3) CONSULTATION.—In developing the plan under paragraph (1), the Secretary shall—

(A) consult with relevant affected parties; and

(B) consider experience with such demonstrations that the Secretary determines are relevant to the value-based purchasing program described in paragraph (1).

(4) REPORT TO CONGRESS.—Not later than October 1, 2011, the Secretary shall submit to Congress a report containing the plan developed under paragraph (1).

SEC. 3007. VALUE-BASED PAYMENT MODIFIER UNDER THE PHYSICIAN FEE SCHEDULE.

Section 1848 of the Social Security Act (42 U.S.C. 1395w–4) is amended—

(1) in subsection (b)(1), by inserting "subject to subsection (p)," after "1998,"; and

(2) by adding at the end the following new subsection:

"(p) ESTABLISHMENT OF VALUE-BASED PAYMENT MODIFIER.—

"(1) IN GENERAL.—The Secretary shall establish a payment modifier that provides for differential payment to a physician or a group of physicians under the fee schedule established under subsection (b) based upon the quality of care furnished compared to cost (as determined under paragraphs (2) and (3), respectively) during a performance period. Such payment modifier shall be separate from the geographic adjustment factors established under subsection (e).

"(2) QUALITY.—

"(A) IN GENERAL.—For purposes of paragraph (1), quality of care shall be evaluated, to the extent practicable, based on a composite of measures of the quality of care furnished (as established by the Secretary under subparagraph (B)).

"(B) MEASURES.—

"(i) The Secretary shall establish appropriate measures of the quality of care furnished by a physician or group of physicians to individuals enrolled under this part, such as measures that reflect health outcomes. Such measures shall be risk adjusted as determined appropriate by the Secretary.

"(ii) The Secretary shall seek endorsement of the measures established under this subparagraph by the entity with a contract under section 1890(a).

"(3) COSTS.—For purposes of paragraph (1), costs shall be evaluated, to the extent practicable, based on a composite of appropriate measures of costs established by the Secretary (such as the composite measure under the methodology established under subsection (n)(9)(C)(iii)) that eliminate the effect of geographic adjustments in payment rates (as described in subsection (e)), and take into account risk factors (such as socioeconomic and demographic characteristics, ethnicity, and health status of individuals (such as to recognize that less healthy individuals may require more intensive interventions) and other factors determined appropriate by the Secretary.

"(4) IMPLEMENTATION.—

"(A) PUBLICATION OF MEASURES, DATES OF IMPLEMENTATION, PERFORMANCE PERIOD.—Not later than January 1, 2012, the Secretary shall publish the following:

"(i) The measures of quality of care and costs established under paragraphs (2) and (3), respectively.

"(ii) The dates for implementation of the payment modifier (as determined under subparagraph (B)).

"(iii) The initial performance period (as specified under subparagraph (B)(ii)).

"(B) DEADLINES FOR IMPLEMENTATION.—

"(i) INITIAL IMPLEMENTATION.—Subject to the preceding provisions of this subparagraph, the Secretary shall begin implementing the payment modifier established under this subsection through the rulemaking process during 2013 for the physician fee schedule established under subsection (b).

"(ii) INITIAL PERFORMANCE PERIOD.—

"(I) IN GENERAL.—The Secretary shall specify an initial performance period for application of the payment modifier established under this subsection with respect to 2015.

"(II) PROVISION OF INFORMATION DURING INITIAL PERFORMANCE PERIOD.—During the initial performance period, the Secretary shall, to the extent practicable, provide information to physicians and groups of physicians about the quality of care furnished by the physician or group of physicians to individuals enrolled under this part compared to cost (as determined under paragraphs (2) and (3), respectively) with respect to the performance period.

"(iii) APPLICATION.—The Secretary shall apply the payment modifier established under this subsection for items and services furnished—

"(I) beginning on January 1, 2015, with respect to specific physicians and groups of physicians the Secretary determines appropriate; and

"(II) beginning not later than January 1, 2017, with respect to all physicians and groups of physicians.

"(C) BUDGET NEUTRALITY.—The payment modifier established under this subsection shall be implemented in a budget neutral manner.

"(5) SYSTEMS-BASED CARE.—The Secretary shall, as appropriate, apply the payment modifier established under this subsection in a manner that promotes systems-based care.

"(6) CONSIDERATION OF SPECIAL CIRCUMSTANCES OF CERTAIN PROVIDERS.—In applying the payment modifier under this subsection, the Secretary shall, as appropriate, take into account the special circumstances of physicians or groups of physicians in rural areas and other underserved communities.

"(7) APPLICATION.—For purposes of the initial application of the payment modifier established under this subsection during the period beginning on January 1, 2015, and ending on December 31, 2016, the term 'physician' has the meaning given such term in section 1861(r). On or after January 1, 2017, the Secretary may apply this subsection to eligible professionals (as defined in subsection (k)(3)(B)) as the Secretary determines appropriate.

"(8) DEFINITIONS.—For purposes of this subsection:

"(A) COSTS.—The term 'costs' means expenditures per individual as determined appropriate by the Secretary. In making the determination under the preceding sentence, the Secretary may take into account the amount of growth in expenditures per individual for a physician compared to the amount of such growth for other physicians.

"(B) PERFORMANCE PERIOD.—The term 'performance period' means a period specified by the Secretary.

"(9) COORDINATION WITH OTHER VALUE-BASED PURCHASING REFORMS.—The Secretary shall coordinate the value-based payment modifier established under this subsection with the Physician Feedback Program under subsection (n) and, as the Secretary determines appropriate, other similar provisions of this title.

"(10) LIMITATIONS ON REVIEW.—There shall be no administrative or judicial review under section 1869, section 1878, or otherwise of—

"(A) the establishment of the value-based payment modifier under this subsection;

"(B) the evaluation of quality of care under paragraph (2), including the establishment of appropriate measures of the quality of care under paragraph (2)(B);

"(C) the evaluation of costs under paragraph (3), including the establishment of appropriate measures of costs under such paragraph;

"(D) the dates for implementation of the value-based payment modifier;

"(E) the specification of the initial performance period and any other performance period under paragraphs (4)(B)(ii) and (8)(B), respectively;

"(F) the application of the value-based payment modifier under paragraph (7); and

"(G) the determination of costs under paragraph (8)(A).".

SEC. 3008. PAYMENT ADJUSTMENT FOR CONDITIONS ACQUIRED IN HOSPITALS.

(a) IN GENERAL.—Section 1886 of the Social Security Act (42 U.S.C. 1395ww), as amended by section 3001, is amended by adding at the end the following new subsection:

"(p) ADJUSTMENT TO HOSPITAL PAYMENTS FOR HOSPITAL ACQUIRED CONDITIONS.—

"(1) IN GENERAL.—In order to provide an incentive for applicable hospitals to reduce hospital acquired conditions under this title, with respect to discharges from an applicable hospital occurring during fiscal year 2015 or a subsequent fiscal year, the amount of payment under this section or section 1814(b)(3), as applicable, for such discharges during the fiscal year shall be equal to 99 percent of the amount of payment that would otherwise apply to such discharges under this section or section 1814(b)(3) (determined after the application of subsections (o) and (q) and section 1814(l)(4) but without regard to this subsection).

"(2) APPLICABLE HOSPITALS.—

"(A) IN GENERAL.—For purposes of this subsection, the term 'applicable hospital' means a subsection (d) hospital that meets the criteria described in subparagraph (B).

"(B) CRITERIA DESCRIBED.—

"(i) IN GENERAL.—The criteria described in this subparagraph, with respect to a subsection (d) hospital, is that the subsection (d) hospital is in the top quartile of all subsection (d) hospitals, relative to the national average, of hospital acquired conditions during the applicable period, as determined by the Secretary.

"(ii) RISK ADJUSTMENT.—In carrying out clause (i), the Secretary shall establish and apply an appropriate risk adjustment methodology.

"(C) EXEMPTION.—In the case of a hospital that is paid under section 1814(b)(3), the Secretary may exempt such hospital from the application of this subsection if the State which is paid under such section submits an annual report to the Secretary describing how a similar program in the State for a participating hospital or hospitals achieves or surpasses the measured results in terms of patient health outcomes and cost savings established under this subsection.

"(3) HOSPITAL ACQUIRED CONDITIONS.—For purposes of this subsection, the term 'hospital acquired condition' means a condition identified for purposes of subsection (d)(4)(D)(iv) and any other condition determined appropriate by the Secretary that an individual acquires during a stay in an applicable hospital, as determined by the Secretary.

"(4) APPLICABLE PERIOD.—In this subsection, the term 'applicable period' means, with respect to a fiscal year, a period specified by the Secretary.

"(5) REPORTING TO HOSPITALS.—Prior to fiscal year 2015 and each subsequent fiscal year, the Secretary shall provide confidential reports to applicable hospitals with respect to hospital acquired conditions of the applicable hospital during the applicable period.

"(6) REPORTING HOSPITAL SPECIFIC INFORMATION.—

"(A) IN GENERAL.—The Secretary shall make information available to the public regarding hospital acquired conditions of each applicable hospital.

"(B) OPPORTUNITY TO REVIEW AND SUBMIT CORRECTIONS.—The Secretary shall ensure that an applicable hospital has the opportunity to review, and submit corrections for, the information to be made public with respect to the hospital under subparagraph (A) prior to such information being made public.

"(C) WEBSITE.—Such information shall be posted on the Hospital Compare Internet website in an easily understandable format.

"(7) LIMITATIONS ON REVIEW.—There shall be no administrative or judicial review under section 1869, section 1878, or otherwise of the following:

"(A) The criteria described in paragraph (2)(A).

"(B) The specification of hospital acquired conditions under paragraph (3).

"(C) The specification of the applicable period under paragraph (4).

"(D) The provision of reports to applicable hospitals under paragraph (5) and the information made available to the public under paragraph (6).".

(b) STUDY AND REPORT ON EXPANSION OF HEALTHCARE ACQUIRED CONDITIONS POLICY TO OTHER PROVIDERS.—

(1) STUDY.—The Secretary of Health and Human Services shall conduct a study on expanding the healthcare acquired conditions policy under subsection (d)(4)(D) of section 1886 of the Social Security Act (42 U.S.C. 1395ww) to payments made to other facilities under the Medicare program under title XVIII of the Social Security Act, including such payments made to inpatient rehabilitation facilities, long-term care hospitals (as described in subsection(d)(1)(B)(iv) of such section), hospital outpatient departments, and other hospitals excluded from the inpatient prospective payment system under such section, skilled nursing facilities, ambulatory surgical centers, and health clinics. Such study shall include an analysis of

how such policies could impact quality of patient care, patient safety, and spending under the Medicare program.

(2) REPORT.—Not later than January 1, 2012, the Secretary shall submit to Congress a report containing the results of the study conducted under paragraph (1), together with recommendations for such legislation and administrative action as the Secretary determines appropriate.

PART II—NATIONAL STRATEGY TO IMPROVE HEALTH CARE QUALITY

SEC. 3011. NATIONAL STRATEGY.

Title III of the Public Health Service Act (42 U.S.C. 241 et seq.) is amended by adding at the end the following:

"PART S—HEALTH CARE QUALITY PROGRAMS

"Subpart I—National Strategy for Quality Improvement in Health Care

"SEC. 399HH. NATIONAL STRATEGY FOR QUALITY IMPROVEMENT IN HEALTH CARE.

"(a) ESTABLISHMENT OF NATIONAL STRATEGY AND PRIORITIES.—

"(1) NATIONAL STRATEGY.—The Secretary, through a transparent collaborative process, shall establish a national strategy to improve the delivery of health care services, patient health outcomes, and population health.

"(2) IDENTIFICATION OF PRIORITIES.—

"(A) IN GENERAL.—The Secretary shall identify national priorities for improvement in developing the strategy under paragraph (1).

"(B) REQUIREMENTS.—The Secretary shall ensure that priorities identified under subparagraph (A) will—

"(i) have the greatest potential for improving the health outcomes, efficiency, and patient-centeredness of health care for all populations, including children and vulnerable populations;

"(ii) identify areas in the delivery of health care services that have the potential for rapid improvement in the quality and efficiency of patient care;

"(iii) address gaps in quality, efficiency, comparative effectiveness information, and health outcomes measures and data aggregation techniques;

"(iv) improve Federal payment policy to emphasize quality and efficiency;

"(v) enhance the use of health care data to improve quality, efficiency, transparency, and outcomes;

"(vi) address the health care provided to patients with high-cost chronic diseases;

"(vii) improve research and dissemination of strategies and best practices to improve patient safety and reduce medical errors, preventable admissions and readmissions, and health care-associated infections;

"(viii) reduce health disparities across health disparity populations (as defined in section 485E) and geographic areas; and "(ix) address other areas as determined appropriate by the Secretary.

"(C) CONSIDERATIONS.—In identifying priorities under subparagraph (A), the Secretary shall take into consideration the recommendations submitted by the entity with a contract under section 1890(a) of the Social Security Act and other stakeholders.

"(D) COORDINATION WITH STATE AGENCIES.—The Secretary shall collaborate, coordinate, and consult with State agencies responsible for administering the Medicaid program under title XIX of the Social Security Act and the Children's Health Insurance Program under title XXI of such Act with respect to developing and disseminating strategies, goals, models, and timetables that are consistent with the national priorities identified under subparagraph (A).

"(b) STRATEGIC PLAN.—

"(1) IN GENERAL.—The national strategy shall include a comprehensive strategic plan to achieve the priorities described in subsection (a).

"(2) REQUIREMENTS.—The strategic plan shall include provisions for addressing, at a minimum, the following:

"(A) Coordination among agencies within the Department, which shall include steps to minimize duplication of efforts and utilization of common quality measures, where available. Such common quality measures shall be measures identified by the Secretary under section 1139A or 1139B of the Social Security Act or endorsed under section 1890 of such Act.

"(B) Agency-specific strategic plans to achieve national priorities.

"(C) Establishment of annual benchmarks for each relevant agency to achieve national priorities.

"(D) A process for regular reporting by the agencies to the Secretary on the implementation of the strategic plan.

"(E) Strategies to align public and private payers with regard to quality and patient safety efforts.

"(F) Incorporating quality improvement and measurement in the strategic plan for health information technology required by the American Recovery and Reinvestment Act of 2009 (Public Law 111–5).

"(c) PERIODIC UPDATE OF NATIONAL STRATEGY.—The Secretary shall update the national strategy not less than annually. Any such update shall include a review of short- and long-term goals.

"(d) SUBMISSION AND AVAILABILITY OF NATIONAL STRATEGY AND UPDATES.—

"(1) DEADLINE FOR INITIAL SUBMISSION OF NATIONAL STRATEGY.—Not later than January 1, 2011, the Secretary shall submit to the relevant committees of Congress the national strategy described in subsection (a).

"(2) UPDATES.—

"(A) IN GENERAL.—The Secretary shall submit to the relevant committees of Congress an annual update to the strategy described in paragraph (1).

"(B) INFORMATION SUBMITTED.—Each update submitted under subparagraph (A) shall include—

"(i) a review of the short- and long-term goals of the national strategy and any gaps in such strategy;

"(ii) an analysis of the progress, or lack of progress, in meeting such goals and any barriers to such progress;

"(iii) the information reported under section 1139A of the Social Security Act, consistent with the reporting requirements of such section; and

"(iv) in the case of an update required to be submitted on or after January 1, 2014, the information reported under section 1139B(b)(4) of the Social Security Act, consistent with the reporting requirements of such section.

"(C) SATISFACTION OF OTHER REPORTING REQUIREMENTS.—Compliance with the requirements of clauses (iii) and (iv) of subparagraph (B) shall satisfy the reporting requirements under sections 1139A(a)(6) and 1139B(b)(4), respectively, of the Social Security Act.

"(e) HEALTH CARE QUALITY INTERNET WEBSITE.—Not later than January 1, 2011, the Secretary shall create an Internet website to make public information regarding—

"(1) the national priorities for health care quality improvement established under subsection (a)(2);

"(2) the agency-specific strategic plans for health care quality described in subsection (b)(2)(B); and

"(3) other information, as the Secretary determines to be appropriate.".

SEC. 3012. INTERAGENCY WORKING GROUP ON HEALTH CARE QUALITY.

(a) IN GENERAL.—The President shall convene a working group to be known as the Interagency Working Group on Health Care Quality (referred to in this section as the "Working Group").

(b) GOALS.—The goals of the Working Group shall be to achieve the following:

(1) Collaboration, cooperation, and consultation between Federal departments and agencies with respect to developing and disseminating strategies, goals, models, and timetables that are consistent with the national priorities identified under section 399HH(a)(2) of the Public Health Service Act (as added by section 3011).

(2) Avoidance of inefficient duplication of quality improvement efforts and resources, where practicable, and a streamlined process for quality reporting and compliance requirements.

(3) Assess alignment of quality efforts in the public sector with private sector initiatives.

(c) COMPOSITION.—

(1) IN GENERAL.—The Working Group shall be composed of senior level representatives of—

(A) the Department of Health and Human Services;

(B) the Centers for Medicare & Medicaid Services;

(C) the National Institutes of Health;

(D) the Centers for Disease Control and Prevention;

(E) the Food and Drug Administration;

(F) the Health Resources and Services Administration;

(G) the Agency for Healthcare Research and Quality;

(H) the Office of the National Coordinator for Health Information Technology;

(I) the Substance Abuse and Mental Health Services Administration;

(J) the Administration for Children and Families;

(K) the Department of Commerce;

(L) the Office of Management and Budget;

(M) the United States Coast Guard;

(N) the Federal Bureau of Prisons;

(O) the National Highway Traffic Safety Administration;

(P) the Federal Trade Commission;

(Q) the Social Security Administration;

(R) the Department of Labor;

(S) the United States Office of Personnel Management;

(T) the Department of Defense;

(U) the Department of Education;

(V) the Department of Veterans Affairs;

(W) the Veterans Health Administration; and

(X) any other Federal agencies and departments with activities relating to improving health care quality and safety, as determined by the President.

(2) CHAIR AND VICE-CHAIR.—

(A) CHAIR.—The Working Group shall be chaired by the Secretary of Health and Human Services.

(B) VICE CHAIR.—Members of the Working Group, other than the Secretary of Health and Human Services, shall serve as Vice Chair of the Group on a rotating basis, as determined by the Group.

(d) REPORT TO CONGRESS.—Not later than December 31, 2010, and annually thereafter, the Working Group shall submit to the relevant Committees of Congress, and make public on an Internet website, a report describing the progress and recommendations of the Working Group in meeting the goals described in subsection (b).

SEC. 3013. QUALITY MEASURE DEVELOPMENT.

(a) PUBLIC HEALTH SERVICE ACT.—Title IX of the Public Health Service Act (42 U.S.C. 299 et seq.) is amended—

(1) by redesignating part D as part E;

(2) by redesignating sections 931 through 938 as sections 941 through 948, respectively;

(3) in section 948(1), as so redesignated, by striking "931" and inserting "941"; and

(4) by inserting after section 926 the following:

"PART D—HEALTH CARE QUALITY IMPROVEMENT

"Subpart I—Quality Measure Development

"SEC. 931. QUALITY MEASURE DEVELOPMENT.

"(a) QUALITY MEASURE.—In this subpart, the term 'quality measure' means a standard for measuring the performance and improvement of population health or of health plans, providers of services, and other clinicians in the delivery of health care services.

"(b) IDENTIFICATION OF QUALITY MEASURES.—

"(1) IDENTIFICATION.—The Secretary, in consultation with the Director of the Agency for Healthcare Research and Quality and the Administrator of the Centers for Medicare & Medicaid Services, shall identify, not less often than triennially, gaps where no quality measures exist and existing quality measures that need improvement, updating, or expansion, consistent with the national strategy under section 399HH, to the extent available, for use in Federal health programs. In identifying such gaps and existing quality measures that need improvement, the Secretary shall take into consideration—

"(A) the gaps identified by the entity with a contract under section 1890(a) of the Social Security Act and other stakeholders;

"(B) quality measures identified by the pediatric quality measures program under section 1139A of the Social Security Act; and

"(C) quality measures identified through the Medicaid Quality Measurement Program under section 1139B of the Social Security Act.

"(2) PUBLICATION.—The Secretary shall make available to the public on an Internet website a report on any gaps identified under paragraph (1) and the process used to make such identification.

"(c) GRANTS OR CONTRACTS FOR QUALITY MEASURE DEVELOPMENT.—

"(1) IN GENERAL.—The Secretary shall award grants, contracts, or intergovernmental agreements to eligible entities for purposes of developing, improving, updating, or expanding quality measures identified under subsection (b).

"(2) PRIORITIZATION IN THE DEVELOPMENT OF QUALITY MEASURES.—In awarding grants, contracts, or agreements under this subsection, the Secretary shall give priority to the development of quality measures that allow the assessment of—

"(A) health outcomes and functional status of patients;

"(B) the management and coordination of health care across episodes of care and care transitions for patients across the continuum of providers, health care settings, and health plans;

"(C) the experience, quality, and use of information provided to and used by patients, caregivers, and authorized representatives to inform decisionmaking about treatment options, including the use of shared decisionmaking tools and preference sensitive care (as defined in section 936);

"(D) the meaningful use of health information technology;

"(E) the safety, effectiveness, patient-centeredness, appropriateness, and timeliness of care;

"(F) the efficiency of care;

"(G) the equity of health services and health disparities across health disparity populations (as defined in section 485E) and geographic areas;

"(H) patient experience and satisfaction;

"(I) the use of innovative strategies and methodologies identified under section 933; and

"(J) other areas determined appropriate by the Secretary.

"(3) ELIGIBLE ENTITIES.—To be eligible for a grant or contract under this subsection, an entity shall—

"(A) have demonstrated expertise and capacity in the development and evaluation of quality measures;

"(B) have adopted procedures to include in the quality measure development process—

"(i) the views of those providers or payers whose performance will be assessed by the measure; and

"(ii) the views of other parties who also will use the quality measures (such as patients, consumers, and health care purchasers);

"(C) collaborate with the entity with a contract under section 1890(a) of the Social Security Act and other stakeholders, as practicable, and the Secretary so that quality measures developed by the eligible entity will meet the requirements to be considered for endorsement by the entity with a contract under such section 1890(a);

"(D) have transparent policies regarding governance and conflicts of interest; and

"(E) submit an application to the Secretary at such time and in such manner, as the Secretary may require.

"(4) USE OF FUNDS.—An entity that receives a grant, contract, or agreement under this subsection shall use such award to develop quality measures that meet the following requirements:

"(A) Such measures support measures required to be reported under the Social Security Act, where applicable, and in support of gaps and existing quality measures that need improvement, as described in subsection (b)(1)(A).

"(B) Such measures support measures developed under section 1139A of the Social Security Act and the Medicaid Quality Measurement Program under section 1139B of such Act, where applicable.

"(C) To the extent practicable, data on such quality measures is able to be collected using health information technologies.

"(D) Each quality measure is free of charge to users of such measure.

"(E) Each quality measure is publicly available on an Internet website.

"(d) OTHER ACTIVITIES BY THE SECRETARY.—The Secretary may use amounts available under this section to update and test, where applicable, quality measures endorsed by the entity with a contract under section 1890(a) of the Social Security Act or adopted by the Secretary.

"(e) COORDINATION OF GRANTS.—The Secretary shall ensure that grants or contracts awarded under this section are coordinated with grants and contracts awarded under sections 1139A(5) and 1139B(4)(A) of the Social Security Act.".

(b) SOCIAL SECURITY ACT.—Section 1890A of the Social Security Act, as added by section 3014(b), is amended by adding at the end the following new subsection:

"(e) DEVELOPMENT OF QUALITY MEASURES.—The Administrator of the Center for Medicare & Medicaid Services shall through contracts develop quality measures (as determined appropriate by the Administrator) for use under this Act. In developing such measures, the Administrator shall consult with the Director of the Agency for Healthcare Research and Quality.".

(c) FUNDING.—There are authorized to be appropriated to the Secretary of Health and Human Services to carry out this section, $75,000,000 for each of fiscal years 2010 through 2014. Of the amounts appropriated under the preceding sentence in a fiscal year, not less than 50 percent of such amounts shall be used pursuant to subsection (e) of section 1890A of the Social Security Act, as added by subsection (b), with respect to programs under such Act. Amounts appropriated under this subsection for a fiscal year shall remain available until expended.

SEC. 3014. QUALITY MEASUREMENT.

(a) NEW DUTIES FOR CONSENSUS-BASED ENTITY.—

(1) MULTI-STAKEHOLDER GROUP INPUT.—Section 1890(b) of the Social Security Act (42 U.S.C. 1395aaa(b)), as amended by section 3003, is amended by adding at the end the following new paragraphs:

"(7) CONVENING MULTI-STAKEHOLDER GROUPS.—

"(A) IN GENERAL.—The entity shall convene multi-stakeholder groups to provide input on—

"(i) the selection of quality measures described in subparagraph (B), from among—

"(I) such measures that have been endorsed by the entity; and

"(II) such measures that have not been considered for endorsement by such entity but are used or proposed to be used by the Secretary for the collection or reporting of quality measures; and

"(ii) national priorities (as identified under section 399HH of the Public Health Service Act) for improvement in population health and in the delivery of health care services for consideration under the national strategy established under section 399HH of the Public Health Service Act.

"(B) QUALITY MEASURES.—

"(i) IN GENERAL.—Subject to clause (ii), the quality measures described in this subparagraph are quality measures—

"(I) for use pursuant to sections 1814(i)(5)(D), 1833(i)(7), 1833(t)(17), 1848(k)(2)(C), 1866(k)(3), 1881(h)(2)(A)(iii), 1886(b)(3)(B)(viii), 1886(j)(7)(D), 1886(m)(5)(D), 1886(o)(2), and 1895(b)(3)(B)(v);

"(II) for use in reporting performance information to the public; and

"(III) for use in health care programs other than for use under this Act.

"(ii) EXCLUSION.—Data sets (such as the outcome and assessment information set for home health services and the minimum data set for skilled nursing facility services) that are used for purposes of classification systems used in establishing payment rates under this title shall not be quality measures described in this subparagraph.

"(C) REQUIREMENT FOR TRANSPARENCY IN PROCESS.—

"(i) IN GENERAL.—In convening multi-stakeholder groups under subparagraph (A) with respect to the selection of quality measures, the entity shall provide for an open and transparent process for the activities conducted pursuant to such convening.

"(ii) SELECTION OF ORGANIZATIONS PARTICIPATING IN MULTI-STAKEHOLDER GROUPS.—The process described in clause (i) shall ensure that the selection of representatives comprising such groups provides for public nominations for, and the opportunity for public comment on, such selection.

"(D) MULTI-STAKEHOLDER GROUP DEFINED.—In this paragraph, the term 'multi-stakeholder group' means, with respect to a quality measure, a voluntary collaborative of organizations representing a broad group of stakeholders interested in or affected by the use of such quality measure.

"(8) TRANSMISSION OF MULTI-STAKEHOLDER INPUT.—Not later than February 1 of each year (beginning with 2012), the entity shall transmit to the Secretary the input of multi-stakeholder groups provided under paragraph (7).".

(2) ANNUAL REPORT.—Section 1890(b)(5)(A) of the Social Security Act (42 U.S.C. 1395aaa(b)(5)(A)) is amended—

(A) in clause (ii), by striking "and" at the end;

(B) in clause (iii), by striking the period at the end and inserting a semicolon; and

(C) by adding at the end the following new clauses:

"(iv) gaps in endorsed quality measures, which shall include measures that are within priority areas identified by the Secretary under the national strategy established under section 399HH of the Public Health Service Act, and where quality measures are unavailable or inadequate to identify or address such gaps;

"(v) areas in which evidence is insufficient to support endorsement of quality measures in priority areas identified by the Secretary under the national strategy established under section 399HH of the Public Health Service Act and where targeted research may address such gaps; and

"(vi) the matters described in clauses (i) and (ii) of paragraph (7)(A).".

(b) MULTI-STAKEHOLDER GROUP INPUT INTO SELECTION OF QUALITY MEASURES.—Title XVIII of the Social Security Act (42 U.S.C. 1395 et seq.) is amended by inserting after section 1890 the following:

"QUALITY MEASUREMENT

"SEC. 1890A. (a) MULTI-STAKEHOLDER GROUP INPUT INTO SELECTION OF QUALITY MEASURES.—The Secretary shall establish a pre-rulemaking process under which the following steps occur with respect to the selection of quality measures described in section 1890(b)(7)(B):

"(1) INPUT.—Pursuant to section 1890(b)(7), the entity with a contract under section 1890 shall convene multi-stakeholder groups to provide input to the Secretary on the selection of quality measures described in subparagraph (B) of such paragraph.

"(2) PUBLIC AVAILABILITY OF MEASURES CONSIDERED FOR SELECTION.—Not later than December 1 of each year (beginning with 2011), the Secretary shall make available to the public a list of quality measures described in section 1890(b)(7)(B) that the Secretary is considering under this title.

"(3) TRANSMISSION OF MULTI-STAKEHOLDER INPUT.—Pursuant to section 1890(b)(8), not later than February 1 of each year (beginning with 2012), the entity shall transmit to the Secretary the input of multi-stakeholder groups described in paragraph (1).

"(4) CONSIDERATION OF MULTI-STAKEHOLDER INPUT.—The Secretary shall take into consideration the input from multi-stakeholder groups described in paragraph (1) in selecting quality measures described in section 1890(b)(7)(B) that have been endorsed by the entity with a contract under section 1890 and measures that have not been endorsed by such entity.

"(5) RATIONALE FOR USE OF QUALITY MEASURES.—The Secretary shall publish in the Federal Register the rationale for the use of any quality measure described in section 1890(b)(7)(B) that has not been endorsed by the entity with a contract under section 1890.

"(6) ASSESSMENT OF IMPACT.—Not later than March 1, 2012, and at least once every three years thereafter, the Secretary shall—

"(A) conduct an assessment of the quality impact of the use of endorsed measures described in section 1890(b)(7)(B); and

"(B) make such assessment available to the public.

"(b) PROCESS FOR DISSEMINATION OF MEASURES USED BY THE SECRETARY.—

"(1) IN GENERAL.—The Secretary shall establish a process for disseminating quality measures used by the Secretary. Such process shall include the following:

"(A) The incorporation of such measures, where applicable, in workforce programs, training curricula, and any other means of dissemination determined appropriate by the Secretary.

"(B) The dissemination of such quality measures through the national strategy developed under section 399HH of the Public Health Service Act.

"(2) EXISTING METHODS.—To the extent practicable, the Secretary shall utilize and expand existing dissemination methods in disseminating quality measures under the process established under paragraph (1).

"(c) REVIEW OF QUALITY MEASURES USED BY THE SECRETARY.—

"(1) IN GENERAL.—The Secretary shall—

"(A) periodically (but in no case less often than once every 3 years) review quality measures described in section 1890(b)(7)(B); and

"(B) with respect to each such measure, determine whether to—

"(i) maintain the use of such measure; or

"(ii) phase out such measure.

"(2) CONSIDERATIONS.—In conducting the review under paragraph (1), the Secretary shall take steps to—

"(A) seek to avoid duplication of measures used; and

"(B) take into consideration current innovative methodologies and strategies for quality improvement practices in the delivery of health care services that represent best practices for such quality improvement and measures endorsed by the entity with a contract under section 1890 since the previous review by the Secretary.

"(d) RULE OF CONSTRUCTION.—Nothing in this section shall preclude a State from using the quality measures identified under sections 1139A and 1139B.".

(c) FUNDING.—For purposes of carrying out the amendments made by this section, the Secretary shall provide for the transfer, from the Federal Hospital Insurance Trust Fund under section 1817 of the Social Security Act (42 U.S.C. 1395i) and the Federal Supplementary Medical Insurance Trust Fund under section 1841 of such Act (42 U.S.C. 1395t), in such proportion as the Secretary determines appropriate, of $20,000,000, to the Centers for Medicare & Medicaid Services Program Management Account for each of fiscal years 2010 through 2014. Amounts transferred under the preceding sentence shall remain available until expended.

SEC. 3015. DATA COLLECTION; PUBLIC REPORTING.

Title III of the Public Health Service Act (42 U.S.C. 241 et seq.), as amended by section 3011, is further amended by adding at the end the following:

"SEC. 399II. COLLECTION AND ANALYSIS OF DATA FOR QUALITY AND RESOURCE USE MEASURES.

"(a) IN GENERAL.—The Secretary shall collect and aggregate consistent data on quality and resource use measures from information systems used to support health care delivery to implement the public reporting of performance information, as described in section 399JJ, and may award grants or contracts for this purpose. The Secretary shall ensure that such collection, aggregation, and analysis systems span an increasingly broad range of patient populations, providers, and geographic areas over time.

"(b) GRANTS OR CONTRACTS FOR DATA COLLECTION.—

"(1) IN GENERAL.—The Secretary may award grants or contracts to eligible entities to support new, or improve existing, efforts to collect and aggregate quality and resource use measures described under subsection (c).

"(2) ELIGIBLE ENTITIES.—To be eligible for a grant or contract under this subsection, an entity shall—

"(A) be—

"(i) a multi-stakeholder entity that coordinates the development of methods and implementation plans for the consistent reporting of summary quality and cost information;

"(ii) an entity capable of submitting such summary data for a particular population and providers, such as a disease registry, regional collaboration, health plan collaboration, or other population-wide source; or

"(iii) a Federal Indian Health Service program or a health program operated by an Indian tribe (as defined in section 4 of the Indian Health Care Improvement Act);

"(B) promote the use of the systems that provide data to improve and coordinate patient care;

"(C) support the provision of timely, consistent quality and resource use information to health care providers, and other groups and organizations as appropriate, with an opportunity for providers to correct inaccurate measures; and

"(D) agree to report, as determined by the Secretary, measures on quality and resource use to the public in accordance with the public reporting process established under section 399JJ.

"(c) CONSISTENT DATA AGGREGATION.—The Secretary may award grants or contracts under this section only to entities that enable summary data that can be integrated and compared across multiple sources. The Secretary shall provide standards for the protection of the security and privacy of patient data.

"(d) MATCHING FUNDS.—The Secretary may not award a grant or contract under this section to an entity unless the entity agrees that it will make available (directly or through contributions from other public or private entities) non-Federal contributions toward the activities to be carried out under the grant or contract in an amount equal to $1 for each $5 of Federal funds provided under the grant or contract. Such non-Federal matching funds may be provided directly or through donations from public or private entities and may be in cash or in-kind, fairly evaluated, including plant, equipment, or services.

"(e) AUTHORIZATION OF APPROPRIATIONS.—To carry out this section, there are authorized to be appropriated such sums as may be necessary for fiscal years 2010 through 2014.

"SEC. 399JJ. PUBLIC REPORTING OF PERFORMANCE INFORMATION.

"(a) DEVELOPMENT OF PERFORMANCE WEBSITES.—The Secretary shall make available to the public, through standardized Internet websites, performance information summarizing data on quality measures. Such information shall be tailored to respond to the differing needs of hospitals and other institutional health care providers, physicians and other clinicians, patients, consumers, researchers, policymakers, States, and other stakeholders, as the Secretary may specify.

"(b) INFORMATION ON CONDITIONS.—The performance information made publicly available on an Internet website, as described in subsection (a), shall include information regarding clinical conditions to the extent such information is available, and the information shall, where appropriate, be provider-specific and sufficiently disaggregated and specific to meet the needs of patients with different clinical conditions.

"(c) CONSULTATION.—

"(1) IN GENERAL.—In carrying out this section, the Secretary shall consult with the entity with a contract under section 1890(a) of the Social Security Act, and other entities, as appropriate, to determine the type of information that is useful to stakeholders and the format that best facilitates use of the reports and of performance reporting Internet websites.

"(2) CONSULTATION WITH STAKEHOLDERS.—The entity with a contract under section 1890(a) of the Social Security Act shall convene multi-stakeholder groups, as described in such section, to review the design and format of each Internet website made available under subsection (a) and shall transmit to the Secretary the views of such multi-stakeholder groups with respect to each such design and format.

"(d) COORDINATION.—Where appropriate, the Secretary shall coordinate the manner in which data are presented through Internet websites described in subsection (a) and for public reporting of other quality measures by the Secretary, including such quality measures under title XVIII of the Social Security Act.

"(e) AUTHORIZATION OF APPROPRIATIONS.—To carry out this section, there are authorized to be appropriated such sums as may be necessary for fiscal years 2010 through 2014.".

PART III—ENCOURAGING DEVELOPMENT OF NEW PATIENT CARE MODELS

SEC. 3021. ESTABLISHMENT OF CENTER FOR MEDICARE AND MEDICAID INNOVATION WITHIN CMS.

(a) IN GENERAL.—Title XI of the Social Security Act is amended by inserting after section 1115 the following new section:

"CENTER FOR MEDICARE AND MEDICAID INNOVATION

"SEC. 1115A. (a) CENTER FOR MEDICARE AND MEDICAID INNOVATION ESTABLISHED.—

"(1) IN GENERAL.—There is created within the Centers for Medicare & Medicaid Services a Center for Medicare and Medicaid Innovation (in this section referred to as the 'CMI') to carry out the duties described in this section. The purpose of the CMI is to test innovative payment and service delivery models to reduce program expenditures under the applicable titles while preserving or enhancing the quality of care furnished to individuals under such titles. In selecting such models, the Secretary shall give preference to models that also improve the coordination, quality, and efficiency of health care services furnished to applicable individuals defined in paragraph (4)(A).

"(2) DEADLINE.—The Secretary shall ensure that the CMI is carrying out the duties described in this section by not later than January 1, 2011.

"(3) CONSULTATION.—In carrying out the duties under this section, the CMI shall consult representatives of relevant Federal agencies, and clinical and analytical experts with expertise in medicine and health care management. The CMI shall use open door forums or other mechanisms to seek input from interested parties.

"(4) DEFINITIONS.—In this section:

"(A) APPLICABLE INDIVIDUAL.—The term 'applicable individual' means—

"(i) an individual who is entitled to, or enrolled for, benefits under part A of title XVIII or enrolled for benefits under part B of such title;

"(ii) an individual who is eligible for medical assistance under title XIX, under a State plan or waiver; or

"(iii) an individual who meets the criteria of both clauses (i) and (ii).

"(B) APPLICABLE TITLE.—The term 'applicable title' means title XVIII, title XIX, or both.

"(b) TESTING OF MODELS (PHASE I).—

"(1) IN GENERAL.—The CMI shall test payment and service delivery models in accordance with selection criteria under paragraph (2) to determine the effect of applying such models under the applicable title (as defined in subsection (a)(4)(B)) on program expenditures under such titles and the quality of care received by individuals receiving benefits under such title.

"(2) SELECTION OF MODELS TO BE TESTED.—

"(A) IN GENERAL.—The Secretary shall select models to be tested from models where the Secretary determines that there is evidence that the model addresses a defined population for which there are deficits in care leading to poor clinical outcomes or potentially avoidable expenditures. The models selected under the preceding sentence may include the models described in subparagraph (B).

"(B) OPPORTUNITIES.—The models described in this subparagraph are the following models:

"(i) Promoting broad payment and practice reform in primary care, including patient-centered medical home models for high-need applicable individuals, medical homes that address women's unique health care needs, and models that transition primary care practices away from fee-for-service based reimbursement and toward comprehensive payment or salary-based payment.

"(ii) Contracting directly with groups of providers of services and suppliers to promote innovative care delivery models, such as through risk-based comprehensive payment or salary-based payment.

"(iii) Utilizing geriatric assessments and comprehensive care plans to coordinate the care (including through interdisciplinary teams) of applicable individuals with multiple chronic conditions and at least one of the following:

"(I) An inability to perform 2 or more activities of daily living.

"(II) Cognitive impairment, including dementia.

"(iv) Promote care coordination between providers of services and suppliers that transition health care providers away from fee-for-service based reimbursement and toward salary-based payment.

"(v) Supporting care coordination for chronically-ill applicable individuals at high risk of hospitalization through a health information technology-enabled provider network that includes care coordinators, a chronic disease registry, and home tele-health technology.

"(vi) Varying payment to physicians who order advanced diagnostic imaging services (as defined in section 1834(e)(1)(B)) according to the physician's adherence to appropriateness criteria for the ordering of such services, as determined in consultation with physician specialty groups and other relevant stakeholders.

"(vii) Utilizing medication therapy management services, such as those described in section 935 of the Public Health Service Act.

"(viii) Establishing community-based health teams to support small-practice medical homes by assisting the primary care practitioner in chronic care management, including patient self-management, activities.

"(ix) Assisting applicable individuals in making informed health care choices by paying providers of services and suppliers for using patient decision-support tools, including tools that meet the standards developed and identified under section 936(c)(2)(A) of the Public Health Service Act, that improve applicable individual and caregiver understanding of medical treatment options.

"(x) Allowing States to test and evaluate fully integrating care for dual eligible individuals in the State, including the management and oversight of all funds under the applicable titles with respect to such individuals.

"(xi) Allowing States to test and evaluate systems of all-payer payment reform for the medical care of residents of the State, including dual eligible individuals.

"(xii) Aligning nationally recognized, evidence-based guidelines of cancer care with payment incentives under title XVIII in the areas of treatment planning and follow-up care planning for applicable individuals described in clause (i) or (iii) of subsection (a)(4)(A) with cancer, including the identification of gaps in applicable quality measures.

"(xiii) Improving post-acute care through continuing care hospitals that offer inpatient rehabilitation, long-term care hospitals, and home health or skilled nursing care during an inpatient stay and the 30 days immediately following discharge.

"(xiv) Funding home health providers who offer chronic care management services to applicable individuals in cooperation with interdisciplinary teams.

"(xv) Promoting improved quality and reduced cost by developing a collaborative of high-quality, low-cost health care institutions that is responsible for—

"(I) developing, documenting, and disseminating best practices and proven care methods;

"(II) implementing such best practices and proven care methods within such institutions to demonstrate further improvements in quality and efficiency; and

"(III) providing assistance to other health care institutions on how best to employ such best practices and proven care methods to improve health care quality and lower costs.

"(xvi) Facilitate inpatient care, including intensive care, of hospitalized applicable individuals at their local hospital through the use of electronic monitoring by specialists, including intensivists and critical care specialists, based at integrated health systems.

"(xvii) Promoting greater efficiencies and timely access to outpatient services (such as outpatient physical therapy services) through models that do not require a physician or other health professional to refer the service or be involved in establishing the plan of care for the service, when such service is furnished by a health professional who has the authority to furnish the service under existing State law.

"(xviii) Establishing comprehensive payments to Healthcare Innovation Zones, consisting of groups of providers that include a teaching hospital, physicians, and other clinical entities, that, through their structure, operations, and joint-activity deliver a full spectrum of integrated and comprehensive health care services to applicable individuals while also incorporating innovative methods for the clinical training of future health care professionals.

"(C) ADDITIONAL FACTORS FOR CONSIDERATION.—In selecting models for testing under subparagraph (A), the CMI may consider the following additional factors:

"(i) Whether the model includes a regular process for monitoring and updating patient care plans in a manner that is consistent with the needs and preferences of applicable individuals.

"(ii) Whether the model places the applicable individual, including family members and other informal caregivers of the applicable individual, at the center of the care team of the applicable individual.

"(iii) Whether the model provides for in-person contact with applicable individuals.

"(iv) Whether the model utilizes technology, such as electronic health records and patient-based remote monitoring systems, to coordinate care over time and across settings.

"(v) Whether the model provides for the maintenance of a close relationship between care coordinators, primary care practitioners, specialist physicians, community-based organizations, and other providers of services and suppliers.

"(vi) Whether the model relies on a team-based approach to interventions, such as comprehensive care assessments, care planning, and self-management coaching.

"(vii) Whether, under the model, providers of services and suppliers are able to share information with patients, caregivers, and other providers of services and suppliers on a real time basis.

"(3) BUDGET NEUTRALITY.—

"(A) INITIAL PERIOD.—The Secretary shall not require, as a condition for testing a model under paragraph (1), that the design of such model ensure that such model is budget neutral initially with respect to expenditures under the applicable title.

"(B) TERMINATION OR MODIFICATION.—The Secretary shall terminate or modify the design and implementation of a model unless the Secretary determines (and the Chief Actuary of the Centers for Medicare & Medicaid Services, with respect to program spending under the applicable title, certifies), after testing has begun, that the model is expected to—

"(i) improve the quality of care (as determined by the Administrator of the Centers for Medicare & Medicaid Services) without increasing spending under the applicable title;

"(ii) reduce spending under the applicable title without reducing the quality of care; or

"(iii) improve the quality of care and reduce spending.

Such termination may occur at any time after such testing has begun and before completion of the testing.

"(4) EVALUATION.—

"(A) IN GENERAL.—The Secretary shall conduct an evaluation of each model tested under this subsection. Such evaluation shall include an analysis of—

"(i) the quality of care furnished under the model, including the measurement of patient-level outcomes and patient-centeredness criteria determined appropriate by the Secretary; and

"(ii) the changes in spending under the applicable titles by reason of the model.

"(B) INFORMATION.—The Secretary shall make the results of each evaluation under this paragraph available to the public in a timely fashion and may establish requirements for States and other entities participating in the testing of models under this section to collect and report information that the Secretary determines is necessary to monitor and evaluate such models.

"(c) EXPANSION OF MODELS (PHASE II).—Taking into account the evaluation under subsection (b)(4), the Secretary may, through rulemaking, expand (including implementation on a nationwide basis) the duration and the scope of a model that is being tested under subsection (b) or a demonstration project under section 1866C, to the extent determined appropriate by the Secretary, if—

"(1) the Secretary determines that such expansion is expected to—

"(A) reduce spending under applicable title without reducing the quality of care; or

"(B) improve the quality of care and reduce spending; and

"(2) the Chief Actuary of the Centers for Medicare & Medicaid Services certifies that such expansion would reduce program spending under applicable titles.

"(d) IMPLEMENTATION.—

"(1) WAIVER AUTHORITY.—The Secretary may waive such requirements of titles XI and XVIII and of sections 1902(a)(1), 1902(a)(13), and 1903(m)(2)(A)(iii) as may be necessary solely for purposes of carrying out this section with respect to testing models described in subsection (b).

"(2) LIMITATIONS ON REVIEW.—There shall be no administrative or judicial review under section 1869, section 1878, or otherwise of—

"(A) the selection of models for testing or expansion under this section;

"(B) the selection of organizations, sites, or participants to test those models selected;

"(C) the elements, parameters, scope, and duration of such models for testing or dissemination;

"(D) determinations regarding budget neutrality under subsection (b)(3);

"(E) the termination or modification of the design and implementation of a model under subsection (b)(3)(B); and

"(F) determinations about expansion of the duration and scope of a model under subsection (c), including the determination that a model is not expected to meet criteria described in paragraph (1) or (2) of such subsection.

"(3) ADMINISTRATION.—Chapter 35 of title 44, United States Code, shall not apply to the testing and evaluation of models or expansion of such models under this section.

"(e) APPLICATION TO CHIP.—The Center may carry out activities under this section with respect to title XXI in the same manner as provided under this section with respect to the program under the applicable titles.

"(f) FUNDING.—

"(1) IN GENERAL.—There are appropriated, from amounts in the Treasury not otherwise appropriated—

"(A) $5,000,000 for the design, implementation, and evaluation of models under subsection (b) for fiscal year 2010;

"(B) $10,000,000,000 for the activities initiated under this section for the period of fiscal years 2011 through 2019; and

"(C) the amount described in subparagraph (B) for the activities initiated under this section for each subsequent 10-year fiscal period (beginning with the 10-year fiscal period beginning with fiscal year 2020).

Amounts appropriated under the preceding sentence shall remain available until expended.

"(2) USE OF CERTAIN FUNDS.—Out of amounts appropriated under subparagraphs (B) and (C) of paragraph (1), not less than $25,000,000 shall be made available each such fiscal year to design, implement, and evaluate models under subsection (b).

"(g) REPORT TO CONGRESS.—Beginning in 2012, and not less than once every other year thereafter, the Secretary shall submit to Congress a report on activities under this section. Each such report shall describe the models tested under subsection (b), including the number of individuals described in subsection (a)(4)(A)(i) and of individuals described in subsection (a)(4)(A)(ii) participating in such models and payments made under applicable titles for services on behalf of such individuals, any models chosen for expansion under subsection (c), and the results from evaluations under subsection (b)(4). In addition, each such report shall provide such recommendations as the Secretary determines are appropriate for legislative action to facilitate the development and expansion of successful payment models.".

(b) MEDICAID CONFORMING AMENDMENT.—Section 1902(a) of the Social Security Act (42 U.S.C. 1396a(a)), as amended by section 8002(b), is amended—

(1) in paragraph (81), by striking "and" at the end;

(2) in paragraph (82), by striking the period at the end and inserting "; and"; and

(3) by inserting after paragraph (82) the following new paragraph:

"(83) provide for implementation of the payment models specified by the Secretary under section 1115A(c) for implementation on a nationwide basis unless the State demonstrates to the satisfaction of the Secretary that implementation would not be administratively feasible or appropriate to the health care delivery system of the State.".

(c) REVISIONS TO HEALTH CARE QUALITY DEMONSTRATION PROGRAM.—Subsections (b) and (f) of section 1866C of the Social Security Act (42 U.S.C. 1395cc–3) are amended by striking "5-year" each place it appears.

SEC. 3022. MEDICARE SHARED SAVINGS PROGRAM.

Title XVIII of the Social Security Act (42 U.S.C. 1395 et seq.) is amended by adding at the end the following new section:

"SHARED SAVINGS PROGRAM

"SEC. 1899. (a) ESTABLISHMENT.—

"(1) IN GENERAL.—Not later than January 1, 2012, the Secretary shall establish a shared savings program (in this section referred to as the 'program') that promotes accountability for a patient population and coordinates items and services under parts A and B, and encourages investment in infrastructure and redesigned care processes for high quality and efficient service delivery. Under such program—

"(A) groups of providers of services and suppliers meeting criteria specified by the Secretary may work together to manage and coordinate care for Medicare fee-for-service beneficiaries through an accountable care organization (referred to in this section as an 'ACO'); and

"(B) ACOs that meet quality performance standards established by the Secretary are eligible to receive payments for shared savings under subsection (d)(2).

"(b) ELIGIBLE ACOs.—

"(1) IN GENERAL.—Subject to the succeeding provisions of this subsection, as determined appropriate by the Secretary, the following groups of providers of services and suppliers which have established a mechanism for shared governance are eligible to participate as ACOs under the program under this section:

"(A) ACO professionals in group practice arrangements.

"(B) Networks of individual practices of ACO professionals.

"(C) Partnerships or joint venture arrangements between hospitals and ACO professionals.

"(D) Hospitals employing ACO professionals.

"(E) Such other groups of providers of services and suppliers as the Secretary determines appropriate.

"(2) REQUIREMENTS.—An ACO shall meet the following requirements:

"(A) The ACO shall be willing to become accountable for the quality, cost, and overall care of the Medicare fee-for-service beneficiaries assigned to it.

"(B) The ACO shall enter into an agreement with the Secretary to participate in the program for not less than a 3-year period (referred to in this section as the 'agreement period').

"(C) The ACO shall have a formal legal structure that would allow the organization to receive and distribute payments for shared savings under subsection (d)(2) to participating providers of services and suppliers.

"(D) The ACO shall include primary care ACO professionals that are sufficient for the number of Medicare fee-for-service beneficiaries assigned to the ACO under subsection (c). At a minimum, the ACO shall have at least 5,000 such beneficiaries assigned to it under subsection (c) in order to be eligible to participate in the ACO program.

"(E) The ACO shall provide the Secretary with such information regarding ACO professionals participating in the ACO as the Secretary determines necessary to support the assignment of Medicare fee-for-service beneficiaries to an ACO, the implementation of quality and other reporting requirements under paragraph (3), and the determination of payments for shared savings under subsection (d)(2).

"(F) The ACO shall have in place a leadership and management structure that includes clinical and administrative systems.

"(G) The ACO shall define processes to promote evidence-based medicine and patient engagement, report on quality and cost measures, and coordinate care, such as through the use of telehealth, remote patient monitoring, and other such enabling technologies.

"(H) The ACO shall demonstrate to the Secretary that it meets patient-centeredness criteria specified by the Secretary, such as the use of patient and caregiver assessments or the use of individualized care plans.

"(3) QUALITY AND OTHER REPORTING REQUIREMENTS.—

"(A) IN GENERAL.—The Secretary shall determine appropriate measures to assess the quality of care furnished by the ACO, such as measures of—

"(i) clinical processes and outcomes;

"(ii) patient and, where practicable, caregiver experience of care; and

"(iii) utilization (such as rates of hospital admissions for ambulatory care sensitive conditions).

"(B) REPORTING REQUIREMENTS.—An ACO shall submit data in a form and manner specified by the Secretary on measures the Secretary determines necessary for the ACO to report in order to evaluate the quality of care furnished by the ACO. Such data may include care transitions across health care settings, including hospital discharge planning and post-hospital discharge follow-up by ACO professionals, as the Secretary determines appropriate.

"(C) QUALITY PERFORMANCE STANDARDS.—The Secretary shall establish quality performance standards to assess the quality of care furnished by ACOs. The Secretary shall seek to improve the quality of care furnished by

ACOs over time by specifying higher standards, new measures, or both for purposes of assessing such quality of care.

"(D) OTHER REPORTING REQUIREMENTS.—The Secretary may, as the Secretary determines appropriate, incorporate reporting requirements and incentive payments related to the physician quality reporting initiative (PQRI) under section 1848, including such requirements and such payments related to electronic prescribing, electronic health records, and other similar initiatives under section 1848, and may use alternative criteria than would otherwise apply under such section for determining whether to make such payments. The incentive payments described in the preceding sentence shall not be taken into consideration when calculating any payments otherwise made under subsection (d).

"(4) NO DUPLICATION IN PARTICIPATION IN SHARED SAVINGS PROGRAMS.—A provider of services or supplier that participates in any of the following shall not be eligible to participate in an ACO under this section:

"(A) A model tested or expanded under section 1115A that involves shared savings under this title, or any other program or demonstration project that involves such shared savings.

"(B) The independence at home medical practice pilot program under section 1866E.

"(c) ASSIGNMENT OF MEDICARE FEE-FOR-SERVICE BENEFICIARIES TO ACOS.—The Secretary shall determine an appropriate method to assign Medicare fee-for-service beneficiaries to an ACO based on their utilization of primary care services provided under this title by an ACO professional described in subsection (h)(1)(A).

"(d) PAYMENTS AND TREATMENT OF SAVINGS.—

"(1) PAYMENTS.—

"(A) IN GENERAL.—Under the program, subject to paragraph (3), payments shall continue to be made to providers of services and suppliers participating in an ACO under the original Medicare fee-for-service program under parts A and B in the same manner as they would otherwise be made except that a participating ACO is eligible to receive payment for shared savings under paragraph (2) if—

"(i) the ACO meets quality performance standards established by the Secretary under subsection (b)(3); and

"(ii) the ACO meets the requirement under subparagraph (B)(i).

"(B) SAVINGS REQUIREMENT AND BENCHMARK.—

"(i) DETERMINING SAVINGS.—In each year of the agreement period, an ACO shall be eligible to receive payment for shared savings under paragraph (2) only if the estimated average per capita Medicare expenditures under the ACO for Medicare fee-for-service beneficiaries for parts A and B services, adjusted for beneficiary characteristics, is at least the percent specified by the Secretary below the applicable benchmark under clause (ii). The Secretary shall determine the appropriate percent described in the preceding sentence to account for normal variation in expenditures under this title, based upon the number of Medicare fee-for-service beneficiaries assigned to an ACO.

"(ii) ESTABLISH AND UPDATE BENCHMARK.—The Secretary shall estimate a benchmark for each agreement period for each ACO using the most recent available 3 years of per-beneficiary expenditures for parts A and B services for Medicare fee-for-service beneficiaries assigned to the ACO. Such benchmark shall be adjusted for beneficiary characteristics and such other factors as the Secretary determines appropriate and updated by the projected absolute amount of growth in national per capita expenditures for parts A and B services under the original Medicare fee-for-service program, as estimated by the Secretary. Such benchmark shall be reset at the start of each agreement period.

"(2) PAYMENTS FOR SHARED SAVINGS.—Subject to performance with respect to the quality performance standards established by the Secretary under subsection (b)(3), if an ACO meets the requirements under paragraph (1), a percent (as determined appropriate by the Secretary) of the difference between such estimated average per capita Medicare expenditures in a year, adjusted for beneficiary characteristics, under the ACO and such benchmark for the ACO may be paid to the ACO as shared savings and the remainder of such difference shall be retained by the program under this title. The Secretary shall establish limits on the total amount of shared savings that may be paid to an ACO under this paragraph.

"(3) MONITORING AVOIDANCE OF AT-RISK PATIENTS.—If the Secretary determines that an ACO has taken steps to avoid patients at risk in order to reduce the likelihood of increasing costs to the ACO the Secretary may impose an appropriate sanction on the ACO, including termination from the program.

"(4) TERMINATION.—The Secretary may terminate an agreement with an ACO if it does not meet the quality performance standards established by the Secretary under subsection (b)(3).

"(e) ADMINISTRATION.—Chapter 35 of title 44, United States Code, shall not apply to the program.

"(f) WAIVER AUTHORITY.—The Secretary may waive such requirements of sections 1128A and 1128B and title XVIII of this Act as may be necessary to carry out the provisions of this section.

"(g) LIMITATIONS ON REVIEW.—There shall be no administrative or judicial review under section 1869, section 1878, or otherwise of—

"(1) the specification of criteria under subsection (a)(1)(B);

"(2) the assessment of the quality of care furnished by an ACO and the establishment of performance standards under subsection (b)(3);

"(3) the assignment of Medicare fee-for-service beneficiaries to an ACO under subsection (c);

"(4) the determination of whether an ACO is eligible for shared savings under subsection (d)(2) and the amount of such shared savings, including the determination of the estimated average per capita Medicare expenditures under the ACO for Medicare fee-for-service beneficiaries assigned to the ACO and the average benchmark for the ACO under subsection (d)(1)(B);

“(5) the percent of shared savings specified by the Secretary under subsection (d)(2) and any limit on the total amount of shared savings established by the Secretary under such subsection; and

“(6) the termination of an ACO under subsection (d)(4).

“(h) DEFINITIONS.—In this section:

“(1) ACO PROFESSIONAL.—The term ‘ACO professional’ means—

“(A) a physician (as defined in section 1861(r)(1)); and

“(B) a practitioner described in section 1842(b)(18)(C)(i).

“(2) HOSPITAL.—The term ‘hospital’ means a subsection (d) hospital (as defined in section 1886(d)(1)(B)).

“(3) MEDICARE FEE-FOR-SERVICE BENEFICIARY.—The term ‘Medicare fee-for-service beneficiary’ means an individual who is enrolled in the original Medicare fee-for-service program under parts A and B and is not enrolled in an MA plan under part C, an eligible organization under section 1876, or a PACE program under section 1894.”.

SEC. 3023. NATIONAL PILOT PROGRAM ON PAYMENT BUNDLING.

Title XVIII of the Social Security Act, as amended by section 3021, is amended by inserting after section 1886C the following new section:

“NATIONAL PILOT PROGRAM ON PAYMENT BUNDLING

“SEC. 1866D. (a) IMPLEMENTATION.—

“(1) IN GENERAL.—The Secretary shall establish a pilot program for integrated care during an episode of care provided to an applicable beneficiary around a hospitalization in order to improve the coordination, quality, and efficiency of health care services under this title.

“(2) DEFINITIONS.—In this section:

“(A) APPLICABLE BENEFICIARY.—The term ‘applicable beneficiary’ means an individual who—

“(i) is entitled to, or enrolled for, benefits under part A and enrolled for benefits under part B of such title, but not enrolled under part C or a PACE program under section 1894; and

“(ii) is admitted to a hospital for an applicable condition.

“(B) APPLICABLE CONDITION.—The term ‘applicable condition’ means 1 or more of 8 conditions selected by the Secretary. In selecting conditions under the preceding sentence, the Secretary shall take into consideration the following factors:

“(i) Whether the conditions selected include a mix of chronic and acute conditions.

“(ii) Whether the conditions selected include a mix of surgical and medical conditions.

“(iii) Whether a condition is one for which there is evidence of an opportunity for providers of services and suppliers to improve the quality of care furnished while reducing total expenditures under this title.

“(iv) Whether a condition has significant variation in—

“(I) the number of readmissions; and

"(II) the amount of expenditures for post-acute care spending under this title.

"(v) Whether a condition is high-volume and has high post-acute care expenditures under this title.

"(vi) Which conditions the Secretary determines are most amenable to bundling across the spectrum of care given practice patterns under this title.

"(C) APPLICABLE SERVICES.—The term 'applicable services' means the following:

"(i) Acute care inpatient services.

"(ii) Physicians' services delivered in and outside of an acute care hospital setting.

"(iii) Outpatient hospital services, including emergency department services.

"(iv) Post-acute care services, including home health services, skilled nursing services, inpatient rehabilitation services, and inpatient hospital services furnished by a long-term care hospital.

"(v) Other services the Secretary determines appropriate.

"(D) EPISODE OF CARE.—

"(i) IN GENERAL.—Subject to clause (ii), the term 'episode of care' means, with respect to an applicable condition and an applicable beneficiary, the period that includes—

"(I) the 3 days prior to the admission of the applicable beneficiary to a hospital for the applicable condition;

"(II) the length of stay of the applicable beneficiary in such hospital; and

"(III) the 30 days following the discharge of the applicable beneficiary from such hospital.

"(ii) ESTABLISHMENT OF PERIOD BY THE SECRETARY.—The Secretary, as appropriate, may establish a period (other than the period described in clause (i)) for an episode of care under the pilot program.

"(E) PHYSICIANS' SERVICES.—The term 'physicians' services' has the meaning given such term in section 1861(q).

"(F) PILOT PROGRAM.—The term 'pilot program' means the pilot program under this section.

"(G) PROVIDER OF SERVICES.—The term 'provider of services' has the meaning given such term in section 1861(u).

"(H) READMISSION.—The term 'readmission' has the meaning given such term in section 1886(q)(5)(E).

"(I) SUPPLIER.—The term 'supplier' has the meaning given such term in section 1861(d).

"(3) DEADLINE FOR IMPLEMENTATION.—The Secretary shall establish the pilot program not later than January 1, 2013.

"(b) DEVELOPMENTAL PHASE.—

"(1) DETERMINATION OF PATIENT ASSESSMENT INSTRUMENT.—The Secretary shall determine which patient assessment instrument (such as the Continuity Assessment Record and Evaluation (CARE) tool) shall be used under the pilot program to evaluate the applicable condition of an applicable beneficiary for purposes of determining the most clinically appropriate site for the provision of post-acute care to the applicable beneficiary.

"(2) DEVELOPMENT OF QUALITY MEASURES FOR AN EPISODE OF CARE AND FOR POST-ACUTE CARE.—

"(A) IN GENERAL.—The Secretary, in consultation with the Agency for Healthcare Research and Quality and the entity with a contract under section 1890(a) of the Social Security Act, shall develop quality measures for use in the pilot program—

"(i) for episodes of care; and

"(ii) for post-acute care.

"(B) SITE-NEUTRAL POST-ACUTE CARE QUALITY MEASURES.—Any quality measures developed under subparagraph (A)(ii) shall be site-neutral.

"(C) COORDINATION WITH QUALITY MEASURE DEVELOPMENT AND ENDORSEMENT PROCEDURES.—The Secretary shall ensure that the development of quality measures under subparagraph (A) is done in a manner that is consistent with the measures developed and endorsed under section 1890 and 1890A that are applicable to all post-acute care settings.

"(c) DETAILS.—

"(1) DURATION.—

"(A) IN GENERAL.—Subject to subparagraph (B), the pilot program shall be conducted for a period of 5 years.

"(B) EXTENSION.—The Secretary may extend the duration of the pilot program for providers of services and suppliers participating in the pilot program as of the day before the end of the 5-year period described in subparagraph (A), for a period determined appropriate by the Secretary, if the Secretary determines that such extension will result in improving or not reducing the quality of patient care and reducing spending under this title.

"(2) PARTICIPATING PROVIDERS OF SERVICES AND SUPPLIERS.—

"(A) IN GENERAL.—An entity comprised of providers of services and suppliers, including a hospital, a physician group, a skilled nursing facility, and a home health agency, who are otherwise participating under this title, may submit an application to the Secretary to provide applicable services to applicable individuals under this section.

"(B) REQUIREMENTS.—The Secretary shall develop requirements for entities to participate in the pilot program under this section. Such requirements shall ensure that applicable beneficiaries have an adequate choice of providers of services and suppliers under the pilot program.

"(3) PAYMENT METHODOLOGY.—

"(A) IN GENERAL.—

"(i) ESTABLISHMENT OF PAYMENT METHODS.—The Secretary shall develop payment methods for the pilot program for entities participating in the pilot program. Such payment methods may include bundled payments and bids from entities for episodes of care. The Secretary shall make payments to the entity for services covered under this section.

"(ii) NO ADDITIONAL PROGRAM EXPENDITURES.—Payments under this section for applicable items and services under this title (including payment for services described in subparagraph (B)) for applicable beneficiaries for a year shall be established in a manner that does not result in spending more for such entity for such beneficiaries than would otherwise be expended for such entity for such beneficiaries for such year if the pilot program were not implemented, as estimated by the Secretary.

"(B) INCLUSION OF CERTAIN SERVICES.—A payment methodology tested under the pilot program shall include payment for the furnishing of applicable services and other appropriate services, such as care coordination, medication reconciliation, discharge planning, transitional care services, and other patient-centered activities as determined appropriate by the Secretary.

"(C) BUNDLED PAYMENTS.—

"(i) IN GENERAL.—A bundled payment under the pilot program shall—

"(I) be comprehensive, covering the costs of applicable services and other appropriate services furnished to an individual during an episode of care (as determined by the Secretary); and

"(II) be made to the entity which is participating in the pilot program.

"(ii) REQUIREMENT FOR PROVISION OF APPLICABLE SERVICES AND OTHER APPROPRIATE SERVICES.—Applicable services and other appropriate services for which payment is made under this subparagraph shall be furnished or directed by the entity which is participating in the pilot program.

"(D) PAYMENT FOR POST-ACUTE CARE SERVICES AFTER THE EPISODE OF CARE.—The Secretary shall establish procedures, in the case where an applicable beneficiary requires continued post-acute care services after the last day of the episode of care, under which payment for such services shall be made.

"(4) QUALITY MEASURES.—

"(A) IN GENERAL.—The Secretary shall establish quality measures (including quality measures of process, outcome, and structure) related to care provided by entities participating in the pilot program. Quality measures established under the preceding sentence shall include measures of the following:

"(i) Functional status improvement.

"(ii) Reducing rates of avoidable hospital readmissions.

"(iii) Rates of discharge to the community.

"(iv) Rates of admission to an emergency room after a hospitalization.

"(v) Incidence of health care acquired infections.

"(vi) Efficiency measures.

"(vii) Measures of patient-centeredness of care.

"(viii) Measures of patient perception of care.

"(ix) Other measures, including measures of patient outcomes, determined appropriate by the Secretary.

"(B) REPORTING ON QUALITY MEASURES.—

"(i) IN GENERAL.—A entity shall submit data to the Secretary on quality measures established under subparagraph (A) during each year of the pilot program (in a form and manner, subject to clause (iii), specified by the Secretary).

"(ii) SUBMISSION OF DATA THROUGH ELECTRONIC HEALTH RECORD.—To the extent practicable, the Secretary shall specify that data on measures be submitted under clause (i) through the use of an qualified electronic health record (as defined in section 3000(13) of the Public Health Service Act (42 U.S.C. 300jj–11(13)) in a manner specified by the Secretary.

"(d) WAIVER.—The Secretary may waive such provisions of this title and title XI as may be necessary to carry out the pilot program.

"(e) INDEPENDENT EVALUATION AND REPORTS ON PILOT PROGRAM.—

"(1) INDEPENDENT EVALUATION.—The Secretary shall conduct an independent evaluation of the pilot program, including the extent to which the pilot program has—

"(A) improved quality measures established under subsection (c)(4)(A);

"(B) improved health outcomes;

"(C) improved applicable beneficiary access to care; and

"(D) reduced spending under this title.

"(2) REPORTS.—

"(A) INTERIM REPORT.—Not later than 2 years after the implementation of the pilot program, the Secretary shall submit to Congress a report on the initial results of the independent evaluation conducted under paragraph (1).

"(B) FINAL REPORT.—Not later than 3 years after the implementation of the pilot program, the Secretary shall submit to Congress a report on the final results of the independent evaluation conducted under paragraph (1).

"(f) CONSULTATION.—The Secretary shall consult with representatives of small rural hospitals, including critical access hospitals (as defined in section 1861(mm)(1)), regarding their participation in the pilot program. Such consultation shall include consideration of innovative methods of implementing bundled payments in hospitals described in the preceding sentence, taking into consideration any difficulties in doing so as a result of the low volume of services provided by such hospitals.

"(g) IMPLEMENTATION PLAN.—

"(1) IN GENERAL.—Not later than January 1, 2016, the Secretary shall submit a plan for the implementation of an expansion of the pilot program if the Secretary determines that such expansion will result in improving or not reducing the quality of patient care and reducing spending under this title.

"(h) ADMINISTRATION.—Chapter 35 of title 44, United States Code, shall not apply to the selection, testing, and evaluation of models or the expansion of such models under this section.".

SEC. 3024. INDEPENDENCE AT HOME DEMONSTRATION PROGRAM.

Title XVIII of the Social Security Act is amended by inserting after section 1866D, as inserted by section 3023, the following new section:

"INDEPENDENCE AT HOME MEDICAL PRACTICE DEMONSTRATION PROGRAM

"SEC. 1866D. (a) ESTABLISHMENT.—

"(1) IN GENERAL.—The Secretary shall conduct a demonstration program (in this section referred to as the 'demonstration program') to test a payment incentive and service delivery model that utilizes physician and nurse practitioner directed home-based primary care teams designed to reduce expenditures and improve health outcomes in the provision of items and services under this title to applicable beneficiaries (as defined in subsection (d)).

"(2) REQUIREMENT.—The demonstration program shall test whether a model described in paragraph (1), which is accountable for providing comprehensive, coordinated, continuous, and accessible care to high-need populations at home and coordinating health care across all treatment settings, results in—

"(A) reducing preventable hospitalizations;

"(B) preventing hospital readmissions;

"(C) reducing emergency room visits;

"(D) improving health outcomes commensurate with the beneficiaries' stage of chronic illness;

"(E) improving the efficiency of care, such as by reducing duplicative diagnostic and laboratory tests;

"(F) reducing the cost of health care services covered under this title; and

"(G) achieving beneficiary and family caregiver satisfaction.

"(b) INDEPENDENCE AT HOME MEDICAL PRACTICE.—

"(1) INDEPENDENCE AT HOME MEDICAL PRACTICE DEFINED.— In this section:

"(A) IN GENERAL.—The term 'independence at home medical practice' means a legal entity that—

"(i) is comprised of an individual physician or nurse practitioner or group of physicians and nurse practitioners that provides care as part of a team that includes physicians, nurses, physician assistants, pharmacists, and other health and social services staff as appropriate who have experience providing home-based primary care to applicable beneficiaries, make in-home visits, and are available 24 hours per day, 7 days per week to carry out plans of care that are tailored to the individual beneficiary's chronic conditions and designed to achieve the results in subsection (a);

"(ii) is organized at least in part for the purpose of providing physicians' services;

"(iii) has documented experience in providing home-based primary care services to high-cost chronically ill beneficiaries, as determined appropriate by the Secretary;

"(iv) furnishes services to at least 200 applicable beneficiaries (as defined in subsection (d)) during each year of the demonstration program;

"(v) has entered into an agreement with the Secretary;

"(vi) uses electronic health information systems, remote monitoring, and mobile diagnostic technology; and

"(vii) meets such other criteria as the Secretary determines to be appropriate to participate in the demonstration program.

The entity shall report on quality measures (in such form, manner, and frequency as specified by the Secretary, which may be for the group, for providers of services and suppliers, or both) and report to the Secretary (in a form, manner, and frequency as specified by the Secretary) such data as the Secretary determines appropriate to monitor and evaluate the demonstration program.

"(B) PHYSICIAN.—The term 'physician' includes, except as the Secretary may otherwise provide, any individual who furnishes services for which payment may be made as physicians' services and has the medical training or experience to fulfill the physician's role described in subparagraph (A)(i).

"(2) PARTICIPATION OF NURSE PRACTITIONERS AND PHYSICIAN ASSISTANTS.—Nothing in this section shall be construed to prevent a nurse practitioner or physician assistant from participating in, or leading, a home-based primary care team as part of an independence at home medical practice if—

"(A) all the requirements of this section are met;

"(B) the nurse practitioner or physician assistant, as the case may be, is acting consistent with State law; and

"(C) the nurse practitioner or physician assistant has the medical training or experience to fulfill the nurse practitioner or physician assistant role described in paragraph (1)(A)(i).

"(3) INCLUSION OF PROVIDERS AND PRACTITIONERS.—Nothing in this subsection shall be construed as preventing an independence at home medical practice from including a provider of services or a participating practitioner described in section 1842(b)(18)(C) that is affiliated with the practice under an arrangement structured so that such provider of services or practitioner participates in the demonstration program and shares in any savings under the demonstration program.

"(4) QUALITY AND PERFORMANCE STANDARDS.—The Secretary shall develop quality performance standards for independence at home medical practices participating in the demonstration program.

"(c) PAYMENT METHODOLOGY.—

"(1) ESTABLISHMENT OF TARGET SPENDING LEVEL.—The Secretary shall establish an estimated annual spending target, for the amount the Secretary estimates would have been spent in the absence of the demonstration, for items and services covered under parts A and B furnished to applicable beneficiaries for each qualifying independence at home medical practice under this section. Such spending targets shall be determined on a per capita basis. Such spending targets shall include a risk corridor that takes into account normal variation in expenditures for items and services covered under parts A and B furnished to such beneficiaries with the size of the corridor being related to the number of applicable beneficiaries furnished services by each independence at home medical practice. The spending targets may also be adjusted for other factors as the Secretary determines appropriate.

"(2) INCENTIVE PAYMENTS.—Subject to performance on quality measures, a qualifying independence at home medical practice is eligible to receive an incentive payment under this section if actual expenditures for a year for the applicable beneficiaries it enrolls are less than the estimated spending target established under paragraph (1) for such year. An incentive payment for such year shall be equal to a portion (as determined by the Secretary) of the amount by which actual expenditures (including incentive payments under this paragraph) for applicable beneficiaries under parts A and B for such year are estimated to be less than 5 percent less than the estimated spending target for such year, as determined under paragraph (1).

"(d) APPLICABLE BENEFICIARIES.—

"(1) DEFINITION.—In this section, the term 'applicable beneficiary' means, with respect to a qualifying independence at home medical practice, an individual who the practice has determined—

"(A) is entitled to benefits under part A and enrolled for benefits under part B;

"(B) is not enrolled in a Medicare Advantage plan under part C or a PACE program under section 1894;

"(C) has 2 or more chronic illnesses, such as congestive heart failure, diabetes, other dementias designated by the Secretary, chronic obstructive pulmonary disease, ischemic heart disease, stroke, Alzheimer's Disease and neurodegenerative diseases, and other diseases and conditions designated by the Secretary which result in high costs under this title;

"(D) within the past 12 months has had a nonelective hospital admission;

"(E) within the past 12 months has received acute or subacute rehabilitation services;

"(F) has 2 or more functional dependencies requiring the assistance of another person (such as bathing, dressing, toileting, walking, or feeding); and

"(G) meets such other criteria as the Secretary determines appropriate.

"(2) PATIENT ELECTION TO PARTICIPATE.—The Secretary shall determine an appropriate method of ensuring that applicable beneficiaries have agreed to enroll in an independence at home medical practice under the demonstration program. Enrollment in the demonstration program shall be voluntary.

"(3) BENEFICIARY ACCESS TO SERVICES.—Nothing in this section shall be construed as encouraging physicians or nurse practitioners to limit applicable beneficiary access to services covered under this title and applicable beneficiaries shall not be required to relinquish access to any benefit under this title as a condition of receiving services from an independence at home medical practice.

"(e) IMPLEMENTATION.—

"(1) STARTING DATE.—The demonstration program shall begin no later than January 1, 2012. An agreement with an independence at home medical practice under the demonstration program may cover not more than a 3-year period.

"(2) NO PHYSICIAN DUPLICATION IN DEMONSTRATION PARTICIPATION.—The Secretary shall not pay an independence at home medical practice under this section that participates in section 1899.

"(3) NO BENEFICIARY DUPLICATION IN DEMONSTRATION PARTICIPATION.—The Secretary shall ensure that no applicable beneficiary enrolled in an independence at home medical practice under this section is participating in the programs under section 1899.

"(4) PREFERENCE.—In approving an independence at home medical practice, the Secretary shall give preference to practices that are—

"(A) located in high-cost areas of the country;

"(B) have experience in furnishing health care services to applicable beneficiaries in the home; and

"(C) use electronic medical records, health information technology, and individualized plans of care.

"(5) LIMITATION ON NUMBER OF PRACTICES.—In selecting qualified independence at home medical practices to participate under the demonstration program, the Secretary shall limit the number of such practices so that the number of applicable beneficiaries that may participate in the demonstration program does not exceed 10,000.

"(6) WAIVER.—The Secretary may waive such provisions of this title and title XI as the Secretary determines necessary in order to implement the demonstration program.

"(7) ADMINISTRATION.—Chapter 35 of title 44, United States Code, shall not apply to this section.

"(f) EVALUATION AND MONITORING.—

"(1) IN GENERAL.—The Secretary shall evaluate each independence at home medical practice under the demonstration program to assess whether the practice achieved the results described in subsection (a).

"(2) MONITORING APPLICABLE BENEFICIARIES.—The Secretary may monitor data on expenditures and quality of services under this title after an applicable beneficiary discontinues receiving services under this title through a qualifying independence at home medical practice.

"(g) REPORTS TO CONGRESS.—The Secretary shall conduct an independent evaluation of the demonstration program and submit to Congress a final report, including best practices under the demonstration program. Such report shall include an analysis of the demonstration program on coordination of care, expenditures under this title, applicable beneficiary access to services, and the quality of health care services provided to applicable beneficiaries.

"(h) FUNDING.—For purposes of administering and carrying out the demonstration program, other than for payments for items and services furnished under this title and incentive payments under subsection (c), in addition to funds otherwise appropriated, there shall be transferred to the Secretary for the Center for Medicare & Medicaid Services Program Management Account from the Federal Hospital Insurance Trust Fund under section 1817 and the Federal Supplementary Medical Insurance Trust Fund under section 1841 (in proportions determined appropriate by the Secretary) $5,000,000 for each of fiscal years 2010 through 2015. Amounts transferred under this subsection for a fiscal year shall be available until expended.

"(i) TERMINATION.—

"(1) MANDATORY TERMINATION.—The Secretary shall terminate an agreement with an independence at home medical practice if—

"(A) the Secretary estimates or determines that such practice will not receive an incentive payment for the second of 2 consecutive years under the demonstration program; or

"(B) such practice fails to meet quality standards during any year of the demonstration program.

"(2) PERMISSIVE TERMINATION.—The Secretary may terminate an agreement with an independence at home medical practice for such other reasons determined appropriate by the Secretary.".

SEC. 3025. HOSPITAL READMISSIONS REDUCTION PROGRAM.

(a) IN GENERAL.—Section 1886 of the Social Security Act (42 U.S.C. 1395ww), as amended by sections 3001 and 3008, is amended by adding at the end the following new subsection:

"(q) HOSPITAL READMISSIONS REDUCTION PROGRAM.—

"(1) IN GENERAL.—With respect to payment for discharges from an applicable hospital (as defined in paragraph (5)(C)) occurring during a fiscal year beginning on or after October 1, 2012, in order to account for excess readmissions in the hospital, the Secretary shall reduce the payments that would otherwise be made to such hospital under subsection (d) (or section 1814(b)(3), as the case may be) for such a discharge by an amount equal to the product of—

"(A) the base operating DRG payment amount (as defined in paragraph (2)) for the discharge; and

"(B) the adjustment factor (described in paragraph (3)(A)) for the hospital for the fiscal year.

"(2) BASE OPERATING DRG PAYMENT AMOUNT DEFINED.—

"(A) IN GENERAL.—Except as provided in subparagraph (B), in this subsection, the term 'base operating DRG payment amount' means, with respect to a hospital for a fiscal year—

"(i) the payment amount that would otherwise be made under subsection (d) (determined without regard to subsection (o)) for a discharge if this subsection did not apply; reduced by

"(ii) any portion of such payment amount that is attributable to payments under paragraphs (5)(A), (5)(B), (5)(F), and (12) of subsection (d).

"(B) SPECIAL RULES FOR CERTAIN HOSPITALS.—

"(i) SOLE COMMUNITY HOSPITALS AND MEDICARE-DEPENDENT, SMALL RURAL HOSPITALS.—In the case of a medicare-dependent, small rural hospital (with respect to discharges occurring during fiscal years 2012 and 2013) or a sole community hospital, in applying subparagraph (A)(i), the payment amount that would otherwise be made under subsection (d) shall be determined without regard to subparagraphs (I) and (L) of subsection (b)(3) and subparagraphs (D) and (G) of subsection (d)(5).

"(ii) HOSPITALS PAID UNDER SECTION 1814.—In the case of a hospital that is paid under section 1814(b)(3), the Secretary may exempt such hospitals provided that States paid under such section submit an annual report to the Secretary describing how a similar program in the State for a participating hospital or hospitals achieves or surpasses the measured results in terms of patient health outcomes and cost savings established herein with respect to this section.

"(3) ADJUSTMENT FACTOR.—

"(A) IN GENERAL.—For purposes of paragraph (1), the adjustment factor under this paragraph for an applicable hospital for a fiscal year is equal to the greater of—

"(i) the ratio described in subparagraph (B) for the hospital for the applicable period (as defined in paragraph (5)(D)) for such fiscal year; or

"(ii) the floor adjustment factor specified in subparagraph (C).

"(B) RATIO.—The ratio described in this subparagraph for a hospital for an applicable period is equal to 1 minus the ratio of—

"(i) the aggregate payments for excess readmissions (as defined in paragraph (4)(A)) with respect to an applicable hospital for the applicable period; and

"(ii) the aggregate payments for all discharges (as defined in paragraph (4)(B)) with respect to such applicable hospital for such applicable period.

"(C) FLOOR ADJUSTMENT FACTOR.—For purposes of subparagraph (A), the floor adjustment factor specified in this subparagraph for—

"(i) fiscal year 2013 is 0.99;

"(ii) fiscal year 2014 is 0.98; or

"(iii) fiscal year 2015 and subsequent fiscal years is 0.97.

"(4) AGGREGATE PAYMENTS, EXCESS READMISSION RATIO DEFINED.—For purposes of this subsection:

"(A) AGGREGATE PAYMENTS FOR EXCESS READMISSIONS.—The term 'aggregate payments for excess readmissions' means, for a hospital for an applicable period, the sum, for applicable conditions (as defined in paragraph (5)(A)), of the product, for each applicable condition, of—

"(i) the base operating DRG payment amount for such hospital for such applicable period for such condition;

"(ii) the number of admissions for such condition for such hospital for such applicable period; and

"(iii) the excess readmissions ratio (as defined in subparagraph (C)) for such hospital for such applicable period minus 1.

"(B) AGGREGATE PAYMENTS FOR ALL DISCHARGES.—The term 'aggregate payments for all discharges' means, for a hospital for an applicable period, the sum of the base operating DRG payment amounts for all discharges for all conditions from such hospital for such applicable period.

"(C) EXCESS READMISSION RATIO.—

"(i) IN GENERAL.—Subject to clause (ii), the term 'excess readmissions ratio' means, with respect to an applicable condition for a hospital for an applicable period, the ratio (but not less than 1.0) of—

"(I) the risk adjusted readmissions based on actual readmissions, as determined consistent with a readmission measure methodology that has been endorsed under paragraph (5)(A)(ii)(I), for an applicable hospital for such condition with respect to such applicable period; to

"(II) the risk adjusted expected readmissions (as determined consistent with such a methodology) for such hospital for such condition with respect to such applicable period.

"(ii) EXCLUSION OF CERTAIN READMISSIONS.—For purposes of clause (i), with respect to a hospital, excess readmissions shall not include readmissions for an applicable condition for which there are fewer than a minimum number (as determined by the Secretary) of discharges for such applicable condition for the applicable period and such hospital.

"(5) DEFINITIONS.—For purposes of this subsection:

"(A) APPLICABLE CONDITION.—The term 'applicable condition' means, subject to subparagraph (B), a condition or procedure selected by the Secretary among conditions and procedures for which—

"(i) readmissions (as defined in subparagraph (E)) that represent conditions or procedures that are high volume or high expenditures under this title (or other criteria specified by the Secretary); and

"(ii) measures of such readmissions—

"(I) have been endorsed by the entity with a contract under section 1890(a); and

"(II) such endorsed measures have exclusions for readmissions that are unrelated to the prior discharge (such as a planned readmission or transfer to another applicable hospital).

"(B) EXPANSION OF APPLICABLE CONDITIONS.—Beginning with fiscal year 2015, the Secretary shall, to the extent practicable, expand the applicable conditions beyond the 3 conditions for which measures have been endorsed as described in subparagraph (A)(ii)(I) as of the date of the enactment of this subsection to the additional 4 conditions that have been identified by the Medicare Payment Advisory Commission in its report to Congress in June 2007 and to other conditions and procedures as determined appropriate by the Secretary. In expanding such applicable conditions, the Secretary shall seek the endorsement described in subparagraph (A)(ii)(I) but may apply such measures without such an endorsement in the case of a specified area or medical topic determined appropriate by the Secretary for which a feasible and practical measure has not been endorsed by the entity with a contract under section 1890(a) as long as due consideration is given to measures that have been endorsed or adopted by a consensus organization identified by the Secretary.

"(C) APPLICABLE HOSPITAL.—The term 'applicable hospital' means a subsection (d) hospital or a hospital that is paid under section 1814(b)(3), as the case may be.

"(D) APPLICABLE PERIOD.—The term 'applicable period' means, with respect to a fiscal year, such period as the Secretary shall specify.

"(E) READMISSION.—The term 'readmission' means, in the case of an individual who is discharged from an applicable hospital, the admission of the individual to the same or another applicable hospital within a time period specified by the Secretary from the date of such discharge. Insofar as the discharge relates to an applicable condition for which there is an endorsed measure described in subparagraph (A)(ii)(I), such time period (such as 30 days) shall be consistent with the time period specified for such measure.

"(6) REPORTING HOSPITAL SPECIFIC INFORMATION.—

"(A) IN GENERAL.—The Secretary shall make information available to the public regarding readmission rates of each subsection (d) hospital under the program.

"(B) OPPORTUNITY TO REVIEW AND SUBMIT CORRECTIONS.—The Secretary shall ensure that a subsection (d) hospital has the opportunity to review, and submit corrections for, the information to be made public with respect to the hospital under subparagraph (A) prior to such information being made public.

"(C) WEBSITE.—Such information shall be posted on the Hospital Compare Internet website in an easily understandable format.

"(7) LIMITATIONS ON REVIEW.—There shall be no administrative or judicial review under section 1869, section 1878, or otherwise of the following:

"(A) The determination of base operating DRG payment amounts.

"(B) The methodology for determining the adjustment factor under paragraph (3), including excess readmissions ratio under paragraph (4)(C), aggregate payments for excess readmissions under paragraph (4)(A), and aggregate payments for all discharges under paragraph (4)(B), and applicable periods and applicable conditions under paragraph (5).

"(C) The measures of readmissions as described in paragraph (5)(A)(ii).

"(8) READMISSION RATES FOR ALL PATIENTS.—

"(A) CALCULATION OF READMISSION.—The Secretary shall calculate readmission rates for all patients (as defined in subparagraph (D)) for a specified hospital (as defined in subparagraph (D)(ii)) for an applicable condition (as defined in paragraph (5)(B)) and other conditions deemed appropriate by the Secretary for an applicable period (as defined in paragraph (5)(D)) in the same manner as used to calculate such readmission rates for hospitals with respect to this title and posted on the CMS Hospital Compare website.

"(B) POSTING OF HOSPITAL SPECIFIC ALL PATIENT READMISSION RATES.—The Secretary shall make information on all patient readmission rates calculated under subparagraph (A) available on the CMS Hospital Compare website in a form and manner determined appropriate by the Secretary. The Secretary may also make other information determined appropriate by the Secretary available on such website.

"(C) HOSPITAL SUBMISSION OF ALL PATIENT DATA.—

"(i) Except as provided for in clause (ii), each specified hospital (as defined in subparagraph (D)(ii)) shall submit to the Secretary, in a form, manner and time specified by the Secretary, data and information determined necessary by the Secretary for the Secretary to calculate the all patient readmission rates described in subparagraph (A).

"(ii) Instead of a specified hospital submitting to the Secretary the data and information described in clause (i), such data and information may be submitted to the Secretary, on behalf of such a specified hospital, by a state or an entity determined appropriate by the Secretary.

"(D) DEFINITIONS.—For purposes of this paragraph:

"(i) The term 'all patients' means patients who are treated on an inpatient basis and discharged from a specified hospital (as defined in clause (ii)).

"(ii) The term 'specified hospital' means a subsection (d) hospital, hospitals described in clauses (i) through (v) of subsection (d)(1)(B) and, as determined feasible and appropriate by the Secretary, other hospitals not otherwise described in this subparagraph.".

(b) QUALITY IMPROVEMENT.—Part S of title III of the Public Health Service Act, as amended by section 3015, is further amended by adding at the end the following:

"SEC. 399KK. QUALITY IMPROVEMENT PROGRAM FOR HOSPITALS WITH A HIGH SEVERITY ADJUSTED READMISSION RATE.

"(a) ESTABLISHMENT.—

"(1) IN GENERAL.—Not later than 2 years after the date of enactment of this section, the Secretary shall make available a program for eligible hospitals to improve their readmission rates through the use of patient safety organizations (as defined in section 921(4)).

"(2) ELIGIBLE HOSPITAL DEFINED.—In this subsection, the term 'eligible hospital' means a hospital that the Secretary determines has a high rate of risk adjusted readmissions for the conditions described in section 1886(q)(8)(A) of the Social Security Act and has not taken appropriate steps to reduce such readmissions and improve patient safety as evidenced through historically high rates of readmissions, as determined by the Secretary.

"(3) RISK ADJUSTMENT.—The Secretary shall utilize appropriate risk adjustment measures to determine eligible hospitals.

"(b) REPORT TO THE SECRETARY.—As determined appropriate by the Secretary, eligible hospitals and patient safety organizations working with those hospitals shall report to the Secretary on the processes employed by the hospital to improve readmission rates and the impact of such processes on readmission rates.".

SEC. 3026. COMMUNITY-BASED CARE TRANSITIONS PROGRAM.

(a) IN GENERAL.—The Secretary shall establish a Community-Based Care Transitions Program under which the Secretary provides funding to eligible entities that furnish improved care transition services to high-risk Medicare beneficiaries.

(b) DEFINITIONS.—In this section:

(1) ELIGIBLE ENTITY.—The term "eligible entity" means the following:

(A) A subsection (d) hospital (as defined in section 1886(d)(1)(B) of the Social Security Act (42 U.S.C. 1395ww(d)(1)(B))) identified by the Secretary as having a high readmission rate, such as under section 1886(q) of the Social Security Act, as added by section 3025.

(B) An appropriate community-based organization that provides care transition services under this section across a continuum of care through arrangements with subsection (d) hospitals (as so defined) to furnish the services described in subsection (c)(2)(B)(i) and whose governing body includes sufficient representation of multiple health care stakeholders (including consumers).

(2) HIGH-RISK MEDICARE BENEFICIARY.—The term "high-risk Medicare beneficiary" means a Medicare beneficiary who has attained a minimum hierarchical condition category score, as determined by the Secretary, based on a diagnosis of multiple chronic conditions or other risk factors associated with a hospital readmission or substandard transition into post-hospitalization care, which may include 1 or more of the following:

(A) Cognitive impairment.

(B) Depression.

(C) A history of multiple readmissions.

(D) Any other chronic disease or risk factor as determined by the Secretary.

(3) MEDICARE BENEFICIARY.—The term "Medicare beneficiary" means an individual who is entitled to benefits under part A of title XVIII of the Social Security Act (42 U.S.C. 1395 et seq.) and enrolled under part B of such title, but not enrolled under part C of such title.

(4) PROGRAM.—The term "program" means the program conducted under this section.

(5) READMISSION.—The term "readmission" has the meaning given such term in section 1886(q)(5)(E) of the Social Security Act, as added by section 3025.

(6) SECRETARY.—The term "Secretary" means the Secretary of Health and Human Services.

(c) REQUIREMENTS.—

(1) DURATION.—

(A) IN GENERAL.—The program shall be conducted for a 5-year period, beginning January 1, 2011.

(B) EXPANSION.—The Secretary may expand the duration and the scope of the program, to the extent determined appropriate by the Secretary, if the Secretary determines (and the Chief Actuary of the Centers for Medicare & Medicaid Services, with respect to spending under this title, certifies) that such expansion would reduce spending under this title without reducing quality.

(2) APPLICATION; PARTICIPATION.—

(A) IN GENERAL.—

(i) APPLICATION.—An eligible entity seeking to participate in the program shall submit an application to the Secretary at such time, in such manner, and containing such information as the Secretary may require.

(ii) PARTNERSHIP.—If an eligible entity is a hospital, such hospital shall enter into a partnership with a community-based organization to participate in the program.

(B) INTERVENTION PROPOSAL.—Subject to subparagraph (C), an application submitted under subparagraph (A)(i) shall include a detailed proposal for at least 1 care transition intervention, which may include the following:

(i) Initiating care transition services for a high-risk Medicare beneficiary not later than 24 hours prior to the discharge of the beneficiary from the eligible entity.

(ii) Arranging timely post-discharge follow-up services to the high-risk Medicare beneficiary to provide the beneficiary (and, as appropriate, the primary caregiver of the beneficiary) with information regarding responding to symptoms that may indicate additional health problems or a deteriorating condition.

(iii) Providing the high-risk Medicare beneficiary (and, as appropriate, the primary caregiver of the beneficiary) with assistance to ensure productive and timely interactions between patients and post-acute and outpatient providers.

(iv) Assessing and actively engaging with a high-risk Medicare beneficiary (and, as appropriate, the primary caregiver of the beneficiary) through the provision of self-management support and relevant information that is specific to the beneficiary's condition.

(v) Conducting comprehensive medication review and management (including, if appropriate, counseling and self-management support).

(C) LIMITATION.—A care transition intervention proposed under subparagraph (B) may not include payment for services required under the discharge planning process described in section 1861(ee) of the Social Security Act (42 U.S.C. 1395x(ee)).

(3) SELECTION.—In selecting eligible entities to participate in the program, the Secretary shall give priority to eligible entities that—

(A) participate in a program administered by the Administration on Aging to provide concurrent care transitions interventions with multiple hospitals and practitioners; or

(B) provide services to medically underserved populations, small communities, and rural areas.

(d) IMPLEMENTATION.—Notwithstanding any other provision of law, the Secretary may implement the provisions of this section by program instruction or otherwise.

(e) WAIVER AUTHORITY.—The Secretary may waive such requirements of titles XI and XVIII of the Social Security Act as may be necessary to carry out the program.

(f) FUNDING.—For purposes of carrying out this section, the Secretary of Health and Human Services shall provide for the transfer, from the Federal Hospital Insurance Trust Fund under section 1817 of the Social Security Act (42 U.S.C. 1395i) and the Federal Supplementary Medical Insurance Trust Fund under section 1841 of such Act (42 U.S.C. 1395t), in such proportion as the Secretary determines appropriate, of $500,000,000, to the Centers for Medicare & Medicaid Services Program Management Account for the period of fiscal years 2011 through 2015. Amounts transferred under the preceding sentence shall remain available until expended.

SEC. 3027. EXTENSION OF GAINSHARING DEMONSTRATION.

(a) IN GENERAL.—Subsection (d)(3) of section 5007 of the Deficit Reduction Act of 2005 (Public Law 109–171) is amended by inserting "(or September 30, 2011, in the case of a demonstration project in operation as of October 1, 2008)" after "December 31, 2009".

(b) FUNDING.—

(1) IN GENERAL.—Subsection (f)(1) of such section is amended by inserting "and for fiscal year 2010, $1,600,000," after "$6,000,000,".

(2) AVAILABILITY.—Subsection (f)(2) of such section is amended by striking "2010" and inserting "2014 or until expended".

(c) REPORTS.—

(1) QUALITY IMPROVEMENT AND SAVINGS.—Subsection (e)(3) of such section is amended by striking "December 1, 2008" and inserting "March 31, 2011".

(2) FINAL REPORT.—Subsection (e)(4) of such section is amended by striking "May 1, 2010" and inserting "March 31, 2013".

Subtitle B—Improving Medicare for Patients and Providers

PART I—ENSURING BENEFICIARY ACCESS TO PHYSICIAN CARE AND OTHER SERVICES

SEC. 3101. INCREASE IN THE PHYSICIAN PAYMENT UPDATE.

Section 1848(d) of the Social Security Act (42 U.S.C. 1395w–4(d)) is amended by adding at the end the following new paragraph:

"(10) UPDATE FOR 2010.—

"(A) IN GENERAL.—Subject to paragraphs (7)(B), (8)(B), and (9)(B), in lieu of the update to the single conversion factor established in paragraph (1)(C) that would otherwise apply for 2010, the update to the single conversion factor shall be 0.5 percent.

"(B) NO EFFECT ON COMPUTATION OF CONVERSION FACTOR FOR 2011 AND SUBSEQUENT YEARS.—The conversion factor under this subsection shall be computed under paragraph (1)(A) for 2011 and subsequent years as if subparagraph (A) had never applied.".

SEC. 3102. EXTENSION OF THE WORK GEOGRAPHIC INDEX FLOOR AND REVISIONS TO THE PRACTICE EXPENSE GEOGRAPHIC ADJUSTMENT UNDER THE MEDICARE PHYSICIAN FEE SCHEDULE.

(a) EXTENSION OF WORK GPCI FLOOR.—Section 1848(e)(1)(E) of the Social Security Act (42 U.S.C. 1395w–4(e)(1)(E)) is amended by striking "before January 1, 2010" and inserting "before January 1, 2011".

(b) PRACTICE EXPENSE GEOGRAPHIC ADJUSTMENT FOR 2010 AND SUBSEQUENT YEARS.—Section 1848(e)(1) of the Social Security Act (42 U.S.C. 1395w4(e)(1)) is amended—

(1) in subparagraph (A), by striking "and (G)" and inserting "(G), and (H)"; and

(2) by adding at the end the following new subparagraph:

"(H) PRACTICE EXPENSE GEOGRAPHIC ADJUSTMENT FOR 2010 AND SUBSEQUENT YEARS.—

"(i) FOR 2010.—Subject to clause (iii), for services furnished during 2010, the employee wage and rent portions of the practice expense geographic index described in subparagraph (A)(i) shall reflect 3/4 of the difference between the relative costs of employee wages and rents in each of the different fee schedule areas and the national average of such employee wages and rents.

"(ii) FOR 2011.—Subject to clause (iii), for services furnished during 2011, the employee wage and rent portions of the practice expense geographic index described in subparagraph (A)(i) shall reflect 1/2 of the difference between the relative costs of employee wages and rents in each of the different fee schedule areas and the national average of such employee wages and rents.

"(iii) HOLD HARMLESS.—The practice expense portion of the geographic adjustment factor applied in a fee schedule area for services furnished in 2010 or 2011 shall not, as a result of the application of clause (i) or (ii), be reduced below the practice expense portion of the geographic adjustment factor under subparagraph (A)(i) (as calculated prior to the application of such clause (i) or (ii), respectively) for such area for such year.

"(iv) ANALYSIS.—The Secretary shall analyze current methods of establishing practice expense geographic adjustments under subparagraph (A)(i) and evaluate data that fairly and reliably establishes distinctions in the costs of operating a medical practice in the different fee schedule areas. Such analysis shall include an evaluation of the following:

"(I) The feasibility of using actual data or reliable survey data developed by medical organizations on the costs of operating a medical practice, including office rents and non-physician staff wages, in different fee schedule areas.

"(II) The office expense portion of the practice expense geographic adjustment described in subparagraph (A)(i), including the extent to which types of office expenses are determined in local markets instead of national markets.

"(III) The weights assigned to each of the categories within the practice expense geographic adjustment described in subparagraph (A)(i).

"(v) REVISION FOR 2012 AND SUBSEQUENT YEARS.—As a result of the analysis described in clause (iv), the Secretary shall, not later than January 1, 2012, make appropriate adjustments to the practice expense geographic adjustment described in subparagraph (A)(i) to ensure accurate geographic adjustments across fee schedule areas, including—

"(I) basing the office rents component and its weight on office expenses that vary among fee schedule areas; and

"(II) considering a representative range of professional and non-professional personnel employed in a medical office based on the use of the American Community Survey data or other reliable data for wage adjustments.

Such adjustments shall be made without regard to adjustments made pursuant to clauses (i) and (ii) and shall be made in a budget neutral manner.".

SEC. 3103. EXTENSION OF EXCEPTIONS PROCESS FOR MEDICARE THERAPY CAPS.

Section 1833(g)(5) of the Social Security Act (42 U.S.C. 1395l(g)(5)) is amended by striking "December 31, 2009" and inserting "December 31, 2010".

SEC. 3104. EXTENSION OF PAYMENT FOR TECHNICAL COMPONENT OF CERTAIN PHYSICIAN PATHOLOGY SERVICES.

Section 542(c) of the Medicare, Medicaid, and SCHIP Benefits Improvement and Protection Act of 2000 (as enacted into law by section 1(a)(6) of Public Law 106–554), as amended by section 732 of the Medicare Prescription Drug, Improvement, and Modernization Act of 2003 (42 U.S.C. 1395w–4 note), section 104 of division B of the Tax Relief and Health Care Act of 2006 (42 U.S.C. 1395w–4 note), section 104 of the Medicare, Medicaid, and SCHIP Extension Act of 2007 (Public Law 110–173), and section 136 of the Medicare Improvements for Patients and Providers Act of 2008 (Public Law 110–275), is amended by striking "and 2009" and inserting "2009, and 2010".

SEC. 3105. EXTENSION OF AMBULANCE ADD-ONS.

(a) GROUND AMBULANCE.—Section 1834(l)(13)(A) of the Social Security Act (42 U.S.C. 1395m(l)(13)(A)) is amended—

(1) in the matter preceding clause (i)—

(A) by striking "2007, and for" and inserting "2007, for"; and

(B) by striking "2010" and inserting "2010, and for such services furnished on or after April 1, 2010, and before January 1, 2011,"; and

(2) in each of clauses (i) and (ii), by inserting ", and on or after April 1, 2010, and before January 1, 2011" after "January 1, 2010" each place it appears.

(b) AIR AMBULANCE.—Section 146(b)(1) of the Medicare Improvements for Patients and Providers Act of 2008 (Public Law

110–275) is amended by striking "December 31, 2009" and inserting "December 31, 2009, and during the period beginning on April 1, 2010, and ending on January 1, 2011".

(c) SUPER RURAL AMBULANCE.—Section 1834(l)(12)(A) of the Social Security Act (42 U.S.C. 1395m(l)(12)(A)) is amended by striking "2010" and inserting "2010, and on or after April 1, 2010, and before January 1, 2011".

SEC. 3106. EXTENSION OF CERTAIN PAYMENT RULES FOR LONG-TERM CARE HOSPITAL SERVICES AND OF MORATORIUM ON THE ESTABLISHMENT OF CERTAIN HOSPITALS AND FACILITIES.

(a) EXTENSION OF CERTAIN PAYMENT RULES.—Section 114(c) of the Medicare, Medicaid, and SCHIP Extension Act of 2007 (42 U.S.C. 1395ww note), as amended by section 4302(a) of the American Recovery and Reinvestment Act (Public Law 111–5), is further amended by striking "3-year period" each place it appears and inserting "4-year period".

(b) EXTENSION OF MORATORIUM.—Section 114(d)(1) of such Act (42 U.S.C. 1395ww note), in the matter preceding subparagraph (A), is amended by striking "3-year period" and inserting "4-year period".

SEC. 3107. EXTENSION OF PHYSICIAN FEE SCHEDULE MENTAL HEALTH ADD-ON.

Section 138(a)(1) of the Medicare Improvements for Patients and Providers Act of 2008 (Public Law 110–275) is amended by striking "December 31, 2009" and inserting "December 31, 2010".

SEC. 3108. PERMITTING PHYSICIAN ASSISTANTS TO ORDER POST-HOSPITAL EXTENDED CARE SERVICES.

(a) ORDERING POST-HOSPITAL EXTENDED CARE SERVICES.—

(1) IN GENERAL.—Section 1814(a)(2) of the Social Security Act (42 U.S.C. 1395f(a)(2)), in the matter preceding subparagraph (A), is amended by striking "or clinical nurse specialist" and inserting ", a clinical nurse specialist, or a physician assistant (as those terms are defined in section 1861(aa)(5))" after "nurse practitioner".

(2) CONFORMING AMENDMENT.—Section 1814(a) of the Social Security Act (42 U.S.C. 1395f(a)) is amended, in the second sentence, by striking "or clinical nurse specialist" and inserting "clinical nurse specialist, or physician assistant" after "nurse practitioner,".

(b) EFFECTIVE DATE.—The amendments made by this section shall apply to items and services furnished on or after January 1, 2011.

SEC. 3109. EXEMPTION OF CERTAIN PHARMACIES FROM ACCREDITATION REQUIREMENTS.

(a) IN GENERAL.—Section 1834(a)(20) of the Social Security Act (42 U.S.C. 1395m(a)(20)), as added by section 154(b)(1)(A) of the Medicare Improvements for Patients and Providers Act of 2008 (Public Law 100–275), is amended—

(1) in subparagraph (F)(i)—

(A) by inserting "and subparagraph (G)" after "clause (ii)"; and

(B) by inserting ", except that the Secretary shall not require a pharmacy to have submitted to the Secretary such evidence of accreditation prior to January 1, 2011" before the semicolon at the end; and

(2) by adding at the end the following new subparagraph:

"(G) APPLICATION OF ACCREDITATION REQUIREMENT TO CERTAIN PHARMACIES.—

"(i) IN GENERAL.—With respect to items and services furnished on or after January 1, 2011, in implementing quality standards under this paragraph—

"(I) subject to subclause (II), in applying such standards and the accreditation requirement of subparagraph (F)(i) with respect to pharmacies described in clause (ii) furnishing such items and services, such standards and accreditation requirement shall not apply to such pharmacies; and

"(II) the Secretary may apply to such pharmacies an alternative accreditation requirement established by the Secretary if the Secretary determines such alternative accreditation requirement is more appropriate for such pharmacies.

"(ii) PHARMACIES DESCRIBED.—A pharmacy described in this clause is a pharmacy that meets each of the following criteria:

"(I) The total billings by the pharmacy for such items and services under this title are less than 5 percent of total pharmacy sales, as determined based on the average total pharmacy sales for the previous 3 calendar years, 3 fiscal years, or other yearly period specified by the Secretary.

"(II) The pharmacy has been enrolled under section 1866(j) as a supplier of durable medical equipment, prosthetics, orthotics, and supplies, has been issued (which may include the renewal of) a provider number for at least 5 years, and for which a final adverse action (as defined in section 424.57(a) of title 42, Code of Federal Regulations) has not been imposed in the past 5 years.

"(III) The pharmacy submits to the Secretary an attestation, in a form and manner, and at a time, specified by the Secretary, that the pharmacy meets the criteria described in subclauses (I) and (II). Such attestation shall be subject to section 1001 of title 18, United States Code.

"(IV) The pharmacy agrees to submit materials as requested by the Secretary, or during the course of an audit conducted on a random sample of pharmacies selected annually, to verify that the pharmacy meets the criteria described in subclauses (I) and (II). Materials submitted under the preceding sentence shall include a certification by an accountant on behalf of the pharmacy or the submission of tax returns filed by the pharmacy during the relevant periods, as requested by the Secretary.".

(b) ADMINISTRATION.—Notwithstanding any other provision of law, the Secretary may implement the amendments made by subsection (a) by program instruction or otherwise.

(c) RULE OF CONSTRUCTION.—Nothing in the provisions of or amendments made by this section shall be construed as affecting the application of an accreditation requirement for pharmacies to qualify for bidding in a competitive acquisition area under section 1847 of the Social Security Act (42 U.S.C. 1395w–3).

SEC. 3110. PART B SPECIAL ENROLLMENT PERIOD FOR DISABLED TRICARE BENEFICIARIES.

(a) IN GENERAL.—

(1) IN GENERAL.—Section 1837 of the Social Security Act (42 U.S.C. 1395p) is amended by adding at the end the following new subsection:

"(l)(1) In the case of any individual who is a covered beneficiary (as defined in section 1072(5) of title 10, United States Code) at the time the individual is entitled to part A under section 226(b) or section 226A and who is eligible to enroll but who has elected not to enroll (or to be deemed enrolled) during the individual's initial enrollment period, there shall be a special enrollment period described in paragraph (2).

"(2) The special enrollment period described in this paragraph, with respect to an individual, is the 12-month period beginning on the day after the last day of the initial enrollment period of the individual or, if later, the 12-month period beginning with the month the individual is notified of enrollment under this section.

"(3) In the case of an individual who enrolls during the special enrollment period provided under paragraph (1), the coverage period under this part shall begin on the first day of the month in which the individual enrolls, or, at the option of the individual, the first month after the end of the individual's initial enrollment period.

"(4) An individual may only enroll during the special enrollment period provided under paragraph (1) one time during the individual's lifetime.

"(5) The Secretary shall ensure that the materials relating to coverage under this part that are provided to an individual described in paragraph (1) prior to the individual's initial enrollment period contain information concerning the impact of not enrolling under this part, including the impact on health care benefits under the TRICARE program under chapter 55 of title 10, United States Code.

"(6) The Secretary of Defense shall collaborate with the Secretary of Health and Human Services and the Commissioner of Social Security to provide for the accurate identification of individuals described in paragraph (1). The Secretary of Defense shall provide such individuals with notification with respect to this subsection. The Secretary of Defense shall collaborate with the Secretary of Health and Human Services and the Commissioner of Social Security to ensure appropriate follow up pursuant to any notification provided under the preceding sentence.".

(2) EFFECTIVE DATE.—The amendment made by paragraph (1) shall apply to elections made with respect to initial enrollment periods that end after the date of the enactment of this Act.

(b) WAIVER OF INCREASE OF PREMIUM.—Section 1839(b) of the Social Security Act (42 U.S.C. 1395r(b)) is amended by striking "section 1837(i)(4)" and inserting "subsection (i)(4) or (l) of section 1837".

SEC. 3111. PAYMENT FOR BONE DENSITY TESTS.

(a) PAYMENT.—

(1) IN GENERAL.—Section 1848 of the Social Security Act (42 U.S.C. 1395w–4) is amended—

(A) in subsection (b)—

(i) in paragraph (4)(B), by inserting ", and for 2010 and 2011, dual-energy x-ray absorptiometry services (as described in paragraph (6))" before the period at the end; and

(ii) by adding at the end the following new paragraph:

"(6) TREATMENT OF BONE MASS SCANS.—For dual-energy x-ray absorptiometry services (identified in 2006 by HCPCS codes 76075 and 76077 (and any succeeding codes)) furnished during 2010 and 2011, instead of the payment amount that would otherwise be determined under this section for such years, the payment amount shall be equal to 70 percent of the product of—

"(A) the relative value for the service (as determined in subsection (c)(2)) for 2006;

"(B) the conversion factor (established under subsection (d)) for 2006; and

"(C) the geographic adjustment factor (established under subsection (e)(2)) for the service for the fee schedule area for 2010 and 2011, respectively."; and

(B) in subsection (c)(2)(B)(iv)—

(i) in subclause (II), by striking "and" at the end;

(ii) in subclause (III), by striking the period at the end and inserting "; and"; and

(iii) by adding at the end the following new subclause:

"(IV) subsection (b)(6) shall not be taken into account in applying clause (ii)(II) for 2010 or 2011.".

(2) IMPLEMENTATION.—Notwithstanding any other provision of law, the Secretary may implement the amendments made by paragraph (1) by program instruction or otherwise.

(b) STUDY AND REPORT BY THE INSTITUTE OF MEDICINE.—

(1) IN GENERAL.—The Secretary of Health and Human Services is authorized to enter into an agreement with the Institute of Medicine of the National Academies to conduct a study on the ramifications of Medicare payment reductions for dual-energy x-ray absorptiometry (as described in section 1848(b)(6) of the Social Security Act, as added by subsection (a)(1)) during 2007, 2008, and 2009 on beneficiary access to bone mass density tests.

(2) REPORT.—An agreement entered into under paragraph (1) shall provide for the Institute of Medicine to submit to the Secretary and to Congress a report containing the results of the study conducted under such paragraph.

SEC. 3112. REVISION TO THE MEDICARE IMPROVEMENT FUND.

Section 1898(b)(1)(A) of the Social Security Act (42 U.S.C. 1395iii) is amended by striking "$22,290,000,000" and inserting "$0".

SEC. 3113. TREATMENT OF CERTAIN COMPLEX DIAGNOSTIC LABORATORY TESTS.

(a) DEMONSTRATION PROJECT.—

(1) IN GENERAL.—The Secretary of Health and Human Services (in this section referred to as the "Secretary") shall conduct a demonstration project under part B title XVIII of the Social Security Act under which separate payments are made under such part for complex diagnostic laboratory tests provided to individuals under such part. Under the demonstration project, the Secretary shall establish appropriate payment rates for such tests.

(2) COVERED COMPLEX DIAGNOSTIC LABORATORY TEST DEFINED.—In this section, the term "complex diagnostic laboratory test" means a diagnostic laboratory test—

(A) that is an analysis of gene protein expression, topographic genotyping, or a cancer chemotherapy sensitivity assay;

(B) that is determined by the Secretary to be a laboratory test for which there is not an alternative test having equivalent performance characteristics;

(C) which is billed using a Health Care Procedure Coding System (HCPCS) code other than a not otherwise classified code under such Coding System;

(D) which is approved or cleared by the Food and Drug Administration or is covered under title XVIII of the Social Security Act; and

(E) is described in section 1861(s)(3) of the Social Security Act (42 U.S.C. 1395x(s)(3)).

(3) SEPARATE PAYMENT DEFINED.—In this section, the term "separate payment" means direct payment to a laboratory (including a hospital-based or independent laboratory) that performs a complex diagnostic laboratory test with respect to a specimen collected from an individual during a period in which the individual is a patient of a hospital if the test is performed after such period of hospitalization and if separate payment would not otherwise be made under title XVIII of the Social Security Act by reason of sections 1862(a)(14) and 1866(a)(1)(H)(i) of the such Act (42 U.S.C. 1395y(a)(14); 42 U.S.C. 1395cc(a)(1)(H)(i)).

(b) DURATION.—Subject to subsection (c)(2), the Secretary shall conduct the demonstration project under this section for the 2-year period beginning on July 1, 2011.

(c) PAYMENTS AND LIMITATION.—Payments under the demonstration project under this section shall—

(1) be made from the Federal Supplemental Medical Insurance Trust Fund under section 1841 of the Social Security Act (42 U.S.C. 1395t); and

(2) may not exceed $100,000,000.

(d) REPORT.—Not later than 2 years after the completion of the demonstration project under this section, the Secretary shall submit to Congress a report on the project. Such report shall include—

(1) an assessment of the impact of the demonstration project on access to care, quality of care, health outcomes, and expenditures under title XVIII of the Social Security Act (including any savings under such title); and

(2) such recommendations as the Secretary determines appropriate.

(e) IMPLEMENTATION FUNDING.—For purposes of administering this section (including preparing and submitting the report under subsection (d)), the Secretary shall provide for the transfer, from the Federal Supplemental Medical Insurance Trust Fund under section 1841 of the Social Security Act (42 U.S.C. 1395t), to the Centers for Medicare & Medicaid Services Program Management Account, of $5,000,000. Amounts transferred under the preceding sentence shall remain available until expended.

SEC. 3114. IMPROVED ACCESS FOR CERTIFIED NURSE-MIDWIFE SERVICES.

Section 1833(a)(1)(K) of the Social Security Act (42 U.S.C. 1395l(a)(1)(K)) is amended by inserting "(or 100 percent for services furnished on or after January 1, 2011)" after "1992, 65 percent".

PART II—RURAL PROTECTIONS

SEC. 3121. EXTENSION OF OUTPATIENT HOLD HARMLESS PROVISION.

(a) IN GENERAL.—Section 1833(t)(7)(D)(i) of the Social Security Act (42 U.S.C. 1395l(t)(7)(D)(i)) is amended—

(1) in subclause (II)—

(A) in the first sentence, by striking "2010"and inserting "2011"; and

(B) in the second sentence, by striking "or 2009" and inserting ", 2009, or 2010"; and

(2) in subclause (III), by striking "January 1, 2010" and inserting "January 1, 2011".

(b) PERMITTING ALL SOLE COMMUNITY HOSPITALS TO BE ELIGIBLE FOR HOLD HARMLESS.—Section 1833(t)(7)(D)(i)(III) of the Social Security Act (42 U.S.C. 1395l(t)(7)(D)(i)(III)) is amended by adding at the end the following new sentence: "In the case of covered OPD services furnished on or after January 1, 2010, and before January 1, 2011, the preceding sentence shall be applied without regard to the 100-bed limitation.".

SEC. 3122. EXTENSION OF MEDICARE REASONABLE COSTS PAYMENTS FOR CERTAIN CLINICAL DIAGNOSTIC LABORATORY TESTS FURNISHED TO HOSPITAL PATIENTS IN CERTAIN RURAL AREAS.

Section 416(b) of the Medicare Prescription Drug, Improvement, and Modernization Act of 2003 (42 U.S.C. 1395l–4), as amended by section 105 of division B of the Tax Relief and Health Care Act of 2006 (42 U.S.C. 1395l note) and section 107 of the Medicare, Medicaid, and SCHIP Extension Act of 2007 (42 U.S.C. 1395l note), is amended by inserting "or during the 1-year period beginning on July 1, 2010" before the period at the end.

SEC. 3123. EXTENSION OF THE RURAL COMMUNITY HOSPITAL DEMONSTRATION PROGRAM.

(a) ONE-YEAR EXTENSION.—Section 410A of the Medicare Prescription Drug, Improvement, and Modernization Act of 2003 (Public Law 108–173; 117 Stat. 2272) is amended by adding at the end the following new subsection:

"(g) ONE-YEAR EXTENSION OF DEMONSTRATION PROGRAM.—

"(1) IN GENERAL.—Subject to the succeeding provisions of this subsection, the Secretary shall conduct the demonstration program under this section for an additional 1-year period (in this section referred to as the '1-year extension period') that begins on the date immediately following the last day of the initial 5-year period under subsection (a)(5).

"(2) EXPANSION OF DEMONSTRATION STATES.—Notwithstanding subsection (a)(2), during the 1-year extension period, the Secretary shall expand the number of States with low population densities determined by the Secretary under such subsection to 20. In determining which States to include in such expansion, the Secretary shall use the same criteria and data that the Secretary used to determine the States under such subsection for purposes of the initial 5-year period.

"(3) INCREASE IN MAXIMUM NUMBER OF HOSPITALS PARTICIPATING IN THE DEMONSTRATION PROGRAM.—Notwithstanding subsection (a)(4), during the 1-year extension period, not more than 30 rural community hospitals may participate in the demonstration program under this section.

"(4) NO AFFECT ON HOSPITALS IN DEMONSTRATION PROGRAM ON DATE OF ENACTMENT.—In the case of a rural community hospital that is participating in the demonstration program under this section as of the last day of the initial 5-year period, the Secretary shall provide for the continued participation of such rural community hospital in the demonstration program during the 1-year extension period unless the rural community hospital makes an election, in such form and manner as the Secretary may specify, to discontinue such participation.".

(b) CONFORMING AMENDMENTS.—Subsection (a)(5) of section 410A of the Medicare Prescription Drug, Improvement, and Modernization Act of 2003 (Public Law 108–173; 117 Stat. 2272) is amended by inserting "(in this section referred to as the 'initial 5-year period') and, as provided in subsection (g), for the 1-year extension period" after "5-year period".

(c) TECHNICAL AMENDMENTS.—

(1) Subsection (b) of section 410A of the Medicare Prescription Drug, Improvement, and Modernization Act of 2003 (Public Law 108–173; 117 Stat. 2272) is amended—

(A) in paragraph (1)(B)(ii), by striking "2)" and inserting "2))"; and

(B) in paragraph (2), by inserting "cost" before "reporting period" the first place such term appears in each of subparagraphs (A) and (B).

(2) Subsection (f)(1) of section 410A of the Medicare Prescription Drug, Improvement, and Modernization Act of 2003 (Public Law 108–173; 117 Stat. 2272) is amended—

(A) in subparagraph (A)(ii), by striking "paragraph (2)" and inserting "subparagraph (B)"; and

(B) in subparagraph (B), by striking "paragraph (1)(B)" and inserting "subparagraph (A)(ii)".

SEC. 3124. EXTENSION OF THE MEDICARE-DEPENDENT HOSPITAL (MDH) PROGRAM.

(a) EXTENSION OF PAYMENT METHODOLOGY.—Section 1886(d)(5)(G) of the Social Security Act (42 U.S.C. 1395ww(d)(5)(G)) is amended—

(1) in clause (i), by striking "October 1, 2011" and inserting "October 1, 2012"; and

(2) in clause (ii)(II), by striking "October 1, 2011" and inserting "October 1, 2012".

(b) CONFORMING AMENDMENTS.—

(1) EXTENSION OF TARGET AMOUNT.—Section 1886(b)(3)(D) of the Social Security Act (42 U.S.C. 1395ww(b)(3)(D)) is amended—

(A) in the matter preceding clause (i), by striking "October 1, 2011" and inserting "October 1, 2012"; and

(B) in clause (iv), by striking "through fiscal year 2011" and inserting "through fiscal year 2012".

(2) PERMITTING HOSPITALS TO DECLINE RECLASSIFICATION.—Section 13501(e)(2) of the Omnibus Budget Reconciliation Act of 1993 (42 U.S.C. 1395ww note) is amended by striking "through fiscal year 2011" and inserting "through fiscal year 2012".

SEC. 3125. TEMPORARY IMPROVEMENTS TO THE MEDICARE INPATIENT HOSPITAL PAYMENT ADJUSTMENT FOR LOW-VOLUME HOSPITALS.

Section 1886(d)(12) of the Social Security Act (42 U.S.C. 1395ww(d)(12)) is amended—

(1) in subparagraph (A), by inserting "or (D)" after "subparagraph (B)";

(2) in subparagraph (B), in the matter preceding clause (i), by striking "The Secretary" and inserting "For discharges occurring in fiscal years 2005 through 2010 and for discharges occurring in fiscal year 2013 and subsequent fiscal years, the Secretary";

(3) in subparagraph (C)(i)—

(A) by inserting "(or, with respect to fiscal years 2011 and 2012, 15 road miles)" after "25 road miles"; and

(B) by inserting "(or, with respect to fiscal years 2011 and 2012, 1,500 discharges of individuals entitled to, or enrolled for, benefits under part A)" after "800 discharges"; and

(4) by adding at the end the following new subparagraph:

"(D) TEMPORARY APPLICABLE PERCENTAGE INCREASE.—For discharges occurring in fiscal years 2011 and 2012, the Secretary shall determine an applicable percentage increase for purposes of subparagraph (A) using a continuous linear sliding scale ranging from 25 percent for low-volume hospitals with 200 or fewer discharges of individuals entitled to, or enrolled for, benefits under part A in the fiscal year to 0 percent for low-volume hospitals with greater than 1,500 discharges of such individuals in the fiscal year.".

SEC. 3126. IMPROVEMENTS TO THE DEMONSTRATION PROJECT ON COMMUNITY HEALTH INTEGRATION MODELS IN CERTAIN RURAL COUNTIES.

(a) REMOVAL OF LIMITATION ON NUMBER OF ELIGIBLE COUNTIES SELECTED.—Subsection (d)(3) of section 123 of the Medicare Improvements for Patients and Providers Act of 2008 (42 U.S.C. 1395i–4 note) is amended by striking "not more than 6".

(b) REMOVAL OF REFERENCES TO RURAL HEALTH CLINIC SERVICES AND INCLUSION OF PHYSICIANS' SERVICES IN SCOPE OF DEMONSTRATION PROJECT.—Such section 123 is amended—

(1) in subsection (d)(4)(B)(i)(3), by striking subclause (III); and

(2) in subsection (j)—

(A) in paragraph (8), by striking subparagraph (B) and inserting the following:

"(B) Physicians' services (as defined in section 1861(q) of the Social Security Act (42 U.S.C. 1395x(q)).";

(B) by striking paragraph (9); and

(C) by redesignating paragraph (10) as paragraph (9).

SEC. 3127. MEDPAC STUDY ON ADEQUACY OF MEDICARE PAYMENTS FOR HEALTH CARE PROVIDERS SERVING IN RURAL AREAS.

(a) STUDY.—The Medicare Payment Advisory Commission shall conduct a study on the adequacy of payments for items and services furnished by providers of services and suppliers in rural areas under the Medicare program under title XVIII of the Social Security Act (42 U.S.C. 1395 et seq.). Such study shall include an analysis of—

(1) any adjustments in payments to providers of services and suppliers that furnish items and services in rural areas;

(2) access by Medicare beneficiaries to items and services in rural areas;

(3) the adequacy of payments to providers of services and suppliers that furnish items and services in rural areas; and

(4) the quality of care furnished in rural areas.

(b) REPORT.—Not later than January 1, 2011, the Medicare Payment Advisory Commission shall submit to Congress a report containing the results of the study conducted under subsection (a). Such report shall include recommendations on appropriate modifications to any adjustments in payments to providers of services and suppliers that furnish items and services in rural areas, together with recommendations for such legislation and administrative action as the Medicare Payment Advisory Commission determines appropriate.

SEC. 3128. TECHNICAL CORRECTION RELATED TO CRITICAL ACCESS HOSPITAL SERVICES.

(a) IN GENERAL.—Subsections (g)(2)(A) and (l)(8) of section 1834 of the Social Security Act (42 U.S.C. 1395m) are each amended by inserting "101 percent of" before "the reasonable costs".

(b) EFFECTIVE DATE.—The amendments made by subsection (a) shall take effect as if included in the enactment of section 405(a) of the Medicare Prescription Drug, Improvement, and Modernization Act of 2003 (Public Law 108–173; 117 Stat. 2266).

SEC. 3129. EXTENSION OF AND REVISIONS TO MEDICARE RURAL HOSPITAL FLEXIBILITY PROGRAM.

(a) AUTHORIZATION.—Section 1820(j) of the Social Security Act (42 U.S.C. 1395i–4(j)) is amended—

(1) by striking "2010, and for" and inserting "2010, for"; and

(2) by inserting "and for making grants to all States under subsection (g), such sums as may be necessary in each of fiscal years 2011 and 2012, to remain available until expended" before the period at the end.

(b) USE OF FUNDS.—Section 1820(g)(3) of the Social Security Act (42 U.S.C. 1395i–4(g)(3)) is amended—

(1) in subparagraph (A), by inserting "and to assist such hospitals in participating in delivery system reforms under the provisions of and amendments made by the Patient Protection and Affordable Care Act, such as value-based purchasing programs, accountable care organizations under section 1899, the National pilot program on payment bundling under section 1866D, and other delivery system reform programs determined appropriate by the Secretary" before the period at the end; and

(2) in subparagraph (E)—

(A) by striking ", and to offset" and inserting ", to offset"; and

(B) by inserting "and to participate in delivery system reforms under the provisions of and amendments made by the Patient Protection and Affordable Care Act, such as value-based purchasing programs, accountable care organizations under section 1899, the National pilot program on payment bundling under section 1866D, and other delivery system reform programs determined appropriate by the Secretary" before the period at the end.

(c) EFFECTIVE DATE.—The amendments made by this section shall apply to grants made on or after January 1, 2010.

PART III—IMPROVING PAYMENT ACCURACY

SEC. 3131. PAYMENT ADJUSTMENTS FOR HOME HEALTH CARE.

(a) REBASING HOME HEALTH PROSPECTIVE PAYMENT AMOUNT.—

(1) IN GENERAL.—Section 1895(b)(3)(A) of the Social Security Act (42 U.S.C. 1395fff(b)(3)(A)) is amended—

(A) in clause (i)(III), by striking "For periods" and inserting "Subject to clause (iii), for periods"; and

(B) by adding at the end the following new clause:

"(iii) ADJUSTMENT FOR 2013 AND SUBSEQUENT YEARS.—

"(I) IN GENERAL.—Subject to subclause (II), for 2013 and subsequent years, the amount (or amounts) that would otherwise be applicable under clause (i)(III) shall be adjusted by a percentage determined appropriate by the Secretary to reflect such factors as changes in the number of visits in an episode, the mix of services in an episode, the level of intensity of services in an episode, the average cost of providing care per episode, and other factors that the Secretary considers to be relevant. In conducting the analysis under the preceding sentence, the Secretary may consider differences between hospital-based and freestanding agencies, between for-profit and nonprofit agencies, and between the resource costs of urban and rural agencies. Such adjustment shall be made before the update under subparagraph (B) is applied for the year.

"(II) TRANSITION.—The Secretary shall provide for a 4-year phase-in (in equal increments) of the adjustment under subclause (I), with such adjustment being fully implemented for 2016. During each year of such phase-in, the amount of any adjustment under subclause (I) for the year may not exceed 3.5 percent of the amount (or amounts) applicable under clause (i)(III) as of the date of enactment of the Patient Protection and Affordable Care Act.".

(2) MEDPAC STUDY AND REPORT.—

(A) STUDY.—The Medicare Payment Advisory Commission shall conduct a study on the implementation of the amendments made by paragraph (1). Such study shall include an analysis of the impact of such amendments on—

(i) access to care;

(ii) quality outcomes;

(iii) the number of home health agencies; and

(iv) rural agencies, urban agencies, for-profit agencies, and nonprofit agencies.

(B) REPORT.—Not later than January 1, 2015, the Medicare Payment Advisory Commission shall submit to Congress a report on the study conducted under subparagraph (A), together with recommendations for such legislation and administrative action as the Commission determines appropriate.

(b) PROGRAM-SPECIFIC OUTLIER CAP.—Section 1895(b) of the Social Security Act (42 U.S.C. 1395fff(b)) is amended—

(1) in paragraph (3)(C), by striking "the aggregate" and all that follows through the period at the end and inserting "5 percent of the total payments estimated to be made based on the prospective payment system under this subsection for the period."; and

(2) in paragraph (5)—

(A) by striking "OUTLIERS.—The Secretary" and inserting the following: "OUTLIERS.—

"(A) IN GENERAL.—Subject to subparagraph (B), the Secretary";

(B) in subparagraph (A), as added by subparagraph (A), by striking "5 percent" and inserting "2.5 percent"; and

(C) by adding at the end the following new subparagraph:

"(B) PROGRAM SPECIFIC OUTLIER CAP.—The estimated total amount of additional payments or payment adjustments made under subparagraph (A) with respect to a home health agency for a year (beginning with 2011) may not exceed an amount equal to 10 percent of the estimated total amount of payments made under this section (without regard to this paragraph) with respect to the home health agency for the year.".

(c) APPLICATION OF THE MEDICARE RURAL HOME HEALTH ADD-ON POLICY.—Section 421 of the Medicare Prescription Drug, Improvement, and Modernization Act of 2003 (Public Law 108–173; 117 Stat. 2283), as amended by section 5201(b) of the Deficit Reduction Act of 2005 (Public Law 109–171; 120 Stat. 46), is amended—

(1) in the section heading, by striking "**ONE-YEAR**" and inserting "**TEMPORARY**"; and

(2) in subsection (a)—

(A) by striking ", and episodes" and inserting ", episodes";

(B) by inserting "and episodes and visits ending on or after April 1, 2010, and before January 1, 2016," after "January 1, 2007,"; and

(C) by inserting "(or, in the case of episodes and visits ending on or after April 1, 2010, and before January 1, 2016, 3 percent)" before the period at the end.

(d) STUDY AND REPORT ON THE DEVELOPMENT OF HOME HEALTH PAYMENT REFORMS IN ORDER TO ENSURE ACCESS TO CARE AND QUALITY SERVICES.—

(1) IN GENERAL.—The Secretary of Health and Human Services (in this section referred to as the "Secretary") shall conduct a study to evaluate the costs and quality of care among efficient home health agencies relative to other such agencies in providing ongoing access to care and in treating Medicare beneficiaries with varying severity levels of illness. Such study shall include an analysis of the following:

(A) Methods to revise the home health prospective payment system under section 1895 of the Social Security Act (42 U.S.C. 1395fff) to more accurately account for the costs related to patient severity of illness or to improving beneficiary access to care, including—

(i) payment adjustments for services that may be under- or over-valued;

(ii) necessary changes to reflect the resource use relative to providing home health services to low-income Medicare beneficiaries or Medicare beneficiaries living in medically underserved areas;

(iii) ways the outlier payment may be improved to more accurately reflect the cost of treating Medicare beneficiaries with high severity levels of illness;

(iv) the role of quality of care incentives and penalties in driving provider and patient behavior;

(v) improvements in the application of a wage index; and

(vi) other areas determined appropriate by the Secretary.

(B) The validity and reliability of responses on the OASIS instrument with particular emphasis on questions that relate to higher payment under the home health prospective payment system and higher outcome scores under Home Care Compare.

(C) Additional research or payment revisions under the home health prospective payment system that may be necessary to set the payment rates for home health services based on costs of high-quality and efficient home health agencies or to improve Medicare beneficiary access to care.

(D) A timetable for implementation of any appropriate changes based on the analysis of the matters described in subparagraphs (A), (B), and (C).

(E) Other areas determined appropriate by the Secretary.

(2) CONSIDERATIONS.—In conducting the study under paragraph (1), the Secretary shall consider whether certain factors

should be used to measure patient severity of illness and access to care, such as—

(A) population density and relative patient access to care;

(B) variations in service costs for providing care to individuals who are dually eligible under the Medicare and Medicaid programs;

(C) the presence of severe or chronic diseases, as evidenced by multiple, discontinuous home health episodes;

(D) poverty status, as evidenced by the receipt of Supplemental Security Income under title XVI of the Social Security Act;

(E) the absence of caregivers;

(F) language barriers;

(G) atypical transportation costs;

(H) security costs; and

(I) other factors determined appropriate by the Secretary.

(3) REPORT.—Not later than March 1, 2011, the Secretary shall submit to Congress a report on the study conducted under paragraph (1), together with recommendations for such legislation and administrative action as the Secretary determines appropriate.

(4) CONSULTATIONS.—In conducting the study under paragraph (1) and preparing the report under paragraph (3), the Secretary shall consult with—

(A) stakeholders representing home health agencies;

(B) groups representing Medicare beneficiaries;

(C) the Medicare Payment Advisory Commission;

(D) the Inspector General of the Department of Health and Human Services; and

(E) the Comptroller General of the United States.

SEC. 3132. HOSPICE REFORM.

(a) HOSPICE CARE PAYMENT REFORMS.—

(1) IN GENERAL.—Section 1814(i) of the Social Security Act (42 U.S.C. 1395f(i)), as amended by section 3004(c), is amended—

(A) by redesignating paragraph (6) as paragraph (7); and

(B) by inserting after paragraph (5) the following new paragraph:

"(6)(A) The Secretary shall collect additional data and information as the Secretary determines appropriate to revise payments for hospice care under this subsection pursuant to subparagraph (D) and for other purposes as determined appropriate by the Secretary. The Secretary shall begin to collect such data by not later than January 1, 2011.

"(B) The additional data and information to be collected under subparagraph (A) may include data and information on—

"(i) charges and payments;

"(ii) the number of days of hospice care which are attributable to individuals who are entitled to, or enrolled for, benefits under part A; and

"(iii) with respect to each type of service included in hospice care—

"(I) the number of days of hospice care attributable to the type of service;

"(II) the cost of the type of service; and

"(III) the amount of payment for the type of service;

"(iv) charitable contributions and other revenue of the hospice program;

"(v) the number of hospice visits;

"(vi) the type of practitioner providing the visit; and

"(vii) the length of the visit and other basic information with respect to the visit.

"(C) The Secretary may collect the additional data and information under subparagraph (A) on cost reports, claims, or other mechanisms as the Secretary determines to be appropriate.

"(D)(i) Notwithstanding the preceding paragraphs of this subsection, not earlier than October 1, 2013, the Secretary shall, by regulation, implement revisions to the methodology for determining the payment rates for routine home care and other services included in hospice care under this part, as the Secretary determines to be appropriate. Such revisions may be based on an analysis of data and information collected under subparagraph (A). Such revisions may include adjustments to per diem payments that reflect changes in resource intensity in providing such care and services during the course of the entire episode of hospice care.

"(ii) Revisions in payment implemented pursuant to clause (i) shall result in the same estimated amount of aggregate expenditures under this title for hospice care furnished in the fiscal year in which such revisions in payment are implemented as would have been made under this title for such care in such fiscal year if such revisions had not been implemented.

"(E) The Secretary shall consult with hospice programs and the Medicare Payment Advisory Commission regarding the additional data and information to be collected under subparagraph (A) and the payment revisions under subparagraph (D).".

(2) CONFORMING AMENDMENTS.—Section 1814(i)(1)(C) of the Social Security Act (42 U.S.C. 1395f(i)(1)(C)) is amended—

(A) in clause (ii)—

(i) in the matter preceding subclause (I), by inserting "(before the first fiscal year in which the payment revisions described in paragraph (6)(D) are implemented)" after "subsequent fiscal year"; and

(ii) in subclause (VII), by inserting "(before the first fiscal year in which the payment revisions described in paragraph (6)(D) are implemented), subject to clause (iv)," after "subsequent fiscal year"; and

(B) by adding at the end the following new clause:

"(iii) With respect to routine home care and other services included in hospice care furnished during fiscal years subsequent to the first fiscal year in which payment revisions described in paragraph (6)(D) are implemented, the payment rates for such care and services shall be the payment rates in effect under this clause during the preceding fiscal year increased by, subject to clause (iv), the market basket percentage increase (as defined in section 1886(b)(3)(B)(iii)) for the fiscal year.”.

(b) ADOPTION OF MEDPAC HOSPICE PROGRAM ELIGIBILITY RECERTIFICATION RECOMMENDATIONS.—Section 1814(a)(7) of the Social Security Act (42 U.S.C. 1395f(a)(7)) is amended—

(1) in subparagraph (B), by striking “and” at the end; and

(2) by adding at the end the following new subparagraph:

“(D) on and after January 1, 2011—

“(i) a hospice physician or nurse practitioner has a face-to-face encounter with the individual to determine continued eligibility of the individual for hospice care prior to the 180th-day recertification and each subsequent recertification under subparagraph (A)(ii) and attests that such visit took place (in accordance with procedures established by the Secretary); and

“(ii) in the case of hospice care provided an individual for more than 180 days by a hospice program for which the number of such cases for such program comprises more than a percent (specified by the Secretary) of the total number of such cases for all programs under this title, the hospice care provided to such individual is medically reviewed (in accordance with procedures established by the Secretary); and”.

SEC. 3133. IMPROVEMENT TO MEDICARE DISPROPORTIONATE SHARE HOSPITAL (DSH) PAYMENTS.

Section 1886 of the Social Security Act (42 U.S.C. 1395ww), as amended by sections 3001, 3008, and 3025, is amended—

(1) in subsection (d)(5)(F)(i), by striking “For” and inserting “Subject to subsection (r), for”; and

(2) by adding at the end the following new subsection:

“(r) ADJUSTMENTS TO MEDICARE DSH PAYMENTS.—

“(1) EMPIRICALLY JUSTIFIED DSH PAYMENTS.—For fiscal year 2015 and each subsequent fiscal year, instead of the amount of disproportionate share hospital payment that would otherwise be made under subsection (d)(5)(F) to a subsection (d) hospital for the fiscal year, the Secretary shall pay to the subsection (d) hospital 25 percent of such amount (which represents the empirically justified amount for such payment, as determined by the Medicare Payment Advisory Commission in its March 2007 Report to the Congress).

“(2) ADDITIONAL PAYMENT.—In addition to the payment made to a subsection (d) hospital under paragraph (1), for fiscal year 2015 and each subsequent fiscal year, the Secretary shall pay to such subsection (d) hospitals an additional amount equal to the product of the following factors:

“(A) FACTOR ONE.—A factor equal to the difference between—

“(i) the aggregate amount of payments that would be made to subsection (d) hospitals under subsection (d)(5)(F) if this subsection did not apply for such fiscal year (as estimated by the Secretary); and

“(ii) the aggregate amount of payments that are made to subsection (d) hospitals under paragraph (1) for such fiscal year (as so estimated).

“(B) FACTOR TWO.—

"(i) FISCAL YEARS 2015, 2016, AND 2017.—For each of fiscal years 2015, 2016, and 2017, a factor equal to 1 minus the percent change (divided by 100) in the percent of individuals under the age of 65 who are uninsured, as determined by comparing the percent of such individuals—

"(I) who are uninsured in 2012, the last year before coverage expansion under the Patient Protection and Affordable Care Act (as calculated by the Secretary based on the most recent estimates available from the Director of the Congressional Budget Office before a vote in either House on such Act that, if determined in the affirmative, would clear such Act for enrollment); and

"(II) who are uninsured in the most recent period for which data is available (as so calculated).

"(ii) 2018 AND SUBSEQUENT YEARS.—For fiscal year 2018 and each subsequent fiscal year, a factor equal to 1 minus the percent change (divided by 100) in the percent of individuals who are uninsured, as determined by comparing the percent of individuals—

"(I) who are uninsured in 2012 (as estimated by the Secretary, based on data from the Census Bureau or other sources the Secretary determines appropriate, and certified by the Chief Actuary of the Centers for Medicare & Medicaid Services); and

"(II) who are uninsured in the most recent period for which data is available (as so estimated and certified).

"(C) FACTOR THREE.—A factor equal to the percent, for each subsection (d) hospital, that represents the quotient of—

"(i) the amount of uncompensated care for such hospital for a period selected by the Secretary (as estimated by the Secretary, based on appropriate data (including, in the case where the Secretary determines that alternative data is available which is a better proxy for the costs of subsection (d) hospitals for treating the uninsured, the use of such alternative data)); and

"(ii) the aggregate amount of uncompensated care for all subsection (d) hospitals that receive a payment under this subsection for such period (as so estimated, based on such data).

"(3) LIMITATIONS ON REVIEW.—There shall be no administrative or judicial review under section 1869, section 1878, or otherwise of the following:

"(A) Any estimate of the Secretary for purposes of determining the factors described in paragraph (2).

"(B) Any period selected by the Secretary for such purposes.".

SEC. 3134. MISVALUED CODES UNDER THE PHYSICIAN FEE SCHEDULE.

(a) IN GENERAL.—Section 1848(c)(2) of the Social Security Act (42 U.S.C. 1395w–4(c)(2)) is amended by adding at the end the following new subparagraphs:

"(K) POTENTIALLY MISVALUED CODES.—

"(i) IN GENERAL.—The Secretary shall—

"(I) periodically identify services as being potentially misvalued using criteria specified in clause (ii); and

"(II) review and make appropriate adjustments to the relative values established under this paragraph for services identified as being potentially misvalued under subclause (I).

"(ii) IDENTIFICATION OF POTENTIALLY MISVALUED CODES.—For purposes of identifying potentially misvalued services pursuant to clause (i)(I), the Secretary shall examine (as the Secretary determines to be appropriate) codes (and families of codes as appropriate) for which there has been the fastest growth; codes (and families of codes as appropriate) that have experienced substantial changes in practice expenses; codes for new technologies or services within an appropriate period (such as 3 years) after the relative values are initially established for such codes; multiple codes that are frequently billed in conjunction with furnishing a single service; codes with low relative values, particularly those that are often billed multiple times for a single treatment; codes which have not been subject to review since the implementation of the RBRVS (the so-called 'Harvard-valued codes'); and such other codes determined to be appropriate by the Secretary.

"(iii) REVIEW AND ADJUSTMENTS.—

"(I) The Secretary may use existing processes to receive recommendations on the review and appropriate adjustment of potentially misvalued services described in clause (i)(II).

"(II) The Secretary may conduct surveys, other data collection activities, studies, or other analyses as the Secretary determines to be appropriate to facilitate the review and appropriate adjustment described in clause (i)(II).

"(III) The Secretary may use analytic contractors to identify and analyze services identified under clause (i)(I), conduct surveys or collect data, and make recommendations on the review and appropriate adjustment of services described in clause (i)(II).

"(IV) The Secretary may coordinate the review and appropriate adjustment described in clause (i)(II) with the periodic review described in subparagraph (B).

"(V) As part of the review and adjustment described in clause (i)(II), including with respect to codes with low relative values described in clause (ii), the Secretary may make appropriate coding revisions (including using existing processes for consideration of coding changes) which may include consolidation of individual services into bundled codes for payment under the fee schedule under subsection (b).

"(VI) The provisions of subparagraph (B)(ii)(II) shall apply to adjustments to relative value units made pursuant to this subparagraph in the same manner as such provisions apply to adjustments under subparagraph (B)(ii)(II).

"(L) VALIDATING RELATIVE VALUE UNITS.—

"(i) IN GENERAL.—The Secretary shall establish a process to validate relative value units under the fee schedule under subsection (b).

"(ii) COMPONENTS AND ELEMENTS OF WORK.—The process described in clause (i) may include validation of work elements (such as time, mental effort and professional judgment, technical skill and physical effort, and stress due to risk) involved with furnishing a service and may include validation of the pre-, post-, and intra-service components of work.

"(iii) SCOPE OF CODES.—The validation of work relative value units shall include a sampling of codes for services that is the same as the codes listed under subparagraph (K)(ii).

"(iv) METHODS.—The Secretary may conduct the validation under this subparagraph using methods described in subclauses (I) through (V) of subparagraph (K)(iii) as the Secretary determines to be appropriate.

"(v) ADJUSTMENTS.—The Secretary shall make appropriate adjustments to the work relative value units under the fee schedule under subsection (b). The provisions of subparagraph (B)(ii)(II) shall apply to adjustments to relative value units made pursuant to this subparagraph in the same manner as such provisions apply to adjustments under subparagraph (B)(ii)(II).".

(b) IMPLEMENTATION.—

(1) ADMINISTRATION.—

(A) Chapter 35 of title 44, United States Code and the provisions of the Federal Advisory Committee Act (5 U.S.C. App.) shall not apply to this section or the amendment made by this section.

(B) Notwithstanding any other provision of law, the Secretary may implement subparagraphs (K) and (L) of 1848(c)(2) of the Social Security Act, as added by subsection (a), by program instruction or otherwise.

(C) Section 4505(d) of the Balanced Budget Act of 1997 is repealed.

(D) Except for provisions related to confidentiality of information, the provisions of the Federal Acquisition Regulation shall not apply to this section or the amendment made by this section.

(2) FOCUSING CMS RESOURCES ON POTENTIALLY OVERVALUED CODES.—Section 1868(a) of the Social Security Act (42 U.S.C. 1395ee(a)) is repealed.

SEC. 3135. MODIFICATION OF EQUIPMENT UTILIZATION FACTOR FOR ADVANCED IMAGING SERVICES.

(a) ADJUSTMENT IN PRACTICE EXPENSE TO REFLECT HIGHER PRESUMED UTILIZATION.—Section 1848 of the Social Security Act (42 U.S.C. 1395w–4) is amended—

(1) in subsection (b)(4)—

(A) in subparagraph (B), by striking "subparagraph (A)" and inserting "this paragraph"; and

(B) by adding at the end the following new subparagraph:

"(C) ADJUSTMENT IN PRACTICE EXPENSE TO REFLECT HIGHER PRESUMED UTILIZATION.—Consistent with the methodology for computing the number of practice expense relative value units under subsection (c)(2)(C)(ii) with respect to advanced diagnostic imaging services (as defined in section 1834(e)(1)(B)) furnished on or after January 1, 2010, the Secretary shall adjust such number of units so it reflects—

"(i) in the case of services furnished on or after January 1, 2010, and before January 1, 2013, a 65 percent (rather than 50 percent) presumed rate of utilization of imaging equipment;

"(ii) in the case of services furnished on or after January 1, 2013, and before January 1, 2014, a 70 percent (rather than 50 percent) presumed rate of utilization of imaging equipment; and

"(iii) in the case of services furnished on or after January 1, 2014, a 75 percent (rather than 50 percent) presumed rate of utilization of imaging equipment."; and

(2) in subsection (c)(2)(B)(v), by adding at the end the following new subclauses:

"(III) CHANGE IN PRESUMED UTILIZATION LEVEL OF CERTAIN ADVANCED DIAGNOSTIC IMAGING SERVICES FOR 2010 THROUGH 2012.—Effective for fee schedules established beginning with 2010 and ending with 2012, reduced expenditures attributable to the presumed rate of utilization of imaging equipment of 65 percent under subsection (b)(4)(C)(i) instead of a presumed rate of utilization of such equipment of 50 percent.

"(IV) CHANGE IN PRESUMED UTILIZATION LEVEL OF CERTAIN ADVANCED DIAGNOSTIC IMAGING SERVICES FOR 2013.—Effective for fee schedules established for 2013, reduced expenditures attributable to the presumed rate of utilization of imaging equipment of 70 percent under subsection (b)(4)(C)(ii) instead of a presumed rate of utilization of such equipment of 50 percent.

"(V) CHANGE IN PRESUMED UTILIZATION LEVEL OF CERTAIN ADVANCED DIAGNOSTIC IMAGING SERVICES FOR 2014 AND SUBSEQUENT YEARS.—Effective for fee schedules established beginning with 2014, reduced expenditures attributable to the presumed rate of utilization of imaging equipment of 75 percent under subsection (b)(4)(C)(iii) instead of a presumed rate of utilization of such equipment of 50 percent.".

(b) ADJUSTMENT IN TECHNICAL COMPONENT "DISCOUNT" ON SINGLE-SESSION IMAGING TO CONSECUTIVE BODY PARTS.—Section 1848 of the Social Security Act (42 U.S.C. 1395w–4), as amended by subsection (a), is amended—

(1) in subsection (b)(4), by adding at the end the following new subparagraph:

"(D) ADJUSTMENT IN TECHNICAL COMPONENT DISCOUNT ON SINGLE-SESSION IMAGING INVOLVING CONSECUTIVE BODY PARTS.—For services furnished on or after July 1, 2010, the Secretary shall increase the reduction in payments attributable to the multiple procedure payment reduction applicable to the technical component for imaging under the final rule published by the Secretary in the Federal Register on November 21, 2005 (part 405 of title 42, Code of Federal Regulations) from 25 percent to 50 percent."; and

(2) in subsection (c)(2)(B)(v), by adding at the end the following new subclause:

"(VI) ADDITIONAL REDUCED PAYMENT FOR MULTIPLE IMAGING PROCEDURES.—Effective for fee schedules established beginning with 2010 (but not applied for services furnished prior to July 1, 2010), reduced expenditures attributable to the increase in the multiple procedure payment reduction from 25 to 50 percent (as described in subsection (b)(4)(D)).".

(c) ANALYSIS BY THE CHIEF ACTUARY OF THE CENTERS FOR MEDICARE & MEDICAID SERVICES.—Not later than January 1, 2013, the Chief Actuary of the Centers for Medicare & Medicaid Services shall make publicly available an analysis of whether, for the period of 2010 through 2019, the cumulative expenditure reductions under title XVIII of the Social Security Act that are attributable to the adjustments under the amendments made by this section are projected to exceed $3,000,000,000.

SEC. 3136. REVISION OF PAYMENT FOR POWER-DRIVEN WHEELCHAIRS.

(a) IN GENERAL.—Section 1834(a)(7)(A) of the Social Security Act (42 U.S.C. 1395m(a)(7)(A)) is amended—

(1) in clause (i)—

(A) in subclause (II), by inserting "subclause (III) and" after "Subject to"; and

(B) by adding at the end the following new subclause:

"(III) SPECIAL RULE FOR POWER-DRIVEN WHEELCHAIRS.—For purposes of payment for power-driven wheelchairs, subclause (II) shall be applied by substituting '15 percent' and '6 percent' for '10 percent' and '7.5 percent', respectively."; and

(2) in clause (iii)—

(A) in the heading, by inserting "COMPLEX, REHABILITATIVE" before "POWER-DRIVEN"; and

(B) by inserting "complex, rehabilitative" before "power-driven".

(b) TECHNICAL AMENDMENT.—Section 1834(a)(7)(C)(ii)(II) of the Social Security Act (42 U.S.C. 1395m(a)(7)(C)(ii)(II)) is amended by striking "(A)(ii) or".

(c) EFFECTIVE DATE.—

(1) IN GENERAL.—Subject to paragraph (2), the amendments made by subsection (a) shall take effect on January 1, 2011, and shall apply to power-driven wheelchairs furnished on or after such date.

(2) APPLICATION TO COMPETITIVE BIDDING.—The amendments made by subsection (a) shall not apply to payment made for items and services furnished pursuant to contracts entered into under section 1847 of the Social Security Act (42 U.S.C. 1395w–3) prior to January 1, 2011, pursuant to the implementation of subsection (a)(1)(B)(i)(I) of such section 1847.

SEC. 3137. HOSPITAL WAGE INDEX IMPROVEMENT.

(a) EXTENSION OF SECTION 508 HOSPITAL RECLASSIFICATIONS.—

(1) IN GENERAL.—Subsection (a) of section 106 of division B of the Tax Relief and Health Care Act of 2006 (42 U.S.C. 1395 note), as amended by section 117 of the Medicare, Medicaid, and SCHIP Extension Act of 2007 (Public Law 110–173) and section 124 of the Medicare Improvements for Patients and Providers Act of 2008 (Public Law 110–275), is amended by striking "September 30, 2009" and inserting "September 30, 2010".

(2) USE OF PARTICULAR WAGE INDEX IN FISCAL YEAR 2010.—For purposes of implementation of the amendment made by this subsection during fiscal year 2010, the Secretary shall use the hospital wage index that was promulgated by the Secretary in the Federal Register on August 27, 2009 (74 Fed. Reg. 43754), and any subsequent corrections.

(b) PLAN FOR REFORMING THE MEDICARE HOSPITAL WAGE INDEX SYSTEM.—

(1) IN GENERAL.—Not later than December 31, 2011, the Secretary of Health and Human Services (in this section referred to as the "Secretary") shall submit to Congress a report that includes a plan to reform the hospital wage index system under section 1886 of the Social Security Act.

(2) DETAILS.—In developing the plan under paragraph (1), the Secretary shall take into account the goals for reforming such system set forth in the Medicare Payment Advisory Commission June 2007 report entitled "Report to Congress: Promoting Greater Efficiency in Medicare", including establishing a new hospital compensation index system that—

(A) uses Bureau of Labor Statistics data, or other data or methodologies, to calculate relative wages for each geographic area involved;

(B) minimizes wage index adjustments between and within metropolitan statistical areas and statewide rural areas;

(C) includes methods to minimize the volatility of wage index adjustments that result from implementation of policy, while maintaining budget neutrality in applying such adjustments;

(D) takes into account the effect that implementation of the system would have on health care providers and on each region of the country;

(E) addresses issues related to occupational mix, such as staffing practices and ratios, and any evidence on the effect on quality of care or patient safety as a result of the implementation of the system; and

(F) provides for a transition.

(3) CONSULTATION.—In developing the plan under paragraph (1), the Secretary shall consult with relevant affected parties.

(c) USE OF PARTICULAR CRITERIA FOR DETERMINING RECLASSIFICATIONS.—Notwithstanding any other provision of law, in making decisions on applications for reclassification of a subsection (d) hospital (as defined in paragraph (1)(B) of section 1886(d) of the Social Security Act (42 U.S.C. 1395ww(d)) for the purposes described in paragraph (10)(D)(v) of such section for fiscal year 2011 and each subsequent fiscal year (until the first fiscal year beginning on or after the date that is 1 year after the Secretary of Health and Human Services submits the report to Congress under subsection (b)), the Geographic Classification Review Board established under paragraph (10) of such section shall use the average hourly wage comparison criteria used in making such decisions as of September 30, 2008. The preceding sentence shall be effected in a budget neutral manner.

SEC. 3138. TREATMENT OF CERTAIN CANCER HOSPITALS.

Section 1833(t) of the Social Security Act (42 U.S.C. 1395l(t)) is amended by adding at the end the following new paragraph:

"(18) AUTHORIZATION OF ADJUSTMENT FOR CANCER HOSPITALS.—

"(A) STUDY.—The Secretary shall conduct a study to determine if, under the system under this subsection, costs incurred by hospitals described in section 1886(d)(1)(B)(v) with respect to ambulatory payment classification groups exceed those costs incurred by other hospitals furnishing services under this subsection (as determined appropriate by the Secretary). In conducting the study under this subparagraph, the Secretary shall take into consideration the cost of drugs and biologicals incurred by such hospitals.

"(B) AUTHORIZATION OF ADJUSTMENT.—Insofar as the Secretary determines under subparagraph (A) that costs incurred by hospitals described in section 1886(d)(1)(B)(v) exceed those costs incurred by other hospitals furnishing services under this subsection, the Secretary shall provide for an appropriate adjustment under paragraph (2)(E) to reflect those higher costs effective for services furnished on or after January 1, 2011.".

SEC. 3139. PAYMENT FOR BIOSIMILAR BIOLOGICAL PRODUCTS.

(a) IN GENERAL.—Section 1847A of the Social Security Act (42 U.S.C. 1395w–3a) is amended—

(1) in subsection (b)—

(A) in paragraph (1)—

(i) in subparagraph (A), by striking "or" at the end;

(ii) in subparagraph (B), by striking the period at the end and inserting "; or"; and

(iii) by adding at the end the following new subparagraph:

"(C) in the case of a biosimilar biological product (as defined in subsection (c)(6)(H)), the amount determined under paragraph (8)."; and

(B) by adding at the end the following new paragraph:

"(8) BIOSIMILAR BIOLOGICAL PRODUCT.—The amount specified in this paragraph for a biosimilar biological product described in paragraph (1)(C) is the sum of—

"(A) the average sales price as determined using the methodology described under paragraph (6) applied to a biosimilar biological product for all National Drug Codes assigned to such product in the same manner as such paragraph is applied to drugs described in such paragraph; and

"(B) 6 percent of the amount determined under paragraph (4) for the reference biological product (as defined in subsection (c)(6)(I))."; and

(2) in subsection (c)(6), by adding at the end the following new subparagraph:

"(H) BIOSIMILAR BIOLOGICAL PRODUCT.—The term 'biosimilar biological product' means a biological product approved under an abbreviated application for a license of a biological product that relies in part on data or information in an application for another biological product licensed under section 351 of the Public Health Service Act.

"(I) REFERENCE BIOLOGICAL PRODUCT.—The term 'reference biological product' means the biological product licensed under such section 351 that is referred to in the application described in subparagraph (H) of the biosimilar biological product.".

(b) EFFECTIVE DATE.—The amendments made by subsection (a) shall apply to payments for biosimilar biological products beginning with the first day of the second calendar quarter after enactment of legislation providing for a biosimilar pathway (as determined by the Secretary).

SEC. 3140. MEDICARE HOSPICE CONCURRENT CARE DEMONSTRATION PROGRAM.

(a) ESTABLISHMENT.—

(1) IN GENERAL.—The Secretary of Health and Human Services (in this section referred to as the "Secretary") shall establish a Medicare Hospice Concurrent Care demonstration program at participating hospice programs under which Medicare beneficiaries are furnished, during the same period, hospice care and any other items or services covered under title XVIII of the Social Security Act (42 U.S.C. 1395 et seq.) from funds otherwise paid under such title to such hospice programs.

(2) DURATION.—The demonstration program under this section shall be conducted for a 3-year period.

(3) SITES.—The Secretary shall select not more than 15 hospice programs at which the demonstration program under this section shall be conducted. Such hospice programs shall be located in urban and rural areas.

(b) INDEPENDENT EVALUATION AND REPORTS.—

(1) INDEPENDENT EVALUATION.—The Secretary shall provide for the conduct of an independent evaluation of the demonstration program under this section. Such independent evaluation shall determine whether the demonstration program

has improved patient care, quality of life, and cost-effectiveness for Medicare beneficiaries participating in the demonstration program.

(2) REPORTS.—The Secretary shall submit to Congress a report containing the results of the evaluation conducted under paragraph (1), together with such recommendations as the Secretary determines appropriate.

(c) BUDGET NEUTRALITY.—With respect to the 3-year period of the demonstration program under this section, the Secretary shall ensure that the aggregate expenditures under title XVIII for such period shall not exceed the aggregate expenditures that would have been expended under such title if the demonstration program under this section had not been implemented.

SEC. 3141. APPLICATION OF BUDGET NEUTRALITY ON A NATIONAL BASIS IN THE CALCULATION OF THE MEDICARE HOSPITAL WAGE INDEX FLOOR.

In the case of discharges occurring on or after October 1, 2010, for purposes of applying section 4410 of the Balanced Budget Act of 1997 (42 U.S.C. 1395ww note) and paragraph (h)(4) of section 412.64 of title 42, Code of Federal Regulations, the Secretary of Health and Human Services shall administer subsection (b) of such section 4410 and paragraph (e) of such section 412.64 in the same manner as the Secretary administered such subsection (b) and paragraph (e) for discharges occurring during fiscal year 2008 (through a uniform, national adjustment to the area wage index).

SEC. 3142. HHS STUDY ON URBAN MEDICARE-DEPENDENT HOSPITALS.

(a) STUDY.—

(1) IN GENERAL.—The Secretary of Health and Human Services (in this section referred to as the "Secretary") shall conduct a study on the need for an additional payment for urban Medicare-dependent hospitals for inpatient hospital services under section 1886 of the Social Security Act (42 U.S.C. 1395ww). Such study shall include an analysis of—

(A) the Medicare inpatient margins of urban Medicare-dependent hospitals, as compared to other hospitals which receive 1 or more additional payments or adjustments under such section (including those payments or adjustments described in paragraph (2)(A)); and

(B) whether payments to medicare-dependent, small rural hospitals under subsection (d)(5)(G) of such section should be applied to urban Medicare-dependent hospitals.

(2) URBAN MEDICARE-DEPENDENT HOSPITAL DEFINED.—For purposes of this section, the term "urban Medicare-dependent hospital" means a subsection (d) hospital (as defined in subsection (d)(1)(B) of such section) that—

(A) does not receive any additional payment or adjustment under such section, such as payments for indirect medical education costs under subsection (d)(5)(B) of such section, disproportionate share payments under subsection (d)(5)(A) of such section, payments to a rural referral center under subsection (d)(5)(C) of such section, payments to a critical access hospital under section 1814(l) of such Act (42 U.S.C. 1395f(l)), payments to a sole community hospital under subsection (d)(5)(D) of such section 1886, or payments to a medicare-dependent, small rural hospital under subsection (d)(5)(G) of such section 1886; and

(B) for which more than 60 percent of its inpatient days or discharges during 2 of the 3 most recently audited cost reporting periods for which the Secretary has a settled cost report were attributable to inpatients entitled to benefits under part A of title XVIII of such Act.

(b) REPORT.—Not later than 9 months after the date of enactment of this Act, the Secretary shall submit to Congress a report containing the results of the study conducted under subsection (a), together with recommendations for such legislation and administrative action as the Secretary determines appropriate.

SEC. 3143. PROTECTING HOME HEALTH BENEFITS.

Nothing in the provisions of, or amendments made by, this Act shall result in the reduction of guaranteed home health benefits under title XVIII of the Social Security Act.

Subtitle C—Provisions Relating to Part C

SEC. 3201. MEDICARE ADVANTAGE PAYMENT.

(a) MA BENCHMARK BASED ON PLAN'S COMPETITIVE BIDS.—

(1) IN GENERAL.—Section 1853(j) of the Social Security Act (42 U.S.C. 1395w–23(j)) is amended—

(A) by striking "AMOUNTS.—For purposes" and inserting "AMOUNTS.—

"(1) IN GENERAL.—For purposes";

(B) by redesignating paragraphs (1) and (2) as subparagraphs (A) and (B), respectively, and indenting the subparagraphs appropriately;

(C) in subparagraph (A), as redesignated by subparagraph (B)—

(i) by redesignating subparagraphs (A) and (B) as clauses (i) and (ii), respectively, and indenting the clauses appropriately; and

(ii) in clause (i), as redesignated by clause (i), by striking "an amount equal to" and all that follows through the end and inserting "an amount equal to—

"(I) for years before 2007, $\frac{1}{12}$ of the annual MA capitation rate under section 1853(c)(1) for the area for the year, adjusted as appropriate for the purpose of risk adjustment;

"(II) for 2007 through 2011, $\frac{1}{12}$ of the applicable amount determined under subsection (k)(1) for the area for the year;

"(III) for 2012, the sum of—

"(aa) $\frac{2}{3}$ of the quotient of—

"(AA) the applicable amount determined under subsection (k)(1) for the area for the year; and

"(BB) 12; and

"(bb) $\frac{1}{3}$ of the MA competitive benchmark amount (determined under paragraph (2)) for the area for the month;

"(IV) for 2013, the sum of—

"(aa) $\frac{1}{3}$ of the quotient of—

"(AA) the applicable amount determined under subsection (k)(1) for the area for the year; and

"(BB) 12; and

"(bb) 2/3 of the MA competitive benchmark amount (as so determined) for the area for the month;

"(V) for 2014, the MA competitive benchmark amount for the area for a month in 2013 (as so determined), increased by the national per capita MA growth percentage, described in subsection (c)(6) for 2014, but not taking into account any adjustment under subparagraph (C) of such subsection for a year before 2004; and

"(VI) for 2015 and each subsequent year, the MA competitive benchmark amount (as so determined) for the area for the month; or";

(iii) in clause (ii), as redesignated by clause (i), by striking "subparagraph (A)" and inserting "clause (i)";

(D) by adding at the end the following new paragraphs:

"(2) COMPUTATION OF MA COMPETITIVE BENCHMARK AMOUNT.—

"(A) IN GENERAL.—Subject to subparagraph (B) and paragraph (3), for months in each year (beginning with 2012) for each MA payment area the Secretary shall compute an MA competitive benchmark amount equal to the weighted average of the unadjusted MA statutory non-drug monthly bid amount (as defined in section 1854(b)(2)(E)) for each MA plan in the area, with the weight for each plan being equal to the average number of beneficiaries enrolled under such plan in the reference month (as defined in section 1858(f)(4), except that, in applying such definition for purposes of this paragraph, 'to compute the MA competitive benchmark amount under section 1853(j)(2)' shall be substituted for 'to compute the percentage specified in subparagraph (A) and other relevant percentages under this part').

"(B) WEIGHTING RULES.—

"(i) SINGLE PLAN RULE.—In the case of an MA payment area in which only a single MA plan is being offered, the weight under subparagraph (A) shall be equal to 1.

"(ii) USE OF SIMPLE AVERAGE AMONG MULTIPLE PLANS IF NO PLANS OFFERED IN PREVIOUS YEAR.—In the case of an MA payment area in which no MA plan was offered in the previous year and more than 1 MA plan is offered in the current year, the Secretary shall use a simple average of the unadjusted MA statutory non-drug monthly bid amount (as so defined) for purposes of computing the MA competitive benchmark amount under subparagraph (A).

"(3) CAP ON MA COMPETITIVE BENCHMARK AMOUNT.—In no case shall the MA competitive benchmark amount for an area for a month in a year be greater than the applicable amount that would (but for the application of this subsection) be determined under subsection (k)(1) for the area for the month in the year.''; and

(E) in subsection (k)(2)(B)(ii)(III), by striking ''(j)(1)(A)'' and inserting ''(j)(1)(A)(i)''.

(2) CONFORMING AMENDMENTS.—

(A) Section 1853(k)(2) of the Social Security Act (42 U.S.C. 1395w–23(k)(2)) is amended—

(i) in subparagraph (A), by striking ''through 2010'' and inserting ''and subsequent years''; and

(ii) in subparagraph (C)—

(I) in clause (iii), by striking ''and'' at the end;

(II) in clause (iv), by striking the period at the end and inserting ''; and''; and

(III) by adding at the end the following new clause:

''(v) for 2011 and subsequent years, 0.00.''.

(B) Section 1854(b) of the Social Security Act (42 U.S.C. 1395w–24(b)) is amended—

(i) in paragraph (3)(B)(i), by striking ''1853(j)(1)'' and inserting ''1853(j)(1)(A)''; and

(ii) in paragraph (4)(B)(i), by striking ''1853(j)(2)'' and inserting ''1853(j)(1)(B)''.

(C) Section 1858(f) of the Social Security Act (42 U.S.C. 1395w–27(f)) is amended—

(i) in paragraph (1), by striking ''1853(j)(2)'' and inserting ''1853(j)(1)(B)''; and

(ii) in paragraph (3)(A), by striking ''1853(j)(1)(A)'' and inserting ''1853(j)(1)(A)(i)''.

(D) Section 1860C–1(d)(1)(A) of the Social Security Act (42 U.S.C. 1395w–29(d)(1)(A)) is amended by striking ''1853(j)(1)(A)'' and inserting ''1853(j)(1)(A)(i)''.

(b) REDUCTION OF NATIONAL PER CAPITA GROWTH PERCENTAGE FOR 2011.—Section 1853(c)(6) of the Social Security Act (42 U.S.C. 1395w–23(c)(6)) is amended—

(1) in clause (v), by striking ''and'' at the end;

(2) in clause (vi)—

(A) by striking ''for a year after 2002'' and inserting ''for 2003 through 2010''; and

(B) by striking the period at the end and inserting a comma; and

(C) by adding at the end the following new clauses:

''(vii) for 2011, 3 percentage points; and

''(viii) for a year after 2011, 0 percentage points.''.

(c) ENHANCEMENT OF BENEFICIARY REBATES.—Section 1854(b)(1)(C)(i) of the Social Security Act (42 U.S.C. 1395w–24(b)(1)(C)(i)) is amended by inserting ''(or 100 percent in the case of plan years beginning on or after January 1, 2014)'' after ''75 percent''.

(d) BIDDING RULES.—

(1) REQUIREMENTS FOR INFORMATION SUBMITTED.—Section 1854(a)(6)(A) of the Social Security Act (42 U.S.C. 1395w–24(a)(6)(A)) is amended, in the flush matter following clause (v), by adding at the end the following sentence: ''Information to be submitted under this paragraph shall be certified by a qualified member of the American Academy of Actuaries

and shall meet actuarial guidelines and rules established by the Secretary under subparagraph (B)(v).".

(2) ESTABLISHMENT OF ACTUARIAL GUIDELINES.—Section 1854(a)(6)(B) of the Social Security Act (42 U.S.C. 1395w–24(a)(6)(B)) is amended—

(A) in clause (i), by striking "(iii) and (iv)" and inserting "(iii), (iv), and (v)"; and

(B) by adding at the end the following new clause:

"(v) ESTABLISHMENT OF ACTUARIAL GUIDELINES.—

"(I) IN GENERAL.—In order to establish fair MA competitive benchmarks under section 1853(j)(1)(A)(i), the Secretary, acting through the Chief Actuary of the Centers for Medicare & Medicaid Services (in this clause referred to as the 'Chief Actuary'), shall establish—

"(aa) actuarial guidelines for the submission of bid information under this paragraph; and

"(bb) bidding rules that are appropriate to ensure accurate bids and fair competition among MA plans.

"(II) DENIAL OF BID AMOUNTS.—The Secretary shall deny monthly bid amounts submitted under subparagraph (A) that do not meet the actuarial guidelines and rules established under subclause (I).

"(III) REFUSAL TO ACCEPT CERTAIN BIDS DUE TO MISREPRESENTATIONS AND FAILURES TO ADEQUATELY MEET REQUIREMENTS.—In the case where the Secretary determines that information submitted by an MA organization under subparagraph (A) contains consistent misrepresentations and failures to adequately meet requirements of the organization, the Secretary may refuse to accept any additional such bid amounts from the organization for the plan year and the Chief Actuary shall, if the Chief Actuary determines that the actuaries of the organization were complicit in those misrepresentations and failures, report those actuaries to the Actuarial Board for Counseling and Discipline.".

(3) EFFECTIVE DATE.—The amendments made by this subsection shall apply to bid amounts submitted on or after January 1, 2012.

(e) MA LOCAL PLAN SERVICE AREAS.—

(1) IN GENERAL.—Section 1853(d) of the Social Security Act (42 U.S.C. 1395w–23(d)) is amended—

(A) in the subsection heading, by striking "MA REGION" and inserting "MA REGION; MA LOCAL PLAN SERVICE AREA";

(B) in paragraph (1), by striking subparagraph (A) and inserting the following:

"(A) with respect to an MA local plan—

"(i) for years before 2012, an MA local area (as defined in paragraph (2)); and "(ii) for 2012 and succeeding years, a service area that is an entire urban or rural area, as applicable (as described in paragraph (5)); and"; and

(C) by adding at the end the following new paragraph:

"(5) MA LOCAL PLAN SERVICE AREA.—For 2012 and succeeding years, the service area for an MA local plan shall be an entire urban or rural area in each State as follows:

"(A) URBAN AREAS.—

"(i) IN GENERAL.—Subject to clause (ii) and subparagraphs (C) and (D), the service area for an MA local plan in an urban area shall be the Core Based Statistical Area (in this paragraph referred to as a 'CBSA') or, if applicable, a conceptually similar alternative classification, as defined by the Director of the Office of Management and Budget.

"(ii) CBSA COVERING MORE THAN ONE STATE.—In the case of a CBSA (or alternative classification) that covers more than one State, the Secretary shall divide the CBSA (or alternative classification) into separate service areas with respect to each State covered by the CBSA (or alternative classification).

"(B) RURAL AREAS.—Subject to subparagraphs (C) and (D), the service area for an MA local plan in a rural area shall be a county that does not qualify for inclusion in a CBSA (or alternative classification), as defined by the Director of the Office of Management and Budget.

"(C) REFINEMENTS TO SERVICE AREAS.—For 2015 and succeeding years, in order to reflect actual patterns of health care service utilization, the Secretary may adjust the boundaries of service areas for MA local plans in urban areas and rural areas under subparagraphs (A) and (B), respectively, but may only do so based on recent analyses of actual patterns of care.

"(D) ADDITIONAL AUTHORITY TO MAKE LIMITED EXCEPTIONS TO SERVICE AREA REQUIREMENTS FOR MA LOCAL PLANS.—The Secretary may, in addition to any adjustments under subparagraph (C), make limited exceptions to service area requirements otherwise applicable under this part for MA local plans that have in effect (as of the date of enactment of the Patient Protection and Affordable Care Act)—

"(i) agreements with another MA organization or MA plan that preclude the offering of benefits throughout an entire service area; or

"(ii) limitations in their structural capacity to support adequate networks throughout an entire service area as a result of the delivery system model of the MA local plan.".

(2) CONFORMING AMENDMENTS.—

(A) IN GENERAL.—

(i) Section 1851(b)(1) of the Social Security Act (42 U.S.C. 1395w–21(b)(1)) is amended by striking subparagraph (C).

(ii) Section 1853(b)(1)(B)(i) of such Act (42 U.S.C. 1395w–23(b)(1)(B)(i))—

(I) in the matter preceding subclause (I), by striking "MA payment area" and inserting "MA local area (as defined in subsection (d)(2))"; and

(II) in subclause (I), by striking "MA payment area" and inserting "MA local area (as so defined)".

(iii) Section 1853(b)(4) of such Act (42 U.S.C. 1395w–23(b)(4)) is amended by striking "Medicare Advantage payment area" and inserting "MA local area (as so defined)".

(iv) Section 1853(c)(1) of such Act (42 U.S.C. 1395w–23(c)(1)) is amended—

(I) in the matter preceding subparagraph (A), by striking "a Medicare Advantage payment area that is"; and

(II) in subparagraph (D)(i), by striking "MA payment area" and inserting "MA local area (as defined in subsection (d)(2))".

(v) Section 1854 of such Act (42 U.S.C. 1395w–24) is amended by striking subsection (h).

(B) EFFECTIVE DATE.—The amendments made by this paragraph shall take effect on January 1, 2012.

(f) PERFORMANCE BONUSES.—

(1) MA PLANS.—

(A) IN GENERAL.—Section 1853 of the Social Security Act (42 U.S.C. 1395w–23) is amended by adding at the end the following new subsection:

"(n) PERFORMANCE BONUSES.—

"(1) CARE COORDINATION AND MANAGEMENT PERFORMANCE BONUS.—

"(A) IN GENERAL.—For years beginning with 2014, subject to subparagraph (B), in the case of an MA plan that conducts 1 or more programs described in subparagraph (C) with respect to the year, the Secretary shall, in addition to any other payment provided under this part, make monthly payments, with respect to coverage of an individual under this part, to the MA plan in an amount equal to the product of—

"(i) 0.5 percent of the national monthly per capita cost for expenditures for individuals enrolled under the original medicare fee-for-service program for the year; and

"(ii) the total number of programs described in clauses (i) through (ix) of subparagraph (C) that the Secretary determines the plan is conducting for the year under such subparagraph.

"(B) LIMITATION.—In no case may the total amount of payment with respect to a year under subparagraph (A) be greater than 2 percent of the national monthly per capita cost for expenditures for individuals enrolled under the original medicare fee-for-service program for the year, as determined prior to the application of risk adjustment under paragraph (4).

"(C) PROGRAMS DESCRIBED.—The following programs are described in this paragraph:

"(i) Care management programs that—

"(I) target individuals with 1 or more chronic conditions;

"(II) identify gaps in care; and

"(III) facilitate improved care by using additional resources like nurses, nurse practitioners, and physician assistants.

"(ii) Programs that focus on patient education and self-management of health conditions, including interventions that—

"(I) help manage chronic conditions;

"(II) reduce declines in health status; and

"(III) foster patient and provider collaboration.

"(iii) Transitional care interventions that focus on care provided around a hospital inpatient episode, including programs that target post-discharge patient care in order to reduce unnecessary health complications and readmissions.

"(iv) Patient safety programs, including provisions for hospital-based patient safety programs in contracts that the Medicare Advantage organization offering the MA plan has with hospitals.

"(v) Financial policies that promote systematic coordination of care by primary care physicians across the full spectrum of specialties and sites of care, such as medical homes, capitation arrangements, or pay-for-performance programs.

"(vi) Programs that address, identify, and ameliorate health care disparities among principal at-risk subpopulations.

"(vii) Medication therapy management programs that are more extensive than is required under section 1860D–4(c) (as determined by the Secretary).

"(viii) Health information technology programs, including clinical decision support and other tools to facilitate data collection and ensure patient-centered, appropriate care.

"(ix) Such other care management and coordination programs as the Secretary determines appropriate.

"(D) CONDUCT OF PROGRAM IN URBAN AND RURAL AREAS.—An MA plan may conduct a program described in subparagraph (C) in a manner appropriate for an urban or rural area, as applicable.

"(E) REPORTING OF DATA.—Each Medicare Advantage organization shall provide to the Secretary the information needed to determine whether they are eligible for a care coordination and management performance bonus at a time and in a manner specified by the Secretary.

"(F) PERIODIC AUDITING.—The Secretary shall provide for the annual auditing of programs described in subparagraph (C) for which an MA plan receives a care coordination and management performance bonus under this paragraph. The Comptroller General shall monitor auditing activities conducted under this subparagraph.

"(2) QUALITY PERFORMANCE BONUSES.—

"(A) QUALITY BONUS.—For years beginning with 2014, the Secretary shall, in addition to any other payment provided under this part, make monthly payments, with respect to coverage of an individual under this part, to an MA plan that achieves at least a 3 star rating (or comparable rating) on a rating system described in subparagraph (C) in an amount equal to—

"(i) in the case of a plan that achieves a 3 star rating (or comparable rating) on such system 2 percent of the national monthly per capita cost for expenditures for individuals enrolled under the original medicare fee-for-service program for the year; and

"(ii) in the case of a plan that achieves a 4 or 5 star rating (or comparable rating on such system, 4 percent of such national monthly per capita cost for the year.

"(B) IMPROVED QUALITY BONUS.—For years beginning with 2014, in the case of an MA plan that does not receive a quality bonus under subparagraph (A) and is an improved quality MA plan with respect to the year (as identified by the Secretary), the Secretary shall, in addition to any other payment provided under this part, make monthly payments, with respect to coverage of an individual under this part, to the MA plan in an amount equal to 1 percent of such national monthly per capita cost for the year.

"(C) USE OF RATING SYSTEM.—For purposes of subparagraph (A), a rating system described in this paragraph is—

"(i) a rating system that uses up to 5 stars to rate clinical quality and enrollee satisfaction and performance at the Medicare Advantage contract or MA plan level; or

"(ii) such other system established by the Secretary that provides for the determination of a comparable quality performance rating to the rating system described in clause (i).

"(D) DATA USED IN DETERMINING SCORE.—

"(i) IN GENERAL.—The rating of an MA plan under the rating system described in subparagraph (C) with respect to a year shall be based on based on the most recent data available.

"(ii) PLANS THAT FAIL TO REPORT DATA.—An MA plan which does not report data that enables the Secretary to rate the plan for purposes of subparagraph (A) or identify the plan for purposes of subparagraph (B) shall be counted, for purposes of such rating or identification, as having the lowest plan performance rating and the lowest percentage improvement, respectively.

"(3) QUALITY BONUS FOR NEW AND LOW ENROLLMENT MA PLANS.—

"(A) NEW MA PLANS.—For years beginning with 2014, in the case of an MA plan that first submits a bid under section 1854(a)(1)(A) for 2012 or a subsequent year, only receives enrollments made during the coverage election periods described in section 1851(e), and is not able to receive a bonus under subparagraph (A) or (B) of paragraph (2) for the year, the Secretary shall, in addition to any other payment provided under this part, make monthly payments, with respect to coverage of an individual under this part, to the MA plan in an amount equal to 2 percent of national monthly per capita cost for expenditures for individuals enrolled under the original medicare fee-for-service program for the year. In its fourth year of operation, the MA plan shall be paid in the same manner as other MA plans with comparable enrollment.

"(B) LOW ENROLLMENT PLANS.—For years beginning with 2014, in the case of an MA plan that has low enrollment (as defined by the Secretary) and would not otherwise be able to receive a bonus under subparagraph (A) or (B) of paragraph (2) or subparagraph (A) of this paragraph for the year (referred to in this subparagraph as a 'low enrollment plan'), the Secretary shall use a regional or local mean of the rating of all MA plans in the region or local area, as determined appropriate by the Secretary, on measures used to determine whether MA plans are eligible for a quality or an improved quality bonus, as applicable, to determine whether the low enrollment plan is eligible for a bonus under such a subparagraph.

"(4) RISK ADJUSTMENT.—The Secretary shall risk adjust a performance bonus under this subsection in the same manner as the Secretary risk adjusts beneficiary rebates described in section 1854(b)(1)(C).

"(5) NOTIFICATION.—The Secretary, in the annual announcement required under subsection (b)(1)(B) for 2014 and each succeeding year, shall notify the Medicare Advantage organization of any performance bonus (including a care coordination and management performance bonus under paragraph (1), a quality performance bonus under paragraph (2), and a quality bonus for new and low enrollment plans under paragraph (3)) that the organization will receive under this subsection with respect to the year. The Secretary shall provide for the publication of the information described in the previous sentence on the Internet website of the Centers for Medicare & Medicaid Services."

(B) CONFORMING AMENDMENT.—Section 1853(a)(1)(B) of the Social Security Act (42 U.S.C. 1395w–23(a)(1)(B)) is amended—

(i) in clause (i), by inserting "and any performance bonus under subsection (n)" before the period at the end; and

(ii) in clause (ii), by striking "(G)" and inserting "(G), plus the amount (if any) of any performance bonus under subsection (n)".

(2) APPLICATION OF PERFORMANCE BONUSES TO MA REGIONAL PLANS.—Section 1858 of the Social Security Act (42 U.S.C. 1395w–27a) is amended—

(A) in subsection (f)(1), by striking "subsection (e)" and inserting "subsections (e) and (i)"; and

(B) by adding at the end the following new subsection:

"(i) APPLICATION OF PERFORMANCE BONUSES TO MA REGIONAL PLANS.—For years beginning with 2014, the Secretary shall apply the performance bonuses under section 1853(n) (relating to bonuses for care coordination and management, quality performance, and new and low enrollment MA plans) to MA regional plans in a similar manner as such performance bonuses apply to MA plans under such subsection.".

(g) GRANDFATHERING SUPPLEMENTAL BENEFITS FOR CURRENT ENROLLEES AFTER IMPLEMENTATION OF COMPETITIVE BIDDING.—

Section 1853 of the Social Security Act (42 U.S.C. 1395w–23), as amended by subsection (f), is amended by adding at the end the following new subsection:

"(o) GRANDFATHERING SUPPLEMENTAL BENEFITS FOR CURRENT ENROLLES AFTER IMPLEMENTATION OF COMPETITIVE BIDDING.—

"(1) IDENTIFICATION OF AREAS.—The Secretary shall identify MA local areas in which, with respect to 2009, average bids submitted by an MA organization under section 1854(a) for MA local plans in the area are not greater than 75 percent of the adjusted average per capita cost for the year involved, determined under section 1876(a)(4), for the area for individuals who are not enrolled in an MA plan under this part for the year, but adjusted to exclude costs attributable to payments under section 1848(o), 1886(n), and 1886(h).

"(2) ELECTION TO PROVIDE REBATES TO GRANDFATHERED ENROLLEES.—

"(A) IN GENERAL.—For years beginning with 2012, each Medicare Advantage organization offering an MA local plan in an area identified by the Secretary under paragraph (1) may elect to provide rebates to grandfathered enrollees under section 1854(b)(1)(C). In the case where an MA organization makes such an election, the monthly per capita dollar amount of such rebates shall not exceed the applicable amount for the year (as defined in subparagraph (B)).

"(B) APPLICABLE AMOUNT.—For purposes of this subsection, the term 'applicable amount' means—

"(i) for 2012, the monthly per capita dollar amount of such rebates provided to enrollees under the MA local plan with respect to 2011; and

"(ii) for a subsequent year, 95 percent of the amount determined under this subparagraph for the preceding year.

"(3) SPECIAL RULES FOR PLANS IN IDENTIFIED AREAS.—Notwithstanding any other provision of this part, the following shall apply with respect to each Medicare Advantage organization offering an MA local plan in an area identified by the Secretary under paragraph (1) that makes an election described in paragraph (2):

"(A) PAYMENTS.—The amount of the monthly payment under this section to the Medicare Advantage organization, with respect to coverage of a grandfathered enrollee under this part in the area for a month, shall be equal to—

"(i) for 2012 and 2013, the sum of—

"(I) the bid amount under section 1854(a) for the MA local plan; and

"(II) the applicable amount (as defined in paragraph (2)(B)) for the MA local plan for the year.

"(ii) for 2014 and subsequent years, the sum of—

"(I) the MA competitive benchmark amount under subsection (j)(1)(A)(i) for the area for the month, adjusted, only to the extent the Secretary determines necessary, to account for induced utilization as a result of rebates provided to grandfathered enrollees (except that such adjustment shall not exceed 0.5 percent of such MA competitive benchmark amount); and

"(II) the applicable amount (as so defined) for the MA local plan for the year.

"(B) REQUIREMENT TO SUBMIT BIDS UNDER COMPETITIVE BIDDING.—The Medicare Advantage organization shall submit a single bid amount under section 1854(a) for the MA local plan. The Medicare Advantage organization shall remove from such bid amount any effects of induced demand for care that may result from the higher rebates available to grandfathered enrollees under this subsection.

"(C) NONAPPLICATION OF BONUS PAYMENTS AND ANY OTHER REBATES.—The Medicare Advantage organization offering the MA local plan shall not be eligible for any bonus payment under subsection (n) or any rebate under this part (other than as provided under this subsection) with respect to grandfathered enrollees.

"(D) NONAPPLICATION OF UNIFORM BID AND PREMIUM AMOUNTS TO GRANDFATHERED ENROLLEES.—Section 1854(c) shall not apply with respect to the MA local plan.

"(E) NONAPPLICATION OF LIMITATION ON APPLICATION OF PLAN REBATES TOWARD PAYMENT OF PART B PREMIUM.—Notwithstanding clause (iii) of section 1854(b)(1)(C), in the case of a grandfathered enrollee, a rebate under such section may be used for the purpose described in clause (ii)(III) of such section.

"(F) RISK ADJUSTMENT.—The Secretary shall risk adjust rebates to grandfathered enrollees under this subsection in the same manner as the Secretary risk adjusts beneficiary rebates described in section 1854(b)(1)(C).

"(4) DEFINITION OF GRANDFATHERED ENROLLEE.—In this subsection, the term 'grandfathered enrollee' means an individual who is enrolled (effective as of the date of enactment of this subsection) in an MA local plan in an area that is identified by the Secretary under paragraph (1).".

(h) TRANSITIONAL EXTRA BENEFITS.—Section 1853 of the Social Security Act (42 U.S.C. 1395w–23), as amended by subsections (f) and (g), is amended by adding at the end the following new subsection:

"(p) TRANSITIONAL EXTRA BENEFITS.—

"(1) IN GENERAL.—For years beginning with 2012, the Secretary shall provide transitional rebates under section 1854(b)(1)(C) for the provision of extra benefits (as specified by the Secretary) to enrollees described in paragraph (2).

"(2) ENROLLEES DESCRIBED.—An enrollee described in this paragraph is an individual who—

"(A) enrolls in an MA local plan in an applicable area; and

"(B) experiences a significant reduction in extra benefits described in clause (ii) of section 1854(b)(1)(C) as a result of competitive bidding under this part (as determined by the Secretary).

"(3) APPLICABLE AREAS.—In this subsection, the term 'applicable area' means the following:

"(A) The 2 largest metropolitan statistical areas, if the Secretary determines that the total amount of such extra benefits for each enrollee for the month in those areas is greater than $100.

"(B) A county where—

"(i) the MA area-specific non-drug monthly benchmark amount for a month in 2011 is equal to the legacy urban floor amount (as described in subsection (c)(1)(B)(iii)), as determined by the Secretary for the area for 2011;

"(ii) the percentage of Medicare Advantage eligible beneficiaries in the county who are enrolled in an MA plan for 2009 is greater than 30 percent (as determined by the Secretary); and

"(iii) average bids submitted by an MA organization under section 1854(a) for MA local plans in the county for 2011 are not greater than the adjusted average per capita cost for the year involved, determined under section 1876(a)(4), for the county for individuals who are not enrolled in an MA plan under this part for the year, but adjusted to exclude costs attributable to payments under section 1848(o), 1886(n), and 1886(h).

"(C) If the Secretary determines appropriate, a county contiguous to an area or county described in subparagraph (A) or (B), respectively.

"(4) REVIEW OF PLAN BIDS.—In the case of a bid submitted by an MA organization under section 1854(a) for an MA local plan in an applicable area, the Secretary shall review such bid in order to ensure that extra benefits (as specified by the Secretary) are provided to enrollees described in paragraph (2).

"(5) FUNDING.—The Secretary shall provide for the transfer from the Federal Hospital Insurance Trust Fund under section 1817 and the Federal Supplementary Medical Insurance Trust Fund established under section 1841, in such proportion as the Secretary determines appropriate, of an amount not to exceed $5,000,000,000 for the period of fiscal years 2012 through 2019 for the purpose of providing transitional rebates under section 1854(b)(1)(C) for the provision of extra benefits under this subsection.".

(i) NONAPPLICATION OF COMPETITIVE BIDDING AND RELATED PROVISIONS AND CLARIFICATION OF MA PAYMENT AREA FOR PACE PROGRAMS.—

(1) NONAPPLICATION OF COMPETITIVE BIDDING AND RELATED PROVISIONS FOR PACE PROGRAMS.—Section 1894 of the Social Security Act (42 U.S.C. 1395eee) is amended—

(A) by redesignating subsections (h) and (i) as subsections (i) and (j), respectively;

(B) by inserting after subsection (g) the following new subsection:

"(h) NONAPPLICATION OF COMPETITIVE BIDDING AND RELATED PROVISIONS UNDER PART C.—With respect to a PACE program under this section, the following provisions (and regulations relating to such provisions) shall not apply:

"(1) Section 1853(j)(1)(A)(i), relating to MA area-specific non-drug monthly benchmark amount being based on competitive bids.

"(2) Section 1853(d)(5), relating to the establishment of MA local plan service areas.

"(3) Section 1853(n), relating to the payment of performance bonuses.

"(4) Section 1853(o), relating to grandfathering supplemental benefits for current enrollees after implementation of competitive bidding.

"(5) Section 1853(p), relating to transitional extra benefits.".

(2) SPECIAL RULE FOR MA PAYMENT AREA FOR PACE PROGRAMS.—Section 1853(d) of the Social Security Act (42 U.S.C. 1395w–23(d)), as amended by subsection (e), is amended by adding at the end the following new paragraph:

"(6) SPECIAL RULE FOR MA PAYMENT AREA FOR PACE PROGRAMS.—For years beginning with 2012, in the case of a PACE program under section 1894, the MA payment area shall be the MA local area (as defined in paragraph (2)).".

SEC. 3202. BENEFIT PROTECTION AND SIMPLIFICATION.

(a) LIMITATION ON VARIATION OF COST SHARING FOR CERTAIN BENEFITS.—

(1) IN GENERAL.—Section 1852(a)(1)(B) of the Social Security Act (42 U.S.C. 1395w–22(a)(1)(B)) is amended—

(A) in clause (i), by inserting ", subject to clause (iii)," after "and B or"; and

(B) by adding at the end the following new clauses:

"(iii) LIMITATION ON VARIATION OF COST SHARING FOR CERTAIN BENEFITS.—Subject to clause (v), cost-sharing for services described in clause (iv) shall not exceed the cost-sharing required for those services under parts A and B.

"(iv) SERVICES DESCRIBED.—The following services are described in this clause:

"(I) Chemotherapy administration services.

"(II) Renal dialysis services (as defined in section 1881(b)(14)(B)).

"(III) Skilled nursing care.

"(IV) Such other services that the Secretary determines appropriate (including services that the Secretary determines require a high level of predictability and transparency for beneficiaries).

"(v) EXCEPTION.—In the case of services described in clause (iv) for which there is no cost-sharing required under parts A and B, cost-sharing may be required for those services in accordance with clause (i).".

(2) EFFECTIVE DATE.—The amendments made by this subsection shall apply to plan years beginning on or after January 1, 2011.

(b) APPLICATION OF REBATES, PERFORMANCE BONUSES, AND PREMIUMS.—

(1) APPLICATION OF REBATES.—Section 1854(b)(1)(C) of the Social Security Act (42 U.S.C. 1395w–24(b)(1)(C)) is amended—

(A) in clause (ii), by striking "REBATE.—A rebate" and inserting "REBATE FOR PLAN YEARS BEFORE 2012.—For plan years before 2012, a rebate";

(B) by redesignating clauses (iii) and (iv) as clauses (iv) and (v); and

(C) by inserting after clause (ii) the following new clause:

"(iii) FORM OF REBATE FOR PLAN YEAR 2012 AND SUBSEQUENT PLAN YEARS.—For plan years beginning on or after January 1, 2012, a rebate required under this subparagraph may not be used for the purpose described in clause (ii)(III) and shall be provided through the application of the amount of the rebate in the following priority order:

"(I) First, to use the most significant share to meaningfully reduce cost-sharing otherwise applicable for benefits under the original medicare fee-for-service program under parts A and B and for qualified prescription drug coverage under part D, including the reduction of any deductibles, copayments, and maximum limitations on out-of-pocket expenses otherwise applicable. Any reduction of maximum limitations on out-of-pocket expenses under the preceding sentence shall apply to all benefits under the original medicare fee-for-service program option. The Secretary may provide guidance on meaningfully reducing cost-sharing under this subclause, except that such guidance may not require a particular amount of cost-sharing or reduction in cost-sharing.

"(II) Second, to use the next most significant share to meaningfully provide coverage of preventive and wellness health care benefits (as defined by the Secretary) which are not benefits under the original medicare fee-for-service program, such as smoking cessation, a free flu shot, and an annual physical examination.

"(III) Third, to use the remaining share to meaningfully provide coverage of other health care benefits which are not benefits under the original medicare fee-for-service program, such as eye examinations and dental coverage, and are not benefits described in subclause (II).".

(2) APPLICATION OF PERFORMANCE BONUSES.—Section 1853(n) of the Social Security Act, as added by section 3201(f), is amended by adding at the end the following new paragraph:

"(6) APPLICATION OF PERFORMANCE BONUSES.—For plan years beginning on or after January 1, 2014, any performance bonus paid to an MA plan under this subsection shall be used for the purposes, and in the priority order, described in subclauses (I) through (III) of section 1854(b)(1)(C)(iii).".

(3) APPLICATION OF MA MONTHLY SUPPLEMENTARY BENEFICIARY PREMIUM.—Section 1854(b)(2)(C) of the Social Security Act (42 U.S.C. 1395w–24(b)(2)(C)) is amended—

(A) by striking "PREMIUM.—The term" and inserting "PREMIUM.—

"(i) IN GENERAL.—The term"; and

(B) by adding at the end the following new clause:

"(ii) APPLICATION OF MA MONTHLY SUPPLEMENTARY BENEFICIARY PREMIUM.—For plan years beginning on or after January 1, 2012, any MA monthly supplementary beneficiary premium charged to an individual enrolled in an MA plan shall be used for the purposes, and in the priority order, described in subclauses (I) through (III) of paragraph (1)(C)(iii).".

SEC. 3203. APPLICATION OF CODING INTENSITY ADJUSTMENT DURING MA PAYMENT TRANSITION.

Section 1853(a)(1)(C) of the Social Security Act (42 U.S.C. 1395w–23(a)(1)(C)) is amended by adding at the end the following new clause:

"(iii) APPLICATION OF CODING INTENSITY ADJUSTMENT FOR 2011 AND SUBSEQUENT YEARS.—

"(I) REQUIREMENT TO APPLY IN 2011 THROUGH 2013.—In order to ensure payment accuracy, the Secretary shall conduct an analysis of the differences described in clause (ii)(I). The Secretary shall ensure that the results of such analysis are incorporated into the risk scores for 2011, 2012, and 2013.

"(II) AUTHORITY TO APPLY IN 2014 AND SUBSEQUENT YEARS.—The Secretary may, as appropriate, incorporate the results of such analysis into the risk scores for 2014 and subsequent years.".

SEC. 3204. SIMPLIFICATION OF ANNUAL BENEFICIARY ELECTION PERIODS.

(a) ANNUAL 45-DAY PERIOD FOR DISENROLLMENT FROM MA PLANS TO ELECT TO RECEIVE BENEFITS UNDER THE ORIGINAL MEDICARE FEE-FOR-SERVICE PROGRAM.—

(1) IN GENERAL.—Section 1851(e)(2)(C) of the Social Security Act (42 U.S.C. 1395w–1(e)(2)(C)) is amended to read as follows:

"(C) ANNUAL 45-DAY PERIOD FOR DISENROLLMENT FROM MA PLANS TO ELECT TO RECEIVE BENEFITS UNDER THE ORIGINAL MEDICARE FEE-FOR-SERVICE PROGRAM.—Subject to subparagraph (D), at any time during the first 45 days of a year (beginning with 2011), an individual who is enrolled in a Medicare Advantage plan may change the election under subsection (a)(1), but only with respect to coverage under the original medicare fee-for-service program under parts A and B, and may elect qualified prescription drug coverage in accordance with section 1860D–1.".

(2) EFFECTIVE DATE.—The amendment made by paragraph (1) shall apply with respect to 2011 and succeeding years.

(b) TIMING OF THE ANNUAL, COORDINATED ELECTION PERIOD UNDER PARTS C AND D.—Section 1851(e)(3)(B) of the Social Security Act (42 U.S.C. 1395w–1(e)(3)(B)) is amended—

(1) in clause (iii), by striking "and" at the end;

(2) in clause (iv)—

(A) by striking "and succeeding years" and inserting ", 2008, 2009, and 2010"; and

(B) by striking the period at the end and inserting "; and"; and

(3) by adding at the end the following new clause:

"(v) with respect to 2012 and succeeding years, the period beginning on October 15 and ending on December 7 of the year before such year.".

SEC. 3205. EXTENSION FOR SPECIALIZED MA PLANS FOR SPECIAL NEEDS INDIVIDUALS.

(a) EXTENSION OF SNP AUTHORITY.—Section 1859(f)(1) of the Social Security Act (42 U.S.C. 1395w–28(f)(1)), as amended by section 164(a) of the Medicare Improvements for Patients and Providers Act of 2008 (Public Law 110–275), is amended by striking "2011" and inserting "2014".

(b) AUTHORITY TO APPLY FRAILTY ADJUSTMENT UNDER PACE PAYMENT RULES.—Section 1853(a)(1)(B) of the Social Security Act (42 U.S.C. 1395w–23(a)(1)(B)) is amended by adding at the end the following new clause:

"(iv) AUTHORITY TO APPLY FRAILTY ADJUSTMENT UNDER PACE PAYMENT RULES FOR CERTAIN SPECIALIZED MA PLANS FOR SPECIAL NEEDS INDIVIDUALS.—

"(I) IN GENERAL.—Notwithstanding the preceding provisions of this paragraph, for plan year 2011 and subsequent plan years, in the case of a plan described in subclause (II), the Secretary may apply the payment rules under section 1894(d) (other than paragraph (3) of such section) rather than the payment rules that would otherwise apply under this part, but only to the extent necessary to reflect the costs of treating high concentrations of frail individuals.

"(II) PLAN DESCRIBED.—A plan described in this subclause is a specialized MA plan for special needs individuals described in section 1859(b)(6)(B)(ii) that is fully integrated with capitated contracts with States for Medicaid benefits, including long-term care, and that have similar average levels of frailty (as determined by the Secretary) as the PACE program.".

(c) TRANSITION AND EXCEPTION REGARDING RESTRICTION ON ENROLLMENT.—Section 1859(f) of the Social Security Act (42 U.S.C. 1395w–28(f)) is amended by adding at the end the following new paragraph:

"(6) TRANSITION AND EXCEPTION REGARDING RESTRICTION ON ENROLLMENT.—

"(A) IN GENERAL.—Subject to subparagraph (C), the Secretary shall establish procedures for the transition of applicable individuals to—

"(i) a Medicare Advantage plan that is not a specialized MA plan for special needs individuals (as defined in subsection (b)(6)); or

"(ii) the original medicare fee-for-service program under parts A and B.

"(B) APPLICABLE INDIVIDUALS.—For purposes of clause (i), the term 'applicable individual' means an individual who—

"(i) is enrolled under a specialized MA plan for special needs individuals (as defined in subsection (b)(6)); and

"(ii) is not within the 1 or more of the classes of special needs individuals to which enrollment under the plan is restricted to.

"(C) EXCEPTION.—The Secretary shall provide for an exception to the transition described in subparagraph (A) for a limited period of time for individuals enrolled under a specialized MA plan for special needs individuals described in subsection (b)(6)(B)(ii) who are no longer eligible for medical assistance under title XIX.

"(D) TIMELINE FOR INITIAL TRANSITION.—The Secretary shall ensure that applicable individuals enrolled in a specialized MA plan for special needs individuals (as defined in subsection (b)(6)) prior to January 1, 2010, are transitioned to a plan or the program described in subparagraph (A) by not later than January 1, 2013.".

(d) TEMPORARY EXTENSION OF AUTHORITY TO OPERATE BUT NO SERVICE AREA EXPANSION FOR DUAL SPECIAL NEEDS PLANS THAT DO NOT MEET CERTAIN REQUIREMENTS.—Section 164(c)(2) of the Medicare Improvements for Patients and Providers Act of 2008 (Public Law 110–275) is amended by striking "December 31, 2010" and inserting "December 31, 2012".

(e) AUTHORITY TO REQUIRE SPECIAL NEEDS PLANS BE NCQA APPROVED.—Section 1859(f) of the Social Security Act (42 U.S.C. 1395w–28(f)), as amended by subsections (a) and (c), is amended—

(1) in paragraph (2), by adding at the end the following new subparagraph:

"(C) If applicable, the plan meets the requirement described in paragraph (7).";

(2) in paragraph (3), by adding at the end the following new subparagraph:

"(E) If applicable, the plan meets the requirement described in paragraph (7).";

(3) in paragraph (4), by adding at the end the following new subparagraph:

"(C) If applicable, the plan meets the requirement described in paragraph (7)."; and

(4) by adding at the end the following new paragraph:

"(7) AUTHORITY TO REQUIRE SPECIAL NEEDS PLANS BE NCQA APPROVED.—For 2012 and subsequent years, the Secretary shall require that a Medicare Advantage organization offering a specialized MA plan for special needs individuals be approved by the National Committee for Quality Assurance (based on standards established by the Secretary).".

(f) RISK ADJUSTMENT.—Section 1853(a)(1)(C) of the Social Security Act (42 U.S.C. 1395i–23(a)(1)(C)) is amended by adding at the end the following new clause:

"(iii) IMPROVEMENTS TO RISK ADJUSTMENT FOR SPECIAL NEEDS INDIVIDUALS WITH CHRONIC HEALTH CONDITIONS.—

"(I) IN GENERAL.—For 2011 and subsequent years, for purposes of the adjustment under clause (i) with respect to individuals described in subclause (II), the Secretary shall use a risk score that reflects the known underlying risk profile and chronic health status of similar individuals. Such risk score shall be used instead of the default risk score for new enrollees in Medicare Advantage plans that are not specialized MA plans for special needs individuals (as defined in section 1859(b)(6)).

"(II) INDIVIDUALS DESCRIBED.—An individual described in this subclause is a special needs individual described in subsection (b)(6)(B)(iii) who enrolls in a specialized MA plan for special needs individuals on or after January 1, 2011.

"(III) EVALUATION.—For 2011 and periodically thereafter, the Secretary shall evaluate and revise the risk adjustment system under this subparagraph in order to, as accurately as possible, account for higher medical and care coordination costs associated with frailty, individuals with multiple, comorbid chronic conditions, and individuals with a diagnosis of mental illness, and also to account for costs that may be associated with higher concentrations of beneficiaries with those conditions.

"(IV) PUBLICATION OF EVALUATION AND REVISIONS.—The Secretary shall publish, as part of an announcement under subsection (b), a description of any evaluation conducted under subclause (III) during the preceding year and any revisions made under such subclause as a result of such evaluation.".

(g) TECHNICAL CORRECTION.—Section 1859(f)(5) of the Social Security Act (42 U.S.C. 1395w–28(f)(5)) is amended, in the matter preceding subparagraph (A), by striking "described in subsection (b)(6)(B)(i)".

SEC. 3206. EXTENSION OF REASONABLE COST CONTRACTS.

Section 1876(h)(5)(C)(ii) of the Social Security Act (42 U.S.C. 1395mm(h)(5)(C)(ii)) is amended, in the matter preceding subclause (I), by striking "January 1, 2010" and inserting "January 1, 2013".

SEC. 3207. TECHNICAL CORRECTION TO MA PRIVATE FEE-FOR-SERVICE PLANS.

For plan year 2011 and subsequent plan years, to the extent that the Secretary of Health and Human Services is applying the 2008 service area extension waiver policy (as modified in the April 11, 2008, Centers for Medicare & Medicaid Services' memorandum with the subject "2009 Employer Group Waiver-Modification of the 2008 Service Area Extension Waiver Granted to Certain MA Local Coordinated Care Plans") to Medicare Advantage coordinated care plans, the Secretary shall extend the application of such waiver policy to employers who contract directly with the Secretary as a Medicare Advantage private fee-for-service plan under section 1857(i)(2) of the Social Security Act (42 U.S.C. 1395w–27(i)(2)) and that had enrollment as of October 1, 2009.

SEC. 3208. MAKING SENIOR HOUSING FACILITY DEMONSTRATION PERMANENT.

(a) IN GENERAL.—Section 1859 of the Social Security Act (42 U.S.C. 1395w–28) is amended by adding at the end the following new subsection:

"(g) SPECIAL RULES FOR SENIOR HOUSING FACILITY PLANS.—

"(1) IN GENERAL.—In the case of a Medicare Advantage senior housing facility plan described in paragraph (2), notwithstanding any other provision of this part to the contrary and in accordance with regulations of the Secretary, the service area of such plan may be limited to a senior housing facility in a geographic area.

"(2) MEDICARE ADVANTAGE SENIOR HOUSING FACILITY PLAN DESCRIBED.—For purposes of this subsection, a Medicare Advantage senior housing facility plan is a Medicare Advantage plan that—

"(A) restricts enrollment of individuals under this part to individuals who reside in a continuing care retirement community (as defined in section 1852(l)(4)(B));

"(B) provides primary care services onsite and has a ratio of accessible physicians to beneficiaries that the Secretary determines is adequate;

"(C) provides transportation services for beneficiaries to specialty providers outside of the facility; and

"(D) has participated (as of December 31, 2009) in a demonstration project established by the Secretary under which such a plan was offered for not less than 1 year.".

(b) EFFECTIVE DATE.—The amendment made by this section shall take effect on January 1, 2010, and shall apply to plan years beginning on or after such date.

SEC. 3209. AUTHORITY TO DENY PLAN BIDS.

(a) IN GENERAL.—Section 1854(a)(5) of the Social Security Act (42 U.S.C. 1395w–24(a)(5)) is amended by adding at the end the following new subparagraph:

"(C) REJECTION OF BIDS.—

"(i) IN GENERAL.—Nothing in this section shall be construed as requiring the Secretary to accept any or every bid submitted by an MA organization under this subsection.

"(ii) AUTHORITY TO DENY BIDS THAT PROPOSE SIGNIFICANT INCREASES IN COST SHARING OR DECREASES IN BENEFITS.—The Secretary may deny a bid submitted by an MA organization for an MA plan if it proposes significant increases in cost sharing or decreases in benefits offered under the plan.".

(b) APPLICATION UNDER PART D.—Section 1860D–11(d) of such Act (42 U.S.C. 1395w–111(d)) is amended by adding at the end the following new paragraph:

"(3) REJECTION OF BIDS.—Paragraph (5)(C) of section 1854(a) shall apply with respect to bids submitted by a PDP sponsor under subsection (b) in the same manner as such paragraph applies to bids submitted by an MA organization under such section 1854(a).".

(c) EFFECTIVE DATE.—The amendments made by this section shall apply to bids submitted for contract years beginning on or after January 1, 2011.

SEC. 3210. DEVELOPMENT OF NEW STANDARDS FOR CERTAIN MEDIGAP PLANS.

(a) IN GENERAL.—Section 1882 of the Social Security Act (42 U.S.C. 1395ss) is amended by adding at the end the following new subsection:

"(y) DEVELOPMENT OF NEW STANDARDS FOR CERTAIN MEDICARE SUPPLEMENTAL POLICIES.—

"(1) IN GENERAL.—The Secretary shall request the National Association of Insurance Commissioners to review and revise the standards for benefit packages described in paragraph (2) under subsection (p)(1), to otherwise update standards to include requirements for nominal cost sharing to encourage the use of appropriate physicians' services under part B. Such revisions shall be based on evidence published in peer-reviewed journals or current examples used by integrated delivery systems and made consistent with the rules applicable under subsection (p)(1)(E) with the reference to the '1991 NAIC Model Regulation' deemed a reference to the NAIC Model Regulation as published in the Federal Register on December 4, 1998, and as subsequently updated by the National Association of Insurance Commissioners to reflect previous changes in law and the reference to 'date of enactment of this subsection' deemed a reference to the date of enactment of the Patient Protection and Affordable Care Act. To the extent practicable, such revision shall provide for the implementation of revised standards for benefit packages as of January 1, 2015.

"(2) BENEFIT PACKAGES DESCRIBED.—The benefit packages described in this paragraph are benefit packages classified as 'C' and 'F'.".

(b) CONFORMING AMENDMENT.—Section 1882(o)(1) of the Social Security Act (42 U.S.C. 1395ss(o)(1)) is amended by striking ", and (w)" and inserting "(w), and (y)".

Subtitle D—Medicare Part D Improvements for Prescription Drug Plans and MA–PD Plans

SEC. 3301. MEDICARE COVERAGE GAP DISCOUNT PROGRAM.

(a) CONDITION FOR COVERAGE OF DRUGS UNDER PART D.—Part D of Title XVIII of the Social Security Act (42 U.S.C. 1395w–101 et seq.), is amended by adding at the end the following new section:

"CONDITION FOR COVERAGE OF DRUGS UNDER THIS PART

"SEC. 1860D–43. (a) IN GENERAL.—In order for coverage to be available under this part for covered part D drugs (as defined in section 1860D–2(e)) of a manufacturer, the manufacturer must—

"(1) participate in the Medicare coverage gap discount program under section 1860D–14A;

"(2) have entered into and have in effect an agreement described in subsection (b) of such section with the Secretary; and

"(3) have entered into and have in effect, under terms and conditions specified by the Secretary, a contract with a third party that the Secretary has entered into a contract with under subsection (d)(3) of such section.

"(b) EFFECTIVE DATE.—Subsection (a) shall apply to covered part D drugs dispensed under this part on or after July 1, 2010.

"(c) AUTHORIZING COVERAGE FOR DRUGS NOT COVERED UNDER AGREEMENTS.—Subsection (a) shall not apply to the dispensing of a covered part D drug if—

"(1) the Secretary has made a determination that the availability of the drug is essential to the health of beneficiaries under this part; or

"(2) the Secretary determines that in the period beginning on July 1, 2010, and ending on December 31, 2010, there were extenuating circumstances.

"(d) DEFINITION OF MANUFACTURER.—In this section, the term 'manufacturer' has the meaning given such term in section 1860D–14A(g)(5).".

(b) MEDICARE COVERAGE GAP DISCOUNT PROGRAM.—Part D of title XVIII of the Social Security Act (42 U.S.C. 1395w–101) is amended by inserting after section 1860D–14 the following new section:

"MEDICARE COVERAGE GAP DISCOUNT PROGRAM

"SEC. 1860D–14A. (a) ESTABLISHMENT.—The Secretary shall establish a Medicare coverage gap discount program (in this section referred to as the 'program') by not later than July 1, 2010. Under the program, the Secretary shall enter into agreements described in subsection (b) with manufacturers and provide for the performance of the duties described in subsection (c)(1). The Secretary shall establish a model agreement for use under the program by not later than April 1, 2010, in consultation with manufacturers, and allow for comment on such model agreement.

"(b) TERMS OF AGREEMENT.—

"(1) IN GENERAL.—

"(A) AGREEMENT.—An agreement under this section shall require the manufacturer to provide applicable beneficiaries access to discounted prices for applicable drugs of the manufacturer.

"(B) PROVISION OF DISCOUNTED PRICES AT THE POINT-OF-SALE.—Except as provided in subsection (c)(1)(A)(iii), such discounted prices shall be provided to the applicable beneficiary at the pharmacy or by the mail order service at the point-of-sale of an applicable drug.

"(C) TIMING OF AGREEMENT.—

"(i) SPECIAL RULE FOR 2010 AND 2011.—In order for an agreement with a manufacturer to be in effect under this section with respect to the period beginning on July 1, 2010, and ending on December 31, 2011, the manufacturer shall enter into such agreement not later than May 1, 2010.

"(ii) 2012 AND SUBSEQUENT YEARS.—In order for an agreement with a manufacturer to be in effect under this section with respect to plan year 2012 or a subsequent plan year, the manufacturer shall enter into such agreement (or such agreement shall be renewed under paragraph (4)(A)) not later than January 30 of the preceding year.

"(2) PROVISION OF APPROPRIATE DATA.—Each manufacturer with an agreement in effect under this section shall collect and have available appropriate data, as determined by the Secretary, to ensure that it can demonstrate to the Secretary compliance with the requirements under the program.

"(3) COMPLIANCE WITH REQUIREMENTS FOR ADMINISTRATION OF PROGRAM.—Each manufacturer with an agreement in effect under this section shall comply with requirements imposed by the Secretary or a third party with a contract under subsection (d)(3), as applicable, for purposes of administering the program, including any determination under clause (i) of subsection (c)(1)(A) or procedures established under such subsection (c)(1)(A).

"(4) LENGTH OF AGREEMENT.—

"(A) IN GENERAL.—An agreement under this section shall be effective for an initial period of not less than 18 months and shall be automatically renewed for a period of not less than 1 year unless terminated under subparagraph (B).

"(B) TERMINATION.—

"(i) BY THE SECRETARY.—The Secretary may provide for termination of an agreement under this section for a knowing and willful violation of the requirements of the agreement or other good cause shown. Such termination shall not be effective earlier than 30 days after the date of notice to the manufacturer of such termination. The Secretary shall provide, upon request, a manufacturer with a hearing concerning such a termination, and such hearing shall take place prior to the effective date of the termination with sufficient time for such effective date to be repealed if the Secretary determines appropriate.

"(ii) BY A MANUFACTURER.—A manufacturer may terminate an agreement under this section for any reason. Any such termination shall be effective, with respect to a plan year—

"(I) if the termination occurs before January 30 of a plan year, as of the day after the end of the plan year; and

"(II) if the termination occurs on or after January 30 of a plan year, as of the day after the end of the succeeding plan year.

"(iii) EFFECTIVENESS OF TERMINATION.—Any termination under this subparagraph shall not affect discounts for applicable drugs of the manufacturer that are due under the agreement before the effective date of its termination.

"(iv) NOTICE TO THIRD PARTY.—The Secretary shall provide notice of such termination to a third party with a contract under subsection (d)(3) within not less than 30 days before the effective date of such termination.

"(c) DUTIES DESCRIBED AND SPECIAL RULE FOR SUPPLEMENTAL BENEFITS.—

"(1) DUTIES DESCRIBED.—The duties described in this subsection are the following:

"(A) ADMINISTRATION OF PROGRAM.—Administering the program, including—

"(i) the determination of the amount of the discounted price of an applicable drug of a manufacturer;

"(ii) except as provided in clause (iii), the establishment of procedures under which discounted prices are provided to applicable beneficiaries at pharmacies or by mail order service at the point-of-sale of an applicable drug;

"(iii) in the case where, during the period beginning on July 1, 2010, and ending on December 31, 2011, it is not practicable to provide such discounted prices at the point-of-sale (as described in clause (ii)), the establishment of procedures to provide such discounted prices as soon as practicable after the point-of-sale;

"(iv) the establishment of procedures to ensure that, not later than the applicable number of calendar days after the dispensing of an applicable drug by a pharmacy or mail order service, the pharmacy or mail order service is reimbursed for an amount equal to the difference between—

"(I) the negotiated price of the applicable drug; and

"(II) the discounted price of the applicable drug;

"(v) the establishment of procedures to ensure that the discounted price for an applicable drug under this section is applied before any coverage or financial assistance under other health benefit plans or programs that provide coverage or financial assistance for the purchase or provision of prescription drug coverage on behalf of applicable beneficiaries as the Secretary may specify;

"(vi) the establishment of procedures to implement the special rule for supplemental benefits under paragraph (2); and

"(vii) providing a reasonable dispute resolution mechanism to resolve disagreements between manufacturers, applicable beneficiaries, and the third party with a contract under subsection (d)(3).

"(B) MONITORING COMPLIANCE.—

"(i) IN GENERAL.—The Secretary shall monitor compliance by a manufacturer with the terms of an agreement under this section.

"(ii) NOTIFICATION.—If a third party with a contract under subsection (d)(3) determines that the manufacturer is not in compliance with such agreement, the third party shall notify the Secretary of such noncompliance for appropriate enforcement under subsection (e).

"(C) COLLECTION OF DATA FROM PRESCRIPTION DRUG PLANS AND MA–PD PLANS.—The Secretary may collect appropriate data from prescription drug plans and MA–PD plans in a timeframe that allows for discounted prices to be provided for applicable drugs under this section.

"(2) SPECIAL RULE FOR SUPPLEMENTAL BENEFITS.—For plan year 2010 and each subsequent plan year, in the case where an applicable beneficiary has supplemental benefits with respect to applicable drugs under the prescription drug plan or MA–PD plan that the applicable beneficiary is enrolled in, the applicable beneficiary shall not be provided a discounted price for an applicable drug under this section until after such supplemental benefits have been applied with respect to the applicable drug.

"(d) ADMINISTRATION.—

"(1) IN GENERAL.—Subject to paragraph (2), the Secretary shall provide for the implementation of this section, including the performance of the duties described in subsection (c)(1).

"(2) LIMITATION.—

"(A) IN GENERAL.—Subject to subparagraph (B), in providing for such implementation, the Secretary shall not receive or distribute any funds of a manufacturer under the program.

"(B) EXCEPTION.—The limitation under subparagraph (A) shall not apply to the Secretary with respect to drugs dispensed during the period beginning on July 1, 2010, and ending on December 31, 2010, but only if the Secretary determines that the exception to such limitation under this subparagraph is necessary in order for the Secretary to begin implementation of this section and provide applicable beneficiaries timely access to discounted prices during such period.

"(3) CONTRACT WITH THIRD PARTIES.—The Secretary shall enter into a contract with 1 or more third parties to administer the requirements established by the Secretary in order to carry out this section. At a minimum, the contract with a third party under the preceding sentence shall require that the third party—

"(A) receive and transmit information between the Secretary, manufacturers, and other individuals or entities the Secretary determines appropriate;

"(B) receive, distribute, or facilitate the distribution of funds of manufacturers to appropriate individuals or entities in order to meet the obligations of manufacturers under agreements under this section;

"(C) provide adequate and timely information to manufacturers, consistent with the agreement with the manufacturer under this section, as necessary for the manufacturer to fulfill its obligations under this section; and

"(D) permit manufacturers to conduct periodic audits, directly or through contracts, of the data and information used by the third party to determine discounts for applicable drugs of the manufacturer under the program.

"(4) PERFORMANCE REQUIREMENTS.—The Secretary shall establish performance requirements for a third party with a contract under paragraph (3) and safeguards to protect the independence and integrity of the activities carried out by the third party under the program under this section.

"(5) IMPLEMENTATION.—The Secretary may implement the program under this section by program instruction or otherwise.

"(6) ADMINISTRATION.—Chapter 35 of title 44, United States Code, shall not apply to the program under this section.

"(e) ENFORCEMENT.—

"(1) AUDITS.—Each manufacturer with an agreement in effect under this section shall be subject to periodic audit by the Secretary.

"(2) CIVIL MONEY PENALTY.—

"(A) IN GENERAL.—The Secretary shall impose a civil money penalty on a manufacturer that fails to provide applicable beneficiaries discounts for applicable drugs of the manufacturer in accordance with such agreement for each such failure in an amount the Secretary determines is commensurate with the sum of—

"(i) the amount that the manufacturer would have paid with respect to such discounts under the agreement, which will then be used to pay the discounts which the manufacturer had failed to provide; and

"(ii) 25 percent of such amount.

"(B) APPLICATION.—The provisions of section 1128A (other than subsections (a) and (b)) shall apply to a civil money penalty under this paragraph in the same manner as such provisions apply to a penalty or proceeding under section 1128A(a).

"(f) CLARIFICATION REGARDING AVAILABILITY OF OTHER COVERED PART D DRUGS.—Nothing in this section shall prevent an applicable beneficiary from purchasing a covered part D drug that is not an applicable drug (including a generic drug or a drug that is not on the formulary of the prescription drug plan or MA–PD plan that the applicable beneficiary is enrolled in).

"(g) DEFINITIONS.—In this section:

"(1) APPLICABLE BENEFICIARY.—The term 'applicable beneficiary' means an individual who, on the date of dispensing an applicable drug—

"(A) is enrolled in a prescription drug plan or an MA–PD plan;

"(B) is not enrolled in a qualified retiree prescription drug plan;

"(C) is not entitled to an income-related subsidy under section 1860D–14(a);

"(D) is not subject to a reduction in premium subsidy under section 1839(i); and

"(E) who—

"(i) has reached or exceeded the initial coverage limit under section 1860D–2(b)(3) during the year; and

"(ii) has not incurred costs for covered part D drugs in the year equal to the annual out-of-pocket threshold specified in section 1860D–2(b)(4)(B).

"(2) APPLICABLE DRUG.—The term 'applicable drug' means, with respect to an applicable beneficiary, a covered part D drug—

"(A) approved under a new drug application under section 505(b) of the Federal Food, Drug, and Cosmetic Act or, in the case of a biologic product, licensed under section 351 of the Public Health Service Act (other than a product licensed under subsection (k) of such section 351); and

"(B)(i) if the PDP sponsor of the prescription drug plan or the MA organization offering the MA–PD plan uses a formulary, which is on the formulary of the prescription drug plan or MA–PD plan that the applicable beneficiary is enrolled in;

"(ii) if the PDP sponsor of the prescription drug plan or the MA organization offering the MA–PD plan does not use a formulary, for which benefits are available under the prescription drug plan or MA–PD plan that the applicable beneficiary is enrolled in; or

"(iii) is provided through an exception or appeal.

"(3) APPLICABLE NUMBER OF CALENDAR DAYS.—The term 'applicable number of calendar days' means—

“(A) with respect to claims for reimbursement submitted electronically, 14 days; and

“(B) with respect to claims for reimbursement submitted otherwise, 30 days.

“(4) DISCOUNTED PRICE.—

“(A) IN GENERAL.—The term ‘discounted price’ means 50 percent of the negotiated price of the applicable drug of a manufacturer.

“(B) CLARIFICATION.—Nothing in this section shall be construed as affecting the responsibility of an applicable beneficiary for payment of a dispensing fee for an applicable drug.

“(C) SPECIAL CASE FOR CERTAIN CLAIMS.—In the case where the entire amount of the negotiated price of an individual claim for an applicable drug with respect to an applicable beneficiary does not fall at or above the initial coverage limit under section 1860D–2(b)(3) and below the annual out-of-pocket threshold specified in section 1860D–2(b)(4)(B) for the year, the manufacturer of the applicable drug shall provide the discounted price under this section on only the portion of the negotiated price of the applicable drug that falls at or above such initial coverage limit and below such annual out-of-pocket threshold.

“(5) MANUFACTURER.—The term ‘manufacturer’ means any entity which is engaged in the production, preparation, propagation, compounding, conversion, or processing of prescription drug products, either directly or indirectly by extraction from substances of natural origin, or independently by means of chemical synthesis, or by a combination of extraction and chemical synthesis. Such term does not include a wholesale distributor of drugs or a retail pharmacy licensed under State law.

“(6) NEGOTIATED PRICE.—The term ‘negotiated price’ has the meaning given such term in section 423.100 of title 42, Code of Federal Regulations (as in effect on the date of enactment of this section), except that such negotiated price shall not include any dispensing fee for the applicable drug.

“(7) QUALIFIED RETIREE PRESCRIPTION DRUG PLAN.—The term ‘qualified retiree prescription drug plan’ has the meaning given such term in section 1860D–22(a)(2).”.

(c) INCLUSION IN INCURRED COSTS.—

(1) IN GENERAL.—Section 1860D–2(b)(4) of the Social Security Act (42 U.S.C. 1395w–102(b)(4)) is amended—

(A) in subparagraph (C), in the matter preceding clause (i), by striking “In applying” and inserting “Except as provided in subparagraph (E), in applying”; and

(B) by adding at the end the following new subparagraph:

“(E) INCLUSION OF COSTS OF APPLICABLE DRUGS UNDER MEDICARE COVERAGE GAP DISCOUNT PROGRAM.—In applying subparagraph (A), incurred costs shall include the negotiated price (as defined in paragraph (6) of section 1860D–14A(g)) of an applicable drug (as defined in paragraph (2) of such section) of a manufacturer that is furnished to an applicable beneficiary (as defined in paragraph (1) of such section) under the Medicare coverage gap discount program under section 1860D–14A, regardless of whether part of such costs were paid by a manufacturer under such program.".

(2) EFFECTIVE DATE.—The amendments made by this subsection shall apply to costs incurred on or after July 1, 2010.

(d) CONFORMING AMENDMENT PERMITTING PRESCRIPTION DRUG DISCOUNTS.—

(1) IN GENERAL.—Section 1128B(b)(3) of the Social Security Act (42 U.S.C. 1320a–7b(b)(3)) is amended—

(A) by striking "and" at the end of subparagraph (G);

(B) in the subparagraph (H) added by section 237(d) of the Medicare Prescription Drug, Improvement, and Modernization Act of 2003 (Public Law 108–173; 117 Stat. 2213)—

(i) by moving such subparagraph 2 ems to the left; and

(ii) by striking the period at the end and inserting a semicolon;

(C) in the subparagraph (H) added by section 431(a) of such Act (117 Stat. 2287)—

(i) by redesignating such subparagraph as subparagraph (I);

(ii) by moving such subparagraph 2 ems to the left; and

(iii) by striking the period at the end and inserting "; and"; and

(D) by adding at the end the following new subparagraph:

"(J) a discount in the price of an applicable drug (as defined in paragraph (2) of section 1860D–14A(g)) of a manufacturer that is furnished to an applicable beneficiary (as defined in paragraph (1) of such section) under the Medicare coverage gap discount program under section 1860D–14A.".

(2) CONFORMING AMENDMENT TO DEFINITION OF BEST PRICE UNDER MEDICAID.—Section 1927(c)(1)(C)(i)(VI) of the Social Security Act (42 U.S.C. 1396r–8(c)(1)(C)(i)(VI)) is amended by inserting ", or any discounts provided by manufacturers under the Medicare coverage gap discount program under section 1860D–14A" before the period at the end.

(3) EFFECTIVE DATE.—The amendments made by this subsection shall apply to drugs dispensed on or after July 1, 2010.

SEC. 3302. IMPROVEMENT IN DETERMINATION OF MEDICARE PART D LOW-INCOME BENCHMARK PREMIUM.

(a) IN GENERAL.—Section 1860D–14(b)(2)(B)(iii) of the Social Security Act (42 U.S.C. 1395w–114(b)(2)(B)(iii)) is amended by inserting ", determined without regard to any reduction in such premium as a result of any beneficiary rebate under section 1854(b)(1)(C) or bonus payment under section 1853(n)" before the period at the end.

(b) EFFECTIVE DATE.—The amendment made by subsection (a) shall apply to premiums for months beginning on or after January 1, 2011.

SEC. 3303. VOLUNTARY DE MINIMIS POLICY FOR SUBSIDY ELIGIBLE INDIVIDUALS UNDER PRESCRIPTION DRUG PLANS AND MA-PD PLANS.

(a) IN GENERAL.—Section 1860D–14(a) of the Social Security Act (42 U.S.C. 1395w–114(a)) is amended by adding at the end the following new paragraph:

"(5) WAIVER OF DE MINIMIS PREMIUMS.—The Secretary shall, under procedures established by the Secretary, permit a prescription drug plan or an MA–PD plan to waive the monthly beneficiary premium for a subsidy eligible individual if the amount of such premium is de minimis. If such premium is waived under the plan, the Secretary shall not reassign subsidy eligible individuals enrolled in the plan to other plans based on the fact that the monthly beneficiary premium under the plan was greater than the low-income benchmark premium amount.".

(b) AUTHORIZING THE SECRETARY TO AUTO-ENROLL SUBSIDY ELIGIBLE INDIVIDUALS IN PLANS THAT WAIVE DE MINIMIS PREMIUMS.—Section 1860D–1(b)(1) of the Social Security Act (42 U.S.C. 1395w–101(b)(1)) is amended—

(1) in subparagraph (C), by inserting "except as provided in subparagraph (D)," after "shall include,"

(2) by adding at the end the following new subparagraph:

"(D) SPECIAL RULE FOR PLANS THAT WAIVE DE MINIMIS PREMIUMS.—The process established under subparagraph (A) may include, in the case of a part D eligible individual who is a subsidy eligible individual (as defined in section 1860D–14(a)(3)) who has failed to enroll in a prescription drug plan or an MA–PD plan, for the enrollment in a prescription drug plan or MA–PD plan that has waived the monthly beneficiary premium for such subsidy eligible individual under section 1860D–14(a)(5). If there is more than one such plan available, the Secretary shall enroll such an individual under the preceding sentence on a random basis among all such plans in the PDP region. Nothing in the previous sentence shall prevent such an individual from declining or changing such enrollment.".

(c) EFFECTIVE DATE.—The amendments made by this subsection shall apply to premiums for months, and enrollments for plan years, beginning on or after January 1, 2011.

SEC. 3304. SPECIAL RULE FOR WIDOWS AND WIDOWERS REGARDING ELIGIBILITY FOR LOW-INCOME ASSISTANCE.

(a) IN GENERAL.—Section 1860D–14(a)(3)(B) of the Social Security Act (42 U.S.C. 1395w–114(a)(3)(B)) is amended by adding at the end the following new clause:

"(vi) SPECIAL RULE FOR WIDOWS AND WIDOWERS.—Notwithstanding the preceding provisions of this subparagraph, in the case of an individual whose spouse dies during the effective period for a determination or redetermination that has been made under this subparagraph, such effective period shall be extended through the date that is 1 year after the date on which the determination or redetermination would (but for the application of this clause) otherwise cease to be effective.".

(b) EFFECTIVE DATE.—The amendment made by subsection (a) shall take effect on January 1, 2011.

SEC. 3305. IMPROVED INFORMATION FOR SUBSIDY ELIGIBLE INDIVIDUALS REASSIGNED TO PRESCRIPTION DRUG PLANS AND MA–PD PLANS.

Section 1860D–14 of the Social Security Act (42 U.S.C. 1395w–114) is amended—

(1) by redesignating subsection (d) as subsection (e); and

(2) by inserting after subsection (c) the following new subsection:

"(d) FACILITATION OF REASSIGNMENTS.—Beginning not later than January 1, 2011, the Secretary shall, in the case of a subsidy eligible individual who is enrolled in one prescription drug plan and is subsequently reassigned by the Secretary to a new prescription drug plan, provide the individual, within 30 days of such reassignment, with—

"(1) information on formulary differences between the individual's former plan and the plan to which the individual is reassigned with respect to the individual's drug regimens; and

"(2) a description of the individual's right to request a coverage determination, exception, or reconsideration under section 1860D–4(g), bring an appeal under section 1860D–4(h), or resolve a grievance under section 1860D–4(f).".

SEC. 3306. FUNDING OUTREACH AND ASSISTANCE FOR LOW-INCOME PROGRAMS.

(a) ADDITIONAL FUNDING FOR STATE HEALTH INSURANCE PROGRAMS.—Subsection (a)(1)(B) of section 119 of the Medicare Improvements for Patients and Providers Act of 2008 (42 U.S.C. 1395b–3 note) is amended by striking "(42 U.S.C. 1395w–23(f))" and all that follows through the period at the end and inserting "(42 U.S.C. 1395w–23(f)), to the Centers for Medicare & Medicaid Services Program Management Account—

"(i) for fiscal year 2009, of $7,500,000; and

"(ii) for the period of fiscal years 2010 through 2012, of $15,000,000.

Amounts appropriated under this subparagraph shall remain available until expended.".

(b) ADDITIONAL FUNDING FOR AREA AGENCIES ON AGING.—Subsection (b)(1)(B) of such section 119 is amended by striking "(42 U.S.C. 1395w–23(f))" and all that follows through the period at the end and inserting "(42 U.S.C. 1395w–23(f)), to the Administration on Aging—

"(i) for fiscal year 2009, of $7,500,000; and

"(ii) for the period of fiscal years 2010 through 2012, of $15,000,000.

Amounts appropriated under this subparagraph shall remain available until expended.".

(c) ADDITIONAL FUNDING FOR AGING AND DISABILITY RESOURCE CENTERS.—Subsection (c)(1)(B) of such section 119 is amended by striking "(42 U.S.C. 1395w–23(f))" and all that follows through the period at the end and inserting "(42 U.S.C. 1395w–23(f)), to the Administration on Aging—

"(i) for fiscal year 2009, of $5,000,000; and

"(ii) for the period of fiscal years 2010 through 2012, of $10,000,000.

Amounts appropriated under this subparagraph shall remain available until expended.".

(d) ADDITIONAL FUNDING FOR CONTRACT WITH THE NATIONAL CENTER FOR BENEFITS AND OUTREACH ENROLLMENT.—Subsection (d)(2) of such section 119 is amended by striking "(42 U.S.C. 1395w–23(f))" and all that follows through the period at the end and inserting "(42 U.S.C. 1395w–23(f)), to the Administration on Aging—

"(i) for fiscal year 2009, of $5,000,000; and

"(ii) for the period of fiscal years 2010 through 2012, of $5,000,000.

Amounts appropriated under this subparagraph shall remain available until expended.".

(e) SECRETARIAL AUTHORITY TO ENLIST SUPPORT IN CONDUCTING CERTAIN OUTREACH ACTIVITIES.—Such section 119 is amended by adding at the end the following new subsection:

"(g) SECRETARIAL AUTHORITY TO ENLIST SUPPORT IN CONDUCTING CERTAIN OUTREACH ACTIVITIES.—The Secretary may request that an entity awarded a grant under this section support the conduct of outreach activities aimed at preventing disease and promoting wellness. Notwithstanding any other provision of this section, an entity may use a grant awarded under this subsection to support the conduct of activities described in the preceding sentence.".

SEC. 3307. IMPROVING FORMULARY REQUIREMENTS FOR PRESCRIPTION DRUG PLANS AND MA–PD PLANS WITH RESPECT TO CERTAIN CATEGORIES OR CLASSES OF DRUGS.

(a) IMPROVING FORMULARY REQUIREMENTS.—Section 1860D–4(b)(3)(G) of the Social Security Act is amended to read as follows:

"(G) REQUIRED INCLUSION OF DRUGS IN CERTAIN CATEGORIES AND CLASSES.—

"(i) FORMULARY REQUIREMENTS.—

"(I) IN GENERAL.—Subject to subclause (II), a PDP sponsor offering a prescription drug plan shall be required to include all covered part D drugs in the categories and classes identified by the Secretary under clause (ii)(I).

"(II) EXCEPTIONS.—The Secretary may establish exceptions that permit a PDP sponsor offering a prescription drug plan to exclude from its formulary a particular covered part D drug in a category or class that is otherwise required to be included in the formulary under subclause (I) (or to otherwise limit access to such a drug, including through prior authorization or utilization management).

"(ii) IDENTIFICATION OF DRUGS IN CERTAIN CATEGORIES AND CLASSES.—

"(I) IN GENERAL.—Subject to clause (iv), the Secretary shall identify, as appropriate, categories and classes of drugs for which the Secretary determines are of clinical concern.

"(II) CRITERIA.—The Secretary shall use criteria established by the Secretary in making any determination under subclause (I).

"(iii) IMPLEMENTATION.—The Secretary shall establish the criteria under clause (ii)(II) and any exceptions under clause (i)(II) through the promulgation of a regulation which includes a public notice and comment period.

"(iv) REQUIREMENT FOR CERTAIN CATEGORIES AND CLASSES UNTIL CRITERIA ESTABLISHED.—Until such time as the Secretary establishes the criteria under clause (ii)(II) the following categories and classes of drugs shall be identified under clause (ii)(I):

"(I) Anticonvulsants.

"(II) Antidepressants.

"(III) Antineoplastics.

"(IV) Antipsychotics.

"(V) Antiretrovirals.

"(VI) Immunosuppressants for the treatment of transplant rejection.".

(b) EFFECTIVE DATE.—The amendments made by this section shall apply to plan year 2011 and subsequent plan years.

SEC. 3308. REDUCING PART D PREMIUM SUBSIDY FOR HIGH-INCOME BENEFICIARIES.

(a) INCOME-RELATED INCREASE IN PART D PREMIUM.—

(1) IN GENERAL.—Section 1860D–13(a) of the Social Security Act (42 U.S.C. 1395w–113(a)) is amended by adding at the end the following new paragraph:

"(7) INCREASE IN BASE BENEFICIARY PREMIUM BASED ON INCOME.—

"(A) IN GENERAL.—In the case of an individual whose modified adjusted gross income exceeds the threshold amount applicable under paragraph (2) of section 1839(i) (including application of paragraph (5) of such section) for the calendar year, the monthly amount of the beneficiary premium applicable under this section for a month after December 2010 shall be increased by the monthly adjustment amount specified in subparagraph (B).

"(B) MONTHLY ADJUSTMENT AMOUNT.—The monthly adjustment amount specified in this subparagraph for an individual for a month in a year is equal to the product of—

"(i) the quotient obtained by dividing—

"(I) the applicable percentage determined under paragraph (3)(C) of section 1839(i) (including application of paragraph (5) of such section) for the individual for the calendar year reduced by 25.5 percent; by

"(II) 25.5 percent; and

"(ii) the base beneficiary premium (as computed under paragraph (2)).

"(C) MODIFIED ADJUSTED GROSS INCOME.—For purposes of this paragraph, the term 'modified adjusted gross income' has the meaning given such term in subparagraph (A) of section 1839(i)(4), determined for the taxable year applicable under subparagraphs (B) and (C) of such section.

"(D) DETERMINATION BY COMMISSIONER OF SOCIAL SECURITY.—The Commissioner of Social Security shall make any determination necessary to carry out the income-related increase in the base beneficiary premium under this paragraph.

"(E) PROCEDURES TO ASSURE CORRECT INCOME-RELATED INCREASE IN BASE BENEFICIARY PREMIUM.—

"(i) DISCLOSURE OF BASE BENEFICIARY PREMIUM.—Not later than September 15 of each year beginning with 2010, the Secretary shall disclose to the Commissioner of Social Security the amount of the base beneficiary premium (as computed under paragraph (2)) for the purpose of carrying out the income-related increase in the base beneficiary premium under this paragraph with respect to the following year.

"(ii) ADDITIONAL DISCLOSURE.—Not later than October 15 of each year beginning with 2010, the Secretary shall disclose to the Commissioner of Social Security the following information for the purpose of carrying out the income-related increase in the base beneficiary premium under this paragraph with respect to the following year:

"(I) The modified adjusted gross income threshold applicable under paragraph (2) of section 1839(i) (including application of paragraph (5) of such section).

"(II) The applicable percentage determined under paragraph (3)(C) of section 1839(i) (including application of paragraph (5) of such section).

"(III) The monthly adjustment amount specified in subparagraph (B).

"(IV) Any other information the Commissioner of Social Security determines necessary to carry out the income-related increase in the base beneficiary premium under this paragraph.

"(F) RULE OF CONSTRUCTION.—The formula used to determine the monthly adjustment amount specified under subparagraph (B) shall only be used for the purpose of determining such monthly adjustment amount under such subparagraph.".

(2) COLLECTION OF MONTHLY ADJUSTMENT AMOUNT.—Section 1860D–13(c) of the Social Security Act (42 U.S.C. 1395w–113(c)) is amended—

(A) in paragraph (1), by striking "(2) and (3)" and inserting "(2), (3), and (4)"; and

(B) by adding at the end the following new paragraph:

"(4) COLLECTION OF MONTHLY ADJUSTMENT AMOUNT.—

"(A) IN GENERAL.—Notwithstanding any provision of this subsection or section 1854(d)(2), subject to subparagraph (B), the amount of the income-related increase in the base beneficiary premium for an individual for a month (as determined under subsection (a)(7)) shall be paid through withholding from benefit payments in the manner provided under section 1840.

"(B) AGREEMENTS.—In the case where the monthly benefit payments of an individual that are withheld under subparagraph (A) are insufficient to pay the amount described in such subparagraph, the Commissioner of Social Security shall enter into agreements with the Secretary, the Director of the Office of Personnel Management, and the Railroad Retirement Board as necessary in order to allow other agencies to collect the amount described in subparagraph (A) that was not withheld under such subparagraph.".

(b) CONFORMING AMENDMENTS.—

(1) MEDICARE.—Section 1860D–13(a)(1) of the Social Security Act (42 U.S.C. 1395w–113(a)(1)) is amended—

(A) by redesignating subparagraph (F) as subparagraph (G);

(B) in subparagraph (G), as redesignated by subparagraph (A), by striking "(D) and (E)" and inserting "(D), (E), and (F)"; and

(C) by inserting after subparagraph (E) the following new subparagraph:

"(F) INCREASE BASED ON INCOME.—The monthly beneficiary premium shall be increased pursuant to paragraph (7).".

(2) INTERNAL REVENUE CODE.—Section 6103(l)(20) of the Internal Revenue Code of 1986 (relating to disclosure of return information to carry out Medicare part B premium subsidy adjustment) is amended—

(A) in the heading, by inserting "AND PART D BASE BENEFICIARY PREMIUM INCREASE" after "PART B PREMIUM SUBSIDY ADJUSTMENT";

(B) in subparagraph (A)—

(i) in the matter preceding clause (i), by inserting "or increase under section 1860D–13(a)(7)" after "1839(i)"; and

(ii) in clause (vii), by inserting after "subsection (i) of such section" the following: "or increase under section 1860D–13(a)(7) of such Act"; and

(C) in subparagraph (B)—

(i) by striking "Return information" and inserting the following:

"(i) IN GENERAL.—Return information";

(ii) by inserting "or increase under such section 1860D–13(a)(7)" before the period at the end;

(iii) as amended by clause (i), by inserting "or for the purpose of resolving taxpayer appeals with respect to any such premium adjustment or increase" before the period at the end; and

(iv) by adding at the end the following new clause:

"(ii) DISCLOSURE TO OTHER AGENCIES.—Officers, employees, and contractors of the Social Security Administration may disclose—

"(I) the taxpayer identity information and the amount of the premium subsidy adjustment or premium increase with respect to a taxpayer described in subparagraph (A) to officers, employees, and contractors of the Centers for Medicare and Medicaid Services, to the extent that such disclosure is necessary for the collection of the premium subsidy amount or the increased premium amount,

"(II) the taxpayer identity information and the amount of the premium subsidy adjustment or the increased premium amount with respect to a taxpayer described in subparagraph (A) to officers and employees of the Office of Personnel Management and the Railroad Retirement Board, to the extent that such disclosure is necessary for the collection of the premium subsidy amount or the increased premium amount,

"(III) return information with respect to a taxpayer described in subparagraph (A) to officers and employees of the Department of Health and Human Services to the extent necessary to resolve administrative appeals of such premium subsidy adjustment or increased premium, and

"(IV) return information with respect to a taxpayer described in subparagraph (A) to officers and employees of the Department of Justice for use in judicial proceedings to the extent necessary to carry out the purposes described in clause (i).".

SEC. 3309. ELIMINATION OF COST SHARING FOR CERTAIN DUAL ELIGIBLE INDIVIDUALS.

Section 1860D–14(a)(1)(D)(i) of the Social Security Act (42 U.S.C. 1395w–114(a)(1)(D)(i)) is amended by inserting "or, effective on a date specified by the Secretary (but in no case earlier than January 1, 2012), who would be such an institutionalized individual or couple, if the full-benefit dual eligible individual were not receiving services under a home and community-based waiver authorized for a State under section 1115 or subsection (c) or (d) of section 1915 or under a State plan amendment under subsection (i) of such section or services provided through enrollment in a medicaid managed care organization with a contract under section 1903(m) or under section 1932" after "1902(q)(1)(B))".

SEC. 3310. REDUCING WASTEFUL DISPENSING OF OUTPATIENT PRESCRIPTION DRUGS IN LONG-TERM CARE FACILITIES UNDER PRESCRIPTION DRUG PLANS AND MA–PD PLANS.

(a) IN GENERAL.—Section 1860D–4(c) of the Social Security Act (42 U.S.C. 1395w–104(c)) is amended by adding at the end the following new paragraph:

"(3) REDUCING WASTEFUL DISPENSING OF OUTPATIENT PRESCRIPTION DRUGS IN LONG-TERM CARE FACILITIES.—The Secretary shall require PDP sponsors of prescription drug plans to utilize specific, uniform dispensing techniques, as determined by the Secretary, in consultation with relevant stakeholders (including representatives of nursing facilities, residents of nursing facilities, pharmacists, the pharmacy industry (including retail and long-term care pharmacy), prescription drug plans, MA–PD plans, and any other stakeholders the Secretary determines appropriate), such as weekly, daily, or automated dose dispensing, when dispensing covered part D drugs to enrollees who reside in a long-term care facility in order to reduce waste associated with 30-day fills.".

(b) EFFECTIVE DATE.—The amendment made by subsection (a) shall apply to plan years beginning on or after January 1, 2012.

SEC. 3311. IMPROVED MEDICARE PRESCRIPTION DRUG PLAN AND MA–PD PLAN COMPLAINT SYSTEM.

(a) IN GENERAL.—The Secretary shall develop and maintain a complaint system, that is widely known and easy to use, to collect and maintain information on MA–PD plan and prescription drug plan complaints that are received (including by telephone, letter, e-mail, or any other means) by the Secretary (including by a regional office of the Department of Health and Human Services, the Medicare Beneficiary Ombudsman, a subcontractor, a carrier, a fiscal intermediary, and a Medicare administrative contractor under section 1874A of the Social Security Act (42 U.S.C. 1395kk)) through the date on which the complaint is resolved. The system shall be able to report and initiate appropriate interventions and monitoring based on substantial complaints and to guide quality improvement.

(b) MODEL ELECTRONIC COMPLAINT FORM.—The Secretary shall develop a model electronic complaint form to be used for reporting plan complaints under the system. Such form shall be prominently displayed on the front page of the Medicare.gov Internet website and on the Internet website of the Medicare Beneficiary Ombudsman.

(c) ANNUAL REPORTS BY THE SECRETARY.—The Secretary shall submit to Congress annual reports on the system. Such reports shall include an analysis of the number and types of complaints reported in the system, geographic variations in such complaints, the timeliness of agency or plan responses to such complaints, and the resolution of such complaints.

(d) DEFINITIONS.—In this section:

(1) MA–PD PLAN.—The term "MA–PD plan" has the meaning given such term in section 1860D–41(a)(9) of such Act (42 U.S.C. 1395w–151(a)(9)).

(2) PRESCRIPTION DRUG PLAN.—The term "prescription drug plan" has the meaning given such term in section 1860D–41(a)(14) of such Act (42 U.S.C. 1395w–151(a)(14)).

(3) SECRETARY.—The term "Secretary" means the Secretary of Health and Human Services.

(4) SYSTEM.—The term "system" means the plan complaint system developed and maintained under subsection (a).

SEC. 3312. UNIFORM EXCEPTIONS AND APPEALS PROCESS FOR PRESCRIPTION DRUG PLANS AND MA–PD PLANS.

(a) IN GENERAL.—Section 1860D–4(b)(3) of the Social Security Act (42 U.S.C. 1395w–104(b)(3)) is amended by adding at the end the following new subparagraph:

"(H) USE OF SINGLE, UNIFORM EXCEPTIONS AND APPEALS PROCESS.—Notwithstanding any other provision of this part, each PDP sponsor of a prescription drug plan shall—

"(i) use a single, uniform exceptions and appeals process (including, to the extent the Secretary determines feasible, a single, uniform model form for use under such process) with respect to the determination of prescription drug coverage for an enrollee under the plan; and

"(ii) provide instant access to such process by enrollees through a toll-free telephone number and an Internet website.".

(b) EFFECTIVE DATE.—The amendment made by subsection (a) shall apply to exceptions and appeals on or after January 1, 2012.

SEC. 3313. OFFICE OF THE INSPECTOR GENERAL STUDIES AND REPORTS.

(a) STUDY AND ANNUAL REPORT ON PART D FORMULARIES' INCLUSION OF DRUGS COMMONLY USED BY DUAL ELIGIBLES.—

(1) STUDY.—The Inspector General of the Department of Health and Human Services shall conduct a study of the extent to which formularies used by prescription drug plans and MA–PD plans under part D include drugs commonly used by full-benefit dual eligible individuals (as defined in section 1935(c)(6) of the Social Security Act (42 U.S.C. 1396u–5(c)(6))).

(2) ANNUAL REPORTS.—Not later than July 1 of each year (beginning with 2011), the Inspector General shall submit to Congress a report on the study conducted under paragraph (1), together with such recommendations as the Inspector General determines appropriate.

(b) STUDY AND REPORT ON PRESCRIPTION DRUG PRICES UNDER MEDICARE PART D AND MEDICAID.—

(1) STUDY.—

(A) IN GENERAL.—The Inspector General of the Department of Health and Human Services shall conduct a study on prices for covered part D drugs under the Medicare prescription drug program under part D of title XVIII of the Social Security Act and for covered outpatient drugs under title XIX. Such study shall include the following:

(i) A comparison, with respect to the 200 most frequently dispensed covered part D drugs under such program and covered outpatient drugs under such title (as determined by the Inspector General based on volume and expenditures), of—

(I) the prices paid for covered part D drugs by PDP sponsors of prescription drug plans and Medicare Advantage organizations offering MA–PD plans; and

(II) the prices paid for covered outpatient drugs by a State plan under title XIX.

(ii) An assessment of—

(I) the financial impact of any discrepancies in such prices on the Federal Government; and

(II) the financial impact of any such discrepancies on enrollees under part D or individuals eligible for medical assistance under a State plan under title XIX.

(B) PRICE.—For purposes of subparagraph (A), the price of a covered part D drug or a covered outpatient drug shall include any rebate or discount under such program or such title, respectively, including any negotiated price concession described in section 1860D–2(d)(1)(B) of the Social Security Act (42 U.S.C. 1395w–102(d)(1)(B)) or rebate under an agreement under section 1927 of the Social Security Act (42 U.S.C. 1396r–8).

(C) AUTHORITY TO COLLECT ANY NECESSARY INFORMATION.—Notwithstanding any other provision of law, the Inspector General of the Department of Health and Human Services shall be able to collect any information related to the prices of covered part D drugs under such program and covered outpatient drugs under such title XIX necessary to carry out the comparison under subparagraph (A).

(2) REPORT.—

(A) IN GENERAL.—Not later than October 1, 2011, subject to subparagraph (B), the Inspector General shall submit to Congress a report containing the results of the study conducted under paragraph (1), together with recommendations for such legislation and administrative action as the Inspector General determines appropriate.

(B) LIMITATION ON INFORMATION CONTAINED IN REPORT.—The report submitted under subparagraph (A) shall not include any information that the Inspector General determines is proprietary or is likely to negatively impact the ability of a PDP sponsor or a State plan under title XIX to negotiate prices for covered part D drugs or covered outpatient drugs, respectively.

(3) DEFINITIONS.—In this section:

(A) COVERED PART D DRUG.—The term "covered part D drug" has the meaning given such term in section 1860D–2(e) of the Social Security Act (42 U.S.C. 1395w–102(e)).

(B) COVERED OUTPATIENT DRUG.—The term "covered outpatient drug" has the meaning given such term in section 1927(k) of such Act (42 U.S.C. 1396r(k)).

(C) MA–PD PLAN.—The term "MA–PD plan" has the meaning given such term in section 1860D–41(a)(9) of such Act (42 U.S.C. 1395w–151(a)(9)).

(D) MEDICARE ADVANTAGE ORGANIZATION.—The term "Medicare Advantage organization" has the meaning given such term in section 1859(a)(1) of such Act (42 U.S.C. 1395w–28)(a)(1)).

(E) PDP SPONSOR.—The term "PDP sponsor" has the meaning given such term in section 1860D–41(a)(13) of such Act (42 U.S.C. 1395w–151(a)(13)).

(F) PRESCRIPTION DRUG PLAN.—The term "prescription drug plan" has the meaning given such term in section 1860D–41(a)(14) of such Act (42 U.S.C. 1395w–151(a)(14)).

SEC. 3314. INCLUDING COSTS INCURRED BY AIDS DRUG ASSISTANCE PROGRAMS AND INDIAN HEALTH SERVICE IN PROVIDING PRESCRIPTION DRUGS TOWARD THE ANNUAL OUT-OF-POCKET THRESHOLD UNDER PART D.

(a) IN GENERAL.—Section 1860D–2(b)(4)(C) of the Social Security Act (42 U.S.C. 1395w–102(b)(4)(C)) is amended—

(1) in clause (i), by striking "and" at the end;

(2) in clause (ii)—

(A) by striking "such costs shall be treated as incurred only if" and inserting "subject to clause (iii), such costs shall be treated as incurred only if";

(B) by striking ", under section 1860D–14, or under a State Pharmaceutical Assistance Program"; and

(C) by striking the period at the end and inserting "; and"; and

(3) by inserting after clause (ii) the following new clause:

"(iii) such costs shall be treated as incurred and shall not be considered to be reimbursed under clause (ii) if such costs are borne or paid—

"(I) under section 1860D–14;

"(II) under a State Pharmaceutical Assistance Program;

"(III) by the Indian Health Service, an Indian tribe or tribal organization, or an urban Indian organization (as defined in section 4 of the Indian Health Care Improvement Act); or

"(IV) under an AIDS Drug Assistance Program under part B of title XXVI of the Public Health Service Act.".

(b) EFFECTIVE DATE.—The amendments made by subsection (a) shall apply to costs incurred on or after January 1, 2011.

SEC. 3315. IMMEDIATE REDUCTION IN COVERAGE GAP IN 2010.

Section 1860D–2(b) of the Social Security Act (42 U.S.C. 1395w–102(b)) is amended—

(1) in paragraph (3)(A), by striking "paragraph (4)" and inserting "paragraphs (4) and (7)"; and

(2) by adding at the end the following new paragraph:

"(7) INCREASE IN INITIAL COVERAGE LIMIT IN 2010.—

"(A) IN GENERAL.—For the plan year beginning on January 1, 2010, the initial coverage limit described in paragraph (3)(B) otherwise applicable shall be increased by $500.

"(B) APPLICATION.—In applying subparagraph (A)—

"(i) except as otherwise provided in this subparagraph, there shall be no change in the premiums, bids, or any other parameters under this part or part C;

"(ii) costs that would be treated as incurred costs for purposes of applying paragraph (4) but for the application of subparagraph (A) shall continue to be treated as incurred costs;

"(iii) the Secretary shall establish procedures, which may include a reconciliation process, to fully reimburse PDP sponsors with respect to prescription drug plans and MA organizations with respect to MA–PD plans for the reduction in beneficiary cost sharing associated with the application of subparagraph (A);

"(iv) the Secretary shall develop an estimate of the additional increased costs attributable to the application of this paragraph for increased drug utilization and financing and administrative costs and shall use such estimate to adjust payments to PDP sponsors with respect to prescription drug plans under this part and MA organizations with respect to MA–PD plans under part C; and

"(v) the Secretary shall establish procedures for retroactive reimbursement of part D eligible individuals who are covered under such a plan for costs which are incurred before the date of initial implementation of subparagraph (A) and which would be reimbursed under such a plan if such implementation occurred as of January 1, 2010.

"(C) NO EFFECT ON SUBSEQUENT YEARS.—The increase under subparagraph (A) shall only apply with respect to the plan year beginning on January 1, 2010, and the initial coverage limit for plan years beginning on or after January

1, 2011, shall be determined as if subparagraph (A) had never applied.".

Subtitle E—Ensuring Medicare Sustainability

SEC. 3401. REVISION OF CERTAIN MARKET BASKET UPDATES AND INCORPORATION OF PRODUCTIVITY IMPROVEMENTS INTO MARKET BASKET UPDATES THAT DO NOT ALREADY INCORPORATE SUCH IMPROVEMENTS.

(a) INPATIENT ACUTE HOSPITALS.—Section 1886(b)(3)(B) of the Social Security Act (42 U.S.C. 1395ww(b)(3)(B)), as amended by section 3001(a)(3), is further amended—

(1) in clause (i)(XX), by striking "clause (viii)" and inserting "clauses (viii), (ix), (xi), and (xii)";

(2) in the first sentence of clause (viii), by inserting "of such applicable percentage increase (determined without regard to clause (ix), (xi), or (xii))" after "one-quarter";

(3) in the first sentence of clause (ix)(I), by inserting "(determined without regard to clause (viii), (xi), or (xii))" after "clause (i)" the second time it appears; and

(4) by adding at the end the following new clauses:

"(xi)(I) For 2012 and each subsequent fiscal year, after determining the applicable percentage increase described in clause (i) and after application of clauses (viii) and (ix), such percentage increase shall be reduced by the productivity adjustment described in subclause (II).

"(II) The productivity adjustment described in this subclause, with respect to a percentage, factor, or update for a fiscal year, year, cost reporting period, or other annual period, is a productivity adjustment equal to the 10-year moving average of changes in annual economy-wide private nonfarm business multi-factor productivity (as projected by the Secretary for the 10-year period ending with the applicable fiscal year, year, cost reporting period, or other annual period).

"(III) The application of subclause (I) may result in the applicable percentage increase described in clause (i) being less than 0.0 for a fiscal year, and may result in payment rates under this section for a fiscal year being less than such payment rates for the preceding fiscal year.

"(xii) After determining the applicable percentage increase described in clause (i), and after application of clauses (viii), (ix), and (xi), the Secretary shall reduce such applicable percentage increase—

"(I) for each of fiscal years 2010 and 2011, by 0.25 percentage point; and

"(II) subject to clause (xiii), for each of fiscal years 2012 through 2019, by 0.2 percentage point.

The application of this clause may result in the applicable percentage increase described in clause (i) being less than 0.0 for a fiscal year, and may result in payment rates under this section for a fiscal year being less than such payment rates for the preceding fiscal year.

"(xiii) Clause (xii) shall be applied with respect to any of fiscal years 2014 through 2019 by substituting '0.0 percentage points' for '0.2 percentage point', if for such fiscal year—

"(I) the excess (if any) of—

"(aa) the total percentage of the non-elderly insured population for the preceding fiscal year (based on the most recent estimates available from the Director of the Congressional Budget Office before a vote in either House on the Patient Protection and Affordable Care Act that, if determined in the affirmative, would clear such Act for enrollment); over

"(bb) the total percentage of the non-elderly insured population for such preceding fiscal year (as estimated by the Secretary); exceeds

"(II) 5 percentage points.".

(b) SKILLED NURSING FACILITIES.—Section 1888(e)(5)(B) of the Social Security Act (42 U.S.C. 1395yy(e)(5)(B)) is amended—

(1) by striking "PERCENTAGE.—The term" and inserting "PERCENTAGE.—

"(i) IN GENERAL.—Subject to clause (ii), the term"; and

(2) by adding at the end the following new clause:

"(ii) ADJUSTMENT.—For fiscal year 2012 and each subsequent fiscal year, after determining the percentage described in clause (i), the Secretary shall reduce such percentage by the productivity adjustment described in section 1886(b)(3)(B)(xi)(II). The application of the preceding sentence may result in such percentage being less than 0.0 for a fiscal year, and may result in payment rates under this subsection for a fiscal year being less than such payment rates for the preceding fiscal year.".

(c) LONG-TERM CARE HOSPITALS.—Section 1886(m) of the Social Security Act (42 U.S.C. 1395ww(m)) is amended by adding at the end the following new paragraphs:

"(3) IMPLEMENTATION FOR RATE YEAR 2010 AND SUBSEQUENT YEARS.—

"(A) IN GENERAL.—In implementing the system described in paragraph (1) for rate year 2010 and each subsequent rate year, any annual update to a standard Federal rate for discharges for the hospital during the rate year, shall be reduced—

"(i) for rate year 2012 and each subsequent rate year, by the productivity adjustment described in section 1886(b)(3)(B)(xi)(II); and

"(ii) for each of rate years 2010 through 2019, by the other adjustment described in paragraph (4).

"(B) SPECIAL RULE.—The application of this paragraph may result in such annual update being less than 0.0 for a rate year, and may result in payment rates under the system described in paragraph (1) for a rate year being less than such payment rates for the preceding rate year.

"(4) OTHER ADJUSTMENT.—

"(A) IN GENERAL.—For purposes of paragraph (3)(A)(ii), the other adjustment described in this paragraph is—

"(i) for each of rate years 2010 and 2011, 0.25 percentage point; and

"(ii) subject to subparagraph (B), for each of rate years 2012 through 2019, 0.2 percentage point.

"(B) REDUCTION OF OTHER ADJUSTMENT.—Subparagraph (A)(ii) shall be applied with respect to any of rate years 2014 through 2019 by substituting '0.0 percentage points' for '0.2 percentage point', if for such rate year—

"(i) the excess (if any) of—

"(I) the total percentage of the non-elderly insured population for the preceding rate year (based on the most recent estimates available from the Director of the Congressional Budget Office before a vote in either House on the Patient Protection and Affordable Care Act that, if determined in the affirmative, would clear such Act for enrollment); over

"(II) the total percentage of the non-elderly insured population for such preceding rate year (as estimated by the Secretary); exceeds

"(ii) 5 percentage points.".

(d) INPATIENT REHABILITATION FACILITIES.—Section 1886(j)(3) of the Social Security Act (42 U.S.C. 1395ww(j)(3)) is amended—

(1) in subparagraph (C)—

(A) by striking "FACTOR.—For purposes" and inserting "FACTOR.—

"(i) IN GENERAL.—For purposes";

(B) by inserting "subject to clause (ii)" before the period at the end of the first sentence of clause (i), as added by paragraph (1); and

(C) by adding at the end the following new clause:

"(ii) PRODUCTIVITY AND OTHER ADJUSTMENT.—After establishing the increase factor described in clause (i) for a fiscal year, the Secretary shall reduce such increase factor—

"(I) for fiscal year 2012 and each subsequent fiscal year, by the productivity adjustment described in section 1886(b)(3)(B)(xi)(II); and

"(II) for each of fiscal years 2010 through 2019, by the other adjustment described in subparagraph (D).

The application of this clause may result in the increase factor under this subparagraph being less than 0.0 for a fiscal year, and may result in payment rates under this subsection for a fiscal year being less than such payment rates for the preceding fiscal year."; and

(2) by adding at the end the following new subparagraph:

"(D) OTHER ADJUSTMENT.—

"(i) IN GENERAL.—For purposes of subparagraph (C)(ii)(II), the other adjustment described in this subparagraph is—

"(I) for each of fiscal years 2010 and 2011, 0.25 percentage point; and

"(II) subject to clause (ii), for each of fiscal years 2012 through 2019, 0.2 percentage point.

"(ii) REDUCTION OF OTHER ADJUSTMENT.—Clause (i)(II) shall be applied with respect to any of fiscal years 2014 through 2019 by substituting '0.0 percentage points' for '0.2 percentage point', if for such fiscal year—

"(I) the excess (if any) of—

"(aa) the total percentage of the non-elderly insured population for the preceding fiscal year (based on the most recent estimates available from the Director of the Congressional Budget Office before a vote in either House on the Patient Protection and Affordable Care Act that, if determined in the affirmative, would clear such Act for enrollment); over

"(bb) the total percentage of the non-elderly insured population for such preceding fiscal year (as estimated by the Secretary); exceeds

"(II) 5 percentage points.".

(e) HOME HEALTH AGENCIES.—Section 1895(b)(3)(B) of the Social Security Act (42 U.S.C. 1395fff(b)(3)(B)) is amended—

(1) in clause (ii)(V), by striking "clause (v)" and inserting "clauses (v) and (vi)"; and

(2) by adding at the end the following new clause:

"(vi) ADJUSTMENTS.—After determining the home health market basket percentage increase under clause (iii), and after application of clause (v), the Secretary shall reduce such percentage—

"(I) for 2015 and each subsequent year, by the productivity adjustment described in section 1886(b)(3)(B)(xi)(II); and

"(II) for each of 2011 and 2012, by 1 percentage point.

The application of this clause may result in the home health market basket percentage increase under clause (iii) being less than 0.0 for a year, and may result in payment rates under the system under this subsection for a year being less than such payment rates for the preceding year.".

(f) PSYCHIATRIC HOSPITALS.—Section 1886 of the Social Security Act, as amended by sections 3001, 3008, 3025, and 3133, is amended by adding at the end the following new subsection:

"(s) PROSPECTIVE PAYMENT FOR PSYCHIATRIC HOSPITALS.—

"(1) REFERENCE TO ESTABLISHMENT AND IMPLEMENTATION OF SYSTEM.—For provisions related to the establishment and implementation of a prospective payment system for payments under this title for inpatient hospital services furnished by psychiatric hospitals (as described in clause (i) of subsection (d)(1)(B)) and psychiatric units (as described in the matter following clause (v) of such subsection), see section 124 of the Medicare, Medicaid, and SCHIP Balanced Budget Refinement Act of 1999.

"(2) IMPLEMENTATION FOR RATE YEAR BEGINNING IN 2010 AND SUBSEQUENT RATE YEARS.—

"(A) IN GENERAL.—In implementing the system described in paragraph (1) for the rate year beginning in 2010 and any subsequent rate year, any update to a base rate for days during the rate year for a psychiatric hospital or unit, respectively, shall be reduced—

"(i) for the rate year beginning in 2012 and each subsequent rate year, by the productivity adjustment described in section 1886(b)(3)(B)(xi)(II); and

"(ii) for each of the rate years beginning in 2010 through 2019, by the other adjustment described in paragraph (3).

"(B) SPECIAL RULE.—The application of this paragraph may result in such update being less than 0.0 for a rate year, and may result in payment rates under the system described in paragraph (1) for a rate year being less than such payment rates for the preceding rate year.

"(3) OTHER ADJUSTMENT.—

"(A) IN GENERAL.—For purposes of paragraph (2)(A)(ii), the other adjustment described in this paragraph is—

"(i) for each of the rate years beginning in 2010 and 2011, 0.25 percentage point; and

"(ii) subject to subparagraph (B), for each of the rate years beginning in 2012 through 2019, 0.2 percentage point.

"(B) REDUCTION OF OTHER ADJUSTMENT.—Subparagraph (A)(ii) shall be applied with respect to any of rate years 2014 through 2019 by substituting '0.0 percentage points' for '0.2 percentage point', if for such rate year—

"(i) the excess (if any) of—

"(I) the total percentage of the non-elderly insured population for the preceding rate year (based on the most recent estimates available from the Director of the Congressional Budget Office before a vote in either House on the Patient Protection and Affordable Care Act that, if determined in the affirmative, would clear such Act for enrollment); over

"(II) the total percentage of the non-elderly insured population for such preceding rate year (as estimated by the Secretary); exceeds

"(ii) 5 percentage points.".

(g) HOSPICE CARE.—Section 1814(i)(1)(C) of the Social Security Act (42 U.S.C. 1395f(i)(1)(C)), as amended by section 3132, is amended by adding at the end the following new clauses:

"(iv) After determining the market basket percentage increase under clause (ii)(VII) or (iii), as applicable, with respect to fiscal year 2013 and each subsequent fiscal year, the Secretary shall reduce such percentage—

"(I) for 2013 and each subsequent fiscal year, by the productivity adjustment described in section 1886(b)(3)(B)(xi)(II); and

"(II) subject to clause (v), for each of fiscal years 2013 through 2019, by 0.5 percentage point.

The application of this clause may result in the market basket percentage increase under clause (ii)(VII) or (iii), as applicable, being less than 0.0 for a fiscal year, and may result in payment rates under this subsection for a fiscal year being less than such payment rates for the preceding fiscal year.

"(v) Clause (iv)(II) shall be applied with respect to any of fiscal years 2014 through 2019 by substituting '0.0 percentage points' for '0.5 percentage point', if for such fiscal year—

"(I) the excess (if any) of—

"(aa) the total percentage of the non-elderly insured population for the preceding fiscal year (based on the most recent estimates available from the Director of the Congressional Budget Office before a vote in either House on the Patient Protection and Affordable Care Act that, if determined in the affirmative, would clear such Act for enrollment); over

"(bb) the total percentage of the non-elderly insured population for such preceding fiscal year (as estimated by the Secretary); exceeds

"(II) 5 percentage points.".

(h) DIALYSIS.—Section 1881(b)(14)(F) of the Social Security Act (42 U.S.C. 1395rr(b)(14)(F)) is amended—

(1) in clause (i)—

(A) by inserting "(I)" after "(F)(i)"

(B) in subclause (I), as inserted by subparagraph (A)—

(i) by striking "clause (ii)" and inserting "subclause (II) and clause (ii)"; and

(ii) by striking "minus 1.0 percentage point"; and

(C) by adding at the end the following new subclause:

"(II) For 2012 and each subsequent year, after determining the increase factor described in subclause (I), the Secretary shall reduce such increase factor by the productivity adjustment described in section 1886(b)(3)(B)(xi)(II). The application of the preceding sentence may result in such increase factor being less than 0.0 for a year, and may result in payment rates under the payment system under this paragraph for a year being less than such payment rates for the preceding year."; and

(2) in clause (ii)(II)—

(A) by striking "The" and inserting "Subject to clause (i)(II), the"; and

(B) by striking "clause (i) minus 1.0 percentage point" and inserting "clause (i)(I)".

(i) OUTPATIENT HOSPITALS.—Section 1833(t)(3) of the Social Security Act (42 U.S.C. 1395l(t)(3)) is amended—

(1) in subparagraph (C)(iv), by inserting "and subparagraph (F) of this paragraph" after "(17)"; and

(2) by adding at the end the following new subparagraphs:

"(F) PRODUCTIVITY AND OTHER ADJUSTMENT.—After determining the OPD fee schedule increase factor under subparagraph (C)(iv), the Secretary shall reduce such increase factor—

"(i) for 2012 and subsequent years, by the productivity adjustment described in section 1886(b)(3)(B)(xi)(II); and

"(ii) for each of 2010 through 2019, by the adjustment described in subparagraph (G).

The application of this subparagraph may result in the increase factor under subparagraph (C)(iv) being less than 0.0 for a year, and may result in payment rates under the payment system under this subsection for a year being less than such payment rates for the preceding year.

"(G) OTHER ADJUSTMENT.—

"(i) ADJUSTMENT.—For purposes of subparagraph (F)(ii), the adjustment described in this subparagraph is—

"(I) for each of 2010 and 2011, 0.25 percentage point; and

"(II) subject to clause (ii), for each of 2012 through 2019, 0.2 percentage point.

"(ii) REDUCTION OF OTHER ADJUSTMENT.—Clause (i)(II) shall be applied with respect to any of 2014 through 2019 by substituting '0.0 percentage points' for '0.2 percentage point', if for such year—

"(I) the excess (if any) of—

"(aa) the total percentage of the non-elderly insured population for the preceding year (based on the most recent estimates available from the Director of the Congressional Budget Office before a vote in either House on the Patient Protection and Affordable Care Act that, if determined in the affirmative, would clear such Act for enrollment); over

"(bb) the total percentage of the non-elderly insured population for such preceding year (as estimated by the Secretary); exceeds

"(II) 5 percentage points.".

(j) AMBULANCE SERVICES.—Section 1834(l)(3) of the Social Security Act (42 U.S.C. 1395m(l)(3)) is amended—

(1) in subparagraph (A), by striking "and" at the end;

(2) in subparagraph (B)—

(A) by inserting ", subject to subparagraph (C) and the succeeding sentence of this paragraph," after "increased"; and

(B) by striking the period at the end and inserting "; and";

(3) by adding at the end the following new subparagraph:

"(C) for 2011 and each subsequent year, after determining the percentage increase under subparagraph (B) for the year, reduce such percentage increase by the productivity adjustment described in section 1886(b)(3)(B)(xi)(II)."; and

(4) by adding at the end the following flush sentence: "The application of subparagraph (C) may result in the percentage increase under subparagraph (B) being less than 0.0 for a year, and may result in payment rates under the fee schedule under this subsection for a year being less than such payment rates for the preceding year.".

(k) AMBULATORY SURGICAL CENTER SERVICES.—Section 1833(i)(2)(D) of the Social Security Act (42 U.S.C. 1395l(i)(2)(D)) is amended—

(1) by redesignating clause (v) as clause (vi); and

(2) by inserting after clause (iv) the following new clause:

"(v) In implementing the system described in clause (i) for 2011 and each subsequent year, any annual update under such system for the year, after application of clause (iv), shall be reduced by the productivity adjustment described in section 1886(b)(3)(B)(xi)(II). The application of the preceding sentence may result in such update being less than 0.0 for a year, and may result in payment rates under the system described in clause (i) for a year being less than such payment rates for the preceding year.".

(l) LABORATORY SERVICES.—Section 1833(h)(2)(A) of the Social Security Act (42 U.S.C. 1395l(h)(2)(A)) is amended—

(1) in clause (i)—

(A) by inserting ", subject to clause (iv)," after "year) by"; and

(B) by striking "through 2013" and inserting "and 2010"; and

(2) by adding at the end the following new clause:

"(iv) After determining the adjustment to the fee schedules under clause (i), the Secretary shall reduce such adjustment—

"(I) for 2011 and each subsequent year, by the productivity adjustment described in section 1886(b)(3)(B)(xi)(II); and

"(II) for each of 2011 through 2015, by 1.75 percentage points.

Subclause (I) shall not apply in a year where the adjustment to the fee schedules determined under clause (i) is 0.0 or a percentage decrease for a year. The application of the productivity adjustment under subclause (I) shall not result in an adjustment to the fee schedules under clause (i) being less than 0.0 for a year. The application of subclause (II) may result in an adjustment to the fee schedules under clause (i) being less than 0.0 for a year, and may result in payment rates for a year being less than such payment rates for the preceding year.".

(m) CERTAIN DURABLE MEDICAL EQUIPMENT.—Section 1834(a)(14) of the Social Security Act (42 U.S.C. 1395m(a)(14)) is amended—

(1) in subparagraph (K)—

(A) by striking "2011, 2012, and 2013,"; and

(B) by inserting "and" after the semicolon at the end;

(2) by striking subparagraphs (L) and (M) and inserting the following new subparagraph:

"(L) for 2011 and each subsequent year—

"(i) the percentage increase in the consumer price index for all urban consumers (United States city average) for the 12-month period ending with June of the previous year, reduced by—

"(ii) the productivity adjustment described in section 1886(b)(3)(B)(xi)(II)."; and

(3) by adding at the end the following flush sentence: "The application of subparagraph (L)(ii) may result in the covered item update under this paragraph being less than 0.0 for a year, and may result in payment rates under this subsection for a year being less than such payment rates for the preceding year.".

(n) PROSTHETIC DEVICES, ORTHOTICS, AND PROSTHETICS.—Section 1834(h)(4) of the Social Security Act (42 U.S.C. 1395m(h)(4)) is amended—

(1) in subparagraph (A)—

(A) in clause (ix), by striking "and" at the end;

(B) in clause (x)—

(i) by striking "a subsequent year" and inserting "for each of 2007 through 2010"; and

(ii) by inserting "and" after the semicolon at the end;

(C) by adding at the end the following new clause:

"(xi) for 2011 and each subsequent year—

"(I) the percentage increase in the consumer price index for all urban consumers (United States city average) for the 12-month period ending with June of the previous year, reduced by—

"(II) the productivity adjustment described in section 1886(b)(3)(B)(xi)(II)."; and

(D) by adding at the end the following flush sentence: "The application of subparagraph (A)(xi)(II) may result in the applicable percentage increase under subparagraph (A) being less than 0.0 for a year, and may result in payment rates under this subsection for a year being less than such payment rates for the preceding year.".

(o) OTHER ITEMS.—Section 1842(s)(1) of the Social Security Act (42 U.S.C. 1395u(s)(1)) is amended—

(1) in the first sentence, by striking "Subject to" and inserting "(A) Subject to";

(2) by striking the second sentence and inserting the following new subparagraph:

"(B) Any fee schedule established under this paragraph for such item or service shall be updated—

"(i) for years before 2011—

"(I) subject to subclause (II), by the percentage increase in the consumer price index for all urban consumers (United States city average) for the 12-month period ending with June of the preceding year; and

"(II) for items and services described in paragraph (2)(D) for 2009, section 1834(a)(14)(J) shall apply under this paragraph instead of the percentage increase otherwise applicable; and

"(ii) for 2011 and subsequent years—

"(I) the percentage increase in the consumer price index for all urban consumers (United States city average) for the 12-month period ending with June of the previous year, reduced by—

"(II) the productivity adjustment described in section 1886(b)(3)(B)(xi)(II)."; and

(3) by adding at the end the following flush sentence: "The application of subparagraph (B)(ii)(II) may result in the update under this paragraph being less than 0.0 for a year, and may result in payment rates under any fee schedule established under this paragraph for a year being less than such payment rates for the preceding year.".

(p) NO APPLICATION PRIOR TO APRIL 1, 2010.—Notwithstanding the preceding provisions of this section, the amendments made by subsections (a), (c), and (d) shall not apply to discharges occurring before April 1, 2010.

SEC. 3402. TEMPORARY ADJUSTMENT TO THE CALCULATION OF PART B PREMIUMS.

Section 1839(i) of the Social Security Act (42 U.S.C. 1395r(i)) is amended—

(1) in paragraph (2), in the matter preceding subparagraph (A), by inserting "subject to paragraph (6)," after "subsection,";

(2) in paragraph (3)(A)(i), by striking "The applicable" and inserting "Subject to paragraph (6), the applicable";

(3) by redesignating paragraph (6) as paragraph (7); and

(4) by inserting after paragraph (5) the following new paragraph:

"(6) TEMPORARY ADJUSTMENT TO INCOME THRESHOLDS.—Notwithstanding any other provision of this subsection, during the period beginning on January 1, 2011, and ending on December 31, 2019—

"(A) the threshold amount otherwise applicable under paragraph (2) shall be equal to such amount for 2010; and

"(B) the dollar amounts otherwise applicable under paragraph (3)(C)(i) shall be equal to such dollar amounts for 2010.".

SEC. 3403. INDEPENDENT MEDICARE ADVISORY BOARD.

(a) BOARD.—

(1) IN GENERAL.—Title XVIII of the Social Security Act (42 U.S.C. 1395 et seq.), as amended by section 3022, is amended by adding at the end the following new section:

"INDEPENDENT MEDICARE ADVISORY BOARD

"SEC. 1899A. (a) ESTABLISHMENT.—There is established an independent board to be known as the 'Independent Medicare Advisory Board'.

"(b) PURPOSE.—It is the purpose of this section to, in accordance with the following provisions of this section, reduce the per capita rate of growth in Medicare spending—

"(1) by requiring the Chief Actuary of the Centers for Medicare & Medicaid Services to determine in each year to which this section applies (in this section referred to as 'a determination year') the projected per capita growth rate under Medicare for the second year following the determination year (in this section referred to as 'an implementation year');

"(2) if the projection for the implementation year exceeds the target growth rate for that year, by requiring the Board to develop and submit during the first year following the determination year (in this section referred to as 'a proposal year') a proposal containing recommendations to reduce the Medicare per capita growth rate to the extent required by this section; and

"(3) by requiring the Secretary to implement such proposals unless Congress enacts legislation pursuant to this section.

"(c) BOARD PROPOSALS.—

"(1) DEVELOPMENT.—

"(A) IN GENERAL.—The Board shall develop detailed and specific proposals related to the Medicare program in accordance with the succeeding provisions of this section.

"(B) ADVISORY REPORTS.—Beginning January 15, 2014, the Board may develop and submit to Congress advisory reports on matters related to the Medicare program, regardless of whether or not the Board submitted a proposal for such year. Such a report may, for years prior to 2020, include recommendations regarding improvements to payment systems for providers of services and suppliers who are not otherwise subject to the scope of the Board's recommendations in a proposal under this section. Any advisory report submitted under this subparagraph shall not be subject to the rules for congressional consideration under subsection (d).

"(2) PROPOSALS.—

"(A) REQUIREMENTS.—Each proposal submitted under this section in a proposal year shall meet each of the following requirements:

"(i) If the Chief Actuary of the Centers for Medicare & Medicaid Services has made a determination under paragraph (7)(A) in the determination year, the proposal shall include recommendations so that the proposal as a whole (after taking into account recommendations under clause (v)) will result in a net reduction in total Medicare program spending in the implementation year that is at least equal to the applicable savings target established under paragraph (7)(B) for such implementation year. In determining whether a proposal meets the requirement of the preceding sentence, reductions in Medicare program spending during the 3-month period immediately preceding the implementation year shall be counted to the extent that such reductions are a result of the implementation of recommendations contained in the proposal for a change in the payment rate for an item or service that was effective during such period pursuant to subsection (e)(2)(A).

"(ii) The proposal shall not include any recommendation to ration health care, raise revenues or Medicare beneficiary premiums under section 1818, 1818A, or 1839, increase Medicare beneficiary cost-sharing (including deductibles, coinsurance, and copayments), or otherwise restrict benefits or modify eligibility criteria.

"(iii) In the case of proposals submitted prior to December 31, 2018, the proposal shall not include any recommendation that would reduce payment rates for items and services furnished, prior to December 31, 2019, by providers of services (as defined in section 1861(u)) and suppliers (as defined in section 1861(d)) scheduled, pursuant to the amendments made by section 3401 of the Patient Protection and Affordable Care Act, to receive a reduction to the inflationary payment updates of such providers of services and suppliers in excess of a reduction due to productivity in a year in which such recommendations would take effect.

"(iv) As appropriate, the proposal shall include recommendations to reduce Medicare payments under parts C and D, such as reductions in direct subsidy payments to Medicare Advantage and prescription drug plans specified under paragraph (1) and (2) of section 1860D–15(a) that are related to administrative expenses (including profits) for basic coverage, denying high bids or removing high bids for prescription drug coverage from the calculation of the national average monthly bid amount under section 1860D–13(a)(4), and reductions in payments to Medicare Advantage plans under clauses (i) and (ii) of section 1853(a)(1)(B) that are related to administrative expenses (including profits) and performance bonuses for Medicare Advantage plans under section 1853(n). Any such recommendation shall not affect the base beneficiary premium percentage specified under 1860D–13(a).

"(v) The proposal shall include recommendations with respect to administrative funding for the Secretary to carry out the recommendations contained in the proposal.

"(vi) The proposal shall only include recommendations related to the Medicare program.

"(B) ADDITIONAL CONSIDERATIONS.—In developing and submitting each proposal under this section in a proposal year, the Board shall, to the extent feasible—

"(i) give priority to recommendations that extend Medicare solvency;

"(ii) include recommendations that—

"(I) improve the health care delivery system and health outcomes, including by promoting integrated care, care coordination, prevention and wellness, and quality and efficiency improvement; and

"(II) protect and improve Medicare beneficiaries' access to necessary and evidence-based items and services, including in rural and frontier areas;

"(iii) include recommendations that target reductions in Medicare program spending to sources of excess cost growth;

"(iv) consider the effects on Medicare beneficiaries of changes in payments to providers of services (as defined in section 1861(u)) and suppliers (as defined in section 1861(d));

"(v) consider the effects of the recommendations on providers of services and suppliers with actual or projected negative cost margins or payment updates; and

"(vi) consider the unique needs of Medicare beneficiaries who are dually eligible for Medicare and the Medicaid program under title XIX.

"(C) NO INCREASE IN TOTAL MEDICARE PROGRAM SPENDING.—Each proposal submitted under this section shall be designed in such a manner that implementation of the recommendations contained in the proposal would not be expected to result, over the 10-year period starting with the implementation year, in any increase in the total amount of net Medicare program spending relative to the total amount of net Medicare program spending that would have occurred absent such implementation.

"(D) CONSULTATION WITH MEDPAC.—The Board shall submit a draft copy of each proposal to be submitted under this section to the Medicare Payment Advisory Commission established under section 1805 for its review. The Board shall submit such draft copy by not later than September 1 of the determination year.

"(E) REVIEW AND COMMENT BY THE SECRETARY.—The Board shall submit a draft copy of each proposal to be submitted to Congress under this section to the Secretary for the Secretary's review and comment. The Board shall submit such draft copy by not later than September 1 of the determination year. Not later than March 1 of the submission year, the Secretary shall submit a report to Congress on the results of such review, unless the Secretary submits a proposal under paragraph (5)(A) in that year.

"(F) CONSULTATIONS.—In carrying out its duties under this section, the Board shall engage in regular consultations with the Medicaid and CHIP Payment and Access Commission under section 1900.

"(3) TRANSMISSION OF BOARD PROPOSAL TO PRESIDENT.—

"(A) IN GENERAL.—

"(i) IN GENERAL.—Except as provided in clause (ii) and subsection (f)(3)(B), the Board shall transmit a proposal under this section to the President on January 15 of each year (beginning with 2014).

"(ii) EXCEPTION.—The Board shall not submit a proposal under clause (i) in a proposal year if the year is—

"(I) a year for which the Chief Actuary of the Centers for Medicare & Medicaid Services makes a determination in the determination year under paragraph (6)(A) that the growth rate described in clause (i) of such paragraph does not exceed the growth rate described in clause (ii) of such paragraph;

"(II) a year in which the Chief Actuary of the Centers for Medicare & Medicaid Services makes a determination in the determination year that the projected percentage increase (if any) for the medical care expenditure category of the Consumer Price Index for All Urban Consumers (United States city average) for the implementation year is less than the projected percentage increase (if any) in the Consumer Price Index for All Urban Consumers (all items; United States city average) for such implementation year; or

"(III) for proposal year 2019 and subsequent proposal years, a year in which the Chief Actuary of the Centers for Medicare & Medicaid Services makes a determination in the determination year that the growth rate described in paragraph (8) exceeds the growth rate described in paragraph (6)(A)(i).

"(iii) START-UP PERIOD.—The Board may not submit a proposal under clause (i) prior to January 15, 2014.

"(B) REQUIRED INFORMATION.—Each proposal submitted by the Board under subparagraph (A)(i) shall include—

"(i) the recommendations described in paragraph (2)(A)(i);

"(ii) an explanation of each recommendation contained in the proposal and the reasons for including such recommendation;

"(iii) an actuarial opinion by the Chief Actuary of the Centers for Medicare & Medicaid Services certifying that the proposal meets the requirements of subparagraphs (A)(i) and (C) of paragraph (2);

"(iv) a legislative proposal that implements the recommendations; and

"(v) other information determined appropriate by the Board.

"(4) PRESIDENTIAL SUBMISSION TO CONGRESS.—Upon receiving a proposal from the Board under paragraph (3)(A)(i) or the Secretary under paragraph (5), the President shall immediately submit such proposal to Congress.

"(5) CONTINGENT SECRETARIAL DEVELOPMENT OF PROPOSAL.—If, with respect to a proposal year, the Board is required, to but fails, to submit a proposal to the President by the deadline applicable under paragraph (3)(A)(i), the Secretary shall develop a detailed and specific proposal that satisfies the requirements of subparagraphs (A) and (C) (and, to the extent feasible, subparagraph (B)) of paragraph (2) and contains the information required paragraph (3)(B)). By not later than January 25 of the year, the Secretary shall transmit—

"(A) such proposal to the President; and

"(B) a copy of such proposal to the Medicare Payment Advisory Commission for its review.

"(6) PER CAPITA GROWTH RATE PROJECTIONS BY CHIEF ACTUARY.—

"(A) IN GENERAL.—Subject to subsection (f)(3)(A), not later than April 30, 2013, and annually thereafter, the Chief Actuary of the Centers for Medicare & Medicaid Services shall determine in each such year whether—

"(i) the projected Medicare per capita growth rate for the implementation year (as determined under subparagraph (B)); exceeds

"(ii) the projected Medicare per capita target growth rate for the implementation year (as determined under subparagraph (C)).

"(B) MEDICARE PER CAPITA GROWTH RATE.—

"(i) IN GENERAL.—For purposes of this section, the Medicare per capita growth rate for an implementation year shall be calculated as the projected 5-year average (ending with such year) of the growth in Medicare program spending per unduplicated enrollee.

"(ii) REQUIREMENT.—The projection under clause (i) shall—

"(I) to the extent that there is projected to be a negative update to the single conversion factor applicable to payments for physicians' services under section 1848(d) furnished in the proposal year or the implementation year, assume that such update for such services is 0 percent rather than the negative percent that would otherwise apply; and

"(II) take into account any delivery system reforms or other payment changes that have been enacted or published in final rules but not yet implemented as of the making of such calculation.

"(C) MEDICARE PER CAPITA TARGET GROWTH RATE.—For purposes of this section, the Medicare per capita target growth rate for an implementation year shall be calculated as the projected 5-year average (ending with such year) percentage increase in—

"(i) with respect to a determination year that is prior to 2018, the average of the projected percentage increase (if any) in—

"(I) the Consumer Price Index for All Urban Consumers (all items; United States city average); and

"(II) the medical care expenditure category of the Consumer Price Index for All Urban Consumers (United States city average); and

"(ii) with respect to a determination year that is after 2017, the nominal gross domestic product per capita plus 1.0 percentage point.

"(7) SAVINGS REQUIREMENT.—

"(A) IN GENERAL.—If, with respect to a determination year, the Chief Actuary of the Centers for Medicare & Medicaid Services makes a determination under paragraph (6)(A) that the growth rate described in clause (i) of such paragraph exceeds the growth rate described in clause (ii) of such paragraph, the Chief Actuary shall establish an applicable savings target for the implementation year.

"(B) APPLICABLE SAVINGS TARGET.—For purposes of this section, the applicable savings target for an implementation year shall be an amount equal to the product of—

"(i) the total amount of projected Medicare program spending for the proposal year; and

"(ii) the applicable percent for the implementation year.

"(C) APPLICABLE PERCENT.—For purposes of subparagraph (B), the applicable percent for an implementation year is the lesser of—

"(i) in the case of—

"(I) implementation year 2015, 0.5 percent;

"(II) implementation year 2016, 1.0 percent;

"(III) implementation year 2017, 1.25 percent; and

"(IV) implementation year 2018 or any subsequent implementation year, 1.5 percent; and

"(ii) the projected excess for the implementation year (expressed as a percent) determined under subparagraph (A).

"(8) PER CAPITA RATE OF GROWTH IN NATIONAL HEALTH EXPENDITURES.—In each determination year (beginning in 2018), the Chief Actuary of the Centers for Medicare & Medicaid Services shall project the per capita rate of growth in national health expenditures for the implementation year. Such rate of growth for an implementation year shall be calculated as the projected 5-year average (ending with such year) percentage increase in national health care expenditures.

"(d) CONGRESSIONAL CONSIDERATION.—

"(1) INTRODUCTION.—

"(A) IN GENERAL.—On the day on which a proposal is submitted by the President to the House of Representatives and the Senate under subsection (c)(4), the legislative proposal (described in subsection (c)(3)(B)(iv)) contained in the proposal shall be introduced (by request) in the Senate by the majority leader of the Senate or by Members of the Senate designated by the majority leader of the Senate and shall be introduced (by request) in the House by the majority leader of the House or by Members of the House designated by the majority leader of the House.

"(B) NOT IN SESSION.—If either House is not in session on the day on which such legislative proposal is submitted, the legislative proposal shall be introduced in that House, as provided in subparagraph (A), on the first day thereafter on which that House is in session.

"(C) ANY MEMBER.—If the legislative proposal is not introduced in either House within 5 days on which that House is in session after the day on which the legislative proposal is submitted, then any Member of that House may introduce the legislative proposal.

"(D) REFERRAL.—The legislation introduced under this paragraph shall be referred by the Presiding Officers of the respective Houses to the Committee on Finance in the Senate and to the Committee on Energy and Commerce and the Committee on Ways and Means in the House of Representatives.

"(2) COMMITTEE CONSIDERATION OF PROPOSAL.—

"(A) REPORTING BILL.—Not later than April 1 of any proposal year in which a proposal is submitted by the President to Congress under this section, the Committee on Ways and Means and the Committee on Energy and Commerce of the House of Representatives and the Committee on Finance of the Senate may report the bill referred to the Committee under paragraph (1)(D) with committee amendments related to the Medicare program.

"(B) CALCULATIONS.—In determining whether a committee amendment meets the requirement of subparagraph (A), the reductions in Medicare program spending during the 3-month period immediately preceding the implementation year shall be counted to the extent that such reductions are a result of the implementation provisions in the committee amendment for a change in the payment rate for an item or service that was effective during such period pursuant to such amendment.

"(C) COMMITTEE JURISDICTION.—Notwithstanding rule XV of the Standing Rules of the Senate, a committee amendment described in subparagraph (A) may include matter not within the jurisdiction of the Committee on Finance if that matter is relevant to a proposal contained in the bill submitted under subsection (c)(3).

"(D) DISCHARGE.—If, with respect to the House involved, the committee has not reported the bill by the date required by subparagraph (A), the committee shall be discharged from further consideration of the proposal.

"(3) LIMITATION ON CHANGES TO THE BOARD RECOMMENDATIONS.—

"(A) IN GENERAL.—It shall not be in order in the Senate or the House of Representatives to consider any bill, resolution, or amendment, pursuant to this subsection or conference report thereon, that fails to satisfy the requirements of subparagraphs (A)(i) and (C) of subsection (c)(2).

"(B) LIMITATION ON CHANGES TO THE BOARD RECOMMENDATIONS IN OTHER LEGISLATION.—It shall not be in order in the Senate or the House of Representatives to consider any bill, resolution, amendment, or conference report (other than pursuant to this section) that would repeal or otherwise change the recommendations of the Board if that change would fail to satisfy the requirements of subparagraphs (A)(i) and (C) of subsection (c)(2).

"(C) LIMITATION ON CHANGES TO THIS SUBSECTION.—It shall not be in order in the Senate or the House of Representatives to consider any bill, resolution, amendment, or conference report that would repeal or otherwise change this subsection.

"(D) WAIVER.—This paragraph may be waived or suspended in the Senate only by the affirmative vote of three-fifths of the Members, duly chosen and sworn.

"(E) APPEALS.—An affirmative vote of three-fifths of the Members of the Senate, duly chosen and sworn, shall be required in the Senate to sustain an appeal of the ruling of the Chair on a point of order raised under this paragraph.

"(4) EXPEDITED PROCEDURE.—

"(A) CONSIDERATION.—A motion to proceed to the consideration of the bill in the Senate is not debatable.

"(B) AMENDMENT.—

"(i) TIME LIMITATION.—Debate in the Senate on any amendment to a bill under this section shall be limited to 1 hour, to be equally divided between, and controlled by, the mover and the manager of the bill, and debate on any amendment to an amendment, debatable motion, or appeal shall be limited to 30 minutes, to be equally divided between, and controlled by, the mover and the manager of the bill, except that in the event the manager of the bill is in favor of any such amendment, motion, or appeal, the time in opposition thereto shall be controlled by the minority leader or such leader's designee.

"(ii) GERMANE.—No amendment that is not germane to the provisions of such bill shall be received.

"(iii) ADDITIONAL TIME.—The leaders, or either of them, may, from the time under their control on the passage of the bill, allot additional time to any Senator during the consideration of any amendment, debatable motion, or appeal.

"(iv) AMENDMENT NOT IN ORDER.—It shall not be in order to consider an amendment that would cause the bill to result in a net reduction in total Medicare program spending in the implementation year that is less than the applicable savings target established under subsection (c)(7)(B) for such implementation year.

"(v) WAIVER AND APPEALS.—This paragraph may be waived or suspended in the Senate only by the affirmative vote of three-fifths of the Members, duly chosen and sworn. An affirmative vote of three-fifths of the Members of the Senate, duly chosen and sworn, shall be required in the Senate to sustain an appeal of the ruling of the Chair on a point of order raised under this section.

"(C) CONSIDERATION BY THE OTHER HOUSE.—

"(i) IN GENERAL.—The expedited procedures provided in this subsection for the consideration of a bill introduced pursuant to paragraph (1) shall not apply to such a bill that is received by one House from the other House if such a bill was not introduced in the receiving House.

"(ii) BEFORE PASSAGE.—If a bill that is introduced pursuant to paragraph (1) is received by one House from the other House, after introduction but before disposition of such a bill in the receiving House, then the following shall apply:

"(I) The receiving House shall consider the bill introduced in that House through all stages of consideration up to, but not including, passage.

"(II) The question on passage shall be put on the bill of the other House as amended by the language of the receiving House.

"(iii) AFTER PASSAGE.—If a bill introduced pursuant to paragraph (1) is received by one House from the other House, after such a bill is passed by the receiving House, then the vote on passage of the bill that originates in the receiving House shall be considered to be the vote on passage of the bill received from the other House as amended by the language of the receiving House.

"(iv) DISPOSITION.—Upon disposition of a bill introduced pursuant to paragraph (1) that is received by one House from the other House, it shall no longer be in order to consider the bill that originates in the receiving House.

"(v) LIMITATION.—Clauses (ii), (iii), and (iv) shall apply only to a bill received by one House from the other House if the bill—

"(I) is related only to the program under this title; and

"(II) satisfies the requirements of subparagraphs (A)(i) and (C) of subsection (c)(2).

"(D) SENATE LIMITS ON DEBATE.—

"(i) IN GENERAL.—In the Senate, consideration of the bill and on all debatable motions and appeals in connection therewith shall not exceed a total of 30 hours, which shall be divided equally between the majority and minority leaders or their designees.

"(ii) MOTION TO FURTHER LIMIT DEBATE.—A motion to further limit debate on the bill is in order and is not debatable.

"(iii) MOTION OR APPEAL.—Any debatable motion or appeal is debatable for not to exceed 1 hour, to be divided equally between those favoring and those opposing the motion or appeal.

"(iv) FINAL DISPOSITION.—After 30 hours of consideration, the Senate shall proceed, without any further debate on any question, to vote on the final disposition thereof to the exclusion of all amendments not then pending before the Senate at that time and to the exclusion of all motions, except a motion to table, or to reconsider and one quorum call on demand to establish the presence of a quorum (and motions required to establish a quorum) immediately before the final vote begins.

"(E) CONSIDERATION IN CONFERENCE.—

"(i) IN GENERAL.—Consideration in the Senate and the House of Representatives on the conference report or any messages between Houses shall be limited to 10 hours, equally divided and controlled by the majority and minority leaders of the Senate or their designees and the Speaker of the House of Representatives and the minority leader of the House of Representatives or their designees.

"(ii) TIME LIMITATION.—Debate in the Senate on any amendment under this subparagraph shall be limited to 1 hour, to be equally divided between, and controlled by, the mover and the manager of the bill, and debate on any amendment to an amendment, debatable motion, or appeal shall be limited to 30 minutes, to be equally divided between, and controlled by, the mover and the manager of the bill, except that in the event the manager of the bill is in favor of any such amendment, motion, or appeal, the time in opposition thereto shall be controlled by the minority leader or such leader's designee.

"(iii) FINAL DISPOSITION.—After 10 hours of consideration, the Senate shall proceed, without any further debate on any question, to vote on the final disposition thereof to the exclusion of all motions not then pending before the Senate at that time or necessary to resolve the differences between the Houses and to the exclusion of all other motions, except a motion to table, or to reconsider and one quorum call on demand to establish the presence of a quorum (and motions required to establish a quorum) immediately before the final vote begins.

"(iv) LIMITATION.—Clauses (i) through (iii) shall only apply to a conference report, message or the amendments thereto if the conference report, message, or an amendment thereto—

"(I) is related only to the program under this title; and

"(II) satisfies the requirements of subparagraphs (A)(i) and (C) of subsection (c)(2).

"(F) VETO.—If the President vetoes the bill debate on a veto message in the Senate under this subsection shall be 1 hour equally divided between the majority and minority leaders or their designees.

"(5) RULES OF THE SENATE AND HOUSE OF REPRESENTATIVES.—This subsection and subsection (f)(2) are enacted by Congress—

"(A) as an exercise of the rulemaking power of the Senate and the House of Representatives, respectively, and is deemed to be part of the rules of each House, respectively, but applicable only with respect to the procedure to be followed in that House in the case of bill under this section, and it supersedes other rules only to the extent that it is inconsistent with such rules; and

"(B) with full recognition of the constitutional right of either House to change the rules (so far as they relate to the procedure of that House) at any time, in the same manner, and to the same extent as in the case of any other rule of that House.

"(e) IMPLEMENTATION OF PROPOSAL.—

"(1) IN GENERAL.—Notwithstanding any other provision of law, the Secretary shall, except as provided in paragraph (3), implement the recommendations contained in a proposal submitted by the President to Congress pursuant to this section on August 15 of the year in which the proposal is so submitted.

"(2) APPLICATION.—

"(A) IN GENERAL.—A recommendation described in paragraph (1) shall apply as follows:

"(i) In the case of a recommendation that is a change in the payment rate for an item or service under Medicare in which payment rates change on a fiscal year basis (or a cost reporting period basis that relates to a fiscal year), on a calendar year basis (or a cost reporting period basis that relates to a calendar year), or on a rate year basis (or a cost reporting period basis that relates to a rate year), such recommendation shall apply to items and services furnished on the first day of the first fiscal year, calendar year, or rate year (as the case may be) that begins after such August 15.

"(ii) In the case of a recommendation relating to payments to plans under parts C and D, such recommendation shall apply to plan years beginning on the first day of the first calendar year that begins after such August 15.

"(iii) In the case of any other recommendation, such recommendation shall be addressed in the regular regulatory process timeframe and shall apply as soon as practicable.

"(B) INTERIM FINAL RULEMAKING.—The Secretary may use interim final rulemaking to implement any recommendation described in paragraph (1).

"(3) EXCEPTION.—The Secretary shall not be required to implement the recommendations contained in a proposal submitted in a proposal year by the President to Congress pursuant to this section if—

"(A) prior to August 15 of the proposal year, Federal legislation is enacted that includes the following provision: 'This Act supercedes the recommendations of the Board contained in the proposal submitted, in the year which includes the date of enactment of this Act, to Congress under section 1899A of the Social Security Act.'; and

"(B) in the case of implementation year 2020 and subsequent implementation years, a joint resolution described in subsection (f)(1) is enacted not later than August 15, 2017.

"(4) NO AFFECT ON AUTHORITY TO IMPLEMENT CERTAIN PROVISIONS.—Nothing in paragraph (3) shall be construed to affect the authority of the Secretary to implement any recommendation contained in a proposal or advisory report under this section to the extent that the Secretary otherwise has the authority to implement such recommendation administratively.

"(5) LIMITATION ON REVIEW.—There shall be no administrative or judicial review under section 1869, section 1878, or otherwise of the implementation by the Secretary under this subsection of the recommendations contained in a proposal.

"(f) JOINT RESOLUTION REQUIRED TO DISCONTINUE THE BOARD.—

"(1) IN GENERAL.—For purposes of subsection (e)(3)(B), a joint resolution described in this paragraph means only a joint resolution—

"(A) that is introduced in 2017 by not later than February 1 of such year;

"(B) which does not have a preamble;

"(C) the title of which is as follows: 'Joint resolution approving the discontinuation of the process for consideration and automatic implementation of the annual proposal of the Independent Medicare Advisory Board under section 1899A of the Social Security Act'; and

"(D) the matter after the resolving clause of which is as follows: 'That Congress approves the discontinuation of the process for consideration and automatic implementation of the annual proposal of the Independent Medicare Advisory Board under section 1899A of the Social Security Act.'.

"(2) PROCEDURE.—

"(A) REFERRAL.—A joint resolution described in paragraph (1) shall be referred to the Committee on Ways and Means and the Committee on Energy and Commerce of the House of Representatives and the Committee on Finance of the Senate.

"(B) DISCHARGE.—In the Senate, if the committee to which is referred a joint resolution described in paragraph (1) has not reported such joint resolution (or an identical joint resolution) at the end of 20 days after the joint resolution described in paragraph (1) is introduced, such committee may be discharged from further consideration of such joint resolution upon a petition supported in writing by 30 Members of the Senate, and such joint resolution shall be placed on the calendar.

"(C) CONSIDERATION.—

"(i) IN GENERAL.—In the Senate, when the committee to which a joint resolution is referred has reported, or when a committee is discharged (under subparagraph (C)) from further consideration of a joint resolution described in paragraph (1), it is at any time thereafter in order (even though a previous motion to the same effect has been disagreed to) for a motion to proceed to the consideration of the joint resolution to be made, and all points of order against the joint resolution (and against consideration of the joint resolution) are waived, except for points of order under the Congressional Budget act of 1974 or under budget resolutions pursuant to that Act. The motion is not debatable. A motion to reconsider the vote by which the motion is agreed to or disagreed to shall not be in order. If a motion to proceed to the consideration of the joint resolution is agreed to, the joint resolution shall remain the unfinished business of the Senate until disposed of.

"(ii) DEBATE LIMITATION.—In the Senate, consideration of the joint resolution, and on all debatable motions and appeals in connection therewith, shall be limited to not more than 10 hours, which shall be divided equally between the majority leader and the minority leader, or their designees. A motion further to limit debate is in order and not debatable. An amendment to, or a motion to postpone, or a motion to proceed to the consideration of other business, or a motion to recommit the joint resolution is not in order.

"(iii) PASSAGE.—In the Senate, immediately following the conclusion of the debate on a joint resolution described in paragraph (1), and a single quorum call at the conclusion of the debate if requested in accordance with the rules of the Senate, the vote on passage of the joint resolution shall occur.

"(iv) APPEALS.—Appeals from the decisions of the Chair relating to the application of the rules of the Senate to the procedure relating to a joint resolution described in paragraph (1) shall be decided without debate.

"(D) OTHER HOUSE ACTS FIRST.—If, before the passage by 1 House of a joint resolution of that House described in paragraph (1), that House receives from the other House a joint resolution described in paragraph (1), then the following procedures shall apply:

"(i) The joint resolution of the other House shall not be referred to a committee.

"(ii) With respect to a joint resolution described in paragraph (1) of the House receiving the joint resolution—

"(I) the procedure in that House shall be the same as if no joint resolution had been received from the other House; but

"(II) the vote on final passage shall be on the joint resolution of the other House.

"(E) EXCLUDED DAYS.—For purposes of determining the period specified in subparagraph (B), there shall be excluded any days either House of Congress is adjourned for more than 3 days during a session of Congress.

"(F) MAJORITY REQUIRED FOR ADOPTION.—A joint resolution considered under this subsection shall require an affirmative vote of three-fifths of the Members, duly chosen and sworn, for adoption.

"(3) TERMINATION.—If a joint resolution described in paragraph (1) is enacted not later than August 15, 2017—

"(A) the Chief Actuary of the Medicare & Medicaid Services shall not—

"(i) make any determinations under subsection (c)(6) after May 1, 2017; or

"(ii) provide any opinion pursuant to subsection (c)(3)(B)(iii) after January 16, 2018;

"(B) the Board shall not submit any proposals or advisory reports to Congress under this section after January 16, 2018; and

"(C) the Board and the consumer advisory council under subsection (k) shall terminate on August 16, 2018.

"(g) BOARD MEMBERSHIP; TERMS OF OFFICE; CHAIRPERSON; REMOVAL.—

"(1) MEMBERSHIP.—

"(A) IN GENERAL.—The Board shall be composed of—

"(i) 15 members appointed by the President, by and with the advice and consent of the Senate; and

"(ii) the Secretary, the Administrator of the Center for Medicare & Medicaid Services, and the Administrator of the Health Resources and Services Administration, all of whom shall serve ex officio as nonvoting members of the Board.

"(B) QUALIFICATIONS.—

"(i) IN GENERAL.—The appointed membership of the Board shall include individuals with national recognition for their expertise in health finance and economics, actuarial science, health facility management, health plans and integrated delivery systems, reimbursement of health facilities, allopathic and osteopathic physicians, and other providers of health services, and other related fields, who provide a mix of different professionals, broad geographic representation, and a balance between urban and rural representatives.

"(ii) INCLUSION.—The appointed membership of the Board shall include (but not be limited to) physicians and other health professionals, experts in the area of pharmaco-economics or prescription drug benefit programs, employers, third-party payers, individuals skilled in the conduct and interpretation of biomedical, health services, and health economics research and expertise in outcomes and effectiveness research and technology assessment. Such membership shall also include representatives of consumers and the elderly.

"(iii) MAJORITY NONPROVIDERS.—Individuals who are directly involved in the provision or management of the delivery of items and services covered under this title shall not constitute a majority of the appointed membership of the Board.

"(C) ETHICAL DISCLOSURE.—The President shall establish a system for public disclosure by appointed members of the Board of financial and other potential conflicts of interest relating to such members. Appointed members of the Board shall be treated as officers in the executive branch for purposes of applying title I of the Ethics in Government Act of 1978 (Public Law 95–521).

"(D) CONFLICTS OF INTEREST.—No individual may serve as an appointed member if that individual engages in any other business, vocation, or employment.

"(E) CONSULTATION WITH CONGRESS.—In selecting individuals for nominations for appointments to the Board, the President shall consult with—

"(i) the majority leader of the Senate concerning the appointment of 3 members;

"(ii) the Speaker of the House of Representatives concerning the appointment of 3 members;

"(iii) the minority leader of the Senate concerning the appointment of 3 members; and

"(iv) the minority leader of the House of Representatives concerning the appointment of 3 members.

"(2) TERM OF OFFICE.—Each appointed member shall hold office for a term of 6 years except that—

"(A) a member may not serve more than 2 full consecutive terms (but may be reappointed to 2 full consecutive terms after being appointed to fill a vacancy on the Board);

"(B) a member appointed to fill a vacancy occurring prior to the expiration of the term for which that member's predecessor was appointed shall be appointed for the remainder of such term;

"(C) a member may continue to serve after the expiration of the member's term until a successor has taken office; and

"(D) of the members first appointed under this section, 5 shall be appointed for a term of 1 year, 5 shall be appointed for a term of 3 years, and 5 shall be appointed for a term of 6 years, the term of each to be designated by the President at the time of nomination.

"(3) CHAIRPERSON.—

"(A) IN GENERAL.—The Chairperson shall be appointed by the President, by and with the advice and consent of the Senate, from among the members of the Board.

"(B) DUTIES.—The Chairperson shall be the principal executive officer of the Board, and shall exercise all of the executive and administrative functions of the Board, including functions of the Board with respect to—

"(i) the appointment and supervision of personnel employed by the Board;

"(ii) the distribution of business among personnel appointed and supervised by the Chairperson and among administrative units of the Board; and

"(iii) the use and expenditure of funds.

"(C) GOVERNANCE.—In carrying out any of the functions under subparagraph (B), the Chairperson shall be governed by the general policies established by the Board and by the decisions, findings, and determinations the Board shall by law be authorized to make.

"(D) REQUESTS FOR APPROPRIATIONS.—Requests or estimates for regular, supplemental, or deficiency appropriations on behalf of the Board may not be submitted by the Chairperson without the prior approval of a majority vote of the Board.

"(4) REMOVAL.—Any appointed member may be removed by the President for neglect of duty or malfeasance in office, but for no other cause.

"(h) VACANCIES; QUORUM; SEAL; VICE CHAIRPERSON; VOTING ON REPORTS.—

"(1) VACANCIES.—No vacancy on the Board shall impair the right of the remaining members to exercise all the powers of the Board.

"(2) QUORUM.—A majority of the appointed members of the Board shall constitute a quorum for the transaction of business, but a lesser number of members may hold hearings.

"(3) SEAL.—The Board shall have an official seal, of which judicial notice shall be taken.

"(4) VICE CHAIRPERSON.—The Board shall annually elect a Vice Chairperson to act in the absence or disability of the Chairperson or in case of a vacancy in the office of the Chairperson.

"(5) VOTING ON PROPOSALS.—Any proposal of the Board must be approved by the majority of appointed members present.

"(i) POWERS OF THE BOARD.—

"(1) HEARINGS.—The Board may hold such hearings, sit and act at such times and places, take such testimony, and receive such evidence as the Board considers advisable to carry out this section.

"(2) AUTHORITY TO INFORM RESEARCH PRIORITIES FOR DATA COLLECTION.—The Board may advise the Secretary on priorities for health services research, particularly as such priorities pertain to necessary changes and issues regarding payment reforms under Medicare.

"(3) OBTAINING OFFICIAL DATA.—The Board may secure directly from any department or agency of the United States information necessary to enable it to carry out this section. Upon request of the Chairperson, the head of that department or agency shall furnish that information to the Board on an agreed upon schedule.

"(4) POSTAL SERVICES.—The Board may use the United States mails in the same manner and under the same conditions as other departments and agencies of the Federal Government.

"(5) GIFTS.—The Board may accept, use, and dispose of gifts or donations of services or property.

"(6) OFFICES.—The Board shall maintain a principal office and such field offices as it determines necessary, and may meet and exercise any of its powers at any other place.

"(j) PERSONNEL MATTERS.—

"(1) COMPENSATION OF MEMBERS AND CHAIRPERSON.—Each appointed member, other than the Chairperson, shall be compensated at a rate equal to the annual rate of basic pay prescribed for level III of the Executive Schedule under section 5315 of title 5, United States Code. The Chairperson shall be compensated at a rate equal to the daily equivalent of the annual rate of basic pay prescribed for level II of the

Executive Schedule under section 5315 of title 5, United States Code.

"(2) TRAVEL EXPENSES.—The appointed members shall be allowed travel expenses, including per diem in lieu of subsistence, at rates authorized for employees of agencies under subchapter I of chapter 57 of title 5, United States Code, while away from their homes or regular places of business in the performance of services for the Board.

"(3) STAFF.—

"(A) IN GENERAL.—The Chairperson may, without regard to the civil service laws and regulations, appoint and terminate an executive director and such other additional personnel as may be necessary to enable the Board to perform its duties. The employment of an executive director shall be subject to confirmation by the Board.

"(B) COMPENSATION.—The Chairperson may fix the compensation of the executive director and other personnel without regard to chapter 51 and subchapter III of chapter 53 of title 5, United States Code, relating to classification of positions and General Schedule pay rates, except that the rate of pay for the executive director and other personnel may not exceed the rate payable for level V of the Executive Schedule under section 5316 of such title.

"(4) DETAIL OF GOVERNMENT EMPLOYEES.—Any Federal Government employee may be detailed to the Board without reimbursement, and such detail shall be without interruption or loss of civil service status or privilege.

"(5) PROCUREMENT OF TEMPORARY AND INTERMITTENT SERVICES.—The Chairperson may procure temporary and intermittent services under section 3109(b) of title 5, United States Code, at rates for individuals which do not exceed the daily equivalent of the annual rate of basic pay prescribed for level V of the Executive Schedule under section 5316 of such title.

"(k) CONSUMER ADVISORY COUNCIL.—

"(1) IN GENERAL.—There is established a consumer advisory council to advise the Board on the impact of payment policies under this title on consumers.

"(2) MEMBERSHIP.—

"(A) NUMBER AND APPOINTMENT.—The consumer advisory council shall be composed of 10 consumer representatives appointed by the Comptroller General of the United States, 1 from among each of the 10 regions established by the Secretary as of the date of enactment of this section.

"(B) QUALIFICATIONS.—The membership of the council shall represent the interests of consumers and particular communities.

"(3) DUTIES.—The consumer advisory council shall, subject to the call of the Board, meet not less frequently than 2 times each year in the District of Columbia.

"(4) OPEN MEETINGS.—Meetings of the consumer advisory council shall be open to the public.

"(5) ELECTION OF OFFICERS.—Members of the consumer advisory council shall elect their own officers.

"(6) APPLICATION OF FACA.—The Federal Advisory Committee Act (5 U.S.C. App.) shall apply to the consumer advisory council except that section 14 of such Act shall not apply.

"(l) DEFINITIONS.—In this section:

"(1) BOARD; CHAIRPERSON; MEMBER.—The terms 'Board', 'Chairperson', and 'Member' mean the Independent Medicare Advisory Board established under subsection (a) and the Chairperson and any Member thereof, respectively.

"(2) MEDICARE.—The term 'Medicare' means the program established under this title, including parts A, B, C, and D.

"(3) MEDICARE BENEFICIARY.—The term 'Medicare beneficiary' means an individual who is entitled to, or enrolled for, benefits under part A or enrolled for benefits under part B.

"(4) MEDICARE PROGRAM SPENDING.—The term 'Medicare program spending' means program spending under parts A, B, and D net of premiums.

"(m) FUNDING.—

"(1) IN GENERAL.—There are appropriated to the Board to carry out its duties and functions—

"(A) for fiscal year 2012, $15,000,000; and

"(B) for each subsequent fiscal year, the amount appropriated under this paragraph for the previous fiscal year increased by the annual percentage increase in the Consumer Price Index for All Urban Consumers (all items; United States city average) as of June of the previous fiscal year.

"(2) FROM TRUST FUNDS.—Sixty percent of amounts appropriated under paragraph (1) shall be derived by transfer from the Federal Hospital Insurance Trust Fund under section 1817 and 40 percent of amounts appropriated under such paragraph shall be derived by transfer from the Federal Supplementary Medical Insurance Trust Fund under section 1841.".

(2) LOBBYING COOLING-OFF PERIOD FOR MEMBERS OF THE INDEPENDENT MEDICARE ADVISORY BOARD.—Section 207(c) of title 18, United States Code, is amended by inserting at the end the following:

"(3) MEMBERS OF THE INDEPENDENT MEDICARE ADVISORY BOARD.—

"(A) IN GENERAL.—Paragraph (1) shall apply to a member of the Independent Medicare Advisory Board under section 1899A.

"(B) AGENCIES AND CONGRESS.—For purposes of paragraph (1), the agency in which the individual described in subparagraph (A) served shall be considered to be the Independent Medicare Advisory Board, the Department of Health and Human Services, and the relevant committees of jurisdiction of Congress, including the Committee on Ways and Means and the Committee on Energy and Commerce of the House of Representatives and the Committee on Finance of the Senate.".

(b) GAO STUDY AND REPORT ON DETERMINATION AND IMPLEMENTATION OF PAYMENT AND COVERAGE POLICIES UNDER THE MEDICARE PROGRAM.—

(1) INITIAL STUDY AND REPORT.—

(A) STUDY.—The Comptroller General of the United States (in this section referred to as the "Comptroller General") shall conduct a study on changes to payment policies, methodologies, and rates and coverage policies and methodologies under the Medicare program under title XVIII of the Social Security Act as a result of the recommendations contained in the proposals made by the Independent Medicare Advisory Board under section 1899A of such Act (as added by subsection (a)), including an analysis of the effect of such recommendations on—

(i) Medicare beneficiary access to providers and items and services;

(ii) the affordability of Medicare premiums and cost-sharing (including deductibles, coinsurance, and copayments);

(iii) the potential impact of changes on other government or private-sector purchasers and payers of care; and

(iv) quality of patient care, including patient experience, outcomes, and other measures of care.

(B) REPORT.—Not later than July 1, 2015, the Comptroller General shall submit to Congress a report containing the results of the study conducted under subparagraph (A), together with recommendations for such legislation and administrative action as the Comptroller General determines appropriate.

(2) SUBSEQUENT STUDIES AND REPORTS.—The Comptroller General shall periodically conduct such additional studies and submit reports to Congress on changes to Medicare payments policies, methodologies, and rates and coverage policies and methodologies as the Comptroller General determines appropriate, in consultation with the Committee on Ways and Means and the Committee on Energy and Commerce of the House of Representatives and the Committee on Finance of the Senate.

(c) CONFORMING AMENDMENTS.—Section 1805(b) of the Social Security Act (42 U.S.C. 1395b–6(b)) is amended—

(1) by redesignating paragraphs (4) through (8) as paragraphs (5) through (9), respectively; and

(2) by inserting after paragraph (3) the following:

"(4) REVIEW AND COMMENT ON THE INDEPENDENT MEDICARE ADVISORY BOARD OR SECRETARIAL PROPOSAL.—If the Independent Medicare Advisory Board (as established under subsection (a) of section 1899A) or the Secretary submits a proposal to the Commission under such section in a year, the Commission shall review the proposal and, not later than March 1 of that year, submit to the Committee on Ways and Means and the Committee on Energy and Commerce of the House of Representatives and the Committee on Finance of the Senate written comments on such proposal. Such comments may include such recommendations as the Commission deems appropriate.".

Subtitle F—Health Care Quality Improvements

SEC. 3501. HEALTH CARE DELIVERY SYSTEM RESEARCH; QUALITY IMPROVEMENT TECHNICAL ASSISTANCE.

Part D of title IX of the Public Health Service Act, as amended by section 3013, is further amended by adding at the end the following:

"Subpart II—Health Care Quality Improvement Programs

"SEC. 933. HEALTH CARE DELIVERY SYSTEM RESEARCH.

"(a) PURPOSE.—The purposes of this section are to—

"(1) enable the Director to identify, develop, evaluate, disseminate, and provide training in innovative methodologies and strategies for quality improvement practices in the delivery of health care services that represent best practices (referred to as 'best practices') in health care quality, safety, and value; and

"(2) ensure that the Director is accountable for implementing a model to pursue such research in a collaborative manner with other related Federal agencies.

"(b) GENERAL FUNCTIONS OF THE CENTER.—The Center for Quality Improvement and Patient Safety of the Agency for Healthcare Research and Quality (referred to in this section as the 'Center'), or any other relevant agency or department designated by the Director, shall—

"(1) carry out its functions using research from a variety of disciplines, which may include epidemiology, health services, sociology, psychology, human factors engineering, biostatistics, health economics, clinical research, and health informatics;

"(2) conduct or support activities consistent with the purposes described in subsection (a), and for—

"(A) best practices for quality improvement practices in the delivery of health care services; and

"(B) that include changes in processes of care and the redesign of systems used by providers that will reliably result in intended health outcomes, improve patient safety, and reduce medical errors (such as skill development for health care providers in team-based health care delivery and rapid cycle process improvement) and facilitate adoption of improved workflow;

"(3) identify health care providers, including health care systems, single institutions, and individual providers, that—

"(A) deliver consistently high-quality, efficient health care services (as determined by the Secretary); and

"(B) employ best practices that are adaptable and scalable to diverse health care settings or effective in improving care across diverse settings;

"(4) assess research, evidence, and knowledge about what strategies and methodologies are most effective in improving health care delivery;

"(5) find ways to translate such information rapidly and effectively into practice, and document the sustainability of those improvements;

"(6) create strategies for quality improvement through the development of tools, methodologies, and interventions that can successfully reduce variations in the delivery of health care;

"(7) identify, measure, and improve organizational, human, or other causative factors, including those related to the culture and system design of a health care organization, that contribute to the success and sustainability of specific quality improvement and patient safety strategies;

"(8) provide for the development of best practices in the delivery of health care services that—

"(A) have a high likelihood of success, based on structured review of empirical evidence;

"(B) are specified with sufficient detail of the individual processes, steps, training, skills, and knowledge required for implementation and incorporation into workflow of health care practitioners in a variety of settings;

"(C) are designed to be readily adapted by health care providers in a variety of settings; and

"(D) where applicable, assist health care providers in working with other health care providers across the continuum of care and in engaging patients and their families in improving the care and patient health outcomes;

"(9) provide for the funding of the activities of organizations with recognized expertise and excellence in improving the delivery of health care services, including children's health care, by involving multiple disciplines, managers of health care entities, broad development and training, patients, caregivers and families, and frontline health care workers, including activities for the examination of strategies to share best quality improvement practices and to promote excellence in the delivery of health care services; and

"(10) build capacity at the State and community level to lead quality and safety efforts through education, training, and mentoring programs to carry out the activities under paragraphs (1) through (9).

"(c) RESEARCH FUNCTIONS OF CENTER.—

"(1) IN GENERAL.—The Center shall support, such as through a contract or other mechanism, research on health care delivery system improvement and the development of tools to facilitate adoption of best practices that improve the quality, safety, and efficiency of health care delivery services. Such support may include establishing a Quality Improvement Network Research Program for the purpose of testing, scaling, and disseminating of interventions to improve quality and efficiency in health care. Recipients of funding under the Program may include national, State, multi-State, or multi-site quality improvement networks.

"(2) RESEARCH REQUIREMENTS.—The research conducted pursuant to paragraph (1) shall—

"(A) address the priorities identified by the Secretary in the national strategic plan established under section 399HH;

"(B) identify areas in which evidence is insufficient to identify strategies and methodologies, taking into consideration areas of insufficient evidence identified by the entity with a contract under section 1890(a) of the Social Security Act in the report required under section 399JJ;

"(C) address concerns identified by health care institutions and providers and communicated through the Center pursuant to subsection (d);

"(D) reduce preventable morbidity, mortality, and associated costs of morbidity and mortality by building capacity for patient safety research;

"(E) support the discovery of processes for the reliable, safe, efficient, and responsive delivery of health care, taking into account discoveries from clinical research and comparative effectiveness research;

"(F) allow communication of research findings and translate evidence into practice recommendations that are adaptable to a variety of settings, and which, as soon as practicable after the establishment of the Center, shall include—

"(i) the implementation of a national application of Intensive Care Unit improvement projects relating to the adult (including geriatric), pediatric, and neonatal patient populations;

"(ii) practical methods for addressing health care associated infections, including Methicillin-Resistant Staphylococcus Aureus and Vancomycin-Resistant Entercoccus infections and other emerging infections; and

"(iii) practical methods for reducing preventable hospital admissions and readmissions;

"(G) expand demonstration projects for improving the quality of children's health care and the use of health information technology, such as through Pediatric Quality Improvement Collaboratives and Learning Networks, consistent with provisions of section 1139A of the Social Security Act for assessing and improving quality, where applicable;

"(H) identify and mitigate hazards by—

"(i) analyzing events reported to patient safety reporting systems and patient safety organizations; and

"(ii) using the results of such analyses to develop scientific methods of response to such events;

"(I) include the conduct of systematic reviews of existing practices that improve the quality, safety, and efficiency of health care delivery, as well as new research on improving such practices; and

"(J) include the examination of how to measure and evaluate the progress of quality and patient safety activities.

"(d) DISSEMINATION OF RESEARCH FINDINGS.—

"(1) PUBLIC AVAILABILITY.—The Director shall make the research findings of the Center available to the public through multiple media and appropriate formats to reflect the varying needs of health care providers and consumers and diverse levels of health literacy.

"(2) LINKAGE TO HEALTH INFORMATION TECHNOLOGY.—The Secretary shall ensure that research findings and results generated by the Center are shared with the Office of the National Coordinator of Health Information Technology and used to inform the activities of the health information technology extension program under section 3012, as well as any relevant standards, certification criteria, or implementation specifications.

"(e) PRIORITIZATION.—The Director shall identify and regularly update a list of processes or systems on which to focus research and dissemination activities of the Center, taking into account—

"(1) the cost to Federal health programs;

"(2) consumer assessment of health care experience;

"(3) provider assessment of such processes or systems and opportunities to minimize distress and injury to the health care workforce;

"(4) the potential impact of such processes or systems on health status and function of patients, including vulnerable populations including children;

"(5) the areas of insufficient evidence identified under subsection (c)(2)(B); and

"(6) the evolution of meaningful use of health information technology, as defined in section 3000.

"(f) COORDINATION.—The Center shall coordinate its activities with activities conducted by the Center for Medicare and Medicaid Innovation established under section 1115A of the Social Security Act.

"(g) FUNDING.—There is authorized to be appropriated to carry out this section $20,000,000 for fiscal years 2010 through 2014.

"SEC. 934. QUALITY IMPROVEMENT TECHNICAL ASSISTANCE AND IMPLEMENTATION.

"(a) IN GENERAL.—The Director, through the Center for Quality Improvement and Patient Safety of the Agency for Healthcare Research and Quality (referred to in this section as the 'Center'), shall award—

"(1) technical assistance grants or contracts to eligible entities to provide technical support to institutions that deliver health care and health care providers (including rural and urban providers of services and suppliers with limited infrastructure and financial resources to implement and support quality improvement activities, providers of services and suppliers with poor performance scores, and providers of services and suppliers for which there are disparities in care among subgroups of patients) so that such institutions and providers understand, adapt, and implement the models and practices identified in the research conducted by the Center, including the Quality Improvement Networks Research Program; and

"(2) implementation grants or contracts to eligible entities to implement the models and practices described under paragraph (1).

"(b) ELIGIBLE ENTITIES.—

"(1) TECHNICAL ASSISTANCE AWARD.—To be eligible to receive a technical assistance grant or contract under subsection (a)(1), an entity—

"(A) may be a health care provider, health care provider association, professional society, health care worker organization, Indian health organization, quality improvement organization, patient safety organization, local quality improvement collaborative, the Joint Commission, academic health center, university, physician-based research network, primary care extension program established under section 399W, a Federal Indian Health Service program or a health program operated by an Indian tribe (as defined in section 4 of the Indian Health Care Improvement Act), or any other entity identified by the Secretary; and

"(B) shall have demonstrated expertise in providing information and technical support and assistance to health care providers regarding quality improvement.

"(2) IMPLEMENTATION AWARD.—To be eligible to receive an implementation grant or contract under subsection (a)(2), an entity—

"(A) may be a hospital or other health care provider or consortium or providers, as determined by the Secretary; and

"(B) shall have demonstrated expertise in providing information and technical support and assistance to health care providers regarding quality improvement.

"(c) APPLICATION.—

"(1) TECHNICAL ASSISTANCE AWARD.—To receive a technical assistance grant or contract under subsection (a)(1), an eligible entity shall submit an application to the Secretary at such time, in such manner, and containing—

"(A) a plan for a sustainable business model that may include a system of—

"(i) charging fees to institutions and providers that receive technical support from the entity; and

"(ii) reducing or eliminating such fees for such institutions and providers that serve low-income populations; and

"(B) such other information as the Director may require.

"(2) IMPLEMENTATION AWARD.—To receive a grant or contract under subsection (a)(2), an eligible entity shall submit an application to the Secretary at such time, in such manner, and containing—

"(A) a plan for implementation of a model or practice identified in the research conducted by the Center including—

"(i) financial cost, staffing requirements, and timeline for implementation; and

"(ii) pre- and projected post-implementation quality measure performance data in targeted improvement areas identified by the Secretary; and

"(B) such other information as the Director may require.

"(d) MATCHING FUNDS.—The Director may not award a grant or contract under this section to an entity unless the entity agrees that it will make available (directly or through contributions from other public or private entities) non-Federal contributions toward the activities to be carried out under the grant or contract in an amount equal to $1 for each $5 of Federal funds provided under the grant or contract. Such non-Federal matching funds may be provided directly or through donations from public or private entities and may be in cash or in-kind, fairly evaluated, including plant, equipment, or services.

"(e) EVALUATION.—

"(1) IN GENERAL.—The Director shall evaluate the performance of each entity that receives a grant or contract under this section. The evaluation of an entity shall include a study of—

"(A) the success of such entity in achieving the implementation, by the health care institutions and providers assisted by such entity, of the models and practices identified in the research conducted by the Center under section 933;

"(B) the perception of the health care institutions and providers assisted by such entity regarding the value of the entity; and

"(C) where practicable, better patient health outcomes and lower cost resulting from the assistance provided by such entity.

"(2) EFFECT OF EVALUATION.—Based on the outcome of the evaluation of the entity under paragraph (1), the Director shall determine whether to renew a grant or contract with such entity under this section.

"(f) COORDINATION.—The entities that receive a grant or contract under this section shall coordinate with health information technology regional extension centers under section 3012(c) and the primary care extension program established under section 399W regarding the dissemination of quality improvement, system delivery reform, and best practices information.".

SEC. 3502. ESTABLISHING COMMUNITY HEALTH TEAMS TO SUPPORT THE PATIENT-CENTERED MEDICAL HOME.

(a) IN GENERAL.—The Secretary of Health and Human Services (referred to in this section as the "Secretary") shall establish a program to provide grants to or enter into contracts with eligible entities to establish community-based interdisciplinary, interprofessional teams (referred to in this section as "health teams") to support primary care practices, including obstetrics and gynecology practices, within the hospital service areas served by the eligible entities. Grants or contracts shall be used to—

(1) establish health teams to provide support services to primary care providers; and

(2) provide capitated payments to primary care providers as determined by the Secretary.

(b) ELIGIBLE ENTITIES.—To be eligible to receive a grant or contract under subsection (a), an entity shall—

(1)(A) be a State or State-designated entity; or

(B) be an Indian tribe or tribal organization, as defined in section 4 of the Indian Health Care Improvement Act;

(2) submit a plan for achieving long-term financial sustainability within 3 years;

(3) submit a plan for incorporating prevention initiatives and patient education and care management resources into the delivery of health care that is integrated with community-based prevention and treatment resources, where available;

(4) ensure that the health team established by the entity includes an interdisciplinary, interprofessional team of health care providers, as determined by the Secretary; such team may include medical specialists, nurses, pharmacists, nutritionists, dieticians, social workers, behavioral and mental health providers (including substance use disorder prevention and treatment providers), doctors of chiropractic, licensed complementary and alternative medicine practitioners, and physicians' assistants;

(5) agree to provide services to eligible individuals with chronic conditions, as described in section 1945 of the Social Security Act (as added by section 2703), in accordance with the payment methodology established under subsection (c) of such section; and

(6) submit to the Secretary an application at such time, in such manner, and containing such information as the Secretary may require.

(c) REQUIREMENTS FOR HEALTH TEAMS.—A health team established pursuant to a grant or contract under subsection (a) shall—

(1) establish contractual agreements with primary care providers to provide support services;

(2) support patient-centered medical homes, defined as a mode of care that includes—

(A) personal physicians;

(B) whole person orientation;

(C) coordinated and integrated care;

(D) safe and high-quality care through evidence-informed medicine, appropriate use of health information technology, and continuous quality improvements;

(E) expanded access to care; and

(F) payment that recognizes added value from additional components of patient-centered care;

(3) collaborate with local primary care providers and existing State and community based resources to coordinate disease prevention, chronic disease management, transitioning between health care providers and settings and case management for patients, including children, with priority given to those amenable to prevention and with chronic diseases or conditions identified by the Secretary;

(4) in collaboration with local health care providers, develop and implement interdisciplinary, interprofessional care plans that integrate clinical and community preventive and health promotion services for patients, including children, with a priority given to those amenable to prevention and with chronic diseases or conditions identified by the Secretary;

(5) incorporate health care providers, patients, caregivers, and authorized representatives in program design and oversight;

(6) provide support necessary for local primary care providers to—

(A) coordinate and provide access to high-quality health care services;

(B) coordinate and provide access to preventive and health promotion services;

(C) provide access to appropriate specialty care and inpatient services;

(D) provide quality-driven, cost-effective, culturally appropriate, and patient- and family-centered health care;

(E) provide access to pharmacist-delivered medication management services, including medication reconciliation;

(F) provide coordination of the appropriate use of complementary and alternative (CAM) services to those who request such services;

(G) promote effective strategies for treatment planning, monitoring health outcomes and resource use, sharing information, treatment decision support, and organizing care to avoid duplication of service and other medical management approaches intended to improve quality and value of health care services;

(H) provide local access to the continuum of health care services in the most appropriate setting, including access to individuals that implement the care plans of patients and coordinate care, such as integrative health care practitioners;

(I) collect and report data that permits evaluation of the success of the collaborative effort on patient outcomes, including collection of data on patient experience of care, and identification of areas for improvement; and

(J) establish a coordinated system of early identification and referral for children at risk for developmental or behavioral problems such as through the use of infolines, health information technology, or other means as determined by the Secretary;

(7) provide 24-hour care management and support during transitions in care settings including—

(A) a transitional care program that provides onsite visits from the care coordinator, assists with the development of discharge plans and medication reconciliation upon admission to and discharge from the hospitals, nursing home, or other institution setting;

(B) discharge planning and counseling support to providers, patients, caregivers, and authorized representatives;

(C) assuring that post-discharge care plans include medication management, as appropriate;

(D) referrals for mental and behavioral health services, which may include the use of infolines; and

(E) transitional health care needs from adolescence to adulthood;

(8) serve as a liaison to community prevention and treatment programs;

(9) demonstrate a capacity to implement and maintain health information technology that meets the requirements of certified EHR technology (as defined in section 3000 of the Public Health Service Act (42 U.S.C. 300jj)) to facilitate coordination among members of the applicable care team and affiliated primary care practices; and

(10) where applicable, report to the Secretary information on quality measures used under section 399JJ of the Public Health Service Act.

(d) REQUIREMENT FOR PRIMARY CARE PROVIDERS.—A provider who contracts with a care team shall—

(1) provide a care plan to the care team for each patient participant;

(2) provide access to participant health records; and

(3) meet regularly with the care team to ensure integration of care.

(e) REPORTING TO SECRETARY.—An entity that receives a grant or contract under subsection (a) shall submit to the Secretary a report that describes and evaluates, as requested by the Secretary, the activities carried out by the entity under subsection (c).

(f) DEFINITION OF PRIMARY CARE.—In this section, the term "primary care" means the provision of integrated, accessible health care services by clinicians who are accountable for addressing a large majority of personal health care needs, developing a sustained partnership with patients, and practicing in the context of family and community.

SEC. 3503. MEDICATION MANAGEMENT SERVICES IN TREATMENT OF CHRONIC DISEASE.

Title IX of the Public Health Service Act (42 U.S.C. 299 et seq.), as amended by section 3501, is further amended by inserting after section 934 the following:

"SEC. 935. GRANTS OR CONTRACTS TO IMPLEMENT MEDICATION MANAGEMENT SERVICES IN TREATMENT OF CHRONIC DISEASES.

"(a) IN GENERAL.—The Secretary, acting through the Patient Safety Research Center established in section 933 (referred to in this section as the 'Center'), shall establish a program to provide grants or contracts to eligible entities to implement medication management (referred to in this section as 'MTM') services provided by licensed pharmacists, as a collaborative, multidisciplinary, interprofessional approach to the treatment of chronic diseases for targeted individuals, to improve the quality of care and reduce overall cost in the treatment of such diseases. The Secretary shall commence the program under this section not later than May 1, 2010.

"(b) ELIGIBLE ENTITIES.—To be eligible to receive a grant or contract under subsection (a), an entity shall—

"(1) provide a setting appropriate for MTM services, as recommended by the experts described in subsection (e);

"(2) submit to the Secretary a plan for achieving long-term financial sustainability;

"(3) where applicable, submit a plan for coordinating MTM services through local community health teams established in section 3502 of the Patient Protection and Affordable Care Act or in collaboration with primary care extension programs established in section 399W;

"(4) submit a plan for meeting the requirements under subsection (c); and

"(5) submit to the Secretary such other information as the Secretary may require.

"(c) MTM SERVICES TO TARGETED INDIVIDUALS.—The MTM services provided with the assistance of a grant or contract awarded under subsection (a) shall, as allowed by State law including applicable collaborative pharmacy practice agreements, include—

"(1) performing or obtaining necessary assessments of the health and functional status of each patient receiving such MTM services;

"(2) formulating a medication treatment plan according to therapeutic goals agreed upon by the prescriber and the patient or caregiver or authorized representative of the patient;

"(3) selecting, initiating, modifying, recommending changes to, or administering medication therapy;

"(4) monitoring, which may include access to, ordering, or performing laboratory assessments, and evaluating the response of the patient to therapy, including safety and effectiveness;

"(5) performing an initial comprehensive medication review to identify, resolve, and prevent medication-related problems, including adverse drug events, quarterly targeted medication reviews for ongoing monitoring, and additional followup interventions on a schedule developed collaboratively with the prescriber;

"(6) documenting the care delivered and communicating essential information about such care, including a summary of the medication review, and the recommendations of the pharmacist to other appropriate health care providers of the patient in a timely fashion;

"(7) providing education and training designed to enhance the understanding and appropriate use of the medications by the patient, caregiver, and other authorized representative;

"(8) providing information, support services, and resources and strategies designed to enhance patient adherence with therapeutic regimens;

"(9) coordinating and integrating MTM services within the broader health care management services provided to the patient; and

"(10) such other patient care services allowed under pharmacist scopes of practice in use in other Federal programs that have implemented MTM services.

"(d) TARGETED INDIVIDUALS.—MTM services provided by licensed pharmacists under a grant or contract awarded under subsection (a) shall be offered to targeted individuals who—

"(1) take 4 or more prescribed medications (including over-the-counter medications and dietary supplements);

"(2) take any 'high risk' medications;

"(3) have 2 or more chronic diseases, as identified by the Secretary; or

"(4) have undergone a transition of care, or other factors, as determined by the Secretary, that are likely to create a high risk of medication-related problems.

"(e) CONSULTATION WITH EXPERTS.—In designing and implementing MTM services provided under grants or contracts awarded under subsection (a), the Secretary shall consult with Federal, State, private, public-private, and academic entities, pharmacy and pharmacist organizations, health care organizations, consumer advocates, chronic disease groups, and other stakeholders involved with the research, dissemination, and implementation of pharmacist-delivered MTM services, as the Secretary determines appropriate. The Secretary, in collaboration with this group, shall determine whether it is possible to incorporate rapid cycle process improvement concepts in use in other Federal programs that have implemented MTM services.

"(f) REPORTING TO THE SECRETARY.—An entity that receives a grant or contract under subsection (a) shall submit to the Secretary a report that describes and evaluates, as requested by the Secretary, the activities carried out under subsection (c), including quality measures endorsed by the entity with a contract under section 1890 of the Social Security Act, as determined by the Secretary.

"(g) EVALUATION AND REPORT.—The Secretary shall submit to the relevant committees of Congress a report which shall—

"(1) assess the clinical effectiveness of pharmacist-provided services under the MTM services program, as compared to usual care, including an evaluation of whether enrollees maintained better health with fewer hospitalizations and emergency room visits than similar patients not enrolled in the program;

"(2) assess changes in overall health care resource use by targeted individuals;

"(3) assess patient and prescriber satisfaction with MTM services;

"(4) assess the impact of patient-cost sharing requirements on medication adherence and recommendations for modifications;

"(5) identify and evaluate other factors that may impact clinical and economic outcomes, including demographic characteristics, clinical characteristics, and health services use of the patient, as well as characteristics of the regimen, pharmacy benefit, and MTM services provided; and

"(6) evaluate the extent to which participating pharmacists who maintain a dispensing role have a conflict of interest in the provision of MTM services, and if such conflict is found, provide recommendations on how such a conflict might be appropriately addressed.

"(h) GRANTS OR CONTRACTS TO FUND DEVELOPMENT OF PERFORMANCE MEASURES.—The Secretary may, through the quality measure development program under section 931 of the Public Health Service Act, award grants or contracts to eligible entities for the purpose of funding the development of performance measures that assess the use and effectiveness of medication therapy management services.".

SEC. 3504. DESIGN AND IMPLEMENTATION OF REGIONALIZED SYSTEMS FOR EMERGENCY CARE.

(a) IN GENERAL.—Title XII of the Public Health Service Act (42 U.S.C. 300d et seq.) is amended—

(1) in section 1203—

(A) in the section heading, by inserting "**FOR TRAUMA SYSTEMS**" after "**GRANTS**"; and

(B) in subsection (a), by striking "Administrator of the Health Resources and Services Administration" and inserting "Assistant Secretary for Preparedness and Response";

(2) by inserting after section 1203 the following:

"SEC. 1204. COMPETITIVE GRANTS FOR REGIONALIZED SYSTEMS FOR EMERGENCY CARE RESPONSE.

"(a) IN GENERAL.—The Secretary, acting through the Assistant Secretary for Preparedness and Response, shall award not fewer than 4 multiyear contracts or competitive grants to eligible entities to support pilot projects that design, implement, and evaluate innovative models of regionalized, comprehensive, and accountable emergency care and trauma systems.

"(b) ELIGIBLE ENTITY; REGION.—In this section:

"(1) ELIGIBLE ENTITY.—The term 'eligible entity' means—

"(A) a State or a partnership of 1 or more States and 1 or more local governments; or

"(B) an Indian tribe (as defined in section 4 of the Indian Health Care Improvement Act) or a partnership of 1 or more Indian tribes.

"(2) REGION.—The term 'region' means an area within a State, an area that lies within multiple States, or a similar area (such as a multicounty area), as determined by the Secretary.

"(3) EMERGENCY SERVICES.—The term 'emergency services' includes acute, prehospital, and trauma care.

"(c) PILOT PROJECTS.—The Secretary shall award a contract or grant under subsection (a) to an eligible entity that proposes a pilot project to design, implement, and evaluate an emergency medical and trauma system that—

"(1) coordinates with public health and safety services, emergency medical services, medical facilities, trauma centers, and other entities in a region to develop an approach to emergency medical and trauma system access throughout the region, including 9–1–1 Public Safety Answering Points and emergency medical dispatch;

"(2) includes a mechanism, such as a regional medical direction or transport communications system, that operates throughout the region to ensure that the patient is taken to the medically appropriate facility (whether an initial facility or a higher-level facility) in a timely fashion;

"(3) allows for the tracking of prehospital and hospital resources, including inpatient bed capacity, emergency department capacity, trauma center capacity, on-call specialist coverage, ambulance diversion status, and the coordination of such tracking with regional communications and hospital destination decisions; and

"(4) includes a consistent region-wide prehospital, hospital, and interfacility data management system that—

"(A) submits data to the National EMS Information System, the National Trauma Data Bank, and others;

"(B) reports data to appropriate Federal and State databanks and registries; and

"(C) contains information sufficient to evaluate key elements of prehospital care, hospital destination decisions, including initial hospital and interfacility decisions, and relevant health outcomes of hospital care.

"(d) APPLICATION.—

"(1) IN GENERAL.—An eligible entity that seeks a contract or grant described in subsection (a) shall submit to the Secretary an application at such time and in such manner as the Secretary may require.

"(2) APPLICATION INFORMATION.—Each application shall include—

"(A) an assurance from the eligible entity that the proposed system—

"(i) has been coordinated with the applicable State Office of Emergency Medical Services (or equivalent State office);

"(ii) includes consistent indirect and direct medical oversight of prehospital, hospital, and interfacility transport throughout the region;

"(iii) coordinates prehospital treatment and triage, hospital destination, and interfacility transport throughout the region;

"(iv) includes a categorization or designation system for special medical facilities throughout the region that is integrated with transport and destination protocols;

"(v) includes a regional medical direction, patient tracking, and resource allocation system that supports day-to-day emergency care and surge capacity and is integrated with other components of the national and State emergency preparedness system; and

"(vi) addresses pediatric concerns related to integration, planning, preparedness, and coordination of emergency medical services for infants, children and adolescents; and

"(B) such other information as the Secretary may require.

"(e) REQUIREMENT OF MATCHING FUNDS.—

"(1) IN GENERAL.—The Secretary may not make a grant under this section unless the State (or consortia of States) involved agrees, with respect to the costs to be incurred by the State (or consortia) in carrying out the purpose for which such grant was made, to make available non-Federal contributions (in cash or in kind under paragraph (2)) toward such costs in an amount equal to not less than $1 for each $3 of Federal funds provided in the grant. Such contributions may be made directly or through donations from public or private entities.

"(2) NON-FEDERAL CONTRIBUTIONS.—Non-Federal contributions required in paragraph (1) may be in cash or in kind, fairly evaluated, including equipment or services (and excluding indirect or overhead costs). Amounts provided by the Federal Government, or services assisted or subsidized to any significant extent by the Federal Government, may not be included in determining the amount of such non-Federal contributions.

"(f) PRIORITY.—The Secretary shall give priority for the award of the contracts or grants described in subsection (a) to any eligible entity that serves a population in a medically underserved area (as defined in section 330(b)(3)).

"(g) REPORT.—Not later than 90 days after the completion of a pilot project under subsection (a), the recipient of such contract or grant described in shall submit to the Secretary a report containing the results of an evaluation of the program, including an identification of—

"(1) the impact of the regional, accountable emergency care and trauma system on patient health outcomes for various critical care categories, such as trauma, stroke, cardiac emergencies, neurological emergencies, and pediatric emergencies;

"(2) the system characteristics that contribute to the effectiveness and efficiency of the program (or lack thereof);

"(3) methods of assuring the long-term financial sustainability of the emergency care and trauma system;

"(4) the State and local legislation necessary to implement and to maintain the system;

"(5) the barriers to developing regionalized, accountable emergency care and trauma systems, as well as the methods to overcome such barriers; and

"(6) recommendations on the utilization of available funding for future regionalization efforts.

"(h) DISSEMINATION OF FINDINGS.—The Secretary shall, as appropriate, disseminate to the public and to the appropriate Committees of the Congress, the information contained in a report made under subsection (g)."; and

(3) in section 1232—

(A) in subsection (a), by striking "appropriated" and all that follows through the period at the end and inserting "appropriated $24,000,000 for each of fiscal years 2010 through 2014."; and

(B) by inserting after subsection (c) the following:

"(d) AUTHORITY.—For the purpose of carrying out parts A through C, beginning on the date of enactment of the Patient Protection and Affordable Care Act, the Secretary shall transfer authority in administering grants and related authorities under such parts from the Administrator of the Health Resources and Services Administration to the Assistant Secretary for Preparedness and Response.".

(b) SUPPORT FOR EMERGENCY MEDICINE RESEARCH.—Part H of title IV of the Public Health Service Act (42 U.S.C. 289 et seq.) is amended by inserting after the section 498C the following:

"SEC. 498D. SUPPORT FOR EMERGENCY MEDICINE RESEARCH.

"(a) EMERGENCY MEDICAL RESEARCH.—The Secretary shall support Federal programs administered by the National Institutes of Health, the Agency for Healthcare Research and Quality, the Health Resources and Services Administration, the Centers for Disease Control and Prevention, and other agencies involved in improving the emergency care system to expand and accelerate research in emergency medical care systems and emergency medicine, including—

"(1) the basic science of emergency medicine;

"(2) the model of service delivery and the components of such models that contribute to enhanced patient health outcomes;

"(3) the translation of basic scientific research into improved practice; and

"(4) the development of timely and efficient delivery of health services.

"(b) PEDIATRIC EMERGENCY MEDICAL RESEARCH.—The Secretary shall support Federal programs administered by the National Institutes of Health, the Agency for Healthcare Research and Quality, the Health Resources and Services Administration, the Centers for Disease Control and Prevention, and other agencies to coordinate and expand research in pediatric emergency medical care systems and pediatric emergency medicine, including—

"(1) an examination of the gaps and opportunities in pediatric emergency care research and a strategy for the optimal organization and funding of such research;

"(2) the role of pediatric emergency services as an integrated component of the overall health system;

"(3) system-wide pediatric emergency care planning, preparedness, coordination, and funding;

"(4) pediatric training in professional education; and

"(5) research in pediatric emergency care, specifically on the efficacy, safety, and health outcomes of medications used for infants, children, and adolescents in emergency care settings in order to improve patient safety.

"(c) IMPACT RESEARCH.—The Secretary shall support research to determine the estimated economic impact of, and savings that result from, the implementation of coordinated emergency care systems.

"(d) AUTHORIZATION OF APPROPRIATIONS.—There are authorized to be appropriated to carry out this section such sums as may be necessary for each of fiscal years 2010 through 2014.".

SEC. 3505. TRAUMA CARE CENTERS AND SERVICE AVAILABILITY.

(a) TRAUMA CARE CENTERS.—

(1) GRANTS FOR TRAUMA CARE CENTERS.—Section 1241 of the Public Health Service Act (42 U.S.C. 300d–41) is amended by striking subsections (a) and (b) and inserting the following:

"(a) IN GENERAL.—The Secretary shall establish 3 programs to award grants to qualified public, nonprofit Indian Health Service, Indian tribal, and urban Indian trauma centers—

"(1) to assist in defraying substantial uncompensated care costs;

"(2) to further the core missions of such trauma centers, including by addressing costs associated with patient stabilization and transfer, trauma education and outreach, coordination with local and regional trauma systems, essential personnel and other fixed costs, and expenses associated with employee and non-employee physician services; and

"(3) to provide emergency relief to ensure the continued and future availability of trauma services.

"(b) MINIMUM QUALIFICATIONS OF TRAUMA CENTERS.—

"(1) PARTICIPATION IN TRAUMA CARE SYSTEM OPERATING UNDER CERTAIN PROFESSIONAL GUIDELINES.—Except as provided in paragraph (2), the Secretary may not award a grant to a trauma center under subsection (a) unless the trauma center is a participant in a trauma system that substantially complies with section 1213.

"(2) EXEMPTION.—Paragraph (1) shall not apply to trauma centers that are located in States with no existing trauma care system.

"(3) QUALIFICATION FOR SUBSTANTIAL UNCOMPENSATED CARE COSTS.—The Secretary shall award substantial uncompensated care grants under subsection (a)(1) only to trauma centers meeting at least 1 of the criteria in 1 of the following 3 categories:

"(A) CATEGORY A.—The criteria for category A are as follows:

"(i) At least 40 percent of the visits in the emergency department of the hospital in which the trauma center is located were charity or self-pay patients.

"(ii) At least 50 percent of the visits in such emergency department were Medicaid (under title XIX of the Social Security Act (42 U.S.C. 1396 et seq.)) and charity and self-pay patients combined.

"(B) CATEGORY B.—The criteria for category B are as follows:

"(i) At least 35 percent of the visits in the emergency department were charity or self-pay patients.

"(ii) At least 50 percent of the visits in the emergency department were Medicaid and charity and self-pay patients combined.

"(C) CATEGORY C.—The criteria for category C are as follows:

"(i) At least 20 percent of the visits in the emergency department were charity or self-pay patients.

"(ii) At least 30 percent of the visits in the emergency department were Medicaid and charity and self-pay patients combined.

"(4) TRAUMA CENTERS IN 1115 WAIVER STATES.—Notwithstanding paragraph (3), the Secretary may award a substantial uncompensated care grant to a trauma center under subsection (a)(1) if the trauma center qualifies for funds under a Low Income Pool or Safety Net Care Pool established through a waiver approved under section 1115 of the Social Security Act (42 U.S.C. 1315).

"(5) DESIGNATION.—The Secretary may not award a grant to a trauma center unless such trauma center is verified by the American College of Surgeons or designated by an equivalent State or local agency.

"(c) ADDITIONAL REQUIREMENTS.—The Secretary may not award a grant to a trauma center under subsection (a)(1) unless such trauma center—

"(1) submits to the Secretary a plan satisfactory to the Secretary that demonstrates a continued commitment to serving trauma patients regardless of their ability to pay; and

"(2) has policies in place to assist patients who cannot pay for part or all of the care they receive, including a sliding fee scale, and to ensure fair billing and collection practices.".

(2) CONSIDERATIONS IN MAKING GRANTS.—Section 1242 of the Public Health Service Act (42 U.S.C. 300d–42) is amended by striking subsections (a) and (b) and inserting the following:

"(a) SUBSTANTIAL UNCOMPENSATED CARE AWARDS.—

"(1) IN GENERAL.—The Secretary shall establish an award basis for each eligible trauma center for grants under section 1241(a)(1) according to the percentage described in paragraph (2), subject to the requirements of section 1241(b)(3).

"(2) PERCENTAGES.—The applicable percentages are as follows:

"(A) With respect to a category A trauma center, 100 percent of the uncompensated care costs.

"(B) With respect to a category B trauma center, not more than 75 percent of the uncompensated care costs.

"(C) With respect to a category C trauma center, not more than 50 percent of the uncompensated care costs.

"(b) CORE MISSION AWARDS.—

"(1) IN GENERAL.—In awarding grants under section 1241(a)(2), the Secretary shall—

"(A) reserve 25 percent of the amount allocated for core mission awards for Level III and Level IV trauma centers; and

"(B) reserve 25 percent of the amount allocated for core mission awards for large urban Level I and II trauma centers—

"(i) that have at least 1 graduate medical education fellowship in trauma or trauma related specialties for which demand is exceeding supply;

"(ii) for which—

"(I) annual uncompensated care costs exceed $10,000,000; or

"(II) at least 20 percent of emergency department visits are charity or self-pay or Medicaid patients; and

"(iii) that are not eligible for substantial uncompensated care awards under section 1241(a)(1).

“(c) EMERGENCY AWARDS.—In awarding grants under section 1241(a)(3), the Secretary shall—

“(1) give preference to any application submitted by a trauma center that provides trauma care in a geographic area in which the availability of trauma care has significantly decreased or will significantly decrease if the center is forced to close or downgrade service or growth in demand for trauma services exceeds capacity; and

“(2) reallocate any emergency awards funds not obligated due to insufficient, or a lack of qualified, applications to the significant uncompensated care award program.”.

(3) CERTAIN AGREEMENTS.—Section 1243 of the Public Health Service Act (42 U.S.C. 300d–43) is amended by striking subsections (a), (b), and (c) and inserting the following:

“(a) MAINTENANCE OF FINANCIAL SUPPORT.—The Secretary may require a trauma center receiving a grant under section 1241(a) to maintain access to trauma services at comparable levels to the prior year during the grant period.

“(b) TRAUMA CARE REGISTRY.—The Secretary may require the trauma center receiving a grant under section 1241(a) to provide data to a national and centralized registry of trauma cases, in accordance with guidelines developed by the American College of Surgeons, and as the Secretary may otherwise require.”.

(4) GENERAL PROVISIONS.—Section 1244 of the Public Health Service Act (42 U.S.C. 300d–44) is amended by striking subsections (a), (b), and (c) and inserting the following:

“(a) APPLICATION.—The Secretary may not award a grant to a trauma center under section 1241(a) unless such center submits an application for the grant to the Secretary and the application is in such form, is made in such manner, and contains such agreements, assurances, and information as the Secretary determines to be necessary to carry out this part.

“(b) LIMITATION ON DURATION OF SUPPORT.—The period during which a trauma center receives payments under a grant under section 1241(a)(3) shall be for 3 fiscal years, except that the Secretary may waive such requirement for a center and authorize such center to receive such payments for 1 additional fiscal year.

“(c) LIMITATION ON AMOUNT OF GRANT.—Notwithstanding section 1242(a), a grant under section 1241 may not be made in an amount exceeding $2,000,000 for each fiscal year.

“(d) ELIGIBILITY.—Except as provided in section 1242(b)(1)(B)(iii), acquisition of, or eligibility for, a grant under section 1241(a) shall not preclude a trauma center from being eligible for other grants described in such section.

“(e) FUNDING DISTRIBUTION.—Of the total amount appropriated for a fiscal year under section 1245, 70 percent shall be used for substantial uncompensated care awards under section 1241(a)(1), 20 percent shall be used for core mission awards under section 1241(a)(2), and 10 percent shall be used for emergency awards under section 1241(a)(3).

“(f) MINIMUM ALLOWANCE.—Notwithstanding subsection (e), if the amount appropriated for a fiscal year under section 1245 is less than $25,000,000, all available funding for such fiscal year shall be used for substantial uncompensated care awards under section 1241(a)(1).

“(g) SUBSTANTIAL UNCOMPENSATED CARE AWARD DISTRIBUTION AND PROPORTIONAL SHARE.—Notwithstanding section 1242(a), of the amount appropriated for substantial uncompensated care grants for a fiscal year, the Secretary shall—

"(1) make available—

"(A) 50 percent of such funds for category A trauma center grantees;

"(B) 35 percent of such funds for category B trauma center grantees; and

"(C) 15 percent of such funds for category C trauma center grantees; and

"(2) provide available funds within each category in a manner proportional to the award basis specified in section 1242(a)(2) to each eligible trauma center.

"(h) REPORT.—Beginning 2 years after the date of enactment of the Patient Protection and Affordable Care Act, and every 2 years thereafter, the Secretary shall biennially report to Congress regarding the status of the grants made under section 1241 and on the overall financial stability of trauma centers.".

(5) AUTHORIZATION OF APPROPRIATIONS.—Section 1245 of the Public Health Service Act (42 U.S.C. 300d–45) is amended to read as follows:

"SEC. 1245. AUTHORIZATION OF APPROPRIATIONS.

"For the purpose of carrying out this part, there are authorized to be appropriated $100,000,000 for fiscal year 2009, and such sums as may be necessary for each of fiscal years 2010 through 2015. Such authorization of appropriations is in addition to any other authorization of appropriations or amounts that are available for such purpose.".

(6) DEFINITION.—Part D of title XII of the Public Health Service Act (42 U.S.C. 300d–41 et seq.) is amended by adding at the end the following:

"SEC. 1246. DEFINITION.

"In this part, the term 'uncompensated care costs' means unreimbursed costs from serving self-pay, charity, or Medicaid patients, without regard to payment under section 1923 of the Social Security Act, all of which are attributable to emergency care and trauma care, including costs related to subsequent inpatient admissions to the hospital.".

(b) TRAUMA SERVICE AVAILABILITY.—Title XII of the Public Health Service Act (42 U.S.C. 300d et seq.) is amended by adding at the end the following:

"PART H—TRAUMA SERVICE AVAILABILITY

"SEC. 1281. GRANTS TO STATES.

"(a) ESTABLISHMENT.—To promote universal access to trauma care services provided by trauma centers and trauma-related physician specialties, the Secretary shall provide funding to States to enable such States to award grants to eligible entities for the purposes described in this section.

"(b) AWARDING OF GRANTS BY STATES.—Each State may award grants to eligible entities within the State for the purposes described in subparagraph (d).

"(c) ELIGIBILITY.—

"(1) IN GENERAL.—To be eligible to receive a grant under subsection (b) an entity shall—

"(A) be—

"(i) a public or nonprofit trauma center or consortium thereof that meets that requirements of paragraphs (1), (2), and (5) of section 1241(b);

"(ii) a safety net public or nonprofit trauma center that meets the requirements of paragraphs (1) through (5) of section 1241(b); or

"(iii) a hospital in an underserved area (as defined by the State) that seeks to establish new trauma services; and

"(B) submit to the State an application at such time, in such manner, and containing such information as the State may require.

"(2) LIMITATION.—A State shall use at least 40 percent of the amount available to the State under this part for a fiscal year to award grants to safety net trauma centers described in paragraph (1)(A)(ii).

"(d) USE OF FUNDS.—The recipient of a grant under subsection (b) shall carry out 1 or more of the following activities consistent with subsection (b):

"(1) Providing trauma centers with funding to support physician compensation in trauma-related physician specialties where shortages exist in the region involved, with priority provided to safety net trauma centers described in subsection (c)(1)(A)(ii).

"(2) Providing for individual safety net trauma center fiscal stability and costs related to having service that is available 24 hours a day, 7 days a week, with priority provided to safety net trauma centers described in subsection (c)(1)(A)(ii) located in urban, border, and rural areas.

"(3) Reducing trauma center overcrowding at specific trauma centers related to throughput of trauma patients.

"(4) Establishing new trauma services in underserved areas as defined by the State.

"(5) Enhancing collaboration between trauma centers and other hospitals and emergency medical services personnel related to trauma service availability.

"(6) Making capital improvements to enhance access and expedite trauma care, including providing helipads and associated safety infrastructure.

"(7) Enhancing trauma surge capacity at specific trauma centers.

"(8) Ensuring expedient receipt of trauma patients transported by ground or air to the appropriate trauma center.

"(9) Enhancing interstate trauma center collaboration.

"(e) LIMITATION.—

"(1) IN GENERAL.—A State may use not more than 20 percent of the amount available to the State under this part for a fiscal year for administrative costs associated with awarding grants and related costs.

"(2) MAINTENANCE OF EFFORT.—The Secretary may not provide funding to a State under this part unless the State agrees that such funds will be used to supplement and not supplant State funding otherwise available for the activities and costs described in this part.

"(f) DISTRIBUTION OF FUNDS.—The following shall apply with respect to grants provided in this part:

"(1) LESS THAN $10,000,000.—If the amount of appropriations for this part in a fiscal year is less than $10,000,000, the Secretary shall divide such funding evenly among only those States that have 1 or more trauma centers eligible for funding under section 1241(b)(3)(A).

"(2) LESS THAN $20,000,000.—If the amount of appropriations in a fiscal year is less than $20,000,000, the Secretary shall divide such funding evenly among only those States that have 1 or more trauma centers eligible for funding under subparagraphs (A) and (B) of section 1241(b)(3).

"(3) LESS THAN $30,000,000.—If the amount of appropriations for this part in a fiscal year is less than $30,000,000, the Secretary shall divide such funding evenly among only those States that have 1 or more trauma centers eligible for funding under section 1241(b)(3).

"(4) $30,000,000 OR MORE.—If the amount of appropriations for this part in a fiscal year is $30,000,000 or more, the Secretary shall divide such funding evenly among all States.

"SEC. 1282. AUTHORIZATION OF APPROPRIATIONS.

"For the purpose of carrying out this part, there is authorized to be appropriated $100,000,000 for each of fiscal years 2010 through 2015.".

SEC. 3506. PROGRAM TO FACILITATE SHARED DECISIONMAKING.

Part D of title IX of the Public Health Service Act, as amended by section 3503, is further amended by adding at the end the following:

"SEC. 936. PROGRAM TO FACILITATE SHARED DECISIONMAKING.

"(a) PURPOSE.—The purpose of this section is to facilitate collaborative processes between patients, caregivers or authorized representatives, and clinicians that engages the patient, caregiver or authorized representative in decisionmaking, provides patients, caregivers or authorized representatives with information about trade-offs among treatment options, and facilitates the incorporation of patient preferences and values into the medical plan.

"(b) DEFINITIONS.—In this section:

"(1) PATIENT DECISION AID.—The term 'patient decision aid' means an educational tool that helps patients, caregivers or authorized representatives understand and communicate their beliefs and preferences related to their treatment options, and to decide with their health care provider what treatments are best for them based on their treatment options, scientific evidence, circumstances, beliefs, and preferences.

"(2) PREFERENCE SENSITIVE CARE.—The term 'preference sensitive care' means medical care for which the clinical evidence does not clearly support one treatment option such that the appropriate course of treatment depends on the values of the patient or the preferences of the patient, caregivers or authorized representatives regarding the benefits, harms and scientific evidence for each treatment option, the use of such care should depend on the informed patient choice among clinically appropriate treatment options.

"(c) ESTABLISHMENT OF INDEPENDENT STANDARDS FOR PATIENT DECISION AIDS FOR PREFERENCE SENSITIVE CARE.—

"(1) CONTRACT WITH ENTITY TO ESTABLISH STANDARDS AND CERTIFY PATIENT DECISION AIDS.—

"(A) IN GENERAL.—For purposes of supporting consensus-based standards for patient decision aids for preference sensitive care and a certification process for patient decision aids for use in the Federal health programs and by other interested parties, the Secretary shall have in effect a contract with the entity with a contract under section 1890 of the Social Security Act. Such contract shall provide that the entity perform the duties described in paragraph (2).

"(B) TIMING FOR FIRST CONTRACT.—As soon as practicable after the date of the enactment of this section, the Secretary shall enter into the first contract under subparagraph (A).

"(C) PERIOD OF CONTRACT.—A contract under subparagraph (A) shall be for a period of 18 months (except such contract may be renewed after a subsequent bidding process).

"(2) DUTIES.—The following duties are described in this paragraph:

"(A) DEVELOP AND IDENTIFY STANDARDS FOR PATIENT DECISION AIDS.—The entity shall synthesize evidence and convene a broad range of experts and key stakeholders to develop and identify consensus-based standards to evaluate patient decision aids for preference sensitive care.

"(B) ENDORSE PATIENT DECISION AIDS.—The entity shall review patient decision aids and develop a certification process whether patient decision aids meet the standards developed and identified under subparagraph (A). The entity shall give priority to the review and certification of patient decision aids for preference sensitive care.

"(d) PROGRAM TO DEVELOP, UPDATE AND PATIENT DECISION AIDS TO ASSIST HEALTH CARE PROVIDERS AND PATIENTS.—

"(1) IN GENERAL.—The Secretary, acting through the Director, and in coordination with heads of other relevant agencies, such as the Director of the Centers for Disease Control and Prevention and the Director of the National Institutes of Health, shall establish a program to award grants or contracts—

"(A) to develop, update, and produce patient decision aids for preference sensitive care to assist health care providers in educating patients, caregivers, and authorized representatives concerning the relative safety, relative effectiveness (including possible health outcomes and impact on functional status), and relative cost of treatment or, where appropriate, palliative care options;

"(B) to test such materials to ensure such materials are balanced and evidence based in aiding health care providers and patients, caregivers, and authorized representatives to make informed decisions about patient care and can be easily incorporated into a broad array of practice settings; and

"(C) to educate providers on the use of such materials, including through academic curricula.

"(2) REQUIREMENTS FOR PATIENT DECISION AIDS.—Patient decision aids developed and produced pursuant to a grant or contract under paragraph (1)—

"(A) shall be designed to engage patients, caregivers, and authorized representatives in informed decisionmaking with health care providers;

"(B) shall present up-to-date clinical evidence about the risks and benefits of treatment options in a form and manner that is age-appropriate and can be adapted for patients, caregivers, and authorized representatives from a variety of cultural and educational backgrounds to reflect the varying needs of consumers and diverse levels of health literacy;

"(C) shall, where appropriate, explain why there is a lack of evidence to support one treatment option over another; and

"(D) shall address health care decisions across the age span, including those affecting vulnerable populations including children.

"(3) DISTRIBUTION.—The Director shall ensure that patient decision aids produced with grants or contracts under this section are available to the public.

"(4) NONDUPLICATION OF EFFORTS.—The Director shall ensure that the activities under this section of the Agency and other agencies, including the Centers for Disease Control and Prevention and the National Institutes of Health, are free of unnecessary duplication of effort.

"(e) GRANTS TO SUPPORT SHARED DECISIONMAKING IMPLEMENTATION.—

"(1) IN GENERAL.—The Secretary shall establish a program to provide for the phased-in development, implementation, and evaluation of shared decisionmaking using patient decision aids to meet the objective of improving the understanding of patients of their medical treatment options.

"(2) SHARED DECISIONMAKING RESOURCE CENTERS.—

"(A) IN GENERAL.—The Secretary shall provide grants for the establishment and support of Shared Decisionmaking Resource Centers (referred to in this subsection as 'Centers') to provide technical assistance to providers and to develop and disseminate best practices and other information to support and accelerate adoption, implementation, and effective use of patient decision aids and shared decisionmaking by providers.

"(B) OBJECTIVES.—The objective of a Center is to enhance and promote the adoption of patient decision aids and shared decisionmaking through—

"(i) providing assistance to eligible providers with the implementation and effective use of, and training on, patient decision aids; and

"(ii) the dissemination of best practices and research on the implementation and effective use of patient decision aids.

"(3) SHARED DECISIONMAKING PARTICIPATION GRANTS.—

"(A) IN GENERAL.—The Secretary shall provide grants to health care providers for the development and implementation of shared decisionmaking techniques and to assess the use of such techniques.

"(B) PREFERENCE.—In order to facilitate the use of best practices, the Secretary shall provide a preference in making grants under this subsection to health care providers who participate in training by Shared Decision-making Resource Centers or comparable training.

"(C) LIMITATION.—Funds under this paragraph shall not be used to purchase or implement use of patient decision aids other than those certified under the process identified in subsection (c).

"(4) GUIDANCE.—The Secretary may issue guidance to eligible grantees under this subsection on the use of patient decision aids.

"(f) FUNDING.—For purposes of carrying out this section there are authorized to be appropriated such sums as may be necessary for fiscal year 2010 and each subsequent fiscal year.".

SEC. 3507. PRESENTATION OF PRESCRIPTION DRUG BENEFIT AND RISK INFORMATION.

(a) IN GENERAL.—The Secretary of Health and Human Services (referred to in this section as the "Secretary"), acting through the Commissioner of Food and Drugs, shall determine whether the addition of quantitative summaries of the benefits and risks of prescription drugs in a standardized format (such as a table or drug facts box) to the promotional labeling or print advertising of such drugs would improve health care decisionmaking by clinicians and patients and consumers.

(b) REVIEW AND CONSULTATION.—In making the determination under subsection (a), the Secretary shall review all available scientific evidence and research on decisionmaking and social and cognitive psychology and consult with drug manufacturers, clinicians, patients and consumers, experts in health literacy, representatives of racial and ethnic minorities, and experts in women's and pediatric health.

(c) REPORT.—Not later than 1 year after the date of enactment of this Act, the Secretary shall submit to Congress a report that provides—

(1) the determination by the Secretary under subsection (a); and

(2) the reasoning and analysis underlying that determination.

(d) AUTHORITY.—If the Secretary determines under subsection (a) that the addition of quantitative summaries of the benefits and risks of prescription drugs in a standardized format (such as a table or drug facts box) to the promotional labeling or print advertising of such drugs would improve health care decisionmaking by clinicians and patients and consumers, then the Secretary, not later than 3 years after the date of submission of the report under subsection (c), shall promulgate proposed regulations as necessary to implement such format.

(e) CLARIFICATION.—Nothing in this section shall be construed to restrict the existing authorities of the Secretary with respect to benefit and risk information.

SEC. 3508. DEMONSTRATION PROGRAM TO INTEGRATE QUALITY IMPROVEMENT AND PATIENT SAFETY TRAINING INTO CLINICAL EDUCATION OF HEALTH PROFESSIONALS.

(a) IN GENERAL.—The Secretary may award grants to eligible entities or consortia under this section to carry out demonstration projects to develop and implement academic curricula that integrates quality improvement and patient safety in the clinical education of health professionals. Such awards shall be made on a competitive basis and pursuant to peer review.

(b) ELIGIBILITY.—To be eligible to receive a grant under subsection (a), an entity or consortium shall—

(1) submit to the Secretary an application at such time, in such manner, and containing such information as the Secretary may require;

(2) be or include—

(A) a health professions school;

(B) a school of public health;

(C) a school of social work;

(D) a school of nursing;

(E) a school of pharmacy;

(F) an institution with a graduate medical education program; or

(G) a school of health care administration;

(3) collaborate in the development of curricula described in subsection (a) with an organization that accredits such school or institution;

(4) provide for the collection of data regarding the effectiveness of the demonstration project; and

(5) provide matching funds in accordance with subsection (c).

(c) MATCHING FUNDS.—

(1) IN GENERAL.—The Secretary may award a grant to an entity or consortium under this section only if the entity or consortium agrees to make available non-Federal contributions toward the costs of the program to be funded under the grant in an amount that is not less than $1 for each $5 of Federal funds provided under the grant.

(2) DETERMINATION OF AMOUNT CONTRIBUTED.—Non-Federal contributions under paragraph (1) may be in cash or in-kind, fairly evaluated, including equipment or services. Amounts provided by the Federal Government, or services assisted or subsidized to any significant extent by the Federal Government, may not be included in determining the amount of such contributions.

(d) EVALUATION.—The Secretary shall take such action as may be necessary to evaluate the projects funded under this section and publish, make publicly available, and disseminate the results of such evaluations on as wide a basis as is practicable.

(e) REPORTS.—Not later than 2 years after the date of enactment of this section, and annually thereafter, the Secretary shall submit to the Committee on Health, Education, Labor, and Pensions and the Committee on Finance of the Senate and the Committee on Energy and Commerce and the Committee on Ways and Means of the House of Representatives a report that—

(1) describes the specific projects supported under this section; and

(2) contains recommendations for Congress based on the evaluation conducted under subsection (d).

SEC. 3509. IMPROVING WOMEN'S HEALTH.

(a) HEALTH AND HUMAN SERVICES OFFICE ON WOMEN'S HEALTH.—

(1) ESTABLISHMENT.—Part A of title II of the Public Health Service Act (42 U.S.C. 202 et seq.) is amended by adding at the end the following:

"SEC. 229. HEALTH AND HUMAN SERVICES OFFICE ON WOMEN'S HEALTH.

"(a) ESTABLISHMENT OF OFFICE.—There is established within the Office of the Secretary, an Office on Women's Health (referred to in this section as the 'Office'). The Office shall be headed by a Deputy Assistant Secretary for Women's Health who may report to the Secretary.

"(b) DUTIES.—The Secretary, acting through the Office, with respect to the health concerns of women, shall—

"(1) establish short-range and long-range goals and objectives within the Department of Health and Human Services and, as relevant and appropriate, coordinate with other appropriate offices on activities within the Department that relate to disease prevention, health promotion, service delivery, research, and public and health care professional education, for issues of particular concern to women throughout their lifespan;

"(2) provide expert advice and consultation to the Secretary concerning scientific, legal, ethical, and policy issues relating to women's health;

"(3) monitor the Department of Health and Human Services' offices, agencies, and regional activities regarding women's health and identify needs regarding the coordination of activities, including intramural and extramural multidisciplinary activities;

"(4) establish a Department of Health and Human Services Coordinating Committee on Women's Health, which shall be chaired by the Deputy Assistant Secretary for Women's Health and composed of senior level representatives from each of the agencies and offices of the Department of Health and Human Services;

"(5) establish a National Women's Health Information Center to—

"(A) facilitate the exchange of information regarding matters relating to health information, health promotion, preventive health services, research advances, and education in the appropriate use of health care;

"(B) facilitate access to such information;

"(C) assist in the analysis of issues and problems relating to the matters described in this paragraph; and

"(D) provide technical assistance with respect to the exchange of information (including facilitating the development of materials for such technical assistance);

"(6) coordinate efforts to promote women's health programs and policies with the private sector; and

"(7) through publications and any other means appropriate, provide for the exchange of information between the Office and recipients of grants, contracts, and agreements under subsection (c), and between the Office and health professionals and the general public.

"(c) GRANTS AND CONTRACTS REGARDING DUTIES.—

"(1) AUTHORITY.—In carrying out subsection (b), the Secretary may make grants to, and enter into cooperative agreements, contracts, and interagency agreements with, public and private entities, agencies, and organizations.

"(2) EVALUATION AND DISSEMINATION.—The Secretary shall directly or through contracts with public and private entities, agencies, and organizations, provide for evaluations of projects carried out with financial assistance provided under paragraph (1) and for the dissemination of information developed as a result of such projects.

"(d) REPORTS.—Not later than 1 year after the date of enactment of this section, and every second year thereafter, the Secretary shall prepare and submit to the appropriate committees of Congress a report describing the activities carried out under this section during the period for which the report is being prepared.

"(e) AUTHORIZATION OF APPROPRIATIONS.—For the purpose of carrying out this section, there are authorized to be appropriated such sums as may be necessary for each of the fiscal years 2010 through 2014.".

(2) TRANSFER OF FUNCTIONS.—There are transferred to the Office on Women's Health (established under section 229 of the Public Health Service Act, as added by this section), all functions exercised by the Office on Women's Health of the Public Health Service prior to the date of enactment of this section, including all personnel and compensation authority, all delegation and assignment authority, and all remaining appropriations. All orders, determinations, rules, regulations, permits, agreements, grants, contracts, certificates, licenses, registrations, privileges, and other administrative actions that—

(A) have been issued, made, granted, or allowed to become effective by the President, any Federal agency or official thereof, or by a court of competent jurisdiction, in the performance of functions transferred under this paragraph; and

(B) are in effect at the time this section takes effect, or were final before the date of enactment of this section and are to become effective on or after such date,

shall continue in effect according to their terms until modified, terminated, superseded, set aside, or revoked in accordance with law by the President, the Secretary, or other authorized official, a court of competent jurisdiction, or by operation of law.

(b) CENTERS FOR DISEASE CONTROL AND PREVENTION OFFICE OF WOMEN'S HEALTH.—Part A of title III of the Public Health Service Act (42 U.S.C. 241 et seq.) is amended by adding at the end the following:

"SEC. 310A. CENTERS FOR DISEASE CONTROL AND PREVENTION OFFICE OF WOMEN'S HEALTH.

"(a) ESTABLISHMENT.—There is established within the Office of the Director of the Centers for Disease Control and Prevention, an office to be known as the Office of Women's Health (referred to in this section as the 'Office'). The Office shall be headed by a director who shall be appointed by the Director of such Centers.

"(b) PURPOSE.—The Director of the Office shall—

"(1) report to the Director of the Centers for Disease Control and Prevention on the current level of the Centers' activity regarding women's health conditions across, where appropriate, age, biological, and sociocultural contexts, in all aspects of the Centers' work, including prevention programs, public and professional education, services, and treatment;

"(2) establish short-range and long-range goals and objectives within the Centers for women's health and, as relevant and appropriate, coordinate with other appropriate offices on activities within the Centers that relate to prevention, research, education and training, service delivery, and policy development, for issues of particular concern to women;

"(3) identify projects in women's health that should be conducted or supported by the Centers;

"(4) consult with health professionals, nongovernmental organizations, consumer organizations, women's health professionals, and other individuals and groups, as appropriate, on the policy of the Centers with regard to women; and

"(5) serve as a member of the Department of Health and Human Services Coordinating Committee on Women's Health (established under section 229(b)(4)).

"(c) DEFINITION.—As used in this section, the term 'women's health conditions', with respect to women of all age, ethnic, and racial groups, means diseases, disorders, and conditions—

"(1) unique to, significantly more serious for, or significantly more prevalent in women; and

"(2) for which the factors of medical risk or type of medical intervention are different for women, or for which there is reasonable evidence that indicates that such factors or types may be different for women.

"(d) AUTHORIZATION OF APPROPRIATIONS.—For the purpose of carrying out this section, there are authorized to be appropriated such sums as may be necessary for each of the fiscal years 2010 through 2014.".

(c) OFFICE OF WOMEN'S HEALTH RESEARCH.—Section 486(a) of the Public Health Service Act (42 U.S.C. 287d(a)) is amended by inserting "and who shall report directly to the Director" before the period at the end thereof.

(d) SUBSTANCE ABUSE AND MENTAL HEALTH SERVICES ADMINISTRATION.—Section 501(f) of the Public Health Service Act (42 U.S.C. 290aa(f)) is amended—

(1) in paragraph (1), by inserting "who shall report directly to the Administrator" before the period;

(2) by redesignating paragraph (4) as paragraph (5); and

(3) by inserting after paragraph (3), the following:

"(4) OFFICE.—Nothing in this subsection shall be construed to preclude the Secretary from establishing within the Substance Abuse and Mental Health Administration an Office of Women's Health.".

(e) AGENCY FOR HEALTHCARE RESEARCH AND QUALITY ACTIVITIES REGARDING WOMEN'S HEALTH.—Part C of title IX of the Public Health Service Act (42 U.S.C. 299c et seq.) is amended—

(1) by redesignating sections 925 and 926 as sections 926 and 927, respectively; and

(2) by inserting after section 924 the following:

"SEC. 925. ACTIVITIES REGARDING WOMEN'S HEALTH.

"(a) ESTABLISHMENT.—There is established within the Office of the Director, an Office of Women's Health and Gender-Based Research (referred to in this section as the 'Office'). The Office shall be headed by a director who shall be appointed by the Director of Healthcare and Research Quality.

"(b) PURPOSE.—The official designated under subsection (a) shall—

"(1) report to the Director on the current Agency level of activity regarding women's health, across, where appropriate, age, biological, and sociocultural contexts, in all aspects of Agency work, including the development of evidence reports and clinical practice protocols and the conduct of research into patient outcomes, delivery of health care services, quality of care, and access to health care;

"(2) establish short-range and long-range goals and objectives within the Agency for research important to women's health and, as relevant and appropriate, coordinate with other appropriate offices on activities within the Agency that relate to health services and medical effectiveness research, for issues of particular concern to women;

"(3) identify projects in women's health that should be conducted or supported by the Agency;

"(4) consult with health professionals, nongovernmental organizations, consumer organizations, women's health professionals, and other individuals and groups, as appropriate, on Agency policy with regard to women; and

"(5) serve as a member of the Department of Health and Human Services Coordinating Committee on Women's Health (established under section 229(b)(4)).".

"(c) AUTHORIZATION OF APPROPRIATIONS.—For the purpose of carrying out this section, there are authorized to be appropriated such sums as may be necessary for each of the fiscal years 2010 through 2014.".

(f) HEALTH RESOURCES AND SERVICES ADMINISTRATION OFFICE OF WOMEN'S HEALTH.—Title VII of the Social Security Act (42 U.S.C. 901 et seq.) is amended by adding at the end the following:

"SEC. 713. OFFICE OF WOMEN'S HEALTH.

"(a) ESTABLISHMENT.—The Secretary shall establish within the Office of the Administrator of the Health Resources and Services Administration, an office to be known as the Office of Women's Health. The Office shall be headed by a director who shall be appointed by the Administrator.

"(b) PURPOSE.—The Director of the Office shall—

"(1) report to the Administrator on the current Administration level of activity regarding women's health across, where appropriate, age, biological, and sociocultural contexts;

"(2) establish short-range and long-range goals and objectives within the Health Resources and Services Administration for women's health and, as relevant and appropriate, coordinate with other appropriate offices on activities within the Administration that relate to health care provider training, health service delivery, research, and demonstration projects, for issues of particular concern to women;

"(3) identify projects in women's health that should be conducted or supported by the bureaus of the Administration;

"(4) consult with health professionals, nongovernmental organizations, consumer organizations, women's health professionals, and other individuals and groups, as appropriate, on Administration policy with regard to women; and

"(5) serve as a member of the Department of Health and Human Services Coordinating Committee on Women's Health (established under section 229(b)(4) of the Public Health Service Act).

"(c) CONTINUED ADMINISTRATION OF EXISTING PROGRAMS.—The Director of the Office shall assume the authority for the development, implementation, administration, and evaluation of any projects carried out through the Health Resources and Services Administration relating to women's health on the date of enactment of this section.

"(d) DEFINITIONS.—For purposes of this section:

"(1) ADMINISTRATION.—The term 'Administration' means the Health Resources and Services Administration.

"(2) ADMINISTRATOR.—The term 'Administrator' means the Administrator of the Health Resources and Services Administration.

"(3) OFFICE.—The term 'Office' means the Office of Women's Health established under this section in the Administration.

"(e) AUTHORIZATION OF APPROPRIATIONS.—For the purpose of carrying out this section, there are authorized to be appropriated such sums as may be necessary for each of the fiscal years 2010 through 2014.".

(g) FOOD AND DRUG ADMINISTRATION OFFICE OF WOMEN'S HEALTH.—Chapter X of the Federal Food, Drug, and Cosmetic Act (21 U.S.C. 391 et seq.) is amended by adding at the end the following:

"SEC. 1011. OFFICE OF WOMEN'S HEALTH.

"(a) ESTABLISHMENT.—There is established within the Office of the Commissioner, an office to be known as the Office of Women's Health (referred to in this section as the 'Office'). The Office shall be headed by a director who shall be appointed by the Commissioner of Food and Drugs.

"(b) PURPOSE.—The Director of the Office shall—

"(1) report to the Commissioner of Food and Drugs on current Food and Drug Administration (referred to in this section as the 'Administration') levels of activity regarding women's participation in clinical trials and the analysis of data by sex in the testing of drugs, medical devices, and biological products across, where appropriate, age, biological, and sociocultural contexts;

"(2) establish short-range and long-range goals and objectives within the Administration for issues of particular concern to women's health within the jurisdiction of the Administration, including, where relevant and appropriate, adequate inclusion of women and analysis of data by sex in Administration protocols and policies;

"(3) provide information to women and health care providers on those areas in which differences between men and women exist;

"(4) consult with pharmaceutical, biologics, and device manufacturers, health professionals with expertise in women's issues, consumer organizations, and women's health professionals on Administration policy with regard to women;

"(5) make annual estimates of funds needed to monitor clinical trials and analysis of data by sex in accordance with needs that are identified; and

"(6) serve as a member of the Department of Health and Human Services Coordinating Committee on Women's Health (established under section 229(b)(4) of the Public Health Service Act).

"(c) AUTHORIZATION OF APPROPRIATIONS.—For the purpose of carrying out this section, there are authorized to be appropriated such sums as may be necessary for each of the fiscal years 2010 through 2014.".

(h) NO NEW REGULATORY AUTHORITY.—Nothing in this section and the amendments made by this section may be construed as establishing regulatory authority or modifying any existing regulatory authority.

(i) LIMITATION ON TERMINATION.—Notwithstanding any other provision of law, a Federal office of women's health (including the Office of Research on Women's Health of the National Institutes of Health) or Federal appointive position with primary responsibility over women's health issues (including the Associate Administrator for Women's Services under the Substance Abuse and Mental Health Services Administration) that is in existence on the date of enactment of this section shall not be terminated, reorganized, or have any of it's powers or duties transferred unless such termination, reorganization, or transfer is approved by Congress through the adoption of a concurrent resolution of approval.

(j) RULE OF CONSTRUCTION.—Nothing in this section (or the amendments made by this section) shall be construed to limit the authority of the Secretary of Health and Human Services with respect to women's health, or with respect to activities carried out through the Department of Health and Human Services on the date of enactment of this section.

SEC. 3510. PATIENT NAVIGATOR PROGRAM.

Section 340A of the Public Health Service Act (42 U.S.C. 256a) is amended—

(1) by striking subsection (d)(3) and inserting the following:

"(3) LIMITATIONS ON GRANT PERIOD.—In carrying out this section, the Secretary shall ensure that the total period of a grant does not exceed 4 years.";

(2) in subsection (e), by adding at the end the following:

"(3) MINIMUM CORE PROFICIENCIES.—The Secretary shall not award a grant to an entity under this section unless such entity provides assurances that patient navigators recruited, assigned, trained, or employed using grant funds meet minimum core proficiencies, as defined by the entity that submits the application, that are tailored for the main focus or intervention of the navigator involved."; and

(3) in subsection (m)—

(A) in paragraph (1), by striking "and $3,500,000 for fiscal year 2010." and inserting "$3,500,000 for fiscal year 2010, and such sums as may be necessary for each of fiscal years 2011 through 2015."; and

(B) in paragraph (2), by striking "2010" and inserting "2015".

SEC. 3511. AUTHORIZATION OF APPROPRIATIONS.

Except where otherwise provided in this subtitle (or an amendment made by this subtitle), there is authorized to be appropriated such sums as may be necessary to carry out this subtitle (and such amendments made by this subtitle).

Subtitle G—Protecting and Improving Guaranteed Medicare Benefits

SEC. 3601. PROTECTING AND IMPROVING GUARANTEED MEDICARE BENEFITS.

(a) PROTECTING GUARANTEED MEDICARE BENEFITS.—Nothing in the provisions of, or amendments made by, this Act shall result in a reduction of guaranteed benefits under title XVIII of the Social Security Act.

(b) ENSURING THAT MEDICARE SAVINGS BENEFIT THE MEDICARE PROGRAM AND MEDICARE BENEFICIARIES.—Savings generated for the Medicare program under title XVIII of the Social Security Act under the provisions of, and amendments made by, this Act shall extend the solvency of the Medicare trust funds, reduce Medicare premiums and other cost-sharing for beneficiaries, and improve or expand guaranteed Medicare benefits and protect access to Medicare providers.

SEC. 3602. NO CUTS IN GUARANTEED BENEFITS.

Nothing in this Act shall result in the reduction or elimination of any benefits guaranteed by law to participants in Medicare Advantage plans.

TITLE IV—PREVENTION OF CHRONIC DISEASE AND IMPROVING PUBLIC HEALTH

Subtitle A—Modernizing Disease Prevention and Public Health Systems

SEC. 4001. NATIONAL PREVENTION, HEALTH PROMOTION AND PUBLIC HEALTH COUNCIL.

(a) ESTABLISHMENT.—The President shall establish, within the Department of Health and Human Services, a council to be known as the "National Prevention, Health Promotion and Public Health Council" (referred to in this section as the "Council").

(b) CHAIRPERSON.—The President shall appoint the Surgeon General to serve as the chairperson of the Council.

(c) COMPOSITION.—The Council shall be composed of—

(1) the Secretary of Health and Human Services;

(2) the Secretary of Agriculture;

(3) the Secretary of Education;

(4) the Chairman of the Federal Trade Commission;

(5) the Secretary of Transportation;

(6) the Secretary of Labor;

(7) the Secretary of Homeland Security;

(8) the Administrator of the Environmental Protection Agency;

(9) the Director of the Office of National Drug Control Policy;

(10) the Director of the Domestic Policy Council;

(11) the Assistant Secretary for Indian Affairs;

(12) the Chairman of the Corporation for National and Community Service; and

(13) the head of any other Federal agency that the chairperson determines is appropriate.

(d) PURPOSES AND DUTIES.—The Council shall—

(1) provide coordination and leadership at the Federal level, and among all Federal departments and agencies, with respect to prevention, wellness and health promotion practices, the public health system, and integrative health care in the United States;

(2) after obtaining input from relevant stakeholders, develop a national prevention, health promotion, public health, and integrative health care strategy that incorporates the most effective and achievable means of improving the health status of Americans and reducing the incidence of preventable illness and disability in the United States;

(3) provide recommendations to the President and Congress concerning the most pressing health issues confronting the United States and changes in Federal policy to achieve national wellness, health promotion, and public health goals, including the reduction of tobacco use, sedentary behavior, and poor nutrition;

(4) consider and propose evidence-based models, policies, and innovative approaches for the promotion of transformative models of prevention, integrative health, and public health on individual and community levels across the United States;

(5) establish processes for continual public input, including input from State, regional, and local leadership communities and other relevant stakeholders, including Indian tribes and tribal organizations;

(6) submit the reports required under subsection (g); and

(7) carry out other activities determined appropriate by the President.

(e) MEETINGS.—The Council shall meet at the call of the Chairperson.

(f) ADVISORY GROUP.—

(1) IN GENERAL.—The President shall establish an Advisory Group to the Council to be known as the "Advisory Group on Prevention, Health Promotion, and Integrative and Public Health" (hereafter referred to in this section as the "Advisory Group"). The Advisory Group shall be within the Department of Health and Human Services and report to the Surgeon General.

(2) COMPOSITION.—

(A) IN GENERAL.—The Advisory Group shall be composed of not more than 25 non-Federal members to be appointed by the President.

(B) REPRESENTATION.—In appointing members under subparagraph (A), the President shall ensure that the Advisory Group includes a diverse group of licensed health professionals, including integrative health practitioners who have expertise in—

(i) worksite health promotion;

(ii) community services, including community health centers;

(iii) preventive medicine;

(iv) health coaching;

(v) public health education;

(vi) geriatrics; and

(vii) rehabilitation medicine.

(3) PURPOSES AND DUTIES.—The Advisory Group shall develop policy and program recommendations and advise the Council on lifestyle-based chronic disease prevention and management, integrative health care practices, and health promotion.

(g) NATIONAL PREVENTION AND HEALTH PROMOTION STRATEGY.—Not later than 1 year after the date of enactment of this Act, the Chairperson, in consultation with the Council, shall develop and make public a national prevention, health promotion and public health strategy, and shall review and revise such strategy periodically. Such strategy shall—

(1) set specific goals and objectives for improving the health of the United States through federally-supported prevention, health promotion, and public health programs, consistent with ongoing goal setting efforts conducted by specific agencies;

(2) establish specific and measurable actions and timelines to carry out the strategy, and determine accountability for meeting those timelines, within and across Federal departments and agencies; and

(3) make recommendations to improve Federal efforts relating to prevention, health promotion, public health, and integrative health care practices to ensure Federal efforts are consistent with available standards and evidence.

(h) REPORT.—Not later than July 1, 2010, and annually thereafter through January 1, 2015, the Council shall submit to the President and the relevant committees of Congress, a report that—

(1) describes the activities and efforts on prevention, health promotion, and public health and activities to develop a national strategy conducted by the Council during the period for which the report is prepared;

(2) describes the national progress in meeting specific prevention, health promotion, and public health goals defined in the strategy and further describes corrective actions recommended by the Council and taken by relevant agencies and organizations to meet these goals;

(3) contains a list of national priorities on health promotion and disease prevention to address lifestyle behavior modification (smoking cessation, proper nutrition, appropriate exercise, mental health, behavioral health, substance use disorder, and domestic violence screenings) and the prevention measures for the 5 leading disease killers in the United States;

(4) contains specific science-based initiatives to achieve the measurable goals of Healthy People 2010 regarding nutrition, exercise, and smoking cessation, and targeting the 5 leading disease killers in the United States;

(5) contains specific plans for consolidating Federal health programs and Centers that exist to promote healthy behavior

and reduce disease risk (including eliminating programs and offices determined to be ineffective in meeting the priority goals of Healthy People 2010);

(6) contains specific plans to ensure that all Federal health care programs are fully coordinated with science-based prevention recommendations by the Director of the Centers for Disease Control and Prevention; and

(7) contains specific plans to ensure that all non-Department of Health and Human Services prevention programs are based on the science-based guidelines developed by the Centers for Disease Control and Prevention under paragraph (4).

(i) PERIODIC REVIEWS.—The Secretary and the Comptroller General of the United States shall jointly conduct periodic reviews, not less than every 5 years, and evaluations of every Federal disease prevention and health promotion initiative, program, and agency. Such reviews shall be evaluated based on effectiveness in meeting metrics-based goals with an analysis posted on such agencies' public Internet websites.

SEC. 4002. PREVENTION AND PUBLIC HEALTH FUND.

(a) PURPOSE.—It is the purpose of this section to establish a Prevention and Public Health Fund (referred to in this section as the "Fund"), to be administered through the Department of Health and Human Services, Office of the Secretary, to provide for expanded and sustained national investment in prevention and public health programs to improve health and help restrain the rate of growth in private and public sector health care costs.

(b) FUNDING.—There are hereby authorized to be appropriated, and appropriated, to the Fund, out of any monies in the Treasury not otherwise appropriated—

(1) for fiscal year 2010, $500,000,000;

(2) for fiscal year 2011, $750,000,000;

(3) for fiscal year 2012, $1,000,000,000;

(4) for fiscal year 2013, $1,250,000,000;

(5) for fiscal year 2014, $1,500,000,000; and

(6) for fiscal year 2015, and each fiscal year thereafter, $2,000,000,000.

(c) USE OF FUND.—The Secretary shall transfer amounts in the Fund to accounts within the Department of Health and Human Services to increase funding, over the fiscal year 2008 level, for programs authorized by the Public Health Service Act, for prevention, wellness, and public health activities including prevention research and health screenings, such as the Community Transformation grant program, the Education and Outreach Campaign for Preventive Benefits, and immunization programs.

(d) TRANSFER AUTHORITY.—The Committee on Appropriations of the Senate and the Committee on Appropriations of the House of Representatives may provide for the transfer of funds in the Fund to eligible activities under this section, subject to subsection (c).

SEC. 4003. CLINICAL AND COMMUNITY PREVENTIVE SERVICES.

(a) PREVENTIVE SERVICES TASK FORCE.—Section 915 of the Public Health Service Act (42 U.S.C. 299b–4) is amended by striking subsection (a) and inserting the following:

"(a) PREVENTIVE SERVICES TASK FORCE.—

"(1) ESTABLISHMENT AND PURPOSE.—The Director shall convene an independent Preventive Services Task Force (referred to in this subsection as the 'Task Force') to be composed of individuals with appropriate expertise. Such Task Force shall review the scientific evidence related to the effectiveness, appropriateness, and cost-effectiveness of clinical preventive services for the purpose of developing recommendations for the health care community, and updating previous clinical preventive recommendations, to be published in the Guide to Clinical Preventive Services (referred to in this section as the 'Guide'), for individuals and organizations delivering clinical services, including primary care professionals, health care systems, professional societies, employers, community organizations, non-profit organizations, Congress and other policy-makers, governmental public health agencies, health care quality organizations, and organizations developing national health objectives. Such recommendations shall consider clinical preventive best practice recommendations from the Agency for Healthcare Research and Quality, the National Institutes of Health, the Centers for Disease Control and Prevention, the Institute of Medicine, specialty medical associations, patient groups, and scientific societies.

"(2) DUTIES.—The duties of the Task Force shall include—

"(A) the development of additional topic areas for new recommendations and interventions related to those topic areas, including those related to specific sub-populations and age groups;

"(B) at least once during every 5-year period, review interventions and update recommendations related to existing topic areas, including new or improved techniques to assess the health effects of interventions;

"(C) improved integration with Federal Government health objectives and related target setting for health improvement;

"(D) the enhanced dissemination of recommendations;

"(E) the provision of technical assistance to those health care professionals, agencies and organizations that request help in implementing the Guide recommendations; and

"(F) the submission of yearly reports to Congress and related agencies identifying gaps in research, such as preventive services that receive an insufficient evidence statement, and recommending priority areas that deserve further examination, including areas related to populations and age groups not adequately addressed by current recommendations.

"(3) ROLE OF AGENCY.—The Agency shall provide ongoing administrative, research, and technical support for the operations of the Task Force, including coordinating and supporting the dissemination of the recommendations of the Task Force, ensuring adequate staff resources, and assistance to those organizations requesting it for implementation of the Guide's recommendations.

"(4) COORDINATION WITH COMMUNITY PREVENTIVE SERVICES TASK FORCE.—The Task Force shall take appropriate steps to coordinate its work with the Community Preventive Services Task Force and the Advisory Committee on Immunization Practices, including the examination of how each task force's recommendations interact at the nexus of clinic and community.

"(5) OPERATION.—Operation. In carrying out the duties under paragraph (2), the Task Force is not subject to the provisions of Appendix 2 of title 5, United States Code.

"(6) INDEPENDENCE.—All members of the Task Force convened under this subsection, and any recommendations made by such members, shall be independent and, to the extent practicable, not subject to political pressure.

"(7) AUTHORIZATION OF APPROPRIATIONS.—There are authorized to be appropriated such sums as may be necessary for each fiscal year to carry out the activities of the Task Force.".

(b) COMMUNITY PREVENTIVE SERVICES TASK FORCE.—

(1) IN GENERAL.—Part P of title III of the Public Health Service Act, as amended by paragraph (2), is amended by adding at the end the following:

"SEC. 399U. COMMUNITY PREVENTIVE SERVICES TASK FORCE.

"(a) ESTABLISHMENT AND PURPOSE.—The Director of the Centers for Disease Control and Prevention shall convene an independent Community Preventive Services Task Force (referred to in this subsection as the 'Task Force') to be composed of individuals with appropriate expertise. Such Task Force shall review the scientific evidence related to the effectiveness, appropriateness, and cost-effectiveness of community preventive interventions for the purpose of developing recommendations, to be published in the Guide to Community Preventive Services (referred to in this section as the 'Guide'), for individuals and organizations delivering population-based services, including primary care professionals, health care systems, professional societies, employers, community organizations, non-profit organizations, schools, governmental public health agencies, Indian tribes, tribal organizations and urban Indian organizations, medical groups, Congress and other policymakers. Community preventive services include any policies, programs, processes or activities designed to affect or otherwise affecting health at the population level.

"(b) DUTIES.—The duties of the Task Force shall include—

"(1) the development of additional topic areas for new recommendations and interventions related to those topic areas, including those related to specific populations and age groups, as well as the social, economic and physical environments that can have broad effects on the health and disease of populations and health disparities among sub-populations and age groups;

"(2) at least once during every 5-year period, review interventions and update recommendations related to existing topic areas, including new or improved techniques to assess the health effects of interventions, including health impact assessment and population health modeling;

"(3) improved integration with Federal Government health objectives and related target setting for health improvement;

"(4) the enhanced dissemination of recommendations;

"(5) the provision of technical assistance to those health care professionals, agencies, and organizations that request help in implementing the Guide recommendations; and

"(6) providing yearly reports to Congress and related agencies identifying gaps in research and recommending priority areas that deserve further examination, including areas related to populations and age groups not adequately addressed by current recommendations.

"(c) ROLE OF AGENCY.—The Director shall provide ongoing administrative, research, and technical support for the operations of the Task Force, including coordinating and supporting the dissemination of the recommendations of the Task Force, ensuring adequate staff resources, and assistance to those organizations requesting it for implementation of Guide recommendations.

"(d) COORDINATION WITH PREVENTIVE SERVICES TASK FORCE.—The Task Force shall take appropriate steps to coordinate its work with the U.S. Preventive Services Task Force and the Advisory Committee on Immunization Practices, including the examination of how each task force's recommendations interact at the nexus of clinic and community.

"(e) OPERATION.—In carrying out the duties under subsection (b), the Task Force shall not be subject to the provisions of Appendix 2 of title 5, United States Code.

"(f) AUTHORIZATION OF APPROPRIATIONS.—There are authorized to be appropriated such sums as may be necessary for each fiscal year to carry out the activities of the Task Force.".

(2) TECHNICAL AMENDMENTS.—

(A) Section 399R of the Public Health Service Act (as added by section 2 of the ALS Registry Act (Public Law 110–373; 122 Stat. 4047)) is redesignated as section 399S.

(B) Section 399R of such Act (as added by section 3 of the Prenatally and Postnatally Diagnosed Conditions Awareness Act (Public Law 110–374; 122 Stat. 4051)) is redesignated as section 399T.

SEC. 4004. EDUCATION AND OUTREACH CAMPAIGN REGARDING PREVENTIVE BENEFITS.

(a) IN GENERAL.—The Secretary of Health and Human Services (referred to in this section as the "Secretary") shall provide for the planning and implementation of a national public–private partnership for a prevention and health promotion outreach and education campaign to raise public awareness of health improvement across the life span. Such campaign shall include the dissemination of information that—

(1) describes the importance of utilizing preventive services to promote wellness, reduce health disparities, and mitigate chronic disease;

(2) promotes the use of preventive services recommended by the United States Preventive Services Task Force and the Community Preventive Services Task Force;

(3) encourages healthy behaviors linked to the prevention of chronic diseases;

(4) explains the preventive services covered under health plans offered through a Gateway;

(5) describes additional preventive care supported by the Centers for Disease Control and Prevention, the Health Resources and Services Administration, the Substance Abuse and Mental Health Services Administration, the Advisory Committee on Immunization Practices, and other appropriate agencies; and

(6) includes general health promotion information.

(b) CONSULTATION.—In coordinating the campaign under subsection (a), the Secretary shall consult with the Institute of Medicine to provide ongoing advice on evidence-based scientific information for policy, program development, and evaluation.

(c) MEDIA CAMPAIGN.—

(1) IN GENERAL.—Not later than 1 year after the date of enactment of this Act, the Secretary, acting through the Director of the Centers for Disease Control and Prevention, shall establish and implement a national science-based media campaign on health promotion and disease prevention.

(2) REQUIREMENT OF CAMPAIGN.—The campaign implemented under paragraph (1)—

(A) shall be designed to address proper nutrition, regular exercise, smoking cessation, obesity reduction, the 5 leading disease killers in the United States, and secondary prevention through disease screening promotion;

(B) shall be carried out through competitively bid contracts awarded to entities providing for the professional production and design of such campaign;

(C) may include the use of television, radio, Internet, and other commercial marketing venues and may be targeted to specific age groups based on peer-reviewed social research;

(D) shall not be duplicative of any other Federal efforts relating to health promotion and disease prevention; and

(E) may include the use of humor and nationally recognized positive role models.

(3) EVALUATION.—The Secretary shall ensure that the campaign implemented under paragraph (1) is subject to an independent evaluation every 2 years and shall report every 2 years to Congress on the effectiveness of such campaigns towards meeting science-based metrics.

(d) WEBSITE.—The Secretary, in consultation with private-sector experts, shall maintain or enter into a contract to maintain an Internet website to provide science-based information on guidelines for nutrition, regular exercise, obesity reduction, smoking cessation, and specific chronic disease prevention. Such website shall be designed to provide information to health care providers and consumers.

(e) DISSEMINATION OF INFORMATION THROUGH PROVIDERS.—The Secretary, acting through the Centers for Disease Control and Prevention, shall develop and implement a plan for the dissemination of health promotion and disease prevention information consistent with national priorities, to health care providers who participate in Federal programs, including programs administered by the Indian Health Service, the Department of Veterans Affairs, the Department of Defense, and the Health Resources and Services Administration, and Medicare and Medicaid.

(f) PERSONALIZED PREVENTION PLANS.—

(1) CONTRACT.—The Secretary, acting through the Director of the Centers for Disease Control and Prevention, shall enter into a contract with a qualified entity for the development and operation of a Federal Internet website personalized prevention plan tool.

(2) USE.—The website developed under paragraph (1) shall be designed to be used as a source of the most up-to-date scientific evidence relating to disease prevention for use by

individuals. Such website shall contain a component that enables an individual to determine their disease risk (based on personal health and family history, BMI, and other relevant information) relating to the 5 leading diseases in the United States, and obtain personalized suggestions for preventing such diseases.

(g) INTERNET PORTAL.—The Secretary shall establish an Internet portal for accessing risk-assessment tools developed and maintained by private and academic entities.

(h) PRIORITY FUNDING.—Funding for the activities authorized under this section shall take priority over funding provided through the Centers for Disease Control and Prevention for grants to States and other entities for similar purposes and goals as provided for in this section. Not to exceed $500,000,000 shall be expended on the campaigns and activities required under this section.

(i) PUBLIC AWARENESS OF PREVENTIVE AND OBESITY-RELATED SERVICES.—

(1) INFORMATION TO STATES.—The Secretary of Health and Human Services shall provide guidance and relevant information to States and health care providers regarding preventive and obesity-related services that are available to Medicaid enrollees, including obesity screening and counseling for children and adults.

(2) INFORMATION TO ENROLLEES.—Each State shall design a public awareness campaign to educate Medicaid enrollees regarding availability and coverage of such services, with the goal of reducing incidences of obesity.

(3) REPORT.—Not later than January 1, 2011, and every 3 years thereafter through January 1, 2017, the Secretary of Health and Human Services shall report to Congress on the status and effectiveness of efforts under paragraphs (1) and (2), including summaries of the States' efforts to increase awareness of coverage of obesity-related services.

(j) AUTHORIZATION OF APPROPRIATIONS.—There are authorized to be appropriated such sums as may be necessary to carry out this section.

Subtitle B—Increasing Access to Clinical Preventive Services

SEC. 4101. SCHOOL-BASED HEALTH CENTERS.

(a) GRANTS FOR THE ESTABLISHMENT OF SCHOOL-BASED HEALTH CENTERS.—

(1) PROGRAM.—The Secretary of Health and Human Services (in this subsection referred to as the "Secretary") shall establish a program to award grants to eligible entities to support the operation of school-based health centers.

(2) ELIGIBILITY.—To be eligible for a grant under this subsection, an entity shall—

(A) be a school-based health center or a sponsoring facility of a school-based health center; and

(B) submit an application at such time, in such manner, and containing such information as the Secretary may require, including at a minimum an assurance that funds awarded under the grant shall not be used to provide any service that is not authorized or allowed by Federal, State, or local law.

(3) PREFERENCE.—In awarding grants under this section, the Secretary shall give preference to awarding grants for school-based health centers that serve a large population of children eligible for medical assistance under the State Medicaid plan under title XIX of the Social Security Act or under a waiver of such plan or children eligible for child health assistance under the State child health plan under title XXI of that Act (42 U.S.C. 1397aa et seq.).

(4) LIMITATION ON USE OF FUNDS.—An eligible entity shall use funds provided under a grant awarded under this subsection only for expenditures for facilities (including the acquisition or improvement of land, or the acquisition, construction, expansion, replacement, or other improvement of any building or other facility), equipment, or similar expenditures, as specified by the Secretary. No funds provided under a grant awarded under this section shall be used for expenditures for personnel or to provide health services.

(5) APPROPRIATIONS.—Out of any funds in the Treasury not otherwise appropriated, there is appropriated for each of fiscal years 2010 through 2013, $50,000,000 for the purpose of carrying out this subsection. Funds appropriated under this paragraph shall remain available until expended.

(6) DEFINITIONS.—In this subsection, the terms "school-based health center" and "sponsoring facility" have the meanings given those terms in section 2110(c)(9) of the Social Security Act (42 U.S.C. 1397jj(c)(9)).

(b) GRANTS FOR THE OPERATION OF SCHOOL-BASED HEALTH CENTERS.—Part Q of title III of the Public Health Service Act (42 U.S.C. 280h et seq.) is amended by adding at the end the following:

"SEC. 399Z–1. SCHOOL-BASED HEALTH CENTERS.

"(a) DEFINITIONS; ESTABLISHMENT OF CRITERIA.—In this section:

"(1) COMPREHENSIVE PRIMARY HEALTH SERVICES.—The term 'comprehensive primary health services' means the core services offered by school-based health centers, which shall include the following:

"(A) PHYSICAL.—Comprehensive health assessments, diagnosis, and treatment of minor, acute, and chronic medical conditions, and referrals to, and follow-up for, specialty care and oral health services.

"(B) MENTAL HEALTH.—Mental health and substance use disorder assessments, crisis intervention, counseling, treatment, and referral to a continuum of services including emergency psychiatric care, community support programs, inpatient care, and outpatient programs.

"(2) MEDICALLY UNDERSERVED CHILDREN AND ADOLESCENTS.—

"(A) IN GENERAL.—The term 'medically underserved children and adolescents' means a population of children and adolescents who are residents of an area designated as a medically underserved area or a health professional shortage area by the Secretary.

"(B) CRITERIA.—The Secretary shall prescribe criteria for determining the specific shortages of personal health services for medically underserved children and adolescents under subparagraph (A) that shall—

"(i) take into account any comments received by the Secretary from the chief executive officer of a State and local officials in a State; and

"(ii) include factors indicative of the health status of such children and adolescents of an area, including the ability of the residents of such area to pay for health services, the accessibility of such services, the availability of health professionals to such children and adolescents, and other factors as determined appropriate by the Secretary.

"(3) SCHOOL-BASED HEALTH CENTER.—The term 'school-based health center' means a health clinic that—

"(A) meets the definition of a school-based health center under section 2110(c)(9)(A) of the Social Security Act and is administered by a sponsoring facility (as defined in section 2110(c)(9)(B) of the Social Security Act);

"(B) provides, at a minimum, comprehensive primary health services during school hours to children and adolescents by health professionals in accordance with established standards, community practice, reporting laws, and other State laws, including parental consent and notification laws that are not inconsistent with Federal law; and

"(C) does not perform abortion services.

"(b) AUTHORITY TO AWARD GRANTS.—The Secretary shall award grants for the costs of the operation of school-based health centers (referred to in this section as 'SBHCs') that meet the requirements of this section.

"(c) APPLICATIONS.—To be eligible to receive a grant under this section, an entity shall—

"(1) be an SBHC (as defined in subsection (a)(3)); and

"(2) submit to the Secretary an application at such time, in such manner, and containing—

"(A) evidence that the applicant meets all criteria necessary to be designated an SBHC;

"(B) evidence of local need for the services to be provided by the SBHC;

"(C) an assurance that—

"(i) SBHC services will be provided to those children and adolescents for whom parental or guardian consent has been obtained in cooperation with Federal, State, and local laws governing health care service provision to children and adolescents;

"(ii) the SBHC has made and will continue to make every reasonable effort to establish and maintain collaborative relationships with other health care providers in the catchment area of the SBHC;

"(iii) the SBHC will provide on-site access during the academic day when school is in session and 24-hour coverage through an on-call system and through its backup health providers to ensure access to services on a year-round basis when the school or the SBHC is closed;

"(iv) the SBHC will be integrated into the school environment and will coordinate health services with school personnel, such as administrators, teachers, nurses, counselors, and support personnel, as well as with other community providers co-located at the school;

"(v) the SBHC sponsoring facility assumes all responsibility for the SBHC administration, operations, and oversight; and

"(vi) the SBHC will comply with Federal, State, and local laws concerning patient privacy and student records, including regulations promulgated under the Health Insurance Portability and Accountability Act of 1996 and section 444 of the General Education Provisions Act; and

"(D) such other information as the Secretary may require.

"(d) PREFERENCES AND CONSIDERATION.—In reviewing applications:

"(1) The Secretary may give preference to applicants who demonstrate an ability to serve the following:

"(A) Communities that have evidenced barriers to primary health care and mental health and substance use disorder prevention services for children and adolescents.

"(B) Communities with high per capita numbers of children and adolescents who are uninsured, underinsured, or enrolled in public health insurance programs.

"(C) Populations of children and adolescents that have historically demonstrated difficulty in accessing health and mental health and substance use disorder prevention services.

"(2) The Secretary may give consideration to whether an applicant has received a grant under subsection (a) of section 4101 of the Patient Protection and Affordable Care Act.

"(e) WAIVER OF REQUIREMENTS.—The Secretary may—

"(1) under appropriate circumstances, waive the application of all or part of the requirements of this subsection with respect to an SBHC for not to exceed 2 years; and

"(2) upon a showing of good cause, waive the requirement that the SBHC provide all required comprehensive primary health services for a designated period of time to be determined by the Secretary.

"(f) USE OF FUNDS.—

"(1) FUNDS.—Funds awarded under a grant under this section—

"(A) may be used for—

"(i) acquiring and leasing equipment (including the costs of amortizing the principle of, and paying interest on, loans for such equipment);

"(ii) providing training related to the provision of required comprehensive primary health services and additional health services;

"(iii) the management and operation of health center programs;

"(iv) the payment of salaries for physicians, nurses, and other personnel of the SBHC; and

"(B) may not be used to provide abortions.

"(2) CONSTRUCTION.—The Secretary may award grants which may be used to pay the costs associated with expanding and modernizing existing buildings for use as an SBHC, including the purchase of trailers or manufactured buildings to install on the school property.

"(3) LIMITATIONS.—

"(A) IN GENERAL.—Any provider of services that is determined by a State to be in violation of a State law described in subsection (a)(3)(B) with respect to activities carried out at a SBHC shall not be eligible to receive additional funding under this section.

"(B) NO OVERLAPPING GRANT PERIOD.—No entity that has received funding under section 330 for a grant period shall be eligible for a grant under this section for with respect to the same grant period.

"(g) MATCHING REQUIREMENT.—

"(1) IN GENERAL.—Each eligible entity that receives a grant under this section shall provide, from non-Federal sources, an amount equal to 20 percent of the amount of the grant (which may be provided in cash or in-kind) to carry out the activities supported by the grant.

"(2) WAIVER.—The Secretary may waive all or part of the matching requirement described in paragraph (1) for any fiscal year for the SBHC if the Secretary determines that applying the matching requirement to the SBHC would result in serious hardship or an inability to carry out the purposes of this section.

"(h) SUPPLEMENT, NOT SUPPLANT.—Grant funds provided under this section shall be used to supplement, not supplant, other Federal or State funds.

"(i) EVALUATION.—The Secretary shall develop and implement a plan for evaluating SBHCs and monitoring quality performance under the awards made under this section.

"(j) AGE APPROPRIATE SERVICES.—An eligible entity receiving funds under this section shall only provide age appropriate services through a SBHC funded under this section to an individual.

"(k) PARENTAL CONSENT.—An eligible entity receiving funds under this section shall not provide services through a SBHC funded under this section to an individual without the consent of the parent or guardian of such individual if such individual is considered a minor under applicable State law.

"(l) AUTHORIZATION OF APPROPRIATIONS.—For purposes of carrying out this section, there are authorized to be appropriated such sums as may be necessary for each of the fiscal years 2010 through 2014.".

SEC. 4102. ORAL HEALTHCARE PREVENTION ACTIVITIES.

(a) IN GENERAL.—Title III of the Public Health Service Act (42 U.S.C. 241 et seq.), as amended by section 3025, is amended by adding at the end the following:

"PART T—ORAL HEALTHCARE PREVENTION ACTIVITIES

"SEC. 399LL. ORAL HEALTHCARE PREVENTION EDUCATION CAMPAIGN.

"(a) ESTABLISHMENT.—The Secretary, acting through the Director of the Centers for Disease Control and Prevention and in consultation with professional oral health organizations, shall, subject to the availability of appropriations, establish a 5-year national, public education campaign (referred to in this section as the 'campaign') that is focused on oral healthcare prevention and education, including prevention of oral disease such as early childhood and other caries, periodontal disease, and oral cancer.

"(b) REQUIREMENTS.—In establishing the campaign, the Secretary shall—

"(1) ensure that activities are targeted towards specific populations such as children, pregnant women, parents, the elderly, individuals with disabilities, and ethnic and racial minority populations, including Indians, Alaska Natives and Native Hawaiians (as defined in section 4(c) of the Indian Health Care Improvement Act) in a culturally and linguistically appropriate manner; and

"(2) utilize science-based strategies to convey oral health prevention messages that include, but are not limited to, community water fluoridation and dental sealants.

"(c) PLANNING AND IMPLEMENTATION.—Not later than 2 years after the date of enactment of this section, the Secretary shall begin implementing the 5-year campaign. During the 2-year period referred to in the previous sentence, the Secretary shall conduct planning activities with respect to the campaign.

"SEC. 399LL–1. RESEARCH-BASED DENTAL CARIES DISEASE MANAGEMENT.

"(a) IN GENERAL.—The Secretary, acting through the Director of the Centers for Disease Control and Prevention, shall award demonstration grants to eligible entities to demonstrate the effectiveness of research-based dental caries disease management activities.

"(b) ELIGIBILITY.—To be eligible for a grant under this section, an entity shall—

"(1) be a community-based provider of dental services (as defined by the Secretary), including a Federally-qualified health center, a clinic of a hospital owned or operated by a State (or by an instrumentality or a unit of government within a State), a State or local department of health, a dental program of the Indian Health Service, an Indian tribe or tribal organization, or an urban Indian organization (as such terms are defined in section 4 of the Indian Health Care Improvement Act), a health system provider, a private provider of dental services, medical, dental, public health, nursing, nutrition educational institutions, or national organizations involved in improving children's oral health; and

"(2) submit to the Secretary an application at such time, in such manner, and containing such information as the Secretary may require.

"(c) USE OF FUNDS.—A grantee shall use amounts received under a grant under this section to demonstrate the effectiveness of research-based dental caries disease management activities.

"(d) USE OF INFORMATION.—The Secretary shall utilize information generated from grantees under this section in planning and implementing the public education campaign under section 399LL.

"SEC. 399LL–2. AUTHORIZATION OF APPROPRIATIONS.

"There is authorized to be appropriated to carry out this part, such sums as may be necessary.".

(b) SCHOOL-BASED SEALANT PROGRAMS.—Section 317M(c)(1) of the Public Health Service Act (42 U.S.C. 247b–14(c)(1)) is amended by striking "may award grants to States and Indian tribes" and inserting "shall award a grant to each of the 50 States and territories and to Indians, Indian tribes, tribal organizations and urban Indian organizations (as such terms are defined in section 4 of the Indian Health Care Improvement Act)".

(c) ORAL HEALTH INFRASTRUCTURE.—Section 317M of the Public Health Service Act (42 U.S.C. 247b–14) is amended—

(1) by redesignating subsections (d) and (e) as subsections (e) and (f), respectively; and

(2) by inserting after subsection (c), the following:

"(d) ORAL HEALTH INFRASTRUCTURE.—

"(1) COOPERATIVE AGREEMENTS.—The Secretary, acting through the Director of the Centers for Disease Control and Prevention, shall enter into cooperative agreements with State, territorial, and Indian tribes or tribal organizations (as those terms are defined in section 4 of the Indian Health Care Improvement Act) to establish oral health leadership and program guidance, oral health data collection and interpretation, (including determinants of poor oral health among vulnerable populations), a multi-dimensional delivery system for oral health, and to implement science-based programs (including dental sealants and community water fluoridation) to improve oral health.

"(2) AUTHORIZATION OF APPROPRIATIONS.—There is authorized to be appropriated such sums as necessary to carry out this subsection for fiscal years 2010 through 2014.".

(d) UPDATING NATIONAL ORAL HEALTHCARE SURVEILLANCE ACTIVITIES.—

(1) PRAMS.—

(A) IN GENERAL.—The Secretary of Health and Human Services (referred to in this subsection as the "Secretary") shall carry out activities to update and improve the Pregnancy Risk Assessment Monitoring System (referred to in this section as "PRAMS") as it relates to oral healthcare.

(B) STATE REPORTS AND MANDATORY MEASUREMENTS.—

(i) IN GENERAL.—Not later than 5 years after the date of enactment of this Act, and every 5 years thereafter, a State shall submit to the Secretary a report concerning activities conducted within the State under PRAMS.

(ii) MEASUREMENTS.—The oral healthcare measurements developed by the Secretary for use under PRAMS shall be mandatory with respect to States for purposes of the State reports under clause (i).

(C) FUNDING.—There is authorized to be appropriated to carry out this paragraph, such sums as may be necessary.

(2) NATIONAL HEALTH AND NUTRITION EXAMINATION SURVEY.—The Secretary shall develop oral healthcare components that shall include tooth-level surveillance for inclusion in the National Health and Nutrition Examination Survey. Such components shall be updated by the Secretary at least every 6 years. For purposes of this paragraph, the term "tooth-level surveillance" means a clinical examination where an examiner looks at each dental surface, on each tooth in the mouth and as expanded by the Division of Oral Health of the Centers for Disease Control and Prevention.

(3) MEDICAL EXPENDITURES PANEL SURVEY.—The Secretary shall ensure that the Medical Expenditures Panel Survey by the Agency for Healthcare Research and Quality includes the verification of dental utilization, expenditure, and coverage findings through conduct of a look-back analysis.

(4) NATIONAL ORAL HEALTH SURVEILLANCE SYSTEM.—

(A) APPROPRIATIONS.—There is authorized to be appropriated, such sums as may be necessary for each of fiscal years 2010 through 2014 to increase the participation of States in the National Oral Health Surveillance System from 16 States to all 50 States, territories, and District of Columbia.

(B) REQUIREMENTS.—The Secretary shall ensure that the National Oral Health Surveillance System include the measurement of early childhood caries.

SEC. 4103. MEDICARE COVERAGE OF ANNUAL WELLNESS VISIT PROVIDING A PERSONALIZED PREVENTION PLAN.

(a) COVERAGE OF PERSONALIZED PREVENTION PLAN SERVICES.—

(1) IN GENERAL.—Section 1861(s)(2) of the Social Security Act (42 U.S.C. 1395x(s)(2)) is amended—

(A) in subparagraph (DD), by striking "and" at the end;

(B) in subparagraph (EE), by adding "and" at the end; and

(C) by adding at the end the following new subparagraph:

"(FF) personalized prevention plan services (as defined in subsection (hhh));".

(2) CONFORMING AMENDMENTS.—Clauses (i) and (ii) of section 1861(s)(2)(K) of the Social Security Act (42 U.S.C. 1395x(s)(2)(K)) are each amended by striking "subsection (ww)(1)" and inserting "subsections (ww)(1) and (hhh)".

(b) PERSONALIZED PREVENTION PLAN SERVICES DEFINED.—Section 1861 of the Social Security Act (42 U.S.C. 1395x) is amended by adding at the end the following new subsection:

"Annual Wellness Visit

"(hhh)(1) The term 'personalized prevention plan services' means the creation of a plan for an individual—

"(A) that includes a health risk assessment (that meets the guidelines established by the Secretary under paragraph (4)(A)) of the individual that is completed prior to or as part of the same visit with a health professional described in paragraph (3); and

"(B) that—

"(i) takes into account the results of the health risk assessment; and

"(ii) may contain the elements described in paragraph (2).

"(2) Subject to paragraph (4)(H), the elements described in this paragraph are the following:

"(A) The establishment of, or an update to, the individual's medical and family history.

"(B) A list of current providers and suppliers that are regularly involved in providing medical care to the individual (including a list of all prescribed medications).

"(C) A measurement of height, weight, body mass index (or waist circumference, if appropriate), blood pressure, and other routine measurements.

"(D) Detection of any cognitive impairment.

"(E) The establishment of, or an update to, the following:

"(i) A screening schedule for the next 5 to 10 years, as appropriate, based on recommendations of the United States Preventive Services Task Force and the Advisory Committee on Immunization Practices, and the individual's health status, screening history, and age-appropriate preventive services covered under this title.

"(ii) A list of risk factors and conditions for which primary, secondary, or tertiary prevention interventions are recommended or are underway, including any mental health conditions or any such risk factors or conditions that have been identified through an initial preventive physical examination (as described under subsection (ww)(1)), and a list of treatment options and their associated risks and benefits.

"(F) The furnishing of personalized health advice and a referral, as appropriate, to health education or preventive counseling services or programs aimed at reducing identified risk factors and improving self-management, or community-based lifestyle interventions to reduce health risks and promote self-management and wellness, including weight loss, physical activity, smoking cessation, fall prevention, and nutrition.

"(G) Any other element determined appropriate by the Secretary.

"(3) A health professional described in this paragraph is—

"(A) a physician;

"(B) a practitioner described in clause (i) of section 1842(b)(18)(C); or

"(C) a medical professional (including a health educator, registered dietitian, or nutrition professional) or a team of medical professionals, as determined appropriate by the Secretary, under the supervision of a physician.

"(4)(A) For purposes of paragraph (1)(A), the Secretary, not later than 1 year after the date of enactment of this subsection, shall establish publicly available guidelines for health risk assessments. Such guidelines shall be developed in consultation with relevant groups and entities and shall provide that a health risk assessment—

"(i) identify chronic diseases, injury risks, modifiable risk factors, and urgent health needs of the individual; and

"(ii) may be furnished—

"(I) through an interactive telephonic or web-based program that meets the standards established under subparagraph (B);

"(II) during an encounter with a health care professional;

"(III) through community-based prevention programs; or

"(IV) through any other means the Secretary determines appropriate to maximize accessibility and ease of use by beneficiaries, while ensuring the privacy of such beneficiaries.

"(B) Not later than 1 year after the date of enactment of this subsection, the Secretary shall establish standards for interactive telephonic or web-based programs used to furnish health risk assessments under subparagraph (A)(ii)(I). The Secretary may utilize any health risk assessment developed under section 4004(f) of the Patient Protection and Affordable Care Act as part of the requirement to develop a personalized prevention plan to comply with this subparagraph.

"(C)(i) Not later than 18 months after the date of enactment of this subsection, the Secretary shall develop and make available to the public a health risk assessment model. Such model shall meet the guidelines under subparagraph (A) and may be used to meet the requirement under paragraph (1)(A).

"(ii) Any health risk assessment that meets the guidelines under subparagraph (A) and is approved by the Secretary may be used to meet the requirement under paragraph (1)(A).

"(D) The Secretary may coordinate with community-based entities (including State Health Insurance Programs, Area Agencies on Aging, Aging and Disability Resource Centers, and the Administration on Aging) to—

"(i) ensure that health risk assessments are accessible to beneficiaries; and

"(ii) provide appropriate support for the completion of health risk assessments by beneficiaries.

"(E) The Secretary shall establish procedures to make beneficiaries and providers aware of the requirement that a beneficiary complete a health risk assessment prior to or at the same time as receiving personalized prevention plan services.

"(F) To the extent practicable, the Secretary shall encourage the use of, integration with, and coordination of health information technology (including use of technology that is compatible with electronic medical records and personal health records) and may experiment with the use of personalized technology to aid in the development of self-management skills and management of and adherence to provider recommendations in order to improve the health status of beneficiaries.

"(G)(i) A beneficiary shall only be eligible to receive an initial preventive physical examination (as defined under subsection (ww)(1)) at any time during the 12-month period after the date that the beneficiary's coverage begins under part B and shall be eligible to receive personalized prevention plan services under this subsection provided that the beneficiary has not received such services within the preceding 12-month period.

"(ii) The Secretary shall establish procedures to make beneficiaries aware of the option to select an initial preventive physical examination or personalized prevention plan services during the period of 12 months after the date that a beneficiary's coverage begins under part B, which shall include information regarding any relevant differences between such services.

"(H) The Secretary shall issue guidance that—

"(i) identifies elements under paragraph (2) that are required to be provided to a beneficiary as part of their first visit for personalized prevention plan services; and

"(ii) establishes a yearly schedule for appropriate provision of such elements thereafter.".

(c) PAYMENT AND ELIMINATION OF COST-SHARING.—

(1) PAYMENT AND ELIMINATION OF COINSURANCE.—Section 1833(a)(1) of the Social Security Act (42 U.S.C. 1395l(a)(1)) is amended—

(A) in subparagraph (N), by inserting "other than personalized prevention plan services (as defined in section 1861(hhh)(1))" after "(as defined in section 1848(j)(3))";

(B) by striking "and" before "(W)"; and

(C) by inserting before the semicolon at the end the following: ", and (X) with respect to personalized prevention plan services (as defined in section 1861(hhh)(1)), the amount paid shall be 100 percent of the lesser of the actual charge for the services or the amount determined under the payment basis determined under section 1848".

(2) PAYMENT UNDER PHYSICIAN FEE SCHEDULE.—Section 1848(j)(3) of the Social Security Act (42 U.S.C. 1395w–4(j)(3)) is amended by inserting "(2)(FF) (including administration of the health risk assessment) ," after "(2)(EE),".

(3) ELIMINATION OF COINSURANCE IN OUTPATIENT HOSPITAL SETTINGS.—

(A) EXCLUSION FROM OPD FEE SCHEDULE.—Section 1833(t)(1)(B)(iv) of the Social Security Act (42 U.S.C. 1395l(t)(1)(B)(iv)) is amended by striking "and diagnostic mammography" and inserting ", diagnostic mammography, or personalized prevention plan services (as defined in section 1861(hhh)(1))".

(B) CONFORMING AMENDMENTS.—Section 1833(a)(2) of the Social Security Act (42 U.S.C. 1395l(a)(2)) is amended—

(i) in subparagraph (F), by striking "and" at the end;

(ii) in subparagraph (G)(ii), by striking the comma at the end and inserting "; and"; and

(iii) by inserting after subparagraph (G)(ii) the following new subparagraph:

"(H) with respect to personalized prevention plan services (as defined in section 1861(hhh)(1)) furnished by an outpatient department of a hospital, the amount determined under paragraph (1)(X),".

(4) WAIVER OF APPLICATION OF DEDUCTIBLE.—The first sentence of section 1833(b) of the Social Security Act (42 U.S.C. 1395l(b)) is amended—

(A) by striking "and" before "(9)"; and

(B) by inserting before the period the following: ", and (10) such deductible shall not apply with respect to personalized prevention plan services (as defined in section 1861(hhh)(1))".

(d) FREQUENCY LIMITATION.—Section 1862(a) of the Social Security Act (42 U.S.C. 1395y(a)) is amended—

(1) in paragraph (1)—

(A) in subparagraph (N), by striking "and" at the end;

(B) in subparagraph (O), by striking the semicolon at the end and inserting ", and"; and

(C) by adding at the end the following new subparagraph:

"(P) in the case of personalized prevention plan services (as defined in section 1861(hhh)(1)), which are performed more frequently than is covered under such section;"; and

(2) in paragraph (7), by striking "or (K)" and inserting "(K), or (P)".

(e) EFFECTIVE DATE.—The amendments made by this section shall apply to services furnished on or after January 1, 2011.

SEC. 4104. REMOVAL OF BARRIERS TO PREVENTIVE SERVICES IN MEDICARE.

(a) DEFINITION OF PREVENTIVE SERVICES.—Section 1861(ddd) of the Social Security Act (42 U.S.C. 1395x(ddd)) is amended—

(1) in the heading, by inserting "; Preventive Services" after "Services";

(2) in paragraph (1), by striking "not otherwise described in this title" and inserting "not described in subparagraph (A) or (C) of paragraph (3)"; and

(3) by adding at the end the following new paragraph:

"(3) The term 'preventive services' means the following:

"(A) The screening and preventive services described in subsection (ww)(2) (other than the service described in subparagraph (M) of such subsection).

"(B) An initial preventive physical examination (as defined in subsection (ww)).

"(C) Personalized prevention plan services (as defined in subsection (hhh)(1)).".

(b) COINSURANCE.—

(1) GENERAL APPLICATION.—

(A) IN GENERAL.—Section 1833(a)(1) of the Social Security Act (42 U.S.C. 1395l(a)(1)), as amended by section 4103(c)(1), is amended—

(i) in subparagraph (T), by inserting "(or 100 percent if such services are recommended with a grade of A or B by the United States Preventive Services Task Force for any indication or population and are appropriate for the individual)" after "80 percent";

(ii) in subparagraph (W)—

(I) in clause (i), by inserting "(if such subparagraph were applied, by substituting '100 percent' for '80 percent')" after "subparagraph (D)"; and

(II) in clause (ii), by striking "80 percent" and inserting "100 percent";

(iii) by striking "and" before "(X)"; and

(iv) by inserting before the semicolon at the end the following: ", and (Y) with respect to preventive services described in subparagraphs (A) and (B) of section 1861(ddd)(3) that are appropriate for the individual and, in the case of such services described in subparagraph (A), are recommended with a grade of A or B by the United States Preventive Services Task Force for any indication or population, the amount paid shall be 100 percent of the lesser of the actual charge for the services or the amount determined under the fee schedule that applies to such services under this part".

(2) ELIMINATION OF COINSURANCE IN OUTPATIENT HOSPITAL SETTINGS.—

(A) EXCLUSION FROM OPD FEE SCHEDULE.—Section 1833(t)(1)(B)(iv) of the Social Security Act (42 U.S.C.

1395l(t)(1)(B)(iv)), as amended by section 4103(c)(3)(A), is amended—

(i) by striking "or" before "personalized prevention plan services"; and

(ii) by inserting before the period the following: ", or preventive services described in subparagraphs (A) and (B) of section 1861(ddd)(3) that are appropriate for the individual and, in the case of such services described in subparagraph (A), are recommended with a grade of A or B by the United States Preventive Services Task Force for any indication or population".

(B) CONFORMING AMENDMENTS.—Section 1833(a)(2) of the Social Security Act (42 U.S.C. 1395l(a)(2)), as amended by section 4103(c)(3)(B), is amended—

(i) in subparagraph (G)(ii), by striking "and" after the semicolon at the end;

(ii) in subparagraph (H), by striking the comma at the end and inserting "; and"; and

(iii) by inserting after subparagraph (H) the following new subparagraph:

"(I) with respect to preventive services described in subparagraphs (A) and (B) of section 1861(ddd)(3) that are appropriate for the individual and are furnished by an outpatient department of a hospital and, in the case of such services described in subparagraph (A), are recommended with a grade of A or B by the United States Preventive Services Task Force for any indication or population, the amount determined under paragraph (1)(W) or (1)(Y),".

(c) WAIVER OF APPLICATION OF DEDUCTIBLE FOR PREVENTIVE SERVICES AND COLORECTAL CANCER SCREENING TESTS.—Section 1833(b) of the Social Security Act (42 U.S.C. 1395l(b)), as amended by section 4103(c)(4), is amended—

(1) in paragraph (1), by striking "items and services described in section 1861(s)(10)(A)" and inserting "preventive services described in subparagraph (A) of section 1861(ddd)(3) that are recommended with a grade of A or B by the United States Preventive Services Task Force for any indication or population and are appropriate for the individual."; and

(2) by adding at the end the following new sentence: "Paragraph (1) of the first sentence of this subsection shall apply with respect to a colorectal cancer screening test regardless of the code that is billed for the establishment of a diagnosis as a result of the test, or for the removal of tissue or other matter or other procedure that is furnished in connection with, as a result of, and in the same clinical encounter as the screening test.".

(d) EFFECTIVE DATE.—The amendments made by this section shall apply to items and services furnished on or after January 1, 2011.

SEC. 4105. EVIDENCE-BASED COVERAGE OF PREVENTIVE SERVICES IN MEDICARE.

(a) AUTHORITY TO MODIFY OR ELIMINATE COVERAGE OF CERTAIN PREVENTIVE SERVICES.—Section 1834 of the Social Security Act (42 U.S.C. 1395m) is amended by adding at the end the following new subsection:

"(n) AUTHORITY TO MODIFY OR ELIMINATE COVERAGE OF CERTAIN PREVENTIVE SERVICES.—Notwithstanding any other provision of this title, effective beginning on January 1, 2010, if the Secretary determines appropriate, the Secretary may—

"(1) modify—

"(A) the coverage of any preventive service described in subparagraph (A) of section 1861(ddd)(3) to the extent that such modification is consistent with the recommendations of the United States Preventive Services Task Force; and

"(B) the services included in the initial preventive physical examination described in subparagraph (B) of such section; and

"(2) provide that no payment shall be made under this title for a preventive service described in subparagraph (A) of such section that has not received a grade of A, B, C, or I by such Task Force.".

(b) CONSTRUCTION.—Nothing in the amendment made by paragraph (1) shall be construed to affect the coverage of diagnostic or treatment services under title XVIII of the Social Security Act.

SEC. 4106. IMPROVING ACCESS TO PREVENTIVE SERVICES FOR ELIGIBLE ADULTS IN MEDICAID.

(a) CLARIFICATION OF INCLUSION OF SERVICES.—Section 1905(a)(13) of the Social Security Act (42 U.S.C. 1396d(a)(13)) is amended to read as follows:

"(13) other diagnostic, screening, preventive, and rehabilitative services, including—

"(A) any clinical preventive services that are assigned a grade of A or B by the United States Preventive Services Task Force;

"(B) with respect to an adult individual, approved vaccines recommended by the Advisory Committee on Immunization Practices (an advisory committee established by the Secretary, acting through the Director of the Centers for Disease Control and Prevention) and their administration; and

"(C) any medical or remedial services (provided in a facility, a home, or other setting) recommended by a physician or other licensed practitioner of the healing arts within the scope of their practice under State law, for the maximum reduction of physical or mental disability and restoration of an individual to the best possible functional level;".

(b) INCREASED FMAP.—Section 1905(b) of the Social Security Act (42 U.S.C. 1396d(b)), as amended by sections 2001(a)(3)(A) and 2004(c)(1), is amended in the first sentence—

(1) by striking ", and (4)" and inserting ", (4)"; and

(2) by inserting before the period the following: ", and (5) in the case of a State that provides medical assistance for services and vaccines described in subparagraphs (A) and (B) of subsection (a)(13), and prohibits cost-sharing for such services and vaccines, the Federal medical assistance percentage, as determined under this subsection and subsection (y) (without regard to paragraph (1)(C) of such subsection), shall be increased by 1 percentage point with respect to medical

assistance for such services and vaccines and for items and services described in subsection (a)(4)(D)”.

(c) EFFECTIVE DATE.—The amendments made under this section shall take effect on January 1, 2013.

SEC. 4107. COVERAGE OF COMPREHENSIVE TOBACCO CESSATION SERVICES FOR PREGNANT WOMEN IN MEDICAID.

(a) REQUIRING COVERAGE OF COUNSELING AND PHARMACOTHERAPY FOR CESSATION OF TOBACCO USE BY PREGNANT WOMEN.—Section 1905 of the Social Security Act (42 U.S.C. 1396d), as amended by sections 2001(a)(3)(B) and 2303, is further amended—

(1) in subsection (a)(4)—

(A) by striking “and” before “(C)”; and

(B) by inserting before the semicolon at the end the following new subparagraph: “; and (D) counseling and pharmacotherapy for cessation of tobacco use by pregnant women (as defined in subsection (bb))”; and

(2) by adding at the end the following:

“(bb)(1) For purposes of this title, the term ‘counseling and pharmacotherapy for cessation of tobacco use by pregnant women’ means diagnostic, therapy, and counseling services and pharmacotherapy (including the coverage of prescription and non-prescription tobacco cessation agents approved by the Food and Drug Administration) for cessation of tobacco use by pregnant women who use tobacco products or who are being treated for tobacco use that is furnished—

“(A) by or under the supervision of a physician; or

“(B) by any other health care professional who—

“(i) is legally authorized to furnish such services under State law (or the State regulatory mechanism provided by State law) of the State in which the services are furnished; and

“(ii) is authorized to receive payment for other services under this title or is designated by the Secretary for this purpose.

“(2) Subject to paragraph (3), such term is limited to—

“(A) services recommended with respect to pregnant women in ‘Treating Tobacco Use and Dependence: 2008 Update: A Clinical Practice Guideline’, published by the Public Health Service in May 2008, or any subsequent modification of such Guideline; and

“(B) such other services that the Secretary recognizes to be effective for cessation of tobacco use by pregnant women.

“(3) Such term shall not include coverage for drugs or biologicals that are not otherwise covered under this title.”.

(b) EXCEPTION FROM OPTIONAL RESTRICTION UNDER MEDICAID PRESCRIPTION DRUG COVERAGE.—Section 1927(d)(2)(F) of the Social Security Act (42 U.S.C. 1396r–8(d)(2)(F)), as redesignated by section 2502(a), is amended by inserting before the period at the end the following: “, except, in the case of pregnant women when recommended in accordance with the Guideline referred to in section 1905(bb)(2)(A), agents approved by the Food and Drug Administration under the over-the-counter monograph process for purposes of promoting, and when used to promote, tobacco cessation”.

(c) REMOVAL OF COST-SHARING FOR COUNSELING AND PHARMACOTHERAPY FOR CESSATION OF TOBACCO USE BY PREGNANT WOMEN.—

(1) GENERAL COST-SHARING LIMITATIONS.—Section 1916 of the Social Security Act (42 U.S.C. 1396o) is amended in each of subsections (a)(2)(B) and (b)(2)(B) by inserting ", and counseling and pharmacotherapy for cessation of tobacco use by pregnant women (as defined in section 1905(bb)) and covered outpatient drugs (as defined in subsection (k)(2) of section 1927 and including nonprescription drugs described in subsection (d)(2) of such section) that are prescribed for purposes of promoting, and when used to promote, tobacco cessation by pregnant women in accordance with the Guideline referred to in section 1905(bb)(2)(A)" after "complicate the pregnancy".

(2) APPLICATION TO ALTERNATIVE COST-SHARING.—Section 1916A(b)(3)(B)(iii) of such Act (42 U.S.C. 1396o–1(b)(3)(B)(iii)) is amended by inserting ", and counseling and pharmacotherapy for cessation of tobacco use by pregnant women (as defined in section 1905(bb))" after "complicate the pregnancy".

(d) EFFECTIVE DATE.—The amendments made by this section shall take effect on October 1, 2010.

SEC. 4108. INCENTIVES FOR PREVENTION OF CHRONIC DISEASES IN MEDICAID.

(a) INITIATIVES.—

(1) ESTABLISHMENT.—

(A) IN GENERAL.—The Secretary shall award grants to States to carry out initiatives to provide incentives to Medicaid beneficiaries who—

(i) successfully participate in a program described in paragraph (3); and

(ii) upon completion of such participation, demonstrate changes in health risk and outcomes, including the adoption and maintenance of healthy behaviors by meeting specific targets (as described in subsection (c)(2)).

(B) PURPOSE.—The purpose of the initiatives under this section is to test approaches that may encourage behavior modification and determine scalable solutions.

(2) DURATION.—

(A) INITIATION OF PROGRAM; RESOURCES.—The Secretary shall awards grants to States beginning on January 1, 2011, or beginning on the date on which the Secretary develops program criteria, whichever is earlier. The Secretary shall develop program criteria for initiatives under this section using relevant evidence-based research and resources, including the Guide to Community Preventive Services, the Guide to Clinical Preventive Services, and the National Registry of Evidence-Based Programs and Practices.

(B) DURATION OF PROGRAM.—A State awarded a grant to carry out initiatives under this section shall carry out such initiatives within the 5-year period beginning on January 1, 2011, or beginning on the date on which the Secretary develops program criteria, whichever is earlier. Initiatives under this section shall be carried out by a State for a period of not less than 3 years.

(3) PROGRAM DESCRIBED.—

(A) IN GENERAL.—A program described in this paragraph is a comprehensive, evidence-based, widely available, and easily accessible program, proposed by the State and approved by the Secretary, that is designed and uniquely suited to address the needs of Medicaid beneficiaries and has demonstrated success in helping individuals achieve one or more of the following:

(i) Ceasing use of tobacco products.

(ii) Controlling or reducing their weight.

(iii) Lowering their cholesterol.

(iv) Lowering their blood pressure.

(v) Avoiding the onset of diabetes or, in the case of a diabetic, improving the management of that condition.

(B) CO-MORBIDITIES.—A program under this section may also address co-morbidities (including depression) that are related to any of the conditions described in subparagraph (A).

(C) WAIVER AUTHORITY.—The Secretary may waive the requirements of section 1902(a)(1) (relating to statewideness) of the Social Security Act for a State awarded a grant to conduct an initiative under this section and shall ensure that a State makes any program described in subparagraph (A) available and accessible to Medicaid beneficiaries.

(D) FLEXIBILITY IN IMPLEMENTATION.—A State may enter into arrangements with providers participating in Medicaid, community-based organizations, faith-based organizations, public-private partnerships, Indian tribes, or similar entities or organizations to carry out programs described in subparagraph (A).

(4) APPLICATION.—Following the development of program criteria by the Secretary, a State may submit an application, in such manner and containing such information as the Secretary may require, that shall include a proposal for programs described in paragraph (3)(A) and a plan to make Medicaid beneficiaries and providers participating in Medicaid who reside in the State aware and informed about such programs.

(b) EDUCATION AND OUTREACH CAMPAIGN.—

(1) STATE AWARENESS.—The Secretary shall conduct an outreach and education campaign to make States aware of the grants under this section.

(2) PROVIDER AND BENEFICIARY EDUCATION.—A State awarded a grant to conduct an initiative under this section shall conduct an outreach and education campaign to make Medicaid beneficiaries and providers participating in Medicaid who reside in the State aware of the programs described in subsection (a)(3) that are to be carried out by the State under the grant.

(c) IMPACT.—A State awarded a grant to conduct an initiative under this section shall develop and implement a system to—

(1) track Medicaid beneficiary participation in the program and validate changes in health risk and outcomes with clinical data, including the adoption and maintenance of health behaviors by such beneficiaries;

(2) to the extent practicable, establish standards and health status targets for Medicaid beneficiaries participating in the program and measure the degree to which such standards and targets are met;

(3) evaluate the effectiveness of the program and provide the Secretary with such evaluations;

(4) report to the Secretary on processes that have been developed and lessons learned from the program; and

(5) report on preventive services as part of reporting on quality measures for Medicaid managed care programs.

(d) EVALUATIONS AND REPORTS.—

(1) INDEPENDENT ASSESSMENT.—The Secretary shall enter into a contract with an independent entity or organization to conduct an evaluation and assessment of the initiatives carried out by States under this section, for the purpose of determining—

(A) the effect of such initiatives on the use of health care services by Medicaid beneficiaries participating in the program;

(B) the extent to which special populations (including adults with disabilities, adults with chronic illnesses, and children with special health care needs) are able to participate in the program;

(C) the level of satisfaction of Medicaid beneficiaries with respect to the accessibility and quality of health care services provided through the program; and

(D) the administrative costs incurred by State agencies that are responsible for administration of the program.

(2) STATE REPORTING.—A State awarded a grant to carry out initiatives under this section shall submit reports to the Secretary, on a semi-annual basis, regarding the programs that are supported by the grant funds. Such report shall include information, as specified by the Secretary, regarding—

(A) the specific uses of the grant funds;

(B) an assessment of program implementation and lessons learned from the programs;

(C) an assessment of quality improvements and clinical outcomes under such programs; and

(D) estimates of cost savings resulting from such programs.

(3) INITIAL REPORT.—Not later than January 1, 2014, the Secretary shall submit to Congress an initial report on such initiatives based on information provided by States through reports required under paragraph (2). The initial report shall include an interim evaluation of the effectiveness of the initiatives carried out with grants awarded under this section and a recommendation regarding whether funding for expanding or extending the initiatives should be extended beyond January 1, 2016.

(4) FINAL REPORT.—Not later than July 1, 2016, the Secretary shall submit to Congress a final report on the program that includes the results of the independent assessment required under paragraph (1), together with recommendations for such legislation and administrative action as the Secretary determines appropriate.

(e) NO EFFECT ON ELIGIBILITY FOR, OR AMOUNT OF, MEDICAID OR OTHER BENEFITS.—Any incentives provided to a Medicaid beneficiary participating in a program described in subsection (a)(3) shall not be taken into account for purposes of determining the beneficiary's eligibility for, or amount of, benefits under the Medicaid program or any program funded in whole or in part with Federal funds.

(f) FUNDING.—Out of any funds in the Treasury not otherwise appropriated, there are appropriated for the 5-year period beginning on January 1, 2011, $100,000,000 to the Secretary to carry out this section. Amounts appropriated under this subsection shall remain available until expended.

(g) DEFINITIONS.—In this section:

(1) MEDICAID BENEFICIARY.—The term "Medicaid beneficiary" means an individual who is eligible for medical assistance under a State plan or waiver under title XIX of the Social Security Act (42 U.S.C. 1396 et seq.) and is enrolled in such plan or waiver.

(2) STATE.—The term "State" has the meaning given that term for purposes of title XIX of the Social Security Act (42 U.S.C. 1396 et seq.).

Subtitle C—Creating Healthier Communities

SEC. 4201. COMMUNITY TRANSFORMATION GRANTS.

(a) IN GENERAL.—The Secretary of Health and Human Services (referred to in this section as the "Secretary"), acting through the Director of the Centers for Disease Control and Prevention (referred to in this section as the "Director"), shall award competitive grants to State and local governmental agencies and community-based organizations for the implementation, evaluation, and dissemination of evidence-based community preventive health activities in order to reduce chronic disease rates, prevent the development of secondary conditions, address health disparities, and develop a stronger evidence-base of effective prevention programming.

(b) ELIGIBILITY.—To be eligible to receive a grant under subsection (a), an entity shall—

(1) be—

(A) a State governmental agency;

(B) a local governmental agency;

(C) a national network of community-based organizations;

(D) a State or local non-profit organization; or

(E) an Indian tribe; and

(2) submit to the Director an application at such time, in such a manner, and containing such information as the Director may require, including a description of the program to be carried out under the grant; and

(3) demonstrate a history or capacity, if funded, to develop relationships necessary to engage key stakeholders from multiple sectors within and beyond health care and across a community, such as healthy futures corps and health care providers.

(c) USE OF FUNDS.—

(1) IN GENERAL.—An eligible entity shall use amounts received under a grant under this section to carry out programs described in this subsection.

(2) COMMUNITY TRANSFORMATION PLAN.—

(A) IN GENERAL.—An eligible entity that receives a grant under this section shall submit to the Director (for approval) a detailed plan that includes the policy, environmental, programmatic, and as appropriate infrastructure changes needed to promote healthy living and reduce disparities.

(B) ACTIVITIES.—Activities within the plan may focus on (but not be limited to)—

(i) creating healthier school environments, including increasing healthy food options, physical activity opportunities, promotion of healthy lifestyle, emotional wellness, and prevention curricula, and activities to prevent chronic diseases;

(ii) creating the infrastructure to support active living and access to nutritious foods in a safe environment;

(iii) developing and promoting programs targeting a variety of age levels to increase access to nutrition, physical activity and smoking cessation, improve social and emotional wellness, enhance safety in a community, or address any other chronic disease priority area identified by the grantee;

(iv) assessing and implementing worksite wellness programming and incentives;

(v) working to highlight healthy options at restaurants and other food venues;

(vi) prioritizing strategies to reduce racial and ethnic disparities, including social, economic, and geographic determinants of health; and

(vii) addressing special populations needs, including all age groups and individuals with disabilities, and individuals in both urban and rural areas.

(3) COMMUNITY-BASED PREVENTION HEALTH ACTIVITIES.—

(A) IN GENERAL.—An eligible entity shall use amounts received under a grant under this section to implement a variety of programs, policies, and infrastructure improvements to promote healthier lifestyles.

(B) ACTIVITIES.—An eligible entity shall implement activities detailed in the community transformation plan under paragraph (2).

(C) IN-KIND SUPPORT.—An eligible entity may provide in-kind resources such as staff, equipment, or office space in carrying out activities under this section.

(4) EVALUATION.—

(A) IN GENERAL.—An eligible entity shall use amounts provided under a grant under this section to conduct activities to measure changes in the prevalence of chronic disease risk factors among community members participating in preventive health activities

(B) TYPES OF MEASURES.—In carrying out subparagraph (A), the eligible entity shall, with respect to residents in the community, measure—

(i) changes in weight;

(ii) changes in proper nutrition;

(iii) changes in physical activity;

(iv) changes in tobacco use prevalence;

(v) changes in emotional well-being and overall mental health;

(vi) other factors using community-specific data from the Behavioral Risk Factor Surveillance Survey; and

(vii) other factors as determined by the Secretary.

(C) REPORTING.—An eligible entity shall annually submit to the Director a report containing an evaluation of activities carried out under the grant.

(5) DISSEMINATION.—A grantee under this section shall—

(A) meet at least annually in regional or national meetings to discuss challenges, best practices, and lessons learned with respect to activities carried out under the grant; and

(B) develop models for the replication of successful programs and activities and the mentoring of other eligible entities.

(d) TRAINING.—

(1) IN GENERAL.—The Director shall develop a program to provide training for eligible entities on effective strategies for the prevention and control of chronic disease and the link between physical, emotional, and social well-being.

(2) COMMUNITY TRANSFORMATION PLAN.—The Director shall provide appropriate feedback and technical assistance to grantees to establish community transformation plans

(3) EVALUATION.—The Director shall provide a literature review and framework for the evaluation of programs conducted as part of the grant program under this section, in addition to working with academic institutions or other entities with expertise in outcome evaluation.

(e) PROHIBITION.—A grantee shall not use funds provided under a grant under this section to create video games or to carry out any other activities that may lead to higher rates of obesity or inactivity.

(f) AUTHORIZATION OF APPROPRIATIONS.—There are authorized to be appropriated to carry out this section, such sums as may be necessary for each fiscal years 2010 through 2014.

SEC. 4202. HEALTHY AGING, LIVING WELL; EVALUATION OF COMMUNITY-BASED PREVENTION AND WELLNESS PROGRAMS FOR MEDICARE BENEFICIARIES.

(a) HEALTHY AGING, LIVING WELL.—

(1) IN GENERAL.—The Secretary of Health and Human Services (referred to in this section as the “Secretary”), acting through the Director of the Centers for Disease Control and Prevention, shall award grants to State or local health departments and Indian tribes to carry out 5-year pilot programs to provide public health community interventions, screenings, and where necessary, clinical referrals for individuals who are between 55 and 64 years of age.

(2) ELIGIBILITY.—To be eligible to receive a grant under paragraph (1), an entity shall—

(A) be—

(i) a State health department;

(ii) a local health department; or

(iii) an Indian tribe;

(B) submit to the Secretary an application at such time, in such manner, and containing such information as the Secretary may require including a description of the program to be carried out under the grant;

(C) design a strategy for improving the health of the 55-to-64 year-old population through community-based public health interventions; and

(D) demonstrate the capacity, if funded, to develop the relationships necessary with relevant health agencies, health care providers, community-based organizations, and insurers to carry out the activities described in paragraph (3), such relationships to include the identification of a community-based clinical partner, such as a community health center or rural health clinic.

(3) USE OF FUNDS.—

(A) IN GENERAL.—A State or local health department shall use amounts received under a grant under this subsection to carry out a program to provide the services described in this paragraph to individuals who are between 55 and 64 years of age.

(B) PUBLIC HEALTH INTERVENTIONS.—

(i) IN GENERAL.—In developing and implementing such activities, a grantee shall collaborate with the Centers for Disease Control and Prevention and the Administration on Aging, and relevant local agencies and organizations.

(ii) TYPES OF INTERVENTION ACTIVITIES.—Intervention activities conducted under this subparagraph may include efforts to improve nutrition, increase physical activity, reduce tobacco use and substance abuse, improve mental health, and promote healthy lifestyles among the target population.

(C) COMMUNITY PREVENTIVE SCREENINGS.—

(i) IN GENERAL.—In addition to community-wide public health interventions, a State or local health department shall use amounts received under a grant under this subsection to conduct ongoing health screening to identify risk factors for cardiovascular disease, cancer, stroke, and diabetes among individuals in both urban and rural areas who are between 55 and 64 years of age.

(ii) TYPES OF SCREENING ACTIVITIES.—Screening activities conducted under this subparagraph may include—

(I) mental health/behavioral health and substance use disorders;

(II) physical activity, smoking, and nutrition; and

(III) any other measures deemed appropriate by the Secretary.

(iii) MONITORING.—Grantees under this section shall maintain records of screening results under this subparagraph to establish the baseline data for monitoring the targeted population

(D) CLINICAL REFERRAL/TREATMENT FOR CHRONIC DISEASES.—

(i) IN GENERAL.—A State or local health department shall use amounts received under a grant under this subsection to ensure that individuals between 55 and 64 years of age who are found to have chronic disease risk factors through the screening activities described in subparagraph (C)(ii), receive clinical referral/treatment for follow-up services to reduce such risk.

(ii) MECHANISM.—

(I) IDENTIFICATION AND DETERMINATION OF STATUS.—With respect to each individual with risk factors for or having heart disease, stroke, diabetes, or any other condition for which such individual was screened under subparagraph (C), a grantee under this section shall determine whether or not such individual is covered under any public or private health insurance program.

(II) INSURED INDIVIDUALS.—An individual determined to be covered under a health insurance program under subclause (I) shall be referred by the grantee to the existing providers under such program or, if such individual does not have a current provider, to a provider who is in-network with respect to the program involved.

(III) UNINSURED INDIVIDUALS.—With respect to an individual determined to be uninsured under subclause (I), the grantee's community-based clinical partner described in paragraph (4)(D) shall assist the individual in determining eligibility for available public coverage options and identify other appropriate community health care resources and assistance programs.

(iii) PUBLIC HEALTH INTERVENTION PROGRAM.—A State or local health department shall use amounts received under a grant under this subsection to enter into contracts with community health centers or rural health clinics and mental health and substance use disorder service providers to assist in the referral/treatment of at risk patients to community resources for clinical follow-up and help determine eligibility for other public programs.

(E) GRANTEE EVALUATION.—An eligible entity shall use amounts provided under a grant under this subsection to conduct activities to measure changes in the prevalence of chronic disease risk factors among participants.

(4) PILOT PROGRAM EVALUATION.—The Secretary shall conduct an annual evaluation of the effectiveness of the pilot program under this subsection. In determining such effectiveness, the Secretary shall consider changes in the prevalence of uncontrolled chronic disease risk factors among new Medicare enrollees (or individuals nearing enrollment, including those who are 63 and 64 years of age) who reside in States or localities receiving grants under this section as compared with national and historical data for those States and localities for the same population.

(5) AUTHORIZATION OF APPROPRIATIONS.—There are authorized to be appropriated to carry out this subsection, such sums as may be necessary for each of fiscal years 2010 through 2014.

(b) EVALUATION AND PLAN FOR COMMUNITY-BASED PREVENTION AND WELLNESS PROGRAMS FOR MEDICARE BENEFICIARIES.—

(1) IN GENERAL.—The Secretary shall conduct an evaluation of community-based prevention and wellness programs and develop a plan for promoting healthy lifestyles and chronic disease self-management for Medicare beneficiaries.

(2) MEDICARE EVALUATION OF PREVENTION AND WELLNESS PROGRAMS.—

(A) IN GENERAL.—The Secretary shall evaluate community prevention and wellness programs including those that are sponsored by the Administration on Aging, are evidence-based, and have demonstrated potential to help Medicare beneficiaries (particularly beneficiaries that have attained 65 years of age) reduce their risk of disease, disability, and injury by making healthy lifestyle choices, including exercise, diet, and self-management of chronic diseases.

(B) EVALUATION.—The evaluation under subparagraph (A) shall consist of the following:

(i) EVIDENCE REVIEW.—The Secretary shall review available evidence, literature, best practices, and resources that are relevant to programs that promote healthy lifestyles and reduce risk factors for the Medicare population. The Secretary may determine the scope of the evidence review and such issues to be considered, which shall include, at a minimum—

(I) physical activity, nutrition, and obesity;

(II) falls;

(III) chronic disease self-management; and

(IV) mental health.

(ii) INDEPENDENT EVALUATION OF EVIDENCE-BASED COMMUNITY PREVENTION AND WELLNESS PROGRAMS.—The Administrator of the Centers for Medicare & Medicaid Services, in consultation with the Assistant Secretary for Aging, shall, to the extent feasible and practicable, conduct an evaluation of existing community prevention and wellness programs that are sponsored by the Administration on Aging to assess the extent to which Medicare beneficiaries who participate in such programs—

(I) reduce their health risks, improve their health outcomes, and adopt and maintain healthy behaviors;

(II) improve their ability to manage their chronic conditions; and

(III) reduce their utilization of health services and associated costs under the Medicare program for conditions that are amenable to improvement under such programs.

(3) REPORT.—Not later than September 30, 2013, the Secretary shall submit to Congress a report that includes—

(A) recommendations for such legislation and administrative action as the Secretary determines appropriate to promote healthy lifestyles and chronic disease self-management for Medicare beneficiaries;

(B) any relevant findings relating to the evidence review under paragraph (2)(B)(i); and

(C) the results of the evaluation under paragraph (2)(B)(ii).

(4) FUNDING.—For purposes of carrying out this subsection, the Secretary shall provide for the transfer, from the Federal Hospital Insurance Trust Fund under section 1817 of the Social Security Act (42 U.S.C. 1395i) and the Federal Supplemental Medical Insurance Trust Fund under section 1841 of such Act (42 U.S.C. 1395t), in such proportion as the Secretary determines appropriate, of $50,000,000 to the Centers for Medicare & Medicaid Services Program Management Account. Amounts transferred under the preceding sentence shall remain available until expended.

(5) ADMINISTRATION.—Chapter 35 of title 44, United States Code shall not apply to the this subsection.

(6) MEDICARE BENEFICIARY.—In this subsection, the term "Medicare beneficiary" means an individual who is entitled to benefits under part A of title XVIII of the Social Security Act and enrolled under part B of such title.

SEC. 4203. REMOVING BARRIERS AND IMPROVING ACCESS TO WELLNESS FOR INDIVIDUALS WITH DISABILITIES.

Title V of the Rehabilitation Act of 1973 (29 U.S.C. 791 et seq.) is amended by adding at the end of the following:

"SEC. 510. ESTABLISHMENT OF STANDARDS FOR ACCESSIBLE MEDICAL DIAGNOSTIC EQUIPMENT.

"(a) STANDARDS.—Not later than 24 months after the date of enactment of the Affordable Health Choices Act, the Architectural and Transportation Barriers Compliance Board shall, in consultation with the Commissioner of the Food and Drug Administration, promulgate regulatory standards in accordance with the Administrative Procedure Act (2 U.S.C. 551 et seq.) setting forth the minimum technical criteria for medical diagnostic equipment used in (or in conjunction with) physician's offices, clinics, emergency rooms, hospitals, and other medical settings. The standards shall ensure that such equipment is accessible to, and usable by, individuals with accessibility needs, and shall allow independent entry to, use of, and exit from the equipment by such individuals to the maximum extent possible.

"(b) MEDICAL DIAGNOSTIC EQUIPMENT COVERED.—The standards issued under subsection (a) for medical diagnostic equipment shall apply to equipment that includes examination tables, examination chairs (including chairs used for eye examinations or procedures, and dental examinations or procedures), weight scales, mammography equipment, x-ray machines, and other radiological equipment commonly used for diagnostic purposes by health professionals.

"(c) REVIEW AND AMENDMENT.—The Architectural and Transportation Barriers Compliance Board, in consultation with the Commissioner of the Food and Drug Administration, shall periodically review and, as appropriate, amend the standards in accordance with the Administrative Procedure Act (2 U.S.C. 551 et seq.).".

SEC. 4204. IMMUNIZATIONS.

(a) STATE AUTHORITY TO PURCHASE RECOMMENDED VACCINES FOR ADULTS.—Section 317 of the Public Health Service Act (42 U.S.C. 247b) is amended by adding at the end the following:

"(l) AUTHORITY TO PURCHASE RECOMMENDED VACCINES FOR ADULTS.—

"(1) IN GENERAL.—The Secretary may negotiate and enter into contracts with manufacturers of vaccines for the purchase and delivery of vaccines for adults as provided for under subsection (e).

"(2) STATE PURCHASE.—A State may obtain additional quantities of such adult vaccines (subject to amounts specified to the Secretary by the State in advance of negotiations) through the purchase of vaccines from manufacturers at the applicable price negotiated by the Secretary under this subsection.".

(b) DEMONSTRATION PROGRAM TO IMPROVE IMMUNIZATION COVERAGE.—Section 317 of the Public Health Service Act (42 U.S.C. 247b), as amended by subsection (a), is further amended by adding at the end the following:

"(m) DEMONSTRATION PROGRAM TO IMPROVE IMMUNIZATION COVERAGE.—

"(1) IN GENERAL.—The Secretary, acting through the Director of the Centers for Disease Control and Prevention, shall establish a demonstration program to award grants to States to improve the provision of recommended immunizations for children, adolescents, and adults through the use of evidence-based, population-based interventions for high-risk populations.

"(2) STATE PLAN.—To be eligible for a grant under paragraph (1), a State shall submit to the Secretary an application at such time, in such manner, and containing such information as the Secretary may require, including a State plan that describes the interventions to be implemented under the grant and how such interventions match with local needs and capabilities, as determined through consultation with local authorities.

"(3) USE OF FUNDS.—Funds received under a grant under this subsection shall be used to implement interventions that are recommended by the Task Force on Community Preventive Services (as established by the Secretary, acting through the Director of the Centers for Disease Control and Prevention) or other evidence-based interventions, including—

"(A) providing immunization reminders or recalls for target populations of clients, patients, and consumers;

"(B) educating targeted populations and health care providers concerning immunizations in combination with one or more other interventions;

"(C) reducing out-of-pocket costs for families for vaccines and their administration;

"(D) carrying out immunization-promoting strategies for participants or clients of public programs, including assessments of immunization status, referrals to health care providers, education, provision of on-site immunizations, or incentives for immunization;

"(E) providing for home visits that promote immunization through education, assessments of need, referrals, provision of immunizations, or other services;

"(F) providing reminders or recalls for immunization providers;

"(G) conducting assessments of, and providing feedback to, immunization providers;

"(H) any combination of one or more interventions described in this paragraph; or

"(I) immunization information systems to allow all States to have electronic databases for immunization records.

"(4) CONSIDERATION.—In awarding grants under this subsection, the Secretary shall consider any reviews or recommendations of the Task Force on Community Preventive Services.

"(5) EVALUATION.—Not later than 3 years after the date on which a State receives a grant under this subsection, the State shall submit to the Secretary an evaluation of progress made toward improving immunization coverage rates among high-risk populations within the State.

"(6) REPORT TO CONGRESS.—Not later than 4 years after the date of enactment of the Affordable Health Choices Act, the Secretary shall submit to Congress a report concerning the effectiveness of the demonstration program established under this subsection together with recommendations on whether to continue and expand such program.

"(7) AUTHORIZATION OF APPROPRIATIONS.—There is authorized to be appropriated to carry out this subsection, such sums as may be necessary for each of fiscal years 2010 through 2014.".

(c) REAUTHORIZATION OF IMMUNIZATION PROGRAM.—Section 317(j) of the Public Health Service Act (42 U.S.C. 247b(j)) is amended—

(1) in paragraph (1), by striking "for each of the fiscal years 1998 through 2005"; and

(2) in paragraph (2), by striking "after October 1, 1997,".

(d) RULE OF CONSTRUCTION REGARDING ACCESS TO IMMUNIZATIONS.—Nothing in this section (including the amendments made by this section), or any other provision of this Act (including any amendments made by this Act) shall be construed to decrease children's access to immunizations.

(e) GAO STUDY AND REPORT ON MEDICARE BENEFICIARY ACCESS TO VACCINES.—

(1) STUDY.—The Comptroller General of the United States (in this section referred to as the "Comptroller General") shall conduct a study on the ability of Medicare beneficiaries who were 65 years of age or older to access routinely recommended vaccines covered under the prescription drug program under part D of title XVIII of the Social Security Act over the period since the establishment of such program. Such study shall include the following:

(A) An analysis and determination of—

(i) the number of Medicare beneficiaries who were 65 years of age or older and were eligible for a routinely recommended vaccination that was covered under part D;

(ii) the number of such beneficiaries who actually received a routinely recommended vaccination that was covered under part D; and

(iii) any barriers to access by such beneficiaries to routinely recommended vaccinations that were covered under part D.

(B) A summary of the findings and recommendations by government agencies, departments, and advisory bodies (as well as relevant professional organizations) on the impact of coverage under part D of routinely recommended adult immunizations for access to such immunizations by Medicare beneficiaries.

(2) REPORT.—Not later than June 1, 2011, the Comptroller General shall submit to the appropriate committees of jurisdiction of the House of Representatives and the Senate a report containing the results of the study conducted under paragraph (1), together with recommendations for such legislation and administrative action as the Comptroller General determines appropriate.

(3) FUNDING.—Out of any funds in the Treasury not otherwise appropriated, there are appropriated $1,000,000 for fiscal year 2010 to carry out this subsection.

SEC. 4205. NUTRITION LABELING OF STANDARD MENU ITEMS AT CHAIN RESTAURANTS.

(a) TECHNICAL AMENDMENTS.—Section 403(q)(5)(A) of the Federal Food, Drug, and Cosmetic Act (21 U.S.C. 343(q)(5)(A)) is amended—

(1) in subitem (i), by inserting at the beginning "except as provided in clause (H)(ii)(III),"; and

(2) in subitem (ii), by inserting at the beginning "except as provided in clause (H)(ii)(III),".

(b) LABELING REQUIREMENTS.—Section 403(q)(5) of the Federal Food, Drug, and Cosmetic Act (21 U.S.C. 343(q)(5)) is amended by adding at the end the following:

"(H) RESTAURANTS, RETAIL FOOD ESTABLISHMENTS, AND VENDING MACHINES.—

"(i) GENERAL REQUIREMENTS FOR RESTAURANTS AND SIMILAR RETAIL FOOD ESTABLISHMENTS.—Except for food described in subclause (vii), in the case of food that is a standard menu item that is offered for sale in a restaurant or similar retail food establishment that is part of a chain with 20 or more locations doing business under the same name (regardless of the type of ownership of the locations) and offering for sale substantially the same menu items, the restaurant or similar retail food establishment shall disclose the information described in subclauses (ii) and (iii).

"(ii) INFORMATION REQUIRED TO BE DISCLOSED BY RESTAURANTS AND RETAIL FOOD ESTABLISHMENTS.—Except as provided in subclause (vii), the restaurant or similar retail food establishment shall disclose in a clear and conspicuous manner—

"(I)(aa) in a nutrient content disclosure statement adjacent to the name of the standard menu item, so as to be clearly associated with the standard menu item, on the menu listing the item for sale, the number of calories contained in the standard menu item, as usually prepared and offered for sale; and

"(bb) a succinct statement concerning suggested daily caloric intake, as specified by the Secretary by regulation and posted prominently on the menu and designed to enable the public to understand, in the context of a total daily diet, the significance of the caloric information that is provided on the menu;

"(II)(aa) in a nutrient content disclosure statement adjacent to the name of the standard menu item, so as to be clearly associated with the standard menu item, on the menu board, including a drive-through menu board, the number of calories contained in the standard menu item, as usually prepared and offered for sale; and

"(bb) a succinct statement concerning suggested daily caloric intake, as specified by the Secretary by regulation and posted prominently on the menu board, designed to enable the public to understand, in the context of a total daily diet, the significance of the nutrition information that is provided on the menu board;

"(III) in a written form, available on the premises of the restaurant or similar retail establishment and to the consumer upon request, the nutrition information required under clauses (C) and (D) of subparagraph (1); and

"(IV) on the menu or menu board, a prominent, clear, and conspicuous statement regarding the availability of the information described in item (III).

"(iii) SELF-SERVICE FOOD AND FOOD ON DISPLAY.—Except as provided in subclause (vii), in the case of food sold at a salad bar, buffet line, cafeteria line, or similar self-service facility, and for self-service beverages or food that is on display and that is visible to customers, a restaurant or similar retail food establishment shall place adjacent to each food offered a sign that lists calories per displayed food item or per serving.

"(iv) REASONABLE BASIS.—For the purposes of this clause, a restaurant or similar retail food establishment shall have a reasonable basis for its nutrient content disclosures, including nutrient databases, cookbooks, laboratory analyses, and other reasonable means, as described in section 101.10 of title 21, Code of Federal Regulations (or any successor regulation) or in a related guidance of the Food and Drug Administration.

"(v) MENU VARIABILITY AND COMBINATION MEALS.—The Secretary shall establish by regulation standards for determining and disclosing the nutrient content for standard menu items that come in different flavors, varieties, or combinations, but which are listed as a single menu item, such as soft drinks, ice cream, pizza, doughnuts, or children's combination meals, through means determined by the Secretary, including ranges, averages, or other methods.

"(vi) ADDITIONAL INFORMATION.—If the Secretary determines that a nutrient, other than a nutrient required under subclause (ii)(III), should be disclosed for the purpose of providing information to assist consumers in maintaining healthy dietary practices, the Secretary may require, by regulation, disclosure of such nutrient in the written form required under subclause (ii)(III).

"(vii) NONAPPLICABILITY TO CERTAIN FOOD.—

"(I) IN GENERAL.—Subclauses (i) through (vi) do not apply to—

"(aa) items that are not listed on a menu or menu board (such as condiments and other items placed on the table or counter for general use);

"(bb) daily specials, temporary menu items appearing on the menu for less than 60 days per calendar year, or custom orders; or

"(cc) such other food that is part of a customary market test appearing on the menu for less than 90 days, under terms and conditions established by the Secretary.

"(II) WRITTEN FORMS.—Subparagraph (5)(C) shall apply to any regulations promulgated under subclauses (ii)(III) and (vi).

"(viii) VENDING MACHINES.—

"(I) IN GENERAL.—In the case of an article of food sold from a vending machine that—

"(aa) does not permit a prospective purchaser to examine the Nutrition Facts Panel before purchasing the article or does not otherwise provide visible nutrition information at the point of purchase; and

"(bb) is operated by a person who is engaged in the business of owning or operating 20 or more vending machines,

the vending machine operator shall provide a sign in close proximity to each article of food or the selection button that includes a clear and conspicuous statement disclosing the number of calories contained in the article.

"(ix) VOLUNTARY PROVISION OF NUTRITION INFORMATION.—

"(I) IN GENERAL.—An authorized official of any restaurant or similar retail food establishment or vending machine operator not subject to the requirements of this clause may elect to be subject to the requirements of such clause, by registering biannually the name and address of such restaurant or similar retail food establishment or vending machine operator with the Secretary, as specified by the Secretary by regulation.

"(II) REGISTRATION.—Within 120 days of enactment of this clause, the Secretary shall publish a notice in the Federal Register specifying the terms and conditions for implementation of item (I), pending promulgation of regulations.

"(III) RULE OF CONSTRUCTION.—Nothing in this subclause shall be construed to authorize the Secretary to require an application, review, or licensing process for any entity to register with the Secretary, as described in such item.

"(x) REGULATIONS.—

"(I) PROPOSED REGULATION.—Not later than 1 year after the date of enactment of this clause, the Secretary shall promulgate proposed regulations to carry out this clause.

"(II) CONTENTS.—In promulgating regulations, the Secretary shall—

"(aa) consider standardization of recipes and methods of preparation, reasonable variation in serving size and formulation of menu items, space on menus and menu boards, inadvertent human error, training of food service workers, variations in ingredients, and other factors, as the Secretary determines; and

"(bb) specify the format and manner of the nutrient content disclosure requirements under this subclause.

"(III) REPORTING.—The Secretary shall submit to the Committee on Health, Education, Labor, and Pensions of the Senate and the Committee on Energy and Commerce of the House of Representatives a quarterly report that describes the Secretary's progress toward promulgating final regulations under this subparagraph.

"(xi) DEFINITION.—In this clause, the term 'menu' or 'menu board' means the primary writing of the restaurant or other similar retail food establishment from which a consumer makes an order selection."

(c) NATIONAL UNIFORMITY.—Section 403A(a)(4) of the Federal Food, Drug, and Cosmetic Act (21 U.S.C. 343–1(a)(4)) is amended by striking "except a requirement for nutrition labeling of food which is exempt under subclause (i) or (ii) of section 403(q)(5)(A)" and inserting "except that this paragraph does not apply to food that is offered for sale in a restaurant or similar retail food establishment that is not part of a chain with 20 or more locations doing business under the same name (regardless of the type of ownership of the locations) and offering for sale substantially the same menu items unless such restaurant or similar retail food establishment complies with the voluntary provision of nutrition information requirements under section 403(q)(5)(H)(ix)".

(d) RULE OF CONSTRUCTION.—Nothing in the amendments made by this section shall be construed—

(1) to preempt any provision of State or local law, unless such provision establishes or continues into effect nutrient content disclosures of the type required under section 403(q)(5)(H) of the Federal Food, Drug, and Cosmetic Act (as added by subsection (b)) and is expressly preempted under subsection (a)(4) of such section;

(2) to apply to any State or local requirement respecting a statement in the labeling of food that provides for a warning concerning the safety of the food or component of the food; or

(3) except as provided in section 403(q)(5)(H)(ix) of the Federal Food, Drug, and Cosmetic Act (as added by subsection (b)), to apply to any restaurant or similar retail food establishment other than a restaurant or similar retail food establishment described in section 403(q)(5)(H)(i) of such Act.

SEC. 4206. DEMONSTRATION PROJECT CONCERNING INDIVIDUALIZED WELLNESS PLAN.

Section 330 of the Public Health Service Act (42 U.S.C. 245b) is amended by adding at the end the following:

"(s) DEMONSTRATION PROGRAM FOR INDIVIDUALIZED WELLNESS PLANS.—

"(1) IN GENERAL.—The Secretary shall establish a pilot program to test the impact of providing at-risk populations who utilize community health centers funded under this section an individualized wellness plan that is designed to reduce risk factors for preventable conditions as identified by a comprehensive risk-factor assessment.

"(2) AGREEMENTS.—The Secretary shall enter into agreements with not more than 10 community health centers funded under this section to conduct activities under the pilot program under paragraph (1).

"(3) WELLNESS PLANS.—

"(A) IN GENERAL.—An individualized wellness plan prepared under the pilot program under this subsection may include one or more of the following as appropriate to the individual's identified risk factors:

"(i) Nutritional counseling.

"(ii) A physical activity plan.

"(iii) Alcohol and smoking cessation counseling and services.

"(iv) Stress management.

"(v) Dietary supplements that have health claims approved by the Secretary.

"(vi) Compliance assistance provided by a community health center employee.

"(B) RISK FACTORS.—Wellness plan risk factors shall include—

"(i) weight;

"(ii) tobacco and alcohol use;

"(iii) exercise rates;

"(iv) nutritional status; and

"(v) blood pressure.

"(C) COMPARISONS.—Individualized wellness plans shall make comparisons between the individual involved and a control group of individuals with respect to the risk factors described in subparagraph (B).

"(4) AUTHORIZATION OF APPROPRIATIONS.—There is authorized to be appropriated to carry out this subsection, such sums as may be necessary.".

SEC. 4207. REASONABLE BREAK TIME FOR NURSING MOTHERS.

Section 7 of the Fair Labor Standards Act of 1938 (29 U.S.C. 207) is amended by adding at the end the following:

"(r)(1) An employer shall provide—

"(A) a reasonable break time for an employee to express breast milk for her nursing child for 1 year after the child's birth each time such employee has need to express the milk; and

"(B) a place, other than a bathroom, that is shielded from view and free from intrusion from coworkers and the public, which may be used by an employee to express breast milk.

"(2) An employer shall not be required to compensate an employee receiving reasonable break time under paragraph (1) for any work time spent for such purpose.

"(3) An employer that employs less than 50 employees shall not be subject to the requirements of this subsection, if such requirements would impose an undue hardship by causing the employer significant difficulty or expense when considered in relation to the size, financial resources, nature, or structure of the employer's business.

"(4) Nothing in this subsection shall preempt a State law that provides greater protections to employees than the protections provided for under this subsection.".

Subtitle D—Support for Prevention and Public Health Innovation

SEC. 4301. RESEARCH ON OPTIMIZING THE DELIVERY OF PUBLIC HEALTH SERVICES.

(a) IN GENERAL.—The Secretary of Health and Human Services (referred to in this section as the "Secretary"), acting through the Director of the Centers for Disease Control and Prevention, shall provide funding for research in the area of public health services and systems.

(b) REQUIREMENTS OF RESEARCH.—Research supported under this section shall include—

(1) examining evidence-based practices relating to prevention, with a particular focus on high priority areas as identified by the Secretary in the National Prevention Strategy or Healthy People 2020, and including comparing community-based public health interventions in terms of effectiveness and cost;

(2) analyzing the translation of interventions from academic settings to real world settings; and

(3) identifying effective strategies for organizing, financing, or delivering public health services in real world community settings, including comparing State and local health department structures and systems in terms of effectiveness and cost.

(c) EXISTING PARTNERSHIPS.—Research supported under this section shall be coordinated with the Community Preventive Services Task Force and carried out by building on existing partnerships within the Federal Government while also considering initiatives at the State and local levels and in the private sector.

(d) ANNUAL REPORT.—The Secretary shall, on an annual basis, submit to Congress a report concerning the activities and findings with respect to research supported under this section.

SEC. 4302. UNDERSTANDING HEALTH DISPARITIES: DATA COLLECTION AND ANALYSIS.

(a) UNIFORM CATEGORIES AND COLLECTION REQUIREMENTS.—The Public Health Service Act (42 U.S.C. 201 et seq.) is amended by adding at the end the following:

"TITLE XXXI—DATA COLLECTION, ANALYSIS, AND QUALITY

"SEC. 3101. DATA COLLECTION, ANALYSIS, AND QUALITY.

"(a) DATA COLLECTION.—

"(1) IN GENERAL.—The Secretary shall ensure that, by not later than 2 years after the date of enactment of this title, any federally conducted or supported health care or public health program, activity or survey (including Current Population Surveys and American Community Surveys conducted by the Bureau of Labor Statistics and the Bureau of the Census) collects and reports, to the extent practicable—

"(A) data on race, ethnicity, sex, primary language, and disability status for applicants, recipients, or participants;

"(B) data at the smallest geographic level such as State, local, or institutional levels if such data can be aggregated;

"(C) sufficient data to generate statistically reliable estimates by racial, ethnic, sex, primary language, and disability status subgroups for applicants, recipients or participants using, if needed, statistical oversamples of these subpopulations; and

"(D) any other demographic data as deemed appropriate by the Secretary regarding health disparities.

"(2) COLLECTION STANDARDS.—In collecting data described in paragraph (1), the Secretary or designee shall—

"(A) use Office of Management and Budget standards, at a minimum, for race and ethnicity measures;

"(B) develop standards for the measurement of sex, primary language, and disability status;

"(C) develop standards for the collection of data described in paragraph (1) that, at a minimum—

"(i) collects self-reported data by the applicant, recipient, or participant; and

"(ii) collects data from a parent or legal guardian if the applicant, recipient, or participant is a minor or legally incapacitated;

"(D) survey health care providers and establish other procedures in order to assess access to care and treatment for individuals with disabilities and to identify—

"(i) locations where individuals with disabilities access primary, acute (including intensive), and long-term care;

"(ii) the number of providers with accessible facilities and equipment to meet the needs of the individuals with disabilities, including medical diagnostic equipment that meets the minimum technical criteria set forth in section 510 of the Rehabilitation Act of 1973; and

"(iii) the number of employees of health care providers trained in disability awareness and patient care of individuals with disabilities; and

"(E) require that any reporting requirement imposed for purposes of measuring quality under any ongoing or federally conducted or supported health care or public health program, activity, or survey includes requirements for the collection of data on individuals receiving health care items or services under such programs activities by race, ethnicity, sex, primary language, and disability status.

"(3) DATA MANAGEMENT.—In collecting data described in paragraph (1), the Secretary, acting through the National Coordinator for Health Information Technology shall—

"(A) develop national standards for the management of data collected; and

"(B) develop interoperability and security systems for data management.

"(b) DATA ANALYSIS.—

"(1) IN GENERAL.—For each federally conducted or supported health care or public health program or activity, the Secretary shall analyze data collected under paragraph (a) to detect and monitor trends in health disparities (as defined for purposes of section 485E) at the Federal and State levels.

"(c) DATA REPORTING AND DISSEMINATION.—

"(1) IN GENERAL.—The Secretary shall make the analyses described in (b) available to—

"(A) the Office of Minority Health;

"(B) the National Center on Minority Health and Health Disparities;

"(C) the Agency for Healthcare Research and Quality;

"(D) the Centers for Disease Control and Prevention;

"(E) the Centers for Medicare & Medicaid Services;

"(F) the Indian Health Service and epidemiology centers funded under the Indian Health Care Improvement Act;

"(G) the Office of Rural health;

"(H) other agencies within the Department of Health and Human Services; and

"(I) other entities as determined appropriate by the Secretary.

"(2) REPORTING OF DATA.—The Secretary shall report data and analyses described in (a) and (b) through—

"(A) public postings on the Internet websites of the Department of Health and Human Services; and

"(B) any other reporting or dissemination mechanisms determined appropriate by the Secretary.

"(3) AVAILABILITY OF DATA.—The Secretary may make data described in (a) and (b) available for additional research, analyses, and dissemination to other Federal agencies, non-governmental entities, and the public, in accordance with any Federal agency's data user agreements.

"(d) LIMITATIONS ON USE OF DATA.—Nothing in this section shall be construed to permit the use of information collected under this section in a manner that would adversely affect any individual.

"(e) PROTECTION AND SHARING OF DATA.—

"(1) PRIVACY AND OTHER SAFEGUARDS.—The Secretary shall ensure (through the promulgation of regulations or otherwise) that—

"(A) all data collected pursuant to subsection (a) is protected—

"(i) under privacy protections that are at least as broad as those that the Secretary applies to other health data under the regulations promulgated under section 264(c) of the Health Insurance Portability and Accountability Act of 1996 (Public Law 104–191; 110 Stat. 2033); and

"(ii) from all inappropriate internal use by any entity that collects, stores, or receives the data, including use of such data in determinations of eligibility (or continued eligibility) in health plans, and from other inappropriate uses, as defined by the Secretary; and

"(B) all appropriate information security safeguards are used in the collection, analysis, and sharing of data collected pursuant to subsection (a).

"(2) DATA SHARING.—The Secretary shall establish procedures for sharing data collected pursuant to subsection (a), measures relating to such data, and analyses of such data, with other relevant Federal and State agencies including the agencies, centers, and entities within the Department of Health and Human Services specified in subsection (c)(1)..

"(f) DATA ON RURAL UNDERSERVED POPULATIONS.—The Secretary shall ensure that any data collected in accordance with this section regarding racial and ethnic minority groups are also collected regarding underserved rural and frontier populations.

"(g) AUTHORIZATION OF APPROPRIATIONS.—For the purpose of carrying out this section, there are authorized to be appropriated such sums as may be necessary for each of fiscal years 2010 through 2014.

"(h) REQUIREMENT FOR IMPLEMENTATION.—Notwithstanding any other provision of this section, data may not be collected under this section unless funds are directly appropriated for such purpose in an appropriations Act.

"(i) CONSULTATION.—The Secretary shall consult with the Director of the Office of Personnel Management, the Secretary of Defense, the Secretary of Veterans Affairs, the Director of the Bureau of the Census, the Commissioner of Social Security, and the head of other appropriate Federal agencies in carrying out this section.".

(b) ADDRESSING HEALTH CARE DISPARITIES IN MEDICAID AND CHIP.—

(1) STANDARDIZED COLLECTION REQUIREMENTS INCLUDED IN STATE PLANS.—

(A) MEDICAID.—Section 1902(a) of the Social Security Act (42 U.S.C. 1396a(a)), as amended by section 2001(d), is amended—

(i) in paragraph 4), by striking "and" at the end;

(ii) in paragraph (75), by striking the period at the end and inserting "; and"; and

(iii) by inserting after paragraph (75) the following new paragraph:

"(76) provide that any data collected under the State plan meets the requirements of section 3101 of the Public Health Service Act.".

(B) CHIP.—Section 2108(e) of the Social Security Act (42 U.S.C. 1397hh(e)) is amended by adding at the end the following new paragraph:

"(7) Data collected and reported in accordance with section 3101 of the Public Health Service Act, with respect to individuals enrolled in the State child health plan (and, in the case of enrollees under 19 years of age, their parents or legal guardians), including data regarding the primary language of such individuals, parents, and legal guardians.".

(2) EXTENDING MEDICARE REQUIREMENT TO ADDRESS HEALTH DISPARITIES DATA COLLECTION TO MEDICAID AND CHIP.—Title XIX of the Social Security Act (42 U.S.C. 1396 et seq.), as amended by section 2703 is amended by adding at the end the following new section:

“SEC. 1946. ADDRESSING HEALTH CARE DISPARITIES.

“(a) EVALUATING DATA COLLECTION APPROACHES.—The Secretary shall evaluate approaches for the collection of data under this title and title XXI, to be performed in conjunction with existing quality reporting requirements and programs under this title and title XXI, that allow for the ongoing, accurate, and timely collection and evaluation of data on disparities in health care services and performance on the basis of race, ethnicity, sex, primary language, and disability status. In conducting such evaluation, the Secretary shall consider the following objectives:

“(1) Protecting patient privacy.

“(2) Minimizing the administrative burdens of data collection and reporting on States, providers, and health plans participating under this title or title XXI.

“(3) Improving program data under this title and title XXI on race, ethnicity, sex, primary language, and disability status.

“(b) REPORTS TO CONGRESS.—

“(1) REPORT ON EVALUATION.—Not later than 18 months after the date of the enactment of this section, the Secretary shall submit to Congress a report on the evaluation conducted under subsection (a). Such report shall, taking into consideration the results of such evaluation—

“(A) identify approaches (including defining methodologies) for identifying and collecting and evaluating data on health care disparities on the basis of race, ethnicity, sex, primary language, and disability status for the programs under this title and title XXI; and

“(B) include recommendations on the most effective strategies and approaches to reporting HEDIS quality measures as required under section 1852(e)(3) and other nationally recognized quality performance measures, as appropriate, on such bases.

“(2) REPORTS ON DATA ANALYSES.—Not later than 4 years after the date of the enactment of this section, and 4 years thereafter, the Secretary shall submit to Congress a report that includes recommendations for improving the identification of health care disparities for beneficiaries under this title and under title XXI based on analyses of the data collected under subsection (c).

“(c) IMPLEMENTING EFFECTIVE APPROACHES.—Not later than 24 months after the date of the enactment of this section, the Secretary shall implement the approaches identified in the report submitted under subsection (b)(1) for the ongoing, accurate, and timely collection and evaluation of data on health care disparities on the basis of race, ethnicity, sex, primary language, and disability status.”.

SEC. 4303. CDC AND EMPLOYER-BASED WELLNESS PROGRAMS.

Title III of the Public Health Service Act (42 U.S.C. 241 et seq.), by section 4102, is further amended by adding at the end the following:

"PART U—EMPLOYER-BASED WELLNESS PROGRAM

"SEC. 399MM. TECHNICAL ASSISTANCE FOR EMPLOYER-BASED WELLNESS PROGRAMS.

"In order to expand the utilization of evidence-based prevention and health promotion approaches in the workplace, the Director shall—

"(1) provide employers (including small, medium, and large employers, as determined by the Director) with technical assistance, consultation, tools, and other resources in evaluating such employers' employer-based wellness programs, including—

"(A) measuring the participation and methods to increase participation of employees in such programs;

"(B) developing standardized measures that assess policy, environmental and systems changes necessary to have a positive health impact on employees' health behaviors, health outcomes, and health care expenditures; and

"(C) evaluating such programs as they relate to changes in the health status of employees, the absenteeism of employees, the productivity of employees, the rate of workplace injury, and the medical costs incurred by employees; and

"(2) build evaluation capacity among workplace staff by training employers on how to evaluate employer-based wellness programs by ensuring evaluation resources, technical assistance, and consultation are available to workplace staff as needed through such mechanisms as web portals, call centers, or other means.

"SEC. 399MM–1. NATIONAL WORKSITE HEALTH POLICIES AND PROGRAMS STUDY.

"(a) IN GENERAL.—In order to assess, analyze, and monitor over time data about workplace policies and programs, and to develop instruments to assess and evaluate comprehensive workplace chronic disease prevention and health promotion programs, policies and practices, not later than 2 years after the date of enactment of this part, and at regular intervals (to be determined by the Director) thereafter, the Director shall conduct a national worksite health policies and programs survey to assess employer-based health policies and programs.

"(b) REPORT.—Upon the completion of each study under subsection (a), the Director shall submit to Congress a report that includes the recommendations of the Director for the implementation of effective employer-based health policies and programs.

"SEC. 399MM–2. PRIORITIZATION OF EVALUATION BY SECRETARY.

"The Secretary shall evaluate, in accordance with this part, all programs funded through the Centers for Disease Control and Prevention before conducting such an evaluation of privately funded programs unless an entity with a privately funded wellness program requests such an evaluation.

"SEC. 399MM–3. PROHIBITION OF FEDERAL WORKPLACE WELLNESS REQUIREMENTS.

"Notwithstanding any other provision of this part, any recommendations, data, or assessments carried out under this part shall not be used to mandate requirements for workplace wellness programs.".

SEC. 4304. EPIDEMIOLOGY-LABORATORY CAPACITY GRANTS.

Title XXVIII of the Public Health Service Act (42 U.S.C. 300hh et seq.) is amended by adding at the end the following:

"Subtitle C—Strengthening Public Health Surveillance Systems

"SEC. 2821. EPIDEMIOLOGY-LABORATORY CAPACITY GRANTS.

"(a) IN GENERAL.—Subject to the availability of appropriations, the Secretary, acting through the Director of the Centers for Disease Control and Prevention, shall establish an Epidemiology and Laboratory Capacity Grant Program to award grants to State health departments as well as local health departments and tribal jurisdictions that meet such criteria as the Director determines appropriate. Academic centers that assist State and eligible local and tribal health departments may also be eligible for funding under this section as the Director determines appropriate. Grants shall be awarded under this section to assist public health agencies in improving surveillance for, and response to, infectious diseases and other conditions of public health importance by—

"(1) strengthening epidemiologic capacity to identify and monitor the occurrence of infectious diseases and other conditions of public health importance;

"(2) enhancing laboratory practice as well as systems to report test orders and results electronically;

"(3) improving information systems including developing and maintaining an information exchange using national guidelines and complying with capacities and functions determined by an advisory council established and appointed by the Director; and

"(4) developing and implementing prevention and control strategies.

"(b) AUTHORIZATION OF APPROPRIATIONS.—There are authorized to be appropriated to carry out this section $190,000,000 for each of fiscal years 2010 through 2013, of which—

"(1) not less than $95,000,000 shall be made available each such fiscal year for activities under paragraphs (1) and (4) of subsection (a);

"(2) not less than $60,000,000 shall be made available each such fiscal year for activities under subsection (a)(3); and

"(3) not less than $32,000,000 shall be made available each such fiscal year for activities under subsection (a)(2).".

SEC. 4305. ADVANCING RESEARCH AND TREATMENT FOR PAIN CARE MANAGEMENT.

(a) INSTITUTE OF MEDICINE CONFERENCE ON PAIN.—

(1) CONVENING.—Not later than 1 year after funds are appropriated to carry out this subsection, the Secretary of Health and Human Services shall seek to enter into an agreement with the Institute of Medicine of the National Academies to convene a Conference on Pain (in this subsection referred to as "the Conference").

(2) PURPOSES.—The purposes of the Conference shall be to—

(A) increase the recognition of pain as a significant public health problem in the United States;

(B) evaluate the adequacy of assessment, diagnosis, treatment, and management of acute and chronic pain in the general population, and in identified racial, ethnic, gender, age, and other demographic groups that may be disproportionately affected by inadequacies in the assessment, diagnosis, treatment, and management of pain;

(C) identify barriers to appropriate pain care;

(D) establish an agenda for action in both the public and private sectors that will reduce such barriers and significantly improve the state of pain care research, education, and clinical care in the United States.

(3) OTHER APPROPRIATE ENTITY.—If the Institute of Medicine declines to enter into an agreement under paragraph (1), the Secretary of Health and Human Services may enter into such agreement with another appropriate entity.

(4) REPORT.—A report summarizing the Conference's findings and recommendations shall be submitted to the Congress not later than June 30, 2011.

(5) AUTHORIZATION OF APPROPRIATIONS.—For the purpose of carrying out this subsection, there is authorized to be appropriated such sums as may be necessary for each of fiscal years 2010 and 2011.

(b) PAIN RESEARCH AT NATIONAL INSTITUTES OF HEALTH.—Part B of title IV of the Public Health Service Act (42 U.S.C. 284 et seq.) is amended by adding at the end the following:

"SEC. 409J. PAIN RESEARCH.

"(a) RESEARCH INITIATIVES.—

"(1) IN GENERAL.—The Director of NIH is encouraged to continue and expand, through the Pain Consortium, an aggressive program of basic and clinical research on the causes of and potential treatments for pain.

"(2) ANNUAL RECOMMENDATIONS.—Not less than annually, the Pain Consortium, in consultation with the Division of Program Coordination, Planning, and Strategic Initiatives, shall develop and submit to the Director of NIH recommendations on appropriate pain research initiatives that could be undertaken with funds reserved under section 402A(c)(1) for the Common Fund or otherwise available for such initiatives.

"(3) DEFINITION.—In this subsection, the term 'Pain Consortium' means the Pain Consortium of the National Institutes of Health or a similar trans-National Institutes of Health coordinating entity designated by the Secretary for purposes of this subsection.

"(b) INTERAGENCY PAIN RESEARCH COORDINATING COMMITTEE.—

"(1) ESTABLISHMENT.—The Secretary shall establish not later than 1 year after the date of the enactment of this section and as necessary maintain a committee, to be known as the Interagency Pain Research Coordinating Committee (in this section referred to as the 'Committee'), to coordinate all efforts within the Department of Health and Human Services and other Federal agencies that relate to pain research.

"(2) MEMBERSHIP.—

"(A) IN GENERAL.—The Committee shall be composed of the following voting members:

"(i) Not more than 7 voting Federal representatives appoint by the Secretary from agencies that conduct pain care research and treatment.

"(ii) 12 additional voting members appointed under subparagraph (B).

"(B) ADDITIONAL MEMBERS.—The Committee shall include additional voting members appointed by the Secretary as follows:

"(i) 6 non-Federal members shall be appointed from among scientists, physicians, and other health professionals.

"(ii) 6 members shall be appointed from members of the general public, who are representatives of leading research, advocacy, and service organizations for individuals with pain-related conditions.

"(C) NONVOTING MEMBERS.—The Committee shall include such nonvoting members as the Secretary determines to be appropriate.

"(3) CHAIRPERSON.—The voting members of the Committee shall select a chairperson from among such members. The selection of a chairperson shall be subject to the approval of the Director of NIH.

"(4) MEETINGS.—The Committee shall meet at the call of the chairperson of the Committee or upon the request of the Director of NIH, but in no case less often than once each year.

"(5) DUTIES.—The Committee shall—

"(A) develop a summary of advances in pain care research supported or conducted by the Federal agencies relevant to the diagnosis, prevention, and treatment of pain and diseases and disorders associated with pain;

"(B) identify critical gaps in basic and clinical research on the symptoms and causes of pain;

"(C) make recommendations to ensure that the activities of the National Institutes of Health and other Federal agencies are free of unnecessary duplication of effort;

"(D) make recommendations on how best to disseminate information on pain care; and

"(E) make recommendations on how to expand partnerships between public entities and private entities to expand collaborative, cross-cutting research.

"(6) REVIEW.—The Secretary shall review the necessity of the Committee at least once every 2 years.".

(c) PAIN CARE EDUCATION AND TRAINING.—Part D of title VII of the Public Health Service Act (42 U.S.C. 294 et seq.) is amended by adding at the end the following new section:

"SEC. 759. PROGRAM FOR EDUCATION AND TRAINING IN PAIN CARE.

"(a) IN GENERAL.—The Secretary may make awards of grants, cooperative agreements, and contracts to health professions schools, hospices, and other public and private entities for the development and implementation of programs to provide education and training to health care professionals in pain care.

"(b) CERTAIN TOPICS.—An award may be made under subsection (a) only if the applicant for the award agrees that the program carried out with the award will include information and education on—

"(1) recognized means for assessing, diagnosing, treating, and managing pain and related signs and symptoms, including the medically appropriate use of controlled substances;

"(2) applicable laws, regulations, rules, and policies on controlled substances, including the degree to which misconceptions and concerns regarding such laws, regulations, rules, and policies, or the enforcement thereof, may create barriers to patient access to appropriate and effective pain care;

"(3) interdisciplinary approaches to the delivery of pain care, including delivery through specialized centers providing comprehensive pain care treatment expertise;

"(4) cultural, linguistic, literacy, geographic, and other barriers to care in underserved populations; and

"(5) recent findings, developments, and improvements in the provision of pain care.

"(c) EVALUATION OF PROGRAMS.—The Secretary shall (directly or through grants or contracts) provide for the evaluation of programs implemented under subsection (a) in order to determine the effect of such programs on knowledge and practice of pain care.

"(d) PAIN CARE DEFINED.—For purposes of this section the term 'pain care' means the assessment, diagnosis, treatment, or management of acute or chronic pain regardless of causation or body location.

"(e) AUTHORIZATION OF APPROPRIATIONS.—There is authorized to be appropriated to carry out this section, such sums as may be necessary for each of the fiscal years 2010 through 2012. Amounts appropriated under this subsection shall remain available until expended.".

SEC. 4306. FUNDING FOR CHILDHOOD OBESITY DEMONSTRATION PROJECT.

Section 1139A(e)(8) of the Social Security Act (42 U.S.C. 1320b–9a(e)(8)) is amended to read as follows:

"(8) APPROPRIATION.—Out of any funds in the Treasury not otherwise appropriated, there is appropriated to carry out this subsection, $25,000,000 for the period of fiscal years 2010 through 2014.".

Subtitle E—Miscellaneous Provisions

SEC. 4401. SENSE OF THE SENATE CONCERNING CBO SCORING.

(a) FINDING.—The Senate finds that the costs of prevention programs are difficult to estimate due in part because prevention initiatives are hard to measure and results may occur outside the 5 and 10 year budget windows.

(b) SENSE OF CONGRESS.—It is the sense of the Senate that Congress should work with the Congressional Budget Office to develop better methodologies for scoring progress to be made in prevention and wellness programs.

SEC. 4402. EFFECTIVENESS OF FEDERAL HEALTH AND WELLNESS INITIATIVES.

To determine whether existing Federal health and wellness initiatives are effective in achieving their stated goals, the Secretary of Health and Human Services shall—

(1) conduct an evaluation of such programs as they relate to changes in health status of the American public and specifically on the health status of the Federal workforce, including absenteeism of employees, the productivity of employees, the rate of workplace injury, and the medical costs incurred by employees, and health conditions, including workplace fitness, healthy food and beverages, and incentives in the Federal Employee Health Benefits Program; and

(2) submit to Congress a report concerning such evaluation, which shall include conclusions concerning the reasons that such existing programs have proven successful or not successful and what factors contributed to such conclusions.

TITLE V—HEALTH CARE WORKFORCE

Subtitle A—Purpose and Definitions

SEC. 5001. PURPOSE.

The purpose of this title is to improve access to and the delivery of health care services for all individuals, particularly low income, underserved, uninsured, minority, health disparity, and rural populations by—

(1) gathering and assessing comprehensive data in order for the health care workforce to meet the health care needs of individuals, including research on the supply, demand, distribution, diversity, and skills needs of the health care workforce;

(2) increasing the supply of a qualified health care workforce to improve access to and the delivery of health care services for all individuals;

(3) enhancing health care workforce education and training to improve access to and the delivery of health care services for all individuals; and

(4) providing support to the existing health care workforce to improve access to and the delivery of health care services for all individuals.

SEC. 5002. DEFINITIONS.

(a) THIS TITLE.—In this title:

(1) ALLIED HEALTH PROFESSIONAL.—The term "allied health professional" means an allied health professional as defined in section 799B(5) of the Public Heath Service Act (42 U.S.C. 295p(5)) who—

(A) has graduated and received an allied health professions degree or certificate from an institution of higher education; and

(B) is employed with a Federal, State, local or tribal public health agency, or in a setting where patients might require health care services, including acute care facilities, ambulatory care facilities, personal residences, and other settings located in health professional shortage areas, medically underserved areas, or medically underserved populations, as recognized by the Secretary of Health and Human Services.

(2) HEALTH CARE CAREER PATHWAY.—The term "healthcare career pathway" means a rigorous, engaging, and high quality set of courses and services that—

(A) includes an articulated sequence of academic and career courses, including 21st century skills;

(B) is aligned with the needs of healthcare industries in a region or State;

(C) prepares students for entry into the full range of postsecondary education options, including registered apprenticeships, and careers;

(D) provides academic and career counseling in student-to-counselor ratios that allow students to make informed decisions about academic and career options;

(E) meets State academic standards, State requirements for secondary school graduation and is aligned with requirements for entry into postsecondary education, and applicable industry standards; and

(F) leads to 2 or more credentials, including—

(i) a secondary school diploma; and

(ii) a postsecondary degree, an apprenticeship or other occupational certification, a certificate, or a license.

(3) INSTITUTION OF HIGHER EDUCATION.—The term "institution of higher education" has the meaning given the term in sections 101 and 102 of the Higher Education Act of 1965 (20 U.S.C. 1001 and 1002).

(4) LOW INCOME INDIVIDUAL, STATE WORKFORCE INVESTMENT BOARD, AND LOCAL WORKFORCE INVESTMENT BOARD.—

(A) LOW-INCOME INDIVIDUAL.—The term "low-income individual" has the meaning given that term in section 101 of the Workforce investment Act of 1998 (29 U.S.C. 2801).

(B) STATE WORKFORCE INVESTMENT BOARD; LOCAL WORKFORCE INVESTMENT BOARD.—The terms "State workforce investment board" and "local workforce investment board", refer to a State workforce investment board established under section 111 of the Workforce Investment Act of 1998 (29 U.S.C. 2821) and a local workforce investment board established under section 117 of such Act (29 U.S.C. 2832), respectively.

(5) POSTSECONDARY EDUCATION.—The term "postsecondary education" means—

(A) a 4-year program of instruction, or not less than a 1-year program of instruction that is acceptable for credit toward an associate or a baccalaureate degree, offered by an institution of higher education; or

(B) a certificate or registered apprenticeship program at the postsecondary level offered by an institution of higher education or a non-profit educational institution.

(6) REGISTERED APPRENTICESHIP PROGRAM.—The term "registered apprenticeship program" means an industry skills training program at the postsecondary level that combines technical and theoretical training through structure on the job

learning with related instruction (in a classroom or through distance learning) while an individual is employed, working under the direction of qualified personnel or a mentor, and earning incremental wage increases aligned to enhance job proficiency, resulting in the acquisition of a nationally recognized and portable certificate, under a plan approved by the Office of Apprenticeship or a State agency recognized by the Department of Labor.

(b) TITLE VII OF THE PUBLIC HEALTH SERVICE ACT.—Section 799B of the Public Health Service Act (42 U.S.C. 295p) is amended—

(1) by striking paragraph (3) and inserting the following:

"(3) PHYSICIAN ASSISTANT EDUCATION PROGRAM.—The term 'physician assistant education program' means an educational program in a public or private institution in a State that—

"(A) has as its objective the education of individuals who, upon completion of their studies in the program, be qualified to provide primary care medical services with the supervision of a physician; and

"(B) is accredited by the Accreditation Review Commission on Education for the Physician Assistant."; and

(2) by adding at the end the following:

"(12) AREA HEALTH EDUCATION CENTER.—The term 'area health education center' means a public or nonprofit private organization that has a cooperative agreement or contract in effect with an entity that has received an award under subsection (a)(1) or (a)(2) of section 751, satisfies the requirements in section 751(d)(1), and has as one of its principal functions the operation of an area health education center. Appropriate organizations may include hospitals, health organizations with accredited primary care training programs, accredited physician assistant educational programs associated with a college or university, and universities or colleges not operating a school of medicine or osteopathic medicine.

"(13) AREA HEALTH EDUCATION CENTER PROGRAM.—The term 'area health education center program' means cooperative program consisting of an entity that has received an award under subsection (a)(1) or (a)(2) of section 751 for the purpose of planning, developing, operating, and evaluating an area health education center program and one or more area health education centers, which carries out the required activities described in section 751(c), satisfies the program requirements in such section, has as one of its principal functions identifying and implementing strategies and activities that address health care workforce needs in its service area, in coordination with the local workforce investment boards.

"(14) CLINICAL SOCIAL WORKER.—The term 'clinical social worker' has the meaning given the term in section 1861(hh)(1) of the Social Security Act (42 U.S.C. 1395x(hh)(1)).

"(15) CULTURAL COMPETENCY.—The term 'cultural competency' shall be defined by the Secretary in a manner consistent with section 1707(d)(3).

"(16) DIRECT CARE WORKER.—The term 'direct care worker' has the meaning given that term in the 2010 Standard Occupational Classifications of the Department of Labor for Home Health Aides [31–1011], Psychiatric Aides [31–1013], Nursing Assistants [31–1014], and Personal Care Aides [39–9021].

"(17) FEDERALLY QUALIFIED HEALTH CENTER.—The term 'Federally qualified health center' has the meaning given that term in section 1861(aa) of the Social Security Act (42 U.S.C. 1395x(aa)).

"(18) FRONTIER HEALTH PROFESSIONAL SHORTAGE AREA.—The term 'frontier health professional shortage area' means an area—

"(A) with a population density less than 6 persons per square mile within the service area; and

"(B) with respect to which the distance or time for the population to access care is excessive.

"(19) GRADUATE PSYCHOLOGY.—The term 'graduate psychology' means an accredited program in professional psychology.

"(20) HEALTH DISPARITY POPULATION.—The term 'health disparity population' has the meaning given such term in section 903(d)(1).

"(21) HEALTH LITERACY.—The term 'health literacy' means the degree to which an individual has the capacity to obtain, communicate, process, and understand health information and services in order to make appropriate health decisions.

"(22) MENTAL HEALTH SERVICE PROFESSIONAL.—The term 'mental health service professional' means an individual with a graduate or postgraduate degree from an accredited institution of higher education in psychiatry, psychology, school psychology, behavioral pediatrics, psychiatric nursing, social work, school social work, substance abuse disorder prevention and treatment, marriage and family counseling, school counseling, or professional counseling.

"(23) ONE-STOP DELIVERY SYSTEM CENTER.—The term 'one-stop delivery system' means a one-stop delivery system described in section 134(c) of the Workforce Investment Act of 1998 (29 U.S.C. 2864(c)).

"(24) PARAPROFESSIONAL CHILD AND ADOLESCENT MENTAL HEALTH WORKER.—The term 'paraprofessional child and adolescent mental health worker' means an individual who is not a mental or behavioral health service professional, but who works at the first stage of contact with children and families who are seeking mental or behavioral health services, including substance abuse prevention and treatment services.

"(25) RACIAL AND ETHNIC MINORITY GROUP; RACIAL AND ETHNIC MINORITY POPULATION.—The terms 'racial and ethnic minority group' and 'racial and ethnic minority population' have the meaning given the term 'racial and ethnic minority group' in section 1707.

"(26) RURAL HEALTH CLINIC.—The term 'rural health clinic' has the meaning given that term in section 1861(aa) of the Social Security Act (42 U.S.C. 1395x(aa)).".

(c) TITLE VIII OF THE PUBLIC HEALTH SERVICE ACT.—Section 801 of the Public Health Service Act (42 U.S.C. 296) is amended—

(1) in paragraph (2)—

(A) by striking "means a" and inserting "means an accredited (as defined in paragraph 6)"; and

(B) by striking the period as inserting the following: "where graduates are—

"(A) authorized to sit for the National Council Licensure EXamination-Registered Nurse (NCLEX–RN); or

"(B) licensed registered nurses who will receive a graduate or equivalent degree or training to become an advanced education nurse as defined by section 811(b)."; and

(2) by adding at the end the following:

"(16) ACCELERATED NURSING DEGREE PROGRAM.—The term 'accelerated nursing degree program' means a program of education in professional nursing offered by an accredited school of nursing in which an individual holding a bachelors degree in another discipline receives a BSN or MSN degree in an accelerated time frame as determined by the accredited school of nursing.

"(17) BRIDGE OR DEGREE COMPLETION PROGRAM.—The term 'bridge or degree completion program' means a program of education in professional nursing offered by an accredited school of nursing, as defined in paragraph (2), that leads to a baccalaureate degree in nursing. Such programs may include, Registered Nurse (RN) to Bachelor's of Science of Nursing (BSN) programs, RN to MSN (Master of Science of Nursing) programs, or BSN to Doctoral programs.".

Subtitle B—Innovations in the Health Care Workforce

SEC. 5101. NATIONAL HEALTH CARE WORKFORCE COMMISSION.

(a) PURPOSE.—It is the purpose of this section to establish a National Health Care Workforce Commission that—

(1) serves as a national resource for Congress, the President, States, and localities;

(2) communicates and coordinates with the Departments of Health and Human Services, Labor, Veterans Affairs, Homeland Security, and Education on related activities administered by one or more of such Departments;

(3) develops and commissions evaluations of education and training activities to determine whether the demand for health care workers is being met;

(4) identifies barriers to improved coordination at the Federal, State, and local levels and recommend ways to address such barriers; and

(5) encourages innovations to address population needs, constant changes in technology, and other environmental factors.

(b) ESTABLISHMENT.—There is hereby established the National Health Care Workforce Commission (in this section referred to as the "Commission").

(c) MEMBERSHIP.—

(1) NUMBER AND APPOINTMENT.—The Commission shall be composed of 15 members to be appointed by the Comptroller General, without regard to section 5 of the Federal Advisory Committee Act (5 U.S.C. App.).

(2) QUALIFICATIONS.—

(A) IN GENERAL.—The membership of the Commission shall include individuals—

(i) with national recognition for their expertise in health care labor market analysis, including health care workforce analysis; health care finance and economics; health care facility management; health care plans and integrated delivery systems; health care workforce education and training; health care philanthropy; providers of health care services; and other related fields; and

(ii) who will provide a combination of professional perspectives, broad geographic representation, and a balance between urban, suburban, rural, and frontier representatives.

(B) INCLUSION.—

(i) IN GENERAL.—The membership of the Commission shall include no less than one representative of—

(I) the health care workforce and health professionals;

(II) employers;

(III) third-party payers;

(IV) individuals skilled in the conduct and interpretation of health care services and health economics research;

(V) representatives of consumers;

(VI) labor unions;

(VII) State or local workforce investment boards; and

(VIII) educational institutions (which may include elementary and secondary institutions, institutions of higher education, including 2 and 4 year institutions, or registered apprenticeship programs).

(ii) ADDITIONAL MEMBERS.—The remaining membership may include additional representatives from clause (i) and other individuals as determined appropriate by the Comptroller General of the United States.

(C) MAJORITY NON-PROVIDERS.—Individuals who are directly involved in health professions education or practice shall not constitute a majority of the membership of the Commission.

(D) ETHICAL DISCLOSURE.—The Comptroller General shall establish a system for public disclosure by members of the Commission of financial and other potential conflicts of interest relating to such members. Members of the Commission shall be treated as employees of Congress for purposes of applying title I of the Ethics in Government Act of 1978. Members of the Commission shall not be treated as special government employees under title 18, United States Code.

(3) TERMS.—

(A) IN GENERAL.—The terms of members of the Commission shall be for 3 years except that the Comptroller General shall designate staggered terms for the members first appointed.

(B) VACANCIES.—Any member appointed to fill a vacancy occurring before the expiration of the term for which the member's predecessor was appointed shall be appointed only for the remainder of that term. A member may serve after the expiration of that member's term until a successor has taken office. A vacancy in the Commission shall be filled in the manner in which the original appointment was made.

(C) INITIAL APPOINTMENTS.—The Comptroller General shall make initial appointments of members to the Commission not later than September 30, 2010.

(4) COMPENSATION.—While serving on the business of the Commission (including travel time), a member of the Commission shall be entitled to compensation at the per diem equivalent of the rate provided for level IV of the Executive Schedule under section 5315 of tile 5, United States Code, and while so serving away from home and the member's regular place of business, a member may be allowed travel expenses, as authorized by the Chairman of the Commission. Physicians serving as personnel of the Commission may be provided a physician comparability allowance by the Commission in the same manner as Government physicians may be provided such an allowance by an agency under section 5948 of title 5, United States Code, and for such purpose subsection (i) of such section shall apply to the Commission in the same manner as it applies to the Tennessee Valley Authority. For purposes of pay (other than pay of members of the Commission) and employment benefits, rights, and privileges, all personnel of the Commission shall be treated as if they were employees of the United States Senate. Personnel of the Commission shall not be treated as employees of the Government Accountability Office for any purpose.

(5) CHAIRMAN, VICE CHAIRMAN.—The Comptroller General shall designate a member of the Commission, at the time of appointment of the member, as Chairman and a member as Vice Chairman for that term of appointment, except that in the case of vacancy of the chairmanship or vice chairmanship, the Comptroller General may designate another member for the remainder of that member's term.

(6) MEETINGS.—The Commission shall meet at the call of the chairman, but no less frequently than on a quarterly basis.

(d) DUTIES.—

(1) RECOGNITION, DISSEMINATION, AND COMMUNICATION.—The Commission shall—

(A) recognize efforts of Federal, State, and local partnerships to develop and offer health care career pathways of proven effectiveness;

(B) disseminate information on promising retention practices for health care professionals; and

(C) communicate information on important policies and practices that affect the recruitment, education and training, and retention of the health care workforce.

(2) REVIEW OF HEALTH CARE WORKFORCE AND ANNUAL REPORTS.—In order to develop a fiscally sustainable integrated workforce that supports a high-quality, readily accessible health care delivery system that meets the needs of patients and populations, the Commission, in consultation with relevant Federal, State, and local agencies, shall—

(A) review current and projected health care workforce supply and demand, including the topics described in paragraph (3);

(B) make recommendations to Congress and the Administration concerning national health care workforce priorities, goals, and policies;

(C) by not later than October 1 of each year (beginning with 2011), submit a report to Congress and the Administration containing the results of such reviews and recommendations concerning related policies; and

(D) by not later than April 1 of each year (beginning with 2011), submit a report to Congress and the Administration containing a review of, and recommendations on, at a minimum one high priority area as described in paragraph (4).

(3) SPECIFIC TOPICS TO BE REVIEWED.—The topics described in this paragraph include—

(A) current health care workforce supply and distribution, including demographics, skill sets, and demands, with projected demands during the subsequent 10 and 25 year periods;

(B) health care workforce education and training capacity, including the number of students who have completed education and training, including registered apprenticeships; the number of qualified faculty; the education and training infrastructure; and the education and training demands, with projected demands during the subsequent 10 and 25 year periods;

(C) the education loan and grant programs in titles VII and VIII of the Public Health Service Act (42 U.S.C. 292 et seq. and 296 et seq.), with recommendations on whether such programs should become part of the Higher Education Act of 1965 (20 U.S.C. 1001 et seq);

(D) the implications of new and existing Federal policies which affect the health care workforce, including Medicare and Medicaid graduate medical education policies, titles VII and VIII of the Public Health Service Act (42 U.S.C. 292 et seq. and 296 et seq.), the National Health Service Corps (with recommendations for aligning such programs with national health workforce priorities and goals), and other health care workforce programs, including those supported through the Workforce Investment Act of 1998 (29 U.S.C. 2801 et seq.), the Carl D. Perkins Career and Technical Education Act of 2006 (20 U.S.C. 2301 et seq.), the Higher Education Act of 1965 (20 U.S.C. 1001 et seq.), and any other Federal health care workforce programs;

(E) the health care workforce needs of special populations, such as minorities, rural populations, medically underserved populations, gender specific needs, individuals with disabilities, and geriatric and pediatric populations with recommendations for new and existing Federal policies to meet the needs of these special populations; and

(F) recommendations creating or revising national loan repayment programs and scholarship programs to require low-income, minority medical students to serve in their home communities, if designated as medical underserved community.

(4) HIGH PRIORITY AREAS.—

(A) IN GENERAL.—The initial high priority topics described in this paragraph include each of the following:

(i) Integrated health care workforce planning that identifies health care professional skills needed and maximizes the skill sets of health care professionals across disciplines.

(ii) An analysis of the nature, scopes of practice, and demands for health care workers in the enhanced information technology and management workplace.

(iii) An analysis of how to align Medicare and Medicaid graduate medical education policies with national workforce goals.

(iv) The education and training capacity, projected demands, and integration with the health care delivery system of each of the following:

(I) Nursing workforce capacity at all levels.

(II) Oral health care workforce capacity at all levels.

(III) Mental and behavioral health care workforce capacity at all levels.

(IV) Allied health and public health care workforce capacity at all levels.

(V) Emergency medical service workforce capacity, including the retention and recruitment of the volunteer workforce, at all levels.

(VI) The geographic distribution of health care providers as compared to the identified health care workforce needs of States and regions.

(B) FUTURE DETERMINATIONS.—The Commission may require that additional topics be included under subparagraph (A). The appropriate committees of Congress may recommend to the Commission the inclusion of other topics for health care workforce development areas that require special attention.

(5) GRANT PROGRAM.—The Commission shall—

(A) review implementation progress reports on, and report to Congress about, the State Health Care Workforce Development Grant program established in section 5102;

(B) in collaboration with the Department of Labor and in coordination with the Department of Education and other relevant Federal agencies, make recommendations to the fiscal and administrative agent under section 5102(b) for grant recipients under section 5102;

(C) assess the implementation of the grants under such section; and

(D) collect performance and report information, including identified models and best practices, on grants from the fiscal and administrative agent under such section and distribute this information to Congress, relevant Federal agencies, and to the public.

(6) STUDY.—The Commission shall study effective mechanisms for financing education and training for careers in health care, including public health and allied health.

(7) RECOMMENDATIONS.—The Commission shall submit recommendations to Congress, the Department of Labor, and the Department of Health and Human Services about improving

safety, health, and worker protections in the workplace for the health care workforce.

(8) ASSESSMENT.—The Commission shall assess and receive reports from the National Center for Health Care Workforce Analysis established under section 761(b) of the Public Service Health Act (as amended by section 5103).

(e) CONSULTATION WITH FEDERAL, STATE, AND LOCAL AGENCIES, CONGRESS, AND OTHER ORGANIZATIONS.—

(1) IN GENERAL.—The Commission shall consult with Federal agencies (including the Departments of Health and Human Services, Labor, Education, Commerce, Agriculture, Defense, and Veterans Affairs and the Environmental Protection Agency), Congress, the Medicare Payment Advisory Commission, the Medicaid and CHIP Payment and Access Commission, and, to the extent practicable, with State and local agencies, Indian tribes, voluntary health care organizations, professional societies, and other relevant public-private health care partnerships.

(2) OBTAINING OFFICIAL DATA.—The Commission, consistent with established privacy rules, may secure directly from any department or agency of the Executive Branch information necessary to enable the Commission to carry out this section.

(3) DETAIL OF FEDERAL GOVERNMENT EMPLOYEES.—An employee of the Federal Government may be detailed to the Commission without reimbursement. The detail of such an employee shall be without interruption or loss of civil service status.

(f) DIRECTOR AND STAFF; EXPERTS AND CONSULTANTS.—Subject to such review as the Comptroller General of the United States determines to be necessary to ensure the efficient administration of the Commission, the Commission may—

(1) employ and fix the compensation of an executive director that shall not exceed the rate of basic pay payable for level V of the Executive Schedule and such other personnel as may be necessary to carry out its duties (without regard to the provisions of title 5, United States Code, governing appointments in the competitive service);

(2) seek such assistance and support as may be required in the performance of its duties from appropriate Federal departments and agencies;

(3) enter into contracts or make other arrangements, as may be necessary for the conduct of the work of the Commission (without regard to section 3709 of the Revised Statutes (41 U.S.C. 5));

(4) make advance, progress, and other payments which relate to the work of the Commission;

(5) provide transportation and subsistence for persons serving without compensation; and

(6) prescribe such rules and regulations as the Commission determines to be necessary with respect to the internal organization and operation of the Commission.

(g) POWERS.—

(1) DATA COLLECTION.—In order to carry out its functions under this section, the Commission shall—

(A) utilize existing information, both published and unpublished, where possible, collected and assessed either by its own staff or under other arrangements made in accordance with this section, including coordination with the Bureau of Labor Statistics;

(B) carry out, or award grants or contracts for the carrying out of, original research and development, where existing information is inadequate, and

(C) adopt procedures allowing interested parties to submit information for the Commission's use in making reports and recommendations.

(2) ACCESS OF THE GOVERNMENT ACCOUNTABILITY OFFICE TO INFORMATION.—The Comptroller General of the United States shall have unrestricted access to all deliberations, records, and data of the Commission, immediately upon request.

(3) PERIODIC AUDIT.—The Commission shall be subject to periodic audit by an independent public accountant under contract to the Commission.

(h) AUTHORIZATION OF APPROPRIATIONS.—

(1) REQUEST FOR APPROPRIATIONS.—The Commission shall submit requests for appropriations in the same manner as the Comptroller General of the United States submits requests for appropriations. Amounts so appropriated for the Commission shall be separate from amounts appropriated for the Comptroller General.

(2) AUTHORIZATION.—There are authorized to be appropriated such sums as may be necessary to carry out this section.

(3) GIFTS AND SERVICES.—The Commission may not accept gifts, bequeaths, or donations of property, but may accept and use donations of services for purposes of carrying out this section.

(i) DEFINITIONS.—In this section:

(1) HEALTH CARE WORKFORCE.—The term "health care workforce" includes all health care providers with direct patient care and support responsibilities, such as physicians, nurses, nurse practitioners, primary care providers, preventive medicine physicians, optometrists, ophthalmologists, physician assistants, pharmacists, dentists, dental hygienists, and other oral healthcare professionals, allied health professionals, doctors of chiropractic, community health workers, health care paraprofessionals, direct care workers, psychologists and other behavioral and mental health professionals (including substance abuse prevention and treatment providers), social workers, physical and occupational therapists, certified nurse midwives, podiatrists, the EMS workforce (including professional and volunteer ambulance personnel and firefighters who perform emergency medical services), licensed complementary and alternative medicine providers, integrative health practitioners, public health professionals, and any other health professional that the Comptroller General of the United States determines appropriate.

(2) HEALTH PROFESSIONALS.—The term "health professionals" includes—

(A) dentists, dental hygienists, primary care providers, specialty physicians, nurses, nurse practitioners, physician assistants, psychologists and other behavioral and mental health professionals (including substance abuse prevention and treatment providers), social workers, physical and occupational therapists, public health professionals, clinical pharmacists, allied health professionals, doctors of chiropractic, community health workers, school nurses, certified nurse midwives, podiatrists, licensed complementary and alternative medicine providers, the EMS workforce (including professional and volunteer ambulance personnel and firefighters who perform emergency medical services), and integrative health practitioners;

(B) national representatives of health professionals;

(C) representatives of schools of medicine, osteopathy, nursing, dentistry, optometry, pharmacy, chiropractic, allied health, educational programs for public health professionals, behavioral and mental health professionals (as so defined), social workers, pharmacists, physical and occupational therapists, oral health care industry dentistry and dental hygiene, and physician assistants;

(D) representatives of public and private teaching hospitals, and ambulatory health facilities, including Federal medical facilities; and

(E) any other health professional the Comptroller General of the United States determines appropriate.

SEC. 5102. STATE HEALTH CARE WORKFORCE DEVELOPMENT GRANTS.

(a) ESTABLISHMENT.—There is established a competitive health care workforce development grant program (referred to in this section as the "program") for the purpose of enabling State partnerships to complete comprehensive planning and to carry out activities leading to coherent and comprehensive health care workforce development strategies at the State and local levels.

(b) FISCAL AND ADMINISTRATIVE AGENT.—The Health Resources and Services Administration of the Department of Health and Human Services (referred to in this section as the "Administration") shall be the fiscal and administrative agent for the grants awarded under this section. The Administration is authorized to carry out the program, in consultation with the National Health Care Workforce Commission (referred to in this section as the "Commission"), which shall review reports on the development, implementation, and evaluation activities of the grant program, including—

(1) administering the grants;

(2) providing technical assistance to grantees; and

(3) reporting performance information to the Commission.

(c) PLANNING GRANTS.—

(1) AMOUNT AND DURATION.—A planning grant shall be awarded under this subsection for a period of not more than one year and the maximum award may not be more than $150,000.

(2) ELIGIBILITY.—To be eligible to receive a planning grant, an entity shall be an eligible partnership. An eligible partnership shall be a State workforce investment board, if it includes or modifies the members to include at least one representative from each of the following: health care employer, labor organization, a public 2-year institution of higher education, a public 4-year institution of higher education, the recognized State federation of labor, the State public secondary education agency, the State P–16 or P–20 Council if such a council exists, and a philanthropic organization that is actively engaged in providing learning, mentoring, and work opportunities to recruit,

educate, and train individuals for, and retain individuals in, careers in health care and related industries.

(3) FISCAL AND ADMINISTRATIVE AGENT.—The Governor of the State receiving a planning grant has the authority to appoint a fiscal and an administrative agency for the partnership.

(4) APPLICATION.—Each State partnership desiring a planning grant shall submit an application to the Administrator of the Administration at such time and in such manner, and accompanied by such information as the Administrator may reasonable require. Each application submitted for a planning grant shall describe the members of the State partnership, the activities for which assistance is sought, the proposed performance benchmarks to be used to measure progress under the planning grant, a budget for use of the funds to complete the required activities described in paragraph (5), and such additional assurance and information as the Administrator determines to be essential to ensure compliance with the grant program requirements.

(5) REQUIRED ACTIVITIES.—A State partnership receiving a planning grant shall carry out the following:

(A) Analyze State labor market information in order to create health care career pathways for students and adults, including dislocated workers.

(B) Identify current and projected high demand State or regional health care sectors for purposes of planning career pathways.

(C) Identify existing Federal, State, and private resources to recruit, educate or train, and retain a skilled health care workforce and strengthen partnerships.

(D) Describe the academic and health care industry skill standards for high school graduation, for entry into postsecondary education, and for various credentials and licensure.

(E) Describe State secondary and postsecondary education and training policies, models, or practices for the health care sector, including career information and guidance counseling.

(F) Identify Federal or State policies or rules to developing a coherent and comprehensive health care workforce development strategy and barriers and a plan to resolve these barriers.

(G) Participate in the Administration's evaluation and reporting activities.

(6) PERFORMANCE AND EVALUATION.—Before the State partnership receives a planning grant, such partnership and the Administrator of the Administration shall jointly determine the performance benchmarks that will be established for the purposes of the planning grant.

(7) MATCH.—Each State partnership receiving a planning grant shall provide an amount, in cash or in kind, that is not less that 15 percent of the amount of the grant, to carry out the activities supported by the grant. The matching requirement may be provided from funds available under other Federal, State, local or private sources to carry out the activities.

(8) REPORT.—

(A) REPORT TO ADMINISTRATION.—Not later than 1 year after a State partnership receives a planning grant, the partnership shall submit a report to the Administration on the State's performance of the activities under the grant, including the use of funds, including matching funds, to carry out required activities, and a description of the progress of the State workforce investment board in meeting the performance benchmarks.

(B) REPORT TO CONGRESS.—The Administration shall submit a report to Congress analyzing the planning activities, performance, and fund utilization of each State grant recipient, including an identification of promising practices and a profile of the activities of each State grant recipient.

(d) IMPLEMENTATION GRANTS.—

(1) IN GENERAL.—The Administration shall—

(A) competitively award implementation grants to State partnerships to enable such partnerships to implement activities that will result in a coherent and comprehensive plan for health workforce development that will address current and projected workforce demands within the State; and

(B) inform the Commission and Congress about the awards made.

(2) DURATION.—An implementation grant shall be awarded for a period of no more than 2 years, except in those cases where the Administration determines that the grantee is high performing and the activities supported by the grant warrant up to 1 additional year of funding.

(3) ELIGIBILITY.—To be eligible for an implementation grant, a State partnership shall have—

(A) received a planning grant under subsection (c) and completed all requirements of such grant; or

(B) completed a satisfactory application, including a plan to coordinate with required partners and complete the required activities during the 2 year period of the implementation grant.

(4) FISCAL AND ADMINISTRATIVE AGENT.—A State partnership receiving an implementation grant shall appoint a fiscal and an administration agent for the implementation of such grant.

(5) APPLICATION.—Each eligible State partnership desiring an implementation grant shall submit an application to the Administration at such time, in such manner, and accompanied by such information as the Administration may reasonably require. Each application submitted shall include—

(A) a description of the members of the State partnership;

(B) a description of how the State partnership completed the required activities under the planning grant, if applicable;

(C) a description of the activities for which implementation grant funds are sought, including grants to regions by the State partnership to advance coherent and comprehensive regional health care workforce planning activities;

(D) a description of how the State partnership will coordinate with required partners and complete the required partnership activities during the duration of an implementation grant;

(E) a budget proposal of the cost of the activities supported by the implementation grant and a timeline for the provision of matching funds required;

(F) proposed performance benchmarks to be used to assess and evaluate the progress of the partnership activities;

(G) a description of how the State partnership will collect data to report progress in grant activities; and

(H) such additional assurances as the Administration determines to be essential to ensure compliance with grant requirements.

(6) REQUIRED ACTIVITIES.—

(A) IN GENERAL.—A State partnership that receives an implementation grant may reserve not less than 60 percent of the grant funds to make grants to be competitively awarded by the State partnership, consistent with State procurement rules, to encourage regional partnerships to address health care workforce development needs and to promote innovative health care workforce career pathway activities, including career counseling, learning, and employment.

(B) ELIGIBLE PARTNERSHIP DUTIES.—An eligible State partnership receiving an implementation grant shall—

(i) identify and convene regional leadership to discuss opportunities to engage in statewide health care workforce development planning, including the potential use of competitive grants to improve the development, distribution, and diversity of the regional health care workforce; the alignment of curricula for health care careers; and the access to quality career information and guidance and education and training opportunities;

(ii) in consultation with key stakeholders and regional leaders, take appropriate steps to reduce Federal, State, or local barriers to a comprehensive and coherent strategy, including changes in State or local policies to foster coherent and comprehensive health care workforce development activities, including health care career pathways at the regional and State levels, career planning information, retraining for dislocated workers, and as appropriate, requests for Federal program or administrative waivers;

(iii) develop, disseminate, and review with key stakeholders a preliminary statewide strategy that addresses short- and long-term health care workforce development supply versus demand;

(iv) convene State partnership members on a regular basis, and at least on a semiannual basis;

(v) assist leaders at the regional level to form partnerships, including technical assistance and capacity building activities;

(vi) collect and assess data on and report on the performance benchmarks selected by the State partnership and the Administration for implementation activities carried out by regional and State partnerships; and

(vii) participate in the Administration's evaluation and reporting activities.

(7) PERFORMANCE AND EVALUATION.—Before the State partnership receives an implementation grant, it and the Administrator shall jointly determine the performance benchmarks that shall be established for the purposes of the implementation grant.

(8) MATCH.—Each State partnership receiving an implementation grant shall provide an amount, in cash or in kind that is not less than 25 percent of the amount of the grant, to carry out the activities supported by the grant. The matching funds may be provided from funds available from other Federal, State, local, or private sources to carry out such activities.

(9) REPORTS.—

(A) REPORT TO ADMINISTRATION.—For each year of the implementation grant, the State partnership receiving the implementation grant shall submit a report to the Administration on the performance of the State of the grant activities, including a description of the use of the funds, including matched funds, to complete activities, and a description of the performance of the State partnership in meeting the performance benchmarks.

(B) REPORT TO CONGRESS.—The Administration shall submit a report to Congress analyzing implementation activities, performance, and fund utilization of the State grantees, including an identification of promising practices and a profile of the activities of each State grantee.

(e) AUTHORIZATION FOR APPROPRIATIONS.—

(1) PLANNING GRANTS.—There are authorized to be appropriated to award planning grants under subsection (c) $8,000,000 for fiscal year 2010, and such sums as may be necessary for each subsequent fiscal year.

(2) IMPLEMENTATION GRANTS.—There are authorized to be appropriated to award implementation grants under subsection (d), $150,000,000 for fiscal year 2010, and such sums as may be necessary for each subsequent fiscal year.

SEC. 5103. HEALTH CARE WORKFORCE ASSESSMENT.

(a) IN GENERAL.—Section 761 of the Public Health Service Act (42 U.S.C. 294m) is amended—

(1) by redesignating subsection (c) as subsection (e);

(2) by striking subsection (b) and inserting the following:

"(b) NATIONAL CENTER FOR HEALTH CARE WORKFORCE ANALYSIS.—

"(1) ESTABLISHMENT.—The Secretary shall establish the National Center for Health Workforce Analysis (referred to in this section as the 'National Center').

"(2) PURPOSES.—The National Center, in coordination to the extent practicable with the National Health Care Workforce

Commission (established in section 5101 of the Patient Protection and Affordable Care Act), and relevant regional and State centers and agencies, shall—

"(A) provide for the development of information describing and analyzing the health care workforce and workforce related issues;

"(B) carry out the activities under section 792(a);

"(C) annually evaluate programs under this title;

"(D) develop and publish performance measures and benchmarks for programs under this title; and

"(E) establish, maintain, and publicize a national Internet registry of each grant awarded under this title and a database to collect data from longitudinal evaluations (as described in subsection (d)(2)) on performance measures (as developed under sections 749(d)(3), 757(d)(3), and 762(a)(3)).

"(3) COLLABORATION AND DATA SHARING.—

"(A) IN GENERAL.—The National Center shall collaborate with Federal agencies and relevant professional and educational organizations or societies for the purpose of linking data regarding grants awarded under this title.

"(B) CONTRACTS FOR HEALTH WORKFORCE ANALYSIS.—For the purpose of carrying out the activities described in subparagraph (A), the National Center may enter into contracts with relevant professional and educational organizations or societies.

"(c) STATE AND REGIONAL CENTERS FOR HEALTH WORKFORCE ANALYSIS.—

"(1) IN GENERAL.—The Secretary shall award grants to, or enter into contracts with, eligible entities for purposes of—

"(A) collecting, analyzing, and reporting data regarding programs under this title to the National Center and to the public; and

"(B) providing technical assistance to local and regional entities on the collection, analysis, and reporting of data.

"(2) ELIGIBLE ENTITIES.—To be eligible for a grant or contract under this subsection, an entity shall—

"(A) be a State, a State workforce investment board, a public health or health professions school, an academic health center, or an appropriate public or private nonprofit entity; and

"(B) submit to the Secretary an application at such time, in such manner, and containing such information as the Secretary may require.

"(d) INCREASE IN GRANTS FOR LONGITUDINAL EVALUATIONS.—

"(1) IN GENERAL.—The Secretary shall increase the amount awarded to an eligible entity under this title for a longitudinal evaluation of individuals who have received education, training, or financial assistance from programs under this title.

"(2) CAPABILITY.—A longitudinal evaluation shall be capable of—

"(A) studying practice patterns; and

"(B) collecting and reporting data on performance measures developed under sections 749(d)(3), 757(d)(3), and 762(a)(3).

"(3) GUIDELINES.—A longitudinal evaluation shall comply with guidelines issued under sections 749(d)(4), 757(d)(4), and 762(a)(4).

"(4) ELIGIBLE ENTITIES.—To be eligible to obtain an increase under this section, an entity shall be a recipient of a grant or contract under this title."; and

(3) in subsection (e), as so redesignated—

(A) by striking paragraph (1) and inserting the following:

"(1) IN GENERAL.—

"(A) NATIONAL CENTER.—To carry out subsection (b), there are authorized to be appropriated $7,500,000 for each of fiscal years 2010 through 2014.

"(B) STATE AND REGIONAL CENTERS.—To carry out subsection (c), there are authorized to be appropriated $4,500,000 for each of fiscal years 2010 through 2014.

"(C) GRANTS FOR LONGITUDINAL EVALUATIONS.—To carry out subsection (d), there are authorized to be appropriated such sums as may be necessary for fiscal years 2010 through 2014."; and

(4) in paragraph (2), by striking "subsection (a)" and inserting "paragraph (1)".

(b) TRANSFERS.—Not later than 180 days after the date of enactment of this Act, the responsibilities and resources of the National Center for Health Workforce Analysis, as in effect on the date before the date of enactment of this Act, shall be transferred to the National Center for Health Care Workforce Analysis established under section 761 of the Public Health Service Act, as amended by subsection (a).

(c) USE OF LONGITUDINAL EVALUATIONS.—Section 791(a)(1) of the Public Health Service Act (42 U.S.C. 295j(a)(1)) is amended—

(1) in subparagraph (A), by striking "or" at the end;

(2) in subparagraph (B), by striking the period and inserting "; or"; and

(3) by adding at the end the following:

"(C) utilizes a longitudinal evaluation (as described in section 761(d)(2)) and reports data from such system to the national workforce database (as established under section 761(b)(2)(E)).".

(d) PERFORMANCE MEASURES; GUIDELINES FOR LONGITUDINAL EVALUATIONS.—

(1) ADVISORY COMMITTEE ON TRAINING IN PRIMARY CARE MEDICINE AND DENTISTRY.—Section 748(d) of the Public Health Service Act is amended—

(A) in paragraph (1), by striking "and" at the end;

(B) in paragraph (2), by striking the period and inserting a semicolon; and

(C) by adding at the end the following:

"(3) develop, publish, and implement performance measures for programs under this part;

"(4) develop and publish guidelines for longitudinal evaluations (as described in section 761(d)(2)) for programs under this part; and

"(5) recommend appropriation levels for programs under this part.".

(2) ADVISORY COMMITTEE ON INTERDISCIPLINARY, COMMUNITY-BASED LINKAGES.—Section 756(d) of the Public Health Service Act is amended—

(A) in paragraph (1), by striking "and" at the end;

(B) in paragraph (2), by striking the period and inserting a semicolon; and

(C) by adding at the end the following:

"(3) develop, publish, and implement performance measures for programs under this part;

"(4) develop and publish guidelines for longitudinal evaluations (as described in section 761(d)(2)) for programs under this part; and

"(5) recommend appropriation levels for programs under this part.".

(3) ADVISORY COUNCIL ON GRADUATE MEDICAL EDUCATION.—Section 762(a) of the Public Health Service Act (42 U.S.C. 294o(a)) is amended—

(A) in paragraph (1), by striking "and" at the end;

(B) in paragraph (2), by striking the period and inserting a semicolon; and

(C) by adding at the end the following:

"(3) develop, publish, and implement performance measures for programs under this title, except for programs under part C or D;

"(4) develop and publish guidelines for longitudinal evaluations (as described in section 761(d)(2)) for programs under this title, except for programs under part C or D; and

"(5) recommend appropriation levels for programs under this title, except for programs under part C or D.".

Subtitle C—Increasing the Supply of the Health Care Workforce

SEC. 5201. FEDERALLY SUPPORTED STUDENT LOAN FUNDS.

(a) MEDICAL SCHOOLS AND PRIMARY HEALTH CARE.—Section 723 of the Public Health Service Act (42 U.S.C. 292s) is amended—

(1) in subsection (a)—

(A) in paragraph (1), by striking subparagraph (B) and inserting the following:

"(B) to practice in such care for 10 years (including residency training in primary health care) or through the date on which the loan is repaid in full, whichever occurs first."; and

(B) by striking paragraph (3) and inserting the following:

"(3) NONCOMPLIANCE BY STUDENT.—Each agreement entered into with a student pursuant to paragraph (1) shall provide that, if the student fails to comply with such agreement, the loan involved will begin to accrue interest at a rate of 2 percent per year greater than the rate at which the student would pay if compliant in such year."; and

(2) by adding at the end the following:

"(d) SENSE OF CONGRESS.—It is the sense of Congress that funds repaid under the loan program under this section should not be transferred to the Treasury of the United States or otherwise used for any other purpose other than to carry out this section.".

(b) STUDENT LOAN GUIDELINES.—The Secretary of Health and Human Services shall not require parental financial information for an independent student to determine financial need under section 723 of the Public Health Service Act (42 U.S.C. 292s) and the determination of need for such information shall be at the discretion of applicable school loan officer. The Secretary shall amend guidelines issued by the Health Resources and Services Administration in accordance with the preceding sentence.

SEC. 5202. NURSING STUDENT LOAN PROGRAM.

(a) LOAN AGREEMENTS.—Section 836(a) of the Public Health Service Act (42 U.S.C. 297b(a)) is amended—

(1) by striking "$2,500" and inserting "$3,300";

(2) by striking "$4,000" and inserting "$5,200"; and

(3) by striking "$13,000" and all that follows through the period and inserting "$17,000 in the case of any student during fiscal years 2010 and 2011. After fiscal year 2011, such amounts shall be adjusted to provide for a cost-of-attendance increase for the yearly loan rate and the aggregate of the loans.".

(b) LOAN PROVISIONS.—Section 836(b) of the Public Health Service Act (42 U.S.C. 297b(b)) is amended—

(1) in paragraph (1)(C), by striking "1986" and inserting "2000"; and

(2) in paragraph (3), by striking "the date of enactment of the Nurse Training Amendments of 1979" and inserting "September 29, 1995".

SEC. 5203. HEALTH CARE WORKFORCE LOAN REPAYMENT PROGRAMS.

Part E of title VII of the Public Health Service Act (42 U.S.C. 294n et seq.) is amended by adding at the end the following:

"Subpart 3—Recruitment and Retention Programs

"SEC. 775. INVESTMENT IN TOMORROW'S PEDIATRIC HEALTH CARE WORKFORCE.

"(a) ESTABLISHMENT.—The Secretary shall establish and carry out a pediatric specialty loan repayment program under which the eligible individual agrees to be employed full-time for a specified period (which shall not be less than 2 years) in providing pediatric medical subspecialty, pediatric surgical specialty, or child and adolescent mental and behavioral health care, including substance abuse prevention and treatment services.

"(b) PROGRAM ADMINISTRATION.—Through the program established under this section, the Secretary shall enter into contracts with qualified health professionals under which—

"(1) such qualified health professionals will agree to provide pediatric medical subspecialty, pediatric surgical specialty, or child and adolescent mental and behavioral health care in an area with a shortage of the specified pediatric subspecialty that has a sufficient pediatric population to support such pediatric subspecialty, as determined by the Secretary; and

"(2) the Secretary agrees to make payments on the principal and interest of undergraduate, graduate, or graduate medical education loans of professionals described in paragraph (1) of not more than $35,000 a year for each year of agreed upon service under such paragraph for a period of not more than 3 years during the qualified health professional's—

"(A) participation in an accredited pediatric medical subspecialty, pediatric surgical specialty, or child and adolescent mental health subspecialty residency or fellowship; or

"(B) employment as a pediatric medical subspecialist, pediatric surgical specialist, or child and adolescent mental health professional serving an area or population described in such paragraph.

"(c) IN GENERAL.—

"(1) ELIGIBLE INDIVIDUALS.—

"(A) PEDIATRIC MEDICAL SPECIALISTS AND PEDIATRIC SURGICAL SPECIALISTS.—For purposes of contracts with respect to pediatric medical specialists and pediatric surgical specialists, the term 'qualified health professional' means a licensed physician who—

"(i) is entering or receiving training in an accredited pediatric medical subspecialty or pediatric surgical specialty residency or fellowship; or

"(ii) has completed (but not prior to the end of the calendar year in which this section is enacted) the training described in subparagraph (B).

"(B) CHILD AND ADOLESCENT MENTAL AND BEHAVIORAL HEALTH.—For purposes of contracts with respect to child and adolescent mental and behavioral health care, the term 'qualified health professional' means a health care professional who—

"(i) has received specialized training or clinical experience in child and adolescent mental health in psychiatry, psychology, school psychology, behavioral pediatrics, psychiatric nursing, social work, school social work, substance abuse disorder prevention and treatment, marriage and family therapy, school counseling, or professional counseling;

"(ii) has a license or certification in a State to practice allopathic medicine, osteopathic medicine, psychology, school psychology, psychiatric nursing, social work, school social work, marriage and family therapy, school counseling, or professional counseling; or

"(iii) is a mental health service professional who completed (but not before the end of the calendar year in which this section is enacted) specialized training or clinical experience in child and adolescent mental health described in clause (i).

"(2) ADDITIONAL ELIGIBILITY REQUIREMENTS.—The Secretary may not enter into a contract under this subsection with an eligible individual unless—

"(A) the individual agrees to work in, or for a provider serving, a health professional shortage area or medically underserved area, or to serve a medically underserved population;

"(B) the individual is a United States citizen or a permanent legal United States resident; and

"(C) if the individual is enrolled in a graduate program, the program is accredited, and the individual has an acceptable level of academic standing (as determined by the Secretary).

"(d) PRIORITY.—In entering into contracts under this subsection, the Secretary shall give priority to applicants who—

"(1) are or will be working in a school or other pre-kindergarten, elementary, or secondary education setting;

"(2) have familiarity with evidence-based methods and cultural and linguistic competence health care services; and

"(3) demonstrate financial need.

"(e) AUTHORIZATION OF APPROPRIATIONS.—There is authorized to be appropriated $30,000,000 for each of fiscal years 2010 through 2014 to carry out subsection (c)(1)(A) and $20,000,000 for each of fiscal years 2010 through 2013 to carry out subsection (c)(1)(B).".

SEC. 5204. PUBLIC HEALTH WORKFORCE RECRUITMENT AND RETENTION PROGRAMS.

Part E of title VII of the Public Health Service Act (42 U.S.C. 294n et seq.), as amended by section 5203, is further amended by adding at the end the following:

"SEC. 776. PUBLIC HEALTH WORKFORCE LOAN REPAYMENT PROGRAM.

"(a) ESTABLISHMENT.—The Secretary shall establish the Public Health Workforce Loan Repayment Program (referred to in this section as the 'Program') to assure an adequate supply of public health professionals to eliminate critical public health workforce shortages in Federal, State, local, and tribal public health agencies.

"(b) ELIGIBILITY.—To be eligible to participate in the Program, an individual shall—

"(1)(A) be accepted for enrollment, or be enrolled, as a student in an accredited academic educational institution in a State or territory in the final year of a course of study or program leading to a public health or health professions degree or certificate; and have accepted employment with a Federal, State, local, or tribal public health agency, or a related training fellowship, as recognized by the Secretary, to commence upon graduation;

"(B)(i) have graduated, during the preceding 10-year period, from an accredited educational institution in a State or territory and received a public health or health professions degree or certificate; and

"(ii) be employed by, or have accepted employment with, a Federal, State, local, or tribal public health agency or a related training fellowship, as recognized by the Secretary;

"(2) be a United States citizen; and

"(3)(A) submit an application to the Secretary to participate in the Program;

"(B) execute a written contract as required in subsection (c); and

"(4) not have received, for the same service, a reduction of loan obligations under section 455(m), 428J, 428K, 428L, or 460 of the Higher Education Act of 1965.

"(c) CONTRACT.—The written contract (referred to in this section as the 'written contract') between the Secretary and an individual shall contain—

"(1) an agreement on the part of the Secretary that the Secretary will repay on behalf of the individual loans incurred by the individual in the pursuit of the relevant degree or certificate in accordance with the terms of the contract;

"(2) an agreement on the part of the individual that the individual will serve in the full-time employment of a Federal,

State, local, or tribal public health agency or a related fellowship program in a position related to the course of study or program for which the contract was awarded for a period of time (referred to in this section as the 'period of obligated service') equal to the greater of—

"(A) 3 years; or

"(B) such longer period of time as determined appropriate by the Secretary and the individual;

"(3) an agreement, as appropriate, on the part of the individual to relocate to a priority service area (as determined by the Secretary) in exchange for an additional loan repayment incentive amount to be determined by the Secretary;

"(4) a provision that any financial obligation of the United States arising out of a contract entered into under this section and any obligation of the individual that is conditioned thereon, is contingent on funds being appropriated for loan repayments under this section;

"(5) a statement of the damages to which the United States is entitled, under this section for the individual's breach of the contract; and

"(6) such other statements of the rights and liabilities of the Secretary and of the individual, not inconsistent with this section.

"(d) PAYMENTS.—

"(1) IN GENERAL.—A loan repayment provided for an individual under a written contract under the Program shall consist of payment, in accordance with paragraph (2), on behalf of the individual of the principal, interest, and related expenses on government and commercial loans received by the individual regarding the undergraduate or graduate education of the individual (or both), which loans were made for tuition expenses incurred by the individual.

"(2) PAYMENTS FOR YEARS SERVED.—For each year of obligated service that an individual contracts to serve under subsection (c) the Secretary may pay up to $35,000 on behalf of the individual for loans described in paragraph (1). With respect to participants under the Program whose total eligible loans are less than $105,000, the Secretary shall pay an amount that does not exceed ⅓ of the eligible loan balance for each year of obligated service of the individual.

"(3) TAX LIABILITY.—For the purpose of providing reimbursements for tax liability resulting from payments under paragraph (2) on behalf of an individual, the Secretary shall, in addition to such payments, make payments to the individual in an amount not to exceed 39 percent of the total amount of loan repayments made for the taxable year involved.

"(e) POSTPONING OBLIGATED SERVICE.—With respect to an individual receiving a degree or certificate from a health professions or other related school, the date of the initiation of the period of obligated service may be postponed as approved by the Secretary.

"(f) BREACH OF CONTRACT.—An individual who fails to comply with the contract entered into under subsection (c) shall be subject to the same financial penalties as provided for under section 338E for breaches of loan repayment contracts under section 338B.

"(g) AUTHORIZATION OF APPROPRIATIONS.—There is authorized to be appropriated to carry out this section $195,000,000 for fiscal year 2010, and such sums as may be necessary for each of fiscal years 2011 through 2015.".

SEC. 5205. ALLIED HEALTH WORKFORCE RECRUITMENT AND RETENTION PROGRAMS.

(a) PURPOSE.—The purpose of this section is to assure an adequate supply of allied health professionals to eliminate critical allied health workforce shortages in Federal, State, local, and tribal public health agencies or in settings where patients might require health care services, including acute care facilities, ambulatory care facilities, personal residences and other settings, as recognized by the Secretary of Health and Human Services by authorizing an Allied Health Loan Forgiveness Program.

(b) ALLIED HEALTH WORKFORCE RECRUITMENT AND RETENTION PROGRAM.—Section 428K of the Higher Education Act of 1965 (20 U.S.C. 1078–11) is amended—

(1) in subsection (b), by adding at the end the following:

"(18) ALLIED HEALTH PROFESSIONALS.—The individual is employed full-time as an allied health professional—

"(A) in a Federal, State, local, or tribal public health agency; or

"(B) in a setting where patients might require health care services, including acute care facilities, ambulatory care facilities, personal residences and other settings located in health professional shortage areas, medically underserved areas, or medically underserved populations, as recognized by the Secretary of Health and Human Services."; and

(2) in subsection (g)—

(A) by redesignating paragraphs (1) through (9) as paragraphs (2) through (10), respectively; and

(B) by inserting before paragraph (2) (as redesignated by subparagraph (A)) the following:

"(1) ALLIED HEALTH PROFESSIONAL.—The term 'allied health professional' means an allied health professional as defined in section 799B(5) of the Public Heath Service Act (42 U.S.C. 295p(5)) who—

"(A) has graduated and received an allied health professions degree or certificate from an institution of higher education; and

"(B) is employed with a Federal, State, local or tribal public health agency, or in a setting where patients might require health care services, including acute care facilities, ambulatory care facilities, personal residences and other settings located in health professional shortage areas, medically underserved areas, or medically underserved populations, as recognized by the Secretary of Health and Human Services.".

SEC. 5206. GRANTS FOR STATE AND LOCAL PROGRAMS.

(a) IN GENERAL.—Section 765(d) of the Public Health Service Act (42 U.S.C. 295(d)) is amended—

(1) in paragraph (7), by striking "; or" and inserting a semicolon;

(2) by redesignating paragraph (8) as paragraph (9); and

(3) by inserting after paragraph (7) the following:

"(8) public health workforce loan repayment programs; or".

(b) TRAINING FOR MID-CAREER PUBLIC HEALTH PROFESSIONALS.—Part E of title VII of the Public Health Service Act (42 U.S.C. 294n et seq.), as amended by section 5204, is further amended by adding at the end the following:

"SEC. 777. TRAINING FOR MID-CAREER PUBLIC AND ALLIED HEALTH PROFESSIONALS.

"(a) IN GENERAL.—The Secretary may make grants to, or enter into contracts with, any eligible entity to award scholarships to eligible individuals to enroll in degree or professional training programs for the purpose of enabling mid-career professionals in the public health and allied health workforce to receive additional training in the field of public health and allied health.

"(b) ELIGIBILITY.—

"(1) ELIGIBLE ENTITY.—The term 'eligible entity' indicates an accredited educational institution that offers a course of study, certificate program, or professional training program in public or allied health or a related discipline, as determined by the Secretary

"(2) ELIGIBLE INDIVIDUALS.—The term 'eligible individuals' includes those individuals employed in public and allied health positions at the Federal, State, tribal, or local level who are interested in retaining or upgrading their education.

"(c) AUTHORIZATION OF APPROPRIATIONS.—There is authorized to be appropriated to carry out this section, $60,000,000 for fiscal year 2010 and such sums as may be necessary for each of fiscal years 2011 through 2015. Fifty percent of appropriated funds shall be allotted to public health mid-career professionals and 50 percent shall be allotted to allied health mid-career professionals.".

SEC. 5207. FUNDING FOR NATIONAL HEALTH SERVICE CORPS.

Section 338H(a) of the Public Health Service Act (42 U.S.C. 254q(a)) is amended to read as follows:

"(a) AUTHORIZATION OF APPROPRIATIONS.—For the purpose of carrying out this section, there is authorized to be appropriated, out of any funds in the Treasury not otherwise appropriated, the following:

"(1) For fiscal year 2010, $320,461,632.

"(2) For fiscal year 2011, $414,095,394.

"(3) For fiscal year 2012, $535,087,442.

"(4) For fiscal year 2013, $691,431,432.

"(5) For fiscal year 2014, $893,456,433.

"(6) For fiscal year 2015, $1,154,510,336.

"(7) For fiscal year 2016, and each subsequent fiscal year, the amount appropriated for the preceding fiscal year adjusted by the product of—

"(A) one plus the average percentage increase in the costs of health professions education during the prior fiscal year; and

"(B) one plus the average percentage change in the number of individuals residing in health professions shortage areas designated under section 333 during the prior fiscal year, relative to the number of individuals residing in such areas during the previous fiscal year.".

SEC. 5208. NURSE-MANAGED HEALTH CLINICS.

(a) PURPOSE.—The purpose of this section is to fund the development and operation of nurse-managed health clinics.

(b) GRANTS.—Subpart 1 of part D of title III of the Public Health Service Act (42 U.S.C. 254b et seq.) is amended by inserting after section 330A the following:

"SEC. 330A–1. GRANTS TO NURSE-MANAGED HEALTH CLINICS.

"(a) DEFINITIONS.—

"(1) COMPREHENSIVE PRIMARY HEALTH CARE SERVICES.—In this section, the term 'comprehensive primary health care services' means the primary health services described in section 330(b)(1).

"(2) NURSE-MANAGED HEALTH CLINIC.—The term 'nurse-managed health clinic' means a nurse-practice arrangement, managed by advanced practice nurses, that provides primary care or wellness services to underserved or vulnerable populations and that is associated with a school, college, university or department of nursing, federally qualified health center, or independent nonprofit health or social services agency.

"(b) AUTHORITY TO AWARD GRANTS.—The Secretary shall award grants for the cost of the operation of nurse-managed health clinics that meet the requirements of this section.

"(c) APPLICATIONS.—To be eligible to receive a grant under this section, an entity shall—

"(1) be an NMHC; and

"(2) submit to the Secretary an application at such time, in such manner, and containing—

"(A) assurances that nurses are the major providers of services at the NMHC and that at least 1 advanced practice nurse holds an executive management position within the organizational structure of the NMHC;

"(B) an assurance that the NMHC will continue providing comprehensive primary health care services or wellness services without regard to income or insurance status of the patient for the duration of the grant period; and

"(C) an assurance that, not later than 90 days of receiving a grant under this section, the NMHC will establish a community advisory committee, for which a majority of the members shall be individuals who are served by the NMHC.

"(d) GRANT AMOUNT.—The amount of any grant made under this section for any fiscal year shall be determined by the Secretary, taking into account—

"(1) the financial need of the NMHC, considering State, local, and other operational funding provided to the NMHC; and

"(2) other factors, as the Secretary determines appropriate.

"(e) AUTHORIZATION OF APPROPRIATIONS.—For the purposes of carrying out this section, there are authorized to be appropriated $50,000,000 for the fiscal year 2010 and such sums as may be necessary for each of the fiscal years 2011 through 2014.".

SEC. 5209. ELIMINATION OF CAP ON COMMISSIONED CORPS.

Section 202 of the Department of Health and Human Services Appropriations Act, 1993 (Public Law 102–394) is amended by striking "not to exceed 2,800".

SEC. 5210. ESTABLISHING A READY RESERVE CORPS.

Section 203 of the Public Health Service Act (42 U.S.C. 204) is amended to read as follows:

"SEC. 203. COMMISSIONED CORPS AND READY RESERVE CORPS.

"(a) ESTABLISHMENT.—

"(1) IN GENERAL.—There shall be in the Service a commissioned Regular Corps and a Ready Reserve Corps for service in time of national emergency.

"(2) REQUIREMENT.—All commissioned officers shall be citizens of the United States and shall be appointed without regard to the civil-service laws and compensated without regard to the Classification Act of 1923, as amended.

"(3) APPOINTMENT.—Commissioned officers of the Ready Reserve Corps shall be appointed by the President and commissioned officers of the Regular Corps shall be appointed by the President with the advice and consent of the Senate.

"(4) ACTIVE DUTY.—Commissioned officers of the Ready Reserve Corps shall at all times be subject to call to active duty by the Surgeon General, including active duty for the purpose of training.

"(5) WARRANT OFFICERS.—Warrant officers may be appointed to the Service for the purpose of providing support to the health and delivery systems maintained by the Service and any warrant officer appointed to the Service shall be considered for purposes of this Act and title 37, United States Code, to be a commissioned officer within the Commissioned Corps of the Service.

"(b) ASSIMILATING RESERVE CORP OFFICERS INTO THE REGULAR CORPS.—Effective on the date of enactment of the Patient Protection and Affordable Care Act, all individuals classified as officers in the Reserve Corps under this section (as such section existed on the day before the date of enactment of such Act) and serving on active duty shall be deemed to be commissioned officers of the Regular Corps.

"(c) PURPOSE AND USE OF READY RESEARCH.—

"(1) PURPOSE.—The purpose of the Ready Reserve Corps is to fulfill the need to have additional Commissioned Corps personnel available on short notice (similar to the uniformed service's reserve program) to assist regular Commissioned Corps personnel to meet both routine public health and emergency response missions.

"(2) USES.—The Ready Reserve Corps shall—

"(A) participate in routine training to meet the general and specific needs of the Commissioned Corps;

"(B) be available and ready for involuntary calls to active duty during national emergencies and public health crises, similar to the uniformed service reserve personnel;

"(C) be available for backfilling critical positions left vacant during deployment of active duty Commissioned Corps members, as well as for deployment to respond to public health emergencies, both foreign and domestic; and

"(D) be available for service assignment in isolated, hardship, and medically underserved communities (as defined in section 799B) to improve access to health services.

"(d) FUNDING.—For the purpose of carrying out the duties and responsibilities of the Commissioned Corps under this section, there are authorized to be appropriated $5,000,000 for each of fiscal years 2010 through 2014 for recruitment and training and $12,500,000 for each of fiscal years 2010 through 2014 for the Ready Reserve Corps.".

Subtitle D—Enhancing Health Care Workforce Education and Training

SEC. 5301. TRAINING IN FAMILY MEDICINE, GENERAL INTERNAL MEDICINE, GENERAL PEDIATRICS, AND PHYSICIAN ASSISTANTSHIP.

Part C of title VII (42 U.S.C. 293k et seq.) is amended by striking section 747 and inserting the following:

"SEC. 747. PRIMARY CARE TRAINING AND ENHANCEMENT.

"(a) SUPPORT AND DEVELOPMENT OF PRIMARY CARE TRAINING PROGRAMS.—

"(1) IN GENERAL.—The Secretary may make grants to, or enter into contracts with, an accredited public or nonprofit private hospital, school of medicine or osteopathic medicine, academically affiliated physician assistant training program, or a public or private nonprofit entity which the Secretary has determined is capable of carrying out such grant or contract—

"(A) to plan, develop, operate, or participate in an accredited professional training program, including an accredited residency or internship program in the field of family medicine, general internal medicine, or general pediatrics for medical students, interns, residents, or practicing physicians as defined by the Secretary;

"(B) to provide need-based financial assistance in the form of traineeships and fellowships to medical students, interns, residents, practicing physicians, or other medical personnel, who are participants in any such program, and who plan to specialize or work in the practice of the fields defined in subparagraph (A);

"(C) to plan, develop, and operate a program for the training of physicians who plan to teach in family medicine, general internal medicine, or general pediatrics training programs;

"(D) to plan, develop, and operate a program for the training of physicians teaching in community-based settings;

"(E) to provide financial assistance in the form of traineeships and fellowships to physicians who are participants in any such programs and who plan to teach or conduct research in a family medicine, general internal medicine, or general pediatrics training program;

"(F) to plan, develop, and operate a physician assistant education program, and for the training of individuals who will teach in programs to provide such training;

"(G) to plan, develop, and operate a demonstration program that provides training in new competencies, as recommended by the Advisory Committee on Training in

Primary Care Medicine and Dentistry and the National Health Care Workforce Commission established in section 5101 of the Patient Protection and Affordable Care Act, which may include—

"(i) providing training to primary care physicians relevant to providing care through patient-centered medical homes (as defined by the Secretary for purposes of this section);

"(ii) developing tools and curricula relevant to patient-centered medical homes; and

"(iii) providing continuing education to primary care physicians relevant to patient-centered medical homes; and

"(H) to plan, develop, and operate joint degree programs to provide interdisciplinary and interprofessional graduate training in public health and other health professions to provide training in environmental health, infectious disease control, disease prevention and health promotion, epidemiological studies and injury control.

"(2) DURATION OF AWARDS.—The period during which payments are made to an entity from an award of a grant or contract under this subsection shall be 5 years.

"(b) CAPACITY BUILDING IN PRIMARY CARE.—

"(1) IN GENERAL.—The Secretary may make grants to or enter into contracts with accredited schools of medicine or osteopathic medicine to establish, maintain, or improve—

"(A) academic units or programs that improve clinical teaching and research in fields defined in subsection (a)(1)(A); or

"(B) programs that integrate academic administrative units in fields defined in subsection (a)(1)(A) to enhance interdisciplinary recruitment, training, and faculty development.

"(2) PREFERENCE IN MAKING AWARDS UNDER THIS SUBSECTION.—In making awards of grants and contracts under paragraph (1), the Secretary shall give preference to any qualified applicant for such an award that agrees to expend the award for the purpose of—

"(A) establishing academic units or programs in fields defined in subsection (a)(1)(A); or

"(B) substantially expanding such units or programs.

"(3) PRIORITIES IN MAKING AWARDS.—In awarding grants or contracts under paragraph (1), the Secretary shall give priority to qualified applicants that—

"(A) proposes a collaborative project between academic administrative units of primary care;

"(B) proposes innovative approaches to clinical teaching using models of primary care, such as the patient centered medical home, team management of chronic disease, and interprofessional integrated models of health care that incorporate transitions in health care settings and integration physical and mental health provision;

"(C) have a record of training the greatest percentage of providers, or that have demonstrated significant improvements in the percentage of providers trained, who enter and remain in primary care practice;

"(D) have a record of training individuals who are from underrepresented minority groups or from a rural or disadvantaged background;

"(E) provide training in the care of vulnerable populations such as children, older adults, homeless individuals, victims of abuse or trauma, individuals with mental health or substance-related disorders, individuals with HIV/AIDS, and individuals with disabilities;

"(F) establish formal relationships and submit joint applications with federally qualified health centers, rural health clinics, area health education centers, or clinics located in underserved areas or that serve underserved populations;

"(G) teach trainees the skills to provide interprofessional, integrated care through collaboration among health professionals;

"(H) provide training in enhanced communication with patients, evidence-based practice, chronic disease management, preventive care, health information technology, or other competencies as recommended by the Advisory Committee on Training in Primary Care Medicine and Dentistry and the National Health Care Workforce Commission established in section 5101 of the Patient Protection and Affordable Care Act; or

"(I) provide training in cultural competency and health literacy.

"(4) DURATION OF AWARDS.—The period during which payments are made to an entity from an award of a grant or contract under this subsection shall be 5 years.

"(c) AUTHORIZATION OF APPROPRIATIONS.—

"(1) IN GENERAL.—For purposes of carrying out this section (other than subsection (b)(1)(B)), there are authorized to be appropriated $125,000,000 for fiscal year 2010, and such sums as may be necessary for each of fiscal years 2011 through 2014.

"(2) TRAINING PROGRAMS.—Fifteen percent of the amount appropriated pursuant to paragraph (1) in each such fiscal year shall be allocated to the physician assistant training programs described in subsection (a)(1)(F), which prepare students for practice in primary care.

"(3) INTEGRATING ACADEMIC ADMINISTRATIVE UNITS.—For purposes of carrying out subsection (b)(1)(B), there are authorized to be appropriated $750,000 for each of fiscal years 2010 through 2014.".

SEC. 5302. TRAINING OPPORTUNITIES FOR DIRECT CARE WORKERS.

Part C of title VII of the Public Health Service Act (42 U.S.C. 293k et seq.) is amended by inserting after section 747, as amended by section 5301, the following:

"SEC. 747A. TRAINING OPPORTUNITIES FOR DIRECT CARE WORKERS.

"(a) IN GENERAL.—The Secretary shall award grants to eligible entities to enable such entities to provide new training opportunities for direct care workers who are employed in long-term care settings such as nursing homes (as defined in section 1908(e)(1) of the Social Security Act (42 U.S.C. 1396g(e)(1)), assisted living facilities and skilled nursing facilities, intermediate care facilities for individuals with mental retardation, home and community based settings, and any other setting the Secretary determines to be appropriate.

"(b) ELIGIBILITY.—To be eligible to receive a grant under this section, an entity shall—

"(1) be an institution of higher education (as defined in section 102 of the Higher Education Act of 1965 (20 U.S.C. 1002)) that—

"(A) is accredited by a nationally recognized accrediting agency or association listed under section 101(c) of the Higher Education Act of 1965 (20 U.S.C. 1001(c)); and

"(B) has established a public-private educational partnership with a nursing home or skilled nursing facility, agency or entity providing home and community based services to individuals with disabilities, or other long-term care provider; and

"(2) submit to the Secretary an application at such time, in such manner, and containing such information as the Secretary may require.

"(c) USE OF FUNDS.—An eligible entity shall use amounts awarded under a grant under this section to provide assistance to eligible individuals to offset the cost of tuition and required fees for enrollment in academic programs provided by such entity.

"(d) ELIGIBLE INDIVIDUAL.—

"(1) ELIGIBILITY.—To be eligible for assistance under this section, an individual shall be enrolled in courses provided by a grantee under this subsection and maintain satisfactory academic progress in such courses.

"(2) CONDITION OF ASSISTANCE.—As a condition of receiving assistance under this section, an individual shall agree that, following completion of the assistance period, the individual will work in the field of geriatrics, disability services, long term services and supports, or chronic care management for a minimum of 2 years under guidelines set by the Secretary.

"(e) AUTHORIZATION OF APPROPRIATIONS.—There is authorized to be appropriated to carry out this section, $10,000,000 for the period of fiscal years 2011 through 2013.".

SEC. 5303. TRAINING IN GENERAL, PEDIATRIC, AND PUBLIC HEALTH DENTISTRY.

Part C of Title VII of the Public Health Service Act (42 U.S.C. 293k et seq.) is amended by—

(1) redesignating section 748, as amended by section 5103 of this Act, as section 749; and

(2) inserting after section 747A, as added by section 5302, the following:

"SEC. 748. TRAINING IN GENERAL, PEDIATRIC, AND PUBLIC HEALTH DENTISTRY.

"(a) SUPPORT AND DEVELOPMENT OF DENTAL TRAINING PROGRAMS.—

"(1) IN GENERAL.—The Secretary may make grants to, or enter into contracts with, a school of dentistry, public or nonprofit private hospital, or a public or private nonprofit entity which the Secretary has determined is capable of carrying out such grant or contract—

"(A) to plan, develop, and operate, or participate in, an approved professional training program in the field of general dentistry, pediatric dentistry, or public health dentistry for dental students, residents, practicing dentists, dental hygienists, or other approved primary care dental trainees, that emphasizes training for general, pediatric, or public health dentistry;

"(B) to provide financial assistance to dental students, residents, practicing dentists, and dental hygiene students who are in need thereof, who are participants in any such program, and who plan to work in the practice of general, pediatric, public heath dentistry, or dental hygiene;

"(C) to plan, develop, and operate a program for the training of oral health care providers who plan to teach in general, pediatric, public health dentistry, or dental hygiene;

"(D) to provide financial assistance in the form of traineeships and fellowships to dentists who plan to teach or are teaching in general, pediatric, or public health dentistry;

"(E) to meet the costs of projects to establish, maintain, or improve dental faculty development programs in primary care (which may be departments, divisions or other units);

"(F) to meet the costs of projects to establish, maintain, or improve predoctoral and postdoctoral training in primary care programs;

"(G) to create a loan repayment program for faculty in dental programs; and

"(H) to provide technical assistance to pediatric training programs in developing and implementing instruction regarding the oral health status, dental care needs, and risk-based clinical disease management of all pediatric populations with an emphasis on underserved children.

"(2) FACULTY LOAN REPAYMENT.—

"(A) IN GENERAL.—A grant or contract under subsection (a)(1)(G) may be awarded to a program of general, pediatric, or public health dentistry described in such subsection to plan, develop, and operate a loan repayment program under which—

"(i) individuals agree to serve full-time as faculty members; and

"(ii) the program of general, pediatric or public health dentistry agrees to pay the principal and interest on the outstanding student loans of the individuals.

"(B) MANNER OF PAYMENTS.—With respect to the payments described in subparagraph (A)(ii), upon completion by an individual of each of the first, second, third, fourth, and fifth years of service, the program shall pay an amount equal to 10, 15, 20, 25, and 30 percent, respectively, of the individual's student loan balance as calculated based on principal and interest owed at the initiation of the agreement.

"(b) ELIGIBLE ENTITY.—For purposes of this subsection, entities eligible for such grants or contracts in general, pediatric, or public health dentistry shall include entities that have programs in dental or dental hygiene schools, or approved residency or advanced education programs in the practice of general, pediatric, or public health dentistry. Eligible entities may partner with schools of public health to permit the education of dental students, residents, and dental hygiene students for a master's year in public health at a school of public health.

"(c) PRIORITIES IN MAKING AWARDS.—With respect to training provided for under this section, the Secretary shall give priority in awarding grants or contracts to the following:

"(1) Qualified applicants that propose collaborative projects between departments of primary care medicine and departments of general, pediatric, or public health dentistry.

"(2) Qualified applicants that have a record of training the greatest percentage of providers, or that have demonstrated significant improvements in the percentage of providers, who enter and remain in general, pediatric, or public health dentistry.

"(3) Qualified applicants that have a record of training individuals who are from a rural or disadvantaged background, or from underrepresented minorities.

"(4) Qualified applicants that establish formal relationships with Federally qualified health centers, rural health centers, or accredited teaching facilities and that conduct training of students, residents, fellows, or faculty at the center or facility.

"(5) Qualified applicants that conduct teaching programs targeting vulnerable populations such as older adults, homeless individuals, victims of abuse or trauma, individuals with mental health or substance-related disorders, individuals with disabilities, and individuals with HIV/AIDS, and in the risk-based clinical disease management of all populations.

"(6) Qualified applicants that include educational activities in cultural competency and health literacy.

"(7) Qualified applicants that have a high rate for placing graduates in practice settings that serve underserved areas or health disparity populations, or who achieve a significant increase in the rate of placing graduates in such settings.

"(8) Qualified applicants that intend to establish a special populations oral health care education center or training program for the didactic and clinical education of dentists, dental health professionals, and dental hygienists who plan to teach oral health care for people with developmental disabilities, cognitive impairment, complex medical problems, significant physical limitations, and vulnerable elderly.

"(d) APPLICATION.—An eligible entity desiring a grant under this section shall submit to the Secretary an application at such time, in such manner, and containing such information as the Secretary may require.

"(e) DURATION OF AWARD.—The period during which payments are made to an entity from an award of a grant or contract under subsection (a) shall be 5 years. The provision of such payments shall be subject to annual approval by the Secretary and subject to the availability of appropriations for the fiscal year involved to make the payments.

"(f) AUTHORIZATIONS OF APPROPRIATIONS.—For the purpose of carrying out subsections (a) and (b), there is authorized to be appropriated $30,000,000 for fiscal year 2010 and such sums as may be necessary for each of fiscal years 2011 through 2015.

"(g) CARRYOVER FUNDS.—An entity that receives an award under this section may carry over funds from 1 fiscal year to another without obtaining approval from the Secretary. In no case may any funds be carried over pursuant to the preceding sentence for more than 3 years.''.

SEC. 5304. ALTERNATIVE DENTAL HEALTH CARE PROVIDERS DEMONSTRATION PROJECT.

Subpart X of part D of title III of the Public Health Service Act (42 U.S.C. 256f et seq.) is amended by adding at the end the following:

''SEC. 340G–1. DEMONSTRATION PROGRAM.

''(a) IN GENERAL.—

''(1) AUTHORIZATION.—The Secretary is authorized to award grants to 15 eligible entities to enable such entities to establish a demonstration program to establish training programs to train, or to employ, alternative dental health care providers in order to increase access to dental health care services in rural and other underserved communities.

''(2) DEFINITION.—The term 'alternative dental health care providers' includes community dental health coordinators, advance practice dental hygienists, independent dental hygienists, supervised dental hygienists, primary care physicians, dental therapists, dental health aides, and any other health professional that the Secretary determines appropriate.

''(b) TIMEFRAME.—The demonstration projects funded under this section shall begin not later than 2 years after the date of enactment of this section, and shall conclude not later than 7 years after such date of enactment.

''(c) ELIGIBLE ENTITIES.—To be eligible to receive a grant under subsection (a), an entity shall—

''(1) be—

''(A) an institution of higher education, including a community college;

''(B) a public-private partnership;

''(C) a federally qualified health center;

''(D) an Indian Health Service facility or a tribe or tribal organization (as such terms are defined in section 4 of the Indian Self-Determination and Education Assistance Act);

''(E) a State or county public health clinic, a health facility operated by an Indian tribe or tribal organization, or urban Indian organization providing dental services; or

''(F) a public hospital or health system;

''(2) be within a program accredited by the Commission on Dental Accreditation or within a dental education program in an accredited institution; and

''(3) shall submit an application to the Secretary at such time, in such manner, and containing such information as the Secretary may require.

''(d) ADMINISTRATIVE PROVISIONS.—

''(1) AMOUNT OF GRANT.—Each grant under this section shall be in an amount that is not less than $4,000,000 for the 5-year period during which the demonstration project being conducted.

''(2) DISBURSEMENT OF FUNDS.—

''(A) PRELIMINARY DISBURSEMENTS.—Beginning 1 year after the enactment of this section, the Secretary may disperse to any entity receiving a grant under this section not more than 20 percent of the total funding awarded to such entity under such grant, for the purpose of enabling the entity to plan the demonstration project to be conducted under such grant.

"(B) SUBSEQUENT DISBURSEMENTS.—The remaining amount of grant funds not dispersed under subparagraph (A) shall be dispersed such that not less than 15 percent of such remaining amount is dispersed each subsequent year.

"(e) COMPLIANCE WITH STATE REQUIREMENTS.—Each entity receiving a grant under this section shall certify that it is in compliance with all applicable State licensing requirements.

"(f) EVALUATION.—The Secretary shall contract with the Director of the Institute of Medicine to conduct a study of the demonstration programs conducted under this section that shall provide analysis, based upon quantitative and qualitative data, regarding access to dental health care in the United States.

"(g) CLARIFICATION REGARDING DENTAL HEALTH AIDE PROGRAM.—Nothing in this section shall prohibit a dental health aide training program approved by the Indian Health Service from being eligible for a grant under this section.

"(h) AUTHORIZATION OF APPROPRIATIONS.—There is authorized to be appropriated such sums as may be necessary to carry out this section.".

SEC. 5305. GERIATRIC EDUCATION AND TRAINING; CAREER AWARDS; COMPREHENSIVE GERIATRIC EDUCATION.

(a) WORKFORCE DEVELOPMENT; CAREER AWARDS.—Section 753 of the Public Health Service Act (42 U.S.C. 294c) is amended by adding at the end the following:

"(d) GERIATRIC WORKFORCE DEVELOPMENT.—

"(1) IN GENERAL.—The Secretary shall award grants or contracts under this subsection to entities that operate a geriatric education center pursuant to subsection (a)(1).

"(2) APPLICATION.—To be eligible for an award under paragraph (1), an entity described in such paragraph shall submit to the Secretary an application at such time, in such manner, and containing such information as the Secretary may require.

"(3) USE OF FUNDS.—Amounts awarded under a grant or contract under paragraph (1) shall be used to—

"(A) carry out the fellowship program described in paragraph (4); and

"(B) carry out 1 of the 2 activities described in paragraph (5).

"(4) FELLOWSHIP PROGRAM.—

"(A) IN GENERAL.—Pursuant to paragraph (3), a geriatric education center that receives an award under this subsection shall use such funds to offer short-term intensive courses (referred to in this subsection as a 'fellowship') that focus on geriatrics, chronic care management, and long-term care that provide supplemental training for faculty members in medical schools and other health professions schools with programs in psychology, pharmacy, nursing, social work, dentistry, public health, allied health, or other health disciplines, as approved by the Secretary. Such a fellowship shall be open to current faculty, and appropriately credentialed volunteer faculty and practitioners, who do not have formal training in geriatrics, to upgrade their knowledge and clinical skills for the care of older adults and adults with functional limitations and to enhance their interdisciplinary teaching skills.

"(B) LOCATION.—A fellowship shall be offered either at the geriatric education center that is sponsoring the course, in collaboration with other geriatric education centers, or at medical schools, schools of dentistry, schools of nursing, schools of pharmacy, schools of social work, graduate programs in psychology, or allied health and other health professions schools approved by the Secretary with which the geriatric education centers are affiliated.

"(C) CME CREDIT.—Participation in a fellowship under this paragraph shall be accepted with respect to complying with continuing health profession education requirements. As a condition of such acceptance, the recipient shall agree to subsequently provide a minimum of 18 hours of voluntary instructional support through a geriatric education center that is providing clinical training to students or trainees in long-term care settings.

"(5) ADDITIONAL REQUIRED ACTIVITIES DESCRIBED.—Pursuant to paragraph (3), a geriatric education center that receives an award under this subsection shall use such funds to carry out 1 of the following 2 activities.

"(A) FAMILY CAREGIVER AND DIRECT CARE PROVIDER TRAINING.—A geriatric education center that receives an award under this subsection shall offer at least 2 courses each year, at no charge or nominal cost, to family caregivers and direct care providers that are designed to provide practical training for supporting frail elders and individuals with disabilities. The Secretary shall require such Centers to work with appropriate community partners to develop training program content and to publicize the availability of training courses in their service areas. All family caregiver and direct care provider training programs shall include instruction on the management of psychological and behavioral aspects of dementia, communication techniques for working with individuals who have dementia, and the appropriate, safe, and effective use of medications for older adults.

"(B) INCORPORATION OF BEST PRACTICES.—A geriatric education center that receives an award under this subsection shall develop and include material on depression and other mental disorders common among older adults, medication safety issues for older adults, and management of the psychological and behavioral aspects of dementia and communication techniques with individuals who have dementia in all training courses, where appropriate.

"(6) TARGETS.—A geriatric education center that receives an award under this subsection shall meet targets approved by the Secretary for providing geriatric training to a certain number of faculty or practitioners during the term of the award, as well as other parameters established by the Secretary.

"(7) AMOUNT OF AWARD.—An award under this subsection shall be in an amount of $150,000. Not more than 24 geriatric education centers may receive an award under this subsection.

“(8) MAINTENANCE OF EFFORT.—A geriatric education center that receives an award under this subsection shall provide assurances to the Secretary that funds provided to the geriatric education center under this subsection will be used only to supplement, not to supplant, the amount of Federal, State, and local funds otherwise expended by the geriatric education center.

“(9) AUTHORIZATION OF APPROPRIATIONS.—In addition to any other funding available to carry out this section, there is authorized to be appropriated to carry out this subsection, $10,800,000 for the period of fiscal year 2011 through 2014.

“(e) GERIATRIC CAREER INCENTIVE AWARDS.—

“(1) IN GENERAL.—The Secretary shall award grants or contracts under this section to individuals described in paragraph (2) to foster greater interest among a variety of health professionals in entering the field of geriatrics, long-term care, and chronic care management.

“(2) ELIGIBLE INDIVIDUALS.—To be eligible to received an award under paragraph (1), an individual shall—

“(A) be an advanced practice nurse, a clinical social worker, a pharmacist, or student of psychology who is pursuing a doctorate or other advanced degree in geriatrics or related fields in an accredited health professions school; and

“(B) submit to the Secretary an application at such time, in such manner, and containing such information as the Secretary may require.

“(3) CONDITION OF AWARD.—As a condition of receiving an award under this subsection, an individual shall agree that, following completion of the award period, the individual will teach or practice in the field of geriatrics, long-term care, or chronic care management for a minimum of 5 years under guidelines set by the Secretary.

“(4) AUTHORIZATION OF APPROPRIATIONS.—There is authorized to be appropriated to carry out this subsection, $10,000,000 for the period of fiscal years 2011 through 2013.”.

(b) EXPANSION OF ELIGIBILITY FOR GERIATRIC ACADEMIC CAREER AWARDS; PAYMENT TO INSTITUTION.—Section 753(c) of the Public Health Service Act 294(c)) is amended—

(1) by redesignating paragraphs (4) and (5) as paragraphs (5) and (6), respectively;

(2) by striking paragraph (2) through paragraph (3) and inserting the following:

“(2) ELIGIBLE INDIVIDUALS.—To be eligible to receive an Award under paragraph (1), an individual shall—

“(A) be board certified or board eligible in internal medicine, family practice, psychiatry, or licensed dentistry, or have completed any required training in a discipline and employed in an accredited health professions school that is approved by the Secretary;

“(B) have completed an approved fellowship program in geriatrics or have completed specialty training in geriatrics as required by the discipline and any addition geriatrics training as required by the Secretary; and

“(C) have a junior (non-tenured) faculty appointment at an accredited (as determined by the Secretary) school of medicine, osteopathic medicine, nursing, social work, psychology, dentistry, pharmacy, or other allied health disciplines in an accredited health professions school that is approved by the Secretary.

"(3) LIMITATIONS.—No Award under paragraph (1) may be made to an eligible individual unless the individual—

"(A) has submitted to the Secretary an application, at such time, in such manner, and containing such information as the Secretary may require, and the Secretary has approved such application;

"(B) provides, in such form and manner as the Secretary may require, assurances that the individual will meet the service requirement described in paragraph (6); and

"(C) provides, in such form and manner as the Secretary may require, assurances that the individual has a full-time faculty appointment in a health professions institution and documented commitment from such institution to spend 75 percent of the total time of such individual on teaching and developing skills in interdisciplinary education in geriatrics.

"(4) MAINTENANCE OF EFFORT.—An eligible individual that receives an Award under paragraph (1) shall provide assurances to the Secretary that funds provided to the eligible individual under this subsection will be used only to supplement, not to supplant, the amount of Federal, State, and local funds otherwise expended by the eligible individual."; and

(3) in paragraph (5), as so designated—

(A) in subparagraph (A)—

(i) by inserting "for individuals who are physicians" after "this section"; and

(ii) by inserting after the period at the end the following: "The Secretary shall determine the amount of an Award under this section for individuals who are not physicians."; and

(B) by adding at the end the following:

"(C) PAYMENT TO INSTITUTION.—The Secretary shall make payments to institutions which include schools of medicine, osteopathic medicine, nursing, social work, psychology, dentistry, and pharmacy, or other allied health discipline in an accredited health professions school that is approved by the Secretary.".

(c) COMPREHENSIVE GERIATRIC EDUCATION.—Section 855 of the Public Health Service Act (42 U.S.C. 298) is amended—

(1) in subsection (b)—

(A) in paragraph (3), by striking "or" at the end;

(B) in paragraph (4), by striking the period and inserting "; or"; and

(C) by adding at the end the following:

"(5) establish traineeships for individuals who are preparing for advanced education nursing degrees in geriatric nursing, long-term care, gero-psychiatric nursing or other nursing areas that specialize in the care of the elderly population."; and

(2) in subsection (e), by striking "2003 through 2007" and inserting "2010 through 2014".

SEC. 5306. MENTAL AND BEHAVIORAL HEALTH EDUCATION AND TRAINING GRANTS.

(a) IN GENERAL.—Part D of title VII (42 U.S.C. 294 et seq.) is amended by—

(1) striking section 757;

(2) redesignating section 756 (as amended by section 5103) as section 757; and

(3) inserting after section 755 the following:

"SEC. 756. MENTAL AND BEHAVIORAL HEALTH EDUCATION AND TRAINING GRANTS.

"(a) GRANTS AUTHORIZED.—The Secretary may award grants to eligible institutions of higher education to support the recruitment of students for, and education and clinical experience of the students in—

"(1) baccalaureate, master's, and doctoral degree programs of social work, as well as the development of faculty in social work;

"(2) accredited master's, doctoral, internship, and post-doctoral residency programs of psychology for the development and implementation of interdisciplinary training of psychology graduate students for providing behavioral and mental health services, including substance abuse prevention and treatment services;

"(3) accredited institutions of higher education or accredited professional training programs that are establishing or expanding internships or other field placement programs in child and adolescent mental health in psychiatry, psychology, school psychology, behavioral pediatrics, psychiatric nursing, social work, school social work, substance abuse prevention and treatment, marriage and family therapy, school counseling, or professional counseling; and

"(4) State-licensed mental health nonprofit and for-profit organizations to enable such organizations to pay for programs for preservice or in-service training of paraprofessional child and adolescent mental health workers.

"(b) ELIGIBILITY REQUIREMENTS.—To be eligible for a grant under this section, an institution shall demonstrate—

"(1) participation in the institutions' programs of individuals and groups from different racial, ethnic, cultural, geographic, religious, linguistic, and class backgrounds, and different genders and sexual orientations;

"(2) knowledge and understanding of the concerns of the individuals and groups described in subsection (a);

"(3) any internship or other field placement program assisted under the grant will prioritize cultural and linguistic competency;

"(4) the institution will provide to the Secretary such data, assurances, and information as the Secretary may require; and

"(5) with respect to any violation of the agreement between the Secretary and the institution, the institution will pay such liquidated damages as prescribed by the Secretary by regulation.

"(c) INSTITUTIONAL REQUIREMENT.—For grants authorized under subsection (a)(1), at least 4 of the grant recipients shall be historically black colleges or universities or other minority-serving institutions.

"(d) PRIORITY.—

"(1) In selecting the grant recipients in social work under subsection (a)(1), the Secretary shall give priority to applicants that—

"(A) are accredited by the Council on Social Work Education;

"(B) have a graduation rate of not less than 80 percent for social work students; and

"(C) exhibit an ability to recruit social workers from and place social workers in areas with a high need and high demand population.

"(2) In selecting the grant recipients in graduate psychology under subsection (a)(2), the Secretary shall give priority to institutions in which training focuses on the needs of vulnerable groups such as older adults and children, individuals with mental health or substance-related disorders, victims of abuse or trauma and of combat stress disorders such as posttraumatic stress disorder and traumatic brain injuries, homeless individuals, chronically ill persons, and their families.

"(3) In selecting the grant recipients in training programs in child and adolescent mental health under subsections (a)(3) and (a)(4), the Secretary shall give priority to applicants that—

"(A) have demonstrated the ability to collect data on the number of students trained in child and adolescent mental health and the populations served by such students after graduation or completion of preservice or in-service training;

"(B) have demonstrated familiarity with evidence-based methods in child and adolescent mental health services, including substance abuse prevention and treatment services;

"(C) have programs designed to increase the number of professionals and paraprofessionals serving high-priority populations and to applicants who come from high-priority communities and plan to serve medically underserved populations, in health professional shortage areas, or in medically underserved areas;

"(D) offer curriculum taught collaboratively with a family on the consumer and family lived experience or the importance of family-professional or family-paraprofessional partnerships; and

"(E) provide services through a community mental health program described in section 1913(b)(1).

"(e) AUTHORIZATION OF APPROPRIATION.—For the fiscal years 2010 through 2013, there is authorized to be appropriated to carry out this section—

"(1) $8,000,000 for training in social work in subsection (a)(1);

"(2) $12,000,000 for training in graduate psychology in subsection (a)(2), of which not less than $10,000,000 shall be allocated for doctoral, postdoctoral, and internship level training;

"(3) $10,000,000 for training in professional child and adolescent mental health in subsection (a)(3); and

"(4) $5,000,000 for training in paraprofessional child and adolescent work in subsection (a)(4).".

(b) CONFORMING AMENDMENTS.—Section 757(b)(2) of the Public Health Service Act, as redesignated by subsection (a), is amended by striking "sections 751(a)(1)(A), 751(a)(1)(B), 753(b), 754(3)(A), and 755(b)" and inserting "sections 751(b)(1)(A), 753(b), and 755(b)".

SEC. 5307. CULTURAL COMPETENCY, PREVENTION, AND PUBLIC HEALTH AND INDIVIDUALS WITH DISABILITIES TRAINING.

(a) TITLE VII.—Section 741 of the Public Health Service Act (42 U.S.C. 293e) is amended—

(1) in subsection (a)—

(A) by striking the subsection heading and inserting "CULTURAL COMPETENCY, PREVENTION, AND PUBLIC HEALTH AND INDIVIDUALS WITH DISABILITY GRANTS"; and

(B) in paragraph (1), by striking "for the purpose of" and all that follows through the period at the end and inserting "for the development, evaluation, and dissemination of research, demonstration projects, and model curricula for cultural competency, prevention, public health proficiency, reducing health disparities, and aptitude for working with individuals with disabilities training for use in health professions schools and continuing education programs, and for other purposes determined as appropriate by the Secretary."; and

(2) by striking subsection (b) and inserting the following:

"(b) COLLABORATION.—In carrying out subsection (a), the Secretary shall collaborate with health professional societies, licensing and accreditation entities, health professions schools, and experts in minority health and cultural competency, prevention, and public health and disability groups, community-based organizations, and other organizations as determined appropriate by the Secretary. The Secretary shall coordinate with curricula and research and demonstration projects developed under section 807.

"(c) DISSEMINATION.—

"(1) IN GENERAL.—Model curricula developed under this section shall be disseminated through the Internet Clearinghouse under section 270 and such other means as determined appropriate by the Secretary.

"(2) EVALUATION.—The Secretary shall evaluate the adoption and the implementation of cultural competency, prevention, and public health, and working with individuals with a disability training curricula, and the facilitate inclusion of these competency measures in quality measurement systems as appropriate.

"(d) AUTHORIZATION OF APPROPRIATIONS.—There is authorized to be appropriated to carry out this section such sums as may be necessary for each of fiscal years 2010 through 2015.".

(b) TITLE VIII.—Section 807 of the Public Health Service Act (42 U.S.C. 296e–1) is amended—

(1) in subsection (a)—

(A) by striking the subsection heading and inserting "CULTURAL COMPETENCY, PREVENTION, AND PUBLIC HEALTH AND INDIVIDUALS WITH DISABILITY GRANTS"; and

(B) by striking "for the purpose of" and all that follows through "health care." and inserting "for the development, evaluation, and dissemination of research, demonstration projects, and model curricula for cultural competency, prevention, public health proficiency, reducing health disparities, and aptitude for working with individuals with disabilities training for use in health professions schools and continuing education programs, and for other purposes determined as appropriate by the Secretary."; and

(2) by redesignating subsection (b) as subsection (d);

(3) by inserting after subsection (a) the following:

"(b) COLLABORATION.—In carrying out subsection (a), the Secretary shall collaborate with the entities described in section 741(b). The Secretary shall coordinate with curricula and research and demonstration projects developed under such section 741.

"(c) DISSEMINATION.—Model curricula developed under this section shall be disseminated and evaluated in the same manner as model curricula developed under section 741, as described in subsection (c) of such section."; and

(4) in subsection (d), as so redesignated—

(A) by striking "subsection (a)" and inserting "this section"; and

(B) by striking "2001 through 2004" and inserting "2010 through 2015".

SEC. 5308. ADVANCED NURSING EDUCATION GRANTS.

Section 811 of the Public Health Service Act (42 U.S.C. 296j) is amended—

(1) in subsection (c)—

(A) in the subsection heading, by striking "AND NURSE MIDWIFERY PROGRAMS"; and

(B) by striking "and nurse midwifery";

(2) in subsection (f)—

(A) by striking paragraph (2); and

(B) by redesignating paragraph (3) as paragraph (2); and

(3) by redesignating subsections (d), (e), and (f) as subsections (e), (f), and (g), respectively; and

(4) by inserting after subsection (c), the following:

"(d) AUTHORIZED NURSE-MIDWIFERY PROGRAMS.—Midwifery programs that are eligible for support under this section are educational programs that—

"(1) have as their objective the education of midwives; and

"(2) are accredited by the American College of Nurse-Midwives Accreditation Commission for Midwifery Education.".

SEC. 5309. NURSE EDUCATION, PRACTICE, AND RETENTION GRANTS.

(a) IN GENERAL.—Section 831 of the Public Health Service Act (42 U.S.C. 296p) is amended—

(1) in the section heading, by striking "**RETENTION**" and inserting "**QUALITY**";

(2) in subsection (a)—

(A) in paragraph (1), by adding "or" after the semicolon;

(B) by striking paragraph (2); and

(C) by redesignating paragraph (3) as paragraph (2);

(3) in subsection (b)(3), by striking "managed care, quality improvement" and inserting "coordinated care";

(4) in subsection (g), by inserting ", as defined in section 801(2)," after "school of nursing"; and

(5) in subsection (h), by striking "2003 through 2007" and inserting "2010 through 2014".

(b) NURSE RETENTION GRANTS.—Title VIII of the Public Health Service Act is amended by inserting after section 831 (42 U.S.C. 296b) the following:

"SEC. 831A. NURSE RETENTION GRANTS.

"(a) RETENTION PRIORITY AREAS.—The Secretary may award grants to, and enter into contracts with, eligible entities to enhance the nursing workforce by initiating and maintaining nurse retention programs pursuant to subsection (b) or (c).

"(b) GRANTS FOR CAREER LADDER PROGRAM.—The Secretary may award grants to, and enter into contracts with, eligible entities for programs—

"(1) to promote career advancement for individuals including licensed practical nurses, licensed vocational nurses, certified nurse assistants, home health aides, diploma degree or associate degree nurses, to become baccalaureate prepared registered nurses or advanced education nurses in order to meet the needs of the registered nurse workforce;

"(2) developing and implementing internships and residency programs in collaboration with an accredited school of nursing, as defined by section 801(2), to encourage mentoring and the development of specialties; or

"(3) to assist individuals in obtaining education and training required to enter the nursing profession and advance within such profession.

"(c) ENHANCING PATIENT CARE DELIVERY SYSTEMS.—

"(1) GRANTS.—The Secretary may award grants to eligible entities to improve the retention of nurses and enhance patient care that is directly related to nursing activities by enhancing collaboration and communication among nurses and other health care professionals, and by promoting nurse involvement in the organizational and clinical decision-making processes of a health care facility.

"(2) PRIORITY.—In making awards of grants under this subsection, the Secretary shall give preference to applicants that have not previously received an award under this subsection (or section 831(c) as such section existed on the day before the date of enactment of this section).

"(3) CONTINUATION OF AN AWARD.—The Secretary shall make continuation of any award under this subsection beyond the second year of such award contingent on the recipient of such award having demonstrated to the Secretary measurable and substantive improvement in nurse retention or patient care.

"(d) OTHER PRIORITY AREAS.—The Secretary may award grants to, or enter into contracts with, eligible entities to address other areas that are of high priority to nurse retention, as determined by the Secretary.

"(e) REPORT.—The Secretary shall submit to the Congress before the end of each fiscal year a report on the grants awarded and the contracts entered into under this section. Each such report shall identify the overall number of such grants and contracts and provide an explanation of why each such grant or contract will meet the priority need of the nursing workforce.

“(f) ELIGIBLE ENTITY.—For purposes of this section, the term ‘eligible entity’ includes an accredited school of nursing, as defined by section 801(2), a health care facility, or a partnership of such a school and facility.

“(g) AUTHORIZATION OF APPROPRIATIONS.—There are authorized to be appropriated to carry out this section such sums as may be necessary for each of fiscal years 2010 through 2012.”.

SEC. 5310. LOAN REPAYMENT AND SCHOLARSHIP PROGRAM.

(a) LOAN REPAYMENTS AND SCHOLARSHIPS.—Section 846(a)(3) of the Public Health Service Act (42 U.S.C. 297n(a)(3)) is amended by inserting before the semicolon the following: “, or in a accredited school of nursing, as defined by section 801(2), as nurse faculty”.

(b) TECHNICAL AND CONFORMING AMENDMENTS.—Title VIII (42 U.S.C. 296 et seq.) is amended—

(1) by redesignating section 810 (relating to prohibition against discrimination by schools on the basis of sex) as section 809 and moving such section so that it follows section 808;

(2) in sections 835, 836, 838, 840, and 842, by striking the term “this subpart” each place it appears and inserting “this part”;

(3) in section 836(h), by striking the last sentence;

(4) in section 836, by redesignating subsection (l) as subsection (k);

(5) in section 839, by striking “839” and all that follows through “(a)” and inserting “839. (a)”;

(6) in section 835(b), by striking “841” each place it appears and inserting “871”;

(7) by redesignating section 841 as section 871, moving part F to the end of the title, and redesignating such part as part I;

(8) in part G—

(A) by redesignating section 845 as section 851; and

(B) by redesignating part G as part F;

(9) in part H—

(A) by redesignating sections 851 and 852 as sections 861 and 862, respectively; and

(B) by redesignating part H as part G; and

(10) in part I—

(A) by redesignating section 855, as amended by section 5305, as section 865; and

(B) by redesignating part I as part H.

SEC. 5311. NURSE FACULTY LOAN PROGRAM.

(a) IN GENERAL.—Section 846A of the Public Health Service Act (42 U.S.C. 297n–1) is amended—

(1) in subsection (a)—

(A) in the subsection heading, by striking “ESTABLISHMENT” and inserting “SCHOOL OF NURSING STUDENT LOAN FUND”; and

(B) by inserting “accredited” after “agreement with any”;

(2) in subsection (c)—

(A) in paragraph (2), by striking “$30,000” and all that follows through the semicolon and inserting “$35,500, during fiscal years 2010 and 2011 fiscal years (after fiscal year 2011, such amounts shall be adjusted to provide for a cost-of-attendance increase for the yearly loan rate and the aggregate loan;"; and

(B) in paragraph (3)(A), by inserting "an accredited" after "faculty member in";

(3) in subsection (e), by striking "a school" and inserting "an accredited school"; and

(4) in subsection (f), by striking "2003 through 2007" and inserting "2010 through 2014".

(b) ELIGIBLE INDIVIDUAL STUDENT LOAN REPAYMENT.—Title VIII of the Public Health Service Act is amended by inserting after section 846A (42 U.S.C. 297n–1) the following:

"SEC. 847. ELIGIBLE INDIVIDUAL STUDENT LOAN REPAYMENT.

"(a) IN GENERAL.—The Secretary, acting through the Administrator of the Health Resources and Services Administration, may enter into an agreement with eligible individuals for the repayment of education loans, in accordance with this section, to increase the number of qualified nursing faculty.

"(b) AGREEMENTS.—Each agreement entered into under this subsection shall require that the eligible individual shall serve as a full-time member of the faculty of an accredited school of nursing, for a total period, in the aggregate, of at least 4 years during the 6-year period beginning on the later of—

"(1) the date on which the individual receives a master's or doctorate nursing degree from an accredited school of nursing; or

"(2) the date on which the individual enters into an agreement under this subsection.

"(c) AGREEMENT PROVISIONS.—Agreements entered into pursuant to subsection (b) shall be entered into on such terms and conditions as the Secretary may determine, except that—

"(1) not more than 10 months after the date on which the 6-year period described under subsection (b) begins, but in no case before the individual starts as a full-time member of the faculty of an accredited school of nursing the Secretary shall begin making payments, for and on behalf of that individual, on the outstanding principal of, and interest on, any loan of that individual obtained to pay for such degree;

"(2) for an individual who has completed a master's in nursing or equivalent degree in nursing—

"(A) payments may not exceed $10,000 per calendar year; and

"(B) total payments may not exceed $40,000 during the 2010 and 2011 fiscal years (after fiscal year 2011, such amounts shall be adjusted to provide for a cost-of-attendance increase for the yearly loan rate and the aggregate loan); and

"(3) for an individual who has completed a doctorate or equivalent degree in nursing—

"(A) payments may not exceed $20,000 per calendar year; and

"(B) total payments may not exceed $80,000 during the 2010 and 2011 fiscal years (adjusted for subsequent fiscal years as provided for in the same manner as in paragraph (2)(B)).

"(d) BREACH OF AGREEMENT.—

"(1) IN GENERAL.—In the case of any agreement made under subsection (b), the individual is liable to the Federal Government for the total amount paid by the Secretary under such agreement, and for interest on such amount at the maximum legal prevailing rate, if the individual fails to meet the agreement terms required under such subsection.

"(2) WAIVER OR SUSPENSION OF LIABILITY.—In the case of an individual making an agreement for purposes of paragraph (1), the Secretary shall provide for the waiver or suspension of liability under such paragraph if compliance by the individual with the agreement involved is impossible or would involve extreme hardship to the individual or if enforcement of the agreement with respect to the individual would be unconscionable.

"(3) DATE CERTAIN FOR RECOVERY.—Subject to paragraph (2), any amount that the Federal Government is entitled to recover under paragraph (1) shall be paid to the United States not later than the expiration of the 3-year period beginning on the date the United States becomes so entitled.

"(4) AVAILABILITY.—Amounts recovered under paragraph (1) shall be available to the Secretary for making loan repayments under this section and shall remain available for such purpose until expended.

"(e) ELIGIBLE INDIVIDUAL DEFINED.—For purposes of this section, the term 'eligible individual' means an individual who—

"(1) is a United States citizen, national, or lawful permanent resident;

"(2) holds an unencumbered license as a registered nurse; and

"(3) has either already completed a master's or doctorate nursing program at an accredited school of nursing or is currently enrolled on a full-time or part-time basis in such a program.

"(f) PRIORITY.—For the purposes of this section and section 846A, funding priority will be awarded to School of Nursing Student Loans that support doctoral nursing students or Individual Student Loan Repayment that support doctoral nursing students.

"(g) AUTHORIZATION OF APPROPRIATIONS.—There are authorized to be appropriated to carry out this section such sums as may be necessary for each of fiscal years 2010 through 2014.".

SEC. 5312. AUTHORIZATION OF APPROPRIATIONS FOR PARTS B THROUGH D OF TITLE VIII.

Section 871 of the Public Health Service Act, as redesignated and moved by section 5310, is amended to read as follows:

"SEC. 871. AUTHORIZATION OF APPROPRIATIONS.

"For the purpose of carrying out parts B, C, and D (subject to section 851(g)), there are authorized to be appropriated $338,000,000 for fiscal year 2010, and such sums as may be necessary for each of the fiscal years 2011 through 2016.".

SEC. 5313. GRANTS TO PROMOTE THE COMMUNITY HEALTH WORKFORCE.

(a) IN GENERAL.—Part P of title III of the Public Health Service Act (42 U.S.C. 280g et seq.) is amended by adding at the end the following:

"SEC. 399V. GRANTS TO PROMOTE POSITIVE HEALTH BEHAVIORS AND OUTCOMES.

"(a) GRANTS AUTHORIZED.—The Director of the Centers for Disease Control and Prevention, in collaboration with the Secretary, shall award grants to eligible entities to promote positive health behaviors and outcomes for populations in medically underserved communities through the use of community health workers.

"(b) USE OF FUNDS.—Grants awarded under subsection (a) shall be used to support community health workers—

"(1) to educate, guide, and provide outreach in a community setting regarding health problems prevalent in medically underserved communities, particularly racial and ethnic minority populations;

"(2) to educate and provide guidance regarding effective strategies to promote positive health behaviors and discourage risky health behaviors;

"(3) to educate and provide outreach regarding enrollment in health insurance including the Children's Health Insurance Program under title XXI of the Social Security Act, Medicare under title XVIII of such Act and Medicaid under title XIX of such Act;

"(4) to identify, educate, refer, and enroll underserved populations to appropriate healthcare agencies and community-based programs and organizations in order to increase access to quality healthcare services and to eliminate duplicative care; or

"(5) to educate, guide, and provide home visitation services regarding maternal health and prenatal care.

"(c) APPLICATION.—Each eligible entity that desires to receive a grant under subsection (a) shall submit an application to the Secretary, at such time, in such manner, and accompanied by such information as the Secretary may require.

"(d) PRIORITY.—In awarding grants under subsection (a), the Secretary shall give priority to applicants that—

"(1) propose to target geographic areas—

"(A) with a high percentage of residents who are eligible for health insurance but are uninsured or underinsured;

"(B) with a high percentage of residents who suffer from chronic diseases; or

"(C) with a high infant mortality rate;

"(2) have experience in providing health or health-related social services to individuals who are underserved with respect to such services; and

"(3) have documented community activity and experience with community health workers.

"(e) COLLABORATION WITH ACADEMIC INSTITUTIONS AND THE ONE-STOP DELIVERY SYSTEM.—The Secretary shall encourage community health worker programs receiving funds under this section to collaborate with academic institutions and one-stop delivery systems under section 134(c) of the Workforce Investment Act of 1998. Nothing in this section shall be construed to require such collaboration.

"(f) EVIDENCE-BASED INTERVENTIONS.—The Secretary shall encourage community health worker programs receiving funding under this section to implement a process or an outcome-based payment system that rewards community health workers for connecting underserved populations with the most appropriate services at the most appropriate time. Nothing in this section shall be construed to require such a payment.

"(g) QUALITY ASSURANCE AND COST EFFECTIVENESS.—The Secretary shall establish guidelines for assuring the quality of the training and supervision of community health workers under the programs funded under this section and for assuring the cost-effectiveness of such programs.

"(h) MONITORING.—The Secretary shall monitor community health worker programs identified in approved applications under this section and shall determine whether such programs are in compliance with the guidelines established under subsection (g).

"(i) TECHNICAL ASSISTANCE.—The Secretary may provide technical assistance to community health worker programs identified in approved applications under this section with respect to planning, developing, and operating programs under the grant.

"(j) AUTHORIZATION OF APPROPRIATIONS.—There are authorized to be appropriated, such sums as may be necessary to carry out this section for each of fiscal years 2010 through 2014.

"(k) DEFINITIONS.—In this section:

"(1) COMMUNITY HEALTH WORKER.—The term 'community health worker', as defined by the Department of Labor as Standard Occupational Classification [21–1094] means an individual who promotes health or nutrition within the community in which the individual resides—

"(A) by serving as a liaison between communities and healthcare agencies;

"(B) by providing guidance and social assistance to community residents;

"(C) by enhancing community residents' ability to effectively communicate with healthcare providers;

"(D) by providing culturally and linguistically appropriate health or nutrition education;

"(E) by advocating for individual and community health;

"(F) by providing referral and follow-up services or otherwise coordinating care; and

"(G) by proactively identifying and enrolling eligible individuals in Federal, State, local, private or nonprofit health and human services programs.

"(2) COMMUNITY SETTING.—The term 'community setting' means a home or a community organization located in the neighborhood in which a participant in the program under this section resides.

"(3) ELIGIBLE ENTITY.—The term 'eligible entity' means a public or nonprofit private entity (including a State or public subdivision of a State, a public health department, a free health clinic, a hospital, or a Federally-qualified health center (as defined in section 1861(aa) of the Social Security Act)), or a consortium of any such entities.

"(4) MEDICALLY UNDERSERVED COMMUNITY.—The term 'medically underserved community' means a community identified by a State—

"(A) that has a substantial number of individuals who are members of a medically underserved population, as defined by section 330(b)(3); and

"(B) a significant portion of which is a health professional shortage area as designated under section 332.".

SEC. 5314. FELLOWSHIP TRAINING IN PUBLIC HEALTH.

Part E of title VII of the Public Health Service Act (42 U.S.C. 294n et seq.), as amended by section 5206, is further amended by adding at the end the following:

"SEC. 778. FELLOWSHIP TRAINING IN APPLIED PUBLIC HEALTH EPIDEMIOLOGY, PUBLIC HEALTH LABORATORY SCIENCE, PUBLIC HEALTH INFORMATICS, AND EXPANSION OF THE EPIDEMIC INTELLIGENCE SERVICE.

"(a) IN GENERAL.—The Secretary may carry out activities to address documented workforce shortages in State and local health departments in the critical areas of applied public health epidemiology and public health laboratory science and informatics and may expand the Epidemic Intelligence Service.

"(b) SPECIFIC USES.—In carrying out subsection (a), the Secretary shall provide for the expansion of existing fellowship programs operated through the Centers for Disease Control and Prevention in a manner that is designed to alleviate shortages of the type described in subsection (a).

"(c) OTHER PROGRAMS.—The Secretary may provide for the expansion of other applied epidemiology training programs that meet objectives similar to the objectives of the programs described in subsection (b).

"(d) WORK OBLIGATION.—Participation in fellowship training programs under this section shall be deemed to be service for purposes of satisfying work obligations stipulated in contracts under section 338I(j).

"(e) GENERAL SUPPORT.—Amounts may be used from grants awarded under this section to expand the Public Health Informatics Fellowship Program at the Centers for Disease Control and Prevention to better support all public health systems at all levels of government.

"(f) AUTHORIZATION OF APPROPRIATIONS.—There are authorized to be appropriated to carry out this section $39,500,000 for each of fiscal years 2010 through 2013, of which—

"(1) $5,000,000 shall be made available in each such fiscal year for epidemiology fellowship training program activities under subsections (b) and (c);

"(2) $5,000,000 shall be made available in each such fiscal year for laboratory fellowship training programs under subsection (b);

"(3) $5,000,000 shall be made available in each such fiscal year for the Public Health Informatics Fellowship Program under subsection (e); and

"(4) $24,500,000 shall be made available for expanding the Epidemic Intelligence Service under subsection (a).".

SEC. 5315. UNITED STATES PUBLIC HEALTH SCIENCES TRACK.

Title II of the Public Health Service Act (42 U.S.C. 202 et seq.) is amended by adding at the end the following:

"PART D—UNITED STATES PUBLIC HEALTH SCIENCES TRACK

"SEC. 271. ESTABLISHMENT.

"(a) UNITED STATES PUBLIC HEALTH SERVICES TRACK.—

"(1) IN GENERAL.—There is hereby authorized to be established a United States Public Health Sciences Track (referred to in this part as the 'Track'), at sites to be selected by the Secretary, with authority to grant appropriate advanced degrees in a manner that uniquely emphasizes team-based service, public health, epidemiology, and emergency preparedness and response. It shall be so organized as to graduate not less than—

"(A) 150 medical students annually, 10 of whom shall be awarded studentships to the Uniformed Services University of Health Sciences;

"(B) 100 dental students annually;

"(C) 250 nursing students annually;

"(D) 100 public health students annually;

"(E) 100 behavioral and mental health professional students annually;

"(F) 100 physician assistant or nurse practitioner students annually; and

"(G) 50 pharmacy students annually.

"(2) LOCATIONS.—The Track shall be located at existing and accredited, affiliated health professions education training programs at academic health centers located in regions of the United States determined appropriate by the Surgeon General, in consultation with the National Health Care Workforce Commission established in section 5101 of the Patient Protection and Affordable Care Act.

"(b) NUMBER OF GRADUATES.—Except as provided in subsection (a), the number of persons to be graduated from the Track shall be prescribed by the Secretary. In so prescribing the number of persons to be graduated from the Track, the Secretary shall institute actions necessary to ensure the maximum number of first-year enrollments in the Track consistent with the academic capacity of the affiliated sites and the needs of the United States for medical, dental, and nursing personnel.

"(c) DEVELOPMENT.—The development of the Track may be by such phases as the Secretary may prescribe subject to the requirements of subsection (a).

"(d) INTEGRATED LONGITUDINAL PLAN.—The Surgeon General shall develop an integrated longitudinal plan for health professions continuing education throughout the continuum of health-related education, training, and practice. Training under such plan shall emphasize patient-centered, interdisciplinary, and care coordination skills. Experience with deployment of emergency response teams shall be included during the clinical experiences.

"(e) FACULTY DEVELOPMENT.—The Surgeon General shall develop faculty development programs and curricula in decentralized venues of health care, to balance urban, tertiary, and inpatient venues.

"SEC. 272. ADMINISTRATION.

"(a) IN GENERAL.—The business of the Track shall be conducted by the Surgeon General with funds appropriated for and provided by the Department of Health and Human Services. The National Health Care Workforce Commission shall assist the Surgeon General in an advisory capacity.

"(b) FACULTY.—

"(1) IN GENERAL.—The Surgeon General, after considering the recommendations of the National Health Care Workforce Commission, shall obtain the services of such professors, instructors, and administrative and other employees as may be necessary to operate the Track, but utilize when possible, existing affiliated health professions training institutions. Members of the faculty and staff shall be employed under salary schedules and granted retirement and other related benefits prescribed by the Secretary so as to place the employees of the Track faculty on a comparable basis with the employees of fully accredited schools of the health professions within the United States.

"(2) TITLES.—The Surgeon General may confer academic titles, as appropriate, upon the members of the faculty.

"(3) NONAPPLICATION OF PROVISIONS.—The limitations in section 5373 of title 5, United States Code, shall not apply to the authority of the Surgeon General under paragraph (1) to prescribe salary schedules and other related benefits.

"(c) AGREEMENTS.—The Surgeon General may negotiate agreements with agencies of the Federal Government to utilize on a reimbursable basis appropriate existing Federal medical resources located in the United States (or locations selected in accordance with section 271(a)(2)). Under such agreements the facilities concerned will retain their identities and basic missions. The Surgeon General may negotiate affiliation agreements with accredited universities and health professions training institutions in the United States. Such agreements may include provisions for payments for educational services provided students participating in Department of Health and Human Services educational programs.

"(d) PROGRAMS.—The Surgeon General may establish the following educational programs for Track students:

"(1) Postdoctoral, postgraduate, and technological programs.

"(2) A cooperative program for medical, dental, physician assistant, pharmacy, behavioral and mental health, public health, and nursing students.

"(3) Other programs that the Surgeon General determines necessary in order to operate the Track in a cost-effective manner.

"(e) CONTINUING MEDICAL EDUCATION.—The Surgeon General shall establish programs in continuing medical education for members of the health professions to the end that high standards of health care may be maintained within the United States.

"(f) AUTHORITY OF THE SURGEON GENERAL.—

"(1) IN GENERAL.—The Surgeon General is authorized—

"(A) to enter into contracts with, accept grants from, and make grants to any nonprofit entity for the purpose of carrying out cooperative enterprises in medical, dental, physician assistant, pharmacy, behavioral and mental health, public health, and nursing research, consultation, and education;

"(B) to enter into contracts with entities under which the Surgeon General may furnish the services of such professional, technical, or clerical personnel as may be necessary to fulfill cooperative enterprises undertaken by the Track;

"(C) to accept, hold, administer, invest, and spend any gift, devise, or bequest of personal property made to the Track, including any gift, devise, or bequest for the support of an academic chair, teaching, research, or demonstration project;

"(D) to enter into agreements with entities that may be utilized by the Track for the purpose of enhancing the activities of the Track in education, research, and technological applications of knowledge; and

"(E) to accept the voluntary services of guest scholars and other persons.

"(2) LIMITATION.—The Surgeon General may not enter into any contract with an entity if the contract would obligate the Track to make outlays in advance of the enactment of budget authority for such outlays.

"(3) SCIENTISTS.—Scientists or other medical, dental, or nursing personnel utilized by the Track under an agreement described in paragraph (1) may be appointed to any position within the Track and may be permitted to perform such duties within the Track as the Surgeon General may approve.

"(4) VOLUNTEER SERVICES.—A person who provides voluntary services under the authority of subparagraph (E) of paragraph (1) shall be considered to be an employee of the Federal Government for the purposes of chapter 81 of title 5, relating to compensation for work-related injuries, and to be an employee of the Federal Government for the purposes of chapter 171 of title 28, relating to tort claims. Such a person who is not otherwise employed by the Federal Government shall not be considered to be a Federal employee for any other purpose by reason of the provision of such services.

"SEC. 273. STUDENTS; SELECTION; OBLIGATION.

"(a) STUDENT SELECTION.—

"(1) IN GENERAL.—Medical, dental, physician assistant, pharmacy, behavioral and mental health, public health, and nursing students at the Track shall be selected under procedures prescribed by the Surgeon General. In so prescribing, the Surgeon General shall consider the recommendations of the National Health Care Workforce Commission.

"(2) PRIORITY.—In developing admissions procedures under paragraph (1), the Surgeon General shall ensure that such procedures give priority to applicant medical, dental, physician assistant, pharmacy, behavioral and mental health, public health, and nursing students from rural communities and underrepresented minorities.

"(b) CONTRACT AND SERVICE OBLIGATION.—

"(1) CONTRACT.—Upon being admitted to the Track, a medical, dental, physician assistant, pharmacy, behavioral and mental health, public health, or nursing student shall enter into a written contract with the Surgeon General that shall contain—

"(A) an agreement under which—

"(i) subject to subparagraph (B), the Surgeon General agrees to provide the student with tuition (or tuition remission) and a student stipend (described in paragraph (2)) in each school year for a period of years (not to exceed 4 school years) determined by the student, during which period the student is enrolled in the Track at an affiliated or other participating health professions institution pursuant to an agreement between the Track and such institution; and

"(ii) subject to subparagraph (B), the student agrees—

"(I) to accept the provision of such tuition and student stipend to the student;

"(II) to maintain enrollment at the Track until the student completes the course of study involved;

"(III) while enrolled in such course of study, to maintain an acceptable level of academic standing (as determined by the Surgeon General);

"(IV) if pursuing a degree from a school of medicine or osteopathic medicine, dental, public health, or nursing school or a physician assistant, pharmacy, or behavioral and mental health professional program, to complete a residency or internship in a specialty that the Surgeon General determines is appropriate; and

"(V) to serve for a period of time (referred to in this part as the 'period of obligated service') within the Commissioned Corps of the Public Health Service equal to 2 years for each school year during which such individual was enrolled at the College, reduced as provided for in paragraph (3);

"(B) a provision that any financial obligation of the United States arising out of a contract entered into under this part and any obligation of the student which is conditioned thereon, is contingent upon funds being appropriated to carry out this part;

"(C) a statement of the damages to which the United States is entitled for the student's breach of the contract; and

"(D) such other statements of the rights and liabilities of the Secretary and of the individual, not inconsistent with the provisions of this part.

"(2) TUITION AND STUDENT STIPEND.—

"(A) TUITION REMISSION RATES.—The Surgeon General, based on the recommendations of the National Health Care Workforce Commission, shall establish Federal tuition remission rates to be used by the Track to provide reimbursement to affiliated and other participating health professions institutions for the cost of educational services provided by such institutions to Track students. The agreement entered into by such participating institutions under paragraph (1)(A)(i) shall contain an agreement to accept as payment in full the established remission rate under this subparagraph.

"(B) STIPEND.—The Surgeon General, based on the recommendations of the National Health Care Workforce

Commission, shall establish and update Federal stipend rates for payment to students under this part.

"(3) REDUCTIONS IN THE PERIOD OF OBLIGATED SERVICE.—The period of obligated service under paragraph (1)(A)(ii)(V) shall be reduced—

"(A) in the case of a student who elects to participate in a high-needs speciality residency (as determined by the National Health Care Workforce Commission), by 3 months for each year of such participation (not to exceed a total of 12 months); and

"(B) in the case of a student who, upon completion of their residency, elects to practice in a Federal medical facility (as defined in section 781(e)) that is located in a health professional shortage area (as defined in section 332), by 3 months for year of full-time practice in such a facility (not to exceed a total of 12 months).

"(c) SECOND 2 YEARS OF SERVICE.—During the third and fourth years in which a medical, dental, physician assistant, pharmacy, behavioral and mental health, public health, or nursing student is enrolled in the Track, training should be designed to prioritize clinical rotations in Federal medical facilities in health professional shortage areas, and emphasize a balance of hospital and community-based experiences, and training within interdisciplinary teams.

"(d) DENTIST, PHYSICIAN ASSISTANT, PHARMACIST, BEHAVIORAL AND MENTAL HEALTH PROFESSIONAL, PUBLIC HEALTH PROFESSIONAL, AND NURSE TRAINING.—The Surgeon General shall establish provisions applicable with respect to dental, physician assistant, pharmacy, behavioral and mental health, public health, and nursing students that are comparable to those for medical students under this section, including service obligations, tuition support, and stipend support. The Surgeon General shall give priority to health professions training institutions that train medical, dental, physician assistant, pharmacy, behavioral and mental health, public health, and nursing students for some significant period of time together, but at a minimum have a discrete and shared core curriculum.

"(e) ELITE FEDERAL DISASTER TEAMS.—The Surgeon General, in consultation with the Secretary, the Director of the Centers for Disease Control and Prevention, and other appropriate military and Federal government agencies, shall develop criteria for the appointment of highly qualified Track faculty, medical, dental, physician assistant, pharmacy, behavioral and mental health, public health, and nursing students, and graduates to elite Federal disaster preparedness teams to train and to respond to public health emergencies, natural disasters, bioterrorism events, and other emergencies.

"(f) STUDENT DROPPED FROM TRACK IN AFFILIATE SCHOOL.—A medical, dental, physician assistant, pharmacy, behavioral and mental health, public health, or nursing student who, under regulations prescribed by the Surgeon General, is dropped from the Track in an affiliated school for deficiency in conduct or studies, or for other reasons, shall be liable to the United States for all tuition and stipend support provided to the student.

"SEC. 274. FUNDING.

"Beginning with fiscal year 2010, the Secretary shall transfer from the Public Health and Social Services Emergency Fund such sums as may be necessary to carry out this part.".

Subtitle E—Supporting the Existing Health Care Workforce

SEC. 5401. CENTERS OF EXCELLENCE.

Section 736 of the Public Health Service Act (42 U.S.C. 293) is amended by striking subsection (h) and inserting the following:

"(h) FORMULA FOR ALLOCATIONS.—

"(1) ALLOCATIONS.—Based on the amount appropriated under subsection (i) for a fiscal year, the following subparagraphs shall apply as appropriate:

"(A) IN GENERAL.—If the amounts appropriated under subsection (i) for a fiscal year are $24,000,000 or less—

"(i) the Secretary shall make available $12,000,000 for grants under subsection (a) to health professions schools that meet the conditions described in subsection (c)(2)(A); and

"(ii) and available after grants are made with funds under clause (i), the Secretary shall make available—

"(I) 60 percent of such amount for grants under subsection (a) to health professions schools that meet the conditions described in paragraph (3) or (4) of subsection (c) (including meeting the conditions under subsection (e)); and

"(II) 40 percent of such amount for grants under subsection (a) to health professions schools that meet the conditions described in subsection (c)(5).

"(B) FUNDING IN EXCESS OF $24,000,000.—If amounts appropriated under subsection (i) for a fiscal year exceed $24,000,000 but are less than $30,000,000—

"(i) 80 percent of such excess amounts shall be made available for grants under subsection (a) to health professions schools that meet the requirements described in paragraph (3) or (4) of subsection (c) (including meeting conditions pursuant to subsection (e)); and

"(ii) 20 percent of such excess amount shall be made available for grants under subsection (a) to health professions schools that meet the conditions described in subsection (c)(5).

"(C) FUNDING IN EXCESS OF $30,000,000.—If amounts appropriated under subsection (i) for a fiscal year exceed $30,000,000 but are less than $40,000,000, the Secretary shall make available—

"(i) not less than $12,000,000 for grants under subsection (a) to health professions schools that meet the conditions described in subsection (c)(2)(A);

"(ii) not less than $12,000,000 for grants under subsection (a) to health professions schools that meet the conditions described in paragraph (3) or (4) of subsection (c) (including meeting conditions pursuant to subsection (e));

"(iii) not less than $6,000,000 for grants under subsection (a) to health professions schools that meet the conditions described in subsection (c)(5); and

"(iv) after grants are made with funds under clauses (i) through (iii), any remaining excess amount for grants under subsection (a) to health professions schools that meet the conditions described in paragraph (2)(A), (3), (4), or (5) of subsection (c).

"(D) FUNDING IN EXCESS OF $40,000,000.—If amounts appropriated under subsection (i) for a fiscal year are $40,000,000 or more, the Secretary shall make available—

"(i) not less than $16,000,000 for grants under subsection (a) to health professions schools that meet the conditions described in subsection (c)(2)(A);

"(ii) not less than $16,000,000 for grants under subsection (a) to health professions schools that meet the conditions described in paragraph (3) or (4) of subsection (c) (including meeting conditions pursuant to subsection (e));

"(iii) not less than $8,000,000 for grants under subsection (a) to health professions schools that meet the conditions described in subsection (c)(5); and

"(iv) after grants are made with funds under clauses (i) through (iii), any remaining funds for grants under subsection (a) to health professions schools that meet the conditions described in paragraph (2)(A), (3), (4), or (5) of subsection (c).

"(2) NO LIMITATION.—Nothing in this subsection shall be construed as limiting the centers of excellence referred to in this section to the designated amount, or to preclude such entities from competing for grants under this section.

"(3) MAINTENANCE OF EFFORT.—

"(A) IN GENERAL.—With respect to activities for which a grant made under this part are authorized to be expended, the Secretary may not make such a grant to a center of excellence for any fiscal year unless the center agrees to maintain expenditures of non-Federal amounts for such activities at a level that is not less than the level of such expenditures maintained by the center for the fiscal year preceding the fiscal year for which the school receives such a grant.

"(B) USE OF FEDERAL FUNDS.—With respect to any Federal amounts received by a center of excellence and available for carrying out activities for which a grant under this part is authorized to be expended, the center shall, before expending the grant, expend the Federal amounts obtained from sources other than the grant, unless given prior approval from the Secretary.

"(i) AUTHORIZATION OF APPROPRIATIONS.—There are authorized to be appropriated to carry out this section—

"(1) $50,000,000 for each of the fiscal years 2010 through 2015; and

"(2) and such sums as are necessary for each subsequent fiscal year.".

SEC. 5402. HEALTH CARE PROFESSIONALS TRAINING FOR DIVERSITY.

(a) LOAN REPAYMENTS AND FELLOWSHIPS REGARDING FACULTY POSITIONS.—Section 738(a)(1) of the Public Health Service Act (42 U.S.C. 293b(a)(1)) is amended by striking "$20,000 of the principal and interest of the educational loans of such individuals." and inserting "$30,000 of the principal and interest of the educational loans of such individuals.".

(b) SCHOLARSHIPS FOR DISADVANTAGED STUDENTS.—Section 740(a) of such Act (42 U.S.C. 293d(a)) is amended by striking "$37,000,000" and all that follows through "2002" and inserting "$51,000,000 for fiscal year 2010, and such sums as may be necessary for each of the fiscal years 2011 through 2014".

(c) REAUTHORIZATION FOR LOAN REPAYMENTS AND FELLOWSHIPS REGARDING FACULTY POSITIONS.—Section 740(b) of such Act (42 U.S.C. 293d(b)) is amended by striking "appropriated" and all that follows through the period at the end and inserting "appropriated, $5,000,000 for each of the fiscal years 2010 through 2014.".

(d) REAUTHORIZATION FOR EDUCATIONAL ASSISTANCE IN THE HEALTH PROFESSIONS REGARDING INDIVIDUALS FROM A DISADVANTAGED BACKGROUND.—Section 740(c) of such Act (42 U.S.C. 293d(c)) is amended by striking the first sentence and inserting the following: "For the purpose of grants and contracts under section 739(a)(1), there is authorized to be appropriated $60,000,000 for fiscal year 2010 and such sums as may be necessary for each of the fiscal years 2011 through 2014."

SEC. 5403. INTERDISCIPLINARY, COMMUNITY-BASED LINKAGES.

(a) AREA HEALTH EDUCATION CENTERS.—Section 751 of the Public Health Service Act (42 U.S.C. 294a) is amended to read as follows:

"SEC. 751. AREA HEALTH EDUCATION CENTERS.

"(a) ESTABLISHMENT OF AWARDS.—The Secretary shall make the following 2 types of awards in accordance with this section:

"(1) INFRASTRUCTURE DEVELOPMENT AWARD.—The Secretary shall make awards to eligible entities to enable such entities to initiate health care workforce educational programs or to continue to carry out comparable programs that are operating at the time the award is made by planning, developing, operating, and evaluating an area health education center program.

"(2) POINT OF SERVICE MAINTENANCE AND ENHANCEMENT AWARD.—The Secretary shall make awards to eligible entities to maintain and improve the effectiveness and capabilities of an existing area health education center program, and make other modifications to the program that are appropriate due to changes in demographics, needs of the populations served, or other similar issues affecting the area health education center program. For the purposes of this section, the term 'Program' refers to the area health education center program.

"(b) ELIGIBLE ENTITIES; APPLICATION.—

"(1) ELIGIBLE ENTITIES.—

"(A) INFRASTRUCTURE DEVELOPMENT.—For purposes of subsection (a)(1), the term 'eligible entity' means a school of medicine or osteopathic medicine, an incorporated consortium of such schools, or the parent institutions of such a school. With respect to a State in which no area health education center program is in operation, the Secretary may award a grant or contract under subsection (a)(1) to a school of nursing.

"(B) POINT OF SERVICE MAINTENANCE AND ENHANCEMENT.—For purposes of subsection (a)(2), the term 'eligible entity' means an entity that has received funds under this section, is operating an area health education center program, including an area health education center or centers, and has a center or centers that are no longer eligible to receive financial assistance under subsection (a)(1).

"(2) APPLICATION.—An eligible entity desiring to receive an award under this section shall submit to the Secretary an application at such time, in such manner, and containing such information as the Secretary may require.

"(c) USE OF FUNDS.—

"(1) REQUIRED ACTIVITIES.—An eligible entity shall use amounts awarded under a grant under subsection (a)(1) or (a)(2) to carry out the following activities:

"(A) Develop and implement strategies, in coordination with the applicable one-stop delivery system under section 134(c) of the Workforce Investment Act of 1998, to recruit individuals from underrepresented minority populations or from disadvantaged or rural backgrounds into health professions, and support such individuals in attaining such careers.

"(B) Develop and implement strategies to foster and provide community-based training and education to individuals seeking careers in health professions within underserved areas for the purpose of developing and maintaining a diverse health care workforce that is prepared to deliver high-quality care, with an emphasis on primary care, in underserved areas or for health disparity populations, in collaboration with other Federal and State health care workforce development programs, the State workforce agency, and local workforce investment boards, and in health care safety net sites.

"(C) Prepare individuals to more effectively provide health services to underserved areas and health disparity populations through field placements or preceptorships in conjunction with community-based organizations, accredited primary care residency training programs, Federally qualified health centers, rural health clinics, public health departments, or other appropriate facilities.

"(D) Conduct and participate in interdisciplinary training that involves physicians, physician assistants, nurse practitioners, nurse midwives, dentists, psychologists, pharmacists, optometrists, community health workers, public and allied health professionals, or other health professionals, as practicable.

"(E) Deliver or facilitate continuing education and information dissemination programs for health care professionals, with an emphasis on individuals providing care in underserved areas and for health disparity populations.

"(F) Propose and implement effective program and outcomes measurement and evaluation strategies.

"(G) Establish a youth public health program to expose and recruit high school students into health careers, with a focus on careers in public health.

"(2) INNOVATIVE OPPORTUNITIES.—An eligible entity may use amounts awarded under a grant under subsection (a)(1) or subsection (a)(2) to carry out any of the following activities:

"(A) Develop and implement innovative curricula in collaboration with community-based accredited primary care residency training programs, Federally qualified health centers, rural health clinics, behavioral and mental health facilities, public health departments, or other appropriate facilities, with the goal of increasing the number of primary care physicians and other primary care providers prepared to serve in underserved areas and health disparity populations.

"(B) Coordinate community-based participatory research with academic health centers, and facilitate rapid flow and dissemination of evidence-based health care information, research results, and best practices to improve quality, efficiency, and effectiveness of health care and health care systems within community settings.

"(C) Develop and implement other strategies to address identified workforce needs and increase and enhance the health care workforce in the area served by the area health education center program.

"(d) REQUIREMENTS.—

"(1) AREA HEALTH EDUCATION CENTER PROGRAM.—In carrying out this section, the Secretary shall ensure the following:

"(A) An entity that receives an award under this section shall conduct at least 10 percent of clinical education required for medical students in community settings that are removed from the primary teaching facility of the contracting institution for grantees that operate a school of medicine or osteopathic medicine. In States in which an entity that receives an award under this section is a nursing school or its parent institution, the Secretary shall alternatively ensure that—

"(i) the nursing school conducts at least 10 percent of clinical education required for nursing students in community settings that are remote from the primary teaching facility of the school; and

"(ii) the entity receiving the award maintains a written agreement with a school of medicine or osteopathic medicine to place students from that school in training sites in the area health education center program area.

"(B) An entity receiving funds under subsection (a)(2) does not distribute such funding to a center that is eligible to receive funding under subsection (a)(1).

"(2) AREA HEALTH EDUCATION CENTER.—The Secretary shall ensure that each area health education center program includes at least 1 area health education center, and that each such center—

"(A) is a public or private organization whose structure, governance, and operation is independent from the awardee and the parent institution of the awardee;

"(B) is not a school of medicine or osteopathic medicine, the parent institution of such a school, or a branch campus or other subunit of a school of medicine or osteopathic medicine or its parent institution, or a consortium of such entities;

"(C) designates an underserved area or population to be served by the center which is in a location removed from the main location of the teaching facilities of the schools participating in the program with such center and does not duplicate, in whole or in part, the geographic area or population served by any other center;

"(D) fosters networking and collaboration among communities and between academic health centers and community-based centers;

"(E) serves communities with a demonstrated need of health professionals in partnership with academic medical centers;

"(F) addresses the health care workforce needs of the communities served in coordination with the public workforce investment system; and

"(G) has a community-based governing or advisory board that reflects the diversity of the communities involved.

"(e) MATCHING FUNDS.—With respect to the costs of operating a program through a grant under this section, to be eligible for financial assistance under this section, an entity shall make available (directly or through contributions from State, county or municipal governments, or the private sector) recurring non-Federal contributions in cash or in kind, toward such costs in an amount that is equal to not less than 50 percent of such costs. At least 25 percent of the total required non-Federal contributions shall be in cash. An entity may apply to the Secretary for a waiver of not more than 75 percent of the matching fund amount required by the entity for each of the first 3 years the entity is funded through a grant under subsection (a)(1).

"(f) LIMITATION.—Not less than 75 percent of the total amount provided to an area health education center program under subsection (a)(1) or (a)(2) shall be allocated to the area health education centers participating in the program under this section. To provide needed flexibility to newly funded area health education center programs, the Secretary may waive the requirement in the sentence for the first 2 years of a new area health education center program funded under subsection (a)(1).

"(g) AWARD.—An award to an entity under this section shall be not less than $250,000 annually per area health education center included in the program involved. If amounts appropriated to carry out this section are not sufficient to comply with the preceding sentence, the Secretary may reduce the per center amount provided for in such sentence as necessary, provided the distribution established in subsection (j)(2) is maintained.

"(h) PROJECT TERMS.—

"(1) IN GENERAL.—Except as provided in paragraph (2), the period during which payments may be made under an award under subsection (a)(1) may not exceed—

"(A) in the case of a program, 12 years; or

"(B) in the case of a center within a program, 6 years.

"(2) EXCEPTION.—The periods described in paragraph (1) shall not apply to programs receiving point of service maintenance and enhancement awards under subsection (a)(2) to maintain existing centers and activities.

"(i) INAPPLICABILITY OF PROVISION.—Notwithstanding any other provision of this title, section 791(a) shall not apply to an area health education center funded under this section.

"(j) AUTHORIZATION OF APPROPRIATIONS.—

"(1) IN GENERAL.—There is authorized to be appropriated to carry out this section $125,000,000 for each of the fiscal years 2010 through 2014.

"(2) REQUIREMENTS.—Of the amounts appropriated for a fiscal year under paragraph (1)—

"(A) not more than 35 percent shall be used for awards under subsection (a)(1);

"(B) not less than 60 percent shall be used for awards under subsection (a)(2);

"(C) not more than 1 percent shall be used for grants and contracts to implement outcomes evaluation for the area health education centers; and

"(D) not more than 4 percent shall be used for grants and contracts to provide technical assistance to entities receiving awards under this section.

"(3) CARRYOVER FUNDS.—An entity that receives an award under this section may carry over funds from 1 fiscal year to another without obtaining approval from the Secretary. In no case may any funds be carried over pursuant to the preceding sentence for more than 3 years.

"(k) SENSE OF CONGRESS.—It is the sense of the Congress that every State have an area health education center program in effect under this section.".

(b) CONTINUING EDUCATIONAL SUPPORT FOR HEALTH PROFESSIONALS SERVING IN UNDERSERVED COMMUNITIES.—Part D of title VII of the Public Health Service Act (42 U.S.C. 294 et seq.) is amended by striking section 752 and inserting the following:

"SEC. 752. CONTINUING EDUCATIONAL SUPPORT FOR HEALTH PROFESSIONALS SERVING IN UNDERSERVED COMMUNITIES.

"(a) IN GENERAL.—The Secretary shall make grants to, and enter into contracts with, eligible entities to improve health care, increase retention, increase representation of minority faculty members, enhance the practice environment, and provide information dissemination and educational support to reduce professional isolation through the timely dissemination of research findings using relevant resources.

"(b) ELIGIBLE ENTITIES.—For purposes of this section, the term 'eligible entity' means an entity described in section 799(b).

"(c) APPLICATION.—An eligible entity desiring to receive an award under this section shall submit to the Secretary an application at such time, in such manner, and containing such information as the Secretary may require.

"(d) USE OF FUNDS.—An eligible entity shall use amounts awarded under a grant or contract under this section to provide innovative supportive activities to enhance education through distance learning, continuing educational activities, collaborative conferences, and electronic and telelearning activities, with priority for primary care.

"(e) AUTHORIZATION.—There is authorized to be appropriated to carry out this section $5,000,000 for each of the fiscal years 2010 through 2014, and such sums as may be necessary for each subsequent fiscal year.".

SEC. 5404. WORKFORCE DIVERSITY GRANTS.

Section 821 of the Public Health Service Act (42 U.S.C. 296m) is amended—

(1) in subsection (a)—

(A) by striking "The Secretary may" and inserting the following:

"(1) AUTHORITY.—The Secretary may";

(B) by striking "pre-entry preparation, and retention activities" and inserting the following: "stipends for diploma or associate degree nurses to enter a bridge or degree completion program, student scholarships or stipends for accelerated nursing degree programs, pre-entry preparation, advanced education preparation, and retention activities"; and

(2) in subsection (b)—

(A) by striking "First" and all that follows through "including the" and inserting "National Advisory Council on Nurse Education and Practice and consult with nursing associations including the National Coalition of Ethnic Minority Nurse Associations,"; and

(B) by inserting before the period the following: ", and other organizations determined appropriate by the Secretary".

SEC. 5405. PRIMARY CARE EXTENSION PROGRAM.

Part P of title III of the Public Health Service Act (42 U.S.C. 280g et seq.), as amended by section 5313, is further amended by adding at the end the following:

"SEC. 399W. PRIMARY CARE EXTENSION PROGRAM.

"(a) ESTABLISHMENT, PURPOSE AND DEFINITION.—

"(1) IN GENERAL.—The Secretary, acting through the Director of the Agency for Healthcare Research and Quality, shall establish a Primary Care Extension Program.

"(2) PURPOSE.—The Primary Care Extension Program shall provide support and assistance to primary care providers to educate providers about preventive medicine, health promotion, chronic disease management, mental and behavioral health services (including substance abuse prevention and treatment services), and evidence-based and evidence-informed therapies and techniques, in order to enable providers to incorporate such matters into their practice and to improve community health by working with community-based health connectors (referred to in this section as 'Health Extension Agents').

"(3) DEFINITIONS.—In this section:

"(A) HEALTH EXTENSION AGENT.—The term 'Health Extension Agent' means any local, community-based health worker who facilitates and provides assistance to primary care practices by implementing quality improvement or system redesign, incorporating the principles of the patient-centered medical home to provide high-quality, effective, efficient, and safe primary care and to provide guidance to patients in culturally and linguistically appropriate ways, and linking practices to diverse health system resources.

"(B) PRIMARY CARE PROVIDER.—The term 'primary care provider' means a clinician who provides integrated, accessible health care services and who is accountable for addressing a large majority of personal health care needs, including providing preventive and health promotion services for men, women, and children of all ages, developing a sustained partnership with patients, and practicing in the context of family and community, as recognized by a State licensing or regulatory authority, unless otherwise specified in this section.

"(b) GRANTS TO ESTABLISH STATE HUBS AND LOCAL PRIMARY CARE EXTENSION AGENCIES.—

"(1) GRANTS.—The Secretary shall award competitive grants to States for the establishment of State- or multistate-level primary care Primary Care Extension Program State Hubs (referred to in this section as 'Hubs').

"(2) COMPOSITION OF HUBS.—A Hub established by a State pursuant to paragraph (1)—

"(A) shall consist of, at a minimum, the State health department, the entity responsible for administering the State Medicaid program (if other than the State health department), the State-level entity administering the Medicare program, and the departments of 1 or more health professions schools in the State that train providers in primary care; and

"(B) may include entities such as hospital associations, primary care practice-based research networks, health professional societies, State primary care associations, State licensing boards, organizations with a contract with the Secretary under section 1153 of the Social Security Act, consumer groups, and other appropriate entities.

"(c) STATE AND LOCAL ACTIVITIES.—

"(1) HUB ACTIVITIES.—Hubs established under a grant under subsection (b) shall—

"(A) submit to the Secretary a plan to coordinate functions with quality improvement organizations and area health education centers if such entities are members of the Hub not described in subsection (b)(2)(A);

"(B) contract with a county- or local-level entity that shall serve as the Primary Care Extension Agency to administer the services described in paragraph (2);

"(C) organize and administer grant funds to county- or local-level Primary Care Extension Agencies that serve a catchment area, as determined by the State; and

"(D) organize State-wide or multistate networks of local-level Primary Care Extension Agencies to share and disseminate information and practices.

"(2) LOCAL PRIMARY CARE EXTENSION AGENCY ACTIVITIES.—

"(A) REQUIRED ACTIVITIES.—Primary Care Extension Agencies established by a Hub under paragraph (1) shall—

"(i) assist primary care providers to implement a patient-centered medical home to improve the accessibility, quality, and efficiency of primary care services, including health homes;

"(ii) develop and support primary care learning communities to enhance the dissemination of research findings for evidence-based practice, assess implementation of practice improvement, share best practices, and involve community clinicians in the generation of new knowledge and identification of important questions for research;

"(iii) participate in a national network of Primary Care Extension Hubs and propose how the Primary Care Extension Agency will share and disseminate lessons learned and best practices; and

"(iv) develop a plan for financial sustainability involving State, local, and private contributions, to provide for the reduction in Federal funds that is expected after an initial 6-year period of program establishment, infrastructure development, and planning.

"(B) DISCRETIONARY ACTIVITIES.—Primary Care Extension Agencies established by a Hub under paragraph (1) may—

"(i) provide technical assistance, training, and organizational support for community health teams established under section 3602 of the Patient Protection and Affordable Care Act;

"(ii) collect data and provision of primary care provider feedback from standardized measurements of processes and outcomes to aid in continuous performance improvement;

"(iii) collaborate with local health departments, community health centers, tribes and tribal entities, and other community agencies to identify community health priorities and local health workforce needs, and participate in community-based efforts to address the social and primary determinants of health, strengthen the local primary care workforce, and eliminate health disparities;

"(iv) develop measures to monitor the impact of the proposed program on the health of practice enrollees and of the wider community served; and

"(v) participate in other activities, as determined appropriate by the Secretary.

"(d) FEDERAL PROGRAM ADMINISTRATION.—

"(1) GRANTS; TYPES.—Grants awarded under subsection (b) shall be—

"(A) program grants, that are awarded to State or multistate entities that submit fully-developed plans for the implementation of a Hub, for a period of 6 years; or

"(B) planning grants, that are awarded to State or multistate entities with the goal of developing a plan for a Hub, for a period of 2 years.

"(2) APPLICATIONS.—To be eligible for a grant under subsection (b), a State or multistate entity shall submit to the

Secretary an application, at such time, in such manner, and containing such information as the Secretary may require.

"(3) EVALUATION.—A State that receives a grant under subsection (b) shall be evaluated at the end of the grant period by an evaluation panel appointed by the Secretary.

"(4) CONTINUING SUPPORT.—After the sixth year in which assistance is provided to a State under a grant awarded under subsection (b), the State may receive additional support under this section if the State program has received satisfactory evaluations with respect to program performance and the merits of the State sustainability plan, as determined by the Secretary.

"(5) LIMITATION.—A State shall not use in excess of 10 percent of the amount received under a grant to carry out administrative activities under this section. Funds awarded pursuant to this section shall not be used for funding direct patient care.

"(e) REQUIREMENTS ON THE SECRETARY.—In carrying out this section, the Secretary shall consult with the heads of other Federal agencies with demonstrated experience and expertise in health care and preventive medicine, such as the Centers for Disease Control and Prevention, the Substance Abuse and Mental Health Administration, the Health Resources and Services Administration, the National Institutes of Health, the Office of the National Coordinator for Health Information Technology, the Indian Health Service, the Agricultural Cooperative Extension Service of the Department of Agriculture, and other entities, as the Secretary determines appropriate.

"(f) AUTHORIZATION OF APPROPRIATIONS.—To awards grants as provided in subsection (d), there are authorized to be appropriated $120,000,000 for each of fiscal years 2011 and 2012, and such sums as may be necessary to carry out this section for each of fiscal years 2013 through 2014.".

Subtitle F—Strengthening Primary Care and Other Workforce Improvements

SEC. 5501. EXPANDING ACCESS TO PRIMARY CARE SERVICES AND GENERAL SURGERY SERVICES.

(a) INCENTIVE PAYMENT PROGRAM FOR PRIMARY CARE SERVICES.—

(1) IN GENERAL.—Section 1833 of the Social Security Act (42 U.S.C. 1395l) is amended by adding at the end the following new subsection:

"(x) INCENTIVE PAYMENTS FOR PRIMARY CARE SERVICES.—

"(1) IN GENERAL.—In the case of primary care services furnished on or after January 1, 2011, and before January 1, 2016, by a primary care practitioner, in addition to the amount of payment that would otherwise be made for such services under this part, there also shall be paid (on a monthly or quarterly basis) an amount equal to 10 percent of the payment amount for the service under this part.

"(2) DEFINITIONS.—In this subsection:

"(A) PRIMARY CARE PRACTITIONER.—The term 'primary care practitioner' means an individual—

"(i) who—

"(I) is a physician (as described in section 1861(r)(1)) who has a primary specialty designation of family medicine, internal medicine, geriatric medicine, or pediatric medicine; or

"(II) is a nurse practitioner, clinical nurse specialist, or physician assistant (as those terms are defined in section 1861(aa)(5)); and

"(ii) for whom primary care services accounted for at least 60 percent of the allowed charges under this part for such physician or practitioner in a prior period as determined appropriate by the Secretary.

"(B) PRIMARY CARE SERVICES.—The term 'primary care services' means services identified, as of January 1, 2009, by the following HCPCS codes (and as subsequently modified by the Secretary):

"(i) 99201 through 99215.

"(ii) 99304 through 99340.

"(iii) 99341 through 99350.

"(3) COORDINATION WITH OTHER PAYMENTS.—The amount of the additional payment for a service under this subsection and subsection (m) shall be determined without regard to any additional payment for the service under subsection (m) and this subsection, respectively.

"(4) LIMITATION ON REVIEW.—There shall be no administrative or judicial review under section 1869, 1878, or otherwise, respecting the identification of primary care practitioners under this subsection.".

(2) CONFORMING AMENDMENT.—Section 1834(g)(2)(B) of the Social Security Act (42 U.S.C. 1395m(g)(2)(B)) is amended by adding at the end the following sentence: "Section 1833(x) shall not be taken into account in determining the amounts that would otherwise be paid pursuant to the preceding sentence.".

(b) INCENTIVE PAYMENT PROGRAM FOR MAJOR SURGICAL PROCEDURES FURNISHED IN HEALTH PROFESSIONAL SHORTAGE AREAS.—

(1) IN GENERAL.—Section 1833 of the Social Security Act (42 U.S.C. 1395l), as amended by subsection (a)(1), is amended by adding at the end the following new subsection:

"(y) INCENTIVE PAYMENTS FOR MAJOR SURGICAL PROCEDURES FURNISHED IN HEALTH PROFESSIONAL SHORTAGE AREAS.—

"(1) IN GENERAL.—In the case of major surgical procedures furnished on or after January 1, 2011, and before January 1, 2016, by a general surgeon in an area that is designated (under section 332(a)(1)(A) of the Public Health Service Act) as a health professional shortage area as identified by the Secretary prior to the beginning of the year involved, in addition to the amount of payment that would otherwise be made for such services under this part, there also shall be paid (on a monthly or quarterly basis) an amount equal to 10 percent of the payment amount for the service under this part.

"(2) DEFINITIONS.—In this subsection:

"(A) GENERAL SURGEON.—In this subsection, the term 'general surgeon' means a physician (as described in section 1861(r)(1)) who has designated CMS specialty code 02–General Surgery as their primary specialty code in the physician's enrollment under section 1866(j).

"(B) MAJOR SURGICAL PROCEDURES.—The term 'major surgical procedures' means physicians' services which are surgical procedures for which a 10-day or 90-day global period is used for payment under the fee schedule under section 1848(b).

"(3) COORDINATION WITH OTHER PAYMENTS.—The amount of the additional payment for a service under this subsection and subsection (m) shall be determined without regard to any additional payment for the service under subsection (m) and this subsection, respectively.

"(4) APPLICATION.—The provisions of paragraph (2) and (4) of subsection (m) shall apply to the determination of additional payments under this subsection in the same manner as such provisions apply to the determination of additional payments under subsection (m).".

(2) CONFORMING AMENDMENT.—Section 1834(g)(2)(B) of the Social Security Act (42 U.S.C. 1395m(g)(2)(B)), as amended by subsection (a)(2), is amended by striking "Section 1833(x)" and inserting "Subsections (x) and (y) of section 1833" in the last sentence.

(c) BUDGET-NEUTRALITY ADJUSTMENT.—Section 1848(c)(2)(B) of the Social Security Act (42 U.S.C. 1395w–4(c)(2)(B)) is amended by adding at the end the following new clause:

"(vii) ADJUSTMENT FOR CERTAIN PHYSICIAN INCENTIVE PAYMENTS.—Fifty percent of the additional expenditures under this part attributable to subsections (x) and (y) of section 1833 for a year (as estimated by the Secretary) shall be taken into account in applying clause (ii)(II) for 2011 and subsequent years. In lieu of applying the budget-neutrality adjustments required under clause (ii)(II) to relative value units to account for such costs for the year, the Secretary shall apply such budget-neutrality adjustments to the conversion factor otherwise determined for the year. For 2011 and subsequent years, the Secretary shall increase the incentive payment otherwise applicable under section 1833(m) by a percent estimated to be equal to the additional expenditures estimated under the first sentence of this clause for such year that is applicable to physicians who primarily furnish services in areas designated (under section 332(a)(1)(A) of the Public Health Service Act) as health professional shortage areas.".

SEC. 5502. MEDICARE FEDERALLY QUALIFIED HEALTH CENTER IMPROVEMENTS.

(a) EXPANSION OF MEDICARE-COVERED PREVENTIVE SERVICES AT FEDERALLY QUALIFIED HEALTH CENTERS.—

(1) IN GENERAL.—Section 1861(aa)(3)(A) of the Social Security Act (42 U.S.C. 1395w (aa)(3)(A)) is amended to read as follows:

"(A) services of the type described subparagraphs (A) through (C) of paragraph (1) and preventive services (as defined in section 1861(ddd)(3)); and".

(2) EFFECTIVE DATE.—The amendment made by paragraph (1) shall apply to services furnished on or after January 1, 2011.

(b) PROSPECTIVE PAYMENT SYSTEM FOR FEDERALLY QUALIFIED HEALTH CENTERS.—Section 1834 of the Social Security Act (42

U.S.C. 1395m) is amended by adding at the end the following new subsection:

"(n) DEVELOPMENT AND IMPLEMENTATION OF PROSPECTIVE PAYMENT SYSTEM.—

"(1) DEVELOPMENT.—

"(A) IN GENERAL.—The Secretary shall develop a prospective payment system for payment for Federally qualified health services furnished by Federally qualified health centers under this title. Such system shall include a process for appropriately describing the services furnished by Federally qualified health centers.

"(B) COLLECTION OF DATA AND EVALUATION.—The Secretary shall require Federally qualified health centers to submit to the Secretary such information as the Secretary may require in order to develop and implement the prospective payment system under this paragraph and paragraph (2), respectively, including the reporting of services using HCPCS codes.

"(2) IMPLEMENTATION.—

"(A) IN GENERAL.—Notwithstanding section 1833(a)(3)(B), the Secretary shall provide, for cost reporting periods beginning on or after October 1, 2014, for payments for Federally qualified health services furnished by Federally qualified health centers under this title in accordance with the prospective payment system developed by the Secretary under paragraph (1).

"(B) PAYMENTS.—

"(i) INITIAL PAYMENTS.—The Secretary shall implement such prospective payment system so that the estimated amount of expenditures under this title for Federally qualified health services in the first year that the prospective payment system is implemented is equal to 103 percent of the estimated amount of expenditures under this title that would have occurred for such services in such year if the system had not been implemented.

"(ii) PAYMENTS IN SUBSEQUENT YEARS.—In the year after the first year of implementation of such system, and in each subsequent year, the payment rate for Federally qualified health services furnished in the year shall be equal to the payment rate established for such services furnished in the preceding year under this subparagraph increased by the percentage increase in the MEI (as defined in 1842(i)(3)) for the year involved.".

SEC. 5503. DISTRIBUTION OF ADDITIONAL RESIDENCY POSITIONS.

(a) IN GENERAL.—Section 1886(h) of the Social Security Act (42 U.S.C. 1395ww(h)) is amended—

(1) in paragraph (4)(F)(i), by striking "paragraph (7)" and inserting "paragraphs (7) and (8)";

(2) in paragraph (4)(H)(i), by striking "paragraph (7)" and inserting "paragraphs (7) and (8)";

(3) in paragraph (7)(E), by inserting "or paragraph (8)" before the period at the end; and

(4) by adding at the end the following new paragraph:

"(8) DISTRIBUTION OF ADDITIONAL RESIDENCY POSITIONS.—

"(A) REDUCTIONS IN LIMIT BASED ON UNUSED POSITIONS.—

"(i) IN GENERAL.—Except as provided in clause (ii), if a hospital's reference resident level (as defined in subparagraph (H)(i)) is less than the otherwise applicable resident limit (as defined in subparagraph (H)(iii)), effective for portions of cost reporting periods occurring on or after July 1, 2011, the otherwise applicable resident limit shall be reduced by 65 percent of the difference between such otherwise applicable resident limit and such reference resident level.

"(ii) EXCEPTIONS.—This subparagraph shall not apply to—

"(I) a hospital located in a rural area (as defined in subsection (d)(2)(D)(ii)) with fewer than 250 acute care inpatient beds;

"(II) a hospital that was part of a qualifying entity which had a voluntary residency reduction plan approved under paragraph (6)(B) or under the authority of section 402 of Public Law 90–248, if the hospital demonstrates to the Secretary that it has a specified plan in place for filling the unused positions by not later than 2 years after the date of enactment of this paragraph; or

"(III) a hospital described in paragraph (4)(H)(v).

"(B) DISTRIBUTION.—

"(i) IN GENERAL.—The Secretary shall increase the otherwise applicable resident limit for each qualifying hospital that submits an application under this subparagraph by such number as the Secretary may approve for portions of cost reporting periods occurring on or after July 1, 2011. The aggregate number of increases in the otherwise applicable resident limit under this subparagraph shall be equal to the aggregate reduction in such limits attributable to subparagraph (A) (as estimated by the Secretary).

"(ii) REQUIREMENTS.—Subject to clause (iii), a hospital that receives an increase in the otherwise applicable resident limit under this subparagraph shall ensure, during the 5-year period beginning on the date of such increase, that—

"(I) the number of full-time equivalent primary care residents, as defined in paragraph (5)(H) (as determined by the Secretary), excluding any additional positions under subclause (II), is not less than the average number of full-time equivalent primary care residents (as so determined) during the 3 most recent cost reporting periods ending prior to the date of enactment of this paragraph; and

"(II) not less than 75 percent of the positions attributable to such increase are in a primary care or general surgery residency (as determined by the Secretary).

The Secretary may determine whether a hospital has met the requirements under this clause during such 5-year period in such manner and at such time as the Secretary determines appropriate, including at the end of such 5-year period.

"(iii) REDISTRIBUTION OF POSITIONS IF HOSPITAL NO LONGER MEETS CERTAIN REQUIREMENTS.—In the case where the Secretary determines that a hospital described in clause (ii) does not meet either of the requirements under subclause (I) or (II) of such clause, the Secretary shall—

"(I) reduce the otherwise applicable resident limit of the hospital by the amount by which such limit was increased under this paragraph; and

"(II) provide for the distribution of positions attributable to such reduction in accordance with the requirements of this paragraph.

"(C) CONSIDERATIONS IN REDISTRIBUTION.—In determining for which hospitals the increase in the otherwise applicable resident limit is provided under subparagraph (B), the Secretary shall take into account—

"(i) the demonstration likelihood of the hospital filling the positions made available under this paragraph within the first 3 cost reporting periods beginning on or after July 1, 2011, as determined by the Secretary; and

"(ii) whether the hospital has an accredited rural training track (as described in paragraph (4)(H)(iv)).

"(D) PRIORITY FOR CERTAIN AREAS.—In determining for which hospitals the increase in the otherwise applicable resident limit is provided under subparagraph (B), subject to subparagraph (E), the Secretary shall distribute the increase to hospitals based on the following factors:

"(i) Whether the hospital is located in a State with a resident-to-population ratio in the lowest quartile (as determined by the Secretary).

"(ii) Whether the hospital is located in a State, a territory of the United States, or the District of Columbia that is among the top 10 States, territories, or Districts in terms of the ratio of—

"(I) the total population of the State, territory, or District living in an area designated (under such section 332(a)(1)(A)) as a health professional shortage area (as of the date of enactment of this paragraph); to

"(II) the total population of the State, territory, or District (as determined by the Secretary based on the most recent available population data published by the Bureau of the Census).

"(iii) Whether the hospital is located in a rural area (as defined in subsection (d)(2)(D)(ii)).

"(E) RESERVATION OF POSITIONS FOR CERTAIN HOSPITALS.—

"(i) IN GENERAL.—Subject to clause (ii), the Secretary shall reserve the positions available for distribution under this paragraph as follows:

"(I) 70 percent of such positions for distribution to hospitals described in clause (i) of subparagraph (D).

"(II) 30 percent of such positions for distribution to hospitals described in clause (ii) and (iii) of such subparagraph.

"(ii) EXCEPTION IF POSITIONS NOT REDISTRIBUTED BY JULY 1, 2011.—In the case where the Secretary does not distribute positions to hospitals in accordance with clause (i) by July 1, 2011, the Secretary shall distribute such positions to other hospitals in accordance with the considerations described in subparagraph (C) and the priority described in subparagraph (D).

"(F) LIMITATION.—A hospital may not receive more than 75 full-time equivalent additional residency positions under this paragraph.

"(G) APPLICATION OF PER RESIDENT AMOUNTS FOR PRIMARY CARE AND NONPRIMARY CARE.—With respect to additional residency positions in a hospital attributable to the increase provided under this paragraph, the approved FTE per resident amounts are deemed to be equal to the hospital per resident amounts for primary care and nonprimary care computed under paragraph (2)(D) for that hospital.

"(H) DEFINITIONS.—In this paragraph:

"(i) REFERENCE RESIDENT LEVEL.—The term 'reference resident level' means, with respect to a hospital, the highest resident level for any of the 3 most recent cost reporting periods (ending before the date of the enactment of this paragraph) of the hospital for which a cost report has been settled (or, if not, submitted (subject to audit)), as determined by the Secretary.

"(ii) RESIDENT LEVEL.—The term 'resident level' has the meaning given such term in paragraph (7)(C)(i).

"(iii) OTHERWISE APPLICABLE RESIDENT LIMIT.—The term 'otherwise applicable resident limit' means, with respect to a hospital, the limit otherwise applicable under subparagraphs (F)(i) and (H) of paragraph (4) on the resident level for the hospital determined without regard to this paragraph but taking into account paragraph (7)(A).".

(b) IME.—

(1) IN GENERAL.—Section 1886(d)(5)(B)(v) of the Social Security Act (42 U.S.C. 1395ww(d)(5)(B)(v)), in the second sentence, is amended—

(A) by striking "subsection (h)(7)" and inserting "subsections (h)(7) and (h)(8)"; and

(B) by striking "it applies" and inserting "they apply".

(2) CONFORMING AMENDMENT.—Section 1886(d)(5)(B) of the Social Security Act (42 U.S.C. 1395ww(d)(5)(B)) is amended by adding at the end the following clause:

"(x) For discharges occurring on or after July 1, 2011, insofar as an additional payment amount under this subparagraph is attributable to resident positions distributed to a hospital under subsection (h)(8)(B), the indirect teaching adjustment factor shall be computed in the same manner as provided under clause (ii) with respect to such resident positions.".

(c) CONFORMING AMENDMENT.—Section 422(b)(2) of the Medicare Prescription Drug, Improvement, and Modernization Act of 2003 (Public Law 108–173) is amended by striking "section 1886(h)(7)" and all that follows and inserting "paragraphs (7) and (8) of subsection (h) of section 1886 of the Social Security Act".

SEC. 5504. COUNTING RESIDENT TIME IN NONPROVIDER SETTINGS.

(a) GME.—Section 1886(h)(4)(E) of the Social Security Act (42 U.S.C. 1395ww(h)(4)(E)) is amended—

(1) by striking "shall be counted and that all the time" and inserting "shall be counted and that—

"(i) effective for cost reporting periods beginning before July 1, 2010, all the time;";

(2) in clause (i), as inserted by paragraph (1), by striking the period at the end and inserting "; and";

(3) by inserting after clause (i), as so inserted, the following new clause:

"(ii) effective for cost reporting periods beginning on or after July 1, 2010, all the time so spent by a resident shall be counted towards the determination of full-time equivalency, without regard to the setting in which the activities are performed, if a hospital incurs the costs of the stipends and fringe benefits of the resident during the time the resident spends in that setting. If more than one hospital incurs these costs, either directly or through a third party, such hospitals shall count a proportional share of the time, as determined by written agreement between the hospitals, that a resident spends training in that setting."; and

(4) by adding at the end the following flush sentence: "Any hospital claiming under this subparagraph for time spent in a nonprovider setting shall maintain and make available to the Secretary records regarding the amount of such time and such amount in comparison with amounts of such time in such base year as the Secretary shall specify.".

(b) IME.—Section 1886(d)(5)(B)(iv) of the Social Security Act (42 U.S.C. 1395ww(d)(5)) is amended—

(1) by striking "(iv) Effective for discharges occurring on or after October 1, 1997" and inserting "(iv)(I) Effective for discharges occurring on or after October 1, 1997, and before July 1, 2010"; and

(2) by inserting after clause (I), as inserted by paragraph (1), the following new subparagraph:

"(II) Effective for discharges occurring on or after July 1, 2010, all the time spent by an intern or resident in patient care activities in a nonprovider setting shall be counted towards the determination of full-time equivalency if a hospital incurs the costs of the stipends and fringe benefits of the intern or resident during the time the intern or resident spends in that setting. If more than one hospital incurs these costs, either directly or through a third party, such hospitals shall count a proportional share of the time, as determined by written agreement between the hospitals, that a resident spends training in that setting.".

(c) APPLICATION.—The amendments made by this section shall not be applied in a manner that requires reopening of any settled hospital cost reports as to which there is not a jurisdictionally proper appeal pending as of the date of the enactment of this Act on the issue of payment for indirect costs of medical education under section 1886(d)(5)(B) of the Social Security Act (42 U.S.C. 1395ww(d)(5)(B)) or for direct graduate medical education costs under section 1886(h) of such Act (42 U.S.C. 1395ww(h)).

SEC. 5505. RULES FOR COUNTING RESIDENT TIME FOR DIDACTIC AND SCHOLARLY ACTIVITIES AND OTHER ACTIVITIES.

(a) GME.—Section 1886(h) of the Social Security Act (42 U.S.C. 1395ww(h)), as amended by section 5504, is amended—

(1) in paragraph (4)—

(A) in subparagraph (E), by striking "Such rules" and inserting "Subject to subparagraphs (J) and (K), such rules"; and

(B) by adding at the end the following new subparagraphs:

"(J) TREATMENT OF CERTAIN NONPROVIDER AND DIDACTIC ACTIVITIES.—Such rules shall provide that all time spent by an intern or resident in an approved medical residency training program in a nonprovider setting that is primarily engaged in furnishing patient care (as defined in paragraph (5)(K)) in non-patient care activities, such as didactic conferences and seminars, but not including research not associated with the treatment or diagnosis of a particular patient, as such time and activities are defined by the Secretary, shall be counted toward the determination of full-time equivalency.

"(K) TREATMENT OF CERTAIN OTHER ACTIVITIES.—In determining the hospital's number of full-time equivalent residents for purposes of this subsection, all the time that is spent by an intern or resident in an approved medical residency training program on vacation, sick leave, or other approved leave, as such time is defined by the Secretary, and that does not prolong the total time the resident is participating in the approved program beyond the normal duration of the program shall be counted toward the determination of full-time equivalency."; and

(2) in paragraph (5), by adding at the end the following new subparagraph:

"(K) NONPROVIDER SETTING THAT IS PRIMARILY ENGAGED IN FURNISHING PATIENT CARE.—The term 'nonprovider setting that is primarily engaged in furnishing patient care' means a nonprovider setting in which the primary activity is the care and treatment of patients, as defined by the Secretary.".

(b) IME DETERMINATIONS.—Section 1886(d)(5)(B) of such Act (42 U.S.C. 1395ww(d)(5)(B)) is amended by adding at the end the following new clause:

"(x)(I) The provisions of subparagraph (K) of subsection (h)(4) shall apply under this subparagraph in the same manner as they apply under such subsection.

"(II) In determining the hospital's number of full-time equivalent residents for purposes of this subparagraph, all the time spent by an intern or resident in an approved medical residency training program in non-patient care activities, such as didactic conferences and seminars, as such time and activities are defined by the Secretary, that occurs in the hospital shall be counted toward the determination of full-time equivalency if the hospital—

"(aa) is recognized as a subsection (d) hospital;

"(bb) is recognized as a subsection (d) Puerto Rico hospital;

"(cc) is reimbursed under a reimbursement system authorized under section 1814(b)(3); or

"(dd) is a provider-based hospital outpatient department.

"(III) In determining the hospital's number of full-time equivalent residents for purposes of this subparagraph, all the time spent by an intern or resident in an approved medical residency training program in research activities that are not associated with the treatment or diagnosis of a particular patient, as such time and activities are defined by the Secretary, shall not be counted toward the determination of full-time equivalency.".

(c) EFFECTIVE DATES.—

(1) IN GENERAL.—Except as otherwise provided, the Secretary of Health and Human Services shall implement the amendments made by this section in a manner so as to apply to cost reporting periods beginning on or after January 1, 1983.

(2) GME.—Section 1886(h)(4)(J) of the Social Security Act, as added by subsection (a)(1)(B), shall apply to cost reporting periods beginning on or after July 1, 2009.

(3) IME.—Section 1886(d)(5)(B)(x)(III) of the Social Security Act, as added by subsection (b), shall apply to cost reporting periods beginning on or after October 1, 2001. Such section, as so added, shall not give rise to any inference as to how the law in effect prior to such date should be interpreted.

SEC. 5506. PRESERVATION OF RESIDENT CAP POSITIONS FROM CLOSED HOSPITALS.

(a) GME.—Section 1886(h)(4)(H) of the Social Security Act (42 U.S.C. Section 1395ww(h)(4)(H)) is amended by adding at the end the following new clause:

"(vi) REDISTRIBUTION OF RESIDENCY SLOTS AFTER A HOSPITAL CLOSES.—

"(I) IN GENERAL.—Subject to the succeeding provisions of this clause, the Secretary shall, by regulation, establish a process under which, in the case where a hospital (other than a hospital described in clause (v)) with an approved medical residency program closes on or after a date that is 2 years before the date of enactment of this clause, the Secretary shall increase the otherwise applicable resident limit under this paragraph for other hospitals in accordance with this clause.

"(II) PRIORITY FOR HOSPITALS IN CERTAIN AREAS.—Subject to the succeeding provisions of this clause, in determining for which hospitals the increase in the otherwise applicable resident limit is provided under such process, the Secretary shall distribute the increase to hospitals in the following priority order (with preference given within each category to hospitals that are members of the same affiliated group (as defined by the Secretary under clause (ii)) as the closed hospital):

"(aa) First, to hospitals located in the same core-based statistical area as, or a core-based statistical area contiguous to, the hospital that closed.

"(bb) Second, to hospitals located in the same State as the hospital that closed.

"(cc) Third, to hospitals located in the same region of the country as the hospital that closed.

"(dd) Fourth, only if the Secretary is not able to distribute the increase to hospitals described in item (cc), to qualifying hospitals in accordance with the provisions of paragraph (8).

"(III) REQUIREMENT HOSPITAL LIKELY TO FILL POSITION WITHIN CERTAIN TIME PERIOD.—The Secretary may only increase the otherwise applicable resident limit of a hospital under such process if the Secretary determines the hospital has demonstrated a likelihood of filling the positions made available under this clause within 3 years.

"(IV) LIMITATION.—The aggregate number of increases in the otherwise applicable resident limits for hospitals under this clause shall be equal to the number of resident positions in the approved medical residency programs that closed on or after the date described in subclause (I).

"(V) ADMINISTRATION.—Chapter 35 of title 44, United States Code, shall not apply to the implementation of this clause.".

(b) IME.—Section 1886(d)(5)(B)(v) of the Social Security Act (42 U.S.C. 1395ww(d)(5)(B)(v)), in the second sentence, as amended by section 5503, is amended by striking "subsections (h)(7) and (h)(8)" and inserting "subsections (h)(4)(H)(vi), (h)(7), and (h)(8)".

(c) APPLICATION.—The amendments made by this section shall not be applied in a manner that requires reopening of any settled hospital cost reports as to which there is not a jurisdictionally proper appeal pending as of the date of the enactment of this Act on the issue of payment for indirect costs of medical education under section 1886(d)(5)(B) of the Social Security Act (42 U.S.C. 1395ww(d)(5)(B)) or for direct graduate medical education costs under section 1886(h) of such Act (42 U.S.C. Section 1395ww(h)).

(d) EFFECT ON TEMPORARY FTE CAP ADJUSTMENTS.—The Secretary of Health and Human Services shall give consideration to the effect of the amendments made by this section on any temporary adjustment to a hospital's FTE cap under section 413.79(h) of title 42, Code of Federal Regulations (as in effect on the date of enactment of this Act) in order to ensure that there is no duplication of FTE slots. Such amendments shall not affect the application of section 1886(h)(4)(H)(v) of the Social Security Act (42 U.S.C. 1395ww(h)(4)(H)(v)).

(e) CONFORMING AMENDMENT.—Section 1886(h)(7)(E) of the Social Security Act (42 U.S.C. 1395ww(h)(7)(E)), as amended by section 5503(a), is amended by striking "paragraph or paragraph (8)" and inserting "this paragraph, paragraph (8), or paragraph (4)(H)(vi)".

SEC. 5507. DEMONSTRATION PROJECTS TO ADDRESS HEALTH PROFESSIONS WORKFORCE NEEDS; EXTENSION OF FAMILY-TO-FAMILY HEALTH INFORMATION CENTERS.

(a) AUTHORITY TO CONDUCT DEMONSTRATION PROJECTS.—Title XX of the Social Security Act (42 U.S.C. 1397 et seq.) is amended by adding at the end the following:

"SEC. 2008. DEMONSTRATION PROJECTS TO ADDRESS HEALTH PROFESSIONS WORKFORCE NEEDS.

"(a) DEMONSTRATION PROJECTS TO PROVIDE LOW-INCOME INDIVIDUALS WITH OPPORTUNITIES FOR EDUCATION, TRAINING, AND CAREER ADVANCEMENT TO ADDRESS HEALTH PROFESSIONS WORKFORCE NEEDS.—

"(1) AUTHORITY TO AWARD GRANTS.—The Secretary, in consultation with the Secretary of Labor, shall award grants to eligible entities to conduct demonstration projects that are designed to provide eligible individuals with the opportunity to obtain education and training for occupations in the health care field that pay well and are expected to either experience labor shortages or be in high demand.

"(2) REQUIREMENTS.—

"(A) AID AND SUPPORTIVE SERVICES.—

"(i) IN GENERAL.—A demonstration project conducted by an eligible entity awarded a grant under this section shall, if appropriate, provide eligible individuals participating in the project with financial aid, child care, case management, and other supportive services.

"(ii) TREATMENT.—Any aid, services, or incentives provided to an eligible beneficiary participating in a demonstration project under this section shall not be considered income, and shall not be taken into account for purposes of determining the individual's eligibility for, or amount of, benefits under any means-tested program.

"(B) CONSULTATION AND COORDINATION.—An eligible entity applying for a grant to carry out a demonstration project under this section shall demonstrate in the application that the entity has consulted with the State agency responsible for administering the State TANF program, the local workforce investment board in the area in which the project is to be conducted (unless the applicant is such board), the State workforce investment board established under section 111 of the Workforce Investment Act of 1998, and the State Apprenticeship Agency recognized under the Act of August 16, 1937 (commonly known as the 'National Apprenticeship Act') (or if no agency has been recognized in the State, the Office of Apprenticeship of the Department of Labor) and that the project will be carried out in coordination with such entities.

"(C) ASSURANCE OF OPPORTUNITIES FOR INDIAN POPULATIONS.—The Secretary shall award at least 3 grants under this subsection to an eligible entity that is an Indian tribe, tribal organization, or Tribal College or University.

"(3) REPORTS AND EVALUATION.—

"(A) ELIGIBLE ENTITIES.—An eligible entity awarded a grant to conduct a demonstration project under this subsection shall submit interim reports to the Secretary on the activities carried out under the project and a final report on such activities upon the conclusion of the entities' participation in the project. Such reports shall include assessments of the effectiveness of such activities with respect to improving outcomes for the eligible individuals participating in the project and with respect to addressing health professions workforce needs in the areas in which the project is conducted.

"(B) EVALUATION.—The Secretary shall, by grant, contract, or interagency agreement, evaluate the demonstration projects conducted under this subsection. Such evaluation shall include identification of successful activities for creating opportunities for developing and sustaining, particularly with respect to low-income individuals and other entry-level workers, a health professions workforce that has accessible entry points, that meets high standards for education, training, certification, and professional development, and that provides increased wages and affordable benefits, including health care coverage, that are responsive to the workforce's needs.

"(C) REPORT TO CONGRESS.—The Secretary shall submit interim reports and, based on the evaluation conducted under subparagraph (B), a final report to Congress on the demonstration projects conducted under this subsection.

"(4) DEFINITIONS.—In this subsection:

"(A) ELIGIBLE ENTITY.—The term 'eligible entity' means a State, an Indian tribe or tribal organization, an institution of higher education, a local workforce investment board established under section 117 of the Workforce Investment Act of 1998, a sponsor of an apprenticeship program registered under the National Apprenticeship Act or a community-based organization.

"(B) ELIGIBLE INDIVIDUAL.—

"(i) IN GENERAL.—The term 'eligible individual' means a individual receiving assistance under the State TANF program.

"(ii) OTHER LOW-INCOME INDIVIDUALS.—Such term may include other low-income individuals described by the eligible entity in its application for a grant under this section.

"(C) INDIAN TRIBE; TRIBAL ORGANIZATION.—The terms 'Indian tribe' and 'tribal organization' have the meaning given such terms in section 4 of the Indian Self-Determination and Education Assistance Act (25 U.S.C. 450b).

"(D) INSTITUTION OF HIGHER EDUCATION.—The term 'institution of higher education' has the meaning given that term in section 101 of the Higher Education Act of 1965 (20 U.S.C. 1001).

"(E) STATE.—The term 'State' means each of the 50 States, the District of Columbia, the Commonwealth of Puerto Rico, the United States Virgin Islands, Guam, and American Samoa.

"(F) STATE TANF PROGRAM.—The term 'State TANF program' means the temporary assistance for needy families program funded under part A of title IV.

"(G) TRIBAL COLLEGE OR UNIVERSITY.—The term 'Tribal College or University' has the meaning given that term in section 316(b) of the Higher Education Act of 1965 (20 U.S.C. 1059c(b)).

"(b) DEMONSTRATION PROJECT TO DEVELOP TRAINING AND CERTIFICATION PROGRAMS FOR PERSONAL OR HOME CARE AIDES.—

"(1) AUTHORITY TO AWARD GRANTS.—Not later than 18 months after the date of enactment of this section, the Secretary shall award grants to eligible entities that are States to conduct demonstration projects for purposes of developing core training competencies and certification programs for personal or home care aides. The Secretary shall—

"(A) evaluate the efficacy of the core training competencies described in paragraph (3)(A) for newly hired personal or home care aides and the methods used by States to implement such core training competencies in accordance with the issues specified in paragraph (3)(B); and

"(B) ensure that the number of hours of training provided by States under the demonstration project with respect to such core training competencies are not less than the number of hours of training required under any applicable State or Federal law or regulation.

"(2) DURATION.—A demonstration project shall be conducted under this subsection for not less than 3 years.

"(3) CORE TRAINING COMPETENCIES FOR PERSONAL OR HOME CARE AIDES.—

"(A) IN GENERAL.—The core training competencies for personal or home care aides described in this subparagraph include competencies with respect to the following areas:

"(i) The role of the personal or home care aide (including differences between a personal or home care aide employed by an agency and a personal or home care aide employed directly by the health care consumer or an independent provider).

"(ii) Consumer rights, ethics, and confidentiality (including the role of proxy decision-makers in the case where a health care consumer has impaired decision-making capacity).

"(iii) Communication, cultural and linguistic competence and sensitivity, problem solving, behavior management, and relationship skills.

"(iv) Personal care skills.

"(v) Health care support.

"(vi) Nutritional support.

"(vii) Infection control.

"(viii) Safety and emergency training.

"(ix) Training specific to an individual consumer's needs (including older individuals, younger individuals with disabilities, individuals with developmental disabilities, individuals with dementia, and individuals with mental and behavioral health needs).

"(x) Self-Care.

"(B) IMPLEMENTATION.—The implementation issues specified in this subparagraph include the following:

"(i) The length of the training.

"(ii) The appropriate trainer to student ratio.

"(iii) The amount of instruction time spent in the classroom as compared to on-site in the home or a facility.

"(iv) Trainer qualifications.

"(v) Content for a 'hands-on' and written certification exam.

"(vi) Continuing education requirements.

"(4) APPLICATION AND SELECTION CRITERIA.—

"(A) IN GENERAL.—

"(i) NUMBER OF STATES.—The Secretary shall enter into agreements with not more than 6 States to conduct demonstration projects under this subsection.

"(ii) REQUIREMENTS FOR STATES.—An agreement entered into under clause (i) shall require that a participating State—

"(I) implement the core training competencies described in paragraph (3)(A); and

"(II) develop written materials and protocols for such core training competencies, including the development of a certification test for personal or home care aides who have completed such training competencies.

"(iii) CONSULTATION AND COLLABORATION WITH COMMUNITY AND VOCATIONAL COLLEGES.—The Secretary shall encourage participating States to consult with community and vocational colleges regarding the development of curricula to implement the project with respect to activities, as applicable, which may include consideration of such colleges as partners in such implementation.

"(B) APPLICATION AND ELIGIBILITY.—A State seeking to participate in the project shall—

"(i) submit an application to the Secretary containing such information and at such time as the Secretary may specify;

"(ii) meet the selection criteria established under subparagraph (C); and

"(iii) meet such additional criteria as the Secretary may specify.

"(C) SELECTION CRITERIA.—In selecting States to participate in the program, the Secretary shall establish criteria to ensure (if applicable with respect to the activities involved)—

"(i) geographic and demographic diversity;

"(ii) that participating States offer medical assistance for personal care services under the State Medicaid plan;

"(iii) that the existing training standards for personal or home care aides in each participating State—

"(I) are different from such standards in the other participating States; and

"(II) are different from the core training competencies described in paragraph (3)(A);

"(iv) that participating States do not reduce the number of hours of training required under applicable State law or regulation after being selected to participate in the project; and

"(v) that participating States recruit a minimum number of eligible health and long-term care providers to participate in the project.

"(D) TECHNICAL ASSISTANCE.—The Secretary shall provide technical assistance to States in developing written materials and protocols for such core training competencies.

"(5) EVALUATION AND REPORT.—

"(A) EVALUATION.—The Secretary shall develop an experimental or control group testing protocol in consultation with an independent evaluation contractor selected by the Secretary. Such contractor shall evaluate—

"(i) the impact of core training competencies described in paragraph (3)(A), including curricula developed to implement such core training competencies, for personal or home care aides within each participating State on job satisfaction, mastery of job skills, beneficiary and family caregiver satisfaction with services, and additional measures determined by the Secretary in consultation with the expert panel;

"(ii) the impact of providing such core training competencies on the existing training infrastructure and resources of States; and

"(iii) whether a minimum number of hours of initial training should be required for personal or home care aides and, if so, what minimum number of hours should be required.

"(B) REPORTS.—

"(i) REPORT ON INITIAL IMPLEMENTATION.—Not later than 2 years after the date of enactment of this section, the Secretary shall submit to Congress a report on the initial implementation of activities conducted under the demonstration project, including any available results of the evaluation conducted under subparagraph (A) with respect to such activities, together with such recommendations for legislation or administrative action as the Secretary determines appropriate.

"(ii) FINAL REPORT.—Not later than 1 year after the completion of the demonstration project, the Secretary shall submit to Congress a report containing the results of the evaluation conducted under subparagraph (A), together with such recommendations for legislation or administrative action as the Secretary determines appropriate.

"(6) DEFINITIONS.—In this subsection:

"(A) ELIGIBLE HEALTH AND LONG-TERM CARE PROVIDER.—The term 'eligible health and long-term care provider' means a personal or home care agency (including personal or home care public authorities), a nursing home, a home health agency (as defined in section 1861(o)), or any other health care provider the Secretary determines appropriate which—

"(i) is licensed or authorized to provide services in a participating State; and

"(ii) receives payment for services under title XIX.

"(B) PERSONAL CARE SERVICES.—The term 'personal care services' has the meaning given such term for purposes of title XIX.

"(C) PERSONAL OR HOME CARE AIDE.—The term 'personal or home care aide' means an individual who helps individuals who are elderly, disabled, ill, or mentally disabled (including an individual with Alzheimer's disease or other dementia) to live in their own home or a residential care facility (such as a nursing home, assisted living facility, or any other facility the Secretary determines appropriate) by providing routine personal care services and other appropriate services to the individual.

"(D) STATE.—The term 'State' has the meaning given that term for purposes of title XIX.

"(c) FUNDING.—

"(1) IN GENERAL.—Subject to paragraph (2), out of any funds in the Treasury not otherwise appropriated, there are appropriated to the Secretary to carry out subsections (a) and (b), $85,000,000 for each of fiscal years 2010 through 2014.

"(2) TRAINING AND CERTIFICATION PROGRAMS FOR PERSONAL AND HOME CARE AIDES.—With respect to the demonstration projects under subsection (b), the Secretary shall use $5,000,000 of the amount appropriated under paragraph (1) for each of fiscal years 2010 through 2012 to carry out such projects. No funds appropriated under paragraph (1) shall be used to carry out demonstration projects under subsection (b) after fiscal year 2012.

"(d) NONAPPLICATION.—

"(1) IN GENERAL.—Except as provided in paragraph (2), the preceding sections of this title shall not apply to grant awarded under this section.

"(2) LIMITATIONS ON USE OF GRANTS.—Section 2005(a) (other than paragraph (6)) shall apply to a grant awarded under this section to the same extent and in the same manner as such section applies to payments to States under this title.".

(b) EXTENSION OF FAMILY-TO-FAMILY HEALTH INFORMATION CENTERS.—Section 501(c)(1)(A)(iii) of the Social Security Act (42 U.S.C. 701(c)(1)(A)(iii)) is amended by striking "fiscal year 2009" and inserting "each of fiscal years 2009 through 2012".

SEC. 5508. INCREASING TEACHING CAPACITY.

(a) TEACHING HEALTH CENTERS TRAINING AND ENHANCEMENT.—Part C of title VII of the Public Health Service Act (42 U.S.C. 293k et. seq.), as amended by section 5303, is further amended by inserting after section 749 the following:

"SEC. 749A. TEACHING HEALTH CENTERS DEVELOPMENT GRANTS.

"(a) PROGRAM AUTHORIZED.—The Secretary may award grants under this section to teaching health centers for the purpose of establishing new accredited or expanded primary care residency programs.

"(b) AMOUNT AND DURATION.—Grants awarded under this section shall be for a term of not more than 3 years and the maximum award may not be more than $500,000.

"(c) USE OF FUNDS.—Amounts provided under a grant under this section shall be used to cover the costs of—

"(1) establishing or expanding a primary care residency training program described in subsection (a), including costs associated with—

"(A) curriculum development;

"(B) recruitment, training and retention of residents and faculty:

"(C) accreditation by the Accreditation Council for Graduate Medical Education (ACGME), the American Dental Association (ADA), or the American Osteopathic Association (AOA); and

"(D) faculty salaries during the development phase; and

"(2) technical assistance provided by an eligible entity.

"(d) APPLICATION.—A teaching health center seeking a grant under this section shall submit an application to the Secretary at such time, in such manner, and containing such information as the Secretary may require.

"(e) PREFERENCE FOR CERTAIN APPLICATIONS.—In selecting recipients for grants under this section, the Secretary shall give preference to any such application that documents an existing affiliation agreement with an area health education center program as defined in sections 751 and 799B.

"(f) DEFINITIONS.—In this section:

"(1) ELIGIBLE ENTITY.—The term 'eligible entity' means an organization capable of providing technical assistance including an area health education center program as defined in sections 751 and 799B.

"(2) PRIMARY CARE RESIDENCY PROGRAM.—The term 'primary care residency program' means an approved graduate medical residency training program (as defined in section 340H) in family medicine, internal medicine, pediatrics, internal medicine-pediatrics, obstetrics and gynecology, psychiatry, general dentistry, pediatric dentistry, and geriatrics.

"(3) TEACHING HEALTH CENTER.—

"(A) IN GENERAL.—The term 'teaching health center' means an entity that—

"(i) is a community based, ambulatory patient care center; and

"(ii) operates a primary care residency program.

"(B) INCLUSION OF CERTAIN ENTITIES.—Such term includes the following:

"(i) A Federally qualified health center (as defined in section 1905(l)(2)(B), of the Social Security Act).

"(ii) A community mental health center (as defined in section 1861(ff)(3)(B) of the Social Security Act).

"(iii) A rural health clinic, as defined in section 1861(aa) of the Social Security Act.

"(iv) A health center operated by the Indian Health Service, an Indian tribe or tribal organization, or an urban Indian organization (as defined in section 4 of the Indian Health Care Improvement Act).

"(v) An entity receiving funds under title X of the Public Health Service Act.

"(g) AUTHORIZATION OF APPROPRIATIONS.—There is authorized to be appropriated, $25,000,000 for fiscal year 2010, $50,000,000 for fiscal year 2011, $50,000,000 for fiscal year 2012, and such sums as may be necessary for each fiscal year thereafter to carry out this section. Not to exceed $5,000,000 annually may be used for technical assistance program grants.".

(b) NATIONAL HEALTH SERVICE CORPS TEACHING CAPACITY.—Section 338C(a) of the Public Health Service Act (42 U.S.C. 254m(a)) is amended to read as follows:

"(a) SERVICE IN FULL-TIME CLINICAL PRACTICE.—Except as provided in section 338D, each individual who has entered into a written contract with the Secretary under section 338A or 338B shall provide service in the full-time clinical practice of such individual's profession as a member of the Corps for the period of obligated service provided in such contract. For the purpose of calculating time spent in full-time clinical practice under this subsection, up to 50 percent of time spent teaching by a member of the Corps may be counted toward his or her service obligation.".

(c) PAYMENTS TO QUALIFIED TEACHING HEALTH CENTERS.—Part D of title III of the Public Health Service Act (42 U.S.C. 254b et seq.) is amended by adding at the end the following:

"Subpart XI—Support of Graduate Medical Education in Qualified Teaching Health Centers

"SEC. 340H. PROGRAM OF PAYMENTS TO TEACHING HEALTH CENTERS THAT OPERATE GRADUATE MEDICAL EDUCATION PROGRAMS.

"(a) PAYMENTS.—Subject to subsection (h)(2), the Secretary shall make payments under this section for direct expenses and for indirect expenses to qualified teaching health centers that are listed as sponsoring institutions by the relevant accrediting body for expansion of existing or establishment of new approved graduate medical residency training programs.

"(b) AMOUNT OF PAYMENTS.—

"(1) IN GENERAL.—Subject to paragraph (2), the amounts payable under this section to qualified teaching health centers for an approved graduate medical residency training program for a fiscal year are each of the following amounts:

"(A) DIRECT EXPENSE AMOUNT.—The amount determined under subsection (c) for direct expenses associated with sponsoring approved graduate medical residency training programs.

"(B) INDIRECT EXPENSE AMOUNT.—The amount determined under subsection (d) for indirect expenses associated with the additional costs relating to teaching residents in such programs.

"(2) CAPPED AMOUNT.—

"(A) IN GENERAL.—The total of the payments made to qualified teaching health centers under paragraph (1)(A) or paragraph (1)(B) in a fiscal year shall not exceed the amount of funds appropriated under subsection (g) for such payments for that fiscal year.

"(B) LIMITATION.—The Secretary shall limit the funding of full-time equivalent residents in order to ensure the direct and indirect payments as determined under subsection (c) and (d) do not exceed the total amount of funds appropriated in a fiscal year under subsection (g).

"(c) AMOUNT OF PAYMENT FOR DIRECT GRADUATE MEDICAL EDUCATION.—

"(1) IN GENERAL.—The amount determined under this subsection for payments to qualified teaching health centers for direct graduate expenses relating to approved graduate medical residency training programs for a fiscal year is equal to the product of—

"(A) the updated national per resident amount for direct graduate medical education, as determined under paragraph (2); and

"(B) the average number of full-time equivalent residents in the teaching health center's graduate approved medical residency training programs as determined under section 1886(h)(4) of the Social Security Act (without regard to the limitation under subparagraph (F) of such section) during the fiscal year.

"(2) UPDATED NATIONAL PER RESIDENT AMOUNT FOR DIRECT GRADUATE MEDICAL EDUCATION.—The updated per resident amount for direct graduate medical education for a qualified teaching health center for a fiscal year is an amount determined as follows:

"(A) DETERMINATION OF QUALIFIED TEACHING HEALTH CENTER PER RESIDENT AMOUNT.—The Secretary shall compute for each individual qualified teaching health center a per resident amount—

"(i) by dividing the national average per resident amount computed under section 340E(c)(2)(D) into a wage-related portion and a non-wage related portion by applying the proportion determined under subparagraph (B);

"(ii) by multiplying the wage-related portion by the factor applied under section 1886(d)(3)(E) of the Social Security Act (but without application of section 4410 of the Balanced Budget Act of 1997 (42 U.S.C. 1395ww note)) during the preceding fiscal year for the teaching health center's area; and

"(iii) by adding the non-wage-related portion to the amount computed under clause (ii).

"(B) UPDATING RATE.—The Secretary shall update such per resident amount for each such qualified teaching health center as determined appropriate by the Secretary.

"(d) AMOUNT OF PAYMENT FOR INDIRECT MEDICAL EDUCATION.—

"(1) IN GENERAL.—The amount determined under this subsection for payments to qualified teaching health centers for indirect expenses associated with the additional costs of teaching residents for a fiscal year is equal to an amount determined appropriate by the Secretary.

"(2) FACTORS.—In determining the amount under paragraph (1), the Secretary shall—

"(A) evaluate indirect training costs relative to supporting a primary care residency program in qualified teaching health centers; and

"(B) based on this evaluation, assure that the aggregate of the payments for indirect expenses under this section and the payments for direct graduate medical education as determined under subsection (c) in a fiscal year do not exceed the amount appropriated for such expenses as determined in subsection (g).

"(3) INTERIM PAYMENT.—Before the Secretary makes a payment under this subsection pursuant to a determination of indirect expenses under paragraph (1), the Secretary may provide to qualified teaching health centers a payment, in addition to any payment made under subsection (c), for expected indirect expenses associated with the additional costs of teaching residents for a fiscal year, based on an estimate by the Secretary.

"(e) CLARIFICATION REGARDING RELATIONSHIP TO OTHER PAYMENTS FOR GRADUATE MEDICAL EDUCATION.—Payments under this section—

"(1) shall be in addition to any payments—

"(A) for the indirect costs of medical education under section 1886(d)(5)(B) of the Social Security Act;

"(B) for direct graduate medical education costs under section 1886(h) of such Act; and

"(C) for direct costs of medical education under section 1886(k) of such Act;

"(2) shall not be taken into account in applying the limitation on the number of total full-time equivalent residents under subparagraphs (F) and (G) of section 1886(h)(4) of such Act and clauses (v), (vi)(I), and (vi)(II) of section 1886(d)(5)(B) of such Act for the portion of time that a resident rotates to a hospital; and

"(3) shall not include the time in which a resident is counted toward full-time equivalency by a hospital under paragraph (2) or under section 1886(d)(5)(B)(iv) of the Social Security Act, section 1886(h)(4)(E) of such Act, or section 340E of this Act.

"(f) RECONCILIATION.—The Secretary shall determine any changes to the number of residents reported by a hospital in the application of the hospital for the current fiscal year to determine the final amount payable to the hospital for the current fiscal year for both direct expense and indirect expense amounts. Based on such determination, the Secretary shall recoup any overpayments made to pay any balance due to the extent possible. The final amount so determined shall be considered a final intermediary determination for the purposes of section 1878 of the Social Security Act and shall be subject to administrative and judicial review under that section in the same manner as the amount of payment under section 1186(d) of such Act is subject to review under such section.

"(g) FUNDING.—To carry out this section, there are appropriated such sums as may be necessary, not to exceed $230,000,000, for the period of fiscal years 2011 through 2015.

"(h) ANNUAL REPORTING REQUIRED.—

"(1) ANNUAL REPORT.—The report required under this paragraph for a qualified teaching health center for a fiscal year is a report that includes (in a form and manner specified by the Secretary) the following information for the residency academic year completed immediately prior to such fiscal year:

"(A) The types of primary care resident approved training programs that the qualified teaching health center provided for residents.

"(B) The number of approved training positions for residents described in paragraph (4).

"(C) The number of residents described in paragraph (4) who completed their residency training at the end of such residency academic year and care for vulnerable populations living in underserved areas.

"(D) Other information as deemed appropriate by the Secretary.

"(2) AUDIT AUTHORITY; LIMITATION ON PAYMENT.—

"(A) AUDIT AUTHORITY.—The Secretary may audit a qualified teaching health center to ensure the accuracy and completeness of the information submitted in a report under paragraph (1).

"(B) LIMITATION ON PAYMENT.—A teaching health center may only receive payment in a cost reporting period for a number of such resident positions that is greater than the base level of primary care resident positions, as determined by the Secretary. For purposes of this subparagraph, the 'base level of primary care residents' for a teaching health center is the level of such residents as of a base period.

"(3) REDUCTION IN PAYMENT FOR FAILURE TO REPORT.—

"(A) IN GENERAL.—The amount payable under this section to a qualified teaching health center for a fiscal year shall be reduced by at least 25 percent if the Secretary determines that—

"(i) the qualified teaching health center has failed to provide the Secretary, as an addendum to the qualified teaching health center's application under this section for such fiscal year, the report required under paragraph (1) for the previous fiscal year; or

"(ii) such report fails to provide complete and accurate information required under any subparagraph of such paragraph.

"(B) NOTICE AND OPPORTUNITY TO PROVIDE ACCURATE AND MISSING INFORMATION.—Before imposing a reduction under subparagraph (A) on the basis of a qualified teaching health center's failure to provide complete and accurate information described in subparagraph (A)(ii), the Secretary shall provide notice to the teaching health center of such failure and the Secretary's intention to impose such reduction and shall provide the teaching health center with the opportunity to provide the required information within the period of 30 days beginning on the date of such notice. If the teaching health center provides such information within such period, no reduction shall be made under subparagraph (A) on the basis of the previous failure to provide such information.

"(4) RESIDENTS.—The residents described in this paragraph are those who are in part-time or full-time equivalent resident training positions at a qualified teaching health center in any approved graduate medical residency training program.

"(i) REGULATIONS.—The Secretary shall promulgate regulations to carry out this section.

"(j) DEFINITIONS.—In this section:

"(1) APPROVED GRADUATE MEDICAL RESIDENCY TRAINING PROGRAM.—The term 'approved graduate medical residency training program' means a residency or other postgraduate medical training program—

"(A) participation in which may be counted toward certification in a specialty or subspecialty and includes formal postgraduate training programs in geriatric medicine approved by the Secretary; and

"(B) that meets criteria for accreditation (as established by the Accreditation Council for Graduate Medical Education, the American Osteopathic Association, or the American Dental Association).

"(2) PRIMARY CARE RESIDENCY PROGRAM.—The term 'primary care residency program' has the meaning given that term in section 749A.

"(3) QUALIFIED TEACHING HEALTH CENTER.—The term 'qualified teaching health center' has the meaning given the term 'teaching health center' in section 749A.".

SEC. 5509. GRADUATE NURSE EDUCATION DEMONSTRATION.

(a) IN GENERAL.—

(1) ESTABLISHMENT.—

(A) IN GENERAL.—The Secretary shall establish a graduate nurse education demonstration under title XVIII of the Social Security Act (42 U.S.C. 1395 et seq.) under which an eligible hospital may receive payment for the hospital's reasonable costs (described in paragraph (2)) for the provision of qualified clinical training to advance practice nurses.

(B) NUMBER.—The demonstration shall include up to 5 eligible hospitals.

(C) WRITTEN AGREEMENTS.—Eligible hospitals selected to participate in the demonstration shall enter into written agreements pursuant to subsection (b) in order to reimburse the eligible partners of the hospital the share of the costs attributable to each partner.

(2) COSTS DESCRIBED.—

(A) IN GENERAL.—Subject to subparagraph (B) and subsection (d), the costs described in this paragraph are the reasonable costs (as described in section 1861(v) of the Social Security Act (42 U.S.C. 1395x(v))) of each eligible hospital for the clinical training costs (as determined by the Secretary) that are attributable to providing advanced practice registered nurses with qualified training.

(B) LIMITATION.—With respect to a year, the amount reimbursed under subparagraph (A) may not exceed the amount of costs described in subparagraph (A) that are attributable to an increase in the number of advanced practice registered nurses enrolled in a program that provides qualified training during the year and for which the hospital is being reimbursed under the demonstration, as compared to the average number of advanced practice registered nurses who graduated in each year during the period beginning on January 1, 2006, and ending on December 31, 2010 (as determined by the Secretary) from the graduate nursing education program operated by the applicable school of nursing that is an eligible partner of the hospital for purposes of the demonstration.

(3) WAIVER AUTHORITY.—The Secretary may waive such requirements of titles XI and XVIII of the Social Security Act as may be necessary to carry out the demonstration.

(4) ADMINISTRATION.—Chapter 35 of title 44, United States Code, shall not apply to the implementation of this section.

(b) WRITTEN AGREEMENTS WITH ELIGIBLE PARTNERS.—No payment shall be made under this section to an eligible hospital unless such hospital has in effect a written agreement with the eligible partners of the hospital. Such written agreement shall describe, at a minimum—

(1) the obligations of the eligible partners with respect to the provision of qualified training; and

(2) the obligation of the eligible hospital to reimburse such eligible partners applicable (in a timely manner) for the costs of such qualified training attributable to partner.

(c) EVALUATION.—Not later than October 17, 2017, the Secretary shall submit to Congress a report on the demonstration. Such report shall include an analysis of the following:

(1) The growth in the number of advanced practice registered nurses with respect to a specific base year as a result of the demonstration.

(2) The growth for each of the specialties described in subparagraphs (A) through (D) of subsection (e)(1).

(3) The costs to the Medicare program under title XVIII of the Social Security Act as a result of the demonstration.

(4) Other items the Secretary determines appropriate and relevant.

(d) FUNDING.—

(1) IN GENERAL.—There is hereby appropriated to the Secretary, out of any funds in the Treasury not otherwise appropriated, $50,000,000 for each of fiscal years 2012 through 2015 to carry out this section, including the design, implementation, monitoring, and evaluation of the demonstration.

(2) PRORATION.—If the aggregate payments to eligible hospitals under the demonstration exceed $50,000,000 for a fiscal year described in paragraph (1), the Secretary shall prorate the payment amounts to each eligible hospital in order to ensure that the aggregate payments do not exceed such amount.

(3) WITHOUT FISCAL YEAR LIMITATION.—Amounts appropriated under this subsection shall remain available without fiscal year limitation.

(e) DEFINITIONS.—In this section:

(1) ADVANCED PRACTICE REGISTERED NURSE.—The term "advanced practice registered nurse" includes the following:

(A) A clinical nurse specialist (as defined in subsection (aa)(5) of section 1861 of the Social Security Act (42 U.S.C. 1395x)).

(B) A nurse practitioner (as defined in such subsection).

(C) A certified registered nurse anesthetist (as defined in subsection (bb)(2) of such section).

(D) A certified nurse-midwife (as defined in subsection (gg)(2) of such section).

(2) APPLICABLE NON-HOSPITAL COMMUNITY-BASED CARE SETTING.—The term "applicable non-hospital community-based care setting" means a non-hospital community-based care setting which has entered into a written agreement (as described in subsection (b)) with the eligible hospital participating in the

demonstration. Such settings include Federally qualified health centers, rural health clinics, and other non-hospital settings as determined appropriate by the Secretary.

(3) APPLICABLE SCHOOL OF NURSING.—The term "applicable school of nursing" means an accredited school of nursing (as defined in section 801 of the Public Health Service Act) which has entered into a written agreement (as described in subsection (b)) with the eligible hospital participating in the demonstration.

(4) DEMONSTRATION.—The term "demonstration" means the graduate nurse education demonstration established under subsection (a).

(5) ELIGIBLE HOSPITAL.—The term "eligible hospital" means a hospital (as defined in subsection (e) of section 1861 of the Social Security Act (42 U.S.C. 1395x)) or a critical access hospital (as defined in subsection (mm)(1) of such section) that has a written agreement in place with—

(A) 1 or more applicable schools of nursing; and

(B) 2 or more applicable non-hospital community-based care settings.

(6) ELIGIBLE PARTNERS.—The term "eligible partners" includes the following:

(A) An applicable non-hospital community-based care setting.

(B) An applicable school of nursing.

(7) QUALIFIED TRAINING.—

(A) IN GENERAL.—The term "qualified training" means training—

(i) that provides an advanced practice registered nurse with the clinical skills necessary to provide primary care, preventive care, transitional care, chronic care management, and other services appropriate for individuals entitled to, or enrolled for, benefits under part A of title XVIII of the Social Security Act, or enrolled under part B of such title; and

(ii) subject to subparagraph (B), at least half of which is provided in a non-hospital community-based care setting.

(B) WAIVER OF REQUIREMENT HALF OF TRAINING BE PROVIDED IN NON-HOSPITAL COMMUNITY-BASED CARE SETTING IN CERTAIN AREAS.—The Secretary may waive the requirement under subparagraph (A)(ii) with respect to eligible hospitals located in rural or medically underserved areas.

(8) SECRETARY.—The term "Secretary" means the Secretary of Health and Human Services.

Subtitle G—Improving Access to Health Care Services

SEC. 5601. SPENDING FOR FEDERALLY QUALIFIED HEALTH CENTERS (FQHCS).

(a) IN GENERAL.—Section 330(r) of the Public Health Service Act (42 U.S.C. 254b(r)) is amended by striking paragraph (1) and inserting the following:

"(1) GENERAL AMOUNTS FOR GRANTS.—For the purpose of carrying out this section, in addition to the amounts authorized to be appropriated under subsection (d), there is authorized to be appropriated the following:

"(A) For fiscal year 2010, $2,988,821,592.

"(B) For fiscal year 2011, $3,862,107,440.

"(C) For fiscal year 2012, $4,990,553,440.

"(D) For fiscal year 2013, $6,448,713,307.

"(E) For fiscal year 2014, $7,332,924,155.

"(F) For fiscal year 2015, $8,332,924,155.

"(G) For fiscal year 2016, and each subsequent fiscal year, the amount appropriated for the preceding fiscal year adjusted by the product of—

"(i) one plus the average percentage increase in costs incurred per patient served; and

"(ii) one plus the average percentage increase in the total number of patients served.".

(b) RULE OF CONSTRUCTION.—Section 330(r) of the Public Health Service Act (42 U.S.C. 254b(r)) is amended by adding at the end the following:

"(4) RULE OF CONSTRUCTION WITH RESPECT TO RURAL HEALTH CLINICS.—

"(A) IN GENERAL.—Nothing in this section shall be construed to prevent a community health center from contracting with a Federally certified rural health clinic (as defined in section 1861(aa)(2) of the Social Security Act), a low-volume hospital (as defined for purposes of section 1886 of such Act), a critical access hospital, a sole community hospital (as defined for purposes of section 1886(d)(5)(D)(iii) of such Act), or a medicare-dependent share hospital (as defined for purposes of section 1886(d)(5)(G)(iv) of such Act) for the delivery of primary health care services that are available at the clinic or hospital to individuals who would otherwise be eligible for free or reduced cost care if that individual were able to obtain that care at the community health center. Such services may be limited in scope to those primary health care services available in that clinic or hospitals.

"(B) ASSURANCES.—In order for a clinic or hospital to receive funds under this section through a contract with a community health center under subparagraph (A), such clinic or hospital shall establish policies to ensure—

"(i) nondiscrimination based on the ability of a patient to pay; and

"(ii) the establishment of a sliding fee scale for low-income patients.".

SEC. 5602. NEGOTIATED RULEMAKING FOR DEVELOPMENT OF METHODOLOGY AND CRITERIA FOR DESIGNATING MEDICALLY UNDERSERVED POPULATIONS AND HEALTH PROFESSIONS SHORTAGE AREAS.

(a) ESTABLISHMENT.—

(1) IN GENERAL.—The Secretary of Health and Human Services (in this section referred to as the "Secretary") shall establish, through a negotiated rulemaking process under subchapter 3 of chapter 5 of title 5, United States Code, a comprehensive methodology and criteria for designation of—

(A) medically underserved populations in accordance with section 330(b)(3) of the Public Health Service Act (42 U.S.C. 254b(b)(3));

(B) health professions shortage areas under section 332 of the Public Health Service Act (42 U.S.C. 254e).

(2) FACTORS TO CONSIDER.—In establishing the methodology and criteria under paragraph (1), the Secretary—

(A) shall consult with relevant stakeholders who will be significantly affected by a rule (such as national, State and regional organizations representing affected entities), State health offices, community organizations, health centers and other affected entities, and other interested parties; and

(B) shall take into account—

(i) the timely availability and appropriateness of data used to determine a designation to potential applicants for such designations;

(ii) the impact of the methodology and criteria on communities of various types and on health centers and other safety net providers;

(iii) the degree of ease or difficulty that will face potential applicants for such designations in securing the necessary data; and

(iv) the extent to which the methodology accurately measures various barriers that confront individuals and population groups in seeking health care services.

(b) PUBLICATION OF NOTICE.—In carrying out the rulemaking process under this subsection, the Secretary shall publish the notice provided for under section 564(a) of title 5, United States Code, by not later than 45 days after the date of the enactment of this Act.

(c) TARGET DATE FOR PUBLICATION OF RULE.—As part of the notice under subsection (b), and for purposes of this subsection, the "target date for publication", as referred to in section 564(a)(5) of title 5, United Sates Code, shall be July 1, 2010.

(d) APPOINTMENT OF NEGOTIATED RULEMAKING COMMITTEE AND FACILITATOR.—The Secretary shall provide for—

(1) the appointment of a negotiated rulemaking committee under section 565(a) of title 5, United States Code, by not later than 30 days after the end of the comment period provided for under section 564(c) of such title; and

(2) the nomination of a facilitator under section 566(c) of such title 5 by not later than 10 days after the date of appointment of the committee.

(e) PRELIMINARY COMMITTEE REPORT.—The negotiated rulemaking committee appointed under subsection (d) shall report to the Secretary, by not later than April 1, 2010, regarding the committee's progress on achieving a consensus with regard to the rulemaking proceeding and whether such consensus is likely to occur before one month before the target date for publication of the rule. If the committee reports that the committee has failed to make significant progress toward such consensus or is unlikely to reach such consensus by the target date, the Secretary may terminate such process and provide for the publication of a rule under this section through such other methods as the Secretary may provide.

(f) Final Committee Report.—If the committee is not terminated under subsection (e), the rulemaking committee shall submit a report containing a proposed rule by not later than one month before the target publication date.

(g) Interim Final Effect.—The Secretary shall publish a rule under this section in the Federal Register by not later than the target publication date. Such rule shall be effective and final immediately on an interim basis, but is subject to change and revision after public notice and opportunity for a period (of not less than 90 days) for public comment. In connection with such rule, the Secretary shall specify the process for the timely review and approval of applications for such designations pursuant to such rules and consistent with this section.

(h) Publication of Rule After Public Comment.—The Secretary shall provide for consideration of such comments and republication of such rule by not later than 1 year after the target publication date.

SEC. 5603. REAUTHORIZATION OF THE WAKEFIELD EMERGENCY MEDICAL SERVICES FOR CHILDREN PROGRAM.

Section 1910 of the Public Health Service Act (42 U.S.C. 300w–9) is amended—

(1) in subsection (a), by striking "3-year period (with an optional 4th year" and inserting "4-year period (with an optional 5th year"; and

(2) in subsection (d)—

(A) by striking "and such sums" and inserting "such sums"; and

(B) by inserting before the period the following: ", $25,000,000 for fiscal year 2010, $26,250,000 for fiscal year 2011, $27,562,500 for fiscal year 2012, $28,940,625 for fiscal year 2013, and $30,387,656 for fiscal year 2014".

SEC. 5604. CO-LOCATING PRIMARY AND SPECIALTY CARE IN COMMUNITY-BASED MENTAL HEALTH SETTINGS.

Subpart 3 of part B of title V of the Public Health Service Act (42 U.S.C. 290bb–31 et seq.) is amended by adding at the end the following:

"SEC. 520K. AWARDS FOR CO-LOCATING PRIMARY AND SPECIALTY CARE IN COMMUNITY-BASED MENTAL HEALTH SETTINGS.

"(a) Definitions.—In this section:

"(1) Eligible entity.—The term 'eligible entity' means a qualified community mental health program defined under section 1913(b)(1).

"(2) Special populations.—The term 'special populations' means adults with mental illnesses who have co-occurring primary care conditions and chronic diseases.

"(b) Program Authorized.—The Secretary, acting through the Administrator shall award grants and cooperative agreements to eligible entities to establish demonstration projects for the provision of coordinated and integrated services to special populations through the co-location of primary and specialty care services in community-based mental and behavioral health settings.

"(c) Application.—To be eligible to receive a grant or cooperative agreement under this section, an eligible entity shall submit an application to the Administrator at such time, in such manner, and accompanied by such information as the Administrator may require, including a description of partnerships, or other arrangements with local primary care providers, including community health centers, to provide services to special populations.

"(d) USE OF FUNDS.—

"(1) IN GENERAL.—For the benefit of special populations, an eligible entity shall use funds awarded under this section for—

"(A) the provision, by qualified primary care professionals, of on site primary care services;

"(B) reasonable costs associated with medically necessary referrals to qualified specialty care professionals, other coordinators of care or, if permitted by the terms of the grant or cooperative agreement, by qualified specialty care professionals on a reasonable cost basis on site at the eligible entity;

"(C) information technology required to accommodate the clinical needs of primary and specialty care professionals; or

"(D) facility modifications needed to bring primary and specialty care professionals on site at the eligible entity.

"(2) LIMITATION.—Not to exceed 15 percent of grant or cooperative agreement funds may be used for activities described in subparagraphs (C) and (D) of paragraph (1).

"(e) EVALUATION.—Not later than 90 days after a grant or cooperative agreement awarded under this section expires, an eligible entity shall submit to the Secretary the results of an evaluation to be conducted by the entity concerning the effectiveness of the activities carried out under the grant or agreement.

"(f) AUTHORIZATION OF APPROPRIATIONS.—There are authorized to be appropriated to carry out this section, $50,000,000 for fiscal year 2010 and such sums as may be necessary for each of fiscal years 2011 through 2014.".

SEC. 5605. KEY NATIONAL INDICATORS.

(a) DEFINITIONS.—In this section:

(1) ACADEMY.—The term "Academy" means the National Academy of Sciences.

(2) COMMISSION.—The term "Commission" means the Commission on Key National Indicators established under subsection (b).

(3) INSTITUTE.—The term "Institute" means a Key National Indicators Institute as designated under subsection (c)(3).

(b) COMMISSION ON KEY NATIONAL INDICATORS.—

(1) ESTABLISHMENT.—There is established a "Commission on Key National Indicators".

(2) MEMBERSHIP.—

(A) NUMBER AND APPOINTMENT.—The Commission shall be composed of 8 members, to be appointed equally by the majority and minority leaders of the Senate and the Speaker and minority leader of the House of Representatives.

(B) PROHIBITED APPOINTMENTS.—Members of the Commission shall not include Members of Congress or other elected Federal, State, or local government officials.

(C) QUALIFICATIONS.—In making appointments under subparagraph (A), the majority and minority leaders of the Senate and the Speaker and minority leader of the House of Representatives shall appoint individuals who have shown a dedication to improving civic dialogue and decision-making through the wide use of scientific evidence and factual information.

(D) PERIOD OF APPOINTMENT.—Each member of the Commission shall be appointed for a 2-year term, except that 1 initial appointment shall be for 3 years. Any vacancies shall not affect the power and duties of the Commission but shall be filled in the same manner as the original appointment and shall last only for the remainder of that term.

(E) DATE.—Members of the Commission shall be appointed by not later than 30 days after the date of enactment of this Act.

(F) INITIAL ORGANIZING PERIOD.—Not later than 60 days after the date of enactment of this Act, the Commission shall develop and implement a schedule for completion of the review and reports required under subsection (d).

(G) CO-CHAIRPERSONS.—The Commission shall select 2 Co-Chairpersons from among its members.

(c) DUTIES OF THE COMMISSION.—

(1) IN GENERAL.—The Commission shall—

(A) conduct comprehensive oversight of a newly established key national indicators system consistent with the purpose described in this subsection;

(B) make recommendations on how to improve the key national indicators system;

(C) coordinate with Federal Government users and information providers to assure access to relevant and quality data; and

(D) enter into contracts with the Academy.

(2) REPORTS.—

(A) ANNUAL REPORT TO CONGRESS.—Not later than 1 year after the selection of the 2 Co-Chairpersons of the Commission, and each subsequent year thereafter, the Commission shall prepare and submit to the appropriate Committees of Congress and the President a report that contains a detailed statement of the recommendations, findings, and conclusions of the Commission on the activities of the Academy and a designated Institute related to the establishment of a Key National Indicator System.

(B) ANNUAL REPORT TO THE ACADEMY.—

(i) IN GENERAL.—Not later than 6 months after the selection of the 2 Co-Chairpersons of the Commission, and each subsequent year thereafter, the Commission shall prepare and submit to the Academy and a designated Institute a report making recommendations concerning potential issue areas and key indicators to be included in the Key National Indicators.

(ii) LIMITATION.—The Commission shall not have the authority to direct the Academy or, if established, the Institute, to adopt, modify, or delete any key indicators.

(3) CONTRACT WITH THE NATIONAL ACADEMY OF SCIENCES.—

(A) IN GENERAL.—As soon as practicable after the selection of the 2 Co-Chairpersons of the Commission, the

Co-Chairpersons shall enter into an arrangement with the National Academy of Sciences under which the Academy shall—

(i) review available public and private sector research on the selection of a set of key national indicators;

(ii) determine how best to establish a key national indicator system for the United States, by either creating its own institutional capability or designating an independent private nonprofit organization as an Institute to implement a key national indicator system;

(iii) if the Academy designates an independent Institute under clause (ii), provide scientific and technical advice to the Institute and create an appropriate governance mechanism that balances Academy involvement and the independence of the Institute; and

(iv) provide an annual report to the Commission addressing scientific and technical issues related to the key national indicator system and, if established, the Institute, and governance of the Institute's budget and operations.

(B) PARTICIPATION.—In executing the arrangement under subparagraph (A), the National Academy of Sciences shall convene a multi-sector, multi-disciplinary process to define major scientific and technical issues associated with developing, maintaining, and evolving a Key National Indicator System and, if an Institute is established, to provide it with scientific and technical advice.

(C) ESTABLISHMENT OF A KEY NATIONAL INDICATOR SYSTEM.—

(i) IN GENERAL.—In executing the arrangement under subparagraph (A), the National Academy of Sciences shall enable the establishment of a key national indicator system by—

(I) creating its own institutional capability; or

(II) partnering with an independent private nonprofit organization as an Institute to implement a key national indicator system.

(ii) INSTITUTE.—If the Academy designates an Institute under clause (i)(II), such Institute shall be a non-profit entity (as defined for purposes of section 501(c)(3) of the Internal Revenue Code of 1986) with an educational mission, a governance structure that emphasizes independence, and characteristics that make such entity appropriate for establishing a key national indicator system.

(iii) RESPONSIBILITIES.—Either the Academy or the Institute designated under clause (i)(II) shall be responsible for the following:

(I) Identifying and selecting issue areas to be represented by the key national indicators.

(II) Identifying and selecting the measures used for key national indicators within the issue areas under subclause (I).

(III) Identifying and selecting data to populate the key national indicators described under subclause (II).

(IV) Designing, publishing, and maintaining a public website that contains a freely accessible database allowing public access to the key national indicators.

(V) Developing a quality assurance framework to ensure rigorous and independent processes and the selection of quality data.

(VI) Developing a budget for the construction and management of a sustainable, adaptable, and evolving key national indicator system that reflects all Commission funding of Academy and, if an Institute is established, Institute activities.

(VII) Reporting annually to the Commission regarding its selection of issue areas, key indicators, data, and progress toward establishing a web-accessible database.

(VIII) Responding directly to the Commission in response to any Commission recommendations and to the Academy regarding any inquiries by the Academy.

(iv) GOVERNANCE.—Upon the establishment of a key national indicator system, the Academy shall create an appropriate governance mechanism that incorporates advisory and control functions. If an Institute is designated under clause (i)(II), the governance mechanism shall balance appropriate Academy involvement and the independence of the Institute.

(v) MODIFICATION AND CHANGES.—The Academy shall retain the sole discretion, at any time, to alter its approach to the establishment of a key national indicator system or, if an Institute is designated under clause (i)(II), to alter any aspect of its relationship with the Institute or to designate a different non-profit entity to serve as the Institute.

(vi) CONSTRUCTION.—Nothing in this section shall be construed to limit the ability of the Academy or the Institute designated under clause (i)(II) to receive private funding for activities related to the establishment of a key national indicator system.

(D) ANNUAL REPORT.—As part of the arrangement under subparagraph (A), the National Academy of Sciences shall, not later than 270 days after the date of enactment of this Act, and annually thereafter, submit to the Co-Chairpersons of the Commission a report that contains the findings and recommendations of the Academy.

(d) GOVERNMENT ACCOUNTABILITY OFFICE STUDY AND REPORT.—

(1) GAO STUDY.—The Comptroller General of the United States shall conduct a study of previous work conducted by all public agencies, private organizations, or foreign countries with respect to best practices for a key national indicator system. The study shall be submitted to the appropriate authorizing committees of Congress.

(2) GAO FINANCIAL AUDIT.—If an Institute is established under this section, the Comptroller General shall conduct an annual audit of the financial statements of the Institute, in accordance with generally accepted government auditing standards and submit a report on such audit to the Commission and the appropriate authorizing committees of Congress.

(3) GAO PROGRAMMATIC REVIEW.—The Comptroller General of the United States shall conduct programmatic assessments of the Institute established under this section as determined necessary by the Comptroller General and report the findings to the Commission and to the appropriate authorizing committees of Congress.

(e) AUTHORIZATION OF APPROPRIATIONS.—

(1) IN GENERAL.—There are authorized to be appropriated to carry out the purposes of this section, $10,000,000 for fiscal year 2010, and $7,500,000 for each of fiscal year 2011 through 2018.

(2) AVAILABILITY.—Amounts appropriated under paragraph (1) shall remain available until expended.

Subtitle H—General Provisions

SEC. 5701. REPORTS.

(a) REPORTS BY SECRETARY OF HEALTH AND HUMAN SERVICES.—On an annual basis, the Secretary of Health and Human Services shall submit to the appropriate Committees of Congress a report on the activities carried out under the amendments made by this title, and the effectiveness of such activities.

(b) REPORTS BY RECIPIENTS OF FUNDS.—The Secretary of Health and Human Services may require, as a condition of receiving funds under the amendments made by this title, that the entity receiving such award submit to such Secretary such reports as the such Secretary may require on activities carried out with such award, and the effectiveness of such activities.

TITLE VI—TRANSPARENCY AND PROGRAM INTEGRITY

Subtitle A—Physician Ownership and Other Transparency

SEC. 6001. LIMITATION ON MEDICARE EXCEPTION TO THE PROHIBITION ON CERTAIN PHYSICIAN REFERRALS FOR HOSPITALS.

(a) IN GENERAL.—Section 1877 of the Social Security Act (42 U.S.C. 1395nn) is amended—

(1) in subsection (d)(2)—

(A) in subparagraph (A), by striking "and" at the end;

(B) in subparagraph (B), by striking the period at the end and inserting "; and"; and

(C) by adding at the end the following new subparagraph:

"(C) in the case where the entity is a hospital, the hospital meets the requirements of paragraph (3)(D).";

(2) in subsection (d)(3)—

(A) in subparagraph (B), by striking "and" at the end;

(B) in subparagraph (C), by striking the period at the end and inserting "; and"; and

(C) by adding at the end the following new subparagraph:

"(D) the hospital meets the requirements described in subsection (i)(1) not later than 18 months after the date of the enactment of this subparagraph."; and

(3) by adding at the end the following new subsection:

"(i) REQUIREMENTS FOR HOSPITALS TO QUALIFY FOR RURAL PROVIDER AND HOSPITAL EXCEPTION TO OWNERSHIP OR INVESTMENT PROHIBITION.—

"(1) REQUIREMENTS DESCRIBED.—For purposes of subsection (d)(3)(D), the requirements described in this paragraph for a hospital are as follows:

"(A) PROVIDER AGREEMENT.—The hospital had—

"(i) physician ownership or investment on February 1, 2010; and

"(ii) a provider agreement under section 1866 in effect on such date.

"(B) LIMITATION ON EXPANSION OF FACILITY CAPACITY.—Except as provided in paragraph (3), the number of operating rooms, procedure rooms, and beds for which the hospital is licensed at any time on or after the date of the enactment of this subsection is no greater than the number of operating rooms, procedure rooms, and beds for which the hospital is licensed as of such date.

"(C) PREVENTING CONFLICTS OF INTEREST.—

"(i) The hospital submits to the Secretary an annual report containing a detailed description of—

"(I) the identity of each physician owner or investor and any other owners or investors of the hospital; and

"(II) the nature and extent of all ownership and investment interests in the hospital.

"(ii) The hospital has procedures in place to require that any referring physician owner or investor discloses to the patient being referred, by a time that permits the patient to make a meaningful decision regarding the receipt of care, as determined by the Secretary—

"(I) the ownership or investment interest, as applicable, of such referring physician in the hospital; and

"(II) if applicable, any such ownership or investment interest of the treating physician.

"(iii) The hospital does not condition any physician ownership or investment interests either directly or indirectly on the physician owner or investor making or influencing referrals to the hospital or otherwise generating business for the hospital.

"(iv) The hospital discloses the fact that the hospital is partially owned or invested in by physicians—

"(I) on any public website for the hospital; and

"(II) in any public advertising for the hospital.

"(D) ENSURING BONA FIDE INVESTMENT.—

"(i) The percentage of the total value of the ownership or investment interests held in the hospital, or in an entity whose assets include the hospital, by physician owners or investors in the aggregate does not exceed such percentage as of the date of enactment of this subsection.

"(ii) Any ownership or investment interests that the hospital offers to a physician owner or investor are not offered on more favorable terms than the terms offered to a person who is not a physician owner or investor.

"(iii) The hospital (or any owner or investor in the hospital) does not directly or indirectly provide loans or financing for any investment in the hospital by a physician owner or investor.

"(iv) The hospital (or any owner or investor in the hospital) does not directly or indirectly guarantee a loan, make a payment toward a loan, or otherwise subsidize a loan, for any individual physician owner or investor or group of physician owners or investors that is related to acquiring any ownership or investment interest in the hospital.

"(v) Ownership or investment returns are distributed to each owner or investor in the hospital in an amount that is directly proportional to the ownership or investment interest of such owner or investor in the hospital.

"(vi) Physician owners and investors do not receive, directly or indirectly, any guaranteed receipt of or right to purchase other business interests related to the hospital, including the purchase or lease of any property under the control of other owners or investors in the hospital or located near the premises of the hospital.

"(vii) The hospital does not offer a physician owner or investor the opportunity to purchase or lease any property under the control of the hospital or any other owner or investor in the hospital on more favorable terms than the terms offered to an individual who is not a physician owner or investor.

"(E) PATIENT SAFETY.—

"(i) Insofar as the hospital admits a patient and does not have any physician available on the premises to provide services during all hours in which the hospital is providing services to such patient, before admitting the patient—

"(I) the hospital discloses such fact to a patient; and

"(II) following such disclosure, the hospital receives from the patient a signed acknowledgment that the patient understands such fact.

"(ii) The hospital has the capacity to—

"(I) provide assessment and initial treatment for patients; and

"(II) refer and transfer patients to hospitals with the capability to treat the needs of the patient involved.

"(F) LIMITATION ON APPLICATION TO CERTAIN CONVERTED FACILITIES.—The hospital was not converted from an ambulatory surgical center to a hospital on or after the date of enactment of this subsection.

"(2) PUBLICATION OF INFORMATION REPORTED.—The Secretary shall publish, and update on an annual basis, the information submitted by hospitals under paragraph (1)(C)(i) on the public Internet website of the Centers for Medicare & Medicaid Services.

"(3) EXCEPTION TO PROHIBITION ON EXPANSION OF FACILITY CAPACITY.—

"(A) PROCESS.—

"(i) ESTABLISHMENT.—The Secretary shall establish and implement a process under which an applicable hospital (as defined in subparagraph (E)) may apply for an exception from the requirement under paragraph (1)(B).

"(ii) OPPORTUNITY FOR COMMUNITY INPUT.—The process under clause (i) shall provide individuals and entities in the community in which the applicable hospital applying for an exception is located with the opportunity to provide input with respect to the application.

"(iii) TIMING FOR IMPLEMENTATION.—The Secretary shall implement the process under clause (i) on August 1, 2011.

"(iv) REGULATIONS.—Not later than July 1, 2011, the Secretary shall promulgate regulations to carry out the process under clause (i).

"(B) FREQUENCY.—The process described in subparagraph (A) shall permit an applicable hospital to apply for an exception up to once every 2 years.

"(C) PERMITTED INCREASE.—

"(i) IN GENERAL.—Subject to clause (ii) and subparagraph (D), an applicable hospital granted an exception under the process described in subparagraph (A) may increase the number of operating rooms, procedure rooms, and beds for which the applicable hospital is licensed above the baseline number of operating rooms, procedure rooms, and beds of the applicable hospital (or, if the applicable hospital has been granted a previous exception under this paragraph, above the number of operating rooms, procedure rooms, and beds for which the hospital is licensed after the application of the most recent increase under such an exception).

"(ii) 100 PERCENT INCREASE LIMITATION.—The Secretary shall not permit an increase in the number of operating rooms, procedure rooms, and beds for which an applicable hospital is licensed under clause (i) to the extent such increase would result in the number of operating rooms, procedure rooms, and beds for which the applicable hospital is licensed exceeding 200 percent of the baseline number of operating rooms, procedure rooms, and beds of the applicable hospital.

"(iii) BASELINE NUMBER OF OPERATING ROOMS, PROCEDURE ROOMS, AND BEDS.—In this paragraph, the term 'baseline number of operating rooms, procedure rooms, and beds' means the number of operating rooms, procedure rooms, and beds for which the applicable hospital is licensed as of the date of enactment of this subsection.

"(D) INCREASE LIMITED TO FACILITIES ON THE MAIN CAMPUS OF THE HOSPITAL.—Any increase in the number of operating rooms, procedure rooms, and beds for which an applicable hospital is licensed pursuant to this paragraph may only occur in facilities on the main campus of the applicable hospital.

"(E) APPLICABLE HOSPITAL.—In this paragraph, the term 'applicable hospital' means a hospital—

"(i) that is located in a county in which the percentage increase in the population during the most recent 5-year period (as of the date of the application under subparagraph (A)) is at least 150 percent of the percentage increase in the population growth of the State in which the hospital is located during that period, as estimated by Bureau of the Census;

"(ii) whose annual percent of total inpatient admissions that represent inpatient admissions under the program under title XIX is equal to or greater than the average percent with respect to such admissions for all hospitals located in the county in which the hospital is located;

"(iii) that does not discriminate against beneficiaries of Federal health care programs and does not permit physicians practicing at the hospital to discriminate against such beneficiaries;

"(iv) that is located in a State in which the average bed capacity in the State is less than the national average bed capacity; and

"(v) that has an average bed occupancy rate that is greater than the average bed occupancy rate in the State in which the hospital is located.

"(F) PROCEDURE ROOMS.—In this subsection, the term 'procedure rooms' includes rooms in which catheterizations, angiographies, angiograms, and endoscopies are performed, except such term shall not include emergency rooms or departments (exclusive of rooms in which catheterizations, angiographies, angiograms, and endoscopies are performed).

"(G) PUBLICATION OF FINAL DECISIONS.—Not later than 60 days after receiving a complete application under this paragraph, the Secretary shall publish in the Federal Register the final decision with respect to such application.

"(H) LIMITATION ON REVIEW.—There shall be no administrative or judicial review under section 1869, section 1878, or otherwise of the process under this paragraph (including the establishment of such process).

"(4) COLLECTION OF OWNERSHIP AND INVESTMENT INFORMATION.—For purposes of subparagraphs (A)(i) and (D)(i) of paragraph (1), the Secretary shall collect physician ownership and investment information for each hospital.

"(5) PHYSICIAN OWNER OR INVESTOR DEFINED.—For purposes of this subsection, the term 'physician owner or investor' means a physician (or an immediate family member of such physician) with a direct or an indirect ownership or investment interest in the hospital.

"(6) CLARIFICATION.—Nothing in this subsection shall be construed as preventing the Secretary from revoking a hospital's provider agreement if not in compliance with regulations implementing section 1866.".

(b) ENFORCEMENT.—

(1) ENSURING COMPLIANCE.—The Secretary of Health and Human Services shall establish policies and procedures to ensure compliance with the requirements described in subsection (i)(1) of section 1877 of the Social Security Act, as added by subsection (a)(3), beginning on the date such requirements first apply. Such policies and procedures may include unannounced site reviews of hospitals.

(2) AUDITS.—Beginning not later than November 1, 2011, the Secretary of Health and Human Services shall conduct audits to determine if hospitals violate the requirements referred to in paragraph (1).

SEC. 6002. TRANSPARENCY REPORTS AND REPORTING OF PHYSICIAN OWNERSHIP OR INVESTMENT INTERESTS.

Part A of title XI of the Social Security Act (42 U.S.C. 1301 et seq.) is amended by inserting after section 1128F the following new section:

"SEC. 1128G. TRANSPARENCY REPORTS AND REPORTING OF PHYSICIAN OWNERSHIP OR INVESTMENT INTERESTS.

"(a) TRANSPARENCY REPORTS.—

"(1) PAYMENTS OR OTHER TRANSFERS OF VALUE.—

"(A) IN GENERAL.—On March 31, 2013, and on the 90th day of each calendar year beginning thereafter, any applicable manufacturer that provides a payment or other transfer of value to a covered recipient (or to an entity or individual at the request of or designated on behalf of a covered recipient), shall submit to the Secretary, in such electronic form as the Secretary shall require, the following information with respect to the preceding calendar year:

"(i) The name of the covered recipient.

"(ii) The business address of the covered recipient and, in the case of a covered recipient who is a physician, the specialty and National Provider Identifier of the covered recipient.

"(iii) The amount of the payment or other transfer of value.

"(iv) The dates on which the payment or other transfer of value was provided to the covered recipient.

"(v) A description of the form of the payment or other transfer of value, indicated (as appropriate for all that apply) as—

"(I) cash or a cash equivalent;

"(II) in-kind items or services;

"(III) stock, a stock option, or any other ownership interest, dividend, profit, or other return on investment; or

"(IV) any other form of payment or other transfer of value (as defined by the Secretary).

"(vi) A description of the nature of the payment or other transfer of value, indicated (as appropriate for all that apply) as—

"(I) consulting fees;

"(II) compensation for services other than consulting;

"(III) honoraria;

"(IV) gift;

"(V) entertainment;

"(VI) food;

"(VII) travel (including the specified destinations);

"(VIII) education;

"(IX) research;

"(X) charitable contribution;

"(XI) royalty or license;

"(XII) current or prospective ownership or investment interest;

"(XIII) direct compensation for serving as faculty or as a speaker for a medical education program;

"(XIV) grant; or

"(XV) any other nature of the payment or other transfer of value (as defined by the Secretary).

"(vii) If the payment or other transfer of value is related to marketing, education, or research specific to a covered drug, device, biological, or medical supply, the name of that covered drug, device, biological, or medical supply.

"(viii) Any other categories of information regarding the payment or other transfer of value the Secretary determines appropriate.

"(B) SPECIAL RULE FOR CERTAIN PAYMENTS OR OTHER TRANSFERS OF VALUE.—In the case where an applicable manufacturer provides a payment or other transfer of value to an entity or individual at the request of or designated on behalf of a covered recipient, the applicable manufacturer shall disclose that payment or other transfer of value under the name of the covered recipient.

"(2) PHYSICIAN OWNERSHIP.—In addition to the requirement under paragraph (1)(A), on March 31, 2013, and on the 90th day of each calendar year beginning thereafter, any applicable manufacturer or applicable group purchasing organization shall submit to the Secretary, in such electronic form as the Secretary shall require, the following information regarding any ownership or investment interest (other than an ownership or investment interest in a publicly traded security and mutual fund, as described in section 1877(c)) held by a physician (or an immediate family member of such physician (as defined for purposes of section 1877(a))) in the applicable manufacturer or applicable group purchasing organization during the preceding year:

"(A) The dollar amount invested by each physician holding such an ownership or investment interest.

"(B) The value and terms of each such ownership or investment interest.

"(C) Any payment or other transfer of value provided to a physician holding such an ownership or investment interest (or to an entity or individual at the request of or designated on behalf of a physician holding such an ownership or investment interest), including the information described in clauses (i) through (viii) of paragraph (1)(A), except that in applying such clauses, 'physician' shall be substituted for 'covered recipient' each place it appears.

"(D) Any other information regarding the ownership or investment interest the Secretary determines appropriate.

"(b) PENALTIES FOR NONCOMPLIANCE.—

"(1) FAILURE TO REPORT.—

"(A) IN GENERAL.—Subject to subparagraph (B) except as provided in paragraph (2), any applicable manufacturer or applicable group purchasing organization that fails to submit information required under subsection (a) in a timely manner in accordance with rules or regulations promulgated to carry out such subsection, shall be subject to a civil money penalty of not less than $1,000, but not more than $10,000, for each payment or other transfer of value or ownership or investment interest not reported as required under such subsection. Such penalty shall be imposed and collected in the same manner as civil money penalties under subsection (a) of section 1128A are imposed and collected under that section.

"(B) LIMITATION.—The total amount of civil money penalties imposed under subparagraph (A) with respect to each annual submission of information under subsection (a) by an applicable manufacturer or applicable group purchasing organization shall not exceed $150,000.

"(2) KNOWING FAILURE TO REPORT.—

"(A) IN GENERAL.—Subject to subparagraph (B), any applicable manufacturer or applicable group purchasing organization that knowingly fails to submit information required under subsection (a) in a timely manner in accordance with rules or regulations promulgated to carry out such subsection, shall be subject to a civil money penalty of not less than $10,000, but not more than $100,000, for each payment or other transfer of value or ownership or investment interest not reported as required under such subsection. Such penalty shall be imposed and collected in the same manner as civil money penalties under subsection (a) of section 1128A are imposed and collected under that section.

"(B) LIMITATION.—The total amount of civil money penalties imposed under subparagraph (A) with respect to each annual submission of information under subsection (a) by an applicable manufacturer or applicable group purchasing organization shall not exceed $1,000,000.

"(3) USE OF FUNDS.—Funds collected by the Secretary as a result of the imposition of a civil money penalty under this subsection shall be used to carry out this section.

"(c) PROCEDURES FOR SUBMISSION OF INFORMATION AND PUBLIC AVAILABILITY.—

"(1) IN GENERAL.—

"(A) ESTABLISHMENT.—Not later than October 1, 2011, the Secretary shall establish procedures—

"(i) for applicable manufacturers and applicable group purchasing organizations to submit information to the Secretary under subsection (a); and

"(ii) for the Secretary to make such information submitted available to the public.

"(B) DEFINITION OF TERMS.—The procedures established under subparagraph (A) shall provide for the definition of terms (other than those terms defined in subsection (e)), as appropriate, for purposes of this section.

"(C) PUBLIC AVAILABILITY.—Except as provided in subparagraph (E), the procedures established under subparagraph (A)(ii) shall ensure that, not later than September 30, 2013, and on June 30 of each calendar year beginning thereafter, the information submitted under subsection (a) with respect to the preceding calendar year is made available through an Internet website that—

"(i) is searchable and is in a format that is clear and understandable;

"(ii) contains information that is presented by the name of the applicable manufacturer or applicable group purchasing organization, the name of the covered recipient, the business address of the covered recipient, the specialty of the covered recipient, the value of the payment or other transfer of value, the date on which the payment or other transfer of value was provided to the covered recipient, the form of the payment or other transfer of value, indicated (as appropriate) under subsection (a)(1)(A)(v), the nature of the payment or other transfer of value, indicated (as appropriate) under subsection (a)(1)(A)(vi), and the name of the covered drug, device, biological, or medical supply, as applicable;

"(iii) contains information that is able to be easily aggregated and downloaded;

"(iv) contains a description of any enforcement actions taken to carry out this section, including any penalties imposed under subsection (b), during the preceding year;

"(v) contains background information on industry-physician relationships;

"(vi) in the case of information submitted with respect to a payment or other transfer of value described in subparagraph (E)(i), lists such information separately from the other information submitted under subsection (a) and designates such separately listed information as funding for clinical research;

"(vii) contains any other information the Secretary determines would be helpful to the average consumer;

"(viii) does not contain the National Provider Identifier of the covered recipient, and

"(ix) subject to subparagraph (D), provides the applicable manufacturer, applicable group purchasing organization, or covered recipient an opportunity to review and submit corrections to the information submitted with respect to the applicable manufacturer, applicable group purchasing organization, or covered recipient, respectively, for a period of not less than 45 days prior to such information being made available to the public.

"(D) CLARIFICATION OF TIME PERIOD FOR REVIEW AND CORRECTIONS.—In no case may the 45-day period for review and submission of corrections to information under subparagraph (C)(ix) prevent such information from being made available to the public in accordance with the dates described in the matter preceding clause (i) in subparagraph (C).

"(E) DELAYED PUBLICATION FOR PAYMENTS MADE PURSUANT TO PRODUCT RESEARCH OR DEVELOPMENT AGREEMENTS AND CLINICAL INVESTIGATIONS.—

"(i) IN GENERAL.—In the case of information submitted under subsection (a) with respect to a payment or other transfer of value made to a covered recipient by an applicable manufacturer pursuant to a product research or development agreement for services furnished in connection with research on a potential new medical technology or a new application of an existing medical technology or the development of a new drug, device, biological, or medical supply, or by an applicable manufacturer in connection with a clinical investigation regarding a new drug, device, biological, or medical supply, the procedures established under subparagraph (A)(ii) shall provide that such information is made available to the public on the first date described in the matter preceding clause (i) in subparagraph (C) after the earlier of the following:

"(I) The date of the approval or clearance of the covered drug, device, biological, or medical supply by the Food and Drug Administration.

"(II) Four calendar years after the date such payment or other transfer of value was made.

"(ii) CONFIDENTIALITY OF INFORMATION PRIOR TO PUBLICATION.—Information described in clause (i) shall be considered confidential and shall not be subject to disclosure under section 552 of title 5, United States Code, or any other similar Federal, State, or local law, until on or after the date on which the information is made available to the public under such clause.

"(2) CONSULTATION.—In establishing the procedures under paragraph (1), the Secretary shall consult with the Inspector General of the Department of Health and Human Services, affected industry, consumers, consumer advocates, and other interested parties in order to ensure that the information made available to the public under such paragraph is presented in the appropriate overall context.

"(d) ANNUAL REPORTS AND RELATION TO STATE LAWS.—

"(1) ANNUAL REPORT TO CONGRESS.—Not later than April 1 of each year beginning with 2013, the Secretary shall submit to Congress a report that includes the following:

"(A) The information submitted under subsection (a) during the preceding year, aggregated for each applicable manufacturer and applicable group purchasing organization that submitted such information during such year (except, in the case of information submitted with respect to a payment or other transfer of value described in subsection (c)(1)(E)(i), such information shall be included in the first report submitted to Congress after the date on which such information is made available to the public under such subsection).

"(B) A description of any enforcement actions taken to carry out this section, including any penalties imposed under subsection (b), during the preceding year.

"(2) ANNUAL REPORTS TO STATES.—Not later than September 30, 2013 and on June 30 of each calendar year thereafter, the Secretary shall submit to States a report that includes a summary of the information submitted under subsection (a) during the preceding year with respect to covered recipients in the State (except, in the case of information submitted with respect to a payment or other transfer of value described in subsection (c)(1)(E)(i), such information shall be included in the first report submitted to States after the date on which such information is made available to the public under such subsection).

"(3) RELATION TO STATE LAWS.—

"(A) IN GENERAL.—In the case of a payment or other transfer of value provided by an applicable manufacturer that is received by a covered recipient (as defined in subsection (e)) on or after January 1, 2012, subject to subparagraph (B), the provisions of this section shall preempt any statute or regulation of a State or of a political subdivision of a State that requires an applicable manufacturer (as so defined) to disclose or report, in any format, the type of information (as described in subsection (a)) regarding such payment or other transfer of value.

"(B) NO PREEMPTION OF ADDITIONAL REQUIREMENTS.—Subparagraph (A) shall not preempt any statute or regulation of a State or of a political subdivision of a State that requires the disclosure or reporting of information—

"(i) not of the type required to be disclosed or reported under this section;

"(ii) described in subsection (e)(10)(B), except in the case of information described in clause (i) of such subsection;

"(iii) by any person or entity other than an applicable manufacturer (as so defined) or a covered recipient (as defined in subsection (e)); or

"(iv) to a Federal, State, or local governmental agency for public health surveillance, investigation, or other public health purposes or health oversight purposes.

"(C) Nothing in subparagraph (A) shall be construed to limit the discovery or admissibility of information described in such subparagraph in a criminal, civil, or administrative proceeding.

"(4) CONSULTATION.—The Secretary shall consult with the Inspector General of the Department of Health and Human Services on the implementation of this section.

"(e) DEFINITIONS.—In this section:

"(1) APPLICABLE GROUP PURCHASING ORGANIZATION.—The term 'applicable group purchasing organization' means a group purchasing organization (as defined by the Secretary) that purchases, arranges for, or negotiates the purchase of a covered drug, device, biological, or medical supply which is operating in the United States, or in a territory, possession, or commonwealth of the United States.

"(2) APPLICABLE MANUFACTURER.—The term 'applicable manufacturer' means a manufacturer of a covered drug, device, biological, or medical supply which is operating in the United States, or in a territory, possession, or commonwealth of the United States.

"(3) CLINICAL INVESTIGATION.—The term 'clinical investigation' means any experiment involving 1 or more human subjects, or materials derived from human subjects, in which a drug or device is administered, dispensed, or used.

"(4) COVERED DEVICE.—The term 'covered device' means any device for which payment is available under title XVIII or a State plan under title XIX or XXI (or a waiver of such a plan).

"(5) COVERED DRUG, DEVICE, BIOLOGICAL, OR MEDICAL SUPPLY.—The term 'covered drug, device, biological, or medical supply' means any drug, biological product, device, or medical supply for which payment is available under title XVIII or a State plan under title XIX or XXI (or a waiver of such a plan).

"(6) COVERED RECIPIENT.—

"(A) IN GENERAL.—Except as provided in subparagraph (B), the term 'covered recipient' means the following:

"(i) A physician.

"(ii) A teaching hospital.

"(B) EXCLUSION.—Such term does not include a physician who is an employee of the applicable manufacturer that is required to submit information under subsection (a).

"(7) EMPLOYEE.—The term 'employee' has the meaning given such term in section 1877(h)(2).

"(8) KNOWINGLY.—The term 'knowingly' has the meaning given such term in section 3729(b) of title 31, United States Code.

"(9) MANUFACTURER OF A COVERED DRUG, DEVICE, BIOLOGICAL, OR MEDICAL SUPPLY.—The term 'manufacturer of a covered drug, device, biological, or medical supply' means any entity which is engaged in the production, preparation, propagation, compounding, or conversion of a covered drug, device, biological, or medical supply (or any entity under common ownership with such entity which provides assistance or support to such entity with respect to the production, preparation, propagation, compounding, conversion, marketing, promotion, sale, or distribution of a covered drug, device, biological, or medical supply).

"(10) PAYMENT OR OTHER TRANSFER OF VALUE.—

"(A) IN GENERAL.—The term 'payment or other transfer of value' means a transfer of anything of value. Such term does not include a transfer of anything of value that is made indirectly to a covered recipient through a third party in connection with an activity or service in the case where the applicable manufacturer is unaware of the identity of the covered recipient.

"(B) EXCLUSIONS.—An applicable manufacturer shall not be required to submit information under subsection (a) with respect to the following:

"(i) A transfer of anything the value of which is less than $10, unless the aggregate amount transferred to, requested by, or designated on behalf of the covered recipient by the applicable manufacturer during the calendar year exceeds $100. For calendar years after 2012, the dollar amounts specified in the preceding sentence shall be increased by the same percentage as the percentage increase in the consumer price index for all urban consumers (all items; U.S. city average) for the 12-month period ending with June of the previous year.

"(ii) Product samples that are not intended to be sold and are intended for patient use.

"(iii) Educational materials that directly benefit patients or are intended for patient use.

"(iv) The loan of a covered device for a short-term trial period, not to exceed 90 days, to permit evaluation of the covered device by the covered recipient.

"(v) Items or services provided under a contractual warranty, including the replacement of a covered device, where the terms of the warranty are set forth in the purchase or lease agreement for the covered device.

"(vi) A transfer of anything of value to a covered recipient when the covered recipient is a patient and not acting in the professional capacity of a covered recipient.

"(vii) Discounts (including rebates).

"(viii) In-kind items used for the provision of charity care.

"(ix) A dividend or other profit distribution from, or ownership or investment interest in, a publicly traded security and mutual fund (as described in section 1877(c)).

"(x) In the case of an applicable manufacturer who offers a self-insured plan, payments for the provision of health care to employees under the plan.

"(xi) In the case of a covered recipient who is a licensed non-medical professional, a transfer of anything of value to the covered recipient if the transfer is payment solely for the non-medical professional services of such licensed non-medical professional.

"(xii) In the case of a covered recipient who is a physician, a transfer of anything of value to the covered recipient if the transfer is payment solely for the services of the covered recipient with respect to a civil or criminal action or an administrative proceeding.

"(11) PHYSICIAN.—The term 'physician' has the meaning given that term in section 1861(r).".

SEC. 6003. DISCLOSURE REQUIREMENTS FOR IN-OFFICE ANCILLARY SERVICES EXCEPTION TO THE PROHIBITION ON PHYSICIAN SELF-REFERRAL FOR CERTAIN IMAGING SERVICES.

(a) IN GENERAL.—Section 1877(b)(2) of the Social Security Act (42 U.S.C. 1395nn(b)(2)) is amended by adding at the end the following new sentence: "Such requirements shall, with respect to magnetic resonance imaging, computed tomography, positron emission tomography, and any other designated health services specified under subsection (h)(6)(D) that the Secretary determines appropriate, include a requirement that the referring physician inform the individual in writing at the time of the referral that the individual may obtain the services for which the individual is being referred from a person other than a person described in subparagraph (A)(i) and provide such individual with a written list of suppliers (as defined in section 1861(d)) who furnish such services in the area in which such individual resides.".

(b) EFFECTIVE DATE.—The amendment made by this section shall apply to services furnished on or after January 1, 2010.

SEC. 6004. PRESCRIPTION DRUG SAMPLE TRANSPARENCY.

Part A of title XI of the Social Security Act (42 U.S.C. 1301 et seq.), as amended by section 6002, is amended by inserting after section 1128G the following new section:

"SEC. 1128H. REPORTING OF INFORMATION RELATING TO DRUG SAMPLES.

"(a) IN GENERAL.—Not later than April 1 of each year (beginning with 2012), each manufacturer and authorized distributor of record of an applicable drug shall submit to the Secretary (in a form and manner specified by the Secretary) the following information with respect to the preceding year:

"(1) In the case of a manufacturer or authorized distributor of record which makes distributions by mail or common carrier under subsection (d)(2) of section 503 of the Federal Food, Drug, and Cosmetic Act (21 U.S.C. 353), the identity and quantity of drug samples requested and the identity and quantity of drug samples distributed under such subsection during that year, aggregated by—

"(A) the name, address, professional designation, and signature of the practitioner making the request under subparagraph (A)(i) of such subsection, or of any individual who makes or signs for the request on behalf of the practitioner; and

"(B) any other category of information determined appropriate by the Secretary.

"(2) In the case of a manufacturer or authorized distributor of record which makes distributions by means other than mail or common carrier under subsection (d)(3) of such section 503, the identity and quantity of drug samples requested and the identity and quantity of drug samples distributed under such subsection during that year, aggregated by—

"(A) the name, address, professional designation, and signature of the practitioner making the request under subparagraph (A)(i) of such subsection, or of any individual who makes or signs for the request on behalf of the practitioner; and

"(B) any other category of information determined appropriate by the Secretary.

"(b) DEFINITIONS.—In this section:

"(1) APPLICABLE DRUG.—The term 'applicable drug' means a drug—

"(A) which is subject to subsection (b) of such section 503; and

"(B) for which payment is available under title XVIII or a State plan under title XIX or XXI (or a waiver of such a plan).

"(2) AUTHORIZED DISTRIBUTOR OF RECORD.—The term 'authorized distributor of record' has the meaning given that term in subsection (e)(3)(A) of such section.

"(3) MANUFACTURER.—The term 'manufacturer' has the meaning given that term for purposes of subsection (d) of such section.".

SEC. 6005. PHARMACY BENEFIT MANAGERS TRANSPARENCY REQUIREMENTS.

Part A of title XI of the Social Security Act (42 U.S.C. 1301 et seq.) is amended by inserting after section 1150 the following new section:

"SEC. 1150A. PHARMACY BENEFIT MANAGERS TRANSPARENCY REQUIREMENTS.

"(a) PROVISION OF INFORMATION.—A health benefits plan or any entity that provides pharmacy benefits management services on behalf of a health benefits plan (in this section referred to as a 'PBM') that manages prescription drug coverage under a contract with—

"(1) a PDP sponsor of a prescription drug plan or an MA organization offering an MA–PD plan under part D of title XVIII; or

"(2) a qualified health benefits plan offered through an exchange established by a State under section 1311 of the Patient Protection and Affordable Care Act,

shall provide the information described in subsection (b) to the Secretary and, in the case of a PBM, to the plan with which the PBM is under contract with, at such times, and in such form and manner, as the Secretary shall specify.

"(b) INFORMATION DESCRIBED.—The information described in this subsection is the following with respect to services provided by a health benefits plan or PBM for a contract year:

"(1) The percentage of all prescriptions that were provided through retail pharmacies compared to mail order pharmacies, and the percentage of prescriptions for which a generic drug was available and dispensed (generic dispensing rate), by pharmacy type (which includes an independent pharmacy, chain pharmacy, supermarket pharmacy, or mass merchandiser pharmacy that is licensed as a pharmacy by the State and that dispenses medication to the general public), that is paid by the health benefits plan or PBM under the contract.

"(2) The aggregate amount, and the type of rebates, discounts, or price concessions (excluding bona fide service fees, which include but are not limited to distribution service fees, inventory management fees, product stocking allowances, and fees associated with administrative services agreements and patient care programs (such as medication compliance programs and patient education programs)) that the PBM negotiates that are attributable to patient utilization under the plan, and the aggregate amount of the rebates, discounts, or price concessions that are passed through to the plan sponsor, and the total number of prescriptions that were dispensed.

"(3) The aggregate amount of the difference between the amount the health benefits plan pays the PBM and the amount that the PBM pays retail pharmacies, and mail order pharmacies, and the total number of prescriptions that were dispensed.

"(c) CONFIDENTIALITY.—Information disclosed by a health benefits plan or PBM under this section is confidential and shall not be disclosed by the Secretary or by a plan receiving the information, except that the Secretary may disclose the information in a form which does not disclose the identity of a specific PBM, plan, or prices charged for drugs, for the following purposes:

"(1) As the Secretary determines to be necessary to carry out this section or part D of title XVIII.

"(2) To permit the Comptroller General to review the information provided.

"(3) To permit the Director of the Congressional Budget Office to review the information provided.

"(4) To States to carry out section 1311 of the Patient Protection and Affordable Care Act.

"(d) PENALTIES.—The provisions of subsection (b)(3)(C) of section 1927 shall apply to a health benefits plan or PBM that fails to provide information required under subsection (a) on a timely basis or that knowingly provides false information in the same manner as such provisions apply to a manufacturer with an agreement under that section.".

Subtitle B—Nursing Home Transparency and Improvement

PART I—IMPROVING TRANSPARENCY OF INFORMATION

SEC. 6101. REQUIRED DISCLOSURE OF OWNERSHIP AND ADDITIONAL DISCLOSABLE PARTIES INFORMATION.

(a) IN GENERAL.—Section 1124 of the Social Security Act (42 U.S.C. 1320a–3) is amended by adding at the end the following new subsection:

"(c) REQUIRED DISCLOSURE OF OWNERSHIP AND ADDITIONAL DISCLOSABLE PARTIES INFORMATION.—

"(1) DISCLOSURE.—A facility shall have the information described in paragraph (2) available—

"(A) during the period beginning on the date of the enactment of this subsection and ending on the date such information is made available to the public under section 6101(b) of the Patient Protection and Affordable Care Act for submission to the Secretary, the Inspector General of the Department of Health and Human Services, the State in which the facility is located, and the State long-term care ombudsman in the case where the Secretary, the

Inspector General, the State, or the State long-term care ombudsman requests such information; and

"(B) beginning on the effective date of the final regulations promulgated under paragraph (3)(A), for reporting such information in accordance with such final regulations.

Nothing in subparagraph (A) shall be construed as authorizing a facility to dispose of or delete information described in such subparagraph after the effective date of the final regulations promulgated under paragraph (3)(A).

"(2) INFORMATION DESCRIBED.—

"(A) IN GENERAL.—The following information is described in this paragraph:

"(i) The information described in subsections (a) and (b), subject to subparagraph (C).

"(ii) The identity of and information on—

"(I) each member of the governing body of the facility, including the name, title, and period of service of each such member;

"(II) each person or entity who is an officer, director, member, partner, trustee, or managing employee of the facility, including the name, title, and period of service of each such person or entity; and

"(III) each person or entity who is an additional disclosable party of the facility.

"(iii) The organizational structure of each additional disclosable party of the facility and a description of the relationship of each such additional disclosable party to the facility and to one another.

"(B) SPECIAL RULE WHERE INFORMATION IS ALREADY REPORTED OR SUBMITTED.—To the extent that information reported by a facility to the Internal Revenue Service on Form 990, information submitted by a facility to the Securities and Exchange Commission, or information otherwise submitted to the Secretary or any other Federal agency contains the information described in clauses (i), (ii), or (iii) of subparagraph (A), the facility may provide such Form or such information submitted to meet the requirements of paragraph (1).

"(C) SPECIAL RULE.—In applying subparagraph (A)(i)—

"(i) with respect to subsections (a) and (b), 'ownership or control interest' shall include direct or indirect interests, including such interests in intermediate entities; and

"(ii) subsection (a)(3)(A)(ii) shall include the owner of a whole or part interest in any mortgage, deed of trust, note, or other obligation secured, in whole or in part, by the entity or any of the property or assets thereof, if the interest is equal to or exceeds 5 percent of the total property or assets of the entirety.

"(3) REPORTING.—

"(A) IN GENERAL.—Not later than the date that is 2 years after the date of the enactment of this subsection, the Secretary shall promulgate final regulations requiring, effective on the date that is 90 days after the date on which such final regulations are published in the Federal Register, a facility to report the information described in paragraph (2) to the Secretary in a standardized format, and such other regulations as are necessary to carry out this subsection. Such final regulations shall ensure that the facility certifies, as a condition of participation and payment under the program under title XVIII or XIX, that the information reported by the facility in accordance with such final regulations is, to the best of the facility's knowledge, accurate and current.

"(B) GUIDANCE.—The Secretary shall provide guidance and technical assistance to States on how to adopt the standardized format under subparagraph (A).

"(4) NO EFFECT ON EXISTING REPORTING REQUIREMENTS.— Nothing in this subsection shall reduce, diminish, or alter any reporting requirement for a facility that is in effect as of the date of the enactment of this subsection.

"(5) DEFINITIONS.—In this subsection:

"(A) ADDITIONAL DISCLOSABLE PARTY.—The term 'additional disclosable party' means, with respect to a facility, any person or entity who—

"(i) exercises operational, financial, or managerial control over the facility or a part thereof, or provides policies or procedures for any of the operations of the facility, or provides financial or cash management services to the facility;

"(ii) leases or subleases real property to the facility, or owns a whole or part interest equal to or exceeding 5 percent of the total value of such real property; or

"(iii) provides management or administrative services, management or clinical consulting services, or accounting or financial services to the facility.

"(B) FACILITY.—The term 'facility' means a disclosing entity which is—

"(i) a skilled nursing facility (as defined in section 1819(a)); or

"(ii) a nursing facility (as defined in section 1919(a)).

"(C) MANAGING EMPLOYEE.—The term 'managing employee' means, with respect to a facility, an individual (including a general manager, business manager, administrator, director, or consultant) who directly or indirectly manages, advises, or supervises any element of the practices, finances, or operations of the facility.

"(D) ORGANIZATIONAL STRUCTURE.—The term 'organizational structure' means, in the case of—

"(i) a corporation, the officers, directors, and shareholders of the corporation who have an ownership interest in the corporation which is equal to or exceeds 5 percent;

"(ii) a limited liability company, the members and managers of the limited liability company (including, as applicable, what percentage each member and manager has of the ownership interest in the limited liability company);

"(iii) a general partnership, the partners of the general partnership;

"(iv) a limited partnership, the general partners and any limited partners of the limited partnership who have an ownership interest in the limited partnership which is equal to or exceeds 10 percent;

"(v) a trust, the trustees of the trust;

"(vi) an individual, contact information for the individual; and

"(vii) any other person or entity, such information as the Secretary determines appropriate.".

(b) PUBLIC AVAILABILITY OF INFORMATION.—Not later than the date that is 1 year after the date on which the final regulations promulgated under section 1124(c)(3)(A) of the Social Security Act, as added by subsection (a), are published in the Federal Register, the Secretary of Health and Human Services shall make the information reported in accordance with such final regulations available to the public in accordance with procedures established by the Secretary.

(c) CONFORMING AMENDMENTS.—

(1) IN GENERAL.—

(A) SKILLED NURSING FACILITIES.—Section 1819(d)(1) of the Social Security Act (42 U.S.C. 1395i–3(d)(1)) is amended by striking subparagraph (B) and redesignating subparagraph (C) as subparagraph (B).

(B) NURSING FACILITIES.—Section 1919(d)(1) of the Social Security Act (42 U.S.C. 1396r(d)(1)) is amended by striking subparagraph (B) and redesignating subparagraph (C) as subparagraph (B).

(2) EFFECTIVE DATE.—The amendments made by paragraph (1) shall take effect on the date on which the Secretary makes the information described in subsection (b)(1) available to the public under such subsection.

SEC. 6102. ACCOUNTABILITY REQUIREMENTS FOR SKILLED NURSING FACILITIES AND NURSING FACILITIES.

Part A of title XI of the Social Security Act (42 U.S.C. 1301 et seq.), as amended by sections 6002 and 6004, is amended by inserting after section 1128H the following new section:

"SEC. 1128I. ACCOUNTABILITY REQUIREMENTS FOR FACILITIES.

"(a) DEFINITION OF FACILITY.—In this section, the term 'facility' means—

"(1) a skilled nursing facility (as defined in section 1819(a)); or

"(2) a nursing facility (as defined in section 1919(a)).

"(b) EFFECTIVE COMPLIANCE AND ETHICS PROGRAMS.—

"(1) REQUIREMENT.—On or after the date that is 36 months after the date of the enactment of this section, a facility shall, with respect to the entity that operates the facility (in this subparagraph referred to as the 'operating organization' or 'organization'), have in operation a compliance and ethics program that is effective in preventing and detecting criminal, civil, and administrative violations under this Act and in promoting quality of care consistent with regulations developed under paragraph (2).

"(2) DEVELOPMENT OF REGULATIONS.—

"(A) IN GENERAL.—Not later than the date that is 2 years after such date of the enactment, the Secretary, working jointly with the Inspector General of the Department of Health and Human Services, shall promulgate regulations for an effective compliance and ethics program for operating organizations, which may include a model compliance program.

"(B) DESIGN OF REGULATIONS.—Such regulations with respect to specific elements or formality of a program shall, in the case of an organization that operates 5 or more facilities, vary with the size of the organization, such that larger organizations should have a more formal program and include established written policies defining the standards and procedures to be followed by its employees. Such requirements may specifically apply to the corporate level management of multi unit nursing home chains.

"(C) EVALUATION.—Not later than 3 years after the date of the promulgation of regulations under this paragraph, the Secretary shall complete an evaluation of the compliance and ethics programs required to be established under this subsection. Such evaluation shall determine if such programs led to changes in deficiency citations, changes in quality performance, or changes in other metrics of patient quality of care. The Secretary shall submit to Congress a report on such evaluation and shall include in such report such recommendations regarding changes in the requirements for such programs as the Secretary determines appropriate.

"(3) REQUIREMENTS FOR COMPLIANCE AND ETHICS PROGRAMS.—In this subsection, the term 'compliance and ethics program' means, with respect to a facility, a program of the operating organization that—

"(A) has been reasonably designed, implemented, and enforced so that it generally will be effective in preventing and detecting criminal, civil, and administrative violations under this Act and in promoting quality of care; and

"(B) includes at least the required components specified in paragraph (4).

"(4) REQUIRED COMPONENTS OF PROGRAM.—The required components of a compliance and ethics program of an operating organization are the following:

"(A) The organization must have established compliance standards and procedures to be followed by its employees and other agents that are reasonably capable of reducing the prospect of criminal, civil, and administrative violations under this Act.

"(B) Specific individuals within high-level personnel of the organization must have been assigned overall responsibility to oversee compliance with such standards and procedures and have sufficient resources and authority to assure such compliance.

"(C) The organization must have used due care not to delegate substantial discretionary authority to individuals whom the organization knew, or should have known through the exercise of due diligence, had a propensity to engage in criminal, civil, and administrative violations under this Act.

"(D) The organization must have taken steps to communicate effectively its standards and procedures to all employees and other agents, such as by requiring participation in training programs or by disseminating publications that explain in a practical manner what is required.

"(E) The organization must have taken reasonable steps to achieve compliance with its standards, such as by utilizing monitoring and auditing systems reasonably designed to detect criminal, civil, and administrative violations under this Act by its employees and other agents and by having in place and publicizing a reporting system whereby employees and other agents could report violations by others within the organization without fear of retribution.

"(F) The standards must have been consistently enforced through appropriate disciplinary mechanisms, including, as appropriate, discipline of individuals responsible for the failure to detect an offense.

"(G) After an offense has been detected, the organization must have taken all reasonable steps to respond appropriately to the offense and to prevent further similar offenses, including any necessary modification to its program to prevent and detect criminal, civil, and administrative violations under this Act.

"(H) The organization must periodically undertake reassessment of its compliance program to identify changes necessary to reflect changes within the organization and its facilities.

"(c) QUALITY ASSURANCE AND PERFORMANCE IMPROVEMENT PROGRAM.—

"(1) IN GENERAL.—Not later than December 31, 2011, the Secretary shall establish and implement a quality assurance and performance improvement program (in this subparagraph referred to as the 'QAPI program') for facilities, including multi unit chains of facilities. Under the QAPI program, the Secretary shall establish standards relating to quality assurance and performance improvement with respect to facilities and provide technical assistance to facilities on the development of best practices in order to meet such standards. Not later than 1 year after the date on which the regulations are promulgated under paragraph (2), a facility must submit to the Secretary a plan for the facility to meet such standards and implement such best practices, including how to coordinate the implementation of such plan with quality assessment and assurance activities conducted under sections 1819(b)(1)(B) and 1919(b)(1)(B), as applicable.

"(2) REGULATIONS.—The Secretary shall promulgate regulations to carry out this subsection.".

SEC. 6103. NURSING HOME COMPARE MEDICARE WEBSITE.

(a) SKILLED NURSING FACILITIES.—

(1) IN GENERAL.—Section 1819 of the Social Security Act (42 U.S.C. 1395i–3) is amended—

(A) by redesignating subsection (i) as subsection (j); and

(B) by inserting after subsection (h) the following new subsection:

"(i) NURSING HOME COMPARE WEBSITE.—

"(1) INCLUSION OF ADDITIONAL INFORMATION.—

"(A) IN GENERAL.—The Secretary shall ensure that the Department of Health and Human Services includes, as part of the information provided for comparison of nursing homes on the official Internet website of the Federal Government for Medicare beneficiaries (commonly referred to as the 'Nursing Home Compare' Medicare website) (or a successor website), the following information in a manner that is prominent, updated on a timely basis, easily accessible, readily understandable to consumers of long-term care services, and searchable:

"(i) Staffing data for each facility (including resident census data and data on the hours of care provided per resident per day) based on data submitted under section 1128I(g), including information on staffing turnover and tenure, in a format that is clearly understandable to consumers of long-term care services and allows such consumers to compare differences in staffing between facilities and State and national averages for the facilities. Such format shall include—

"(I) concise explanations of how to interpret the data (such as a plain English explanation of data reflecting 'nursing home staff hours per resident day');

"(II) differences in types of staff (such as training associated with different categories of staff);

"(III) the relationship between nurse staffing levels and quality of care; and

"(IV) an explanation that appropriate staffing levels vary based on patient case mix.

"(ii) Links to State Internet websites with information regarding State survey and certification programs, links to Form 2567 State inspection reports (or a successor form) on such websites, information to guide consumers in how to interpret and understand such reports, and the facility plan of correction or other response to such report. Any such links shall be posted on a timely basis.

"(iii) The standardized complaint form developed under section 1128I(f), including explanatory material on what complaint forms are, how they are used, and how to file a complaint with the State survey and certification program and the State long-term care ombudsman program.

"(iv) Summary information on the number, type, severity, and outcome of substantiated complaints.

"(v) The number of adjudicated instances of criminal violations by a facility or the employees of a facility—

"(I) that were committed inside the facility;

"(II) with respect to such instances of violations or crimes committed inside of the facility that were the violations or crimes of abuse, neglect, and exploitation, criminal sexual abuse, or other violations or crimes that resulted in serious bodily injury; and

"(III) the number of civil monetary penalties levied against the facility, employees, contractors, and other agents.

"(B) DEADLINE FOR PROVISION OF INFORMATION.—

"(i) IN GENERAL.—Except as provided in clause (ii), the Secretary shall ensure that the information described in subparagraph (A) is included on such website (or a successor website) not later than 1 year after the date of the enactment of this subsection.

"(ii) EXCEPTION.—The Secretary shall ensure that the information described in subparagraph (A)(i) is included on such website (or a successor website) not later than the date on which the requirements under section 1128I(g) are implemented.

"(2) REVIEW AND MODIFICATION OF WEBSITE.—

"(A) IN GENERAL.—The Secretary shall establish a process—

"(i) to review the accuracy, clarity of presentation, timeliness, and comprehensiveness of information reported on such website as of the day before the date of the enactment of this subsection; and

"(ii) not later than 1 year after the date of the enactment of this subsection, to modify or revamp such website in accordance with the review conducted under clause (i).

"(B) CONSULTATION.—In conducting the review under subparagraph (A)(i), the Secretary shall consult with—

"(i) State long-term care ombudsman programs;

"(ii) consumer advocacy groups;

"(iii) provider stakeholder groups; and

"(iv) any other representatives of programs or groups the Secretary determines appropriate.".

(2) TIMELINESS OF SUBMISSION OF SURVEY AND CERTIFICATION INFORMATION.—

(A) IN GENERAL.—Section 1819(g)(5) of the Social Security Act (42 U.S.C. 1395i–3(g)(5)) is amended by adding at the end the following new subparagraph:

"(E) SUBMISSION OF SURVEY AND CERTIFICATION INFORMATION TO THE SECRETARY.—In order to improve the timeliness of information made available to the public under subparagraph (A) and provided on the Nursing Home Compare Medicare website under subsection (i), each State shall submit information respecting any survey or certification made respecting a skilled nursing facility (including any enforcement actions taken by the State) to the Secretary not later than the date on which the State sends such information to the facility. The Secretary shall use the information submitted under the preceding sentence to update the information provided on the Nursing Home Compare Medicare website as expeditiously as practicable but not less frequently than quarterly.".

(B) EFFECTIVE DATE.—The amendment made by this paragraph shall take effect 1 year after the date of the enactment of this Act.

(3) SPECIAL FOCUS FACILITY PROGRAM.—Section 1819(f) of the Social Security Act (42 U.S.C. 1395i–3(f)) is amended by adding at the end the following new paragraph:

"(8) SPECIAL FOCUS FACILITY PROGRAM.—

"(A) IN GENERAL.—The Secretary shall conduct a special focus facility program for enforcement of requirements for skilled nursing facilities that the Secretary has identified as having substantially failed to meet applicable requirement of this Act.

"(B) PERIODIC SURVEYS.—Under such program the Secretary shall conduct surveys of each facility in the program not less than once every 6 months.".

(b) NURSING FACILITIES.—

(1) IN GENERAL.—Section 1919 of the Social Security Act (42 U.S.C. 1396r) is amended—

(A) by redesignating subsection (i) as subsection (j); and

(B) by inserting after subsection (h) the following new subsection:

"(i) NURSING HOME COMPARE WEBSITE.—

"(1) INCLUSION OF ADDITIONAL INFORMATION.—

"(A) IN GENERAL.—The Secretary shall ensure that the Department of Health and Human Services includes, as part of the information provided for comparison of nursing homes on the official Internet website of the Federal Government for Medicare beneficiaries (commonly referred to as the 'Nursing Home Compare' Medicare website) (or a successor website), the following information in a manner that is prominent, updated on a timely basis, easily accessible, readily understandable to consumers of long-term care services, and searchable:

"(i) Staffing data for each facility (including resident census data and data on the hours of care provided per resident per day) based on data submitted under section 1128I(g), including information on staffing turnover and tenure, in a format that is clearly understandable to consumers of long-term care services and allows such consumers to compare differences in staffing between facilities and State and national averages for the facilities. Such format shall include—

"(I) concise explanations of how to interpret the data (such as plain English explanation of data reflecting 'nursing home staff hours per resident day');

"(II) differences in types of staff (such as training associated with different categories of staff);

"(III) the relationship between nurse staffing levels and quality of care; and

"(IV) an explanation that appropriate staffing levels vary based on patient case mix.

"(ii) Links to State Internet websites with information regarding State survey and certification programs, links to Form 2567 State inspection reports (or a successor form) on such websites, information to guide consumers in how to interpret and understand such reports, and the facility plan of correction or other response to such report. Any such links shall be posted on a timely basis.

"(iii) The standardized complaint form developed under section 1128I(f), including explanatory material on what complaint forms are, how they are used, and how to file a complaint with the State survey and certification program and the State long-term care ombudsman program.

"(iv) Summary information on the number, type, severity, and outcome of substantiated complaints.

"(v) The number of adjudicated instances of criminal violations by a facility or the employees of a facility—

"(I) that were committed inside of the facility; and

"(II) with respect to such instances of violations or crimes committed outside of the facility, that were violations or crimes that resulted in the serious bodily injury of an elder.

"(B) DEADLINE FOR PROVISION OF INFORMATION.—

"(i) IN GENERAL.—Except as provided in clause (ii), the Secretary shall ensure that the information described in subparagraph (A) is included on such website (or a successor website) not later than 1 year after the date of the enactment of this subsection.

"(ii) EXCEPTION.—The Secretary shall ensure that the information described in subparagraph (A)(i) is included on such website (or a successor website) not later than the date on which the requirements under section 1128I(g) are implemented.

"(2) REVIEW AND MODIFICATION OF WEBSITE.—

"(A) IN GENERAL.—The Secretary shall establish a process—

"(i) to review the accuracy, clarity of presentation, timeliness, and comprehensiveness of information reported on such website as of the day before the date of the enactment of this subsection; and

"(ii) not later than 1 year after the date of the enactment of this subsection, to modify or revamp such website in accordance with the review conducted under clause (i).

"(B) CONSULTATION.—In conducting the review under subparagraph (A)(i), the Secretary shall consult with—

"(i) State long-term care ombudsman programs;

"(ii) consumer advocacy groups;

"(iii) provider stakeholder groups;

"(iv) skilled nursing facility employees and their representatives; and

"(v) any other representatives of programs or groups the Secretary determines appropriate.".

(2) TIMELINESS OF SUBMISSION OF SURVEY AND CERTIFICATION INFORMATION.—

(A) IN GENERAL.—Section 1919(g)(5) of the Social Security Act (42 U.S.C. 1396r(g)(5)) is amended by adding at the end the following new subparagraph:

"(E) SUBMISSION OF SURVEY AND CERTIFICATION INFORMATION TO THE SECRETARY.—In order to improve the timeliness of information made available to the public under subparagraph (A) and provided on the Nursing Home

Compare Medicare website under subsection (i), each State shall submit information respecting any survey or certification made respecting a nursing facility (including any enforcement actions taken by the State) to the Secretary not later than the date on which the State sends such information to the facility. The Secretary shall use the information submitted under the preceding sentence to update the information provided on the Nursing Home Compare Medicare website as expeditiously as practicable but not less frequently than quarterly.".

(B) EFFECTIVE DATE.—The amendment made by this paragraph shall take effect 1 year after the date of the enactment of this Act.

(3) SPECIAL FOCUS FACILITY PROGRAM.—Section 1919(f) of the Social Security Act (42 U.S.C. 1396r(f)) is amended by adding at the end of the following new paragraph:

"(10) SPECIAL FOCUS FACILITY PROGRAM.—

"(A) IN GENERAL.—The Secretary shall conduct a special focus facility program for enforcement of requirements for nursing facilities that the Secretary has identified as having substantially failed to meet applicable requirements of this Act.

"(B) PERIODIC SURVEYS.—Under such program the Secretary shall conduct surveys of each facility in the program not less often than once every 6 months.".

(c) AVAILABILITY OF REPORTS ON SURVEYS, CERTIFICATIONS, AND COMPLAINT INVESTIGATIONS.—

(1) SKILLED NURSING FACILITIES.—Section 1819(d)(1) of the Social Security Act (42 U.S.C. 1395i–3(d)(1)), as amended by section 6101, is amended by adding at the end the following new subparagraph:

"(C) AVAILABILITY OF SURVEY, CERTIFICATION, AND COMPLAINT INVESTIGATION REPORTS.—A skilled nursing facility must—

"(i) have reports with respect to any surveys, certifications, and complaint investigations made respecting the facility during the 3 preceding years available for any individual to review upon request; and

"(ii) post notice of the availability of such reports in areas of the facility that are prominent and accessible to the public.

The facility shall not make available under clause (i) identifying information about complainants or residents.".

(2) NURSING FACILITIES.—Section 1919(d)(1) of the Social Security Act (42 U.S.C. 1396r(d)(1)), as amended by section 6101, is amended by adding at the end the following new subparagraph:

"(V) AVAILABILITY OF SURVEY, CERTIFICATION, AND COMPLAINT INVESTIGATION REPORTS.—A nursing facility must—

"(i) have reports with respect to any surveys, certifications, and complaint investigations made respecting the facility during the 3 preceding years available for any individual to review upon request; and "(ii) post notice of the availability of such reports in areas of the facility that are prominent and accessible to the public.

The facility shall not make available under clause (i) identifying information about complainants or residents.".

(3) EFFECTIVE DATE.—The amendments made by this subsection shall take effect 1 year after the date of the enactment of this Act.

(d) GUIDANCE TO STATES ON FORM 2567 STATE INSPECTION REPORTS AND COMPLAINT INVESTIGATION REPORTS.—

(1) GUIDANCE.—The Secretary of Health and Human Services (in this subtitle referred to as the "Secretary") shall provide guidance to States on how States can establish electronic links to Form 2567 State inspection reports (or a successor form), complaint investigation reports, and a facility's plan of correction or other response to such Form 2567 State inspection reports (or a successor form) on the Internet website of the State that provides information on skilled nursing facilities and nursing facilities and the Secretary shall, if possible, include such information on Nursing Home Compare.

(2) REQUIREMENT.—Section 1902(a)(9) of the Social Security Act (42 U.S.C. 1396a(a)(9)) is amended—

(A) by striking "and" at the end of subparagraph (B);

(B) by striking the semicolon at the end of subparagraph (C) and inserting ", and"; and

(C) by adding at the end the following new subparagraph:

"(D) that the State maintain a consumer-oriented website providing useful information to consumers regarding all skilled nursing facilities and all nursing facilities in the State, including for each facility, Form 2567 State inspection reports (or a successor form), complaint investigation reports, the facility's plan of correction, and such other information that the State or the Secretary considers useful in assisting the public to assess the quality of long term care options and the quality of care provided by individual facilities;".

(3) DEFINITIONS.—In this subsection:

(A) NURSING FACILITY.—The term "nursing facility" has the meaning given such term in section 1919(a) of the Social Security Act (42 U.S.C. 1396r(a)).

(B) SECRETARY.—The term "Secretary" means the Secretary of Health and Human Services.

(C) SKILLED NURSING FACILITY.—The term "skilled nursing facility" has the meaning given such term in section 1819(a) of the Social Security Act (42 U.S.C. 1395i–3(a)).

(e) DEVELOPMENT OF CONSUMER RIGHTS INFORMATION PAGE ON NURSING HOME COMPARE WEBSITE.—Not later than 1 year after the date of enactment of this Act, the Secretary shall ensure that the Department of Health and Human Services, as part of the information provided for comparison of nursing facilities on the Nursing Home Compare Medicare website develops and includes a consumer rights information page that contains links to descriptions of, and information with respect to, the following:

(1) The documentation on nursing facilities that is available to the public.

(2) General information and tips on choosing a nursing facility that meets the needs of the individual.

(3) General information on consumer rights with respect to nursing facilities.

(4) The nursing facility survey process (on a national and State-specific basis).

(5) On a State-specific basis, the services available through the State long-term care ombudsman for such State.

SEC. 6104. REPORTING OF EXPENDITURES.

Section 1888 of the Social Security Act (42 U.S.C. 1395yy) is amended by adding at the end the following new subsection:

"(f) REPORTING OF DIRECT CARE EXPENDITURES.—

"(1) IN GENERAL.—For cost reports submitted under this title for cost reporting periods beginning on or after the date that is 2 years after the date of the enactment of this subsection, skilled nursing facilities shall separately report expenditures for wages and benefits for direct care staff (breaking out (at a minimum) registered nurses, licensed professional nurses, certified nurse assistants, and other medical and therapy staff).

"(2) MODIFICATION OF FORM.—The Secretary, in consultation with private sector accountants experienced with Medicare and Medicaid nursing facility home cost reports, shall redesign such reports to meet the requirement of paragraph (1) not later than 1 year after the date of the enactment of this subsection.

"(3) CATEGORIZATION BY FUNCTIONAL ACCOUNTS.—Not later than 30 months after the date of the enactment of this subsection, the Secretary, working in consultation with the Medicare Payment Advisory Commission, the Medicaid and CHIP Payment and Access Commission, the Inspector General of the Department of Health and Human Services, and other expert parties the Secretary determines appropriate, shall take the expenditures listed on cost reports, as modified under paragraph (1), submitted by skilled nursing facilities and categorize such expenditures, regardless of any source of payment for such expenditures, for each skilled nursing facility into the following functional accounts on an annual basis:

"(A) Spending on direct care services (including nursing, therapy, and medical services).

"(B) Spending on indirect care (including housekeeping and dietary services).

"(C) Capital assets (including building and land costs).

"(D) Administrative services costs.

"(4) AVAILABILITY OF INFORMATION SUBMITTED.—The Secretary shall establish procedures to make information on expenditures submitted under this subsection readily available to interested parties upon request, subject to such requirements as the Secretary may specify under the procedures established under this paragraph.".

SEC. 6105. STANDARDIZED COMPLAINT FORM.

(a) IN GENERAL.—Section 1128I of the Social Security Act, as added and amended by this Act, is amended by adding at the end the following new subsection:

"(f) STANDARDIZED COMPLAINT FORM.—

"(1) DEVELOPMENT BY THE SECRETARY.—The Secretary shall develop a standardized complaint form for use by a resident (or a person acting on the resident's behalf) in filing a complaint with a State survey and certification agency and a State long-term care ombudsman program with respect to a facility.

"(2) COMPLAINT FORMS AND RESOLUTION PROCESSES.—

"(A) COMPLAINT FORMS.—The State must make the standardized complaint form developed under paragraph (1) available upon request to—

"(i) a resident of a facility; and

"(ii) any person acting on the resident's behalf.

"(B) COMPLAINT RESOLUTION PROCESS.—The State must establish a complaint resolution process in order to ensure that the legal representative of a resident of a facility or other responsible party is not denied access to such resident or otherwise retaliated against if they have complained about the quality of care provided by the facility or other issues relating to the facility. Such complaint resolution process shall include—

"(i) procedures to assure accurate tracking of complaints received, including notification to the complainant that a complaint has been received;

"(ii) procedures to determine the likely severity of a complaint and for the investigation of the complaint; and

"(iii) deadlines for responding to a complaint and for notifying the complainant of the outcome of the investigation.

"(3) RULE OF CONSTRUCTION.—Nothing in this subsection shall be construed as preventing a resident of a facility (or a person acting on the resident's behalf) from submitting a complaint in a manner or format other than by using the standardized complaint form developed under paragraph (1) (including submitting a complaint orally).".

(b) EFFECTIVE DATE.—The amendment made by this section shall take effect 1 year after the date of the enactment of this Act.

SEC. 6106. ENSURING STAFFING ACCOUNTABILITY.

Section 1128I of the Social Security Act, as added and amended by this Act, is amended by adding at the end the following new subsection:

"(g) SUBMISSION OF STAFFING INFORMATION BASED ON PAYROLL DATA IN A UNIFORM FORMAT.—Beginning not later than 2 years after the date of the enactment of this subsection, and after consulting with State long-term care ombudsman programs, consumer advocacy groups, provider stakeholder groups, employees and their representatives, and other parties the Secretary deems appropriate, the Secretary shall require a facility to electronically submit to the Secretary direct care staffing information (including information with respect to agency and contract staff) based on payroll and other verifiable and auditable data in a uniform format (according to specifications established by the Secretary in consultation with such programs, groups, and parties). Such specifications shall require that the information submitted under the preceding sentence—

"(1) specify the category of work a certified employee performs (such as whether the employee is a registered nurse, licensed practical nurse, licensed vocational nurse, certified nursing assistant, therapist, or other medical personnel);

"(2) include resident census data and information on resident case mix;

"(3) include a regular reporting schedule; and

"(4) include information on employee turnover and tenure and on the hours of care provided by each category of certified employees referenced in paragraph (1) per resident per day.

Nothing in this subsection shall be construed as preventing the Secretary from requiring submission of such information with respect to specific categories, such as nursing staff, before other categories of certified employees. Information under this subsection with respect to agency and contract staff shall be kept separate from information on employee staffing.".

SEC. 6107. GAO STUDY AND REPORT ON FIVE-STAR QUALITY RATING SYSTEM.

(a) STUDY.—The Comptroller General of the United States (in this section referred to as the "Comptroller General") shall conduct a study on the Five-Star Quality Rating System for nursing homes of the Centers for Medicare & Medicaid Services. Such study shall include an analysis of—

(1) how such system is being implemented;

(2) any problems associated with such system or its implementation; and

(3) how such system could be improved.

(b) REPORT.—Not later than 2 years after the date of enactment of this Act, the Comptroller General shall submit to Congress a report containing the results of the study conducted under subsection (a), together with recommendations for such legislation and administrative action as the Comptroller General determines appropriate.

PART II—TARGETING ENFORCEMENT

SEC. 6111. CIVIL MONEY PENALTIES.

(a) SKILLED NURSING FACILITIES.—

(1) IN GENERAL.—Section 1819(h)(2)(B)(ii) of the Social Security Act (42 U.S.C. 1395i–3(h)(2)(B)(ii)) is amended—

(A) by striking "PENALTIES.—The Secretary" and inserting "PENALTIES.—

"(I) IN GENERAL.—Subject to subclause (II), the Secretary"; and

(B) by adding at the end the following new subclauses:

"(II) REDUCTION OF CIVIL MONEY PENALTIES IN CERTAIN CIRCUMSTANCES.—Subject to subclause (III), in the case where a facility self-reports and promptly corrects a deficiency for which a penalty was imposed under this clause not later than 10 calendar days after the date of such imposition, the Secretary may reduce the amount of the penalty imposed by not more than 50 percent.

"(III) PROHIBITIONS ON REDUCTION FOR CERTAIN DEFICIENCIES.—

"(aa) REPEAT DEFICIENCIES.—The Secretary may not reduce the amount of a penalty under subclause (II) if the Secretary had reduced a penalty imposed on the facility in the preceding year under such subclause with respect to a repeat deficiency.

"(bb) CERTAIN OTHER DEFICIENCIES.—The Secretary may not reduce the amount of a penalty under subclause (II) if the penalty is imposed on the facility for a deficiency that is found to result in a pattern of harm or widespread harm, immediately jeopardizes the health or safety of a resident or residents of the facility, or results in the death of a resident of the facility.

"(IV) COLLECTION OF CIVIL MONEY PENALTIES.—In the case of a civil money penalty imposed under this clause, the Secretary shall issue regulations that—

"(aa) subject to item (cc), not later than 30 days after the imposition of the penalty, provide for the facility to have the opportunity to participate in an independent informal dispute resolution process which generates a written record prior to the collection of such penalty;

"(bb) in the case where the penalty is imposed for each day of noncompliance, provide that a penalty may not be imposed for any day during the period beginning on the initial day of the imposition of the penalty and ending on the day on which the informal dispute resolution process under item (aa) is completed;

"(cc) may provide for the collection of such civil money penalty and the placement of such amounts collected in an escrow account under the direction of the Secretary on the earlier of the date on which the informal dispute resolution process under item (aa) is completed or the date that is 90 days after the date of the imposition of the penalty;

"(dd) may provide that such amounts collected are kept in such account pending the resolution of any subsequent appeals;

"(ee) in the case where the facility successfully appeals the penalty, may provide for the return of such amounts collected (plus interest) to the facility; and

"(ff) in the case where all such appeals are unsuccessful, may provide that some portion of such amounts collected may be used to support activities that benefit residents, including assistance to support and protect residents of a facility that closes (voluntarily or involuntarily) or is decertified (including offsetting costs of relocating residents to home and community-based settings or another facility), projects that support resident and family councils and other consumer involvement in assuring quality care in facilities, and facility improvement initiatives approved by the Secretary (including joint training of facility staff and surveyors, technical assistance for facilities implementing quality assurance programs, the appointment of temporary management firms, and other activities approved by the Secretary).".

(2) CONFORMING AMENDMENT.—The second sentence of section 1819(h)(5) of the Social Security Act (42 U.S.C. 1395i–3(h)(5)) is amended by inserting "(ii)(IV)," after "(i),".

(b) NURSING FACILITIES.—

(1) IN GENERAL.—Section 1919(h)(3)(C)(ii) of the Social Security Act (42 U.S.C. 1396r(h)(3)(C)) is amended—

(A) by striking "PENALTIES.—The Secretary" and inserting "PENALTIES.—

"(I) IN GENERAL.—Subject to subclause (II), the Secretary"; and

(B) by adding at the end the following new subclauses:

"(II) REDUCTION OF CIVIL MONEY PENALTIES IN CERTAIN CIRCUMSTANCES.—Subject to subclause (III), in the case where a facility self-reports and promptly corrects a deficiency for which a penalty was imposed under this clause not later than 10 calendar days after the date of such imposition, the Secretary may reduce the amount of the penalty imposed by not more than 50 percent.

"(III) PROHIBITIONS ON REDUCTION FOR CERTAIN DEFICIENCIES.—

"(aa) REPEAT DEFICIENCIES.—The Secretary may not reduce the amount of a penalty under subclause (II) if the Secretary had reduced a penalty imposed on the facility in the preceding year under such subclause with respect to a repeat deficiency.

"(bb) CERTAIN OTHER DEFICIENCIES.—The Secretary may not reduce the amount of a penalty under subclause (II) if the penalty is imposed on the facility for a deficiency that is found to result in a pattern of harm or widespread harm, immediately jeopardizes the health or safety of a resident or residents of the facility, or results in the death of a resident of the facility.

"(IV) COLLECTION OF CIVIL MONEY PENALTIES.—In the case of a civil money penalty imposed under this clause, the Secretary shall issue regulations that—

"(aa) subject to item (cc), not later than 30 days after the imposition of the penalty, provide for the facility to have the opportunity to participate in an independent informal dispute resolution process which generates a written record prior to the collection of such penalty;

"(bb) in the case where the penalty is imposed for each day of noncompliance, provide that a penalty may not be imposed for any day during the period beginning on the initial day of the imposition of the penalty and ending on the day on which the informal dispute resolution process under item (aa) is completed;

"(cc) may provide for the collection of such civil money penalty and the placement of such amounts collected in an escrow account under the direction of the Secretary on the earlier of the date on which the informal dispute resolution process under item (aa) is completed or the date that is 90 days after the date of the imposition of the penalty;

"(dd) may provide that such amounts collected are kept in such account pending the resolution of any subsequent appeals;

"(ee) in the case where the facility successfully appeals the penalty, may provide for the return of such amounts collected (plus interest) to the facility; and

"(ff) in the case where all such appeals are unsuccessful, may provide that some portion of such amounts collected may be used to support activities that benefit residents, including assistance to support and protect residents of a facility that closes (voluntarily or involuntarily) or is decertified (including offsetting costs of relocating residents to home and community-based settings or another facility), projects that support resident and family councils and other consumer involvement in assuring quality care in facilities, and facility improvement initiatives approved by the Secretary (including joint training of facility staff and surveyors, technical assistance for facilities implementing quality assurance programs, the appointment of temporary management firms, and other activities approved by the Secretary).".

(2) CONFORMING AMENDMENT.—Section 1919(h)(5)(8) of the Social Security Act (42 U.S.C. 1396r(h)(5)(8)) is amended by inserting "(ii)(IV)," after "(i),".

(c) EFFECTIVE DATE.—The amendments made by this section shall take effect 1 year after the date of the enactment of this Act.

SEC. 6112. NATIONAL INDEPENDENT MONITOR DEMONSTRATION PROJECT.

(a) ESTABLISHMENT.—

(1) IN GENERAL.—The Secretary, in consultation with the Inspector General of the Department of Health and Human Services, shall conduct a demonstration project to develop, test, and implement an independent monitor program to oversee

interstate and large intrastate chains of skilled nursing facilities and nursing facilities.

(2) SELECTION.—The Secretary shall select chains of skilled nursing facilities and nursing facilities described in paragraph (1) to participate in the demonstration project under this section from among those chains that submit an application to the Secretary at such time, in such manner, and containing such information as the Secretary may require.

(3) DURATION.—The Secretary shall conduct the demonstration project under this section for a 2-year period.

(4) IMPLEMENTATION.—The Secretary shall implement the demonstration project under this section not later than 1 year after the date of the enactment of this Act.

(b) REQUIREMENTS.—The Secretary shall evaluate chains selected to participate in the demonstration project under this section based on criteria selected by the Secretary, including where evidence suggests that a number of the facilities of the chain are experiencing serious safety and quality of care problems. Such criteria may include the evaluation of a chain that includes a number of facilities participating in the "Special Focus Facility" program (or a successor program) or multiple facilities with a record of repeated serious safety and quality of care deficiencies.

(c) RESPONSIBILITIES.—An independent monitor that enters into a contract with the Secretary to participate in the conduct of the demonstration project under this section shall—

(1) conduct periodic reviews and prepare root-cause quality and deficiency analyses of a chain to assess if facilities of the chain are in compliance with State and Federal laws and regulations applicable to the facilities;

(2) conduct sustained oversight of the efforts of the chain, whether publicly or privately held, to achieve compliance by facilities of the chain with State and Federal laws and regulations applicable to the facilities;

(3) analyze the management structure, distribution of expenditures, and nurse staffing levels of facilities of the chain in relation to resident census, staff turnover rates, and tenure;

(4) report findings and recommendations with respect to such reviews, analyses, and oversight to the chain and facilities of the chain, to the Secretary, and to relevant States; and

(5) publish the results of such reviews, analyses, and oversight.

(d) IMPLEMENTATION OF RECOMMENDATIONS.—

(1) RECEIPT OF FINDING BY CHAIN.—Not later than 10 days after receipt of a finding of an independent monitor under subsection (c)(4), a chain participating in the demonstration project shall submit to the independent monitor a report—

(A) outlining corrective actions the chain will take to implement the recommendations in such report; or

(B) indicating that the chain will not implement such recommendations, and why it will not do so.

(2) RECEIPT OF REPORT BY INDEPENDENT MONITOR.—Not later than 10 days after receipt of a report submitted by a chain under paragraph (1), an independent monitor shall finalize its recommendations and submit a report to the chain and facilities of the chain, the Secretary, and the State or States, as appropriate, containing such final recommendations.

(e) COST OF APPOINTMENT.—A chain shall be responsible for a portion of the costs associated with the appointment of independent monitors under the demonstration project under this section. The chain shall pay such portion to the Secretary (in an amount and in accordance with procedures established by the Secretary).

(f) WAIVER AUTHORITY.—The Secretary may waive such requirements of titles XVIII and XIX of the Social Security Act (42 U.S.C. 1395 et seq.; 1396 et seq.) as may be necessary for the purpose of carrying out the demonstration project under this section.

(g) AUTHORIZATION OF APPROPRIATIONS.—There are authorized to be appropriated such sums as may be necessary to carry out this section.

(h) DEFINITIONS.—In this section:

(1) ADDITIONAL DISCLOSABLE PARTY.—The term "additional disclosable party" has the meaning given such term in section 1124(c)(5)(A) of the Social Security Act, as added by section 4201(a).

(2) FACILITY.—The term "facility" means a skilled nursing facility or a nursing facility.

(3) NURSING FACILITY.—The term "nursing facility" has the meaning given such term in section 1919(a) of the Social Security Act (42 U.S.C. 1396r(a)).

(4) SECRETARY.—The term "Secretary" means the Secretary of Health and Human Services, acting through the Assistant Secretary for Planning and Evaluation.

(5) SKILLED NURSING FACILITY.—The term "skilled nursing facility" has the meaning given such term in section 1819(a) of the Social Security Act (42 U.S.C. 1395(a)).

(i) EVALUATION AND REPORT.—

(1) EVALUATION.—The Secretary, in consultation with the Inspector General of the Department of Health and Human Services, shall evaluate the demonstration project conducted under this section.

(2) REPORT.—Not later than 180 days after the completion of the demonstration project under this section, the Secretary shall submit to Congress a report containing the results of the evaluation conducted under paragraph (1), together with recommendations—

(A) as to whether the independent monitor program should be established on a permanent basis;

(B) if the Secretary recommends that such program be so established, on appropriate procedures and mechanisms for such establishment; and

(C) for such legislation and administrative action as the Secretary determines appropriate.

SEC. 6113. NOTIFICATION OF FACILITY CLOSURE.

(a) IN GENERAL.—Section 1128I of the Social Security Act, as added and amended by this Act, is amended by adding at the end the following new subsection:

"(h) NOTIFICATION OF FACILITY CLOSURE.—

"(1) IN GENERAL.—Any individual who is the administrator of a facility must—

"(A) submit to the Secretary, the State long-term care ombudsman, residents of the facility, and the legal representatives of such residents or other responsible parties, written notification of an impending closure—

"(i) subject to clause (ii), not later than the date that is 60 days prior to the date of such closure; and

"(ii) in the case of a facility where the Secretary terminates the facility's participation under this title, not later than the date that the Secretary determines appropriate;

"(B) ensure that the facility does not admit any new residents on or after the date on which such written notification is submitted; and

"(C) include in the notice a plan for the transfer and adequate relocation of the residents of the facility by a specified date prior to closure that has been approved by the State, including assurances that the residents will be transferred to the most appropriate facility or other setting in terms of quality, services, and location, taking into consideration the needs, choice, and best interests of each resident.

"(2) RELOCATION.—

"(A) IN GENERAL.—The State shall ensure that, before a facility closes, all residents of the facility have been successfully relocated to another facility or an alternative home and community-based setting.

"(B) CONTINUATION OF PAYMENTS UNTIL RESIDENTS RELOCATED.—The Secretary may, as the Secretary determines appropriate, continue to make payments under this title with respect to residents of a facility that has submitted a notification under paragraph (1) during the period beginning on the date such notification is submitted and ending on the date on which the resident is successfully relocated.

"(3) SANCTIONS.—Any individual who is the administrator of a facility that fails to comply with the requirements of paragraph (1)—

"(A) shall be subject to a civil monetary penalty of up to $100,000;

"(B) may be subject to exclusion from participation in any Federal health care program (as defined in section 1128B(f)); and

"(C) shall be subject to any other penalties that may be prescribed by law.

"(4) PROCEDURE.—The provisions of section 1128A (other than subsections (a) and (b) and the second sentence of subsection (f)) shall apply to a civil money penalty or exclusion under paragraph (3) in the same manner as such provisions apply to a penalty or proceeding under section 1128A(a).".

(b) CONFORMING AMENDMENTS.—Section 1819(h)(4) of the Social Security Act (42 U.S.C. 1395i–3(h)(4)) is amended—

(1) in the first sentence, by striking "the Secretary shall terminate" and inserting "the Secretary, subject to section 1128I(h), shall terminate"; and

(2) in the second sentence, by striking "subsection (c)(2)" and inserting "subsection (c)(2) and section 1128I(h)".

(c) EFFECTIVE DATE.—The amendments made by this section shall take effect 1 year after the date of the enactment of this Act.

SEC. 6114. NATIONAL DEMONSTRATION PROJECTS ON CULTURE CHANGE AND USE OF INFORMATION TECHNOLOGY IN NURSING HOMES.

(a) IN GENERAL.—The Secretary shall conduct 2 demonstration projects, 1 for the development of best practices in skilled nursing facilities and nursing facilities that are involved in the culture change movement (including the development of resources for facilities to find and access funding in order to undertake culture change) and 1 for the development of best practices in skilled nursing facilities and nursing facilities for the use of information technology to improve resident care.

(b) CONDUCT OF DEMONSTRATION PROJECTS.—

(1) GRANT AWARD.—Under each demonstration project conducted under this section, the Secretary shall award 1 or more grants to facility-based settings for the development of best practices described in subsection (a) with respect to the demonstration project involved. Such award shall be made on a competitive basis and may be allocated in 1 lump-sum payment.

(2) CONSIDERATION OF SPECIAL NEEDS OF RESIDENTS.—Each demonstration project conducted under this section shall take into consideration the special needs of residents of skilled nursing facilities and nursing facilities who have cognitive impairment, including dementia.

(c) DURATION AND IMPLEMENTATION.—

(1) DURATION.—The demonstration projects shall each be conducted for a period not to exceed 3 years.

(2) IMPLEMENTATION.—The demonstration projects shall each be implemented not later than 1 year after the date of the enactment of this Act.

(d) DEFINITIONS.—In this section:

(1) NURSING FACILITY.—The term "nursing facility" has the meaning given such term in section 1919(a) of the Social Security Act (42 U.S.C. 1396r(a)).

(2) SECRETARY.—The term "Secretary" means the Secretary of Health and Human Services.

(3) SKILLED NURSING FACILITY.—The term "skilled nursing facility" has the meaning given such term in section 1819(a) of the Social Security Act (42 U.S.C. 1395(a)).

(e) AUTHORIZATION OF APPROPRIATIONS.—There are authorized to be appropriated such sums as may be necessary to carry out this section.

(f) REPORT.—Not later than 9 months after the completion of the demonstration project, the Secretary shall submit to Congress a report on such project, together with recommendations for such legislation and administrative action as the Secretary determines appropriate.

PART III—IMPROVING STAFF TRAINING

SEC. 6121. DEMENTIA AND ABUSE PREVENTION TRAINING.

(a) SKILLED NURSING FACILITIES.—

(1) IN GENERAL.—Section 1819(f)(2)(A)(i)(I) of the Social Security Act (42 U.S.C. 1395i–3(f)(2)(A)(i)(I)) is amended by

inserting “(including, in the case of initial training and, if the Secretary determines appropriate, in the case of ongoing training, dementia management training, and patient abuse prevention training” before “, (II)”.

(2) CLARIFICATION OF DEFINITION OF NURSE AIDE.—Section 1819(b)(5)(F) of the Social Security Act (42 U.S.C. 1395i–3(b)(5)(F)) is amended by adding at the end the following flush sentence:

“Such term includes an individual who provides such services through an agency or under a contract with the facility.”.

(b) NURSING FACILITIES.—

(1) IN GENERAL.—Section 1919(f)(2)(A)(i)(I) of the Social Security Act (42 U.S.C. 1396r(f)(2)(A)(i)(I)) is amended by inserting “(including, in the case of initial training and, if the Secretary determines appropriate, in the case of ongoing training, dementia management training, and patient abuse prevention training” before “, (II)”.

(2) CLARIFICATION OF DEFINITION OF NURSE AIDE.—Section 1919(b)(5)(F) of the Social Security Act (42 U.S.C. 1396r(b)(5)(F)) is amended by adding at the end the following flush sentence:

“Such term includes an individual who provides such services through an agency or under a contract with the facility.”.

(c) EFFECTIVE DATE.—The amendments made by this section shall take effect 1 year after the date of the enactment of this Act.

Subtitle C—Nationwide Program for National and State Background Checks on Direct Patient Access Employees of Long-term Care Facilities and Providers

SEC. 6201. NATIONWIDE PROGRAM FOR NATIONAL AND STATE BACKGROUND CHECKS ON DIRECT PATIENT ACCESS EMPLOYEES OF LONG-TERM CARE FACILITIES AND PROVIDERS.

(a) IN GENERAL.—The Secretary of Health and Human Services (in this section referred to as the “Secretary”), shall establish a program to identify efficient, effective, and economical procedures for long term care facilities or providers to conduct background checks on prospective direct patient access employees on a nationwide basis (in this subsection, such program shall be referred to as the “nationwide program”). Except for the following modifications, the Secretary shall carry out the nationwide program under similar terms and conditions as the pilot program under section 307 of the Medicare Prescription Drug, Improvement, and Modernization Act of 2003 (Public Law 108–173; 117 Stat. 2257), including the prohibition on hiring abusive workers and the authorization of the imposition of penalties by a participating State under subsection (b)(3)(A) and (b)(6), respectively, of such section 307:

(1) AGREEMENTS.—

(A) NEWLY PARTICIPATING STATES.—The Secretary shall enter into agreements with each State—

(i) that the Secretary has not entered into an agreement with under subsection (c)(1) of such section 307;

(ii) that agrees to conduct background checks under the nationwide program on a Statewide basis; and

(iii) that submits an application to the Secretary containing such information and at such time as the Secretary may specify.

(B) CERTAIN PREVIOUSLY PARTICIPATING STATES.—The Secretary shall enter into agreements with each State—

(i) that the Secretary has entered into an agreement with under such subsection (c)(1), but only in the case where such agreement did not require the State to conduct background checks under the program established under subsection (a) of such section 307 on a Statewide basis;

(ii) that agrees to conduct background checks under the nationwide program on a Statewide basis; and

(iii) that submits an application to the Secretary containing such information and at such time as the Secretary may specify.

(2) NONAPPLICATION OF SELECTION CRITERIA.—The selection criteria required under subsection (c)(3)(B) of such section 307 shall not apply.

(3) REQUIRED FINGERPRINT CHECK AS PART OF CRIMINAL HISTORY BACKGROUND CHECK.—The procedures established under subsection (b)(1) of such section 307 shall—

(A) require that the long-term care facility or provider (or the designated agent of the long-term care facility or provider) obtain State and national criminal history background checks on the prospective employee through such means as the Secretary determines appropriate, efficient, and effective that utilize a search of State-based abuse and neglect registries and databases, including the abuse and neglect registries of another State in the case where a prospective employee previously resided in that State, State criminal history records, the records of any proceedings in the State that may contain disqualifying information about prospective employees (such as proceedings conducted by State professional licensing and disciplinary boards and State Medicaid Fraud Control Units), and Federal criminal history records, including a fingerprint check using the Integrated Automated Fingerprint Identification System of the Federal Bureau of Investigation;

(B) require States to describe and test methods that reduce duplicative fingerprinting, including providing for the development of "rap back" capability by the State such that, if a direct patient access employee of a long-term care facility or provider is convicted of a crime following the initial criminal history background check conducted with respect to such employee, and the employee's fingerprints match the prints on file with the State law enforcement department, the department will immediately inform the State and the State will immediately inform the long-term care facility or provider which employs the direct patient access employee of such conviction; and

(C) require that criminal history background checks conducted under the nationwide program remain valid for a period of time specified by the Secretary.

(4) STATE REQUIREMENTS.—An agreement entered into under paragraph (1) shall require that a participating State—

(A) be responsible for monitoring compliance with the requirements of the nationwide program;

(B) have procedures in place to—

(i) conduct screening and criminal history background checks under the nationwide program in accordance with the requirements of this section;

(ii) monitor compliance by long-term care facilities and providers with the procedures and requirements of the nationwide program;

(iii) as appropriate, provide for a provisional period of employment by a long-term care facility or provider of a direct patient access employee, not to exceed 60 days, pending completion of the required criminal history background check and, in the case where the employee has appealed the results of such background check, pending completion of the appeals process, during which the employee shall be subject to direct on-site supervision (in accordance with procedures established by the State to ensure that a long-term care facility or provider furnishes such direct on-site supervision);

(iv) provide an independent process by which a provisional employee or an employee may appeal or dispute the accuracy of the information obtained in a background check performed under the nationwide program, including the specification of criteria for appeals for direct patient access employees found to have disqualifying information which shall include consideration of the passage of time, extenuating circumstances, demonstration of rehabilitation, and relevancy of the particular disqualifying information with respect to the current employment of the individual;

(v) provide for the designation of a single State agency as responsible for—

(I) overseeing the coordination of any State and national criminal history background checks requested by a long-term care facility or provider (or the designated agent of the long-term care facility or provider) utilizing a search of State and Federal criminal history records, including a fingerprint check of such records;

(II) overseeing the design of appropriate privacy and security safeguards for use in the review of the results of any State or national criminal history background checks conducted regarding a prospective direct patient access employee to determine whether the employee has any conviction for a relevant crime;

(III) immediately reporting to the long-term care facility or provider that requested the criminal history background check the results of such review; and

(IV) in the case of an employee with a conviction for a relevant crime that is subject to reporting under section 1128E of the Social Security Act (42 U.S.C. 1320a–7e), reporting the existence of such conviction to the database established under that section;

(vi) determine which individuals are direct patient access employees (as defined in paragraph (6)(B)) for purposes of the nationwide program;

(vii) as appropriate, specify offenses, including convictions for violent crimes, for purposes of the nationwide program; and

(viii) describe and test methods that reduce duplicative fingerprinting, including providing for the development of "rap back" capability such that, if a direct patient access employee of a long-term care facility or provider is convicted of a crime following the initial criminal history background check conducted with respect to such employee, and the employee's fingerprints match the prints on file with the State law enforcement department—

(I) the department will immediately inform the State agency designated under clause (v) and such agency will immediately inform the facility or provider which employs the direct patient access employee of such conviction; and

(II) the State will provide, or will require the facility to provide, to the employee a copy of the results of the criminal history background check conducted with respect to the employee at no charge in the case where the individual requests such a copy.

(5) PAYMENTS.—

(A) NEWLY PARTICIPATING STATES.—

(i) IN GENERAL.—As part of the application submitted by a State under paragraph (1)(A)(iii), the State shall guarantee, with respect to the costs to be incurred by the State in carrying out the nationwide program, that the State will make available (directly or through donations from public or private entities) a particular amount of non-Federal contributions, as a condition of receiving the Federal match under clause (ii).

(ii) FEDERAL MATCH.—The payment amount to each State that the Secretary enters into an agreement with under paragraph (1)(A) shall be 3 times the amount that the State guarantees to make available under clause (i), except that in no case may the payment amount exceed $3,000,000.

(B) PREVIOUSLY PARTICIPATING STATES.—

(i) IN GENERAL.—As part of the application submitted by a State under paragraph (1)(B)(iii), the State shall guarantee, with respect to the costs to be incurred by the State in carrying out the nationwide program, that the State will make available (directly or through donations from public or private entities) a particular amount of non-Federal contributions, as a condition of receiving the Federal match under clause (ii).

(ii) FEDERAL MATCH.—The payment amount to each State that the Secretary enters into an agreement with under paragraph (1)(B) shall be 3 times the amount that the State guarantees to make available under clause (i), except that in no case may the payment amount exceed $1,500,000.

(6) DEFINITIONS.—Under the nationwide program:

(A) CONVICTION FOR A RELEVANT CRIME.—The term "conviction for a relevant crime" means any Federal or State criminal conviction for—

(i) any offense described in section 1128(a) of the Social Security Act (42 U.S.C. 1320a–7); or

(ii) such other types of offenses as a participating State may specify for purposes of conducting the program in such State.

(B) DISQUALIFYING INFORMATION.—The term "disqualifying information" means a conviction for a relevant crime or a finding of patient or resident abuse.

(C) FINDING OF PATIENT OR RESIDENT ABUSE.—The term "finding of patient or resident abuse" means any substantiated finding by a State agency under section 1819(g)(1)(C) or 1919(g)(1)(C) of the Social Security Act (42 U.S.C. 1395i–3(g)(1)(C), 1396r(g)(1)(C)) or a Federal agency that a direct patient access employee has committed—

(i) an act of patient or resident abuse or neglect or a misappropriation of patient or resident property; or

(ii) such other types of acts as a participating State may specify for purposes of conducting the program in such State.

(D) DIRECT PATIENT ACCESS EMPLOYEE.—The term "direct patient access employee" means any individual who has access to a patient or resident of a long-term care facility or provider through employment or through a contract with such facility or provider and has duties that involve (or may involve) one-on-one contact with a patient or resident of the facility or provider, as determined by the State for purposes of the nationwide program. Such term does not include a volunteer unless the volunteer has duties that are equivalent to the duties of a direct patient access employee and those duties involve (or may involve) one-on-one contact with a patient or resident of the long-term care facility or provider.

(E) LONG-TERM CARE FACILITY OR PROVIDER.—The term "long-term care facility or provider" means the following facilities or providers which receive payment for services under title XVIII or XIX of the Social Security Act:

(i) A skilled nursing facility (as defined in section 1819(a) of the Social Security Act (42 U.S.C. 1395i–3(a))).

(ii) A nursing facility (as defined in section 1919(a) of such Act (42 U.S.C. 1396r(a))).

(iii) A home health agency.

(iv) A provider of hospice care (as defined in section 1861(dd)(1) of such Act (42 U.S.C. 1395x(dd)(1))).

(v) A long-term care hospital (as described in section 1886(d)(1)(B)(iv) of such Act (42 U.S.C. 1395ww(d)(1)(B)(iv))).

(vi) A provider of personal care services.

(vii) A provider of adult day care.

(viii) A residential care provider that arranges for, or directly provides, long-term care services, including an assisted living facility that provides a level of care established by the Secretary.

(ix) An intermediate care facility for the mentally retarded (as defined in section 1905(d) of such Act (42 U.S.C. 1396d(d))).

(x) Any other facility or provider of long-term care services under such titles as the participating State determines appropriate.

(7) EVALUATION AND REPORT.—

(A) EVALUATION.—

(i) IN GENERAL.—The Inspector General of the Department of Health and Human Services shall conduct an evaluation of the nationwide program.

(ii) INCLUSION OF SPECIFIC TOPICS.—The evaluation conducted under clause (i) shall include the following:

(I) A review of the various procedures implemented by participating States for long-term care facilities or providers, including staffing agencies, to conduct background checks of direct patient access employees under the nationwide program and identification of the most appropriate, efficient, and effective procedures for conducting such background checks.

(II) An assessment of the costs of conducting such background checks (including start up and administrative costs).

(III) A determination of the extent to which conducting such background checks leads to any unintended consequences, including a reduction in the available workforce for long-term care facilities or providers.

(IV) An assessment of the impact of the nationwide program on reducing the number of incidents of neglect, abuse, and misappropriation of resident property to the extent practicable.

(V) An evaluation of other aspects of the nationwide program, as determined appropriate by the Secretary.

(B) REPORT.—Not later than 180 days after the completion of the nationwide program, the Inspector General of the Department of Health and Human Services shall submit a report to Congress containing the results of the evaluation conducted under subparagraph (A).

(b) FUNDING.—

(1) NOTIFICATION.—The Secretary of Health and Human Services shall notify the Secretary of the Treasury of the amount necessary to carry out the nationwide program under this section for the period of fiscal years 2010 through 2012, except that in no case shall such amount exceed $160,000,000.

(2) TRANSFER OF FUNDS.—

(A) IN GENERAL.—Out of any funds in the Treasury not otherwise appropriated, the Secretary of the Treasury shall provide for the transfer to the Secretary of Health and Human Services of the amount specified as necessary to carry out the nationwide program under paragraph (1). Such amount shall remain available until expended.

(B) RESERVATION OF FUNDS FOR CONDUCT OF EVALUATION.—The Secretary may reserve not more than $3,000,000 of the amount transferred under subparagraph (A) to provide for the conduct of the evaluation under subsection (a)(7)(A).

Subtitle D—Patient-Centered Outcomes Research

SEC. 6301. PATIENT-CENTERED OUTCOMES RESEARCH.

(a) IN GENERAL.—Title XI of the Social Security Act (42 U.S.C. 1301 et seq.) is amended by adding at the end the following new part:

"PART D—COMPARATIVE CLINICAL EFFECTIVENESS RESEARCH

"COMPARATIVE CLINICAL EFFECTIVENESS RESEARCH

"SEC. 1181. (a) DEFINITIONS.—In this section:

"(1) BOARD.—The term 'Board' means the Board of Governors established under subsection (f).

"(2) COMPARATIVE CLINICAL EFFECTIVENESS RESEARCH; RESEARCH.—

"(A) IN GENERAL.—The terms 'comparative clinical effectiveness research' and 'research' mean research evaluating and comparing health outcomes and the clinical effectiveness, risks, and benefits of 2 or more medical treatments, services, and items described in subparagraph (B).

"(B) MEDICAL TREATMENTS, SERVICES, AND ITEMS DESCRIBED.—The medical treatments, services, and items described in this subparagraph are health care interventions, protocols for treatment, care management, and delivery, procedures, medical devices, diagnostic tools, pharmaceuticals (including drugs and biologicals), integrative health practices, and any other strategies or items being used in the treatment, management, and diagnosis of, or prevention of illness or injury in, individuals.

"(3) CONFLICT OF INTEREST.—The term 'conflict of interest' means an association, including a financial or personal association, that have the potential to bias or have the appearance of biasing an individual's decisions in matters related to the Institute or the conduct of activities under this section.

"(4) REAL CONFLICT OF INTEREST.—The term 'real conflict of interest' means any instance where a member of the Board, the methodology committee established under subsection (d)(6), or an advisory panel appointed under subsection (d)(4), or a close relative of such member, has received or could receive either of the following:

"(A) A direct financial benefit of any amount deriving from the result or findings of a study conducted under this section.

"(B) A financial benefit from individuals or companies that own or manufacture medical treatments, services, or items to be studied under this section that in the aggregate exceeds $10,000 per year. For purposes of the preceding sentence, a financial benefit includes honoraria, fees, stock, or other financial benefit and the current value of the member or close relative's already existing stock holdings, in addition to any direct financial benefit deriving from the results or findings of a study conducted under this section.

"(b) PATIENT-CENTERED OUTCOMES RESEARCH INSTITUTE.—

"(1) ESTABLISHMENT.—There is authorized to be established a nonprofit corporation, to be known as the 'Patient-Centered Outcomes Research Institute' (referred to in this section as the 'Institute') which is neither an agency nor establishment of the United States Government.

"(2) APPLICATION OF PROVISIONS.—The Institute shall be subject to the provisions of this section, and, to the extent consistent with this section, to the District of Columbia Nonprofit Corporation Act.

"(3) FUNDING OF COMPARATIVE CLINICAL EFFECTIVENESS RESEARCH.—For fiscal year 2010 and each subsequent fiscal year, amounts in the Patient-Centered Outcomes Research Trust Fund (referred to in this section as the 'PCORTF') under section 9511 of the Internal Revenue Code of 1986 shall be available, without further appropriation, to the Institute to carry out this section.

"(c) PURPOSE.—The purpose of the Institute is to assist patients, clinicians, purchasers, and policy-makers in making informed health decisions by advancing the quality and relevance of evidence concerning the manner in which diseases, disorders, and other health conditions can effectively and appropriately be prevented, diagnosed, treated, monitored, and managed through research and evidence synthesis that considers variations in patient subpopulations, and the dissemination of research findings with respect to the relative health outcomes, clinical effectiveness, and appropriateness of the medical treatments, services, and items described in subsection (a)(2)(B).

"(d) DUTIES.—

"(1) IDENTIFYING RESEARCH PRIORITIES AND ESTABLISHING RESEARCH PROJECT AGENDA.—

"(A) IDENTIFYING RESEARCH PRIORITIES.—The Institute shall identify national priorities for research, taking into account factors of disease incidence, prevalence, and burden in the United States (with emphasis on chronic conditions), gaps in evidence in terms of clinical outcomes, practice variations and health disparities in terms of delivery and outcomes of care, the potential for new evidence to improve patient health, well-being, and the quality of care, the effect on national expenditures associated with a health care treatment, strategy, or health conditions, as well as patient needs, outcomes, and preferences, the relevance to patients and clinicians in making informed health decisions, and priorities in the National Strategy for quality care established under section 399H of the Public Health Service Act that are consistent with this section.

"(B) ESTABLISHING RESEARCH PROJECT AGENDA.—The Institute shall establish and update a research project agenda for research to address the priorities identified under subparagraph (A), taking into consideration the types of research that might address each priority and the relative value (determined based on the cost of conducting research compared to the potential usefulness of the information produced by research) associated with the different types of research, and such other factors as the Institute determines appropriate.

"(2) CARRYING OUT RESEARCH PROJECT AGENDA.—

"(A) RESEARCH.—The Institute shall carry out the research project agenda established under paragraph (1)(B) in accordance with the methodological standards adopted under paragraph (9) using methods, including the following:

"(i) Systematic reviews and assessments of existing and future research and evidence including original research conducted subsequent to the date of the enactment of this section.

"(ii) Primary research, such as randomized clinical trials, molecularly informed trials, and observational studies.

"(iii) Any other methodologies recommended by the methodology committee established under paragraph (6) that are adopted by the Board under paragraph (9).

"(B) CONTRACTS FOR THE MANAGEMENT OF FUNDING AND CONDUCT OF RESEARCH.—

"(i) CONTRACTS.—

"(I) IN GENERAL.—In accordance with the research project agenda established under paragraph (1)(B), the Institute shall enter into contracts for the management of funding and conduct of research in accordance with the following:

"(aa) Appropriate agencies and instrumentalities of the Federal Government.

"(bb) Appropriate academic research, private sector research, or study-conducting entities.

"(II) PREFERENCE.—In entering into contracts under subclause (I), the Institute shall give preference to the Agency for Healthcare Research and Quality and the National Institutes of Health, but only if the research to be conducted or managed under such contract is authorized by the governing statutes of such Agency or Institutes.

"(ii) CONDITIONS FOR CONTRACTS.—A contract entered into under this subparagraph shall require that the agency, instrumentality, or other entity—

"(I) abide by the transparency and conflicts of interest requirements under subsection (h) that apply to the Institute with respect to the research managed or conducted under such contract;

"(II) comply with the methodological standards adopted under paragraph (9) with respect to such research;

"(III) consult with the expert advisory panels for clinical trials and rare disease appointed under clauses (ii) and (iii), respectively, of paragraph (4)(A);

"(IV) subject to clause (iv), permit a researcher who conducts original research under the contract for the agency, instrumentality, or other entity to have such research published in a peer-reviewed journal or other publication;

"(V) have appropriate processes in place to manage data privacy and meet ethical standards for the research;

"(VI) comply with the requirements of the Institute for making the information available to the public under paragraph (8); and

"(VII) comply with other terms and conditions determined necessary by the Institute to carry out the research agenda adopted under paragraph (2).

"(iii) COVERAGE OF COPAYMENTS OR COINSURANCE.—A contract entered into under this subparagraph may allow for the coverage of copayments or coinsurance, or allow for other appropriate measures, to the extent that such coverage or other measures are necessary to preserve the validity of a research project, such as in the case where the research project must be blinded.

"(iv) REQUIREMENTS FOR PUBLICATION OF RESEARCH.—Any research published under clause (ii)(IV) shall be within the bounds of and entirely consistent with the evidence and findings produced under the contract with the Institute under this subparagraph. If the Institute determines that those requirements are not met, the Institute shall not enter into another contract with the agency, instrumentality, or entity which managed or conducted such research for a period determined appropriate by the Institute (but not less than 5 years).

"(C) REVIEW AND UPDATE OF EVIDENCE.—The Institute shall review and update evidence on a periodic basis as appropriate.

"(D) TAKING INTO ACCOUNT POTENTIAL DIFFERENCES.—Research shall be designed, as appropriate, to take into account the potential for differences in the effectiveness of health care treatments, services, and items as used with various subpopulations, such as racial and ethnic minorities, women, age, and groups of individuals with different comorbidities, genetic and molecular sub-types, or quality of life preferences and include members of such subpopulations as subjects in the research as feasible and appropriate.

"(E) DIFFERENCES IN TREATMENT MODALITIES.—Research shall be designed, as appropriate, to take into account different characteristics of treatment modalities that may affect research outcomes, such as the phase of the treatment modality in the innovation cycle and the impact of the skill of the operator of the treatment modality.

"(3) DATA COLLECTION.—

"(A) IN GENERAL.—The Secretary shall, with appropriate safeguards for privacy, make available to the Institute such data collected by the Centers for Medicare & Medicaid Services under the programs under titles XVIII, XIX, and XXI, as well as provide access to the data networks developed under section 937(f) of the Public Health Service Act, as the Institute and its contractors may require to carry out this section. The Institute may also request and obtain data from Federal, State, or private entities, including data from clinical databases and registries.

"(B) USE OF DATA.—The Institute shall only use data provided to the Institute under subparagraph (A) in accordance with laws and regulations governing the release and use of such data, including applicable confidentiality and privacy standards.

"(4) APPOINTING EXPERT ADVISORY PANELS.—

"(A) APPOINTMENT.—

"(i) IN GENERAL.—The Institute may appoint permanent or ad hoc expert advisory panels as determined appropriate to assist in identifying research priorities and establishing the research project agenda under paragraph (1) and for other purposes.

"(ii) EXPERT ADVISORY PANELS FOR CLINICAL TRIALS.—The Institute shall appoint expert advisory panels in carrying out randomized clinical trials under the research project agenda under paragraph (2)(A)(ii). Such expert advisory panels shall advise the Institute and the agency, instrumentality, or entity conducting the research on the research question involved and the research design or protocol, including important patient subgroups and other parameters of the research. Such panels shall be available as a resource for technical questions that may arise during the conduct of such research.

"(iii) EXPERT ADVISORY PANEL FOR RARE DISEASE.—In the case of a research study for rare disease, the Institute shall appoint an expert advisory panel for purposes of assisting in the design of the research study and determining the relative value and feasibility of conducting the research study.

"(B) COMPOSITION.—An expert advisory panel appointed under subparagraph (A) shall include representatives of practicing and research clinicians, patients, and experts in scientific and health services research, health services delivery, and evidence-based medicine who have experience in the relevant topic, and as appropriate, experts in integrative health and primary prevention strategies. The Institute may include a technical expert of each manufacturer or each medical technology that is included under the relevant topic, project, or category for which the panel is established.

"(5) SUPPORTING PATIENT AND CONSUMER REPRESENTATIVES.—The Institute shall provide support and resources to help patient and consumer representatives effectively participate on the Board and expert advisory panels appointed by the Institute under paragraph (4).

"(6) ESTABLISHING METHODOLOGY COMMITTEE.—

"(A) IN GENERAL.—The Institute shall establish a standing methodology committee to carry out the functions described in subparagraph (C).

"(B) APPOINTMENT AND COMPOSITION.—The methodology committee established under subparagraph (A) shall be composed of not more than 15 members appointed by the Comptroller General of the United States. Members appointed to the methodology committee shall be experts in their scientific field, such as health services research, clinical research, comparative clinical effectiveness research, biostatistics, genomics, and research methodologies. Stakeholders with such expertise may be appointed to the methodology committee. In addition to the members appointed under the first sentence, the Directors of the National Institutes of Health and the Agency for Healthcare Research and Quality (or their designees) shall each be included as members of the methodology committee.

"(C) FUNCTIONS.—Subject to subparagraph (D), the methodology committee shall work to develop and improve the science and methods of comparative clinical effectiveness research by, not later than 18 months after the establishment of the Institute, directly or through subcontract, developing and periodically updating the following:

"(i) Methodological standards for research. Such methodological standards shall provide specific criteria for internal validity, generalizability, feasibility, and timeliness of research and for health outcomes measures, risk adjustment, and other relevant aspects of research and assessment with respect to the design of research. Any methodological standards developed and updated under this subclause shall be scientifically based and include methods by which new information, data, or advances in technology are considered and incorporated into ongoing research projects by the Institute, as appropriate. The process for developing and updating such standards shall include input from relevant experts, stakeholders, and decisionmakers, and shall provide opportunities for public comment. Such standards shall also include methods by which patient subpopulations can be accounted for and evaluated in different types of research. As appropriate, such standards shall build on existing work on methodological standards for defined categories of health interventions and for each of the major categories of comparative clinical effectiveness research methods (determined as of the date of enactment of the Patient Protection and Affordable Care Act).

"(ii) A translation table that is designed to provide guidance and act as a reference for the Board to determine research methods that are most likely to address each specific research question.

"(D) CONSULTATION AND CONDUCT OF EXAMINATIONS.—The methodology committee may consult and contract with the Institute of Medicine of the National Academies and academic, nonprofit, or other private and governmental entities with relevant expertise to carry out activities described in subparagraph (C) and may consult with relevant stakeholders to carry out such activities.

"(E) REPORTS.—The methodology committee shall submit reports to the Board on the committee's performance of the functions described in subparagraph (C). Reports shall contain recommendations for the Institute to adopt methodological standards developed and updated by the methodology committee as well as other actions deemed necessary to comply with such methodological standards.

"(7) PROVIDING FOR A PEER-REVIEW PROCESS FOR PRIMARY RESEARCH.—

"(A) IN GENERAL.—The Institute shall ensure that there is a process for peer review of primary research described in subparagraph (A)(ii) of paragraph (2) that is conducted under such paragraph. Under such process—

"(i) evidence from such primary research shall be reviewed to assess scientific integrity and adherence to methodological standards adopted under paragraph (9); and

"(ii) a list of the names of individuals contributing to any peer-review process during the preceding year or years shall be made public and included in annual reports in accordance with paragraph (10)(D).

"(B) COMPOSITION.—Such peer-review process shall be designed in a manner so as to avoid bias and conflicts of interest on the part of the reviewers and shall be composed of experts in the scientific field relevant to the research under review.

"(C) USE OF EXISTING PROCESSES.—

"(i) PROCESSES OF ANOTHER ENTITY.—In the case where the Institute enters into a contract or other agreement with another entity for the conduct or management of research under this section, the Institute may utilize the peer-review process of such entity if such process meets the requirements under subparagraphs (A) and (B).

"(ii) PROCESSES OF APPROPRIATE MEDICAL JOURNALS.—The Institute may utilize the peer-review process of appropriate medical journals if such process meets the requirements under subparagraphs (A) and (B).

"(8) RELEASE OF RESEARCH FINDINGS.—

"(A) IN GENERAL.—The Institute shall, not later than 90 days after the conduct or receipt of research findings under this part, make such research findings available to clinicians, patients, and the general public. The Institute shall ensure that the research findings—

"(i) convey the findings of research in a manner that is comprehensible and useful to patients and providers in making health care decisions;

"(ii) fully convey findings and discuss considerations specific to certain subpopulations, risk factors, and comorbidities, as appropriate;

"(iii) include limitations of the research and what further research may be needed as appropriate;

"(iv) not be construed as mandates for practice guidelines, coverage recommendations, payment, or policy recommendations; and

"(v) not include any data which would violate the privacy of research participants or any confidentiality agreements made with respect to the use of data under this section.

"(B) DEFINITION OF RESEARCH FINDINGS.—In this paragraph, the term 'research findings' means the results of a study or assessment.

"(9) ADOPTION.—Subject to subsection (h)(1), the Institute shall adopt the national priorities identified under paragraph (1)(A), the research project agenda established under paragraph (1)(B), the methodological standards developed and updated by the methodology committee under paragraph (6)(C)(i), and any peer-review process provided under paragraph (7) by majority vote. In the case where the Institute does not adopt such processes in accordance with the preceding sentence, the processes shall be referred to the appropriate staff or entity within the Institute (or, in the case of the methodological standards, the methodology committee) for further review.

"(10) ANNUAL REPORTS.—The Institute shall submit an annual report to Congress and the President, and shall make the annual report available to the public. Such report shall contain—

"(A) a description of the activities conducted under this section, research priorities identified under paragraph (1)(A) and methodological standards developed and updated by the methodology committee under paragraph (6)(C)(i) that are adopted under paragraph (9) during the preceding year;

"(B) the research project agenda and budget of the Institute for the following year;

"(C) any administrative activities conducted by the Institute during the preceding year;

"(D) the names of individuals contributing to any peer-review process under paragraph (7), without identifying them with a particular research project; and

"(E) any other relevant information (including information on the membership of the Board, expert advisory panels, methodology committee, and the executive staff of the Institute, any conflicts of interest with respect to these individuals, and any bylaws adopted by the Board during the preceding year).

"(e) ADMINISTRATION.—

"(1) IN GENERAL.—Subject to paragraph (2), the Board shall carry out the duties of the Institute.

"(2) NONDELEGABLE DUTIES.—The activities described in subsections (d)(1) and (d)(9) are nondelegable.

"(f) BOARD OF GOVERNORS.—

"(1) IN GENERAL.—The Institute shall have a Board of Governors, which shall consist of the following members:

"(A) The Director of Agency for Healthcare Research and Quality (or the Director's designee).

"(B) The Director of the National Institutes of Health (or the Director's designee).

"(C) Seventeen members appointed, not later than 6 months after the date of enactment of this section, by the Comptroller General of the United States as follows:

"(i) 3 members representing patients and health care consumers.

"(ii) 5 members representing physicians and providers, including at least 1 surgeon, nurse, State-licensed integrative health care practitioner, and representative of a hospital.

"(iii) 3 members representing private payers, of whom at least 1 member shall represent health insurance issuers and at least 1 member shall represent employers who self-insure employee benefits.

"(iv) 3 members representing pharmaceutical, device, and diagnostic manufacturers or developers.

"(v) 1 member representing quality improvement or independent health service researchers.

"(vi) 2 members representing the Federal Government or the States, including at least 1 member representing a Federal health program or agency.

"(2) QUALIFICATIONS.—The Board shall represent a broad range of perspectives and collectively have scientific expertise in clinical health sciences research, including epidemiology, decisions sciences, health economics, and statistics. In appointing the Board, the Comptroller General of the United States shall consider and disclose any conflicts of interest in accordance with subsection (h)(4)(B). Members of the Board shall be recused from relevant Institute activities in the case where the member (or an immediate family member of such member) has a real conflict of interest directly related to the research project or the matter that could affect or be affected by such participation.

"(3) TERMS; VACANCIES.—A member of the Board shall be appointed for a term of 6 years, except with respect to the members first appointed, whose terms of appointment shall be staggered evenly over 2-year increments. No individual shall be appointed to the Board for more than 2 terms. Vacancies shall be filled in the same manner as the original appointment was made.

"(4) CHAIRPERSON AND VICE-CHAIRPERSON.—The Comptroller General of the United States shall designate a Chairperson and Vice Chairperson of the Board from among the members of the Board. Such members shall serve as Chairperson or Vice Chairperson for a period of 3 years.

"(5) COMPENSATION.—Each member of the Board who is not an officer or employee of the Federal Government shall be entitled to compensation (equivalent to the rate provided for level IV of the Executive Schedule under section 5315 of title 5, United States Code) and expenses incurred while performing the duties of the Board. An officer or employee of the Federal government who is a member of the Board shall be exempt from compensation.

"(6) DIRECTOR AND STAFF; EXPERTS AND CONSULTANTS.—The Board may employ and fix the compensation of an Executive Director and such other personnel as may be necessary to carry out the duties of the Institute and may seek such assistance and support of, or contract with, experts and consultants that may be necessary for the performance of the duties of the Institute.

"(7) MEETINGS AND HEARINGS.—The Board shall meet and hold hearings at the call of the Chairperson or a majority of its members. Meetings not solely concerning matters of personnel shall be advertised at least 7 days in advance and open to the public. A majority of the Board members shall constitute a quorum, but a lesser number of members may meet and hold hearings.

"(g) FINANCIAL AND GOVERNMENTAL OVERSIGHT.—

"(1) CONTRACT FOR AUDIT.—The Institute shall provide for the conduct of financial audits of the Institute on an annual basis by a private entity with expertise in conducting financial audits.

"(2) REVIEW AND ANNUAL REPORTS.—

"(A) REVIEW.—The Comptroller General of the United States shall review the following:

"(i) Not less frequently than on an annual basis, the financial audits conducted under paragraph (1).

"(ii) Not less frequently than every 5 years, the processes established by the Institute, including the research priorities and the conduct of research projects, in order to determine whether information produced by such research projects is objective and credible, is produced in a manner consistent with the requirements under this section, and is developed through a transparent process.

"(iii) Not less frequently than every 5 years, the dissemination and training activities and data networks established under section 937 of the Public Health Service Act, including the methods and products used to disseminate research, the types of training conducted and supported, and the types and functions of the data networks established, in order to determine whether the activities and data are produced in a manner consistent with the requirements under such section.

"(iv) Not less frequently than every 5 years, the overall effectiveness of activities conducted under this section and the dissemination, training, and capacity building activities conducted under section 937 of the Public Health Service Act. Such review shall include an analysis of the extent to which research findings are used by health care decision-makers, the effect of the dissemination of such findings on reducing practice variation and disparities in health care, and the effect of the research conducted and disseminated on innovation and the health care economy of the United States.

"(v) Not later than 8 years after the date of enactment of this section, the adequacy and use of the funding for the Institute and the activities conducted under section 937 of the Public Health Service Act, including a determination as to whether, based on the utilization of research findings by public and private payers, funding sources for the Patient-Centered Outcomes Research Trust Fund under section 9511 of the Internal Revenue Code of 1986 are appropriate and whether such sources of funding should be continued or adjusted.

"(B) ANNUAL REPORTS.—Not later than April 1 of each year, the Comptroller General of the United States shall submit to Congress a report containing the results of the review conducted under subparagraph (A) with respect to the preceding year (or years, if applicable), together with recommendations for such legislation and administrative action as the Comptroller General determines appropriate.

"(h) ENSURING TRANSPARENCY, CREDIBILITY, AND ACCESS.—The Institute shall establish procedures to ensure that the following requirements for ensuring transparency, credibility, and access are met:

"(1) PUBLIC COMMENT PERIODS.—The Institute shall provide for a public comment period of not less than 45 days and not more than 60 days prior to the adoption under subsection (d)(9) of the national priorities identified under subsection (d)(1)(A), the research project agenda established under subsection (d)(1)(B), the methodological standards developed and updated by the methodology committee under subsection (d)(6)(C)(i), and the peer-review process provided under paragraph (7), and after the release of draft findings with respect to systematic reviews of existing research and evidence.

"(2) ADDITIONAL FORUMS.—The Institute shall support forums to increase public awareness and obtain and incorporate public input and feedback through media (such as an Internet website) on research priorities, research findings, and other duties, activities, or processes the Institute determines appropriate.

"(3) PUBLIC AVAILABILITY.—The Institute shall make available to the public and disclose through the official public Internet website of the Institute the following:

"(A) Information contained in research findings as specified in subsection (d)(9).

"(B) The process and methods for the conduct of research, including the identity of the entity and the investigators conducing such research and any conflicts of interests of such parties, any direct or indirect links the entity has to industry, and research protocols, including measures taken, methods of research and analysis, research results, and such other information the Institute determines appropriate) concurrent with the release of research findings.

"(C) Notice of public comment periods under paragraph (1), including deadlines for public comments.

"(D) Subsequent comments received during each of the public comment periods.

"(E) In accordance with applicable laws and processes and as the Institute determines appropriate, proceedings of the Institute.

"(4) DISCLOSURE OF CONFLICTS OF INTEREST.—

"(A) IN GENERAL.—A conflict of interest shall be disclosed in the following manner:

"(i) By the Institute in appointing members to an expert advisory panel under subsection (d)(4), in selecting individuals to contribute to any peer-review process under subsection (d)(7), and for employment as executive staff of the Institute.

"(ii) By the Comptroller General in appointing members of the methodology committee under subsection (d)(6);

"(iii) By the Institute in the annual report under subsection (d)(10), except that, in the case of individuals contributing to any such peer review process, such description shall be in a manner such that those individuals cannot be identified with a particular research project.

"(B) MANNER OF DISCLOSURE.—Conflicts of interest shall be disclosed as described in subparagraph (A) as soon as practicable on the Internet web site of the Institute and of the Government Accountability Office. The information disclosed under the preceding sentence shall include the type, nature, and magnitude of the interests of the individual involved, except to the extent that the individual recuses himself or herself from participating in the consideration of or any other activity with respect to the study as to which the potential conflict exists.

"(i) RULES.—The Institute, its Board or staff, shall be prohibited from accepting gifts, bequeaths, or donations of services or property. In addition, the Institute shall be prohibited from establishing a corporation or generating revenues from activities other than as provided under this section.

"(j) RULES OF CONSTRUCTION.—

"(1) COVERAGE.—Nothing in this section shall be construed—

"(A) to permit the Institute to mandate coverage, reimbursement, or other policies for any public or private payer; or

"(B) as preventing the Secretary from covering the routine costs of clinical care received by an individual entitled to, or enrolled for, benefits under title XVIII, XIX, or XXI in the case where such individual is participating in a clinical trial and such costs would otherwise be covered under such title with respect to the beneficiary.".

(b) DISSEMINATION AND BUILDING CAPACITY FOR RESEARCH.—Title IX of the Public Health Service Act (42 U.S.C. 299 et seq.), as amended by section 3606, is further amended by inserting after section 936 the following:

"SEC. 937. DISSEMINATION AND BUILDING CAPACITY FOR RESEARCH.

"(a) IN GENERAL.—

"(1) DISSEMINATION.—The Office of Communication and Knowledge Transfer (referred to in this section as the 'Office') at the Agency for Healthcare Research and Quality (or any other relevant office designated by Agency for Healthcare Research and Quality), in consultation with the National Institutes of Health, shall broadly disseminate the research findings that are published by the Patient Centered Outcomes Research Institute established under section 1181(b) of the Social Security Act (referred to in this section as the 'Institute') and other government-funded research relevant to comparative clinical effectiveness research. The Office shall create informational tools that organize and disseminate research findings for physicians, health care providers, patients, payers, and policy makers. The Office shall also develop a publicly available resource database that collects and contains government-funded evidence and research from public, private, not-for profit, and academic sources.

"(2) REQUIREMENTS.—The Office shall provide for the dissemination of the Institute's research findings and government-funded research relevant to comparative clinical effectiveness research to physicians, health care providers, patients, vendors of health information technology focused on clinical decision support, appropriate professional associations, and Federal and private health plans. Materials, forums, and media used to disseminate the findings, informational tools, and resource databases shall—

"(A) include a description of considerations for specific subpopulations, the research methodology, and the limitations of the research, and the names of the entities, agencies, instrumentalities, and individuals who conducted any research which was published by the Institute; and

"(B) not be construed as mandates, guidelines, or recommendations for payment, coverage, or treatment.

"(b) INCORPORATION OF RESEARCH FINDINGS.—The Office, in consultation with relevant medical and clinical associations, shall assist users of health information technology focused on clinical decision support to promote the timely incorporation of research findings disseminated under subsection (a) into clinical practices and to promote the ease of use of such incorporation.

"(c) FEEDBACK.—The Office shall establish a process to receive feedback from physicians, health care providers, patients, and vendors of health information technology focused on clinical decision support, appropriate professional associations, and Federal and private health plans about the value of the information disseminated and the assistance provided under this section.

"(d) RULE OF CONSTRUCTION.—Nothing in this section shall preclude the Institute from making its research findings publicly available as required under section 1181(d)(8) of the Social Security Act.

"(e) TRAINING OF RESEARCHERS.—The Agency for Health Care Research and Quality, in consultation with the National Institutes of Health, shall build capacity for comparative clinical effectiveness research by establishing a grant program that provides for the training of researchers in the methods used to conduct such research, including systematic reviews of existing research and primary research such as clinical trials. At a minimum, such training shall be in methods that meet the methodological standards adopted under section 1181(d)(9) of the Social Security Act.

"(f) BUILDING DATA FOR RESEARCH.—The Secretary shall provide for the coordination of relevant Federal health programs to build data capacity for comparative clinical effectiveness research, including the development and use of clinical registries and health outcomes research data networks, in order to develop and maintain a comprehensive, interoperable data network to collect, link, and analyze data on outcomes and effectiveness from multiple sources, including electronic health records.

"(g) AUTHORITY TO CONTRACT WITH THE INSTITUTE.—Agencies and instrumentalities of the Federal Government may enter into agreements with the Institute, and accept and retain funds, for the conduct and support of research described in this part, provided that the research to be conducted or supported under such agreements is authorized under the governing statutes of such agencies and instrumentalities.".

(c) IN GENERAL.—Part D of title XI of the Social Security Act, as added by subsection (a), is amended by adding at the end the following new section:

"LIMITATIONS ON CERTAIN USES OF COMPARATIVE CLINICAL EFFECTIVENESS RESEARCH

"SEC. 1182. (a) The Secretary may only use evidence and findings from research conducted under section 1181 to make a determination regarding coverage under title XVIII if such use is through an iterative and transparent process which includes public comment and considers the effect on subpopulations.

"(b) Nothing in section 1181 shall be construed as—

"(1) superceding or modifying the coverage of items or services under title XVIII that the Secretary determines are reasonable and necessary under section 1862(l)(1); or

"(2) authorizing the Secretary to deny coverage of items or services under such title solely on the basis of comparative clinical effectiveness research.

"(c)(1) The Secretary shall not use evidence or findings from comparative clinical effectiveness research conducted under section 1181 in determining coverage, reimbursement, or incentive programs under title XVIII in a manner that treats extending the life of an elderly, disabled, or terminally ill individual as of lower value than extending the life of an individual who is younger, nondisabled, or not terminally ill.

"(2) Paragraph (1) shall not be construed as preventing the Secretary from using evidence or findings from such comparative clinical effectiveness research in determining coverage, reimbursement, or incentive programs under title XVIII based upon a comparison of the difference in the effectiveness of alternative treatments in extending an individual's life due to the individual's age, disability, or terminal illness.

"(d)(1) The Secretary shall not use evidence or findings from comparative clinical effectiveness research conducted under section 1181 in determining coverage, reimbursement, or incentive programs under title XVIII in a manner that precludes, or with the intent to discourage, an individual from choosing a health care treatment based on how the individual values the tradeoff between extending the length of their life and the risk of disability.

"(2)(A) Paragraph (1) shall not be construed to—

"(i) limit the application of differential copayments under title XVIII based on factors such as cost or type of service; or

"(ii) prevent the Secretary from using evidence or findings from such comparative clinical effectiveness research in determining coverage, reimbursement, or incentive programs under such title based upon a comparison of the difference in the effectiveness of alternative health care treatments in extending an individual's life due to that individual's age, disability, or terminal illness.

"(3) Nothing in the provisions of, or amendments made by the Patient Protection and Affordable Care Act, shall be construed to limit comparative clinical effectiveness research or any other research, evaluation, or dissemination of information concerning the likelihood that a health care treatment will result in disability.

"(e) The Patient-Centered Outcomes Research Institute established under section 1181(b)(1) shall not develop or employ a dollars-per-quality adjusted life year (or similar measure that discounts the value of a life because of an individual's disability) as a threshold to establish what type of health care is cost effective or recommended. The Secretary shall not utilize such an adjusted life year (or such a similar measure) as a threshold to determine coverage, reimbursement, or incentive programs under title XVIII.".

(d) IN GENERAL.—Part D of title XI of the Social Security Act, as added by subsection (a) and amended by subsection (c), is amended by adding at the end the following new section:

"TRUST FUND TRANSFERS TO PATIENT-CENTERED OUTCOMES RESEARCH TRUST FUND

"SEC. 1183. (a) IN GENERAL.—The Secretary shall provide for the transfer, from the Federal Hospital Insurance Trust Fund under section 1817 and the Federal Supplementary Medical Insurance Trust Fund under section 1841, in proportion (as estimated by the Secretary) to the total expenditures during such fiscal year that are made under title XVIII from the respective trust fund, to the Patient-Centered Outcomes Research Trust Fund (referred to in this section as the 'PCORTF') under section 9511 of the Internal Revenue Code of 1986, of the following:

"(1) For fiscal year 2013, an amount equal to $1 multiplied by the average number of individuals entitled to benefits under part A, or enrolled under part B, of title XVIII during such fiscal year.

"(2) For each of fiscal years 2014, 2015, 2016, 2017, 2018, and 2019, an amount equal to $2 multiplied by the average number of individuals entitled to benefits under part A, or enrolled under part B, of title XVIII during such fiscal year.

"(b) ADJUSTMENTS FOR INCREASES IN HEALTH CARE SPENDING.—In the case of any fiscal year beginning after September 30, 2014, the dollar amount in effect under subsection (a)(2) for such fiscal year shall be equal to the sum of such dollar amount for the previous fiscal year (determined after the application of this subsection), plus an amount equal to the product of—

"(1) such dollar amount for the previous fiscal year, multiplied by

"(2) the percentage increase in the projected per capita amount of National Health Expenditures, as most recently published by the Secretary before the beginning of the fiscal year.".

(e) PATIENT-CENTERED OUTCOMES RESEARCH TRUST FUND; FINANCING FOR TRUST FUND.—

(1) ESTABLISHMENT OF TRUST FUND.—

(A) IN GENERAL.—Subchapter A of chapter 98 of the Internal Revenue Code of 1986 (relating to establishment of trust funds) is amended by adding at the end the following new section:

"SEC. 9511. PATIENT-CENTERED OUTCOMES RESEARCH TRUST FUND.

"(a) CREATION OF TRUST FUND.—There is established in the Treasury of the United States a trust fund to be known as the 'Patient-Centered Outcomes Research Trust Fund' (hereafter in this section referred to as the 'PCORTF'), consisting of such amounts as may be appropriated or credited to such Trust Fund as provided in this section and section 9602(b).

"(b) TRANSFERS TO FUND.—

"(1) APPROPRIATION.—There are hereby appropriated to the Trust Fund the following:

"(A) For fiscal year 2010, $10,000,000.

"(B) For fiscal year 2011, $50,000,000.

"(C) For fiscal year 2012, $150,000,000.

"(D) For fiscal year 2013—

"(i) an amount equivalent to the net revenues received in the Treasury from the fees imposed under subchapter B of chapter 34 (relating to fees on health insurance and self-insured plans) for such fiscal year; and

"(ii) $150,000,000.

"(E) For each of fiscal years 2014, 2015, 2016, 2017, 2018, and 2019—

"(i) an amount equivalent to the net revenues received in the Treasury from the fees imposed under subchapter B of chapter 34 (relating to fees on health insurance and self-insured plans) for such fiscal year; and

"(ii) $150,000,000.

The amounts appropriated under subparagraphs (A), (B), (C), (D)(ii), and (E)(ii) shall be transferred from the general fund of the Treasury, from funds not otherwise appropriated.

"(2) TRUST FUND TRANSFERS.—In addition to the amounts appropriated under paragraph (1), there shall be credited to the PCORTF the amounts transferred under section 1183 of the Social Security Act.

"(3) LIMITATION ON TRANSFERS TO PCORTF.—No amount may be appropriated or transferred to the PCORTF on and after the date of any expenditure from the PCORTF which is not an expenditure permitted under this section. The determination of whether an expenditure is so permitted shall be made without regard to—

"(A) any provision of law which is not contained or referenced in this chapter or in a revenue Act, and

"(B) whether such provision of law is a subsequently enacted provision or directly or indirectly seeks to waive the application of this paragraph.

"(c) TRUSTEE.—The Secretary of the Treasury shall be a trustee of the PCORTF.

“(d) EXPENDITURES FROM FUND.—

“(1) AMOUNTS AVAILABLE TO THE PATIENT-CENTERED OUTCOMES RESEARCH INSTITUTE.—Subject to paragraph (2), amounts in the PCORTF are available, without further appropriation, to the Patient-Centered Outcomes Research Institute established under section 1181(b) of the Social Security Act for carrying out part D of title XI of the Social Security Act (as in effect on the date of enactment of such Act).

“(2) TRANSFER OF FUNDS.—

“(A) IN GENERAL.—The trustee of the PCORTF shall provide for the transfer from the PCORTF of 20 percent of the amounts appropriated or credited to the PCORTF for each of fiscal years 2011 through 2019 to the Secretary of Health and Human Services to carry out section 937 of the Public Health Service Act.

“(B) AVAILABILITY.—Amounts transferred under subparagraph (A) shall remain available until expended.

“(C) REQUIREMENTS.—Of the amounts transferred under subparagraph (A) with respect to a fiscal year, the Secretary of Health and Human Services shall distribute—

“(i) 80 percent to the Office of Communication and Knowledge Transfer of the Agency for Healthcare Research and Quality (or any other relevant office designated by Agency for Healthcare Research and Quality) to carry out the activities described in section 937 of the Public Health Service Act; and

“(ii) 20 percent to the Secretary to carry out the activities described in such section 937.

“(e) NET REVENUES.—For purposes of this section, the term ‘net revenues’ means the amount estimated by the Secretary of the Treasury based on the excess of—

“(1) the fees received in the Treasury under subchapter B of chapter 34, over

“(2) the decrease in the tax imposed by chapter 1 resulting from the fees imposed by such subchapter.

“(f) TERMINATION.—No amounts shall be available for expenditure from the PCORTF after September 30, 2019, and any amounts in such Trust Fund after such date shall be transferred to the general fund of the Treasury.”.

(B) CLERICAL AMENDMENT.—The table of sections for subchapter A of chapter 98 of such Code is amended by adding at the end the following new item:

“Sec. 9511. Patient-centered outcomes research trust fund.”.

(2) FINANCING FOR FUND FROM FEES ON INSURED AND SELF-INSURED HEALTH PLANS.—

(A) GENERAL RULE.—Chapter 34 of the Internal Revenue Code of 1986 is amended by adding at the end the following new subchapter:

“Subchapter B—Insured and Self-Insured Health Plans

“Sec. 4375. Health insurance.
“Sec. 4376. Self-insured health plans.
“Sec. 4377. Definitions and special rules.

“SEC. 4375. HEALTH INSURANCE.

“(a) IMPOSITION OF FEE.—There is hereby imposed on each specified health insurance policy for each policy year ending after

September 30, 2012, a fee equal to the product of $2 ($1 in the case of policy years ending during fiscal year 2013) multiplied by the average number of lives covered under the policy.

"(b) LIABILITY FOR FEE.—The fee imposed by subsection (a) shall be paid by the issuer of the policy.

"(c) SPECIFIED HEALTH INSURANCE POLICY.—For purposes of this section:

"(1) IN GENERAL.—Except as otherwise provided in this section, the term 'specified health insurance policy' means any accident or health insurance policy (including a policy under a group health plan) issued with respect to individuals residing in the United States.

"(2) EXEMPTION FOR CERTAIN POLICIES.—The term 'specified health insurance policy' does not include any insurance if substantially all of its coverage is of excepted benefits described in section 9832(c).

"(3) TREATMENT OF PREPAID HEALTH COVERAGE ARRANGEMENTS.—

"(A) IN GENERAL.—In the case of any arrangement described in subparagraph (B), such arrangement shall be treated as a specified health insurance policy, and the person referred to in such subparagraph shall be treated as the issuer.

"(B) DESCRIPTION OF ARRANGEMENTS.—An arrangement is described in this subparagraph if under such arrangement fixed payments or premiums are received as consideration for any person's agreement to provide or arrange for the provision of accident or health coverage to residents of the United States, regardless of how such coverage is provided or arranged to be provided.

"(d) ADJUSTMENTS FOR INCREASES IN HEALTH CARE SPENDING.—In the case of any policy year ending in any fiscal year beginning after September 30, 2014, the dollar amount in effect under subsection (a) for such policy year shall be equal to the sum of such dollar amount for policy years ending in the previous fiscal year (determined after the application of this subsection), plus an amount equal to the product of—

"(1) such dollar amount for policy years ending in the previous fiscal year, multiplied by

"(2) the percentage increase in the projected per capita amount of National Health Expenditures, as most recently published by the Secretary before the beginning of the fiscal year.

"(e) TERMINATION.—This section shall not apply to policy years ending after September 30, 2019.

"SEC. 4376. SELF-INSURED HEALTH PLANS.

"(a) IMPOSITION OF FEE.—In the case of any applicable self-insured health plan for each plan year ending after September 30, 2012, there is hereby imposed a fee equal to $2 ($1 in the case of plan years ending during fiscal year 2013) multiplied by the average number of lives covered under the plan.

"(b) LIABILITY FOR FEE.—

"(1) IN GENERAL.—The fee imposed by subsection (a) shall be paid by the plan sponsor.

"(2) PLAN SPONSOR.—For purposes of paragraph (1) the term 'plan sponsor' means—

"(A) the employer in the case of a plan established or maintained by a single employer,

"(B) the employee organization in the case of a plan established or maintained by an employee organization,

"(C) in the case of—

"(i) a plan established or maintained by 2 or more employers or jointly by 1 or more employers and 1 or more employee organizations,

"(ii) a multiple employer welfare arrangement, or

"(iii) a voluntary employees' beneficiary association described in section 501(c)(9), the association, committee, joint board of trustees, or other similar group of representatives of the parties who establish or maintain the plan, or

"(D) the cooperative or association described in subsection (c)(2)(F) in the case of a plan established or maintained by such a cooperative or association.

"(c) APPLICABLE SELF-INSURED HEALTH PLAN.—For purposes of this section, the term 'applicable self-insured health plan' means any plan for providing accident or health coverage if—

"(1) any portion of such coverage is provided other than through an insurance policy, and

"(2) such plan is established or maintained—

"(A) by 1 or more employers for the benefit of their employees or former employees,

"(B) by 1 or more employee organizations for the benefit of their members or former members,

"(C) jointly by 1 or more employers and 1 or more employee organizations for the benefit of employees or former employees,

"(D) by a voluntary employees' beneficiary association described in section 501(c)(9),

"(E) by any organization described in section 501(c)(6), or

"(F) in the case of a plan not described in the preceding subparagraphs, by a multiple employer welfare arrangement (as defined in section 3(40) of Employee Retirement Income Security Act of 1974), a rural electric cooperative (as defined in section 3(40)(B)(iv) of such Act), or a rural telephone cooperative association (as defined in section 3(40)(B)(v) of such Act).

"(d) ADJUSTMENTS FOR INCREASES IN HEALTH CARE SPENDING.—In the case of any plan year ending in any fiscal year beginning after September 30, 2014, the dollar amount in effect under subsection (a) for such plan year shall be equal to the sum of such dollar amount for plan years ending in the previous fiscal year (determined after the application of this subsection), plus an amount equal to the product of—

"(1) such dollar amount for plan years ending in the previous fiscal year, multiplied by

"(2) the percentage increase in the projected per capita amount of National Health Expenditures, as most recently published by the Secretary before the beginning of the fiscal year.

"(e) TERMINATION.—This section shall not apply to plan years ending after September 30, 2019.

"SEC. 4377. DEFINITIONS AND SPECIAL RULES.

"(a) DEFINITIONS.—For purposes of this subchapter—

"(1) ACCIDENT AND HEALTH COVERAGE.—The term 'accident and health coverage' means any coverage which, if provided by an insurance policy, would cause such policy to be a specified health insurance policy (as defined in section 4375(c)).

"(2) INSURANCE POLICY.—The term 'insurance policy' means any policy or other instrument whereby a contract of insurance is issued, renewed, or extended.

"(3) UNITED STATES.—The term 'United States' includes any possession of the United States.

"(b) TREATMENT OF GOVERNMENTAL ENTITIES.—

"(1) IN GENERAL.—For purposes of this subchapter—

"(A) the term 'person' includes any governmental entity, and

"(B) notwithstanding any other law or rule of law, governmental entities shall not be exempt from the fees imposed by this subchapter except as provided in paragraph (2).

"(2) TREATMENT OF EXEMPT GOVERNMENTAL PROGRAMS.—In the case of an exempt governmental program, no fee shall be imposed under section 4375 or section 4376 on any covered life under such program.

"(3) EXEMPT GOVERNMENTAL PROGRAM DEFINED.—For purposes of this subchapter, the term 'exempt governmental program' means—

"(A) any insurance program established under title XVIII of the Social Security Act,

"(B) the medical assistance program established by title XIX or XXI of the Social Security Act,

"(C) any program established by Federal law for providing medical care (other than through insurance policies) to individuals (or the spouses and dependents thereof) by reason of such individuals being members of the Armed Forces of the United States or veterans, and

"(D) any program established by Federal law for providing medical care (other than through insurance policies) to members of Indian tribes (as defined in section 4(d) of the Indian Health Care Improvement Act).

"(c) TREATMENT AS TAX.—For purposes of subtitle F, the fees imposed by this subchapter shall be treated as if they were taxes.

"(d) NO COVER OVER TO POSSESSIONS.—Notwithstanding any other provision of law, no amount collected under this subchapter shall be covered over to any possession of the United States.".

(B) CLERICAL AMENDMENTS.—

(i) Chapter 34 of such Code is amended by striking the chapter heading and inserting the following:

"CHAPTER 34—TAXES ON CERTAIN INSURANCE POLICIES

"Subchapter A—Policies Issued By Foreign Insurers".

(ii) The table of chapters for subtitle D of such Code is amended by striking the item relating to chapter 34 and inserting the following new item:

"CHAPTER 34—TAXES ON CERTAIN INSURANCE POLICIES".

(f) TAX-EXEMPT STATUS OF THE PATIENT-CENTERED OUTCOMES RESEARCH INSTITUTE.—Subsection 501(l) of the Internal Revenue Code of 1986 is amended by adding at the end the following new paragraph:

"(4) The Patient-Centered Outcomes Research Institute established under section 1181(b) of the Social Security Act.".

SEC. 6302. FEDERAL COORDINATING COUNCIL FOR COMPARATIVE EFFECTIVENESS RESEARCH.

Notwithstanding any other provision of law, the Federal Coordinating Council for Comparative Effectiveness Research established under section 804 of Division A of the American Recovery and Reinvestment Act of 2009 (42 U.S.C. 299b–8), including the requirement under subsection (e)(2) of such section, shall terminate on the date of enactment of this Act.

Subtitle E—Medicare, Medicaid, and CHIP Program Integrity Provisions

SEC. 6401. PROVIDER SCREENING AND OTHER ENROLLMENT REQUIREMENTS UNDER MEDICARE, MEDICAID, AND CHIP.

(a) MEDICARE.—Section 1866(j) of the Social Security Act (42 U.S.C. 1395cc(j)) is amended—

(1) in paragraph (1)(A), by adding at the end the following: "Such process shall include screening of providers and suppliers in accordance with paragraph (2), a provisional period of enhanced oversight in accordance with paragraph (3), disclosure requirements in accordance with paragraph (4), the imposition of temporary enrollment moratoria in accordance with paragraph (5), and the establishment of compliance programs in accordance with paragraph (6).";

(2) by redesignating paragraph (2) as paragraph (7); and

(3) by inserting after paragraph (1) the following:

"(2) PROVIDER SCREENING.—

"(A) PROCEDURES.—Not later than 180 days after the date of enactment of this paragraph, the Secretary, in consultation with the Inspector General of the Department of Health and Human Services, shall establish procedures under which screening is conducted with respect to providers of medical or other items or services and suppliers under the program under this title, the Medicaid program under title XIX, and the CHIP program under title XXI.

"(B) LEVEL OF SCREENING.—The Secretary shall determine the level of screening conducted under this paragraph according to the risk of fraud, waste, and abuse, as determined by the Secretary, with respect to the category of provider of medical or other items or services or supplier. Such screening—

"(i) shall include a licensure check, which may include such checks across States; and

"(ii) may, as the Secretary determines appropriate based on the risk of fraud, waste, and abuse described in the preceding sentence, include—

"(I) a criminal background check;

"(II) fingerprinting;

"(III) unscheduled and unannounced site visits, including preenrollment site visits;

"(IV) database checks (including such checks across States); and

"(V) such other screening as the Secretary determines appropriate.

"(C) APPLICATION FEES.—

"(i) INDIVIDUAL PROVIDERS.—Except as provided in clause (iii), the Secretary shall impose a fee on each individual provider of medical or other items or services or supplier (such as a physician, physician assistant, nurse practitioner, or clinical nurse specialist) with respect to which screening is conducted under this paragraph in an amount equal to—

"(I) for 2010, $200; and

"(II) for 2011 and each subsequent year, the amount determined under this clause for the preceding year, adjusted by the percentage change in the consumer price index for all urban consumers (all items; United States city average) for the 12-month period ending with June of the previous year.

"(ii) INSTITUTIONAL PROVIDERS.—Except as provided in clause (iii), the Secretary shall impose a fee on each institutional provider of medical or other items or services or supplier (such as a hospital or skilled nursing facility) with respect to which screening is conducted under this paragraph in an amount equal to—

"(I) for 2010, $500; and

"(II) for 2011 and each subsequent year, the amount determined under this clause for the preceding year, adjusted by the percentage change in the consumer price index for all urban consumers (all items; United States city average) for the 12-month period ending with June of the previous year.

"(iii) HARDSHIP EXCEPTION; WAIVER FOR CERTAIN MEDICAID PROVIDERS.—The Secretary may, on a case-by-case basis, exempt a provider of medical or other items or services or supplier from the imposition of an application fee under this subparagraph if the Secretary determines that the imposition of the application fee would result in a hardship. The Secretary may waive the application fee under this subparagraph for providers enrolled in a State Medicaid program for whom the State demonstrates that imposition of the fee would impede beneficiary access to care.

"(iv) USE OF FUNDS.—Amounts collected as a result of the imposition of a fee under this subparagraph shall be used by the Secretary for program integrity efforts, including to cover the costs of conducting screening under this paragraph and to carry out this subsection and section 1128J.

"(D) APPLICATION AND ENFORCEMENT.—

"(i) NEW PROVIDERS OF SERVICES AND SUPPLIERS.—The screening under this paragraph shall apply, in the case of a provider of medical or other items or services or supplier who is not enrolled in the program under this title, title XIX , or title XXI as of the date of enactment of this paragraph, on or after the date that is 1 year after such date of enactment.

"(ii) CURRENT PROVIDERS OF SERVICES AND SUPPLIERS.—The screening under this paragraph shall apply, in the case of a provider of medical or other items or services or supplier who is enrolled in the program under this title, title XIX, or title XXI as of such date of enactment, on or after the date that is 2 years after such date of enactment.

"(iii) REVALIDATION OF ENROLLMENT.—Effective beginning on the date that is 180 days after such date of enactment, the screening under this paragraph shall apply with respect to the revalidation of enrollment of a provider of medical or other items or services or supplier in the program under this title, title XIX, or title XXI.

"(iv) LIMITATION ON ENROLLMENT AND REVALIDATION OF ENROLLMENT.—In no case may a provider of medical or other items or services or supplier who has not been screened under this paragraph be initially enrolled or reenrolled in the program under this title, title XIX, or title XXI on or after the date that is 3 years after such date of enactment.

"(E) EXPEDITED RULEMAKING.—The Secretary may promulgate an interim final rule to carry out this paragraph.

"(3) PROVISIONAL PERIOD OF ENHANCED OVERSIGHT FOR NEW PROVIDERS OF SERVICES AND SUPPLIERS.—

"(A) IN GENERAL.—The Secretary shall establish procedures to provide for a provisional period of not less than 30 days and not more than 1 year during which new providers of medical or other items or services and suppliers, as the Secretary determines appropriate, including categories of providers or suppliers, would be subject to enhanced oversight, such as prepayment review and payment caps, under the program under this title, the Medicaid program under title XIX. and the CHIP program under title XXI.

"(B) IMPLEMENTATION.—The Secretary may establish by program instruction or otherwise the procedures under this paragraph.

"(4) INCREASED DISCLOSURE REQUIREMENTS.—

"(A) DISCLOSURE.—A provider of medical or other items or services or supplier who submits an application for enrollment or revalidation of enrollment in the program under this title, title XIX, or title XXI on or after the date that is 1 year after the date of enactment of this paragraph shall disclose (in a form and manner and at such time as determined by the Secretary) any current or previous affiliation (directly or indirectly) with a provider of medical or other items or services or supplier that has uncollected debt, has been or is subject to a payment suspension under a Federal health care program (as defined in section 1128B(f)), has been excluded from participation under the program under this title, the Medicaid program under title XIX, or the CHIP program under title XXI, or has had its billing privileges denied or revoked.

"(B) AUTHORITY TO DENY ENROLLMENT.—If the Secretary determines that such previous affiliation poses an undue risk of fraud, waste, or abuse, the Secretary may deny such application. Such a denial shall be subject to appeal in accordance with paragraph (7).

"(5) AUTHORITY TO ADJUST PAYMENTS OF PROVIDERS OF SERVICES AND SUPPLIERS WITH THE SAME TAX IDENTIFICATION NUMBER FOR PAST-DUE OBLIGATIONS.—

"(A) IN GENERAL.—Notwithstanding any other provision of this title, in the case of an applicable provider of services or supplier, the Secretary may make any necessary adjustments to payments to the applicable provider of services or supplier under the program under this title in order to satisfy any past-due obligations described in subparagraph (B)(ii) of an obligated provider of services or supplier.

"(B) DEFINITIONS.—In this paragraph:

"(i) IN GENERAL.—The term 'applicable provider of services or supplier' means a provider of services or supplier that has the same taxpayer identification number assigned under section 6109 of the Internal Revenue Code of 1986 as is assigned to the obligated provider of services or supplier under such section, regardless of whether the applicable provider of services or supplier is assigned a different billing number or national provider identification number under the program under this title than is assigned to the obligated provider of services or supplier.

"(ii) OBLIGATED PROVIDER OF SERVICES OR SUPPLIER.—The term 'obligated provider of services or supplier' means a provider of services or supplier that owes a past-due obligation under the program under this title (as determined by the Secretary).

"(6) TEMPORARY MORATORIUM ON ENROLLMENT OF NEW PROVIDERS.—

"(A) IN GENERAL.—The Secretary may impose a temporary moratorium on the enrollment of new providers of services and suppliers, including categories of providers of services and suppliers, in the program under this title, under the Medicaid program under title XIX, or under the CHIP program under title XXI if the Secretary determines such moratorium is necessary to prevent or combat fraud, waste, or abuse under either such program.

"(B) LIMITATION ON REVIEW.—There shall be no judicial review under section 1869, section 1878, or otherwise, of a temporary moratorium imposed under subparagraph (A).

"(7) COMPLIANCE PROGRAMS.—

"(A) IN GENERAL.—On or after the date of implementation determined by the Secretary under subparagraph (C), a provider of medical or other items or services or supplier within a particular industry sector or category shall, as a condition of enrollment in the program under this title, title XIX, or title XXI, establish a compliance program that contains the core elements established under subparagraph (B) with respect to that provider or supplier and industry or category.

"(B) ESTABLISHMENT OF CORE ELEMENTS.—The Secretary, in consultation with the Inspector General of the Department of Health and Human Services, shall establish core elements for a compliance program under subparagraph (A) for providers or suppliers within a particular industry or category.

"(C) TIMELINE FOR IMPLEMENTATION.—The Secretary shall determine the timeline for the establishment of the core elements under subparagraph (B) and the date of the implementation of subparagraph (A) for providers or suppliers within a particular industry or category. The Secretary shall, in determining such date of implementation, consider the extent to which the adoption of compliance programs by a provider of medical or other items or services or supplier is widespread in a particular industry sector or with respect to a particular provider or supplier category.".

(b) MEDICAID.—

(1) STATE PLAN AMENDMENT.—Section 1902(a) of the Social Security Act (42 U.S.C. 1396a(a)), as amended by section 4302(b), is amended—

(A) in subsection (a)—

(i) by striking "and" at the end of paragraph (75);

(ii) by striking the period at the end of paragraph (76) and inserting a semicolon; and

(iii) by inserting after paragraph (76) the following:

"(77) provide that the State shall comply with provider and supplier screening, oversight, and reporting requirements in accordance with subsection (ii);"; and

(B) by adding at the end the following:

"(ii) PROVIDER AND SUPPLIER SCREENING, OVERSIGHT, AND REPORTING REQUIREMENTS.—For purposes of subsection (a)(77), the requirements of this subsection are the following:

"(1) SCREENING.—The State complies with the process for screening providers and suppliers under this title, as established by the Secretary under section 1886(j)(2).

"(2) PROVISIONAL PERIOD OF ENHANCED OVERSIGHT FOR NEW PROVIDERS AND SUPPLIERS.—The State complies with procedures to provide for a provisional period of enhanced oversight for new providers and suppliers under this title, as established by the Secretary under section 1886(j)(3).

"(3) DISCLOSURE REQUIREMENTS.—The State requires providers and suppliers under the State plan or under a waiver of the plan to comply with the disclosure requirements established by the Secretary under section 1886(j)(4).

"(4) TEMPORARY MORATORIUM ON ENROLLMENT OF NEW PROVIDERS OR SUPPLIERS.—

"(A) TEMPORARY MORATORIUM IMPOSED BY THE SECRETARY.—

"(i) IN GENERAL.—Subject to clause (ii), the State complies with any temporary moratorium on the enrollment of new providers or suppliers imposed by the Secretary under section 1886(j)(6).

"(ii) EXCEPTION.—A State shall not be required to comply with a temporary moratorium described in clause (i) if the State determines that the imposition of such temporary moratorium would adversely impact beneficiaries' access to medical assistance.

"(B) MORATORIUM ON ENROLLMENT OF PROVIDERS AND SUPPLIERS.—At the option of the State, the State imposes, for purposes of entering into participation agreements with providers or suppliers under the State plan or under a waiver of the plan, periods of enrollment moratoria, or numerical caps or other limits, for providers or suppliers identified by the Secretary as being at high-risk for fraud, waste, or abuse as necessary to combat fraud, waste, or abuse, but only if the State determines that the imposition of any such period, cap, or other limits would not adversely impact beneficiaries' access to medical assistance.

"(5) COMPLIANCE PROGRAMS.—The State requires providers and suppliers under the State plan or under a waiver of the plan to establish, in accordance with the requirements of section 1866(j)(7), a compliance program that contains the core elements established under subparagraph (B) of that section 1866(j)(7) for providers or suppliers within a particular industry or category.

"(6) REPORTING OF ADVERSE PROVIDER ACTIONS.—The State complies with the national system for reporting criminal and civil convictions, sanctions, negative licensure actions, and other adverse provider actions to the Secretary, through the Administrator of the Centers for Medicare & Medicaid Services, in accordance with regulations of the Secretary.

"(7) ENROLLMENT AND NPI OF ORDERING OR REFERRING PROVIDERS.—The State requires—

"(A) all ordering or referring physicians or other professionals to be enrolled under the State plan or under a waiver of the plan as a participating provider; and

"(B) the national provider identifier of any ordering or referring physician or other professional to be specified on any claim for payment that is based on an order or referral of the physician or other professional.

"(8) OTHER STATE OVERSIGHT.—Nothing in this subsection shall be interpreted to preclude or limit the ability of a State to engage in provider and supplier screening or enhanced provider and supplier oversight activities beyond those required by the Secretary.".

(2) DISCLOSURE OF MEDICARE TERMINATED PROVIDERS AND SUPPLIERS TO STATES.—The Administrator of the Centers for

Medicare & Medicaid Services shall establish a process for making available to the each State agency with responsibility for administering a State Medicaid plan (or a waiver of such plan) under title XIX of the Social Security Act or a child health plan under title XXI the name, national provider identifier, and other identifying information for any provider of medical or other items or services or supplier under the Medicare program under title XVIII or under the CHIP program under title XXI that is terminated from participation under that program within 30 days of the termination (and, with respect to all such providers or suppliers who are terminated from the Medicare program on the date of enactment of this Act, within 90 days of such date).

(3) CONFORMING AMENDMENT.—Section 1902(a)(23) of the Social Security Act (42 U.S.C. 1396a), is amended by inserting before the semicolon at the end the following: "or by a provider or supplier to which a moratorium under subsection (ii)(4) is applied during the period of such moratorium".

(c) CHIP.—Section 2107(e)(1) of the Social Security Act (42 U.S.C. 1397gg(e)(1)), as amended by section 2101(d), is amended—

(1) by redesignating subparagraphs (D) through (M) as subparagraphs (E) through (N), respectively; and

(2) by inserting after subparagraph (C), the following:

"(D) Subsections (a)(77) and (ii) of section 1902 (relating to provider and supplier screening, oversight, and reporting requirements).".

SEC. 6402. ENHANCED MEDICARE AND MEDICAID PROGRAM INTEGRITY PROVISIONS.

(a) IN GENERAL.—Part A of title XI of the Social Security Act (42 U.S.C. 1301 et seq.), as amended by sections 6002, 6004, and 6102, is amended by inserting after section 1128I the following new section:

"SEC. 1128J. MEDICARE AND MEDICAID PROGRAM INTEGRITY PROVISIONS.

"(a) DATA MATCHING.—

"(1) INTEGRATED DATA REPOSITORY.—

"(A) INCLUSION OF CERTAIN DATA.—

"(i) IN GENERAL.—The Integrated Data Repository of the Centers for Medicare & Medicaid Services shall include, at a minimum, claims and payment data from the following:

"(I) The programs under titles XVIII and XIX (including parts A, B, C, and D of title XVIII).

"(II) The program under title XXI.

"(III) Health-related programs administered by the Secretary of Veterans Affairs.

"(IV) Health-related programs administered by the Secretary of Defense.

"(V) The program of old-age, survivors, and disability insurance benefits established under title II.

"(VI) The Indian Health Service and the Contract Health Service program.

"(ii) PRIORITY FOR INCLUSION OF CERTAIN DATA.—Inclusion of the data described in subclause (I) of such clause in the Integrated Data Repository shall be a priority. Data described in subclauses (II) through (VI) of such clause shall be included in the Integrated Data Repository as appropriate.

"(B) DATA SHARING AND MATCHING.—

"(i) IN GENERAL.—The Secretary shall enter into agreements with the individuals described in clause (ii) under which such individuals share and match data in the system of records of the respective agencies of such individuals with data in the system of records of the Department of Health and Human Services for the purpose of identifying potential fraud, waste, and abuse under the programs under titles XVIII and XIX.

"(ii) INDIVIDUALS DESCRIBED.—The following individuals are described in this clause:

"(I) The Commissioner of Social Security.

"(II) The Secretary of Veterans Affairs.

"(III) The Secretary of Defense.

"(IV) The Director of the Indian Health Service.

"(iii) DEFINITION OF SYSTEM OF RECORDS.—For purposes of this paragraph, the term 'system of records' has the meaning given such term in section 552a(a)(5) of title 5, United States Code.

"(2) ACCESS TO CLAIMS AND PAYMENT DATABASES.—For purposes of conducting law enforcement and oversight activities and to the extent consistent with applicable information, privacy, security, and disclosure laws, including the regulations promulgated under the Health Insurance Portability and Accountability Act of 1996 and section 552a of title 5, United States Code, and subject to any information systems security requirements under such laws or otherwise required by the Secretary, the Inspector General of the Department of Health and Human Services and the Attorney General shall have access to claims and payment data of the Department of Health and Human Services and its contractors related to titles XVIII, XIX, and XXI.

"(b) OIG AUTHORITY TO OBTAIN INFORMATION.—

"(1) IN GENERAL.—Notwithstanding and in addition to any other provision of law, the Inspector General of the Department of Health and Human Services may, for purposes of protecting the integrity of the programs under titles XVIII and XIX, obtain information from any individual (including a beneficiary provided all applicable privacy protections are followed) or entity that—

"(A) is a provider of medical or other items or services, supplier, grant recipient, contractor, or subcontractor; or

"(B) directly or indirectly provides, orders, manufactures, distributes, arranges for, prescribes, supplies, or receives medical or other items or services payable by any Federal health care program (as defined in section 1128B(f)) regardless of how the item or service is paid for, or to whom such payment is made.

"(2) INCLUSION OF CERTAIN INFORMATION.—Information which the Inspector General may obtain under paragraph (1) includes any supporting documentation necessary to validate claims for payment or payments under title XVIII or XIX, including a prescribing physician's medical records for an individual who is prescribed an item or service which is covered under part B of title XVIII, a covered part D drug (as defined in section 1860D–2(e)) for which payment is made under an MA–PD plan under part C of such title, or a prescription drug plan under part D of such title, and any records necessary for evaluation of the economy, efficiency, and effectiveness of the programs under titles XVIII and XIX.

"(c) ADMINISTRATIVE REMEDY FOR KNOWING PARTICIPATION BY BENEFICIARY IN HEALTH CARE FRAUD SCHEME.—

"(1) IN GENERAL.—In addition to any other applicable remedies, if an applicable individual has knowingly participated in a Federal health care fraud offense or a conspiracy to commit a Federal health care fraud offense, the Secretary shall impose an appropriate administrative penalty commensurate with the offense or conspiracy.

"(2) APPLICABLE INDIVIDUAL.—For purposes of paragraph (1), the term 'applicable individual' means an individual—

"(A) entitled to, or enrolled for, benefits under part A of title XVIII or enrolled under part B of such title;

"(B) eligible for medical assistance under a State plan under title XIX or under a waiver of such plan; or

"(C) eligible for child health assistance under a child health plan under title XXI.

"(d) REPORTING AND RETURNING OF OVERPAYMENTS.—

"(1) IN GENERAL.—If a person has received an overpayment, the person shall—

"(A) report and return the overpayment to the Secretary, the State, an intermediary, a carrier, or a contractor, as appropriate, at the correct address; and

"(B) notify the Secretary, State, intermediary, carrier, or contractor to whom the overpayment was returned in writing of the reason for the overpayment.

"(2) DEADLINE FOR REPORTING AND RETURNING OVERPAYMENTS.—An overpayment must be reported and returned under paragraph (1) by the later of—

"(A) the date which is 60 days after the date on which the overpayment was identified; or

"(B) the date any corresponding cost report is due, if applicable.

"(3) ENFORCEMENT.—Any overpayment retained by a person after the deadline for reporting and returning the overpayment under paragraph (2) is an obligation (as defined in section 3729(b)(3) of title 31, United States Code) for purposes of section 3729 of such title.

"(4) DEFINITIONS.—In this subsection:

"(A) KNOWING AND KNOWINGLY.—The terms 'knowing' and 'knowingly' have the meaning given those terms in section 3729(b) of title 31, United States Code.

"(B) OVERPAYMENT.—The term "overpayment" means any funds that a person receives or retains under title XVIII or XIX to which the person, after applicable reconciliation, is not entitled under such title.

"(C) PERSON.—

"(i) IN GENERAL.—The term 'person' means a provider of services, supplier, medicaid managed care organization (as defined in section 1903(m)(1)(A)),

Medicare Advantage organization (as defined in section 1859(a)(1)), or PDP sponsor (as defined in section 1860D–41(a)(13)).

"(ii) EXCLUSION.—Such term does not include a beneficiary.

"(e) INCLUSION OF NATIONAL PROVIDER IDENTIFIER ON ALL APPLICATIONS AND CLAIMS.—The Secretary shall promulgate a regulation that requires, not later than January 1, 2011, all providers of medical or other items or services and suppliers under the programs under titles XVIII and XIX that qualify for a national provider identifier to include their national provider identifier on all applications to enroll in such programs and on all claims for payment submitted under such programs.".

(b) ACCESS TO DATA.—

(1) MEDICARE PART D.—Section 1860D–15(f)(2) of the Social Security Act (42 U.S.C. 1395w–116(f)(2)) is amended by striking "may be used by" and all that follows through the period at the end and inserting "may be used—

"(A) by officers, employees, and contractors of the Department of Health and Human Services for the purposes of, and to the extent necessary in—

"(i) carrying out this section; and

"(ii) conducting oversight, evaluation, and enforcement under this title; and

"(B) by the Attorney General and the Comptroller General of the United States for the purposes of, and to the extent necessary in, carrying out health oversight activities.".

(2) DATA MATCHING.—Section 552a(a)(8)(B) of title 5, United States Code, is amended—

(A) in clause (vii), by striking "or" at the end;

(B) in clause (viii), by inserting "or" after the semicolon; and

(C) by adding at the end the following new clause:

"(ix) matches performed by the Secretary of Health and Human Services or the Inspector General of the Department of Health and Human Services with respect to potential fraud, waste, and abuse, including matches of a system of records with non-Federal records;".

(3) MATCHING AGREEMENTS WITH THE COMMISSIONER OF SOCIAL SECURITY.—Section 205(r) of the Social Security Act (42 U.S.C. 405(r)) is amended by adding at the end the following new paragraph:

"(9)(A) The Commissioner of Social Security shall, upon the request of the Secretary or the Inspector General of the Department of Health and Human Services—

"(i) enter into an agreement with the Secretary or such Inspector General for the purpose of matching data in the system of records of the Social Security Administration and the system of records of the Department of Health and Human Services; and

"(ii) include in such agreement safeguards to assure the maintenance of the confidentiality of any information disclosed.

"(B) For purposes of this paragraph, the term 'system of records' has the meaning given such term in section 552a(a)(5) of title 5, United States Code.".

(c) WITHHOLDING OF FEDERAL MATCHING PAYMENTS FOR STATES THAT FAIL TO REPORT ENROLLEE ENCOUNTER DATA IN THE MEDICAID STATISTICAL INFORMATION SYSTEM.—Section 1903(i) of the Social Security Act (42 U.S.C. 1396b(i)) is amended—

(1) in paragraph (23), by striking "or" at the end;

(2) in paragraph (24), by striking the period at the end and inserting "; or"; and

(3) by adding at the end the following new paragraph:.

"(25) with respect to any amounts expended for medical assistance for individuals for whom the State does not report enrollee encounter data (as defined by the Secretary) to the Medicaid Statistical Information System (MSIS) in a timely manner (as determined by the Secretary).".

(d) PERMISSIVE EXCLUSIONS AND CIVIL MONETARY PENALTIES.—

(1) PERMISSIVE EXCLUSIONS.—Section 1128(b) of the Social Security Act (42 U.S.C. 1320a–7(b)) is amended by adding at the end the following new paragraph:

"(16) MAKING FALSE STATEMENTS OR MISREPRESENTATION OF MATERIAL FACTS.—Any individual or entity that knowingly makes or causes to be made any false statement, omission, or misrepresentation of a material fact in any application, agreement, bid, or contract to participate or enroll as a provider of services or supplier under a Federal health care program (as defined in section 1128B(f)), including Medicare Advantage organizations under part C of title XVIII, prescription drug plan sponsors under part D of title XVIII, medicaid managed care organizations under title XIX, and entities that apply to participate as providers of services or suppliers in such managed care organizations and such plans.".

(2) CIVIL MONETARY PENALTIES.—

(A) IN GENERAL.—Section 1128A(a) of the Social Security Act (42 U.S.C. 1320a–7a(a)) is amended—

(i) in paragraph (1)(D), by striking "was excluded" and all that follows through the period at the end and inserting "was excluded from the Federal health care program (as defined in section 1128B(f)) under which the claim was made pursuant to Federal law.";

(ii) in paragraph (6), by striking "or" at the end;

(iii) by inserting after paragraph (7), the following new paragraphs:

"(8) orders or prescribes a medical or other item or service during a period in which the person was excluded from a Federal health care program (as so defined), in the case where the person knows or should know that a claim for such medical or other item or service will be made under such a program;

"(9) knowingly makes or causes to be made any false statement, omission, or misrepresentation of a material fact in any application, bid, or contract to participate or enroll as a provider of services or a supplier under a Federal health care program (as so defined), including Medicare Advantage organizations under part C of title XVIII, prescription drug plan sponsors under part D of title XVIII, medicaid managed care organizations under title XIX, and entities that apply to participate as providers of services or suppliers in such managed care organizations and such plans;

"(10) knows of an overpayment (as defined in paragraph (4) of section 1128J(d)) and does not report and return the overpayment in accordance with such section;";

(iv) in the first sentence—

(I) by striking the "or" after "prohibited relationship occurs;"; and

(II) by striking "act)" and inserting "act; or in cases under paragraph (9), $50,000 for each false statement or misrepresentation of a material fact)"; and

(v) in the second sentence, by striking "purpose)" and inserting "purpose; or in cases under paragraph (9), an assessment of not more than 3 times the total amount claimed for each item or service for which payment was made based upon the application containing the false statement or misrepresentation of a material fact)".

(B) CLARIFICATION OF TREATMENT OF CERTAIN CHARITABLE AND OTHER INNOCUOUS PROGRAMS.—Section 1128A(i)(6) of the Social Security Act (42 U.S.C. 1320a–7a(i)(6)) is amended—

(i) in subparagraph (C), by striking "or" at the end;

(ii) in subparagraph (D), as redesignated by section 4331(e) of the Balanced Budget Act of 1997 (Public Law 105–33), by striking the period at the end and inserting a semicolon;

(iii) by redesignating subparagraph (D), as added by section 4523(c) of such Act, as subparagraph (E) and striking the period at the end and inserting "; or"; and

(iv) by adding at the end the following new subparagraphs:

"(F) any other remuneration which promotes access to care and poses a low risk of harm to patients and Federal health care programs (as defined in section 1128B(f) and designated by the Secretary under regulations);

"(G) the offer or transfer of items or services for free or less than fair market value by a person, if—

"(i) the items or services consist of coupons, rebates, or other rewards from a retailer;

"(ii) the items or services are offered or transferred on equal terms available to the general public, regardless of health insurance status; and

"(iii) the offer or transfer of the items or services is not tied to the provision of other items or services reimbursed in whole or in part by the program under title XVIII or a State health care program (as defined in section 1128(h));

"(H) the offer or transfer of items or services for free or less than fair market value by a person, if—

"(i) the items or services are not offered as part of any advertisement or solicitation;

"(ii) the items or services are not tied to the provision of other services reimbursed in whole or in part by the program under title XVIII or a State health care program (as so defined);

"(iii) there is a reasonable connection between the items or services and the medical care of the individual; and

"(iv) the person provides the items or services after determining in good faith that the individual is in financial need; or

"(I) effective on a date specified by the Secretary (but not earlier than January 1, 2011), the waiver by a PDP sponsor of a prescription drug plan under part D of title XVIII or an MA organization offering an MA–PD plan under part C of such title of any copayment for the first fill of a covered part D drug (as defined in section 1860D–2(e)) that is a generic drug for individuals enrolled in the prescription drug plan or MA–PD plan, respectively.".

(e) TESTIMONIAL SUBPOENA AUTHORITY IN EXCLUSION-ONLY CASES.—Section 1128(f) of the Social Security Act (42 U.S.C. 1320a–7(f)) is amended by adding at the end the following new paragraph:

"(4) The provisions of subsections (d) and (e) of section 205 shall apply with respect to this section to the same extent as they are applicable with respect to title II. The Secretary may delegate the authority granted by section 205(d) (as made applicable to this section) to the Inspector General of the Department of Health and Human Services for purposes of any investigation under this section.".

(f) HEALTH CARE FRAUD.—

(1) KICKBACKS.—Section 1128B of the Social Security Act (42 U.S.C. 1320a–7b) is amended by adding at the end the following new subsection:

"(g) In addition to the penalties provided for in this section or section 1128A, a claim that includes items or services resulting from a violation of this section constitutes a false or fraudulent claim for purposes of subchapter III of chapter 37 of title 31, United States Code.".

(2) REVISING THE INTENT REQUIREMENT.—Section 1128B of the Social Security Act (42 U.S.C. 1320a–7b), as amended by paragraph (1), is amended by adding at the end the following new subsection:

"(h) With respect to violations of this section, a person need not have actual knowledge of this section or specific intent to commit a violation of this section.".

(g) SURETY BOND REQUIREMENTS.—

(1) DURABLE MEDICAL EQUIPMENT.—Section 1834(a)(16)(B) of the Social Security Act (42 U.S.C. 1395m(a)(16)(B)) is amended by inserting "that the Secretary determines is commensurate with the volume of the billing of the supplier" before the period at the end.

(2) HOME HEALTH AGENCIES.—Section 1861(o)(7)(C) of the Social Security Act (42 U.S.C. 1395x(o)(7)(C)) is amended by inserting "that the Secretary determines is commensurate with the volume of the billing of the home health agency" before the semicolon at the end.

(3) REQUIREMENTS FOR CERTAIN OTHER PROVIDERS OF SERVICES AND SUPPLIERS.—Section 1862 of the Social Security Act

(42 U.S.C. 1395y) is amended by adding at the end the following new subsection:

"(n) REQUIREMENT OF A SURETY BOND FOR CERTAIN PROVIDERS OF SERVICES AND SUPPLIERS.—

"(1) IN GENERAL.—The Secretary may require a provider of services or supplier described in paragraph (2) to provide the Secretary on a continuing basis with a surety bond in a form specified by the Secretary in an amount (not less than $50,000) that the Secretary determines is commensurate with the volume of the billing of the provider of services or supplier. The Secretary may waive the requirement of a bond under the preceding sentence in the case of a provider of services or supplier that provides a comparable surety bond under State law.

"(2) PROVIDER OF SERVICES OR SUPPLIER DESCRIBED.—A provider of services or supplier described in this paragraph is a provider of services or supplier the Secretary determines appropriate based on the level of risk involved with respect to the provider of services or supplier, and consistent with the surety bond requirements under sections 1834(a)(16)(B) and 1861(o)(7)(C).".

(h) SUSPENSION OF MEDICARE AND MEDICAID PAYMENTS PENDING INVESTIGATION OF CREDIBLE ALLEGATIONS OF FRAUD.—

(1) MEDICARE.—Section 1862 of the Social Security Act (42 U.S.C. 1395y), as amended by subsection (g)(3), is amended by adding at the end the following new subsection:

"(o) SUSPENSION OF PAYMENTS PENDING INVESTIGATION OF CREDIBLE ALLEGATIONS OF FRAUD.—

"(1) IN GENERAL.—The Secretary may suspend payments to a provider of services or supplier under this title pending an investigation of a credible allegation of fraud against the provider of services or supplier, unless the Secretary determines there is good cause not to suspend such payments.

"(2) CONSULTATION.—The Secretary shall consult with the Inspector General of the Department of Health and Human Services in determining whether there is a credible allegation of fraud against a provider of services or supplier.

"(3) PROMULGATION OF REGULATIONS.—The Secretary shall promulgate regulations to carry out this subsection and section 1903(i)(2)(C).".

(2) MEDICAID.—Section 1903(i)(2) of such Act (42 U.S.C. 1396b(i)(2)) is amended—

(A) in subparagraph (A), by striking "or" at the end; and

(B) by inserting after subparagraph (B), the following:

"(C) by any individual or entity to whom the State has failed to suspend payments under the plan during any period when there is pending an investigation of a credible allegation of fraud against the individual or entity, as determined by the State in accordance with regulations promulgated by the Secretary for purposes of section 1862(o) and this subparagraph, unless the State determines in accordance with such regulations there is good cause not to suspend such payments; or".

(i) INCREASED FUNDING TO FIGHT FRAUD AND ABUSE.—

(1) IN GENERAL.—Section 1817(k) of the Social Security Act (42 U.S.C. 1395i(k)) is amended—

(A) by adding at the end the following new paragraph:

"(7) ADDITIONAL FUNDING.—In addition to the funds otherwise appropriated to the Account from the Trust Fund under paragraphs (3) and (4) and for purposes described in paragraphs (3)(C) and (4)(A), there are hereby appropriated an additional $10,000,000 to such Account from such Trust Fund for each of fiscal years 2011 through 2020. The funds appropriated under this paragraph shall be allocated in the same proportion as the total funding appropriated with respect to paragraphs (3)(A) and (4)(A) was allocated with respect to fiscal year 2010, and shall be available without further appropriation until expended."; and

(B) in paragraph (4)(A), by inserting "until expended" after "appropriation".

(2) INDEXING OF AMOUNTS APPROPRIATED.—

(A) DEPARTMENTS OF HEALTH AND HUMAN SERVICES AND JUSTICE.—Section 1817(k)(3)(A)(i) of the Social Security Act (42 U.S.C. 1395i(k)(3)(A)(i)) is amended—

(i) in subclause (III), by inserting "and" at the end;

(ii) in subclause (IV)—

(I) by striking "for each of fiscal years 2007, 2008, 2009, and 2010" and inserting "for each fiscal year after fiscal year 2006"; and

(II) by striking "; and" and inserting a period; and

(iii) by striking subclause (V).

(B) OFFICE OF THE INSPECTOR GENERAL OF THE DEPARTMENT OF HEALTH AND HUMAN SERVICES.—Section 1817(k)(3)(A)(ii) of such Act (42 U.S.C. 1395i(k)(3)(A)(ii)) is amended—

(i) in subclause (VIII), by inserting "and" at the end;

(ii) in subclause (IX)—

(I) by striking "for each of fiscal years 2008, 2009, and 2010" and inserting "for each fiscal year after fiscal year 2007"; and

(II) by striking "; and" and inserting a period; and

(iii) by striking subclause (X).

(C) FEDERAL BUREAU OF INVESTIGATION.—Section 1817(k)(3)(B) of the Social Security Act (42 U.S.C. 1395i(k)(3)(B)) is amended—

(i) in clause (vii), by inserting "and" at the end;

(ii) in clause (viii)—

(I) by striking "for each of fiscal years 2007, 2008, 2009, and 2010" and inserting "for each fiscal year after fiscal year 2006"; and

(II) by striking "; and" and inserting a period; and

(iii) by striking clause (ix).

(D) MEDICARE INTEGRITY PROGRAM.—Section 1817(k)(4)(C) of the Social Security Act (42 U.S.C. 1395i(k)(4)(C)) is amended by adding at the end the following new clause:

"(ii) For each fiscal year after 2010, by the percentage increase in the consumer price index for all urban consumers (all items; United States city average) over the previous year.".

(j) MEDICARE INTEGRITY PROGRAM AND MEDICAID INTEGRITY PROGRAM.—

(1) MEDICARE INTEGRITY PROGRAM.—

(A) REQUIREMENT TO PROVIDE PERFORMANCE STATISTICS.—Section 1893(c) of the Social Security Act (42 U.S.C. 1395ddd(c)) is amended—

(i) in paragraph (3), by striking "and" at the end;

(ii) by redesignating paragraph (4) as paragraph (5); and

(iii) by inserting after paragraph (3) the following new paragraph:

"(4) the entity agrees to provide the Secretary and the Inspector General of the Department of Health and Human Services with such performance statistics (including the number and amount of overpayments recovered, the number of fraud referrals, and the return on investment of such activities by the entity) as the Secretary or the Inspector General may request; and".

(B) EVALUATIONS AND ANNUAL REPORT.—Section 1893 of the Social Security Act (42 U.S.C. 1395ddd) is amended by adding at the end the following new subsection:

"(i) EVALUATIONS AND ANNUAL REPORT.—

"(1) EVALUATIONS.—The Secretary shall conduct evaluations of eligible entities which the Secretary contracts with under the Program not less frequently than every 3 years.

"(2) ANNUAL REPORT.—Not later than 180 days after the end of each fiscal year (beginning with fiscal year 2011), the Secretary shall submit a report to Congress which identifies—

"(A) the use of funds, including funds transferred from the Federal Hospital Insurance Trust Fund under section 1817 and the Federal Supplementary Insurance Trust Fund under section 1841, to carry out this section; and

"(B) the effectiveness of the use of such funds.".

(C) FLEXIBILITY IN PURSUING FRAUD AND ABUSE.—Section 1893(a) of the Social Security Act (42 U.S.C. 1395ddd(a)) is amended by inserting ", or otherwise," after "entities".

(2) MEDICAID INTEGRITY PROGRAM.—

(A) REQUIREMENT TO PROVIDE PERFORMANCE STATISTICS.—Section 1936(c)(2) of the Social Security Act (42 U.S.C. 1396u–6(c)(2)) is amended—

(i) by redesignating subparagraph (D) as subparagraph (E); and

(ii) by inserting after subparagraph (C) the following new subparagraph:

"(D) The entity agrees to provide the Secretary and the Inspector General of the Department of Health and Human Services with such performance statistics (including the number and amount of overpayments recovered, the number of fraud referrals, and the return on investment of such activities by the entity) as the Secretary or the Inspector General may request.".

(B) EVALUATIONS AND ANNUAL REPORT.—Section 1936(e) of the Social Security Act (42 U.S.C. 1396u–7(e)) is amended—

(i) by redesignating paragraph (4) as paragraph (5); and

(ii) by inserting after paragraph (3) the following new paragraph:

"(4) EVALUATIONS.—The Secretary shall conduct evaluations of eligible entities which the Secretary contracts with under the Program not less frequently than every 3 years.".

(k) EXPANDED APPLICATION OF HARDSHIP WAIVERS FOR EXCLUSIONS.—Section 1128(c)(3)(B) of the Social Security Act (42 U.S.C. 1320a–7(c)(3)(B)) is amended by striking "individuals entitled to benefits under part A of title XVIII or enrolled under part B of such title, or both" and inserting "beneficiaries (as defined in section 1128A(i)(5)) of that program".

SEC. 6403. ELIMINATION OF DUPLICATION BETWEEN THE HEALTHCARE INTEGRITY AND PROTECTION DATA BANK AND THE NATIONAL PRACTITIONER DATA BANK.

(a) INFORMATION REPORTED BY FEDERAL AGENCIES AND HEALTH PLANS.—Section 1128E of the Social Security Act (42 U.S.C. 1320a–7e) is amended—

(1) by striking subsection (a) and inserting the following:

"(a) IN GENERAL.—The Secretary shall maintain a national health care fraud and abuse data collection program under this section for the reporting of certain final adverse actions (not including settlements in which no findings of liability have been made) against health care providers, suppliers, or practitioners as required by subsection (b), with access as set forth in subsection (d), and shall furnish the information collected under this section to the National Practitioner Data Bank established pursuant to the Health Care Quality Improvement Act of 1986 (42 U.S.C. 11101 et seq.).";

(2) by striking subsection (d) and inserting the following:

"(d) ACCESS TO REPORTED INFORMATION.—

"(1) AVAILABILITY.—The information collected under this section shall be available from the National Practitioner Data Bank to the agencies, authorities, and officials which are provided under section 1921(b) information reported under section 1921(a).

"(2) FEES FOR DISCLOSURE.—The Secretary may establish or approve reasonable fees for the disclosure of information under this section. The amount of such a fee may not exceed the costs of processing the requests for disclosure and of providing such information. Such fees shall be available to the Secretary to cover such costs.";

(3) by striking subsection (f) and inserting the following:

"(f) APPROPRIATE COORDINATION.—In implementing this section, the Secretary shall provide for the maximum appropriate coordination with part B of the Health Care Quality Improvement Act of 1986 (42 U.S.C. 11131 et seq.) and section 1921."; and

(4) in subsection (g)—

(A) in paragraph (1)(A)—

(i) in clause (iii)—

(I) by striking "or State" each place it appears;

(II) by redesignating subclauses (II) and (III) as subclauses (III) and (IV), respectively; and

(III) by inserting after subclause (I) the following new subclause:

"(II) any dismissal or closure of the proceedings by reason of the provider, supplier, or practitioner surrendering their license or leaving the State or jurisdiction"; and

(ii) by striking clause (iv) and inserting the following:

"(iv) Exclusion from participation in a Federal health care program (as defined in section 1128B(f)).";

(B) in paragraph (3)—

(i) by striking subparagraphs (D) and (E); and

(ii) by redesignating subparagraph (F) as subparagraph (D); and

(C) in subparagraph (D) (as so redesignated), by striking "or State".

(b) INFORMATION REPORTED BY STATE LAW OR FRAUD ENFORCEMENT AGENCIES.—Section 1921 of the Social Security Act (42 U.S.C. 1396r–2) is amended—

(1) in subsection (a)—

(A) in paragraph (1)—

(i) by striking "SYSTEM.—The State" and all that follows through the semicolon and inserting SYSTEM.—

"(A) LICENSING OR CERTIFICATION ACTIONS.—The State must have in effect a system of reporting the following information with respect to formal proceedings (as defined by the Secretary in regulations) concluded against a health care practitioner or entity by a State licensing or certification agency:";

(ii) by redesignating subparagraphs (A) through (D) as clauses (i) through (iv), respectively, and indenting appropriately;

(iii) in subparagraph (A)(iii) (as so redesignated)—

(I) by striking "the license of" and inserting "license or the right to apply for, or renew, a license by"; and

(II) by inserting "nonrenewability," after "voluntary surrender,"; and

(iv) by adding at the end the following new subparagraph:

"(B) OTHER FINAL ADVERSE ACTIONS.—The State must have in effect a system of reporting information with respect to any final adverse action (not including settlements in which no findings of liability have been made) taken against a health care provider, supplier, or practitioner by a State law or fraud enforcement agency."; and

(B) in paragraph (2), by striking "the authority described in paragraph (1)" and inserting "a State licensing or certification agency or State law or fraud enforcement agency";

(2) in subsection (b)—

(A) by striking paragraph (2) and inserting the following:

"(2) to State licensing or certification agencies and Federal agencies responsible for the licensing and certification of health care providers, suppliers, and licensed health care practitioners;";

(B) in each of paragraphs (4) and (6), by inserting ", but only with respect to information provided pursuant to subsection (a)(1)(A)" before the comma at the end;

(C) by striking paragraph (5) and inserting the following:

"(5) to State law or fraud enforcement agencies,";

(D) by redesignating paragraphs (7) and (8) as paragraphs (8) and (9), respectively; and

(E) by inserting after paragraph (6) the following new paragraph:

"(7) to health plans (as defined in section 1128C(c));";

(3) by redesignating subsection (d) as subsection (h), and by inserting after subsection (c) the following new subsections:

"(d) DISCLOSURE AND CORRECTION OF INFORMATION.—

"(1) DISCLOSURE.—With respect to information reported pursuant to subsection (a)(1), the Secretary shall—

"(A) provide for disclosure of the information, upon request, to the health care practitioner who, or the entity that, is the subject of the information reported; and

"(B) establish procedures for the case where the health care practitioner or entity disputes the accuracy of the information reported.

"(2) CORRECTIONS.—Each State licensing or certification agency and State law or fraud enforcement agency shall report corrections of information already reported about any formal proceeding or final adverse action described in subsection (a), in such form and manner as the Secretary prescribes by regulation.

"(e) FEES FOR DISCLOSURE.—The Secretary may establish or approve reasonable fees for the disclosure of information under this section. The amount of such a fee may not exceed the costs of processing the requests for disclosure and of providing such information. Such fees shall be available to the Secretary to cover such costs.

"(f) PROTECTION FROM LIABILITY FOR REPORTING.—No person or entity, including any agency designated by the Secretary in subsection (b), shall be held liable in any civil action with respect to any reporting of information as required under this section, without knowledge of the falsity of the information contained in the report.

"(g) REFERENCES.—For purposes of this section:

"(1) STATE LICENSING OR CERTIFICATION AGENCY.—The term 'State licensing or certification agency' includes any authority of a State (or of a political subdivision thereof) responsible for the licensing of health care practitioners (or any peer review organization or private accreditation entity reviewing the services provided by health care practitioners) or entities.

"(2) STATE LAW OR FRAUD ENFORCEMENT AGENCY.—The term 'State law or fraud enforcement agency' includes—

"(A) a State law enforcement agency; and

"(B) a State medicaid fraud control unit (as defined in section 1903(q)).

"(3) FINAL ADVERSE ACTION.—

"(A) IN GENERAL.—Subject to subparagraph (B), the term 'final adverse action' includes—

"(i) civil judgments against a health care provider, supplier, or practitioner in State court related to the delivery of a health care item or service;

"(ii) State criminal convictions related to the delivery of a health care item or service;

"(iii) exclusion from participation in State health care programs (as defined in section 1128(h));

"(iv) any licensing or certification action described in subsection (a)(1)(A) taken against a supplier by a State licensing or certification agency; and

"(v) any other adjudicated actions or decisions that the Secretary shall establish by regulation.

"(B) EXCEPTION.—Such term does not include any action with respect to a malpractice claim."; and

(4) in subsection (h), as so redesignated, by striking "The Secretary" and all that follows through the period at the end and inserting "In implementing this section, the Secretary shall provide for the maximum appropriate coordination with part B of the Health Care Quality Improvement Act of 1986 (42 U.S.C. 11131 et seq.) and section 1128E.".

(c) CONFORMING AMENDMENT.—Section 1128C(a)(1) of the Social Security Act (42 U.S.C. 1320a–7c(a)(1)) is amended—

(1) in subparagraph (C), by adding "and" after the comma at the end;

(2) in subparagraph (D), by striking ", and" and inserting a period; and

(3) by striking subparagraph (E).

(d) TRANSITION PROCESS; EFFECTIVE DATE.—

(1) IN GENERAL.—Effective on the date of enactment of this Act, the Secretary of Health and Human Services (in this section referred to as the "Secretary") shall implement a transition process under which, by not later than the end of the transition period described in paragraph (5), the Secretary shall cease operating the Healthcare Integrity and Protection Data Bank established under section 1128E of the Social Security Act (as in effect before the effective date specified in paragraph (6)) and shall transfer all data collected in the Healthcare Integrity and Protection Data Bank to the National Practitioner Data Bank established pursuant to the Health Care Quality Improvement Act of 1986 (42 U.S.C. 11101 et seq.). During such transition process, the Secretary shall have in effect appropriate procedures to ensure that data collection and access to the Healthcare Integrity and Protection Data Bank and the National Practitioner Data Bank are not disrupted.

(2) REGULATIONS.—The Secretary shall promulgate regulations to carry out the amendments made by subsections (a) and (b).

(3) FUNDING.—

(A) AVAILABILITY OF FEES.—Fees collected pursuant to section 1128E(d)(2) of the Social Security Act prior to the effective date specified in paragraph (6) for the disclosure of information in the Healthcare Integrity and Protection Data Bank shall be available to the Secretary, without fiscal year limitation, for payment of costs related to the transition process described in paragraph (1). Any such fees remaining after the transition period is complete shall be available to the Secretary, without fiscal year limitation, for payment of the costs of operating the National Practitioner Data Bank.

(B) AVAILABILITY OF ADDITIONAL FUNDS.—In addition to the fees described in subparagraph (A), any funds available to the Secretary or to the Inspector General of the Department of Health and Human Services for a purpose related to combating health care fraud, waste, or abuse shall be available to the extent necessary for operating the Healthcare Integrity and Protection Data Bank during the transition period, including systems testing and other activities necessary to ensure that information formerly reported to the Healthcare Integrity and Protection Data Bank will be accessible through the National Practitioner Data Bank after the end of such transition period.

(4) SPECIAL PROVISION FOR ACCESS TO THE NATIONAL PRACTITIONER DATA BANK BY THE DEPARTMENT OF VETERANS AFFAIRS.—

(A) IN GENERAL.—Notwithstanding any other provision of law, during the 1-year period that begins on the effective date specified in paragraph (6), the information described in subparagraph (B) shall be available from the National Practitioner Data Bank to the Secretary of Veterans Affairs without charge.

(B) INFORMATION DESCRIBED.—For purposes of subparagraph (A), the information described in this subparagraph is the information that would, but for the amendments made by this section, have been available to the Secretary of Veterans Affairs from the Healthcare Integrity and Protection Data Bank.

(5) TRANSITION PERIOD DEFINED.—For purposes of this subsection, the term "transition period" means the period that begins on the date of enactment of this Act and ends on the later of—

(A) the date that is 1 year after such date of enactment; or

(B) the effective date of the regulations promulgated under paragraph (2).

(6) EFFECTIVE DATE.—The amendments made by subsections (a), (b), and (c) shall take effect on the first day after the final day of the transition period.

SEC. 6404. MAXIMUM PERIOD FOR SUBMISSION OF MEDICARE CLAIMS REDUCED TO NOT MORE THAN 12 MONTHS.

(a) REDUCING MAXIMUM PERIOD FOR SUBMISSION.—

(1) PART A.—Section 1814(a) of the Social Security Act (42 U.S.C. 1395f(a)(1)) is amended—

(A) in paragraph (1), by striking "period of 3 calendar years" and all that follows through the semicolon and inserting "period ending 1 calendar year after the date of service;"; and

(B) by adding at the end the following new sentence: "In applying paragraph (1), the Secretary may specify exceptions to the 1 calendar year period specified in such paragraph."

(2) PART B.—

(A) Section 1842(b)(3) of such Act (42 U.S.C. 1395u(b)(3)(B)) is amended—

(i) in subparagraph (B), in the flush language following clause (ii), by striking "close of the calendar year following the year in which such service is furnished (deeming any service furnished in the last 3 months of any calendar year to have been furnished in the succeeding calendar year)" and inserting "period ending 1 calendar year after the date of service"; and

(ii) by adding at the end the following new sentence: "In applying subparagraph (B), the Secretary may specify exceptions to the 1 calendar year period specified in such subparagraph."

(B) Section 1835(a) of such Act (42 U.S.C. 1395n(a)) is amended—

(i) in paragraph (1), by striking "period of 3 calendar years" and all that follows through the semicolon and inserting "period ending 1 calendar year after the date of service;"; and

(ii) by adding at the end the following new sentence: "In applying paragraph (1), the Secretary may specify exceptions to the 1 calendar year period specified in such paragraph."

(b) EFFECTIVE DATE.—

(1) IN GENERAL.—The amendments made by subsection (a) shall apply to services furnished on or after January 1, 2010.

(2) SERVICES FURNISHED BEFORE 2010.—In the case of services furnished before January 1, 2010, a bill or request for payment under section 1814(a)(1), 1842(b)(3)(B), or 1835(a) shall be filed not later that December 31, 2010.

SEC. 6405. PHYSICIANS WHO ORDER ITEMS OR SERVICES REQUIRED TO BE MEDICARE ENROLLED PHYSICIANS OR ELIGIBLE PROFESSIONALS.

(a) DME.—Section 1834(a)(11)(B) of the Social Security Act (42 U.S.C. 1395m(a)(11)(B)) is amended by striking "physician" and inserting "physician enrolled under section 1866(j) or an eligible professional under section 1848(k)(3)(B) that is enrolled under section 1866(j)".

(b) HOME HEALTH SERVICES.—

(1) PART A.—Section 1814(a)(2) of such Act (42 U.S.C. 1395(a)(2)) is amended in the matter preceding subparagraph (A) by inserting "in the case of services described in subparagraph (C), a physician enrolled under section 1866(j) or an eligible professional under section 1848(k)(3)(B)," before "or, in the case of services".

(2) PART B.—Section 1835(a)(2) of such Act (42 U.S.C. 1395n(a)(2)) is amended in the matter preceding subparagraph (A) by inserting ", or in the case of services described in subparagraph (A), a physician enrolled under section 1866(j) or an eligible professional under section 1848(k)(3)(B)," after "a physician".

(c) APPLICATION TO OTHER ITEMS OR SERVICES.—The Secretary may extend the requirement applied by the amendments made by subsections (a) and (b) to durable medical equipment and home health services (relating to requiring certifications and written orders to be made by enrolled physicians and health professions) to all other categories of items or services under title XVIII of the Social Security Act (42 U.S.C. 1395 et seq.), including covered part D drugs as defined in section 1860D–2(e) of such Act (42 U.S.C. 1395w–102), that are ordered, prescribed, or referred by a physician enrolled under section 1866(j) of such Act (42 U.S.C. 1395cc(j)) or an eligible professional under section 1848(k)(3)(B) of such Act (42 U.S.C. 1395w–4(k)(3)(B)).

(d) EFFECTIVE DATE.—The amendments made by this section shall apply to written orders and certifications made on or after July 1, 2010.

SEC. 6406. REQUIREMENT FOR PHYSICIANS TO PROVIDE DOCUMENTATION ON REFERRALS TO PROGRAMS AT HIGH RISK OF WASTE AND ABUSE.

(a) PHYSICIANS AND OTHER SUPPLIERS.—Section 1842(h) of the Social Security Act (42 U.S.C. 1395u(h)) is amended by adding at the end the following new paragraph:

"(9) The Secretary may revoke enrollment, for a period of not more than one year for each act, for a physician or supplier under section 1866(j) if such physician or supplier fails to maintain and, upon request of the Secretary, provide access to documentation relating to written orders or requests for payment for durable medical equipment, certifications for home health services, or referrals for other items or services written or ordered by such physician or supplier under this title, as specified by the Secretary.".

(b) PROVIDERS OF SERVICES.—Section 1866(a)(1) of such Act (42 U.S.C. 1395cc) is further amended—

(1) in subparagraph (U), by striking at the end "and";

(2) in subparagraph (V), by striking the period at the end and adding "; and"; and

(3) by adding at the end the following new subparagraph:

"(W) maintain and, upon request of the Secretary, provide access to documentation relating to written orders or requests for payment for durable medical equipment, certifications for home health services, or referrals for other items or services written or ordered by the provider under this title, as specified by the Secretary.".

(c) OIG PERMISSIVE EXCLUSION AUTHORITY.—Section 1128(b)(11) of the Social Security Act (42 U.S.C. 1320a–7(b)(11)) is amended by inserting ", ordering, referring for furnishing, or certifying the need for" after "furnishing".

(d) EFFECTIVE DATE.—The amendments made by this section shall apply to orders, certifications, and referrals made on or after January 1, 2010.

SEC. 6407. FACE TO FACE ENCOUNTER WITH PATIENT REQUIRED BEFORE PHYSICIANS MAY CERTIFY ELIGIBILITY FOR HOME HEALTH SERVICES OR DURABLE MEDICAL EQUIPMENT UNDER MEDICARE.

(a) CONDITION OF PAYMENT FOR HOME HEALTH SERVICES.—

(1) PART A.—Section 1814(a)(2)(C) of such Act is amended—

(A) by striking "and such services" and inserting "such services"; and

(B) by inserting after "care of a physician" the following: ", and, in the case of a certification made by a physician after January 1, 2010, prior to making such certification the physician must document that the physician himself or herself has had a face-to-face encounter (including through use of telehealth, subject to the requirements in section 1834(m), and other than with respect to encounters that are incident to services involved) with the individual within a reasonable timeframe as determined by the Secretary".

(2) PART B.—Section 1835(a)(2)(A) of the Social Security Act is amended—

(A) by striking "and" before "(iii)"; and

(B) by inserting after "care of a physician" the following: ", and (iv) in the case of a certification after January 1, 2010, prior to making such certification the physician must document that the physician has had a face-to-face encounter (including through use of telehealth and other than with respect to encounters that are incident to services involved) with the individual during the 6-month period preceding such certification, or other reasonable timeframe as determined by the Secretary".

(b) CONDITION OF PAYMENT FOR DURABLE MEDICAL EQUIPMENT.—Section 1834(a)(11)(B) of the Social Security Act (42 U.S.C. 1395m(a)(11)(B)) is amended—

(1) by striking "ORDER.—The Secretary" and inserting "ORDER.—

"(i) IN GENERAL.—The Secretary"; and

(2) by adding at the end the following new clause:

"(ii) REQUIREMENT FOR FACE TO FACE ENCOUNTER.—The Secretary shall require that such an order be written pursuant to the physician documenting that a physician, a physician assistant, a nurse practitioner, or a clinical nurse specialist (as those terms are defined in section 1861(aa)(5)) has had a face-to-face encounter (including through use of telehealth under subsection (m) and other than with respect to encounters that are incident to services involved) with the individual involved during the 6-month period preceding such written order, or other reasonable timeframe as determined by the Secretary.".

(c) APPLICATION TO OTHER AREAS UNDER MEDICARE.—The Secretary may apply the face-to-face encounter requirement described in the amendments made by subsections (a) and (b) to other items and services for which payment is provided under title XVIII of the Social Security Act based upon a finding that such an decision would reduce the risk of waste, fraud, or abuse.

(d) APPLICATION TO MEDICAID.—The requirements pursuant to the amendments made by subsections (a) and (b) shall apply in the case of physicians making certifications for home health services under title XIX of the Social Security Act in the same manner and to the same extent as such requirements apply in the case of physicians making such certifications under title XVIII of such Act.

SEC. 6408. ENHANCED PENALTIES.

(a) CIVIL MONETARY PENALTIES FOR FALSE STATEMENTS OR DELAYING INSPECTIONS.—Section 1128A(a) of the Social Security Act (42 U.S.C. 1320a–7a(a)), as amended by section 5002(d)(2)(A), is amended—

(1) in paragraph (6), by striking "or" at the end; and

(2) by inserting after paragraph (7) the following new paragraphs:

"(8) knowingly makes, uses, or causes to be made or used, a false record or statement material to a false or fraudulent claim for payment for items and services furnished under a Federal health care program; or

"(9) fails to grant timely access, upon reasonable request (as defined by the Secretary in regulations), to the Inspector General of the Department of Health and Human Services, for the purpose of audits, investigations, evaluations, or other statutory functions of the Inspector General of the Department of Health and Human Services;"; and

(3) in the first sentence—

(A) by striking "or in cases under paragraph (7)" and inserting "in cases under paragraph (7)"; and

(B) by striking "act)" and inserting "act, in cases under paragraph (8), $50,000 for each false record or statement, or in cases under paragraph (9), $15,000 for each day of the failure described in such paragraph)".

(b) MEDICARE ADVANTAGE AND PART D PLANS.—

(1) ENSURING TIMELY INSPECTIONS RELATING TO CONTRACTS WITH MA ORGANIZATIONS.—Section 1857(d)(2) of such Act (42 U.S.C. 1395w–27(d)(2)) is amended—

(A) in subparagraph (A), by inserting "timely" before "inspect"; and

(B) in subparagraph (B), by inserting "timely" before "audit and inspect".

(2) MARKETING VIOLATIONS.—Section 1857(g)(1) of the Social Security Act (42 U.S.C. 1395w–27(g)(1)) is amended—

(A) in subparagraph (F), by striking "or" at the end;

(B) by inserting after subparagraph (G) the following new subparagraphs:

"(H) except as provided under subparagraph (C) or (D) of section 1860D–1(b)(1), enrolls an individual in any plan under this part without the prior consent of the individual or the designee of the individual;

"(I) transfers an individual enrolled under this part from one plan to another without the prior consent of the individual or the designee of the individual or solely for the purpose of earning a commission;

"(J) fails to comply with marketing restrictions described in subsections (h) and (j) of section 1851 or applicable implementing regulations or guidance; or

"(K) employs or contracts with any individual or entity who engages in the conduct described in subparagraphs (A) through (J) of this paragraph;"; and

(C) by adding at the end the following new sentence: "The Secretary may provide, in addition to any other remedies authorized by law, for any of the remedies described in paragraph (2), if the Secretary determines that any employee or agent of such organization, or any provider or supplier who contracts with such organization, has engaged in any conduct described in subparagraphs (A) through (K) of this paragraph.".

(3) PROVISION OF FALSE INFORMATION.—Section 1857(g)(2)(A) of the Social Security Act (42 U.S.C. 1395w–

27(g)(2)(A)) is amended by inserting "except with respect to a determination under subparagraph (E), an assessment of not more than the amount claimed by such plan or plan sponsor based upon the misrepresentation or falsified information involved," after "for each such determination,".

(c) OBSTRUCTION OF PROGRAM AUDITS.—Section 1128(b)(2) of the Social Security Act (42 U.S.C. 1320a–7(b)(2)) is amended—

(1) in the heading, by inserting "OR AUDIT" after "INVESTIGATION"; and

(2) by striking "investigation into" and all that follows through the period and inserting "investigation or audit related to—"

"(i) any offense described in paragraph (1) or in subsection (a); or

"(ii) the use of funds received, directly or indirectly, from any Federal health care program (as defined in section 1128B(f)).".

(d) EFFECTIVE DATE.—

(1) IN GENERAL.—Except as provided in paragraph (2), the amendments made by this section shall apply to acts committed on or after January 1, 2010.

(2) EXCEPTION.—The amendments made by subsection (b)(1) take effect on the date of enactment of this Act.

SEC. 6409. MEDICARE SELF-REFERRAL DISCLOSURE PROTOCOL.

(a) DEVELOPMENT OF SELF-REFERRAL DISCLOSURE PROTOCOL.—

(1) IN GENERAL.—The Secretary of Health and Human Services, in cooperation with the Inspector General of the Department of Health and Human Services, shall establish, not later than 6 months after the date of the enactment of this Act, a protocol to enable health care providers of services and suppliers to disclose an actual or potential violation of section 1877 of the Social Security Act (42 U.S.C. 1395nn) pursuant to a self-referral disclosure protocol (in this section referred to as an "SRDP"). The SRDP shall include direction to health care providers of services and suppliers on—

(A) a specific person, official, or office to whom such disclosures shall be made; and

(B) instruction on the implication of the SRDP on corporate integrity agreements and corporate compliance agreements.

(2) PUBLICATION ON INTERNET WEBSITE OF SRDP INFORMATION.—The Secretary of Health and Human Services shall post information on the public Internet website of the Centers for Medicare & Medicaid Services to inform relevant stakeholders of how to disclose actual or potential violations pursuant to an SRDP.

(3) RELATION TO ADVISORY OPINIONS.—The SRDP shall be separate from the advisory opinion process set forth in regulations implementing section 1877(g) of the Social Security Act.

(b) REDUCTION IN AMOUNTS OWED.—The Secretary of Health and Human Services is authorized to reduce the amount due and owing for all violations under section 1877 of the Social Security Act to an amount less than that specified in subsection (g) of such section. In establishing such amount for a violation, the Secretary may consider the following factors:

(1) The nature and extent of the improper or illegal practice.

(2) The timeliness of such self-disclosure.

(3) The cooperation in providing additional information related to the disclosure.

(4) Such other factors as the Secretary considers appropriate.

(c) REPORT.—Not later than 18 months after the date on which the SRDP protocol is established under subsection (a)(1), the Secretary shall submit to Congress a report on the implementation of this section. Such report shall include—

(1) the number of health care providers of services and suppliers making disclosures pursuant to the SRDP;

(2) the amounts collected pursuant to the SRDP;

(3) the types of violations reported under the SRDP; and

(4) such other information as may be necessary to evaluate the impact of this section.

SEC. 6410. ADJUSTMENTS TO THE MEDICARE DURABLE MEDICAL EQUIPMENT, PROSTHETICS, ORTHOTICS, AND SUPPLIES COMPETITIVE ACQUISITION PROGRAM.

(a) EXPANSION OF ROUND 2 OF THE DME COMPETITIVE BIDDING PROGRAM.—Section 1847(a)(1) of the Social Security Act (42 U.S.C. 1395w–3(a)(1)) is amended—

(1) in subparagraph (B)(i)(II), by striking "70" and inserting "91"; and

(2) in subparagraph (D)(ii)—

(A) in subclause (I), by striking "and" at the end;

(B) by redesignating subclause (II) as subclause (III); and

(C) by inserting after subclause (I) the following new subclause:

"(II) the Secretary shall include the next 21 largest metropolitan statistical areas by total population (after those selected under subclause (I)) for such round; and".

(b) REQUIREMENT TO EITHER COMPETITIVELY BID AREAS OR USE COMPETITIVE BID PRICES BY 2016.—Section 1834(a)(1)(F) of the Social Security Act (42 U.S.C. 1395m(a)(1)(F)) is amended—

(1) in clause (i), by striking "and" at the end;

(2) in clause (ii)—

(A) by inserting "(and, in the case of covered items furnished on or after January 1, 2016, subject to clause (iii), shall)" after "may"; and

(B) by striking the period at the end and inserting "; and"; and

(3) by adding at the end the following new clause:

"(iii) in the case of covered items furnished on or after January 1, 2016, the Secretary shall continue to make such adjustments described in clause (ii) as, under such competitive acquisition programs, additional covered items are phased in or information is updated as contracts under section 1847 are recompeted in accordance with section 1847(b)(3)(B).".

SEC. 6411. EXPANSION OF THE RECOVERY AUDIT CONTRACTOR (RAC) PROGRAM.

(a) EXPANSION TO MEDICAID.—

(1) STATE PLAN AMENDMENT.—Section 1902(a)(42) of the Social Security Act (42 U.S.C. 1396a(a)(42)) is amended—

(A) by striking "that the records" and inserting "that— "(A) the records";

(B) by inserting "and" after the semicolon; and

(C) by adding at the end the following:

"(B) not later than December 31, 2010, the State shall—

"(i) establish a program under which the State contracts (consistent with State law and in the same manner as the Secretary enters into contracts with recovery audit contractors under section 1893(h), subject to such exceptions or requirements as the Secretary may require for purposes of this title or a particular State) with 1 or more recovery audit contractors for the purpose of identifying underpayments and overpayments and recouping overpayments under the State plan and under any waiver of the State plan with respect to all services for which payment is made to any entity under such plan or waiver; and

"(ii) provide assurances satisfactory to the Secretary that—

"(I) under such contracts, payment shall be made to such a contractor only from amounts recovered;

"(II) from such amounts recovered, payment—

"(aa) shall be made on a contingent basis for collecting overpayments; and

"(bb) may be made in such amounts as the State may specify for identifying underpayments;

"(III) the State has an adequate process for entities to appeal any adverse determination made by such contractors; and

"(IV) such program is carried out in accordance with such requirements as the Secretary shall specify, including—

"(aa) for purposes of section 1903(a)(7), that amounts expended by the State to carry out the program shall be considered amounts expended as necessary for the proper and efficient administration of the State plan or a waiver of the plan;

"(bb) that section 1903(d) shall apply to amounts recovered under the program; and

"(cc) that the State and any such contractors under contract with the State shall coordinate such recovery audit efforts with other contractors or entities performing audits of entities receiving payments under the State plan or waiver in the State, including efforts with Federal and State law enforcement with respect to the Department of Justice, including the Federal Bureau of Investigations, the Inspector General of the Department of Health and Human Services, and the State medicaid fraud control unit; and".

(2) COORDINATION; REGULATIONS.—

(A) IN GENERAL.—The Secretary of Health and Human Services, acting through the Administrator of the Centers for Medicare & Medicaid Services, shall coordinate the expansion of the Recovery Audit Contractor program to Medicaid with States, particularly with respect to each State that enters into a contract with a recovery audit contractor for purposes of the State's Medicaid program prior to December 31, 2010.

(B) REGULATIONS.—The Secretary of Health and Human Services shall promulgate regulations to carry out this subsection and the amendments made by this subsection, including with respect to conditions of Federal financial participation, as specified by the Secretary.

(b) EXPANSION TO MEDICARE PARTS C AND D.—Section 1893(h) of the Social Security Act (42 U.S.C. 1395ddd(h)) is amended—

(1) in paragraph (1), in the matter preceding subparagraph (A), by striking "part A or B" and inserting "this title";

(2) in paragraph (2), by striking "parts A and B" and inserting "this title";

(3) in paragraph (3), by inserting "(not later than December 31, 2010, in the case of contracts relating to payments made under part C or D)" after "2010";

(4) in paragraph (4), in the matter preceding subparagraph (A), by striking "part A or B" and inserting "this title"; and

(5) by adding at the end the following:

"(9) SPECIAL RULES RELATING TO PARTS C AND D.—The Secretary shall enter into contracts under paragraph (1) to require recovery audit contractors to—

"(A) ensure that each MA plan under part C has an anti-fraud plan in effect and to review the effectiveness of each such anti-fraud plan;

"(B) ensure that each prescription drug plan under part D has an anti-fraud plan in effect and to review the effectiveness of each such anti-fraud plan;

"(C) examine claims for reinsurance payments under section 1860D–15(b) to determine whether prescription drug plans submitting such claims incurred costs in excess of the allowable reinsurance costs permitted under paragraph (2) of that section; and

"(D) review estimates submitted by prescription drug plans by private plans with respect to the enrollment of high cost beneficiaries (as defined by the Secretary) and to compare such estimates with the numbers of such beneficiaries actually enrolled by such plans.".

(c) ANNUAL REPORT.—The Secretary of Health and Human Services, acting through the Administrator of the Centers for Medicare & Medicaid Services, shall submit an annual report to Congress concerning the effectiveness of the Recovery Audit Contractor program under Medicaid and Medicare and shall include such reports recommendations for expanding or improving the program.

Subtitle F—Additional Medicaid Program Integrity Provisions

SEC. 6501. TERMINATION OF PROVIDER PARTICIPATION UNDER MEDICAID IF TERMINATED UNDER MEDICARE OR OTHER STATE PLAN.

Section 1902(a)(39) of the Social Security Act (42 U.S.C. 42 U.S.C. 1396a(a)) is amended by inserting after "1128A," the following: "terminate the participation of any individual or entity in such program if (subject to such exceptions as are permitted with respect to exclusion under sections 1128(c)(3)(B) and 1128(d)(3)(B)) participation of such individual or entity is terminated under title XVIII or any other State plan under this title,".

SEC. 6502. MEDICAID EXCLUSION FROM PARTICIPATION RELATING TO CERTAIN OWNERSHIP, CONTROL, AND MANAGEMENT AFFILIATIONS.

Section 1902(a) of the Social Security Act (42 U.S.C. 1396a(a)), as amended by section 6401(b), is amended by inserting after paragraph (77) the following:

"(78) provide that the State agency described in paragraph (9) exclude, with respect to a period, any individual or entity from participation in the program under the State plan if such individual or entity owns, controls, or manages an entity that (or if such entity is owned, controlled, or managed by an individual or entity that)—

"(A) has unpaid overpayments (as defined by the Secretary) under this title during such period determined by the Secretary or the State agency to be delinquent;

"(B) is suspended or excluded from participation under or whose participation is terminated under this title during such period; or

"(C) is affiliated with an individual or entity that has been suspended or excluded from participation under this title or whose participation is terminated under this title during such period;".

SEC. 6503. BILLING AGENTS, CLEARINGHOUSES, OR OTHER ALTERNATE PAYEES REQUIRED TO REGISTER UNDER MEDICAID.

(a) In General.—Section 1902(a) of the Social Security Act (42 U.S.C. 42 U.S.C. 1396a(a)), as amended by section 6502(a), is amended by inserting after paragraph (78), the following:

"(79) provide that any agent, clearinghouse, or other alternate payee (as defined by the Secretary) that submits claims on behalf of a health care provider must register with the State and the Secretary in a form and manner specified by the Secretary;".

SEC. 6504. REQUIREMENT TO REPORT EXPANDED SET OF DATA ELEMENTS UNDER MMIS TO DETECT FRAUD AND ABUSE.

(a) In General.—Section 1903(r)(1)(F) of the Social Security Act (42 U.S.C. 1396b(r)(1)(F)) is amended by inserting after "necessary" the following: "and including, for data submitted to the Secretary on or after January 1, 2010, data elements from the automated data system that the Secretary determines to be necessary for program integrity, program oversight, and administration, at such frequency as the Secretary shall determine".

(b) MANAGED CARE ORGANIZATIONS.—

(1) IN GENERAL.—Section 1903(m)(2)(A)(xi) of the Social Security Act (42 U.S.C. 1396b(m)(2)(A)(xi)) is amended by inserting "and for the provision of such data to the State at a frequency and level of detail to be specified by the Secretary" after "patients".

(2) EFFECTIVE DATE.—The amendment made by paragraph (1) shall apply with respect to contract years beginning on or after January 1, 2010.

SEC. 6505. PROHIBITION ON PAYMENTS TO INSTITUTIONS OR ENTITIES LOCATED OUTSIDE OF THE UNITED STATES.

Section 1902(a) of the Social Security Act (42 U.S.C. 1396b(a)), as amended by section 6503, is amended by inserting after paragraph (79) the following new paragraph:

"(80) provide that the State shall not provide any payments for items or services provided under the State plan or under a waiver to any financial institution or entity located outside of the United States;".

SEC. 6506. OVERPAYMENTS.

(a) EXTENSION OF PERIOD FOR COLLECTION OF OVERPAYMENTS DUE TO FRAUD.—

(1) IN GENERAL.—Section 1903(d)(2) of the Social Security Act (42 U.S.C. 1396b(d)(2)) is amended—

(A) in subparagraph (C)—

(i) in the first sentence, by striking "60 days" and inserting "1 year"; and

(ii) in the second sentence, by striking "60 days" and inserting "1-year period"; and

(B) in subparagraph (D)—

(i) in inserting "(i)" after "(D)"; and

(ii) by adding at the end the following:

"(ii) In any case where the State is unable to recover a debt which represents an overpayment (or any portion thereof) made to a person or other entity due to fraud within 1 year of discovery because there is not a final determination of the amount of the overpayment under an administrative or judicial process (as applicable), including as a result of a judgment being under appeal, no adjustment shall be made in the Federal payment to such State on account of such overpayment (or portion thereof) before the date that is 30 days after the date on which a final judgment (including, if applicable, a final determination on an appeal) is made.".

(2) EFFECTIVE DATE.—The amendments made by this subsection take effect on the date of enactment of this Act and apply to overpayments discovered on or after that date.

(b) CORRECTIVE ACTION.—The Secretary shall promulgate regulations that require States to correct Federally identified claims overpayments, of an ongoing or recurring nature, with new Medicaid Management Information System (MMIS) edits, audits, or other appropriate corrective action.

SEC. 6507. MANDATORY STATE USE OF NATIONAL CORRECT CODING INITIATIVE.

Section 1903(r) of the Social Security Act (42 U.S.C. 1396b(r)) is amended—

(1) in paragraph (1)(B)—

(A) in clause (ii), by striking "and" at the end;

(B) in clause (iii), by adding "and" after the semicolon; and

(C) by adding at the end the following new clause:

"(iv) effective for claims filed on or after October 1, 2010, incorporate compatible methodologies of the National Correct Coding Initiative administered by the Secretary (or any successor initiative to promote correct coding and to control improper coding leading to inappropriate payment) and such other methodologies of that Initiative (or such other national correct coding methodologies) as the Secretary identifies in accordance with paragraph (4);"; and

(2) by adding at the end the following new paragraph:

"(4) For purposes of paragraph (1)(B)(iv), the Secretary shall do the following:

"(A) Not later than September 1, 2010:

"(i) Identify those methodologies of the National Correct Coding Initiative administered by the Secretary (or any successor initiative to promote correct coding and to control improper coding leading to inappropriate payment) which are compatible to claims filed under this title.

"(ii) Identify those methodologies of such Initiative (or such other national correct coding methodologies) that should be incorporated into claims filed under this title with respect to items or services for which States provide medical assistance under this title and no national correct coding methodologies have been established under such Initiative with respect to title XVIII.

"(iii) Notify States of—

"(I) the methodologies identified under subparagraphs (A) and (B) (and of any other national correct coding methodologies identified under subparagraph (B)); and

"(II) how States are to incorporate such methodologies into claims filed under this title.

"(B) Not later than March 1, 2011, submit a report to Congress that includes the notice to States under clause (iii) of subparagraph (A) and an analysis supporting the identification of the methodologies made under clauses (i) and (ii) of subparagraph (A).".

SEC. 6508. GENERAL EFFECTIVE DATE.

(a) IN GENERAL.—Except as otherwise provided in this subtitle, this subtitle and the amendments made by this subtitle take effect on January 1, 2011, without regard to whether final regulations to carry out such amendments and subtitle have been promulgated by that date.

(b) DELAY IF STATE LEGISLATION REQUIRED.—In the case of a State plan for medical assistance under title XIX of the Social Security Act or a child health plan under title XXI of such Act which the Secretary of Health and Human Services determines requires State legislation (other than legislation appropriating funds) in order for the plan to meet the additional requirement imposed by the amendments made by this subtitle, the State plan or child health plan shall not be regarded as failing to comply with the requirements of such title solely on the basis of its failure to meet this additional requirement before the first day of the first calendar quarter beginning after the close of the first regular session of the State legislature that begins after the date of the enactment of this Act. For purposes of the previous sentence, in the case of a State that has a 2-year legislative session, each year of such session shall be deemed to be a separate regular session of the State legislature.

Subtitle G—Additional Program Integrity Provisions

SEC. 6601. PROHIBITION ON FALSE STATEMENTS AND REPRESENTATIONS.

(a) PROHIBITION.—Part 5 of subtitle B of title I of the Employee Retirement Income Security Act of 1974 (29 U.S.C. 1131 et seq.) is amended by adding at the end the following:

"SEC. 519. PROHIBITION ON FALSE STATEMENTS AND REPRESENTATIONS.

"No person, in connection with a plan or other arrangement that is multiple employer welfare arrangement described in section 3(40), shall make a false statement or false representation of fact, knowing it to be false, in connection with the marketing or sale of such plan or arrangement, to any employee, any member of an employee organization, any beneficiary, any employer, any employee organization, the Secretary, or any State, or the representative or agent of any such person, State, or the Secretary, concerning—

"(1) the financial condition or solvency of such plan or arrangement;

"(2) the benefits provided by such plan or arrangement;

"(3) the regulatory status of such plan or other arrangement under any Federal or State law governing collective bargaining, labor management relations, or intern union affairs; or

"(4) the regulatory status of such plan or other arrangement regarding exemption from state regulatory authority under this Act.

This section shall not apply to any plan or arrangement that does not fall within the meaning of the term 'multiple employer welfare arrangement' under section 3(40)(A).".

(b) CRIMINAL PENALTIES.—Section 501 of the Employee Retirement Income Security Act of 1974 (29 U.S.C. 1131) is amended—

(1) by inserting "(a)" before "Any person"; and

(2) by adding at the end the following:

"(b) Any person that violates section 519 shall upon conviction be imprisoned not more than 10 years or fined under title 18, United States Code, or both.".

(c) CONFORMING AMENDMENT.—The table of sections for part 5 of subtitle B of title I of the Employee Retirement Income Security Act of 1974 is amended by adding at the end the following:

"Sec. 519. Prohibition on false statement and representations.".

SEC. 6602. CLARIFYING DEFINITION.

Section 24(a)(2) of title 18, United States Code, is amended by inserting "or section 411, 518, or 511 of the Employee Retirement Income Security Act of 1974," after "1954 of this title".

SEC. 6603. DEVELOPMENT OF MODEL UNIFORM REPORT FORM.

Part C of title XXVII of the Public Health Service Act (42 U.S.C. 300gg–91 et seq.) is amended by adding at the end the following:

"SEC. 2794. UNIFORM FRAUD AND ABUSE REFERRAL FORMAT.

"The Secretary shall request the National Association of Insurance Commissioners to develop a model uniform report form for private health insurance issuer seeking to refer suspected fraud and abuse to State insurance departments or other responsible State agencies for investigation. The Secretary shall request that the National Association of Insurance Commissioners develop recommendations for uniform reporting standards for such referrals.".

SEC. 6604. APPLICABILITY OF STATE LAW TO COMBAT FRAUD AND ABUSE.

(a) IN GENERAL.—Part 5 of subtitle B of title I of the Employee Retirement Income Security Act of 1974 (29 U.S.C. 1131 et seq.), as amended by section 6601, is further amended by adding at the end the following:

"SEC. 520. APPLICABILITY OF STATE LAW TO COMBAT FRAUD AND ABUSE.

"The Secretary may, for the purpose of identifying, preventing, or prosecuting fraud and abuse, adopt regulatory standards establishing, or issue an order relating to a specific person establishing, that a person engaged in the business of providing insurance through a multiple employer welfare arrangement described in section 3(40) is subject to the laws of the States in which such person operates which regulate insurance in such State, notwithstanding section 514(b)(6) of this Act or the Liability Risk Retention Act of 1986, and regardless of whether the law of the State is otherwise preempted under any of such provisions. This section shall not apply to any plan or arrangement that does not fall within the meaning of the term 'multiple employer welfare arrangement' under section 3(40)(A).".

(b) CONFORMING AMENDMENT.—The table of sections for part 5 of subtitle B of title I of the Employee Retirement Income Security Act of 1974, as amended by section 6601, is further amended by adding at the end the following:

SEC. 6605. ENABLING THE DEPARTMENT OF LABOR TO ISSUE ADMINISTRATIVE SUMMARY CEASE AND DESIST ORDERS AND SUMMARY SEIZURES ORDERS AGAINST PLANS THAT ARE IN FINANCIALLY HAZARDOUS CONDITION.

(a) IN GENERAL.—Part 5 of subtitle B of title I of the Employee Retirement Income Security Act of 1974 (29 U.S.C. 1131 et seq.), as amended by section 6604, is further amended by adding at the end the following:

"SEC. 521. ADMINISTRATIVE SUMMARY CEASE AND DESIST ORDERS AND SUMMARY SEIZURE ORDERS AGAINST MULTIPLE EMPLOYER WELFARE ARRANGEMENTS IN FINANCIALLY HAZARDOUS CONDITION.

"(a) IN GENERAL.—The Secretary may issue a cease and desist (ex parte) order under this title if it appears to the Secretary that the alleged conduct of a multiple employer welfare arrangement described in section 3(40), other than a plan or arrangement described in subsection (g), is fraudulent, or creates an immediate danger to the public safety or welfare, or is causing or can be reasonably expected to cause significant, imminent, and irreparable public injury.

"(b) HEARING.—A person that is adversely affected by the issuance of a cease and desist order under subsection (a) may request a hearing by the Secretary regarding such order. The Secretary may require that a proceeding under this section, including all related information and evidence, be conducted in a confidential manner.

"(c) BURDEN OF PROOF.—The burden of proof in any hearing conducted under subsection (b) shall be on the party requesting the hearing to show cause why the cease and desist order should be set aside.

"(d) DETERMINATION.—Based upon the evidence presented at a hearing under subsection (b), the cease and desist order involved may be affirmed, modified, or set aside by the Secretary in whole or in part.

"(e) SEIZURE.—The Secretary may issue a summary seizure order under this title if it appears that a multiple employer welfare arrangement is in a financially hazardous condition.

"(f) REGULATIONS.—The Secretary may promulgate such regulations or other guidance as may be necessary or appropriate to carry out this section.

"(g) EXCEPTION.—This section shall not apply to any plan or arrangement that does not fall within the meaning of the term 'multiple employer welfare arrangement' under section 3(40)(A).".

(b) CONFORMING AMENDMENT.—The table of sections for part 5 of subtitle B of title I of the Employee Retirement Income Security Act of 1974, as amended by section 6604, is further amended by adding at the end the following:

"Sec. 521. Administrative summary cease and desist orders and summary seizure orders against health plans in financially hazardous condition.".

SEC. 6606. MEWA PLAN REGISTRATION WITH DEPARTMENT OF LABOR.

Section 101(g) of the Employee Retirement Income Security Act of 1974 (29 U.S.C. 1021(g)) is amended—

(1) by striking "Secretary may" and inserting "Secretary shall"; and

(2) by inserting "to register with the Secretary prior to operating in a State and may, by regulation, require such multiple employer welfare arrangements" after "not group health plans".

SEC. 6607. PERMITTING EVIDENTIARY PRIVILEGE AND CONFIDENTIAL COMMUNICATIONS.

Section 504 of the Employee Retirement Income Security Act of 1974 (29 U.S.C. 1134) is amended by adding at the end the following:

"(d) The Secretary may promulgate a regulation that provides an evidentiary privilege for, and provides for the confidentiality of communications between or among, any of the following entities or their agents, consultants, or employees:

"(1) A State insurance department.

"(2) A State attorney general.

"(3) The National Association of Insurance Commissioners.

"(4) The Department of Labor.

"(5) The Department of the Treasury.

"(6) The Department of Justice.

"(7) The Department of Health and Human Services.

"(8) Any other Federal or State authority that the Secretary determines is appropriate for the purposes of enforcing the provisions of this title.

"(e) The privilege established under subsection (d) shall apply to communications related to any investigation, audit, examination, or inquiry conducted or coordinated by any of the agencies. A communication that is privileged under subsection (d) shall not waive any privilege otherwise available to the communicating agency or to any person who provided the information that is communicated.".

Subtitle H—Elder Justice Act

SEC. 6701. SHORT TITLE OF SUBTITLE.

This subtitle may be cited as the "Elder Justice Act of 2009".

SEC. 6702. DEFINITIONS.

Except as otherwise specifically provided, any term that is defined in section 2011 of the Social Security Act (as added by section 6703(a)) and is used in this subtitle has the meaning given such term by such section.

SEC. 6703. ELDER JUSTICE.

(a) ELDER JUSTICE.—

(1) IN GENERAL.—Title XX of the Social Security Act (42 U.S.C. 1397 et seq.) is amended—

(A) in the heading, by inserting "**AND ELDER JUSTICE**" after "**SOCIAL SERVICES**";

(B) by inserting before section 2001 the following:

"Subtitle A—Block Grants to States for Social Services";

and

(C) by adding at the end the following:

"Subtitle B—Elder Justice

"SEC. 2011. DEFINITIONS.

"In this subtitle:

"(1) ABUSE.—The term 'abuse' means the knowing infliction of physical or psychological harm or the knowing deprivation of goods or services that are necessary to meet essential needs or to avoid physical or psychological harm.

"(2) ADULT PROTECTIVE SERVICES.—The term 'adult protective services' means such services provided to adults as the Secretary may specify and includes services such as—

"(A) receiving reports of adult abuse, neglect, or exploitation;

"(B) investigating the reports described in subparagraph (A);

"(C) case planning, monitoring, evaluation, and other case work and services; and

"(D) providing, arranging for, or facilitating the provision of medical, social service, economic, legal, housing, law enforcement, or other protective, emergency, or support services.

"(3) CAREGIVER.—The term 'caregiver' means an individual who has the responsibility for the care of an elder, either voluntarily, by contract, by receipt of payment for care, or as a result of the operation of law, and means a family member or other individual who provides (on behalf of such individual or of a public or private agency, organization, or institution) compensated or uncompensated care to an elder who needs supportive services in any setting.

"(4) DIRECT CARE.—The term 'direct care' means care by an employee or contractor who provides assistance or long-term care services to a recipient.

"(5) ELDER.—The term 'elder' means an individual age 60 or older.

"(6) ELDER JUSTICE.—The term 'elder justice' means—

"(A) from a societal perspective, efforts to—

"(i) prevent, detect, treat, intervene in, and prosecute elder abuse, neglect, and exploitation; and

"(ii) protect elders with diminished capacity while maximizing their autonomy; and

"(B) from an individual perspective, the recognition of an elder's rights, including the right to be free of abuse, neglect, and exploitation.

"(7) ELIGIBLE ENTITY.—The term 'eligible entity' means a State or local government agency, Indian tribe or tribal organization, or any other public or private entity that is engaged in and has expertise in issues relating to elder justice or in a field necessary to promote elder justice efforts.

"(8) EXPLOITATION.—The term 'exploitation' means the fraudulent or otherwise illegal, unauthorized, or improper act or process of an individual, including a caregiver or fiduciary, that uses the resources of an elder for monetary or personal benefit, profit, or gain, or that results in depriving an elder of rightful access to, or use of, benefits, resources, belongings, or assets.

"(9) FIDUCIARY.—The term 'fiduciary'—

"(A) means a person or entity with the legal responsibility—

"(i) to make decisions on behalf of and for the benefit of another person; and

"(ii) to act in good faith and with fairness; and

"(B) includes a trustee, a guardian, a conservator, an executor, an agent under a financial power of attorney or health care power of attorney, or a representative payee.

"(10) GRANT.—The term 'grant' includes a contract, cooperative agreement, or other mechanism for providing financial assistance.

"(11) GUARDIANSHIP.—The term 'guardianship' means—

"(A) the process by which a State court determines that an adult individual lacks capacity to make decisions about self-care or property, and appoints another individual or entity known as a guardian, as a conservator, or by a similar term, as a surrogate decisionmaker;

"(B) the manner in which the court-appointed surrogate decisionmaker carries out duties to the individual and the court; or

"(C) the manner in which the court exercises oversight of the surrogate decisionmaker.

"(12) INDIAN TRIBE.—

"(A) IN GENERAL.—The term 'Indian tribe' has the meaning given such term in section 4 of the Indian Self-Determination and Education Assistance Act (25 U.S.C. 450b).

"(B) INCLUSION OF PUEBLO AND RANCHERIA.—The term 'Indian tribe' includes any Pueblo or Rancheria.

"(13) LAW ENFORCEMENT.—The term 'law enforcement' means the full range of potential responders to elder abuse, neglect, and exploitation including—

"(A) police, sheriffs, detectives, public safety officers, and corrections personnel;

"(B) prosecutors;

"(C) medical examiners;

"(D) investigators; and

"(E) coroners.

"(14) LONG-TERM CARE.—

"(A) IN GENERAL.—The term 'long-term care' means supportive and health services specified by the Secretary for individuals who need assistance because the individuals have a loss of capacity for self-care due to illness, disability, or vulnerability.

"(B) LOSS OF CAPACITY FOR SELF-CARE.—For purposes of subparagraph (A), the term 'loss of capacity for self-care' means an inability to engage in 1 or more activities of daily living, including eating, dressing, bathing, management of one's financial affairs, and other activities the Secretary determines appropriate.

"(15) LONG-TERM CARE FACILITY.—The term 'long-term care facility' means a residential care provider that arranges for, or directly provides, long-term care.

"(16) NEGLECT.—The term 'neglect' means—

"(A) the failure of a caregiver or fiduciary to provide the goods or services that are necessary to maintain the health or safety of an elder; or

"(B) self-neglect.

"(17) NURSING FACILITY.—

"(A) IN GENERAL.—The term 'nursing facility' has the meaning given such term under section 1919(a).

"(B) INCLUSION OF SKILLED NURSING FACILITY.—The term 'nursing facility' includes a skilled nursing facility (as defined in section 1819(a)).

"(18) SELF-NEGLECT.—The term 'self-neglect' means an adult's inability, due to physical or mental impairment or diminished capacity, to perform essential self-care tasks including—

"(A) obtaining essential food, clothing, shelter, and medical care;

"(B) obtaining goods and services necessary to maintain physical health, mental health, or general safety; or

"(C) managing one's own financial affairs.

"(19) SERIOUS BODILY INJURY.—

"(A) IN GENERAL.—The term 'serious bodily injury' means an injury—

"(i) involving extreme physical pain;

"(ii) involving substantial risk of death;

"(iii) involving protracted loss or impairment of the function of a bodily member, organ, or mental faculty; or

"(iv) requiring medical intervention such as surgery, hospitalization, or physical rehabilitation.

"(B) CRIMINAL SEXUAL ABUSE.—Serious bodily injury shall be considered to have occurred if the conduct causing the injury is conduct described in section 2241 (relating to aggravated sexual abuse) or 2242 (relating to sexual abuse) of title 18, United States Code, or any similar offense under State law.

"(20) SOCIAL.—The term 'social', when used with respect to a service, includes adult protective services.

"(21) STATE LEGAL ASSISTANCE DEVELOPER.—The term 'State legal assistance developer' means an individual described in section 731 of the Older Americans Act of 1965.

"(22) STATE LONG-TERM CARE OMBUDSMAN.—The term 'State Long-Term Care Ombudsman' means the State Long-Term Care Ombudsman described in section 712(a)(2) of the Older Americans Act of 1965.

"SEC. 2012. GENERAL PROVISIONS.

"(a) PROTECTION OF PRIVACY.—In pursuing activities under this subtitle, the Secretary shall ensure the protection of individual health privacy consistent with the regulations promulgated under section 264(c) of the Health Insurance Portability and Accountability Act of 1996 and applicable State and local privacy regulations.

"(b) RULE OF CONSTRUCTION.—Nothing in this subtitle shall be construed to interfere with or abridge an elder's right to practice his or her religion through reliance on prayer alone for healing when this choice—

"(1) is contemporaneously expressed, either orally or in writing, with respect to a specific illness or injury which the elder has at the time of the decision by an elder who is competent at the time of the decision;

"(2) is previously set forth in a living will, health care proxy, or other advance directive document that is validly executed and applied under State law; or

"(3) may be unambiguously deduced from the elder's life history.

“PART I—NATIONAL COORDINATION OF ELDER JUSTICE ACTIVITIES AND RESEARCH

“Subpart A—Elder Justice Coordinating Council and Advisory Board on Elder Abuse, Neglect, and Exploitation

“SEC. 2021. ELDER JUSTICE COORDINATING COUNCIL.

“(a) ESTABLISHMENT.—There is established within the Office of the Secretary an Elder Justice Coordinating Council (in this section referred to as the ‘Council’).

“(b) MEMBERSHIP.—

“(1) IN GENERAL.—The Council shall be composed of the following members:

“(A) The Secretary (or the Secretary’s designee).

“(B) The Attorney General (or the Attorney General’s designee).

“(C) The head of each Federal department or agency or other governmental entity identified by the Chair referred to in subsection (d) as having responsibilities, or administering programs, relating to elder abuse, neglect, and exploitation.

“(2) REQUIREMENT.—Each member of the Council shall be an officer or employee of the Federal Government.

“(c) VACANCIES.—Any vacancy in the Council shall not affect its powers, but shall be filled in the same manner as the original appointment was made.

“(d) CHAIR.—The member described in subsection (b)(1)(A) shall be Chair of the Council.

“(e) MEETINGS.—The Council shall meet at least 2 times per year, as determined by the Chair.

“(f) DUTIES.—

“(1) IN GENERAL.—The Council shall make recommendations to the Secretary for the coordination of activities of the Department of Health and Human Services, the Department of Justice, and other relevant Federal, State, local, and private agencies and entities, relating to elder abuse, neglect, and exploitation and other crimes against elders.

“(2) REPORT.—Not later than the date that is 2 years after the date of enactment of the Elder Justice Act of 2009 and every 2 years thereafter, the Council shall submit to the Committee on Finance of the Senate and the Committee on Ways and Means and the Committee on Energy and Commerce of the House of Representatives a report that—

“(A) describes the activities and accomplishments of, and challenges faced by—

“(i) the Council; and

“(ii) the entities represented on the Council; and

“(B) makes such recommendations for legislation, model laws, or other action as the Council determines to be appropriate.

“(g) POWERS OF THE COUNCIL.—

“(1) INFORMATION FROM FEDERAL AGENCIES.—Subject to the requirements of section 2012(a), the Council may secure directly from any Federal department or agency such information as the Council considers necessary to carry out this section. Upon request of the Chair of the Council, the head of such department or agency shall furnish such information to the Council.

"(2) POSTAL SERVICES.—The Council may use the United States mails in the same manner and under the same conditions as other departments and agencies of the Federal Government.

"(h) TRAVEL EXPENSES.—The members of the Council shall not receive compensation for the performance of services for the Council. The members shall be allowed travel expenses, including per diem in lieu of subsistence, at rates authorized for employees of agencies under subchapter I of chapter 57 of title 5, United States Code, while away from their homes or regular places of business in the performance of services for the Council. Notwithstanding section 1342 of title 31, United States Code, the Secretary may accept the voluntary and uncompensated services of the members of the Council.

"(i) DETAIL OF GOVERNMENT EMPLOYEES.—Any Federal Government employee may be detailed to the Council without reimbursement, and such detail shall be without interruption or loss of civil service status or privilege.

"(j) STATUS AS PERMANENT COUNCIL.—Section 14 of the Federal Advisory Committee Act (5 U.S.C. App.) shall not apply to the Council.

"(k) AUTHORIZATION OF APPROPRIATIONS.—There are authorized to be appropriated such sums as are necessary to carry out this section.

"SEC. 2022. ADVISORY BOARD ON ELDER ABUSE, NEGLECT, AND EXPLOITATION.

"(a) ESTABLISHMENT.—There is established a board to be known as the 'Advisory Board on Elder Abuse, Neglect, and Exploitation' (in this section referred to as the 'Advisory Board') to create short- and long-term multidisciplinary strategic plans for the development of the field of elder justice and to make recommendations to the Elder Justice Coordinating Council established under section 2021.

"(b) COMPOSITION.—The Advisory Board shall be composed of 27 members appointed by the Secretary from among members of the general public who are individuals with experience and expertise in elder abuse, neglect, and exploitation prevention, detection, treatment, intervention, or prosecution.

"(c) SOLICITATION OF NOMINATIONS.—The Secretary shall publish a notice in the Federal Register soliciting nominations for the appointment of members of the Advisory Board under subsection (b).

"(d) TERMS.—

"(1) IN GENERAL.—Each member of the Advisory Board shall be appointed for a term of 3 years, except that, of the members first appointed—

"(A) 9 shall be appointed for a term of 3 years;

"(B) 9 shall be appointed for a term of 2 years; and

"(C) 9 shall be appointed for a term of 1 year.

"(2) VACANCIES.—

"(A) IN GENERAL.—Any vacancy on the Advisory Board shall not affect its powers, but shall be filled in the same manner as the original appointment was made.

"(B) FILLING UNEXPIRED TERM.—An individual chosen to fill a vacancy shall be appointed for the unexpired term of the member replaced.

"(3) EXPIRATION OF TERMS.—The term of any member shall not expire before the date on which the member's successor takes office.

"(e) ELECTION OF OFFICERS.—The Advisory Board shall elect a Chair and Vice Chair from among its members. The Advisory Board shall elect its initial Chair and Vice Chair at its initial meeting.

"(f) DUTIES.—

"(1) ENHANCE COMMUNICATION ON PROMOTING QUALITY OF, AND PREVENTING ABUSE, NEGLECT, AND EXPLOITATION IN, LONG-TERM CARE.—The Advisory Board shall develop collaborative and innovative approaches to improve the quality of, including preventing abuse, neglect, and exploitation in, long-term care.

"(2) COLLABORATIVE EFFORTS TO DEVELOP CONSENSUS AROUND THE MANAGEMENT OF CERTAIN QUALITY-RELATED FACTORS.—

"(A) IN GENERAL.—The Advisory Board shall establish multidisciplinary panels to address, and develop consensus on, subjects relating to improving the quality of long-term care. At least 1 such panel shall address, and develop consensus on, methods for managing resident-to-resident abuse in long-term care.

"(B) ACTIVITIES CONDUCTED.—The multidisciplinary panels established under subparagraph (A) shall examine relevant research and data, identify best practices with respect to the subject of the panel, determine the best way to carry out those best practices in a practical and feasible manner, and determine an effective manner of distributing information on such subject.

"(3) REPORT.—Not later than the date that is 18 months after the date of enactment of the Elder Justice Act of 2009, and annually thereafter, the Advisory Board shall prepare and submit to the Elder Justice Coordinating Council, the Committee on Finance of the Senate, and the Committee on Ways and Means and the Committee on Energy and Commerce of the House of Representatives a report containing—

"(A) information on the status of Federal, State, and local public and private elder justice activities;

"(B) recommendations (including recommended priorities) regarding—

"(i) elder justice programs, research, training, services, practice, enforcement, and coordination;

"(ii) coordination between entities pursuing elder justice efforts and those involved in related areas that may inform or overlap with elder justice efforts, such as activities to combat violence against women and child abuse and neglect; and

"(iii) activities relating to adult fiduciary systems, including guardianship and other fiduciary arrangements;

"(C) recommendations for specific modifications needed in Federal and State laws (including regulations) or for programs, research, and training to enhance prevention, detection, and treatment (including diagnosis) of, intervention in (including investigation of), and prosecution of elder abuse, neglect, and exploitation;

"(D) recommendations on methods for the most effective coordinated national data collection with respect to elder justice, and elder abuse, neglect, and exploitation; and

"(E) recommendations for a multidisciplinary strategic plan to guide the effective and efficient development of the field of elder justice.

"(g) POWERS OF THE ADVISORY BOARD.—

"(1) INFORMATION FROM FEDERAL AGENCIES.—Subject to the requirements of section 2012(a), the Advisory Board may secure directly from any Federal department or agency such information as the Advisory Board considers necessary to carry out this section. Upon request of the Chair of the Advisory Board, the head of such department or agency shall furnish such information to the Advisory Board.

"(2) SHARING OF DATA AND REPORTS.—The Advisory Board may request from any entity pursuing elder justice activities under the Elder Justice Act of 2009 or an amendment made by that Act, any data, reports, or recommendations generated in connection with such activities.

"(3) POSTAL SERVICES.—The Advisory Board may use the United States mails in the same manner and under the same conditions as other departments and agencies of the Federal Government.

"(h) TRAVEL EXPENSES.—The members of the Advisory Board shall not receive compensation for the performance of services for the Advisory Board. The members shall be allowed travel expenses for up to 4 meetings per year, including per diem in lieu of subsistence, at rates authorized for employees of agencies under subchapter I of chapter 57 of title 5, United States Code, while away from their homes or regular places of business in the performance of services for the Advisory Board. Notwithstanding section 1342 of title 31, United States Code, the Secretary may accept the voluntary and uncompensated services of the members of the Advisory Board.

"(i) DETAIL OF GOVERNMENT EMPLOYEES.—Any Federal Government employee may be detailed to the Advisory Board without reimbursement, and such detail shall be without interruption or loss of civil service status or privilege.

"(j) STATUS AS PERMANENT ADVISORY COMMITTEE.—Section 14 of the Federal Advisory Committee Act (5 U.S.C. App.) shall not apply to the advisory board.

"(k) AUTHORIZATION OF APPROPRIATIONS.—There are authorized to be appropriated such sums as are necessary to carry out this section.

"SEC. 2023. RESEARCH PROTECTIONS.

"(a) GUIDELINES.—The Secretary shall promulgate guidelines to assist researchers working in the area of elder abuse, neglect, and exploitation, with issues relating to human subject protections.

"(b) DEFINITION OF LEGALLY AUTHORIZED REPRESENTATIVE FOR APPLICATION OF REGULATIONS.—For purposes of the application of subpart A of part 46 of title 45, Code of Federal Regulations, to research conducted under this subpart, the term 'legally authorized representative' means, unless otherwise provided by law, the individual or judicial or other body authorized under the applicable law to consent to medical treatment on behalf of another person.

"SEC. 2024. AUTHORIZATION OF APPROPRIATIONS.

"There are authorized to be appropriated to carry out this subpart—

"(1) for fiscal year 2011, $6,500,000; and

"(2) for each of fiscal years 2012 through 2014, $7,000,000.

"Subpart B—Elder Abuse, Neglect, and Exploitation Forensic Centers

"SEC. 2031. ESTABLISHMENT AND SUPPORT OF ELDER ABUSE, NEGLECT, AND EXPLOITATION FORENSIC CENTERS.

"(a) IN GENERAL.—The Secretary, in consultation with the Attorney General, shall make grants to eligible entities to establish and operate stationary and mobile forensic centers, to develop forensic expertise regarding, and provide services relating to, elder abuse, neglect, and exploitation.

"(b) STATIONARY FORENSIC CENTERS.—The Secretary shall make 4 of the grants described in subsection (a) to institutions of higher education with demonstrated expertise in forensics or commitment to preventing or treating elder abuse, neglect, or exploitation, to establish and operate stationary forensic centers.

"(c) MOBILE CENTERS.—The Secretary shall make 6 of the grants described in subsection (a) to appropriate entities to establish and operate mobile forensic centers.

"(d) AUTHORIZED ACTIVITIES.—

"(1) DEVELOPMENT OF FORENSIC MARKERS AND METHODOLOGIES.—An eligible entity that receives a grant under this section shall use funds made available through the grant to assist in determining whether abuse, neglect, or exploitation occurred and whether a crime was committed and to conduct research to describe and disseminate information on—

"(A) forensic markers that indicate a case in which elder abuse, neglect, or exploitation may have occurred; and

"(B) methodologies for determining, in such a case, when and how health care, emergency service, social and protective services, and legal service providers should intervene and when the providers should report the case to law enforcement authorities.

"(2) DEVELOPMENT OF FORENSIC EXPERTISE.—An eligible entity that receives a grant under this section shall use funds made available through the grant to develop forensic expertise regarding elder abuse, neglect, and exploitation in order to provide medical and forensic evaluation, therapeutic intervention, victim support and advocacy, case review, and case tracking.

"(3) COLLECTION OF EVIDENCE.—The Secretary, in coordination with the Attorney General, shall use data made available by grant recipients under this section to develop the capacity of geriatric health care professionals and law enforcement to collect forensic evidence, including collecting forensic evidence relating to a potential determination of elder abuse, neglect, or exploitation.

"(e) APPLICATION.—To be eligible to receive a grant under this section, an entity shall submit an application to the Secretary at such time, in such manner, and containing such information as the Secretary may require.

"(f) AUTHORIZATION OF APPROPRIATIONS.—There are authorized to be appropriated to carry out this section—

"(1) for fiscal year 2011, $4,000,000;

"(2) for fiscal year 2012, $6,000,000; and

"(3) for each of fiscal years 2013 and 2014, $8,000,000.

"PART II—PROGRAMS TO PROMOTE ELDER JUSTICE

"SEC. 2041. ENHANCEMENT OF LONG-TERM CARE.

"(a) GRANTS AND INCENTIVES FOR LONG-TERM CARE STAFFING.—

"(1) IN GENERAL.—The Secretary shall carry out activities, including activities described in paragraphs (2) and (3), to provide incentives for individuals to train for, seek, and maintain employment providing direct care in long-term care.

"(2) SPECIFIC PROGRAMS TO ENHANCE TRAINING, RECRUITMENT, AND RETENTION OF STAFF.—

"(A) COORDINATION WITH SECRETARY OF LABOR TO RECRUIT AND TRAIN LONG-TERM CARE STAFF.—The Secretary shall coordinate activities under this subsection with the Secretary of Labor in order to provide incentives for individuals to train for and seek employment providing direct care in long-term care.

"(B) CAREER LADDERS AND WAGE OR BENEFIT INCREASES TO INCREASE STAFFING IN LONG-TERM CARE.—

"(i) IN GENERAL.—The Secretary shall make grants to eligible entities to carry out programs through which the entities—

"(I) offer, to employees who provide direct care to residents of an eligible entity or individuals receiving community-based long-term care from an eligible entity, continuing training and varying levels of certification, based on observed clinical care practices and the amount of time the employees spend providing direct care; and

"(II) provide, or make arrangements to provide, bonuses or other increased compensation or benefits to employees who achieve certification under such a program.

"(ii) APPLICATION.—To be eligible to receive a grant under this subparagraph, an eligible entity shall submit an application to the Secretary at such time, in such manner, and containing such information as the Secretary may require (which may include evidence of consultation with the State in which the eligible entity is located with respect to carrying out activities funded under the grant).

"(iii) AUTHORITY TO LIMIT NUMBER OF APPLICANTS.—Nothing in this subparagraph shall be construed as prohibiting the Secretary from limiting the number of applicants for a grant under this subparagraph.

"(3) SPECIFIC PROGRAMS TO IMPROVE MANAGEMENT PRACTICES.—

"(A) IN GENERAL.—The Secretary shall make grants to eligible entities to enable the entities to provide training and technical assistance.

"(B) AUTHORIZED ACTIVITIES.—An eligible entity that receives a grant under subparagraph (A) shall use funds made available through the grant to provide training and technical assistance regarding management practices using methods that are demonstrated to promote retention of individuals who provide direct care, such as—

"(i) the establishment of standard human resource policies that reward high performance, including policies that provide for improved wages and benefits on the basis of job reviews;

"(ii) the establishment of motivational and thoughtful work organization practices;

"(iii) the creation of a workplace culture that respects and values caregivers and their needs;

"(iv) the promotion of a workplace culture that respects the rights of residents of an eligible entity or individuals receiving community-based long-term care from an eligible entity and results in improved care for the residents or the individuals; and

"(v) the establishment of other programs that promote the provision of high quality care, such as a continuing education program that provides additional hours of training, including on-the-job training, for employees who are certified nurse aides.

"(C) APPLICATION.—To be eligible to receive a grant under this paragraph, an eligible entity shall submit an application to the Secretary at such time, in such manner, and containing such information as the Secretary may require (which may include evidence of consultation with the State in which the eligible entity is located with respect to carrying out activities funded under the grant).

"(D) AUTHORITY TO LIMIT NUMBER OF APPLICANTS.—Nothing in this paragraph shall be construed as prohibiting the Secretary from limiting the number of applicants for a grant under this paragraph.

"(4) ACCOUNTABILITY MEASURES.—The Secretary shall develop accountability measures to ensure that the activities conducted using funds made available under this subsection benefit individuals who provide direct care and increase the stability of the long-term care workforce.

"(5) DEFINITIONS.—In this subsection:

"(A) COMMUNITY-BASED LONG-TERM CARE.—The term 'community-based long-term care' has the meaning given such term by the Secretary.

"(B) ELIGIBLE ENTITY.—The term 'eligible entity' means the following:

"(i) A long-term care facility.

"(ii) A community-based long-term care entity (as defined by the Secretary).

"(b) CERTIFIED EHR TECHNOLOGY GRANT PROGRAM.—

"(1) GRANTS AUTHORIZED.—The Secretary is authorized to make grants to long-term care facilities for the purpose of assisting such entities in offsetting the costs related to purchasing, leasing, developing, and implementing certified EHR technology (as defined in section 1848(o)(4)) designed to improve patient safety and reduce adverse events and health care complications resulting from medication errors.

"(2) USE OF GRANT FUNDS.—Funds provided under grants under this subsection may be used for any of the following:

"(A) Purchasing, leasing, and installing computer software and hardware, including handheld computer technologies.

"(B) Making improvements to existing computer software and hardware.

"(C) Making upgrades and other improvements to existing computer software and hardware to enable e-prescribing.

"(D) Providing education and training to eligible long-term care facility staff on the use of such technology to implement the electronic transmission of prescription and patient information.

"(3) APPLICATION.—

"(A) IN GENERAL.—To be eligible to receive a grant under this subsection, a long-term care facility shall submit an application to the Secretary at such time, in such manner, and containing such information as the Secretary may require (which may include evidence of consultation with the State in which the long-term care facility is located with respect to carrying out activities funded under the grant).

"(B) AUTHORITY TO LIMIT NUMBER OF APPLICANTS.—Nothing in this subsection shall be construed as prohibiting the Secretary from limiting the number of applicants for a grant under this subsection.

"(4) PARTICIPATION IN STATE HEALTH EXCHANGES.—A long-term care facility that receives a grant under this subsection shall, where available, participate in activities conducted by a State or a qualified State-designated entity (as defined in section 3013(f) of the Public Health Service Act) under a grant under section 3013 of the Public Health Service Act to coordinate care and for other purposes determined appropriate by the Secretary.

"(5) ACCOUNTABILITY MEASURES.—The Secretary shall develop accountability measures to ensure that the activities conducted using funds made available under this subsection help improve patient safety and reduce adverse events and health care complications resulting from medication errors.

"(c) ADOPTION OF STANDARDS FOR TRANSACTIONS INVOLVING CLINICAL DATA BY LONG-TERM CARE FACILITIES.—

"(1) STANDARDS AND COMPATIBILITY.—The Secretary shall adopt electronic standards for the exchange of clinical data by long-term care facilities, including, where available, standards for messaging and nomenclature. Standards adopted by the Secretary under the preceding sentence shall be compatible with standards established under part C of title XI, standards established under subsections (b)(2)(B)(i) and (e)(4) of section 1860D–4, standards adopted under section 3004 of the Public Health Service Act, and general health information technology standards.

"(2) ELECTRONIC SUBMISSION OF DATA TO THE SECRETARY.—

"(A) IN GENERAL.—Not later than 10 years after the date of enactment of the Elder Justice Act of 2009, the Secretary shall have procedures in place to accept the optional electronic submission of clinical data by long-term care facilities pursuant to the standards adopted under paragraph (1).

"(B) RULE OF CONSTRUCTION.—Nothing in this subsection shall be construed to require a long-term care facility to submit clinical data electronically to the Secretary.

"(3) REGULATIONS.—The Secretary shall promulgate regulations to carry out this subsection. Such regulations shall require a State, as a condition of the receipt of funds under this part, to conduct such data collection and reporting as the Secretary determines are necessary to satisfy the requirements of this subsection.

"(d) AUTHORIZATION OF APPROPRIATIONS.—There are authorized to be appropriated to carry out this section—

"(1) for fiscal year 2011, $20,000,000;

"(2) for fiscal year 2012, $17,500,000; and

"(3) for each of fiscal years 2013 and 2014, $15,000,000.

"SEC. 2042. ADULT PROTECTIVE SERVICES FUNCTIONS AND GRANT PROGRAMS.

"(a) SECRETARIAL RESPONSIBILITIES.—

"(1) IN GENERAL.—The Secretary shall ensure that the Department of Health and Human Services—

"(A) provides funding authorized by this part to State and local adult protective services offices that investigate reports of the abuse, neglect, and exploitation of elders;

"(B) collects and disseminates data annually relating to the abuse, exploitation, and neglect of elders in coordination with the Department of Justice;

"(C) develops and disseminates information on best practices regarding, and provides training on, carrying out adult protective services;

"(D) conducts research related to the provision of adult protective services; and

"(E) provides technical assistance to States and other entities that provide or fund the provision of adult protective services, including through grants made under subsections (b) and (c).

"(2) AUTHORIZATION OF APPROPRIATIONS.—There are authorized to be appropriated to carry out this subsection, $3,000,000 for fiscal year 2011 and $4,000,000 for each of fiscal years 2012 through 2014.

"(b) GRANTS TO ENHANCE THE PROVISION OF ADULT PROTECTIVE SERVICES.—

"(1) ESTABLISHMENT.—There is established an adult protective services grant program under which the Secretary shall annually award grants to States in the amounts calculated under paragraph (2) for the purposes of enhancing adult protective services provided by States and local units of government.

"(2) AMOUNT OF PAYMENT.—

"(A) IN GENERAL.—Subject to the availability of appropriations and subparagraphs (B) and (C), the amount paid to a State for a fiscal year under the program under this subsection shall equal the amount appropriated for that year to carry out this subsection multiplied by the percentage of the total number of elders who reside in the United States who reside in that State.

"(B) GUARANTEED MINIMUM PAYMENT AMOUNT.—

"(i) 50 STATES.—Subject to clause (ii), if the amount determined under subparagraph (A) for a State for a fiscal year is less than 0.75 percent of the amount appropriated for such year, the Secretary shall increase such determined amount so that the total amount paid under this subsection to the State for the year is equal to 0.75 percent of the amount so appropriated.

"(ii) TERRITORIES.—In the case of a State other than 1 of the 50 States, clause (i) shall be applied as if each reference to '0.75' were a reference to '0.1'.

"(C) PRO RATA REDUCTIONS.—The Secretary shall make such pro rata reductions to the amounts described in subparagraph (A) as are necessary to comply with the requirements of subparagraph (B).

"(3) AUTHORIZED ACTIVITIES.—

"(A) ADULT PROTECTIVE SERVICES.—Funds made available pursuant to this subsection may only be used by States and local units of government to provide adult protective services and may not be used for any other purpose.

"(B) USE BY AGENCY.—Each State receiving funds pursuant to this subsection shall provide such funds to the agency or unit of State government having legal responsibility for providing adult protective services within the State.

"(C) SUPPLEMENT NOT SUPPLANT.—Each State or local unit of government shall use funds made available pursuant to this subsection to supplement and not supplant other Federal, State, and local public funds expended to provide adult protective services in the State.

"(4) STATE REPORTS.—Each State receiving funds under this subsection shall submit to the Secretary, at such time and in such manner as the Secretary may require, a report on the number of elders served by the grants awarded under this subsection.

"(5) AUTHORIZATION OF APPROPRIATIONS.—There are authorized to be appropriated to carry out this subsection, $100,000,000 for each of fiscal years 2011 through 2014.

"(c) STATE DEMONSTRATION PROGRAMS.—

"(1) ESTABLISHMENT.—The Secretary shall award grants to States for the purposes of conducting demonstration programs in accordance with paragraph (2).

"(2) DEMONSTRATION PROGRAMS.—Funds made available pursuant to this subsection may be used by States and local units of government to conduct demonstration programs that test—

"(A) training modules developed for the purpose of detecting or preventing elder abuse;

"(B) methods to detect or prevent financial exploitation of elders;

"(C) methods to detect elder abuse;

"(D) whether training on elder abuse forensics enhances the detection of elder abuse by employees of the State or local unit of government; or

"(E) other matters relating to the detection or prevention of elder abuse.

"(3) APPLICATION.—To be eligible to receive a grant under this subsection, a State shall submit an application to the Secretary at such time, in such manner, and containing such information as the Secretary may require.

"(4) STATE REPORTS.—Each State that receives funds under this subsection shall submit to the Secretary a report at such time, in such manner, and containing such information as the Secretary may require on the results of the demonstration program conducted by the State using funds made available under this subsection.

"(5) AUTHORIZATION OF APPROPRIATIONS.—There are authorized to be appropriated to carry out this subsection, $25,000,000 for each of fiscal years 2011 through 2014.

"SEC. 2043. LONG-TERM CARE OMBUDSMAN PROGRAM GRANTS AND TRAINING.

"(a) GRANTS TO SUPPORT THE LONG-TERM CARE OMBUDSMAN PROGRAM.—

"(1) IN GENERAL.—The Secretary shall make grants to eligible entities with relevant expertise and experience in abuse and neglect in long-term care facilities or long-term care ombudsman programs and responsibilities, for the purpose of—

"(A) improving the capacity of State long-term care ombudsman programs to respond to and resolve complaints about abuse and neglect;

"(B) conducting pilot programs with State long-term care ombudsman offices or local ombudsman entities; and

"(C) providing support for such State long-term care ombudsman programs and such pilot programs (such as through the establishment of a national long-term care ombudsman resource center).

"(2) AUTHORIZATION OF APPROPRIATIONS.—There are authorized to be appropriated to carry out this subsection—

"(A) for fiscal year 2011, $5,000,000;

"(B) for fiscal year 2012, $7,500,000; and

"(C) for each of fiscal years 2013 and 2014, $10,000,000.

"(b) OMBUDSMAN TRAINING PROGRAMS.—

"(1) IN GENERAL.—The Secretary shall establish programs to provide and improve ombudsman training with respect to elder abuse, neglect, and exploitation for national organizations and State long-term care ombudsman programs.

"(2) AUTHORIZATION OF APPROPRIATIONS.—There are authorized to be appropriated to carry out this subsection, for each of fiscal years 2011 through 2014, $10,000,000.

"SEC. 2044. PROVISION OF INFORMATION REGARDING, AND EVALUATIONS OF, ELDER JUSTICE PROGRAMS.

"(a) PROVISION OF INFORMATION.—To be eligible to receive a grant under this part, an applicant shall agree—

"(1) except as provided in paragraph (2), to provide the eligible entity conducting an evaluation under subsection (b) of the activities funded through the grant with such information as the eligible entity may require in order to conduct such evaluation; or

"(2) in the case of an applicant for a grant under section 2041(b), to provide the Secretary with such information as the Secretary may require to conduct an evaluation or audit under subsection (c).

"(b) USE OF ELIGIBLE ENTITIES TO CONDUCT EVALUATIONS.—

"(1) EVALUATIONS REQUIRED.—Except as provided in paragraph (2), the Secretary shall—

"(A) reserve a portion (not less than 2 percent) of the funds appropriated with respect to each program carried out under this part; and

"(B) use the funds reserved under subparagraph (A) to provide assistance to eligible entities to conduct evaluations of the activities funded under each program carried out under this part.

"(2) CERTIFIED EHR TECHNOLOGY GRANT PROGRAM NOT INCLUDED.—The provisions of this subsection shall not apply to the certified EHR technology grant program under section 2041(b).

"(3) AUTHORIZED ACTIVITIES.—A recipient of assistance described in paragraph (1)(B) shall use the funds made available through the assistance to conduct a validated evaluation of the effectiveness of the activities funded under a program carried out under this part.

"(4) APPLICATIONS.—To be eligible to receive assistance under paragraph (1)(B), an entity shall submit an application to the Secretary at such time, in such manner, and containing such information as the Secretary may require, including a proposal for the evaluation.

"(5) REPORTS.—Not later than a date specified by the Secretary, an eligible entity receiving assistance under paragraph (1)(B) shall submit to the Secretary, the Committee on Ways and Means and the Committee on Energy and Commerce of the House of Representatives, and the Committee on Finance of the Senate a report containing the results of the evaluation conducted using such assistance together with such recommendations as the entity determines to be appropriate.

"(c) EVALUATIONS AND AUDITS OF CERTIFIED EHR TECHNOLOGY GRANT PROGRAM BY THE SECRETARY.—

"(1) EVALUATIONS.—The Secretary shall conduct an evaluation of the activities funded under the certified EHR technology grant program under section 2041(b). Such evaluation shall include an evaluation of whether the funding provided under the grant is expended only for the purposes for which it is made.

"(2) AUDITS.—The Secretary shall conduct appropriate audits of grants made under section 2041(b).

"SEC. 2045. REPORT.

"Not later than October 1, 2014, the Secretary shall submit to the Elder Justice Coordinating Council established under section 2021, the Committee on Ways and Means and the Committee on Energy and Commerce of the House of Representatives, and the Committee on Finance of the Senate a report—

"(1) compiling, summarizing, and analyzing the information contained in the State reports submitted under subsections (b)(4) and (c)(4) of section 2042; and

"(2) containing such recommendations for legislative or administrative action as the Secretary determines to be appropriate.

"SEC. 2046. RULE OF CONSTRUCTION.

"Nothing in this subtitle shall be construed as—

"(1) limiting any cause of action or other relief related to obligations under this subtitle that is available under the law of any State, or political subdivision thereof; or

"(2) creating a private cause of action for a violation of this subtitle.".

(2) OPTION FOR STATE PLAN UNDER PROGRAM FOR TEMPORARY ASSISTANCE FOR NEEDY FAMILIES.—

(A) IN GENERAL.—Section 402(a)(1)(B) of the Social Security Act (42 U.S.C. 602(a)(1)(B)) is amended by adding at the end the following new clause:

"(v) The document shall indicate whether the State intends to assist individuals to train for, seek, and maintain employment—

"(I) providing direct care in a long-term care facility (as such terms are defined under section 2011); or

"(II) in other occupations related to elder care determined appropriate by the State for which the State identifies an unmet need for service personnel,

and, if so, shall include an overview of such assistance.".

(B) EFFECTIVE DATE.—The amendment made by subparagraph (A) shall take effect on January 1, 2011.

(b) PROTECTING RESIDENTS OF LONG-TERM CARE FACILITIES.—

(1) NATIONAL TRAINING INSTITUTE FOR SURVEYORS.—

(A) IN GENERAL.—The Secretary of Health and Human Services shall enter into a contract with an entity for the purpose of establishing and operating a National Training Institute for Federal and State surveyors. Such Institute shall provide and improve the training of surveyors with respect to investigating allegations of abuse, neglect, and misappropriation of property in programs and long-term care facilities that receive payments under title XVIII or XIX of the Social Security Act.

(B) ACTIVITIES CARRIED OUT BY THE INSTITUTE.—The contract entered into under subparagraph (A) shall require the Institute established and operated under such contract to carry out the following activities:

(i) Assess the extent to which State agencies use specialized surveyors for the investigation of reported allegations of abuse, neglect, and misappropriation of property in such programs and long-term care facilities.

(ii) Evaluate how the competencies of surveyors may be improved to more effectively investigate reported allegations of such abuse, neglect, and misappropriation of property, and provide feedback to Federal and State agencies on the evaluations conducted.

(iii) Provide a national program of training, tools, and technical assistance to Federal and State surveyors on investigating reports of such abuse, neglect, and misappropriation of property.

(iv) Develop and disseminate information on best practices for the investigation of such abuse, neglect, and misappropriation of property.

(v) Assess the performance of State complaint intake systems, in order to ensure that the intake of complaints occurs 24 hours per day, 7 days a week (including holidays).

(vi) To the extent approved by the Secretary of Health and Human Services, provide a national 24 hours per day, 7 days a week (including holidays), back-up system to State complaint intake systems in order to ensure optimum national responsiveness to complaints of such abuse, neglect, and misappropriation of property.

(vii) Analyze and report annually on the following:

(I) The total number and sources of complaints of such abuse, neglect, and misappropriation of property.

(II) The extent to which such complaints are referred to law enforcement agencies.

(III) General results of Federal and State investigations of such complaints.

(viii) Conduct a national study of the cost to State agencies of conducting complaint investigations of skilled nursing facilities and nursing facilities under sections 1819 and 1919, respectively, of the Social Security Act (42 U.S.C. 1395i–3; 1396r), and making recommendations to the Secretary of Health and Human Services with respect to options to increase the efficiency and cost-effectiveness of such investigations.

(C) AUTHORIZATION.—There are authorized to be appropriated to carry out this paragraph, for the period of fiscal years 2011 through 2014, $12,000,000.

(2) GRANTS TO STATE SURVEY AGENCIES.—

(A) IN GENERAL.—The Secretary of Health and Human Services shall make grants to State agencies that perform surveys of skilled nursing facilities or nursing facilities under sections 1819 or 1919, respectively, of the Social Security Act (42 U.S.C. 1395i–3; 1395r).

(B) USE OF FUNDS.—A grant awarded under subparagraph (A) shall be used for the purpose of designing and implementing complaint investigations systems that—

(i) promptly prioritize complaints in order to ensure a rapid response to the most serious and urgent complaints;

(ii) respond to complaints with optimum effectiveness and timeliness; and

(iii) optimize the collaboration between local authorities, consumers, and providers, including—

(I) such State agency;

(II) the State Long-Term Care Ombudsman;

(III) local law enforcement agencies;

(IV) advocacy and consumer organizations;

(V) State aging units;

(VI) Area Agencies on Aging; and

(VII) other appropriate entities.

(C) AUTHORIZATION.—There are authorized to be appropriated to carry out this paragraph, for each of fiscal years 2011 through 2014, $5,000,000.

(3) REPORTING OF CRIMES IN FEDERALLY FUNDED LONG-TERM CARE FACILITIES.—Part A of title XI of the Social Security Act (42 U.S.C. 1301 et seq.), as amended by section 6005, is amended by inserting after section 1150A the following new section:

"REPORTING TO LAW ENFORCEMENT OF CRIMES OCCURRING IN FEDERALLY FUNDED LONG-TERM CARE FACILITIES

"SEC. 1150B. (a) DETERMINATION AND NOTIFICATION.—

"(1) DETERMINATION.—The owner or operator of each long-term care facility that receives Federal funds under this Act shall annually determine whether the facility received at least $10,000 in such Federal funds during the preceding year.

"(2) NOTIFICATION.—If the owner or operator determines under paragraph (1) that the facility received at least $10,000 in such Federal funds during the preceding year, such owner or operator shall annually notify each covered individual (as defined in paragraph (3)) of that individual's obligation to comply with the reporting requirements described in subsection (b).

"(3) COVERED INDIVIDUAL DEFINED.—In this section, the term 'covered individual' means each individual who is an owner, operator, employee, manager, agent, or contractor of a long-term care facility that is the subject of a determination described in paragraph (1).

"(b) REPORTING REQUIREMENTS.—

"(1) IN GENERAL.—Each covered individual shall report to the Secretary and 1 or more law enforcement entities for the political subdivision in which the facility is located any reasonable suspicion of a crime (as defined by the law of the applicable political subdivision) against any individual who is a resident of, or is receiving care from, the facility.

"(2) TIMING.—If the events that cause the suspicion—

"(A) result in serious bodily injury, the individual shall report the suspicion immediately, but not later than 2 hours after forming the suspicion; and

"(B) do not result in serious bodily injury, the individual shall report the suspicion not later than 24 hours after forming the suspicion.

"(c) PENALTIES.—

"(1) IN GENERAL.—If a covered individual violates subsection (b)—

"(A) the covered individual shall be subject to a civil money penalty of not more than $200,000; and

"(B) the Secretary may make a determination in the same proceeding to exclude the covered individual from participation in any Federal health care program (as defined in section 1128B(f)).

"(2) INCREASED HARM.—If a covered individual violates subsection (b) and the violation exacerbates the harm to the victim of the crime or results in harm to another individual—

"(A) the covered individual shall be subject to a civil money penalty of not more than $300,000; and

"(B) the Secretary may make a determination in the same proceeding to exclude the covered individual from participation in any Federal health care program (as defined in section 1128B(f)).

"(3) EXCLUDED INDIVIDUAL.—During any period for which a covered individual is classified as an excluded individual under paragraph (1)(B) or (2)(B), a long-term care facility that employs such individual shall be ineligible to receive Federal funds under this Act.

"(4) EXTENUATING CIRCUMSTANCES.—

"(A) IN GENERAL.—The Secretary may take into account the financial burden on providers with underserved populations in determining any penalty to be imposed under this subsection.

"(B) UNDERSERVED POPULATION DEFINED.—In this paragraph, the term 'underserved population' means the population of an area designated by the Secretary as an area with a shortage of elder justice programs or a population group designated by the Secretary as having a shortage of such programs. Such areas or groups designated by the Secretary may include—

"(i) areas or groups that are geographically isolated (such as isolated in a rural area);

"(ii) racial and ethnic minority populations; and

"(iii) populations underserved because of special needs (such as language barriers, disabilities, alien status, or age).

"(d) ADDITIONAL PENALTIES FOR RETALIATION.—

"(1) IN GENERAL.—A long-term care facility may not—

"(A) discharge, demote, suspend, threaten, harass, or deny a promotion or other employment-related benefit to an employee, or in any other manner discriminate against an employee in the terms and conditions of employment because of lawful acts done by the employee; or

"(B) file a complaint or a report against a nurse or other employee with the appropriate State professional disciplinary agency because of lawful acts done by the nurse or employee,

for making a report, causing a report to be made, or for taking steps in furtherance of making a report pursuant to subsection (b)(1).

"(2) PENALTIES FOR RETALIATION.—If a long-term care facility violates subparagraph (A) or (B) of paragraph (1) the facility shall be subject to a civil money penalty of not more than $200,000 or the Secretary may classify the entity as an excluded entity for a period of 2 years pursuant to section 1128(b), or both.

"(3) REQUIREMENT TO POST NOTICE.—Each long-term care facility shall post conspicuously in an appropriate location a sign (in a form specified by the Secretary) specifying the rights of employees under this section. Such sign shall include a statement that an employee may file a complaint with the Secretary against a long-term care facility that violates the provisions of this subsection and information with respect to the manner of filing such a complaint.

"(e) PROCEDURE.—The provisions of section 1128A (other than subsections (a) and (b) and the second sentence of subsection (f)) shall apply to a civil money penalty or exclusion under this section in the same manner as such provisions apply to a penalty or proceeding under section 1128A(a).

"(f) DEFINITIONS.—In this section, the terms 'elder justice', 'long-term care facility', and 'law enforcement' have the meanings given those terms in section 2011.".

(c) NATIONAL NURSE AIDE REGISTRY.—

(1) DEFINITION OF NURSE AIDE.—In this subsection, the term "nurse aide" has the meaning given that term in sections 1819(b)(5)(F) and 1919(b)(5)(F) of the Social Security Act (42 U.S.C. 1395i–3(b)(5)(F); 1396r(b)(5)(F)).

(2) STUDY AND REPORT.—

(A) IN GENERAL.—The Secretary, in consultation with appropriate government agencies and private sector organizations, shall conduct a study on establishing a national nurse aide registry.

(B) AREAS EVALUATED.—The study conducted under this subsection shall include an evaluation of—

(i) who should be included in the registry;

(ii) how such a registry would comply with Federal and State privacy laws and regulations;

(iii) how data would be collected for the registry;

(iv) what entities and individuals would have access to the data collected;

(v) how the registry would provide appropriate information regarding violations of Federal and State law by individuals included in the registry;

(vi) how the functions of a national nurse aide registry would be coordinated with the nationwide program for national and State background checks on direct patient access employees of long-term care facilities and providers under section 4301; and

(vii) how the information included in State nurse aide registries developed and maintained under sections 1819(e)(2) and 1919(e)(2) of the Social Security Act (42 U.S.C. 1395i–3(e)(2); 1396r(e)(2)(2)) would be provided as part of a national nurse aide registry.

(C) CONSIDERATIONS.—In conducting the study and preparing the report required under this subsection, the Secretary shall take into consideration the findings and conclusions of relevant reports and other relevant resources, including the following:

(i) The Department of Health and Human Services Office of Inspector General Report, Nurse Aide Registries: State Compliance and Practices (February 2005).

(ii) The General Accounting Office (now known as the Government Accountability Office) Report, Nursing Homes: More Can Be Done to Protect Residents from Abuse (March 2002).

(iii) The Department of Health and Human Services Office of the Inspector General Report, Nurse Aide Registries: Long-Term Care Facility Compliance and Practices (July 2005).

(iv) The Department of Health and Human Services Health Resources and Services Administration Report, Nursing Aides, Home Health Aides, and Related Health Care Occupations—National and Local Workforce Shortages and Associated Data Needs (2004) (in particular with respect to chapter 7 and appendix F).

(v) The 2001 Report to CMS from the School of Rural Public Health, Texas A&M University, Preventing Abuse and Neglect in Nursing Homes: The Role of Nurse Aide Registries.

(vi) Information included in State nurse aide registries developed and maintained under sections 1819(e)(2) and 1919(e)(2) of the Social Security Act (42 U.S.C. 1395i–3(e)(2); 1396r(e)(2)(2)).

(D) REPORT.—Not later than 18 months after the date of enactment of this Act, the Secretary shall submit to the Elder Justice Coordinating Council established under section 2021 of the Social Security Act, as added by section 1805(a), the Committee on Finance of the Senate, and the Committee on Ways and Means and the Committee on Energy and Commerce of the House of Representatives a report containing the findings and recommendations of the study conducted under this paragraph.

(E) FUNDING LIMITATION.—Funding for the study conducted under this subsection shall not exceed $500,000.

(3) CONGRESSIONAL ACTION.—After receiving the report submitted by the Secretary under paragraph (2)(D), the Committee on Finance of the Senate and the Committee on Ways and Means and the Committee on Energy and Commerce of the House of Representatives shall, as they deem appropriate, take action based on the recommendations contained in the report.

(4) AUTHORIZATION OF APPROPRIATIONS.—There are authorized to be appropriated such sums as are necessary for the purpose of carrying out this subsection.

(d) CONFORMING AMENDMENTS.—

(1) TITLE XX.—Title XX of the Social Security Act (42 U.S.C. 1397 et seq.), as amended by section 6703(a), is amended—

(A) in the heading of section 2001, by striking "TITLE" and inserting "SUBTITLE"; and

(B) in subtitle 1, by striking "this title" each place it appears and inserting "this subtitle".

(2) TITLE IV.—Title IV of the Social Security Act (42 U.S.C. 601 et seq.) is amended—

(A) in section 404(d)—

(i) in paragraphs (1)(A), (2)(A), and (3)(B), by inserting "subtitle 1 of" before "title XX" each place it appears;

(ii) in the heading of paragraph (2), by inserting "SUBTITLE 1 OF" before "TITLE XX"; and

(iii) in the heading of paragraph (3)(B), by inserting "SUBTITLE 1 OF" before "TITLE XX"; and

(B) in sections 422(b), 471(a)(4), 472(h)(1), and 473(b)(2), by inserting "subtitle 1 of" before "title XX" each place it appears.

(3) TITLE XI.—Title XI of the Social Security Act (42 U.S.C. 1301 et seq.) is amended—

(A) in section 1128(h)(3)—

(i) by inserting "subtitle 1 of" before "title XX"; and

(ii) by striking "such title" and inserting "such subtitle"; and

(B) in section 1128A(i)(1), by inserting "subtitle 1 of" before "title XX".

Subtitle I—Sense of the Senate Regarding Medical Malpractice

SEC. 6801. SENSE OF THE SENATE REGARDING MEDICAL MALPRACTICE.

It is the sense of the Senate that—

(1) health care reform presents an opportunity to address issues related to medical malpractice and medical liability insurance;

(2) States should be encouraged to develop and test alternatives to the existing civil litigation system as a way of improving patient safety, reducing medical errors, encouraging the efficient resolution of disputes, increasing the availability of prompt and fair resolution of disputes, and improving access to liability insurance, while preserving an individual's right to seek redress in court; and

(3) Congress should consider establishing a State demonstration program to evaluate alternatives to the existing civil litigation system with respect to the resolution of medical malpractice claims.

TITLE VII—IMPROVING ACCESS TO INNOVATIVE MEDICAL THERAPIES

Subtitle A—Biologics Price Competition and Innovation

SEC. 7001. SHORT TITLE.

(a) IN GENERAL.—This subtitle may be cited as the "Biologics Price Competition and Innovation Act of 2009".

(b) SENSE OF THE SENATE.—It is the sense of the Senate that a biosimilars pathway balancing innovation and consumer interests should be established.

SEC. 7002. APPROVAL PATHWAY FOR BIOSIMILAR BIOLOGICAL PRODUCTS.

(a) LICENSURE OF BIOLOGICAL PRODUCTS AS BIOSIMILAR OR INTERCHANGEABLE.—Section 351 of the Public Health Service Act (42 U.S.C. 262) is amended—

(1) in subsection (a)(1)(A), by inserting "under this subsection or subsection (k)" after "biologics license"; and

(2) by adding at the end the following:

"(k) LICENSURE OF BIOLOGICAL PRODUCTS AS BIOSIMILAR OR INTERCHANGEABLE.—

"(1) IN GENERAL.—Any person may submit an application for licensure of a biological product under this subsection.

"(2) CONTENT.—

"(A) IN GENERAL.—

"(i) REQUIRED INFORMATION.—An application submitted under this subsection shall include information demonstrating that—

"(I) the biological product is biosimilar to a reference product based upon data derived from—

"(aa) analytical studies that demonstrate that the biological product is highly similar to the reference product notwithstanding minor differences in clinically inactive components;

"(bb) animal studies (including the assessment of toxicity); and

"(cc) a clinical study or studies (including the assessment of immunogenicity and pharmacokinetics or pharmacodynamics) that are sufficient to demonstrate safety, purity, and potency in 1 or more appropriate conditions of use for which the reference product is licensed and intended to be used and for which licensure is sought for the biological product;

"(II) the biological product and reference product utilize the same mechanism or mechanisms of action for the condition or conditions of use prescribed, recommended, or suggested in the proposed labeling, but only to the extent the mechanism or mechanisms of action are known for the reference product;

"(III) the condition or conditions of use prescribed, recommended, or suggested in the labeling proposed for the biological product have been previously approved for the reference product;

"(IV) the route of administration, the dosage form, and the strength of the biological product are the same as those of the reference product; and

"(V) the facility in which the biological product is manufactured, processed, packed, or held meets standards designed to assure that the biological product continues to be safe, pure, and potent.

"(ii) DETERMINATION BY SECRETARY.—The Secretary may determine, in the Secretary's discretion, that an element described in clause (i)(I) is unnecessary in an application submitted under this subsection.

"(iii) ADDITIONAL INFORMATION.—An application submitted under this subsection—

"(I) shall include publicly-available information regarding the Secretary's previous determination that the reference product is safe, pure, and potent; and

"(II) may include any additional information in support of the application, including publicly-available information with respect to the reference product or another biological product.

"(B) INTERCHANGEABILITY.—An application (or a supplement to an application) submitted under this subsection may include information demonstrating that the biological product meets the standards described in paragraph (4).

"(3) EVALUATION BY SECRETARY.—Upon review of an application (or a supplement to an application) submitted under this subsection, the Secretary shall license the biological product under this subsection if—

"(A) the Secretary determines that the information submitted in the application (or the supplement) is sufficient to show that the biological product—

"(i) is biosimilar to the reference product; or

"(ii) meets the standards described in paragraph (4), and therefore is interchangeable with the reference product; and

"(B) the applicant (or other appropriate person) consents to the inspection of the facility that is the subject of the application, in accordance with subsection (c).

"(4) SAFETY STANDARDS FOR DETERMINING INTERCHANGEABILITY.—Upon review of an application submitted under this subsection or any supplement to such application, the Secretary shall determine the biological product to be interchangeable with the reference product if the Secretary determines that the information submitted in the application (or a supplement to such application) is sufficient to show that—

"(A) the biological product—

"(i) is biosimilar to the reference product; and

"(ii) can be expected to produce the same clinical result as the reference product in any given patient; and

"(B) for a biological product that is administered more than once to an individual, the risk in terms of safety or diminished efficacy of alternating or switching between use of the biological product and the reference product is not greater than the risk of using the reference product without such alternation or switch.

"(5) GENERAL RULES.—

"(A) ONE REFERENCE PRODUCT PER APPLICATION.—A biological product, in an application submitted under this subsection, may not be evaluated against more than 1 reference product.

"(B) REVIEW.—An application submitted under this subsection shall be reviewed by the division within the Food and Drug Administration that is responsible for the review and approval of the application under which the reference product is licensed.

"(C) RISK EVALUATION AND MITIGATION STRATEGIES.—The authority of the Secretary with respect to risk evaluation and mitigation strategies under the Federal Food, Drug, and Cosmetic Act shall apply to biological products licensed under this subsection in the same manner as such authority applies to biological products licensed under subsection (a).

"(6) EXCLUSIVITY FOR FIRST INTERCHANGEABLE BIOLOGICAL PRODUCT.—Upon review of an application submitted under this subsection relying on the same reference product for which a prior biological product has received a determination of interchangeability for any condition of use, the Secretary shall not make a determination under paragraph (4) that the second or subsequent biological product is interchangeable for any condition of use until the earlier of—

"(A) 1 year after the first commercial marketing of the first interchangeable biosimilar biological product to be approved as interchangeable for that reference product;

"(B) 18 months after—

"(i) a final court decision on all patents in suit in an action instituted under subsection (l)(6) against the applicant that submitted the application for the first approved interchangeable biosimilar biological product; or

"(ii) the dismissal with or without prejudice of an action instituted under subsection (l)(6) against the applicant that submitted the application for the first approved interchangeable biosimilar biological product; or

"(C)(i) 42 months after approval of the first interchangeable biosimilar biological product if the applicant that submitted such application has been sued under subsection (l)(6) and such litigation is still ongoing within such 42-month period; or

"(ii) 18 months after approval of the first interchangeable biosimilar biological product if the applicant that submitted such application has not been sued under subsection (l)(6).

For purposes of this paragraph, the term 'final court decision' means a final decision of a court from which no appeal (other than a petition to the United States Supreme Court for a writ of certiorari) has been or can be taken.

"(7) EXCLUSIVITY FOR REFERENCE PRODUCT.—

"(A) EFFECTIVE DATE OF BIOSIMILAR APPLICATION APPROVAL.—Approval of an application under this subsection may not be made effective by the Secretary until the date that is 12 years after the date on which the reference product was first licensed under subsection (a).

"(B) FILING PERIOD.—An application under this subsection may not be submitted to the Secretary until the date that is 4 years after the date on which the reference product was first licensed under subsection (a).

"(C) FIRST LICENSURE.—Subparagraphs (A) and (B) shall not apply to a license for or approval of—

"(i) a supplement for the biological product that is the reference product; or

"(ii) a subsequent application filed by the same sponsor or manufacturer of the biological product that is the reference product (or a licensor, predecessor in interest, or other related entity) for—

"(I) a change (not including a modification to the structure of the biological product) that results in a new indication, route of administration, dosing schedule, dosage form, delivery system, delivery device, or strength; or

"(II) a modification to the structure of the biological product that does not result in a change in safety, purity, or potency.

"(8) GUIDANCE DOCUMENTS.—

"(A) IN GENERAL.—The Secretary may, after opportunity for public comment, issue guidance in accordance, except as provided in subparagraph (B)(i), with section 701(h) of the Federal Food, Drug, and Cosmetic Act with respect to the licensure of a biological product under this subsection. Any such guidance may be general or specific.

"(B) PUBLIC COMMENT.—

"(i) IN GENERAL.—The Secretary shall provide the public an opportunity to comment on any proposed guidance issued under subparagraph (A) before issuing final guidance.

"(ii) INPUT REGARDING MOST VALUABLE GUIDANCE.—The Secretary shall establish a process through which the public may provide the Secretary with input regarding priorities for issuing guidance.

"(C) NO REQUIREMENT FOR APPLICATION CONSIDERATION.—The issuance (or non-issuance) of guidance under subparagraph (A) shall not preclude the review of, or action on, an application submitted under this subsection.

"(D) REQUIREMENT FOR PRODUCT CLASS-SPECIFIC GUIDANCE.—If the Secretary issues product class-specific guidance under subparagraph (A), such guidance shall include a description of—

"(i) the criteria that the Secretary will use to determine whether a biological product is highly similar to a reference product in such product class; and

"(ii) the criteria, if available, that the Secretary will use to determine whether a biological product meets the standards described in paragraph (4).

"(E) CERTAIN PRODUCT CLASSES.—

"(i) GUIDANCE.—The Secretary may indicate in a guidance document that the science and experience, as of the date of such guidance, with respect to a product or product class (not including any recombinant protein) does not allow approval of an application for a license as provided under this subsection for such product or product class.

"(ii) MODIFICATION OR REVERSAL.—The Secretary may issue a subsequent guidance document under subparagraph (A) to modify or reverse a guidance document under clause (i).

"(iii) NO EFFECT ON ABILITY TO DENY LICENSE.—Clause (i) shall not be construed to require the Secretary to approve a product with respect to which the Secretary has not indicated in a guidance document that the science and experience, as described in clause (i), does not allow approval of such an application.

"(l) PATENTS.—

"(1) CONFIDENTIAL ACCESS TO SUBSECTION (k) APPLICATION.—

“(A) APPLICATION OF PARAGRAPH.—Unless otherwise agreed to by a person that submits an application under subsection (k) (referred to in this subsection as the ‘subsection (k) applicant’) and the sponsor of the application for the reference product (referred to in this subsection as the ‘reference product sponsor’), the provisions of this paragraph shall apply to the exchange of information described in this subsection.

“(B) IN GENERAL.—

“(i) PROVISION OF CONFIDENTIAL INFORMATION.—When a subsection (k) applicant submits an application under subsection (k), such applicant shall provide to the persons described in clause (ii), subject to the terms of this paragraph, confidential access to the information required to be produced pursuant to paragraph (2) and any other information that the subsection (k) applicant determines, in its sole discretion, to be appropriate (referred to in this subsection as the ‘confidential information’).

“(ii) RECIPIENTS OF INFORMATION.—The persons described in this clause are the following:

“(I) OUTSIDE COUNSEL.—One or more attorneys designated by the reference product sponsor who are employees of an entity other than the reference product sponsor (referred to in this paragraph as the ‘outside counsel’), provided that such attorneys do not engage, formally or informally, in patent prosecution relevant or related to the reference product.

“(II) IN-HOUSE COUNSEL.—One attorney that represents the reference product sponsor who is an employee of the reference product sponsor, provided that such attorney does not engage, formally or informally, in patent prosecution relevant or related to the reference product.

“(iii) PATENT OWNER ACCESS.—A representative of the owner of a patent exclusively licensed to a reference product sponsor with respect to the reference product and who has retained a right to assert the patent or participate in litigation concerning the patent may be provided the confidential information, provided that the representative informs the reference product sponsor and the subsection (k) applicant of his or her agreement to be subject to the confidentiality provisions set forth in this paragraph, including those under clause (ii).

“(C) LIMITATION ON DISCLOSURE.—No person that receives confidential information pursuant to subparagraph (B) shall disclose any confidential information to any other person or entity, including the reference product sponsor employees, outside scientific consultants, or other outside counsel retained by the reference product sponsor, without the prior written consent of the subsection (k) applicant, which shall not be unreasonably withheld.

“(D) USE OF CONFIDENTIAL INFORMATION.—Confidential information shall be used for the sole and exclusive purpose of determining, with respect to each patent assigned to or exclusively licensed by the reference product sponsor, whether a claim of patent infringement could reasonably be asserted if the subsection (k) applicant engaged in the manufacture, use, offering for sale, sale, or importation into the United States of the biological product that is the subject of the application under subsection (k).

"(E) OWNERSHIP OF CONFIDENTIAL INFORMATION.—The confidential information disclosed under this paragraph is, and shall remain, the property of the subsection (k) applicant. By providing the confidential information pursuant to this paragraph, the subsection (k) applicant does not provide the reference product sponsor or the outside counsel any interest in or license to use the confidential information, for purposes other than those specified in subparagraph (D).

"(F) EFFECT OF INFRINGEMENT ACTION.—In the event that the reference product sponsor files a patent infringement suit, the use of confidential information shall continue to be governed by the terms of this paragraph until such time as a court enters a protective order regarding the information. Upon entry of such order, the subsection (k) applicant may redesignate confidential information in accordance with the terms of that order. No confidential information shall be included in any publicly-available complaint or other pleading. In the event that the reference product sponsor does not file an infringement action by the date specified in paragraph (6), the reference product sponsor shall return or destroy all confidential information received under this paragraph, provided that if the reference product sponsor opts to destroy such information, it will confirm destruction in writing to the subsection (k) applicant.

"(G) RULE OF CONSTRUCTION.—Nothing in this paragraph shall be construed—

"(i) as an admission by the subsection (k) applicant regarding the validity, enforceability, or infringement of any patent; or

"(ii) as an agreement or admission by the subsection (k) applicant with respect to the competency, relevance, or materiality of any confidential information.

"(H) EFFECT OF VIOLATION.—The disclosure of any confidential information in violation of this paragraph shall be deemed to cause the subsection (k) applicant to suffer irreparable harm for which there is no adequate legal remedy and the court shall consider immediate injunctive relief to be an appropriate and necessary remedy for any violation or threatened violation of this paragraph.

"(2) SUBSECTION (k) APPLICATION INFORMATION.—Not later than 20 days after the Secretary notifies the subsection (k) applicant that the application has been accepted for review, the subsection (k) applicant—

"(A) shall provide to the reference product sponsor a copy of the application submitted to the Secretary under subsection (k), and such other information that describes the process or processes used to manufacture the biological product that is the subject of such application; and

"(B) may provide to the reference product sponsor additional information requested by or on behalf of the reference product sponsor.

"(3) LIST AND DESCRIPTION OF PATENTS.—

"(A) LIST BY REFERENCE PRODUCT SPONSOR.—Not later than 60 days after the receipt of the application and information under paragraph (2), the reference product sponsor shall provide to the subsection (k) applicant—

"(i) a list of patents for which the reference product sponsor believes a claim of patent infringement could reasonably be asserted by the reference product sponsor, or by a patent owner that has granted an exclusive license to the reference product sponsor with respect to the reference product, if a person not licensed by the reference product sponsor engaged in the making, using, offering to sell, selling, or importing into the United States of the biological product that is the subject of the subsection (k) application; and

"(ii) an identification of the patents on such list that the reference product sponsor would be prepared to license to the subsection (k) applicant.

"(B) LIST AND DESCRIPTION BY SUBSECTION (k) APPLICANT.—Not later than 60 days after receipt of the list under subparagraph (A), the subsection (k) applicant—

"(i) may provide to the reference product sponsor a list of patents to which the subsection (k) applicant believes a claim of patent infringement could reasonably be asserted by the reference product sponsor if a person not licensed by the reference product sponsor engaged in the making, using, offering to sell, selling, or importing into the United States of the biological product that is the subject of the subsection (k) application;

"(ii) shall provide to the reference product sponsor, with respect to each patent listed by the reference product sponsor under subparagraph (A) or listed by the subsection (k) applicant under clause (i)—

"(I) a detailed statement that describes, on a claim by claim basis, the factual and legal basis of the opinion of the subsection (k) applicant that such patent is invalid, unenforceable, or will not be infringed by the commercial marketing of the biological product that is the subject of the subsection (k) application; or

"(II) a statement that the subsection (k) applicant does not intend to begin commercial marketing of the biological product before the date that such patent expires; and

"(iii) shall provide to the reference product sponsor a response regarding each patent identified by the reference product sponsor under subparagraph (A)(ii).

"(C) DESCRIPTION BY REFERENCE PRODUCT SPONSOR.—Not later than 60 days after receipt of the list and statement under subparagraph (B), the reference product sponsor shall provide to the subsection (k) applicant a detailed statement that describes, with respect to each patent described in subparagraph (B)(ii)(I), on a claim by claim basis, the factual and legal basis of the opinion of the reference product sponsor that such patent will be infringed by the commercial marketing of the biological product that is the subject of the subsection (k) application and a response to the statement concerning validity and enforceability provided under subparagraph (B)(ii)(I).

"(4) PATENT RESOLUTION NEGOTIATIONS.—

"(A) IN GENERAL.—After receipt by the subsection (k) applicant of the statement under paragraph (3)(C), the reference product sponsor and the subsection (k) applicant shall engage in good faith negotiations to agree on which, if any, patents listed under paragraph (3) by the subsection (k) applicant or the reference product sponsor shall be the subject of an action for patent infringement under paragraph (6).

"(B) FAILURE TO REACH AGREEMENT.—If, within 15 days of beginning negotiations under subparagraph (A), the subsection (k) applicant and the reference product sponsor fail to agree on a final and complete list of which, if any, patents listed under paragraph (3) by the subsection (k) applicant or the reference product sponsor shall be the subject of an action for patent infringement under paragraph (6), the provisions of paragraph (5) shall apply to the parties.

"(5) PATENT RESOLUTION IF NO AGREEMENT.—

"(A) NUMBER OF PATENTS.—The subsection (k) applicant shall notify the reference product sponsor of the number of patents that such applicant will provide to the reference product sponsor under subparagraph (B)(i)(I).

"(B) EXCHANGE OF PATENT LISTS.—

"(i) IN GENERAL.—On a date agreed to by the subsection (k) applicant and the reference product sponsor, but in no case later than 5 days after the subsection (k) applicant notifies the reference product sponsor under subparagraph (A), the subsection (k) applicant and the reference product sponsor shall simultaneously exchange—

"(I) the list of patents that the subsection (k) applicant believes should be the subject of an action for patent infringement under paragraph (6); and

"(II) the list of patents, in accordance with clause (ii), that the reference product sponsor believes should be the subject of an action for patent infringement under paragraph (6).

"(ii) NUMBER OF PATENTS LISTED BY REFERENCE PRODUCT SPONSOR.—

"(I) IN GENERAL.—Subject to subclause (II), the number of patents listed by the reference product sponsor under clause (i)(II) may not exceed the number of patents listed by the subsection (k) applicant under clause (i)(I).

"(II) EXCEPTION.—If a subsection (k) applicant does not list any patent under clause (i)(I), the reference product sponsor may list 1 patent under clause (i)(II).

"(6) IMMEDIATE PATENT INFRINGEMENT ACTION.—

"(A) ACTION IF AGREEMENT ON PATENT LIST.—If the subsection (k) applicant and the reference product sponsor agree on patents as described in paragraph (4), not later than 30 days after such agreement, the reference product sponsor shall bring an action for patent infringement with respect to each such patent.

"(B) ACTION IF NO AGREEMENT ON PATENT LIST.—If the provisions of paragraph (5) apply to the parties as described in paragraph (4)(B), not later than 30 days after the exchange of lists under paragraph (5)(B), the reference product sponsor shall bring an action for patent infringement with respect to each patent that is included on such lists.

"(C) NOTIFICATION AND PUBLICATION OF COMPLAINT.—

"(i) NOTIFICATION TO SECRETARY.—Not later than 30 days after a complaint is served to a subsection (k) applicant in an action for patent infringement described under this paragraph, the subsection (k) applicant shall provide the Secretary with notice and a copy of such complaint.

"(ii) PUBLICATION BY SECRETARY.—The Secretary shall publish in the Federal Register notice of a complaint received under clause (i).

"(7) NEWLY ISSUED OR LICENSED PATENTS.—In the case of a patent that—

"(A) is issued to, or exclusively licensed by, the reference product sponsor after the date that the reference product sponsor provided the list to the subsection (k) applicant under paragraph (3)(A); and

"(B) the reference product sponsor reasonably believes that, due to the issuance of such patent, a claim of patent infringement could reasonably be asserted by the reference product sponsor if a person not licensed by the reference product sponsor engaged in the making, using, offering to sell, selling, or importing into the United States of the biological product that is the subject of the subsection (k) application,

not later than 30 days after such issuance or licensing, the reference product sponsor shall provide to the subsection (k) applicant a supplement to the list provided by the reference product sponsor under paragraph (3)(A) that includes such patent, not later than 30 days after such supplement is provided, the subsection (k) applicant shall provide a statement to the reference product sponsor in accordance with paragraph (3)(B), and such patent shall be subject to paragraph (8).

"(8) NOTICE OF COMMERCIAL MARKETING AND PRELIMINARY INJUNCTION.—

"(A) NOTICE OF COMMERCIAL MARKETING.—The subsection (k) applicant shall provide notice to the reference product sponsor not later than 180 days before the date of the first commercial marketing of the biological product licensed under subsection (k).

"(B) PRELIMINARY INJUNCTION.—After receiving the notice under subparagraph (A) and before such date of the first commercial marketing of such biological product, the reference product sponsor may seek a preliminary injunction prohibiting the subsection (k) applicant from engaging in the commercial manufacture or sale of such biological product until the court decides the issue of patent validity, enforcement, and infringement with respect to any patent that is—

"(i) included in the list provided by the reference product sponsor under paragraph (3)(A) or in the list provided by the subsection (k) applicant under paragraph (3)(B); and

"(ii) not included, as applicable, on—

"(I) the list of patents described in paragraph (4); or

"(II) the lists of patents described in paragraph (5)(B).

"(C) REASONABLE COOPERATION.—If the reference product sponsor has sought a preliminary injunction under subparagraph (B), the reference product sponsor and the subsection (k) applicant shall reasonably cooperate to expedite such further discovery as is needed in connection with the preliminary injunction motion.

"(9) LIMITATION ON DECLARATORY JUDGMENT ACTION.—

"(A) SUBSECTION (k) APPLICATION PROVIDED.—If a subsection (k) applicant provides the application and information required under paragraph (2)(A), neither the reference product sponsor nor the subsection (k) applicant may, prior to the date notice is received under paragraph (8)(A), bring any action under section 2201 of title 28, United States Code, for a declaration of infringement, validity, or enforceability of any patent that is described in clauses (i) and (ii) of paragraph (8)(B).

"(B) SUBSEQUENT FAILURE TO ACT BY SUBSECTION (k) APPLICANT.—If a subsection (k) applicant fails to complete an action required of the subsection (k) applicant under paragraph (3)(B)(ii), paragraph (5), paragraph (6)(C)(i), paragraph (7), or paragraph (8)(A), the reference product sponsor, but not the subsection (k) applicant, may bring an action under section 2201 of title 28, United States Code, for a declaration of infringement, validity, or enforceability of any patent included in the list described in paragraph (3)(A), including as provided under paragraph (7).

"(C) SUBSECTION (k) APPLICATION NOT PROVIDED.—If a subsection (k) applicant fails to provide the application and information required under paragraph (2)(A), the reference product sponsor, but not the subsection (k) applicant, may bring an action under section 2201 of title 28, United States Code, for a declaration of infringement, validity, or enforceability of any patent that claims the biological product or a use of the biological product.".

(b) DEFINITIONS.—Section 351(i) of the Public Health Service Act (42 U.S.C. 262(i)) is amended—

(1) by striking "In this section, the term 'biological product' means" and inserting the following: "In this section:

"(1) The term 'biological product' means";

(2) in paragraph (1), as so designated, by inserting "protein (except any chemically synthesized polypeptide)," after "allergenic product,"; and

(3) by adding at the end the following:

"(2) The term 'biosimilar' or 'biosimilarity', in reference to a biological product that is the subject of an application under subsection (k), means—

"(A) that the biological product is highly similar to the reference product notwithstanding minor differences in clinically inactive components; and

"(B) there are no clinically meaningful differences between the biological product and the reference product in terms of the safety, purity, and potency of the product.

"(3) The term 'interchangeable' or 'interchangeability', in reference to a biological product that is shown to meet the standards described in subsection (k)(4), means that the biological product may be substituted for the reference product without the intervention of the health care provider who prescribed the reference product.

"(4) The term 'reference product' means the single biological product licensed under subsection (a) against which a biological product is evaluated in an application submitted under subsection (k).".

(c) CONFORMING AMENDMENTS RELATING TO PATENTS.—

(1) PATENTS.—Section 271(e) of title 35, United States Code, is amended—

(A) in paragraph (2)—

(i) in subparagraph (A), by striking "or" at the end;

(ii) in subparagraph (B), by adding "or" at the end; and

(iii) by inserting after subparagraph (B) the following:

"(C)(i) with respect to a patent that is identified in the list of patents described in section 351(l)(3) of the Public Health Service Act (including as provided under section 351(l)(7) of such Act), an application seeking approval of a biological product, or

"(ii) if the applicant for the application fails to provide the application and information required under section 351(l)(2)(A) of such Act, an application seeking approval of a biological product for a patent that could be identified pursuant to section 351(l)(3)(A)(i) of such Act,"; and

(iv) in the matter following subparagraph (C) (as added by clause (iii)), by striking "or veterinary biological product" and inserting ", veterinary biological product, or biological product";

(B) in paragraph (4)—

(i) in subparagraph (B), by—

(I) striking "or veterinary biological product" and inserting ", veterinary biological product, or biological product"; and

(II) striking "and" at the end;

(ii) in subparagraph (C), by—

(I) striking "or veterinary biological product" and inserting ", veterinary biological product, or biological product"; and

(II) striking the period and inserting ", and";

(iii) by inserting after subparagraph (C) the following:

"(D) the court shall order a permanent injunction prohibiting any infringement of the patent by the biological product involved in the infringement until a date which is not earlier than the date of the expiration of the patent that has been infringed under paragraph (2)(C), provided the patent is the subject of a final court decision, as defined in section 351(k)(6) of the Public Health Service Act, in an action for infringement of the patent under section 351(l)(6) of such Act, and the biological product has not yet been approved because of section 351(k)(7) of such Act."; and

(iv) in the matter following subparagraph (D) (as added by clause (iii)), by striking "and (C)" and inserting "(C), and (D)"; and

(C) by adding at the end the following:

"(6)(A) Subparagraph (B) applies, in lieu of paragraph (4), in the case of a patent—

"(i) that is identified, as applicable, in the list of patents described in section 351(l)(4) of the Public Health Service Act or the lists of patents described in section 351(l)(5)(B) of such Act with respect to a biological product; and

"(ii) for which an action for infringement of the patent with respect to the biological product—

"(I) was brought after the expiration of the 30-day period described in subparagraph (A) or (B), as applicable, of section 351(l)(6) of such Act; or

"(II) was brought before the expiration of the 30-day period described in subclause (I), but which was dismissed without prejudice or was not prosecuted to judgment in good faith.

"(B) In an action for infringement of a patent described in subparagraph (A), the sole and exclusive remedy that may be granted by a court, upon a finding that the making, using, offering to sell, selling, or importation into the United States of the biological product that is the subject of the action infringed the patent, shall be a reasonable royalty.

"(C) The owner of a patent that should have been included in the list described in section 351(l)(3)(A) of the Public Health Service Act, including as provided under section 351(l)(7) of such Act for a biological product, but was not timely included in such list, may not bring an action under this section for infringement of the patent with respect to the biological product.".

(2) CONFORMING AMENDMENT UNDER TITLE 28.—Section 2201(b) of title 28, United States Code, is amended by inserting before the period the following: ", or section 351 of the Public Health Service Act".

(d) CONFORMING AMENDMENTS UNDER THE FEDERAL FOOD, DRUG, AND COSMETIC ACT.—

(1) CONTENT AND REVIEW OF APPLICATIONS.—Section 505(b)(5)(B) of the Federal Food, Drug, and Cosmetic Act (21 U.S.C. 355(b)(5)(B)) is amended by inserting before the period at the end of the first sentence the following: "or, with respect to an applicant for approval of a biological product under section 351(k) of the Public Health Service Act, any necessary clinical study or studies".

(2) NEW ACTIVE INGREDIENT.—Section 505B of the Federal Food, Drug, and Cosmetic Act (21 U.S.C. 355c) is amended by adding at the end the following:

"(n) NEW ACTIVE INGREDIENT.—

"(1) NON-INTERCHANGEABLE BIOSIMILAR BIOLOGICAL PRODUCT.—A biological product that is biosimilar to a reference product under section 351 of the Public Health Service Act, and that the Secretary has not determined to meet the standards described in subsection (k)(4) of such section for interchangeability with the reference product, shall be considered to have a new active ingredient under this section.

"(2) INTERCHANGEABLE BIOSIMILAR BIOLOGICAL PRODUCT.—A biological product that is interchangeable with a reference product under section 351 of the Public Health Service Act shall not be considered to have a new active ingredient under this section.".

(e) PRODUCTS PREVIOUSLY APPROVED UNDER SECTION 505.—

(1) REQUIREMENT TO FOLLOW SECTION 351.—Except as provided in paragraph (2), an application for a biological product shall be submitted under section 351 of the Public Health Service Act (42 U.S.C. 262) (as amended by this Act).

(2) EXCEPTION.—An application for a biological product may be submitted under section 505 of the Federal Food, Drug, and Cosmetic Act (21 U.S.C. 355) if—

(A) such biological product is in a product class for which a biological product in such product class is the subject of an application approved under such section 505 not later than the date of enactment of this Act; and

(B) such application—

(i) has been submitted to the Secretary of Health and Human Services (referred to in this subtitle as the "Secretary") before the date of enactment of this Act; or

(ii) is submitted to the Secretary not later than the date that is 10 years after the date of enactment of this Act.

(3) LIMITATION.—Notwithstanding paragraph (2), an application for a biological product may not be submitted under section 505 of the Federal Food, Drug, and Cosmetic Act (21 U.S.C. 355) if there is another biological product approved under subsection (a) of section 351 of the Public Health Service Act that could be a reference product with respect to such application (within the meaning of such section 351) if such application were submitted under subsection (k) of such section 351.

(4) DEEMED APPROVED UNDER SECTION 351.—An approved application for a biological product under section 505 of the Federal Food, Drug, and Cosmetic Act (21 U.S.C. 355) shall be deemed to be a license for the biological product under such section 351 on the date that is 10 years after the date of enactment of this Act.

(5) DEFINITIONS.—For purposes of this subsection, the term "biological product" has the meaning given such term under section 351 of the Public Health Service Act (42 U.S.C. 262) (as amended by this Act).

(f) FOLLOW-ON BIOLOGICS USER FEES.—

(1) DEVELOPMENT OF USER FEES FOR BIOSIMILAR BIOLOGICAL PRODUCTS.—

(A) IN GENERAL.—Beginning not later than October 1, 2010, the Secretary shall develop recommendations to present to Congress with respect to the goals, and plans for meeting the goals, for the process for the review of biosimilar biological product applications submitted under section 351(k) of the Public Health Service Act (as added by this Act) for the first 5 fiscal years after fiscal year 2012. In developing such recommendations, the Secretary shall consult with—

(i) the Committee on Health, Education, Labor, and Pensions of the Senate;

(ii) the Committee on Energy and Commerce of the House of Representatives;

(iii) scientific and academic experts;

(iv) health care professionals;

(v) representatives of patient and consumer advocacy groups; and

(vi) the regulated industry.

(B) PUBLIC REVIEW OF RECOMMENDATIONS.—After negotiations with the regulated industry, the Secretary shall—

(i) present the recommendations developed under subparagraph (A) to the Congressional committees specified in such subparagraph;

(ii) publish such recommendations in the Federal Register;

(iii) provide for a period of 30 days for the public to provide written comments on such recommendations;

(iv) hold a meeting at which the public may present its views on such recommendations; and

(v) after consideration of such public views and comments, revise such recommendations as necessary.

(C) TRANSMITTAL OF RECOMMENDATIONS.—Not later than January 15, 2012, the Secretary shall transmit to Congress the revised recommendations under subparagraph (B), a summary of the views and comments received under such subparagraph, and any changes made to the recommendations in response to such views and comments.

(2) ESTABLISHMENT OF USER FEE PROGRAM.—It is the sense of the Senate that, based on the recommendations transmitted to Congress by the Secretary pursuant to paragraph (1)(C), Congress should authorize a program, effective on October 1, 2012, for the collection of user fees relating to the submission of biosimilar biological product applications under section 351(k) of the Public Health Service Act (as added by this Act).

(3) TRANSITIONAL PROVISIONS FOR USER FEES FOR BIOSIMILAR BIOLOGICAL PRODUCTS.—

(A) APPLICATION OF THE PRESCRIPTION DRUG USER FEE PROVISIONS.—Section 735(1)(B) of the Federal Food, Drug, and Cosmetic Act (21 U.S.C. 379g(1)(B)) is amended by striking "section 351" and inserting "subsection (a) or (k) of section 351".

(B) EVALUATION OF COSTS OF REVIEWING BIOSIMILAR BIOLOGICAL PRODUCT APPLICATIONS.—During the period beginning on the date of enactment of this Act and ending on October 1, 2010, the Secretary shall collect and evaluate data regarding the costs of reviewing applications for biological products submitted under section 351(k) of the

Public Health Service Act (as added by this Act) during such period.

(C) AUDIT.—

(i) IN GENERAL.—On the date that is 2 years after first receiving a user fee applicable to an application for a biological product under section 351(k) of the Public Health Service Act (as added by this Act), and on a biennial basis thereafter until October 1, 2013, the Secretary shall perform an audit of the costs of reviewing such applications under such section 351(k). Such an audit shall compare—

(I) the costs of reviewing such applications under such section 351(k) to the amount of the user fee applicable to such applications; and

(II)(aa) such ratio determined under subclause (I); to

(bb) the ratio of the costs of reviewing applications for biological products under section 351(a) of such Act (as amended by this Act) to the amount of the user fee applicable to such applications under such section 351(a).

(ii) ALTERATION OF USER FEE.—If the audit performed under clause (i) indicates that the ratios compared under subclause (II) of such clause differ by more than 5 percent, then the Secretary shall alter the user fee applicable to applications submitted under such section 351(k) to more appropriately account for the costs of reviewing such applications.

(iii) ACCOUNTING STANDARDS.—The Secretary shall perform an audit under clause (i) in conformance with the accounting principles, standards, and requirements prescribed by the Comptroller General of the United States under section 3511 of title 31, United State Code, to ensure the validity of any potential variability.

(4) AUTHORIZATION OF APPROPRIATIONS.—There is authorized to be appropriated to carry out this subsection such sums as may be necessary for each of fiscal years 2010 through 2012.

(g) PEDIATRIC STUDIES OF BIOLOGICAL PRODUCTS.—

(1) IN GENERAL.—Section 351 of the Public Health Service Act (42 U.S.C. 262) is amended by adding at the end the following:

"(m) PEDIATRIC STUDIES.—

"(1) APPLICATION OF CERTAIN PROVISIONS.—The provisions of subsections (a), (d), (e), (f), (i), (j), (k), (l), (p), and (q) of section 505A of the Federal Food, Drug, and Cosmetic Act shall apply with respect to the extension of a period under paragraphs (2) and (3) to the same extent and in the same manner as such provisions apply with respect to the extension of a period under subsection (b) or (c) of section 505A of the Federal Food, Drug, and Cosmetic Act.

"(2) MARKET EXCLUSIVITY FOR NEW BIOLOGICAL PRODUCTS.—If, prior to approval of an application that is submitted under subsection (a), the Secretary determines that information relating to the use of a new biological product in the pediatric population may produce health benefits in that population, the Secretary makes a written request for pediatric studies (which shall include a timeframe for completing such studies), the applicant agrees to the request, such studies are completed using appropriate formulations for each age group for which the study is requested within any such timeframe, and the reports thereof are submitted and accepted in accordance with section 505A(d)(3) of the Federal Food, Drug, and Cosmetic Act—

"(A) the periods for such biological product referred to in subsection (k)(7) are deemed to be 4 years and 6 months rather than 4 years and 12 years and 6 months rather than 12 years; and

"(B) if the biological product is designated under section 526 for a rare disease or condition, the period for such biological product referred to in section 527(a) is deemed to be 7 years and 6 months rather than 7 years.

"(3) MARKET EXCLUSIVITY FOR ALREADY-MARKETED BIOLOGICAL PRODUCTS.—If the Secretary determines that information relating to the use of a licensed biological product in the pediatric population may produce health benefits in that population and makes a written request to the holder of an approved application under subsection (a) for pediatric studies (which shall include a timeframe for completing such studies), the holder agrees to the request, such studies are completed using appropriate formulations for each age group for which the study is requested within any such timeframe, and the reports thereof are submitted and accepted in accordance with section 505A(d)(3) of the Federal Food, Drug, and Cosmetic Act—

"(A) the periods for such biological product referred to in subsection (k)(7) are deemed to be 4 years and 6 months rather than 4 years and 12 years and 6 months rather than 12 years; and

"(B) if the biological product is designated under section 526 for a rare disease or condition, the period for such biological product referred to in section 527(a) is deemed to be 7 years and 6 months rather than 7 years.

"(4) EXCEPTION.—The Secretary shall not extend a period referred to in paragraph (2)(A), (2)(B), (3)(A), or (3)(B) if the determination under section 505A(d)(3) is made later than 9 months prior to the expiration of such period.".

(2) STUDIES REGARDING PEDIATRIC RESEARCH.—

(A) PROGRAM FOR PEDIATRIC STUDY OF DRUGS.—Subsection (a)(1) of section 409I of the Public Health Service Act (42 U.S.C. 284m) is amended by inserting ", biological products," after "including drugs".

(B) INSTITUTE OF MEDICINE STUDY.—Section 505A(p) of the Federal Food, Drug, and Cosmetic Act (21 U.S.C. 355b(p)) is amended by striking paragraphs (4) and (5) and inserting the following:

"(4) review and assess the number and importance of biological products for children that are being tested as a result of the amendments made by the Biologics Price Competition and Innovation Act of 2009 and the importance for children, health care providers, parents, and others of labeling changes made as a result of such testing;

"(5) review and assess the number, importance, and prioritization of any biological products that are not being tested for pediatric use; and

"(6) offer recommendations for ensuring pediatric testing of biological products, including consideration of any incentives, such as those provided under this section or section 351(m) of the Public Health Service Act.".

(h) ORPHAN PRODUCTS.—If a reference product, as defined in section 351 of the Public Health Service Act (42 U.S.C. 262) (as amended by this Act) has been designated under section 526 of the Federal Food, Drug, and Cosmetic Act (21 U.S.C. 360bb) for a rare disease or condition, a biological product seeking approval for such disease or condition under subsection (k) of such section 351 as biosimilar to, or interchangeable with, such reference product may be licensed by the Secretary only after the expiration for such reference product of the later of—

(1) the 7-year period described in section 527(a) of the Federal Food, Drug, and Cosmetic Act (21 U.S.C. 360cc(a)); and

(2) the 12-year period described in subsection (k)(7) of such section 351.

SEC. 7003. SAVINGS.

(a) DETERMINATION.—The Secretary of the Treasury, in consultation with the Secretary of Health and Human Services, shall for each fiscal year determine the amount of savings to the Federal Government as a result of the enactment of this subtitle.

(b) USE.—Notwithstanding any other provision of this subtitle (or an amendment made by this subtitle), the savings to the Federal Government generated as a result of the enactment of this subtitle shall be used for deficit reduction.

Subtitle B—More Affordable Medicines for Children and Underserved Communities

SEC. 7101. EXPANDED PARTICIPATION IN 340B PROGRAM.

(a) EXPANSION OF COVERED ENTITIES RECEIVING DISCOUNTED PRICES.—Section 340B(a)(4) of the Public Health Service Act (42 U.S.C. 256b(a)(4)) is amended by adding at the end the following:

"(M) A children's hospital excluded from the Medicare prospective payment system pursuant to section 1886(d)(1)(B)(iii) of the Social Security Act, or a free-standing cancer hospital excluded from the Medicare prospective payment system pursuant to section 1886(d)(1)(B)(v) of the Social Security Act, that would meet the requirements of subparagraph (L), including the disproportionate share adjustment percentage requirement under clause (ii) of such subparagraph, if the hospital were a subsection (d) hospital as defined by section 1886(d)(1)(B) of the Social Security Act.

"(N) An entity that is a critical access hospital (as determined under section 1820(c)(2) of the Social Security Act), and that meets the requirements of subparagraph (L)(i).

"(O) An entity that is a rural referral center, as defined by section 1886(d)(5)(C)(i) of the Social Security Act, or a sole community hospital, as defined by section 1886(d)(5)(C)(iii) of such Act, and that both meets the requirements of subparagraph (L)(i) and has a disproportionate share adjustment percentage equal to or greater than 8 percent.".

(b) EXTENSION OF DISCOUNT TO INPATIENT DRUGS.—Section 340B of the Public Health Service Act (42 U.S.C. 256b) is amended—

(1) in paragraphs (2), (5), (7), and (9) of subsection (a), by striking "outpatient" each place it appears; and

(2) in subsection (b)—

(A) by striking "OTHER DEFINITION" and all that follows through "In this section" and inserting the following: "OTHER DEFINITIONS.—

"(1) IN GENERAL.—In this section"; and

(B) by adding at the end the following new paragraph:

"(2) COVERED DRUG.—In this section, the term 'covered drug'—

"(A) means a covered outpatient drug (as defined in section 1927(k)(2) of the Social Security Act); and

"(B) includes, notwithstanding paragraph (3)(A) of section 1927(k) of such Act, a drug used in connection with an inpatient or outpatient service provided by a hospital described in subparagraph (L), (M), (N), or (O) of subsection (a)(4) that is enrolled to participate in the drug discount program under this section.".

(c) PROHIBITION ON GROUP PURCHASING ARRANGEMENTS.—Section 340B(a) of the Public Health Service Act (42 U.S.C. 256b(a)) is amended—

(1) in paragraph (4)(L)—

(A) in clause (i), by adding "and" at the end;

(B) in clause (ii), by striking "; and" and inserting a period; and

(C) by striking clause (iii); and

(2) in paragraph (5), as amended by subsection (b)—

(A) by redesignating subparagraphs (C) and (D) as subparagraphs (D) and (E); respectively; and

(B) by inserting after subparagraph (B), the following:

"(C) PROHIBITION ON GROUP PURCHASING ARRANGEMENTS.—

"(i) IN GENERAL.—A hospital described in subparagraph (L), (M), (N), or (O) of paragraph (4) shall not obtain covered outpatient drugs through a group purchasing organization or other group purchasing arrangement, except as permitted or provided for pursuant to clauses (ii) or (iii).

"(ii) INPATIENT DRUGS.—Clause (i) shall not apply to drugs purchased for inpatient use.

"(iii) EXCEPTIONS.—The Secretary shall establish reasonable exceptions to clause (i)—

"(I) with respect to a covered outpatient drug that is unavailable to be purchased through the program under this section due to a drug shortage problem, manufacturer noncompliance, or any other circumstance beyond the hospital's control;

"(II) to facilitate generic substitution when a generic covered outpatient drug is available at a lower price; or

"(III) to reduce in other ways the administrative burdens of managing both inventories of drugs subject to this section and inventories of drugs that are not subject to this section, so long as the exceptions do not create a duplicate discount problem in violation of subparagraph (A) or a diversion problem in violation of subparagraph (B).

"(iv) PURCHASING ARRANGEMENTS FOR INPATIENT DRUGS.—The Secretary shall ensure that a hospital described in subparagraph (L), (M), (N), or (O) of subsection (a)(4) that is enrolled to participate in the drug discount program under this section shall have multiple options for purchasing covered drugs for inpatients, including by utilizing a group purchasing organization or other group purchasing arrangement, establishing and utilizing its own group purchasing program, purchasing directly from a manufacturer, and any other purchasing arrangements that the Secretary determines is appropriate to ensure access to drug discount pricing under this section for inpatient drugs taking into account the particular needs of small and rural hospitals.".

(d) MEDICAID CREDITS ON INPATIENT DRUGS.—Section 340B of the Public Health Service Act (42 U.S.C. 256b) is amended by striking subsection (c) and inserting the following:

"(c) MEDICAID CREDIT.—Not later than 90 days after the date of filing of the hospital's most recently filed Medicare cost report, the hospital shall issue a credit as determined by the Secretary to the State Medicaid program for inpatient covered drugs provided to Medicaid recipients.".

(e) EFFECTIVE DATES.—

(1) IN GENERAL.—The amendments made by this section and section 7102 shall take effect on January 1, 2010, and shall apply to drugs purchased on or after January 1, 2010.

(2) EFFECTIVENESS.—The amendments made by this section and section 7102 shall be effective and shall be taken into account in determining whether a manufacturer is deemed to meet the requirements of section 340B(a) of the Public Health Service Act (42 U.S.C. 256b(a)), notwithstanding any other provision of law.

SEC. 7102. IMPROVEMENTS TO 340B PROGRAM INTEGRITY.

(a) INTEGRITY IMPROVEMENTS.—Subsection (d) of section 340B of the Public Health Service Act (42 U.S.C. 256b) is amended to read as follows:

"(d) IMPROVEMENTS IN PROGRAM INTEGRITY.—

"(1) MANUFACTURER COMPLIANCE.—

"(A) IN GENERAL.—From amounts appropriated under paragraph (4), the Secretary shall provide for improvements in compliance by manufacturers with the requirements of this section in order to prevent overcharges and other violations of the discounted pricing requirements specified in this section.

"(B) IMPROVEMENTS.—The improvements described in subparagraph (A) shall include the following:

"(i) The development of a system to enable the Secretary to verify the accuracy of ceiling prices calculated by manufacturers under subsection (a)(1) and charged to covered entities, which shall include the following:

"(I) Developing and publishing through an appropriate policy or regulatory issuance, precisely defined standards and methodology for the calculation of ceiling prices under such subsection.

"(II) Comparing regularly the ceiling prices calculated by the Secretary with the quarterly pricing data that is reported by manufacturers to the Secretary.

"(III) Performing spot checks of sales transactions by covered entities.

"(IV) Inquiring into the cause of any pricing discrepancies that may be identified and either taking, or requiring manufacturers to take, such corrective action as is appropriate in response to such price discrepancies.

"(ii) The establishment of procedures for manufacturers to issue refunds to covered entities in the event that there is an overcharge by the manufacturers, including the following:

"(I) Providing the Secretary with an explanation of why and how the overcharge occurred, how the refunds will be calculated, and to whom the refunds will be issued.

"(II) Oversight by the Secretary to ensure that the refunds are issued accurately and within a reasonable period of time, both in routine instances of retroactive adjustment to relevant pricing data and exceptional circumstances such as erroneous or intentional overcharging for covered drugs.

"(iii) The provision of access through the Internet website of the Department of Health and Human Services to the applicable ceiling prices for covered drugs as calculated and verified by the Secretary in accordance with this section, in a manner (such as through the use of password protection) that limits such access to covered entities and adequately assures security and protection of privileged pricing data from unauthorized re-disclosure.

"(iv) The development of a mechanism by which—

"(I) rebates and other discounts provided by manufacturers to other purchasers subsequent to the sale of covered drugs to covered entities are reported to the Secretary; and

"(II) appropriate credits and refunds are issued to covered entities if such discounts or rebates have the effect of lowering the applicable ceiling price for the relevant quarter for the drugs involved.

"(v) Selective auditing of manufacturers and wholesalers to ensure the integrity of the drug discount program under this section.

"(vi) The imposition of sanctions in the form of civil monetary penalties, which—

"(I) shall be assessed according to standards established in regulations to be promulgated by the Secretary not later than 180 days after the date of enactment of the Patient Protection and Affordable Care Act;

"(II) shall not exceed $5,000 for each instance of overcharging a covered entity that may have occurred; and

"(III) shall apply to any manufacturer with an agreement under this section that knowingly and intentionally charges a covered entity a price for purchase of a drug that exceeds the maximum applicable price under subsection (a)(1).

"(2) COVERED ENTITY COMPLIANCE.—

"(A) IN GENERAL.—From amounts appropriated under paragraph (4), the Secretary shall provide for improvements in compliance by covered entities with the requirements of this section in order to prevent diversion and violations of the duplicate discount provision and other requirements specified under subsection (a)(5).

"(B) IMPROVEMENTS.—The improvements described in subparagraph (A) shall include the following:

"(i) The development of procedures to enable and require covered entities to regularly update (at least annually) the information on the Internet website of the Department of Health and Human Services relating to this section.

"(ii) The development of a system for the Secretary to verify the accuracy of information regarding covered entities that is listed on the website described in clause (i).

"(iii) The development of more detailed guidance describing methodologies and options available to covered entities for billing covered drugs to State Medicaid agencies in a manner that avoids duplicate discounts pursuant to subsection (a)(5)(A).

"(iv) The establishment of a single, universal, and standardized identification system by which each covered entity site can be identified by manufacturers, distributors, covered entities, and the Secretary for purposes of facilitating the ordering, purchasing, and delivery of covered drugs under this section, including the processing of chargebacks for such drugs.

"(v) The imposition of sanctions, in appropriate cases as determined by the Secretary, additional to those to which covered entities are subject under subsection (a)(5)(E), through one or more of the following actions:

"(I) Where a covered entity knowingly and intentionally violates subsection (a)(5)(B), the covered entity shall be required to pay a monetary penalty to a manufacturer or manufacturers in the form of interest on sums for which the covered entity is found liable under subsection (a)(5)(E), such interest to be compounded monthly and equal to the current short term interest rate as determined by the Federal Reserve for the time period for which the covered entity is liable.

"(II) Where the Secretary determines a violation of subsection (a)(5)(B) was systematic and egregious as well as knowing and intentional, removing the covered entity from the drug discount program under this section and disqualifying the entity from re-entry into such program for a reasonable period of time to be determined by the Secretary.

"(III) Referring matters to appropriate Federal authorities within the Food and Drug Administration, the Office of Inspector General of Department of Health and Human Services, or other Federal agencies for consideration of appropriate action under other Federal statutes, such as the Prescription Drug Marketing Act (21 U.S.C. 353).

"(3) ADMINISTRATIVE DISPUTE RESOLUTION PROCESS.—

"(A) IN GENERAL.—Not later than 180 days after the date of enactment of the Patient Protection and Affordable Care Act, the Secretary shall promulgate regulations to establish and implement an administrative process for the resolution of claims by covered entities that they have been overcharged for drugs purchased under this section, and claims by manufacturers, after the conduct of audits as authorized by subsection (a)(5)(D), of violations of subsections (a)(5)(A) or (a)(5)(B), including appropriate procedures for the provision of remedies and enforcement of determinations made pursuant to such process through mechanisms and sanctions described in paragraphs (1)(B) and (2)(B).

"(B) DEADLINES AND PROCEDURES.—Regulations promulgated by the Secretary under subparagraph (A) shall—

"(i) designate or establish a decision-making official or decision-making body within the Department of Health and Human Services to be responsible for reviewing and finally resolving claims by covered entities that they have been charged prices for covered drugs in excess of the ceiling price described in subsection (a)(1), and claims by manufacturers that violations of subsection (a)(5)(A) or (a)(5)(B) have occurred;

"(ii) establish such deadlines and procedures as may be necessary to ensure that claims shall be resolved fairly, efficiently, and expeditiously;

"(iii) establish procedures by which a covered entity may discover and obtain such information and documents from manufacturers and third parties as may be relevant to demonstrate the merits of a claim that charges for a manufacturer's product have exceeded the applicable ceiling price under this section, and may submit such documents and information to the administrative official or body responsible for adjudicating such claim;

"(iv) require that a manufacturer conduct an audit of a covered entity pursuant to subsection (a)(5)(D) as a prerequisite to initiating administrative dispute resolution proceedings against a covered entity;

"(v) permit the official or body designated under clause (i), at the request of a manufacturer or manufacturers, to consolidate claims brought by more than one manufacturer against the same covered entity where, in the judgment of such official or body, consolidation is appropriate and consistent with the goals of fairness and economy of resources; and

"(vi) include provisions and procedures to permit multiple covered entities to jointly assert claims of overcharges by the same manufacturer for the same drug or drugs in one administrative proceeding, and permit such claims to be asserted on behalf of covered entities by associations or organizations representing the interests of such covered entities and of which the covered entities are members.

"(C) FINALITY OF ADMINISTRATIVE RESOLUTION.—The administrative resolution of a claim or claims under the regulations promulgated under subparagraph (A) shall be a final agency decision and shall be binding upon the parties involved, unless invalidated by an order of a court of competent jurisdiction.

"(4) AUTHORIZATION OF APPROPRIATIONS.—There are authorized to be appropriated to carry out this subsection, such sums as may be necessary for fiscal year 2010 and each succeeding fiscal year.".

(b) CONFORMING AMENDMENTS.—Section 340B(a) of the Public Health Service Act (42 U.S.C. 256b(a)) is amended—

(1) in subsection (a)(1), by adding at the end the following: "Each such agreement shall require that the manufacturer furnish the Secretary with reports, on a quarterly basis, of the price for each covered drug subject to the agreement that, according to the manufacturer, represents the maximum price that covered entities may permissibly be required to pay for the drug (referred to in this section as the 'ceiling price'), and shall require that the manufacturer offer each covered entity covered drugs for purchase at or below the applicable ceiling price if such drug is made available to any other purchaser at any price."; and

(2) in the first sentence of subsection (a)(5)(E), as redesignated by section 7101(c), by inserting "after audit as described in subparagraph (D) and" after "finds,".

SEC. 7103. GAO STUDY TO MAKE RECOMMENDATIONS ON IMPROVING THE 340B PROGRAM.

(a) REPORT.—Not later than 18 months after the date of enactment of this Act, the Comptroller General of the United States shall submit to Congress a report that examines whether those individuals served by the covered entities under the program under section 340B of the Public Health Service Act (42 U.S.C. 256b) (referred to in this section as the "340B program") are receiving optimal health care services.

(b) RECOMMENDATIONS.—The report under subsection (a) shall include recommendations on the following:

(1) Whether the 340B program should be expanded since it is anticipated that the 47,000,000 individuals who are uninsured as of the date of enactment of this Act will have health care coverage once this Act is implemented.

(2) Whether mandatory sales of certain products by the 340B program could hinder patients access to those therapies through any provider.

(3) Whether income from the 340B program is being used by the covered entities under the program to further the program objectives.

TITLE VIII—CLASS ACT

SEC. 8001. SHORT TITLE OF TITLE.

This title may be cited as the "Community Living Assistance Services and Supports Act" or the "CLASS Act".

SEC. 8002. ESTABLISHMENT OF NATIONAL VOLUNTARY INSURANCE PROGRAM FOR PURCHASING COMMUNITY LIVING ASSISTANCE SERVICES AND SUPPORT.

(a) ESTABLISHMENT OF CLASS PROGRAM.—

(1) IN GENERAL.—The Public Health Service Act (42 U.S.C. 201 et seq.), as amended by section 4302(a), is amended by adding at the end the following:

"TITLE XXXII—COMMUNITY LIVING ASSISTANCE SERVICES AND SUPPORTS

"SEC. 3201. PURPOSE.

"The purpose of this title is to establish a national voluntary insurance program for purchasing community living assistance services and supports in order to—

"(1) provide individuals with functional limitations with tools that will allow them to maintain their personal and financial independence and live in the community through a new financing strategy for community living assistance services and supports;

"(2) establish an infrastructure that will help address the Nation's community living assistance services and supports needs;

"(3) alleviate burdens on family caregivers; and

"(4) address institutional bias by providing a financing mechanism that supports personal choice and independence to live in the community.

"SEC. 3202. DEFINITIONS.

"In this title:

"(1) ACTIVE ENROLLEE.—The term 'active enrollee' means an individual who is enrolled in the CLASS program in accordance with section 3204 and who has paid any premiums due to maintain such enrollment.

"(2) ACTIVELY EMPLOYED.—The term 'actively employed' means an individual who—

"(A) is reporting for work at the individual's usual place of employment or at another location to which the individual is required to travel because of the individual's employment (or in the case of an individual who is a member of the uniformed services, is on active duty and is physically able to perform the duties of the individual's position); and

"(B) is able to perform all the usual and customary duties of the individual's employment on the individual's regular work schedule.

"(3) ACTIVITIES OF DAILY LIVING.—The term 'activities of daily living' means each of the following activities specified in section 7702B(c)(2)(B) of the Internal Revenue Code of 1986:

"(A) Eating.

"(B) Toileting.

"(C) Transferring.

"(D) Bathing.

"(E) Dressing.

"(F) Continence.

"(4) CLASS PROGRAM.—The term 'CLASS program' means the program established under this title.

"(5) ELIGIBILITY ASSESSMENT SYSTEM.—The term 'Eligibility Assessment System' means the entity established by the Secretary under section 3205(a)(2) to make functional eligibility determinations for the CLASS program.

"(6) ELIGIBLE BENEFICIARY.—

"(A) IN GENERAL.—The term 'eligible beneficiary' means any individual who is an active enrollee in the CLASS program and, as of the date described in subparagraph (B)—

"(i) has paid premiums for enrollment in such program for at least 60 months;

"(ii) has earned, with respect to at least 3 calendar years that occur during the first 60 months for which the individual has paid premiums for enrollment in the program, at least an amount equal to the amount of wages and self-employment income which an individual must have in order to be credited with a quarter of coverage under section 213(d) of the Social Security Act for the year; and

"(iii) has paid premiums for enrollment in such program for at least 24 consecutive months, if a lapse in premium payments of more than 3 months has occurred during the period that begins on the date of the individual's enrollment and ends on the date of such determination.

"(B) DATE DESCRIBED.—For purposes of subparagraph (A), the date described in this subparagraph is the date on which the individual is determined to have a functional limitation described in section 3203(a)(1)(C) that is expected to last for a continuous period of more than 90 days.

"(C) REGULATIONS.—The Secretary shall promulgate regulations specifying exceptions to the minimum earnings requirements under subparagraph (A)(ii) for purposes of being considered an eligible beneficiary for certain populations.

"(7) HOSPITAL; NURSING FACILITY; INTERMEDIATE CARE FACILITY FOR THE MENTALLY RETARDED; INSTITUTION FOR

MENTAL DISEASES.—The terms 'hospital', 'nursing facility', 'intermediate care facility for the mentally retarded', and 'institution for mental diseases' have the meanings given such terms for purposes of Medicaid.

"(8) CLASS INDEPENDENCE ADVISORY COUNCIL.—The term 'CLASS Independence Advisory Council' or 'Council' means the Advisory Council established under section 3207 to advise the Secretary.

"(9) CLASS INDEPENDENCE BENEFIT PLAN.—The term 'CLASS Independence Benefit Plan' means the benefit plan developed and designated by the Secretary in accordance with section 3203.

"(10) CLASS INDEPENDENCE FUND.—The term 'CLASS Independence Fund' or 'Fund' means the fund established under section 3206.

"(11) MEDICAID.—The term 'Medicaid' means the program established under title XIX of the Social Security Act (42 U.S.C. 1396 et seq.).

"(12) POVERTY LINE.—The term 'poverty line' has the meaning given that term in section 2110(c)(5) of the Social Security Act (42 U.S.C. 1397jj(c)(5)).

"(13) PROTECTION AND ADVOCACY SYSTEM.—The term 'Protection and Advocacy System' means the system for each State established under section 143 of the Developmental Disabilities Assistance and Bill of Rights Act of 2000 (42 U.S.C. 15043).

"SEC. 3203. CLASS INDEPENDENCE BENEFIT PLAN.

"(a) PROCESS FOR DEVELOPMENT.—

"(1) IN GENERAL.—The Secretary, in consultation with appropriate actuaries and other experts, shall develop at least 3 actuarially sound benefit plans as alternatives for consideration for designation by the Secretary as the CLASS Independence Benefit Plan under which eligible beneficiaries shall receive benefits under this title. Each of the plan alternatives developed shall be designed to provide eligible beneficiaries with the benefits described in section 3205 consistent with the following requirements:

"(A) PREMIUMS.—

"(i) IN GENERAL.—Beginning with the first year of the CLASS program, and for each year thereafter, subject to clauses (ii) and (iii), the Secretary shall establish all premiums to be paid by enrollees for the year based on an actuarial analysis of the 75-year costs of the program that ensures solvency throughout such 75-year period.

"(ii) NOMINAL PREMIUM FOR POOREST INDIVIDUALS AND FULL-TIME STUDENTS.—

"(I) IN GENERAL.—The monthly premium for enrollment in the CLASS program shall not exceed the applicable dollar amount per month determined under subclause (II) for—

"(aa) any individual whose income does not exceed the poverty line; and

"(bb) any individual who has not attained age 22, and is actively employed during any period in which the individual is a full-time student (as determined by the Secretary).

"(II) APPLICABLE DOLLAR AMOUNT.—The applicable dollar amount described in this subclause is the amount equal to $5, increased by the percentage increase in the consumer price index for all urban consumers (U.S. city average) for each year occurring after 2009 and before such year.

"(iii) CLASS INDEPENDENCE FUND RESERVES.—At such time as the CLASS program has been in operation for 10 years, the Secretary shall establish all premiums to be paid by enrollees for the year based on an actuarial analysis that accumulated reserves in the CLASS Independence Fund would not decrease in that year. At such time as the Secretary determines the CLASS program demonstrates a sustained ability to finance expected yearly expenses with expected yearly premiums and interest credited to the CLASS Independence Fund, the Secretary may decrease the required amount of CLASS Independence Fund reserves.

"(B) VESTING PERIOD.—A 5-year vesting period for eligibility for benefits.

"(C) BENEFIT TRIGGERS.—A benefit trigger for provision of benefits that requires a determination that an individual has a functional limitation, as certified by a licensed health care practitioner, described in any of the following clauses that is expected to last for a continuous period of more than 90 days:

"(i) The individual is determined to be unable to perform at least the minimum number (which may be 2 or 3) of activities of daily living as are required under the plan for the provision of benefits without substantial assistance (as defined by the Secretary) from another individual.

"(ii) The individual requires substantial supervision to protect the individual from threats to health and safety due to substantial cognitive impairment.

"(iii) The individual has a level of functional limitation similar (as determined under regulations prescribed by the Secretary) to the level of functional limitation described in clause (i) or (ii).

"(D) CASH BENEFIT.—Payment of a cash benefit that satisfies the following requirements:

"(i) MINIMUM REQUIRED AMOUNT.—The benefit amount provides an eligible beneficiary with not less than an average of $50 per day (as determined based on the reasonably expected distribution of beneficiaries receiving benefits at various benefit levels).

"(ii) AMOUNT SCALED TO FUNCTIONAL ABILITY.—The benefit amount is varied based on a scale of functional ability, with not less than 2, and not more than 6, benefit level amounts.

"(iii) DAILY OR WEEKLY.—The benefit is paid on a daily or weekly basis.

"(iv) NO LIFETIME OR AGGREGATE LIMIT.—The benefit is not subject to any lifetime or aggregate limit.

"(E) COORDINATION WITH SUPPLEMENTAL COVERAGE OBTAINED THROUGH THE EXCHANGE.—The benefits allow for coordination with any supplemental coverage purchased through an Exchange established under section 1311 of the Patient Protection and Affordable Care Act.

"(2) REVIEW AND RECOMMENDATION BY THE CLASS INDEPENDENCE ADVISORY COUNCIL.—The CLASS Independence Advisory Council shall—

"(A) evaluate the alternative benefit plans developed under paragraph (1); and

"(B) recommend for designation as the CLASS Independence Benefit Plan for offering to the public the plan that the Council determines best balances price and benefits to meet enrollees' needs in an actuarially sound manner, while optimizing the probability of the long-term sustainability of the CLASS program.

"(3) DESIGNATION BY THE SECRETARY.—Not later than October 1, 2012, the Secretary, taking into consideration the recommendation of the CLASS Independence Advisory Council under paragraph (2)(B), shall designate a benefit plan as the CLASS Independence Benefit Plan. The Secretary shall publish such designation, along with details of the plan and the reasons for the selection by the Secretary, in a final rule that allows for a period of public comment.

"(b) ADDITIONAL PREMIUM REQUIREMENTS.—

"(1) ADJUSTMENT OF PREMIUMS.—

"(A) IN GENERAL.—Except as provided in subparagraphs (B), (C), (D), and (E), the amount of the monthly premium determined for an individual upon such individual's enrollment in the CLASS program shall remain the same for as long as the individual is an active enrollee in the program.

"(B) RECALCULATED PREMIUM IF REQUIRED FOR PROGRAM SOLVENCY.—

"(i) IN GENERAL.—Subject to clause (ii), if the Secretary determines, based on the most recent report of the Board of Trustees of the CLASS Independence Fund, the advice of the CLASS Independence Advisory Council, and the annual report of the Inspector General of the Department of Health and Human Services, and waste, fraud, and abuse, or such other information as the Secretary determines appropriate, that the monthly premiums and income to the CLASS Independence Fund for a year are projected to be insufficient with respect to the 20-year period that begins with that year, the Secretary shall adjust the monthly premiums for individuals enrolled in the CLASS program as necessary (but maintaining a nominal premium for enrollees whose income is below the poverty line or who are full-time students actively employed).

"(ii) EXEMPTION FROM INCREASE.—Any increase in a monthly premium imposed as result of a determination described in clause (i) shall not apply with respect to the monthly premium of any active enrollee who—

"(I) has attained age 65;

"(II) has paid premiums for enrollment in the program for at least 20 years; and

"(III) is not actively employed.

"(C) RECALCULATED PREMIUM IF REENROLLMENT AFTER MORE THAN A 3-MONTH LAPSE.—

"(i) IN GENERAL.—The reenrollment of an individual after a 90-day period during which the individual failed to pay the monthly premium required to maintain the individual's enrollment in the CLASS program shall be treated as an initial enrollment for purposes of age-adjusting the premium for enrollment in the program.

"(ii) CREDIT FOR PRIOR MONTHS IF REENROLLED WITHIN 5 YEARS.—An individual who reenrolls in the CLASS program after such a 90-day period and before the end of the 5-year period that begins with the first month for which the individual failed to pay the monthly premium required to maintain the individual's enrollment in the program shall be—

"(I) credited with any months of paid premiums that accrued prior to the individual's lapse in enrollment; and

"(II) notwithstanding the total amount of any such credited months, required to satisfy section 3202(6)(A)(ii) before being eligible to receive benefits.

"(D) NO LONGER STATUS AS A FULL-TIME STUDENT.—An individual subject to a nominal premium on the basis of being described in subsection (a)(1)(A)(ii)(I)(bb) who ceases to be described in that subsection, beginning with the first month following the month in which the individual ceases to be so described, shall be subject to the same monthly premium as the monthly premium that applies to an individual of the same age who first enrolls in the program under the most similar circumstances as the individual (such as the first year of eligibility for enrollment in the program or in a subsequent year).

"(E) PENALTY FOR REENOLLMENT AFTER 5-YEAR LAPSE.—In the case of an individual who reenrolls in the CLASS program after the end of the 5-year period described in subparagraph (C)(ii), the monthly premium required for the individual shall be the age-adjusted premium that would be applicable to an initially enrolling individual who is the same age as the reenrolling individual, increased by the greater of—

"(i) an amount that the Secretary determines is actuarially sound for each month that occurs during the period that begins with the first month for which the individual failed to pay the monthly premium required to maintain the individual's enrollment in the CLASS program and ends with the month preceding the month in which the reenollment is effective; or

"(ii) 1 percent of the applicable age-adjusted premium for each such month occurring in such period.

"(2) ADMINISTRATIVE EXPENSES.—In determining the monthly premiums for the CLASS program the Secretary may factor in costs for administering the program, not to exceed for any year in which the program is in effect under this title, an amount equal to 3 percent of all premiums paid during the year.

"(3) NO UNDERWRITING REQUIREMENTS.—No underwriting (other than on the basis of age in accordance with subparagraphs (D) and (E) of paragraph (1)) shall be used to—

"(A) determine the monthly premium for enrollment in the CLASS program; or

"(B) prevent an individual from enrolling in the program.

"(c) SELF-ATTESTATION AND VERIFICATION OF INCOME.—The Secretary shall establish procedures to—

"(1) permit an individual who is eligible for the nominal premium required under subsection (a)(1)(A)(ii), as part of their automatic enrollment in the CLASS program, to self-attest that their income does not exceed the poverty line or that their status as a full-time student who is actively employed;

"(2) verify, using procedures similar to the procedures used by the Commissioner of Social Security under section 1631(e)(1)(B)(ii) of the Social Security Act and consistent with the requirements applicable to the conveyance of data and information under section 1942 of such Act, the validity of such self-attestation; and

"(3) require an individual to confirm, on at least an annual basis, that their income does not exceed the poverty line or that they continue to maintain such status.

"SEC. 3204. ENROLLMENT AND DISENROLLMENT REQUIREMENTS.

"(a) AUTOMATIC ENROLLMENT.—

"(1) IN GENERAL.—Subject to paragraph (2), the Secretary, in coordination with the Secretary of the Treasury, shall establish procedures under which each individual described in subsection (c) may be automatically enrolled in the CLASS program by an employer of such individual in the same manner as an employer may elect to automatically enroll employees in a plan under section 401(k), 403(b), or 457 of the Internal Revenue Code of 1986.

"(2) ALTERNATIVE ENROLLMENT PROCEDURES.—The procedures established under paragraph (1) shall provide for an alternative enrollment process for an individual described in subsection (c) in the case of such an individual—

"(A) who is self-employed;

"(B) who has more than 1 employer; or

"(C) whose employer does not elect to participate in the automatic enrollment process established by the Secretary.

"(3) ADMINISTRATION.—

"(A) IN GENERAL.—The Secretary and the Secretary of the Treasury shall, by regulation, establish procedures to ensure that an individual is not automatically enrolled in the CLASS program by more than 1 employer.

"(B) FORM.—Enrollment in the CLASS program shall be made in such manner as the Secretary may prescribe in order to ensure ease of administration.

"(b) ELECTION TO OPT-OUT.—An individual described in subsection (c) may elect to waive enrollment in the CLASS program at any time in such form and manner as the Secretary and the Secretary of the Treasury shall prescribe.

"(c) INDIVIDUAL DESCRIBED.—For purposes of enrolling in the CLASS program, an individual described in this paragraph is an individual—

"(1) who has attained age 18;

"(2) who—

"(A) receives wages on which there is imposed a tax under section 3201(a) of the Internal Revenue Code of 1986; or

"(B) derives self-employment income on which there is imposed a tax under section 1401(a) of the Internal Revenue Code of 1986;

"(3) who is actively employed; and

"(4) who is not—

"(A) a patient in a hospital or nursing facility, an intermediate care facility for the mentally retarded, or an institution for mental diseases and receiving medical assistance under Medicaid; or

"(B) confined in a jail, prison, other penal institution or correctional facility, or by court order pursuant to conviction of a criminal offense or in connection with a verdict or finding described in section 202(x)(1)(A)(ii) of the Social Security Act (42 U.S.C. 402(x)(1)(A)(ii)).

"(d) RULE OF CONSTRUCTION.—Nothing in this title shall be construed as requiring an active enrollee to continue to satisfy subparagraph (B) or (C) of subsection (c)(1) in order to maintain enrollment in the CLASS program.

"(e) PAYMENT.—

"(1) PAYROLL DEDUCTION.—An amount equal to the monthly premium for the enrollment in the CLASS program of an individual shall be deducted from the wages or self-employment income of such individual in accordance with such procedures as the Secretary, in coordination with the Secretary of the Treasury, shall establish for employers who elect to deduct and withhold such premiums on behalf of enrolled employees.

"(2) ALTERNATIVE PAYMENT MECHANISM.—The Secretary, in coordination with the Secretary of the Treasury, shall establish alternative procedures for the payment of monthly premiums by an individual enrolled in the CLASS program—

"(A) who does not have an employer who elects to deduct and withhold premiums in accordance with subparagraph (A); or

"(B) who does not earn wages or derive self-employment income.

"(f) TRANSFER OF PREMIUMS COLLECTED.—

"(1) IN GENERAL.—During each calendar year the Secretary of the Treasury shall deposit into the CLASS Independence Fund a total amount equal, in the aggregate, to 100 percent of the premiums collected during that year.

"(2) TRANSFERS BASED ON ESTIMATES.—The amount deposited pursuant to paragraph (1) shall be transferred in at least monthly payments to the CLASS Independence Fund on the basis of estimates by the Secretary and certified to the Secretary of the Treasury of the amounts collected in accordance with subparagraphs (A) and (B) of paragraph (5). Proper adjustments shall be made in amounts subsequently transferred to the Fund to the extent prior estimates were in excess of, or were less than, actual amounts collected.

"(g) OTHER ENROLLMENT AND DISENROLLMENT OPPORTUNITIES.—The Secretary, in coordination with the Secretary of the Treasury, shall establish procedures under which—

"(1) an individual who, in the year of the individual's initial eligibility to enroll in the CLASS program, has elected to waive enrollment in the program, is eligible to elect to enroll in the program, in such form and manner as the Secretaries shall establish, only during an open enrollment period established by the Secretaries that is specific to the individual and that may not occur more frequently than biennially after the date on which the individual first elected to waive enrollment in the program; and

"(2) an individual shall only be permitted to disenroll from the program (other than for nonpayment of premiums) during an annual disenrollment period established by the Secretaries and in such form and manner as the Secretaries shall establish.

"SEC. 3205. BENEFITS.

"(a) DETERMINATION OF ELIGIBILITY.—

"(1) APPLICATION FOR RECEIPT OF BENEFITS.—The Secretary shall establish procedures under which an active enrollee shall apply for receipt of benefits under the CLASS Independence Benefit Plan.

"(2) ELIGIBILITY ASSESSMENTS.—

"(A) IN GENERAL.—Not later than January 1, 2012, the Secretary shall—

"(i) establish an Eligibility Assessment System (other than a service with which the Commissioner of Social Security has entered into an agreement, with respect to any State, to make disability determinations for purposes of title II or XVI of the Social Security Act) to provide for eligibility assessments of active enrollees who apply for receipt of benefits;

"(ii) enter into an agreement with the Protection and Advocacy System for each State to provide advocacy services in accordance with subsection (d); and

"(iii) enter into an agreement with public and private entities to provide advice and assistance counseling in accordance with subsection (e).

"(B) REGULATIONS.—The Secretary shall promulgate regulations to develop an expedited nationally equitable eligibility determination process, as certified by a licensed health care practitioner, an appeals process, and a redetermination process, as certified by a licensed health care practitioner, including whether an active enrollee is eligible for a cash benefit under the program and if so, the amount of the cash benefit (in accordance the sliding scale established under the plan).

"(C) PRESUMPTIVE ELIGIBILITY FOR CERTAIN INSTITUTIONALIZED ENROLLEES PLANNING TO DISCHARGE.—An active enrollee shall be deemed presumptively eligible if the enrollee—

"(i) has applied for, and attests is eligible for, the maximum cash benefit available under the sliding scale established under the CLASS Independence Benefit Plan;

"(ii) is a patient in a hospital (but only if the hospitalization is for long-term care), nursing facility, intermediate care facility for the mentally retarded, or an institution for mental diseases; and

"(iii) is in the process of, or about to begin the process of, planning to discharge from the hospital, facility, or institution, or within 60 days from the date of discharge from the hospital, facility, or institution.

"(D) APPEALS.—The Secretary shall establish procedures under which an applicant for benefits under the CLASS Independence Benefit Plan shall be guaranteed the right to appeal an adverse determination.

"(b) BENEFITS.—An eligible beneficiary shall receive the following benefits under the CLASS Independence Benefit Plan:

"(1) CASH BENEFIT.—A cash benefit established by the Secretary in accordance with the requirements of section 3203(a)(1)(D) that—

"(A) the first year in which beneficiaries receive the benefits under the plan, is not less than the average dollar amount specified in clause (i) of such section; and

"(B) for any subsequent year, is not less than the average per day dollar limit applicable under this subparagraph for the preceding year, increased by the percentage increase in the consumer price index for all urban consumers (U.S. city average) over the previous year.

"(2) ADVOCACY SERVICES.—Advocacy services in accordance with subsection (d).

"(3) ADVICE AND ASSISTANCE COUNSELING.—Advice and assistance counseling in accordance with subsection (e).

"(4) ADMINISTRATIVE EXPENSES.—Advocacy services and advise and assistance counseling services under paragraphs (2) and (3) of this subsection shall be included as administrative expenses under section 3203(b)(3).

"(c) PAYMENT OF BENEFITS.—

"(1) LIFE INDEPENDENCE ACCOUNT.—

"(A) IN GENERAL.—The Secretary shall establish procedures for administering the provision of benefits to eligible beneficiaries under the CLASS Independence Benefit Plan, including the payment of the cash benefit for the beneficiary into a Life Independence Account established by the Secretary on behalf of each eligible beneficiary.

"(B) USE OF CASH BENEFITS.—Cash benefits paid into a Life Independence Account of an eligible beneficiary shall be used to purchase nonmedical services and supports that the beneficiary needs to maintain his or her independence at home or in another residential setting of their choice in the community, including (but not limited to) home modifications, assistive technology, accessible transportation, homemaker services, respite care, personal assistance services, home care aides, and nursing support. Nothing in the preceding sentence shall prevent an eligible beneficiary from using cash benefits paid into a Life Independence Account for obtaining assistance with decision making concerning medical care, including the right to accept or refuse medical or surgical treatment and the right to formulate advance directives or other written instructions recognized under State law, such as a living will or durable power of attorney for health care, in the case that an injury or illness causes the individual to be unable to make health care decisions.

"(C) ELECTRONIC MANAGEMENT OF FUNDS.—The Secretary shall establish procedures for—

"(i) crediting an account established on behalf of a beneficiary with the beneficiary's cash daily benefit;

"(ii) allowing the beneficiary to access such account through debit cards; and

"(iii) accounting for withdrawals by the beneficiary from such account.

"(D) PRIMARY PAYOR RULES FOR BENEFICIARIES WHO ARE ENROLLED IN MEDICAID.—In the case of an eligible beneficiary who is enrolled in Medicaid, the following payment rules shall apply:

"(i) INSTITUTIONALIZED BENEFICIARY.—If the beneficiary is a patient in a hospital, nursing facility, intermediate care facility for the mentally retarded, or an institution for mental diseases, the beneficiary shall retain an amount equal to 5 percent of the beneficiary's daily or weekly cash benefit (as applicable) (which shall be in addition to the amount of the beneficiary's personal needs allowance provided under Medicaid), and the remainder of such benefit shall be applied toward the facility's cost of providing the beneficiary's care, and Medicaid shall provide secondary coverage for such care.

"(ii) BENEFICIARIES RECEIVING HOME AND COMMUNITY-BASED SERVICES.—

"(I) 50 PERCENT OF BENEFIT RETAINED BY BENEFICIARY.—Subject to subclause (II), if a beneficiary is receiving medical assistance under Medicaid for home and community based services, the beneficiary shall retain an amount equal to 50 percent of the beneficiary's daily or weekly cash benefit (as applicable), and the remainder of the daily or weekly cash benefit shall be applied toward the cost to the State of providing such assistance (and shall not be used to claim Federal matching funds under Medicaid), and Medicaid shall provide secondary coverage for the remainder of any costs incurred in providing such assistance.

"(II) REQUIREMENT FOR STATE OFFSET.—A State shall be paid the remainder of a beneficiary's daily or weekly cash benefit under subclause (I) only if the State home and community-based waiver under section 1115 of the Social Security Act (42 U.S.C. 1315) or subsection (c) or (d) of section 1915 of such Act (42 U.S.C. 1396n), or the State plan amendment under subsection (i) of such section does not include a waiver of the requirements of section 1902(a)(1) of the Social Security Act (relating to statewideness) or of section 1902(a)(10)(B) of such Act (relating to comparability) and the State offers at a minimum case management services, personal care services, habilitation services, and respite care under such a waiver or State plan amendment.

"(III) DEFINITION OF HOME AND COMMUNITY-BASED SERVICES.—In this clause, the term 'home and community-based services' means any services which may be offered under a home and community-based waiver authorized for a State under section 1115 of the Social Security Act (42 U.S.C. 1315) or subsection (c) or (d) of section 1915 of such Act (42 U.S.C. 1396n) or under a State plan amendment under subsection (i) of such section.

"(iii) BENEFICIARIES ENROLLED IN PROGRAMS OF ALL-INCLUSIVE CARE FOR THE ELDERLY (PACE).—

"(I) IN GENERAL.—Subject to subclause (II), if a beneficiary is receiving medical assistance under Medicaid for PACE program services under section 1934 of the Social Security Act (42 U.S.C. 1396u–4), the beneficiary shall retain an amount equal to 50 percent of the beneficiary's daily or weekly cash benefit (as applicable), and the remainder of the daily or weekly cash benefit shall be applied toward the cost to the State of providing such assistance (and shall not be used to claim Federal matching funds under Medicaid), and Medicaid shall provide secondary coverage for the remainder of any costs incurred in providing such assistance.

"(II) INSTITUTIONALIZED RECIPIENTS OF PACE PROGRAM SERVICES.—If a beneficiary receiving assistance under Medicaid for PACE program services is a patient in a hospital, nursing facility, intermediate care facility for the mentally retarded, or an institution for mental diseases, the beneficiary shall be treated as in institutionalized beneficiary under clause (i).

"(2) AUTHORIZED REPRESENTATIVES.—

"(A) IN GENERAL.—The Secretary shall establish procedures to allow access to a beneficiary's cash benefits by an authorized representative of the eligible beneficiary on whose behalf such benefits are paid.

"(B) QUALITY ASSURANCE AND PROTECTION AGAINST FRAUD AND ABUSE.—The procedures established under subparagraph (A) shall ensure that authorized representatives of eligible beneficiaries comply with standards of conduct established by the Secretary, including standards requiring that such representatives provide quality services on behalf of such beneficiaries, do not have conflicts of interest, and do not misuse benefits paid on behalf of such beneficiaries or otherwise engage in fraud or abuse.

"(3) COMMENCEMENT OF BENEFITS.—Benefits shall be paid to, or on behalf of, an eligible beneficiary beginning with the first month in which an application for such benefits is approved.

"(4) ROLLOVER OPTION FOR LUMP-SUM PAYMENT.—An eligible beneficiary may elect to—

"(A) defer payment of their daily or weekly benefit and to rollover any such deferred benefits from month-to-month, but not from year-to-year; and

"(B) receive a lump-sum payment of such deferred benefits in an amount that may not exceed the lesser of—

"(i) the total amount of the accrued deferred benefits; or

"(ii) the applicable annual benefit.

"(5) PERIOD FOR DETERMINATION OF ANNUAL BENEFITS.—

"(A) IN GENERAL.—The applicable period for determining with respect to an eligible beneficiary the applicable annual benefit and the amount of any accrued deferred benefits is the 12-month period that commences with the first month in which the beneficiary began to receive such benefits, and each 12-month period thereafter.

"(B) INCLUSION OF INCREASED BENEFITS.—The Secretary shall establish procedures under which cash benefits paid to an eligible beneficiary that increase or decrease as a result of a change in the functional status of the beneficiary before the end of a 12-month benefit period shall be included in the determination of the applicable annual benefit paid to the eligible beneficiary.

"(C) RECOUPMENT OF UNPAID, ACCRUED BENEFITS.—

"(i) IN GENERAL.—The Secretary, in coordination with the Secretary of the Treasury, shall recoup any accrued benefits in the event of—

"(I) the death of a beneficiary; or

"(II) the failure of a beneficiary to elect under paragraph (4)(B) to receive such benefits as a lump-sum payment before the end of the 12-month period in which such benefits accrued.

"(ii) PAYMENT INTO CLASS INDEPENDENCE FUND.—Any benefits recouped in accordance with clause (i) shall be paid into the CLASS Independence Fund and used in accordance with section 3206.

"(6) REQUIREMENT TO RECERTIFY ELIGIBILITY FOR RECEIPT OF BENEFITS.—An eligible beneficiary shall periodically, as determined by the Secretary—

"(A) recertify by submission of medical evidence the beneficiary's continued eligibility for receipt of benefits; and

"(B) submit records of expenditures attributable to the aggregate cash benefit received by the beneficiary during the preceding year.

"(7) SUPPLEMENT, NOT SUPPLANT OTHER HEALTH CARE BENEFITS.—Subject to the Medicaid payment rules under paragraph (1)(D), benefits received by an eligible beneficiary shall supplement, but not supplant, other health care benefits for which the beneficiary is eligible under Medicaid or any other Federally funded program that provides health care benefits or assistance.

"(d) ADVOCACY SERVICES.—An agreement entered into under subsection (a)(2)(A)(ii) shall require the Protection and Advocacy System for the State to—

"(1) assign, as needed, an advocacy counselor to each eligible beneficiary that is covered by such agreement and who shall provide an eligible beneficiary with—

"(A) information regarding how to access the appeals process established for the program;

"(B) assistance with respect to the annual recertification and notification required under subsection (c)(6); and

"(C) such other assistance with obtaining services as the Secretary, by regulation, shall require; and

"(2) ensure that the System and such counselors comply with the requirements of subsection (h).

"(e) ADVICE AND ASSISTANCE COUNSELING.—An agreement entered into under subsection (a)(2)(A)(iii) shall require the entity to assign, as requested by an eligible beneficiary that is covered by such agreement, an advice and assistance counselor who shall provide an eligible beneficiary with information regarding—

"(1) accessing and coordinating long-term services and supports in the most integrated setting;

"(2) possible eligibility for other benefits and services;

"(3) development of a service and support plan;

"(4) information about programs established under the Assistive Technology Act of 1998 and the services offered under such programs;

"(5) available assistance with decision making concerning medical care, including the right to accept or refuse medical or surgical treatment and the right to formulate advance directives or other written instructions recognized under State law, such as a living will or durable power of attorney for health care, in the case that an injury or illness causes the individual to be unable to make health care decisions; and

"(6) such other services as the Secretary, by regulation, may require.

"(f) NO EFFECT ON ELIGIBILITY FOR OTHER BENEFITS.—Benefits paid to an eligible beneficiary under the CLASS program shall be disregarded for purposes of determining or continuing the beneficiary's eligibility for receipt of benefits under any other Federal, State, or locally funded assistance program, including benefits paid under titles II, XVI, XVIII, XIX, or XXI of the Social Security Act (42 U.S.C. 401 et seq., 1381 et seq., 1395 et seq., 1396 et seq., 1397aa et seq.), under the laws administered by the Secretary of Veterans Affairs, under low-income housing assistance programs, or under the supplemental nutrition assistance program established under the Food and Nutrition Act of 2008 (7 U.S.C. 2011 et seq.).

"(g) RULE OF CONSTRUCTION.—Nothing in this title shall be construed as prohibiting benefits paid under the CLASS Independence Benefit Plan from being used to compensate a family caregiver for providing community living assistance services and supports to an eligible beneficiary.

"(h) PROTECTION AGAINST CONFLICT OF INTERESTS.—The Secretary shall establish procedures to ensure that the Eligibility Assessment System, the Protection and Advocacy System for a State, advocacy counselors for eligible beneficiaries, and any other entities that provide services to active enrollees and eligible beneficiaries under the CLASS program comply with the following:

"(1) If the entity provides counseling or planning services, such services are provided in a manner that fosters the best interests of the active enrollee or beneficiary.

"(2) The entity has established operating procedures that are designed to avoid or minimize conflicts of interest between the entity and an active enrollee or beneficiary.

"(3) The entity provides information about all services and options available to the active enrollee or beneficiary, to the best of its knowledge, including services available through other entities or providers.

"(4) The entity assists the active enrollee or beneficiary to access desired services, regardless of the provider.

"(5) The entity reports the number of active enrollees and beneficiaries provided with assistance by age, disability, and whether such enrollees and beneficiaries received services from the entity or another entity.

"(6) If the entity provides counseling or planning services, the entity ensures that an active enrollee or beneficiary is informed of any financial interest that the entity has in a service provider.

"(7) The entity provides an active enrollee or beneficiary with a list of available service providers that can meet the needs of the active enrollee or beneficiary.

"SEC. 3206. CLASS INDEPENDENCE FUND.

"(a) ESTABLISHMENT OF CLASS INDEPENDENCE FUND.—There is established in the Treasury of the United States a trust fund to be known as the 'CLASS Independence Fund'. The Secretary of the Treasury shall serve as Managing Trustee of such Fund. The Fund shall consist of all amounts derived from payments into the Fund under sections 3204(f) and 3205(c)(5)(C)(ii), and remaining after investment of such amounts under subsection (b), including additional amounts derived as income from such investments. The amounts held in the Fund are appropriated and shall remain available without fiscal year limitation—

"(1) to be held for investment on behalf of individuals enrolled in the CLASS program;

"(2) to pay the administrative expenses related to the Fund and to investment under subsection (b); and

"(3) to pay cash benefits to eligible beneficiaries under the CLASS Independence Benefit Plan.

"(b) INVESTMENT OF FUND BALANCE.—The Secretary of the Treasury shall invest and manage the CLASS Independence Fund in the same manner, and to the same extent, as the Federal Supplementary Medical Insurance Trust Fund may be invested and managed under subsections (c), (d), and (e) of section 1841(d) of the Social Security Act (42 U.S.C. 1395t).

"(c) BOARD OF TRUSTEES.—

"(1) IN GENERAL.—With respect to the CLASS Independence Fund, there is hereby created a body to be known as the Board of Trustees of the CLASS Independence Fund (hereinafter in this section referred to as the 'Board of Trustees') composed of the Secretary of the Treasury, the Secretary of Labor, and the Secretary of Health and Human Services, all ex officio, and of two members of the public (both of whom may not be from the same political party), who shall be nominated by the President for a term of 4 years and subject to confirmation by the Senate. A member of the Board of Trustees serving as a member of the public and nominated and confirmed to fill a vacancy occurring during a term shall be nominated and confirmed only for the remainder of such term. An individual nominated and confirmed as a member of the public may serve in such position after the expiration of such member's term until the earlier of the time at which the member's successor takes office or the time at which a report of the Board is first issued under paragraph (2) after the expiration of the member's term. The Secretary of the Treasury shall be the Managing Trustee of the Board of Trustees. The Board of Trustees shall meet not less frequently than once each calendar year. A person serving on the Board of Trustees shall not be considered to be a fiduciary and shall not be personally liable for actions taken in such capacity with respect to the Trust Fund.

"(2) DUTIES.—

"(A) IN GENERAL.—It shall be the duty of the Board of Trustees to do the following:

"(i) Hold the CLASS Independence Fund.

"(ii) Report to the Congress not later than the first day of April of each year on the operation and status of the CLASS Independence Fund during the preceding fiscal year and on its expected operation and status during the current fiscal year and the next 2 fiscal years.

"(iii) Report immediately to the Congress whenever the Board is of the opinion that the amount of the CLASS Independence Fund is not actuarially sound in regards to the projection under section 3203(b)(1)(B)(i).

"(iv) Review the general policies followed in managing the CLASS Independence Fund, and recommend changes in such policies, including necessary changes in the provisions of law which govern the way in which the CLASS Independence Fund is to be managed.

"(B) REPORT.—The report provided for in subparagraph (A)(ii) shall—

"(i) include—

"(I) a statement of the assets of, and the disbursements made from, the CLASS Independence Fund during the preceding fiscal year;

"(II) an estimate of the expected income to, and disbursements to be made from, the CLASS Independence Fund during the current fiscal year and each of the next 2 fiscal years;

"(III) a statement of the actuarial status of the CLASS Independence Fund for the current fiscal year, each of the next 2 fiscal years, and as projected over the 75-year period beginning with the current fiscal year; and

"(IV) an actuarial opinion by the Chief Actuary of the Centers for Medicare & Medicaid Services certifying that the techniques and methodologies used are generally accepted within the actuarial profession and that the assumptions and cost estimates used are reasonable; and

"(ii) be printed as a House document of the session of the Congress to which the report is made.

"(C) RECOMMENDATIONS.—If the Board of Trustees determines that enrollment trends and expected future benefit claims on the CLASS Independence Fund are not actuarially sound in regards to the projection under section 3203(b)(1)(B)(i) and are unlikely to be resolved with reasonable premium increases or through other means, the Board of Trustees shall include in the report provided for in subparagraph (A)(ii) recommendations for such legislative action as the Board of Trustees determine to be appropriate, including whether to adjust monthly premiums or impose a temporary moratorium on new enrollments.

"SEC. 3207. CLASS INDEPENDENCE ADVISORY COUNCIL.

"(a) ESTABLISHMENT.—There is hereby created an Advisory Committee to be known as the 'CLASS Independence Advisory Council'.

"(b) MEMBERSHIP.—

"(1) IN GENERAL.—The CLASS Independence Advisory Council shall be composed of not more than 15 individuals, not otherwise in the employ of the United States—

"(A) who shall be appointed by the President without regard to the civil service laws and regulations; and

"(B) a majority of whom shall be representatives of individuals who participate or are likely to participate in the CLASS program, and shall include representatives of older and younger workers, individuals with disabilities, family caregivers of individuals who require services and supports to maintain their independence at home or in another residential setting of their choice in the community, individuals with expertise in long-term care or disability insurance, actuarial science, economics, and other relevant disciplines, as determined by the Secretary.

"(2) TERMS.—

"(A) IN GENERAL.—The members of the CLASS Independence Advisory Council shall serve overlapping terms of 3 years (unless appointed to fill a vacancy occurring prior to the expiration of a term, in which case the individual shall serve for the remainder of the term).

"(B) LIMITATION.—A member shall not be eligible to serve for more than 2 consecutive terms.

"(3) CHAIR.—The President shall, from time to time, appoint one of the members of the CLASS Independence Advisory Council to serve as the Chair.

"(c) DUTIES.—The CLASS Independence Advisory Council shall advise the Secretary on matters of general policy in the administration of the CLASS program established under this title and in the formulation of regulations under this title including with respect to—

"(1) the development of the CLASS Independence Benefit Plan under section 3203;

"(2) the determination of monthly premiums under such plan; and

"(3) the financial solvency of the program.

"(d) APPLICATION OF FACA.—The Federal Advisory Committee Act (5 U.S.C. App.), other than section 14 of that Act, shall apply to the CLASS Independence Advisory Council.

"(e) AUTHORIZATION OF APPROPRIATIONS.—

"(1) IN GENERAL.—There are authorized to be appropriated to the CLASS Independence Advisory Council to carry out its duties under this section, such sums as may be necessary for fiscal year 2011 and for each fiscal year thereafter.

"(2) AVAILABILITY.—Any sums appropriated under the authorization contained in this section shall remain available, without fiscal year limitation, until expended.

"SEC. 3208. SOLVENCY AND FISCAL INDEPENDENCE; REGULATIONS; ANNUAL REPORT.

"(a) SOLVENCY.—The Secretary shall regularly consult with the Board of Trustees of the CLASS Independence Fund and the CLASS Independence Advisory Council, for purposes of ensuring that enrollees premiums are adequate to ensure the financial solvency of the CLASS program, both with respect to fiscal years occurring in the near-term and fiscal years occurring over 20- and 75-year periods, taking into account the projections required for such periods under subsections (a)(1)(A)(i) and (b)(1)(B)(i) of section 3202.

"(b) NO TAXPAYER FUNDS USED TO PAY BENEFITS.—No taxpayer funds shall be used for payment of benefits under a CLASS Independent Benefit Plan. For purposes of this subsection, the term 'taxpayer funds' means any Federal funds from a source other than premiums deposited by CLASS program participants in the CLASS Independence Fund and any associated interest earnings.

"(c) REGULATIONS.—The Secretary shall promulgate such regulations as are necessary to carry out the CLASS program in accordance with this title. Such regulations shall include provisions to prevent fraud and abuse under the program.

"(d) ANNUAL REPORT.—Beginning January 1, 2014, the Secretary shall submit an annual report to Congress on the CLASS program. Each report shall include the following:

"(1) The total number of enrollees in the program.

"(2) The total number of eligible beneficiaries during the fiscal year.

"(3) The total amount of cash benefits provided during the fiscal year.

"(4) A description of instances of fraud or abuse identified during the fiscal year.

"(5) Recommendations for such administrative or legislative action as the Secretary determines is necessary to improve the program, ensure the solvency of the program, or to prevent the occurrence of fraud or abuse.

"SEC. 3209. INSPECTOR GENERAL'S REPORT.

"The Inspector General of the Department of Health and Human Services shall submit an annual report to the Secretary and Congress relating to the overall progress of the CLASS program and of the existence of waste, fraud, and abuse in the CLASS program. Each such report shall include findings in the following areas:

"(1) The eligibility determination process.

"(2) The provision of cash benefits.

"(3) Quality assurance and protection against waste, fraud, and abuse.

"(4) Recouping of unpaid and accrued benefits.

"SEC. 3210. TAX TREATMENT OF PROGRAM.

"The CLASS program shall be treated for purposes of the Internal Revenue Code of 1986 in the same manner as a qualified long-term care insurance contract for qualified long-term care services.".

(2) CONFORMING AMENDMENTS TO MEDICAID.—Section 1902(a) of the Social Security Act (42 U.S.C. 1396a(a)), as amended by section 6505, is amended by inserting after paragraph (80) the following:

"(81) provide that the State will comply with such regulations regarding the application of primary and secondary payor rules with respect to individuals who are eligible for medical assistance under this title and are eligible beneficiaries under the CLASS program established under title XXXII of the Public Health Service Act as the Secretary shall establish; and".

(b) ASSURANCE OF ADEQUATE INFRASTRUCTURE FOR THE PROVISION OF PERSONAL CARE ATTENDANT WORKERS.—Section 1902(a) of the Social Security Act (42 U.S.C. 1396a(a)), as amended by subsection (a)(2), is amended by inserting after paragraph (81) the following:

"(82) provide that, not later than 2 years after the date of enactment of the Community Living Assistance Services and Supports Act, each State shall—

"(A) assess the extent to which entities such as providers of home care, home health services, home and community service providers, public authorities created to provide personal care services to individuals eligible for medical assistance under the State plan, and nonprofit organizations, are serving or have the capacity to serve as fiscal agents for, employers of, and providers of employment-related benefits for, personal care attendant workers who provide personal care services to individuals receiving benefits under the CLASS program established under title XXXII of the Public Health Service Act, including in rural and underserved areas;

"(B) designate or create such entities to serve as fiscal agents for, employers of, and providers of employment-related benefits for, such workers to ensure an adequate supply of the workers for individuals receiving benefits under the CLASS program, including in rural and underserved areas; and

"(C) ensure that the designation or creation of such entities will not negatively alter or impede existing programs, models, methods, or administration of service delivery that provide for consumer controlled or self-directed home and community services and further ensure that such entities will not impede the ability of individuals to direct and control their home and community services, including the ability to select, manage, dismiss, co-employ, or employ such workers or inhibit such individuals from relying on family members for the provision of personal care services.".

(c) PERSONAL CARE ATTENDANTS WORKFORCE ADVISORY PANEL.—

(1) ESTABLISHMENT.—Not later than 90 days after the date of enactment of this Act, the Secretary of Health and Human Services shall establish a Personal Care Attendants Workforce

Advisory Panel for the purpose of examining and advising the Secretary and Congress on workforce issues related to personal care attendant workers, including with respect to the adequacy of the number of such workers, the salaries, wages, and benefits of such workers, and access to the services provided by such workers.

(2) MEMBERSHIP.—In appointing members to the Personal Care Attendants Workforce Advisory Panel, the Secretary shall ensure that such members include the following:

(A) Individuals with disabilities of all ages.

(B) Senior individuals.

(C) Representatives of individuals with disabilities.

(D) Representatives of senior individuals.

(E) Representatives of workforce and labor organizations.

(F) Representatives of home and community-based service providers.

(G) Representatives of assisted living providers.

(d) INCLUSION OF INFORMATION ON SUPPLEMENTAL COVERAGE IN THE NATIONAL CLEARINGHOUSE FOR LONG-TERM CARE INFORMATION; EXTENSION OF FUNDING.—Section 6021(d) of the Deficit Reduction Act of 2005 (42 U.S.C. 1396p note) is amended—

(1) in paragraph (2)(A)—

(A) in clause (ii), by striking "and" at the end;

(B) in clause (iii), by striking the period at the end and inserting "; and"; and

(C) by adding at the end the following:

"(iv) include information regarding the CLASS program established under title XXXII of the Public Health Service Act and coverage available for purchase through a Exchange established under section 1311 of the Patient Protection and Affordable Care Act that is supplemental coverage to the benefits provided under a CLASS Independence Benefit Plan under that program, and information regarding how benefits provided under a CLASS Independence Benefit Plan differ from disability insurance benefits."; and

(2) in paragraph (3), by striking "2010" and inserting "2015".

(e) EFFECTIVE DATE.—The amendments made by subsections (a), (b), and (d) take effect on January 1, 2011.

(f) RULE OF CONSTRUCTION.—Nothing in this title or the amendments made by this title are intended to replace or displace public or private disability insurance benefits, including such benefits that are for income replacement.

TITLE IX—REVENUE PROVISIONS

Subtitle A—Revenue Offset Provisions

SEC. 9001. EXCISE TAX ON HIGH COST EMPLOYER-SPONSORED HEALTH COVERAGE.

(a) IN GENERAL.—Chapter 43 of the Internal Revenue Code of 1986, as amended by section 1513, is amended by adding at the end the following:

"SEC. 4980I. EXCISE TAX ON HIGH COST EMPLOYER-SPONSORED HEALTH COVERAGE.

"(a) IMPOSITION OF TAX.—If—

"(1) an employee is covered under any applicable employer-sponsored coverage of an employer at any time during a taxable period, and

"(2) there is any excess benefit with respect to the coverage,

there is hereby imposed a tax equal to 40 percent of the excess benefit.

"(b) EXCESS BENEFIT.—For purposes of this section—

"(1) IN GENERAL.—The term 'excess benefit' means, with respect to any applicable employer-sponsored coverage made available by an employer to an employee during any taxable period, the sum of the excess amounts determined under paragraph (2) for months during the taxable period.

"(2) MONTHLY EXCESS AMOUNT.—The excess amount determined under this paragraph for any month is the excess (if any) of—

"(A) the aggregate cost of the applicable employer-sponsored coverage of the employee for the month, over

"(B) an amount equal to 1⁄12 of the annual limitation under paragraph (3) for the calendar year in which the month occurs.

"(3) ANNUAL LIMITATION.—For purposes of this subsection—

"(A) IN GENERAL.—The annual limitation under this paragraph for any calendar year is the dollar limit determined under subparagraph (C) for the calendar year.

"(B) APPLICABLE ANNUAL LIMITATION.—The annual limitation which applies for any month shall be determined on the basis of the type of coverage (as determined under subsection (f)(1)) provided to the employee by the employer as of the beginning of the month.

"(C) APPLICABLE DOLLAR LIMIT.—Except as provided in subparagraph (D)—

"(i) 2013.—In the case of 2013, the dollar limit under this subparagraph is—

"(I) in the case of an employee with self-only coverage, $8,500, and

"(II) in the case of an employee with coverage other than self-only coverage, $23,000.

"(ii) EXCEPTION FOR CERTAIN INDIVIDUALS.—In the case of an individual who is a qualified retiree or who participates in a plan sponsored by an employer the majority of whose employees are engaged in a high-risk profession or employed to repair or install electrical or telecommunications lines—

"(I) the dollar amount in clause (i)(I) (determined after the application of subparagraph (D)) shall be increased by $1,350, and

"(II) the dollar amount in clause (i)(II) (determined after the application of subparagraph (D)) shall be increased by $3,000.

"(iii) SUBSEQUENT YEARS.—In the case of any calendar year after 2013, each of the dollar amounts under clauses (i) and (ii) shall be increased to the amount equal to such amount as in effect for the calendar year preceding such year, increased by an amount equal to the product of—

"(I) such amount as so in effect, multiplied by

"(II) the cost-of-living adjustment determined under section 1(f)(3) for such year (determined by substituting the calendar year that is 2 years before such year for '1992' in subparagraph (B) thereof), increased by 1 percentage point.

If any amount determined under this clause is not a multiple of $50, such amount shall be rounded to the nearest multiple of $50.

"(D) TRANSITION RULE FOR STATES WITH HIGHEST COVERAGE COSTS.—

"(i) IN GENERAL.—If an employee is a resident of a high cost State on the first day of any month beginning in 2013, 2014, or 2015, the annual limitation under this paragraph for such month with respect to such employee shall be an amount equal to the applicable percentage of the annual limitation (determined without regard to this subparagraph or subparagraph (C)(ii)).

"(ii) APPLICABLE PERCENTAGE.—The applicable percentage is 120 percent for 2013, 110 percent for 2014, and 105 percent for 2015.

"(iii) HIGH COST STATE.—The term 'high cost State' means each of the 17 States which the Secretary of Health and Human Services, in consultation with the Secretary, estimates had the highest average cost during 2012 for employer-sponsored coverage under health plans. The Secretary's estimate shall be made on the basis of aggregate premiums paid in the State for such health plans, determined using the most recent data available as of August 31, 2012.

"(c) LIABILITY TO PAY TAX.—

"(1) IN GENERAL.—Each coverage provider shall pay the tax imposed by subsection (a) on its applicable share of the excess benefit with respect to an employee for any taxable period.

"(2) COVERAGE PROVIDER.—For purposes of this subsection, the term 'coverage provider' means each of the following:

"(A) HEALTH INSURANCE COVERAGE.—If the applicable employer-sponsored coverage consists of coverage under a group health plan which provides health insurance coverage, the health insurance issuer.

"(B) HSA AND MSA CONTRIBUTIONS.—If the applicable employer-sponsored coverage consists of coverage under an arrangement under which the employer makes contributions described in subsection (b) or (d) of section 106, the employer.

"(C) OTHER COVERAGE.—In the case of any other applicable employer-sponsored coverage, the person that administers the plan benefits.

"(3) APPLICABLE SHARE.—For purposes of this subsection, a coverage provider's applicable share of an excess benefit for any taxable period is the amount which bears the same ratio to the amount of such excess benefit as—

"(A) the cost of the applicable employer-sponsored coverage provided by the provider to the employee during such period, bears to

"(B) the aggregate cost of all applicable employer-sponsored coverage provided to the employee by all coverage providers during such period.

"(4) RESPONSIBILITY TO CALCULATE TAX AND APPLICABLE SHARES.—

"(A) IN GENERAL.—Each employer shall—

"(i) calculate for each taxable period the amount of the excess benefit subject to the tax imposed by subsection (a) and the applicable share of such excess benefit for each coverage provider, and

"(ii) notify, at such time and in such manner as the Secretary may prescribe, the Secretary and each coverage provider of the amount so determined for the provider.

"(B) SPECIAL RULE FOR MULTIEMPLOYER PLANS.—In the case of applicable employer-sponsored coverage made available to employees through a multiemployer plan (as defined in section 414(f)), the plan sponsor shall make the calculations, and provide the notice, required under subparagraph (A).

"(d) APPLICABLE EMPLOYER-SPONSORED COVERAGE; COST.—For purposes of this section—

"(1) APPLICABLE EMPLOYER-SPONSORED COVERAGE.—

"(A) IN GENERAL.—The term 'applicable employer-sponsored coverage' means, with respect to any employee, coverage under any group health plan made available to the employee by an employer which is excludable from the employee's gross income under section 106, or would be so excludable if it were employer-provided coverage (within the meaning of such section 106).

"(B) EXCEPTIONS.—The term 'applicable employer-sponsored coverage' shall not include—

"(i) any coverage (whether through insurance or otherwise) described in section 9832(c)(1)(A) or for long-term care, or

"(ii) any coverage described in section 9832(c)(3) the payment for which is not excludable from gross income and for which a deduction under section 162(l) is not allowable.

"(C) COVERAGE INCLUDES EMPLOYEE PAID PORTION.—Coverage shall be treated as applicable employer-sponsored coverage without regard to whether the employer or employee pays for the coverage.

"(D) SELF-EMPLOYED INDIVIDUAL.—In the case of an individual who is an employee within the meaning of section 401(c)(1), coverage under any group health plan providing health insurance coverage shall be treated as applicable employer-sponsored coverage if a deduction is allowable under section 162(l) with respect to all or any portion of the cost of the coverage.

"(E) GOVERNMENTAL PLANS INCLUDED.—Applicable employer-sponsored coverage shall include coverage under any group health plan established and maintained primarily for its civilian employees by the Government of the United States, by the government of any State or political subdivision thereof, or by any agency or instrumentality of any such government.

"(2) DETERMINATION OF COST.—

"(A) IN GENERAL.—The cost of applicable employer-sponsored coverage shall be determined under rules similar to the rules of section 4980B(f)(4), except that in determining such cost, any portion of the cost of such coverage which is attributable to the tax imposed under this section shall not be taken into account and the amount of such cost shall be calculated separately for self-only coverage and other coverage. In the case of applicable employer-sponsored coverage which provides coverage to retired employees, the plan may elect to treat a retired employee who has not attained the age of 65 and a retired employee who has attained the age of 65 as similarly situated beneficiaries.

"(B) HEALTH FSAS.—In the case of applicable employer-sponsored coverage consisting of coverage under a flexible spending arrangement (as defined in section 106(c)(2)), the cost of the coverage shall be equal to the sum of—

"(i) the amount of employer contributions under any salary reduction election under the arrangement, plus

"(ii) the amount determined under subparagraph (A) with respect to any reimbursement under the arrangement in excess of the contributions described in clause (i).

"(C) ARCHER MSAS AND HSAS.—In the case of applicable employer-sponsored coverage consisting of coverage under an arrangement under which the employer makes contributions described in subsection (b) or (d) of section 106, the cost of the coverage shall be equal to the amount of employer contributions under the arrangement.

"(D) ALLOCATION ON A MONTHLY BASIS.—If cost is determined on other than a monthly basis, the cost shall be allocated to months in a taxable period on such basis as the Secretary may prescribe.

"(e) PENALTY FOR FAILURE TO PROPERLY CALCULATE EXCESS BENEFIT.—

"(1) IN GENERAL.—If, for any taxable period, the tax imposed by subsection (a) exceeds the tax determined under such subsection with respect to the total excess benefit calculated by the employer or plan sponsor under subsection (c)(4)—

"(A) each coverage provider shall pay the tax on its applicable share (determined in the same manner as under subsection (c)(4)) of the excess, but no penalty shall be imposed on the provider with respect to such amount, and

"(B) the employer or plan sponsor shall, in addition to any tax imposed by subsection (a), pay a penalty in an amount equal to such excess, plus interest at the underpayment rate determined under section 6621 for the period beginning on the due date for the payment of tax imposed by subsection (a) to which the excess relates and ending on the date of payment of the penalty.

"(2) LIMITATIONS ON PENALTY.—

"(A) PENALTY NOT TO APPLY WHERE FAILURE NOT DISCOVERED EXERCISING REASONABLE DILIGENCE.—No penalty shall be imposed by paragraph (1)(B) on any failure to properly calculate the excess benefit during any period for which it is established to the satisfaction of the Secretary that the employer or plan sponsor neither knew, nor exercising reasonable diligence would have known, that such failure existed.

"(B) PENALTY NOT TO APPLY TO FAILURES CORRECTED WITHIN 30 DAYS.—No penalty shall be imposed by paragraph (1)(B) on any such failure if—

"(i) such failure was due to reasonable cause and not to willful neglect, and

"(ii) such failure is corrected during the 30-day period beginning on the 1st date that the employer knew, or exercising reasonable diligence would have known, that such failure existed.

"(C) WAIVER BY SECRETARY.—In the case of any such failure which is due to reasonable cause and not to willful neglect, the Secretary may waive part or all of the penalty imposed by paragraph (1), to the extent that the payment of such penalty would be excessive or otherwise inequitable relative to the failure involved.

"(f) OTHER DEFINITIONS AND SPECIAL RULES.—For purposes of this section—

"(1) COVERAGE DETERMINATIONS.—

"(A) IN GENERAL.—Except as provided in subparagraph (B), an employee shall be treated as having self-only coverage with respect to any applicable employer-sponsored coverage of an employer.

"(B) MINIMUM ESSENTIAL COVERAGE.—An employee shall be treated as having coverage other than self-only coverage only if the employee is enrolled in coverage other than self-only coverage in a group health plan which provides minimum essential coverage (as defined in section 5000A(f)) to the employee and at least one other beneficiary, and the benefits provided under such minimum essential coverage do not vary based on whether any individual covered under such coverage is the employee or another beneficiary.

"(2) QUALIFIED RETIREE.—The term 'qualified retiree' means any individual who—

"(A) is receiving coverage by reason of being a retiree,

"(B) has attained age 55, and

"(C) is not entitled to benefits or eligible for enrollment under the Medicare program under title XVIII of the Social Security Act.

"(3) EMPLOYEES ENGAGED IN HIGH-RISK PROFESSION.—The term 'employees engaged in a high-risk profession' means law enforcement officers (as such term is defined in section 1204 of the Omnibus Crime Control and Safe Streets Act of 1968), employees in fire protection activities (as such term is defined in section 3(y) of the Fair Labor Standards Act of 1938), individuals who provide out-of-hospital emergency medical care (including emergency medical technicians, paramedics, and first-responders), and individuals engaged in the construction, mining, agriculture (not including food processing), forestry, and fishing industries. Such term includes an employee who is retired from a high-risk profession described in the preceding sentence, if such employee satisfied the requirements of such sentence for a period of not less than 20 years during the employee's employment.

"(4) GROUP HEALTH PLAN.—The term 'group health plan' has the meaning given such term by section 5000(b)(1).

"(5) HEALTH INSURANCE COVERAGE; HEALTH INSURANCE ISSUER.—

"(A) HEALTH INSURANCE COVERAGE.—The term 'health insurance coverage' has the meaning given such term by section 9832(b)(1) (applied without regard to subparagraph (B) thereof, except as provided by the Secretary in regulations).

"(B) HEALTH INSURANCE ISSUER.—The term 'health insurance issuer' has the meaning given such term by section 9832(b)(2).

"(6) PERSON THAT ADMINISTERS THE PLAN BENEFITS.—The term 'person that administers the plan benefits' shall include the plan sponsor if the plan sponsor administers benefits under the plan.

"(7) PLAN SPONSOR.—The term 'plan sponsor' has the meaning given such term in section 3(16)(B) of the Employee Retirement Income Security Act of 1974.

"(8) TAXABLE PERIOD.—The term 'taxable period' means the calendar year or such shorter period as the Secretary may prescribe. The Secretary may have different taxable periods for employers of varying sizes.

"(9) AGGREGATION RULES.—All employers treated as a single employer under subsection (b), (c), (m), or (o) of section 414 shall be treated as a single employer.

"(10) DENIAL OF DEDUCTION.—For denial of a deduction for the tax imposed by this section, see section 275(a)(6).

"(g) REGULATIONS.—The Secretary shall prescribe such regulations as may be necessary to carry out this section.".

(b) CLERICAL AMENDMENT.—The table of sections for chapter 43 of such Code, as amended by section 1513, is amended by adding at the end the following new item:

"Sec. 4980I. Excise tax on high cost employer-sponsored health coverage.".

(c) EFFECTIVE DATE.—The amendments made by this section shall apply to taxable years beginning after December 31, 2012.

SEC. 9002. INCLUSION OF COST OF EMPLOYER-SPONSORED HEALTH COVERAGE ON W–2.

(a) IN GENERAL.—Section 6051(a) of the Internal Revenue Code of 1986 (relating to receipts for employees) is amended by striking "and" at the end of paragraph (12), by striking the period at the end of paragraph (13) and inserting ", and", and by adding after paragraph (13) the following new paragraph:

"(14) the aggregate cost (determined under rules similar to the rules of section 4980B(f)(4)) of applicable employer-sponsored coverage (as defined in section 4980I(d)(1)), except that this paragraph shall not apply to—

"(A) coverage to which paragraphs (11) and (12) apply, or

"(B) the amount of any salary reduction contributions to a flexible spending arrangement (within the meaning of section 125).".

(b) EFFECTIVE DATE.—The amendments made by this section shall apply to taxable years beginning after December 31, 2010.

SEC. 9003. DISTRIBUTIONS FOR MEDICINE QUALIFIED ONLY IF FOR PRESCRIBED DRUG OR INSULIN.

(a) HSAS.—Subparagraph (A) of section 223(d)(2) of the Internal Revenue Code of 1986 is amended by adding at the end the following: "Such term shall include an amount paid for medicine or a drug only if such medicine or drug is a prescribed drug (determined without regard to whether such drug is available without a prescription) or is insulin.".

(b) ARCHER MSAS.—Subparagraph (A) of section 220(d)(2) of the Internal Revenue Code of 1986 is amended by adding at the end the following: "Such term shall include an amount paid for medicine or a drug only if such medicine or drug is a prescribed drug (determined without regard to whether such drug is available without a prescription) or is insulin.".

(c) HEALTH FLEXIBLE SPENDING ARRANGEMENTS AND HEALTH REIMBURSEMENT ARRANGEMENTS.—Section 106 of the Internal Revenue Code of 1986 is amended by adding at the end the following new subsection:

"(f) REIMBURSEMENTS FOR MEDICINE RESTRICTED TO PRESCRIBED DRUGS AND INSULIN.—For purposes of this section and section 105, reimbursement for expenses incurred for a medicine or a drug shall be treated as a reimbursement for medical expenses only if such medicine or drug is a prescribed drug (determined without regard to whether such drug is available without a prescription) or is insulin.".

(d) EFFECTIVE DATES.—

(1) DISTRIBUTIONS FROM SAVINGS ACCOUNTS.—The amendments made by subsections (a) and (b) shall apply to amounts paid with respect to taxable years beginning after December 31, 2010.

(2) REIMBURSEMENTS.—The amendment made by subsection (c) shall apply to expenses incurred with respect to taxable years beginning after December 31, 2010.

SEC. 9004. INCREASE IN ADDITIONAL TAX ON DISTRIBUTIONS FROM HSAS AND ARCHER MSAS NOT USED FOR QUALIFIED MEDICAL EXPENSES.

(a) HSAS.—Section 223(f)(4)(A) of the Internal Revenue Code of 1986 is amended by striking "10 percent" and inserting "20 percent".

(b) ARCHER MSAS.—Section 220(f)(4)(A) of the Internal Revenue Code of 1986 is amended by striking "15 percent" and inserting "20 percent".

(c) EFFECTIVE DATE.—The amendments made by this section shall apply to distributions made after December 31, 2010.

SEC. 9005. LIMITATION ON HEALTH FLEXIBLE SPENDING ARRANGEMENTS UNDER CAFETERIA PLANS.

(a) IN GENERAL.—Section 125 of the Internal Revenue Code of 1986 is amended—

(1) by redesignating subsections (i) and (j) as subsections (j) and (k), respectively, and

(2) by inserting after subsection (h) the following new subsection:

"(i) LIMITATION ON HEALTH FLEXIBLE SPENDING ARRANGEMENTS.—For purposes of this section, if a benefit is provided under a cafeteria plan through employer contributions to a health flexible spending arrangement, such benefit shall not be treated as a qualified benefit unless the cafeteria plan provides that an employee may not elect for any taxable year to have salary reduction contributions in excess of $2,500 made to such arrangement.".

(b) EFFECTIVE DATE.—The amendments made by this section shall apply to taxable years beginning after December 31, 2010.

SEC. 9006. EXPANSION OF INFORMATION REPORTING REQUIREMENTS.

(a) IN GENERAL.—Section 6041 of the Internal Revenue Code of 1986 is amended by adding at the end the following new subsections:

"(h) APPLICATION TO CORPORATIONS.—Notwithstanding any regulation prescribed by the Secretary before the date of the enactment of this subsection, for purposes of this section the term 'person' includes any corporation that is not an organization exempt from tax under section 501(a).

"(i) REGULATIONS.—The Secretary may prescribe such regulations and other guidance as may be appropriate or necessary to carry out the purposes of this section, including rules to prevent duplicative reporting of transactions.".

(b) PAYMENTS FOR PROPERTY AND OTHER GROSS PROCEEDS.—Subsection (a) of section 6041 of the Internal Revenue Code of 1986 is amended—

(1) by inserting "amounts in consideration for property," after "wages,",

(2) by inserting "gross proceeds," after "emoluments, or other", and

(3) by inserting "gross proceeds," after "setting forth the amount of such".

(c) EFFECTIVE DATE.—The amendments made by this section shall apply to payments made after December 31, 2011.

SEC. 9007. ADDITIONAL REQUIREMENTS FOR CHARITABLE HOSPITALS.

(a) REQUIREMENTS TO QUALIFY AS SECTION 501(C)(3) CHARITABLE HOSPITAL ORGANIZATION.—Section 501 of the Internal Revenue Code of 1986 (relating to exemption from tax on corporations, certain trusts, etc.) is amended by redesignating subsection (r) as subsection (s) and by inserting after subsection (q) the following new subsection:

"(r) ADDITIONAL REQUIREMENTS FOR CERTAIN HOSPITALS.—

"(1) IN GENERAL.—A hospital organization to which this subsection applies shall not be treated as described in subsection (c)(3) unless the organization—

"(A) meets the community health needs assessment requirements described in paragraph (3),

"(B) meets the financial assistance policy requirements described in paragraph (4),

"(C) meets the requirements on charges described in paragraph (5), and

"(D) meets the billing and collection requirement described in paragraph (6).

"(2) HOSPITAL ORGANIZATIONS TO WHICH SUBSECTION APPLIES.—

“(A) IN GENERAL.—This subsection shall apply to—

“(i) an organization which operates a facility which is required by a State to be licensed, registered, or similarly recognized as a hospital, and

“(ii) any other organization which the Secretary determines has the provision of hospital care as its principal function or purpose constituting the basis for its exemption under subsection (c)(3) (determined without regard to this subsection).

“(B) ORGANIZATIONS WITH MORE THAN 1 HOSPITAL FACILITY.—If a hospital organization operates more than 1 hospital facility—

“(i) the organization shall meet the requirements of this subsection separately with respect to each such facility, and

“(ii) the organization shall not be treated as described in subsection (c)(3) with respect to any such facility for which such requirements are not separately met.

“(3) COMMUNITY HEALTH NEEDS ASSESSMENTS.—

“(A) IN GENERAL.—An organization meets the requirements of this paragraph with respect to any taxable year only if the organization—

“(i) has conducted a community health needs assessment which meets the requirements of subparagraph (B) in such taxable year or in either of the 2 taxable years immediately preceding such taxable year, and

“(ii) has adopted an implementation strategy to meet the community health needs identified through such assessment.

“(B) COMMUNITY HEALTH NEEDS ASSESSMENT.—A community health needs assessment meets the requirements of this paragraph if such community health needs assessment—

“(i) takes into account input from persons who represent the broad interests of the community served by the hospital facility, including those with special knowledge of or expertise in public health, and

“(ii) is made widely available to the public.

“(4) FINANCIAL ASSISTANCE POLICY.—An organization meets the requirements of this paragraph if the organization establishes the following policies:

“(A) FINANCIAL ASSISTANCE POLICY.—A written financial assistance policy which includes—

“(i) eligibility criteria for financial assistance, and whether such assistance includes free or discounted care,

“(ii) the basis for calculating amounts charged to patients,

“(iii) the method for applying for financial assistance,

“(iv) in the case of an organization which does not have a separate billing and collections policy, the actions the organization may take in the event of non-payment, including collections action and reporting to credit agencies, and "(v) measures to widely publicize the policy within the community to be served by the organization.

"(B) POLICY RELATING TO EMERGENCY MEDICAL CARE.—A written policy requiring the organization to provide, without discrimination, care for emergency medical conditions (within the meaning of section 1867 of the Social Security Act (42 U.S.C. 1395dd)) to individuals regardless of their eligibility under the financial assistance policy described in subparagraph (A).

"(5) LIMITATION ON CHARGES.—An organization meets the requirements of this paragraph if the organization—

"(A) limits amounts charged for emergency or other medically necessary care provided to individuals eligible for assistance under the financial assistance policy described in paragraph (4)(A) to not more than the lowest amounts charged to individuals who have insurance covering such care, and

"(B) prohibits the use of gross charges.

"(6) BILLING AND COLLECTION REQUIREMENTS.—An organization meets the requirement of this paragraph only if the organization does not engage in extraordinary collection actions before the organization has made reasonable efforts to determine whether the individual is eligible for assistance under the financial assistance policy described in paragraph (4)(A).

"(7) REGULATORY AUTHORITY.—The Secretary shall issue such regulations and guidance as may be necessary to carry out the provisions of this subsection, including guidance relating to what constitutes reasonable efforts to determine the eligibility of a patient under a financial assistance policy for purposes of paragraph (6).".

(b) EXCISE TAX FOR FAILURES TO MEET HOSPITAL EXEMPTION REQUIREMENTS.—

(1) IN GENERAL.—Subchapter D of chapter 42 of the Internal Revenue Code of 1986 (relating to failure by certain charitable organizations to meet certain qualification requirements) is amended by adding at the end the following new section:

"SEC. 4959. TAXES ON FAILURES BY HOSPITAL ORGANIZATIONS.

"If a hospital organization to which section 501(r) applies fails to meet the requirement of section 501(r)(3) for any taxable year, there is imposed on the organization a tax equal to $50,000.".

(2) CONFORMING AMENDMENT.—The table of sections for subchapter D of chapter 42 of such Code is amended by adding at the end the following new item:

"Sec. 4959. Taxes on failures by hospital organizations.".

(c) MANDATORY REVIEW OF TAX EXEMPTION FOR HOSPITALS.—The Secretary of the Treasury or the Secretary's delegate shall review at least once every 3 years the community benefit activities of each hospital organization to which section 501(r) of the Internal Revenue Code of 1986 (as added by this section) applies.

(d) ADDITIONAL REPORTING REQUIREMENTS.—

(1) COMMUNITY HEALTH NEEDS ASSESSMENTS AND AUDITED FINANCIAL STATEMENTS.—Section 6033(b) of the Internal Revenue Code of 1986 (relating to certain organizations described in section 501(c)(3)) is amended by striking "and" at the end

of paragraph (14), by redesignating paragraph (15) as paragraph (16), and by inserting after paragraph (14) the following new paragraph:

"(15) in the case of an organization to which the requirements of section 501(r) apply for the taxable year—

"(A) a description of how the organization is addressing the needs identified in each community health needs assessment conducted under section 501(r)(3) and a description of any such needs that are not being addressed together with the reasons why such needs are not being addressed, and

"(B) the audited financial statements of such organization (or, in the case of an organization the financial statements of which are included in a consolidated financial statement with other organizations, such consolidated financial statement).".

(2) TAXES.—Section 6033(b)(10) of such Code is amended by striking "and" at the end of subparagraph (B), by inserting "and" at the end of subparagraph (C), and by adding at the end the following new subparagraph:

"(D) section 4959 (relating to taxes on failures by hospital organizations),".

(e) REPORTS.—

(1) REPORT ON LEVELS OF CHARITY CARE.—The Secretary of the Treasury, in consultation with the Secretary of Health and Human Services, shall submit to the Committees on Ways and Means, Education and Labor, and Energy and Commerce of the House of Representatives and to the Committees on Finance and Health, Education, Labor, and Pensions of the Senate an annual report on the following:

(A) Information with respect to private tax-exempt, taxable, and government-owned hospitals regarding—

(i) levels of charity care provided,

(ii) bad debt expenses,

(iii) unreimbursed costs for services provided with respect to means-tested government programs, and

(iv) unreimbursed costs for services provided with respect to non-means tested government programs.

(B) Information with respect to private tax-exempt hospitals regarding costs incurred for community benefit activities.

(2) REPORT ON TRENDS.—

(A) STUDY.—The Secretary of the Treasury, in consultation with the Secretary of Health and Human Services, shall conduct a study on trends in the information required to be reported under paragraph (1).

(B) REPORT.—Not later than 5 years after the date of the enactment of this Act, the Secretary of the Treasury, in consultation with the Secretary of Health and Human Services, shall submit a report on the study conducted under subparagraph (A) to the Committees on Ways and Means, Education and Labor, and Energy and Commerce of the House of Representatives and to the Committees on Finance and Health, Education, Labor, and Pensions of the Senate.

(f) EFFECTIVE DATES.—

(1) IN GENERAL.—Except as provided in paragraphs (2) and (3), the amendments made by this section shall apply to taxable years beginning after the date of the enactment of this Act.

(2) COMMUNITY HEALTH NEEDS ASSESSMENT.—The requirements of section 501(r)(3) of the Internal Revenue Code of 1986, as added by subsection (a), shall apply to taxable years beginning after the date which is 2 years after the date of the enactment of this Act.

(3) EXCISE TAX.—The amendments made by subsection (b) shall apply to failures occurring after the date of the enactment of this Act.

SEC. 9008. IMPOSITION OF ANNUAL FEE ON BRANDED PRESCRIPTION PHARMACEUTICAL MANUFACTURERS AND IMPORTERS.

(a) IMPOSITION OF FEE.—

(1) IN GENERAL.—Each covered entity engaged in the business of manufacturing or importing branded prescription drugs shall pay to the Secretary of the Treasury not later than the annual payment date of each calendar year beginning after 2009 a fee in an amount determined under subsection (b).

(2) ANNUAL PAYMENT DATE.—For purposes of this section, the term "annual payment date" means with respect to any calendar year the date determined by the Secretary, but in no event later than September 30 of such calendar year.

(b) DETERMINATION OF FEE AMOUNT.—

(1) IN GENERAL.—With respect to each covered entity, the fee under this section for any calendar year shall be equal to an amount that bears the same ratio to $2,300,000,000 as—

(A) the covered entity's branded prescription drug sales taken into account during the preceding calendar year, bear to

(B) the aggregate branded prescription drug sales of all covered entities taken into account during such preceding calendar year.

(2) SALES TAKEN INTO ACCOUNT.—For purposes of paragraph (1), the branded prescription drug sales taken into account during any calendar year with respect to any covered entity shall be determined in accordance with the following table:

With respect to a covered entity's aggregate branded prescription drug sales during the calendar year that are:	The percentage of such sales taken into account is:
Not more than $5,000,000	0 percent
More than $5,000,000 but not more than $125,000,000.	10 percent
More than $125,000,000 but not more than $225,000,000.	40 percent
More than $225,000,000 but not more than $400,000,000.	75 percent
More than $400,000,000	100 percent.

(3) SECRETARIAL DETERMINATION.—The Secretary of the Treasury shall calculate the amount of each covered entity's fee for any calendar year under paragraph (1). In calculating such amount, the Secretary of the Treasury shall determine such covered entity's branded prescription drug sales on the basis of reports submitted under subsection (g) and through the use of any other source of information available to the Secretary of the Treasury.

(c) TRANSFER OF FEES TO MEDICARE PART B TRUST FUND.—There is hereby appropriated to the Federal Supplementary Medical Insurance Trust Fund established under section 1841 of the Social Security Act an amount equal to the fees received by the Secretary of the Treasury under subsection (a).

(d) COVERED ENTITY.—

(1) IN GENERAL.—For purposes of this section, the term "covered entity" means any manufacturer or importer with gross receipts from branded prescription drug sales.

(2) CONTROLLED GROUPS.—

(A) IN GENERAL.—For purposes of this subsection, all persons treated as a single employer under subsection (a) or (b) of section 52 of the Internal Revenue Code of 1986 or subsection (m) or (o) of section 414 of such Code shall be treated as a single covered entity.

(B) INCLUSION OF FOREIGN CORPORATIONS.—For purposes of subparagraph (A), in applying subsections (a) and (b) of section 52 of such Code to this section, section 1563 of such Code shall be applied without regard to subsection (b)(2)(C) thereof.

(e) BRANDED PRESCRIPTION DRUG SALES.—For purposes of this section—

(1) IN GENERAL.—The term "branded prescription drug sales" means sales of branded prescription drugs to any specified government program or pursuant to coverage under any such program.

(2) BRANDED PRESCRIPTION DRUGS.—

(A) IN GENERAL.—The term "branded prescription drug" means—

(i) any prescription drug the application for which was submitted under section 505(b) of the Federal Food, Drug, and Cosmetic Act (21 U.S.C. 355(b)), or

(ii) any biological product the license for which was submitted under section 351(a) of the Public Health Service Act (42 U.S.C. 262(a)).

(B) PRESCRIPTION DRUG.—For purposes of subparagraph (A)(i), the term "prescription drug" means any drug which is subject to section 503(b) of the Federal Food, Drug, and Cosmetic Act (21 U.S.C. 353(b)).

(3) EXCLUSION OF ORPHAN DRUG SALES.—The term "branded prescription drug sales" shall not include sales of any drug or biological product with respect to which a credit was allowed for any taxable year under section 45C of the Internal Revenue Code of 1986. The preceding sentence shall not apply with respect to any such drug or biological product after the date on which such drug or biological product is approved by the Food and Drug Administration for marketing for any indication other than the treatment of the rare disease or condition with respect to which such credit was allowed.

(4) SPECIFIED GOVERNMENT PROGRAM.—The term "specified government program" means—

(A) the Medicare Part D program under part D of title XVIII of the Social Security Act,

(B) the Medicare Part B program under part B of title XVIII of the Social Security Act,

(C) the Medicaid program under title XIX of the Social Security Act,

(D) any program under which branded prescription drugs are procured by the Department of Veterans Affairs,

(E) any program under which branded prescription drugs are procured by the Department of Defense, or

(F) the TRICARE retail pharmacy program under section 1074g of title 10, United States Code.

(f) TAX TREATMENT OF FEES.—The fees imposed by this section—

(1) for purposes of subtitle F of the Internal Revenue Code of 1986, shall be treated as excise taxes with respect to which only civil actions for refund under procedures of such subtitle shall apply, and

(2) for purposes of section 275 of such Code, shall be considered to be a tax described in section 275(a)(6).

(g) REPORTING REQUIREMENT.—Not later than the date determined by the Secretary of the Treasury following the end of any calendar year, the Secretary of Health and Human Services, the Secretary of Veterans Affairs, and the Secretary of Defense shall report to the Secretary of the Treasury, in such manner as the Secretary of the Treasury prescribes, the total branded prescription drug sales for each covered entity with respect to each specified government program under such Secretary's jurisdiction using the following methodology:

(1) MEDICARE PART D PROGRAM.—The Secretary of Health and Human Services shall report, for each covered entity and for each branded prescription drug of the covered entity covered by the Medicare Part D program, the product of—

(A) the per-unit ingredient cost, as reported to the Secretary of Health and Human Services by prescription drug plans and Medicare Advantage prescription drug plans, minus any per-unit rebate, discount, or other price concession provided by the covered entity, as reported to the Secretary of Health and Human Services by the prescription drug plans and Medicare Advantage prescription drug plans, and

(B) the number of units of the branded prescription drug paid for under the Medicare Part D program.

(2) MEDICARE PART B PROGRAM.—The Secretary of Health and Human Services shall report, for each covered entity and for each branded prescription drug of the covered entity covered by the Medicare Part B program under section 1862(a) of the Social Security Act, the product of—

(A) the per-unit average sales price (as defined in section 1847A(c) of the Social Security Act) or the per-unit Part B payment rate for a separately paid branded prescription drug without a reported average sales price, and

(B) the number of units of the branded prescription drug paid for under the Medicare Part B program.

The Centers for Medicare and Medicaid Services shall establish a process for determining the units and the allocated price for purposes of this section for those branded prescription drugs that are not separately payable or for which National Drug Codes are not reported.

(3) MEDICAID PROGRAM.—The Secretary of Health and Human Services shall report, for each covered entity and for each branded prescription drug of the covered entity covered under the Medicaid program, the product of—

(A) the per-unit ingredient cost paid to pharmacies by States for the branded prescription drug dispensed to Medicaid beneficiaries, minus any per-unit rebate paid by the covered entity under section 1927 of the Social Security Act and any State supplemental rebate, and

(B) the number of units of the branded prescription drug paid for under the Medicaid program.

(4) DEPARTMENT OF VETERANS AFFAIRS PROGRAMS.—The Secretary of Veterans Affairs shall report, for each covered entity and for each branded prescription drug of the covered entity the total amount paid for each such branded prescription drug procured by the Department of Veterans Affairs for its beneficiaries.

(5) DEPARTMENT OF DEFENSE PROGRAMS AND TRICARE.—The Secretary of Defense shall report, for each covered entity and for each branded prescription drug of the covered entity, the sum of—

(A) the total amount paid for each such branded prescription drug procured by the Department of Defense for its beneficiaries, and

(B) for each such branded prescription drug dispensed under the TRICARE retail pharmacy program, the product of—

(i) the per-unit ingredient cost, minus any per-unit rebate paid by the covered entity, and

(ii) the number of units of the branded prescription drug dispensed under such program.

(h) SECRETARY.—For purposes of this section, the term "Secretary" includes the Secretary's delegate.

(i) GUIDANCE.—The Secretary of the Treasury shall publish guidance necessary to carry out the purposes of this section.

(j) APPLICATION OF SECTION.—This section shall apply to any branded prescription drug sales after December 31, 2008.

(k) CONFORMING AMENDMENT.—Section 1841(a) of the Social Security Act is amended by inserting "or section 9008(c) of the Patient Protection and Affordable Care Act of 2009" after "this part".

SEC. 9009. IMPOSITION OF ANNUAL FEE ON MEDICAL DEVICE MANUFACTURERS AND IMPORTERS.

(a) IMPOSITION OF FEE.—

(1) IN GENERAL.—Each covered entity engaged in the business of manufacturing or importing medical devices shall pay to the Secretary not later than the annual payment date of each calendar year beginning after 2009 a fee in an amount determined under subsection (b).

(2) ANNUAL PAYMENT DATE.—For purposes of this section, the term "annual payment date" means with respect to any

calendar year the date determined by the Secretary, but in no event later than September 30 of such calendar year.

(b) DETERMINATION OF FEE AMOUNT.—

(1) IN GENERAL.—With respect to each covered entity, the fee under this section for any calendar year shall be equal to an amount that bears the same ratio to $2,000,000,000 as—

(A) the covered entity's gross receipts from medical device sales taken into account during the preceding calendar year, bear to

(B) the aggregate gross receipts of all covered entities from medical device sales taken into account during such preceding calendar year.

(2) GROSS RECEIPTS FROM SALES TAKEN INTO ACCOUNT.—For purposes of paragraph (1), the gross receipts from medical device sales taken into account during any calendar year with respect to any covered entity shall be determined in accordance with the following table:

With respect to a covered entity's aggregate gross receipts from medical device sales during the calendar year that are:	The percentage of gross receipts taken into account is:
Not more than $5,000,000	0 percent
More than $5,000,000 but not more than $25,000,000.	50 percent
More than $25,000,000	100 percent.

(3) SECRETARIAL DETERMINATION.—The Secretary shall calculate the amount of each covered entity's fee for any calendar year under paragraph (1). In calculating such amount, the Secretary shall determine such covered entity's gross receipts from medical device sales on the basis of reports submitted by the covered entity under subsection (f) and through the use of any other source of information available to the Secretary.

(c) COVERED ENTITY.—

(1) IN GENERAL.—For purposes of this section, the term "covered entity" means any manufacturer or importer with gross receipts from medical device sales.

(2) CONTROLLED GROUPS.—

(A) IN GENERAL.—For purposes of this subsection, all persons treated as a single employer under subsection (a) or (b) of section 52 of the Internal Revenue Code of 1986 or subsection (m) or (o) of section 414 of such Code shall be treated as a single covered entity.

(B) INCLUSION OF FOREIGN CORPORATIONS.—For purposes of subparagraph (A), in applying subsections (a) and (b) of section 52 of such Code to this section, section 1563 of such Code shall be applied without regard to subsection (b)(2)(C) thereof.

(d) MEDICAL DEVICE SALES.—For purposes of this section—

(1) IN GENERAL.—The term "medical device sales" means sales for use in the United States of any medical device, other than the sales of a medical device that—

(A) has been classified in class II under section 513 of the Federal Food, Drug, and Cosmetic Act (21 U.S.C.

360c) and is primarily sold to consumers at retail for not more than $100 per unit, or

(B) has been classified in class I under such section.

(2) UNITED STATES.—For purposes of paragraph (1), the term "United States" means the several States, the District of Columbia, the Commonwealth of Puerto Rico, and the possessions of the United States.

(3) MEDICAL DEVICE.—For purposes of paragraph (1), the term "medical device" means any device (as defined in section 201(h) of the Federal Food, Drug, and Cosmetic Act (21 U.S.C. 321(h))) intended for humans.

(e) TAX TREATMENT OF FEES.—The fees imposed by this section—

(1) for purposes of subtitle F of the Internal Revenue Code of 1986, shall be treated as excise taxes with respect to which only civil actions for refund under procedures of such subtitle shall apply, and

(2) for purposes of section 275 of such Code, shall be considered to be a tax described in section 275(a)(6).

(f) REPORTING REQUIREMENT.—

(1) IN GENERAL.—Not later than the date determined by the Secretary following the end of any calendar year, each covered entity shall report to the Secretary, in such manner as the Secretary prescribes, the gross receipts from medical device sales of such covered entity during such calendar year.

(2) PENALTY FOR FAILURE TO REPORT.—

(A) IN GENERAL.—In the case of any failure to make a report containing the information required by paragraph (1) on the date prescribed therefor (determined with regard to any extension of time for filing), unless it is shown that such failure is due to reasonable cause, there shall be paid by the covered entity failing to file such report, an amount equal to—

(i) $10,000, plus

(ii) the lesser of—

(I) an amount equal to $1,000, multiplied by the number of days during which such failure continues, or

(II) the amount of the fee imposed by this section for which such report was required.

(B) TREATMENT OF PENALTY.—The penalty imposed under subparagraph (A)—

(i) shall be treated as a penalty for purposes of subtitle F of the Internal Revenue Code of 1986,

(ii) shall be paid on notice and demand by the Secretary and in the same manner as tax under such Code, and

(iii) with respect to which only civil actions for refund under procedures of such subtitle F shall apply.

(g) SECRETARY.—For purposes of this section, the term "Secretary" means the Secretary of the Treasury or the Secretary's delegate.

(h) GUIDANCE.—The Secretary shall publish guidance necessary to carry out the purposes of this section, including identification of medical devices described in subsection (d)(1)(A) and with respect to the treatment of gross receipts from sales of medical devices to another covered entity or to another entity by reason of the application of subsection (c)(2).

(i) APPLICATION OF SECTION.—This section shall apply to any medical device sales after December 31, 2008.

SEC. 9010. IMPOSITION OF ANNUAL FEE ON HEALTH INSURANCE PROVIDERS.

(a) IMPOSITION OF FEE.—

(1) IN GENERAL.—Each covered entity engaged in the business of providing health insurance shall pay to the Secretary not later than the annual payment date of each calendar year beginning after 2009 a fee in an amount determined under subsection (b).

(2) ANNUAL PAYMENT DATE.—For purposes of this section, the term "annual payment date" means with respect to any calendar year the date determined by the Secretary, but in no event later than September 30 of such calendar year.

(b) DETERMINATION OF FEE AMOUNT.—

(1) IN GENERAL.—With respect to each covered entity, the fee under this section for any calendar year shall be equal to an amount that bears the same ratio to $6,700,000,000 as—

(A) the sum of—

(i) the covered entity's net premiums written with respect to health insurance for any United States health risk that are taken into account during the preceding calendar year, plus

(ii) 200 percent of the covered entity's third party administration agreement fees that are taken into account during the preceding calendar year, bears to

(B) the sum of—

(i) the aggregate net premiums written with respect to such health insurance of all covered entities that are taken into account during such preceding calendar year, plus

(ii) 200 percent of the aggregate third party administration agreement fees of all covered entities that are taken into account during such preceding calendar year.

(2) AMOUNTS TAKEN INTO ACCOUNT.—For purposes of paragraph (1)—

(A) NET PREMIUMS WRITTEN.—The net premiums written with respect to health insurance for any United States health risk that are taken into account during any calendar year with respect to any covered entity shall be determined in accordance with the following table:

With respect to a covered entity's net premiums written during the calendar year that are:	The percentage of net premiums written that are taken into account is:
Not more than $25,000,000	0 percent
More than $25,000,000 but not more than $50,000,000.	50 percent
More than $50,000,000	100 percent.

(B) THIRD PARTY ADMINISTRATION AGREEMENT FEES.—The third party administration agreement fees that are taken into account during any calendar year with respect to any covered entity shall be determined in accordance with the following table:

With respect to a covered entity's third party administration agreement fees during the calendar year that are:	The percentage of third party administration agreement fees that are taken into account is:
Not more than $5,000,000	0 percent
More than $5,000,000 but not more than $10,000,000.	50 percent
More than $10,000,000	100 percent.

(3) SECRETARIAL DETERMINATION.—The Secretary shall calculate the amount of each covered entity's fee for any calendar year under paragraph (1). In calculating such amount, the Secretary shall determine such covered entity's net premiums written with respect to any United States health risk and third party administration agreement fees on the basis of reports submitted by the covered entity under subsection (g) and through the use of any other source of information available to the Secretary.

(c) COVERED ENTITY.—

(1) IN GENERAL.—For purposes of this section, the term "covered entity" means any entity which provides health insurance for any United States health risk.

(2) EXCLUSION.—Such term does not include—

(A) any employer to the extent that such employer self-insures its employees' health risks, or

(B) any governmental entity (except to the extent such an entity provides health insurance coverage through the community health insurance option under section 1323).

(3) CONTROLLED GROUPS.—

(A) IN GENERAL.—For purposes of this subsection, all persons treated as a single employer under subsection (a) or (b) of section 52 of the Internal Revenue Code of 1986 or subsection (m) or (o) of section 414 of such Code shall be treated as a single covered entity (or employer for purposes of paragraph (2)).

(B) INCLUSION OF FOREIGN CORPORATIONS.—For purposes of subparagraph (A), in applying subsections (a) and (b) of section 52 of such Code to this section, section 1563 of such Code shall be applied without regard to subsection (b)(2)(C) thereof.

(d) UNITED STATES HEALTH RISK.—For purposes of this section, the term "United States health risk" means the health risk of any individual who is—

(1) a United States citizen,

(2) a resident of the United States (within the meaning of section 7701(b)(1)(A) of the Internal Revenue Code of 1986), or

(3) located in the United States, with respect to the period such individual is so located.

(e) THIRD PARTY ADMINISTRATION AGREEMENT FEES.—For purposes of this section, the term "third party administration agreement fees" means, with respect to any covered entity, amounts received from an employer which are in excess of payments made by such covered entity for health benefits under an arrangement under which such employer self-insures the United States health risk of its employees.

(f) TAX TREATMENT OF FEES.—The fees imposed by this section—

(1) for purposes of subtitle F of the Internal Revenue Code of 1986, shall be treated as excise taxes with respect to which only civil actions for refund under procedures of such subtitle shall apply, and

(2) for purposes of section 275 of such Code shall be considered to be a tax described in section 275(a)(6).

(g) REPORTING REQUIREMENT.—

(1) IN GENERAL.—Not later than the date determined by the Secretary following the end of any calendar year, each covered entity shall report to the Secretary, in such manner as the Secretary prescribes, the covered entity's net premiums written with respect to health insurance for any United States health risk and third party administration agreement fees for such calendar year.

(2) PENALTY FOR FAILURE TO REPORT.—

(A) IN GENERAL.—In the case of any failure to make a report containing the information required by paragraph (1) on the date prescribed therefor (determined with regard to any extension of time for filing), unless it is shown that such failure is due to reasonable cause, there shall be paid by the covered entity failing to file such report, an amount equal to—

(i) $10,000, plus

(ii) the lesser of—

(I) an amount equal to $1,000, multiplied by the number of days during which such failure continues, or

(II) the amount of the fee imposed by this section for which such report was required.

(B) TREATMENT OF PENALTY.—The penalty imposed under subparagraph (A)—

(i) shall be treated as a penalty for purposes of subtitle F of the Internal Revenue Code of 1986,

(ii) shall be paid on notice and demand by the Secretary and in the same manner as tax under such Code, and

(iii) with respect to which only civil actions for refund under procedures of such subtitle F shall apply.

(h) ADDITIONAL DEFINITIONS.—For purposes of this section—

(1) SECRETARY.—The term "Secretary" means the Secretary of the Treasury or the Secretary's delegate.

(2) UNITED STATES.—The term "United States" means the several States, the District of Columbia, the Commonwealth of Puerto Rico, and the possessions of the United States.

(3) HEALTH INSURANCE.—The term "health insurance" shall not include insurance for long-term care or disability.

(i) GUIDANCE.—The Secretary shall publish guidance necessary to carry out the purposes of this section.

(j) APPLICATION OF SECTION.—This section shall apply to any net premiums written after December 31, 2008, with respect to health insurance for any United States health risk, and any third party administration agreement fees received after such date.

SEC. 9011. STUDY AND REPORT OF EFFECT ON VETERANS HEALTH CARE.

(a) IN GENERAL.—The Secretary of Veterans Affairs shall conduct a study on the effect (if any) of the provisions of sections 9008, 9009, and 9010 on—

(1) the cost of medical care provided to veterans, and

(2) veterans' access to medical devices and branded prescription drugs.

(b) REPORT.—The Secretary of Veterans Affairs shall report the results of the study under subsection (a) to the Committee on Ways and Means of the House of Representatives and to the Committee on Finance of the Senate not later than December 31, 2012.

SEC. 9012. ELIMINATION OF DEDUCTION FOR EXPENSES ALLOCABLE TO MEDICARE PART D SUBSIDY.

(a) IN GENERAL.—Section 139A of the Internal Revenue Code of 1986 is amended by striking the second sentence.

(b) EFFECTIVE DATE.—The amendment made by this section shall apply to taxable years beginning after December 31, 2010.

SEC. 9013. MODIFICATION OF ITEMIZED DEDUCTION FOR MEDICAL EXPENSES.

(a) IN GENERAL.—Subsection (a) of section 213 of the Internal Revenue Code of 1986 is amended by striking "7.5 percent" and inserting "10 percent".

(b) TEMPORARY WAIVER OF INCREASE FOR CERTAIN SENIORS.—Section 213 of the Internal Revenue Code of 1986 is amended by adding at the end the following new subsection:

"(f) SPECIAL RULE FOR 2013, 2014, 2015, AND 2016.—In the case of any taxable year beginning after December 31, 2012, and ending before January 1, 2017, subsection (a) shall be applied with respect to a taxpayer by substituting '7.5 percent' for '10 percent' if such taxpayer or such taxpayer's spouse has attained age 65 before the close of such taxable year.".

(c) CONFORMING AMENDMENT.—Section 56(b)(1)(B) of the Internal Revenue Code of 1986 is amended by striking "by substituting '10 percent' for '7.5 percent'" and inserting "without regard to subsection (f) of such section".

(d) EFFECTIVE DATE.—The amendments made by this section shall apply to taxable years beginning after December 31, 2012.

SEC. 9014. LIMITATION ON EXCESSIVE REMUNERATION PAID BY CERTAIN HEALTH INSURANCE PROVIDERS.

(a) IN GENERAL.—Section 162(m) of the Internal Revenue Code of 1986 is amended by adding at the end the following new subparagraph:

"(6) SPECIAL RULE FOR APPLICATION TO CERTAIN HEALTH INSURANCE PROVIDERS.—

"(A) IN GENERAL.—No deduction shall be allowed under this chapter—

"(i) in the case of applicable individual remuneration which is for any disqualified taxable year beginning after December 31, 2012, and which is attributable to services performed by an applicable individual during such taxable year, to the extent that the amount of such remuneration exceeds $500,000, or

"(ii) in the case of deferred deduction remuneration for any taxable year beginning after December 31, 2012, which is attributable to services performed by an applicable individual during any disqualified taxable year beginning after December 31, 2009, to the extent that the amount of such remuneration exceeds $500,000 reduced (but not below zero) by the sum of—

"(I) the applicable individual remuneration for such disqualified taxable year, plus

"(II) the portion of the deferred deduction remuneration for such services which was taken into account under this clause in a preceding taxable year (or which would have been taken into account under this clause in a preceding taxable year if this clause were applied by substituting 'December 31, 2009' for 'December 31, 2012' in the matter preceding subclause (I)).

"(B) DISQUALIFIED TAXABLE YEAR.—For purposes of this paragraph, the term 'disqualified taxable year' means, with respect to any employer, any taxable year for which such employer is a covered health insurance provider.

"(C) COVERED HEALTH INSURANCE PROVIDER.—For purposes of this paragraph—

"(i) IN GENERAL.—The term 'covered health insurance provider' means—

"(I) with respect to taxable years beginning after December 31, 2009, and before January 1, 2013, any employer which is a health insurance issuer (as defined in section 9832(b)(2)) and which receives premiums from providing health insurance coverage (as defined in section 9832(b)(1)), and

"(II) with respect to taxable years beginning after December 31, 2012, any employer which is a health insurance issuer (as defined in section 9832(b)(2)) and with respect to which not less than 25 percent of the gross premiums received from providing health insurance coverage (as defined in section 9832(b)(1)) is from minimum essential coverage (as defined in section 5000A(f)).

"(ii) AGGREGATION RULES.—Two or more persons who are treated as a single employer under subsection (b), (c), (m), or (o) of section 414 shall be treated as a single employer, except that in applying section 1563(a) for purposes of any such subsection, paragraphs (2) and (3) thereof shall be disregarded.

"(D) APPLICABLE INDIVIDUAL REMUNERATION.—For purposes of this paragraph, the term 'applicable individual remuneration' means, with respect to any applicable individual for any disqualified taxable year, the aggregate amount allowable as a deduction under this chapter for such taxable year (determined without regard to this subsection) for remuneration (as defined in paragraph (4) without regard to subparagraphs (B), (C), and (D) thereof) for services performed by such individual (whether or not during the taxable year). Such term shall not include any deferred deduction remuneration with respect to services performed during the disqualified taxable year.

"(E) DEFERRED DEDUCTION REMUNERATION.—For purposes of this paragraph, the term 'deferred deduction remuneration' means remuneration which would be applicable individual remuneration for services performed in a disqualified taxable year but for the fact that the deduction under this chapter (determined without regard to this paragraph) for such remuneration is allowable in a subsequent taxable year.

"(F) APPLICABLE INDIVIDUAL.—For purposes of this paragraph, the term 'applicable individual' means, with respect to any covered health insurance provider for any disqualified taxable year, any individual—

"(i) who is an officer, director, or employee in such taxable year, or

"(ii) who provides services for or on behalf of such covered health insurance provider during such taxable year.

"(G) COORDINATION.—Rules similar to the rules of subparagraphs (F) and (G) of paragraph (4) shall apply for purposes of this paragraph.

"(H) REGULATORY AUTHORITY.—The Secretary may prescribe such guidance, rules, or regulations as are necessary to carry out the purposes of this paragraph.".

(b) EFFECTIVE DATE.—The amendment made by this section shall apply to taxable years beginning after December 31, 2009, with respect to services performed after such date.

SEC. 9015. ADDITIONAL HOSPITAL INSURANCE TAX ON HIGH-INCOME TAXPAYERS.

(a) FICA.—

(1) IN GENERAL.—Section 3101(b) of the Internal Revenue Code of 1986 is amended—

(A) by striking "In addition" and inserting the following:

"(1) IN GENERAL.—In addition",

(B) by striking "the following percentages of the" and inserting "1.45 percent of the",

(C) by striking "(as defined in section 3121(b))—" and all that follows and inserting "(as defined in section 3121(b)).", and

(D) by adding at the end the following new paragraph:

"(2) ADDITIONAL TAX.—In addition to the tax imposed by paragraph (1) and the preceding subsection, there is hereby imposed on every taxpayer (other than a corporation, estate, or trust) a tax equal to 0.5 percent of wages which are received with respect to employment (as defined in section 3121(b)) during any taxable year beginning after December 31, 2012, and which are in excess of—

"(A) in the case of a joint return, $250,000, and

"(B) in any other case, $200,000.".

(2) COLLECTION OF TAX.—Section 3102 of the Internal Revenue Code of 1986 is amended by adding at the end the following new subsection:

"(f) SPECIAL RULES FOR ADDITIONAL TAX.—

"(1) IN GENERAL.—In the case of any tax imposed by section 3101(b)(2), subsection (a) shall only apply to the extent to which the taxpayer receives wages from the employer in excess of $200,000, and the employer may disregard the amount of wages received by such taxpayer's spouse.

"(2) COLLECTION OF AMOUNTS NOT WITHHELD.—To the extent that the amount of any tax imposed by section 3101(b)(2) is not collected by the employer, such tax shall be paid by the employee.

"(3) TAX PAID BY RECIPIENT.—If an employer, in violation of this chapter, fails to deduct and withhold the tax imposed by section 3101(b)(2) and thereafter the tax is paid by the employee, the tax so required to be deducted and withheld shall not be collected from the employer, but this paragraph shall in no case relieve the employer from liability for any penalties or additions to tax otherwise applicable in respect of such failure to deduct and withhold.".

(b) SECA.—

(1) IN GENERAL.—Section 1401(b) of the Internal Revenue Code of 1986 is amended—

(A) by striking "In addition" and inserting the following:

"(1) IN GENERAL.—In addition", and

(B) by adding at the end the following new paragraph:

"(2) ADDITIONAL TAX.—

"(A) IN GENERAL.—In addition to the tax imposed by paragraph (1) and the preceding subsection, there is hereby imposed on every taxpayer (other than a corporation, estate, or trust) for each taxable year beginning after December 31, 2012, a tax equal to 0.5 percent of the self-employment income for such taxable year which is in excess of—

"(i) in the case of a joint return, $250,000, and

"(ii) in any other case, $200,000.

"(B) COORDINATION WITH FICA.—The amounts under clauses (i) and (ii) of subparagraph (A) shall be reduced (but not below zero) by the amount of wages taken into account in determining the tax imposed under section 3121(b)(2) with respect to the taxpayer.".

(2) NO DEDUCTION FOR ADDITIONAL TAX.—

(A) IN GENERAL.—Section 164(f) of such Code is amended by inserting "(other than the taxes imposed by section 1401(b)(2))" after "section 1401)".

(B) DEDUCTION FOR NET EARNINGS FROM SELF-EMPLOYMENT.—Subparagraph (B) of section 1402(a)(12) is amended by inserting "(determined without regard to the rate imposed under paragraph (2) of section 1401(b))" after "for such year".

(c) EFFECTIVE DATE.—The amendments made by this section shall apply with respect to remuneration received, and taxable years beginning, after December 31, 2012.

SEC. 9016. MODIFICATION OF SECTION 833 TREATMENT OF CERTAIN HEALTH ORGANIZATIONS.

(a) IN GENERAL.—Subsection (c) of section 833 of the Internal Revenue Code of 1986 is amended by adding at the end the following new paragraph:

"(5) NONAPPLICATION OF SECTION IN CASE OF LOW MEDICAL LOSS RATIO.—Notwithstanding the preceding paragraphs, this section shall not apply to any organization unless such organization's percentage of total premium revenue expended on reimbursement for clinical services provided to enrollees under its policies during such taxable year (as reported under section 2718 of the Public Health Service Act) is not less than 85 percent.".

(b) EFFECTIVE DATE.—The amendment made by this section shall apply to taxable years beginning after December 31, 2009.

SEC. 9017. EXCISE TAX ON ELECTIVE COSMETIC MEDICAL PROCEDURES.

(a) IN GENERAL.—Subtitle D of the Internal Revenue Code of 1986, as amended by this Act, is amended by adding at the end the following new chapter:

"CHAPTER 49—ELECTIVE COSMETIC MEDICAL PROCEDURES

"SEC. 5000B. IMPOSITION OF TAX ON ELECTIVE COSMETIC MEDICAL PROCEDURES.

"(a) IN GENERAL.—There is hereby imposed on any cosmetic surgery and medical procedure a tax equal to 5 percent of the amount paid for such procedure (determined without regard to this section), whether paid by insurance or otherwise.

"(b) COSMETIC SURGERY AND MEDICAL PROCEDURE.—For purposes of this section, the term 'cosmetic surgery and medical procedure' means any cosmetic surgery (as defined in section 213(d)(9)(B)) or other similar procedure which—

"(1) is performed by a licensed medical professional, and

"(2) is not necessary to ameliorate a deformity arising from, or directly related to, a congenital abnormality, a personal injury resulting from an accident or trauma, or disfiguring disease.

"(c) PAYMENT OF TAX.—

"(1) IN GENERAL.—The tax imposed by this section shall be paid by the individual on whom the procedure is performed.

"(2) COLLECTION.—Every person receiving a payment for procedures on which a tax is imposed under subsection (a) shall collect the amount of the tax from the individual on whom the procedure is performed and remit such tax quarterly to the Secretary at such time and in such manner as provided by the Secretary.

"(3) SECONDARY LIABILITY.—Where any tax imposed by subsection (a) is not paid at the time payments for cosmetic surgery and medical procedures are made, then to the extent that such tax is not collected, such tax shall be paid by the person who performs the procedure.".

(b) CLERICAL AMENDMENT.—The table of chapters for subtitle D of the Internal Revenue Code of 1986, as amended by this Act, is amended by inserting after the item relating to chapter 48 the following new item:

"CHAPTER 49—ELECTIVE COSMETIC MEDICAL PROCEDURES".

(c) EFFECTIVE DATE.—The amendments made by this section shall apply to procedures performed on or after January 1, 2010.

Subtitle B—Other Provisions

SEC. 9021. EXCLUSION OF HEALTH BENEFITS PROVIDED BY INDIAN TRIBAL GOVERNMENTS.

(a) IN GENERAL.—Part III of subchapter B of chapter 1 of the Internal Revenue Code of 1986 is amended by inserting after section 139C the following new section:

"SEC. 139D. INDIAN HEALTH CARE BENEFITS.

"(a) GENERAL RULE.—Except as otherwise provided in this section, gross income does not include the value of any qualified Indian health care benefit.

"(b) QUALIFIED INDIAN HEALTH CARE BENEFIT.—For purposes of this section, the term 'qualified Indian health care benefit' means—

"(1) any health service or benefit provided or purchased, directly or indirectly, by the Indian Health Service through a grant to or a contract or compact with an Indian tribe or tribal organization, or through a third-party program funded by the Indian Health Service,

"(2) medical care provided or purchased by, or amounts to reimburse for such medical care provided by, an Indian tribe or tribal organization for, or to, a member of an Indian tribe, including a spouse or dependent of such a member,

"(3) coverage under accident or health insurance (or an arrangement having the effect of accident or health insurance), or an accident or health plan, provided by an Indian tribe or tribal organization for medical care to a member of an Indian tribe, include a spouse or dependent of such a member, and

"(4) any other medical care provided by an Indian tribe or tribal organization that supplements, replaces, or substitutes for a program or service relating to medical care provided by the Federal government to Indian tribes or members of such a tribe.

"(c) DEFINITIONS.—For purposes of this section—

"(1) INDIAN TRIBE.—The term 'Indian tribe' has the meaning given such term by section 45A(c)(6).

"(2) TRIBAL ORGANIZATION.—The term 'tribal organization' has the meaning given such term by section 4(l) of the Indian Self-Determination and Education Assistance Act.

"(3) MEDICAL CARE.—The term 'medical care' has the same meaning as when used in section 213.

"(4) ACCIDENT OR HEALTH INSURANCE; ACCIDENT OR HEALTH PLAN.—The terms 'accident or health insurance' and 'accident or health plan' have the same meaning as when used in section 105.

"(5) DEPENDENT.—The term 'dependent' has the meaning given such term by section 152, determined without regard to subsections (b)(1), (b)(2), and (d)(1)(B) thereof.

"(d) DENIAL OF DOUBLE BENEFIT.—Subsection (a) shall not apply to the amount of any qualified Indian health care benefit which is not includible in gross income of the beneficiary of such benefit under any other provision of this chapter, or to the amount of any such benefit for which a deduction is allowed to such beneficiary under any other provision of this chapter.".

(b) CLERICAL AMENDMENT.—The table of sections for part III of subchapter B of chapter 1 of the Internal Revenue Code of 1986 is amended by inserting after the item relating to section 139C the following new item:

"Sec. 139D. Indian health care benefits.".

(c) EFFECTIVE DATE.—The amendments made by this section shall apply to benefits and coverage provided after the date of the enactment of this Act.

(d) NO INFERENCE.—Nothing in the amendments made by this section shall be construed to create an inference with respect to the exclusion from gross income of—

(1) benefits provided by an Indian tribe or tribal organization that are not within the scope of this section, and

(2) benefits provided prior to the date of the enactment of this Act.

SEC. 9022. ESTABLISHMENT OF SIMPLE CAFETERIA PLANS FOR SMALL BUSINESSES.

(a) IN GENERAL.—Section 125 of the Internal Revenue Code of 1986 (relating to cafeteria plans), as amended by this Act, is amended by redesignating subsections (j) and (k) as subsections (k) and (l), respectively, and by inserting after subsection (i) the following new subsection:

"(j) SIMPLE CAFETERIA PLANS FOR SMALL BUSINESSES.—

"(1) IN GENERAL.—An eligible employer maintaining a simple cafeteria plan with respect to which the requirements of this subsection are met for any year shall be treated as meeting any applicable nondiscrimination requirement during such year.

"(2) SIMPLE CAFETERIA PLAN.—For purposes of this subsection, the term 'simple cafeteria plan' means a cafeteria plan—

"(A) which is established and maintained by an eligible employer, and

"(B) with respect to which the contribution requirements of paragraph (3), and the eligibility and participation requirements of paragraph (4), are met.

"(3) CONTRIBUTION REQUIREMENTS.—

"(A) IN GENERAL.—The requirements of this paragraph are met if, under the plan the employer is required, without regard to whether a qualified employee makes any salary reduction contribution, to make a contribution to provide qualified benefits under the plan on behalf of each qualified employee in an amount equal to—

"(i) a uniform percentage (not less than 2 percent) of the employee's compensation for the plan year, or "(ii) an amount which is not less than the lesser of—

"(I) 6 percent of the employee's compensation for the plan year, or

"(II) twice the amount of the salary reduction contributions of each qualified employee.

"(B) MATCHING CONTRIBUTIONS ON BEHALF OF HIGHLY COMPENSATED AND KEY EMPLOYEES.—The requirements of subparagraph (A)(ii) shall not be treated as met if, under the plan, the rate of contributions with respect to any salary reduction contribution of a highly compensated or key employee at any rate of contribution is greater than that with respect to an employee who is not a highly compensated or key employee.

"(C) ADDITIONAL CONTRIBUTIONS.—Subject to subparagraph (B), nothing in this paragraph shall be treated as prohibiting an employer from making contributions to provide qualified benefits under the plan in addition to contributions required under subparagraph (A).

"(D) DEFINITIONS.—For purposes of this paragraph—

"(i) SALARY REDUCTION CONTRIBUTION.—The term 'salary reduction contribution' means, with respect to a cafeteria plan, any amount which is contributed to the plan at the election of the employee and which is not includible in gross income by reason of this section.

"(ii) QUALIFIED EMPLOYEE.—The term 'qualified employee' means, with respect to a cafeteria plan, any employee who is not a highly compensated or key employee and who is eligible to participate in the plan.

"(iii) HIGHLY COMPENSATED EMPLOYEE.—The term 'highly compensated employee' has the meaning given such term by section 414(q).

"(iv) KEY EMPLOYEE.—The term 'key employee' has the meaning given such term by section 416(i).

"(4) MINIMUM ELIGIBILITY AND PARTICIPATION REQUIREMENTS.—

"(A) IN GENERAL.—The requirements of this paragraph shall be treated as met with respect to any year if, under the plan—

"(i) all employees who had at least 1,000 hours of service for the preceding plan year are eligible to participate, and

"(ii) each employee eligible to participate in the plan may, subject to terms and conditions applicable to all participants, elect any benefit available under the plan.

"(B) CERTAIN EMPLOYEES MAY BE EXCLUDED.—For purposes of subparagraph (A)(i), an employer may elect to exclude under the plan employees—

"(i) who have not attained the age of 21 before the close of a plan year,

"(ii) who have less than 1 year of service with the employer as of any day during the plan year,

"(iii) who are covered under an agreement which the Secretary of Labor finds to be a collective bargaining agreement if there is evidence that the benefits covered under the cafeteria plan were the subject of good faith bargaining between employee representatives and the employer, or

"(iv) who are described in section 410(b)(3)(C) (relating to nonresident aliens working outside the United States).

A plan may provide a shorter period of service or younger age for purposes of clause (i) or (ii).

"(5) ELIGIBLE EMPLOYER.—For purposes of this subsection—

"(A) IN GENERAL.—The term 'eligible employer' means, with respect to any year, any employer if such employer employed an average of 100 or fewer employees on business days during either of the 2 preceding years. For purposes of this subparagraph, a year may only be taken into account if the employer was in existence throughout the year.

"(B) EMPLOYERS NOT IN EXISTENCE DURING PRECEDING YEAR.—If an employer was not in existence throughout the preceding year, the determination under subparagraph (A) shall be based on the average number of employees that it is reasonably expected such employer will employ on business days in the current year.

"(C) GROWING EMPLOYERS RETAIN TREATMENT AS SMALL EMPLOYER.—

"(i) IN GENERAL.—If—

"(I) an employer was an eligible employer for any year (a 'qualified year'), and

"(II) such employer establishes a simple cafeteria plan for its employees for such year,

then, notwithstanding the fact the employer fails to meet the requirements of subparagraph (A) for any subsequent year, such employer shall be treated as an eligible employer for such subsequent year with respect to employees (whether or not employees during a qualified year) of any trade or business which was covered by the plan during any qualified year.

"(ii) EXCEPTION.—This subparagraph shall cease to apply if the employer employs an average of 200 or more employees on business days during any year preceding any such subsequent year.

"(D) SPECIAL RULES.—

"(i) PREDECESSORS.—Any reference in this paragraph to an employer shall include a reference to any predecessor of such employer.

"(ii) AGGREGATION RULES.—All persons treated as a single employer under subsection (a) or (b) of section 52, or subsection (n) or (o) of section 414, shall be treated as one person.

"(6) APPLICABLE NONDISCRIMINATION REQUIREMENT.—For purposes of this subsection, the term 'applicable nondiscrimination requirement' means any requirement under subsection (b) of this section, section 79(d), section 105(h), or paragraph (2), (3), (4), or (8) of section 129(d).

"(7) COMPENSATION.—The term 'compensation' has the meaning given such term by section 414(s).".

(b) EFFECTIVE DATE.—The amendments made by this section shall apply to years beginning after December 31, 2010.

SEC. 9023. QUALIFYING THERAPEUTIC DISCOVERY PROJECT CREDIT.

(a) IN GENERAL.—Subpart E of part IV of subchapter A of chapter 1 of the Internal Revenue Code of 1986 is amended by inserting after section 48C the following new section:

"SEC. 48D. QUALIFYING THERAPEUTIC DISCOVERY PROJECT CREDIT.

"(a) IN GENERAL.—For purposes of section 46, the qualifying therapeutic discovery project credit for any taxable year is an amount equal to 50 percent of the qualified investment for such taxable year with respect to any qualifying therapeutic discovery project of an eligible taxpayer.

"(b) QUALIFIED INVESTMENT.—

"(1) IN GENERAL.—For purposes of subsection (a), the qualified investment for any taxable year is the aggregate amount of the costs paid or incurred in such taxable year for expenses necessary for and directly related to the conduct of a qualifying therapeutic discovery project.

"(2) LIMITATION.—The amount which is treated as qualified investment for all taxable years with respect to any qualifying therapeutic discovery project shall not exceed the amount certified by the Secretary as eligible for the credit under this section.

"(3) EXCLUSIONS.—The qualified investment for any taxable year with respect to any qualifying therapeutic discovery project shall not take into account any cost—

"(A) for remuneration for an employee described in section 162(m)(3),

"(B) for interest expenses,

"(C) for facility maintenance expenses,

"(D) which is identified as a service cost under section 1.263A–1(e)(4) of title 26, Code of Federal Regulations, or

"(E) for any other expense as determined by the Secretary as appropriate to carry out the purposes of this section.

"(4) CERTAIN PROGRESS EXPENDITURE RULES MADE APPLICABLE.—In the case of costs described in paragraph (1) that are paid for property of a character subject to an allowance for depreciation, rules similar to the rules of subsections (c)(4) and (d) of section 46 (as in effect on the day before the date of the enactment of the Revenue Reconciliation Act of 1990) shall apply for purposes of this section.

"(5) APPLICATION OF SUBSECTION.—An investment shall be considered a qualified investment under this subsection only if such investment is made in a taxable year beginning in 2009 or 2010.

"(c) DEFINITIONS.—

"(1) QUALIFYING THERAPEUTIC DISCOVERY PROJECT.—The term 'qualifying therapeutic discovery project' means a project which is designed—

"(A) to treat or prevent diseases or conditions by conducting pre-clinical activities, clinical trials, and clinical studies, or carrying out research protocols, for the purpose of securing approval of a product under section 505(b) of the Federal Food, Drug, and Cosmetic Act or section 351(a) of the Public Health Service Act,

"(B) to diagnose diseases or conditions or to determine molecular factors related to diseases or conditions by developing molecular diagnostics to guide therapeutic decisions, or

"(C) to develop a product, process, or technology to further the delivery or administration of therapeutics.

"(2) ELIGIBLE TAXPAYER.—

"(A) IN GENERAL.—The term 'eligible taxpayer' means a taxpayer which employs not more than 250 employees in all businesses of the taxpayer at the time of the submission of the application under subsection (d)(2).

"(B) AGGREGATION RULES.—All persons treated as a single employer under subsection (a) or (b) of section 52, or subsection (m) or (o) of section 414, shall be so treated for purposes of this paragraph.

"(3) FACILITY MAINTENANCE EXPENSES.—The term 'facility maintenance expenses' means costs paid or incurred to maintain a facility, including—

"(A) mortgage or rent payments,

"(B) insurance payments,

"(C) utility and maintenance costs, and

"(D) costs of employment of maintenance personnel.

"(d) QUALIFYING THERAPEUTIC DISCOVERY PROJECT PROGRAM.—

"(1) ESTABLISHMENT.—

"(A) IN GENERAL.—Not later than 60 days after the date of the enactment of this section, the Secretary, in consultation with the Secretary of Health and Human Services, shall establish a qualifying therapeutic discovery project program to consider and award certifications for qualified investments eligible for credits under this section to qualifying therapeutic discovery project sponsors.

"(B) LIMITATION.—The total amount of credits that may be allocated under the program shall not exceed $1,000,000,000 for the 2-year period beginning with 2009.

"(2) CERTIFICATION.—

"(A) APPLICATION PERIOD.—Each applicant for certification under this paragraph shall submit an application containing such information as the Secretary may require during the period beginning on the date the Secretary establishes the program under paragraph (1).

"(B) TIME FOR REVIEW OF APPLICATIONS.—The Secretary shall take action to approve or deny any application under subparagraph (A) within 30 days of the submission of such application.

"(C) MULTI-YEAR APPLICATIONS.—An application for certification under subparagraph (A) may include a request for an allocation of credits for more than 1 of the years described in paragraph (1)(B).

"(3) SELECTION CRITERIA.—In determining the qualifying therapeutic discovery projects with respect to which qualified investments may be certified under this section, the Secretary—

"(A) shall take into consideration only those projects that show reasonable potential—

"(i) to result in new therapies—

"(I) to treat areas of unmet medical need, or

"(II) to prevent, detect, or treat chronic or acute diseases and conditions, "(ii) to reduce long-term health care costs in the United States, or

"(iii) to significantly advance the goal of curing cancer within the 30-year period beginning on the date the Secretary establishes the program under paragraph (1), and

"(B) shall take into consideration which projects have the greatest potential—

"(i) to create and sustain (directly or indirectly) high quality, high-paying jobs in the United States, and

"(ii) to advance United States competitiveness in the fields of life, biological, and medical sciences.

"(4) DISCLOSURE OF ALLOCATIONS.—The Secretary shall, upon making a certification under this subsection, publicly disclose the identity of the applicant and the amount of the credit with respect to such applicant.

"(e) SPECIAL RULES.—

"(1) BASIS ADJUSTMENT.—For purposes of this subtitle, if a credit is allowed under this section for an expenditure related to property of a character subject to an allowance for depreciation, the basis of such property shall be reduced by the amount of such credit.

"(2) DENIAL OF DOUBLE BENEFIT.—

"(A) BONUS DEPRECIATION.—A credit shall not be allowed under this section for any investment for which bonus depreciation is allowed under section 168(k), 1400L(b)(1), or 1400N(d)(1).

"(B) DEDUCTIONS.—No deduction under this subtitle shall be allowed for the portion of the expenses otherwise allowable as a deduction taken into account in determining the credit under this section for the taxable year which is equal to the amount of the credit determined for such taxable year under subsection (a) attributable to such portion. This subparagraph shall not apply to expenses related to property of a character subject to an allowance for depreciation the basis of which is reduced under paragraph (1), or which are described in section 280C(g).

"(C) CREDIT FOR RESEARCH ACTIVITIES.—

"(i) IN GENERAL.—Except as provided in clause (ii), any expenses taken into account under this section for a taxable year shall not be taken into account for purposes of determining the credit allowable under section 41 or 45C for such taxable year.

"(ii) EXPENSES INCLUDED IN DETERMINING BASE PERIOD RESEARCH EXPENSES.—Any expenses for any taxable year which are qualified research expenses (within the meaning of section 41(b)) shall be taken into account in determining base period research expenses for purposes of applying section 41 to subsequent taxable years.

"(f) COORDINATION WITH DEPARTMENT OF TREASURY GRANTS.—In the case of any investment with respect to which the Secretary makes a grant under section 9023(e) of the Patient Protection and Affordable Care Act of 2009—

"(1) DENIAL OF CREDIT.—No credit shall be determined under this section with respect to such investment for the taxable year in which such grant is made or any subsequent taxable year.

"(2) RECAPTURE OF CREDITS FOR PROGRESS EXPENDITURES MADE BEFORE GRANT.—If a credit was determined under this section with respect to such investment for any taxable year ending before such grant is made—

"(A) the tax imposed under subtitle A on the taxpayer for the taxable year in which such grant is made shall be increased by so much of such credit as was allowed under section 38,

"(B) the general business carryforwards under section 39 shall be adjusted so as to recapture the portion of such credit which was not so allowed, and

"(C) the amount of such grant shall be determined without regard to any reduction in the basis of any property of a character subject to an allowance for depreciation by reason of such credit.

"(3) TREATMENT OF GRANTS.—Any such grant shall not be includible in the gross income of the taxpayer.".

(b) INCLUSION AS PART OF INVESTMENT CREDIT.—Section 46 of the Internal Revenue Code of 1986 is amended—

(1) by adding a comma at the end of paragraph (2),

(2) by striking the period at the end of paragraph (5) and inserting ", and", and

(3) by adding at the end the following new paragraph:

"(6) the qualifying therapeutic discovery project credit.".

(c) CONFORMING AMENDMENTS.—

(1) Section 49(a)(1)(C) of the Internal Revenue Code of 1986 is amended—

(A) by striking "and" at the end of clause (iv),

(B) by striking the period at the end of clause (v) and inserting ", and", and

(C) by adding at the end the following new clause:

"(vi) the basis of any property to which paragraph (1) of section 48D(e) applies which is part of a qualifying therapeutic discovery project under such section 48D.".

(2) Section 280C of such Code is amended by adding at the end the following new subsection:

"(g) QUALIFYING THERAPEUTIC DISCOVERY PROJECT CREDIT.—

"(1) IN GENERAL.—No deduction shall be allowed for that portion of the qualified investment (as defined in section 48D(b)) otherwise allowable as a deduction for the taxable year which—

"(A) would be qualified research expenses (as defined in section 41(b)), basic research expenses (as defined in section 41(e)(2)), or qualified clinical testing expenses (as defined in section 45C(b)) if the credit under section 41 or section 45C were allowed with respect to such expenses for such taxable year, and

"(B) is equal to the amount of the credit determined for such taxable year under section 48D(a), reduced by—

"(i) the amount disallowed as a deduction by reason of section 48D(e)(2)(B), and

"(ii) the amount of any basis reduction under section 48D(e)(1).

"(2) SIMILAR RULE WHERE TAXPAYER CAPITALIZES RATHER THAN DEDUCTS EXPENSES.—In the case of expenses described in paragraph (1)(A) taken into account in determining the credit under section 48D for the taxable year, if—

"(A) the amount of the portion of the credit determined under such section with respect to such expenses, exceeds

"(B) the amount allowable as a deduction for such taxable year for such expenses (determined without regard to paragraph (1)),

the amount chargeable to capital account for the taxable year for such expenses shall be reduced by the amount of such excess.

"(3) CONTROLLED GROUPS.—Paragraph (3) of subsection (b) shall apply for purposes of this subsection.".

(d) CLERICAL AMENDMENT.—The table of sections for subpart E of part IV of subchapter A of chapter 1 of the Internal Revenue Code of 1986 is amended by inserting after the item relating to section 48C the following new item:

"Sec. 48D. Qualifying therapeutic discovery project credit.".

(e) GRANTS FOR QUALIFIED INVESTMENTS IN THERAPEUTIC DISCOVERY PROJECTS IN LIEU OF TAX CREDITS.—

(1) IN GENERAL.—Upon application, the Secretary of the Treasury shall, subject to the requirements of this subsection, provide a grant to each person who makes a qualified investment in a qualifying therapeutic discovery project in the amount of 50 percent of such investment. No grant shall be made under this subsection with respect to any investment unless such investment is made during a taxable year beginning in 2009 or 2010.

(2) APPLICATION.—

(A) IN GENERAL.—At the stated election of the applicant, an application for certification under section 48D(d)(2) of the Internal Revenue Code of 1986 for a credit under such section for the taxable year of the applicant which begins in 2009 shall be considered to be an application for a grant under paragraph (1) for such taxable year.

(B) TAXABLE YEARS BEGINNING IN 2010.—An application for a grant under paragraph (1) for a taxable year beginning in 2010 shall be submitted—

(i) not earlier than the day after the last day of such taxable year, and

(ii) not later than the due date (including extensions) for filing the return of tax for such taxable year.

(C) INFORMATION TO BE SUBMITTED.—An application for a grant under paragraph (1) shall include such information and be in such form as the Secretary may require to state the amount of the credit allowable (but for the receipt of a grant under this subsection) under section 48D for the taxable year for the qualified investment with respect to which such application is made.

(3) TIME FOR PAYMENT OF GRANT.—

(A) IN GENERAL.—The Secretary of the Treasury shall make payment of the amount of any grant under paragraph (1) during the 30-day period beginning on the later of—

(i) the date of the application for such grant, or

(ii) the date the qualified investment for which the grant is being made is made.

(B) REGULATIONS.—In the case of investments of an ongoing nature, the Secretary shall issue regulations to determine the date on which a qualified investment shall be deemed to have been made for purposes of this paragraph.

(4) QUALIFIED INVESTMENT.—For purposes of this subsection, the term "qualified investment" means a qualified investment that is certified under section 48D(d) of the Internal Revenue Code of 1986 for purposes of the credit under such section 48D.

(5) APPLICATION OF CERTAIN RULES.—

(A) IN GENERAL.—In making grants under this subsection, the Secretary of the Treasury shall apply rules similar to the rules of section 50 of the Internal Revenue Code of 1986. In applying such rules, any increase in tax under chapter 1 of such Code by reason of an investment ceasing to be a qualified investment shall be imposed on the person to whom the grant was made.

(B) SPECIAL RULES.—

(i) RECAPTURE OF EXCESSIVE GRANT AMOUNTS.—If the amount of a grant made under this subsection exceeds the amount allowable as a grant under this subsection, such excess shall be recaptured under subparagraph (A) as if the investment to which such excess portion of the grant relates had ceased to be a qualified investment immediately after such grant was made.

(ii) GRANT INFORMATION NOT TREATED AS RETURN INFORMATION.—In no event shall the amount of a grant made under paragraph (1), the identity of the person to whom such grant was made, or a description of the investment with respect to which such grant was made be treated as return information for purposes of section 6103 of the Internal Revenue Code of 1986.

(6) EXCEPTION FOR CERTAIN NON-TAXPAYERS.—The Secretary of the Treasury shall not make any grant under this subsection to—

(A) any Federal, State, or local government (or any political subdivision, agency, or instrumentality thereof),

(B) any organization described in section 501(c) of the Internal Revenue Code of 1986 and exempt from tax under section 501(a) of such Code,

(C) any entity referred to in paragraph (4) of section 54(j) of such Code, or

(D) any partnership or other pass-thru entity any partner (or other holder of an equity or profits interest) of which is described in subparagraph (A), (B) or (C).

In the case of a partnership or other pass-thru entity described in subparagraph (D), partners and other holders of any equity or profits interest shall provide to such partnership or entity such information as the Secretary of the Treasury may require to carry out the purposes of this paragraph.

(7) SECRETARY.—Any reference in this subsection to the Secretary of the Treasury shall be treated as including the Secretary's delegate.

(8) OTHER TERMS.—Any term used in this subsection which is also used in section 48D of the Internal Revenue Code

of 1986 shall have the same meaning for purposes of this subsection as when used in such section.

(9) DENIAL OF DOUBLE BENEFIT.—No credit shall be allowed under section 46(6) of the Internal Revenue Code of 1986 by reason of section 48D of such Code for any investment for which a grant is awarded under this subsection.

(10) APPROPRIATIONS.—There is hereby appropriated to the Secretary of the Treasury such sums as may be necessary to carry out this subsection.

(11) TERMINATION.—The Secretary of the Treasury shall not make any grant to any person under this subsection unless the application of such person for such grant is received before January 1, 2013.

(12) PROTECTING MIDDLE CLASS FAMILIES FROM TAX INCREASES.—It is the sense of the Senate that the Senate should reject any procedural maneuver that would raise taxes on middle class families, such as a motion to commit the pending legislation to the Committee on Finance, which is designed to kill legislation that provides tax cuts for American workers and families, including the affordability tax credit and the small business tax credit.

(f) EFFECTIVE DATE.—The amendments made by subsections (a) through (d) of this section shall apply to amounts paid or incurred after December 31, 2008, in taxable years beginning after such date.

TITLE X—STRENGTHENING QUALITY, AFFORDABLE HEALTH CARE FOR ALL AMERICANS

Subtitle A—Provisions Relating to Title I

SEC. 10101. AMENDMENTS TO SUBTITLE A.

(a) Section 2711 of the Public Health Service Act, as added by section 1001(5) of this Act, is amended to read as follows:

"SEC. 2711. NO LIFETIME OR ANNUAL LIMITS.

"(a) PROHIBITION.—

"(1) IN GENERAL.—A group health plan and a health insurance issuer offering group or individual health insurance coverage may not establish—

"(A) lifetime limits on the dollar value of benefits for any participant or beneficiary; or

"(B) except as provided in paragraph (2), annual limits on the dollar value of benefits for any participant or beneficiary.

"(2) ANNUAL LIMITS PRIOR TO 2014.—With respect to plan years beginning prior to January 1, 2014, a group health plan and a health insurance issuer offering group or individual health insurance coverage may only establish a restricted annual limit on the dollar value of benefits for any participant or beneficiary with respect to the scope of benefits that are essential health benefits under section 1302(b) of the Patient

Protection and Affordable Care Act, as determined by the Secretary. In defining the term 'restricted annual limit' for purposes of the preceding sentence, the Secretary shall ensure that access to needed services is made available with a minimal impact on premiums.

"(b) PER BENEFICIARY LIMITS.—Subsection (a) shall not be construed to prevent a group health plan or health insurance coverage from placing annual or lifetime per beneficiary limits on specific covered benefits that are not essential health benefits under section 1302(b) of the Patient Protection and Affordable Care Act, to the extent that such limits are otherwise permitted under Federal or State law.".

(b) Section 2715(a) of the Public Health Service Act, as added by section 1001(5) of this Act, is amended by striking "and providing to enrollees" and inserting "and providing to applicants, enrollees, and policyholders or certificate holders".

(c) Subpart II of part A of title XXVII of the Public Health Service Act, as added by section 1001(5), is amended by inserting after section 2715, the following:

"SEC. 2715A. PROVISION OF ADDITIONAL INFORMATION.

"A group health plan and a health insurance issuer offering group or individual health insurance coverage shall comply with the provisions of section 1311(e)(3) of the Patient Protection and Affordable Care Act, except that a plan or coverage that is not offered through an Exchange shall only be required to submit the information required to the Secretary and the State insurance commissioner, and make such information available to the public.".

(d) Section 2716 of the Public Health Service Act, as added by section 1001(5) of this Act, is amended to read as follows:

"SEC. 2716. PROHIBITION ON DISCRIMINATION IN FAVOR OF HIGHLY COMPENSATED INDIVIDUALS.

"(a) IN GENERAL.—A group health plan (other than a self-insured plan) shall satisfy the requirements of section 105(h)(2) of the Internal Revenue Code of 1986 (relating to prohibition on discrimination in favor of highly compensated individuals).

"(b) RULES AND DEFINITIONS.—For purposes of this section—

"(1) CERTAIN RULES TO APPLY.—Rules similar to the rules contained in paragraphs (3), (4), and (8) of section 105(h) of such Code shall apply.

"(2) HIGHLY COMPENSATED INDIVIDUAL.—The term 'highly compensated individual' has the meaning given such term by section 105(h)(5) of such Code.".

(e) Section 2717 of the Public Health Service Act, as added by section 1001(5) of this Act, is amended—

(1) by redesignating subsections (c) and (d) as subsections (d) and (e), respectively; and

(2) by inserting after subsection (b), the following:

"(c) PROTECTION OF SECOND AMENDMENT GUN RIGHTS.—

"(1) WELLNESS AND PREVENTION PROGRAMS.—A wellness and health promotion activity implemented under subsection (a)(1)(D) may not require the disclosure or collection of any information relating to—

"(A) the presence or storage of a lawfully-possessed firearm or ammunition in the residence or on the property of an individual; or

"(B) the lawful use, possession, or storage of a firearm or ammunition by an individual.

"(2) LIMITATION ON DATA COLLECTION.—None of the authorities provided to the Secretary under the Patient Protection and Affordable Care Act or an amendment made by that Act shall be construed to authorize or may be used for the collection of any information relating to—

"(A) the lawful ownership or possession of a firearm or ammunition;

"(B) the lawful use of a firearm or ammunition; or

"(C) the lawful storage of a firearm or ammunition.

"(3) LIMITATION ON DATABASES OR DATA BANKS.—None of the authorities provided to the Secretary under the Patient Protection and Affordable Care Act or an amendment made by that Act shall be construed to authorize or may be used to maintain records of individual ownership or possession of a firearm or ammunition.

"(4) LIMITATION ON DETERMINATION OF PREMIUM RATES OR ELIGIBILITY FOR HEALTH INSURANCE.—A premium rate may not be increased, health insurance coverage may not be denied, and a discount, rebate, or reward offered for participation in a wellness program may not be reduced or withheld under any health benefit plan issued pursuant to or in accordance with the Patient Protection and Affordable Care Act or an amendment made by that Act on the basis of, or on reliance upon—

"(A) the lawful ownership or possession of a firearm or ammunition; or

"(B) the lawful use or storage of a firearm or ammunition.

"(5) LIMITATION ON DATA COLLECTION REQUIREMENTS FOR INDIVIDUALS.—No individual shall be required to disclose any information under any data collection activity authorized under the Patient Protection and Affordable Care Act or an amendment made by that Act relating to—

"(A) the lawful ownership or possession of a firearm or ammunition; or

"(B) the lawful use, possession, or storage of a firearm or ammunition.".

(f) Section 2718 of the Public Health Service Act, as added by section 1001(5), is amended to read as follows:

"SEC. 2718. BRINGING DOWN THE COST OF HEALTH CARE COVERAGE.

"(a) CLEAR ACCOUNTING FOR COSTS.—A health insurance issuer offering group or individual health insurance coverage (including a grandfathered health plan) shall, with respect to each plan year, submit to the Secretary a report concerning the ratio of the incurred loss (or incurred claims) plus the loss adjustment expense (or change in contract reserves) to earned premiums. Such report shall include the percentage of total premium revenue, after accounting for collections or receipts for risk adjustment and risk corridors and payments of reinsurance, that such coverage expends—

"(1) on reimbursement for clinical services provided to enrollees under such coverage;

"(2) for activities that improve health care quality; and

"(3) on all other non-claims costs, including an explanation of the nature of such costs, and excluding Federal and State taxes and licensing or regulatory fees.

The Secretary shall make reports received under this section available to the public on the Internet website of the Department of Health and Human Services.

"(b) ENSURING THAT CONSUMERS RECEIVE VALUE FOR THEIR PREMIUM PAYMENTS.—

"(1) REQUIREMENT TO PROVIDE VALUE FOR PREMIUM PAYMENTS.—

"(A) REQUIREMENT.—Beginning not later than January 1, 2011, a health insurance issuer offering group or individual health insurance coverage (including a grandfathered health plan) shall, with respect to each plan year, provide an annual rebate to each enrollee under such coverage, on a pro rata basis, if the ratio of the amount of premium revenue expended by the issuer on costs described in paragraphs (1) and (2) of subsection (a) to the total amount of premium revenue (excluding Federal and State taxes and licensing or regulatory fees and after accounting for payments or receipts for risk adjustment, risk corridors, and reinsurance under sections 1341, 1342, and 1343 of the Patient Protection and Affordable Care Act) for the plan year (except as provided in subparagraph (B)(ii)), is less than—

"(i) with respect to a health insurance issuer offering coverage in the large group market, 85 percent, or such higher percentage as a State may by regulation determine; or

"(ii) with respect to a health insurance issuer offering coverage in the small group market or in the individual market, 80 percent, or such higher percentage as a State may by regulation determine, except that the Secretary may adjust such percentage with respect to a State if the Secretary determines that the application of such 80 percent may destabilize the individual market in such State.

"(B) REBATE AMOUNT.—

"(i) CALCULATION OF AMOUNT.—The total amount of an annual rebate required under this paragraph shall be in an amount equal to the product of—

"(I) the amount by which the percentage described in clause (i) or (ii) of subparagraph (A) exceeds the ratio described in such subparagraph; and

"(II) the total amount of premium revenue (excluding Federal and State taxes and licensing or regulatory fees and after accounting for payments or receipts for risk adjustment, risk corridors, and reinsurance under sections 1341, 1342, and 1343 of the Patient Protection and Affordable Care Act) for such plan year.

"(ii) CALCULATION BASED ON AVERAGE RATIO.— Beginning on January 1, 2014, the determination made under subparagraph (A) for the year involved shall be based on the averages of the premiums expended on the costs described in such subparagraph and total premium revenue for each of the previous 3 years for the plan.

"(2) CONSIDERATION IN SETTING PERCENTAGES.—In determining the percentages under paragraph (1), a State shall seek to ensure adequate participation by health insurance issuers, competition in the health insurance market in the State, and value for consumers so that premiums are used for clinical services and quality improvements.

"(3) ENFORCEMENT.—The Secretary shall promulgate regulations for enforcing the provisions of this section and may provide for appropriate penalties.

"(c) DEFINITIONS.—Not later than December 31, 2010, and subject to the certification of the Secretary, the National Association of Insurance Commissioners shall establish uniform definitions of the activities reported under subsection (a) and standardized methodologies for calculating measures of such activities, including definitions of which activities, and in what regard such activities, constitute activities described in subsection (a)(2). Such methodologies shall be designed to take into account the special circumstances of smaller plans, different types of plans, and newer plans.

"(d) ADJUSTMENTS.—The Secretary may adjust the rates described in subsection (b) if the Secretary determines appropriate on account of the volatility of the individual market due to the establishment of State Exchanges.

"(e) STANDARD HOSPITAL CHARGES.—Each hospital operating within the United States shall for each year establish (and update) and make public (in accordance with guidelines developed by the Secretary) a list of the hospital's standard charges for items and services provided by the hospital, including for diagnosis-related groups established under section 1886(d)(4) of the Social Security Act.".

(g) Section 2719 of the Public Health Service Act, as added by section 1001(4) of this Act, is amended to read as follows:

"SEC. 2719. APPEALS PROCESS.

"(a) INTERNAL CLAIMS APPEALS.—

"(1) IN GENERAL.—A group health plan and a health insurance issuer offering group or individual health insurance coverage shall implement an effective appeals process for appeals of coverage determinations and claims, under which the plan or issuer shall, at a minimum—

"(A) have in effect an internal claims appeal process;

"(B) provide notice to enrollees, in a culturally and linguistically appropriate manner, of available internal and external appeals processes, and the availability of any applicable office of health insurance consumer assistance or ombudsman established under section 2793 to assist such enrollees with the appeals processes; and

"(C) allow an enrollee to review their file, to present evidence and testimony as part of the appeals process, and to receive continued coverage pending the outcome of the appeals process.

"(2) ESTABLISHED PROCESSES.—To comply with paragraph (1)—

"(A) a group health plan and a health insurance issuer offering group health coverage shall provide an internal claims and appeals process that initially incorporates the claims and appeals procedures (including urgent claims) set forth at section 2560.503–1 of title 29, Code of Federal Regulations, as published on November 21, 2000 (65 Fed. Reg. 70256), and shall update such process in accordance with any standards established by the Secretary of Labor for such plans and issuers; and

"(B) a health insurance issuer offering individual health coverage, and any other issuer not subject to subparagraph (A), shall provide an internal claims and appeals process that initially incorporates the claims and appeals procedures set forth under applicable law (as in existence on the date of enactment of this section), and shall update such process in accordance with any standards established by the Secretary of Health and Human Services for such issuers.

"(b) EXTERNAL REVIEW.—A group health plan and a health insurance issuer offering group or individual health insurance coverage—

"(1) shall comply with the applicable State external review process for such plans and issuers that, at a minimum, includes the consumer protections set forth in the Uniform External Review Model Act promulgated by the National Association of Insurance Commissioners and is binding on such plans; or

"(2) shall implement an effective external review process that meets minimum standards established by the Secretary through guidance and that is similar to the process described under paragraph (1)—

"(A) if the applicable State has not established an external review process that meets the requirements of paragraph (1); or

"(B) if the plan is a self-insured plan that is not subject to State insurance regulation (including a State law that establishes an external review process described in paragraph (1)).

"(c) SECRETARY AUTHORITY.—The Secretary may deem the external review process of a group health plan or health insurance issuer, in operation as of the date of enactment of this section, to be in compliance with the applicable process established under subsection (b), as determined appropriate by the Secretary.".

(h) Subpart II of part A of title XVIII of the Public Health Service Act, as added by section 1001(5) of this Act, is amended by inserting after section 2719 the following:

"SEC. 2719A. PATIENT PROTECTIONS.

"(a) CHOICE OF HEALTH CARE PROFESSIONAL.—If a group health plan, or a health insurance issuer offering group or individual health insurance coverage, requires or provides for designation by a participant, beneficiary, or enrollee of a participating primary care provider, then the plan or issuer shall permit each participant, beneficiary, and enrollee to designate any participating primary care provider who is available to accept such individual.

"(b) COVERAGE OF EMERGENCY SERVICES.—

"(1) IN GENERAL.—If a group health plan, or a health insurance issuer offering group or individual health insurance issuer, provides or covers any benefits with respect to services in an emergency department of a hospital, the plan or issuer shall cover emergency services (as defined in paragraph (2)(B))—

"(A) without the need for any prior authorization determination;

"(B) whether the health care provider furnishing such services is a participating provider with respect to such services;

"(C) in a manner so that, if such services are provided to a participant, beneficiary, or enrollee—

"(i) by a nonparticipating health care provider with or without prior authorization; or

"(ii)(I) such services will be provided without imposing any requirement under the plan for prior authorization of services or any limitation on coverage where the provider of services does not have a contractual relationship with the plan for the providing of services that is more restrictive than the requirements or limitations that apply to emergency department services received from providers who do have such a contractual relationship with the plan; and

"(II) if such services are provided out-of-network, the cost-sharing requirement (expressed as a copayment amount or coinsurance rate) is the same requirement that would apply if such services were provided in-network;

"(D) without regard to any other term or condition of such coverage (other than exclusion or coordination of benefits, or an affiliation or waiting period, permitted under section 2701 of this Act, section 701 of the Employee Retirement Income Security Act of 1974, or section 9801 of the Internal Revenue Code of 1986, and other than applicable cost-sharing).

"(2) DEFINITIONS.—In this subsection:

"(A) EMERGENCY MEDICAL CONDITION.—The term 'emergency medical condition' means a medical condition manifesting itself by acute symptoms of sufficient severity (including severe pain) such that a prudent layperson, who possesses an average knowledge of health and medicine, could reasonably expect the absence of immediate medical attention to result in a condition described in clause (i), (ii), or (iii) of section 1867(e)(1)(A) of the Social Security Act.

"(B) EMERGENCY SERVICES.—The term 'emergency services' means, with respect to an emergency medical condition—

"(i) a medical screening examination (as required under section 1867 of the Social Security Act) that is within the capability of the emergency department of a hospital, including ancillary services routinely available to the emergency department to evaluate such emergency medical condition, and

"(ii) within the capabilities of the staff and facilities available at the hospital, such further medical examination and treatment as are required under section 1867 of such Act to stabilize the patient.

"(C) STABILIZE.—The term 'to stabilize', with respect to an emergency medical condition (as defined in subparagraph (A)), has the meaning give in section 1867(e)(3) of the Social Security Act (42 U.S.C. 1395dd(e)(3)).

"(c) ACCESS TO PEDIATRIC CARE.—

"(1) PEDIATRIC CARE.—In the case of a person who has a child who is a participant, beneficiary, or enrollee under a group health plan, or health insurance coverage offered by a health insurance issuer in the group or individual market, if the plan or issuer requires or provides for the designation of a participating primary care provider for the child, the plan or issuer shall permit such person to designate a physician (allopathic or osteopathic) who specializes in pediatrics as the child's primary care provider if such provider participates in the network of the plan or issuer.

"(2) CONSTRUCTION.—Nothing in paragraph (1) shall be construed to waive any exclusions of coverage under the terms and conditions of the plan or health insurance coverage with respect to coverage of pediatric care.

"(d) PATIENT ACCESS TO OBSTETRICAL AND GYNECOLOGICAL CARE.—

"(1) GENERAL RIGHTS.—

"(A) DIRECT ACCESS.—A group health plan, or health insurance issuer offering group or individual health insurance coverage, described in paragraph (2) may not require authorization or referral by the plan, issuer, or any person (including a primary care provider described in paragraph (2)(B)) in the case of a female participant, beneficiary, or enrollee who seeks coverage for obstetrical or gynecological care provided by a participating health care professional who specializes in obstetrics or gynecology. Such professional shall agree to otherwise adhere to such plan's or issuer's policies and procedures, including procedures regarding referrals and obtaining prior authorization and providing services pursuant to a treatment plan (if any) approved by the plan or issuer.

"(B) OBSTETRICAL AND GYNECOLOGICAL CARE.—A group health plan or health insurance issuer described in paragraph (2) shall treat the provision of obstetrical and gynecological care, and the ordering of related obstetrical and gynecological items and services, pursuant to the direct access described under subparagraph (A), by a participating health care professional who specializes in obstetrics or gynecology as the authorization of the primary care provider.

"(2) APPLICATION OF PARAGRAPH.—A group health plan, or health insurance issuer offering group or individual health insurance coverage, described in this paragraph is a group health plan or coverage that—

"(A) provides coverage for obstetric or gynecologic care; and

"(B) requires the designation by a participant, beneficiary, or enrollee of a participating primary care provider.

"(3) CONSTRUCTION.—Nothing in paragraph (1) shall be construed to—

"(A) waive any exclusions of coverage under the terms and conditions of the plan or health insurance coverage with respect to coverage of obstetrical or gynecological care; or

"(B) preclude the group health plan or health insurance issuer involved from requiring that the obstetrical or gynecological provider notify the primary care health care professional or the plan or issuer of treatment decisions.".

(i) Section 2794 of the Public Health Service Act, as added by section 1003 of this Act, is amended—

(1) in subsection (c)(1)—

(A) in subparagraph (A), by striking "and" at the end;

(B) in subparagraph (B), by striking the period and inserting "; and"; and

(C) by adding at the end the following:

"(C) in establishing centers (consistent with subsection (d)) at academic or other nonprofit institutions to collect medical reimbursement information from health insurance issuers, to analyze and organize such information, and to make such information available to such issuers, health care providers, health researchers, health care policy makers, and the general public."; and

(2) by adding at the end the following:

"(d) MEDICAL REIMBURSEMENT DATA CENTERS.—

"(1) FUNCTIONS.—A center established under subsection (c)(1)(C) shall—

"(A) develop fee schedules and other database tools that fairly and accurately reflect market rates for medical services and the geographic differences in those rates;

"(B) use the best available statistical methods and data processing technology to develop such fee schedules and other database tools;

"(C) regularly update such fee schedules and other database tools to reflect changes in charges for medical services;

"(D) make health care cost information readily available to the public through an Internet website that allows consumers to understand the amounts that health care providers in their area charge for particular medical services; and

"(E) regularly publish information concerning the statistical methodologies used by the center to analyze health charge data and make such data available to researchers and policy makers.

"(2) CONFLICTS OF INTEREST.—A center established under subsection (c)(1)(C) shall adopt by-laws that ensures that the center (and all members of the governing board of the center) is independent and free from all conflicts of interest. Such by-laws shall ensure that the center is not controlled or influenced by, and does not have any corporate relation to, any individual or entity that may make or receive payments for health care services based on the center's analysis of health care costs.

"(3) RULE OF CONSTRUCTION.—Nothing in this subsection shall be construed to permit a center established under subsection (c)(1)(C) to compel health insurance issuers to provide data to the center.".

SEC. 10102. AMENDMENTS TO SUBTITLE B.

(a) Section 1102(a)(2)(B) of this Act is amended—

(1) in the matter preceding clause (i), by striking "group health benefits plan" and inserting "group benefits plan providing health benefits"; and

(2) in clause (i)(I), by inserting "or any agency or instrumentality of any of the foregoing" before the closed parenthetical.

(b) Section 1103(a) of this Act is amended—

(1) in paragraph (1), by inserting ", or small business in," after "residents of any"; and

(2) by striking paragraph (2) and inserting the following:

"(2) CONNECTING TO AFFORDABLE COVERAGE.—An Internet website established under paragraph (1) shall, to the extent practicable, provide ways for residents of, and small businesses in, any State to receive information on at least the following coverage options:

"(A) Health insurance coverage offered by health insurance issuers, other than coverage that provides reimbursement only for the treatment or mitigation of—

"(i) a single disease or condition; or

"(ii) an unreasonably limited set of diseases or conditions (as determined by the Secretary).

"(B) Medicaid coverage under title XIX of the Social Security Act.

"(C) Coverage under title XXI of the Social Security Act.

"(D) A State health benefits high risk pool, to the extent that such high risk pool is offered in such State; and

"(E) Coverage under a high risk pool under section 1101.

"(F) Coverage within the small group market for small businesses and their employees, including reinsurance for early retirees under section 1102, tax credits available under section 45R of the Internal Revenue Code of 1986 (as added by section 1421), and other information specifically for small businesses regarding affordable health care options.".

SEC. 10103. AMENDMENTS TO SUBTITLE C.

(a) Section 2701(a)(5) of the Public Health Service Act, as added by section 1201(4) of this Act, is amended by inserting "(other than self-insured group health plans offered in such market)" after "such market".

(b) Section 2708 of the Public Health Service Act, as added by section 1201(4) of this Act, is amended by striking "or individual".

(c) Subpart I of part A of title XXVII of the Public Health Service Act, as added by section 1201(4) of this Act, is amended by inserting after section 2708, the following:

"SEC. 2709. COVERAGE FOR INDIVIDUALS PARTICIPATING IN APPROVED CLINICAL TRIALS.

"(a) COVERAGE.—

"(1) IN GENERAL.—If a group health plan or a health insurance issuer offering group or individual health insurance coverage provides coverage to a qualified individual, then such plan or issuer—

"(A) may not deny the individual participation in the clinical trial referred to in subsection (b)(2);

"(B) subject to subsection (c), may not deny (or limit or impose additional conditions on) the coverage of routine patient costs for items and services furnished in connection with participation in the trial; and

"(C) may not discriminate against the individual on the basis of the individual's participation in such trial.

"(2) ROUTINE PATIENT COSTS.—

"(A) INCLUSION.—For purposes of paragraph (1)(B), subject to subparagraph (B), routine patient costs include all items and services consistent with the coverage provided in the plan (or coverage) that is typically covered for a qualified individual who is not enrolled in a clinical trial.

"(B) EXCLUSION.—For purposes of paragraph (1)(B), routine patient costs does not include—

"(i) the investigational item, device, or service, itself;

"(ii) items and services that are provided solely to satisfy data collection and analysis needs and that are not used in the direct clinical management of the patient; or

"(iii) a service that is clearly inconsistent with widely accepted and established standards of care for a particular diagnosis.

"(3) USE OF IN-NETWORK PROVIDERS.—If one or more participating providers is participating in a clinical trial, nothing in paragraph (1) shall be construed as preventing a plan or issuer from requiring that a qualified individual participate in the trial through such a participating provider if the provider will accept the individual as a participant in the trial.

"(4) USE OF OUT-OF-NETWORK.—Notwithstanding paragraph (3), paragraph (1) shall apply to a qualified individual participating in an approved clinical trial that is conducted outside the State in which the qualified individual resides.

"(b) QUALIFIED INDIVIDUAL DEFINED.—For purposes of subsection (a), the term 'qualified individual' means an individual who is a participant or beneficiary in a health plan or with coverage described in subsection (a)(1) and who meets the following conditions:

"(1) The individual is eligible to participate in an approved clinical trial according to the trial protocol with respect to treatment of cancer or other life-threatening disease or condition.

"(2) Either—

"(A) the referring health care professional is a participating health care provider and has concluded that the individual's participation in such trial would be appropriate based upon the individual meeting the conditions described in paragraph (1); or

"(B) the participant or beneficiary provides medical and scientific information establishing that the individual's participation in such trial would be appropriate based upon the individual meeting the conditions described in paragraph (1).

"(c) LIMITATIONS ON COVERAGE.—This section shall not be construed to require a group health plan, or a health insurance issuer offering group or individual health insurance coverage, to provide benefits for routine patient care services provided outside of the plan's (or coverage's) health care provider network unless out-of-network benefits are otherwise provided under the plan (or coverage).

"(d) APPROVED CLINICAL TRIAL DEFINED.—

"(1) IN GENERAL.—In this section, the term 'approved clinical trial' means a phase I, phase II, phase III, or phase IV clinical trial that is conducted in relation to the prevention, detection, or treatment of cancer or other life-threatening disease or condition and is described in any of the following subparagraphs:

"(A) FEDERALLY FUNDED TRIALS.—The study or investigation is approved or funded (which may include funding through in-kind contributions) by one or more of the following:

"(i) The National Institutes of Health.

"(ii) The Centers for Disease Control and Prevention.

"(iii) The Agency for Health Care Research and Quality.

"(iv) The Centers for Medicare & Medicaid Services.

"(v) cooperative group or center of any of the entities described in clauses (i) through (iv) or the Department of Defense or the Department of Veterans Affairs.

"(vi) A qualified non-governmental research entity identified in the guidelines issued by the National Institutes of Health for center support grants.

"(vii) Any of the following if the conditions described in paragraph (2) are met:

"(I) The Department of Veterans Affairs.

"(II) The Department of Defense.

"(III) The Department of Energy.

"(B) The study or investigation is conducted under an investigational new drug application reviewed by the Food and Drug Administration.

"(C) The study or investigation is a drug trial that is exempt from having such an investigational new drug application.

"(2) CONDITIONS FOR DEPARTMENTS.—The conditions described in this paragraph, for a study or investigation conducted by a Department, are that the study or investigation has been reviewed and approved through a system of peer review that the Secretary determines—

"(A) to be comparable to the system of peer review of studies and investigations used by the National Institutes of Health, and

"(B) assures unbiased review of the highest scientific standards by qualified individuals who have no interest in the outcome of the review.

"(e) LIFE-THREATENING CONDITION DEFINED.—In this section, the term 'life-threatening condition' means any disease or condition from which the likelihood of death is probable unless the course of the disease or condition is interrupted.

"(f) CONSTRUCTION.—Nothing in this section shall be construed to limit a plan's or issuer's coverage with respect to clinical trials.

"(g) APPLICATION TO FEHBP.—Notwithstanding any provision of chapter 89 of title 5, United States Code, this section shall apply to health plans offered under the program under such chapter.

"(h) PREEMPTION.—Notwithstanding any other provision of this Act, nothing in this section shall preempt State laws that require a clinical trials policy for State regulated health insurance plans that is in addition to the policy required under this section.".

(d) Section 1251(a) of this Act is amended—

(1) in paragraph (2), by striking "With" and inserting "Except as provided in paragraph (3), with"; and

(2) by adding at the end the following:

"(3) APPLICATION OF CERTAIN PROVISIONS.—The provisions of sections 2715 and 2718 of the Public Health Service Act (as added by subtitle A) shall apply to grandfathered health plans for plan years beginning on or after the date of enactment of this Act.".

(e) Section 1253 of this Act is amended insert before the period the following: ", except that—

"(1) section 1251 shall take effect on the date of enactment of this Act; and

"(2) the provisions of section 2704 of the Public Health Service Act (as amended by section 1201), as they apply to enrollees who are under 19 years of age, shall become effective for plan years beginning on or after the date that is 6 months after the date of enactment of this Act.".

(f) Subtitle C of title I of this Act is amended—

(1) by redesignating section 1253 as section 1255; and

(2) by inserting after section 1252, the following:

"SEC. 1253. ANNUAL REPORT ON SELF-INSURED PLANS.

"Not later than 1 year after the date of enactment of this Act, and annually thereafter, the Secretary of Labor shall prepare an aggregate annual report, using data collected from the Annual Return/Report of Employee Benefit Plan (Department of Labor Form 5500), that shall include general information on self-insured group health plans (including plan type, number of participants, benefits offered, funding arrangements, and benefit arrangements) as well as data from the financial filings of self-insured employers (including information on assets, liabilities, contributions, investments, and expenses). The Secretary shall submit such reports to the appropriate committees of Congress.

"SEC. 1254. STUDY OF LARGE GROUP MARKET.

"(a) IN GENERAL.—The Secretary of Health and Human Services shall conduct a study of the fully-insured and self-insured group health plan markets to—

"(1) compare the characteristics of employers (including industry, size, and other characteristics as determined appropriate by the Secretary), health plan benefits, financial solvency, capital reserve levels, and the risks of becoming insolvent; and

"(2) determine the extent to which new insurance market reforms are likely to cause adverse selection in the large group market or to encourage small and midsize employers to self-insure.

"(b) COLLECTION OF INFORMATION.—In conducting the study under subsection (a), the Secretary, in coordination with the Secretary of Labor, shall collect information and analyze—

"(1) the extent to which self-insured group health plans can offer less costly coverage and, if so, whether lower costs are due to more efficient plan administration and lower overhead or to the denial of claims and the offering very limited benefit packages;

"(2) claim denial rates, plan benefit fluctuations (to evaluate the extent that plans scale back health benefits during economic downturns), and the impact of the limited recourse options on consumers; and

"(3) any potential conflict of interest as it relates to the health care needs of self-insured enrollees and self-insured employer's financial contribution or profit margin, and the impact of such conflict on administration of the health plan.

"(c) REPORT.—Not later than 1 year after the date of enactment of this Act, the Secretary shall submit to the appropriate committees of Congress a report concerning the results of the study conducted under subsection (a).".

SEC. 10104. AMENDMENTS TO SUBTITLE D.

(a) Section 1301(a) of this Act is amended by striking paragraph (2) and inserting the following:

"(2) INCLUSION OF CO–OP PLANS AND MULTI-STATE QUALIFIED HEALTH PLANS.—Any reference in this title to a qualified health plan shall be deemed to include a qualified health plan offered through the CO–OP program under section 1322, and a multi-State plan under section 1334, unless specifically provided for otherwise.

"(3) TREATMENT OF QUALIFIED DIRECT PRIMARY CARE MEDICAL HOME PLANS.—The Secretary of Health and Human Services shall permit a qualified health plan to provide coverage through a qualified direct primary care medical home plan that meets criteria established by the Secretary, so long as the qualified health plan meets all requirements that are otherwise applicable and the services covered by the medical home plan are coordinated with the entity offering the qualified health plan.

"(4) VARIATION BASED ON RATING AREA.—A qualified health plan, including a multi-State qualified health plan, may as appropriate vary premiums by rating area (as defined in section 2701(a)(2) of the Public Health Service Act).".

(b) Section 1302 of this Act is amended—

(1) in subsection (d)(2)(B), by striking "may issue" and inserting "shall issue"; and

(2) by adding at the end the following:

"(g) PAYMENTS TO FEDERALLY-QUALIFIED HEALTH CENTERS.—If any item or service covered by a qualified health plan is provided by a Federally-qualified health center (as defined in section 1905(l)(2)(B) of the Social Security Act (42 U.S.C. 1396d(l)(2)(B)) to an enrollee of the plan, the offeror of the plan shall pay to the center for the item or service an amount that is not less than the amount of payment that would have been paid to the center under section 1902(bb) of such Act (42 U.S.C. 1396a(bb)) for such item or service.".

(c) Section 1303 of this Act is amended to read as follows:

"SEC. 1303. SPECIAL RULES.

"(a) STATE OPT-OUT OF ABORTION COVERAGE.—

"(1) IN GENERAL.—A State may elect to prohibit abortion coverage in qualified health plans offered through an Exchange in such State if such State enacts a law to provide for such prohibition.

"(2) TERMINATION OF OPT OUT.—A State may repeal a law described in paragraph (1) and provide for the offering of such services through the Exchange.

"(b) SPECIAL RULES RELATING TO COVERAGE OF ABORTION SERVICES.—

"(1) VOLUNTARY CHOICE OF COVERAGE OF ABORTION SERVICES.—

"(A) IN GENERAL.—Notwithstanding any other provision of this title (or any amendment made by this title)—

"(i) nothing in this title (or any amendment made by this title), shall be construed to require a qualified health plan to provide coverage of services described in subparagraph (B)(i) or (B)(ii) as part of its essential health benefits for any plan year; and

"(ii) subject to subsection (a), the issuer of a qualified health plan shall determine whether or not the plan provides coverage of services described in subparagraph (B)(i) or (B)(ii) as part of such benefits for the plan year.

"(B) ABORTION SERVICES.—

"(i) ABORTIONS FOR WHICH PUBLIC FUNDING IS PROHIBITED.—The services described in this clause are abortions for which the expenditure of Federal funds appropriated for the Department of Health and Human Services is not permitted, based on the law as in effect as of the date that is 6 months before the beginning of the plan year involved.

"(ii) ABORTIONS FOR WHICH PUBLIC FUNDING IS ALLOWED.—The services described in this clause are abortions for which the expenditure of Federal funds appropriated for the Department of Health and Human Services is permitted, based on the law as in effect as of the date that is 6 months before the beginning of the plan year involved.

"(2) PROHIBITION ON THE USE OF FEDERAL FUNDS.—

"(A) IN GENERAL.—If a qualified health plan provides coverage of services described in paragraph (1)(B)(i), the issuer of the plan shall not use any amount attributable to any of the following for purposes of paying for such services:

"(i) The credit under section 36B of the Internal Revenue Code of 1986 (and the amount (if any) of the advance payment of the credit under section 1412 of the Patient Protection and Affordable Care Act).

"(ii) Any cost-sharing reduction under section 1402 of the Patient Protection and Affordable Care Act (and the amount (if any) of the advance payment of the reduction under section 1412 of the Patient Protection and Affordable Care Act).

"(B) ESTABLISHMENT OF ALLOCATION ACCOUNTS.—In the case of a plan to which subparagraph (A) applies, the issuer of the plan shall—

"(i) collect from each enrollee in the plan (without regard to the enrollee's age, sex, or family status) a separate payment for each of the following:

"(I) an amount equal to the portion of the premium to be paid directly by the enrollee for coverage under the plan of services other than services described in paragraph (1)(B)(i) (after reduction for credits and cost-sharing reductions described in subparagraph (A)); and

"(II) an amount equal to the actuarial value of the coverage of services described in paragraph (1)(B)(i), and

"(ii) shall deposit all such separate payments into separate allocation accounts as provided in subparagraph (C).

In the case of an enrollee whose premium for coverage under the plan is paid through employee payroll deposit, the separate payments required under this subparagraph shall each be paid by a separate deposit.

"(C) SEGREGATION OF FUNDS.—

"(i) IN GENERAL.—The issuer of a plan to which subparagraph (A) applies shall establish allocation accounts described in clause (ii) for enrollees receiving amounts described in subparagraph (A).

"(ii) ALLOCATION ACCOUNTS.—The issuer of a plan to which subparagraph (A) applies shall deposit—

"(I) all payments described in subparagraph (B)(i)(I) into a separate account that consists solely of such payments and that is used exclusively to pay for services other than services described in paragraph (1)(B)(i); and

"(II) all payments described in subparagraph (B)(i)(II) into a separate account that consists solely of such payments and that is used exclusively to pay for services described in paragraph (1)(B)(i).

"(D) ACTUARIAL VALUE.—

"(i) IN GENERAL.—The issuer of a qualified health plan shall estimate the basic per enrollee, per month cost, determined on an average actuarial basis, for including coverage under the qualified health plan of the services described in paragraph (1)(B)(i).

"(ii) CONSIDERATIONS.—In making such estimate, the issuer—

"(I) may take into account the impact on overall costs of the inclusion of such coverage, but may not take into account any cost reduction estimated to result from such services, including prenatal care, delivery, or postnatal care;

"(II) shall estimate such costs as if such coverage were included for the entire population covered; and

"(III) may not estimate such a cost at less than $1 per enrollee, per month.

"(E) ENSURING COMPLIANCE WITH SEGREGATION REQUIREMENTS.—

"(i) IN GENERAL.—Subject to clause (ii), State health insurance commissioners shall ensure that health plans comply with the segregation requirements in this subsection through the segregation of plan funds in accordance with applicable provisions of generally accepted accounting requirements, circulars on funds management of the Office of Management and Budget, and guidance on accounting of the Government Accountability Office.

"(ii) CLARIFICATION.—Nothing in clause (i) shall prohibit the right of an individual or health plan to appeal such action in courts of competent jurisdiction.

"(3) RULES RELATING TO NOTICE.—

"(A) NOTICE.—A qualified health plan that provides for coverage of the services described in paragraph (1)(B)(i) shall provide a notice to enrollees, only as part of the summary of benefits and coverage explanation, at the time of enrollment, of such coverage.

"(B) RULES RELATING TO PAYMENTS.—The notice described in subparagraph (A), any advertising used by the issuer with respect to the plan, any information provided by the Exchange, and any other information specified by the Secretary shall provide information only with respect to the total amount of the combined payments for services described in paragraph (1)(B)(i) and other services covered by the plan.

"(4) NO DISCRIMINATION ON BASIS OF PROVISION OF ABORTION.—No qualified health plan offered through an Exchange may discriminate against any individual health care provider or health care facility because of its unwillingness to provide, pay for, provide coverage of, or refer for abortions

"(c) APPLICATION OF STATE AND FEDERAL LAWS REGARDING ABORTION.—

"(1) NO PREEMPTION OF STATE LAWS REGARDING ABORTION.—Nothing in this Act shall be construed to preempt or otherwise have any effect on State laws regarding the prohibition of (or requirement of) coverage, funding, or procedural requirements on abortions, including parental notification or consent for the performance of an abortion on a minor.

"(2) NO EFFECT ON FEDERAL LAWS REGARDING ABORTION.—

"(A) IN GENERAL.—Nothing in this Act shall be construed to have any effect on Federal laws regarding—

"(i) conscience protection;

"(ii) willingness or refusal to provide abortion; and

"(iii) discrimination on the basis of the willingness or refusal to provide, pay for, cover, or refer for abortion or to provide or participate in training to provide abortion.

"(3) NO EFFECT ON FEDERAL CIVIL RIGHTS LAW.—Nothing in this subsection shall alter the rights and obligations of employees and employers under title VII of the Civil Rights Act of 1964.

"(d) APPLICATION OF EMERGENCY SERVICES LAWS.—Nothing in this Act shall be construed to relieve any health care provider from providing emergency services as required by State or Federal law, including section 1867 of the Social Security Act (popularly known as 'EMTALA').".

(d) Section 1304 of this Act is amended by adding at the end the following:

"(e) EDUCATED HEALTH CARE CONSUMERS.—The term 'educated health care consumer' means an individual who is knowledgeable about the health care system, and has background or experience in making informed decisions regarding health, medical, and scientific matters.".

(e) Section 1311(d) of this Act is amended—

(1) in paragraph (3)(B), by striking clause (ii) and inserting the following:

"(ii) STATE MUST ASSUME COST.—A State shall make payments—

"(I) to an individual enrolled in a qualified health plan offered in such State; or

"(II) on behalf of an individual described in subclause (I) directly to the qualified health plan in which such individual is enrolled;

to defray the cost of any additional benefits described in clause (i)."; and

(2) in paragraph (6)(A), by inserting "educated" before "health care".

(f) Section 1311(e) of this Act is amended—

(1) in paragraph (2), by striking "may" in the second sentence and inserting "shall"; and

(2) by adding at the end the following:

"(3) TRANSPARENCY IN COVERAGE.—

"(A) IN GENERAL.—The Exchange shall require health plans seeking certification as qualified health plans to submit to the Exchange, the Secretary, the State insurance commissioner, and make available to the public, accurate and timely disclosure of the following information:

"(i) Claims payment policies and practices.

"(ii) Periodic financial disclosures.

"(iii) Data on enrollment.

"(iv) Data on disenrollment.

"(v) Data on the number of claims that are denied.

"(vi) Data on rating practices.

"(vii) Information on cost-sharing and payments with respect to any out-of-network coverage.

"(viii) Information on enrollee and participant rights under this title.

"(ix) Other information as determined appropriate by the Secretary.

"(B) USE OF PLAIN LANGUAGE.—The information required to be submitted under subparagraph (A) shall be provided in plain language. The term 'plain language' means language that the intended audience, including individuals with limited English proficiency, can readily understand and use because that language is concise, well-organized, and follows other best practices of plain language writing. The Secretary and the Secretary of Labor shall jointly develop and issue guidance on best practices of plain language writing.

"(C) COST SHARING TRANSPARENCY.—The Exchange shall require health plans seeking certification as qualified health plans to permit individuals to learn the amount of cost-sharing (including deductibles, copayments, and coinsurance) under the individual's plan or coverage that the individual would be responsible for paying with respect to the furnishing of a specific item or service by a participating provider in a timely manner upon the request of the individual. At a minimum, such information shall be made available to such individual through an Internet website and such other means for individuals without access to the Internet.

"(D) GROUP HEALTH PLANS.—The Secretary of Labor shall update and harmonize the Secretary's rules concerning the accurate and timely disclosure to participants by group health plans of plan disclosure, plan terms and conditions, and periodic financial disclosure with the standards established by the Secretary under subparagraph (A).".

(g) Section 1311(g)(1) of this Act is amended—

(1) in subparagraph (C), by striking "; and" and inserting a semicolon;

(2) in subparagraph (D), by striking the period and inserting "; and"; and

(3) by adding at the end the following:

"(E) the implementation of activities to reduce health and health care disparities, including through the use of language services, community outreach, and cultural competency trainings.".

(h) Section 1311(i)(2)((B) of this Act is amended by striking "small business development centers" and inserting "resource partners of the Small Business Administration".

(i) Section 1312 of this Act is amended—

(1) in subsection (a)(1), by inserting "and for which such individual is eligible" before the period;

(2) in subsection (e)—

(A) in paragraph (1), by inserting "and employers" after "enroll individuals"; and

(B) by striking the flush sentence at the end; and

(3) in subsection (f)(1)(A)(ii), by striking the parenthetical.

(j)(1) Subparagraph (B) of section 1313(a)(6) of this Act is hereby deemed null, void, and of no effect.

(2) Section 3730(e) of title 31, United States Code, is amended by striking paragraph (4) and inserting the following:

"(4)(A) The court shall dismiss an action or claim under this section, unless opposed by the Government, if substantially the same allegations or transactions as alleged in the action or claim were publicly disclosed—

"(i) in a Federal criminal, civil, or administrative hearing in which the Government or its agent is a party;

"(ii) in a congressional, Government Accountability Office, or other Federal report, hearing, audit, or investigation; or

"(iii) from the news media,

unless the action is brought by the Attorney General or the person bringing the action is an original source of the information.

"(B) For purposes of this paragraph, "original source" means an individual who either (i) prior to a public disclosure under subsection (e)(4)(a), has voluntarily disclosed to the

Government the information on which allegations or transactions in a claim are based, or (2) who has knowledge that is independent of and materially adds to the publicly disclosed allegations or transactions, and who has voluntarily provided the information to the Government before filing an action under this section.".

(k) Section 1313(b) of this Act is amended—

(1) in paragraph (3), by striking "and" at the end;

(2) by redesignating paragraph (4) as paragraph (5); and

(3) by inserting after paragraph (3) the following:

"(4) a survey of the cost and affordability of health care insurance provided under the Exchanges for owners and employees of small business concerns (as defined under section 3 of the Small Business Act (15 U.S.C. 632)), including data on enrollees in Exchanges and individuals purchasing health insurance coverage outside of Exchanges; and".

(l) Section 1322(b) of this Act is amended—

(1) by redesignating paragraph (3) as paragraph (4); and

(2) by inserting after paragraph (2), the following:

"(3) REPAYMENT OF LOANS AND GRANTS.—Not later than July 1, 2013, and prior to awarding loans and grants under the CO–OP program, the Secretary shall promulgate regulations with respect to the repayment of such loans and grants in a manner that is consistent with State solvency regulations and other similar State laws that may apply. In promulgating such regulations, the Secretary shall provide that such loans shall be repaid within 5 years and such grants shall be repaid within 15 years, taking into consideration any appropriate State reserve requirements, solvency regulations, and requisite surplus note arrangements that must be constructed in a State to provide for such repayment prior to awarding such loans and grants.".

(m) Part III of subtitle D of title I of this Act is amended by striking section 1323.

(n) Section 1324(a) of this Act is amended by striking ", a community health" and all that follows through "1333(b)" and inserting ", or a multi-State qualified health plan under section 1334".

(o) Section 1331 of this Act is amended—

(1) in subsection (d)(3)(A)(i), by striking "85" and inserting "95"; and

(2) in subsection (e)(1)(B), by inserting before the semicolon the following: ", or, in the case of an alien lawfully present in the United States, whose income is not greater than 133 percent of the poverty line for the size of the family involved but who is not eligible for the Medicaid program under title XIX of the Social Security Act by reason of such alien status".

(p) Section 1333 of this Act is amended by striking subsection (b).

(q) Part IV of subtitle D of title I of this Act is amended by adding at the end the following:

"SEC. 1334. MULTI-STATE PLANS.

"(a) OVERSIGHT BY THE OFFICE OF PERSONNEL MANAGEMENT.—

"(1) IN GENERAL.—The Director of the Office of Personnel Management (referred to in this section as the 'Director') shall enter into contracts with health insurance issuers (which may include a group of health insurance issuers affiliated either by common ownership and control or by the common use of a nationally licensed service mark), without regard to section 5 of title 41, United States Code, or other statutes requiring competitive bidding, to offer at least 2 multi-State qualified health plans through each Exchange in each State. Such plans shall provide individual, or in the case of small employers, group coverage.

"(2) TERMS.—Each contract entered into under paragraph (1) shall be for a uniform term of at least 1 year, but may be made automatically renewable from term to term in the absence of notice of termination by either party. In entering into such contracts, the Director shall ensure that health benefits coverage is provided in accordance with the types of coverage provided for under section 2701(a)(1)(A)(i) of the Public Health Service Act.

"(3) NON-PROFIT ENTITIES.—In entering into contracts under paragraph (1), the Director shall ensure that at least one contract is entered into with a non-profit entity.

"(4) ADMINISTRATION.—The Director shall implement this subsection in a manner similar to the manner in which the Director implements the contracting provisions with respect to carriers under the Federal employees health benefit program under chapter 89 of title 5, United States Code, including (through negotiating with each multi-state plan)—

"(A) a medical loss ratio;

"(B) a profit margin;

"(C) the premiums to be charged; and

"(D) such other terms and conditions of coverage as are in the interests of enrollees in such plans.

"(5) AUTHORITY TO PROTECT CONSUMERS.—The Director may prohibit the offering of any multi-State health plan that does not meet the terms and conditions defined by the Director with respect to the elements described in subparagraphs (A) through (D) of paragraph (4).

"(6) ASSURED AVAILABILITY OF VARIED COVERAGE.—In entering into contracts under this subsection, the Director shall ensure that with respect to multi-State qualified health plans offered in an Exchange, there is at least one such plan that does not provide coverage of services described in section 1303(b)(1)(B)(i).

"(7) WITHDRAWAL.—Approval of a contract under this subsection may be withdrawn by the Director only after notice and opportunity for hearing to the issuer concerned without regard to subchapter II of chapter 5 and chapter 7 of title 5, United States Code.

"(b) ELIGIBILITY.—A health insurance issuer shall be eligible to enter into a contract under subsection (a)(1) if such issuer—

"(1) agrees to offer a multi-State qualified health plan that meets the requirements of subsection (c) in each Exchange in each State;

"(2) is licensed in each State and is subject to all requirements of State law not inconsistent with this section, including the standards and requirements that a State imposes that do not prevent the application of a requirement of part A of title XXVII of the Public Health Service Act or a requirement of this title;

"(3) otherwise complies with the minimum standards prescribed for carriers offering health benefits plans under section 8902(e) of title 5, United States Code, to the extent that such standards do not conflict with a provision of this title; and

"(4) meets such other requirements as determined appropriate by the Director, in consultation with the Secretary.

"(c) REQUIREMENTS FOR MULTI-STATE QUALIFIED HEALTH PLAN.—

"(1) IN GENERAL.—A multi-State qualified health plan meets the requirements of this subsection if, in the determination of the Director—

"(A) the plan offers a benefits package that is uniform in each State and consists of the essential benefits described in section 1302;

"(B) the plan meets all requirements of this title with respect to a qualified health plan, including requirements relating to the offering of the bronze, silver, and gold levels of coverage and catastrophic coverage in each State Exchange;

"(C) except as provided in paragraph (5), the issuer provides for determinations of premiums for coverage under the plan on the basis of the rating requirements of part A of title XXVII of the Public Health Service Act; and

"(D) the issuer offers the plan in all geographic regions, and in all States that have adopted adjusted community rating before the date of enactment of this Act.

"(2) STATES MAY OFFER ADDITIONAL BENEFITS.—Nothing in paragraph (1)(A) shall preclude a State from requiring that benefits in addition to the essential health benefits required under such paragraph be provided to enrollees of a multi-State qualified health plan offered in such State.

"(3) CREDITS.—

"(A) IN GENERAL.—An individual enrolled in a multi-State qualified health plan under this section shall be eligible for credits under section 36B of the Internal Revenue Code of 1986 and cost sharing assistance under section 1402 in the same manner as an individual who is enrolled in a qualified health plan.

"(B) NO ADDITIONAL FEDERAL COST.—A requirement by a State under paragraph (2) that benefits in addition to the essential health benefits required under paragraph (1)(A) be provided to enrollees of a multi-State qualified health plan shall not affect the amount of a premium tax credit provided under section 36B of the Internal Revenue Code of 1986 with respect to such plan.

"(4) STATE MUST ASSUME COST.—A State shall make payments—

"(A) to an individual enrolled in a multi-State qualified health plan offered in such State; or

"(B) on behalf of an individual described in subparagraph (A) directly to the multi-State qualified health plan in which such individual is enrolled;

to defray the cost of any additional benefits described in paragraph (2).

"(5) APPLICATION OF CERTAIN STATE RATING REQUIREMENTS.—With respect to a multi-State qualified health plan that is offered in a State with age rating requirements that are lower than 3:1, the State may require that Exchanges operating in such State only permit the offering of such multi-State qualified health plans if such plans comply with the State's more protective age rating requirements.

"(d) PLANS DEEMED TO BE CERTIFIED.—A multi-State qualified health plan that is offered under a contract under subsection (a) shall be deemed to be certified by an Exchange for purposes of section 1311(d)(4)(A).

"(e) PHASE-IN.—Notwithstanding paragraphs (1) and (2) of subsection (b), the Director shall enter into a contract with a health insurance issuer for the offering of a multi-State qualified health plan under subsection (a) if—

"(1) with respect to the first year for which the issuer offers such plan, such issuer offers the plan in at least 60 percent of the States;

"(2) with respect to the second such year, such issuer offers the plan in at least 70 percent of the States;

"(3) with respect to the third such year, such issuer offers the plan in at least 85 percent of the States; and

"(4) with respect to each subsequent year, such issuer offers the plan in all States.

"(f) APPLICABILITY.—The requirements under chapter 89 of title 5, United States Code, applicable to health benefits plans under such chapter shall apply to multi-State qualified health plans provided for under this section to the extent that such requirements do not conflict with a provision of this title.

"(g) CONTINUED SUPPORT FOR FEHBP.—

"(1) MAINTENANCE OF EFFORT.—Nothing in this section shall be construed to permit the Director to allocate fewer financial or personnel resources to the functions of the Office of Personnel Management related to the administration of the Federal Employees Health Benefit Program under chapter 89 of title 5, United States Code.

"(2) SEPARATE RISK POOL.—Enrollees in multi-State qualified health plans under this section shall be treated as a separate risk pool apart from enrollees in the Federal Employees Health Benefit Program under chapter 89 of title 5, United States Code.

"(3) AUTHORITY TO ESTABLISH SEPARATE ENTITIES.—The Director may establish such separate units or offices within the Office of Personnel Management as the Director determines to be appropriate to ensure that the administration of multi-State qualified health plans under this section does not interfere with the effective administration of the Federal Employees Health Benefit Program under chapter 89 of title 5, United States Code.

"(4) EFFECTIVE OVERSIGHT.—The Director may appoint such additional personnel as may be necessary to enable the Director to carry out activities under this section.

"(5) ASSURANCE OF SEPARATE PROGRAM.—In carrying out this section, the Director shall ensure that the program under this section is separate from the Federal Employees Health Benefit Program under chapter 89 of title 5, United States Code. Premiums paid for coverage under a multi-State qualified health plan under this section shall not be considered to be Federal funds for any purposes.

"(6) FEHBP PLANS NOT REQUIRED TO PARTICIPATE.—Nothing in this section shall require that a carrier offering coverage under the Federal Employees Health Benefit Program under chapter 89 of title 5, United States Code, also offer a multi-State qualified health plan under this section.

"(h) ADVISORY BOARD.—The Director shall establish an advisory board to provide recommendations on the activities described in this section. A significant percentage of the members of such board shall be comprised of enrollees in a multi-State qualified health plan, or representatives of such enrollees.

"(i) AUTHORIZATION OF APPROPRIATIONS.—There is authorized to be appropriated, such sums as may be necessary to carry out this section.".

(r) Section 1341 of this Act is amended—

(1) in the section heading, by striking "**AND SMALL GROUP MARKETS**" and inserting "**MARKET**";

(2) in subsection (b)(2)(B), by striking "paragraph (1)(A)" and inserting "paragraph (1)(B)"; and

(3) in subsection (c)(1)(A), by striking "and small group markets" and inserting "market".

SEC. 10105. AMENDMENTS TO SUBTITLE E.

(a) Section 36B(b)(3)(A)(ii) of the Internal Revenue Code of 1986, as added by section 1401(a) of this Act, is amended by striking "is in excess of" and inserting "equals or exceeds".

(b) Section 36B(c)(1)(A) of the Internal Revenue Code of 1986, as added by section 1401(a) of this Act, is amended by inserting "equals or" before "exceeds".

(c) Section 36B(c)(2)(C)(iv) of the Internal Revenue Code of 1986, as added by section 1401(a) of this Act, is amended by striking "subsection (b)(3)(A)(ii)" and inserting "subsection (b)(3)(A)(iii)".

(d) Section 1401(d) of this Act is amended by adding at the end the following:

"(3) Section 6211(b)(4)(A) of the Internal Revenue Code of 1986 is amended by inserting '36B,' after '36A,'.".

(e)(1) Subparagraph (B) of section 45R(d)(3) of the Internal Revenue Code of 1986, as added by section 1421(a) of this Act, is amended to read as follows:

"(B) DOLLAR AMOUNT.—For purposes of paragraph (1)(B) and subsection (c)(2)—

"(i) 2010, 2011, 2012, AND 2013.—The dollar amount in effect under this paragraph for taxable years beginning in 2010, 2011, 2012, or 2013 is $25,000.

"(ii) SUBSEQUENT YEARS.—In the case of a taxable year beginning in a calendar year after 2013, the dollar amount in effect under this paragraph shall be equal to $25,000, multiplied by the cost-of-living adjustment under section 1(f)(3) for the calendar year, determined by substituting 'calendar year 2012' for 'calendar year 1992' in subparagraph (B) thereof.".

(2) Subsection (g) of section 45R of the Internal Revenue Code of 1986, as added by section 1421(a) of this Act, is amended by striking "2011" both places it appears and inserting "2010, 2011".

(3) Section 280C(h) of the Internal Revenue Code of 1986, as added by section 1421(d)(1) of this Act, is amended by striking "2011" and inserting "2010, 2011".

(4) Section 1421(f) of this Act is amended by striking "2010" both places it appears and inserting "2009".

(5) The amendments made by this subsection shall take effect as if included in the enactment of section 1421 of this Act.

(f) Part I of subtitle E of title I of this Act is amended by adding at the end of subpart B, the following:

"SEC. 1416. STUDY OF GEOGRAPHIC VARIATION IN APPLICATION OF FPL.

"(a) IN GENERAL.—The Secretary shall conduct a study to examine the feasibility and implication of adjusting the application of the Federal poverty level under this subtitle (and the amendments made by this subtitle) for different geographic areas so as to reflect the variations in cost-of-living among different areas within the United States. If the Secretary determines that an adjustment is feasible, the study should include a methodology to make such an adjustment. Not later than January 1, 2013, the Secretary shall submit to Congress a report on such study and shall include such recommendations as the Secretary determines appropriate.

"(b) INCLUSION OF TERRITORIES.—

"(1) IN GENERAL.—The Secretary shall ensure that the study under subsection (a) covers the territories of the United States and that special attention is paid to the disparity that exists among poverty levels and the cost of living in such territories and to the impact of such disparity on efforts to expand health coverage and ensure health care.

"(2) TERRITORIES DEFINED.—In this subsection, the term 'territories of the United States' includes the Commonwealth of Puerto Rico, the United States Virgin Islands, Guam, the Northern Mariana Islands, and any other territory or possession of the United States.".

SEC. 10106. AMENDMENTS TO SUBTITLE F.

(a) Section 1501(a)(2) of this Act is amended to read as follows:

"(2) EFFECTS ON THE NATIONAL ECONOMY AND INTERSTATE COMMERCE.—The effects described in this paragraph are the following:

"(A) The requirement regulates activity that is commercial and economic in nature: economic and financial decisions about how and when health care is paid for, and when health insurance is purchased. In the absence of the requirement, some individuals would make an economic and financial decision to forego health insurance coverage and attempt to self-insure, which increases financial risks to households and medical providers.

"(B) Health insurance and health care services are a significant part of the national economy. National health spending is projected to increase from $2,500,000,000,000, or 17.6 percent of the economy, in 2009 to $4,700,000,000,000 in 2019. Private health insurance spending is projected to be $854,000,000,000 in 2009, and pays for medical supplies, drugs, and equipment that are shipped in interstate commerce. Since most health insurance is sold by national or regional health insurance companies, health insurance is sold in interstate commerce and claims payments flow through interstate commerce.

"(C) The requirement, together with the other provisions of this Act, will add millions of new consumers to the health insurance market, increasing the supply of, and demand for, health care services, and will increase the number and share of Americans who are insured.

"(D) The requirement achieves near-universal coverage by building upon and strengthening the private employer-based health insurance system, which covers 176,000,000 Americans nationwide. In Massachusetts, a similar requirement has strengthened private employer-based coverage: despite the economic downturn, the number of workers offered employer-based coverage has actually increased.

"(E) The economy loses up to $207,000,000,000 a year because of the poorer health and shorter lifespan of the uninsured. By significantly reducing the number of the uninsured, the requirement, together with the other provisions of this Act, will significantly reduce this economic cost.

"(F) The cost of providing uncompensated care to the uninsured was $43,000,000,000 in 2008. To pay for this cost, health care providers pass on the cost to private insurers, which pass on the cost to families. This cost-shifting increases family premiums by on average over $1,000 a year. By significantly reducing the number of the uninsured, the requirement, together with the other provisions of this Act, will lower health insurance premiums.

"(G) 62 percent of all personal bankruptcies are caused in part by medical expenses. By significantly increasing health insurance coverage, the requirement, together with the other provisions of this Act, will improve financial security for families.

"(H) Under the Employee Retirement Income Security Act of 1974 (29 U.S.C. 1001 et seq.), the Public Health Service Act (42 U.S.C. 201 et seq.), and this Act, the Federal Government has a significant role in regulating health insurance. The requirement is an essential part of this larger regulation of economic activity, and the absence of the requirement would undercut Federal regulation of the health insurance market.

"(I) Under sections 2704 and 2705 of the Public Health Service Act (as added by section 1201 of this Act), if there were no requirement, many individuals would wait to purchase health insurance until they needed care. By significantly increasing health insurance coverage, the requirement, together with the other provisions of this Act, will minimize this adverse selection and broaden the health insurance risk pool to include healthy individuals, which will lower health insurance premiums. The requirement is essential to creating effective health insurance markets in which improved health insurance products that are guaranteed issue and do not exclude coverage of pre-existing conditions can be sold.

"(J) Administrative costs for private health insurance, which were $90,000,000,000 in 2006, are 26 to 30 percent of premiums in the current individual and small group markets. By significantly increasing health insurance coverage and the size of purchasing pools, which will increase economies of scale, the requirement, together with the other provisions of this Act, will significantly reduce administrative costs and lower health insurance premiums. The requirement is essential to creating effective health insurance markets that do not require underwriting and eliminate its associated administrative costs.".

(b)(1) Section 5000A(b)(1) of the Internal Revenue Code of 1986, as added by section 1501(b) of this Act, is amended to read as follows:

"(1) IN GENERAL.—If a taxpayer who is an applicable individual, or an applicable individual for whom the taxpayer is liable under paragraph (3), fails to meet the requirement of subsection (a) for 1 or more months, then, except as provided in subsection (e), there is hereby imposed on the taxpayer a penalty with respect to such failures in the amount determined under subsection (c).".

(2) Paragraphs (1) and (2) of section 5000A(c) of the Internal Revenue Code of 1986, as so added, are amended to read as follows:

"(1) IN GENERAL.—The amount of the penalty imposed by this section on any taxpayer for any taxable year with respect to failures described in subsection (b)(1) shall be equal to the lesser of—

"(A) the sum of the monthly penalty amounts determined under paragraph (2) for months in the taxable year during which 1 or more such failures occurred, or

"(B) an amount equal to the national average premium for qualified health plans which have a bronze level of coverage, provide coverage for the applicable family size involved, and are offered through Exchanges for plan years beginning in the calendar year with or within which the taxable year ends.

"(2) MONTHLY PENALTY AMOUNTS.—For purposes of paragraph (1)(A), the monthly penalty amount with respect to any taxpayer for any month during which any failure described in subsection (b)(1) occurred is an amount equal to 1⁄12 of the greater of the following amounts:

"(A) FLAT DOLLAR AMOUNT.—An amount equal to the lesser of—

"(i) the sum of the applicable dollar amounts for all individuals with respect to whom such failure occurred during such month, or

"(ii) 300 percent of the applicable dollar amount (determined without regard to paragraph (3)(C)) for the calendar year with or within which the taxable year ends.

"(B) PERCENTAGE OF INCOME.—An amount equal to the following percentage of the taxpayer's household income for the taxable year:

"(i) 0.5 percent for taxable years beginning in 2014.

"(ii) 1.0 percent for taxable years beginning in 2015.

"(iii) 2.0 percent for taxable years beginning after 2015.".

(3) Section 5000A(c)(3) of the Internal Revenue Code of 1986, as added by section 1501(b) of this Act, is amended by striking "$350" and inserting "$495".

(c) Section 5000A(d)(2)(A) of the Internal Revenue Code of 1986, as added by section 1501(b) of this Act, is amended to read as follows:

"(A) RELIGIOUS CONSCIENCE EXEMPTION.—Such term shall not include any individual for any month if such individual has in effect an exemption under section 1311(d)(4)(H) of the Patient Protection and Affordable Care Act which certifies that such individual is—

"(i) a member of a recognized religious sect or division thereof which is described in section 1402(g)(1), and

"(ii) an adherent of established tenets or teachings of such sect or division as described in such section.".

(d) Section 5000A(e)(1)(C) of the Internal Revenue Code of 1986, as added by section 1501(b) of this Act, is amended to read as follows:

"(C) SPECIAL RULES FOR INDIVIDUALS RELATED TO EMPLOYEES.—For purposes of subparagraph (B)(i), if an applicable individual is eligible for minimum essential coverage through an employer by reason of a relationship to an employee, the determination under subparagraph (A) shall be made by reference to required contribution of the employee.".

(e) Section 4980H(b) of the Internal Revenue Code of 1986, as added by section 1513(a) of this Act, is amended to read as follows:

"(b) LARGE EMPLOYERS WITH WAITING PERIODS EXCEEDING 60 DAYS.—

"(1) IN GENERAL.—In the case of any applicable large employer which requires an extended waiting period to enroll in any minimum essential coverage under an employer-sponsored plan (as defined in section 5000A(f)(2)), there is hereby imposed on the employer an assessable payment of $600 for each full-time employee of the employer to whom the extended waiting period applies.

"(2) EXTENDED WAITING PERIOD.—The term 'extended waiting period' means any waiting period (as defined in section 2701(b)(4) of the Public Health Service Act) which exceeds 60 days.".

(f)(1) Subparagraph (A) of section 4980H(d)(4) of the Internal Revenue Code of 1986, as added by section 1513(a) of this Act, is amended by inserting ", with respect to any month," after "means".

(2) Section 4980H(d)(2) of the Internal Revenue Code of 1986, as added by section 1513(a) of this Act, is amended by adding at the end the following:

"(D) APPLICATION TO CONSTRUCTION INDUSTRY EMPLOYERS.—In the case of any employer the substantial annual gross receipts of which are attributable to the construction industry—

"(i) subparagraph (A) shall be applied by substituting 'who employed an average of at least 5 full-time employees on business days during the preceding calendar year and whose annual payroll expenses exceed $250,000 for such preceding calendar year' for 'who employed an average of at least 50 full-time employees on business days during the preceding calendar year', and

"(ii) subparagraph (B) shall be applied by substituting '5' for '50'.".

(3) The amendment made by paragraph (2) shall apply to months beginning after December 31, 2013.

(g) Section 6056(b) of the Internal Revenue Code of 1986, as added by section 1514(a) of the Act, is amended by adding at the end the following new flush sentence:

"The Secretary shall have the authority to review the accuracy of the information provided under this subsection, including the applicable large employer's share under paragraph (2)(C)(iv).".

SEC. 10107. AMENDMENTS TO SUBTITLE G.

(a) Section 1562 of this Act is amended, in the amendment made by subsection (a)(2)(B)(iii), by striking "subpart 1" and inserting "subparts I and II"; and

(b) Subtitle G of title I of this Act is amended—

(1) by redesignating section 1562 (as amended) as section 1563; and

(2) by inserting after section 1561 the following:

"SEC. 1562. GAO STUDY REGARDING THE RATE OF DENIAL OF COVERAGE AND ENROLLMENT BY HEALTH INSURANCE ISSUERS AND GROUP HEALTH PLANS.

"(a) IN GENERAL.—The Comptroller General of the United States (referred to in this section as the 'Comptroller General') shall conduct a study of the incidence of denials of coverage for medical services and denials of applications to enroll in health insurance plans, as described in subsection (b), by group health plans and health insurance issuers.

"(b) DATA.—

"(1) IN GENERAL.—In conducting the study described in subsection (a), the Comptroller General shall consider samples of data concerning the following:

"(A)(i) denials of coverage for medical services to a plan enrollees, by the types of services for which such coverage was denied; and

"(ii) the reasons such coverage was denied; and

"(B)(i) incidents in which group health plans and health insurance issuers deny the application of an individual to enroll in a health insurance plan offered by such group health plan or issuer; and

"(ii) the reasons such applications are denied.

"(2) SCOPE OF DATA.—

"(A) FAVORABLY RESOLVED DISPUTES.—The data that the Comptroller General considers under paragraph (1) shall include data concerning denials of coverage for medical services and denials of applications for enrollment in a plan by a group health plan or health insurance issuer, where such group health plan or health insurance issuer later approves such coverage or application.

"(B) ALL HEALTH PLANS.—The study under this section shall consider data from varied group health plans and health insurance plans offered by health insurance issuers, including qualified health plans and health plans that are not qualified health plans.

"(c) REPORT.—Not later than one year after the date of enactment of this Act, the Comptroller General shall submit to the Secretaries of Health and Human Services and Labor a report describing the results of the study conducted under this section.

"(d) PUBLICATION OF REPORT.—The Secretaries of Health and Human Services and Labor shall make the report described in subsection (c) available to the public on an Internet website.

"SEC. 1563. SMALL BUSINESS PROCUREMENT.

"Part 19 of the Federal Acquisition Regulation, section 15 of the Small Business Act (15 U.S.C. 644), and any other applicable laws or regulations establishing procurement requirements relating to small business concerns (as defined in section 3 of the Small Business Act (15 U.S.C. 632)) may not be waived with respect to any contract awarded under any program or other authority under this Act or an amendment made by this Act.".

SEC. 10108. FREE CHOICE VOUCHERS.

(a) IN GENERAL.—An offering employer shall provide free choice vouchers to each qualified employee of such employer.

(b) OFFERING EMPLOYER.—For purposes of this section, the term "offering employer" means any employer who—

(1) offers minimum essential coverage to its employees consisting of coverage through an eligible employer-sponsored plan; and

(2) pays any portion of the costs of such plan.

(c) QUALIFIED EMPLOYEE.—For purposes of this section—

(1) IN GENERAL.—The term "qualified employee" means, with respect to any plan year of an offering employer, any employee—

(A) whose required contribution (as determined under section 5000A(e)(1)(B)) for minimum essential coverage through an eligible employer-sponsored plan—

(i) exceeds 8 percent of such employee's household income for the taxable year described in section 1412(b)(1)(B) which ends with or within in the plan year; and

(ii) does not exceed 9.8 percent of such employee's household income for such taxable year;

(B) whose household income for such taxable year is not greater than 400 percent of the poverty line for a family of the size involved; and

(C) who does not participate in a health plan offered by the offering employer.

(2) INDEXING.—In the case of any calendar year beginning after 2014, the Secretary shall adjust the 8 percent under paragraph (1)(A)(i) and 9.8 percent under paragraph (1)(A)(ii) for the calendar year to reflect the rate of premium growth between the preceding calendar year and 2013 over the rate of income growth for such period.

(d) FREE CHOICE VOUCHER.—

(1) AMOUNT.—

(A) IN GENERAL.—The amount of any free choice voucher provided under subsection (a) shall be equal to the monthly portion of the cost of the eligible employer-sponsored plan which would have been paid by the employer if the employee were covered under the plan with respect to which the employer pays the largest portion of the cost of the plan. Such amount shall be equal to the amount the employer would pay for an employee with self-only coverage unless such employee elects family coverage (in which case such amount shall be the amount the employer would pay for family coverage).

(B) DETERMINATION OF COST.—The cost of any health plan shall be determined under the rules similar to the rules of section 2204 of the Public Health Service Act, except that such amount shall be adjusted for age and category of enrollment in accordance with regulations established by the Secretary.

(2) USE OF VOUCHERS.—An Exchange shall credit the amount of any free choice voucher provided under subsection (a) to the monthly premium of any qualified health plan in the Exchange in which the qualified employee is enrolled and the offering employer shall pay any amounts so credited to the Exchange.

(3) PAYMENT OF EXCESS AMOUNTS.—If the amount of the free choice voucher exceeds the amount of the premium of the qualified health plan in which the qualified employee is enrolled for such month, such excess shall be paid to the employee.

(e) OTHER DEFINITIONS.—Any term used in this section which is also used in section 5000A of the Internal Revenue Code of 1986 shall have the meaning given such term under such section 5000A.

(f) EXCLUSION FROM INCOME FOR EMPLOYEE.—

(1) IN GENERAL.—Part III of subchapter B of chapter 1 of the Internal Revenue Code of 1986 is amended by inserting after section 139C the following new section:

"SEC. 139D. FREE CHOICE VOUCHERS.

"Gross income shall not include the amount of any free choice voucher provided by an employer under section 10108 of the Patient Protection and Affordable Care Act to the extent that the amount of such voucher does not exceed the amount paid for a qualified health plan (as defined in section 1301 of such Act) by the taxpayer.".

(2) CLERICAL AMENDMENT.—The table of sections for part III of subchapter B of chapter 1 of such Code is amended by inserting after the item relating to section 139C the following new item:

"Sec. 139D. Free choice vouchers.".

(3) EFFECTIVE DATE.—The amendments made by this subsection shall apply to vouchers provided after December 31, 2013.

(g) DEDUCTION ALLOWED TO EMPLOYER.—

(1) IN GENERAL.—Section 162(a) of the Internal Revenue Code of 1986 is amended by adding at the end the following new sentence: "For purposes of paragraph (1), the amount of a free choice voucher provided under section 10108 of the Patient Protection and Affordable Care Act shall be treated as an amount for compensation for personal services actually rendered.".

(2) EFFECTIVE DATE.—The amendments made by this subsection shall apply to vouchers provided after December 31, 2013.

(h) VOUCHER TAKEN INTO ACCOUNT IN DETERMINING PREMIUM CREDIT.—

(1) IN GENERAL.—Subsection (c)(2) of section 36B of the Internal Revenue Code of 1986, as added by section 1401, is amended by adding at the end the following new subparagraph:

"(D) EXCEPTION FOR INDIVIDUAL RECEIVING FREE CHOICE VOUCHERS.—The term 'coverage month' shall not include any month in which such individual has a free choice voucher provided under section 10108 of the Patient Protection and Affordable Care Act.".

(2) EFFECTIVE DATE.—The amendment made by this subsection shall apply to taxable years beginning after December 31, 2013.

(i) COORDINATION WITH EMPLOYER RESPONSIBILITIES.—

(1) SHARED RESPONSIBILITY PENALTY.—

(A) IN GENERAL.—Subsection (c) of section 4980H of the Internal Revenue Code of 1986, as added by section 1513, is amended by adding at the end the following new paragraph:

"(3) SPECIAL RULES FOR EMPLOYERS PROVIDING FREE CHOICE VOUCHERS.—No assessable payment shall be imposed under paragraph (1) for any month with respect to any employee to whom the employer provides a free choice voucher under section 10108 of the Patient Protection and Affordable Care Act for such month.".

(B) EFFECTIVE DATE.—The amendment made by this paragraph shall apply to months beginning after December 31, 2013.

(2) NOTIFICATION REQUIREMENT.—Section 18B(a)(3) of the Fair Labor Standards Act of 1938, as added by section 1512, is amended—

(A) by inserting "and the employer does not offer a free choice voucher" after "Exchange"; and

(B) by striking "will lose" and inserting "may lose".

(j) EMPLOYER REPORTING.—

(1) IN GENERAL.—Subsection (a) of section 6056 of the Internal Revenue Code of 1986, as added by section 1514, is amended by inserting "and every offering employer" before "shall".

(2) OFFERING EMPLOYERS.—Subsection (f) of section 6056 of such Code, as added by section 1514, is amended to read as follows:

"(f) DEFINITIONS.—For purposes of this section—

"(1) OFFERING EMPLOYER.—

"(A) IN GENERAL.—The term 'offering employer' means any offering employer (as defined in section 10108(b) of the Patient Protection and Affordable Care Act) if the required contribution (within the meaning of section 5000A(e)(1)(B)(i)) of any employee exceeds 8 percent of the wages (as defined in section 3121(a)) paid to such employee by such employer.

"(B) INDEXING.—In the case of any calendar year beginning after 2014, the 8 percent under subparagraph (A) shall be adjusted for the calendar year to reflect the rate of premium growth between the preceding calendar year and 2013 over the rate of income growth for such period.

"(2) OTHER DEFINITIONS.—Any term used in this section which is also used in section 4980H shall have the meaning given such term by section 4980H.".

(3) CONFORMING AMENDMENTS.—

(A) The heading of section 6056 of such Code, as added by section 1514, is amended by striking "**LARGE**" and inserting "**CERTAIN**".

(B) Section 6056(b)(2)(C) of such Code is amended—

(i) by inserting "in the case of an applicable large employer," before "the length" in clause (i);

(ii) by striking "and" at the end of clause (iii);

(iii) by striking "applicable large employer" in clause (iv) and inserting "employer";

(iv) by inserting "and" at the end of clause (iv); and

(v) by inserting at the end the following new clause:

"(v) in the case of an offering employer, the option for which the employer pays the largest portion of the cost of the plan and the portion of the cost paid by the employer in each of the enrollment categories under such option,".

(C) Section 6056(d)(2) of such Code is amended by inserting "or offering employer" after "applicable large employer".

(D) Section 6056(e) of such Code is amended by inserting "or offering employer" after "applicable large employer".

(E) Section 6724(d)(1)(B)(xxv) of such Code, as added by section 1514, is amended by striking "large" and inserting "certain".

(F) Section 6724(d)(2)(HH) of such Code, as added by section 1514, is amended by striking "large" and inserting "certain".

(G) The table of sections for subpart D of part III of subchapter A of chapter 1 of such Code, as amended by section 1514, is amended by striking "Large employers" in the item relating to section 6056 and inserting "Certain employers".

(4) EFFECTIVE DATE.—The amendments made by this subsection shall apply to periods beginning after December 31, 2013.

SEC. 10109. DEVELOPMENT OF STANDARDS FOR FINANCIAL AND ADMINISTRATIVE TRANSACTIONS.

(a) ADDITIONAL TRANSACTION STANDARDS AND OPERATING RULES.—

(1) DEVELOPMENT OF ADDITIONAL TRANSACTION STANDARDS AND OPERATING RULES.—Section 1173(a) of the Social Security Act (42 U.S.C. 1320d–2(a)), as amended by section 1104(b)(2), is amended—

(A) in paragraph (1)(B), by inserting before the period the following: ", and subject to the requirements under paragraph (5)"; and

(B) by adding at the end the following new paragraph:

"(5) CONSIDERATION OF STANDARDIZATION OF ACTIVITIES AND ITEMS.—

"(A) IN GENERAL.—For purposes of carrying out paragraph (1)(B), the Secretary shall solicit, not later than January 1, 2012, and not less than every 3 years thereafter, input from entities described in subparagraph (B) on—

"(i) whether there could be greater uniformity in financial and administrative activities and items, as determined appropriate by the Secretary; and

"(ii) whether such activities should be considered financial and administrative transactions (as described in paragraph (1)(B)) for which the adoption of standards and operating rules would improve the operation of the health care system and reduce administrative costs.

"(B) SOLICITATION OF INPUT.—For purposes of subparagraph (A), the Secretary shall seek input from—

"(i) the National Committee on Vital and Health Statistics, the Health Information Technology Policy Committee, and the Health Information Technology Standards Committee; and

"(ii) standard setting organizations and stakeholders, as determined appropriate by the Secretary.".

(b) ACTIVITIES AND ITEMS FOR INITIAL CONSIDERATION.—For purposes of section 1173(a)(5) of the Social Security Act, as added by subsection (a), the Secretary of Health and Human Services (in this section referred to as the "Secretary") shall, not later than January 1, 2012, seek input on activities and items relating to the following areas:

(1) Whether the application process, including the use of a uniform application form, for enrollment of health care providers by health plans could be made electronic and standardized.

(2) Whether standards and operating rules described in section 1173 of the Social Security Act should apply to the health care transactions of automobile insurance, worker's compensation, and other programs or persons not described in section 1172(a) of such Act (42 U.S.C. 1320d–1(a)).

(3) Whether standardized forms could apply to financial audits required by health plans, Federal and State agencies (including State auditors, the Office of the Inspector General of the Department of Health and Human Services, and the Centers for Medicare & Medicaid Services), and other relevant entities as determined appropriate by the Secretary.

(4) Whether there could be greater transparency and consistency of methodologies and processes used to establish claim edits used by health plans (as described in section 1171(5) of the Social Security Act (42 U.S.C. 1320d(5))).

(5) Whether health plans should be required to publish their timeliness of payment rules.

(c) ICD CODING CROSSWALKS.—

(1) ICD–9 TO ICD–10 CROSSWALK.—The Secretary shall task the ICD–9–CM Coordination and Maintenance Committee to convene a meeting, not later than January 1, 2011, to receive input from appropriate stakeholders (including health plans, health care providers, and clinicians) regarding the crosswalk

between the Ninth and Tenth Revisions of the International Classification of Diseases (ICD–9 and ICD–10, respectively) that is posted on the website of the Centers for Medicare & Medicaid Services, and make recommendations about appropriate revisions to such crosswalk.

(2) REVISION OF CROSSWALK.—For purposes of the crosswalk described in paragraph (1), the Secretary shall make appropriate revisions and post any such revised crosswalk on the website of the Centers for Medicare & Medicaid Services.

(3) USE OF REVISED CROSSWALK.—For purposes of paragraph (2), any revised crosswalk shall be treated as a code set for which a standard has been adopted by the Secretary for purposes of section 1173(c)(1)(B) of the Social Security Act (42 U.S.C. 1320d–2(c)(1)(B)).

(4) SUBSEQUENT CROSSWALKS.—For subsequent revisions of the International Classification of Diseases that are adopted by the Secretary as a standard code set under section 1173(c) of the Social Security Act (42 U.S.C. 1320d–2(c)), the Secretary shall, after consultation with the appropriate stakeholders, post on the website of the Centers for Medicare & Medicaid Services a crosswalk between the previous and subsequent version of the International Classification of Diseases not later than the date of implementation of such subsequent revision.

Subtitle B—Provisions Relating to Title II

PART I—MEDICAID AND CHIP

SEC. 10201. AMENDMENTS TO THE SOCIAL SECURITY ACT AND TITLE II OF THIS ACT.

(a)(1) Section 1902(a)(10)(A)(i)(IX) of the Social Security Act (42 U.S.C. 1396a(a)(10)(A)(i)(IX)), as added by section 2004(a), is amended to read as follows:

"(IX) who—

"(aa) are under 26 years of age;

"(bb) are not described in or enrolled under any of subclauses (I) through (VII) of this clause or are described in any of such subclauses but have income that exceeds the level of income applicable under the State plan for eligibility to enroll for medical assistance under such subclause;

"(cc) were in foster care under the responsibility of the State on the date of attaining 18 years of age or such higher age as the State has elected under section 475(8)(B)(iii); and

"(dd) were enrolled in the State plan under this title or under a waiver of the plan while in such foster care;".

(2) Section 1902(a)(10) of the Social Security Act (42 U.S.C. 1396a(a)(10), as amended by section 2001(a)(5)(A), is amended in the matter following subparagraph (G), by striking "and (XV)" and inserting "(XV)", and by inserting "and (XVI) if an individual is described in subclause (IX) of subparagraph (A)(i) and is also described in subclause (VIII) of that subparagraph, the medical

assistance shall be made available to the individual through subclause (IX) instead of through subclause (VIII)" before the semicolon.

(3) Section 2004(d) of this Act is amended by striking "2019" and inserting "2014".

(b) Section 1902(k)(2) of the Social Security Act (42 U.S.C. 1396a(k)(2)), as added by section 2001(a)(4)(A), is amended by striking "January 1, 2011" and inserting "April 1, 2010".

(c) Section 1905 of the Social Security Act (42 U.S.C. 1396d), as amended by sections 2001(a)(3), 2001(a)(5)(C), 2006, and 4107(a)(2), is amended—

(1) in subsection (a), in the matter preceding paragraph (1), by inserting in clause (xiv), "or 1902(a)(10)(A)(i)(IX)" before the comma;

(2) in subsection (b), in the first sentence, by inserting ", (z)," before "and (aa)";

(3) in subsection (y)—

(A) in paragraph (1)(B)(ii)(II), in the first sentence, by inserting "includes inpatient hospital services," after "100 percent of the poverty line, that"; and

(B) in paragraph (2)(A), by striking "on the date of enactment of the Patient Protection and Affordable Care Act" and inserting "as of December 1, 2009";

(4) by inserting after subsection (y) the following:

"(z) EQUITABLE SUPPORT FOR CERTAIN STATES.—

"(1)(A) During the period that begins on January 1, 2014, and ends on September 30, 2019, notwithstanding subsection (b), the Federal medical assistance percentage otherwise determined under subsection (b) with respect to a fiscal year occurring during that period shall be increased by 2.2 percentage points for any State described in subparagraph (B) for amounts expended for medical assistance for individuals who are not newly eligible (as defined in subsection (y)(2)) individuals described in subclause (VIII) of section 1902(a)(10)(A)(i).

"(B) For purposes of subparagraph (A), a State described in this subparagraph is a State that—

"(i) is an expansion State described in subsection (y)(1)(B)(ii)(II);

"(ii) the Secretary determines will not receive any payments under this title on the basis of an increased Federal medical assistance percentage under subsection (y) for expenditures for medical assistance for newly eligible individuals (as so defined); and

"(iii) has not been approved by the Secretary to divert a portion of the DSH allotment for a State to the costs of providing medical assistance or other health benefits coverage under a waiver that is in effect on July 2009.

"(2)(A) During the period that begins on January 1, 2014, and ends on December 31, 2016, notwithstanding subsection (b), the Federal medical assistance percentage otherwise determined under subsection (b) with respect to all or any portion of a fiscal year occurring during that period shall be increased by .5 percentage point for a State described in subparagraph (B) for amounts expended for medical assistance under the State plan under this title or under a waiver of that plan during that period.

"(B) For purposes of subparagraph (A), a State described in this subparagraph is a State that—

"(i) is described in clauses (i) and (ii) of paragraph (1)(B); and

"(ii) is the State with the highest percentage of its population insured during 2008, based on the Current Population Survey.

"(3) Notwithstanding subsection (b) and paragraphs (1) and (2) of this subsection, the Federal medical assistance percentage otherwise determined under subsection (b) with respect to all or any portion of a fiscal year that begins on or after January 1, 2017, for the State of Nebraska, with respect to amounts expended for newly eligible individuals described in subclause (VIII) of section 1902(a)(10)(A)(i), shall be determined as provided for under subsection (y)(1)(A) (notwithstanding the period provided for in such paragraph).

"(4) The increase in the Federal medical assistance percentage for a State under paragraphs (1), (2), or (3) shall apply only for purposes of this title and shall not apply with respect to—

"(A) disproportionate share hospital payments described in section 1923;

"(B) payments under title IV;

"(C) payments under title XXI; and

"(D) payments under this title that are based on the enhanced FMAP described in section 2105(b).";

(5) in subsection (aa), is amended by striking "without regard to this subsection and subsection (y)" and inserting "without regard to this subsection, subsection (y), subsection (z), and section 10202 of the Patient Protection and Affordable Care Act" each place it appears;

(6) by adding after subsection (bb), the following:

"(cc) REQUIREMENT FOR CERTAIN STATES.—Notwithstanding subsections (y), (z), and (aa), in the case of a State that requires political subdivisions within the State to contribute toward the non-Federal share of expenditures required under the State plan under section 1902(a)(2), the State shall not be eligible for an increase in its Federal medical assistance percentage under such subsections if it requires that political subdivisions pay a greater percentage of the non-Federal share of such expenditures, or a greater percentage of the non-Federal share of payments under section 1923, than the respective percentages that would have been required by the State under the State plan under this title, State law, or both, as in effect on December 31, 2009, and without regard to any such increase. Voluntary contributions by a political subdivision to the non-Federal share of expenditures under the State plan under this title or to the non-Federal share of payments under section 1923, shall not be considered to be required contributions for purposes of this subsection. The treatment of voluntary contributions, and the treatment of contributions required by a State under the State plan under this title, or State law, as provided by this subsection, shall also apply to the increases in the Federal medical assistance percentage under section 5001 of the American Recovery and Reinvestment Act of 2009.".

(d) Section 1108(g)(4)(B) of the Social Security Act (42 U.S.C. 1308(g)(4)(B)), as added by section 2005(b), is amended by striking "income eligibility level in effect for that population under title XIX or under a waiver" and inserting "the highest income eligibility level in effect for parents under the commonwealth's or territory's State plan under title XIX or under a waiver of the plan".

(e)(1) Section 1923(f) of the Social Security Act (42 U.S.C. 1396r–4(f)), as amended by section 2551, is amended—

(A) in paragraph (6)—

(i) by striking the paragraph heading and inserting the following: "ALLOTMENT ADJUSTMENTS"; and

(ii) in subparagraph (B), by adding at the end the following:

"(iii) ALLOTMENT FOR 2D, 3RD, AND 4TH QUARTER OF FISCAL YEAR 2012, FISCAL YEAR 2013, AND SUCCEEDING FISCAL YEARS.—Notwithstanding the table set forth in paragraph (2) or paragraph (7):

"(I) 2D, 3RD, AND 4TH QUARTER OF FISCAL YEAR 2012.—The DSH allotment for Hawaii for the 2d, 3rd, and 4th quarters of fiscal year 2012 shall be $7,500,000.

"(II) TREATMENT AS A LOW-DSH STATE FOR FISCAL YEAR 2013 AND SUCCEEDING FISCAL YEARS.—With respect to fiscal year 2013, and each fiscal year thereafter, the DSH allotment for Hawaii shall be increased in the same manner as allotments for low DSH States are increased for such fiscal year under clause (iii) of paragraph (5)(B).

"(III) CERTAIN HOSPITAL PAYMENTS.—The Secretary may not impose a limitation on the total amount of payments made to hospitals under the QUEST section 1115 Demonstration Project except to the extent that such limitation is necessary to ensure that a hospital does not receive payments in excess of the amounts described in subsection (g), or as necessary to ensure that such payments under the waiver and such payments pursuant to the allotment provided in this clause do not, in the aggregate in any year, exceed the amount that the Secretary determines is equal to the Federal medical assistance percentage component attributable to disproportionate share hospital payment adjustments for such year that is reflected in the budget neutrality provision of the QUEST Demonstration Project."; and

(B) in paragraph (7)—

(i) in subparagraph (A), in the matter preceding clause (i), by striking "subparagraph (E)" and inserting "subparagraphs (E) and (G)";

(ii) in subparagraph (B)—

(I) in clause (i), by striking subclauses (I) and (II), and inserting the following:

"(I) if the State is a low DSH State described in paragraph (5)(B) and has spent not more than 99.90 percent of the DSH allotments for the State on average for the period of fiscal years 2004 through 2008, as of September 30, 2009, the applicable percentage is equal to 25 percent;

"(II) if the State is a low DSH State described in paragraph (5)(B) and has spent more than 99.90 percent of the DSH allotments for the State on average for the period of fiscal years 2004 through

2008, as of September 30, 2009, the applicable percentage is equal to 17.5 percent;

"(III) if the State is not a low DSH State described in paragraph (5)(B) and has spent not more than 99.90 percent of the DSH allotments for the State on average for the period of fiscal years 2004 through 2008, as of September 30, 2009, the applicable percentage is equal to 50 percent; and

"(IV) if the State is not a low DSH State described in paragraph (5)(B) and has spent more than 99.90 percent of the DSH allotments for the State on average for the period of fiscal years 2004 through 2008, as of September 30, 2009, the applicable percentage is equal to 35 percent.";

(II) in clause (ii), by striking subclauses (I) and (II), and inserting the following:

"(I) if the State is a low DSH State described in paragraph (5)(B) and has spent not more than 99.90 percent of the DSH allotments for the State on average for the period of fiscal years 2004 through 2008, as of September 30, 2009, the applicable percentage is equal to the product of the percentage reduction in uncovered individuals for the fiscal year from the preceding fiscal year and 27.5 percent;

"(II) if the State is a low DSH State described in paragraph (5)(B) and has spent more than 99.90 percent of the DSH allotments for the State on average for the period of fiscal years 2004 through 2008, as of September 30, 2009, the applicable percentage is equal to the product of the percentage reduction in uncovered individuals for the fiscal year from the preceding fiscal year and 20 percent;

"(III) if the State is not a low DSH State described in paragraph (5)(B) and has spent not more than 99.90 percent of the DSH allotments for the State on average for the period of fiscal years 2004 through 2008, as of September 30, 2009, the applicable percentage is equal to the product of the percentage reduction in uncovered individuals for the fiscal year from the preceding fiscal year and 55 percent; and

"(IV) if the State is not a low DSH State described in paragraph (5)(B) and has spent more than 99.90 percent of the DSH allotments for the State on average for the period of fiscal years 2004 through 2008, as of September 30, 2009, the applicable percentage is equal to the product of the percentage reduction in uncovered individuals for the fiscal year from the preceding fiscal year and 40 percent.";

(III) in subparagraph (E), by striking "35 percent" and inserting "50 percent"; and

(IV) by adding at the end the following:

"(G) NONAPPLICATION.—The preceding provisions of this paragraph shall not apply to the DSH allotment determined for the State of Hawaii for a fiscal year under paragraph (6).".

(f) Section 2551 of this Act is amended by striking subsection (b).

(g) Section 2105(d)(3)(B) of the Social Security Act (42 U.S.C. 1397ee(d)(3)(B)), as added by section 2101(b)(1), is amended by adding at the end the following: "For purposes of eligibility for premium assistance for the purchase of a qualified health plan under section 36B of the Internal Revenue Code of 1986 and reduced cost-sharing under section 1402 of the Patient Protection and Affordable Care Act, children described in the preceding sentence shall be deemed to be ineligible for coverage under the State child health plan.".

(h) Clause (i) of subparagraph (C) of section 513(b)(2) of the Social Security Act, as added by section 2953 of this Act, is amended to read as follows:

"(i) Healthy relationships, including marriage and family interactions.".

(i) Section 1115 of the Social Security Act (42 U.S.C. 1315) is amended by inserting after subsection (c) the following:

"(d)(1) An application or renewal of any experimental, pilot, or demonstration project undertaken under subsection (a) to promote the objectives of title XIX or XXI in a State that would result in an impact on eligibility, enrollment, benefits, cost-sharing, or financing with respect to a State program under title XIX or XXI (in this subsection referred to as a 'demonstration project') shall be considered by the Secretary in accordance with the regulations required to be promulgated under paragraph (2).

"(2) Not later than 180 days after the date of enactment of this subsection, the Secretary shall promulgate regulations relating to applications for, and renewals of, a demonstration project that provide for—

"(A) a process for public notice and comment at the State level, including public hearings, sufficient to ensure a meaningful level of public input;

"(B) requirements relating to—

"(i) the goals of the program to be implemented or renewed under the demonstration project;

"(ii) the expected State and Federal costs and coverage projections of the demonstration project; and

"(iii) the specific plans of the State to ensure that the demonstration project will be in compliance with title XIX or XXI;

"(C) a process for providing public notice and comment after the application is received by the Secretary, that is sufficient to ensure a meaningful level of public input;

"(D) a process for the submission to the Secretary of periodic reports by the State concerning the implementation of the demonstration project; and

"(E) a process for the periodic evaluation by the Secretary of the demonstration project.

"(3) The Secretary shall annually report to Congress concerning actions taken by the Secretary with respect to applications for demonstration projects under this section.".

(j) Subtitle F of title III of this Act is amended by adding at the end the following:

"SEC. 3512. GAO STUDY AND REPORT ON CAUSES OF ACTION.

"(a) STUDY.—

"(1) IN GENERAL.—The Comptroller General of the United States shall conduct a study of whether the development, recognition, or implementation of any guideline or other standards under a provision described in paragraph (2) would result in the establishment of a new cause of action or claim.

"(2) PROVISIONS DESCRIBED.—The provisions described in this paragraph include the following:

"(A) Section 2701 (adult health quality measures).

"(B) Section 2702 (payment adjustments for health care acquired conditions).

"(C) Section 3001 (Hospital Value-Based Purchase Program).

"(D) Section 3002 (improvements to the Physician Quality Reporting Initiative).

"(E) Section 3003 (improvements to the Physician Feedback Program).

"(F) Section 3007 (value based payment modifier under physician fee schedule).

"(G) Section 3008 (payment adjustment for conditions acquired in hospitals).

"(H) Section 3013 (quality measure development).

"(I) Section 3014 (quality measurement).

"(J) Section 3021 (Establishment of Center for Medicare and Medicaid Innovation).

"(K) Section 3025 (hospital readmission reduction program).

"(L) Section 3501 (health care delivery system research, quality improvement).

"(M) Section 4003 (Task Force on Clinical and Preventive Services).

"(N) Section 4301 (research to optimize deliver of public health services).

"(b) REPORT.—Not later than 2 years after the date of enactment of this Act, the Comptroller General of the United States shall submit to the appropriate committees of Congress, a report containing the findings made by the Comptroller General under the study under subsection (a).".

SEC. 10202. INCENTIVES FOR STATES TO OFFER HOME AND COMMUNITY-BASED SERVICES AS A LONG-TERM CARE ALTERNATIVE TO NURSING HOMES.

(a) STATE BALANCING INCENTIVE PAYMENTS PROGRAM.—Notwithstanding section 1905(b) of the Social Security Act (42 U.S.C. 1396d(b)), in the case of a balancing incentive payment State, as defined in subsection (b), that meets the conditions described in subsection (c), during the balancing incentive period, the Federal medical assistance percentage determined for the State under section 1905(b) of such Act and, if applicable, increased under subsection (z) or (aa) shall be increased by the applicable percentage points determined under subsection (d) with respect to eligible medical assistance expenditures described in subsection (e).

(b) BALANCING INCENTIVE PAYMENT STATE.—A balancing incentive payment State is a State—

(1) in which less than 50 percent of the total expenditures for medical assistance under the State Medicaid program for a fiscal year for long-term services and supports (as defined by the Secretary under subsection (f))(1)) are for non-institutionally-based long-term services and supports described in subsection (f)(1)(B);

(2) that submits an application and meets the conditions described in subsection (c); and

(3) that is selected by the Secretary to participate in the State balancing incentive payment program established under this section.

(c) CONDITIONS.—The conditions described in this subsection are the following:

(1) APPLICATION.—The State submits an application to the Secretary that includes, in addition to such other information as the Secretary shall require—

(A) a proposed budget that details the State's plan to expand and diversify medical assistance for non-institutionally-based long-term services and supports described in subsection (f)(1)(B) under the State Medicaid program during the balancing incentive period and achieve the target spending percentage applicable to the State under paragraph (2), including through structural changes to how the State furnishes such assistance, such as through the establishment of a "no wrong door—single entry point system", optional presumptive eligibility, case management services, and the use of core standardized assessment instruments, and that includes a description of the new or expanded offerings of such services that the State will provide and the projected costs of such services; and

(B) in the case of a State that proposes to expand the provision of home and community-based services under its State Medicaid program through a State plan amendment under section 1915(i) of the Social Security Act, at the option of the State, an election to increase the income eligibility for such services from 150 percent of the poverty line to such higher percentage as the State may establish for such purpose, not to exceed 300 percent of the supplemental security income benefit rate established by section 1611(b)(1) of the Social Security Act (42 U.S.C. 1382(b)(1)).

(2) TARGET SPENDING PERCENTAGES.—

(A) In the case of a balancing incentive payment State in which less than 25 percent of the total expenditures for long-term services and supports under the State Medicaid program for fiscal year 2009 are for home and community-based services, the target spending percentage for the State to achieve by not later than October 1, 2015, is that 25 percent of the total expenditures for long-term services and supports under the State Medicaid program are for home and community-based services.

(B) In the case of any other balancing incentive payment State, the target spending percentage for the State to achieve by not later than October 1, 2015, is that 50 percent of the total expenditures for long-term services and supports under the State Medicaid program are for home and community-based services.

(3) MAINTENANCE OF ELIGIBILITY REQUIREMENTS.—The State does not apply eligibility standards, methodologies, or procedures for determining eligibility for medical assistance for non-institutionally-based long-term services and supports described in subsection (f)(1)(B) under the State Medicaid program that are more restrictive than the eligibility standards, methodologies, or procedures in effect for such purposes on December 31, 2010.

(4) USE OF ADDITIONAL FUNDS.—The State agrees to use the additional Federal funds paid to the State as a result of this section only for purposes of providing new or expanded offerings of non-institutionally-based long-term services and supports described in subsection (f)(1)(B) under the State Medicaid program.

(5) STRUCTURAL CHANGES.—The State agrees to make, not later than the end of the 6-month period that begins on the date the State submits an application under this section, the following changes:

(A) "NO WRONG DOOR—SINGLE ENTRY POINT SYSTEM".—Development of a statewide system to enable consumers to access all long-term services and supports through an agency, organization, coordinated network, or portal, in accordance with such standards as the State shall establish and that shall provide information regarding the availability of such services, how to apply for such services, referral services for services and supports otherwise available in the community, and determinations of financial and functional eligibility for such services and supports, or assistance with assessment processes for financial and functional eligibility.

(B) CONFLICT-FREE CASE MANAGEMENT SERVICES.—Conflict-free case management services to develop a service plan, arrange for services and supports, support the beneficiary (and, if appropriate, the beneficiary's caregivers) in directing the provision of services and supports for the beneficiary, and conduct ongoing monitoring to assure that services and supports are delivered to meet the beneficiary's needs and achieve intended outcomes.

(C) CORE STANDARDIZED ASSESSMENT INSTRUMENTS.—Development of core standardized assessment instruments for determining eligibility for non-institutionally-based long-term services and supports described in subsection (f)(1)(B), which shall be used in a uniform manner throughout the State, to determine a beneficiary's needs for training, support services, medical care, transportation, and other services, and develop an individual service plan to address such needs.

(6) DATA COLLECTION.—The State agrees to collect from providers of services and through such other means as the State determines appropriate the following data:

(A) SERVICES DATA.—Services data from providers of non-institutionally-based long-term services and supports described in subsection (f)(1)(B) on a per-beneficiary basis and in accordance with such standardized coding procedures as the State shall establish in consultation with the Secretary.

(B) QUALITY DATA.—Quality data on a selected set of core quality measures agreed upon by the Secretary and the State that are linked to population-specific outcomes measures and accessible to providers.

(C) OUTCOMES MEASURES.—Outcomes measures data on a selected set of core population-specific outcomes measures agreed upon by the Secretary and the State that are accessible to providers and include—

(i) measures of beneficiary and family caregiver experience with providers;

(ii) measures of beneficiary and family caregiver satisfaction with services; and

(iii) measures for achieving desired outcomes appropriate to a specific beneficiary, including employment, participation in community life, health stability, and prevention of loss in function.

(d) APPLICABLE PERCENTAGE POINTS INCREASE IN FMAP.—The applicable percentage points increase is—

(1) in the case of a balancing incentive payment State subject to the target spending percentage described in subsection (c)(2)(A), 5 percentage points; and

(2) in the case of any other balancing incentive payment State, 2 percentage points.

(e) ELIGIBLE MEDICAL ASSISTANCE EXPENDITURES.—

(1) IN GENERAL.—Subject to paragraph (2), medical assistance described in this subsection is medical assistance for non-institutionally-based long-term services and supports described in subsection (f)(1)(B) that is provided by a balancing incentive payment State under its State Medicaid program during the balancing incentive payment period.

(2) LIMITATION ON PAYMENTS.—In no case may the aggregate amount of payments made by the Secretary to balancing incentive payment States under this section during the balancing incentive period exceed $3,000,000,000.

(f) DEFINITIONS.—In this section:

(1) LONG-TERM SERVICES AND SUPPORTS DEFINED.—The term "long-term services and supports" has the meaning given that term by Secretary and may include any of the following (as defined for purposes of State Medicaid programs):

(A) INSTITUTIONALLY-BASED LONG-TERM SERVICES AND SUPPORTS.—Services provided in an institution, including the following:

(i) Nursing facility services.

(ii) Services in an intermediate care facility for the mentally retarded described in subsection (a)(15) of section 1905 of such Act.

(B) NON-INSTITUTIONALLY-BASED LONG-TERM SERVICES AND SUPPORTS.—Services not provided in an institution, including the following:

(i) Home and community-based services provided under subsection (c), (d), or (i) of section 1915 of such Act or under a waiver under section 1115 of such Act.

(ii) Home health care services.

(iii) Personal care services.

(iv) Services described in subsection (a)(26) of section 1905 of such Act (relating to PACE program services).

(v) Self-directed personal assistance services described in section 1915(j) of such Act.

(2) BALANCING INCENTIVE PERIOD.—The term "balancing incentive period" means the period that begins on October 1, 2011, and ends on September 30, 2015.

(3) POVERTY LINE.—The term "poverty line" has the meaning given that term in section 2110(c)(5) of the Social Security Act (42 U.S.C. 1397jj(c)(5)).

(4) STATE MEDICAID PROGRAM.—The term "State Medicaid program" means the State program for medical assistance provided under a State plan under title XIX of the Social Security Act and under any waiver approved with respect to such State plan.

SEC. 10203. EXTENSION OF FUNDING FOR CHIP THROUGH FISCAL YEAR 2015 AND OTHER CHIP-RELATED PROVISIONS.

(a) Section 1311(c)(1) of this Act is amended by striking "and" at the end of subparagraph (G), by striking the period at the end of subparagraph (H) and inserting "; and", and by adding at the end the following:

"(I) report to the Secretary at least annually and in such manner as the Secretary shall require, pediatric quality reporting measures consistent with the pediatric quality reporting measures established under section 1139A of the Social Security Act.".

(b) Effective as if included in the enactment of the Children's Health Insurance Program Reauthorization Act of 2009 (Public Law 111–3):

(1) Section 1906(e)(2) of the Social Security Act (42 U.S.C. 1396e(e)(2)) is amended by striking "means" and all that follows through the period and inserting "has the meaning given that term in section 2105(c)(3)(A).".

(2)(A) Section 1906A(a) of the Social Security Act (42 U.S.C. 1396e–1(a)), is amended by inserting before the period the following: "and the offering of such a subsidy is cost-effective, as defined for purposes of section 2105(c)(3)(A)".

(B) This Act shall be applied without regard to subparagraph (A) of section 2003(a)(1) of this Act and that subparagraph and the amendment made by that subparagraph are hereby deemed null, void, and of no effect.

(3) Section 2105(c)(10) of the Social Security Act (42 U.S.C. 1397ee(c)(10)) is amended—

(A) in subparagraph (A), in the first sentence, by inserting before the period the following: "if the offering of such a subsidy is cost-effective, as defined for purposes of paragraph (3)(A)";

(B) by striking subparagraph (M); and

(C) by redesignating subparagraph (N) as subparagraph (M).

(4) Section 2105(c)(3)(A) of the Social Security Act (42 U.S.C. 1397ee(c)(3)(A)) is amended—

(A) in the matter preceding clause (i), by striking "to" and inserting "to—"; and

(B) in clause (ii), by striking the period and inserting a semicolon.

(c) Section 2105 of the Social Security Act (42 U.S.C. 1397ee), as amended by section 2101, is amended—

(1) in subsection (b), in the second sentence, by striking "2013" and inserting "2015"; and

(2) in subsection (d)(3)—

(A) in subparagraph (A)—

(i) in the first sentence, by inserting "as a condition of receiving payments under section 1903(a)," after "2019,";

(ii) in clause (i), by striking "or" at the end;

(iii) by redesignating clause (ii) as clause (iii); and

(iv) by inserting after clause (i), the following:

"(ii) after September 30, 2015, enrolling children eligible to be targeted low-income children under the State child health plan in a qualified health plan that has been certified by the Secretary under subparagraph (C); or";

(B) in subparagraph (B), by striking "provided coverage" and inserting "screened for eligibility for medical assistance under the State plan under title XIX or a waiver of that plan and, if found eligible, enrolled in such plan or a waiver. In the case of such children who, as a result of such screening, are determined to not be eligible for medical assistance under the State plan or a waiver under title XIX, the State shall establish procedures to ensure that the children are enrolled in a qualified health plan that has been certified by the Secretary under subparagraph (C) and is offered"; and

(C) by adding at the end the following:

"(C) CERTIFICATION OF COMPARABILITY OF PEDIATRIC COVERAGE OFFERED BY QUALIFIED HEALTH PLANS.—With respect to each State, the Secretary, not later than April 1, 2015, shall review the benefits offered for children and the cost-sharing imposed with respect to such benefits by qualified health plans offered through an Exchange established by the State under section 1311 of the Patient Protection and Affordable Care Act and shall certify those plans that offer benefits for children and impose cost-sharing with respect to such benefits that the Secretary determines are at least comparable to the benefits offered and cost-sharing protections provided under the State child health plan.".

(d)(1) Section 2104(a) of such Act (42 U.S.C. 1397dd(a)) is amended—

(A) in paragraph (15), by striking "and" at the end; and

(B) by striking paragraph (16) and inserting the following:

"(16) for fiscal year 2013, $17,406,000,000;

"(17) for fiscal year 2014, $19,147,000,000; and

"(18) for fiscal year 2015, for purposes of making 2 semi-annual allotments—

"(A) $2,850,000,000 for the period beginning on October 1, 2014, and ending on March 31, 2015, and

"(B) $2,850,000,000 for the period beginning on April 1, 2015, and ending on September 30, 2015.".

(2)(A) Section 2104(m) of such Act (42 U.S.C. 1397dd(m)), as amended by section 2102(a)(1), is amended—

(i) in the subsection heading, by striking "2013" and inserting "2015";

(ii) in paragraph (2)—

(I) in the paragraph heading, by striking "2012" and inserting "2014"; and

(II) by adding at the end the following:

"(B) FISCAL YEARS 2013 AND 2014.—Subject to paragraphs (4) and (6), from the amount made available under paragraphs (16) and (17) of subsection (a) for fiscal years 2013 and 2014, respectively, the Secretary shall compute a State allotment for each State (including the District of Columbia and each commonwealth and territory) for each such fiscal year as follows:

"(i) REBASING IN FISCAL YEAR 2013.—For fiscal year 2013, the allotment of the State is equal to the Federal payments to the State that are attributable to (and countable towards) the total amount of allotments available under this section to the State in fiscal year 2012 (including payments made to the State under subsection (n) for fiscal year 2012 as well as amounts redistributed to the State in fiscal year 2012), multiplied by the allotment increase factor under paragraph (5) for fiscal year 2013.

"(ii) GROWTH FACTOR UPDATE FOR FISCAL YEAR 2014.—For fiscal year 2014, the allotment of the State is equal to the sum of—

"(I) the amount of the State allotment under clause (i) for fiscal year 2013; and

"(II) the amount of any payments made to the State under subsection (n) for fiscal year 2013, multiplied by the allotment increase factor under paragraph (5) for fiscal year 2014.";

(iii) in paragraph (3)—

(I) in the paragraph heading, by striking "2013" and inserting "2015";

(II) in subparagraphs (A) and (B), by striking "paragraph (16)" each place it appears and inserting "paragraph (18)";

(III) in subparagraph (C)—

(aa) by striking "2012" each place it appears and inserting "2014"; and

(bb) by striking "2013" and inserting "2015"; and

(IV) in subparagraph (D)—

(aa) in clause (i)(I), by striking "subsection (a)(16)(A)" and inserting "subsection (a)(18)(A)"; and

(bb) in clause (ii)(II), by striking "subsection (a)(16)(B)" and inserting "subsection (a)(18)(B)";

(iv) in paragraph (4), by striking "2013" and inserting "2015";

(v) in paragraph (6)—

(I) in subparagraph (A), by striking "2013" and inserting "2015"; and

(II) in the flush language after and below subparagraph (B)(ii), by striking "or fiscal year 2012" and inserting ", fiscal year 2012, or fiscal year 2014"; and

(vi) in paragraph (8)—

(I) in the paragraph heading, by striking "2013" and inserting "2015"; and

(II) by striking "2013" and inserting "2015".

(B) Section 2104(n) of such Act (42 U.S.C. 1397dd(n)) is amended—

(i) in paragraph (2)—

(I) in subparagraph (A)(ii)—

(aa) by striking "2012" and inserting "2014"; and

(bb) by striking "2013" and inserting "2015";

(II) in subparagraph (B)—

(aa) by striking "2012" and inserting "2014"; and

(bb) by striking "2013" and inserting "2015"; and

(ii) in paragraph (3)(A), by striking "or a semi-annual allotment period for fiscal year 2013" and inserting "fiscal year 2013, fiscal year 2014, or a semi-annual allotment period for fiscal year 2015".

(C) Section 2105(g)(4) of such Act (42 U.S.C. 1397ee(g)(4)) is amended—

(i) in the paragraph heading, by striking "2013" and inserting "2015"; and

(ii) in subparagraph (A), by striking "2013" and inserting "2015".

(D) Section 2110(b) of such Act (42 U.S.C. 1397jj(b)) is amended—

(i) in paragraph (2)(B), by inserting "except as provided in paragraph (6)," before "a child"; and

(ii) by adding at the end the following new paragraph:

"(6) EXCEPTIONS TO EXCLUSION OF CHILDREN OF EMPLOYEES OF A PUBLIC AGENCY IN THE STATE.—

"(A) IN GENERAL.—A child shall not be considered to be described in paragraph (2)(B) if—

"(i) the public agency that employs a member of the child's family to which such paragraph applies satisfies subparagraph (B); or

"(ii) subparagraph (C) applies to such child.

"(B) MAINTENANCE OF EFFORT WITH RESPECT TO PER PERSON AGENCY CONTRIBUTION FOR FAMILY COVERAGE.—For purposes of subparagraph (A)(i), a public agency satisfies this subparagraph if the amount of annual agency expenditures made on behalf of each employee enrolled in health coverage paid for by the agency that includes dependent coverage for the most recent State fiscal year is not less than the amount of such expenditures made by the agency for the 1997 State fiscal year, increased by the percentage increase in the medical care expenditure category of the Consumer Price Index for All-Urban Consumers (all items: U.S. City Average) for such preceding fiscal year.

"(C) HARDSHIP EXCEPTION.—For purposes of subparagraph (A)(ii), this subparagraph applies to a child if the State determines, on a case-by-case basis, that the annual aggregate amount of premiums and cost-sharing imposed for coverage of the family of the child would exceed 5 percent of such family's income for the year involved.".

(E) Section 2113 of such Act (42 U.S.C. 1397mm) is amended—

(i) in subsection (a)(1), by striking "2013" and inserting "2015"; and

(ii) in subsection (g), by striking "$100,000,000 for the period of fiscal years 2009 through 2013" and inserting "$140,000,000 for the period of fiscal years 2009 through 2015".

(F) Section 108 of Public Law 111–3 is amended by striking "$11,706,000,000" and all that follows through the second sentence and inserting "$15,361,000,000 to accompany the allotment made for the period beginning on October 1, 2014, and ending on March 31, 2015, under section 2104(a)(18)(A) of the Social Security Act (42 U.S.C. 1397dd(a)(18)(A)), to remain available until expended. Such amount shall be used to provide allotments to States under paragraph (3) of section 2104(m) of the Social Security Act (42 U.S.C. 1397dd(m)) for the first 6 months of fiscal year 2015 in the same manner as allotments are provided under subsection (a)(18)(A) of such section 2104 and subject to the same terms and conditions as apply to the allotments provided from such subsection (a)(18)(A).".

PART II—SUPPORT FOR PREGNANT AND PARENTING TEENS AND WOMEN

SEC. 10211. DEFINITIONS.

In this part:

(1) ACCOMPANIMENT.—The term "accompaniment" means assisting, representing, and accompanying a woman in seeking judicial relief for child support, child custody, restraining orders, and restitution for harm to persons and property, and in filing criminal charges, and may include the payment of court costs and reasonable attorney and witness fees associated therewith.

(2) ELIGIBLE INSTITUTION OF HIGHER EDUCATION.—The term "eligible institution of higher education" means an institution of higher education (as such term is defined in section 101 of the Higher Education Act of 1965 (20 U.S.C. 1001)) that has established and operates, or agrees to establish and operate upon the receipt of a grant under this part, a pregnant and parenting student services office.

(3) COMMUNITY SERVICE CENTER.—The term "community service center" means a non-profit organization that provides social services to residents of a specific geographical area via direct service or by contract with a local governmental agency.

(4) HIGH SCHOOL.—The term "high school" means any public or private school that operates grades 10 through 12, inclusive, grades 9 through 12, inclusive or grades 7 through 12, inclusive.

(5) INTERVENTION SERVICES.—The term "intervention services" means, with respect to domestic violence, sexual violence, sexual assault, or stalking, 24-hour telephone hotline services for police protection and referral to shelters.

(6) SECRETARY.—The term "Secretary" means the Secretary of Health and Human Services.

(7) STATE.—The term “State” includes the District of Columbia, any commonwealth, possession, or other territory of the United States, and any Indian tribe or reservation.

(8) SUPPORTIVE SOCIAL SERVICES.—The term “supportive social services” means transitional and permanent housing, vocational counseling, and individual and group counseling aimed at preventing domestic violence, sexual violence, sexual assault, or stalking.

(9) VIOLENCE.—The term “violence” means actual violence and the risk or threat of violence.

SEC. 10212. ESTABLISHMENT OF PREGNANCY ASSISTANCE FUND.

(a) IN GENERAL.—The Secretary, in collaboration and coordination with the Secretary of Education (as appropriate), shall establish a Pregnancy Assistance Fund to be administered by the Secretary, for the purpose of awarding competitive grants to States to assist pregnant and parenting teens and women.

(b) USE OF FUND.—A State may apply for a grant under subsection (a) to carry out any activities provided for in section 10213.

(c) APPLICATIONS.—To be eligible to receive a grant under subsection (a), a State shall submit to the Secretary an application at such time, in such manner, and containing such information as the Secretary may require, including a description of the purposes for which the grant is being requested and the designation of a State agency for receipt and administration of funding received under this part.

SEC. 10213. PERMISSIBLE USES OF FUND.

(a) IN GENERAL.—A State shall use amounts received under a grant under section 10212 for the purposes described in this section to assist pregnant and parenting teens and women.

(b) INSTITUTIONS OF HIGHER EDUCATION.—

(1) IN GENERAL.—A State may use amounts received under a grant under section 10212 to make funding available to eligible institutions of higher education to enable the eligible institutions to establish, maintain, or operate pregnant and parenting student services. Such funding shall be used to supplement, not supplant, existing funding for such services.

(2) APPLICATION.—An eligible institution of higher education that desires to receive funding under this subsection shall submit an application to the designated State agency at such time, in such manner, and containing such information as the State agency may require.

(3) MATCHING REQUIREMENT.—An eligible institution of higher education that receives funding under this subsection shall contribute to the conduct of the pregnant and parenting student services office supported by the funding an amount from non-Federal funds equal to 25 percent of the amount of the funding provided. The non-Federal share may be in cash or in-kind, fairly evaluated, including services, facilities, supplies, or equipment.

(4) USE OF FUNDS FOR ASSISTING PREGNANT AND PARENTING COLLEGE STUDENTS.—An eligible institution of higher education that receives funding under this subsection shall use such funds to establish, maintain or operate pregnant and parenting student services and may use such funding for the following programs and activities:

(A) Conduct a needs assessment on campus and within the local community—

(i) to assess pregnancy and parenting resources, located on the campus or within the local community, that are available to meet the needs described in subparagraph (B); and

(ii) to set goals for—

(I) improving such resources for pregnant, parenting, and prospective parenting students; and

(II) improving access to such resources.

(B) Annually assess the performance of the eligible institution in meeting the following needs of students enrolled in the eligible institution who are pregnant or are parents:

(i) The inclusion of maternity coverage and the availability of riders for additional family members in student health care.

(ii) Family housing.

(iii) Child care.

(iv) Flexible or alternative academic scheduling, such as telecommuting programs, to enable pregnant or parenting students to continue their education or stay in school.

(v) Education to improve parenting skills for mothers and fathers and to strengthen marriages.

(vi) Maternity and baby clothing, baby food (including formula), baby furniture, and similar items to assist parents and prospective parents in meeting the material needs of their children.

(vii) Post-partum counseling.

(C) Identify public and private service providers, located on the campus of the eligible institution or within the local community, that are qualified to meet the needs described in subparagraph (B), and establishes programs with qualified providers to meet such needs.

(D) Assist pregnant and parenting students, fathers or spouses in locating and obtaining services that meet the needs described in subparagraph (B).

(E) If appropriate, provide referrals for prenatal care and delivery, infant or foster care, or adoption, to a student who requests such information. An office shall make such referrals only to service providers that serve the following types of individuals:

(i) Parents.

(ii) Prospective parents awaiting adoption.

(iii) Women who are pregnant and plan on parenting or placing the child for adoption.

(iv) Parenting or prospective parenting couples.

(5) REPORTING.—

(A) ANNUAL REPORT BY INSTITUTIONS.—

(i) IN GENERAL.—For each fiscal year that an eligible institution of higher education receives funds under this subsection, the eligible institution shall prepare and submit to the State, by the date determined by the State, a report that—

(I) itemizes the pregnant and parenting student services office's expenditures for the fiscal year;

(II) contains a review and evaluation of the performance of the office in fulfilling the requirements of this section, using the specific performance criteria or standards established under subparagraph (B)(i); and

(III) describes the achievement of the office in meeting the needs listed in paragraph (4)(B) of the students served by the eligible institution, and the frequency of use of the office by such students.

(ii) PERFORMANCE CRITERIA.—Not later than 180 days before the date the annual report described in clause (i) is submitted, the State—

(I) shall identify the specific performance criteria or standards that shall be used to prepare the report; and

(II) may establish the form or format of the report.

(B) REPORT BY STATE.—The State shall annually prepare and submit a report on the findings under this subsection, including the number of eligible institutions of higher education that were awarded funds and the number of students served by each pregnant and parenting student services office receiving funds under this section, to the Secretary.

(c) SUPPORT FOR PREGNANT AND PARENTING TEENS.—A State may use amounts received under a grant under section 10212 to make funding available to eligible high schools and community service centers to establish, maintain or operate pregnant and parenting services in the same general manner and in accordance with all conditions and requirements described in subsection (b), except that paragraph (3) of such subsection shall not apply for purposes of this subsection.

(d) IMPROVING SERVICES FOR PREGNANT WOMEN WHO ARE VICTIMS OF DOMESTIC VIOLENCE, SEXUAL VIOLENCE, SEXUAL ASSAULT, AND STALKING.—

(1) IN GENERAL.—A State may use amounts received under a grant under section 10212 to make funding available tp its State Attorney General to assist Statewide offices in providing—

(A) intervention services, accompaniment, and supportive social services for eligible pregnant women who are victims of domestic violence, sexual violence, sexual assault, or stalking.

(B) technical assistance and training (as described in subsection (c)) relating to violence against eligible pregnant women to be made available to the following:

(i) Federal, State, tribal, territorial, and local governments, law enforcement agencies, and courts.

(ii) Professionals working in legal, social service, and health care settings.

(iii) Nonprofit organizations.

(iv) Faith-based organizations.

(2) ELIGIBILITY.—To be eligible for a grant under paragraph (1), a State Attorney General shall submit an application to the designated State agency at such time, in such manner, and containing such information, as specified by the State.

(3) TECHNICAL ASSISTANCE AND TRAINING DESCRIBED.—For purposes of paragraph (1)(B), technical assistance and training is—

(A) the identification of eligible pregnant women experiencing domestic violence, sexual violence, sexual assault, or stalking;

(B) the assessment of the immediate and short-term safety of such a pregnant woman, the evaluation of the impact of the violence or stalking on the pregnant woman's health, and the assistance of the pregnant woman in developing a plan aimed at preventing further domestic violence, sexual violence, sexual assault, or stalking, as appropriate;

(C) the maintenance of complete medical or forensic records that include the documentation of any examination, treatment given, and referrals made, recording the location and nature of the pregnant woman's injuries, and the establishment of mechanisms to ensure the privacy and confidentiality of those medical records; and

(D) the identification and referral of the pregnant woman to appropriate public and private nonprofit entities that provide intervention services, accompaniment, and supportive social services.

(4) ELIGIBLE PREGNANT WOMAN.—In this subsection, the term "eligible pregnant woman" means any woman who is pregnant on the date on which such woman becomes a victim of domestic violence, sexual violence, sexual assault, or stalking or who was pregnant during the one-year period before such date.

(e) PUBLIC AWARENESS AND EDUCATION.—A State may use amounts received under a grant under section 10212 to make funding available to increase public awareness and education concerning any services available to pregnant and parenting teens and women under this part, or any other resources available to pregnant and parenting women in keeping with the intent and purposes of this part. The State shall be responsible for setting guidelines or limits as to how much of funding may be utilized for public awareness and education in any funding award.

SEC. 10214. APPROPRIATIONS.

There is authorized to be appropriated, and there are appropriated, $25,000,000 for each of fiscal years 2010 through 2019, to carry out this part.

PART III—INDIAN HEALTH CARE IMPROVEMENT

SEC. 10221. INDIAN HEALTH CARE IMPROVEMENT.

(a) IN GENERAL.—Except as provided in subsection (b), S. 1790 entitled "A bill to amend the Indian Health Care Improvement Act to revise and extend that Act, and for other purposes.", as reported by the Committee on Indian Affairs of the Senate in December 2009, is enacted into law.

(b) AMENDMENTS.—

(1) Section 119 of the Indian Health Care Improvement Act (as amended by section 111 of the bill referred to in subsection (a)) is amended—

(A) in subsection (d)—

(i) in paragraph (2), by striking "In establishing" and inserting "Subject to paragraphs (3) and (4), in establishing"; and

(ii) by adding at the end the following:

"(3) ELECTION OF INDIAN TRIBE OR TRIBAL ORGANIZATION.—

"(A) IN GENERAL.—Subparagraph (B) of paragraph (2) shall not apply in the case of an election made by an Indian tribe or tribal organization located in a State (other than Alaska) in which the use of dental health aide therapist services or midlevel dental health provider services is authorized under State law to supply such services in accordance with State law.

"(B) ACTION BY SECRETARY.—On an election by an Indian tribe or tribal organization under subparagraph (A), the Secretary, acting through the Service, shall facilitate implementation of the services elected.

"(4) VACANCIES.—The Secretary shall not fill any vacancy for a certified dentist in a program operated by the Service with a dental health aide therapist."; and

(B) by adding at the end the following:

"(e) EFFECT OF SECTION.—Nothing in this section shall restrict the ability of the Service, an Indian tribe, or a tribal organization to participate in any program or to provide any service authorized by any other Federal law.".

(2) The Indian Health Care Improvement Act (as amended by section 134(b) of the bill referred to in subsection (a)) is amended by striking section 125 (relating to treatment of scholarships for certain purposes).

(3) Section 806 of the Indian Health Care Improvement Act (25 U.S.C. 1676) is amended—

(A) by striking "Any limitation" and inserting the following:

"(a) HHS APPROPRIATIONS.—Any limitation"; and

(B) by adding at the end the following:

"(b) LIMITATIONS PURSUANT TO OTHER FEDERAL LAW.—Any limitation pursuant to other Federal laws on the use of Federal funds appropriated to the Service shall apply with respect to the performance or coverage of abortions.".

(4) The bill referred to in subsection (a) is amended by striking section 201.

Subtitle C—Provisions Relating to Title III

SEC. 10301. PLANS FOR A VALUE-BASED PURCHASING PROGRAM FOR AMBULATORY SURGICAL CENTERS.

(a) IN GENERAL.—Section 3006 is amended by adding at the end the following new subsection:

"(f) AMBULATORY SURGICAL CENTERS.—

"(1) IN GENERAL.—The Secretary shall develop a plan to implement a value-based purchasing program for payments under the Medicare program under title XVIII of the Social

Security Act for ambulatory surgical centers (as described in section 1833(i) of the Social Security Act (42 U.S.C. 1395l(i))).

"(2) DETAILS.—In developing the plan under paragraph (1), the Secretary shall consider the following issues:

"(A) The ongoing development, selection, and modification process for measures (including under section 1890 of the Social Security Act (42 U.S.C. 1395aaa) and section 1890A of such Act, as added by section 3014), to the extent feasible and practicable, of all dimensions of quality and efficiency in ambulatory surgical centers.

"(B) The reporting, collection, and validation of quality data.

"(C) The structure of value-based payment adjustments, including the determination of thresholds or improvements in quality that would substantiate a payment adjustment, the size of such payments, and the sources of funding for the value-based bonus payments.

"(D) Methods for the public disclosure of information on the performance of ambulatory surgical centers.

"(E) Any other issues determined appropriate by the Secretary.

"(3) CONSULTATION.—In developing the plan under paragraph (1), the Secretary shall—

"(A) consult with relevant affected parties; and

"(B) consider experience with such demonstrations that the Secretary determines are relevant to the value-based purchasing program described in paragraph (1).

"(4) REPORT TO CONGRESS.—Not later than January 1, 2011, the Secretary shall submit to Congress a report containing the plan developed under paragraph (1).".

(b) TECHNICAL.—Section 3006(a)(2)(A) is amended by striking clauses (i) and (ii).

SEC. 10302. REVISION TO NATIONAL STRATEGY FOR QUALITY IMPROVEMENT IN HEALTH CARE.

Section 399HH(a)(2)(B)(iii) of the Public Health Service Act, as added by section 3011, is amended by inserting "(taking into consideration the limitations set forth in subsections (c) and (d) of section 1182 of the Social Security Act)" after "information".

SEC. 10303. DEVELOPMENT OF OUTCOME MEASURES.

(a) DEVELOPMENT.—Section 931 of the Public Health Service Act, as added by section 3013(a), is amended by adding at the end the following new subsection:

"(f) DEVELOPMENT OF OUTCOME MEASURES.—

"(1) IN GENERAL.—The Secretary shall develop, and periodically update (not less than every 3 years), provider-level outcome measures for hospitals and physicians, as well as other providers as determined appropriate by the Secretary.

"(2) CATEGORIES OF MEASURES.—The measures developed under this subsection shall include, to the extent determined appropriate by the Secretary—

"(A) outcome measurement for acute and chronic diseases, including, to the extent feasible, the 5 most prevalent and resource-intensive acute and chronic medical conditions; and

"(B) outcome measurement for primary and preventative care, including, to the extent feasible, measurements that cover provision of such care for distinct patient populations (such as healthy children, chronically ill adults, or infirm elderly individuals).

"(3) GOALS.—In developing such measures, the Secretary shall seek to—

"(A) address issues regarding risk adjustment, accountability, and sample size;

"(B) include the full scope of services that comprise a cycle of care; and

"(C) include multiple dimensions.

"(4) TIMEFRAME.—

"(A) ACUTE AND CHRONIC DISEASES.—Not later than 24 months after the date of enactment of this Act, the Secretary shall develop not less than 10 measures described in paragraph (2)(A).

"(B) PRIMARY AND PREVENTIVE CARE.—Not later than 36 months after the date of enactment of this Act, the Secretary shall develop not less than 10 measures described in paragraph (2)(B).".

(b) HOSPITAL-ACQUIRED CONDITIONS.—Section 1890A of the Social Security Act, as amended by section 3013(b), is amended by adding at the end the following new subsection:

"(f) HOSPITAL ACQUIRED CONDITIONS.—The Secretary shall, to the extent practicable, publicly report on measures for hospital-acquired conditions that are currently utilized by the Centers for Medicare & Medicaid Services for the adjustment of the amount of payment to hospitals based on rates of hospital-acquired infections.".

(c) CLINICAL PRACTICE GUIDELINES.—Section 304(b) of the Medicare Improvements for Patients and Providers Act of 2008 (Public Law 110–275) is amended by adding at the end the following new paragraph:

"(4) IDENTIFICATION.—

"(A) IN GENERAL.—Following receipt of the report submitted under paragraph (2), and not less than every 3 years thereafter, the Secretary shall contract with the Institute to employ the results of the study performed under paragraph (1) and the best methods identified by the Institute for the purpose of identifying existing and new clinical practice guidelines that were developed using such best methods, including guidelines listed in the National Guideline Clearinghouse.

"(B) CONSULTATION.—In carrying out the identification process under subparagraph (A), the Secretary shall allow for consultation with professional societies, voluntary health care organizations, and expert panels.".

SEC. 10304. SELECTION OF EFFICIENCY MEASURES.

Sections 1890(b)(7) and 1890A of the Social Security Act, as added by section 3014, are amended by striking "quality" each place it appears and inserting "quality and efficiency".

SEC. 10305. DATA COLLECTION; PUBLIC REPORTING.

Section 399II(a) of the Public Health Service Act, as added by section 3015, is amended to read as follows:

"(a) IN GENERAL.—

"(1) ESTABLISHMENT OF STRATEGIC FRAMEWORK.—The Secretary shall establish and implement an overall strategic framework to carry out the public reporting of performance information, as described in section 399JJ. Such strategic framework may include methods and related timelines for implementing nationally consistent data collection, data aggregation, and analysis methods.

"(2) COLLECTION AND AGGREGATION OF DATA.—The Secretary shall collect and aggregate consistent data on quality and resource use measures from information systems used to support health care delivery, and may award grants or contracts for this purpose. The Secretary shall align such collection and aggregation efforts with the requirements and assistance regarding the expansion of health information technology systems, the interoperability of such technology systems, and related standards that are in effect on the date of enactment of the Patient Protection and Affordable Care Act.

"(3) SCOPE.—The Secretary shall ensure that the data collection, data aggregation, and analysis systems described in paragraph (1) involve an increasingly broad range of patient populations, providers, and geographic areas over time.".

SEC. 10306. IMPROVEMENTS UNDER THE CENTER FOR MEDICARE AND MEDICAID INNOVATION.

Section 1115A of the Social Security Act, as added by section 3021, is amended—

(1) in subsection (a), by inserting at the end the following new paragraph:

"(5) TESTING WITHIN CERTAIN GEOGRAPHIC AREAS.—For purposes of testing payment and service delivery models under this section, the Secretary may elect to limit testing of a model to certain geographic areas.";

(2) in subsection (b)(2)—

(A) in subparagraph (A)—

(i) in the second sentence, by striking "the preceding sentence may include" and inserting "this subparagraph may include, but are not limited to,"; and

(ii) by inserting after the first sentence the following new sentence: "The Secretary shall focus on models expected to reduce program costs under the applicable title while preserving or enhancing the quality of care received by individuals receiving benefits under such title.";

(B) in subparagraph (B), by adding at the end the following new clauses:

"(xix) Utilizing, in particular in entities located in medically underserved areas and facilities of the Indian Health Service (whether operated by such Service or by an Indian tribe or tribal organization (as those terms are defined in section 4 of the Indian Health Care Improvement Act)), telehealth services—

"(I) in treating behavioral health issues (such as post-traumatic stress disorder) and stroke; and

"(II) to improve the capacity of non-medical providers and non-specialized medical providers to provide health services for patients with chronic complex conditions.

"(xx) Utilizing a diverse network of providers of services and suppliers to improve care coordination for applicable individuals described in subsection (a)(4)(A)(i) with 2 or more chronic conditions and a history of prior-year hospitalization through interventions developed under the Medicare Coordinated Care Demonstration Project under section 4016 of the Balanced Budget Act of 1997 (42 U.S.C. 1395b–1 note)."; and

(C) in subparagraph (C), by adding at the end the following new clause:

"(viii) Whether the model demonstrates effective linkage with other public sector or private sector payers.";

(3) in subsection (b)(4), by adding at the end the following new subparagraph:

"(C) MEASURE SELECTION.—To the extent feasible, the Secretary shall select measures under this paragraph that reflect national priorities for quality improvement and patient-centered care consistent with the measures described in 1890(b)(7)(B)."; and

(4) in subsection (c)—

(A) in paragraph (1)(B), by striking "care and reduce spending; and" and inserting "patient care without increasing spending;";

(B) in paragraph (2), by striking "reduce program spending under applicable titles." and inserting "reduce (or would not result in any increase in) net program spending under applicable titles; and"; and

(C) by adding at the end the following:

"(3) the Secretary determines that such expansion would not deny or limit the coverage or provision of benefits under the applicable title for applicable individuals.

In determining which models or demonstration projects to expand under the preceding sentence, the Secretary shall focus on models and demonstration projects that improve the quality of patient care and reduce spending.".

SEC. 10307. IMPROVEMENTS TO THE MEDICARE SHARED SAVINGS PROGRAM.

Section 1899 of the Social Security Act, as added by section 3022, is amended by adding at the end the following new subsections:

"(i) OPTION TO USE OTHER PAYMENT MODELS.—

"(1) IN GENERAL.—If the Secretary determines appropriate, the Secretary may use any of the payment models described in paragraph (2) or (3) for making payments under the program rather than the payment model described in subsection (d).

"(2) PARTIAL CAPITATION MODEL.—

"(A) IN GENERAL.—Subject to subparagraph (B), a model described in this paragraph is a partial capitation model in which an ACO is at financial risk for some, but not all, of the items and services covered under parts A and B, such as at risk for some or all physicians' services or all items and services under part B. The Secretary may limit a partial capitation model to ACOs that are highly integrated systems of care and to ACOs capable of bearing risk, as determined to be appropriate by the Secretary.

"(B) NO ADDITIONAL PROGRAM EXPENDITURES.—Payments to an ACO for items and services under this title for beneficiaries for a year under the partial capitation model shall be established in a manner that does not result in spending more for such ACO for such beneficiaries than would otherwise be expended for such ACO for such beneficiaries for such year if the model were not implemented, as estimated by the Secretary.

"(3) OTHER PAYMENT MODELS.—

"(A) IN GENERAL.—Subject to subparagraph (B), a model described in this paragraph is any payment model that the Secretary determines will improve the quality and efficiency of items and services furnished under this title.

"(B) NO ADDITIONAL PROGRAM EXPENDITURES.—Subparagraph (B) of paragraph (2) shall apply to a payment model under subparagraph (A) in a similar manner as such subparagraph (B) applies to the payment model under paragraph (2).

"(j) INVOLVEMENT IN PRIVATE PAYER AND OTHER THIRD PARTY ARRANGEMENTS.—The Secretary may give preference to ACOs who are participating in similar arrangements with other payers.

"(k) TREATMENT OF PHYSICIAN GROUP PRACTICE DEMONSTRATION.—During the period beginning on the date of the enactment of this section and ending on the date the program is established, the Secretary may enter into an agreement with an ACO under the demonstration under section 1866A, subject to rebasing and other modifications deemed appropriate by the Secretary.".

SEC. 10308. REVISIONS TO NATIONAL PILOT PROGRAM ON PAYMENT BUNDLING.

(a) IN GENERAL.—Section 1866D of the Social Security Act, as added by section 3023, is amended—

(1) in paragraph (a)(2)(B), in the matter preceding clause (i), by striking "8 conditions" and inserting "10 conditions";

(2) by striking subsection (c)(1)(B) and inserting the following:

"(B) EXPANSION.—The Secretary may, at any point after January 1, 2016, expand the duration and scope of the pilot program, to the extent determined appropriate by the Secretary, if—

"(i) the Secretary determines that such expansion is expected to—

"(I) reduce spending under title XVIII of the Social Security Act without reducing the quality of care; or

"(II) improve the quality of care and reduce spending;

"(ii) the Chief Actuary of the Centers for Medicare & Medicaid Services certifies that such expansion would reduce program spending under such title XVIII; and "(iii) the Secretary determines that such expansion would not deny or limit the coverage or provision of benefits under this title for individuals."; and

(3) by striking subsection (g) and inserting the following new subsection:

"(g) APPLICATION OF PILOT PROGRAM TO CONTINUING CARE HOSPITALS.—

"(1) IN GENERAL.—In conducting the pilot program, the Secretary shall apply the provisions of the program so as to separately pilot test the continuing care hospital model.

"(2) SPECIAL RULES.—In pilot testing the continuing care hospital model under paragraph (1), the following rules shall apply:

"(A) Such model shall be tested without the limitation to the conditions selected under subsection (a)(2)(B).

"(B) Notwithstanding subsection (a)(2)(D), an episode of care shall be defined as the full period that a patient stays in the continuing care hospital plus the first 30 days following discharge from such hospital.

"(3) CONTINUING CARE HOSPITAL DEFINED.—In this subsection, the term 'continuing care hospital' means an entity that has demonstrated the ability to meet patient care and patient safety standards and that provides under common management the medical and rehabilitation services provided in inpatient rehabilitation hospitals and units (as defined in section 1886(d)(1)(B)(ii)), long term care hospitals (as defined in section 1886(d)(1)(B)(iv)(I)), and skilled nursing facilities (as defined in section 1819(a)) that are located in a hospital described in section 1886(d).".

(b) TECHNICAL AMENDMENTS.—

(1) Section 3023 is amended by striking "1886C" and inserting "1866C".

(2) Title XVIII of the Social Security Act is amended by redesignating section 1866D, as added by section 3024, as section 1866E.

SEC. 10309. REVISIONS TO HOSPITAL READMISSIONS REDUCTION PROGRAM.

Section 1886(q)(1) of the Social Security Act, as added by section 3025, in the matter preceding subparagraph (A), is amended by striking "the Secretary shall reduce the payments" and all that follows through "the product of" and inserting "the Secretary shall make payments (in addition to the payments described in paragraph (2)(A)(ii)) for such a discharge to such hospital under subsection (d) (or section 1814(b)(3), as the case may be) in an amount equal to the product of".

SEC. 10310. REPEAL OF PHYSICIAN PAYMENT UPDATE.

The provisions of, and the amendment made by, section 3101 are repealed.

SEC. 10311. REVISIONS TO EXTENSION OF AMBULANCE ADD-ONS.

(a) GROUND AMBULANCE.—Section 1834(l)(13)(A) of the Social Security Act (42 U.S.C. 1395m(l)(13)(A)), as amended by section 3105(a), is further amended—

(1) in the matter preceding clause (i)—

(A) by striking "2007, for" and inserting "2007, and for"; and

(B) by striking "2010, and for such services furnished on or after April 1, 2010, and before January 1, 2011" and inserting "2011"; and

(2) in each of clauses (i) and (ii)—

(A) by striking ", and on or after April 1, 2010, and before January 1, 2011" each place it appears; and

(B) by striking "January 1, 2010" and inserting "January 1, 2011" each place it appears.

(b) AIR AMBULANCE.—Section 146(b)(1) of the Medicare Improvements for Patients and Providers Act of 2008 (Public Law 110–275), as amended by section 3105(b), is further amended by striking "December 31, 2009, and during the period beginning on April 1, 2010, and ending on January 1, 2011" and inserting "December 31, 2010".

(c) SUPER RURAL AMBULANCE.—Section 1834(l)(12)(A) of the Social Security Act (42 U.S.C. 1395m(l)(12)(A)), as amended by section 3105(c), is further amended by striking "2010, and on or after April 1, 2010, and before January 1, 2011" and inserting "2011".

SEC. 10312. CERTAIN PAYMENT RULES FOR LONG-TERM CARE HOSPITAL SERVICES AND MORATORIUM ON THE ESTABLISHMENT OF CERTAIN HOSPITALS AND FACILITIES.

(a) CERTAIN PAYMENT RULES.—Section 114(c) of the Medicare, Medicaid, and SCHIP Extension Act of 2007 (42 U.S.C. 1395ww note), as amended by section 4302(a) of the American Recovery and Reinvestment Act (Public Law 111–5) and section 3106(a) of this Act, is further amended by striking "4-year period" each place it appears and inserting "5-year period".

(b) MORATORIUM.—Section 114(d) of such Act (42 U.S.C. 1395ww note), as amended by section 3106(b) of this Act, in the matter preceding subparagraph (A), is amended by striking "4-year period" and inserting "5-year period".

SEC. 10313. REVISIONS TO THE EXTENSION FOR THE RURAL COMMUNITY HOSPITAL DEMONSTRATION PROGRAM.

(a) IN GENERAL.—Subsection (g) of section 410A of the Medicare Prescription Drug, Improvement, and Modernization Act of 2003 (Public Law 108–173; 117 Stat. 2272), as added by section 3123(a) of this Act, is amended to read as follows:

"(g) FIVE-YEAR EXTENSION OF DEMONSTRATION PROGRAM.—

"(1) IN GENERAL.—Subject to the succeeding provisions of this subsection, the Secretary shall conduct the demonstration program under this section for an additional 5-year period (in this section referred to as the '5-year extension period') that begins on the date immediately following the last day of the initial 5-year period under subsection (a)(5).

"(2) EXPANSION OF DEMONSTRATION STATES.—Notwithstanding subsection (a)(2), during the 5-year extension period, the Secretary shall expand the number of States with low population densities determined by the Secretary under such subsection to 20. In determining which States to include in such expansion, the Secretary shall use the same criteria and data that the Secretary used to determine the States under such subsection for purposes of the initial 5-year period.

"(3) INCREASE IN MAXIMUM NUMBER OF HOSPITALS PARTICIPATING IN THE DEMONSTRATION PROGRAM.—Notwithstanding subsection (a)(4), during the 5-year extension period, not more than 30 rural community hospitals may participate in the demonstration program under this section.

"(4) HOSPITALS IN DEMONSTRATION PROGRAM ON DATE OF ENACTMENT.—In the case of a rural community hospital that is participating in the demonstration program under this section as of the last day of the initial 5-year period, the Secretary—

"(A) shall provide for the continued participation of such rural community hospital in the demonstration program during the 5-year extension period unless the rural community hospital makes an election, in such form and manner as the Secretary may specify, to discontinue such participation; and

"(B) in calculating the amount of payment under subsection (b) to the rural community hospital for covered inpatient hospital services furnished by the hospital during such 5-year extension period, shall substitute, under paragraph (1)(A) of such subsection—

"(i) the reasonable costs of providing such services for discharges occurring in the first cost reporting period beginning on or after the first day of the 5-year extension period, for

"(ii) the reasonable costs of providing such services for discharges occurring in the first cost reporting period beginning on or after the implementation of the demonstration program.".

(b) CONFORMING AMENDMENTS.—Subsection (a)(5) of section 410A of the Medicare Prescription Drug, Improvement, and Modernization Act of 2003 (Public Law 108–173; 117 Stat. 2272), as amended by section 3123(b) of this Act, is amended by striking "1-year extension" and inserting "5-year extension".

SEC. 10314. ADJUSTMENT TO LOW-VOLUME HOSPITAL PROVISION.

Section 1886(d)(12) of the Social Security Act (42 U.S.C. 1395ww(d)(12), as amended by section 3125, is amended—

(1) in subparagraph (C)(i), by striking "1,500 discharges" and inserting "1,600 discharges"; and

(2) in subparagraph (D), by striking "1,500 discharges" and inserting "1,600 discharges".

SEC. 10315. REVISIONS TO HOME HEALTH CARE PROVISIONS.

(a) REBASING.—Section 1895(b)(3)(A)(iii) of the Social Security Act, as added by section 3131, is amended—

(1) in the clause heading, by striking "2013" and inserting "2014";

(2) in subclause (I), by striking "2013" and inserting "2014"; and

(3) in subclause (II), by striking "2016" and inserting "2017".

(b) REVISION OF HOME HEALTH STUDY AND REPORT.—Section 3131(d) is amended to read as follows:

"(d) STUDY AND REPORT ON THE DEVELOPMENT OF HOME HEALTH PAYMENT REVISIONS IN ORDER TO ENSURE ACCESS TO CARE AND PAYMENT FOR SEVERITY OF ILLNESS.—

"(1) IN GENERAL.—The Secretary of Health and Human Services (in this section referred to as the 'Secretary') shall conduct a study on home health agency costs involved with providing ongoing access to care to low-income Medicare beneficiaries or beneficiaries in medically underserved areas, and in treating beneficiaries with varying levels of severity of illness. In conducting the study, the Secretary may analyze items such as the following:

"(A) Methods to potentially revise the home health prospective payment system under section 1895 of the Social Security Act (42 U.S.C. 1395fff) to account for costs related to patient severity of illness or to improving beneficiary access to care, such as—

"(i) payment adjustments for services that may involve additional or fewer resources;

"(ii) changes to reflect resources involved with providing home health services to low-income Medicare beneficiaries or Medicare beneficiaries residing in medically underserved areas;

"(iii) ways outlier payments might be revised to reflect costs of treating Medicare beneficiaries with high levels of severity of illness; and

"(iv) other issues determined appropriate by the Secretary.

"(B) Operational issues involved with potential implementation of potential revisions to the home health payment system, including impacts for both home health agencies and administrative and systems issues for the Centers for Medicare & Medicaid Services, and any possible payment vulnerabilities associated with implementing potential revisions.

"(C) Whether additional research might be needed.

"(D) Other items determined appropriate by the Secretary.

"(2) CONSIDERATIONS.—In conducting the study under paragraph (1), the Secretary may consider whether patient severity of illness and access to care could be measured by factors, such as—

"(A) population density and relative patient access to care;

"(B) variations in service costs for providing care to individuals who are dually eligible under the Medicare and Medicaid programs;

"(C) the presence of severe or chronic diseases, which might be measured by multiple, discontinuous home health episodes;

"(D) poverty status, such as evidenced by the receipt of Supplemental Security Income under title XVI of the Social Security Act; and

"(E) other factors determined appropriate by the Secretary.

"(3) REPORT.—Not later than March 1, 2014, the Secretary shall submit to Congress a report on the study conducted under paragraph (1), together with recommendations for such legislation and administrative action as the Secretary determines appropriate.

"(4) CONSULTATIONS.—In conducting the study under paragraph (1), the Secretary shall consult with appropriate stakeholders, such as groups representing home health agencies and groups representing Medicare beneficiaries.

"(5) MEDICARE DEMONSTRATION PROJECT BASED ON THE RESULTS OF THE STUDY.—

"(A) IN GENERAL.—Subject to subparagraph (D), taking into account the results of the study conducted under paragraph (1), the Secretary may, as determined appropriate, provide for a demonstration project to test whether making payment adjustments for home health services under the Medicare program would substantially improve access to care for patients with high severity levels of illness or for low-income or underserved Medicare beneficiaries.

"(B) WAIVING BUDGET NEUTRALITY.—The Secretary shall not reduce the standard prospective payment amount (or amounts) under section 1895 of the Social Security Act (42 U.S.C. 1395fff) applicable to home health services furnished during a period to offset any increase in payments during such period resulting from the application of the payment adjustments under subparagraph (A).

"(C) NO EFFECT ON SUBSEQUENT PERIODS.—A payment adjustment resulting from the application of subparagraph (A) for a period—

"(i) shall not apply to payments for home health services under title XVIII after such period; and

"(ii) shall not be taken into account in calculating the payment amounts applicable for such services after such period.

"(D) DURATION.—If the Secretary determines it appropriate to conduct the demonstration project under this subsection, the Secretary shall conduct the project for a four year period beginning not later than January 1, 2015.

"(E) FUNDING.—The Secretary shall provide for the transfer from the Federal Hospital Insurance Trust Fund under section 1817 of the Social Security Act (42 U.S.C. 1395i) and the Federal Supplementary Medical Insurance Trust Fund established under section 1841 of such Act (42 U.S.C. 1395t), in such proportion as the Secretary determines appropriate, of $500,000,000 for the period of fiscal years 2015 through 2018. Such funds shall be made available for the study described in paragraph (1) and the design, implementation and evaluation of the demonstration described in this paragraph. Amounts available under this subparagraph shall be available until expended.

"(F) EVALUATION AND REPORT.—If the Secretary determines it appropriate to conduct the demonstration project under this subsection, the Secretary shall—

"(i) provide for an evaluation of the project; and

"(ii) submit to Congress, by a date specified by the Secretary, a report on the project.

"(G) ADMINISTRATION.—Chapter 35 of title 44, United States Code, shall not apply with respect to this subsection.".

SEC. 10316. MEDICARE DSH.

Section 1886(r)(2)(B) of the Social Security Act, as added by section 3133, is amended—

(1) in clause (i)—

(A) in the matter preceding subclause (I), by striking "(divided by 100)";

(B) in subclause (I), by striking "2012" and inserting "2013";

(C) in subclause (II), by striking the period at the end and inserting a comma; and

(D) by adding at the end the following flush matter: "minus 1.5 percentage points.".

(2) in clause (ii)—

(A) in the matter preceding subclause (I), by striking "(divided by 100)";

(B) in subclause (I), by striking "2012" and inserting "2013";

(C) in subclause (II), by striking the period at the end and inserting a comma; and

(D) by adding at the end the following flush matter: "and, for each of 2018 and 2019, minus 1.5 percentage points.".

SEC. 10317. REVISIONS TO EXTENSION OF SECTION 508 HOSPITAL PROVISIONS.

Section 3137(a) is amended to read as follows:

"(a) EXTENSION.—

"(1) IN GENERAL.—Subsection (a) of section 106 of division B of the Tax Relief and Health Care Act of 2006 (42 U.S.C. 1395 note), as amended by section 117 of the Medicare, Medicaid, and SCHIP Extension Act of 2007 (Public Law 110–173) and section 124 of the Medicare Improvements for Patients and Providers Act of 2008 (Public Law 110–275), is amended by striking 'September 30, 2009' and inserting 'September 30, 2010'.

"(2) SPECIAL RULE FOR FISCAL YEAR 2010.—

"(A) IN GENERAL.—Subject to subparagraph (B), for purposes of implementation of the amendment made by paragraph (1), including (notwithstanding paragraph (3) of section 117(a) of the Medicare, Medicaid and SCHIP Extension Act of 2007 (Public Law 110–173), as amended by section 124(b) of the Medicare Improvements for Patients and Providers Act of 2008 (Public Law 110–275)) for purposes of the implementation of paragraph (2) of such section 117(a), during fiscal year 2010, the Secretary of Health and Human Services (in this subsection referred to as the 'Secretary') shall use the hospital wage index that was promulgated by the Secretary in the Federal Register on August 27, 2009 (74 Fed. Reg. 43754), and any subsequent corrections.

"(B) EXCEPTION.—Beginning on April 1, 2010, in determining the wage index applicable to hospitals that qualify for wage index reclassification, the Secretary shall include the average hourly wage data of hospitals whose reclassification was extended pursuant to the amendment made by paragraph (1) only if including such data results in a higher applicable reclassified wage index.

"(3) ADJUSTMENT FOR CERTAIN HOSPITALS IN FISCAL YEAR 2010.—

"(A) IN GENERAL.—In the case of a subsection (d) hospital (as defined in subsection (d)(1)(B) of section 1886 of the Social Security Act (42 U.S.C. 1395ww)) with respect to which—

"(i) a reclassification of its wage index for purposes of such section was extended pursuant to the amendment made by paragraph (1); and

"(ii) the wage index applicable for such hospital for the period beginning on October 1, 2009, and ending on March 31, 2010, was lower than for the period beginning on April 1, 2010, and ending on September 30, 2010, by reason of the application of paragraph (2)(B);

the Secretary shall pay such hospital an additional payment that reflects the difference between the wage index for such periods.

"(B) TIMEFRAME FOR PAYMENTS.—The Secretary shall make payments required under subparagraph by not later than December 31, 2010.".

SEC. 10318. REVISIONS TO TRANSITIONAL EXTRA BENEFITS UNDER MEDICARE ADVANTAGE.

Section 1853(p)(3)(A) of the Social Security Act, as added by section 3201(h), is amended by inserting "in 2009" before the period at the end.

SEC. 10319. REVISIONS TO MARKET BASKET ADJUSTMENTS.

(a) INPATIENT ACUTE HOSPITALS.—Section 1886(b)(3)(B)(xii) of the Social Security Act, as added by section 3401(a), is amended—

(1) in subclause (I), by striking "and" at the end;

(2) by redesignating subclause (II) as subclause (III);

(3) by inserting after subclause (II) the following new subclause:

"(II) for each of fiscal years 2012 and 2013, by 0.1 percentage point; and"; and

(4) in subclause (III), as redesignated by paragraph (2), by striking "2012" and inserting "2014".

(b) LONG-TERM CARE HOSPITALS.—Section 1886(m)(4) of the Social Security Act, as added by section 3401(c), is amended—

(1) in subparagraph (A)—

(A) in clause (i)—

(i) by striking "each of rate years 2010 and 2011" and inserting "rate year 2010"; and

(ii) by striking "and" at the end;

(B) by redesignating clause (ii) as clause (iv);

(C) by inserting after clause (i) the following new clauses:

"(ii) for rate year 2011, 0.50 percentage point;

"(iii) for each of the rate years beginning in 2012 and 2013, 0.1 percentage point; and"; and

(D) in clause (iv), as redesignated by subparagraph (B), by striking "2012" and inserting "2014"; and

(2) in subparagraph (B), by striking "(A)(ii)" and inserting "(A)(iv)".

(c) INPATIENT REHABILITATION FACILITIES.—Section 1886(j)(3)(D)(i) of the Social Security Act, as added by section 3401(d), is amended—

(1) in subclause (I), by striking "and" at the end;

(2) by redesignating subclause (II) as subclause (III);

(3) by inserting after subclause (II) the following new subclause:

"(II) for each of fiscal years 2012 and 2013, 0.1 percentage point; and"; and

(4) in subclause (III), as redesignated by paragraph (2), by striking "2012" and inserting "2014".

(d) HOME HEALTH AGENCIES.—Section 1895(b)(3)(B)(vi)(II) of such Act, as added by section 3401(e), is amended by striking "and 2012" and inserting ", 2012, and 2013".

(e) PSYCHIATRIC HOSPITALS.—Section 1886(s)(3)(A) of the Social Security Act, as added by section 3401(f), is amended—

(1) in clause (i), by striking "and" at the end;

(2) by redesignating clause (ii) as clause (iii);

(3) by inserting after clause (ii) the following new clause:

"(ii) for each of the rate years beginning in 2012 and 2013, 0.1 percentage point; and"; and

(4) in clause (iii), as redesignated by paragraph (2), by striking "2012" and inserting "2014".

(f) HOSPICE CARE.—Section 1814(i)(1)(C) of the Social Security Act (42 U.S.C. 1395f(i)(1)(C)), as amended by section 3401(g), is amended—

(1) in clause (iv)(II), by striking "0.5" and inserting "0.3"; and

(2) in clause (v), in the matter preceding subclause (I), by striking "0.5" and inserting "0.3".

(g) OUTPATIENT HOSPITALS.—Section 1833(t)(3)(G)(i) of the Social Security Act, as added by section 3401(i), is amended—

(1) in subclause (I), by striking "and" at the end;

(2) by redesignating subclause (II) as subclause (III);

(3) by inserting after subclause (II) the following new subclause:

"(II) for each of 2012 and 2013, 0.1 percentage point; and"; and

(4) in subclause (III), as redesignated by paragraph (2), by striking "2012" and inserting "2014".

SEC. 10320. EXPANSION OF THE SCOPE OF, AND ADDITIONAL IMPROVEMENTS TO, THE INDEPENDENT MEDICARE ADVISORY BOARD.

(a) IN GENERAL.—Section 1899A of the Social Security Act, as added by section 3403, is amended—

(1) in subsection (c)—

(A) in paragraph (1)(B), by adding at the end the following new sentence: "In any year (beginning with 2014) that the Board is not required to submit a proposal under this section, the Board shall submit to Congress an advisory report on matters related to the Medicare program.";

(B) in paragraph (2)(A)—

(i) in clause (iv), by inserting "or the full premium subsidy under section 1860D–14(a)" before the period at the end of the last sentence; and

(ii) by adding at the end the following new clause:

"(vii) If the Chief Actuary of the Centers for Medicare & Medicaid Services has made a determination described in subsection (e)(3)(B)(i)(II) in the determination year, the proposal shall be designed to help reduce the growth rate described in paragraph (8) while maintaining or enhancing beneficiary access to quality care under this title.";

(C) in paragraph (2)(B)—

(i) in clause (v), by striking "and" at the end;

(ii) in clause (vi), by striking the period at the end and inserting "; and"; and

(iii) by adding at the end the following new clause:

"(vii) take into account the data and findings contained in the annual reports under subsection (n) in order to develop proposals that can most effectively promote the delivery of efficient, high quality care to Medicare beneficiaries.";

(D) in paragraph (3)—

(i) in the heading, by striking "TRANSMISSION OF BOARD PROPOSAL TO PRESIDENT" and inserting "SUBMISSION OF BOARD PROPOSAL TO CONGRESS AND THE PRESIDENT";

(ii) in subparagraph (A)(i), by striking "transmit a proposal under this section to the President" and insert "submit a proposal under this section to Congress and the President"; and

(iii) in subparagraph (A)(ii)—

(I) in subclause (I), by inserting "or" at the end;

(II) in subclause (II), by striking "; or" and inserting a period; and

(III) by striking subclause (III);

(E) in paragraph (4)—

(i) by striking "the Board under paragraph (3)(A)(i) or"; and

(ii) by striking "immediately" and inserting "within 2 days";

(F) in paragraph (5)—

(i) by striking "to but" and inserting "but"; and

(ii) by inserting "Congress and" after "submit a proposal to"; and

(G) in paragraph (6)(B)(i), by striking "per unduplicated enrollee" and inserting "(calculated as the sum of per capita spending under each of parts A, B, and D)";

(2) in subsection (d)—

(A) in paragraph (1)(A)—

(i) by inserting "the Board or" after "a proposal is submitted by"; and

(ii) by inserting "subsection (c)(3)(A)(i) or" after "the Senate under"; and

(B) in paragraph (2)(A), by inserting "the Board or" after "a proposal is submitted by";

(3) in subsection (e)—

(A) in paragraph (1), by inserting "the Board or" after "a proposal submitted by"; and

(B) in paragraph (3)—

(i) by striking "EXCEPTION.—The Secretary shall not be required to implement the recommendations contained in a proposal submitted in a proposal year by" and inserting "EXCEPTIONS.—

"(A) IN GENERAL.—The Secretary shall not implement the recommendations contained in a proposal submitted in a proposal year by the Board or";

(ii) by redesignating subparagraphs (A) and (B) as clauses (i) and (ii), respectively, and indenting appropriately; and

(iii) by adding at the end the following new subparagraph:

"(B) LIMITED ADDITIONAL EXCEPTION.—

"(i) IN GENERAL.—Subject to clause (ii), the Secretary shall not implement the recommendations contained in a proposal submitted by the Board or the President to Congress pursuant to this section in a proposal year (beginning with proposal year 2019) if—

"(I) the Board was required to submit a proposal to Congress under this section in the year preceding the proposal year; and

"(II) the Chief Actuary of the Centers for Medicare & Medicaid Services makes a determination in the determination year that the growth rate described in subsection (c)(8) exceeds the growth rate described in subsection (c)(6)(A)(i).

"(ii) LIMITED ADDITIONAL EXCEPTION MAY NOT BE APPLIED IN TWO CONSECUTIVE YEARS.—This subparagraph shall not apply if the recommendations contained in a proposal submitted by the Board or the President to Congress pursuant to this section in the year preceding the proposal year were not required to be implemented by reason of this subparagraph.

"(iii) NO AFFECT ON REQUIREMENT TO SUBMIT PROPOSALS OR FOR CONGRESSIONAL CONSIDERATION OF PROPOSALS.—Clause (i) and (ii) shall not affect—

"(I) the requirement of the Board or the President to submit a proposal to Congress in a proposal year in accordance with the provisions of this section; or

"(II) Congressional consideration of a legislative proposal (described in subsection (c)(3)(B)(iv)) contained such a proposal in accordance with subsection (d).";

(4) in subsection (f)(3)(B)—

(A) by striking "or advisory reports to Congress" and inserting ", advisory reports, or advisory recommendations"; and

(B) by inserting "or produce the public report under subsection (n)" after "this section"; and

(5) by adding at the end the following new subsections:

"(n) ANNUAL PUBLIC REPORT.—

"(1) IN GENERAL.—Not later than July 1, 2014, and annually thereafter, the Board shall produce a public report containing standardized information on system-wide health care costs, patient access to care, utilization, and quality-of-care that allows for comparison by region, types of services, types of providers, and both private payers and the program under this title.

"(2) REQUIREMENTS.—Each report produced pursuant to paragraph (1) shall include information with respect to the following areas:

"(A) The quality and costs of care for the population at the most local level determined practical by the Board (with quality and costs compared to national benchmarks and reflecting rates of change, taking into account quality measures described in section 1890(b)(7)(B)).

"(B) Beneficiary and consumer access to care, patient and caregiver experience of care, and the cost-sharing or out-of-pocket burden on patients.

"(C) Epidemiological shifts and demographic changes.

"(D) The proliferation, effectiveness, and utilization of health care technologies, including variation in provider practice patterns and costs.

"(E) Any other areas that the Board determines affect overall spending and quality of care in the private sector.

"(o) ADVISORY RECOMMENDATIONS FOR NON-FEDERAL HEALTH CARE PROGRAMS.—

"(1) IN GENERAL.—Not later than January 15, 2015, and at least once every two years thereafter, the Board shall submit to Congress and the President recommendations to slow the growth in national health expenditures (excluding expenditures under this title and in other Federal health care programs) while preserving or enhancing quality of care, such as recommendations—

"(A) that the Secretary or other Federal agencies can implement administratively;

"(B) that may require legislation to be enacted by Congress in order to be implemented;

"(C) that may require legislation to be enacted by State or local governments in order to be implemented;

"(D) that private sector entities can voluntarily implement; and

"(E) with respect to other areas determined appropriate by the Board.

"(2) COORDINATION.—In making recommendations under paragraph (1), the Board shall coordinate such recommendations with recommendations contained in proposals and advisory reports produced by the Board under subsection (c).

"(3) AVAILABLE TO PUBLIC.—The Board shall make recommendations submitted to Congress and the President under this subsection available to the public.".

(b) NAME CHANGE.—Any reference in the provisions of, or amendments made by, section 3403 to the "Independent Medicare Advisory Board" shall be deemed to be a reference to the "Independent Payment Advisory Board".

(c) RULE OF CONSTRUCTION.—Nothing in the amendments made by this section shall preclude the Independent Medicare Advisory Board, as established under section 1899A of the Social Security Act (as added by section 3403), from solely using data from public or private sources to carry out the amendments made by subsection (a)(4).

SEC. 10321. REVISION TO COMMUNITY HEALTH TEAMS.

Section 3502(c)(2)(A) is amended by inserting "or other primary care providers" after "physicians".

SEC. 10322. QUALITY REPORTING FOR PSYCHIATRIC HOSPITALS.

(a) IN GENERAL.—Section 1886(s) of the Social Security Act, as added by section 3401(f), is amended by adding at the end the following new paragraph:

"(4) QUALITY REPORTING.—

"(A) REDUCTION IN UPDATE FOR FAILURE TO REPORT.—

"(i) IN GENERAL.—Under the system described in paragraph (1), for rate year 2014 and each subsequent rate year, in the case of a psychiatric hospital or psychiatric unit that does not submit data to the Secretary in accordance with subparagraph (C) with respect to such a rate year, any annual update to a standard Federal rate for discharges for the hospital during the rate year, and after application of paragraph (2), shall be reduced by 2 percentage points.

"(ii) SPECIAL RULE.—The application of this subparagraph may result in such annual update being less than 0.0 for a rate year, and may result in payment rates under the system described in paragraph (1) for a rate year being less than such payment rates for the preceding rate year.

"(B) NONCUMULATIVE APPLICATION.—Any reduction under subparagraph (A) shall apply only with respect to the rate year involved and the Secretary shall not take into account such reduction in computing the payment amount under the system described in paragraph (1) for a subsequent rate year.

"(C) SUBMISSION OF QUALITY DATA.—For rate year 2014 and each subsequent rate year, each psychiatric hospital and psychiatric unit shall submit to the Secretary data on quality measures specified under subparagraph (D). Such data shall be submitted in a form and manner, and at a time, specified by the Secretary for purposes of this subparagraph.

"(D) QUALITY MEASURES.—

"(i) IN GENERAL.—Subject to clause (ii), any measure specified by the Secretary under this subparagraph must have been endorsed by the entity with a contract under section 1890(a).

"(ii) EXCEPTION.—In the case of a specified area or medical topic determined appropriate by the Secretary for which a feasible and practical measure has not been endorsed by the entity with a contract under section 1890(a), the Secretary may specify a measure that is not so endorsed as long as due consideration is given to measures that have been endorsed or adopted by a consensus organization identified by the Secretary.

"(iii) TIME FRAME.—Not later than October 1, 2012, the Secretary shall publish the measures selected under this subparagraph that will be applicable with respect to rate year 2014.

"(E) PUBLIC AVAILABILITY OF DATA SUBMITTED.—The Secretary shall establish procedures for making data submitted under subparagraph (C) available to the public. Such procedures shall ensure that a psychiatric hospital and a psychiatric unit has the opportunity to review the data that is to be made public with respect to the hospital or unit prior to such data being made public. The Secretary shall report quality measures that relate to services furnished in inpatient settings in psychiatric hospitals and psychiatric units on the Internet website of the Centers for Medicare & Medicaid Services.".

(b) CONFORMING AMENDMENT.—Section 1890(b)(7)(B)(i)(I) of the Social Security Act, as added by section 3014, is amended by inserting "1886(s)(4)(D)," after "1886(o)(2),".

SEC. 10323. MEDICARE COVERAGE FOR INDIVIDUALS EXPOSED TO ENVIRONMENTAL HEALTH HAZARDS.

(a) IN GENERAL.—Title XVIII of the Social Security Act (42 U.S.C. 1395 et seq.) is amended by inserting after section 1881 the following new section:

"SEC. 1881A. MEDICARE COVERAGE FOR INDIVIDUALS EXPOSED TO ENVIRONMENTAL HEALTH HAZARDS.

"(a) DEEMING OF INDIVIDUALS AS ELIGIBLE FOR MEDICARE BENEFITS.—

"(1) IN GENERAL.—For purposes of eligibility for benefits under this title, an individual determined under subsection (c) to be an environmental exposure affected individual described in subsection (e)(2) shall be deemed to meet the conditions specified in section 226(a).

"(2) DISCRETIONARY DEEMING.—For purposes of eligibility for benefits under this title, the Secretary may deem an individual determined under subsection (c) to be an environmental exposure affected individual described in subsection (e)(3) to meet the conditions specified in section 226(a).

"(3) EFFECTIVE DATE OF COVERAGE.—An Individual who is deemed eligible for benefits under this title under paragraph (1) or (2) shall be—

"(A) entitled to benefits under the program under Part A as of the date of such deeming; and

"(B) eligible to enroll in the program under Part B beginning with the month in which such deeming occurs.

"(b) PILOT PROGRAM FOR CARE OF CERTAIN INDIVIDUALS RESIDING IN EMERGENCY DECLARATION AREAS.—

"(1) PROGRAM; PURPOSE.—

"(A) PRIMARY PILOT PROGRAM.—The Secretary shall establish a pilot program in accordance with this subsection to provide innovative approaches to furnishing comprehensive, coordinated, and cost-effective care under this title to individuals described in paragraph (2)(A).

"(B) OPTIONAL PILOT PROGRAMS.—The Secretary may establish a separate pilot program, in accordance with this subsection, with respect to each geographic area subject to an emergency declaration (other than the declaration of June 17, 2009), in order to furnish such comprehensive, coordinated and cost-effective care to individuals described in subparagraph (2)(B) who reside in each such area.

"(2) INDIVIDUAL DESCRIBED.—For purposes of paragraph (1), an individual described in this paragraph is an individual who enrolls in part B, submits to the Secretary an application to participate in the applicable pilot program under this subsection, and—

"(A) is an environmental exposure affected individual described in subsection (e)(2) who resides in or around the geographic area subject to an emergency declaration made as of June 17, 2009; or

"(B) is an environmental exposure affected individual described in subsection (e)(3) who—

"(i) is deemed under subsection (a)(2); and

"(ii) meets such other criteria or conditions for participation in a pilot program under paragraph (1)(B) as the Secretary specifies.

"(3) FLEXIBLE BENEFITS AND SERVICES.—A pilot program under this subsection may provide for the furnishing of benefits, items, or services not otherwise covered or authorized under this title, if the Secretary determines that furnishing such benefits, items, or services will further the purposes of such pilot program (as described in paragraph (1)).

"(4) INNOVATIVE REIMBURSEMENT METHODOLOGIES.—For purposes of the pilot program under this subsection, the Secretary—

"(A) shall develop and implement appropriate methodologies to reimburse providers for furnishing benefits, items, or services for which payment is not otherwise covered or authorized under this title, if such benefits, items, or services are furnished pursuant to paragraph (3); and

"(B) may develop and implement innovative approaches to reimbursing providers for any benefits, items, or services furnished under this subsection.

"(5) LIMITATION.—Consistent with section 1862(b), no payment shall be made under the pilot program under this subsection with respect to benefits, items, or services furnished to an environmental exposure affected individual (as defined in subsection (e)) to the extent that such individual is eligible to receive such benefits, items, or services through any other public or private benefits plan or legal agreement.

"(6) WAIVER AUTHORITY.—The Secretary may waive such provisions of this title and title XI as are necessary to carry out pilot programs under this subsection.

"(7) FUNDING.—For purposes of carrying out pilot programs under this subsection, the Secretary shall provide for the transfer, from the Federal Hospital Insurance Trust Fund under section 1817 and the Federal Supplementary Medical Insurance Trust Fund under section 1841, in such proportion as the Secretary determines appropriate, of such sums as the Secretary determines necessary, to the Centers for Medicare & Medicaid Services Program Management Account.

"(8) WAIVER OF BUDGET NEUTRALITY.—The Secretary shall not require that pilot programs under this subsection be budget neutral with respect to expenditures under this title.

"(c) DETERMINATIONS.—

"(1) BY THE COMMISSIONER OF SOCIAL SECURITY.—For purposes of this section, the Commissioner of Social Security, in consultation with the Secretary, and using the cost allocation method prescribed in section 201(g), shall determine whether individuals are environmental exposure affected individuals.

"(2) BY THE SECRETARY.—The Secretary shall determine eligibility for pilot programs under subsection (b).

"(d) EMERGENCY DECLARATION DEFINED.—For purposes of this section, the term 'emergency declaration' means a declaration of a public health emergency under section 104(a) of the Comprehensive Environmental Response, Compensation, and Liability Act of 1980.

"(e) ENVIRONMENTAL EXPOSURE AFFECTED INDIVIDUAL DEFINED.—

"(1) IN GENERAL.—For purposes of this section, the term 'environmental exposure affected individual' means—

"(A) an individual described in paragraph (2); and

"(B) an individual described in paragraph (3).

"(2) INDIVIDUAL DESCRIBED.—

"(A) IN GENERAL.—An individual described in this paragraph is any individual who—

"(i) is diagnosed with 1 or more conditions described in subparagraph (B);

"(ii) as demonstrated in such manner as the Secretary determines appropriate, has been present for an aggregate total of 6 months in the geographic area subject to an emergency declaration specified in subsection (b)(2)(A), during a period ending—

"(I) not less than 10 years prior to such diagnosis; and

"(II) prior to the implementation of all the remedial and removal actions specified in the Record of Decision for Operating Unit 4 and the Record of Decision for Operating Unit 7;

"(iii) files an application for benefits under this title (or has an application filed on behalf of the individual), including pursuant to this section; and

"(iv) is determined under this section to meet the criteria in this subparagraph.

"(B) CONDITIONS DESCRIBED.—For purposes of subparagraph (A), the following conditions are described in this subparagraph:

"(i) Asbestosis, pleural thickening, or pleural plaques as established by—

"(I) interpretation by a 'B Reader' qualified physician of a plain chest x-ray or interpretation of a computed tomographic radiograph of the chest by a qualified physician, as determined by the Secretary; or

"(II) such other diagnostic standards as the Secretary specifies,

except that this clause shall not apply to pleural thickening or pleural plaques unless there are symptoms or conditions requiring medical treatment as a result of these diagnoses.

"(ii) Mesothelioma, or malignancies of the lung, colon, rectum, larynx, stomach, esophagus, pharynx, or ovary, as established by—

"(I) pathologic examination of biopsy tissue;

"(II) cytology from bronchioalveolar lavage; or

"(III) such other diagnostic standards as the Secretary specifies.

"(iii) Any other diagnosis which the Secretary, in consultation with the Commissioner of Social Security, determines is an asbestos-related medical condition, as established by such diagnostic standards as the Secretary specifies.

"(3) OTHER INDIVIDUAL DESCRIBED.—An individual described in this paragraph is any individual who—

"(A) is not an individual described in paragraph (2);

"(B) is diagnosed with a medical condition caused by the exposure of the individual to a public health hazard to which an emergency declaration applies, based on such medical conditions, diagnostic standards, and other criteria as the Secretary specifies;

"(C) as demonstrated in such manner as the Secretary determines appropriate, has been present for an aggregate total of 6 months in the geographic area subject to the emergency declaration involved, during a period determined appropriate by the Secretary;

"(D) files an application for benefits under this title (or has an application filed on behalf of the individual), including pursuant to this section; and

"(E) is determined under this section to meet the criteria in this paragraph.".

(b) PROGRAM FOR EARLY DETECTION OF CERTAIN MEDICAL CONDITIONS RELATED TO ENVIRONMENTAL HEALTH HAZARDS.—Title XX of the Social Security Act (42 U.S.C. 1397 et seq.), as amended by section 5507, is amended by adding at the end the following:

"SEC. 2009. PROGRAM FOR EARLY DETECTION OF CERTAIN MEDICAL CONDITIONS RELATED TO ENVIRONMENTAL HEALTH HAZARDS.

"(a) PROGRAM ESTABLISHMENT.—The Secretary shall establish a program in accordance with this section to make competitive grants to eligible entities specified in subsection (b) for the purpose of—

"(1) screening at-risk individuals (as defined in subsection (c)(1)) for environmental health conditions (as defined in subsection (c)(3)); and

"(2) developing and disseminating public information and education concerning—

"(A) the availability of screening under the program under this section;

"(B) the detection, prevention, and treatment of environmental health conditions; and

"(C) the availability of Medicare benefits for certain individuals diagnosed with environmental health conditions under section 1881A.

"(b) ELIGIBLE ENTITIES.—

"(1) IN GENERAL.—For purposes of this section, an eligible entity is an entity described in paragraph (2) which submits an application to the Secretary in such form and manner, and containing such information and assurances, as the Secretary determines appropriate.

"(2) TYPES OF ELIGIBLE ENTITIES.—The entities described in this paragraph are the following:

"(A) A hospital or community health center.

"(B) A Federally qualified health center.

"(C) A facility of the Indian Health Service.

"(D) A National Cancer Institute-designated cancer center.

"(E) An agency of any State or local government.

"(F) A nonprofit organization.

"(G) Any other entity the Secretary determines appropriate.

“(c) DEFINITIONS.—In this section:

“(1) AT-RISK INDIVIDUAL.—The term ‘at-risk individual’ means an individual who—

“(A)(i) as demonstrated in such manner as the Secretary determines appropriate, has been present for an aggregate total of 6 months in the geographic area subject to an emergency declaration specified under paragraph (2), during a period ending—

“(I) not less than 10 years prior to the date of such individual’s application under subparagraph (B); and

“(II) prior to the implementation of all the remedial and removal actions specified in the Record of Decision for Operating Unit 4 and the Record of Decision for Operating Unit 7; or

“(ii) meets such other criteria as the Secretary determines appropriate considering the type of environmental health condition at issue; and

“(B) has submitted an application (or has an application submitted on the individual’s behalf), to an eligible entity receiving a grant under this section, for screening under the program under this section.

“(2) EMERGENCY DECLARATION.—The term ‘emergency declaration’ means a declaration of a public health emergency under section 104(a) of the Comprehensive Environmental Response, Compensation, and Liability Act of 1980.

“(3) ENVIRONMENTAL HEALTH CONDITION.—The term ‘environmental health condition’ means—

“(A) asbestosis, pleural thickening, or pleural plaques, as established by—

“(i) interpretation by a ‘B Reader’ qualified physician of a plain chest x-ray or interpretation of a computed tomographic radiograph of the chest by a qualified physician, as determined by the Secretary; or

“(ii) such other diagnostic standards as the Secretary specifies;

“(B) mesothelioma, or malignancies of the lung, colon, rectum, larynx, stomach, esophagus, pharynx, or ovary, as established by—

“(i) pathologic examination of biopsy tissue;

“(ii) cytology from bronchioalveolar lavage; or

“(iii) such other diagnostic standards as the Secretary specifies; and

“(C) any other medical condition which the Secretary determines is caused by exposure to a hazardous substance or pollutant or contaminant at a Superfund site to which an emergency declaration applies, based on such criteria and as established by such diagnostic standards as the Secretary specifies.

“(4) HAZARDOUS SUBSTANCE; POLLUTANT; CONTAMINANT.—The terms ‘hazardous substance’, ‘pollutant’, and ‘contaminant’ have the meanings given those terms in section 101 of the Comprehensive Environmental Response, Compensation, and Liability Act of 1980 (42 U.S.C. 9601).

“(5) SUPERFUND SITE.—The term ‘Superfund site’ means a site included on the National Priorities List developed by the President in accordance with section 105(a)(8)(B) of the

Comprehensive Environmental Response, Compensation, and Liability Act of 1980 (42 U.S.C. 9605(a)(8)(B)).

"(d) HEALTH COVERAGE UNAFFECTED.—Nothing in this section shall be construed to affect any coverage obligation of a governmental or private health plan or program relating to an at-risk individual.

"(e) FUNDING.—

"(1) IN GENERAL.—Out of any funds in the Treasury not otherwise appropriated, there are appropriated to the Secretary, to carry out the program under this section—

"(A) $23,000,000 for the period of fiscal years 2010 through 2014; and

"(B) $20,000,000 for each 5-fiscal year period thereafter.

"(2) AVAILABILITY.—Funds appropriated under paragraph (1) shall remain available until expended.

"(f) NONAPPLICATION.—

"(1) IN GENERAL.—Except as provided in paragraph (2), the preceding sections of this title shall not apply to grants awarded under this section.

"(2) LIMITATIONS ON USE OF GRANTS.—Section 2005(a) shall apply to a grant awarded under this section to the same extent and in the same manner as such section applies to payments to States under this title, except that paragraph (4) of such section shall not be construed to prohibit grantees from conducting screening for environmental health conditions as authorized under this section.".

SEC. 10324. PROTECTIONS FOR FRONTIER STATES.

(a) FLOOR ON AREA WAGE INDEX FOR HOSPITALS IN FRONTIER STATES.—

(1) IN GENERAL.—Section 1886(d)(3)(E) of the Social Security Act (42 U.S.C. 1395ww(d)(3)(E)) is amended—

(A) in clause (i), by striking "clause (ii)" and inserting "clause (ii) or (iii)"; and

(B) by adding at the end the following new clause:

"(iii) FLOOR ON AREA WAGE INDEX FOR HOSPITALS IN FRONTIER STATES.—

"(I) IN GENERAL.—Subject to subclause (IV), for discharges occurring on or after October 1, 2010, the area wage index applicable under this subparagraph to any hospital which is located in a frontier State (as defined in subclause (II)) may not be less than 1.00.

"(II) FRONTIER STATE DEFINED.—In this clause, the term 'frontier State' means a State in which at least 50 percent of the counties in the State are frontier counties.

"(III) FRONTIER COUNTY DEFINED.—In this clause, the term 'frontier county' means a county in which the population per square mile is less than 6.

"(IV) LIMITATION.—This clause shall not apply to any hospital located in a State that receives a non-labor related share adjustment under paragraph (5)(H).".

(2) WAIVING BUDGET NEUTRALITY.—Section 1886(d)(3)(E) of the Social Security Act (42 U.S.C. 1395ww(d)(3)(E)), as amended by subsection (a), is amended in the third sentence by inserting "and the amendments made by section 10324(a)(1) of the Patient Protection and Affordable Care Act" after "2003".

(b) FLOOR ON AREA WAGE ADJUSTMENT FACTOR FOR HOSPITAL OUTPATIENT DEPARTMENT SERVICES IN FRONTIER STATES.—Section 1833(t) of the Social Security Act (42 U.S.C. 1395l(t)), as amended by section 3138, is amended—

(1) in paragraph (2)(D), by striking "the Secretary" and inserting "subject to paragraph (19), the Secretary"; and

(2) by adding at the end the following new paragraph:

"(19) FLOOR ON AREA WAGE ADJUSTMENT FACTOR FOR HOSPITAL OUTPATIENT DEPARTMENT SERVICES IN FRONTIER STATES.—

"(A) IN GENERAL.—Subject to subparagraph (B), with respect to covered OPD services furnished on or after January 1, 2011, the area wage adjustment factor applicable under the payment system established under this subsection to any hospital outpatient department which is located in a frontier State (as defined in section 1886(d)(3)(E)(iii)(II)) may not be less than 1.00. The preceding sentence shall not be applied in a budget neutral manner.

"(B) LIMITATION.—This paragraph shall not apply to any hospital outpatient department located in a State that receives a non-labor related share adjustment under section 1886(d)(5)(H).".

(c) FLOOR FOR PRACTICE EXPENSE INDEX FOR PHYSICIANS' SERVICES FURNISHED IN FRONTIER STATES.—Section 1848(e)(1) of the Social Security Act (42 U.S.C. 1395w–4(e)(1)), as amended by section 3102, is amended—

(1) in subparagraph (A), by striking "and (H)" and inserting "(H), and (I)"; and

(2) by adding at the end the following new subparagraph:

"(I) FLOOR FOR PRACTICE EXPENSE INDEX FOR SERVICES FURNISHED IN FRONTIER STATES.—

"(i) IN GENERAL.—Subject to clause (ii), for purposes of payment for services furnished in a frontier State (as defined in section 1886(d)(3)(E)(iii)(II)) on or after January 1, 2011, after calculating the practice expense index in subparagraph (A)(i), the Secretary shall increase any such index to 1.00 if such index would otherwise be less that 1.00. The preceding sentence shall not be applied in a budget neutral manner.

"(ii) LIMITATION.—This subparagraph shall not apply to services furnished in a State that receives a non-labor related share adjustment under section 1886(d)(5)(H).".

SEC. 10325. REVISION TO SKILLED NURSING FACILITY PROSPECTIVE PAYMENT SYSTEM.

(a) TEMPORARY DELAY OF RUG–IV.—Notwithstanding any other provision of law, the Secretary of Health and Human Services shall not, prior to October 1, 2011, implement Version 4 of the Resource Utilization Groups (in this subsection refereed to as "RUG–IV") published in the Federal Register on August 11, 2009, entitled "Prospective Payment System and Consolidated Billing for

Skilled Nursing Facilities for FY 2010; Minimum Data Set, Version 3.0 for Skilled Nursing Facilities and Medicaid Nursing Facilities" (74 Fed. Reg. 40288). Beginning on October 1, 2010, the Secretary of Health and Human Services shall implement the change specific to therapy furnished on a concurrent basis that is a component of RUG–IV and changes to the lookback period to ensure that only those services furnished after admission to a skilled nursing facility are used as factors in determining a case mix classification under the skilled nursing facility prospective payment system under section 1888(e) of the Social Security Act (42 U.S.C. 1395yy(e)).

(b) CONSTRUCTION.—Nothing in this section shall be interpreted as delaying the implementation of Version 3.0 of the Minimum Data Sets (MDS 3.0) beyond the planned implementation date of October 1, 2010.

SEC. 10326. PILOT TESTING PAY-FOR-PERFORMANCE PROGRAMS FOR CERTAIN MEDICARE PROVIDERS.

(a) IN GENERAL.—Not later than January 1, 2016, the Secretary of Health and Human Services (in this section referred to as the "Secretary") shall, for each provider described in subsection (b), conduct a separate pilot program under title XVIII of the Social Security Act to test the implementation of a value-based purchasing program for payments under such title for the provider.

(b) PROVIDERS DESCRIBED.—The providers described in this paragraph are the following:

(1) Psychiatric hospitals (as described in clause (i) of section 1886(d)(1)(B) of such Act (42 U.S.C. 1395ww(d)(1)(B))) and psychiatric units (as described in the matter following clause (v) of such section).

(2) Long-term care hospitals (as described in clause (iv) of such section).

(3) Rehabilitation hospitals (as described in clause (ii) of such section).

(4) PPS-exempt cancer hospitals (as described in clause (v) of such section).

(5) Hospice programs (as defined in section 1861(dd)(2) of such Act (42 U.S.C. 1395x(dd)(2))).

(c) WAIVER AUTHORITY.—The Secretary may waive such requirements of titles XI and XVIII of the Social Security Act as may be necessary solely for purposes of carrying out the pilot programs under this section.

(d) NO ADDITIONAL PROGRAM EXPENDITURES.—Payments under this section under the separate pilot program for value based purchasing (as described in subsection (a)) for each provider type described in paragraphs (1) through (5) of subsection (b) for applicable items and services under title XVIII of the Social Security Act for a year shall be established in a manner that does not result in spending more under each such value based purchasing program for such year than would otherwise be expended for such provider type for such year if the pilot program were not implemented, as estimated by the Secretary.

(e) EXPANSION OF PILOT PROGRAM.—The Secretary may, at any point after January 1, 2018, expand the duration and scope of a pilot program conducted under this subsection, to the extent determined appropriate by the Secretary, if—

(1) the Secretary determines that such expansion is expected to—

(A) reduce spending under title XVIII of the Social Security Act without reducing the quality of care; or

(B) improve the quality of care and reduce spending;

(2) the Chief Actuary of the Centers for Medicare & Medicaid Services certifies that such expansion would reduce program spending under such title XVIII; and

(3) the Secretary determines that such expansion would not deny or limit the coverage or provision of benefits under such title XIII for Medicare beneficiaries.

SEC. 10327. IMPROVEMENTS TO THE PHYSICIAN QUALITY REPORTING SYSTEM.

(a) IN GENERAL.—Section 1848(m) of the Social Security Act (42 U.S.C. 1395w–4(m)) is amended by adding at the end the following new paragraph:

"(7) ADDITIONAL INCENTIVE PAYMENT.—

"(A) IN GENERAL.—For 2011 through 2014, if an eligible professional meets the requirements described in subparagraph (B), the applicable quality percent for such year, as described in clauses (iii) and (iv) of paragraph (1)(B), shall be increased by 0.5 percentage points.

"(B) REQUIREMENTS DESCRIBED.—In order to qualify for the additional incentive payment described in subparagraph (A), an eligible professional shall meet the following requirements:

"(i) The eligible professional shall—

"(I) satisfactorily submit data on quality measures for purposes of paragraph (1) for a year; and

"(II) have such data submitted on their behalf through a Maintenance of Certification Program (as defined in subparagraph (C)(i)) that meets—

"(aa) the criteria for a registry (as described in subsection (k)(4)); or

"(bb) an alternative form and manner determined appropriate by the Secretary.

"(ii) The eligible professional, more frequently than is required to qualify for or maintain board certification status—

"(I) participates in such a Maintenance of Certification program for a year; and

"(II) successfully completes a qualified Maintenance of Certification Program practice assessment (as defined in subparagraph (C)(ii)) for such year.

"(iii) A Maintenance of Certification program submits to the Secretary, on behalf of the eligible professional, information—

"(I) in a form and manner specified by the Secretary, that the eligible professional has successfully met the requirements of clause (ii) (which may be in the form of a structural measure);

"(II) if requested by the Secretary, on the survey of patient experience with care (as described in subparagraph (C)(ii)(II)); and

"(III) as the Secretary may require, on the methods, measures, and data used under the Maintenance of Certification Program and the qualified Maintenance of Certification Program practice assessment.

"(C) DEFINITIONS.—For purposes of this paragraph:

"(i) The term 'Maintenance of Certification Program' means a continuous assessment program, such as qualified American Board of Medical Specialties Maintenance of Certification program or an equivalent program (as determined by the Secretary), that advances quality and the lifelong learning and self-assessment of board certified specialty physicians by focusing on the competencies of patient care, medical knowledge, practice-based learning, interpersonal and communication skills and professionalism. Such a program shall include the following:

"(I) The program requires the physician to maintain a valid, unrestricted medical license in the United States.

"(II) The program requires a physician to participate in educational and self-assessment programs that require an assessment of what was learned.

"(III) The program requires a physician to demonstrate, through a formalized, secure examination, that the physician has the fundamental diagnostic skills, medical knowledge, and clinical judgment to provide quality care in their respective specialty.

"(IV) The program requires successful completion of a qualified Maintenance of Certification Program practice assessment as described in clause (ii).

"(ii) The term 'qualified Maintenance of Certification Program practice assessment' means an assessment of a physician's practice that—

"(I) includes an initial assessment of an eligible professional's practice that is designed to demonstrate the physician's use of evidence-based medicine;

"(II) includes a survey of patient experience with care; and

"(III) requires a physician to implement a quality improvement intervention to address a practice weakness identified in the initial assessment under subclause (I) and then to remeasure to assess performance improvement after such intervention.".

(b) AUTHORITY.—Section 3002(c) of this Act is amended by adding at the end the following new paragraph:

"(3) AUTHORITY.—For years after 2014, if the Secretary of Health and Human Services determines it to be appropriate, the Secretary may incorporate participation in a Maintenance of Certification Program and successful completion of a qualified Maintenance of Certification Program practice assessment into the composite of measures of quality of care furnished pursuant to the physician fee schedule payment modifier, as described in section 1848(p)(2) of the Social Security Act (42 U.S.C. 1395w–4(p)(2)).".

(c) ELIMINATION OF MA REGIONAL PLAN STABILIZATION FUND.—

(1) IN GENERAL.—Section 1858 of the Social Security Act (42 U.S.C. 1395w–27a) is amended by striking subsection (e).

(2) TRANSITION.—Any amount contained in the MA Regional Plan Stabilization Fund as of the date of the enactment of this Act shall be transferred to the Federal Supplementary Medical Insurance Trust Fund.

SEC. 10328. IMPROVEMENT IN PART D MEDICATION THERAPY MANAGEMENT (MTM) PROGRAMS.

(a) IN GENERAL.—Section 1860D–4(c)(2) of the Social Security Act (42 U.S.C. 1395w–104(c)(2)) is amended—

(1) by redesignating subparagraphs (C), (D), and (E) as subparagraphs (E), (F), and (G), respectively; and

(2) by inserting after subparagraph (B) the following new subparagraphs:

"(C) REQUIRED INTERVENTIONS.—For plan years beginning on or after the date that is 2 years after the date of the enactment of the Patient Protection and Affordable Care Act, prescription drug plan sponsors shall offer medication therapy management services to targeted beneficiaries described in subparagraph (A)(ii) that include, at a minimum, the following to increase adherence to prescription medications or other goals deemed necessary by the Secretary:

"(i) An annual comprehensive medication review furnished person-to-person or using telehealth technologies (as defined by the Secretary) by a licensed pharmacist or other qualified provider. The comprehensive medication review—

"(I) shall include a review of the individual's medications and may result in the creation of a recommended medication action plan or other actions in consultation with the individual and with input from the prescriber to the extent necessary and practicable; and

"(II) shall include providing the individual with a written or printed summary of the results of the review.

The Secretary, in consultation with relevant stakeholders, shall develop a standardized format for the action plan under subclause (I) and the summary under subclause (II).

"(ii) Follow-up interventions as warranted based on the findings of the annual medication review or the targeted medication enrollment and which may be provided person-to-person or using telehealth technologies (as defined by the Secretary).

"(D) ASSESSMENT.—The prescription drug plan sponsor shall have in place a process to assess, at least on a quarterly basis, the medication use of individuals who are at risk but not enrolled in the medication therapy management program, including individuals who have experienced a transition in care, if the prescription drug plan sponsor has access to that information.

"(E) AUTOMATIC ENROLLMENT WITH ABILITY TO OPT-OUT.—The prescription drug plan sponsor shall have in place a process to—

"(i) subject to clause (ii), automatically enroll targeted beneficiaries described in subparagraph (A)(ii), including beneficiaries identified under subparagraph (D), in the medication therapy management program required under this subsection; and

"(ii) permit such beneficiaries to opt-out of enrollment in such program.".

(b) RULE OF CONSTRUCTION.—Nothing in this section shall limit the authority of the Secretary of Health and Human Services to modify or broaden requirements for a medication therapy management program under part D of title XVIII of the Social Security Act or to study new models for medication therapy management through the Center for Medicare and Medicaid Innovation under section 1115A of such Act, as added by section 3021.

SEC. 10329. DEVELOPING METHODOLOGY TO ASSESS HEALTH PLAN VALUE.

(a) DEVELOPMENT.—The Secretary of Health and Human Services (referred to in this section as the "Secretary"), in consultation with relevant stakeholders including health insurance issuers, health care consumers, employers, health care providers, and other entities determined appropriate by the Secretary, shall develop a methodology to measure health plan value. Such methodology shall take into consideration, where applicable—

(1) the overall cost to enrollees under the plan;

(2) the quality of the care provided for under the plan;

(3) the efficiency of the plan in providing care;

(4) the relative risk of the plan's enrollees as compared to other plans;

(5) the actuarial value or other comparative measure of the benefits covered under the plan; and

(6) other factors determined relevant by the Secretary.

(b) REPORT.—Not later than 18 months after the date of enactment of this Act, the Secretary shall submit to Congress a report concerning the methodology developed under subsection (a).

SEC. 10330. MODERNIZING COMPUTER AND DATA SYSTEMS OF THE CENTERS FOR MEDICARE & MEDICAID SERVICES TO SUPPORT IMPROVEMENTS IN CARE DELIVERY.

(a) IN GENERAL.—The Secretary of Health and Human Services (in this section referred to as the "Secretary") shall develop a plan (and detailed budget for the resources needed to implement such plan) to modernize the computer and data systems of the Centers for Medicare & Medicaid Services (in this section referred to as "CMS").

(b) CONSIDERATIONS.—In developing the plan, the Secretary shall consider how such modernized computer system could—

(1) in accordance with the regulations promulgated under section 264(c) of the Health Insurance Portability and Accountability Act of 1996, make available data in a reliable and timely manner to providers of services and suppliers to support their efforts to better manage and coordinate care furnished to beneficiaries of CMS programs; and

(2) support consistent evaluations of payment and delivery system reforms under CMS programs.

(c) POSTING OF PLAN.—By not later than 9 months after the date of the enactment of this Act, the Secretary shall post on the website of the Centers for Medicare & Medicaid Services the plan described in subsection (a).

SEC. 10331. PUBLIC REPORTING OF PERFORMANCE INFORMATION.

(a) IN GENERAL.—

(1) DEVELOPMENT.—Not later than January 1, 2011, the Secretary shall develop a Physician Compare Internet website with information on physicians enrolled in the Medicare program under section 1866(j) of the Social Security Act (42 U.S.C. 1395cc(j)) and other eligible professionals who participate in the Physician Quality Reporting Initiative under section 1848 of such Act (42 U.S.C. 1395w–4).

(2) PLAN.—Not later than January 1, 2013, and with respect to reporting periods that begin no earlier than January 1, 2012, the Secretary shall also implement a plan for making publicly available through Physician Compare, consistent with subsection (c), information on physician performance that provides comparable information for the public on quality and patient experience measures with respect to physicians enrolled in the Medicare program under such section 1866(j). To the extent scientifically sound measures that are developed consistent with the requirements of this section are available, such information, to the extent practicable, shall include—

(A) measures collected under the Physician Quality Reporting Initiative;

(B) an assessment of patient health outcomes and the functional status of patients;

(C) an assessment of the continuity and coordination of care and care transitions, including episodes of care and risk-adjusted resource use;

(D) an assessment of efficiency;

(E) an assessment of patient experience and patient, caregiver, and family engagement;

(F) an assessment of the safety, effectiveness, and timeliness of care; and

(G) other information as determined appropriate by the Secretary.

(b) OTHER REQUIRED CONSIDERATIONS.—In developing and implementing the plan described in subsection (a)(2), the Secretary shall, to the extent practicable, include—

(1) processes to assure that data made public, either by the Centers for Medicare & Medicaid Services or by other entities, is statistically valid and reliable, including risk adjustment mechanisms used by the Secretary;

(2) processes by which a physician or other eligible professional whose performance on measures is being publicly reported has a reasonable opportunity, as determined by the Secretary, to review his or her individual results before they are made public;

(3) processes by the Secretary to assure that the implementation of the plan and the data made available on Physician Compare provide a robust and accurate portrayal of a physician's performance;

(4) data that reflects the care provided to all patients seen by physicians, under both the Medicare program and,

to the extent practicable, other payers, to the extent such information would provide a more accurate portrayal of physician performance;

(5) processes to ensure appropriate attribution of care when multiple physicians and other providers are involved in the care of a patient;

(6) processes to ensure timely statistical performance feedback is provided to physicians concerning the data reported under any program subject to public reporting under this section; and

(7) implementation of computer and data systems of the Centers for Medicare & Medicaid Services that support valid, reliable, and accurate public reporting activities authorized under this section.

(c) ENSURING PATIENT PRIVACY.—The Secretary shall ensure that information on physician performance and patient experience is not disclosed under this section in a manner that violates sections 552 or 552a of title 5, United States Code, with regard to the privacy of individually identifiable health information.

(d) FEEDBACK FROM MULTI-STAKEHOLDER GROUPS.—The Secretary shall take into consideration input provided by multi-stakeholder groups, consistent with sections 1890(b)(7) and 1890A of the Social Security Act, as added by section 3014 of this Act, in selecting quality measures for use under this section.

(e) CONSIDERATION OF TRANSITION TO VALUE-BASED PURCHASING.—In developing the plan under this subsection (a)(2), the Secretary shall, as the Secretary determines appropriate, consider the plan to transition to a value-based purchasing program for physicians and other practitioners developed under section 131 of the Medicare Improvements for Patients and Providers Act of 2008 (Public Law 110–275).

(f) REPORT TO CONGRESS.—Not later than January 1, 2015, the Secretary shall submit to Congress a report on the Physician Compare Internet website developed under subsection (a)(1). Such report shall include information on the efforts of and plans made by the Secretary to collect and publish data on physician quality and efficiency and on patient experience of care in support of value-based purchasing and consumer choice, together with recommendations for such legislation and administrative action as the Secretary determines appropriate.

(g) EXPANSION.—At any time before the date on which the report is submitted under subsection (f), the Secretary may expand (including expansion to other providers of services and suppliers under title XVIII of the Social Security Act) the information made available on such website.

(h) FINANCIAL INCENTIVES TO ENCOURAGE CONSUMERS TO CHOOSE HIGH QUALITY PROVIDERS.—The Secretary may establish a demonstration program, not later than January 1, 2019, to provide financial incentives to Medicare beneficiaries who are furnished services by high quality physicians, as determined by the Secretary based on factors in subparagraphs (A) through (G) of subsection (a)(2). In no case may Medicare beneficiaries be required to pay increased premiums or cost sharing or be subject to a reduction in benefits under title XVIII of the Social Security Act as a result of such demonstration program. The Secretary shall ensure that any such demonstration program does not disadvantage those beneficiaries without reasonable access to high performing physicians or create financial inequities under such title.

(i) DEFINITIONS.—In this section:

(1) ELIGIBLE PROFESSIONAL.—The term "eligible professional" has the meaning given that term for purposes of the Physician Quality Reporting Initiative under section 1848 of the Social Security Act (42 U.S.C. 1395w–4).

(2) PHYSICIAN.—The term "physician" has the meaning given that term in section 1861(r) of such Act (42 U.S.C. 1395x(r)).

(3) PHYSICIAN COMPARE.—The term "Physician Compare" means the Internet website developed under subsection (a)(1).

(4) SECRETARY.—The term "Secretary" means the Secretary of Health and Human Services.

SEC. 10332. AVAILABILITY OF MEDICARE DATA FOR PERFORMANCE MEASUREMENT.

(a) IN GENERAL.—Section 1874 of the Social Security Act (42 U.S.C. 1395kk) is amended by adding at the end the following new subsection:

"(e) AVAILABILITY OF MEDICARE DATA.—

"(1) IN GENERAL.—Subject to paragraph (4), the Secretary shall make available to qualified entities (as defined in paragraph (2)) data described in paragraph (3) for the evaluation of the performance of providers of services and suppliers.

"(2) QUALIFIED ENTITIES.—For purposes of this subsection, the term 'qualified entity' means a public or private entity that—

"(A) is qualified (as determined by the Secretary) to use claims data to evaluate the performance of providers of services and suppliers on measures of quality, efficiency, effectiveness, and resource use; and

"(B) agrees to meet the requirements described in paragraph (4) and meets such other requirements as the Secretary may specify, such as ensuring security of data.

"(3) DATA DESCRIBED.—The data described in this paragraph are standardized extracts (as determined by the Secretary) of claims data under parts A, B, and D for items and services furnished under such parts for one or more specified geographic areas and time periods requested by a qualified entity. The Secretary shall take such actions as the Secretary deems necessary to protect the identity of individuals entitled to or enrolled for benefits under such parts.

"(4) REQUIREMENTS.—

"(A) FEE.—Data described in paragraph (3) shall be made available to a qualified entity under this subsection at a fee equal to the cost of making such data available. Any fee collected pursuant to the preceding sentence shall be deposited into the Federal Supplementary Medical Insurance Trust Fund under section 1841.

"(B) SPECIFICATION OF USES AND METHODOLOGIES.—A qualified entity requesting data under this subsection shall—

"(i) submit to the Secretary a description of the methodologies that such qualified entity will use to evaluate the performance of providers of services and suppliers using such data;

"(ii)(I) except as provided in subclause (II), if available, use standard measures, such as measures endorsed by the entity with a contract under section 1890(a) and measures developed pursuant to section 931 of the Public Health Service Act; or

"(II) use alternative measures if the Secretary, in consultation with appropriate stakeholders, determines that use of such alternative measures would be more valid, reliable, responsive to consumer preferences, cost-effective, or relevant to dimensions of quality and resource use not addressed by such standard measures;

"(iii) include data made available under this subsection with claims data from sources other than claims data under this title in the evaluation of performance of providers of services and suppliers;

"(iv) only include information on the evaluation of performance of providers and suppliers in reports described in subparagraph (C);

"(v) make available to providers of services and suppliers, upon their request, data made available under this subsection; and

"(vi) prior to their release, submit to the Secretary the format of reports under subparagraph (C).

"(C) REPORTS.—Any report by a qualified entity evaluating the performance of providers of services and suppliers using data made available under this subsection shall—

"(i) include an understandable description of the measures, which shall include quality measures and the rationale for use of other measures described in subparagraph (B)(ii)(II), risk adjustment methods, physician attribution methods, other applicable methods, data specifications and limitations, and the sponsors, so that consumers, providers of services and suppliers, health plans, researchers, and other stakeholders can assess such reports;

"(ii) be made available confidentially, to any provider of services or supplier to be identified in such report, prior to the public release of such report, and provide an opportunity to appeal and correct errors;

"(iii) only include information on a provider of services or supplier in an aggregate form as determined appropriate by the Secretary; and

"(iv) except as described in clause (ii), be made available to the public.

"(D) APPROVAL AND LIMITATION OF USES.—The Secretary shall not make data described in paragraph (3) available to a qualified entity unless the qualified entity agrees to release the information on the evaluation of performance of providers of services and suppliers. Such entity shall only use such data, and information derived from such evaluation, for the reports under subparagraph (C). Data released to a qualified entity under this subsection shall not be subject to discovery or admission as evidence in judicial or administrative proceedings without consent of the applicable provider of services or supplier.”.

(b) EFFECTIVE DATE.—The amendment made by subsection (a) shall take effect on January 1, 2012.

SEC. 10333. COMMUNITY-BASED COLLABORATIVE CARE NETWORKS.

Part D of title III of the Public Health Service Act (42 U.S.C. 254b et seq.) is amended by adding at the end the following new subpart:

“Subpart XI—Community-Based Collaborative Care Network Program

“SEC. 340H. COMMUNITY-BASED COLLABORATIVE CARE NETWORK PROGRAM.

“(a) IN GENERAL.—The Secretary may award grants to eligible entities to support community-based collaborative care networks that meet the requirements of subsection (b).

“(b) COMMUNITY-BASED COLLABORATIVE CARE NETWORKS.—

“(1) DESCRIPTION.—A community-based collaborative care network (referred to in this section as a ‘network’) shall be a consortium of health care providers with a joint governance structure (including providers within a single entity) that provides comprehensive coordinated and integrated health care services (as defined by the Secretary) for low-income populations.

“(2) REQUIRED INCLUSION.—A network shall include the following providers (unless such provider does not exist within the community, declines or refuses to participate, or places unreasonable conditions on their participation):

“(A) A hospital that meets the criteria in section 1923(b)(1) of the Social Security Act; and

“(B) All Federally qualified health centers (as defined in section 1861(aa) of the Social Security Act located in the community.

“(3) PRIORITY.—In awarding grants, the Secretary shall give priority to networks that include—

“(A) the capability to provide the broadest range of services to low-income individuals;

“(B) the broadest range of providers that currently serve a high volume of low-income individuals; and

“(C) a county or municipal department of health.

“(c) APPLICATION.—

“(1) APPLICATION.—A network described in subsection (b) shall submit an application to the Secretary.

“(2) RENEWAL.—In subsequent years, based on the performance of grantees, the Secretary may provide renewal grants to prior year grant recipients.

“(d) USE OF FUNDS.—

“(1) USE BY GRANTEES.—Grant funds may be used for the following activities:

“(A) Assist low-income individuals to—

“(i) access and appropriately use health services;

“(ii) enroll in health coverage programs; and

“(iii) obtain a regular primary care provider or a medical home.

“(B) Provide case management and care management.

"(C) Perform health outreach using neighborhood health workers or through other means.

"(D) Provide transportation.

"(E) Expand capacity, including through telehealth, after-hours services or urgent care.

"(F) Provide direct patient care services.

"(2) GRANT FUNDS TO HRSA GRANTEES.—The Secretary may limit the percent of grant funding that may be spent on direct care services provided by grantees of programs administered by the Health Resources and Services Administration or impose other requirements on such grantees deemed necessary.

"(e) AUTHORIZATION OF APPROPRIATIONS.—There are authorized to be appropriated to carry out this section such sums as may be necessary for each of fiscal years 2011 through 2015.".

SEC. 10334. MINORITY HEALTH.

(a) OFFICE OF MINORITY HEALTH.—

(1) IN GENERAL.—Section 1707 of the Public Health Service Act (42 U.S.C. 300u–6) is amended—

(A) in subsection (a), by striking "within the Office of Public Health and Science" and all that follows through the end and inserting ". The Office of Minority Health as existing on the date of enactment of the Patient Protection and Affordable Care Act shall be transferred to the Office of the Secretary in such manner that there is established in the Office of the Secretary, the Office of Minority Health, which shall be headed by the Deputy Assistant Secretary for Minority Health who shall report directly to the Secretary, and shall retain and strengthen authorities (as in existence on such date of enactment) for the purpose of improving minority health and the quality of health care minorities receive, and eliminating racial and ethnic disparities. In carrying out this subsection, the Secretary, acting through the Deputy Assistant Secretary, shall award grants, contracts, enter into memoranda of understanding, cooperative, interagency, intra-agency and other agreements with public and nonprofit private entities, agencies, as well as Departmental and Cabinet agencies and organizations, and with organizations that are indigenous human resource providers in communities of color to assure improved health status of racial and ethnic minorities, and shall develop measures to evaluate the effectiveness of activities aimed at reducing health disparities and supporting the local community. Such measures shall evaluate community outreach activities, language services, workforce cultural competence, and other areas as determined by the Secretary."; and

(B) by striking subsection (h) and inserting the following:

"(h) AUTHORIZATION OF APPROPRIATIONS.—For the purpose of carrying out this section, there are authorized to be appropriated such sums as may be necessary for each of fiscal years 2011 through 2016.".

(2) TRANSFER OF FUNCTIONS.—There are transferred to the Office of Minority Health in the office of the Secretary of Health and Human Services, all duties, responsibilities, authorities, accountabilities, functions, staff, funds, award

mechanisms, and other entities under the authority of the Office of Minority Health of the Public Health Service as in effect on the date before the date of enactment of this Act, which shall continue in effect according to the terms in effect on the date before such date of enactment, until modified, terminated, superseded, set aside, or revoked in accordance with law by the President, the Secretary, a court of competent jurisdiction, or by operation of law.

(3) REPORTS.—Not later than 1 year after the date of enactment of this section, and biennially thereafter, the Secretary of Health and Human Services shall prepare and submit to the appropriate committees of Congress a report describing the activities carried out under section 1707 of the Public Health Service Act (as amended by this subsection) during the period for which the report is being prepared. Not later than 1 year after the date of enactment of this section, and biennially thereafter, the heads of each of the agencies of the Department of Health and Human Services shall submit to the Deputy Assistant Secretary for Minority Health a report summarizing the minority health activities of each of the respective agencies.

(b) ESTABLISHMENT OF INDIVIDUAL OFFICES OF MINORITY HEALTH WITHIN THE DEPARTMENT OF HEALTH AND HUMAN SERVICES.—

(1) IN GENERAL.—Title XVII of the Public Health Service Act (42 U.S.C. 300u et seq.) is amended by inserting after section 1707 the following section:

"SEC. 1707A. INDIVIDUAL OFFICES OF MINORITY HEALTH WITHIN THE DEPARTMENT.

"(a) IN GENERAL.—The head of each agency specified in subsection (b)(1) shall establish within the agency an office to be known as the Office of Minority Health. The head of each such Office shall be appointed by the head of the agency within which the Office is established, and shall report directly to the head of the agency. The head of such agency shall carry out this section (as this section relates to the agency) acting through such Director.

"(b) SPECIFIED AGENCIES.—The agencies referred to in subsection (a) are the Centers for Disease Control and Prevention, the Health Resources and Services Administration, the Substance Abuse and Mental Health Services Administration, the Agency for Healthcare Research and Quality, the Food and Drug Administration, and the Centers for Medicare & Medicaid Services.

"(c) DIRECTOR; APPOINTMENT.—Each Office of Minority Health established in an agency listed in subsection (a) shall be headed by a director, with documented experience and expertise in minority health services research and health disparities elimination.

"(d) REFERENCES.—Except as otherwise specified, any reference in Federal law to an Office of Minority Health (in the Department of Health and Human Services) is deemed to be a reference to the Office of Minority Health in the Office of the Secretary.

"(e) FUNDING.—

"(1) ALLOCATIONS.—Of the amounts appropriated for a specified agency for a fiscal year, the Secretary must designate an appropriate amount of funds for the purpose of carrying out activities under this section through the minority health office of the agency. In reserving an amount under the preceding sentence for a minority health office for a fiscal year, the Secretary shall reduce, by substantially the same percentage, the amount that otherwise would be available for each of the programs of the designated agency involved.

"(2) AVAILABILITY OF FUNDS FOR STAFFING.—The purposes for which amounts made available under paragraph may be expended by a minority health office include the costs of employing staff for such office.".

(2) NO NEW REGULATORY AUTHORITY.—Nothing in this subsection and the amendments made by this subsection may be construed as establishing regulatory authority or modifying any existing regulatory authority.

(3) LIMITATION ON TERMINATION.—Notwithstanding any other provision of law, a Federal office of minority health or Federal appointive position with primary responsibility over minority health issues that is in existence in an office of agency of the Department of Health and Human Services on the date of enactment of this section shall not be terminated, reorganized, or have any of its power or duties transferred unless such termination, reorganization, or transfer is approved by an Act of Congress.

(c) REDESIGNATION OF NATIONAL CENTER ON MINORITY HEALTH AND HEALTH DISPARITIES.—

(1) REDESIGNATION.—Title IV of the Public Health Service Act (42 U.S.C. 281 et seq.) is amended—

(A) by redesignating subpart 6 of part E as subpart 20;

(B) by transferring subpart 20, as so redesignated, to part C of such title IV;

(C) by inserting subpart 20, as so redesignated, after subpart 19 of such part C; and

(D) in subpart 20, as so redesignated—

(i) by redesignating sections 485E through 485H as sections 464z–3 through 464z–6, respectively;

(ii) by striking "National Center on Minority Health and Health Disparities" each place such term appears and inserting "National Institute on Minority Health and Health Disparities"; and

(iii) by striking "Center" each place such term appears and inserting "Institute".

(2) PURPOSE OF INSTITUTE; DUTIES.—Section 464z–3 of the Public Health Service Act, as so redesignated, is amended—

(A) in subsection (h)(1), by striking "research endowments at centers of excellence under section 736." and inserting the following: "research endowments—

"(1) at centers of excellence under section 736; and

"(2) at centers of excellence under section 464z–4.";

(B) in subsection (h)(2)(A), by striking "average" and inserting "median"; and

(C) by adding at the end the following:

"(h) INTERAGENCY COORDINATION.—The Director of the Institute, as the primary Federal officials with responsibility for coordinating all research and activities conducted or supported by the National Institutes of Health on minority health and health disparities, shall plan, coordinate, review and evaluate research and other activities conducted or supported by the Institutes and Centers of the National Institutes of Health.".

(3) TECHNICAL AND CONFORMING AMENDMENTS.—

(A) Section 401(b)(24) of the Public Health Service Act (42 U.S.C. 281(b)(24)) is amended by striking "Center" and inserting "Institute".

(B) Subsection (d)(1) of section 903 of the Public Health Service Act (42 U.S.C. 299a–1(d)(1)) is amended by striking "section 485E" and inserting "section 464z–3".

SEC. 10335. TECHNICAL CORRECTION TO THE HOSPITAL VALUE-BASED PURCHASING PROGRAM.

Section 1886(o)(2)A) of the Social Security Act, as added by section 3001, is amended, in the first sentence, by inserting ", other than measures of readmissions," after "shall select measures".

SEC. 10336. GAO STUDY AND REPORT ON MEDICARE BENEFICIARY ACCESS TO HIGH-QUALITY DIALYSIS SERVICES.

(a) STUDY.—

(1) IN GENERAL.—The Comptroller General of the United States shall conduct a study on the impact on Medicare beneficiary access to high-quality dialysis services of including specified oral drugs that are furnished to such beneficiaries for the treatment of end stage renal disease in the bundled prospective payment system under section 1881(b)(14) of the Social Security Act (42 U.S.C. 1395rr(b)(14)) (pursuant to the proposed rule published by the Secretary of Health and Human Services in the Federal Register on September 29, 2009 (74 Fed. Reg. 49922 et seq.)). Such study shall include an analysis of—

(A) the ability of providers of services and renal dialysis facilities to furnish specified oral drugs or arrange for the provision of such drugs;

(B) the ability of providers of services and renal dialysis facilities to comply, if necessary, with applicable State laws (such as State pharmacy licensure requirements) in order to furnish specified oral drugs;

(C) whether appropriate quality measures exist to safeguard care for Medicare beneficiaries being furnished specified oral drugs by providers of services and renal dialysis facilities; and

(D) other areas determined appropriate by the Comptroller General.

(2) SPECIFIED ORAL DRUG DEFINED.—For purposes of paragraph (1), the term "specified oral drug" means a drug or biological for which there is no injectable equivalent (or other non-oral form of administration).

(b) REPORT.—Not later than 1 year after the date of the enactment of this Act, the Comptroller General of the United States shall submit to Congress a report containing the results of the study conducted under subsection (a), together with recommendations for such legislation and administrative action as the Comptroller General determines appropriate.

Subtitle D—Provisions Relating to Title IV

SEC. 10401. AMENDMENTS TO SUBTITLE A.

(a) Section 4001(h)(4) and (5) of this Act is amended by striking "2010" each place such appears and inserting "2020".

(b) Section 4002(c) of this Act is amended—

(1) by striking "research and health screenings" and inserting "research, health screenings, and initiatives"; and

(2) by striking "for Preventive" and inserting "Regarding Preventive".

(c) Section 4004(a)(4) of this Act is amended by striking "a Gateway" and inserting "an Exchange".

SEC. 10402. AMENDMENTS TO SUBTITLE B.

(a) Section 399Z–1(a)(1(A) of the Public Health Service Act, as added by section 4101(b) of this Act, is amended by inserting "and vision" after "oral".

(b) Section 1861(hhh)(4)(G) of the Social Security Act, as added by section 4103(b), is amended to read as follows:

"(G) A beneficiary shall be eligible to receive only an initial preventive physical examination (as defined under subsection (ww)(1)) during the 12-month period after the date that the beneficiary's coverage begins under part B and shall be eligible to receive personalized prevention plan services under this subsection each year thereafter provided that the beneficiary has not received either an initial preventive physical examination or personalized prevention plan services within the preceding 12-month period.".

SEC. 10403. AMENDMENTS TO SUBTITLE C.

Section 4201 of this Act is amended—

(1) in subsection (a), by adding before the period the following: ", with not less than 20 percent of such grants being awarded to rural and frontier areas";

(2) in subsection (c)(2)(B)(vii), by striking "both urban and rural areas" and inserting "urban, rural, and frontier areas"; and

(3) in subsection (f), by striking "each fiscal years" and inserting "each of fiscal year".

SEC. 10404. AMENDMENTS TO SUBTITLE D.

Section 399MM(2) of the Public Health Service Act, as added by section 4303 of this Act, is amended by striking "by ensuring" and inserting "and ensuring".

SEC. 10405. AMENDMENTS TO SUBTITLE E.

Subtitle E of title IV of this Act is amended by striking section 4401.

SEC. 10406. AMENDMENT RELATING TO WAIVING COINSURANCE FOR PREVENTIVE SERVICES.

Section 4104(b) of this Act is amended to read as follows:

"(b) PAYMENT AND ELIMINATION OF COINSURANCE IN ALL SETTINGS.—Section 1833(a)(1) of the Social Security Act (42 U.S.C. 1395l(a)(1)), as amended by section 4103(c)(1), is amended—

"(1) in subparagraph (T), by inserting '(or 100 percent if such services are recommended with a grade of A or B by the United States Preventive Services Task Force for any indication or population and are appropriate for the individual)' after '80 percent';

"(2) in subparagraph (W)—

"(A) in clause (i), by inserting '(if such subparagraph were applied, by substituting "100 percent" for "80 percent")' after 'subparagraph (D)'; and

"(B) in clause (ii), by striking '80 percent' and inserting '100 percent';

"(3) by striking 'and' before '(X)'; and

"(4) by inserting before the semicolon at the end the following: ', and (Y) with respect to preventive services described in subparagraphs (A) and (B) of section 1861(ddd)(3) that are appropriate for the individual and, in the case of such services described in subparagraph (A), are recommended with a grade of A or B by the United States Preventive Services Task Force for any indication or population, the amount paid shall be 100 percent of (i) except as provided in clause (ii), the lesser of the actual charge for the services or the amount determined under the fee schedule that applies to such services under this part, and (ii) in the case of such services that are covered OPD services (as defined in subsection (t)(1)(B)), the amount determined under subsection (t)'.".

SEC. 10407. BETTER DIABETES CARE.

(a) SHORT TITLE.—This section may be cited as the "Catalyst to Better Diabetes Care Act of 2009".

(b) NATIONAL DIABETES REPORT CARD.—

(1) IN GENERAL.—The Secretary, in collaboration with the Director of the Centers for Disease Control and Prevention (referred to in this section as the "Director"), shall prepare on a biennial basis a national diabetes report card (referred to in this section as a "Report Card") and, to the extent possible, for each State.

(2) CONTENTS.—

(A) IN GENERAL.—Each Report Card shall include aggregate health outcomes related to individuals diagnosed with diabetes and prediabetes including—

(i) preventative care practices and quality of care;

(ii) risk factors; and

(iii) outcomes.

(B) UPDATED REPORTS.—Each Report Card that is prepared after the initial Report Card shall include trend analysis for the Nation and, to the extent possible, for each State, for the purpose of—

(i) tracking progress in meeting established national goals and objectives for improving diabetes care, costs, and prevalence (including Healthy People 2010); and

(ii) informing policy and program development.

(3) AVAILABILITY.—The Secretary, in collaboration with the Director, shall make each Report Card publicly available, including by posting the Report Card on the Internet.

(c) IMPROVEMENT OF VITAL STATISTICS COLLECTION.—

(1) IN GENERAL.—The Secretary, acting through the Director of the Centers for Disease Control and Prevention and in collaboration with appropriate agencies and States, shall—

(A) promote the education and training of physicians on the importance of birth and death certificate data and how to properly complete these documents, including the collection of such data for diabetes and other chronic diseases;

(B) encourage State adoption of the latest standard revisions of birth and death certificates; and

(C) work with States to re-engineer their vital statistics systems in order to provide cost-effective, timely, and accurate vital systems data.

(2) DEATH CERTIFICATE ADDITIONAL LANGUAGE.—In carrying out this subsection, the Secretary may promote improvements to the collection of diabetes mortality data, including the addition of a question for the individual certifying the cause of death regarding whether the deceased had diabetes.

(d) STUDY ON APPROPRIATE LEVEL OF DIABETES MEDICAL EDUCATION.—

(1) IN GENERAL.—The Secretary shall, in collaboration with the Institute of Medicine and appropriate associations and councils, conduct a study of the impact of diabetes on the practice of medicine in the United States and the appropriateness of the level of diabetes medical education that should be required prior to licensure, board certification, and board recertification.

(2) REPORT.—Not later than 2 years after the date of the enactment of this Act, the Secretary shall submit a report on the study under paragraph (1) to the Committees on Ways and Means and Energy and Commerce of the House of Representatives and the Committees on Finance and Health, Education, Labor, and Pensions of the Senate.

(e) AUTHORIZATION OF APPROPRIATIONS.—There are authorized to be appropriated to carry out this section such sums as may be necessary.

SEC. 10408. GRANTS FOR SMALL BUSINESSES TO PROVIDE COMPREHENSIVE WORKPLACE WELLNESS PROGRAMS.

(a) ESTABLISHMENT.—The Secretary shall award grants to eligible employers to provide their employees with access to comprehensive workplace wellness programs (as described under subsection (c)).

(b) SCOPE.—

(1) DURATION.—The grant program established under this section shall be conducted for a 5-year period.

(2) ELIGIBLE EMPLOYER.—The term "eligible employer" means an employer (including a non-profit employer) that—

(A) employs less than 100 employees who work 25 hours or greater per week; and

(B) does not provide a workplace wellness program as of the date of enactment of this Act.

(c) COMPREHENSIVE WORKPLACE WELLNESS PROGRAMS.—

(1) CRITERIA.—The Secretary shall develop program criteria for comprehensive workplace wellness programs under this section that are based on and consistent with evidence-based research and best practices, including research and practices as provided in the Guide to Community Preventive Services, the Guide to Clinical Preventive Services, and the National Registry for Effective Programs.

(2) REQUIREMENTS.—A comprehensive workplace wellness program shall be made available by an eligible employer to all employees and include the following components:

(A) Health awareness initiatives (including health education, preventive screenings, and health risk assessments).

(B) Efforts to maximize employee engagement (including mechanisms to encourage employee participation).

(C) Initiatives to change unhealthy behaviors and lifestyle choices (including counseling, seminars, online programs, and self-help materials).

(D) Supportive environment efforts (including workplace policies to encourage healthy lifestyles, healthy eating, increased physical activity, and improved mental health).

(d) APPLICATION.—An eligible employer desiring to participate in the grant program under this section shall submit an application to the Secretary, in such manner and containing such information as the Secretary may require, which shall include a proposal for a comprehensive workplace wellness program that meet the criteria and requirements described under subsection (c).

(e) AUTHORIZATION OF APPROPRIATION.—For purposes of carrying out the grant program under this section, there is authorized to be appropriated $200,000,000 for the period of fiscal years 2011 through 2015. Amounts appropriated pursuant to this subsection shall remain available until expended.

SEC. 10409. CURES ACCELERATION NETWORK.

(a) SHORT TITLE.—This section may be cited as the "Cures Acceleration Network Act of 2009".

(b) REQUIREMENT FOR THE DIRECTOR OF NIH TO ESTABLISH A CURES ACCELERATION NETWORK.—Section 402(b) of the Public Health Service Act (42 U.S.C. 282(b)) is amended—

(1) in paragraph (22), by striking "and" at the end;

(2) in paragraph (23), by striking the period and inserting "; and"; and

(3) by inserting after paragraph (23), the following:

"(24) implement the Cures Acceleration Network described in section 402C.".

(c) ACCEPTING GIFTS TO SUPPORT THE CURES ACCELERATION NETWORK.—Section 499(c)(1) of the Public Health Service Act (42 U.S.C. 290b(c)(1)) is amended by adding at the end the following:

"(E) The Cures Acceleration Network described in section 402C.".

(d) ESTABLISHMENT OF THE CURES ACCELERATION NETWORK.—Part A of title IV of the Public Health Service Act is amended by inserting after section 402B (42 U.S.C. 282b) the following:

"SEC. 402C. CURES ACCELERATION NETWORK.

"(a) DEFINITIONS.—In this section:

"(1) BIOLOGICAL PRODUCT.—The term 'biological product' has the meaning given such term in section 351 of the Public Health Service Act.

"(2) DRUG; DEVICE.—The terms 'drug' and 'device' have the meanings given such terms in section 201 of the Federal Food, Drug, and Cosmetic Act.

"(3) HIGH NEED CURE.—The term 'high need cure' means a drug (as that term is defined by section 201(g)(1) of the Federal Food, Drug, and Cosmetic Act, biological product (as that term is defined by section 262(i)), or device (as that term is defined by section 201(h) of the Federal Food, Drug, and

Cosmetic Act) that, in the determination of the Director of NIH—

"(A) is a priority to diagnose, mitigate, prevent, or treat harm from any disease or condition; and

"(B) for which the incentives of the commercial market are unlikely to result in its adequate or timely development.

"(4) MEDICAL PRODUCT.—The term 'medical product' means a drug, device, biological product, or product that is a combination of drugs, devices, and biological products.

"(b) ESTABLISHMENT OF THE CURES ACCELERATION NETWORK.—Subject to the appropriation of funds as described in subsection (g), there is established within the Office of the Director of NIH a program to be known as the Cures Acceleration Network (referred to in this section as 'CAN'), which shall—

"(1) be under the direction of the Director of NIH, taking into account the recommendations of a CAN Review Board (referred to in this section as the 'Board'), described in subsection (d); and

"(2) award grants and contracts to eligible entities, as described in subsection (e), to accelerate the development of high need cures, including through the development of medical products and behavioral therapies.

"(c) FUNCTIONS.—The functions of the CAN are to—

"(1) conduct and support revolutionary advances in basic research, translating scientific discoveries from bench to bedside;

"(2) award grants and contracts to eligible entities to accelerate the development of high need cures;

"(3) provide the resources necessary for government agencies, independent investigators, research organizations, biotechnology companies, academic research institutions, and other entities to develop high need cures;

"(4) reduce the barriers between laboratory discoveries and clinical trials for new therapies; and

"(5) facilitate review in the Food and Drug Administration for the high need cures funded by the CAN, through activities that may include—

"(A) the facilitation of regular and ongoing communication with the Food and Drug Administration regarding the status of activities conducted under this section;

"(B) ensuring that such activities are coordinated with the approval requirements of the Food and Drug Administration, with the goal of expediting the development and approval of countermeasures and products; and

"(C) connecting interested persons with additional technical assistance made available under section 565 of the Federal Food, Drug, and Cosmetic Act.

"(d) CAN BOARD.—

"(1) ESTABLISHMENT.—There is established a Cures Acceleration Network Review Board (referred to in this section as the 'Board'), which shall advise the Director of NIH on the conduct of the activities of the Cures Acceleration Network.

"(2) MEMBERSHIP.—

"(A) IN GENERAL.—

"(i) APPOINTMENT.—The Board shall be comprised of 24 members who are appointed by the Secretary and who serve at the pleasure of the Secretary.

"(ii) CHAIRPERSON AND VICE CHAIRPERSON.—The Secretary shall designate, from among the 24 members appointed under clause (i), one Chairperson of the Board (referred to in this section as the 'Chairperson') and one Vice Chairperson.

"(B) TERMS.—

"(i) IN GENERAL.—Each member shall be appointed to serve a 4-year term, except that any member appointed to fill a vacancy occurring prior to the expiration of the term for which the member's predecessor was appointed shall be appointed for the remainder of such term.

"(ii) CONSECUTIVE APPOINTMENTS; MAXIMUM TERMS.—A member may be appointed to serve not more than 3 terms on the Board, and may not serve more than 2 such terms consecutively.

"(C) QUALIFICATIONS.—

"(i) IN GENERAL.—The Secretary shall appoint individuals to the Board based solely upon the individual's established record of distinguished service in one of the areas of expertise described in clause (ii). Each individual appointed to the Board shall be of distinguished achievement and have a broad range of disciplinary interests.

"(ii) EXPERTISE.—The Secretary shall select individuals based upon the following requirements:

"(I) For each of the fields of—

"(aa) basic research;

"(bb) medicine;

"(cc) biopharmaceuticals;

"(dd) discovery and delivery of medical products;

"(ee) bioinformatics and gene therapy;

"(ff) medical instrumentation; and

"(gg) regulatory review and approval of medical products,

the Secretary shall select at least 1 individual who is eminent in such fields.

"(II) At least 4 individuals shall be recognized leaders in professional venture capital or private equity organizations and have demonstrated experience in private equity investing.

"(III) At least 8 individuals shall represent disease advocacy organizations.

"(3) EX-OFFICIO MEMBERS.—

"(A) APPOINTMENT.—In addition to the 24 Board members described in paragraph (2), the Secretary shall appoint as ex-officio members of the Board—

"(i) a representative of the National Institutes of Health, recommended by the Secretary of the Department of Health and Human Services;

"(ii) a representative of the Office of the Assistant Secretary of Defense for Health Affairs, recommended by the Secretary of Defense;

"(iii) a representative of the Office of the Under Secretary for Health for the Veterans Health Administration, recommended by the Secretary of Veterans Affairs;

"(iv) a representative of the National Science Foundation, recommended by the Chair of the National Science Board; and

"(v) a representative of the Food and Drug Administration, recommended by the Commissioner of Food and Drugs.

"(B) TERMS.—Each ex-officio member shall serve a 3-year term on the Board, except that the Chairperson may adjust the terms of the initial ex-officio members in order to provide for a staggered term of appointment for all such members.

"(4) RESPONSIBILITIES OF THE BOARD AND THE DIRECTOR OF NIH.—

"(A) RESPONSIBILITIES OF THE BOARD.—

"(i) IN GENERAL.—The Board shall advise, and provide recommendations to, the Director of NIH with respect to—

"(I) policies, programs, and procedures for carrying out the duties of the Director of NIH under this section; and

"(II) significant barriers to successful translation of basic science into clinical application (including issues under the purview of other agencies and departments).

"(ii) REPORT.—In the case that the Board identifies a significant barrier, as described in clause (i)(II), the Board shall submit to the Secretary a report regarding such barrier.

"(B) RESPONSIBILITIES OF THE DIRECTOR OF NIH.—With respect to each recommendation provided by the Board under subparagraph (A)(i), the Director of NIH shall respond in writing to the Board, indicating whether such Director will implement such recommendation. In the case that the Director of NIH indicates a recommendation of the Board will not be implemented, such Director shall provide an explanation of the reasons for not implementing such recommendation.

"(5) MEETINGS.—

"(A) IN GENERAL.—The Board shall meet 4 times per calendar year, at the call of the Chairperson.

"(B) QUORUM; REQUIREMENTS; LIMITATIONS.—

"(i) QUORUM.—A quorum shall consist of a total of 13 members of the Board, excluding ex-officio members, with diverse representation as described in clause (iii).

"(ii) CHAIRPERSON OR VICE CHAIRPERSON.—Each meeting of the Board shall be attended by either the Chairperson or the Vice Chairperson.

"(iii) DIVERSE REPRESENTATION.—At each meeting of the Board, there shall be not less than one scientist, one representative of a disease advocacy organization, and one representative of a professional venture capital or private equity organization.

"(6) COMPENSATION AND TRAVEL EXPENSES.—

"(A) COMPENSATION.—Members shall receive compensation at a rate to be fixed by the Chairperson but not to exceed a rate equal to the daily equivalent of the annual rate of basic pay prescribed for level IV of the Executive Schedule under section 5315 of title 5, United States Code, for each day (including travel time) during which the member is engaged in the performance of the duties of the Board. All members of the Board who are officers or employees of the United States shall serve without compensation in addition to that received for their services as officers or employees of the United States.

"(B) TRAVEL EXPENSES.—Members of the Board shall be allowed travel expenses, including per diem in lieu of subsistence, at rates authorized for persons employed intermittently by the Federal Government under section 5703(b) of title 5, United States Code, while away from their homes or regular places of business in the performance of services for the Board.

"(e) GRANT PROGRAM.—

"(1) SUPPORTING INNOVATION.—To carry out the purposes described in this section, the Director of NIH shall award contracts, grants, or cooperative agreements to the entities described in paragraph (2), to—

"(A) promote innovation in technologies supporting the advanced research and development and production of high need cures, including through the development of medical products and behavioral therapies.

"(B) accelerate the development of high need cures, including through the development of medical products, behavioral therapies, and biomarkers that demonstrate the safety or effectiveness of medical products; or

"(C) help the award recipient establish protocols that comply with Food and Drug Administration standards and otherwise permit the recipient to meet regulatory requirements at all stages of development, manufacturing, review, approval, and safety surveillance of a medical product.

"(2) ELIGIBLE ENTITIES.—To receive assistance under paragraph (1), an entity shall—

"(A) be a public or private entity, which may include a private or public research institution, an institution of higher education, a medical center, a biotechnology company, a pharmaceutical company, a disease advocacy organization, a patient advocacy organization, or an academic research institution;

"(B) submit an application containing—

"(i) a detailed description of the project for which the entity seeks such grant or contract;

"(ii) a timetable for such project;

"(iii) an assurance that the entity will submit—

"(I) interim reports describing the entity's—

"(aa) progress in carrying out the project; and

"(bb) compliance with all provisions of this section and conditions of receipt of such grant or contract; and

"(II) a final report at the conclusion of the grant period, describing the outcomes of the project; and

"(iv) a description of the protocols the entity will follow to comply with Food and Drug Administration standards and regulatory requirements at all stages of development, manufacturing, review, approval, and safety surveillance of a medical product; and

"(C) provide such additional information as the Director of NIH may require.

"(3) AWARDS.—

"(A) THE CURES ACCELERATION PARTNERSHIP AWARDS.—

"(i) INITIAL AWARD AMOUNT.—Each award under this subparagraph shall be not more than $15,000,000 per project for the first fiscal year for which the project is funded, which shall be payable in one payment.

"(ii) FUNDING IN SUBSEQUENT FISCAL YEARS.—An eligible entity receiving an award under clause (i) may apply for additional funding for such project by submitting to the Director of NIH the information required under subparagraphs (B) and (C) of paragraph (2). The Director may fund a project of such eligible entity in an amount not to exceed $15,000,000 for a fiscal year subsequent to the initial award under clause (i).

"(iii) MATCHING FUNDS.—As a condition for receiving an award under this subsection, an eligible entity shall contribute to the project non-Federal funds in the amount of $1 for every $3 awarded under clauses (i) and (ii), except that the Director of NIH may waive or modify such matching requirement in any case where the Director determines that the goals and objectives of this section cannot adequately be carried out unless such requirement is waived.

"(B) THE CURES ACCELERATION GRANT AWARDS.—

"(i) INITIAL AWARD AMOUNT.—Each award under this subparagraph shall be not more than $15,000,000 per project for the first fiscal year for which the project is funded, which shall be payable in one payment.

"(ii) FUNDING IN SUBSEQUENT FISCAL YEARS.—An eligible entity receiving an award under clause (i) may apply for additional funding for such project by submitting to the Board the information required under subparagraphs (B) and (C) of paragraph (2). The Director of NIH may fund a project of such eligible entity in an amount not to exceed $15,000,000 for a fiscal year subsequent to the initial award under clause (i).

"(C) THE CURES ACCELERATION FLEXIBLE RESEARCH AWARDS.—If the Director of NIH determines that the goals and objectives of this section cannot adequately be carried out through a contract, grant, or cooperative agreement, the Director of NIH shall have flexible research authority to use other transactions to fund projects in accordance with the terms and conditions of this section. Awards made under such flexible research authority for a fiscal year shall not exceed 20 percent of the total funds appropriated under subsection (g)(1) for such fiscal year.

"(4) SUSPENSION OF AWARDS FOR DEFAULTS, NONCOMPLIANCE WITH PROVISIONS AND PLANS, AND DIVERSION OF FUNDS; REPAYMENT OF FUNDS.—The Director of NIH may suspend the award to any entity upon noncompliance by such entity with provisions and plans under this section or diversion of funds.

"(5) AUDITS.—The Director of NIH may enter into agreements with other entities to conduct periodic audits of the projects funded by grants or contracts awarded under this subsection.

"(6) CLOSEOUT PROCEDURES.—At the end of a grant or contract period, a recipient shall follow the closeout procedures under section 74.71 of title 45, Code of Federal Regulations (or any successor regulation).

"(7) REVIEW.—A determination by the Director of NIH as to whether a drug, device, or biological product is a high need cure (for purposes of subsection (a)(3)) shall not be subject to judicial review.

"(f) COMPETITIVE BASIS OF AWARDS.—Any grant, cooperative agreement, or contract awarded under this section shall be awarded on a competitive basis.

"(g) AUTHORIZATION OF APPROPRIATIONS.—

"(1) IN GENERAL.—For purposes of carrying out this section, there are authorized to be appropriated $500,000,000 for fiscal year 2010, and such sums as may be necessary for subsequent fiscal years. Funds appropriated under this section shall be available until expended.

"(2) LIMITATION ON USE OF FUNDS OTHERWISE APPROPRIATED.—No funds appropriated under this Act, other than funds appropriated under paragraph (1), may be allocated to the Cures Acceleration Network.".

SEC. 10410. CENTERS OF EXCELLENCE FOR DEPRESSION.

(a) SHORT TITLE.—This section may be cited as the "Establishing a Network of Health-Advancing National Centers of Excellence for Depression Act of 2009" or the "ENHANCED Act of 2009".

(b) CENTERS OF EXCELLENCE FOR DEPRESSION.—Subpart 3 of part B of title V of the Public Health Service Act (42 U.S.C. 290bb et seq.) is amended by inserting after section 520A the following:

"SEC. 520B. NATIONAL CENTERS OF EXCELLENCE FOR DEPRESSION.

"(a) DEPRESSIVE DISORDER DEFINED.—In this section, the term 'depressive disorder' means a mental or brain disorder relating to depression, including major depression, bipolar disorder, and related mood disorders.

"(b) GRANT PROGRAM.—

"(1) IN GENERAL.—The Secretary, acting through the Administrator, shall award grants on a competitive basis to eligible entities to establish national centers of excellence for depression (referred to in this section as 'Centers'), which shall engage in activities related to the treatment of depressive disorders.

"(2) ALLOCATION OF AWARDS.—If the funds authorized under subsection (f) are appropriated in the amounts provided for under such subsection, the Secretary shall allocate such amounts so that—

"(A) not later than 1 year after the date of enactment of the ENHANCED Act of 2009, not more than 20 Centers may be established; and

"(B) not later than September 30, 2016, not more than 30 Centers may be established.

"(3) GRANT PERIOD.—

"(A) IN GENERAL.—A grant awarded under this section shall be for a period of 5 years.

"(B) RENEWAL.—A grant awarded under subparagraph (A) may be renewed, on a competitive basis, for 1 additional 5-year period, at the discretion of the Secretary. In determining whether to renew a grant, the Secretary shall consider the report cards issued under subsection (e)(2).

"(4) USE OF FUNDS.—Grant funds awarded under this subsection shall be used for the establishment and ongoing activities of the recipient of such funds.

"(5) ELIGIBLE ENTITIES.—

"(A) REQUIREMENTS.—To be eligible to receive a grant under this section, an entity shall—

"(i) be an institution of higher education or a public or private nonprofit research institution; and

"(ii) submit an application to the Secretary at such time and in such manner as the Secretary may require, as described in subparagraph (B).

"(B) APPLICATION.—An application described in subparagraph (A)(ii) shall include—

"(i) evidence that such entity—

"(I) provides, or is capable of coordinating with other entities to provide, comprehensive health services with a focus on mental health services and subspecialty expertise for depressive disorders;

"(II) collaborates with other mental health providers, as necessary, to address co-occurring mental illnesses;

"(III) is capable of training health professionals about mental health; and

"(ii) such other information, as the Secretary may require.

"(C) PRIORITIES.—In awarding grants under this section, the Secretary shall give priority to eligible entities that meet 1 or more of the following criteria:

"(i) Demonstrated capacity and expertise to serve the targeted population.

"(ii) Existing infrastructure or expertise to provide appropriate, evidence-based and culturally and linguistically competent services.

"(iii) A location in a geographic area with disproportionate numbers of underserved and at-risk populations in medically underserved areas and health professional shortage areas.

"(iv) Proposed innovative approaches for outreach to initiate or expand services.

"(v) Use of the most up-to-date science, practices, and interventions available.

"(vi) Demonstrated capacity to establish cooperative and collaborative agreements with community mental health centers and other community entities to provide mental health, social, and human services to individuals with depressive disorders.

"(6) NATIONAL COORDINATING CENTER.—

"(A) IN GENERAL.—The Secretary, acting through the Administrator, shall designate 1 recipient of a grant under this section to be the coordinating center of excellence for depression (referred to in this section as the 'coordinating center'). The Secretary shall select such coordinating center on a competitive basis, based upon the demonstrated capacity of such center to perform the duties described in subparagraph (C).

"(B) APPLICATION.—A Center that has been awarded a grant under paragraph (1) may apply for designation as the coordinating center by submitting an application to the Secretary at such time, in such manner, and containing such information as the Secretary may require.

"(C) DUTIES.—The coordinating center shall—

"(i) develop, administer, and coordinate the network of Centers under this section;

"(ii) oversee and coordinate the national database described in subsection (d);

"(iii) lead a strategy to disseminate the findings and activities of the Centers through such database; and

"(iv) serve as a liaison with the Administration, the National Registry of Evidence-based Programs and Practices of the Administration, and any Federal interagency or interagency forum on mental health.

"(7) MATCHING FUNDS.—The Secretary may not award a grant or contract under this section to an entity unless the entity agrees that it will make available (directly or through contributions from other public or private entities) non-Federal contributions toward the activities to be carried out under the grant or contract in an amount equal to $1 for each $5 of Federal funds provided under the grant or contract. Such non-Federal matching funds may be provided directly or through donations from public or private entities and may be in cash or in-kind, fairly evaluated, including plant, equipment, or services.

"(c) ACTIVITIES OF THE CENTERS.—Each Center shall carry out the following activities:

"(1) GENERAL ACTIVITIES.—Each Center shall—

"(A) integrate basic, clinical, or health services interdisciplinary research and practice in the development, implementation, and dissemination of evidence-based interventions;

"(B) involve a broad cross-section of stakeholders, such as researchers, clinicians, consumers, families of consumers, and voluntary health organizations, to develop a research agenda and disseminate findings, and to provide support in the implementation of evidence-based practices;

"(C) provide training and technical assistance to mental health professionals, and engage in and disseminate translational research with a focus on meeting the needs of individuals with depressive disorders; and

"(D) educate policy makers, employers, community leaders, and the public about depressive disorders to reduce stigma and raise awareness of treatments.

"(2) IMPROVED TREATMENT STANDARDS, CLINICAL GUIDELINES, DIAGNOSTIC PROTOCOLS, AND CARE COORDINATION PRACTICE.—Each Center shall collaborate with other Centers in the network to—

"(A) develop and implement treatment standards, clinical guidelines, and protocols that emphasize primary prevention, early intervention, treatment for, and recovery from, depressive disorders;

"(B) foster communication with other providers attending to co-occurring physical health conditions such as cardiovascular, diabetes, cancer, and substance abuse disorders;

"(C) leverage available community resources, develop and implement improved self-management programs, and, when appropriate, involve family and other providers of social support in the development and implementation of care plans; and

"(D) use electronic health records and telehealth technology to better coordinate and manage, and improve access to, care, as determined by the coordinating center.

"(3) TRANSLATIONAL RESEARCH THROUGH COLLABORATION OF CENTERS AND COMMUNITY-BASED ORGANIZATIONS.—Each Center shall—

"(A) demonstrate effective use of a public-private partnership to foster collaborations among members of the network and community-based organizations such as community mental health centers and other social and human services providers;

"(B) expand interdisciplinary, translational, and patient-oriented research and treatment; and

"(C) coordinate with accredited academic programs to provide ongoing opportunities for the professional and continuing education of mental health providers.

"(d) NATIONAL DATABASE.—

"(1) IN GENERAL.—The coordinating center shall establish and maintain a national, publicly available database to improve prevention programs, evidence-based interventions, and disease management programs for depressive disorders, using data collected from the Centers, as described in paragraph (2).

"(2) DATA COLLECTION.—Each Center shall submit data gathered at such center, as appropriate, to the coordinating center regarding—

"(A) the prevalence and incidence of depressive disorders;

"(B) the health and social outcomes of individuals with depressive disorders;

"(C) the effectiveness of interventions designed, tested, and evaluated;

"(D) other information, as the Secretary may require.

"(3) SUBMISSION OF DATA TO THE ADMINISTRATOR.—The coordinating center shall submit to the Administrator the data and financial information gathered under paragraph (2).

"(4) PUBLICATION USING DATA FROM THE DATABASE.—A Center, or an individual affiliated with a Center, may publish findings using the data described in paragraph (2) only if such center submits such data to the coordinating center, as required under such paragraph.

"(e) ESTABLISHMENT OF STANDARDS; REPORT CARDS AND RECOMMENDATIONS; THIRD PARTY REVIEW.—

"(1) ESTABLISHMENT OF STANDARDS.—The Secretary, acting through the Administrator, shall establish performance standards for—

"(A) each Center; and

"(B) the network of Centers as a whole.

"(2) REPORT CARDS.—The Secretary, acting through the Administrator, shall—

"(A) for each Center, not later than 3 years after the date on which such center of excellence is established and annually thereafter, issue a report card to the coordinating center to rate the performance of such Center; and

"(B) not later than 3 years after the date on which the first grant is awarded under subsection (b)(1) and annually thereafter, issue a report card to Congress to rate the performance of the network of centers of excellence as a whole.

"(3) RECOMMENDATIONS.—Based upon the report cards described in paragraph (2), the Secretary shall, not later than September 30, 2015—

"(A) make recommendations to the Centers regarding improvements such centers shall make; and

"(B) make recommendations to Congress for expanding the Centers to serve individuals with other types of mental disorders.

"(4) THIRD PARTY REVIEW.—Not later than 3 years after the date on which the first grant is awarded under subsection (b)(1) and annually thereafter, the Secretary shall arrange for an independent third party to conduct an evaluation of the network of Centers to ensure that such centers are meeting the goals of this section.

"(f) AUTHORIZATION OF APPROPRIATIONS.—

"(1) IN GENERAL.—To carry out this section, there are authorized to be appropriated—

"(A) $100,000,000 for each of the fiscal years 2011 through 2015; and

"(B) $150,000,000 for each of the fiscal years 2016 through 2020.

"(2) ALLOCATION OF FUNDS AUTHORIZED.—Of the amount appropriated under paragraph (1) for a fiscal year, the Secretary shall determine the allocation of each Center receiving a grant under this section, but in no case may the allocation be more than $5,000,000, except that the Secretary may allocate not more than $10,000,000 to the coordinating center.".

SEC. 10411. PROGRAMS RELATING TO CONGENITAL HEART DISEASE.

(a) SHORT TITLE.—This subtitle may be cited as the "Congenital Heart Futures Act".

(b) PROGRAMS RELATING TO CONGENITAL HEART DISEASE.—

(1) NATIONAL CONGENITAL HEART DISEASE SURVEILLANCE SYSTEM.—Part P of title III of the Public Health Service Act (42 U.S.C. 280g et seq.), as amended by section 5405, is further amended by adding at the end the following:

"SEC. 399V–2. NATIONAL CONGENITAL HEART DISEASE SURVEILLANCE SYSTEM.

"(a) IN GENERAL.—The Secretary, acting through the Director of the Centers for Disease Control and Prevention, may—

"(1) enhance and expand infrastructure to track the epidemiology of congenital heart disease and to organize such information into a nationally-representative, population-based surveillance system that compiles data concerning actual occurrences of congenital heart disease, to be known as the 'National Congenital Heart Disease Surveillance System'; or

"(2) award a grant to one eligible entity to undertake the activities described in paragraph (1).

"(b) PURPOSE.—The purpose of the Congenital Heart Disease Surveillance System shall be to facilitate further research into the types of health services patients use and to identify possible areas for educational outreach and prevention in accordance with standard practices of the Centers for Disease Control and Prevention.

"(c) CONTENT.—The Congenital Heart Disease Surveillance System—

"(1) may include information concerning the incidence and prevalence of congenital heart disease in the United States;

"(2) may be used to collect and store data on congenital heart disease, including data concerning—

"(A) demographic factors associated with congenital heart disease, such as age, race, ethnicity, sex, and family history of individuals who are diagnosed with the disease;

"(B) risk factors associated with the disease;

"(C) causation of the disease;

"(D) treatment approaches; and

"(E) outcome measures, such that analysis of the outcome measures will allow derivation of evidence-based best practices and guidelines for congenital heart disease patients; and

"(3) may ensure the collection and analysis of longitudinal data related to individuals of all ages with congenital heart disease, including infants, young children, adolescents, and adults of all ages.

"(d) PUBLIC ACCESS.—The Congenital Heart Disease Surveillance System shall be made available to the public, as appropriate, including congenital heart disease researchers.

"(e) PATIENT PRIVACY.—The Secretary shall ensure that the Congenital Heart Disease Surveillance System is maintained in a manner that complies with the regulations promulgated under section 264 of the Health Insurance Portability and Accountability Act of 1996.

"(f) ELIGIBILITY FOR GRANT.—To be eligible to receive a grant under subsection (a)(2), an entity shall—

"(1) be a public or private nonprofit entity with specialized experience in congenital heart disease; and

"(2) submit to the Secretary an application at such time, in such manner, and containing such information as the Secretary may require.".

(2) CONGENITAL HEART DISEASE RESEARCH.—Subpart 2 of part C of title IV of the Public Health Service Act (42 U.S.C. 285b et seq.) is amended by adding at the end the following:

“SEC. 425. CONGENITAL HEART DISEASE.

“(a) IN GENERAL.—The Director of the Institute may expand, intensify, and coordinate research and related activities of the Institute with respect to congenital heart disease, which may include congenital heart disease research with respect to—

“(1) causation of congenital heart disease, including genetic causes;

“(2) long-term outcomes in individuals with congenital heart disease, including infants, children, teenagers, adults, and elderly individuals;

“(3) diagnosis, treatment, and prevention;

“(4) studies using longitudinal data and retrospective analysis to identify effective treatments and outcomes for individuals with congenital heart disease; and

“(5) identifying barriers to life-long care for individuals with congenital heart disease.

“(b) COORDINATION OF RESEARCH ACTIVITIES.—The Director of the Institute may coordinate research efforts related to congenital heart disease among multiple research institutions and may develop research networks.

“(c) MINORITY AND MEDICALLY UNDERSERVED COMMUNITIES.—In carrying out the activities described in this section, the Director of the Institute shall consider the application of such research and other activities to minority and medically underserved communities.”.

(c) AUTHORIZATION OF APPROPRIATIONS.—There are authorized to be appropriated to carry out the amendments made by this section such sums as may be necessary for each of fiscal years 2011 through 2015.

SEC. 10412. AUTOMATED DEFIBRILLATION IN ADAM’S MEMORY ACT.

Section 312 of the Public Health Service Act (42 U.S.C. 244) is amended—

(1) in subsection (c)(6), after “clearinghouse” insert “, that shall be administered by an organization that has substantial expertise in pediatric education, pediatric medicine, and electrophysiology and sudden death,”; and

(2) in the first sentence of subsection (e), by striking “fiscal year 2003” and all that follows through “2006” and inserting “for each of fiscal years 2003 through 2014”.

SEC. 10413. YOUNG WOMEN’S BREAST HEALTH AWARENESS AND SUPPORT OF YOUNG WOMEN DIAGNOSED WITH BREAST CANCER.

(a) SHORT TITLE.—This section may be cited as the “Young Women’s Breast Health Education and Awareness Requires Learning Young Act of 2009” or the “EARLY Act”.

(b) AMENDMENT.—Title III of the Public Health Service Act (42 U.S.C. 241 et seq.), as amended by this Act, is further amended by adding at the end the following:

“PART V—PROGRAMS RELATING TO BREAST HEALTH AND CANCER

“SEC. 399NN. YOUNG WOMEN’S BREAST HEALTH AWARENESS AND SUPPORT OF YOUNG WOMEN DIAGNOSED WITH BREAST CANCER.

“(a) PUBLIC EDUCATION CAMPAIGN.—

“(1) IN GENERAL.—The Secretary, acting through the Director of the Centers for Disease Control and Prevention, shall conduct a national evidence-based education campaign to increase awareness of young women’s knowledge regarding—

“(A) breast health in young women of all racial, ethnic, and cultural backgrounds;

“(B) breast awareness and good breast health habits;

“(C) the occurrence of breast cancer and the general and specific risk factors in women who may be at high risk for breast cancer based on familial, racial, ethnic, and cultural backgrounds such as Ashkenazi Jewish populations;

“(D) evidence-based information that would encourage young women and their health care professional to increase early detection of breast cancers; and

“(E) the availability of health information and other resources for young women diagnosed with breast cancer.

“(2) EVIDENCE-BASED, AGE APPROPRIATE MESSAGES.—The campaign shall provide evidence-based, age-appropriate messages and materials as developed by the Centers for Disease Control and Prevention and the Advisory Committee established under paragraph (4).

“(3) MEDIA CAMPAIGN.—In conducting the education campaign under paragraph (1), the Secretary shall award grants to entities to establish national multimedia campaigns oriented to young women that may include advertising through television, radio, print media, billboards, posters, all forms of existing and especially emerging social networking media, other Internet media, and any other medium determined appropriate by the Secretary.

“(4) ADVISORY COMMITTEE.—

“(A) ESTABLISHMENT.—Not later than 60 days after the date of the enactment of this section, the Secretary, acting through the Director of the Centers for Disease Control and Prevention, shall establish an advisory committee to assist in creating and conducting the education campaigns under paragraph (1) and subsection (b)(1).

“(B) MEMBERSHIP.—The Secretary, acting through the Director of the Centers for Disease Control and Prevention, shall appoint to the advisory committee under subparagraph (A) such members as deemed necessary to properly advise the Secretary, and shall include organizations and individuals with expertise in breast cancer, disease prevention, early detection, diagnosis, public health, social marketing, genetic screening and counseling, treatment, rehabilitation, palliative care, and survivorship in young women.

“(b) HEALTH CARE PROFESSIONAL EDUCATION CAMPAIGN.—The Secretary, acting through the Director of the Centers for Disease

Control and Prevention, and in consultation with the Administrator of the Health Resources and Services Administration, shall conduct an education campaign among physicians and other health care professionals to increase awareness—

"(1) of breast health, symptoms, and early diagnosis and treatment of breast cancer in young women, including specific risk factors such as family history of cancer and women that may be at high risk for breast cancer, such as Ashkenazi Jewish population;

"(2) on how to provide counseling to young women about their breast health, including knowledge of their family cancer history and importance of providing regular clinical breast examinations;

"(3) concerning the importance of discussing healthy behaviors, and increasing awareness of services and programs available to address overall health and wellness, and making patient referrals to address tobacco cessation, good nutrition, and physical activity;

"(4) on when to refer patients to a health care provider with genetics expertise;

"(5) on how to provide counseling that addresses long-term survivorship and health concerns of young women diagnosed with breast cancer; and

"(6) on when to provide referrals to organizations and institutions that provide credible health information and substantive assistance and support to young women diagnosed with breast cancer.

"(c) PREVENTION RESEARCH ACTIVITIES.—The Secretary, acting through—

"(1) the Director of the Centers for Disease Control and Prevention, shall conduct prevention research on breast cancer in younger women, including—

"(A) behavioral, survivorship studies, and other research on the impact of breast cancer diagnosis on young women;

"(B) formative research to assist with the development of educational messages and information for the public, targeted populations, and their families about breast health, breast cancer, and healthy lifestyles;

"(C) testing and evaluating existing and new social marketing strategies targeted at young women; and

"(D) surveys of health care providers and the public regarding knowledge, attitudes, and practices related to breast health and breast cancer prevention and control in high-risk populations; and

"(2) the Director of the National Institutes of Health, shall conduct research to develop and validate new screening tests and methods for prevention and early detection of breast cancer in young women.

"(d) SUPPORT FOR YOUNG WOMEN DIAGNOSED WITH BREAST CANCER.—

"(1) IN GENERAL.—The Secretary shall award grants to organizations and institutions to provide health information from credible sources and substantive assistance directed to young women diagnosed with breast cancer and pre-neoplastic breast diseases.

"(2) PRIORITY.—In making grants under paragraph (1), the Secretary shall give priority to applicants that deal specifically with young women diagnosed with breast cancer and pre-neoplastic breast disease.

"(e) NO DUPLICATION OF EFFORT.—In conducting an education campaign or other program under subsections (a), (b), (c), or (d), the Secretary shall avoid duplicating other existing Federal breast cancer education efforts.

"(f) MEASUREMENT; REPORTING.—The Secretary, acting through the Director of the Centers for Disease Control and Prevention, shall—

"(1) measure—

"(A) young women's awareness regarding breast health, including knowledge of family cancer history, specific risk factors and early warning signs, and young women's proactive efforts at early detection;

"(B) the number or percentage of young women utilizing information regarding lifestyle interventions that foster healthy behaviors;

"(C) the number or percentage of young women receiving regular clinical breast exams; and

"(D) the number or percentage of young women who perform breast self exams, and the frequency of such exams, before the implementation of this section;

"(2) not less than every 3 years, measure the impact of such activities; and

"(3) submit reports to the Congress on the results of such measurements.

"(g) DEFINITION.—In this section, the term 'young women' means women 15 to 44 years of age.

"(h) AUTHORIZATION OF APPROPRIATIONS.—To carry out subsections (a), (b), (c)(1), and (d), there are authorized to be appropriated $9,000,000 for each of the fiscal years 2010 through 2014.".

Subtitle E—Provisions Relating to Title V

SEC. 10501. AMENDMENTS TO THE PUBLIC HEALTH SERVICE ACT, THE SOCIAL SECURITY ACT, AND TITLE V OF THIS ACT.

(a) Section 5101 of this Act is amended—

(1) in subsection (c)(2)(B)(i)(II), by inserting ", including representatives of small business and self-employed individuals" after "employers";

(2) in subsection (d)(4)(A)—

(A) by redesignating clause (iv) as clause (v); and

(B) by inserting after clause (iii) the following:

"(iv) An analysis of, and recommendations for, eliminating the barriers to entering and staying in primary care, including provider compensation."; and

(3) in subsection (i)(2)(B), by inserting "optometrists, ophthalmologists," after "occupational therapists,".

(b) Subtitle B of title V of this Act is amended by adding at the end the following:

"SEC. 5104. INTERAGENCY TASK FORCE TO ASSESS AND IMPROVE ACCESS TO HEALTH CARE IN THE STATE OF ALASKA.

"(a) ESTABLISHMENT.—There is established a task force to be known as the 'Interagency Access to Health Care in Alaska Task Force' (referred to in this section as the 'Task Force').

"(b) DUTIES.—The Task Force shall—

"(1) assess access to health care for beneficiaries of Federal health care systems in Alaska; and

"(2) develop a strategy for the Federal Government to improve delivery of health care to Federal beneficiaries in the State of Alaska.

"(c) MEMBERSHIP.—The Task Force shall be comprised of Federal members who shall be appointed, not later than 45 days after the date of enactment of this Act, as follows:

"(1) The Secretary of Health and Human Services shall appoint one representative of each of the following:

"(A) The Department of Health and Human Services.

"(B) The Centers for Medicare and Medicaid Services.

"(C) The Indian Health Service.

"(2) The Secretary of Defense shall appoint one representative of the TRICARE Management Activity.

"(3) The Secretary of the Army shall appoint one representative of the Army Medical Department.

"(4) The Secretary of the Air Force shall appoint one representative of the Air Force, from among officers at the Air Force performing medical service functions.

"(5) The Secretary of Veterans Affairs shall appoint one representative of each of the following:

"(A) The Department of Veterans Affairs.

"(B) The Veterans Health Administration.

"(6) The Secretary of Homeland Security shall appoint one representative of the United States Coast Guard.

"(d) CHAIRPERSON.—One chairperson of the Task Force shall be appointed by the Secretary at the time of appointment of members under subsection (c), selected from among the members appointed under paragraph (1).

"(e) MEETINGS.—The Task Force shall meet at the call of the chairperson.

"(f) REPORT.—Not later than 180 days after the date of enactment of this Act, the Task Force shall submit to Congress a report detailing the activities of the Task Force and containing the findings, strategies, recommendations, policies, and initiatives developed pursuant to the duty described in subsection (b)(2). In preparing such report, the Task Force shall consider completed and ongoing efforts by Federal agencies to improve access to health care in the State of Alaska.

"(g) TERMINATION.—The Task Force shall be terminated on the date of submission of the report described in subsection (f).".

(c) Section 399V of the Public Health Service Act, as added by section 5313, is amended—

(1) in subsection (b)(4), by striking "identify, educate, refer, and enroll" and inserting "identify and refer"; and

(2) in subsection (k)(1), by striking ", as defined by the Department of Labor as Standard Occupational Classification [21–1094]".

(d) Section 738(a)(3) of the Public Health Service Act (42 U.S.C. 293b(a)(3)) is amended by inserting "schools offering physician assistant education programs," after "public health,".

(e) Subtitle D of title V of this Act is amended by adding at the end the following:

"SEC. 5316. DEMONSTRATION GRANTS FOR FAMILY NURSE PRACTITIONER TRAINING PROGRAMS.

"(a) ESTABLISHMENT OF PROGRAM.—The Secretary of Health and Human Services (referred to in this section as the 'Secretary') shall establish a training demonstration program for family nurse practitioners (referred to in this section as the 'program') to employ and provide 1-year training for nurse practitioners who have graduated from a nurse practitioner program for careers as primary care providers in Federally qualified health centers (referred to in this section as 'FQHCs') and nurse-managed health clinics (referred to in this section as 'NMHCs').

"(b) PURPOSE.—The purpose of the program is to enable each grant recipient to—

"(1) provide new nurse practitioners with clinical training to enable them to serve as primary care providers in FQHCs and NMHCs;

"(2) train new nurse practitioners to work under a model of primary care that is consistent with the principles set forth by the Institute of Medicine and the needs of vulnerable populations; and

"(3) create a model of FQHC and NMHC training for nurse practitioners that may be replicated nationwide.

"(c) GRANTS.—The Secretary shall award 3-year grants to eligible entities that meet the requirements established by the Secretary, for the purpose of operating the nurse practitioner primary care programs described in subsection (a) in such entities.

"(d) ELIGIBLE ENTITIES.—To be eligible to receive a grant under this section, an entity shall—

"(1)(A) be a FQHC as defined in section 1861(aa) of the Social Security Act (42 U.S.C. 1395x(aa)); or

"(B) be a nurse-managed health clinic, as defined in section 330A–1 of the Public Health Service Act (as added by section 5208 of this Act); and

"(2) submit to the Secretary an application at such time, in such manner, and containing such information as the Secretary may require.

"(e) PRIORITY IN AWARDING GRANTS.—In awarding grants under this section, the Secretary shall give priority to eligible entities that—

"(1) demonstrate sufficient infrastructure in size, scope, and capacity to undertake the requisite training of a minimum of 3 nurse practitioners per year, and to provide to each awardee 12 full months of full-time, paid employment and benefits consistent with the benefits offered to other full-time employees of such entity;

"(2) will assign not less than 1 staff nurse practitioner or physician to each of 4 precepted clinics;

"(3) will provide to each awardee specialty rotations, including specialty training in prenatal care and women's health, adult and child psychiatry, orthopedics, geriatrics, and at least 3 other high-volume, high-burden specialty areas;

"(4) provide sessions on high-volume, high-risk health problems and have a record of training health care professionals in the care of children, older adults, and underserved populations; and

"(5) collaborate with other safety net providers, schools, colleges, and universities that provide health professions training.

"(f) ELIGIBILITY OF NURSE PRACTITIONERS.—

"(1) IN GENERAL.—To be eligible for acceptance to a program funded through a grant awarded under this section, an individual shall—

"(A) be licensed or eligible for licensure in the State in which the program is located as an advanced practice registered nurse or advanced practice nurse and be eligible or board-certified as a family nurse practitioner; and

"(B) demonstrate commitment to a career as a primary care provider in a FQHC or in a NMHC.

"(2) PREFERENCE.—In selecting awardees under the program, each grant recipient shall give preference to bilingual candidates that meet the requirements described in paragraph (1).

"(3) DEFERRAL OF CERTAIN SERVICE.—The starting date of required service of individuals in the National Health Service Corps Service program under title II of the Public Health Service Act (42 U.S.C. 202 et seq.) who receive training under this section shall be deferred until the date that is 22 days after the date of completion of the program.

"(g) GRANT AMOUNT.—Each grant awarded under this section shall be in an amount not to exceed $600,000 per year. A grant recipient may carry over funds from 1 fiscal year to another without obtaining approval from the Secretary.

"(h) TECHNICAL ASSISTANCE GRANTS.—The Secretary may award technical assistance grants to 1 or more FQHCs or NMHCs that have demonstrated expertise in establishing a nurse practitioner residency training program. Such technical assistance grants shall be for the purpose of providing technical assistance to other recipients of grants under subsection (c).

"(i) AUTHORIZATION OF APPROPRIATIONS.—To carry out this section, there is authorized to be appropriated such sums as may be necessary for each of fiscal years 2011 through 2014.".

(f)(1) Section 399W of the Public Health Service Act, as added by section 5405, is redesignated as section 399V–1.

(2) Section 399V–1 of the Public Health Service Act, as so redesignated, is amended in subsection (b)(2)(A) by striking "and the departments of 1 or more health professions schools in the State that train providers in primary care" and inserting "and the departments that train providers in primary care in 1 or more health professions schools in the State".

(3) Section 934 of the Public Health Service Act, as added by section 3501, is amended by striking "399W" each place such term appears and inserting "399V–1".

(4) Section 935(b) of the Public Health Service Act, as added by section 3503, is amended by striking "399W" and inserting "399V–1".

(g) Part P of title III of the Public Health Service Act 42 U.S.C. 280g et seq.), as amended by section 10411, is amended by adding at the end the following:

"SEC. 399V–3. NATIONAL DIABETES PREVENTION PROGRAM.

"(a) IN GENERAL.—The Secretary, acting through the Director of the Centers for Disease Control and Prevention, shall establish a national diabetes prevention program (referred to in this section as the 'program') targeted at adults at high risk for diabetes in order to eliminate the preventable burden of diabetes.

"(b) PROGRAM ACTIVITIES.—The program described in subsection (a) shall include—

"(1) a grant program for community-based diabetes prevention program model sites;

"(2) a program within the Centers for Disease Control and Prevention to determine eligibility of entities to deliver community-based diabetes prevention services;

"(3) a training and outreach program for lifestyle intervention instructors; and

"(4) evaluation, monitoring and technical assistance, and applied research carried out by the Centers for Disease Control and Prevention.

"(c) ELIGIBLE ENTITIES.—To be eligible for a grant under subsection (b)(1), an entity shall be a State or local health department, a tribal organization, a national network of community-based non-profits focused on health and wellbeing, an academic institution, or other entity, as the Secretary determines.

"(d) AUTHORIZATION OF APPROPRIATIONS.—For the purpose of carrying out this section, there are authorized to be appropriated such sums as may be necessary for each of fiscal years 2010 through 2014.".

(h) The provisions of, and amendment made by, section 5501(c) of this Act are repealed.

(i)(1) The provisions of, and amendments made by, section 5502 of this Act are repealed.

(2)(A) Section 1861(aa)(3)(A) of the Social Security Act (42 U.S.C. 1395w(aa)(3)(A)) is amended to read as follows:

"(A) services of the type described in subparagraphs (A) through (C) of paragraph (1) and preventive services (as defined in section 1861(ddd)(3)); and".

(B) The amendment made by subparagraph (A) shall apply to services furnished on or after January 1, 2011.

(3)(A) Section 1834 of the Social Security Act (42 U.S.C. 1395m), as amended by section 4105, is amended by adding at the end the following new subsection:

"(o) DEVELOPMENT AND IMPLEMENTATION OF PROSPECTIVE PAYMENT SYSTEM.—

"(1) DEVELOPMENT.—

"(A) IN GENERAL.—The Secretary shall develop a prospective payment system for payment for Federally qualified health center services furnished by Federally qualified health centers under this title. Such system shall include a process for appropriately describing the services furnished by Federally qualified health centers and shall establish payment rates for specific payment codes based on such appropriate descriptions of services. Such system shall be established to take into account the type, intensity, and duration of services furnished by Federally qualified health centers. Such system may include adjustments, including geographic adjustments, determined appropriate by the Secretary.

"(B) COLLECTION OF DATA AND EVALUATION.—By not later than January 1, 2011, the Secretary shall require Federally qualified health centers to submit to the Secretary such information as the Secretary may require in order to develop and implement the prospective payment system under this subsection, including the reporting of services using HCPCS codes.

"(2) IMPLEMENTATION.—

"(A) IN GENERAL.—Notwithstanding section 1833(a)(3)(A), the Secretary shall provide, for cost reporting periods beginning on or after October 1, 2014, for payments of prospective payment rates for Federally qualified health center services furnished by Federally qualified health centers under this title in accordance with the prospective payment system developed by the Secretary under paragraph (1).

"(B) PAYMENTS.—

"(i) INITIAL PAYMENTS.—The Secretary shall implement such prospective payment system so that the estimated aggregate amount of prospective payment rates (determined prior to the application of section 1833(a)(1)(Z)) under this title for Federally qualified health center services in the first year that such system is implemented is equal to 100 percent of the estimated amount of reasonable costs (determined without the application of a per visit payment limit or productivity screen and prior to the application of section 1866(a)(2)(A)(ii)) that would have occurred for such services under this title in such year if the system had not been implemented.

"(ii) PAYMENTS IN SUBSEQUENT YEARS.—Payment rates in years after the year of implementation of such system shall be the payment rates in the previous year increased—

"(I) in the first year after implementation of such system, by the percentage increase in the MEI (as defined in section 1842(i)(3)) for the year involved; and

"(II) in subsequent years, by the percentage increase in a market basket of Federally qualified health center goods and services as promulgated through regulations, or if such an index is not available, by the percentage increase in the MEI (as defined in section 1842(i)(3)) for the year involved.

"(C) PREPARATION FOR PPS IMPLEMENTATION.—Notwithstanding any other provision of law, the Secretary may establish and implement by program instruction or otherwise the payment codes to be used under the prospective payment system under this section.".

(B) Section 1833(a)(1) of the Social Security Act (42 U.S.C. 1395l(a)(1)), as amended by section 4104, is amended—

(i) by striking "and" before "(Y)"; and

(ii) by inserting before the semicolon at the end the following: ", and (Z) with respect to Federally qualified health center services for which payment is made under section 1834(o), the amounts paid shall be 80 percent of the lesser of the actual charge or the amount determined under such section".

(C) Section 1833(a) of the Social Security Act (42 U.S.C. 1395l(a)) is amended—

(i) in paragraph (3)(B)(i)—

(I) by inserting "(I)" after "otherwise been provided"; and

(II) by inserting ", or (II) in the case of such services furnished on or after the implementation date of the prospective payment system under section 1834(o), under such section (calculated as if '100 percent' were substituted for '80 percent' in such section) for such services if the individual had not been so enrolled" after "been so enrolled"; and

(ii) by adding at the end the following flush sentence: "Paragraph (3)(A) shall not apply to Federally qualified health center services furnished on or after the implementation date of the prospective payment system under section 1834(0).".

(j) Section 5505 is amended by adding at the end the following new subsection:

"(d) APPLICATION.—The amendments made by this section shall not be applied in a manner that requires reopening of any settled cost reports as to which there is not a jurisdictionally proper appeal pending as of the date of the enactment of this Act on the issue of payment for indirect costs of medical education under section 1886(d)(5)(B) of the Social Security Act (42 U.S.C. 1395ww(d)(5)(B)) or for direct graduate medical education costs under section 1886(h) of such Act (42 U.S.C. 1395ww(h)).".

(k) Subtitle G of title V of this Act is amended by adding at the end the following:

"SEC. 5606. STATE GRANTS TO HEALTH CARE PROVIDERS WHO PROVIDE SERVICES TO A HIGH PERCENTAGE OF MEDICALLY UNDERSERVED POPULATIONS OR OTHER SPECIAL POPULATIONS.

"(a) IN GENERAL.—A State may award grants to health care providers who treat a high percentage, as determined by such State, of medically underserved populations or other special populations in such State.

"(b) SOURCE OF FUNDS.—A grant program established by a State under subsection (a) may not be established within a department, agency, or other entity of such State that administers the Medicaid program under title XIX of the Social Security Act (42 U.S.C. 1396 et seq.), and no Federal or State funds allocated to such Medicaid program, the Medicare program under title XVIII of the Social Security Act (42 U.S.C. 1395 et seq.), or the TRICARE program under chapter 55 of title 10, United States Code, may be used to award grants or to pay administrative costs associated with a grant program established under subsection (a).".

(l) Part C of title VII of the Public Health Service Act (42 U.S.C. 293k et seq.) is amended—

(1) after the part heading, by inserting the following:

"Subpart I—Medical Training Generally";

and

(2) by inserting at the end the following:

"Subpart II—Training in Underserved Communities

"SEC. 749B. RURAL PHYSICIAN TRAINING GRANTS.

"(a) IN GENERAL.—The Secretary, acting through the Administrator of the Health Resources and Services Administration, shall establish a grant program for the purposes of assisting eligible entities in recruiting students most likely to practice medicine in underserved rural communities, providing rural-focused training and experience, and increasing the number of recent allopathic and osteopathic medical school graduates who practice in underserved rural communities.

"(b) ELIGIBLE ENTITIES.—In order to be eligible to receive a grant under this section, an entity shall—

"(1) be a school of allopathic or osteopathic medicine accredited by a nationally recognized accrediting agency or association approved by the Secretary for this purpose, or any combination or consortium of such schools; and

"(2) submit an application to the Secretary that includes a certification that such entity will use amounts provided to the institution as described in subsection (d)(1).

"(c) PRIORITY.—In awarding grant funds under this section, the Secretary shall give priority to eligible entities that—

"(1) demonstrate a record of successfully training students, as determined by the Secretary, who practice medicine in underserved rural communities;

"(2) demonstrate that an existing academic program of the eligible entity produces a high percentage, as determined by the Secretary, of graduates from such program who practice medicine in underserved rural communities;

"(3) demonstrate rural community institutional partnerships, through such mechanisms as matching or contributory funding, documented in-kind services for implementation, or existence of training partners with interprofessional expertise in community health center training locations or other similar facilities; or

"(4) submit, as part of the application of the entity under subsection (b), a plan for the long-term tracking of where the graduates of such entity practice medicine.

"(d) USE OF FUNDS.—

"(1) ESTABLISHMENT.—An eligible entity receiving a grant under this section shall use the funds made available under such grant to establish, improve, or expand a rural-focused training program (referred to in this section as the 'Program') meeting the requirements described in this subsection and to carry out such program.

"(2) STRUCTURE OF PROGRAM.—An eligible entity shall—

"(A) enroll no fewer than 10 students per class year into the Program; and

"(B) develop criteria for admission to the Program that gives priority to students—

"(i) who have originated from or lived for a period of 2 or more years in an underserved rural community; and

"(ii) who express a commitment to practice medicine in an underserved rural community.

"(3) CURRICULA.—The Program shall require students to enroll in didactic coursework and clinical experience particularly applicable to medical practice in underserved rural communities, including—

"(A) clinical rotations in underserved rural communities, and in applicable specialties, or other coursework or clinical experience deemed appropriate by the Secretary; and

"(B) in addition to core school curricula, additional coursework or training experiences focused on medical issues prevalent in underserved rural communities.

"(4) RESIDENCY PLACEMENT ASSISTANCE.—Where available, the Program shall assist all students of the Program in obtaining clinical training experiences in locations with postgraduate programs offering residency training opportunities in underserved rural communities, or in local residency training programs that support and train physicians to practice in underserved rural communities.

"(5) PROGRAM STUDENT COHORT SUPPORT.—The Program shall provide and require all students of the Program to participate in group activities designed to further develop, maintain, and reinforce the original commitment of such students to practice in an underserved rural community.

"(e) ANNUAL REPORTING.—An eligible entity receiving a grant under this section shall submit an annual report to the Secretary on the success of the Program, based on criteria the Secretary determines appropriate, including the residency program selection of graduating students who participated in the Program.

"(f) REGULATIONS.—Not later than 60 days after the date of enactment of this section, the Secretary shall by regulation define 'underserved rural community' for purposes of this section.

"(g) SUPPLEMENT NOT SUPPLANT.—Any eligible entity receiving funds under this section shall use such funds to supplement, not supplant, any other Federal, State, and local funds that would otherwise be expended by such entity to carry out the activities described in this section.

"(h) MAINTENANCE OF EFFORT.—With respect to activities for which funds awarded under this section are to be expended, the entity shall agree to maintain expenditures of non-Federal amounts for such activities at a level that is not less than the level of such expenditures maintained by the entity for the fiscal year preceding the fiscal year for which the entity receives a grant under this section.

"(i) AUTHORIZATION OF APPROPRIATIONS.—There are authorized to be appropriated $4,000,000 for each of the fiscal years 2010 through 2013.".

(m)(1) Section 768 of the Public Health Service Act (42 U.S.C. 295c) is amended to read as follows:

"SEC. 768. PREVENTIVE MEDICINE AND PUBLIC HEALTH TRAINING GRANT PROGRAM.

"(a) GRANTS.—The Secretary, acting through the Administrator of the Health Resources and Services Administration and in consultation with the Director of the Centers for Disease Control and Prevention, shall award grants to, or enter into contracts with, eligible entities to provide training to graduate medical residents in preventive medicine specialties.

"(b) ELIGIBILITY.—To be eligible for a grant or contract under subsection (a), an entity shall be—

"(1) an accredited school of public health or school of medicine or osteopathic medicine;

"(2) an accredited public or private nonprofit hospital;

"(3) a State, local, or tribal health department; or

"(4) a consortium of 2 or more entities described in paragraphs (1) through (3).

"(c) USE OF FUNDS.—Amounts received under a grant or contract under this section shall be used to—

"(1) plan, develop (including the development of curricula), operate, or participate in an accredited residency or internship program in preventive medicine or public health;

"(2) defray the costs of practicum experiences, as required in such a program; and

"(3) establish, maintain, or improve—

"(A) academic administrative units (including departments, divisions, or other appropriate units) in preventive medicine and public health; or

"(B) programs that improve clinical teaching in preventive medicine and public health.

"(d) REPORT.—The Secretary shall submit to the Congress an annual report on the program carried out under this section.".

(2) Section 770(a) of the Public Health Service Act (42 U.S.C. 295e(a)) is amended to read as follows:

"(a) IN GENERAL.—For the purpose of carrying out this subpart, there is authorized to be appropriated $43,000,000 for fiscal year 2011, and such sums as may be necessary for each of the fiscal years 2012 through 2015.".

(n)(1) Subsection (i) of section 331 of the Public Health Service Act (42 U.S.C. 254d) of the Public Health Service Act is amended—

(A) in paragraph (1), by striking "In carrying out subpart III" and all that follows through the period and inserting "In carrying out subpart III, the Secretary may, in accordance with this subsection, issue waivers to individuals who have entered into a contract for obligated service under the Scholarship Program or the Loan Repayment Program under which the individuals are authorized to satisfy the requirement of obligated service through providing clinical practice that is half time.";

(B) in paragraph (2)—

(i) in subparagraphs (A)(ii) and (B), by striking "less than full time" each place it appears and inserting "half time";

(ii) in subparagraphs (C) and (F), by striking "less than full-time service" each place it appears and inserting "half-time service"; and

(iii) by amending subparagraphs (D) and (E) to read as follows:

"(D) the entity and the Corps member agree in writing that the Corps member will perform half-time clinical practice;

"(E) the Corps member agrees in writing to fulfill all of the service obligations under section 338C through half-time clinical practice and either—

"(i) double the period of obligated service that would otherwise be required; or "(ii) in the case of contracts entered into under section 338B, accept a minimum service obligation of 2 years with an award amount equal to 50 percent of the amount that would otherwise be payable for full-time service; and"; and

(C) in paragraph (3), by striking "In evaluating a demonstration project described in paragraph (1)" and inserting "In evaluating waivers issued under paragraph (1)".

(2) Subsection (j) of section 331 of the Public Health Service Act (42 U.S.C. 254d) is amended by adding at the end the following:

"(5) The terms 'full time' and 'full-time' mean a minimum of 40 hours per week in a clinical practice, for a minimum of 45 weeks per year.

"(6) The terms 'half time' and 'half-time' mean a minimum of 20 hours per week (not to exceed 39 hours per week) in a clinical practice, for a minimum of 45 weeks per year.".

(3) Section 337(b)(1) of the Public Health Service Act (42 U.S.C. 254j(b)(1)) is amended by striking "Members may not be reappointed to the Council.".

(4) Section 338B(g)(2)(A) of the Public Health Service Act (42 U.S.C. 254l–1(g)(2)(A)) is amended by striking "$35,000" and inserting "$50,000, plus, beginning with fiscal year 2012, an amount determined by the Secretary on an annual basis to reflect inflation,".

(5) Subsection (a) of section 338C of the Public Health Service Act (42 U.S.C. 254m), as amended by section 5508, is amended—

(A) by striking the second sentence and inserting the following: "The Secretary may treat teaching as clinical practice for up to 20 percent of such period of obligated service."; and

(B) by adding at the end the following: "Notwithstanding the preceding sentence, with respect to a member of the Corps participating in the teaching health centers graduate medical education program under section 340H, for the purpose of calculating time spent in full-time clinical practice under this section, up to 50 percent of time spent teaching by such member may be counted toward his or her service obligation.".

SEC. 10502. INFRASTRUCTURE TO EXPAND ACCESS TO CARE.

(a) APPROPRIATION.—There are authorized to be appropriated, and there are appropriated to the Department of Health and Human Services, $100,000,000 for fiscal year 2010, to remain available for obligation until September 30, 2011, to be used for debt service on, or direct construction or renovation of, a health care facility that provides research, inpatient tertiary care, or outpatient clinical services. Such facility shall be affiliated with an academic health center at a public research university in the United States that contains a State's sole public academic medical and dental school.

(b) REQUIREMENT.—Amount appropriated under subsection (a) may only be made available by the Secretary of Health and Human Services upon the receipt of an application from the Governor of a State that certifies that—

(1) the new health care facility is critical for the provision of greater access to health care within the State;

(2) such facility is essential for the continued financial viability of the State's sole public medical and dental school and its academic health center;

(3) the request for Federal support represents not more than 40 percent of the total cost of the proposed new facility; and

(4) the State has established a dedicated funding mechanism to provide all remaining funds necessary to complete the construction or renovation of the proposed facility.

SEC. 10503. COMMUNITY HEALTH CENTERS AND THE NATIONAL HEALTH SERVICE CORPS FUND.

(a) PURPOSE.—It is the purpose of this section to establish a Community Health Center Fund (referred to in this section as the "CHC Fund"), to be administered through the Office of the Secretary of the Department of Health and Human Services to provide for expanded and sustained national investment in community health centers under section 330 of the Public Health Service Act and the National Health Service Corps.

(b) FUNDING.—There is authorized to be appropriated, and there is appropriated, out of any monies in the Treasury not otherwise appropriated, to the CHC Fund—

(1) to be transferred to the Secretary of Health and Human Services to provide enhanced funding for the community health center program under section 330 of the Public Health Service Act—

(A) $700,000,000 for fiscal year 2011;

(B) $800,000,000 for fiscal year 2012;

(C) $1,000,000,000 for fiscal year 2013;

(D) $1,600,000,000 for fiscal year 2014; and

(E) $2,900,000,000 for fiscal year 2015; and

(2) to be transferred to the Secretary of Health and Human Services to provide enhanced funding for the National Health Service Corps—

(A) $290,000,000 for fiscal year 2011;

(B) $295,000,000 for fiscal year 2012;

(C) $300,000,000 for fiscal year 2013;

(D) $305,000,000 for fiscal year 2014; and

(E) $310,000,000 for fiscal year 2015.

(c) CONSTRUCTION.—There is authorized to be appropriated, and there is appropriated, out of any monies in the Treasury not otherwise appropriated, $1,500,000,000 to be available for fiscal years 2011 through 2015 to be used by the Secretary of Health and Human Services for the construction and renovation of community health centers.

(d) USE OF FUND.—The Secretary of Health and Human Services shall transfer amounts in the CHC Fund to accounts within the Department of Health and Human Services to increase funding, over the fiscal year 2008 level, for community health centers and the National Health Service Corps.

(e) AVAILABILITY.—Amounts appropriated under subsections (b) and (c) shall remain available until expended.

SEC. 10504. DEMONSTRATION PROJECT TO PROVIDE ACCESS TO AFFORDABLE CARE.

(a) IN GENERAL.—Not later than 6 months after the date of enactment of this Act, the Secretary of Health and Human Services (referred to in this section as the "Secretary"), acting through the Health Resources and Services Administration, shall establish a 3 year demonstration project in up to 10 States to provide access to comprehensive health care services to the uninsured at reduced fees. The Secretary shall evaluate the feasibility of expanding the project to additional States.

(b) ELIGIBILITY.—To be eligible to participate in the demonstration project, an entity shall be a State-based, nonprofit, public-private partnership that provides access to comprehensive health care services to the uninsured at reduced fees. Each State in which a participant selected by the Secretary is located shall receive not more than $2,000,000 to establish and carry out the project for the 3-year demonstration period.

(c) AUTHORIZATION.—There is authorized to be appropriated such sums as may be necessary to carry out this section.

Subtitle F—Provisions Relating to Title VI

SEC. 10601. REVISIONS TO LIMITATION ON MEDICARE EXCEPTION TO THE PROHIBITION ON CERTAIN PHYSICIAN REFERRALS FOR HOSPITALS.

(a) IN GENERAL.—Section 1877(i) of the Social Security Act, as added by section 6001(a), is amended—

(1) in paragraph (1)(A)(i), by striking "February 1, 2010" and inserting "August 1, 2010"; and

(2) in paragraph (3)(A)—

(A) in clause (iii), by striking "August 1, 2011" and inserting "February 1, 2012"; and

(B) in clause (iv), by striking "July 1, 2011" and inserting "January 1, 2012".

(b) CONFORMING AMENDMENT.—Section 6001(b)(2) of this Act is amended by striking "November 1, 2011" and inserting "May 1, 2012".

SEC. 10602. CLARIFICATIONS TO PATIENT-CENTERED OUTCOMES RESEARCH.

Section 1181 of the Social Security Act (as added by section 6301) is amended—

(1) in subsection (d)(2)(B)—

(A) in clause (ii)(IV)—

(i) by inserting ", as described in subparagraph (A)(ii)," after "original research"; and

(ii) by inserting ", as long as the researcher enters into a data use agreement with the Institute for use of the data from the original research, as appropriate" after "publication"; and

(B) by amending clause (iv) to read as follows:

"(iv) SUBSEQUENT USE OF THE DATA.—The Institute shall not allow the subsequent use of data from original research in work-for-hire contracts with individuals, entities, or instrumentalities that have a financial interest in the results, unless approved under a data use agreement with the Institute.";

(2) in subsection (d)(8)(A)(iv), by striking "not be construed as mandates for" and inserting "do not include"; and

(3) in subsection (f)(1)(C), by amending clause (ii) to read as follows:

"(ii) 7 members representing physicians and providers, including 4 members representing physicians (at least 1 of whom is a surgeon), 1 nurse, 1 State-licensed integrative health care practitioner, and 1 representative of a hospital.".

SEC. 10603. STRIKING PROVISIONS RELATING TO INDIVIDUAL PROVIDER APPLICATION FEES.

(a) IN GENERAL.—Section 1866(j)(2)(C) of the Social Security Act, as added by section 6401(a), is amended—

(1) by striking clause (i);

(2) by redesignating clauses (ii) through (iv), respectively, as clauses (i) through (iii); and

(3) in clause (i), as redesignated by paragraph (2), by striking "clause (iii)" and inserting "clause (ii)".

(b) TECHNICAL CORRECTION.—Section 6401(a)(2) of this Act is amended to read as follows:

"(2) by redesignating paragraph (2) as paragraph (8); and".

SEC. 10604. TECHNICAL CORRECTION TO SECTION 6405.

Paragraphs (1) and (2) of section 6405(b) are amended to read as follows:

"(1) PART A.—Section 1814(a)(2) of the Social Security Act (42 U.S.C. 1395(a)(2)) is amended in the matter preceding subparagraph (A) by inserting ', or, in the case of services described in subparagraph (C), a physician enrolled under section 1866(j),' after 'in collaboration with a physician,'.

"(2) PART B.—Section 1835(a)(2) of the Social Security Act (42 U.S.C. 1395n(a)(2)) is amended in the matter preceding subparagraph (A) by inserting ', or, in the case of services described in subparagraph (A), a physician enrolled under section 1866(j),' after 'a physician'.".

SEC. 10605. CERTAIN OTHER PROVIDERS PERMITTED TO CONDUCT FACE TO FACE ENCOUNTER FOR HOME HEALTH SERVICES.

(a) PART A.—Section 1814(a)(2)(C) of the Social Security Act (42 U.S.C. 1395f(a)(2)(C)), as amended by section 6407(a)(1), is amended by inserting ", or a nurse practitioner or clinical nurse specialist (as those terms are defined in section 1861(aa)(5)) who is working in collaboration with the physician in accordance with State law, or a certified nurse-midwife (as defined in section 1861(gg)) as authorized by State law, or a physician assistant (as defined in section 1861(aa)(5)) under the supervision of the physician," after "himself or herself".

(b) PART B.—Section 1835(a)(2)(A)(iv) of the Social Security Act, as added by section 6407(a)(2), is amended by inserting ", or a nurse practitioner or clinical nurse specialist (as those terms are defined in section 1861(aa)(5)) who is working in collaboration with the physician in accordance with State law, or a certified nurse-midwife (as defined in section 1861(gg)) as authorized by State law, or a physician assistant (as defined in section 1861(aa)(5)) under the supervision of the physician," after "must document that the physician".

SEC. 10606. HEALTH CARE FRAUD ENFORCEMENT.

(a) FRAUD SENTENCING GUIDELINES.—

(1) DEFINITION.—In this subsection, the term "Federal health care offense" has the meaning given that term in section 24 of title 18, United States Code, as amended by this Act.

(2) REVIEW AND AMENDMENTS.—Pursuant to the authority under section 994 of title 28, United States Code, and in accordance with this subsection, the United States Sentencing Commission shall—

(A) review the Federal Sentencing Guidelines and policy statements applicable to persons convicted of Federal health care offenses;

(B) amend the Federal Sentencing Guidelines and policy statements applicable to persons convicted of Federal health care offenses involving Government health care programs to provide that the aggregate dollar amount of fraudulent bills submitted to the Government health care program shall constitute prima facie evidence of the amount of the intended loss by the defendant; and

(C) amend the Federal Sentencing Guidelines to provide—

(i) a 2-level increase in the offense level for any defendant convicted of a Federal health care offense relating to a Government health care program which involves a loss of not less than $1,000,000 and less than $7,000,000;

(ii) a 3-level increase in the offense level for any defendant convicted of a Federal health care offense relating to a Government health care program which involves a loss of not less than $7,000,000 and less than $20,000,000;

(iii) a 4-level increase in the offense level for any defendant convicted of a Federal health care offense relating to a Government health care program which involves a loss of not less than $20,000,000; and

(iv) if appropriate, otherwise amend the Federal Sentencing Guidelines and policy statements applicable to persons convicted of Federal health care offenses involving Government health care programs.

(3) REQUIREMENTS.—In carrying this subsection, the United States Sentencing Commission shall—

(A) ensure that the Federal Sentencing Guidelines and policy statements—

(i) reflect the serious harms associated with health care fraud and the need for aggressive and appropriate law enforcement action to prevent such fraud; and

(ii) provide increased penalties for persons convicted of health care fraud offenses in appropriate circumstances;

(B) consult with individuals or groups representing health care fraud victims, law enforcement officials, the health care industry, and the Federal judiciary as part of the review described in paragraph (2);

(C) ensure reasonable consistency with other relevant directives and with other guidelines under the Federal Sentencing Guidelines;

(D) account for any aggravating or mitigating circumstances that might justify exceptions, including circumstances for which the Federal Sentencing Guidelines, as in effect on the date of enactment of this Act, provide sentencing enhancements;

(E) make any necessary conforming changes to the Federal Sentencing Guidelines; and

(F) ensure that the Federal Sentencing Guidelines adequately meet the purposes of sentencing.

(b) INTENT REQUIREMENT FOR HEALTH CARE FRAUD.—Section 1347 of title 18, United States Code, is amended—

(1) by inserting "(a)" before "Whoever knowingly"; and

(2) by adding at the end the following:

"(b) With respect to violations of this section, a person need not have actual knowledge of this section or specific intent to commit a violation of this section.".

(c) HEALTH CARE FRAUD OFFENSE.—Section 24(a) of title 18, United States Code, is amended—

(1) in paragraph (1), by striking the semicolon and inserting "or section 1128B of the Social Security Act (42 U.S.C. 1320a–7b); or"; and

(2) in paragraph (2)—

(A) by inserting "1349," after "1343,"; and

(B) by inserting "section 301 of the Federal Food, Drug, and Cosmetic Act (21 U.S.C. 331), or section 501 of the Employee Retirement Income Security Act of 1974 (29 U.S.C. 1131)," after "title,".

(d) SUBPOENA AUTHORITY RELATING TO HEALTH CARE.—

(1) SUBPOENAS UNDER THE HEALTH INSURANCE PORTABILITY AND ACCOUNTABILITY ACT OF 1996.—Section 1510(b) of title 18, United States Code, is amended—

(A) in paragraph (1), by striking "to the grand jury"; and

(B) in paragraph (2)—

(i) in subparagraph (A), by striking "grand jury subpoena" and inserting "subpoena for records"; and

(ii) in the matter following subparagraph (B), by striking "to the grand jury".

(2) SUBPOENAS UNDER THE CIVIL RIGHTS OF INSTITUTIONALIZED PERSONS ACT.—The Civil Rights of Institutionalized Persons Act (42 U.S.C. 1997 et seq.) is amended by inserting after section 3 the following:

"SEC. 3A. SUBPOENA AUTHORITY.

"(a) AUTHORITY.—The Attorney General, or at the direction of the Attorney General, any officer or employee of the Department of Justice may require by subpoena access to any institution that is the subject of an investigation under this Act and to any document, record, material, file, report, memorandum, policy, procedure, investigation, video or audio recording, or quality assurance report relating to any institution that is the subject of an investigation under this Act to determine whether there are conditions which deprive persons residing in or confined to the institution of any rights, privileges, or immunities secured or protected by the Constitution or laws of the United States.

"(b) ISSUANCE AND ENFORCEMENT OF SUBPOENAS.—

"(1) ISSUANCE.—Subpoenas issued under this section—

"(A) shall bear the signature of the Attorney General or any officer or employee of the Department of Justice as designated by the Attorney General; and

"(B) shall be served by any person or class of persons designated by the Attorney General or a designated officer or employee for that purpose.

"(2) ENFORCEMENT.—In the case of contumacy or failure to obey a subpoena issued under this section, the United States district court for the judicial district in which the institution is located may issue an order requiring compliance. Any failure to obey the order of the court may be punished by the court as a contempt that court.

"(c) PROTECTION OF SUBPOENAED RECORDS AND INFORMATION.—Any document, record, material, file, report, memorandum, policy, procedure, investigation, video or audio recording, or quality assurance report or other information obtained under a subpoena issued under this section—

"(1) may not be used for any purpose other than to protect the rights, privileges, or immunities secured or protected by the Constitution or laws of the United States of persons who reside, have resided, or will reside in an institution;

"(2) may not be transmitted by or within the Department of Justice for any purpose other than to protect the rights, privileges, or immunities secured or protected by the Constitution or laws of the United States of persons who reside, have resided, or will reside in an institution; and

"(3) shall be redacted, obscured, or otherwise altered if used in any publicly available manner so as to prevent the disclosure of any personally identifiable information.".

SEC. 10607. STATE DEMONSTRATION PROGRAMS TO EVALUATE ALTERNATIVES TO CURRENT MEDICAL TORT LITIGATION.

Part P of title III of the Public Health Service Act (42 U.S.C. 280g et seq.), as amended by this Act, is further amended by adding at the end the following:

"SEC. 399V–4. STATE DEMONSTRATION PROGRAMS TO EVALUATE ALTERNATIVES TO CURRENT MEDICAL TORT LITIGATION.

"(a) IN GENERAL.—The Secretary is authorized to award demonstration grants to States for the development, implementation, and evaluation of alternatives to current tort litigation for resolving disputes over injuries allegedly caused by health care providers or health care organizations. In awarding such grants, the Secretary shall ensure the diversity of the alternatives so funded.

"(b) DURATION.—The Secretary may award grants under subsection (a) for a period not to exceed 5 years.

"(c) CONDITIONS FOR DEMONSTRATION GRANTS.—

"(1) REQUIREMENTS.—Each State desiring a grant under subsection (a) shall develop an alternative to current tort litigation that—

"(A) allows for the resolution of disputes over injuries allegedly caused by health care providers or health care organizations; and

"(B) promotes a reduction of health care errors by encouraging the collection and analysis of patient safety data related to disputes resolved under subparagraph (A) by organizations that engage in efforts to improve patient safety and the quality of health care.

"(2) ALTERNATIVE TO CURRENT TORT LITIGATION.—Each State desiring a grant under subsection (a) shall demonstrate how the proposed alternative described in paragraph (1)(A)—

"(A) makes the medical liability system more reliable by increasing the availability of prompt and fair resolution of disputes;

"(B) encourages the efficient resolution of disputes;

"(C) encourages the disclosure of health care errors;

"(D) enhances patient safety by detecting, analyzing, and helping to reduce medical errors and adverse events;

"(E) improves access to liability insurance;

"(F) fully informs patients about the differences in the alternative and current tort litigation;

"(G) provides patients the ability to opt out of or voluntarily withdraw from participating in the alternative at any time and to pursue other options, including litigation, outside the alternative;

"(H) would not conflict with State law at the time of the application in a way that would prohibit the adoption of an alternative to current tort litigation; and

"(I) would not limit or curtail a patient's existing legal rights, ability to file a claim in or access a State's legal system, or otherwise abrogate a patient's ability to file a medical malpractice claim.

"(3) SOURCES OF COMPENSATION.—Each State desiring a grant under subsection (a) shall identify the sources from and methods by which compensation would be paid for claims resolved under the proposed alternative to current tort litigation, which may include public or private funding sources, or a combination of such sources. Funding methods shall to the extent practicable provide financial incentives for activities that improve patient safety.

"(4) SCOPE.—

"(A) IN GENERAL.—Each State desiring a grant under subsection (a) shall establish a scope of jurisdiction (such as Statewide, designated geographic region, a designated area of health care practice, or a designated group of health care providers or health care organizations) for the proposed alternative to current tort litigation that is sufficient to evaluate the effects of the alternative. No scope of jurisdiction shall be established under this paragraph that is based on a health care payer or patient population.

"(B) NOTIFICATION OF PATIENTS.—A State shall demonstrate how patients would be notified that they are receiving health care services that fall within such scope, and the process by which they may opt out of or voluntarily withdraw from participating in the alternative. The decision of the patient whether to participate or continue participating in the alternative process shall be made at any time and shall not be limited in any way.

"(5) PREFERENCE IN AWARDING DEMONSTRATION GRANTS.—In awarding grants under subsection (a), the Secretary shall give preference to States—

"(A) that have developed the proposed alternative through substantive consultation with relevant stakeholders, including patient advocates, health care providers and health care organizations, attorneys with expertise in representing patients and health care providers, medical malpractice insurers, and patient safety experts;

"(B) that make proposals that are likely to enhance patient safety by detecting, analyzing, and helping to reduce medical errors and adverse events; and

"(C) that make proposals that are likely to improve access to liability insurance.

"(d) APPLICATION.—

"(1) IN GENERAL.—Each State desiring a grant under subsection (a) shall submit to the Secretary an application, at such time, in such manner, and containing such information as the Secretary may require.

"(2) REVIEW PANEL.—

"(A) IN GENERAL.—In reviewing applications under paragraph (1), the Secretary shall consult with a review panel composed of relevant experts appointed by the Comptroller General.

"(B) COMPOSITION.—

"(i) NOMINATIONS.—The Comptroller General shall solicit nominations from the public for individuals to serve on the review panel.

"(ii) APPOINTMENT.—The Comptroller General shall appoint, at least 9 but not more than 13, highly qualified and knowledgeable individuals to serve on the review panel and shall ensure that the following entities receive fair representation on such panel:

"(I) Patient advocates.

"(II) Health care providers and health care organizations.

"(III) Attorneys with expertise in representing patients and health care providers.

"(IV) Medical malpractice insurers.

"(V) State officials.

"(VI) Patient safety experts.

"(C) CHAIRPERSON.—The Comptroller General, or an individual within the Government Accountability Office designated by the Comptroller General, shall be the chairperson of the review panel.

"(D) AVAILABILITY OF INFORMATION.—The Comptroller General shall make available to the review panel such information, personnel, and administrative services and assistance as the review panel may reasonably require to carry out its duties.

"(E) INFORMATION FROM AGENCIES.—The review panel may request directly from any department or agency of the United States any information that such panel considers necessary to carry out its duties. To the extent consistent with applicable laws and regulations, the head of such department or agency shall furnish the requested information to the review panel.

"(e) REPORTS.—

"(1) BY STATE.—Each State receiving a grant under subsection (a) shall submit to the Secretary an annual report evaluating the effectiveness of activities funded with grants awarded under such subsection. Such report shall, at a minimum, include the impact of the activities funded on patient safety and on the availability and price of medical liability insurance.

"(2) BY SECRETARY.—The Secretary shall submit to Congress an annual compendium of the reports submitted under paragraph (1) and an analysis of the activities funded under subsection (a) that examines any differences that result from such activities in terms of the quality of care, number and nature of medical errors, medical resources used, length of time for dispute resolution, and the availability and price of liability insurance.

"(f) TECHNICAL ASSISTANCE.—

"(1) IN GENERAL.—The Secretary shall provide technical assistance to the States applying for or awarded grants under subsection (a).

"(2) REQUIREMENTS.—Technical assistance under paragraph (1) shall include—

"(A) guidance on non-economic damages, including the consideration of individual facts and circumstances in determining appropriate payment, guidance on identifying avoidable injuries, and guidance on disclosure to patients of health care errors and adverse events; and

"(B) the development, in consultation with States, of common definitions, formats, and data collection infrastructure for States receiving grants under this section to use in reporting to facilitate aggregation and analysis of data both within and between States.

"(3) USE OF COMMON DEFINITIONS, FORMATS, AND DATA COLLECTION INFRASTRUCTURE.—States not receiving grants under this section may also use the common definitions, formats, and data collection infrastructure developed under paragraph (2)(B).

"(g) EVALUATION.—

"(1) IN GENERAL.—The Secretary, in consultation with the review panel established under subsection (d)(2), shall enter into a contract with an appropriate research organization to conduct an overall evaluation of the effectiveness of grants awarded under subsection (a) and to annually prepare and submit a report to Congress. Such an evaluation shall begin not later than 18 months following the date of implementation of the first program funded by a grant under subsection (a).

"(2) CONTENTS.—The evaluation under paragraph (1) shall include—

"(A) an analysis of the effects of the grants awarded under subsection (a) with regard to the measures described in paragraph (3);

"(B) for each State, an analysis of the extent to which the alternative developed under subsection (c)(1) is effective in meeting the elements described in subsection (c)(2);

"(C) a comparison among the States receiving grants under subsection (a) of the effectiveness of the various alternatives developed by such States under subsection (c)(1);

"(D) a comparison, considering the measures described in paragraph (3), of States receiving grants approved under subsection (a) and similar States not receiving such grants; and

"(E) a comparison, with regard to the measures described in paragraph (3), of—

"(i) States receiving grants under subsection (a);

"(ii) States that enacted, prior to the date of enactment of the Patient Protection and Affordable Care Act, any cap on non-economic damages; and

"(iii) States that have enacted, prior to the date of enactment of the Patient Protection and Affordable Care Act, a requirement that the complainant obtain an opinion regarding the merit of the claim, although the substance of such opinion may have no bearing on whether the complainant may proceed with a case.

"(3) MEASURES.—The evaluations under paragraph (2) shall analyze and make comparisons on the basis of—

"(A) the nature and number of disputes over injuries allegedly caused by health care providers or health care organizations;

"(B) the nature and number of claims in which tort litigation was pursued despite the existence of an alternative under subsection (a);

"(C) the disposition of disputes and claims, including the length of time and estimated costs to all parties;

"(D) the medical liability environment;

"(E) health care quality;

"(F) patient safety in terms of detecting, analyzing, and helping to reduce medical errors and adverse events;

"(G) patient and health care provider and organization satisfaction with the alternative under subsection (a) and with the medical liability environment; and

"(H) impact on utilization of medical services, appropriately adjusted for risk.

"(4) FUNDING.—The Secretary shall reserve 5 percent of the amount appropriated in each fiscal year under subsection (k) to carry out this subsection.

"(h) MEDPAC AND MACPAC REPORTS.—

"(1) MEDPAC.—The Medicare Payment Advisory Commission shall conduct an independent review of the alternatives to current tort litigation that are implemented under grants under subsection (a) to determine the impact of such alternatives on the Medicare program under title XVIII of the Social Security Act, and its beneficiaries.

"(2) MACPAC.—The Medicaid and CHIP Payment and Access Commission shall conduct an independent review of the alternatives to current tort litigation that are implemented under grants under subsection (a) to determine the impact of such alternatives on the Medicaid or CHIP programs under titles XIX and XXI of the Social Security Act, and their beneficiaries.

"(3) REPORTS.—Not later than December 31, 2016, the Medicare Payment Advisory Commission and the Medicaid and CHIP Payment and Access Commission shall each submit to Congress a report that includes the findings and recommendations of each respective Commission based on independent reviews conducted under paragraphs (1) and (2), including an analysis of the impact of the alternatives reviewed on the efficiency and effectiveness of the respective programs.

"(i) OPTION TO PROVIDE FOR INITIAL PLANNING GRANTS.—Of the funds appropriated pursuant to subsection (k), the Secretary may use a portion not to exceed $500,000 per State to provide planning grants to such States for the development of demonstration project applications meeting the criteria described in subsection (c). In selecting States to receive such planning grants, the Secretary shall give preference to those States in which State law at the time of the application would not prohibit the adoption of an alternative to current tort litigation.

"(j) DEFINITIONS.—In this section:

"(1) HEALTH CARE SERVICES.—The term 'health care services' means any services provided by a health care provider, or by any individual working under the supervision of a health care provider, that relate to—

"(A) the diagnosis, prevention, or treatment of any human disease or impairment; or

"(B) the assessment of the health of human beings.

"(2) HEALTH CARE ORGANIZATION.—The term 'health care organization' means any individual or entity which is obligated to provide, pay for, or administer health benefits under any health plan.

"(3) HEALTH CARE PROVIDER.—The term 'health care provider' means any individual or entity—

"(A) licensed, registered, or certified under Federal or State laws or regulations to provide health care services; or

"(B) required to be so licensed, registered, or certified but that is exempted by other statute or regulation.

"(k) AUTHORIZATION OF APPROPRIATIONS.—There are authorized to be appropriated to carry out this section, $50,000,000 for the 5-fiscal year period beginning with fiscal year 2011.

"(l) CURRENT STATE EFFORTS TO ESTABLISH ALTERNATIVE TO TORT LITIGATION.—Nothing in this section shall be construed to limit any prior, current, or future efforts of any State to establish any alternative to tort litigation.

"(m) RULE OF CONSTRUCTION.—Nothing in this section shall be construed as limiting states' authority over or responsibility for their state justice systems.".

SEC. 10608. EXTENSION OF MEDICAL MALPRACTICE COVERAGE TO FREE CLINICS.

(a) IN GENERAL.—Section 224(o)(1) of the Public Health Service Act (42 U.S.C. 233(o)(1)) is amended by inserting after "to an individual" the following: ", or an officer, governing board member, employee, or contractor of a free clinic shall in providing services for the free clinic,".

(b) EFFECTIVE DATE.—The amendment made by this section shall take effect on the date of enactment of this Act and apply to any act or omission which occurs on or after that date.

SEC. 10609. LABELING CHANGES.

Section 505(j) of the Federal Food, Drug, and Cosmetic Act (21 U.S.C. 355(j)) is amended by adding at the end the following:

"(10)(A) If the proposed labeling of a drug that is the subject of an application under this subsection differs from the listed drug due to a labeling revision described under clause (i), the drug that is the subject of such application shall, notwithstanding any other provision of this Act, be eligible for approval and shall not be considered misbranded under section 502 if—

"(i) the application is otherwise eligible for approval under this subsection but for expiration of patent, an exclusivity period, or of a delay in approval described in paragraph (5)(B)(iii), and a revision to the labeling of the listed drug has been approved by the Secretary within 60 days of such expiration;

"(ii) the labeling revision described under clause (i) does not include a change to the 'Warnings' section of the labeling;

"(iii) the sponsor of the application under this subsection agrees to submit revised labeling of the drug that is the subject of such application not later than 60 days after the notification of any changes to such labeling required by the Secretary; and

"(iv) such application otherwise meets the applicable requirements for approval under this subsection.

"(B) If, after a labeling revision described in subparagraph (A)(i), the Secretary determines that the continued presence in interstate commerce of the labeling of the listed drug (as in effect before the revision described in subparagraph (A)(i)) adversely impacts the safe use of the drug, no application under this subsection shall be eligible for approval with such labeling.".

Subtitle G—Provisions Relating to Title VIII

SEC. 10801. PROVISIONS RELATING TO TITLE VIII.

(a) Title XXXII of the Public Health Service Act, as added by section 8002(a)(1), is amended—

(1) in section 3203—

(A) in subsection (a)(1), by striking subparagraph (E);

(B) in subsection (b)(1)(C)(i), by striking "for enrollment" and inserting "for reenrollment"; and

(C) in subsection (c)(1), by striking ", as part of their automatic enrollment in the CLASS program,"; and

(2) in section 3204—

(A) in subsection (c)(2), by striking subparagraph (A) and inserting the following:

"(A) receives wages or income on which there is imposed a tax under section 3101(a) or 3201(a) of the Internal Revenue Code of 1986; or";

(B) in subsection (d), by striking "subparagraph (B) or (C) of subsection (c)(1)" and inserting "subparagraph (A) or (B) of subsection (c)(2)";

(C) in subsection (e)(2)(A), by striking "subparagraph (A)" and inserting "paragraph (1)"; and

(D) in subsection (g)(1), by striking "has elected to waive enrollment" and inserting "has not enrolled".

(b) Section 8002 of this Act is amended in the heading for subsection (d), by striking "INFORMATION ON SUPPLEMENTAL COVERAGE" and inserting "CLASS PROGRAM INFORMATION".

(c) Section 6021(d)(2)(A)(iv) of the Deficit Reduction Act of 2005, as added by section 8002(d) of this Act, is amended by striking "and coverage available" and all that follows through "that program,".

Subtitle H—Provisions Relating to Title IX

SEC. 10901. MODIFICATIONS TO EXCISE TAX ON HIGH COST EMPLOYER-SPONSORED HEALTH COVERAGE.

(a) LONGSHORE WORKERS TREATED AS EMPLOYEES ENGAGED IN HIGH-RISK PROFESSIONS.—Paragraph (3) of section 4980I(f) of the Internal Revenue Code of 1986, as added by section 9001 of this Act, is amended by inserting "individuals whose primary work is longshore work (as defined in section 258(b) of the Immigration and Nationality Act (8 U.S.C. 1288(b)), determined without regard to paragraph (2) thereof)," before "and individuals engaged in the construction, mining".

(b) EXEMPTION FROM HIGH-COST INSURANCE TAX INCLUDES CERTAIN ADDITIONAL EXCEPTED BENEFITS.—Clause (i) of section 4980I(d)(1)(B) of the Internal Revenue Code of 1986, as added by section 9001 of this Act, is amended by striking "section 9832(c)(1)(A)" and inserting "section 9832(c)(1) (other than subparagraph (G) thereof)".

(c) EFFECTIVE DATE.—The amendments made by this section shall apply to taxable years beginning after December 31, 2012.

SEC. 10902. INFLATION ADJUSTMENT OF LIMITATION ON HEALTH FLEXIBLE SPENDING ARRANGEMENTS UNDER CAFETERIA PLANS.

(a) IN GENERAL.—Subsection (i) of section 125 of the Internal Revenue Code of 1986, as added by section 9005 of this Act, is amended to read as follows:

"(i) LIMITATION ON HEALTH FLEXIBLE SPENDING ARRANGEMENTS.—

"(1) IN GENERAL.—For purposes of this section, if a benefit is provided under a cafeteria plan through employer contributions to a health flexible spending arrangement, such benefit shall not be treated as a qualified benefit unless the cafeteria plan provides that an employee may not elect for any taxable year to have salary reduction contributions in excess of $2,500 made to such arrangement.

"(2) ADJUSTMENT FOR INFLATION.—In the case of any taxable year beginning after December 31, 2011, the dollar amount in paragraph (1) shall be increased by an amount equal to—

"(A) such amount, multiplied by

"(B) the cost-of-living adjustment determined under section 1(f)(3) for the calendar year in which such taxable year begins by substituting 'calendar year 2010' for 'calendar year 1992' in subparagraph (B) thereof.

If any increase determined under this paragraph is not a multiple of $50, such increase shall be rounded to the next lowest multiple of $50.".

(b) EFFECTIVE DATE.—The amendment made by this section shall apply to taxable years beginning after December 31, 2010.

SEC. 10903. MODIFICATION OF LIMITATION ON CHARGES BY CHARITABLE HOSPITALS.

(a) IN GENERAL.—Subparagraph (A) of section 501(r)(5) of the Internal Revenue Code of 1986, as added by section 9007 of this Act, is amended by striking "the lowest amounts charged" and inserting "the amounts generally billed".

(b) EFFECTIVE DATE.—The amendment made by this section shall apply to taxable years beginning after the date of the enactment of this Act.

SEC. 10904. MODIFICATION OF ANNUAL FEE ON MEDICAL DEVICE MANUFACTURERS AND IMPORTERS.

(a) IN GENERAL.—Section 9009 of this Act is amended—

(1) by striking "2009" in subsection (a)(1) and inserting "2010",

(2) by inserting "($3,000,000,000 after 2017)" after "$2,000,000,000", and

(3) by striking "2008" in subsection (i) and inserting "2009".

(b) EFFECTIVE DATE.—The amendments made by this section shall take effect as if included in the enactment of section 9009.

SEC. 10905. MODIFICATION OF ANNUAL FEE ON HEALTH INSURANCE PROVIDERS.

(a) DETERMINATION OF FEE AMOUNT.—Subsection (b) of section 9010 of this Act is amended to read as follows:

"(b) DETERMINATION OF FEE AMOUNT.—

"(1) IN GENERAL.—With respect to each covered entity, the fee under this section for any calendar year shall be equal to an amount that bears the same ratio to the applicable amount as—

"(A) the covered entity's net premiums written with respect to health insurance for any United States health risk that are taken into account during the preceding calendar year, bears to

"(B) the aggregate net premiums written with respect to such health insurance of all covered entities that are taken into account during such preceding calendar year.

"(2) AMOUNTS TAKEN INTO ACCOUNT.—For purposes of paragraph (1), the net premiums written with respect to health insurance for any United States health risk that are taken into account during any calendar year with respect to any covered entity shall be determined in accordance with the following table:

"With respect to a covered entity's net premiums written during the calendar year that are:	The percentage of net premiums written that are taken into account is:
Not more than $25,000,000	0 percent
More than $25,000,000 but not more than $50,000,000.	50 percent
More than $50,000,000	100 percent.

"(3) SECRETARIAL DETERMINATION.—The Secretary shall calculate the amount of each covered entity's fee for any calendar year under paragraph (1). In calculating such amount, the Secretary shall determine such covered entity's net premiums written with respect to any United States health risk on the basis of reports submitted by the covered entity under subsection (g) and through the use of any other source of information available to the Secretary.".

(b) APPLICABLE AMOUNT.—Subsection (e) of section 9010 of this Act is amended to read as follows:

"(e) APPLICABLE AMOUNT.—For purposes of subsection (b)(1), the applicable amount shall be determined in accordance with the following table:

"Calendar year	**Applicable amount**
2011	$2,000,000,000
2012	$4,000,000,000

2013	$7,000,000,000
2014, 2015 and 2016	$9,000,000,000
2017 and thereafter	$10,000,000,000.”.

(c) EXEMPTION FROM ANNUAL FEE ON HEALTH INSURANCE FOR CERTAIN NONPROFIT ENTITIES.—Section 9010(c)(2) of this Act is amended by striking “or” at the end of subparagraph (A), by striking the period at the end of subparagraph (B) and inserting a comma, and by adding at the end the following new subparagraphs:

“(C) any entity—

“(i)(I) which is incorporated as, is a wholly owned subsidiary of, or is a wholly owned affiliate of, a nonprofit corporation under a State law, or

“(II) which is described in section 501(c)(4) of the Internal Revenue Code of 1986 and the activities of which consist of providing commercial-type insurance (within the meaning of section 501(m) of such Code),

“(ii) the premium rate increases of which are regulated by a State authority,

“(iii) which, as of the date of the enactment of this section, acts as the insurer of last resort in the State and is subject to State guarantee issue requirements, and

“(iv) for which the medical loss ratio (determined in a manner consistent with the determination of such ratio under section 2718(b)(1)(A) of the Public Health Service Act) with respect to the individual insurance market for such entity for the calendar year is not less than 100 percent,

“(D) any entity—

“(i)(I) which is incorporated as a nonprofit corporation under a State law, or

“(II) which is described in section 501(c)(4) of the Internal Revenue Code of 1986 and the activities of which consist of providing commercial-type insurance (within the meaning of section 501(m) of such Code), and

“(ii) for which the medical loss ratio (as so determined)—

“(I) with respect to each of the individual, small group, and large group insurance markets for such entity for the calendar year is not less than 90 percent, and

“(II) with respect to all such markets for such entity for the calendar year is not less than 92 percent, or

“(E) any entity—

“(i) which is a mutual insurance company,

“(ii) which for the period reported on the 2008 Accident and Health Policy Experience Exhibit of the National Association of Insurance Commissioners had—

“(I) a market share of the insured population of a State of at least 40 but not more than 60 percent, and

"(II) with respect to all markets described in subparagraph (D)(ii)(I), a medical loss ratio of not less than 90 percent, and

"(iii) with respect to annual payment dates in calendar years after 2011, for which the medical loss ratio (determined in a manner consistent with the determination of such ratio under section 2718(b)(1)(A) of the Public Health Service Act) with respect to all such markets for such entity for the preceding calendar year is not less than 89 percent (except that with respect to such annual payment date for 2012, the calculation under 2718(b)(1)(B)(ii) of such Act is determined by reference to the previous year, and with respect to such annual payment date for 2013, such calculation is determined by reference to the average for the previous 2 years).".

(d) CERTAIN INSURANCE EXEMPTED FROM FEE.—Paragraph (3) of section 9010(h) of this Act is amended to read as follows:

"(3) HEALTH INSURANCE.—The term 'health insurance' shall not include—

"(A) any insurance coverage described in paragraph (1)(A) or (3) of section 9832(c) of the Internal Revenue Code of 1986,

"(B) any insurance for long-term care, or

"(C) any medicare supplemental health insurance (as defined in section 1882(g)(1) of the Social Security Act).".

(e) ANTI-AVOIDANCE GUIDANCE.—Subsection (i) of section 9010 of this Act is amended by inserting "and shall prescribe such regulations as are necessary or appropriate to prevent avoidance of the purposes of this section, including inappropriate actions taken to qualify as an exempt entity under subsection (c)(2)" after "section".

(f) CONFORMING AMENDMENTS.—

(1) Section 9010(a)(1) of this Act is amended by striking "2009" and inserting "2010".

(2) Section 9010(c)(2)(B) of this Act is amended by striking "(except" and all that follows through "1323)".

(3) Section 9010(c)(3) of this Act is amended by adding at the end the following new sentence: "If any entity described in subparagraph (C)(i)(I), (D)(i)(I), or (E)(i) of paragraph (2) is treated as a covered entity by reason of the application of the preceding sentence, the net premiums written with respect to health insurance for any United States health risk of such entity shall not be taken into account for purposes of this section.".

(4) Section 9010(g)(1) of this Act is amended by striking "and third party administration agreement fees".

(5) Section 9010(j) of this Act is amended—

(A) by striking "2008" and inserting "2009", and

(B) by striking ", and any third party administration agreement fees received after such date".

(g) EFFECTIVE DATE.—The amendments made by this section shall take effect as if included in the enactment of section 9010.

SEC. 10906. MODIFICATIONS TO ADDITIONAL HOSPITAL INSURANCE TAX ON HIGH-INCOME TAXPAYERS.

(a) FICA.—Section 3101(b)(2) of the Internal Revenue Code of 1986, as added by section 9015(a)(1) of this Act, is amended by striking "0.5 percent" and inserting "0.9 percent".

(b) SECA.—Section 1401(b)(2)(A) of the Internal Revenue Code of 1986, as added by section 9015(b)(1) of this Act, is amended by striking "0.5 percent" and inserting "0.9 percent".

(c) EFFECTIVE DATE.—The amendments made by this section shall apply with respect to remuneration received, and taxable years beginning, after December 31, 2012.

SEC. 10907. EXCISE TAX ON INDOOR TANNING SERVICES IN LIEU OF ELECTIVE COSMETIC MEDICAL PROCEDURES.

(a) IN GENERAL.—The provisions of, and amendments made by, section 9017 of this Act are hereby deemed null, void, and of no effect.

(b) EXCISE TAX ON INDOOR TANNING SERVICES.—Subtitle D of the Internal Revenue Code of 1986, as amended by this Act, is amended by adding at the end the following new chapter:

"CHAPTER 49—COSMETIC SERVICES

"SEC. 5000B. IMPOSITION OF TAX ON INDOOR TANNING SERVICES.

"(a) IN GENERAL.—There is hereby imposed on any indoor tanning service a tax equal to 10 percent of the amount paid for such service (determined without regard to this section), whether paid by insurance or otherwise.

"(b) INDOOR TANNING SERVICE.—For purposes of this section—

"(1) IN GENERAL.—The term 'indoor tanning service' means a service employing any electronic product designed to incorporate 1 or more ultraviolet lamps and intended for the irradiation of an individual by ultraviolet radiation, with wavelengths in air between 200 and 400 nanometers, to induce skin tanning.

"(2) EXCLUSION OF PHOTOTHERAPY SERVICES.—Such term does not include any phototherapy service performed by a licensed medical professional.

"(c) PAYMENT OF TAX.—

"(1) IN GENERAL.—The tax imposed by this section shall be paid by the individual on whom the service is performed.

"(2) COLLECTION.—Every person receiving a payment for services on which a tax is imposed under subsection (a) shall collect the amount of the tax from the individual on whom the service is performed and remit such tax quarterly to the Secretary at such time and in such manner as provided by the Secretary.

"(3) SECONDARY LIABILITY.—Where any tax imposed by subsection (a) is not paid at the time payments for indoor tanning services are made, then to the extent that such tax is not collected, such tax shall be paid by the person who performs the service.".

(c) CLERICAL AMENDMENT.—The table of chapter for subtitle D of the Internal Revenue Code of 1986, as amended by this Act, is amended by inserting after the item relating to chapter 48 the following new item:

"CHAPTER 49—COSMETIC SERVICES".

(d) EFFECTIVE DATE.—The amendments made by this section shall apply to services performed on or after July 1, 2010.

SEC. 10908. EXCLUSION FOR ASSISTANCE PROVIDED TO PARTICIPANTS IN STATE STUDENT LOAN REPAYMENT PROGRAMS FOR CERTAIN HEALTH PROFESSIONALS.

(a) IN GENERAL.—Paragraph (4) of section 108(f) of the Internal Revenue Code of 1986 is amended to read as follows:

"(4) PAYMENTS UNDER NATIONAL HEALTH SERVICE CORPS LOAN REPAYMENT PROGRAM AND CERTAIN STATE LOAN REPAYMENT PROGRAMS.—In the case of an individual, gross income shall not include any amount received under section 338B(g) of the Public Health Service Act, under a State program described in section 338I of such Act, or under any other State loan repayment or loan forgiveness program that is intended to provide for the increased availability of health care services in underserved or health professional shortage areas (as determined by such State).".

(b) EFFECTIVE DATE.—The amendment made by this section shall apply to amounts received by an individual in taxable years beginning after December 31, 2008.

SEC. 10909. EXPANSION OF ADOPTION CREDIT AND ADOPTION ASSISTANCE PROGRAMS.

(a) INCREASE IN DOLLAR LIMITATION.—

(1) ADOPTION CREDIT.—

(A) IN GENERAL.—Paragraph (1) of section 23(b) of the Internal Revenue Code of 1986 (relating to dollar limitation) is amended by striking "$10,000" and inserting "$13,170".

(B) CHILD WITH SPECIAL NEEDS.—Paragraph (3) of section 23(a) of such Code (relating to $10,000 credit for adoption of child with special needs regardless of expenses) is amended—

(i) in the text by striking "$10,000" and inserting "$13,170", and

(ii) in the heading by striking "$10,000" and inserting "$13,170".

(C) CONFORMING AMENDMENT TO INFLATION ADJUSTMENT.—Subsection (h) of section 23 of such Code (relating to adjustments for inflation) is amended to read as follows:

"(h) ADJUSTMENTS FOR INFLATION.—

"(1) DOLLAR LIMITATIONS.—In the case of a taxable year beginning after December 31, 2010, each of the dollar amounts in subsections (a)(3) and (b)(1) shall be increased by an amount equal to—

"(A) such dollar amount, multiplied by

"(B) the cost-of-living adjustment determined under section 1(f)(3) for the calendar year in which the taxable year begins, determined by substituting 'calendar year 2009' for 'calendar year 1992' in subparagraph (B) thereof.

If any amount as increased under the preceding sentence is not a multiple of $10, such amount shall be rounded to the nearest multiple of $10.

"(2) INCOME LIMITATION.—In the case of a taxable year beginning after December 31, 2002, the dollar amount in subsection (b)(2)(A)(i) shall be increased by an amount equal to—

"(A) such dollar amount, multiplied by

"(B) the cost-of-living adjustment determined under section 1(f)(3) for the calendar year in which the taxable year begins, determined by substituting 'calendar year 2001' for 'calendar year 1992' in subparagraph (B) thereof.

If any amount as increased under the preceding sentence is not a multiple of $10, such amount shall be rounded to the nearest multiple of $10.".

(2) ADOPTION ASSISTANCE PROGRAMS.—

(A) IN GENERAL.—Paragraph (1) of section 137(b) of the Internal Revenue Code of 1986 (relating to dollar limitation) is amended by striking "$10,000" and inserting "$13,170".

(B) CHILD WITH SPECIAL NEEDS.—Paragraph (2) of section 137(a) of such Code (relating to $10,000 exclusion for adoption of child with special needs regardless of expenses) is amended—

(i) in the text by striking "$10,000" and inserting "$13,170", and

(ii) in the heading by striking "$10,000" and inserting "$13,170".

(C) CONFORMING AMENDMENT TO INFLATION ADJUSTMENT.—Subsection (f) of section 137 of such Code (relating to adjustments for inflation) is amended to read as follows:

"(f) ADJUSTMENTS FOR INFLATION.—

"(1) DOLLAR LIMITATIONS.—In the case of a taxable year beginning after December 31, 2010, each of the dollar amounts in subsections (a)(2) and (b)(1) shall be increased by an amount equal to—

"(A) such dollar amount, multiplied by

"(B) the cost-of-living adjustment determined under section 1(f)(3) for the calendar year in which the taxable year begins, determined by substituting 'calendar year 2009' for 'calendar year 1992' in subparagraph (B) thereof.

If any amount as increased under the preceding sentence is not a multiple of $10, such amount shall be rounded to the nearest multiple of $10.

"(2) INCOME LIMITATION.—In the case of a taxable year beginning after December 31, 2002, the dollar amount in subsection (b)(2)(A) shall be increased by an amount equal to—

"(A) such dollar amount, multiplied by

"(B) the cost-of-living adjustment determined under section 1(f)(3) for the calendar year in which the taxable year begins, determined by substituting 'calendar year 2001' for 'calendar year 1992' in subparagraph thereof.

If any amount as increased under the preceding sentence is not a multiple of $10, such amount shall be rounded to the nearest multiple of $10.".

(b) CREDIT MADE REFUNDABLE.—

(1) CREDIT MOVED TO SUBPART RELATING TO REFUNDABLE CREDITS.—The Internal Revenue Code of 1986 is amended—

(A) by redesignating section 23, as amended by subsection (a), as section 36C, and

(B) by moving section 36C (as so redesignated) from subpart A of part IV of subchapter A of chapter 1 to the location immediately before section 37 in subpart C of part IV of subchapter A of chapter 1.

(2) CONFORMING AMENDMENTS.—

(A) Section 24(b)(3)(B) of such Code is amended by striking "23,".

(B) Section 25(e)(1)(C) of such Code is amended by striking "23," both places it appears.

(C) Section 25A(i)(5)(B) of such Code is amended by striking "23, 25D," and inserting "25D".

(D) Section 25B(g)(2) of such Code is amended by striking "23,".

(E) Section 26(a)(1) of such Code is amended by striking "23,".

(F) Section 30(c)(2)(B)(ii) of such Code is amended by striking "23, 25D," and inserting "25D".

(G) Section 30B(g)(2)(B)(ii) of such Code is amended by striking "23,".

(H) Section 30D(c)(2)(B)(ii) of such Code is amended by striking "sections 23 and" and inserting "section".

(I) Section 36C of such Code, as so redesignated, is amended—

(i) by striking paragraph (4) of subsection (b), and

(ii) by striking subsection (c).

(J) Section 137 of such Code is amended—

(i) by striking "section 23(d)" in subsection (d) and inserting "section 36C(d)", and

(ii) by striking "section 23" in subsection (e) and inserting "section 36C".

(K) Section 904(i) of such Code is amended by striking "23,".

(L) Section 1016(a)(26) is amended by striking "23(g)" and inserting "36C(g)".

(M) Section 1400C(d) of such Code is amended by striking "23,".

(N) Section 6211(b)(4)(A) of such Code is amended by inserting "36C," before "53(e)".

(O) The table of sections for subpart A of part IV of subchapter A of chapter 1 of such Code of 1986 is amended by striking the item relating to section 23.

(P) Paragraph (2) of section 1324(b) of title 31, United States Code, as amended by this Act, is amended by inserting "36C," after "36B,".

(Q) The table of sections for subpart C of part IV of subchapter A of chapter 1 of the Internal Revenue Code of 1986, as amended by this Act, is amended by inserting after the item relating to section 36B the following new item:

"Sec. 36C. Adoption expenses.".

(c) APPLICATION AND EXTENSION OF EGTRRA SUNSET.—Notwithstanding section 901 of the Economic Growth and Tax Relief Reconciliation Act of 2001, such section shall apply to the amendments made by this section and the amendments made by section 202 of such Act by substituting "December 31, 2011" for "December 31, 2010" in subsection (a)(1) thereof.

(d) EFFECTIVE DATE.—The amendments made by this section shall apply to taxable years beginning after December 31, 2009.

Speaker of the House of Representatives.

Vice President of the United States and
President of the Senate.

H. R. 4872

One Hundred Eleventh Congress of the United States of America

AT THE SECOND SESSION

Begun and held at the City of Washington on Tuesday, the fifth day of January, two thousand and ten

An Act

To provide for reconciliation pursuant to Title II of the concurrent resolution on the budget for fiscal year 2010 (S. Con. Res. 13).

Be it enacted by the Senate and House of Representatives of the United States of America in Congress assembled,

SECTION 1. SHORT TITLE; TABLE OF CONTENTS.

(a) SHORT TITLE.—This Act may be cited as the "Health Care and Education Reconciliation Act of 2010".

(b) TABLE OF CONTENTS.—The table of contents of this Act is as follows:

TITLE I—COVERAGE, MEDICARE, MEDICAID, AND REVENUES

Subtitle A—Coverage

SEC. 1001. TAX CREDITS.

(a) PREMIUM TAX CREDITS.—Section 36B of the Internal Revenue Code of 1986, as added by section 1401 of the Patient Protection and Affordable Care Act and amended by section 10105 of such Act, is amended—

(1) in subsection (b)(3)(A)—

(A) in clause (i), by striking "with respect to any taxpayer" and all that follows up to the end period and inserting: "for any taxable year shall be the percentage such that the applicable percentage for any taxpayer whose household income is within an income tier specified in the following table shall increase, on a sliding scale in a linear manner, from the initial premium percentage to the final premium percentage specified in such table for such income tier:

"In the case of household income (expressed as a percent of poverty line) within the following income tier:	The initial premium percentage is—	The final premium percentage is—
Up to 133%	2.0%	2.0%
133% up to 150%	3.0%	4.0%
150% up to 200%	4.0%	6.3%
200% up to 250%	6.3%	8.05%
250% up to 300%	8.05%	9.5%
300% up to 400%	9.5%	9.5%"; and

(B) by striking clauses (ii) and (iii), and inserting the following:

"(ii) INDEXING.—

"(I) IN GENERAL.—Subject to subclause (II), in the case of taxable years beginning in any calendar year after 2014, the initial and final applicable percentages under clause (i) (as in effect for the preceding calendar year after application of this clause) shall be adjusted to reflect the excess of the rate of premium growth for the preceding calendar year over the rate of income growth for the preceding calendar year.

"(II) ADDITIONAL ADJUSTMENT.—Except as provided in subclause (III), in the case of any calendar year after 2018, the percentages described in subclause (I) shall, in addition to the adjustment under subclause (I), be adjusted to reflect the excess (if any) of the rate of premium growth estimated under subclause (I) for the preceding calendar year over the rate of growth in the consumer price index for the preceding calendar year.

"(III) FAILSAFE.—Subclause (II) shall apply for any calendar year only if the aggregate amount of premium tax credits under this section and cost-sharing reductions under section 1402 of the Patient Protection and Affordable Care Act for the preceding calendar year exceeds an amount equal to 0.504 percent of the gross domestic product for the preceding calendar year."; and

(2) in subsection (c)(2)(C)—

(A) by striking "9.8 percent" in clauses (i)(II) and (iv) and inserting "9.5 percent"; and

(B) by striking "(b)(3)(A)(iii)" in clause (iv) and inserting "(b)(3)(A)(ii)".

(b) COST SHARING.—Section 1402(c) of the Patient Protection and Affordable Care Act is amended—

(1) in paragraph (1)(B)(i)—

(A) in subclause (I), by striking "90" and inserting "94";

(B) in subclause (II)—

(i) by striking "80" and inserting "87"; and

(ii) by striking "and"; and

(C) by striking subclause (III) and inserting the following:

"(III) 73 percent in the case of an eligible insured whose household income is more than 200 percent but not more than 250 percent of the poverty line for a family of the size involved; and

"(IV) 70 percent in the case of an eligible insured whose household income is more than 250 percent but not more than 400 percent of the poverty line for a family of the size involved."; and

(2) in paragraph (2)—

(A) in subparagraph (A)—

(i) by striking "90" and inserting "94"; and

(ii) by striking "and";

(B) in subparagraph (B)—

(i) by striking "80" and inserting "87"; and

(ii) by striking the period and inserting "; and"; and

(C) by inserting after subparagraph (B) the following new subparagraph:

"(C) in the case of an eligible insured whose household income is more than 200 percent but not more than 250 percent of the poverty line for a family of the size involved, increase the plan's share of the total allowed costs of benefits provided under the plan to 73 percent of such costs.".

SEC. 1002. INDIVIDUAL RESPONSIBILITY.

(a) AMOUNTS.—Section 5000A(c) of the Internal Revenue Code of 1986, as added by section 1501(b) of the Patient Protection and Affordable Care Act and amended by section 10106 of such Act, is amended—

(1) in paragraph (2)(B)—

(A) in the matter preceding clause (i), by—

(i) inserting "the excess of" before "the taxpayer's household income"; and

(ii) inserting "for the taxable year over the amount of gross income specified in section 6012(a)(1) with respect to the taxpayer" before "for the taxable year";

(B) in clause (i), by striking "0.5" and inserting "1.0";

(C) in clause (ii), by striking "1.0" and inserting "2.0"; and

(D) in clause (iii), by striking "2.0" and inserting "2.5"; and

(2) in paragraph (3)—

(A) in subparagraph (A), by striking "$750" and inserting "$695";

(B) in subparagraph (B), by striking "$495" and inserting "$325"; and

(C) in subparagraph (D)—

(i) in the matter preceding clause (i), by striking "$750" and inserting "$695"; and

(ii) in clause (i), by striking "$750" and inserting "$695".

(b) THRESHOLD.—Section 5000A of such Code, as so added and amended, is amended—

(1) by striking subsection (c)(4)(D); and

(2) in subsection (e)(2)—

(A) by striking "UNDER 100 PERCENT OF POVERTY LINE" and inserting "BELOW FILING THRESHOLD"; and

(B) by striking all that follows "less than" and inserting "the amount of gross income specified in section 6012(a)(1) with respect to the taxpayer.".

SEC. 1003. EMPLOYER RESPONSIBILITY.

(a) PAYMENT CALCULATION.—Subparagraph (D) of subsection (d)(2) of section 4980H of the Internal Revenue Code of 1986, as added by section 1513 of the Patient Protection and Affordable Care Act and amended by section 10106 of such Act, is amended to read as follows:

"(D) APPLICATION OF EMPLOYER SIZE TO ASSESSABLE PENALTIES.—

"(i) IN GENERAL.—The number of individuals employed by an applicable large employer as full-time employees during any month shall be reduced by 30 solely for purposes of calculating—

"(I) the assessable payment under subsection (a), or

"(II) the overall limitation under subsection (b)(2).

"(ii) AGGREGATION.—In the case of persons treated as 1 employer under subparagraph (C)(i), only 1 reduction under subclause (I) or (II) shall be allowed with respect to such persons and such reduction shall be allocated among such persons ratably on the basis of the number of full-time employees employed by each such person.".

(b) APPLICABLE PAYMENT AMOUNT.—Section 4980H of such Code, as so added and amended, is amended—

(1) in the flush text following subsection (c)(1)(B), by striking "400 percent of the applicable payment amount" and inserting "an amount equal to 1/12 of $3,000";

(2) in subsection (d)(1), by striking "$750" and inserting "$2,000"; and

(3) in subsection (d)(5)(A), in the matter preceding clause (i), by striking "subsection (b)(2) and (d)(1)" and inserting "subsection (b) and paragraph (1)".

(c) COUNTING PART-TIME WORKERS IN SETTING THE THRESHOLD FOR EMPLOYER RESPONSIBILITY.—Section 4980H(d)(2) of such Code, as so added and amended and as amended by subsection (a), is amended by adding at the end the following new subparagraph:

"(E) FULL-TIME EQUIVALENTS TREATED AS FULL-TIME EMPLOYEES.—Solely for purposes of determining whether an employer is an applicable large employer under this paragraph, an employer shall, in addition to the number of full-time employees for any month otherwise determined, include for such month a number of full-time employees determined by dividing the aggregate number of hours of service of employees who are not full-time employees for the month by 120.".

(d) ELIMINATING WAITING PERIOD ASSESSMENT.—Section 4980H of such Code, as so added and amended and as amended by the preceding subsections, is amended by striking subsection (b) and redesignating subsections (c), (d), and (e) as subsections (b), (c), and (d), respectively.

SEC. 1004. INCOME DEFINITIONS.

(a) MODIFIED ADJUSTED GROSS INCOME.—

(1) IN GENERAL.—The following provisions of the Internal Revenue Code of 1986 are each amended by striking "modified gross" each place it appears and inserting "modified adjusted gross":

(A) Clauses (i) and (ii) of section 36B(d)(2)(A), as added by section 1401 of the Patient Protection and Affordable Care Act.

(B) Section 6103(l)(21)(A)(iv), as added by section 1414 of such Act.

(C) Clauses (i) and (ii) of section 5000A(c)(4), as added by section 1501(b) of such Act.

(2) DEFINITION.—

(A) Section 36B(d)(2)(B) of such Code, as so added, is amended to read as follows:

"(B) MODIFIED ADJUSTED GROSS INCOME.—The term 'modified adjusted gross income' means adjusted gross income increased by—

"(i) any amount excluded from gross income under section 911, and

"(ii) any amount of interest received or accrued by the taxpayer during the taxable year which is exempt from tax.".

(B) Section 5000A(c)(4)(C) of such Code, as so added, is amended to read as follows:

"(C) MODIFIED ADJUSTED GROSS INCOME.—The term 'modified adjusted gross income' means adjusted gross income increased by—

"(i) any amount excluded from gross income under section 911, and

"(ii) any amount of interest received or accrued by the taxpayer during the taxable year which is exempt from tax.".

(b) MODIFIED ADJUSTED GROSS INCOME DEFINITION.—

(1) MEDICAID.—Section 1902 of the Social Security Act (42 U.S.C. 1396a) is amended by striking "modified gross income" each place it appears in the text and headings of the following provisions and inserting "modified adjusted gross income":

(A) Paragraph (14) of subsection (e), as added by section 2002(a) of the Patient Protection and Affordable Care Act.

(B) Subsection (gg)(4)(A), as added by section 2001(b) of such Act.

(2) CHIP.—

(A) STATE PLAN REQUIREMENTS.—Section 2102(b)(1)(B)(v) of the Social Security Act (42 U.S.C. 1397bb(b)(1)(B)(v)), as added by section 2101(d)(1) of the Patient Protection and Affordable Care Act, is amended by striking "modified gross income" and inserting "modified adjusted gross income".

(B) PLAN ADMINISTRATION.—Section 2107(e)(1)(E) of the Social Security Act (42 U.S.C. 1397gg(e)(1)(E)), as added by section 2101(d)(2) of the Patient Protection and Affordable Care Act, is amended by striking "modified gross income" and inserting "modified adjusted gross income".

(c) NO EXCESS PAYMENTS.—Section 36B(f) of the Internal Revenue Code of 1986, as added by section 1401(a) of the Patient Protection and Affordable Care Act, is amended by adding at the end the following new paragraph:

"(3) INFORMATION REQUIREMENT.—Each Exchange (or any person carrying out 1 or more responsibilities of an Exchange under section 1311(f)(3) or 1321(c) of the Patient Protection and Affordable Care Act) shall provide the following information to the Secretary and to the taxpayer with respect to any health plan provided through the Exchange:

"(A) The level of coverage described in section 1302(d) of the Patient Protection and Affordable Care Act and the period such coverage was in effect.

"(B) The total premium for the coverage without regard to the credit under this section or cost-sharing reductions under section 1402 of such Act.

"(C) The aggregate amount of any advance payment of such credit or reductions under section 1412 of such Act.

"(D) The name, address, and TIN of the primary insured and the name and TIN of each other individual obtaining coverage under the policy.

"(E) Any information provided to the Exchange, including any change of circumstances, necessary to determine eligibility for, and the amount of, such credit.

"(F) Information necessary to determine whether a taxpayer has received excess advance payments.".

(d) ADULT DEPENDENTS.—

(1) EXCLUSION OF AMOUNTS EXPENDED FOR MEDICAL CARE.—The first sentence of section 105(b) of the Internal Revenue Code of 1986 (relating to amounts expended for medical care) is amended—

(A) by striking "and his dependents" and inserting "his dependents"; and

(B) by inserting before the period the following: ", and any child (as defined in section 152(f)(1)) of the taxpayer who as of the end of the taxable year has not attained age 27".

(2) SELF-EMPLOYED HEALTH INSURANCE DEDUCTION.—Section 162(l)(1) of such Code is amended to read as follows:

"(1) ALLOWANCE OF DEDUCTION.—In the case of a taxpayer who is an employee within the meaning of section 401(c)(1), there shall be allowed as a deduction under this section an amount equal to the amount paid during the taxable year for insurance which constitutes medical care for—

"(A) the taxpayer,

"(B) the taxpayer's spouse,

"(C) the taxpayer's dependents, and

"(D) any child (as defined in section 152(f)(1)) of the taxpayer who as of the end of the taxable year has not attained age 27.".

(3) COVERAGE UNDER SELF-EMPLOYED DEDUCTION.—Section 162(l)(2)(B) of such Code is amended by inserting ", or any dependent, or individual described in subparagraph (D) of paragraph (1) with respect to," after "spouse of".

(4) SICK AND ACCIDENT BENEFITS PROVIDED TO MEMBERS OF A VOLUNTARY EMPLOYEES' BENEFICIARY ASSOCIATION AND

THEIR DEPENDENTS.—Section 501(c)(9) of such Code is amended by adding at the end the following new sentence: "For purposes of providing for the payment of sick and accident benefits to members of such an association and their dependents, the term 'dependent' shall include any individual who is a child (as defined in section 152(f)(1)) of a member who as of the end of the calendar year has not attained age 27.".

(5) MEDICAL AND OTHER BENEFITS FOR RETIRED EMPLOYEES.—Section 401(h) of such Code is amended by adding at the end the following: "For purposes of this subsection, the term 'dependent' shall include any individual who is a child (as defined in section 152(f)(1)) of a retired employee who as of the end of the calendar year has not attained age 27.".

(e) FIVE PERCENT INCOME DISREGARD FOR CERTAIN INDIVIDUALS.—Section 1902(e)(14) of the Social Security Act (42 U.S.C. 1396a(e)(14)), as amended by subsection (b)(1), is further amended—

(1) in subparagraph (B), by striking "No type" and inserting "Subject to subparagraph (I), no type"; and

(2) by adding at the end the following new subparagraph:

"(I) TREATMENT OF PORTION OF MODIFIED ADJUSTED GROSS INCOME.—For purposes of determining the income eligibility of an individual for medical assistance whose eligibility is determined based on the application of modified adjusted gross income under subparagraph (A), the State shall—

"(i) determine the dollar equivalent of the difference between the upper income limit on eligibility for such an individual (expressed as a percentage of the poverty line) and such upper income limit increased by 5 percentage points; and

"(ii) notwithstanding the requirement in subparagraph (A) with respect to use of modified adjusted gross income, utilize as the applicable income of such individual, in determining such income eligibility, an amount equal to the modified adjusted gross income applicable to such individual reduced by such dollar equivalent amount.".

SEC. 1005. IMPLEMENTATION FUNDING.

(a) IN GENERAL.—There is hereby established a Health Insurance Reform Implementation Fund (referred to in this section as the "Fund") within the Department of Health and Human Services to carry out the Patient Protection and Affordable Care Act and this Act (and the amendments made by such Acts).

(b) FUNDING.—There is appropriated to the Fund, out of any funds in the Treasury not otherwise appropriated, $1,000,000,000 for Federal administrative expenses to carry out such Act (and the amendments made by such Acts).

Subtitle B—Medicare

SEC. 1101. CLOSING THE MEDICARE PRESCRIPTION DRUG "DONUT HOLE".

(a) COVERAGE GAP REBATE FOR 2010.—

(1) IN GENERAL.—Section 1860D–42 of the Social Security Act (42 U.S.C. 1395w–152) is amended by adding at the end the following new subsection:

"(c) COVERAGE GAP REBATE FOR 2010.—

"(1) IN GENERAL.—In the case of an individual described in subparagraphs (A) through (D) of section 1860D–14A(g)(1) who as of the last day of a calendar quarter in 2010 has incurred costs for covered part D drugs so that the individual has exceeded the initial coverage limit under section 1860D–2(b)(3) for 2010, the Secretary shall provide for payment from the Medicare Prescription Drug Account of $250 to the individual by not later than the 15th day of the third month following the end of such quarter.

"(2) LIMITATION.—The Secretary shall provide only 1 payment under this subsection with respect to any individual.".

(2) REPEAL OF PROVISION.—Section 3315 of the Patient Protection and Affordable Care Act (including the amendments made by such section) is repealed, and any provision of law amended or repealed by such sections is hereby restored or revived as if such section had not been enacted into law.

(b) CLOSING THE DONUT HOLE.—Part D of title XVIII of the Social Security Act (42 U.S.C. 1395w–101 et seq.), as amended by section 3301 of the Patient Protection and Affordable Care Act, is further amended—

(1) in section 1860D–43—

(A) in subsection (b), by striking "July 1, 2010" and inserting "January 1, 2011"; and

(B) in subsection (c)(2), by striking "July 1, 2010, and ending on December 31, 2010," and inserting "January 1, 2011, and December 31, 2011,";

(2) in section 1860D–14A—

(A) in subsection (a)—

(i) by striking "July 1, 2010" and inserting "January 1, 2011"; and

(ii) by striking "April 1, 2010" and inserting "180 days after the date of the enactment of this section";

(B) in subsection (b)(1)(C)—

(i) in the heading, by striking "2010 AND";

(ii) by striking "July 1, 2010" and inserting "January 1, 2011"; and

(iii) by striking "May 1, 2010" and inserting "not later than 30 days after the date of the establishment of a model agreement under subsection (a)";

(C) in subsection (c)—

(i) in paragraph (1)(A)(iii), by striking "July 1, 2010, and ending on December 31, 2011" and inserting "January 1, 2011, and ending on December 31, 2011"; and

(ii) in paragraph (2), by striking "2010" and inserting "2011";

(D) in subsection (d)(2)(B), by striking "July 1, 2010, and ending on December 31, 2010" and inserting "January 1, 2011, and ending on December 31, 2011"; and

(E) in subsection (g)(1)—

(i) in the matter before subparagraph (A), by striking "an applicable drug" and inserting "a covered part D drug";

(ii) by adding "and" at the end of subparagraph (C);

(iii) by striking subparagraph (D); and

(iv) by redesignating subparagraph (E) as subparagraph (D); and

(3) in section 1860D–2(b)—

(A) in paragraph (2)(A), by striking "The coverage" and inserting "Subject to subparagraphs (C) and (D), the coverage";

(B) in paragraph (2)(B), by striking "subparagraph (A)(ii)" and inserting "subparagraphs (A)(ii), (C), and (D)";

(C) by adding at the end of paragraph (2) the following new subparagraphs:

"(C) COVERAGE FOR GENERIC DRUGS IN COVERAGE GAP.—

"(i) IN GENERAL.—Except as provided in paragraph (4), the coverage for an applicable beneficiary (as defined in section 1860D–14A(g)(1)) has coinsurance (for costs above the initial coverage limit under paragraph (3) and below the out-of-pocket threshold) for covered part D drugs that are not applicable drugs under section 1860D–14A(g)(2) that is—

"(I) equal to the generic-gap coinsurance percentage (specified in clause (ii)) for the year; or

"(II) actuarially equivalent (using processes and methods established under section 1860D–11(c)) to an average expected payment of such percentage of such costs for covered part D drugs that are not applicable drugs under section 1860D–14A(g)(2).

"(ii) GENERIC-GAP COINSURANCE PERCENTAGE.—The generic-gap coinsurance percentage specified in this clause for—

"(I) 2011 is 93 percent;

"(II) 2012 and each succeeding year before 2020 is the generic-gap coinsurance percentage under this clause for the previous year decreased by 7 percentage points; and

"(III) 2020 and each subsequent year is 25 percent.

"(D) COVERAGE FOR APPLICABLE DRUGS IN COVERAGE GAP.—

"(i) IN GENERAL.—Except as provided in paragraph (4), the coverage for an applicable beneficiary (as defined in section 1860D–14A(g)(1)) has coinsurance (for costs above the initial coverage limit under paragraph (3) and below the out-of-pocket threshold) for the negotiated price (as defined in section 1860D–14A(g)(6)) of covered part D drugs that are applicable drugs under section 1860D–14A(g)(2) that is—

"(I) equal to the difference between the applicable gap percentage (specified in clause (ii) for the year) and the discount percentage specified in section 1860D–14A(g)(4)(A) for such applicable drugs; or

"(II) actuarially equivalent (using processes and methods established under section 1860D–11(c)) to an average expected payment of such percentage of such costs, for covered part D drugs that are applicable drugs under section 1860D–14A(g)(2).

"(ii) APPLICABLE GAP PERCENTAGE.—The applicable gap percentage specified in this clause for—

"(I) 2013 and 2014 is 97.5 percent;

"(II) 2015 and 2016 is 95 percent;

"(III) 2017 is 90 percent;

"(IV) 2018 is 85 percent;

"(V) 2019 is 80 percent; and

"(VI) 2020 and each subsequent year is 75 percent.";

(D) in paragraph (3)(A), as restored under subsection (a)(2), by striking "paragraph (4)" and inserting "paragraphs (2)(C), (2)(D), and (4)"; and

(E) in paragraph (4)(E), by inserting before the period at the end the following: ", except that incurred costs shall not include the portion of the negotiated price that represents the reduction in coinsurance resulting from the application of paragraph (2)(D)"; and

(4) in section 1860D–22(a)(2)(A), by inserting before the period at the end the following: ", not taking into account the value of any discount or coverage provided during the gap in prescription drug coverage that occurs between the initial coverage limit under section 1860D–2(b)(3) during the year and the out-of-pocket threshold specified in section 1860D–2(b)(4)(B)".

(c) CONFORMING AMENDMENT TO AMP UNDER MEDICAID.—Section 1927(k)(1)(B)(i) of the Social Security Act (42 U.S.C. 1396r–8(k)(1)(B)(i)), as amended by section 2503(a)(2)(B) of the Patient Protection and Affordable Care Act, is amended—

(1) by striking "and" at the end of subclause (III);

(2) by striking the period at the end of subclause (IV); and

(3) by adding at the end the following new subclause:

"(V) discounts provided by manufacturers under section 1860D–14A.".

(d) REDUCING GROWTH RATE OF OUT-OF-POCKET COST THRESHOLD.—Section 1860D–2(b) of the Social Security Act (42 U.S.C. 1395w–102(b)) is amended—

(1) in paragraph (4)(B)(i)—

(A) in subclause (I), by striking "or" at the end;

(B) by redesignating subclause (II) as subclause (VI); and

(C) by inserting after subclause (I) the following new subclauses:

"(II) for each of years 2007 through 2013, is equal to the amount specified in this subparagraph for the previous year, increased by the annual percentage increase described in paragraph (6) for the year involved;

"(III) for 2014 and 2015, is equal to the amount specified in this subparagraph for the previous year, increased by the annual percentage increase described in paragraph (6) for the year involved, minus 0.25 percentage point;

"(IV) for each of years 2016 through 2019, is equal to the amount specified in this subparagraph for the previous year, increased by the lesser of—

"(aa) the annual percentage increase described in paragraph (7) for the year involved, plus 2 percentage points; or

"(bb) the annual percentage increase described in paragraph (6) for the year;

"(V) for 2020, is equal to the amount that would have been applied under this subparagraph for 2020 if the amendments made by section 1101(d)(1) of the Health Care and Education Reconciliation Act of 2010 had not been enacted; or"; and

(2) by adding at the end the following new paragraph:

"(7) ADDITIONAL ANNUAL PERCENTAGE INCREASE.—The annual percentage increase specified in this paragraph for a year is equal to the annual percentage increase in the consumer price index for all urban consumers (United States city average) for the 12-month period ending in July of the previous year.".

SEC. 1102. MEDICARE ADVANTAGE PAYMENTS.

(a) REPEAL.—Effective as if included in the enactment of the Patient Protection and Affordable Care Act, sections 3201 and 3203 of such Act (and the amendments made by such sections) are repealed.

(b) PHASE-IN OF MODIFIED BENCHMARKS.—Section 1853 of the Social Security Act (42 U.S.C. 1395w–23) is amended—

(1) in subsection (j)(1)(A), by striking "(or, beginning with 2007, 1⁄12 of the applicable amount determined under subsection (k)(1)) for the area for the year" and inserting "for the area for the year (or, for 2007, 2008, 2009, and 2010, 1⁄12 of the applicable amount determined under subsection (k)(1) for the area for the year; for 2011, 1⁄12 of the applicable amount determined under subsection (k)(1) for the area for 2010; and, beginning with 2012, 1⁄12 of the blended benchmark amount determined under subsection (n)(1) for the area for the year)"; and

(2) by adding at the end the following new subsection:

"(n) DETERMINATION OF BLENDED BENCHMARK AMOUNT.—

"(1) IN GENERAL.—For purposes of subsection (j), subject to paragraphs (3), (4), and (5), the term 'blended benchmark amount' means for an area—

"(A) for 2012 the sum of—

"(i) 1⁄2 of the applicable amount for the area and year; and

"(ii) 1⁄2 of the amount specified in paragraph (2)(A) for the area and year; and

"(B) for a subsequent year the amount specified in paragraph (2)(A) for the area and year.

"(2) SPECIFIED AMOUNT.—

"(A) IN GENERAL.—The amount specified in this subparagraph for an area and year is the product of—

"(i) the base payment amount specified in subparagraph (E) for the area and year adjusted to take into account the phase-out in the indirect costs of medical education from capitation rates described in subsection (k)(4); and

"(ii) the applicable percentage for the area for the year specified under subparagraph (B).

"(B) APPLICABLE PERCENTAGE.—Subject to subparagraph (D), the applicable percentage specified in this subparagraph for an area for a year in the case of an area that is ranked—

"(i) in the highest quartile under subparagraph (C) for the previous year is 95 percent;

"(ii) in the second highest quartile under such subparagraph for the previous year is 100 percent;

"(iii) in the third highest quartile under such subparagraph for the previous year is 107.5 percent; or

"(iv) in the lowest quartile under such subparagraph for the previous year is 115 percent.

"(C) PERIODIC RANKING.—For purposes of this paragraph in the case of an area located—

"(i) in 1 of the 50 States or the District of Columbia, the Secretary shall rank such area in each year specified under subsection (c)(1)(D)(ii) based upon the level of the amount specified in subparagraph (A)(i) for such areas; or

"(ii) in a territory, the Secretary shall rank such areas in each such year based upon the level of the amount specified in subparagraph (A)(i) for such area relative to quartile rankings computed under clause (i).

"(D) 1-YEAR TRANSITION FOR CHANGES IN APPLICABLE PERCENTAGE.—If, for a year after 2012, there is a change in the quartile in which an area is ranked compared to the previous year, the applicable percentage for the area in the year shall be the average of—

"(i) the applicable percentage for the area for the previous year; and

"(ii) the applicable percentage that would otherwise apply for the area for the year.

"(E) BASE PAYMENT AMOUNT.—Subject to subparagraph (F), the base payment amount specified in this subparagraph—

"(i) for 2012 is the amount specified in subsection (c)(1)(D) for the area for the year; or

"(ii) for a subsequent year that—

"(I) is not specified under subsection (c)(1)(D)(ii), is the base amount specified in this subparagraph for the area for the previous year, increased by the national per capita MA growth percentage, described in subsection (c)(6) for that succeeding year, but not taking into account any adjustment under subparagraph (C) of such subsection for a year before 2004; and

"(II) is specified under subsection (c)(1)(D)(ii), is the amount specified in subsection (c)(1)(D) for the area for the year.

"(F) APPLICATION OF INDIRECT MEDICAL EDUCATION PHASE-OUT.—The base payment amount specified in subparagraph (E) for a year shall be adjusted in the same manner under paragraph (4) of subsection (k) as the applicable amount is adjusted under such subsection.

"(3) ALTERNATIVE PHASE-INS.—

"(A) 4-YEAR PHASE-IN FOR CERTAIN AREAS.—If the difference between the applicable amount (as defined in subsection (k)) for an area for 2010 and the projected 2010 benchmark amount (as defined in subparagraph (C)) for the area is at least $30 but less than $50, the blended benchmark amount for the area is—

"(i) for 2012 the sum of—

"(I) 3⁄4 of the applicable amount for the area and year; and

"(II) 1⁄4 of the amount specified in paragraph (2)(A) for the area and year;

"(ii) for 2013 the sum of—

"(I) 1⁄2 of the applicable amount for the area and year; and

"(II) 1⁄2 of the amount specified in paragraph (2)(A) for the area and year;

"(iii) for 2014 the sum of—

"(I) 1⁄4 of the applicable amount for the area and year; and

"(II) 3⁄4 of the amount specified in paragraph (2)(A) for the area and year; and

"(iv) for a subsequent year the amount specified in paragraph (2)(A) for the area and year.

"(B) 6-YEAR PHASE-IN FOR CERTAIN AREAS.—If the difference between the applicable amount (as defined in subsection (k)) for an area for 2010 and the projected 2010 benchmark amount (as defined in subparagraph (C)) for the area is at least $50, the blended benchmark amount for the area is—

"(i) for 2012 the sum of—

"(I) 5⁄6 of the applicable amount for the area and year; and

"(II) 1⁄6 of the amount specified in paragraph (2)(A) for the area and year;

"(ii) for 2013 the sum of—

"(I) 2⁄3 of the applicable amount for the area and year; and

"(II) 1⁄3 of the amount specified in paragraph (2)(A) for the area and year;

"(iii) for 2014 the sum of—

"(I) 1⁄2 of the applicable amount for the area and year; and

"(II) 1⁄2 of the amount specified in paragraph (2)(A) for the area and year;

"(iv) for 2015 the sum of—

"(I) 1⁄3 of the applicable amount for the area and year; and

"(II) 2⁄3 of the amount specified in paragraph (2)(A) for the area and year; and

"(v) for 2016 the sum of—

"(I) 1⁄6 of the applicable amount for the area and year; and

"(II) 5⁄6 of the amount specified in paragraph (2)(A) for the area and year; and

"(vi) for a subsequent year the amount specified in paragraph (2)(A) for the area and year.

"(C) PROJECTED 2010 BENCHMARK AMOUNT.—The projected 2010 benchmark amount described in this subparagraph for an area is equal to the sum of—

"(i) 1⁄2 of the applicable amount (as defined in subsection (k)) for the area for 2010; and

"(ii) 1⁄2 of the amount specified in paragraph (2)(A) for the area for 2010 but determined as if there were substituted for the applicable percentage specified in clause (ii) of such paragraph the sum of—

"(I) the applicable percent that would be specified under subparagraph (B) of paragraph (2) (determined without regard to subparagraph (D) of such paragraph) for the area for 2010 if any reference in such paragraph to 'the previous year' were deemed a reference to 2010; and

"(II) the applicable percentage increase that would apply to a qualifying plan in the area under subsection (o) as if any reference in such subsection to 2012 were deemed a reference to 2010 and as if the determination of a qualifying county under paragraph (3)(B) of such subsection were made for 2010.

"(4) CAP ON BENCHMARK AMOUNT.—In no case shall the blended benchmark amount for an area for a year (determined taking into account subsection (o)) be greater than the applicable amount that would (but for the application of this subsection) be determined under subsection (k)(1) for the area for the year.

"(5) NON-APPLICATION TO PACE PLANS.—This subsection shall not apply to payments to a PACE program under section 1894.".

(c) APPLICABLE PERCENTAGE QUALITY INCREASES.—Section 1853 of such Act (42 U.S.C. 1395w–23), as amended by subsection (b), is amended—

(1) in subsection (j), by inserting "subject to subsection (o)," after "For purposes of this part,";

(2) in subsection (n)(2)(B), as added by subsection (b), by inserting ", subject to subsection (o)" after "as follows"; and

(3) by adding at the end the following new subsection:

"(o) APPLICABLE PERCENTAGE QUALITY INCREASES.—

"(1) IN GENERAL.—Subject to the succeeding paragraphs, in the case of a qualifying plan with respect to a year beginning with 2012, the applicable percentage under subsection (n)(2)(B) shall be increased on a plan or contract level, as determined by the Secretary—

"(A) for 2012, by 1.5 percentage points;

"(B) for 2013, by 3.0 percentage points; and

"(C) for 2014 or a subsequent year, by 5.0 percentage points.

"(2) INCREASE FOR QUALIFYING PLANS IN QUALIFYING COUNTIES.—The increase applied under paragraph (1) for a qualifying plan located in a qualifying county for a year shall be doubled.

"(3) QUALIFYING PLANS AND QUALIFYING COUNTY DEFINED; APPLICATION OF INCREASES TO LOW ENROLLMENT AND NEW PLANS.—For purposes of this subsection:

"(A) QUALIFYING PLAN.—

"(i) IN GENERAL.—The term 'qualifying plan' means, for a year and subject to paragraph (4), a plan that had a quality rating under paragraph (4) of 4 stars or higher based on the most recent data available for such year.

"(ii) APPLICATION OF INCREASES TO LOW ENROLLMENT PLANS.—

"(I) 2012.—For 2012, the term 'qualifying plan' includes an MA plan that the Secretary determines is not able to have a quality rating under paragraph (4) because of low enrollment.

"(II) 2013 AND SUBSEQUENT YEARS.—For 2013 and subsequent years, for purposes of determining whether an MA plan with low enrollment (as defined by the Secretary) is included as a qualifying plan, the Secretary shall establish a method to apply to MA plans with low enrollment (as defined by the Secretary) the computation of quality rating and the rating system under paragraph (4).

"(iii) APPLICATION OF INCREASES TO NEW PLANS.—

"(I) IN GENERAL.—A new MA plan that meets criteria specified by the Secretary shall be treated as a qualifying plan, except that in applying paragraph (1), the applicable percentage under subsection (n)(2)(B) shall be increased—

"(aa) for 2012, by 1.5 percentage points;

"(bb) for 2013, by 2.5 percentage points; and

"(cc) for 2014 or a subsequent year, by 3.5 percentage points.

"(II) NEW MA PLAN DEFINED.—The term 'new MA plan' means, with respect to a year, a plan offered by an organization or sponsor that has not had a contract as a Medicare Advantage organization in the preceding 3-year period.

"(B) QUALIFYING COUNTY.—The term 'qualifying county' means, for a year, a county—

"(i) that has an MA capitation rate that, in 2004, was based on the amount specified in subsection (c)(1)(B) for a Metropolitan Statistical Area with a population of more than 250,000;

"(ii) for which, as of December 2009, of the Medicare Advantage eligible individuals residing in the county at least 25 percent of such individuals were enrolled in Medicare Advantage plans; and

"(iii) that has per capita fee-for-service spending that is lower than the national monthly per capita cost for expenditures for individuals enrolled under the original medicare fee-for-service program for the year.

"(4) QUALITY DETERMINATIONS FOR APPLICATION OF INCREASE.—

"(A) QUALITY DETERMINATION.—The quality rating for a plan shall be determined according to a 5-star rating system (based on the data collected under section 1852(e)).

"(B) PLANS THAT FAILED TO REPORT.—An MA plan which does not report data that enables the Secretary to rate the plan for purposes of this paragraph shall be counted as having a rating of fewer than 3.5 stars.

"(5) EXCEPTION FOR PACE PLANS.—This subsection shall not apply to payments to a PACE program under section 1894.".

(4) DETERMINATION OF MEDICARE PART D LOW-INCOME BENCHMARK PREMIUM.—Section 1860D–14(b)(2)(B)(iii) of the Social Security Act (42 U.S.C. 1395w–114(b)(2)(B)(iii)) as amended by section 3302 of the Patient Protection and Affordable Care Act, is amended by striking ", determined without regard to any reduction in such premium as a result of any beneficiary rebate under section 1854(b)(1)(C) or bonus payment under section 1853(n)" and inserting the following: "and determined before the application of the monthly rebate computed under section 1854(b)(1)(C)(i) for that plan and year involved and, in the case of a qualifying plan, before the application of the increase under section 1853(o) for that plan and year involved".

(d) BENEFICIARY REBATES.—Section 1854(b)(1)(C) of such Act (42 U.S.C. 1395w–24(b)(1)(C)), as amended by section 3202(b) of the Patient Protection and Affordable Care Act, is further amended—

(1) in clause (i), by inserting "(or the applicable rebate percentage specified in clause (iii) in the case of plan years beginning on or after January 1, 2012)" after "75 percent"; and

(2) by striking clause (iii), by redesignating clauses (iv) and (v) as clauses (vii) and (viii), respectively, and by inserting after clause (ii) the following new clauses:

"(iii) APPLICABLE REBATE PERCENTAGE.—The applicable rebate percentage specified in this clause for a plan for a year, based on the system under section 1853(o)(4)(A), is the sum of—

"(I) the product of the old phase-in proportion for the year under clause (iv) and 75 percent; and

"(II) the product of the new phase-in proportion for the year under clause (iv) and the final applicable rebate percentage under clause (v).

"(iv) OLD AND NEW PHASE-IN PROPORTIONS.—For purposes of clause (iv)—

"(I) for 2012, the old phase-in proportion is ⅔ and the new phase-in proportion is ⅓;

"(II) for 2013, the old phase-in proportion is ⅓ and the new phase-in proportion is ⅔; and

"(III) for 2014 and any subsequent year, the old phase-in proportion is 0 and the new phase-in proportion is 1.

"(v) FINAL APPLICABLE REBATE PERCENTAGE.—Subject to clause (vi), the final applicable rebate percentage under this clause is—

"(I) in the case of a plan with a quality rating under such system of at least 4.5 stars, 70 percent;

"(II) in the case of a plan with a quality rating under such system of at least 3.5 stars and less than 4.5 stars, 65 percent; and

"(III) in the case of a plan with a quality rating under such system of less than 3.5 stars, 50 percent.

"(vi) TREATMENT OF LOW ENROLLMENT AND NEW PLANS.—For purposes of clause (v)—

"(I) for 2012, in the case of a plan described in subclause (I) of subsection (o)(3)(A)(ii), the plan shall be treated as having a rating of 4.5 stars; and

"(II) for 2012 or a subsequent year, in the case of a new MA plan (as defined under subclause (III) of subsection (o)(3)(A)(iii)) that is treated as a qualifying plan pursuant to subclause (I) of such subsection, the plan shall be treated as having a rating of 3.5 stars.".

(e) CODING INTENSITY ADJUSTMENT.—Section 1853(a)(1)(C)(ii) of such Act (42 U.S.C. 1395w–23(a)(1)(C)(ii)) is amended—

(1) in the heading, by striking "DURING PHASEOUT OF BUDGET NEUTRALITY FACTOR" and inserting "OF CODING ADJUSTMENT";

(2) in the matter before subclause (I), by striking "through 2010" and inserting "and each subsequent year"; and

(3) in subclause (II)—

(A) in the first sentence, by inserting "annually" before "conduct an analysis";

(B) in the second sentence—

(i) by inserting "on a timely basis" after "are incorporated"; and

(ii) by striking "only for 2008, 2009, and 2010" and inserting "for 2008 and subsequent years";

(C) in the third sentence, by inserting "and updated as appropriate" before the period at the end; and

(D) by adding at the end the following new subclauses:

"(III) In calculating each year's adjustment, the adjustment factor shall be for 2014, not less than the adjustment factor applied for 2010, plus 1.3 percentage points; for each of years 2015 through 2018, not less than the adjustment factor applied for the previous year, plus 0.25 percentage point; and for 2019 and each subsequent year, not less than 5.7 percent.

"(IV) Such adjustment shall be applied to risk scores until the Secretary implements risk adjustment using Medicare Advantage diagnostic, cost, and use data.".

(f) REPEAL OF COMPARATIVE COST ADJUSTMENT PROGRAM.—Section 1860C–1 of the Social Security Act (42 U.S.C. 1395w–29), as added by section 241(a) of the Medicare Prescription Drug,

Improvement, and Modernization Act of 2003 (Public Law 108–173), is repealed.

SEC. 1103. SAVINGS FROM LIMITS ON MA PLAN ADMINISTRATIVE COSTS.

Section 1857(e) of the Social Security Act (42 U.S.C. 1395w–27(e)) is amended by adding at the end the following new paragraph:

"(4) REQUIREMENT FOR MINIMUM MEDICAL LOSS RATIO.—If the Secretary determines for a contract year (beginning with 2014) that an MA plan has failed to have a medical loss ratio of at least .85—

"(A) the MA plan shall remit to the Secretary an amount equal to the product of—

"(i) the total revenue of the MA plan under this part for the contract year; and

"(ii) the difference between .85 and the medical loss ratio;

"(B) for 3 consecutive contract years, the Secretary shall not permit the enrollment of new enrollees under the plan for coverage during the second succeeding contract year; and

"(C) the Secretary shall terminate the plan contract if the plan fails to have such a medical loss ratio for 5 consecutive contract years.".

SEC. 1104. DISPROPORTIONATE SHARE HOSPITAL (DSH) PAYMENTS.

Section 1886(r) of the Social Security Act (42 U.S.C. 1395ww(r)), as added by section 3133 of the Patient Protection and Affordable Care Act and as amended by section 10316 of such Act, is amended—

(1) in paragraph (1), by striking "2015" and inserting "2014"; and

(2) in paragraph (2)—

(A) in the matter preceding subparagraph (A), by striking "2015" and inserting "2014";

(B) in subparagraph (B)(i)—

(i) in the heading, by inserting "2014," after "YEARS";

(ii) in the matter preceding subclause (I), by inserting "2014," after "each of fiscal years";

(iii) in subclause (I), by striking "on such Act" and inserting "on the Health Care and Education Reconciliation Act of 2010"; and

(iv) in the matter following subclause (II), by striking "minus 1.5 percentage points" and inserting "minus 0.1 percentage points for fiscal year 2014 and minus 0.2 percentage points for each of fiscal years 2015, 2016, and 2017"; and

(C) in subparagraph (B)(ii), in the matter following subclause (II), by striking "and, for each of 2018 and 2019, minus 1.5 percentage points" and inserting "minus 0.2 percentage points for each of fiscal years 2018 and 2019".

SEC. 1105. MARKET BASKET UPDATES.

(a) IPPS.—Section 1886(b)(3)(B) of the Social Security Act (42 U.S.C. 1395ww(b)(3)(B)), as amended by sections 3401(a)(4) and 10319(a) of the Patient Protection and Affordable Care Act, is amended—

(1) in clause (xii)—

(A) by placing the subclause (II) (inserted by section 10319(a)(3) of the Patient Protection and Affordable Care Act) immediately after subclause (I) and, in such subclause (II), by striking "and" at the end; and

(B) by striking subclause (III) and inserting the following:

"(III) for fiscal year 2014, by 0.3 percentage point;

"(IV) for each of fiscal years 2015 and 2016, by 0.2 percentage point; and

"(V) for each of fiscal years 2017, 2018, and 2019, by 0.75 percentage point."; and

(2) by striking clause (xiii).

(b) LONG-TERM CARE HOSPITALS.—Section 1886(m)(4) of the Social Security Act (42 U.S.C. 1395ww(m)(4)), as added by section 3401(c) of the Patient Protection and Affordable Care Act and amended by section 10319(b) of such Act, is amended—

(1) in subparagraph (A)—

(A) in clause (iii), by striking "and" at the end; and

(B) by striking clause (iv) and inserting the following:

"(iv) for rate year 2014, 0.3 percentage point;

"(v) for each of rate years 2015 and 2016, 0.2 percentage point; and

"(vi) for each of rate years 2017, 2018, and 2019, 0.75 percentage point.";

(2) by striking subparagraph (B); and

(3) by striking "(4) OTHER ADJUSTMENT.—" and all that follows through "For purposes" and inserting "(4) OTHER ADJUSTMENT.—For purposes" (and redesignating clauses (i) through (vi) as subparagraphs (A) through (F), respectively, with appropriate indentation).

(c) INPATIENT REHABILITATION FACILITIES.—Section 1886(j)(3)(D) of the Social Security Act (42 U.S.C. 1395ww(j)(3)(D)), as added by section 3401(d)(2) of the Patient Protection and Affordable Care Act and amended by section 10319(c) of such Act, is amended—

(1) in clause (i)—

(A) by placing the subclause (II) (inserted by section 10319(c)(3) of the Patient Protection and Affordable Care Act) immediately after subclause (I) and, in such subclause (II), by striking "and" at the end; and

(B) by striking subclause (III) and inserting the following:

"(III) for fiscal year 2014, 0.3 percentage point;

"(IV) for each of fiscal years 2015 and 2016, 0.2 percentage point; and

"(V) for each of fiscal years 2017, 2018, and 2019, 0.75 percentage point.";

(2) by striking clause (ii); and

(3) by striking "(D) OTHER ADJUSTMENT.—" and all that follows through "For purposes" and inserting "(D) OTHER ADJUSTMENT.—For purposes" (and redesignating subclauses (I) through (V) as clauses (i) through (v), respectively, with appropriate indentation).

(d) PSYCHIATRIC HOSPITALS.—Section 1886(s)(3) of the Social Security Act, as added by section 3401(f) of the Patient Protection and Affordable Care Act and amended by section 10319(e) of such Act, is amended—

(1) in subparagraph (A)—

(A) by placing the clause (ii) (inserted by section 10319(e)(3) of the Patient Protection and Affordable Care Act) immediately after clause (i) and, in such clause (ii), by striking "and" at the end; and

(B) by striking clause (iii) and inserting the following:

"(iii) for the rate year beginning in 2014, 0.3 percentage point;

"(iv) for each of the rate years beginning in 2015 and 2016, 0.2 percentage point; and

"(v) for each of the rate years beginning in 2017, 2018, and 2019, 0.75 percentage point.";

(2) by striking subparagraph (B); and

(3) by striking "(3) OTHER ADJUSTMENT.—" and all that follows through "For purposes" and inserting "(3) OTHER ADJUSTMENT.—For purposes" (and redesignating clauses (i) through (v) as subparagraphs (A) through (E), respectively, with appropriate indentation).

(e) OUTPATIENT HOSPITALS.—Section 1833(t)(3)(G) of the Social Security Act (42 U.S.C. 1395l(t)(3)(G)), as added by section 3401(i)(2) of the Patient Protection and Affordable Care Act and amended by section 10319(g) of such Act, is amended—

(1) in clause (i)—

(A) by placing the subclause (II) (inserted by section 10319(g)(3) of the Patient Protection and Affordable Care Act) immediately after subclause (I) and, in such subclause (II), by striking "and" at the end; and

(B) by striking subclause (III) and inserting the following:

"(III) for 2014, 0.3 percentage point;

"(IV) for each of 2015 and 2016, 0.2 percentage point; and

"(V) for each of 2017, 2018, and 2019, 0.75 percentage point.";

(2) by striking clause (ii); and

(3) by striking "(G) OTHER ADJUSTMENT.—" and all that follows through "For purposes" and inserting "(G) OTHER ADJUSTMENT.—For purposes" (and redesignating subclauses (I) through (V) as clauses (i) through (v), respectively, with appropriate indentation).

SEC. 1106. PHYSICIAN OWNERSHIP-REFERRAL.

Section 1877(i) of the Social Security Act (42 U.S.C. 1395nn(i)), as added by section 6001(a)(3) of the Patient Protection and Affordable Care Act and as amended by section 10601(a) of such Act, is amended—

(1) in paragraph (1)(A)(i), by striking "August 1, 2010" and inserting "December 31, 2010"; and

(2) in paragraph (3)—

(A) in subparagraph (A)(i), by striking "an applicable hospital (as defined in subparagraph (E))" and inserting "a hospital that is an applicable hospital (as defined in subparagraph (E)) or is a high Medicaid facility described in subparagraph (F)";

(B) in subparagraph (C)(iii), by inserting after "date of enactment of this subsection" the following: "(or, in the case of a hospital that did not have a provider agreement in effect as of such date but does have such an agreement in effect on December 31, 2010, the effective date of such provider agreement)";

(C) by redesignating subparagraphs (F) through (H) as subparagraphs (G) through (I), respectively; and

(D) by inserting after subparagraph (E) the following new subparagraph:

"(F) HIGH MEDICAID FACILITY DESCRIBED.—A high Medicaid facility described in this subparagraph is a hospital that—

"(i) is not the sole hospital in a county;

"(ii) with respect to each of the 3 most recent years for which data are available, has an annual percent of total inpatient admissions that represent inpatient admissions under title XIX that is estimated to be greater than such percent with respect to such admissions for any other hospital located in the county in which the hospital is located; and

"(iii) meets the conditions described in subparagraph (E)(iii).".

SEC. 1107. PAYMENT FOR IMAGING SERVICES.

Section 1848 of the Social Security Act (42 U.S.C. 1395w–4), as amended by section 3135(a) of the Patient Protection and Affordable Care Act, is amended—

(1) in subsection (b)(4)—

(A) in subparagraph (B), by striking "this paragraph" and inserting "subparagraph (A)"; and

(B) by amending subparagraph (C) to read as follows:

"(C) ADJUSTMENT IN IMAGING UTILIZATION RATE.—With respect to fee schedules established for 2011 and subsequent years, in the methodology for determining practice expense relative value units for expensive diagnostic imaging equipment under the final rule published by the Secretary in the Federal Register on November 25, 2009 (42 CFR 410 et al.), the Secretary shall use a 75 percent assumption instead of the utilization rates otherwise established in such final rule."; and

(2) in subsection (c)(2)(B)(v), by striking subclauses (III), (IV), and (V) and inserting the following new subclause:

"(III) CHANGE IN UTILIZATION RATE FOR CERTAIN IMAGING SERVICES.—Effective for fee schedules established beginning with 2011, reduced expenditures attributable to the change in the utilization rate applicable to 2011, as described in subsection (b)(4)(C).".

SEC. 1108. PE GPCI ADJUSTMENT FOR 2010.

Effective as if included in the enactment of the Patient Protection and Affordable Care Act, section 1848(e)(1)(H)(i) of the Social Security Act (42 U.S.C. 1395w–4(e)(1)(H)(i)), as added by section 3102(b)(2) of the Patient Protection and Affordable Care Act, is amended by striking "¾" and inserting "½".

SEC. 1109. PAYMENT FOR QUALIFYING HOSPITALS.

(a) IN GENERAL.—From the amount available under subsection (b), the Secretary of Health and Human Services shall provide for a payment to qualifying hospitals (as defined in subsection (d)) for fiscal years 2011 and 2012 of the amount determined under subsection (c).

(b) AMOUNTS AVAILABLE.—There shall be available from the Federal Hospital Insurance Trust Fund $400,000,000 for payments under this section for fiscal years 2011 and 2012.

(c) PAYMENT AMOUNT.—The amount of payment under this section for a qualifying hospital shall be determined, in a manner consistent with the amount available under subsection (b), in proportion to the portion of the amount of the aggregate payments under section 1886(d) of the Social Security Act to the hospital for fiscal year 2009 bears to the sum of all such payments to all qualifying hospitals for such fiscal year.

(d) QUALIFYING HOSPITAL DEFINED.—In this section, the term "qualifying hospital" means a subsection (d) hospital (as defined for purposes of section 1886(d) of the Social Security Act) that is located in a county that ranks, based upon its ranking in age, sex, and race adjusted spending for benefits under parts A and B under title XVIII of such Act per enrollee, within the lowest quartile of such counties in the United States.

Subtitle C—Medicaid

SEC. 1201. FEDERAL FUNDING FOR STATES.

Section 1905 of the Social Security Act (42 U.S.C. 1396d), as amended by sections 2001(a)(3) and 10201(c) of the Patient Protection and Affordable Care Act, is amended—

(1) in subsection (y)—

(A) by redesignating subclause (II) of paragraph (1)(B)(ii) as paragraph (5) of subsection (z) and realigning the left margins accordingly; and

(B) by striking paragraph (1) and inserting the following:

"(1) AMOUNT OF INCREASE.—Notwithstanding subsection (b), the Federal medical assistance percentage for a State that is one of the 50 States or the District of Columbia, with respect to amounts expended by such State for medical assistance for newly eligible individuals described in subclause (VIII) of section 1902(a)(10)(A)(i), shall be equal to—

"(A) 100 percent for calendar quarters in 2014, 2015, and 2016;

"(B) 95 percent for calendar quarters in 2017;

"(C) 94 percent for calendar quarters in 2018;

"(D) 93 percent for calendar quarters in 2019; and

"(E) 90 percent for calendar quarters in 2020 and each year thereafter."; and

(2) in subsection (z)—

(A) in paragraph (1), by striking "September 30, 2019" and inserting "December 31, 2015" and by striking "subsection (y)(1)(B)(ii)(II)" and inserting "paragraph (3)";

(B) by striking paragraphs (2) through (4) and inserting the following:

"(2)(A) For calendar quarters in 2014 and each year thereafter, the Federal medical assistance percentage otherwise determined under subsection (b) for an expansion State described in paragraph (3) with respect to medical assistance for individuals described in section 1902(a)(10)(A)(i)(VIII) who are nonpregnant childless adults with respect to whom the State may require enrollment in benchmark coverage under section 1937 shall be equal to the percent specified in subparagraph (B)(i) for such year.

"(B)(i) The percent specified in this subparagraph for a State for a year is equal to the Federal medical assistance percentage (as defined in the first sentence of subsection (b)) for the State increased by a number of percentage points equal to the transition percentage (specified in clause (ii) for the year) of the number of percentage points by which—

"(I) such Federal medical assistance percentage for the State, is less than

"(II) the percent specified in subsection (y)(1) for the year.

"(ii) The transition percentage specified in this clause for—

"(I) 2014 is 50 percent;

"(II) 2015 is 60 percent;

"(III) 2016 is 70 percent;

"(IV) 2017 is 80 percent;

"(V) 2018 is 90 percent; and

"(VI) 2019 and each subsequent year is 100 percent."; and

(C) by redesignating paragraph (5) (as added by paragraph (1)(A) of this section) as paragraph (3), realigning the left margins to align with paragraph (2), and striking the heading and all that follows through "a State is" and inserting "A State is".

SEC. 1202. PAYMENTS TO PRIMARY CARE PHYSICIANS.

(a) IN GENERAL.—

(1) FEE-FOR-SERVICE PAYMENTS.—Section 1902 of the Social Security Act (42 U.S.C. 1396a), as amended by section 2303(a)(2) of the Patient Protection and Affordable Care Act, is amended—

(A) in subsection (a)(13)—

(i) by striking "and" at the end of subparagraph (A);

(ii) by adding "and" at the end of subparagraph (B); and

(iii) by adding at the end the following new subparagraph:

"(C) payment for primary care services (as defined in subsection (jj)) furnished in 2013 and 2014 by a physician with a primary specialty designation of family medicine, general internal medicine, or pediatric medicine at a rate not less than 100 percent of the payment rate that applies to such services and physician under part B of title XVIII (or, if greater, the payment rate that would be applicable under such part if the conversion factor under section 1848(d) for the year involved were the conversion factor under such section for 2009);"; and

(B) by adding at the end the following new subsection:

"(jj) PRIMARY CARE SERVICES DEFINED.—For purposes of subsection (a)(13)(C), the term 'primary care services' means—

"(1) evaluation and management services that are procedure codes (for services covered under title XVIII) for services in the category designated Evaluation and Management in the Healthcare Common Procedure Coding System (established by the Secretary under section 1848(c)(5) as of December 31, 2009, and as subsequently modified); and

"(2) services related to immunization administration for vaccines and toxoids for which CPT codes 90465, 90466, 90467, 90468, 90471, 90472, 90473, or 90474 (as subsequently modified) apply under such System.".

(2) UNDER MEDICAID MANAGED CARE PLANS.—Section 1932(f) of such Act (42 U.S.C. 1396u–2(f)) is amended—

(A) in the heading, by adding at the end the following: "; ADEQUACY OF PAYMENT FOR PRIMARY CARE SERVICES"; and

(B) by inserting before the period at the end the following: "and, in the case of primary care services described in section 1902(a)(13)(C), consistent with the minimum payment rates specified in such section (regardless of the manner in which such payments are made, including in the form of capitation or partial capitation)".

(b) INCREASE IN PAYMENT USING INCREASED FMAP.—Section 1905 of the Social Security Act, as amended by section 1004(b) of this Act and section 10201(c)(6) of the Patient Protection and Affordable Care Act, is amended by adding at the end the following new subsection:

"(dd) INCREASED FMAP FOR ADDITIONAL EXPENDITURES FOR PRIMARY CARE SERVICES.—Notwithstanding subsection (b), with respect to the portion of the amounts expended for medical assistance for services described in section 1902(a)(13)(C) furnished on or after January 1, 2013, and before January 1, 2015, that is attributable to the amount by which the minimum payment rate required under such section (or, by application, section 1932(f)) exceeds the payment rate applicable to such services under the State plan as of July 1, 2009, the Federal medical assistance percentage for a State that is one of the 50 States or the District of Columbia shall be equal to 100 percent. The preceding sentence does not prohibit the payment of Federal financial participation based on the Federal medical assistance percentage for amounts in excess of those specified in such sentence.".

SEC. 1203. DISPROPORTIONATE SHARE HOSPITAL PAYMENTS.

(a) IN GENERAL.—Section 1923(f) of the Social Security Act (42 U.S.C. 1396r–4(f)), as amended by sections 2551(a)(4) and 10201(e)(1) of the Patient Protection and Affordable Care Act, is amended—

(1) in paragraph (6)(B)(iii), in the matter preceding subclause (I), by striking "or paragraph (7)"; and

(2) by striking paragraph (7) and inserting the following:

"(7) MEDICAID DSH REDUCTIONS.—

"(A) REDUCTIONS.—

"(i) IN GENERAL.—For each of fiscal years 2014 through 2020 the Secretary shall effect the following reductions:

"(I) REDUCTION IN DSH ALLOTMENTS.—The Secretary shall reduce DSH allotments to States in the amount specified under the DSH health reform methodology under subparagraph (B) for the State for the fiscal year.

"(II) REDUCTIONS IN PAYMENTS.—The Secretary shall reduce payments to States under section 1903(a) for each calendar quarter in the fiscal year, in the manner specified in clause (iii), in an amount equal to 1/4 of the DSH allotment reduction under subclause (I) for the State for the fiscal year.

"(ii) AGGREGATE REDUCTIONS.—The aggregate reductions in DSH allotments for all States under clause (i)(I) shall be equal to—

"(I) $500,000,000 for fiscal year 2014;

"(II) $600,000,000 for fiscal year 2015;

"(III) $600,000,000 for fiscal year 2016;

"(IV) $1,800,000,000 for fiscal year 2017;

"(V) $5,000,000,000 for fiscal year 2018;

"(VI) $5,600,000,000 for fiscal year 2019; and

"(VII) $4,000,000,000 for fiscal year 2020.

The Secretary shall distribute such aggregate reductions among States in accordance with subparagraph (B).

"(iii) MANNER OF PAYMENT REDUCTION.—The amount of the payment reduction under clause (i)(II) for a State for a quarter shall be deemed an overpayment to the State under this title to be disallowed against the State's regular quarterly draw for all spending under section 1903(d)(2). Such a disallowance is not subject to a reconsideration under subsections (d) and (e) of section 1116.

"(iv) DEFINITION.—In this paragraph, the term 'State' means the 50 States and the District of Columbia.

"(B) DSH HEALTH REFORM METHODOLOGY.—The Secretary shall carry out subparagraph (A) through use of a DSH Health Reform methodology that meets the following requirements:

"(i) The methodology imposes the largest percentage reductions on the States that—

"(I) have the lowest percentages of uninsured individuals (determined on the basis of data from the Bureau of the Census, audited hospital cost reports, and other information likely to yield accurate data) during the most recent year for which such data are available; or

"(II) do not target their DSH payments on—

"(aa) hospitals with high volumes of Medicaid inpatients (as defined in subsection (b)(1)(A)); and

"(bb) hospitals that have high levels of uncompensated care (excluding bad debt).

"(ii) The methodology imposes a smaller percentage reduction on low DSH States described in paragraph (5)(B).

"(iii) The methodology takes into account the extent to which the DSH allotment for a State was included in the budget neutrality calculation for a coverage expansion approved under section 1115 as of July 31, 2009.".

(b) EXTENSION OF DSH ALLOTMENT.—Section 1923(f)(6)(A) of the Social Security Act (42 U.S.C. 1396r–4(f)(6)(A)) is amended by adding at the end the following:

"(v) ALLOTMENT FOR 2D, 3RD, AND 4TH QUARTERS OF FISCAL YEAR 2012 AND FOR FISCAL YEAR 2013.—Notwithstanding the table set forth in paragraph (2):

"(I) 2D, 3RD, AND 4TH QUARTERS OF FISCAL YEAR 2012.—In the case of a State that has a DSH allotment of $0 for the 2d, 3rd, and 4th quarters of fiscal year 2012, the DSH allotment shall be $47,200,000 for such quarters.

"(II) FISCAL YEAR 2013.—In the case of a State that has a DSH allotment of $0 for fiscal year 2013, the DSH allotment shall be $53,100,000 for such fiscal year.".

SEC. 1204. FUNDING FOR THE TERRITORIES.

(a) IN GENERAL.—Part III of subtitle D of title I of the Patient Protection and Affordable Care Act, as amended by section 10104(m) of such Act, is amended by inserting after section 1322 the following section:

"SEC. 1323. FUNDING FOR THE TERRITORIES.

"(a) IN GENERAL.—A territory that—

"(1) elects consistent with subsection (b) to establish an Exchange in accordance with part II of this subtitle and establishes such an Exchange in accordance with such part shall be treated as a State for purposes of such part and shall be entitled to payment from the amount allocated to the territory under subsection (c); or

"(2) does not make such election shall be entitled to an increase in the dollar limitation applicable to the territory under subsections (f) and (g) of section 1108 of the Social Security Act (42 U.S.C. 1308) for such period in such amount for such territory and such increase shall not be taken into account in computing any other amount under such subsections.

"(b) TERMS AND CONDITIONS.—An election under subsection (a)(1) shall—

"(1) not be effective unless the election is consistent with section 1321 and is received not later than October 1, 2013; and

"(2) be contingent upon entering into an agreement between the territory and the Secretary that requires that—

"(A) funds provided under the agreement shall be used only to provide premium and cost-sharing assistance to residents of the territory obtaining health insurance coverage through the Exchange; and

"(B) the premium and cost-sharing assistance provided under such agreement shall be structured in such a manner so as to prevent any gap in assistance for individuals between the income level at which medical assistance is available through the territory's Medicaid plan under title XIX of the Social Security Act and the income level at which premium and cost-sharing assistance is available under the agreement.

"(c) APPROPRIATION AND ALLOCATION.—

"(1) APPROPRIATION.—Out of any funds in the Treasury not otherwise appropriated, there is appropriated for purposes of payment pursuant to subsection (a) $1,000,000,000, to be available during the period beginning with 2014 and ending with 2019.

"(2) ALLOCATION.—The Secretary shall allocate the amount appropriated under paragraph (1) among the territories for purposes of carrying out this section as follows:

"(A) For Puerto Rico, $925,000,000.

"(B) For another territory, the portion of $75,000,000 specified by the Secretary.".

(b) MEDICAID FUNDING.—

(1) INCREASE IN FUNDING CAPS.—Section 1108(g) of the Social Security Act (42 U.S.C. 1308(g)), as amended by section 2005(a) of the Patient Protection and Affordable Care Act, is amended—

(A) in paragraph (2), by inserting "and section 1323(a)(2) of the Patient Protection and Affordable Care Act" after "subject to"; and

(B) by striking paragraph (5) and inserting the following:

"(5) ADDITIONAL INCREASE.—The Secretary shall increase the amounts otherwise determined under this subsection for Puerto Rico, the Virgin Islands, Guam, the Northern Mariana Islands, and American Samoa (after the application of subsection (f) and the preceding paragraphs of this subsection) for the period beginning July 1, 2011, and ending on September 30, 2019, by such amounts that the total additional payments under title XIX to such territories equals $6,300,000,000 for such period. The Secretary shall increase such amounts in proportion to the amounts applicable to such territories under this subsection and subsection (f) on the date of enactment of this paragraph.".

(2) DISREGARD OF PAYMENTS; INCREASED FMAP.—Section 2005 of the Patient Protection and Affordable Care Act is amended—

(A) by repealing subsection (b) (and the amendments made by that subsection) and section 1108(g)(4) of the Social Security Act shall be applied as if such amendments had never been enacted; and

(B) in subsection (c)(2), by striking "January" and inserting "July".

SEC. 1205. DELAY IN COMMUNITY FIRST CHOICE OPTION.

Section 1915(k)(1) of the Social Security Act (42 U.S.C. 1396n(k)), as added by section 2401 of the Patient Protection and Affordable Care Act, is amended by striking "October 1, 2010" and inserting "October 1, 2011".

SEC. 1206. DRUG REBATES FOR NEW FORMULATIONS OF EXISTING DRUGS.

(a) TREATMENT OF NEW FORMULATIONS.—Subparagraph (C) of section 1927(c)(2) of the Social Security Act (42 U.S.C. 1396r–8(c)(2)), as added by section 2501(d) of the Patient Protection and Affordable Care Act, is amended to read as follows:

"(C) TREATMENT OF NEW FORMULATIONS.—In the case of a drug that is a line extension of a single source drug or an innovator multiple source drug that is an oral solid dosage form, the rebate obligation with respect to such drug under this section shall be the amount computed under this section for such new drug or, if greater, the product of—

"(i) the average manufacturer price of the line extension of a single source drug or an innovator multiple source drug that is an oral solid dosage form;

"(ii) the highest additional rebate (calculated as a percentage of average manufacturer price) under this section for any strength of the original single source drug or innovator multiple source drug; and

"(iii) the total number of units of each dosage form and strength of the line extension product paid for under the State plan in the rebate period (as reported by the State).

In this subparagraph, the term 'line extension' means, with respect to a drug, a new formulation of the drug, such as an extended release formulation.".

(b) EFFECTIVE DATE.—The amendment made by subsection (a) shall take effect as if included in the enactment of the Patient Protection and Affordable Care Act.

Subtitle D—Reducing Fraud, Waste, and Abuse

SEC. 1301. COMMUNITY MENTAL HEALTH CENTERS.

(a) IN GENERAL.—Section 1861(ff)(3)(B) of the Social Security Act (42 U.S.C. 1395x(ff)(3)(B)) is amended—

(1) in clause (ii), by striking "and" at the end;

(2) by redesignating clause (iii) as clause (iv); and

(3) by inserting after clause (ii) the following:

"(iii) provides at least 40 percent of its services to individuals who are not eligible for benefits under this title; and".

(b) RESTRICTION.—Section 1861(ff)(3)(A) of such Act (42 U.S.C. 1395x(ff)(3)(A)) is amended by inserting "other than in an individual's home or in an inpatient or residential setting" before the period.

(c) EFFECTIVE DATE.—The amendments made by this section shall apply to items and services furnished on or after the first day of the first calendar quarter that begins at least 12 months after the date of the enactment of this Act.

SEC. 1302. MEDICARE PREPAYMENT MEDICAL REVIEW LIMITATIONS.

Section 1874A(h) of the Social Security Act (42 U.S.C. 1395w–3a(h)) is repealed.

SEC. 1303. FUNDING TO FIGHT FRAUD, WASTE, AND ABUSE.

(a) FUNDING TO FIGHT FRAUD, WASTE, AND ABUSE.—

(1) IN GENERAL.—Section 1817(k) of the Social Security Act (42 U.S.C. 1395i(k)), as amended by section 6402(i) of the Patient Protection and Affordable Care Act, is further amended—

(A) by adding at the end the following new paragraph:

"(8) ADDITIONAL FUNDING.—

"(A) IN GENERAL.—In addition to the funds otherwise appropriated to the Account from the Trust Fund under paragraphs (3)(C) and (4)(A) and for purposes described in paragraphs (3)(C) and (4)(A), there are hereby appropriated to such Account from such Trust Fund the following additional amounts:

"(i) For fiscal year 2011, $95,000,000.

"(ii) For fiscal year 2012, $55,000,000.

"(iii) For each of fiscal years 2013 and 2014, $30,000,000.

"(iv) For each of fiscal years 2015 and 2016, $20,000,000.

"(B) ALLOCATION.—The funds appropriated under this paragraph shall be allocated in the same proportion as the total funding appropriated with respect to paragraphs (3)(A) and (4)(A) was allocated with respect to fiscal year 2010, and shall be available without further appropriation until expended."; and

(B) in paragraph (4)(A), by inserting "for activities described in paragraph (3)(C) and" after "necessary".

(b) MEDICAID INTEGRITY PROGRAM.—Section 1936(e)(1) of such Act (42 U.S.C. 1396–u6(e)(1)) is amended—

(1) in subparagraph (B), by striking at the end "and";

(2) in subparagraph (C)—

(A) by striking "for each fiscal year thereafter" and inserting "for each of fiscal years 2009 and 2010"; and

(B) by striking the period and inserting "; and"; and

(3) by adding at the end the following new subparagraph:

"(D) for each fiscal year after fiscal year 2010, the amount appropriated under this paragraph for the previous fiscal year, increased by the percentage increase in the consumer price index for all urban consumers (all items; United States city average) over the previous year.".

SEC. 1304. 90-DAY PERIOD OF ENHANCED OVERSIGHT FOR INITIAL CLAIMS OF DME SUPPLIERS.

Section 1866(j), as amended by section 6401 of the Patient Protection and Affordable Care Act, is further amended—

(1) by redesignating paragraphs (4) through (7) as paragraphs (5) through (8), respectively; and

(2) by inserting after paragraph (3) the following new paragraph:

"(4) 90-DAY PERIOD OF ENHANCED OVERSIGHT FOR INITIAL CLAIMS OF DME SUPPLIERS.—For periods beginning after January 1, 2011, if the Secretary determines that there is a significant risk of fraudulent activity among suppliers of durable medical equipment, in the case of a supplier of durable medical equipment who is within a category or geographic area under title XVIII identified pursuant to such determination and who is initially enrolling under such title, the Secretary shall, notwithstanding sections 1816(c), 1842(c), and 1869(a)(2), withhold payment under such title with respect to durable medical equipment furnished by such supplier during the 90-day period beginning on the date of the first submission of a claim under such title for durable medical equipment furnished by such supplier.".

Subtitle E—Provisions Relating to Revenue

SEC. 1401. HIGH-COST PLAN EXCISE TAX.

(a) IN GENERAL.—Section 4980I of the Internal Revenue Code of 1986, as added by section 9001 of the Patient Protection and Affordable Care Act and amended by section 10901 of such Act, is amended—

(1) in subsection (b)(3)(B)—

(A) by striking "The annual" and inserting the following:

"(i) IN GENERAL.—Except as provided in clause (ii), the annual"; and

(B) by adding at the end the following new clause:

"(ii) MULTIEMPLOYER PLAN COVERAGE.—Any coverage provided under a multiemployer plan (as defined in section 414(f)) shall be treated as coverage other than self-only coverage.";

(2) in subsection (b)(3)(C)—

(A) by striking "Except as provided in subparagraph (D)—";

(B) in clause (i)—

(i) by striking "2013" each place it appears in the heading and the text and inserting "2018";

(ii) by striking "$8,500" in subclause (I) and inserting "$10,200 multiplied by the health cost adjustment percentage (determined by only taking into account self-only coverage)"; and

(iii) by striking "$23,000" in subclause (II) and inserting "$27,500 multiplied by the health cost adjustment percentage (determined by only taking into account coverage other than self-only coverage)";

(C) by redesignating clauses (ii) and (iii) as clauses (iv) and (v), respectively, and by inserting after clause (i) the following new clauses:

"(ii) HEALTH COST ADJUSTMENT PERCENTAGE.—For purposes of clause (i), the health cost adjustment percentage is equal to 100 percent plus the excess (if any) of—

"(I) the percentage by which the per employee cost for providing coverage under the Blue Cross/Blue Shield standard benefit option under the Federal Employees Health Benefits Plan for plan year 2018 (determined by using the benefit package for such coverage in 2010) exceeds such cost for plan year 2010, over

"(II) 55 percent.

"(iii) AGE AND GENDER ADJUSTMENT.—

"(I) IN GENERAL.—The amount determined under subclause (I) or (II) of clause (i), whichever is applicable, for any taxable period shall be increased by the amount determined under subclause (II).

"(II) AMOUNT DETERMINED.—The amount determined under this subclause is an amount equal to the excess (if any) of—

"(aa) the premium cost of the Blue Cross/ Blue Shield standard benefit option under the Federal Employees Health Benefits Plan for the type of coverage provided such individual in such taxable period if priced for the age and gender characteristics of all employees of the individual's employer, over

"(bb) that premium cost for the provision of such coverage under such option in such taxable period if priced for the age and gender characteristics of the national workforce.".

(D) in clause (iv), as redesignated by subparagraph (C)—

(i) by inserting "covered by the plan" after "whose employees"; and

(ii) by striking subclauses (I) and (II) and inserting the following:

"(I) the dollar amount in clause (i)(I) shall be increased by $1,650, and

"(II) the dollar amount in clause (i)(II) shall be increased by $3,450,", and

(E) in clause (v), as redesignated by subparagraph (C)—

(i) by striking "2013" and inserting "2018";

(ii) by striking "clauses (i) and (ii)" and inserting "clauses (i) (after the application of clause (ii)) and (iv)"; and

(iii) by inserting "in the case of determinations for calendar years beginning before 2020" after "1 percentage point" in subclause (II) thereof;

(3) by striking subparagraph (D) of subsection (b)(3);

(4) in subsection (d)(1)(B), by redesignating clause (ii) as clause (iii) and by inserting after clause (i) the following new clause:

"(ii) any coverage under a separate policy, certificate, or contract of insurance which provides benefits substantially all of which are for treatment of the mouth (including any organ or structure within the mouth) or for treatment of the eye, or"; and

(5) in subsection (d), by adding at the end the following new paragraph:

"(3) EMPLOYEE.—The term 'employee' includes any former employee, surviving spouse, or other primary insured individual.".

(b) EFFECTIVE DATES.—

(1) Section 9001(c) of the Patient Protection and Affordable Care Act is amended by striking "2012" and inserting "2017".

(2) Section 10901(c) of the Patient Protection and Affordable Care Act is amended by striking "2012" and inserting "2017".

SEC. 1402. UNEARNED INCOME MEDICARE CONTRIBUTION.

(a) INVESTMENT INCOME.—

(1) IN GENERAL.—Subtitle A of the Internal Revenue Code of 1986 is amended by inserting after chapter 2 the following new chapter:

"CHAPTER 2A—UNEARNED INCOME MEDICARE CONTRIBUTION

"SEC. 1411. IMPOSITION OF TAX.

"(a) IN GENERAL.—Except as provided in subsection (e)—

"(1) APPLICATION TO INDIVIDUALS.—In the case of an individual, there is hereby imposed (in addition to any other tax imposed by this subtitle) for each taxable year a tax equal to 3.8 percent of the lesser of—

"(A) net investment income for such taxable year, or

"(B) the excess (if any) of—

"(i) the modified adjusted gross income for such taxable year, over

"(ii) the threshold amount.

"(2) APPLICATION TO ESTATES AND TRUSTS.—In the case of an estate or trust, there is hereby imposed (in addition to any other tax imposed by this subtitle) for each taxable year a tax of 3.8 percent of the lesser of—

"(A) the undistributed net investment income for such taxable year, or

"(B) the excess (if any) of—

"(i) the adjusted gross income (as defined in section 67(e)) for such taxable year, over

"(ii) the dollar amount at which the highest tax bracket in section 1(e) begins for such taxable year.

"(b) THRESHOLD AMOUNT.—For purposes of this chapter, the term 'threshold amount' means—

"(1) in the case of a taxpayer making a joint return under section 6013 or a surviving spouse (as defined in section 2(a)), $250,000,

"(2) in the case of a married taxpayer (as defined in section 7703) filing a separate return, ½ of the dollar amount determined under paragraph (1), and

"(3) in any other case, $200,000.

"(c) NET INVESTMENT INCOME.—For purposes of this chapter—

"(1) IN GENERAL.—The term 'net investment income' means the excess (if any) of—

"(A) the sum of—

"(i) gross income from interest, dividends, annuities, royalties, and rents, other than such income which is derived in the ordinary course of a trade or business not described in paragraph (2),

"(ii) other gross income derived from a trade or business described in paragraph (2), and

"(iii) net gain (to the extent taken into account in computing taxable income) attributable to the disposition of property other than property held in a trade or business not described in paragraph (2), over

"(B) the deductions allowed by this subtitle which are properly allocable to such gross income or net gain.

"(2) TRADES AND BUSINESSES TO WHICH TAX APPLIES.—A trade or business is described in this paragraph if such trade or business is—

"(A) a passive activity (within the meaning of section 469) with respect to the taxpayer, or

"(B) a trade or business of trading in financial instruments or commodities (as defined in section 475(e)(2)).

"(3) INCOME ON INVESTMENT OF WORKING CAPITAL SUBJECT TO TAX.—A rule similar to the rule of section 469(e)(1)(B) shall apply for purposes of this subsection.

"(4) EXCEPTION FOR CERTAIN ACTIVE INTERESTS IN PARTNERSHIPS AND S CORPORATIONS.—In the case of a disposition of an interest in a partnership or S corporation—

"(A) gain from such disposition shall be taken into account under clause (iii) of paragraph (1)(A) only to the extent of the net gain which would be so taken into account by the transferor if all property of the partnership or S corporation were sold for fair market value immediately before the disposition of such interest, and

"(B) a rule similar to the rule of subparagraph (A) shall apply to a loss from such disposition.

"(5) EXCEPTION FOR DISTRIBUTIONS FROM QUALIFIED PLANS.—The term 'net investment income' shall not include any distribution from a plan or arrangement described in section 401(a), 403(a), 403(b), 408, 408A, or 457(b).

"(6) SPECIAL RULE.—Net investment income shall not include any item taken into account in determining self-employment income for such taxable year on which a tax is imposed by section 1401(b).

"(d) MODIFIED ADJUSTED GROSS INCOME.—For purposes of this chapter, the term 'modified adjusted gross income' means adjusted gross income increased by the excess of—

"(1) the amount excluded from gross income under section 911(a)(1), over

"(2) the amount of any deductions (taken into account in computing adjusted gross income) or exclusions disallowed under section 911(d)(6) with respect to the amounts described in paragraph (1).

"(e) NONAPPLICATION OF SECTION.—This section shall not apply to—

"(1) a nonresident alien, or

"(2) a trust all of the unexpired interests in which are devoted to one or more of the purposes described in section 170(c)(2)(B).".

(2) ESTIMATED TAXES.—Section 6654 of the Internal Revenue Code of 1986 is amended—

(A) in subsection (a), by striking "and the tax under chapter 2" and inserting "the tax under chapter 2, and the tax under chapter 2A"; and

(B) in subsection (f)—

(i) by striking "minus" at the end of paragraph (2) and inserting "plus"; and

(ii) by redesignating paragraph (3) as paragraph (4) and inserting after paragraph (2) the following new paragraph:

"(3) the taxes imposed by chapter 2A, minus".

(3) CLERICAL AMENDMENT.—The table of chapters for subtitle A of chapter 1 of the Internal Revenue Code of 1986 is amended by inserting after the item relating to chapter 2 the following new item:

"CHAPTER 2A—UNEARNED INCOME MEDICARE CONTRIBUTION".

(4) EFFECTIVE DATES.—The amendments made by this subsection shall apply to taxable years beginning after December 31, 2012.

(b) EARNED INCOME.—

(1) THRESHOLD.—

(A) FICA.—Paragraph (2) of section 3101(b) of the Internal Revenue Code of 1986, as added by section 9015 of the Patient Protection and Affordable Care Act and amended by section 10906 of such Act, is amended by striking "and" at the end of subparagraph (A), by redesignating subparagraph (B) as subparagraph (C), and by inserting after subparagraph (A) the following new subparagraph:

"(B) in the case of a married taxpayer (as defined in section 7703) filing a separate return, ½ of the dollar amount determined under subparagraph (A), and".

(B) SECA.—Section 1401(b)(2) of the Internal Revenue Code of 1986, as added by section 9015 of the Patient Protection and Affordable Care Act and amended by section 10906 of such Act, is amended—

(i) in subparagraph (A), by striking "and" at the end of clause (i), by redesignating clause (ii) as clause (iii), and by inserting after clause (i) the following new clause:

"(ii) in the case of a married taxpayer (as defined in section 7703) filing a separate return, ½ of the dollar amount determined under clause (i), and"; and

(ii) in subparagraph (B), by striking "under clauses (i) and (ii)" and inserting "under clause (i), (ii), or (iii) (whichever is applicable)".

(2) ESTIMATED TAXES.—Section 6654 of the Internal Revenue Code of 1986 is amended by redesignating subsection (m) as subsection (n) and by inserting after subsection (l) the following new subsection:

"(m) SPECIAL RULE FOR MEDICARE TAX.—For purposes of this section, the tax imposed under section 3101(b)(2) (to the extent not withheld) shall be treated as a tax imposed under chapter 2.".

(3) EFFECTIVE DATE.—The amendments made by this subsection shall apply with respect to remuneration received, and taxable years beginning after, December 31, 2012.

SEC. 1403. DELAY OF LIMITATION ON HEALTH FLEXIBLE SPENDING ARRANGEMENTS UNDER CAFETERIA PLANS.

(a) IN GENERAL.—Section 10902(b) of the Patient Protection and Affordable Care Act is amended by striking "December 31, 2010" and inserting "December 31, 2012".

(b) INFLATION ADJUSTMENT.—Paragraph (2) of section 125(i) of the Internal Revenue Code of 1986, as added by section 9005 of the Patient Protection and Affordable Care Act and amended by section 10902 of such Act, is amended—

(1) in the matter preceding subparagraph (A), by striking "December 31, 2011" and inserting "December 31, 2013"; and

(2) in subparagraph (B), by striking "2010" and inserting "2012".

SEC. 1404. BRAND NAME PHARMACEUTICALS.

(a) IN GENERAL.—Section 9008 of the Patient Protection and Affordable Care Act is amended—

(1) in subsection (a)(1), by striking "2009" and inserting "2010";

(2) in subsection (b)—

(A) by striking "$2,300,000,000" in paragraph (1) and inserting "the applicable amount"; and

(B) by adding at the end the following new paragraph:

"(4) APPLICABLE AMOUNT.—For purposes of paragraph (1), the applicable amount shall be determined in accordance with the following table:

"Calendar year	Applicable amount
2011	$2,500,000,000
2012	$2,800,000,000
2013	$2,800,000,000
2014	$3,000,000,000
2015	$3,000,000,000
2016	$3,000,000,000
2017	$4,000,000,000
2018	$4,100,000,000
2019 and thereafter	$2,800,000,000.";

(3) in subsection (d), by adding at the end the following new paragraph:

"(3) JOINT AND SEVERAL LIABILITY.—If more than one person is liable for payment of the fee under subsection (a) with respect to a single covered entity by reason of the application of paragraph (2), all such persons shall be jointly and severally liable for payment of such fee."; and

(4) by striking subsection (j) and inserting the following new subsection:

"(j) EFFECTIVE DATE.—This section shall apply to calendar years beginning after December 31, 2010.".

(b) EFFECTIVE DATE.—The amendments made by this section shall take effect as if included in section 9008 of the Patient Protection and Affordable Care Act.

SEC. 1405. EXCISE TAX ON MEDICAL DEVICE MANUFACTURERS.

(a) IN GENERAL.—Chapter 32 of the Internal Revenue Code of 1986 is amended—

(1) by inserting after subchapter D the following new subchapter:

"Subchapter E—Medical Devices

"SEC. 4191. MEDICAL DEVICES.

"(a) IN GENERAL.—There is hereby imposed on the sale of any taxable medical device by the manufacturer, producer, or importer a tax equal to 2.3 percent of the price for which so sold.

"(b) TAXABLE MEDICAL DEVICE.—For purposes of this section—

"(1) IN GENERAL.—The term 'taxable medical device' means any device (as defined in section 201(h) of the Federal Food, Drug, and Cosmetic Act) intended for humans.

"(2) EXEMPTIONS.—Such term shall not include—

"(A) eyeglasses,
"(B) contact lenses,
"(C) hearing aids, and
"(D) any other medical device determined by the Secretary to be of a type which is generally purchased by the general public at retail for individual use.", and

(2) by inserting after the item relating to subchapter D in the table of subchapters for such chapter the following new item:

"SUBCHAPTER E. MEDICAL DEVICES".

(b) CERTAIN EXEMPTIONS NOT TO APPLY.—

(1) Section 4221(a) of the Internal Revenue Code of 1986 is amended by adding at the end the following new sentence: "In the case of the tax imposed by section 4191, paragraphs (3), (4), (5), and (6) shall not apply.".

(2) Section 6416(b)(2) of such Code is amended by adding at the end the following: "In the case of the tax imposed by section 4191, subparagraphs (B), (C), (D), and (E) shall not apply.".

(c) EFFECTIVE DATE.—The amendments made by this section shall apply to sales after December 31, 2012.

(d) REPEAL OF SECTION 9009 OF THE PATIENT PROTECTION AND AFFORDABLE CARE ACT.—Section 9009 of the Patient Protection and Affordable Care Act, as amended by section 10904 of such Act, is repealed effective as of the date of enactment of that Act.

SEC. 1406. HEALTH INSURANCE PROVIDERS.

(a) IN GENERAL.—Section 9010 of the Patient Protection and Affordable Care Act, as amended by section 10905 of such Act, is amended—

(1) in subsection (a)(1), by striking "2010" and inserting "2013";

(2) in subsection (b)(2)—

(A) by striking "For purposes of paragraph (1), the net premiums" and inserting "For purposes of paragraph (1)—

"(A) IN GENERAL.—The net premiums"; and

(B) by adding at the end the following subparagraph:

"(B) PARTIAL EXCLUSION FOR CERTAIN EXEMPT ACTIVITIES.—After the application of subparagraph (A), only 50 percent of the remaining net premiums written with respect to health insurance for any United States health risk that are attributable to the activities (other than activities of an unrelated trade or business as defined in section 513 of the Internal Revenue Code of 1986) of any covered entity qualifying under paragraph (3), (4), (26), or (29) of section 501(c) of such Code and exempt from tax under section 501(a) of such Code shall be taken into account.";

(3) in subsection (c)—

(A) by inserting "during the calendar year in which the fee under this section is due" in paragraph (1) after "risk";

(B) in paragraph (2), by striking subparagraphs (C), (D), and (E) and inserting the following new subparagraphs:

"(C) any entity—

"(i) which is incorporated as a nonprofit corporation under a State law,

"(ii) no part of the net earnings of which inures to the benefit of any private shareholder or individual, no substantial part of the activities of which is carrying on propaganda, or otherwise attempting, to influence legislation (except as otherwise provided in section 501(h) of the Internal Revenue Code of 1986), and which does not participate in, or intervene in (including the publishing or distributing of statements), any political campaign on behalf of (or in opposition to) any candidate for public office, and

"(iii) more than 80 percent of the gross revenues of which is received from government programs that target low-income, elderly, or disabled populations under titles XVIII, XIX, and XXI of the Social Security Act, and

"(D) any entity which is described in section 501(c)(9) of such Code and which is established by an entity (other than by an employer or employers) for purposes of providing health care benefits.";

(C) in paragraph (3)(A), by striking "subparagraph (C)(i)(I), (D)(i)(I), or (E)(i)" and inserting "subparagraph (C) or (D)"; and

(D) by adding at the end the following new paragraph:

"(4) JOINT AND SEVERAL LIABILITY.—If more than one person is liable for payment of the fee under subsection (a) with respect to a single covered entity by reason of the application of paragraph (3), all such persons shall be jointly and severally liable for payment of such fee.";

(4) by striking subsection (e) and inserting the following:

"(e) APPLICABLE AMOUNT.—For purposes of subsection (b)(1)—

"(1) YEARS BEFORE 2019.—In the case of calendar years beginning before 2019, the applicable amount shall be determined in accordance with the following table:

"Calendar year	Applicable amount
2014	$8,000,000,000
2015	$11,300,000,000
2016	$11,300,000,000
2017	$13,900,000,000
2018	$14,300,000,000.

"(2) YEARS AFTER 2018.—In the case of any calendar year beginning after 2018, the applicable amount shall be the applicable amount for the preceding calendar year increased by the rate of premium growth (within the meaning of section 36B(b)(3)(A)(ii) of the Internal Revenue Code of 1986) for such preceding calendar year.";

(5) in subsection (g), by adding at the end the following new paragraphs:

"(3) ACCURACY-RELATED PENALTY.—

"(A) IN GENERAL.—In the case of any understatement of a covered entity's net premiums written with respect to health insurance for any United States health risk for any calendar year, there shall be paid by the covered entity making such understatement, an amount equal to the excess of—

"(i) the amount of the covered entity's fee under this section for the calendar year the Secretary determines should have been paid in the absence of any such understatement, over

"(ii) the amount of such fee the Secretary determined based on such understatement.

"(B) UNDERSTATEMENT.—For purposes of this paragraph, an understatement of a covered entity's net premiums written with respect to health insurance for any United States health risk for any calendar year is the difference between the amount of such net premiums written as reported on the return filed by the covered entity under paragraph (1) and the amount of such net premiums written that should have been reported on such return.

"(C) TREATMENT OF PENALTY.—The penalty imposed under subparagraph (A) shall be subject to the provisions of subtitle F of the Internal Revenue Code of 1986 that apply to assessable penalties imposed under chapter 68 of such Code.

"(4) TREATMENT OF INFORMATION.—Section 6103 of the Internal Revenue Code of 1986 shall not apply to any information reported under this subsection."; and

(6) by striking subsection (j) and inserting the following new subsection:

"(j) EFFECTIVE DATE.—This section shall apply to calendar years beginning after December 31, 2013.".

(b) EFFECTIVE DATE.—The amendments made by this section shall take effect as if included in section 9010 of the Patient Protection and Affordable Care Act.

SEC. 1407. DELAY OF ELIMINATION OF DEDUCTION FOR EXPENSES ALLOCABLE TO MEDICARE PART D SUBSIDY.

Section 9012(b) of the Patient Protection and Affordable Care Act is amended by striking "2010" and inserting "2012".

SEC. 1408. ELIMINATION OF UNINTENDED APPLICATION OF CELLULOSIC BIOFUEL PRODUCER CREDIT.

(a) IN GENERAL.—Section 40(b)(6)(E) of the Internal Revenue Code of 1986 is amended by adding at the end the following new clause:

"(iii) EXCLUSION OF UNPROCESSED FUELS.—The term 'cellulosic biofuel' shall not include any fuel if—

"(I) more than 4 percent of such fuel (determined by weight) is any combination of water and sediment, or

"(II) the ash content of such fuel is more than 1 percent (determined by weight).".

(b) EFFECTIVE DATE.—The amendment made by this section shall apply to fuels sold or used on or after January 1, 2010.

SEC. 1409. CODIFICATION OF ECONOMIC SUBSTANCE DOCTRINE AND PENALTIES.

(a) IN GENERAL.—Section 7701 of the Internal Revenue Code of 1986 is amended by redesignating subsection (o) as subsection (p) and by inserting after subsection (n) the following new subsection:

"(o) CLARIFICATION OF ECONOMIC SUBSTANCE DOCTRINE.—

"(1) APPLICATION OF DOCTRINE.—In the case of any transaction to which the economic substance doctrine is relevant, such transaction shall be treated as having economic substance only if—

"(A) the transaction changes in a meaningful way (apart from Federal income tax effects) the taxpayer's economic position, and

"(B) the taxpayer has a substantial purpose (apart from Federal income tax effects) for entering into such transaction.

"(2) SPECIAL RULE WHERE TAXPAYER RELIES ON PROFIT POTENTIAL.—

"(A) IN GENERAL.—The potential for profit of a transaction shall be taken into account in determining whether the requirements of subparagraphs (A) and (B) of paragraph (1) are met with respect to the transaction only if the present value of the reasonably expected pre-tax profit from the transaction is substantial in relation to the present value of the expected net tax benefits that would be allowed if the transaction were respected.

"(B) TREATMENT OF FEES AND FOREIGN TAXES.—Fees and other transaction expenses shall be taken into account as expenses in determining pre-tax profit under subparagraph (A). The Secretary shall issue regulations requiring foreign taxes to be treated as expenses in determining pre-tax profit in appropriate cases.

"(3) STATE AND LOCAL TAX BENEFITS.—For purposes of paragraph (1), any State or local income tax effect which is related to a Federal income tax effect shall be treated in the same manner as a Federal income tax effect.

"(4) FINANCIAL ACCOUNTING BENEFITS.—For purposes of paragraph (1)(B), achieving a financial accounting benefit shall not be taken into account as a purpose for entering into a transaction if the origin of such financial accounting benefit is a reduction of Federal income tax.

"(5) DEFINITIONS AND SPECIAL RULES.—For purposes of this subsection—

"(A) ECONOMIC SUBSTANCE DOCTRINE.—The term 'economic substance doctrine' means the common law doctrine under which tax benefits under subtitle A with respect to a transaction are not allowable if the transaction does not have economic substance or lacks a business purpose.

"(B) EXCEPTION FOR PERSONAL TRANSACTIONS OF INDIVIDUALS.—In the case of an individual, paragraph (1) shall apply only to transactions entered into in connection with a trade or business or an activity engaged in for the production of income.

"(C) DETERMINATION OF APPLICATION OF DOCTRINE NOT AFFECTED.—The determination of whether the economic substance doctrine is relevant to a transaction shall be made in the same manner as if this subsection had never been enacted.

"(D) TRANSACTION.—The term 'transaction' includes a series of transactions.".

(b) PENALTY FOR UNDERPAYMENTS ATTRIBUTABLE TO TRANSACTIONS LACKING ECONOMIC SUBSTANCE.—

(1) IN GENERAL.—Subsection (b) of section 6662 is amended by inserting after paragraph (5) the following new paragraph:

"(6) Any disallowance of claimed tax benefits by reason of a transaction lacking economic substance (within the meaning of section 7701(o)) or failing to meet the requirements of any similar rule of law.".

(2) INCREASED PENALTY FOR NONDISCLOSED TRANSACTIONS.—Section 6662 is amended by adding at the end the following new subsection:

"(i) INCREASE IN PENALTY IN CASE OF NONDISCLOSED NONECONOMIC SUBSTANCE TRANSACTIONS.—

"(1) IN GENERAL.—In the case of any portion of an underpayment which is attributable to one or more nondisclosed noneconomic substance transactions, subsection (a) shall be applied with respect to such portion by substituting '40 percent' for '20 percent'.

"(2) NONDISCLOSED NONECONOMIC SUBSTANCE TRANSACTIONS.—For purposes of this subsection, the term 'nondisclosed noneconomic substance transaction' means any portion of a transaction described in subsection (b)(6) with respect to which the relevant facts affecting the tax treatment are not adequately disclosed in the return nor in a statement attached to the return.

"(3) SPECIAL RULE FOR AMENDED RETURNS.—In no event shall any amendment or supplement to a return of tax be taken into account for purposes of this subsection if the amendment or supplement is filed after the earlier of the date the taxpayer is first contacted by the Secretary regarding the examination of the return or such other date as is specified by the Secretary.".

(3) CONFORMING AMENDMENT.—Subparagraph (B) of section 6662A(e)(2) is amended—

(A) by striking "section 6662(h)" and inserting "subsections (h) or (i) of section 6662"; and

(B) by striking "GROSS VALUATION MISSTATEMENT PENALTY" in the heading and inserting "CERTAIN INCREASED UNDERPAYMENT PENALTIES".

(c) REASONABLE CAUSE EXCEPTION NOT APPLICABLE TO NONECONOMIC SUBSTANCE TRANSACTIONS.—

(1) REASONABLE CAUSE EXCEPTION FOR UNDERPAYMENTS.—Subsection (c) of section 6664 is amended—

(A) by redesignating paragraphs (2) and (3) as paragraphs (3) and (4), respectively;

(B) by striking "paragraph (2)" in paragraph (4)(A), as so redesignated, and inserting "paragraph (3)"; and

(C) by inserting after paragraph (1) the following new paragraph:

"(2) EXCEPTION.—Paragraph (1) shall not apply to any portion of an underpayment which is attributable to one or more transactions described in section 6662(b)(6).".

(2) REASONABLE CAUSE EXCEPTION FOR REPORTABLE TRANSACTION UNDERSTATEMENTS.—Subsection (d) of section 6664 is amended—

(A) by redesignating paragraphs (2) and (3) as paragraphs (3) and (4), respectively;

(B) by striking "paragraph (2)(C)" in paragraph (4), as so redesignated, and inserting "paragraph (3)(C)"; and

(C) by inserting after paragraph (1) the following new paragraph:

"(2) EXCEPTION.—Paragraph (1) shall not apply to any portion of a reportable transaction understatement which is attributable to one or more transactions described in section 6662(b)(6).".

(d) APPLICATION OF PENALTY FOR ERRONEOUS CLAIM FOR REFUND OR CREDIT TO NONECONOMIC SUBSTANCE TRANSACTIONS.—Section 6676 is amended by redesignating subsection (c) as subsection (d) and inserting after subsection (b) the following new subsection:

"(c) NONECONOMIC SUBSTANCE TRANSACTIONS TREATED AS LACKING REASONABLE BASIS.—For purposes of this section, any excessive amount which is attributable to any transaction described in section 6662(b)(6) shall not be treated as having a reasonable basis.".

(e) EFFECTIVE DATE.—

(1) IN GENERAL.—Except as otherwise provided in this subsection, the amendments made by this section shall apply to transactions entered into after the date of the enactment of this Act.

(2) UNDERPAYMENTS.—The amendments made by subsections (b) and (c)(1) shall apply to underpayments attributable to transactions entered into after the date of the enactment of this Act.

(3) UNDERSTATEMENTS.—The amendments made by subsection (c)(2) shall apply to understatements attributable to transactions entered into after the date of the enactment of this Act.

(4) REFUNDS AND CREDITS.—The amendment made by subsection (d) shall apply to refunds and credits attributable to transactions entered into after the date of the enactment of this Act.

SEC. 1410. TIME FOR PAYMENT OF CORPORATE ESTIMATED TAXES.

The percentage under paragraph (1) of section 202(b) of the Corporate Estimated Tax Shift Act of 2009 in effect on the date of the enactment of this Act is increased by 15.75 percentage points.

Subtitle F—Other Provisions

SEC. 1501. COMMUNITY COLLEGE AND CAREER TRAINING GRANT PROGRAM.

Section 279(b) of the Trade Act of 1974 (19 U.S.C. 2372a(b)) is amended by striking "SUPPLEMENT" and all that follows through "Funds" and inserting "There are" and by striking "pursuant" and all that follows and inserting "$500,000,000 for each of fiscal years 2011, 2012, 2013, and 2014 to carry out this subchapter, except that the limitations contained in section 278(a)(2) shall not apply to such funds and each State shall receive not less than 0.5 percent of the amount appropriated pursuant to this subsection for each such fiscal year.".

TITLE II—EDUCATION AND HEALTH

Subtitle A—Education

SEC. 2001. SHORT TITLE; REFERENCES.

(a) SHORT TITLE.—This subtitle may be cited as the "SAFRA Act".

(b) REFERENCES.—Except as otherwise expressly provided, whenever in this subtitle an amendment or repeal is expressed in terms of an amendment to, or repeal of, a section or other provision, the reference shall be considered to be made to a section or other provision of the Higher Education Act of 1965 (20 U.S.C. 1001 et seq.).

PART I—INVESTING IN STUDENTS AND FAMILIES

SEC. 2101. FEDERAL PELL GRANTS.

(a) AMOUNT OF GRANTS.—Section 401(b) (20 U.S.C. 1070a(b)) is amended—

(1) by amending paragraph (2)(A) to read as follows:

"(A) The amount of the Federal Pell Grant for a student eligible under this part shall be—

"(i) the maximum Federal Pell Grant, as specified in the last enacted appropriation Act applicable to that award year, plus

"(ii) the amount of the increase calculated under paragraph (8)(B) for that year, less

"(iii) an amount equal to the amount determined to be the expected family contribution with respect to that student for that year."; and

(2) in paragraph (8)—

(A) in subparagraph (A)—

(i) in the matter preceding clause (i), by striking ", to carry out subparagraph (B) of this paragraph"; and

(ii) by striking clauses (iii) through (x) and inserting the following:

"(iii) to carry out subparagraph (B) of this paragraph, such sums as may be necessary for fiscal year 2010 and each subsequent fiscal year to provide the amount of increase of the maximum Federal Pell Grant required by clauses (ii) and (iii) of subparagraph (B); and

"(iv) to carry out this section, $13,500,000,000 for fiscal year 2011.";

(B) in subparagraph (B)—

(i) in the matter preceding clause (i), by striking "subparagraph (A)" and inserting "clauses (i) through (iii) of subparagraph (A)";

(ii) in clause (ii), by striking "and 2011–2012" and inserting ", 2011–2012, and 2012–2013"; and

(iii) by striking clause (iii) and inserting the following:

"(iii) the amount determined under subparagraph (C) for each succeeding award year."; and

(C) by striking subparagraph (C) and inserting the following:

"(C) ADJUSTMENT AMOUNTS.—

"(i) AWARD YEAR 2013–2014.—For award year 2013–2014, the amount determined under this subparagraph for purposes of subparagraph (B)(iii) shall be equal to—

"(I) $5,550 or the total maximum Federal Pell Grant for the preceding award year (as determined under clause (v)(II)), whichever is greater, increased by a percentage equal to the annual adjustment percentage for award year 2013–2014, reduced by

"(II) $4,860 or the maximum Federal Pell Grant for which a student was eligible for the preceding award year, as specified in the last enacted appropriation Act applicable to that year, whichever is greater; and

"(III) rounded to the nearest $5.

"(ii) AWARD YEARS 2014–2015 THROUGH 2017–2018.—For each of the award years 2014–2015 through 2017–2018, the amount determined under this subparagraph for purposes of subparagraph (B)(iii) shall be equal to—

"(I) the total maximum Federal Pell Grant for the preceding award year (as determined under clause (v)(II)), increased by a percentage equal to the annual adjustment percentage for the award year for which the amount under this subparagraph is being determined, reduced by

"(II) $4,860 or the maximum Federal Pell Grant for which a student was eligible for the preceding award year, as specified in the last enacted appropriation Act applicable to that year, whichever is greater; and

"(III) rounded to the nearest $5.

"(iii) SUBSEQUENT AWARD YEARS.—For award year 2018–2019 and each subsequent award year, the amount determined under this subparagraph for purposes of subparagraph (B)(iii) shall be equal to the amount determined under clause (ii) for award year 2017–2018.

"(iv) DEFINITIONS.—For purposes of this subparagraph—

"(I) the term 'annual adjustment percentage' as applied to an award year, is equal to the estimated percentage change in the Consumer Price Index (as determined by the Secretary, using the definition in section 478(f)) for the most recent calendar year ending prior to the beginning of that award year; and

"(II) the term 'total maximum Federal Pell Grant' as applied to a preceding award year, is equal to the sum of—

"(aa) the maximum Federal Pell Grant for which a student is eligible during an award year, as specified in the last enacted appropriation Act applicable to that preceding award year; and

"(bb) the amount of the increase in the maximum Federal Pell Grant required by this paragraph for that preceding award year.".

(b) CONFORMING AMENDMENTS.—Title IV (20 U.S.C. 1070 et seq.) is further amended—

(1) in section 401(b) (20 U.S.C. 1070a(b))—

(A) in paragraph (4)—

(i) by striking "maximum basic grant level specified in the appropriate appropriation Act" and inserting "maximum amount of a Federal Pell Grant award determined under paragraph (2)(A)"; and

(ii) by striking "such level" each place it appears and inserting "such Federal Pell Grant amount" in each such place; and

(B) in paragraph (6), by striking "the grant level specified in the appropriate Appropriation Act for this subpart for such year" and inserting "the maximum amount of a Federal Pell Grant award determined under paragraph (2)(A), for which a student is eligible during such award year";

(2) in section 402D(d)(1) (20 U.S.C. 1070a–14(d)(1)), by striking "exceed the maximum" and all that follows through "Grant, for" and inserting "exceed the Federal Pell Grant amount, determined under section 401(b)(2)(A), for which a student is eligible, or be less than the minimum Federal Pell Grant amount described in section 401(b)(4), for";

(3) in section 435(a)(5)(A)(i)(I) (20 U.S.C. 1085(a)(5)(A)(i)(I)), by striking "one-half the maximum Federal Pell Grant award for which a student would be eligible" and inserting "one-half the Federal Pell Grant amount, determined under section 401(b)(2)(A), for which a student would be eligible";

(4) in section 483(e)(3)(A)(ii) (20 U.S.C. 1090(e)(3)(A)(ii)), by striking "based on the maximum Federal Pell Grant award at the time of application" and inserting "based on the Federal Pell Grant amount, determined under section 401(b)(2)(A), for which a student is eligible at the time of application";

(5) in section 485E(b)(1)(A) (20 U.S.C. 1092f(b)(1)(A)), by striking "of such students' potential eligibility for a maximum Federal Pell Grant under subpart 1 of part A" and inserting "of such students' potential eligibility for the Federal Pell Grant amount, determined under section 401(b)(2)(A), for which the student would be eligible"; and

(6) in section 894(f)(2)(C)(ii)(I) (20 U.S.C. 1161y(f)(2)(C)(ii)(I)), by striking "the maximum Federal Pell Grant for each award year" and inserting "the Federal Pell Grant amount, determined under section 401(b)(2)(A), for which a student may be eligible for each award year".

(c) EFFECTIVE DATE.—The amendments made by subsections (a) and (b) shall take effect on July 1, 2010.

SEC. 2102. COLLEGE ACCESS CHALLENGE GRANT PROGRAM.

Section 781 (20 U.S.C. 1141) is amended—

(1) in the first sentence of subsection (a), by striking "$66,000,000" and all that follows through the period and inserting "$150,000,000 for each of the fiscal years 2010 through 2014. The authority to award grants under this section shall expire at the end of fiscal year 2014."; and

(2) in subsection (c)(2), by striking "0.5 percent" and inserting "1.0 percent".

SEC. 2103. INVESTMENT IN HISTORICALLY BLACK COLLEGES AND UNIVERSITIES AND MINORITY-SERVING INSTITUTIONS.

Section 371(b)(1)(A) (20 U.S.C. 1067q(b)(1)(A)) is amended by striking "and 2009." and all that follows and inserting "through 2019. The authority to award grants under this section shall expire at the end of fiscal year 2019.".

PART II—STUDENT LOAN REFORM

SEC. 2201. TERMINATION OF FEDERAL FAMILY EDUCATION LOAN APPROPRIATIONS.

Section 421 (20 U.S.C. 1071) is amended—

(1) in subsection (b), in the first sentence of the matter following paragraph (6), by inserting ", except that no sums may be expended after June 30, 2010, with respect to loans under this part for which the first disbursement is after such date" after "expended"; and

(2) by adding at the end the following new subsection:

"(d) TERMINATION OF AUTHORITY TO MAKE OR INSURE NEW LOANS.—Notwithstanding paragraphs (1) through (6) of subsection (b) or any other provision of law—

"(1) no new loans (including consolidation loans) may be made or insured under this part after June 30, 2010; and

"(2) no funds are authorized to be appropriated, or may be expended, under this Act or any other Act to make or insure loans under this part (including consolidation loans) for which the first disbursement is after June 30, 2010,

except as expressly authorized by an Act of Congress enacted after the date of enactment of the SAFRA Act.".

SEC. 2202. TERMINATION OF FEDERAL LOAN INSURANCE PROGRAM.

Section 424(a) (20 U.S.C. 1074(a)) is amended by striking "September 30, 1976," and all that follows and inserting "September 30, 1976, for each of the succeeding fiscal years ending prior to October 1, 2009, and for the period from October 1, 2009, to June 30, 2010, for loans first disbursed on or before June 30, 2010.".

SEC. 2203. TERMINATION OF APPLICABLE INTEREST RATES.

Section 427A(l) (20 U.S.C. 1077a(l)) is amended—

(1) in the subsection heading, by inserting "AND BEFORE JULY 1, 2010" after "2006";

(2) in paragraph (1), by inserting "and before July 1, 2010," after "July 1, 2006,";

(3) in paragraph (2), by inserting "and before July 1, 2010," after "July 1, 2006,";

(4) in paragraph (3), by inserting "and that was disbursed before July 1, 2010," after "July 1, 2006,"; and

(5) in paragraph (4)—

(A) in the matter preceding subparagraph (A), by striking "July 1, 2012" and inserting "July 1, 2010"; and

(B) by repealing subparagraphs (D) and (E).

SEC. 2204. TERMINATION OF FEDERAL PAYMENTS TO REDUCE STUDENT INTEREST COSTS.

(a) HIGHER EDUCATION ACT OF 1965.—Section 428 (20 U.S.C. 1078) is amended—

(1) in subsection (a)—

(A) in paragraph (1), in the matter preceding subparagraph (A), by inserting "for which the first disbursement is made before July 1, 2010, and" after "eligible institution"; and

(B) in paragraph (5), by striking "September 30, 2014," and all that follows through the period and inserting "June 30, 2010.";

(2) in subsection (b)(1)—

(A) in subparagraph (G)(ii), by inserting "and before July 1, 2010," after "July 1, 2006,"; and

(B) in subparagraph (H)(ii), by inserting "and that are first disbursed before July 1, 2010," after "July 1, 2006,";

(3) in subsection (f)(1)(A)(ii)—

(A) by striking "during fiscal years beginning"; and

(B) by inserting "and first disbursed before July 1, 2010," after "October 1, 2003,"; and

(4) in subsection (j)(1), by inserting ", before July 1, 2010," after "section 435(d)(1)(D) of this Act shall".

(b) COLLEGE COST REDUCTION AND ACCESS ACT.—Section 303 of the College Cost Reduction and Access Act (Public Law 110–84) is repealed.

SEC. 2205. TERMINATION OF FFEL PLUS LOANS.

Section 428B(a)(1) (20 U.S.C. 1078–2(a)(1)) is amended by striking "A graduate" and inserting "Prior to July 1, 2010, a graduate".

SEC. 2206. FEDERAL CONSOLIDATION LOANS.

(a) IN GENERAL.—Section 428C (20 U.S.C. 1078–3) is amended—

(1) in subsection (a)(4)(A), by inserting ", and first disbursed before July 1, 2010" after "under this part";

(2) in subsection (b)—

(A) in paragraph (1)(E), by inserting before the semicolon ", and before July 1, 2010"; and

(B) in paragraph (5), by striking "In the event that" and inserting "If, before July 1, 2010,";

(3) in subsection (c)(1)—

(A) in subparagraph (A)(ii), by inserting "and that is disbursed before July 1, 2010," after "2006,"; and

(B) in subparagraph (C), by inserting "and disbursed before July 1, 2010," after "1994,"; and

(4) in subsection (e), by striking "September 30, 2014." and inserting "June 30, 2010. No loan may be made under this section for which the disbursement is on or after July 1, 2010.".

(b) TEMPORARY LOAN CONSOLIDATION AUTHORITY.—Part D of title IV (20 U.S.C. 1087a et seq.) is amended by inserting after section 459A (20 U.S.C. 1087i) the following:

"SEC. 459B. TEMPORARY LOAN CONSOLIDATION AUTHORITY.

"(a) TEMPORARY LOAN CONSOLIDATION AUTHORITY.—

"(1) IN GENERAL.—A borrower who has 1 or more loans in 2 or more of the categories described in paragraph (2), and who has not yet entered repayment on 1 or more of those loans in any of the categories, may consolidate all of the loans of the borrower that are described in paragraph (2) into a Federal Direct Consolidation Loan during the period described in paragraph (3).

"(2) CATEGORIES OF LOANS THAT MAY BE CONSOLIDATED.— The categories of loans that may be consolidated under paragraph (1) are—

"(A) loans made under this part;

"(B) loans purchased by the Secretary pursuant to section 459A; and

"(C) loans made under part B that are held by an eligible lender, as such term is defined in section 435(d).

"(3) TIME PERIOD IN WHICH LOANS MAY BE CONSOLIDATED.— The Secretary may make a Federal Direct Consolidation Loan under this section to a borrower whose application for such Federal Direct Consolidation Loan is received on or after July 1, 2010, and before July 1, 2011.

"(b) TERMS OF LOANS.—A Federal Direct Consolidation Loan made under this section shall have the same terms and conditions as a Federal Direct Consolidation Loan made under section 455(g), except that—

"(1) in determining the applicable rate of interest on the Federal Direct Consolidation Loan made under this section (other than on a Federal Direct Consolidation Loan described in paragraph (2)), section 427A(l)(3) shall be applied without rounding the weighted average of the interest rate on the loans consolidated to the nearest higher one-eighth of 1 percent as described in subparagraph (A) of section 427A(l)(3); and

"(2) if a Federal Direct Consolidation Loan made under this section that repays a loan which is subject to an interest rate determined under section 427A(g)(2), (j)(2), or (k)(2), then the interest rate for such Federal Direct Consolidation Loan shall be calculated—

"(A) by using the applicable rate of interest described in section 427A(g)(2), (j)(2), or (k)(2), respectively; and

"(B) in accordance with section 427A(l)(3).".

SEC. 2207. TERMINATION OF UNSUBSIDIZED STAFFORD LOANS FOR MIDDLE-INCOME BORROWERS.

Section 428H (20 U.S.C. 1078–8) is amended—

(1) in subsection (a), by inserting "that are first disbursed before July 1, 2010," after "under this part";

(2) in subsection (b)—

(A) by striking "Any student" and inserting "Prior to July 1, 2010, any student"; and

(B) by inserting "for which the first disbursement is made before such date" after "unsubsidized Federal Stafford Loan"; and

(3) in subsection (h), by inserting "and that are first disbursed before July 1, 2010," after "July 1, 2006,".

SEC. 2208. TERMINATION OF SPECIAL ALLOWANCES.

Section 438 (20 U.S.C. 1087–1) is amended—

(1) in subsection (b)(2)(I)—

(A) in the subclause heading, by inserting ", AND BEFORE JULY 1, 2010" after "2000";

(B) in clause (i), by inserting "and before July 1, 2010," after "2000,";

(C) in clause (ii)(II), by inserting "and before July 1, 2010," after "2006,";

(D) in clause (iii), by inserting "and before July 1, 2010," after "2000,";

(E) in clause (iv), by inserting "and that is disbursed before July 1, 2010," after "2000,";

(F) in clause (v)(I), by inserting "and before July 1, 2010," after "2006,"; and

(G) in clause (vi)—

(i) in the clause heading, by inserting ", AND BEFORE JULY 1, 2010" after "2007"; and

(ii) in the matter preceding subclause (I), by inserting "and before July 1, 2010," after "2007,";

(2) in subsection (c)—

(A) in paragraph (2)(B)—

(i) in clause (iii), by inserting "and" after the semicolon;

(ii) in clause (iv), by striking "; and" and inserting a period; and

(iii) by striking clause (v); and

(B) in paragraph (6), by inserting "and first disbursed before July 1, 2010," after "1992,"; and

(3) in subsection (d)(2)(B), by inserting ", and before July 1, 2010" after "2007".

SEC. 2209. ORIGINATION OF DIRECT LOANS AT INSTITUTIONS OUTSIDE THE UNITED STATES.

(a) LOANS FOR STUDENTS ATTENDING INSTITUTIONS OUTSIDE THE UNITED STATES.—Section 452 (20 U.S.C. 1087b) is amended by adding at the end the following:

"(d) INSTITUTIONS OUTSIDE THE UNITED STATES.—Loan funds for students (and parents of students) attending institutions outside the United States shall be disbursed through a financial institution located or operating in the United States and designated by the Secretary to serve as the agent of such institutions with respect to the receipt of the disbursements of such loan funds and the transfer of such funds to such institutions. To be eligible to receive funds under this part, an institution outside the United States shall make arrangements with the agent designated by the Secretary under this subsection to receive funds under this part.".

(b) CONFORMING AMENDMENTS.—

(1) AMENDMENTS.—Section 102 (20 U.S.C. 1002), as amended by section 102 of the Higher Education Opportunity Act (Public Law 110–315) and section 101 of Public Law 111–39, is amended—

(A) by striking "part B" each place the term appears and inserting "part D";

(B) in subsection (a)(1)(C), by inserting ", consistent with the requirements of section 452(d)" before the period at the end; and

(C) in subsection (a)(2)(A)—

(i) in the second sentence of the matter preceding clause (i), by striking “made, insured, or guaranteed” and inserting “made”; and

(ii) in clause (iii)—

(I) in subclause (III), by striking “only Federal Stafford” and all that follows through “section 428B” and inserting “only Federal Direct Stafford Loans under section 455(a)(2)(A), Federal Direct Unsubsidized Stafford Loans under section 455(a)(2)(D), or Federal Direct PLUS Loans under section 455(a)(2)(B)”; and

(II) in subclause (V), by striking “a Federal Stafford” and all that follows through “section 428B” and inserting “a Federal Direct Stafford Loan under section 455(a)(2)(A), a Federal Direct Unsubsidized Stafford Loan under section 455(a)(2)(D), or a Federal Direct PLUS Loan under section 455(a)(2)(B)”.

(2) EFFECTIVE DATE.—The amendments made by subparagraph (C) of paragraph (1) shall be effective on July 1, 2010, as if enacted as part of section 102(a)(1) of the Higher Education Opportunity Act (Public Law 110–315) and subject to section 102(e) of such Act as amended by section 101(a)(2) of Public Law 111–39 (20 U.S.C. 1002 note).

SEC. 2210. CONFORMING AMENDMENTS.

(a) AMENDMENTS.—Section 454 (20 U.S.C. 1087d) is amended—

(1) in subsection (a)—

(A) by striking paragraph (4); and

(B) by redesignating paragraphs (5) through (7) as paragraphs (4) through (6), respectively; and

(2) in subsection (b)(2), by striking “(5), (6), and (7)” and inserting “(5), and (6)”.

(b) EFFECTIVE DATE.—The amendments made by subsection (a) shall take effect on July 1, 2010.

SEC. 2211. TERMS AND CONDITIONS OF LOANS.

(a) IN GENERAL.—Section 455 (20 U.S.C. 1087e) is amended—

(1) in subsection (a)(1), by inserting “, and first disbursed on June 30, 2010,” before “under sections 428”; and

(2) in subsection (g)—

(A) by inserting “, including any loan made under part B and first disbursed before July 1, 2010” after “section 428C(a)(4)”; and

(B) by striking the third sentence.

(b) EFFECTIVE DATE.—The amendment made by subsection (a)(1) shall apply with respect to loans first disbursed under part D of title IV of the Higher Education Act of 1965 (20 U.S.C. 1087a et seq.) on or after July 1, 2010.

SEC. 2212. CONTRACTS; MANDATORY FUNDS.

(a) CONTRACTS.—Section 456 (20 U.S.C. 1087f) is amended—

(1) in subsection (a)—

(A) by inserting after paragraph (3) the following new paragraph:

“(4) SERVICING BY ELIGIBLE NOT-FOR-PROFIT SERVICERS.—

“(A) SERVICING CONTRACTS.—

"(i) IN GENERAL.—The Secretary shall contract with each eligible not-for-profit servicer to service loans originated under this part, if the servicer—

"(I) meets the standards for servicing Federal assets that apply to contracts awarded pursuant to paragraph (1); and

"(II) has the capacity to service the applicable loan volume allocation described in subparagraph (B).

"(ii) COMPETITIVE MARKET RATE DETERMINATION FOR FIRST 100,000 BORROWER ACCOUNTS.—The Secretary shall establish a separate pricing tier for each of the first 100,000 borrower loan accounts at a competitive market rate.

"(iii) INELIGIBILITY.—An eligible not-for-profit servicer shall no longer be eligible for a contract under this paragraph after July 1, 2014, if—

"(I) the servicer has not been awarded such a contract before that date; or

"(II) the servicer's contract was terminated, and the servicer had not reapplied for, and been awarded, a contract under this paragraph.

"(B) ALLOCATIONS.—

"(i) IN GENERAL.—The Secretary shall (except as provided in clause (ii)) allocate to an eligible not-for-profit servicer, subject to the contract of such servicer described in subparagraph (A), the servicing rights for the loan accounts of 100,000 borrowers (including borrowers who borrowed loans in a prior year that were serviced by the servicer).

"(ii) SERVICER ALLOCATION.—The Secretary may reallocate, increase, reduce, or terminate an eligible not-for-profit servicer's allocation of servicing rights under clause (i) based on the performance of such servicer, on the same terms as loan allocations provided by contracts awarded pursuant to paragraph (1)."; and

(2) by adding at the end the following:

"(c) DEFINITION OF ELIGIBLE NOT-FOR-PROFIT SERVICER.—In this section:

"(1) IN GENERAL.—The term 'eligible not-for-profit servicer' means an entity—

"(A) that is not owned or controlled in whole or in part by—

"(i) a for-profit entity; or

"(ii) a nonprofit entity having its principal place of business in another State; and

"(B) that—

"(i) as of July 1, 2009—

"(I) meets the definition of an eligible not-for-profit holder under section 435(p), except that such term does not include eligible lenders described in paragraph (1)(D) of such section; and

"(II) was performing, or had entered into a contract with a third party servicer (as such term is defined in section 481(c)) who was performing, student loan servicing functions for loans made under part B of this title;

"(ii) notwithstanding clause (i), as of July 1, 2009—

"(I) is the sole beneficial owner of a loan for which the special allowance rate is calculated under section 438(b)(2)(I)(vi)(II) because the loan is held by an eligible lender trustee that is an eligible not-for-profit holder as defined under section 435(p)(1)(D); and

"(II) was performing, or had entered into a contract with a third party servicer (as such term is defined in section 481(c)) who was performing, student loan servicing functions for loans made under part B of this title; or

"(iii) is an affiliated entity of an eligible not-for-profit servicer described in clause (i) or (ii) that—

"(I) directly employs, or will directly employ (on or before the date the entity begins servicing loans under a contract awarded by the Secretary pursuant to subsection (a)(3)(A)), the majority of individuals who perform borrower-specific student loan servicing functions; and

"(II) as of July 1, 2009, was performing, or had entered into a contract with a third party servicer (as such term is defined in section 481(c)) who was performing, student loan servicing functions for loans made under part B of this title.

"(2) AFFILIATED ENTITY.—For the purposes of paragraph (1), the term 'affiliated entity'—

"(A) means an entity contracted to perform services for an eligible not-for-profit servicer that—

"(i) is a nonprofit entity or is wholly owned by a nonprofit entity; and

"(ii) is not owned or controlled, in whole or in part, by—

"(I) a for-profit entity; or

"(II) an entity having its principal place of business in another State; and

"(B) may include an affiliated entity that is established by an eligible not-for-profit servicer after the date of enactment of the SAFRA Act, if such affiliated entity is otherwise described in paragraph (1)(B)(iii)(I) and subparagraph (A) of this paragraph.".

(b) MANDATORY FUNDS.—

(1) AMENDMENTS.—Section 458(a) (20 U.S.C. 1087h(a)) is amended—

(A) by redesignating paragraph (5) as paragraph (8);

(B) by redesignating paragraphs (2) through (4) as paragraphs (3) through (5), respectively;

(C) by inserting after paragraph (1) the following new paragraph:

"(2) MANDATORY FUNDS FOR ELIGIBLE NOT-FOR-PROFIT SERVICERS.—For fiscal years 2010 through 2019, there shall be available to the Secretary, in addition to any other amounts appropriated to carry out this paragraph and out of any money in the Treasury not otherwise appropriated, funds to be obligated for administrative costs of servicing contracts with eligible not-for-profit servicers as described in section 456."; and

(D) by inserting after paragraph (5), as redesignated by subparagraph (B) of this paragraph, the following:

"(6) TECHNICAL ASSISTANCE TO INSTITUTIONS OF HIGHER EDUCATION.—

"(A) PROVISION OF ASSISTANCE.—The Secretary shall provide institutions of higher education participating, or seeking to participate, in the loan programs under this part with technical assistance in establishing and administering such programs.

"(B) FUNDS.—There are authorized to be appropriated, and there are appropriated, to carry out this paragraph (in addition to any other amounts appropriated to carry out this paragraph and out of any money in the Treasury not otherwise appropriated), $50,000,000 for fiscal year 2010.

"(C) DEFINITION.—In this paragraph, the term 'assistance' means the provision of technical support, training, materials, technical assistance, and financial assistance.

"(7) ADDITIONAL PAYMENTS.—

"(A) PROVISION OF ASSISTANCE.—The Secretary shall provide payments to loan servicers for retaining jobs at locations in the United States where such servicers were operating under part B on January 1, 2010.

"(B) FUNDS.—There are authorized to be appropriated, and there are appropriated, to carry out this paragraph (in addition to any other amounts appropriated to carry out this paragraph and out of any money in the Treasury not otherwise appropriated), $25,000,000 for each of the fiscal years 2010 and 2011.".

(2) CONFORMING AMENDMENT.—Section 458 (20 U.S.C. 1087h) is further amended by striking "subsection (a)(3)" in subsection (b) and inserting "subsection (a)(4)".

SEC. 2213. INCOME-BASED REPAYMENT.

Section 493C (20 U.S.C. 1098e) is amended by adding at the end the following new subsection:

"(e) SPECIAL TERMS FOR NEW BORROWERS ON AND AFTER JULY 1, 2014.—With respect to any loan made to a new borrower on or after July 1, 2014—

"(1) subsection (a)(3)(B) shall be applied by substituting '10 percent' for '15 percent'; and

"(2) subsection (b)(7)(B) shall be applied by substituting '20 years' for '25 years'.".

Subtitle B—Health

SEC. 2301. INSURANCE REFORMS.

(a) EXTENDING CERTAIN INSURANCE REFORMS TO GRANDFATHERED PLANS.—Section 1251(a) of the Patient Protection and Affordable Care Act, as added by section 10103(d) of such Act, is amended by adding at the end the following:

"(4) APPLICATION OF CERTAIN PROVISIONS.—

"(A) IN GENERAL.—The following provisions of the Public Health Service Act (as added by this title) shall apply to grandfathered health plans for plan years beginning with the first plan year to which such provisions would otherwise apply:

"(i) Section 2708 (relating to excessive waiting periods).

"(ii) Those provisions of section 2711 relating to lifetime limits.

"(iii) Section 2712 (relating to rescissions).

"(iv) Section 2714 (relating to extension of dependent coverage).

"(B) PROVISIONS APPLICABLE ONLY TO GROUP HEALTH PLANS.—

"(i) PROVISIONS DESCRIBED.—Those provisions of section 2711 relating to annual limits and the provisions of section 2704 (relating to pre-existing condition exclusions) of the Public Health Service Act (as added by this subtitle) shall apply to grandfathered health plans that are group health plans for plan years beginning with the first plan year to which such provisions otherwise apply.

"(ii) ADULT CHILD COVERAGE.—For plan years beginning before January 1, 2014, the provisions of section 2714 of the Public Health Service Act (as added by this subtitle) shall apply in the case of an adult child with respect to a grandfathered health plan that is a group health plan only if such adult child is not eligible to enroll in an eligible employer-sponsored health plan (as defined in section 5000A(f)(2) of the Internal Revenue Code of 1986) other than such grandfathered health plan.".

(b) CLARIFICATION REGARDING DEPENDENT COVERAGE.—Section 2714(a) of the Public Health Service Act, as added by section 1001(5) of the Patient Protection and Affordable Care Act, is amended by striking "(who is not married)".

SEC. 2302. DRUGS PURCHASED BY COVERED ENTITIES.

Section 340B of the Public Health Service Act (42 U.S.C. 256b), as amended by sections 7101 and 7102 of the Patient Protection and Affordable Care Act, is amended—

(1) in subsection (a)—

(A) in paragraphs (1), (2), (5), (7), and (9), by striking the terms "covered drug" and "covered drugs" each place either term appears and inserting "covered outpatient drug" or "covered outpatient drugs", respectively;

(B) in paragraph (4)(L)—

(i) in clause (i), by striking "and" at the end;

(ii) in clause (ii), by striking the period and inserting "; and"; and

(iii) by inserting after clause (ii), the following:

"(iii) does not obtain covered outpatient drugs through a group purchasing organization or other group purchasing arrangement."; and

(C) in paragraph (5)—

(i) by striking subparagraph (C);

(ii) by redesignating subparagraphs (D) and (E) as subparagraphs (C) and (D), respectively; and

(iii) in subparagraph (D), as so redesignated, by striking "subparagraph (D)" and inserting "subparagraph (C)";

(2) by striking subsection (c);

(3) in subsection (d)—

(A) by striking "covered drugs" each place it appears and inserting "covered outpatient drugs";

(B) by striking "(a)(5)(D)" each place it appears and inserting "(a)(5)(C)"; and

(C) by striking "(a)(5)(E)" each place it appears and inserting "(a)(5)(D)"; and

(4) by inserting after subsection (d) the following:

"(e) EXCLUSION OF ORPHAN DRUGS FOR CERTAIN COVERED ENTITIES.—For covered entities described in subparagraph (M), (N), or (O) of subsection (a)(4), the term 'covered outpatient drug' shall not include a drug designated by the Secretary under section 526 of the Federal Food, Drug, and Cosmetic Act for a rare disease or condition.".

SEC. 2303. COMMUNITY HEALTH CENTERS.

Section 10503(b)(1) of the Patient Protection and Affordable Care Act is amended—

(1) in subparagraph (A), by striking "700,000,000" and inserting "1,000,000,000";

(2) in subparagraph (B), by striking "800,000,000" and inserting "1,200,000,000";

(3) in subparagraph (C), by striking "1,000,000,000" and inserting "1,500,000,000";

(4) in subparagraph (D), by striking "1,600,000,000" and inserting "2,200,000,000"; and

(5) in subparagraph (E), by striking "2,900,000,000" and inserting "3,600,000,000".

Speaker of the House of Representatives.

Vice President of the United States and
President of the Senate.

TECHNICAL EXPLANATION OF THE REVENUE PROVISIONS OF THE "RECONCILIATON ACT OF 2010," AS AMENDED, IN COMBINATION WITH THE "PATIENT PROTECTION AND AFFORDABLE CARE ACT"

Prepared by the Staff
of the
JOINT COMMITTEE ON TAXATION

March 21, 2010
JCX-18-10

CONTENTS

INTRODUCTION

This document,[1] prepared by the staff of the Joint Committee on Taxation, provides a technical explanation of the revenue provisions contained in the "Reconciliation Act of 2010," as amended, in combination with the "Patient Protection and Affordable Care Act." Unless otherwise indicated, all section references are to the Internal Revenue Code of 1986, as amended. References to the "Senate amendment" refer to the Patient Protection and Affordable Care Act, an amendment to H.R. 3590, the engrossed amendment as agreed to by the Senate. References to the "Reconciliation bill" refer to the Health Care and Education Reconciliation Act of 2010, an amendment in the nature of a substitute to H.R. 4872, the Reconciliation Act of 2010, as amended.

[1] This document may be cited as follows: Joint Committee on Taxation, *Technical Explanation of the Revenue Provisions of the "Reconciliation Act of 2010," as amended, in combination with the "Patient Protection and Affordable Care Act"* (JCX-18-10), March 21, 2010. This document can also be found on our website at www.jct.gov.

TITLE I – QUALITY, AFFORDABLE HEALTH CARE FOR ALL AMERICANS

A. Tax Exemption for Certain Member-Run Health Insurance Issuers (sec. 1322[2] of the Senate amendment, new section 501(c)(29) of the Code, and section 6033 of the Code)

Present Law

In general

Although present law provides that certain limited categories of organizations that offer insurance may qualify for exemption from Federal income tax, present law generally does not provide tax-exempt status for newly established, member-run nonprofit health insurers that are established and funded pursuant to the Consumer Oriented, Not-for-Profit Health Plan program created under the bill and described below.

Taxation of insurance companies

Taxation of stock and mutual companies providing health insurance

Present law provides special rules for determining the taxable income of insurance companies (subchapter L of the Code). Both mutual insurance companies and stock insurance companies are subject to Federal income tax under these rules. Separate sets of rules apply to life insurance companies and to property and casualty insurance companies. Insurance companies are subject to Federal income tax at regular corporate income tax rates.

An insurance company that provides health insurance is subject to Federal income tax as either a life insurance company or as a property and casualty insurance company, depending on its mix of lines of business and on the resulting portion of its reserves that are treated as life insurance reserves. For Federal income tax purposes, an insurance company is treated as a life insurance company if the sum of its (1) life insurance reserves and (2) unearned premiums and unpaid losses on noncancellable life, accident or health contracts not included in life insurance reserves, comprise more than 50 percent of its total reserves.[3]

Life insurance companies

A life insurance company, whether stock or mutual, is taxed at regular corporate rates on its life insurance company taxable income (LICTI). LICTI is life insurance gross income reduced by life insurance deductions.[4] An alternative tax applies if a company has a net capital gain for the taxable year, if such tax is less than the tax that would otherwise apply. Life insurance gross income is the sum of (1) premiums, (2) decreases in reserves, and (3) other

---

[2] Section 1322 of the Senate amendment as amended by section 10104.

[3] Sec. 816(a).

[4] Sec. 801.

amounts generally includible by a taxpayer in gross income. Methods for determining reserves for Federal income tax purposes generally are based on reserves prescribed by the National Association of Insurance Commissioners for purposes of financial reporting under State regulatory rules.

Because deductible reserves might be viewed as being funded proportionately out of taxable and tax-exempt income, the net increase and net decrease in reserves are computed by reducing the ending balance of the reserve items by a portion of tax-exempt interest (known as a proration rule).[5] Similarly, a life insurance company is allowed a dividends-received deduction for intercorporate dividends from nonaffiliates only in proportion to the company's share of such dividends.[6]

Property and casualty insurance companies

The taxable income of a property and casualty insurance company is determined as the sum of the amount earned from underwriting income and from investment income (as well as gains and other income items), reduced by allowable deductions.[7] For this purpose, underwriting income and investment income are computed on the basis of the underwriting and investment exhibit of the annual statement approved by the National Association of Insurance Commissioners.[8]

Underwriting income means premiums earned during the taxable year less losses incurred and expenses incurred.[9] Losses incurred include certain unpaid losses (reported losses that have not been paid, estimates of losses incurred but not reported, resisted claims, and unpaid loss adjustment expenses). Present law limits the deduction for unpaid losses to the amount of discounted unpaid losses, which are discounted using prescribed discount periods and a prescribed interest rate, to take account partially of the time value of money.[10] Any net decrease in the amount of unpaid losses results in income inclusion, and the amount included is computed on a discounted basis.

---

[5] Secs. 807(b)(2)(B) and (b)(1)(B).

[6] Secs. 805(a)(4), 812. Fully deductible dividends from affiliates are excluded from the application of this proration formula (so long as such dividends are not themselves distributions from tax-exempt interest or from dividend income that would not be fully deductible if received directly by the taxpayer). In addition, the proration rule includes in prorated amounts the increase for the taxable year in policy cash values of life insurance policies and annuity and endowment contracts owned by the company (the inside buildup on which is not taxed).

[7] Sec. 832.

[8] Sec. 832(b)(1)(A).

[9] Sec. 832(b)(3). In determining premiums earned, the company deducts from gross premiums the increase in unearned premiums for the year (sec. 832(b)(4)(B)). The company is required to reduce the deduction for increases in unearned premiums by 20 percent, reflecting the matching of deferred expenses to deferred income.

[10] Sec. 846.

In calculating its reserve for losses incurred, a proration rule requires that a property and casualty insurance company must reduce the amount of losses incurred by 15 percent of (1) the insurer's tax-exempt interest, (2) the deductible portion of dividends received (with special rules for dividends from affiliates), and (3) the increase for the taxable year in the cash value of life insurance, endowment, or annuity contracts the company owns (sec. 832(b)(5)). This rule reflects the fact that reserves are generally funded in part from tax-exempt interest, from wholly or partially deductible dividends, or from other untaxed amounts.

Tax exemption for certain organizations

In general

Section 501(a) generally provides for exemption from Federal income tax for certain organizations. These organizations include: (1) qualified pension, profit sharing, and stock bonus plans described in section 401(a); (2) religious and apostolic organizations described in section 501(d); and (3) organizations described in section 501(c). Sections 501(c) describes 28 different categories of exempt organizations, including: charitable organizations (section 501(c)(3)); social welfare organizations (section 501(c)(4)); labor, agricultural, and horticultural organizations (section 501(c)(5)); professional associations (section 501(c)(6)); and social clubs (section 501(c)(7)).[11]

Insurance organizations described in section 501(c)

Although most organizations that engage principally in insurance activities are not exempt from Federal income tax, certain organizations that engage in insurance activities are described in section 501(c) and exempt from tax under section 501(a). Section 501(c)(8), for example, describes certain fraternal beneficiary societies, orders, or associations operating under the lodge system or for the exclusive benefit of their members that provide for the payment of life, sick, accident, or other benefits to the members or their dependents. Section 501(c)(9) describes certain voluntary employees' beneficiary societies that provide for the payment of life,

---

[11] Certain organizations that operate on a cooperative basis are taxed under special rules set forth in Subchapter T of the Code. The two principal criteria for determining whether an entity is operating on a cooperative basis are: (1) ownership of the cooperative by persons who patronize the cooperative (e.g., the farmer members of a cooperative formed to market the farmers' produce); and (2) return of earnings to patrons in proportion to their patronage. In general, cooperative members are those who participate in the management of the cooperative and who share in patronage capital. For Federal income tax purposes, a cooperative that is taxed under the Subchapter T rules generally computes its income as if it were a taxable corporation, with one exception -- the cooperative may deduct from its taxable income distributions of patronage dividends. In general, patronage dividends are the profits of the cooperative that are rebated to its patrons pursuant to a preexisting obligation of the cooperative to do so. Certain farmers' cooperatives described in section 521 are authorized to deduct not only patronage dividends from patronage sources, but also dividends on capital stock and certain distributions to patrons from nonpatronage sources.

Separate from the Subchapter T rules, the Code provides tax exemption for certain cooperatives. Section 501(c)(12), for example, provides that certain rural electric and telephone cooperative are exempt from tax under section 501(a), provided that 85 percent or more of the cooperative's income consists of amounts collected from members for the sole purpose of meeting losses or expenses, and certain other requirements are met.

sick, accident, or other benefits to the members of the association or their dependents or designated beneficiaries. Section 501(c)(12)(A) describes certain benevolent life insurance associations of a purely local character. Section 501(c)(15) describes certain small non-life insurance companies with annual gross receipts of no more than $600,000 ($150,000 in the case of a mutual insurance company). Section 501(c)(26) describes certain membership organizations established to provide health insurance to certain high-risk individuals.[12] Section 501(c)(27) describes certain organizations established to provide workmen's compensation insurance.

Certain section 501(c)(3) organizations

Certain health maintenance organizations (HMOs) have been held to qualify for tax exemption as charitable organizations described in section 501(c)(3). In *Sound Health Association v. Commissioner*,[13] the Tax Court held that a staff model HMO qualified as a charitable organization. A staff model HMO generally employs its own physicians and staff and serves its subscribers at its own facilities. The court concluded that the HMO satisfied the section 501(c)(3) community benefit standard, as its membership was open to almost all members of the community. Although membership was limited to persons who had the money to pay the fixed premiums, the court held that this was not disqualifying, because the HMO had a subsidized premium program for persons of lesser means to be funded through donations and Medicare and Medicaid payments. The HMO also operated an emergency room open to all persons regardless of income. The court rejected the government's contention that the HMO conferred primarily a private benefit to its subscribers, stating that when the potential membership is such a broad segment of the community, benefit to the membership is benefit to the community.

In *Geisinger Health Plan v. Commissioner*,[14] the court applied the section 501(c)(3) community benefit standard to an individual practice association (IPA) model HMO. In the IPA model, health care generally is provided by physicians practicing independently in their own offices, with the IPA usually contracting on behalf of the physicians with the HMO. Reversing a Tax Court decision, the court held that the HMO did not qualify as charitable, because the community benefit standard requires that an HMO be an actual provider of health care rather than merely an arranger or deliverer of health care, which is how the court viewed the IPA model in that case.

---

[12] When section 501(c)(26) was enacted in 1996, the House Ways and Means Committee, in reporting out the bill, stated as its reasons for change: "The Committee believes that eliminating the uncertainty concerning the eligibility of certain State health insurance risk pools for tax-exempt status will assist States in providing medical care coverage for their uninsured high-risk residents." H.R. Rep. No. 104-496, Part I, "Health Coverage Availability and Affordability Act of 1996," 104th Cong., 2d Sess., March 25, 1996, 124. *See also* Joint Committee on Taxation, *General Explanation of Tax Legislation Enacted in the 104th Congress*, JCS-12-96, December 18, 1996, 351.

[13] 71 T.C. 158 (1978), *acq.* 1981-2 C.B. 2.

[14] 985 F.2d 1210 (3rd Cir. 1993), *rev'g* T.C. Memo. 1991-649.

More recently, in *IHC Health Plans, Inc. v. Commissioner*,[15] the court ruled that three affiliated HMOs did not operate primarily for the benefit of the community they served. The organizations in the case did not provide health care directly, but provided group insurance that could be used at both affiliated and non-affiliated providers. The court found that the organizations primarily performed a risk-bearing function and provided virtually no free or below-cost health care services. In denying charitable status, the court held that a health-care provider must make its services available to all in the community plus provide additional community or public benefits.[16] The benefit must either further the function of government-funded institutions or provide a service that would not likely be provided within the community but for the subsidy. Further, the additional public benefit conferred must be sufficient to give rise to a strong inference that the public benefit is the primary purpose for which the organization operates.[17]

<u>Certain organizations providing commercial-type insurance</u>

Section 501(m) provides that an organization may not be exempt from tax under section 501(c)(3) (generally, charitable organizations) or section 501(c)(4) (social welfare organizations) unless no substantial part of its activities consists of providing commercial-type insurance. For this purpose, commercial-type insurance excludes, among other things: (1) insurance provided at substantially below cost to a class of charitable recipients; and (2) incidental health insurance provided by an HMO of a kind customarily provided by such organizations.

When section 501(m) was enacted in 1986, the following reasons for the provision were stated: "The committee is concerned that exempt charitable and social welfare organizations that engaged in insurance activities are engaged in an activity whose nature and scope is so inherently commercial that tax exempt status is inappropriate. The committee believes that the tax-exempt status of organizations engaged in insurance activities provides an unfair competitive advantage to these organizations. The committee further believes that the provision of insurance to the general public at a price sufficient to cover the costs of insurance generally constitutes an activity that is commercial. In addition, the availability of tax-exempt status . . . has allowed some large insurance entities to compete directly with commercial insurance companies. For example, the Blue Cross/Blue Shield organizations historically have been treated as tax-exempt organizations described in sections 501(c)(3) or (4). This group of organizations is now among the largest health care insurers in the United States. Other tax-exempt charitable and social welfare organizations engaged in insurance activities also have a competitive advantage over commercial insurers who do not have tax-exempt status. . . ."[18]

---

[15] 325 F.3d 1188 (10th Cir. 2003).

[16] *Ibid.* at 1198.

[17] *Ibid.*

[18] H.R. Rep. No. 99-426, "Tax Reform Act of 1985," Report of the Committee on Ways and Means, 99th Cong., 1st Sess., December 7, 1985, 664. *See also* Joint Committee on Taxation, *General Explanation of the Tax Reform Act of 1986*, JCS-10-87, May 4, 1987, 584.

Unrelated business income tax

Most organizations that are exempt from tax under section 501(a) are subject to the unrelated business income tax rules of sections 511 through 515. The unrelated business income tax generally applies to income derived from a trade or business regularly carried on by the organization that is not substantially related to the performance of the organization's tax-exempt functions. Certain types of income are specifically exempt from the unrelated business income tax, such as dividends, interest, royalties, and certain rents, unless derived from debt-financed property or from certain 50-percent controlled subsidiaries.

Explanation of Provision

In general

The provision authorizes $6 billion in funding for, and instructs the Secretary of Health and Human Services ("HHS") to establish, the Consumer Operated and Oriented Plan (the "program") to foster the creation of qualified nonprofit health insurance issuers to offer qualified health plans in the individual and small group markets in the States in which the issuers are licensed to offer such plans. Federal funds are to be distributed as loans to assist with start-up costs and grants to assist in meeting State solvency requirements.

Under the provision, the Secretary of HHS must require any person receiving a loan or grant under the program to enter into an agreement with the Secretary of HHS requiring the recipient of funds to meet and continue to meet any requirement under the provision for being treated as a qualified nonprofit health insurance issuer, and any requirements to receive the loan or grant. The provision also requires that the agreement prohibit the use of loan or grant funds for carrying on propaganda or otherwise attempting to influence legislation or for marketing.

If the Secretary of HHS determines that a grant or loan recipient failed to meet the requirements described in the preceding paragraph, and failed to correct such failure within a reasonable period from when the person first knew (or reasonably should have known) of such failure, then such person must repay the Secretary of HHS an amount equal to 110 percent of the aggregate amount of the loans and grants received under the program, plus interest on such amount for the period during which the loans or grants were outstanding. The Secretary of HHS must notify the Secretary of the Treasury of any determination of a failure that results in the termination of the grantee's Federal tax-exempt status.

Qualified nonprofit health insurance issuers

The provision defines a qualified nonprofit health insurance issuer as an organization that meets the following requirements:

1. The organization is organized as a nonprofit, member corporation under State law;

2. Substantially all of its activities consist of the issuance of qualified health plans in the individual and small group markets in each State in which it is licensed to issue such plans;

3. None of the organization, a related entity, or a predecessor of either was a health insurance issuer as of July 16, 2009;

4. The organization is not sponsored by a State or local government, any political subdivision thereof, or any instrumentality of such government or political subdivision;

5. Governance of the organization is subject to a majority vote of its members;

6. The organization's governing documents incorporate ethics and conflict of interest standards protecting against insurance industry involvement and interference;

7. The organization must operate with a strong consumer focus, including timeliness, responsiveness, and accountability to its members, in accordance with regulations to be promulgated by the Secretary of HHS;

8. Any profits made must be used to lower premiums, improve benefits, or for other programs intended to improve the quality of health care delivered to its members;

9. The organization meets all other requirements that other issuers of qualified health plans are required to meet in any State in which it offers a qualified health plan, including solvency and licensure requirements, rules on payments to providers, rules on network adequacy, rate and form filing rules, and any applicable State premium assessments. Additionally, the organization must coordinate with certain other State insurance reforms under the bill; and

10. The organization does not offer a health plan in a State until that State has in effect (or the Secretary of HHS has implemented for the State), the market reforms required by part A of title XXVII of the Public Health Service Act ("PHSA"), as amended by the bill.

Tax exemption for qualified nonprofit health insurance issuers

An organization receiving a grant or loan under the program qualifies for exemption from Federal income tax under section 501(a) of the Code with respect to periods during which the organization is in compliance with the above-described requirements of the program and with the terms of any program grant or loan agreement to which such organization is a party. Such organizations also are subject to organizational and operational requirements applicable to certain section 501(c) organizations, including the prohibitions on private inurement and political activities, the limitation on lobbying activities, taxation of excess benefit transactions (section 4958), and taxation of unrelated business taxable income under section 511.

Program participants are required to file an application for exempt status with the IRS in such manner as the Secretary of the Treasury may require, and are subject to annual information reporting requirements. In addition, such an organization is required to disclose on its annual information return the amount of reserves required by each State in which it operates and the amount of reserves on hand.

Effective Date

The provision is effective on date of enactment.

B. Tax Exemption for Entities Established Pursuant to Transitional Reinsurance Program for Individual Market in Each State (sec. 1341[19] of the Senate amendment)

Present Law

Although present law provides that certain limited categories of organizations that offer insurance may qualify for exemption from Federal income tax, present law does not provide tax-exempt status for transitional nonprofit reinsurance entities created under the Senate bill and described below.

Explanation of Provision

In general, issuers of health benefit plans that are offered in the individual market would be required to contribute to a temporary reinsurance program for individual policies that is administered by a nonprofit reinsurance entity. Such contributions would begin January 1, 2014, and continue for a 36-month period. The provision requires each State, no later than January 1, 2014, to adopt a reinsurance program based on a model regulation and to establish (or enter into a contract with) one or more applicable reinsurance entities to carry out the reinsurance program under the provision. For purposes of the provision, an applicable reinsurance entity is a not-for-profit organization (1) the purpose of which is to help stabilize premiums for coverage in the individual market in a State during the first three years of operation of an exchange for such markets within the State, and (2) the duties of which are to carry out the reinsurance program under the provision by coordinating the funding and operation of the risk-spreading mechanisms designed to implement the reinsurance program. A State may have more than one applicable reinsurance entity to carry out the reinsurance program in the State, and two or more States may enter into agreements to allow a reinsurer to operate the reinsurance program in those States.

An applicable reinsurance entity established under the provision is exempt from Federal income tax. Notwithstanding an applicable reinsurance entity's tax-exempt status, it is subject to tax on unrelated business taxable income under section 511 as if such entity were described in section 511(a)(2).

Effective Date

The provision is effective on the date of enactment.

---

[19] Section 1341 of the Senate amendment as amended by section 10104.

C. Refundable Tax Credit Providing Premium Assistance for Coverage Under a Qualified Health Plan (secs. 1401, 1411, and 1412[20] of the Senate amendment and new sec. 36B of the Code)

Present Law

Currently there is no tax credit that is generally available to low or middle income individuals or families for the purchase of health insurance. Some individuals may be eligible for health coverage through State Medicaid programs which consider income, assets, and family circumstances. However, these Medicaid programs are not in the Code.

Health coverage tax credit

Certain individuals are eligible for the health coverage tax credit ("HCTC"). The HCTC is a refundable tax credit equal to 80 percent of the cost of qualified health coverage paid by an eligible individual. In general, eligible individuals are individuals who receive a trade adjustment allowance (and individuals who would be eligible to receive such an allowance but for the fact that they have not exhausted their regular unemployment benefits), individuals eligible for the alternative trade adjustment assistance program, and individuals over age 55 who receive pension benefits from the Pension Benefit Guaranty Corporation. The HCTC is available for "qualified health insurance," which includes certain employer-based insurance, certain State-based insurance, and in some cases, insurance purchased in the individual market.

The credit is available on an advance basis through a program established and administered by the Treasury Department. The credit generally is delivered as follows: the eligible individual sends his or her portion of the premium to the Treasury, and the Treasury then pays the full premium (the individual's portion and the amount of the refundable tax credit) to the insurer. Alternatively, an eligible individual is also permitted to pay the entire premium during the year and claim the credit on his or her income tax return.

Individuals entitled to Medicare and certain other governmental health programs, covered under certain employer-subsidized health plans, or with certain other specified health coverage are not eligible for the credit.

COBRA continuation coverage premium reduction

The Consolidated Omnibus Reconciliation Act of 1985 ("COBRA")[21] requires that a group health plan must offer continuation coverage to qualified beneficiaries in the case of a qualifying event (such as a loss of employment). A plan may require payment of a premium for any period of continuation coverage. The amount of such premium generally may not exceed 102 percent of the "applicable premium" for such period and the premium must be payable, at the election of the payor, in monthly installments.

---

[20] Sections 1401, 1411 and 1412 of the Senate amendment, as amended by sections 10104, 10105, 10107, are further amended by section 1001 of the Reconciliation bill.

[21] Pub. L. No. 99-272.

Section 3001 of the American Recovery and Reinvestment Act of 2009,[22] as amended by the Department of Defense Appropriations Act, 2010,[23] and the Temporary Extension Act of 2010[24] provides that, for a period not exceeding 15 months, an assistance eligible individual is treated as having paid any premium required for COBRA continuation coverage under a group health plan if the individual pays 35 percent of the premium. Thus, if the assistance eligible individual pays 35 percent of the premium, the group health plan must treat the individual as having paid the full premium required for COBRA continuation coverage, and the individual is entitled to a subsidy for 65 percent of the premium. An assistance eligible individual generally is any qualified beneficiary who elects COBRA continuation coverage and the qualifying event with respect to the covered employee for that qualified beneficiary is a loss of group health plan coverage on account of an involuntary termination of the covered employee's employment (for other than gross misconduct).[25] In addition, the qualifying event must occur during the period beginning September 1, 2008, and ending March 31, 2010.

The COBRA continuation coverage subsidy also applies to temporary continuation coverage elected under the Federal Employees Health Benefits Program and to continuation health coverage under State programs that provide coverage comparable to continuation coverage. The subsidy is generally delivered by requiring employers to pay the subsidized portion of the premium for assistance eligible individuals. The employer then treats the payment of the subsidized portion as a payment of employment taxes and offsets its employment tax liability by the amount of the subsidy. To the extent that the aggregate amount of the subsidy for all assistance eligible individuals for which the employer is entitled to a credit for a quarter exceeds the employer's employment tax liability for the quarter, the employer can request a tax refund or can claim the credit against future employment tax liability.

There is an income limit on the entitlement to the COBRA continuation coverage subsidy. Taxpayers with modified adjusted gross income exceeding $145,000 (or $290,000 for joint filers), must repay any subsidy received by them, their spouse, or their dependant, during the taxable year. For taxpayers with modified adjusted gross incomes between $125,000 and $145,000 (or $250,000 and $290,000 for joint filers), the amount of the subsidy that must be repaid is reduced proportionately. The subsidy is also conditioned on the individual not being eligible for certain other health coverage. To the extent that an eligible individual receives a subsidy during a taxable year to which the individual was not entitled due to income or being eligible for other health coverage, the subsidy overpayment is repaid on the individual's income

---

[22] Pub. L. No. 111-5.

[23] Pub. L. No. 111-118.

[24] Pub. L. No. 111-144.

[25] TEA expanded eligibility for the COBRA subsidy to include individuals who experience a loss of coverage on account of a reduction in hours of employment followed by the involuntary termination of employment of the covered employee. For an individual entitled to COBRA because of a reduction in hours and who is then subsequently involuntarily terminated from employment, the termination is considered a qualifying event for purposes of the COBRA subsidy, as long as the termination occurs during the period beginning on the date following TEA's date of enactment and ending on March 31, 2010.

tax return as additional tax. However, in contrast to the HCTC, the subsidy for COBRA continuation coverage may only be claimed through the employer and cannot be claimed at the end of the year on an individual tax return.

Explanation of Provision

Premium assistance credit

The provision creates a refundable tax credit (the "premium assistance credit") for eligible individuals and families who purchase health insurance through an exchange.[26] The premium assistance credit, which is refundable and payable in advance directly to the insurer, subsidizes the purchase of certain health insurance plans through an exchange.

Under the provision, an eligible individual enrolls in a plan offered through an exchange and reports his or her income to the exchange. Based on the information provided to the exchange, the individual receives a premium assistance credit based on income and the Treasury pays the premium assistance credit amount directly to the insurance plan in which the individual is enrolled. The individual then pays to the plan in which he or she is enrolled the dollar difference between the premium tax credit amount and the total premium charged for the plan.[27] Individuals who fail to pay all or part of the remaining premium amount are given a mandatory three-month grace period prior to an involuntary termination of their participation in the plan. For employed individuals who purchase health insurance through a State exchange, the premium payments are made through payroll deductions. Initial eligibility for the premium assistance credit is based on the individual's income for the tax year ending two years prior to the enrollment period. Individuals (or couples) who experience a change in marital status or other household circumstance, experience a decrease in income of more than 20 percent, or receive unemployment insurance, may update eligibility information or request a redetermination of their tax credit eligibility.

The premium assistance credit is available for individuals (single or joint filers) with household incomes between 100 and 400 percent of the Federal poverty level ("FPL") for the family size involved who do not received health insurance through an employer or a spouse's employer.[28] Household income is defined as the sum of: (1) the taxpayer's modified adjusted gross income, plus (2) the aggregate modified adjusted gross incomes of all other individuals taken into account in determining that taxpayer's family size (but only if such individuals are required to file a tax return for the taxable year). Modified adjusted gross income is defined as

---

[26] Individuals enrolled in multi-state plans, pursuant to section 1334 of the Senate amendment, are also eligible for the credit.

[27] Although the credit is generally payable in advance directly to the insurer, individuals may elect to purchase health insurance out-of-pocket and apply to the IRS for the credit at the end of the taxable year. The amount of the reduction in premium is required to be included with each bill sent to the individual.

[28] Individuals who are lawfully present in the United States but are not eligible for Medicaid because of their immigration status are treated as having a household income equal to 100 percent of FPL (and thus eligible for the premium assistance credit) as long as their household income does not actually exceed 100 percent of FPL.

adjusted gross income increased by: (1) the amount (if any) normally excluded by section 911 (the exclusion from gross income for citizens or residents living abroad), plus (2) any tax-exempt interest received or accrued during the tax year. To be eligible for the premium assistance credit, taxpayers who are married (within the meaning of section 7703) must file a joint return. Individuals who are listed as dependants on a return are ineligible for the premium assistance credit.

As described in Table 1 below, premium assistance credits are available on a sliding scale basis for individuals and families with household incomes between 100 and 400 percent of FPL to help offset the cost of private health insurance premiums. The premium assistance credit amount is determined by the Secretary of HHS based on the percentage of income the cost of premiums represents, rising from two percent of income for those at 100 percent of FPL for the family size involved to 9.5 percent of income for those at 400 percent of FPL for the family size involved. Beginning in 2014, the percentages of income are indexed to the excess of premium growth over income growth for the preceding calendar year (in order to hold steady the share of premiums that enrollees at a given poverty level pay over time). Beginning in 2018, if the aggregate amount of premium assistance credits and cost-sharing reductions[29] exceeds 0.504 percent of the gross domestic product for that year, the percentage of income is also adjusted to reflect the excess (if any) of premium growth over the rate of growth in the consumer price index for the preceding calendar year. For purposes of calculating household size, individuals who are in the country illegally are not included. Individuals who are listed as dependants on a return are ineligible for the premium assistance credit.

Premium assistance credits, or any amounts that are attributable to them, cannot be used to pay for abortions for which federal funding is prohibited. Premium assistance credits are not available for months in which an individual has a free choice voucher (as defined in section 10108 of the Senate amendment).

<u>The low income premium credit phase-out</u>

The premium assistance credit increases, on a sliding scale in a linear manner, as shown in the table below.

---

[29] As described in section 1402 of the Senate amendment.

Household Income (expressed as a percent of poverty line)	Initial Premium (percentage)	Final Premium (percentage)
100% through 133%	2.0	3.0
133% through 150%	3.0	4.0
150% through 200%	4.0	6.3
200% through 250%	6.3	8.05
250% through 300%	8.05	9.5
300% through 400%	9.5	9.5

The premium assistance credit amount is tied to the cost of the second lowest-cost silver plan (adjusted for age) which: (1) is in the rating area where the individual resides, (2) is offered through an exchange in the area in which the individual resides, and (3) provides self-only coverage in the case of an individual who purchases self-only coverage, or family coverage in the case of any other individual. If the plan in which the individual enrolls offers benefits in addition to essential health benefits,[30] even if the State in which the individual resides requires such additional benefits, the portion of the premium that is allocable to those additional benefits is disregarded in determining the premium assistance credit amount.[31] Premium assistance credits may be used for any plan purchased through an exchange, including bronze, silver, gold and platinum level plans and, for those eligible,[32] catastrophic plans.

---

[30] As defined in section 1302(b) of the Senate amendment.

[31] A similar rule applies to additional benefits that are offered in multi-State plans, under section 1334 of the Senate amendment.

[32] Those eligible to purchase catastrophic plans either must have not reached the age of 30 before the beginning of the plan year, or have certification or an affordability or hardship exemption from the individual responsibility payment, as described in new sections 5000A(e)(1) and 5000A(e)(5), respectively.

Minimum essential coverage and employer offer of health insurance coverage

Generally, if an employee is offered minimum essential coverage[33] in the group market, including employer-provided health insurance coverage, the individual is ineligible for the premium tax credit for health insurance purchased through a State exchange.

If an employee is offered unaffordable coverage by his or her employer or the plan's share of provided benefits is less than 60 percent, the employee can be eligible for the premium tax credit, but only if the employee declines to enroll in the coverage and satisfies the conditions for receiving a tax credit through an exchange. Unaffordable is defined as coverage with a premium required to be paid by the employee that is 9.5 percent or more of the employee's household income, based on the type of coverage applicable (e.g., individual or family coverage).[34] The percentage of income that is considered unaffordable is indexed in the same manner as the percentage of income is indexed for purposes of determining eligibility for the credit (as discussed above). The Secretary of the Treasury is informed of the name and employer identification number of every employer that has one or more employees receiving a premium tax credit.

No later than five years after the date of the enactment of the provision the Comptroller General must conduct a study of whether the percentage of household income used for purposes of determining whether coverage is affordable is the appropriate level, and whether such level can be lowered without significantly increasing the costs to the Federal Government and reducing employer-provided health coverage. The Secretary reports the results of such study to the appropriate committees of Congress, including any recommendations for legislative changes.

Procedures for determining eligibility

For purposes of the premium assistance credit, exchange participants must provide information from their tax return from two years prior during the open enrollment period for coverage during the next calendar year. For example, if an individual applies for a premium assistance credit for 2014, the individual must provide a tax return from 2012 during the 2103 open enrollment period. The Internal Revenue Service ("IRS") is authorized to disclose to HHS limited tax return information to verify a taxpayer's income based on the most recent return information available to establish eligibility for the premium tax credit. Existing privacy and safeguard requirements apply. Individuals who do not qualify for the premium tax credit on the basis of their prior year income may apply for the premium tax credit based on specified changes in circumstances. For individuals and families who did not file a tax return in the prior tax year, the Secretary of HHS will establish alternative income documentation that may be provided to determine income eligibility for the premium tax credit.

The Secretary of HHS must establish a program for determining whether or not individuals are eligible to: (1) enroll in an exchange-offered health plan; (2) claim a premium

---

[33] As defined in section 5000A(f) of the Senate amendment.

[34] The 9.5 percent amount is indexed for calendar years beginning after 2014.

assistance credit; and (3) establish that their coverage under an employer-sponsored plan is unaffordable. The program must provide for the following: (1) the details of an individual's application process; (2) the details of how public entities are to make determinations of individuals' eligibility; (3) procedures for deeming individuals to be eligible; and, (4) procedures for allowing individuals with limited English proficiency to have proper access to exchanges.

In applying for enrollment in an exchange-offered health plan, an individual applicant is required to provide individually identifiable information, including name, address, date of birth, and citizenship or immigration status. In the case of an individual claiming a premium assistance credit, the individual is required to submit to the exchange income and family size information and information regarding changes in marital or family status or income. Personal information provided to the exchange is submitted to the Secretary of HHS. In turn, the Secretary of HHS submits the applicable information to the Social Security Commissioner, Homeland Security Secretary, and Treasury Secretary for verification purposes. The Secretary of HHS is notified of the results following verification, and notifies the exchange of such results. The provision specifies actions to be undertaken if inconsistencies are found. The Secretary of HHS, in consultation with the Social Security Commissioner, the Secretary of Homeland Security, and the Treasury Secretary must establish procedures for appealing determinations resulting from the verification process, and redetermining eligibility on a periodic basis.

An employer must be notified if one of its employees is determined to be eligible for a premium assistance credit because the employer does not provide minimal essential coverage through an employer-sponsored plan, or the employer does offer such coverage but it is not affordable. The notice must include information about the employer's potential liability for payments under section 4980H and that terminating or discriminating against an employee because he or she received a credit or subsidy is in violation of the Fair Labor Standards Act.[35] An employer is generally not entitled to information about its employees who qualify for the premium assistance credit. Employers may, however, be notified of the name of the employee and whether his or her income is above or below the threshold used to measure the affordability of the employer's health insurance coverage.

Personal information submitted for verification may be used only to the extent necessary for verification purposes and may not be disclosed to anyone not identified in this provision. Any person, who submits false information due to negligence or disregard of any rule, and without reasonable cause, is subject to a civil penalty of not more than $25,000. Any person who intentionally provides false information will be fined not more than $250,000. Any person who knowingly and willfully uses or discloses confidential applicant information will be fined not more than $25,000. Any fines imposed by this provision may not be collected through a lien or levy against property, and the section does not impose any criminal liability.

The provision requires the Secretary of HHS, in consultation with the Secretaries of the Treasury and Labor, to conduct a study to ensure that the procedures necessary to administer the determination of individuals' eligibility to participate in an exchange, to receive premium

[35] Pub. L. No. 75-718.

assistance credits, and to obtain an individual responsibility exemption, adequately protect employees' rights of privacy and employers' rights to due process. The results of the study must be reported by January 1, 2013, to the appropriate committees of Congress.

Reconciliation

If the premium assistance received through an advance payment exceeds the amount of credit to which the taxpayer is entitled, the excess advance payment is treated as an increase in tax. For persons whose household income is below 400% of the FPL, the amount of the increase in tax is limited to $400. If the premium assistance received through an advance payment is less than the amount of the credit to which the taxpayer is entitled, the shortfall is treated as a reduction in tax.

The eligibility for and amount of premium assistance is determined in advance of the coverage year, on the basis of household income and family size from two years prior, and the monthly premiums for qualified health plans in the individual market in which the taxpayer, spouse and any dependent enroll in an exchange. Any advance premium assistance is paid during the year for which coverage is provided by the exchange. In the subsequent year, the amount of advance premium assistance is required to be reconciled with the allowable refundable credit for the year of coverage. Generally, this would be accomplished on the tax return filed for the year of coverage, based on that year's actual household income, family size, and premiums. Any adjustment to tax resulting from the difference between the advance premium assistance and the allowable refundable tax credit would be assessed as additional tax or a reduction in tax on the tax return.

Separately, the provision requires that the exchange, or any person with whom it contracts to administer the insurance program, must report to the Secretary with respect to any taxpayer's participation in the health plan offered by the Exchange. The information to be reported is information necessary to determine whether a person has received excess advance payments, identifying information about the taxpayer (such as name, taxpayer identification number, months of coverage) and any other person covered by that policy; the level of coverage purchased by the taxpayer; the total premium charged for the coverage, as well as the aggregate advance payments credited to that taxpayer; and information provided to the Exchange for the purpose of establishing eligibility for the program, including changes of circumstances of the taxpayer since first purchasing the coverage. Finally, the party submitting the report must provide a copy to the taxpayer whose information is the subject of the report.

Effective Date

The provision is effective for taxable years ending after December 31, 2013.

D. Reduced Cost-Sharing for Individuals Enrolling in Qualified Health Plans (secs. 1402, 1411, and 1412 of the Senate amendment[36])

Present Law

Currently there is no tax credit that is generally available to low or middle income individuals or families for the purchase of health insurance. Some individuals may be eligible for health coverage through State Medicaid programs which consider income, assets, and family circumstances. However, these Medicaid programs are not in the Code.

Health coverage tax credit

Certain individuals are eligible for the HCTC. The HCTC is a refundable tax credit equal to 80 percent of the cost of qualified health coverage paid by an eligible individual. In general, eligible individuals are individuals who receive a trade adjustment allowance (and individuals who would be eligible to receive such an allowance but for the fact that they have not exhausted their regular unemployment benefits), individuals eligible for the alternative trade adjustment assistance program, and individuals over age 55 who receive pension benefits from the Pension Benefit Guaranty Corporation. The HCTC is available for "qualified health insurance," which includes certain employer-based insurance, certain State-based insurance, and in some cases, insurance purchased in the individual market.

The credit is available on an advance basis through a program established and administered by the Treasury Department. The credit generally is delivered as follows: the eligible individual sends his or her portion of the premium to the Treasury, and the Treasury then pays the full premium (the individual's portion and the amount of the refundable tax credit) to the insurer. Alternatively, an eligible individual is also permitted to pay the entire premium during the year and claim the credit on his or her income tax return.

Individuals entitled to Medicare and certain other governmental health programs, covered under certain employer-subsidized health plans, or with certain other specified health coverage are not eligible for the credit.

COBRA continuation coverage premium reduction

COBRA[37] requires that a group health plan must offer continuation coverage to qualified beneficiaries in the case of a qualifying event (such as a loss of employment). A plan may require payment of a premium for any period of continuation coverage. The amount of such premium generally may not exceed 102 percent of the "applicable premium" for such period and the premium must be payable, at the election of the payor, in monthly installments.

---

[36] Sections 1401, 1411 and 1412 of the Senate amendment, as amended by section 10104, is further amended by section 1001 of the Reconciliation bill.

[37] Pub. L. No. 99-272.

Section 3001 of the American Recovery and Reinvestment Act of 2009,[38] as amended by the Department of Defense Appropriations Act, 2010,[39] and the Temporary Extension Act of 2010[40] provides that, for a period not exceeding 15 months, an assistance eligible individual is treated as having paid any premium required for COBRA continuation coverage under a group health plan if the individual pays 35 percent of the premium. Thus, if the assistance eligible individual pays 35 percent of the premium, the group health plan must treat the individual as having paid the full premium required for COBRA continuation coverage, and the individual is entitled to a subsidy for 65 percent of the premium. An assistance eligible individual generally is any qualified beneficiary who elects COBRA continuation coverage and the qualifying event with respect to the covered employee for that qualified beneficiary is a loss of group health plan coverage on account of an involuntary termination of the covered employee's employment (for other than gross misconduct).[41] In addition, the qualifying event must occur during the period beginning September 1, 2008, and ending March 31, 2010.

The COBRA continuation coverage subsidy also applies to temporary continuation coverage elected under the Federal Employees Health Benefits Program and to continuation health coverage under State programs that provide coverage comparable to continuation coverage. The subsidy is generally delivered by requiring employers to pay the subsidized portion of the premium for assistance eligible individuals. The employer then treats the payment of the subsidized portion as a payment of employment taxes and offsets its employment tax liability by the amount of the subsidy. To the extent that the aggregate amount of the subsidy for all assistance eligible individuals for which the employer is entitled to a credit for a quarter exceeds the employer's employment tax liability for the quarter, the employer can request a tax refund or can claim the credit against future employment tax liability.

There is an income limit on the entitlement to the COBRA continuation coverage subsidy. Taxpayers with modified adjusted gross income exceeding $145,000 (or $290,000 for joint filers), must repay any subsidy received by them, their spouse, or their dependant, during the taxable year. For taxpayers with modified adjusted gross incomes between $125,000 and $145,000 (or $250,000 and $290,000 for joint filers), the amount of the subsidy that must be repaid is reduced proportionately. The subsidy is also conditioned on the individual not being eligible for certain other health coverage. To the extent that an eligible individual receives a subsidy during a taxable year to which the individual was not entitled due to income or being eligible for other health coverage, the subsidy overpayment is repaid on the individual's income

38 Pub. L. No. 111-5.

39 Pub. L. No. 111-118.

40 Pub. L. No. 111-144.

41 TEA expanded eligibility for the COBRA subsidy to include individuals who experience a loss of coverage on account of a reduction in hours of employment followed by the involuntary termination of employment of the covered employee. For an individual entitled to COBRA because of a reduction in hours and who is then subsequently involuntarily terminated from employment, the termination is considered a qualifying event for purposes of the COBRA subsidy, as long as the termination occurs during the period beginning on the date following TEA's date of enactment and ending on March 31, 2010.

tax return as additional tax. However, in contrast to the HCTC, the subsidy for COBRA continuation coverage may only be claimed through the employer and cannot be claimed at the end of the year on an individual tax return.

Explanation of Provision

Cost-sharing subsidy

A cost-sharing subsidy is provided to reduce annual out-of-pocket cost-sharing for individuals and households between 100 and 400 of percent FPL (for the family size involved). The reductions are made in reference to the dollar cap on annual deductibles for high deductable health plans in section 223(c)(2)(A)(ii) (currently $5,000 for self-only coverage and $10,000 for family coverage). For individuals with household income of more than 100 but not more than 200 percent of FPL, the out-of-pocket limit is reduced by two-thirds. For those between 201 and 300 percent of FPL by one-half, and for those between 301 and 400 percent of FPL by one-third.

The cost-sharing subsidy that is provided must buy out any difference in cost-sharing between the qualified health insurance purchased and the actuarial values specified below. For individuals between 100 and 150 percent of FPL (for the family size involved), the subsidy must bring the value of the plan to not more than 94 percent actuarial value. For those between 150 and 200 percent of FPL, the subsidy must bring the value of the plan to not more than 87 percent actuarial value. For those between 201 and 250 percent of FPL, the subsidy must bring the value of the plan to not more than 73 percent actuarial value. For those between 251 and 400 percent of FPL, the subsidy must bring the value of the plan to not more than 70 percent actuarial value. The determination of cost-sharing subsidies will be made based on data from the same taxable year as is used for determining advance credits under section 1412 of the Senate amendment (and not the taxable year used for determining premium assistance credits under section 36B). The amount received by an insurer as a cost-sharing subsidy on behalf of an individual, as well as any out-of-pocket spending by the individual, counts towards the out-of-pocket limit. Individuals enrolled in multi-state plans, pursuant to section 1334 of the Senate amendment, are eligible for the subsidy.

In addition to adjusting actuarial values, plans must further reduce cost-sharing for low-income individuals as specified below. For individuals between 100 and 150 percent of FPL (for the family size involved) the plan's share of the total allowed cost of benefits provided under the plan must be 94 percent. For those between 151 and 200 percent of FPL, the plan's share must be 87 percent, and for those between 201 and 250 percent of FPL the plan's share must be 73 percent.

The cost-sharing subsidy is available only for those months in which an individual receives an affordability credit under new section 36B.[42]

As with the premium assistance credit, if the plan in which the individual enrolls offers benefits in addition to essential health benefits,[43] even if the State in which the individual resides

[42] Section 1401 of the Senate amendment.

requires such additional benefits, the reduction in cost-sharing does not apply to the additional benefits. In addition, individuals enrolled in both a qualified health plan and a pediatric dental plan may not receive a cost-sharing subsidy for the pediatric dental benefits that are included in the essential health benefits required to be provided by the qualified health plan. Cost-sharing subsidies, and any amounts that are attributable to them, cannot be used to pay for abortions for which federal funding is prohibited.

The Secretary of HHS must establish a program for determining whether individuals are eligible to claim a cost-sharing credit. The program must provide for the following: (1) the details of an individual's application process; (2) the details of how public entities are to make determinations of individuals' eligibility; (3) procedures for deeming individuals to be eligible; and, (4) procedures for allowing individuals with limited English proficiency proper access to exchanges.

In applying for enrollment, an individual claiming a cost-sharing subsidy is required to submit to the exchange income and family size information and information regarding changes in marital or family status or income. Personal information provided to the exchange is submitted to the Secretary of HHS. In turn, the Secretary of HHS submits the applicable information to the Social Security Commissioner, Homeland Security Secretary, and Treasury Secretary for verification purposes. The Secretary of HHS is notified of the results following verification, and notifies the exchange of such results. The provision specifies actions to be undertaken if inconsistencies are found. The Secretary of HHS, in consultation with the Treasury Secretary, Homeland Security Secretary, and Social Security Commissioner, must establish procedures for appealing determinations resulting from the verification process, and redetermining eligibility on a periodic basis.

The Secretary notifies the plan that the individual is eligible and the plan reduces the cost-sharing by reducing the out-of-pocket limit under the provision. The plan notifies the Secretary of cost-sharing reductions and the Secretary makes periodic and timely payments to the plan equal to the value of the reductions in cost-sharing. The provision authorizes the Secretary to establish a capitated payment system with appropriate risk adjustments.

An employer must be notified if one of its employees is determined to be eligible for a cost-sharing subsidy. The notice must include information about the employer's potential liability for payments under section 4980H and explicit notice that hiring, terminating, or otherwise discriminating against an employee because he or she received a credit or subsidy is in violation of the Fair Labor Standards Act.[44] An employer is generally not entitled to information about its employees who qualify for the premium assistance credit or the cost-sharing subsidy. Employers may, however, be notified of the name of an employee and whether his or her income is above or below the threshold used to measure the affordability of the employer's health insurance coverage.

---

[43] As defined in section 1302(b) of the Senate amendment.

[44] Pub. Law No. 75-718.

The Secretary of the Treasury is informed of the name and employer identification number of every employer that has one or more employee receiving a cost-sharing subsidy.

The provision implements special rules for Indians (as defined by the Indian Health Care Improvement Act) and undocumented aliens. The provision prohibits cost-sharing reductions for individuals who are not lawfully present in the United States, and such individuals are not taken into account in determining the family size involved.

The provision defines any term used in this section that is also used by section 36B as having the same meaning as defined by the latter. The provision also denies subsidies to dependents, with respect to whom a deduction under section 151 is allowable to another taxpayer for a taxable year beginning in the calendar year in which the individual's taxable year begins. Further, the provision does not permit a subsidy for any month that is not treated as a coverage month.

Effective Date

The provision is effective on date of enactment.

E. Disclosures to Carry Out Eligibility Requirements for Certain Programs (sec. 1414[45] of the Senate amendment and sec. 6103 of the Code)

Present Law

Section 6103 provides that returns and return information are confidential and may not be disclosed by the IRS, other Federal employees, State employees, and certain others having access to such information except as provided in the Internal Revenue Code. Section 6103 contains a number of exceptions to the general rule of nondisclosure that authorize disclosure in specifically identified circumstances. For example, section 6103 provides for the disclosure of certain return information for purposes of establishing the appropriate amount of any Medicare Part B premium subsidy adjustment.

Section 6103(p)(4) requires, as a condition of receiving returns and return information, that Federal and State agencies (and certain other recipients) provide safeguards as prescribed by the Secretary of the Treasury by regulation to be necessary or appropriate to protect the confidentiality of returns or return information. Unauthorized disclosure of a return or return information is a felony punishable by a fine not exceeding $5,000 or imprisonment of not more than five years, or both, together with the costs of prosecution.[46] The unauthorized inspection of a return or return information is punishable by a fine not exceeding $1,000 or imprisonment of not more than one year, or both, together with the costs of prosecution.[47] An action for civil damages also may be brought for unauthorized disclosure or inspection.[48]

Explanation of Provision

Individuals will submit income information to an exchange as part of an application process in order to claim the cost-sharing reduction and the tax credit on an advance basis. The Department of HHS serves as the centralized verification agency for information submitted by individuals to the exchanges with respect to the reduction and the tax credit to the extent provided on an advance basis. The IRS is permitted to substantiate the accuracy of income information that has been provided to HHS for eligibility determination.

Specifically, upon written request of the Secretary of HHS, the IRS is permitted to disclose the following return information of any taxpayer whose income is relevant in determining the amount of the tax credit or cost-sharing reduction, or eligibility for participation in the specified State health subsidy programs (i.e., a State Medicaid program under title XIX of the Social Security Act, a State's children's health insurance program under title XXI of such Act, or a basic health program under section 2228 of such Act): (1) taxpayer identity; (2) the filing status of such taxpayer; (3) the modified adjusted gross income (as defined in new sec.

---

[45] Section 1414 of the Senate amendment is amended by section 1004 of the Reconciliation bill.

[46] Sec. 7213.

[47] Sec. 7213A.

[48] Sec. 7431.

36B of the Code) of such taxpayer, the taxpayer's spouse and of any dependants who are required to file a tax return; (4) such other information as is prescribed by Treasury regulation as might indicate whether such taxpayer is eligible for the credit or subsidy (and the amount thereof); and (5) the taxable year with respect to which the preceding information relates, or if applicable, the fact that such information is not available. HHS is permitted to disclose to an exchange or its contractors, or to the State agency administering the health subsidy programs referenced above (and their contractors) any inconsistency between the information submitted and IRS records.

The disclosed return information may be used only for the purposes of, and only to the extent necessary in, establishing eligibility for participation in the exchange, verifying the appropriate amount of the tax credit, and cost-sharing subsidy, or eligibility for the specified State health subsidy programs.

Recipients of the confidential return information are subject to the safeguard protections and civil and criminal penalties for unauthorized disclosure and inspection. Special rules apply to the disclosure of return information to contractors.

The IRS is required to make an accounting for all disclosures.

Effective Date

The provision is effective on date of enactment.

F. Premium Tax Credit and Cost-Sharing Reduction Payments Disregarded for Federal and Federally Assisted Programs (sec. 1415 of the Senate amendment)

Present Law

There is no tax credit that is generally available to low or middle income individuals or families for the purchase of health insurance.

Explanation of Provision

Any premium assistance tax credits and cost-sharing subsidies provided to an individual under the Senate amendment are disregarded for purposes of determining that individual's eligibility for benefits or assistance, or the amount or extent of benefits and assistance, under any Federal program or under any State or local program financed in whole or in part with Federal funds. Specifically, any amount of premium tax credit provided to an individual is not counted as income, and cannot be taken into account as resources for the month of receipt and the following two months. Any cost sharing subsidy provided on the individual's behalf is treated as made to the health plan in which the individual is enrolled and not to the individual.

Effective Date

The provision is effective on date of enactment.

G. Small Business Tax Credit
(sec. 1421[49] of the Senate amendment and new sec. 45R of the Code)

Present Law

The Code does not provide a tax credit for employers that provide health coverage for their employees. The cost to an employer of providing health coverage for its employees is generally deductible as an ordinary and necessary business expense for employee compensation.[50] In addition, the value of employer-provided health insurance is not subject to employer-paid Federal Insurance Contributions Act ("FICA") tax.

The Code generally provides that employees are not taxed on the value of employer-provided health coverage under an accident or health plan.[51] That is, these benefits are excluded from gross income. In addition, medical care provided under an accident or health plan for employees, their spouses, and their dependents generally is excluded from gross income.[52] Active employees participating in a cafeteria plan may be able to pay their share of premiums on a pre-tax basis through salary reduction.[53] Such salary reduction contributions are treated as employer contributions and thus also are excluded from gross income.

Explanation of Provisions

Small business employers eligible for the credit

Under the provision, a tax credit is provided for a qualified small employer for nonelective contributions to purchase health insurance for its employees. A qualified small business employer for this purpose generally is an employer with no more than 25 full-time equivalent employees ("FTEs") employed during the employer's taxable year, and whose employees have annual full-time equivalent wages that average no more than $50,000. However, the full amount of the credit is available only to an employer with 10 or fewer FTEs and whose employees have average annual fulltime equivalent wages from the employer of less than $25,000. These wage limits are indexed to the Consumer Price Index for Urban Consumers ("CPI-U") for years beginning in 2014.

Under the provision, an employer's FTEs are calculated by dividing the total hours worked by all employees during the employer's tax year by 2080. For this purpose, the maximum number of hours that are counted for any single employee is 2080 (rounded down to the nearest whole number). Wages are defined in the same manner as under section 3121(a) (as

---

[49] Section 1421 of the Senate amendment is amended by section 10105 of the Senate amendment.

[50] Sec. 162. However, see special rules in sections 419 and 419A for the deductibility of contributions to welfare benefit plans with respect to medical benefits for employees and their dependents.

[51] Sec 106.

[52] Sec. 105(b).

[53] Sec. 125.

determined for purposes of FICA taxes but without regard to the dollar limit for covered wages) and the average wage is determined by dividing the total wages paid by the small employer by the number of FTEs (rounded down to the nearest $1,000).

The number of hours of service worked by, and wages paid to, a seasonal worker of an employer is not taken into account in determining the full-time equivalent employees and average annual wages of the employer unless the worker works for the employer on more than 120 days during the taxable year. For purposes of the credit the term 'seasonal worker' means a worker who performs labor or services on a seasonal basis as defined by the Secretary of Labor, including workers covered by 29 CFR sec. 500.20(s)(1) and retail workers employed exclusively during holiday seasons.

The contributions must be provided under an arrangement that requires the eligible small employer to make a nonelective contribution on behalf of each employee who enrolls in certain defined qualifying health insurance offered to employees by the employer equal to a uniform percentage (not less than 50 percent) of the premium cost of the qualifying health plan.

The credit is only available to offset actual tax liability and is claimed on the employer's tax return. The credit is not payable in advance to the taxpayer or refundable. Thus, the employer must pay the employees' premiums during the year and claim the credit at the end of the year on its income tax return. The credit is a general business credit, and can be carried back for one year and carried forward for 20 years. The credit is available for tax liability under the alternative minimum tax.

Years the credit is available

Under the provision, the credit is initially available for any taxable year beginning in 2010, 2011, 2012, or 2013. Qualifying health insurance for claiming the credit for this first phase of the credit is health insurance coverage within the meaning of section 9832, which is generally health insurance coverage purchased from an insurance company licensed under State law.

For taxable years beginning in years after 2013, the credit is only available to a qualified small employer that purchases health insurance coverage for its employees through a State exchange and is only available for a maximum coverage period of two consecutive taxable years beginning with the first year in which the employer or any predecessor first offers one or more qualified plans to its employees through an exchange.[54]

The maximum two-year coverage period does not take into account any taxable years beginning in years before 2014. Thus a qualified small employer could potentially qualify for this credit for six taxable years, four years under the first phase and two years under the second phase.

---

[54] Sec. 1301 of the Senate amendment provides the requirements for a qualified health plan purchased through the exchange.

Calculation of credit amount

The credit is equal to the applicable percentage of the small business employer's contribution to the health insurance premium for each covered employee. Only nonelective contributions by the employer are taken into account in calculating the credit. Therefore, any amount contributed pursuant to a salary reduction arrangement under a cafeteria plan within the meaning of section 125 is not treated as an employer contribution for purposes of this credit. The credit is equal to the lesser of the following two amounts multiplied an applicable tax credit percentage: (1) the amount of contributions the employer made on behalf of the employees during the taxable year for the qualifying health coverage and (2) the amount of contributions that the employer would have made during the taxable year if each employee had enrolled in coverage with a small business benchmark premium. To calculate such contributions under the second of these two amounts, the benchmark premium is multiplied by the number of employees enrolled in coverage and then multiplied by the uniform percentage that applies for calculating the level of coverage selected by the employer. As discussed above, this tax credit is only available if this uniform percentage is at least 50 percent.

For the first phase of the credit (any taxable years beginning in 2010, 2011, 2012, or 2013), the applicable tax credit percentage is 35 percent. The benchmark premium is the average total premium cost in the small group market for employer-sponsored coverage in the employer's State. The premium and the benchmark premium vary based on the type of coverage provided to the employee (i.e., single, adult with child, family or two adults).

For taxable years beginning in years after 2013, the applicable tax credit percentage is 50 percent. The benchmark premium is the average total premium cost in the small group market for employer-sponsored coverage in the employer's State. The premium and the benchmark premium vary based on the type of coverage being provided to the employee (e.g. single or family).

The credit is reduced for employers with more than 10 FTEs but not more than 25 FTEs. The credit is also reduced for an employer for whom the average wages per employee is between $25,000 and $50,000. The amount of this reduction is equal to the amount of the credit (determined before any reduction) multiplied by a fraction, the numerator of which is the average annual wages of the employer in excess of $25,000 and the denominator is $25,000. For an employer with more than 10 FTEs, the percentage is reduced in proportion to the number of FTEs in excess of 10. For an employer with both more than 10 FTEs and average annual wages in excess of $25,000, the reduction is the sum of the amount of the two reductions.

Tax exempt organizations as qualified small employers

Any organization described in section 501(c) which is exempt under section 501(a) that otherwise qualifies for the small business tax credit is eligible to receive the credit. However, for tax-exempt organizations, the applicable percentage for the credit during the first phase of the credit (any taxable year beginning in 2010, 2011, 2012, or 2013) is limited to 25 percent and the applicable percentage for the credit during the second phase (taxable years beginning in years after 2013) is limited to 35 percent. The small business tax credit is otherwise calculated in the same manner for tax-exempt organizations that are qualified small employers as the tax credit is calculated for all other qualified small employers. Tax-exempt organizations are eligible to apply the tax credit against the organization's liability as an employer for payroll taxes for the taxable year to the extent of: (1) the amount of income tax withheld from its employees under section 3401(a); (2) the amount of hospital insurance tax withheld from its employees under section 3101(b); (3) and the amount of the hospital tax imposed on the organization under section 3111(b). However, the organization is not eligible for a credit in excess of the amount of these payroll taxes.

Special rules

The employer is entitled to a deduction under section 162 equal to the amount of the employer contribution minus the dollar amount of the credit. For example, if a qualified small employer pays 100 percent of the cost of its employees' health insurance coverage and the tax credit under this provision is 50 percent of that cost, the employer is able to claim a section 162 deduction for the other 50 percent of the premium cost.

The employer is determined by applying the employer aggregations rules in section 414(b), (c), and (m). In addition, the definition of employee includes a leased employee within the meaning of section 414(n).[55]

Self-employed individuals, including partners and sole proprietors, two percent shareholders of an S Corporation, and five percent owners of the employer (within the meaning of section 416(i)(1)(B)(i)) are not treated as employees for purposes of this credit. Any employee with respect to a self employed individual is not an employee of the employer for purposes of this credit if the employee is not performing services in the trade or business of the employer. Thus, the credit is not available for a domestic employee of a sole proprietor of a business. There is also a special rule to prevent sole proprietorships from receiving the credit for the owner and their family members. Thus, no credit is available for any contribution to the purchase of health insurance for these individuals and the individual is not taken into account in determining the number of FTEs or average full-time equivalent wages.

The Secretary of is directed to prescribe such regulations as may be necessary to carry out the provisions of new section 45R, including regulations to prevent the avoidance of the two-year limit on the credit period for the second phase of the credit through the use of successor entities and the use of the limit on the number of employees and the amount of average wages through the use of multiple entities. The Secretary of Treasury, in consultation with the Secretary of Labor, is directed to prescribe such regulations, rules, and guidance as may be necessary to

---

[55] Section 414(b) provides that, for specified employee benefit purposes, all employees of all corporations which are members of a controlled group of corporations are treated as employed by a single employer. There is a similar rule in section 414(c) under which all employees of trades or businesses (whether or not incorporated) which are under common are treated under regulations as employed by a single employer, and, in section 414(m), under which employees of an affiliated service group (as defined in that section) are treated as employed by a single employer. Section 414(n) provides that leased employees, as defined in that section, are treated as employees of the service recipient for specified purposes. Section 414(o) authorizes the Treasury to issue regulations to prevent avoidance of the certain requirement under section 414(m) and 414(n).

determine the hours of service of an employee for purposes of determining FTEs, including rules for the employees who are not compensated on an hourly basis.

Effective Date

The provision is effective for taxable years beginning after December 31, 2009.

H. Excise Tax on Individuals Without Essential Health Benefits Coverage (sec. 1501[56] of the Senate amendment and new sec. 5000A of the Code)

Present Law

Federal law does not require individuals to have health insurance. Only the Commonwealth of Massachusetts, through its statewide program, requires that individuals have health insurance (although this policy has been considered in other states, such as California, Maryland, Maine, and Washington). All adult residents of Massachusetts are required to have health insurance that meets "minimum creditable coverage" standards if it is deemed "affordable" at their income level under a schedule set by the board of the Commonwealth Health Insurance Connector Authority ("Connector"). Individuals report their insurance status on State income tax forms. Individuals can file hardship exemptions from the mandate; persons for whom there are no affordable insurance options available are not subject to the requirement for insurance coverage.

For taxable year 2007, an individual without insurance and who was not exempt from the requirement did not qualify under Massachusetts law for a State income tax personal exemption. For taxable years beginning on or after January 1, 2008, a penalty is levied for each month an individual is without insurance. The penalty consists of an amount up to 50 percent of the lowest premium available to the individual through the Connector. The penalty is reported and paid by the individual with the individual's Massachusetts State income tax return at the same time and in the same manner as State income taxes. Failure to pay the penalty results in the same interest and penalties as apply to unpaid income tax.

Explanation of Provision

Personal responsibility requirement

Beginning January, 2014, non-exempt U.S. citizens and legal residents are required to maintain minimum essential coverage. Minimum essential coverage includes government sponsored programs, eligible employer-sponsored plans, plans in the individual market, grandfathered group health plans and other coverage as recognized by the Secretary of HHS in coordination with the Secretary of the Treasury. Government sponsored programs include Medicare, Medicaid, Children's Health Insurance Program, coverage for members of the U.S. military,[57] veterans health care,[58] and health care for Peace Corps volunteers.[59] Eligible employer-sponsored plans include: governmental plans,[60] church plans,[61] grandfathered plans

---

[56] Section 1501 of the Senate amendment, as amended by section 10106, is further amended by section 1002 of the Reconciliation bill.

[57] 10 U.S.C. 55 and 38 U.S.C. 1781.

[58] 38 U.S.C. 17.

[59] 22 U.S.C. 2504(e).

[60] ERISA Sec. 3(32), U.S.C. 5: Chapter 89, except a plan described in paragraph (1)(A).

and other group health plans offered in the small or large group market within a State. Minimum essential coverage does not include coverage that consists of certain HIPAA excepted benefits.[62] Other HIPAA excepted benefits that do not constitute minimum essential coverage if offered under a separate policy, certificate or contract of insurance include long term care, limited scope dental and vision benefits, coverage for a disease or specified illness, hospital indemnity or other fixed indemnity insurance or Medicare supplemental health insurance.[63]

Individuals are exempt from the requirement for months they are incarcerated, not legally present in the United States or maintain religious exemptions. Those who are exempt from the requirement due to religious reasons must be members of a recognized religious sect exempting them from self employment taxes[64] and adhere to tenets of the sect. Individuals residing[65] outside of the United States are deemed to maintain minimum essential coverage. If an individual is a dependent[66] of another taxpayer, the other taxpayer is liable for any penalty payment with respect to the individual.

Penalty

Individuals who fail to maintain minimum essential coverage in 2016 are subject to a penalty equal to the greater of: (1) 2.5 percent of household income in excess of the taxpayer's household income for the taxable year over the threshold amount of income required for income tax return filing for that taxpayer under section 6012(a)(1);[67] or (2) $695 per uninsured adult in the household. The fee for an uninsured individual under age 18 is one-half of the adult fee for an adult. The total household penalty may not exceed 300 percent of the per adult penalty ($2,085). The total annual household payment may not exceed the national average annual premium for bronze level health plan offered through the Exchange that year for the household size.

This per adult annual penalty is phased in as follows: $95 for 2014; $325 for 2015; and $695 in 2016. For years after 2016, the $695 amount is indexed to CPI-U, rounded to the next

---

61 ERISA sec. 3(33).

62 U.S.C. 42 sec. 300gg-91(c)(1). HIPAA excepted benefits include: (1) coverage only for accident, or disability income insurance; (2) coverage issued as a supplement to liability insurance; (3) liability insurance, including general liability insurance and automobile liability insurance; (4) workers' compensation or similar insurance; (5) automobile medical payment insurance; (6) credit-only insurance; (7) coverage for on-site medical clinics; and (8) other similar insurance coverage, specified in regulations, under which benefits for medical care are secondary or incidental to other insurance benefits.

63 42 U.S.C. 300gg-91(c)(2-4).

64 Sec. 1402(g)(1).

65 Sec. 911(d)(1).

66 Sec. 152.

67 Generally, in 2010, the filing threshold is $9,350 for a single person or a married person filing separately and is $18,700 for married filing jointly. IR-2009-93, Oct. 15, 2009.

lowest $50. The percentage of income is phased in as follows: one percent for 2014; two percent in 2015; and 2.5 percent beginning after 2015. If a taxpayer files a joint return, the individual and spouse are jointly liable for any penalty payment.

The penalty applies to any period the individual does not maintain minimum essential coverage and is determined monthly. The penalty is assessed through the Code and accounted for as an additional amount of Federal tax owed. However, it is not subject to the enforcement provisions of subtitle F of the Code.[68] The use of liens and seizures otherwise authorized for collection of taxes does not apply to the collection of this penalty. Non-compliance with the personal responsibility requirement to have health coverage is not subject to criminal or civil penalties under the Code and interest does not accrue for failure to pay such assessments in a timely manner.

Individuals who cannot afford coverage because their required contribution for employer-sponsored coverage or the lowest cost bronze plan in the local Exchange exceeds eight percent of household income for the year are exempt from the penalty.[69] In years after 2014, the eight percent exemption is increased by the amount by which premium growth exceeds income growth. If self-only coverage is affordable to an employee, but family coverage is unaffordable, the employee is subject to the mandate penalty if the employee does not maintain minimum essential coverage. However, any individual eligible for employer coverage due to a relationship with an employee (e.g. spouse or child of employee) is exempt from the penalty if that individual does not maintain minimum essential coverage because family coverage is not affordable[70] (i.e., exceeds eight percent of household income). Taxpayers with income below the income tax filing

[68] IRS authority to assess and collect taxes is generally provided in subtitle F, "Procedure and Administration" in the Code. That subtitle establishes the rules governing both how taxpayers are required to report information to the IRS and pay their taxes as well as their rights. It also establishes the duties and authority of the IRS to enforce the Code, including civil and criminal penalties.

[69] In the case of an individual participating in a salary reduction arrangement, the taxpayer's household income is increased by any exclusion from gross income for any portion of the required contribution to the premium. The required contribution to the premium is the individual contribution to coverage through an employer or in the purchase of a bronze plan through the Exchange.

[70] For example, if an employee with a family is offered self-only coverage costing five percent of income and family coverage costing 10 percent of income, the employee is not eligible for the tax credit in the Exchange because self-only coverage costs less than 9.5 percent of household income. The employee is not exempt from the individual responsibility penalty on the grounds of an affordability exemption because the self-only plan costs less than eight percent of income. Although family coverage costs more than 9.5 percent of income, the family does not qualify for a tax credit regardless of whether the employee purchases self-only coverage or does not purchase self-only coverage through the employer. However, if the family of the employee does not maintain minimum essential benefits coverage, the employee's family is exempt from the individual mandate penalty because while self-only coverage is affordable to the employee, family coverage is not considered affordable.

threshold[71] shall also be exempt from the penalty for failure to maintain minimum essential coverage. All members of Indian tribes[72] are exempt from the penalty.

No penalty is assessed for individuals who do not maintain health insurance for a period of three months or less during the taxable year. If an individual exceeds the three month maximum during the taxable year, the penalty for the full duration of the gap during the year is applied. If there are multiple gaps in coverage during a calendar year, the exemption from penalty applies only to the first such gap in coverage. The Secretary of the Treasury shall provide rules when a coverage gap includes months in multiple calendar years. Individuals may also apply to the Secretary of HHS for a hardship exemption due to hardship in obtaining coverage.[73] Residents of the possessions[74] of the United States are treated as being covered by acceptable coverage.

Family size is the number of individuals for whom the taxpayer is allowed a personal exemption. Household income is the sum of the modified adjusted gross incomes of the taxpayer and all individuals accounted for in the family size required to file a tax return for that year. Modified adjusted gross income means adjusted gross income increased by all tax-exempt interest and foreign earned income.[75]

Effective Date

The provision is effective for taxable years beginning after December 31, 2013.

---

[71] Generally, in 2010, the filing threshold is $9,350 for a single person or a married person filing separately and is $18,700 for married filing jointly. IR-2009-93, Oct. 15, 2009.

[72] Tribal membership is defined in section 45A(c)(6).

[73] Sec. 1311(d)(4)(H).

[74] Sec. 937(a).

[75] Sec. 911.

I. Reporting of Health Insurance Coverage (sec. 1502 of the Senate amendment and new sec. 6055 of the Code and sec. 6724(d) of the Code)

Present Law

Insurer reporting of health insurance coverage

No provision.

Penalties for failure to comply with information reporting requirements

Present law imposes a variety of information reporting requirements on participants in certain transactions.[76] These requirements are intended to assist taxpayers in preparing their income tax returns and help the IRS determine whether such returns are correct and complete. Failure to comply with the information reporting requirements may result in penalties, including: a penalty for failure to file the information return,[77] a penalty for failure to furnish payee statements,[78] and a penalty for failure to comply with various other reporting requirements.[79]

The penalty for failure to file an information return generally is $50 for each return for which such failure occurs. The total penalty imposed on a person for all failures during a calendar year cannot exceed $250,000. Additionally, special rules apply to reduce the per-failure and maximum penalty where the failure is corrected within a specified period.

The penalty for failure to provide a correct payee statement is $50 for each statement with respect to which such failure occurs, with the total penalty for a calendar year not to exceed $100,000. Special rules apply that increase the per-statement and total penalties where there is intentional disregard of the requirement to furnish a payee statement.

Explanation of Provision

Under the provision, insurers (including employers who self-insure) that provide minimum essential coverage[80] to any individual during a calendar year must report certain health insurance coverage information to both the covered individual and to the IRS. In the case of coverage provided by a governmental unit, or any agency or instrumentality thereof, the

---

[76] Secs. 6031 through 6060.

[77] Sec. 6721.

[78] Sec. 6722.

[79] Sec. 6723. The penalty for failure to comply timely with a specified information reporting requirement is $50 per failure, not to exceed $100,000 for a calendar year.

[80] As defined in section 5000A of the Senate amendment, as amended by section 10106, as further amended by section 1002 of the Reconciliation bill.

reporting requirement applies to the person or employee who enters into the agreement to provide the health insurance coverage (or their designee).

The information required to be reported includes: (1) the name, address, and taxpayer identification number of the primary insured, and the name and taxpayer identification number of each other individual obtaining coverage under the policy; (2) the dates during which the individual was covered under the policy during the calendar year; (3) whether the coverage is a qualified health plan offered through an exchange; (4) the amount of any premium tax credit or cost-sharing reduction received by the individual with respect to such coverage; and (5) such other information as the Secretary may require.

To the extent health insurance coverage is through an employer-provided group health plan, the insurer is also required to report the name, address and employer identification number of the employer, the portion of the premium, if any, required to be paid by the employer, and any other information the Secretary may require to administer the new tax credit for eligible small employers.

The insurer is required to report the above information, along with the name, address and contact information of the reporting insurer, to the covered individual on or before January 31 of the year following the calendar year for which the information is required to be reported to the IRS.

The provision amends the information reporting provisions of the Code to provide that an insurer who fails to comply with these new reporting requirements is subject to the penalties for failure to file an information return and failure to furnish payee statements, respectively.

The IRS is required, not later than June 30 of each year, in consultation with the Secretary of HHS, to provide annual notice to each individual who files an income tax return and who fails to enroll in minimum essential coverage. The notice is required to include information on the services available through the exchange operating in the individual's State of residence.

Effective Date

The provision is effective for calendar years beginning after 2013.

J. Shared Responsibility for Employers (sec. 1513[81] of the Senate amendment and new sec. 4980H of the Code)

Present Law

Currently, there is no Federal requirement that employers offer health insurance coverage to employees or their families. However, as with other compensation, the cost of employer-provided health coverage is a deductible business expense under section 162 of the Code.[82] In addition, employer-provided health insurance coverage is generally not included in an employee's gross income.[83]

Employees participating in a cafeteria plan may be able to pay the portion of premiums for health insurance coverage not otherwise paid for by their employers on a pre-tax basis through salary reduction.[84] Such salary reduction contributions are treated as employer contributions for purposes of the Code, and are thus excluded from gross income.

One way that employers can offer employer-provided health insurance coverage for purposes of the tax exclusion is to offer to reimburse employees for the premiums for health insurance purchased by employees in the individual health insurance market. The payment or reimbursement of employees' substantiated individual health insurance premiums is excludible from employees' gross income.[85] This reimbursement for individual health insurance premiums can also be paid through salary reduction under a cafeteria plan.[86] However, this offer to reimburse individual health insurance premiums constitutes a group health plan

The Employee Retirement Income Security Act of 1974 ("ERISA")[87] preempts State law relating to certain employee benefit plans, including employer-sponsored health plans. While ERISA specifically provides that its preemption rule does not exempt or relieve any person from any State law which regulates insurance, ERISA also provides that an employee benefit plan is not deemed to be engaged in the business of insurance for purposes of any State law regulating insurance companies or insurance contracts. As a result of this ERISA preemption, self-insured employer-sponsored health plans need not provide benefits that are mandated under State insurance law.

---

[81] Section 1513 of the Senate amendment, as amended by section 10106, is further amended by section 1003 of the Reconciliation bill.

[82] Sec. 162. However see special rules in sections 419 and 419A for the deductibility of contributions to welfare benefit plans with respect to medical benefits for employees and their dependents.

[83] Sec. 106.

[84] Sec. 125.

[85] Rev. Rul. 61-146 (1961-2 CB 25).

[86] Proposed Treas. Reg. sec.1.125-1(m).

[87] Pub. L. 93-406

While ERISA does not require an employer to offer health benefits, it does require compliance if an employer chooses to offer health benefits, such as compliance with plan fiduciary standards, reporting and disclosure requirements, and procedures for appealing denied benefit claims. There are other Federal requirements for health plans which include, for example, rules for health care continuation coverage.[88] The Code imposes an excise tax on group health plans that fail to meet these other requirements.[89] The excise tax generally is equal to $100 per day per failure during the period of noncompliance and is imposed on the employer sponsoring the plan.

Under Medicaid, States may establish "premium assistance" programs, which pay a Medicaid beneficiary's share of premiums for employer-sponsored health coverage. Besides being available to the beneficiary through his or her employer, the coverage must be comprehensive and cost-effective for the State. An individual's enrollment in an employer plan is considered cost-effective if paying the premiums, deductibles, coinsurance and other cost-sharing obligations of the employer plan is less expensive than the State's expected cost of directly providing Medicaid-covered services. States are also required to provide coverage for those Medicaid-covered services that are not included in the private plans. A 2007 analysis showed that 12 States had Medicaid premium assistance programs as authorized under current law.

Explanation of Provision

An applicable large employer that does not offer coverage for all its full-time employees, offers minimum essential coverage that is unaffordable, or offers minimum essential coverage that consists of a plan under which the plan's share of the total allowed cost of benefits is less than 60 percent, is required to pay a penalty if any full-time employee is certified to the employer as having purchased health insurance through a state exchange with respect to which a tax credit or cost-sharing reduction is allowed or paid to the employee.

Applicable large employer

An employer is an applicable large employer with respect to any calendar year if it employed an average of at least 50 full-time employees during the preceding calendar year. For purposes of the provision, "employer" includes any predecessor employer. An employer is not treated as employing more than 50 full-time employees if the employer's workforce exceeds 50 full-time employees for 120 days or fewer during the calendar year and the employees that cause the employer's workforce to exceed 50 full-time employees are seasonal workers. A seasonal worker is a worker who performs labor or services on a seasonal basis (as defined by the Secretary of Labor), including retail workers employed exclusively during the holiday season and workers whose employment is, ordinarily, the kind exclusively performed at certain seasons

---

[88] These rules were added to ERISA and the Code by the Consolidated Omnibus Budget Reconciliation Act of 1985 (Pub. L. No. 99-272).

[89] Sec. 4980B.

or periods of the year and which, from its nature, may not be continuous or carried on throughout the year.[90]

In counting the number of employees for purposes of determining whether an employer is an applicable large employer, a full-time employee (meaning, for any month, an employee working an average of at least 30 hours or more each week) is counted as one employee and all other employees are counted on a pro-rated basis in accordance with regulations prescribed by the Secretary. The number of full-time equivalent employees that must be taken into account for purposes of determining whether the employer exceeds the threshold is equal to the aggregate number of hours worked by non-full-time employees for the month, divided by 120 (or such other number based on an average of 30 hours of service each week as the Secretary may prescribe in regulations).

The Secretary, in consultation with the Secretary of Labor, is directed to issue, as necessary, rules, regulations and guidance to determine an employee's hours of service, including rules that apply to employees who are not compensated on an hourly basis.

The aggregation rules of section 414(b), (c), (m), and (o) apply in determining whether an employer is an applicable large employer. The determination of whether an employer that was not in existence during the preceding calendar year is an applicable large employer is made based on the average number of employees that it is reasonably expected to employ on business days in the current calendar year.

Penalty for employers not offering coverage

An applicable large employer who fails to offer its full-time employees and their dependents the opportunity to enroll in minimum essential coverage under an employer-sponsored plan for any month is subject to a penalty if at least one of its full-time employees is certified to the employer as having enrolled in health insurance coverage purchased through a State exchange with respect to which a premium tax credit or cost-sharing reduction is allowed or paid to such employee or employees. The penalty for any month is an excise tax equal to the number of full-time employees over a 30-employee threshold during the applicable month (regardless of how many employees are receiving a premium tax credit or cost-sharing reduction) multiplied by one-twelfth of $2,000. In the case of persons treated as a single employer under the provision, the 30-employee reduction in full-time employees is made from the total number of full-time employees employed by such persons (i.e., only one 30-person reduction is permitted per controlled group of employers) and is allocated among such persons in relation to the number of full-time employees employed by each such person.

For example, in 2014, Employer A fails to offer minimum essential coverage and has 100 full-time employees, ten of whom receive a tax credit for the year for enrolling in a State exchange-offered plan. For each employee over the 30-employee threshold, the employer owes

---

[90] Section 500.20(s)(1) of title 29, Code of Federal Regulations. Under section 5000.20(s)(1), a worker who moves from one seasonal activity to another, while employed in agriculture or performing agricultural labor, is employed on a seasonal basis even though he may continue to be employed during a major portion of the year.

$2,000, for a total penalty of $140,000 ($2,000 multiplied by 70 ((100-30)). This penalty is assessed on a monthly basis.

For calendar years after 2014, the $2,000 dollar amount is increased by the percentage (if any) by which the average per capita premium for health insurance coverage in the United States for the preceding calendar year (as estimated by the Secretary of HHS no later than October 1 of the preceding calendar year) exceeds the average per capita premium for 2013 (as determined by the Secretary of HHS), rounded down to the nearest $10.

Penalty for employees receiving premium credits

An applicable large employer who offers, for any month, its full-time employees and their dependents the opportunity to enroll in minimum essential coverage under an employer-sponsored plan is subject to a penalty if any full-time employee is certified to the employer as having enrolled in health insurance coverage purchased through a State exchange with respect to which a premium tax credit or cost-sharing reduction is allowed or paid to such employee or employees.

The penalty is an excise tax that is imposed for each employee who receives a premium tax credit or cost-sharing reduction for health insurance purchased through a State exchange. For each full-time employee receiving a premium tax credit or cost-sharing subsidy through a State exchange for any month, the employer is required to pay an amount equal to one-twelfth of $3,000. The penalty for each employer for any month is capped at an amount equal to the number of full-time employees during the month (regardless of how many employees are receiving a premium tax credit or cost-sharing reduction) in excess of 30, multiplied by one-twelfth of $2,000. In the case of persons treated as a single employer under the provision, the 30-employee reduction in full-time employees for purposes of calculating the maximum penalty is made from the total number of full-time employees employed by such persons (i.e., only one 30-person reduction is permitted per controlled group of employers) and is allocated among such persons in relation to the number of full-time employees employed by each such person.

For example, in 2014, Employer A offers health coverage and has 100 full-time employees, 20 of whom receive a tax credit for the year for enrolling in a State exchange offered plan. For each employee receiving a tax credit, the employer owes $3,000, for a total penalty of $60,000. The maximum penalty for this employer is capped at the amount of the penalty that it would have been assessed for a failure to provide coverage, or $140,000 ($2,000 multiplied by 70 ((100-30)). Since the calculated penalty of $60,000 is less than the maximum amount, Employer A pays the $60,000 calculated penalty. This penalty is assessed on a monthly basis.

For calendar years after 2014, the $3,000 and $2,000 dollar amounts are increased by the percentage (if any) by which the average per capita premium for health insurance coverage in the United States for the preceding calendar year (as estimated by the Secretary of HHS no later than October 1 of the preceding calendar year) exceeds the average per capita premium for 2013 (as determined by the Secretary of HHS), rounded down to the nearest $10.

Time for payment, deductibility of excise taxes, restrictions on assessment

The excise taxes imposed under this provision are payable on an annual, monthly or other periodic basis as the Secretary of Treasury may prescribe. The excise taxes imposed under this provision for employees receiving premium tax credits are not deductible under section 162 as a business expense. The restrictions on assessment under section 6213 are not applicable to the excise taxes imposed under the provision.

Employer offer of health insurance coverage

Under the provision, as under current law, an employer is not required to offer health insurance coverage. If an employee is offered health insurance coverage by his or her employer and chooses to enroll in the coverage, the employer-provided portion of the coverage is excluded from gross income. The tax treatment is the same whether the employer offers coverage outside of a State exchange or the employer offers a coverage option through a State exchange.

Definition of coverage

As a general matter, if an employee is offered affordable minimum essential coverage under an employer-sponsored plan, the individual is ineligible for a premium tax credit and cost sharing reductions for health insurance purchased through a State exchange.

Unaffordable coverage

If an employee is offered minimum essential coverage by their employer that is either unaffordable or that consists of a plan under which the plan's share of the total allowed cost of benefits is less than 60 percent, however, the employee is eligible for a premium tax credit and cost sharing reductions, but only if the employee declines to enroll in the coverage and purchases coverage through the exchange instead. Unaffordable is defined as coverage with a premium required to be paid by the employee that is more than 9.5 percent of the employee's household income (as defined for purposes of the premium tax credits provided under the Senate amendment). This percentage of the employee's income is indexed to the per capita growth in premiums for the insured market as determined by the Secretary of HHS. The employee must seek an affordability waiver from the State exchange and provide information as to family income and the lowest cost employer option offered to them. The State exchange then provides the waiver to the employee. The employer penalty applies for any employee(s) receiving an affordability waiver.

For purposes of determining if coverage is unaffordable, required salary reduction contributions are treated as payments required to be made by the employee. However, if an employee is reimbursed by the employer for any portion of the premium for health insurance coverage purchased through the exchange, including any reimbursement through salary reduction contributions under a cafeteria plan, the coverage is employer-provided and the employee is not eligible for premium tax credits or cost-sharing reductions. Thus, an individual is not permitted to purchase coverage through the exchange, apply for the premium tax credit, and pay for the individual's portion of the premium using salary reduction contributions under the cafeteria plan of the individual's employer.

An employer must be notified if one of its employees is determined to be eligible for a premium assistance credit or a cost-sharing reduction because the employer does not provide minimal essential coverage through an employer-sponsored plan, or the employer does offer such coverage but it is not affordable or the plan's share of the total allowed cost of benefits is less than 60 percent. The notice must include information about the employer's potential liability for payments under section 4980H. The employer must also receive notification of the appeals process established for employers notified of potential liability for payments under section 4980H. An employer is generally not entitled to information about its employees who qualify for the premium assistance credit or cost-sharing reductions; however, the appeals process must provide an employer the opportunity to access the data used to make the determination of an employee's eligibility for a premium assistance credit or cost-sharing reduction, to the extent allowable by law.

The Secretary is required to prescribe rules, regulations or guidance for the repayment of any assessable payment (including interest) if the payment is based on the allowance or payment of a premium tax credit or cost-sharing reduction with respect to an employee that is subsequently disallowed and with respect to which the assessable payment would not have been required to have been made in the absence of the allowance or payment.

Effect of medicaid enrollment

A Medicaid-eligible individual can always choose to leave the employer's coverage and enroll in Medicaid, and an employer is not required to pay a penalty for any employees enrolled in Medicaid.

Study and reporting on employer responsibility requirements

The Secretary of Labor is required to study whether employee wages are reduced by reason of the application of the employer responsibility requirements, using the National Compensation Survey published by the Bureau of Labor Statistics. The Secretary of Labor is to report the results of this study to the Committee on Ways and Means of the House of Representatives and the Committee on Finance of the Senate.

Effective Date

The provision is effective for months beginning after December 31, 2013.

K. Reporting of Employer Health Insurance Coverage (sec. 1514 of the Senate amendment and new sec. 6056 of the Code and sec. 6724(d) of the Code)

Present Law

Employer reporting of health insurance coverage

No provision.

Penalties for failure to comply with information reporting requirements

Present law imposes a variety of information reporting requirements on participants in certain transactions.[91] These requirements are intended to assist taxpayers in preparing their income tax returns and help the IRS determine whether such returns are correct and complete. Failure to comply with the information reporting requirements may result in penalties, including: a penalty for failure to file the information return,[92] a penalty for failure to furnish payee statements,[93] and a penalty for failure to comply with various other reporting requirements.[94]

The penalty for failure to file an information return generally is $50 for each return for which such failure occurs. The total penalty imposed on a person for all failures during a calendar year cannot exceed $250,000. Additionally, special rules apply to reduce the per-failure and maximum penalty where the failure is corrected within a specified period.

The penalty for failure to provide a correct payee statement is $50 for each statement with respect to which such failure occurs, with the total penalty for a calendar year not to exceed $100,000. Special rules apply that increase the per-statement and total penalties where there is intentional disregard of the requirement to furnish a payee statement.

Explanation of Provision

Under the provision, each applicable large employer subject to the employer responsibility provisions of new section 4980H and each "offering employer" must report certain health insurance coverage information to both its full-time employees and to the IRS. An offering employer is any employer who offers minimum essential coverage[95] to its employees under an eligible employer-sponsored plan and who pays any portion of the costs of such plan,

---

91 Secs. 6031 through 6060.

92 Sec. 6721.

93 Sec. 6722.

94 Sec. 6723. The penalty for failure to comply timely with a specified information reporting requirement is $50 per failure, not to exceed $100,000 for a calendar year.

95 As defined in section 5000A of the Senate amendment, as amended by section 10106, as further amended by section 1002 of the Reconciliation bill.

but only if the required employer contribution of any employee exceeds eight percent of the wages paid by the employer to the employee. In the case of years after 2014, the eight percent is indexed to reflect the rate of premium growth over income growth between 2013 and the preceding calendar year. In the case of coverage provided by a governmental unit, or any agency or instrumentality thereof, the reporting requirement applies to the person or employee appropriately designated for purposes of making the returns and statements required by the provision.

The information required to be reported includes: (1) the name, address and employer identification number of the employer; (2) a certification as to whether the employer offers its full-time employees and their dependents the opportunity to enroll in minimum essential coverage under an eligible employer-sponsored plan; (3) the number of full-time employees of the employer for each month during the calendar year; (4) the name, address and taxpayer identification number of each full-time employee employed by the employer during the calendar year and the number of months, if any, during which the employee (and any dependents) was covered under a plan sponsored by the employer during the calendar year; and (5) such other information as the Secretary may require.

Employers who offer the opportunity to enroll in minimum essential coverage must also report: (1) in the case of an applicable large employer, the length of any waiting period with respect to such coverage; (2) the months during the calendar year during which the coverage was available; (3) the monthly premium for the lowest cost option in each of the enrollment categories under the plan; (4) the employer's share of the total allowed costs of benefits under the plan; and (5), in the case of an offering employer, the option for which the employer pays the largest position of the cost of the plan and the portion of the cost paid by the employer in each of the enrollment categories under each option.

The employer is required to report to each full-time employee the above information required to be reported with respect to that employee, along with the name, address and contact information of the reporting employer, on or before January 31 of the year following the calendar year for which the information is required to be reported to the IRS.

The provision amends the information reporting provisions of the Code to provide that an employer who fails to comply with these new reporting requirements is subject to the penalties for failure to file an information return and failure to furnish payee statements, respectively.

To the maximum extent feasible, the Secretary may provide that any information return or payee statement required to be provided under the provision may be provided as part of any return or statement required under new sections 6051[96] or 6055[97] and, in the case of an applicable large employer or offering employer offering health insurance coverage of a health insurance issuer, the employer may enter into an agreement with the issuer to include the

---

[96] For additional information on new section 6051, see the explanation of section 9002 of the Senate amendment, "Inclusion of Employer-Sponsored Health Coverage on W-2."

[97] For additional information on new section 6055, see the explanation of section 1502 of the Senate amendment, "Reporting of Health Insurance Coverage."

information required by the provision with the information return and payee statement required under new section 6055.

The Secretary has the authority, in coordination with the Secretary of Labor, to review the accuracy of the information reported by the employer, including the employer's share of the total allowed costs of benefits under the plan.

Effective Date

The provision is effective for periods beginning after December 31, 2013.

L. Offering of Qualified Health Plans Through Cafeteria Plans (sec. 1515 of the Senate amendment and sec. 125 of the Code)

Present Law

Currently, there is no Federal requirement that employers offer health insurance coverage to employees or their families. However, as with other compensation, the cost of employer-provided health coverage is a deductible business expense under section 162 of the Code.[98] In addition, employer-provided health insurance coverage is generally not included in an employee's gross income.[99]

Definition of a cafeteria plan

If an employee receives a qualified benefit (as defined below) based on the employee's election between the qualified benefit and a taxable benefit under a cafeteria plan, the qualified benefit generally is not includable in gross income.[100] However, if a plan offering an employee an election between taxable benefits (including cash) and nontaxable qualified benefits does not meet the requirements for being a cafeteria plan, the election between taxable and nontaxable benefits results in gross income to the employee, regardless of what benefit is elected and when the election is made.[101] A cafeteria plan is a separate written plan under which all participants are employees, and participants are permitted to choose among at least one permitted taxable benefit (for example, current cash compensation) and at least one qualified benefit. Finally, a cafeteria plan must not provide for deferral of compensation, except as specifically permitted in sections 125(d)(2)(B), (C), or (D).

Qualified benefits

Qualified benefits under a cafeteria plan are generally employer-provided benefits that are not includable in gross income under an express provision of the Code. Examples of qualified benefits include employer-provided health insurance coverage, group term life insurance coverage not in excess of $50,000, and benefits under a dependent care assistance program. In order to be excludable, any qualified benefit elected under a cafeteria plan must independently satisfy any requirements under the Code section that provides the exclusion. However, some employer-provided benefits that are not includable in gross income under an express provision of the Code are explicitly not allowed in a cafeteria plan. These benefits are generally referred to as nonqualified benefits. Examples of nonqualified benefits include scholarships[102]; employer-

---

[98] Sec. 162. However see special rules in sections 419 and 419A for the deductibility of contributions to welfare benefit plans with respect to medical benefits for employees and their dependents.

[99] Sec. 106.

[100] Sec. 125(a).

[101] Proposed Treas. Reg. sec. 1.125-1(b).

[102] Sec. 117.

provided meals and lodging;[103] educational assistance;[104] and fringe benefits.[105] A plan offering any nonqualified benefit is not a cafeteria plan.[106]

Payment of health insurance premiums through a cafeteria plan

Employees participating in a cafeteria plan may be able to pay the portion of premiums for health insurance coverage not otherwise paid for by their employers on a pre-tax basis through salary reduction.[107] Such salary reduction contributions are treated as employer contributions for purposes of the Code, and are thus excluded from gross income.

One way that employers can offer employer-provided health insurance coverage for purposes of the tax exclusion is to offer to reimburse employees for the premiums for health insurance purchased by employees in the individual health insurance market. The payment or reimbursement of employees' substantiated individual health insurance premiums is excludible from employees' gross income.[108] This reimbursement for individual health insurance premiums can also be paid for through salary reduction under a cafeteria plan.[109] This offer to reimburse individual health insurance premiums constitutes a group health plan.

Explanation of Provision

Under the provision, reimbursement (or direct payment) for the premiums for coverage under any qualified health plan (as defined in section 1301(a) of the the Senate amendment) offered through an Exchange established under section 1311 of the Senate amendment is a qualified benefit under a cafeteria plan if the employer is a qualified employer. Under section 1312(f)(2) of the Senate amendment, a qualified employer is generally a small employer that elects to make all its full-time employees eligible for one or more qualified plans offered in the small group market through an Exchange.[110] Otherwise, reimbursement (or direct payment) for the premiums for coverage under any qualified health plan offered through an Exchange is not a

---

[103] Sec. 119.

[104] Sec.127.

[105] Sec. 132.

[106] Proposed Treas. Reg. sec. 1.125-1(q). Long-term care services, contributions to Archer Medical Savings Accounts, group term life insurance for an employee's spouse, child or dependent, and elective deferrals to section 403(b) plans are also nonqualified benefits.

[107] Sec. 125.

[108] Rev. Rul. 61-146 (1961-2 CB 25).

[109] Proposed Treas. Reg. sec.1.125-1(m).

[110] Beginning in 2017, each State may allow issuers of health insurance coverage in the large group market in a state to offer qualified plans in the large group market. In that event, a qualified employer includes a small employer that elects to make all its full-time employees eligible for one or more qualified plans offered in the large group market through an Exchange.

qualified benefit under a cafeteria plan. Thus, an employer that is not a qualified employer cannot offer to reimburse an employee for the premium for a qualified plan that the employee purchases through the individual market in an Exchange as a health insurance coverage option under its cafeteria plan.

Effective Date

This provision applies to taxable years beginning after December 31, 2013.

M. Conforming Amendments
(sec. 1562 of the Senate amendment and new sec. 9815 of the Code)

Present Law

The Health Insurance Portability and Accountability Act of 1996 ("HIPAA")[111] imposes a number of requirements with respect to group health coverage that are designed to provide protections to health plan participants. These protections include limitations on exclusions from coverage based on pre-existing conditions; the prohibition of discrimination on the basis of health status; guaranteed renewability in multiemployer plans and certain employer welfare arrangements; standards relating to benefits for mother and newborns; parity in the application of certain limits to mental health benefits; and coverage of dependent students on medically necessary leave of absence. The requirements are enforced through the Code, ERISA,[112] and PHSA.[113] The HIPAA requirements in the Code are in chapter 100 of Subtitle K, Group Health Plan Requirements.

A group health plan is defined as a plan (including a self-insured plan) of, or contributed to by, an employer (including a self-employed person) or employee organization to provide health care (directly or otherwise) to the employees, former employees, the employer, others associated or formerly associated with the employer in a business relationship, or their families.[114]

The Code imposes an excise tax on group health plans which fail to meet the HIPAA requirements.[115] The excise tax is equal to $100 per day during the period of noncompliance and is generally imposed on the employer sponsoring the plan if the plan fails to meet the requirements. The maximum tax that can be imposed during a taxable year cannot exceed the lesser of: (1) 10 percent of the employer's group health plan expenses for the prior year; or (2) $500,000. No tax is imposed if the Secretary of the Treasury determines that the employer did not know, and in exercising reasonable diligence would not have known, that the failure existed.

Explanation of Provision

The provision adds new Code section 9815 which provides that the provisions of part A of title XXVII of the PHSA (as amended by the Senate amendment) apply to group health plans, and health insurance issuers providing health insurance coverage in connection with group health plans, as if included in the HIPAA provisions of the Code. To the extent that any HIPAA provision of the Code conflicts with a provision of part A of title XXVII of the PHSA with

---

[111] Pub. L. No. 104-191.

[112] Pub. L. No. 93-406.

[113] 42 U.S.C. 6A.

[114] The requirements do not apply to any governmental plan or any group health plan that has fewer than two participants who are current employees.

[115] Sec. 4980D.

respect to group health plans, or health insurance issuers providing health insurance coverage in connection with group health plans, the provisions of such part A generally apply.

The provisions of part A of title XXVII of the PHSA added by section 1001 of the Senate amendment that are incorporated by reference in new section 9815 include the following: section 2711 (No lifetime or annual limits); section 2712 (Prohibition on rescissions); section 2713 (Coverage of preventive health services); section 2714 (Extension of dependent coverage); section 2715 (Development and utilization of uniform explanation of coverage documents and standardized definitions); section 2716 (Prohibition of discrimination based on salary); section 2717 (Ensuring the quality of care); section 2718 (Bringing down the cost of health care coverage); and section 2719 (Appeals process). These new sections of the PHSA, which relate to individual and group market reforms, are effective six months after the date of enactment.

The provisions of part A of title XXVII of the PHSA added by section 1201 of the Senate amendment that are incorporated by reference in new section 9815 include the following: section 2704 (Prohibition of preexisting condition exclusions or other discrimination based on health status); section 2701 (Fair health insurance premiums); section 2702 (Guaranteed availability of coverage) section 2703 (Guaranteed renewability of coverage); section 2705 (Prohibiting discrimination against individual participants and beneficiaries based on health status); section 2706 (Non-discrimination in health care); section 2707 (Comprehensive health insurance coverage); and section 2708 (Prohibition on excessive waiting periods). These new sections of the PHSA, which relate to general health insurance reforms, are effective for plan years beginning on or after January 1, 2014.

New section 9815 specifies that section 2716 (Prohibition of discrimination based on salary) and 2718 (Bringing down the cost of health coverage) of title XXVII of the PHSA (as amended by the Senate amendment) do not apply under the Code provisions of HIPAA with respect to self-insured group health plans.

As a result of incorporating these HIPAA provision by reference, the excise tax that applies in the event of a violation of present law HIPAA requirements also applies in the event of a violation of these new requirements.

Effective Date

This provision is effective on the date of enactment.

TITLE III – IMPROVING THE QUALITY AND EFFICIENCY OF HEALTHCARE

A. Disclosures to Carry Out the Reduction of Medicare Part D Subsidies for High Income Beneficiaries (sec. 3308(b)(2) of the Senate amendment and sec. 6103 of the Code)

Present Law

Section 6103 provides that returns and return information are confidential and may not be disclosed by the IRS, other Federal employees, State employees, and certain others having access to such information except as provided in the Code. Section 6103 contains a number of exceptions to the general rule of nondisclosure that authorize disclosure in specifically identified circumstances. For example, section 6103 provides for the disclosure of certain return information for purposes of establishing the appropriate amount of any Medicare Part B premium subsidy adjustment.

Specifically, upon written request from the Commissioner of Social Security, the IRS may disclose the following limited return information of a taxpayer whose premium, according to the records of the Secretary, may be subject to adjustment under section 1839(i) of the Social Security Act (relating to Medicare Part B):

- Taxpayer identity information with respect to such taxpayer;
- The filing status of the taxpayer;
- The adjusted gross income of such taxpayer;
- The amounts excluded from such taxpayer's gross income under sections 135 and 911 to the extent such information is available;
- The interest received or accrued during the taxable year which is exempt from the tax imposed by chapter 1 to the extent such information is available;
- The amounts excluded from such taxpayer's gross income by sections 931 and 933 to the extent such information is available;
- Such other information relating to the liability of the taxpayer as is prescribed by the Secretary by regulation as might indicate that the amount of the premium of the taxpayer may be subject to an adjustment and the amount of such adjustment; and
- The taxable year with respect to which the preceding information relates.

This return information may be used by officers, employees, and contractors of the Social Security Administration only for the purposes of, and to the extent necessary in, establishing the appropriate amount of any Medicare Part B premium subsidy adjustment.

Section 6103(p)(4) requires, as a condition of receiving returns and return information, that Federal and State agencies (and certain other recipients) provide safeguards as prescribed by the Secretary by regulation to be necessary or appropriate to protect the confidentiality of returns or return information. Unauthorized disclosure of a return or return information is a felony punishable by a fine not exceeding $5,000 or imprisonment of not more than five years, or both, together with the costs of prosecution.[116] The unauthorized inspection of a return or return information is punishable by a fine not exceeding $1,000 or imprisonment of not more than one year, or both, together with the costs of prosecution.[117] An action for civil damages also may be brought for unauthorized disclosure or inspection.[118]

Explanation of Provision

Upon written request from the Commissioner of Social Security, the IRS may disclose the following limited return information of a taxpayer whose Medicare Part D premium subsidy, according to the records of the Secretary, may be subject to adjustment:

- Taxpayer identity information with respect to such taxpayer;
- The filing status of the taxpayer;
- The adjusted gross income of such taxpayer;
- The amounts excluded from such taxpayer's gross income under sections 135 and 911 to the extent such information is available;
- The interest received or accrued during the taxable year which is exempt from the tax imposed by chapter 1 to the extent such information is available;
- The amounts excluded from such taxpayer's gross income by sections 931 and 933 to the extent such information is available;
- Such other information relating to the liability of the taxpayer as is prescribed by the Secretary by regulation as might indicate that the amount of the Part D premium of the taxpayer may be subject to an adjustment and the amount of such adjustment; and
- The taxable year with respect to which the preceding information relates.

This return information may be used by officers, employees, and contractors of the Social Security Administration only for the purposes of, and to the extent necessary in, establishing the appropriate amount of any Medicare Part D premium subsidy adjustment.

For purposes of both the Medicare Part B premium subsidy adjustment and the Medicare Part D premium subsidy adjustment, the provision provides that the Social Security Administration may redisclose only taxpayer identity and the amount of premium subsidy adjustment to officers and employees and contractors of the Centers for Medicare and Medicaid Services, and officers and employees of the Office of Personnel Management and the Railroad Retirement Board. This redisclosure is permitted only to the extent necessary for the collection of the premium subsidy amount from the taxpayers under the jurisdiction of the respective agencies.

---

[116] Sec. 7213.

[117] Sec. 7213A.

[118] Sec. 7431.

Further, the Social Security Administration may redisclose the return information received under this provision to officers and employees of the Department of HHS to the extent necessary to resolve administrative appeals of the Part B and Part D subsidy adjustments and to officers and employees of the Department of Justice to the extent necessary for use in judicial proceedings related to establishing and collecting the appropriate amount of any Medicare Part B or Medicare Part D premium subsidy adjustments.

Effective Date

The provision is effective on date of enactment.

TITLE VI – TRANSPARENCY AND PROGRAM INTEGRITY

A. Patient-Centered Outcomes Research Trust Fund; Financing for Trust Fund (sec. 6301 of the Senate amendment and new secs. 4375, 4376, 4377, and 9511 of the Code)

Present Law

No provision.

Explanation of Provision

Patient-Centered Outcomes Research Trust Fund

Under new section 9511, there is established in the Treasury of the United States a trust fund, the Patient Centered Outcomes Research Trust Fund ("PCORTF"), to carry out the provisions in the Senate amendment relating to comparative effectiveness research. The PCORTF is funded in part from fees imposed on health plans under new sections 4375 through 4377.

Fee on insured and self-insured health plans

Insured plans

Under new section 4375, a fee is imposed on each specified health insurance policy. The fee is equal to two dollars (one dollar in the case of policy years ending during fiscal year 2013) multiplied by the average number of lives covered under the policy. For any policy year beginning after September 30, 2014, the dollar amount is equal to the sum of: (1) the dollar amount for policy years ending in the preceding fiscal year, plus (2) an amount equal to the product of (A) the dollar amount for policy years ending in the preceding fiscal year, multiplied by (B) the percentage increase in the projected per capita amount of National Health Expenditures, as most recently published by the Secretary before the beginning of the fiscal year. The issuer of the policy is liable for payment of the fee. A specified health insurance policy includes any accident or health insurance policy[119] issued with respect to individuals residing in the United States.[120] An arrangement under which fixed payments of premiums are received as consideration for a person's agreement to provide, or arrange for the provision of, accident or

[119] A specified health insurance policy does not include insurance if substantially all of the coverage provided under such policy consists of excepted benefits described in section 9832(c). Examples of excepted benefits described in section 9832(c) are coverage for only accident, or disability insurance, or any combination thereof; liability insurance, including general liability insurance and automobile liability insurance; workers' compensation or similar insurance; automobile medical payment insurance; coverage for on-site medical clinics; limited scope dental or vision benefits; benefits for long term care, nursing home care, community based care, or any combination thereof; coverage only for a specified disease or illness; hospital indemnity or other fixed indemnity insurance; and Medicare supplemental coverage.

[120] Under the provision, the United States includes any possession of the United States.

health coverage to residents of the United States, regardless of how such coverage is provided or arranged to be provided, is treated as a specified health insurance policy. The person agreeing to provide or arrange for the provision of coverage is treated as the issuer.

Self -insured plans

In the case of an applicable self-insured health plan, new Code section 4376 imposes a fee equal to two dollars (one dollar in the case of policy years ending during fiscal year 2013) multiplied by the average number of lives covered under the plan. For any policy year beginning after September 30, 2014, the dollar amount is equal to the sum of: (1) the dollar amount for policy years ending in the preceding fiscal year, plus (2) an amount equal to the product of (A) the dollar amount for policy years ending in the preceding fiscal year, multiplied by (B) the percentage increase in the projected per capita amount of National Health Expenditures, as most recently published by the Secretary before the beginning of the fiscal year. The plan sponsor is liable for payment of the fee. For purposes of the provision, the plan sponsor is: the employer in the case of a plan established or maintained by a single employer or the employee organization in the case of a plan established or maintained by an employee organization. In the case of: (1) a plan established or maintained by two or more employers or jointly by one of more employers and one or more employee organizations, (2) a multiple employer welfare arrangement, or (3) a voluntary employees' beneficiary association described in Code section 501(c)(9) ("VEBA"), the plan sponsor is the association, committee, joint board of trustees, or other similar group of representatives of the parties who establish or maintain the plan. In the case of a rural electric cooperative or a rural telephone cooperative, the plan sponsor is the cooperative or association.

Under the provision, an applicable self-insured health plan is any plan providing accident or health coverage if any portion of such coverage is provided other than through an insurance policy and such plan is established or maintained: (1) by one or more employers for the benefit of their employees or former employees, (2) by one or more employee organizations for the benefit of their members or former members, (3) jointly by one or more employers and one or more employee organizations for the benefit of employees or former employees, (4) by a VEBA, (5) by any organization described in section 501(c)(6) of the Code, or (6) in the case of a plan not previously described, by a multiple employer welfare arrangement (as defined in section 3(40) of ERISA, a rural electric cooperative (as defined in section 3(40)(B)(iv) of ERISA), or a rural telephone cooperative association (as defined in section 3(40)(B)(v) of ERISA).

Other special rules

Governmental entities are generally not exempt from the fees imposed under the provision. There is an exception for exempt governmental programs including, Medicare, Medicaid, SCHIP, and any program established by Federal law for proving medical care (other than through insurance policies) to members of the Armed Forces, veterans, or members of Indian tribes.

No amount collected from the fee on health insurance and self-insured plans is covered over to any possession of the United States. For purposes of the Code's procedure and administration rules, the fee imposed under the provision is treated as a tax. The fees imposed under new sections 4375 and 4376 do not apply to plan years ending after September 31, 2019.

Effective Date

The fee on health insurance and self-insured plans is effective with respect to policies and plans for portions of policy or plan years beginning on or after October 1, 2012.

TITLE IX – REVENUE PROVISONS

A. Excise Tax on High Cost Employer-Sponsored Health Coverage (sec. 9001[121] of the Senate amendment and new sec. 4980I of the Code)

Present Law

Taxation of insurance companies

Current law provides special rules for determining the taxable income of insurance companies (subchapter L of the Code). Separate sets of rules apply to life insurance companies and to property and casualty insurance companies. Insurance companies generally are subject to Federal income tax at regular corporate income tax rates.

An insurance company that provides health insurance is subject to Federal income tax as either a life insurance company or as a property insurance company, depending on its mix of lines of business and on the resulting portion of its reserves that are treated as life insurance reserves. For Federal income tax purposes, an insurance company is treated as a life insurance company if the sum of its (1) life insurance reserves and (2) unearned premiums and unpaid losses on noncancellable life, accident or health contracts not included in life insurance reserves, comprise more than 50 percent of its total reserves.[122]

Some insurance providers may be exempt from Federal income tax under section 501(a) if specific requirements are satisfied. Section 501(c)(8), for example, describes certain fraternal beneficiary societies, orders, or associations operating under the lodge system or for the exclusive benefit of their members that provide for the payment of life, sick, accident, or other benefits to the members or their dependents. Section 501(c)(9) describes certain voluntary employees' beneficiary associations that provide for the payment of life, sick, accident, or other benefits to the members of the association or their dependents or designated beneficiaries. Section 501(c)(12)(A) describes certain benevolent life insurance associations of a purely local character. Section 501(c)(15) describes certain small non-life insurance companies with annual gross receipts of no more than $600,000 ($150,000 in the case of a mutual insurance company). Section 501(c)(26) describes certain membership organizations established to provide health insurance to certain high-risk individuals. Section 501(c)(27) describes certain organizations established to provide workmen's compensation insurance. A health maintenance organization that is tax-exempt under section 501(c)(3) or (4) is not treated as providing prohibited[123] commercial-type insurance, in the case of incidental health insurance provided by the health maintenance organization that is of a kind customarily provided by such organizations.

---

[121] Section 9001 of the Senate amendment, as amended by section 10901, is further amended by section 1401 of the Reconciliation bill.

[122] Sec. 816(a).

[123] Sec. 501(m).

Treatment of employer-sponsored health coverage

As with other compensation, the cost of employer-provided health coverage is a deductible business expense under section 162.[124] Employer-provided health insurance coverage is generally not included in an employee's gross income.

In addition, employees participating in a cafeteria plan may be able to pay the portion of premiums for health insurance coverage not otherwise paid for by their employers on a pre-tax basis through salary reduction.[125] Such salary reduction contributions are treated as employer contributions for Federal income purposes, and are thus excluded from gross income.

Employers may agree to reimburse medical expenses of their employees (and their spouses and dependents), not covered by a health insurance plan, through flexible spending arrangements which allow reimbursement not in excess of a specified dollar amount (either elected by an employee under a cafeteria plan or otherwise specified by the employer). Reimbursements under these arrangements are also excludible from gross income as employer-provided health coverage.

A flexible spending arrangement for medical expenses under a cafeteria plan ("Health FSA") is an unfunded arrangement under which employees are given the option to reduce their current cash compensation and instead have the amount made available for use in reimbursing the employee for his or her medical expenses.[126] Health FSAs that are funded on a salary reduction basis are subject to the requirements for cafeteria plans, including a requirement that amounts remaining under a Health FSA at the end of a plan year must be forfeited by the employee (referred to as the "use-it-or-lose-it rule").[127]

Alternatively, the employer may specify a dollar amount that is available for medical expense reimbursement. These arrangements are commonly called Health Reimbursement Arrangements ("HRAs"). Some of the rules applicable to HRAs and Health FSAs are similar (e.g., the amounts in the arrangements can only be used to reimburse medical expenses and not for other purposes), but the rules are not identical. In particular, HRAs cannot be funded on a salary reduction basis and the use-it-or-lose-it rule does not apply. Thus, amounts remaining at

---

[124] Sec. 162. However see special rules in section 419 and 419A for the deductibility of contributions to welfare benefit plans with respect to medical benefits for employees and their dependents.

[125] Sec. 125.

[126] Sec. 125. Prop. Treas. Reg. sec. 1.125-5 provides rules for Health FSAs. There is a similar type of flexible spending arrangement for dependent care expenses.

[127] Sec. 125(d)(2). A cafeteria plan is permitted to allow a grace period not to exceed two and one-half months immediately following the end of the plan year during which unused amounts may be used. Notice 2005-42, 2005-1 C.B. 1204.

the end of the year may be carried forward to be used to reimburse medical expenses in following years.[128]

Current law provides that individuals with a high deductible health plan (and generally no other health plan) may establish and make tax-deductible contributions to a health savings account ("HSA"). An HSA is subject to a condition that the individual is covered under a high deductible health plan (purchased either through the individual market or through an employer). Subject to certain limitations,[129] contributions made to an HSA by an employer, including contributions made through a cafeteria plan through salary reduction, are excluded from income (and from wages for payroll tax purposes). Contributions made by individuals are deductible for income tax purposes, regardless of whether the individuals itemize. Like an HSA, an Archer MSA is a tax-exempt trust or custodial account to which tax-deductible contributions may be made by individuals with a high deductible health plan; however, only self-employed individuals and employees of small employers are eligible to have an Archer MSA. Archer MSAs provide tax benefits similar to, but generally not as favorable as, those provided by HSAs for individuals covered by high deductible health plans.[130]

ERISA[131] preempts State law relating to certain employee benefit plans, including employer-sponsored health plans. While ERISA specifically provides that its preemption rule does not exempt or relieve any person from any State law which regulates insurance, ERISA also provides that an employee benefit plan is not deemed to be engaged in the business of insurance for purposes of any State law regulating insurance companies or insurance contracts. As a result of this ERISA preemption, self-insured employer-sponsored health plans need not provide benefits that are mandated under State insurance law.

While ERISA does not require an employer to offer health benefits, it does require compliance if an employer chooses to offer health benefits, such as compliance with plan fiduciary standards, reporting and disclosure requirements, and procedures for appealing denied benefit claims. ERISA was amended (as well as the PHSA and the Code) by COBRA[132] and

---

[128] Guidance with respect to HRAs, including the interaction of FSAs and HRAs in the case of an individual covered under both, is provided in Notice 2002-45, 2002-2 C.B. 93.

[129] For 2010, the maximum aggregate annual contribution that can be made to an HSA is $3,050 in the case of self-only coverage and $6,150 in the case of family coverage. The annual contribution limits are increased for individuals who have attained age 55 by the end of the taxable year (referred to as "catch-up contributions"). In the case of policyholders and covered spouses who are age 55 or older, the HSA annual contribution limit is greater than the otherwise applicable limit by $1,000 in 2009 and thereafter. Contributions, including catch-up contributions, cannot be made once an individual is enrolled in Medicare.

[130] In addition to being limited to self-employed individuals and employees of small employers, the definition of a high deductible health plan for an Archer MSA differs from that for an HSA. After 2007, no new contributions can be made to Archer MSAs except by or on behalf of individuals who previously had made Archer MSA contributions and employees who are employed by a participating employer.

[131] Pub. L. No. 93-406.

[132] Pub. L. No. 99-272.

HIPAA,[133] which added other Federal requirements for health plans, including rules for health care continuation coverage, limitations on exclusions from coverage based on preexisting conditions, and a few benefit requirements such as minimum hospital stay requirements for mothers following the birth of a child.

COBRA requires that a group health plan offer continuation coverage to qualified beneficiaries in the case of a qualifying event (such as a loss of employment).[134] A plan may require payment of a premium for any period of continuation coverage. The amount of such premium generally may not exceed 102 percent of the "applicable premium" for such period and the premium must be payable, at the election of the payor, in monthly installments. The applicable premium for any period of continuation coverage means the cost to the plan for such period of coverage for similarly situated non-COBRA beneficiaries with respect to whom a qualifying event has not occurred, and is determined without regard to whether the cost is paid by the employer or employee. There are special rules for determining the applicable premium in the case of self-insured plans. Under the special rules for self-insured plans, the applicable premium generally is equal to a reasonable estimate of the cost of providing coverage for similarly situated beneficiaries which is determined on an actuarial basis and takes into account such other factors as the Secretary of Treasury may prescribe in regulations.

Current law imposes an excise tax on group health plans that fail to meet HIPAA and COBRA requirements.[135] The excise tax generally is equal to $100 per day per failure during the period of noncompliance and is imposed on the employer sponsoring the plan.

Deduction for health insurance costs of self-employed individuals

Under current law, self-employed individuals may deduct the cost of health insurance for themselves and their spouses and dependents.[136] The deduction is not available for any month in which the self-employed individual is eligible to participate in an employer-subsidized health plan. Moreover, the deduction may not exceed the individual's earned income from self-employment. The deduction applies only to the cost of insurance (i.e., it does not apply to out-of-pocket expenses that are not reimbursed by insurance). The deduction does not apply for self-employment tax purposes. For purposes of the deduction, a more-than-two-percent-shareholder-employee of an S corporation is treated the same as a self-employed individual. Thus, the exclusion for employer provided health care coverage does not apply to such individuals, but they are entitled to the deduction for health insurance costs as if they were self-employed.

---

[133] Pub. L. No. 104-191.

[134] A group health plan is defined as a plan (including a self-insured plan) of, or contributed to by, an employer (including a self-employed person) or employee organization to provide health care (directly or otherwise) to the employees, former employees, the employer, others associated or formerly associated with the employer in a business relationship, or their families. The COBRA requirements are enforced through the Code, ERISA, and the PHSA.

[135] Secs. 4980B and 4980D.

[136] Sec. 162(l).

Deductibility of excise taxes

In general, excise taxes may be deductible under section 162 of the Code if such taxes are paid or incurred in carrying on a trade or business, and are not within the scope of the disallowance of deductions for certain taxes enumerated in section 275 of the Code.

Explanation of Provision

The provision imposes an excise tax on insurers if the aggregate value of employer-sponsored health insurance coverage for an employee (including, for purposes of the provision, any former employee, surviving spouse and any other primary insured individual) exceeds a threshold amount. The tax is equal to 40 percent of the aggregate value that exceeds the threshold amount. For 2018, the threshold amount is $10,200 for individual coverage and $27,500 for family coverage, multiplied by the health cost adjustment percentage (as defined below) and increased by the age and gender adjusted excess premium amount (as defined below).

The health cost adjustment percentage is designed to increase the thresholds in the event that the actual growth in the cost of U.S. health care between 2010 and 2018 exceeds the projected growth for that period. The health cost adjustment percentage is equal to 100 percent plus the excess, if any, of (1) the percentage by which the per employee cost of coverage under the Blue Cross/Blue Shield standard benefit option under the Federal Employees Health Benefits Plan ("standard FEHBP coverage")[137] for plan year 2018 (as determined using the benefit package for standard FEHBP coverage for plan year 2010) exceeds the per employee cost of standard FEHBP coverage for plan year 2010; over (2) 55 percent. In 2019, the threshold amounts, after application of the health cost adjustment percentage in 2018, if any, are indexed to the CPI-U, as determined by the Department of Labor, plus one percentage point, rounded to the nearest $50. In 2020 and thereafter, the threshold amounts are indexed to the CPI-U as determined by the Department of Labor, rounded to the nearest $50.

For each employee (other than for certain retirees and employees in high risk professions, whose thresholds are adjusted under rules described below), the age and gender adjusted excess premium amount is equal to the excess, if any, of (1) the premium cost of standard FEHBP coverage for the type of coverage provided to the individual if priced for the age and gender characteristics of all employees of the individual's employer over (2) the premium cost, determined under procedures proscribed by the Secretary, for that coverage if priced for the age and gender characteristics of the national workforce.

For example, if the growth in the cost of health care during the period between 2010 and 2018, calculated by reference to the growth in the per employee cost of standard FEHBP

[137] For purposes of determining the health cost adjustment percentage in 2018 and the age and gender adjusted excess premium amount in any year, in the event the standard Blue Cross/Blue Shield option is not available under the Federal Employees Health Benefit Plan for such year, the Secretary will determine the health cost adjustment percentage by reference to a substantially similar option available under the Federal Employees Health Benefit Plan for that year.

coverage during that period (holding benefits under the standard FEBHP plan constant during the period) is 57 percent, the threshold amounts for 2013 will be $10,200 for individual coverage and $27,500 for family coverage, multiplied by 102 percent (100 percent plus the excess of 57 percent over 55 percent), or $10,404 for individual coverage and $28,050 for family coverage. In 2019, the new threshold amounts of $10,404 for individual coverage and $28,050 for family coverage are indexed for CPI-U, plus one percentage point, rounded to the nearest $50. Beginning in 2020, the threshold amounts are indexed to the CPI-U, rounded to the nearest $50.

The new threshold amounts (as indexed) are then increased for any employee by the age and gender adjusted excess premium amount, if any. For an employee with individual coverage in 2019, if standard FEHBP coverage priced for the age and gender characteristics of the workforce of the employee's employer is $11,400 and the Secretary estimates that the premium cost for individual standard FEHBP coverage priced for the age and gender characteristics of the national workforce is $10,500, the threshold for that employee is increased by $900 ($11,400 less $10,500) to $11,304 ($10,404 plus $900).

The excise tax is imposed pro rata on the issuers of the insurance. In the case of a self-insured group health plan, a Health FSA or an HRA, the excise tax is paid by the entity that administers benefits under the plan or arrangement ("plan administrator"). Where the employer acts as plan administrator to a self-insured group health plan, a Health FSA or an HRA, the excise tax is paid by the employer. Where an employer contributes to an HSA or an Archer MSA, the employer is responsible for payment of the excise tax, as the insurer.

Employer-sponsored health insurance coverage is health coverage under any group health plan offered by an employer to an employee without regard to whether the employer provides the coverage (and thus the coverage is excludable from the employee's gross income) or the employee pays for the coverage with after-tax dollars. Employer-sponsored health insurance coverage includes coverage under any group health plan established and maintained primarily for the civilian employees of the Federal government or any of its agencies or instrumentalities and, except as provided below, of any State government or political subdivision thereof or by any of agencies or instrumentalities of such government or subdivision.

Employer-sponsored health insurance coverage includes both fully-insured and self-insured health coverage excludable from the employee's gross income, including, in the self-insured context, on-site medical clinics that offer more than a de minimis amount of medical care to employees and executive physical programs. In the case of a self-employed individual, employer-sponsored health insurance coverage is coverage for any portion of which a deduction is allowable to the self-employed individual under section 162(l).

In determining the amount by which the value of employer-sponsored health insurance coverage exceeds the threshold amount, the aggregate value of all employer-sponsored health insurance coverage is taken into account, including coverage in the form of reimbursements under a Health FSA or an HRA, contributions to an HSA or Archer MSA, and, except as provided below, other supplementary health insurance coverage. The value of employer-sponsored coverage for long term care and the following benefits described in section 9832(c)(1) that are excepted from the portability, access and renewability requirements of HIPAA are not taken into account in the determination of whether the value of health coverage exceeds the threshold amount: (1) coverage only for accident or disability income insurance, or any combination of these coverages; (2) coverage issued as a supplement to liability insurance; (3) liability insurance, including general liability insurance and automobile liability insurance; (4) workers' compensation or similar insurance; (5) automobile medical payment insurance; (5) credit-only insurance; and (6) other similar insurance coverage, specified in regulations, under which benefits for medical care are secondary or incidental to other insurance benefits.

The value of employer-sponsored health insurance coverage does not include the value of independent, noncoordinated coverage described in section 9832(c)(3) as excepted from the portability, access and renewability requirements of HIPAA if that coverage is purchased exclusively by the employee with after-tax dollars (or, in the case of a self-employed individual, for which a deduction under section 162(l) is not allowable). The value of employer-sponsored health insurance coverage does include the value of such coverage if any portion of the coverage is employer-provided (or, in the case of a self-employed individual, if a deduction is allowable for any portion of the payment for the coverage). Coverage described in section 9832(c)(3) is coverage only for a specified disease or illness or for hospital or other fixed indemnity health coverage. Fixed indemnity health coverage pays fixed dollar amounts based on the occurrence of qualifying events, including but not limited to the diagnosis of a specific disease, an accidental injury or a hospitalization, provided that the coverage is not coordinated with other health coverage.

Finally, the value of employer-sponsored health insurance coverage does not include any coverage under a separate policy, certificate, or contract of insurance which provides benefits substantially all of which are for treatment of the mouth (including any organ or structure within the mouth) or for treatment of the eye.

Calculation and proration of excise tax and reporting requirements

Applicable threshold

In general, the individual threshold applies to any employee covered by employer-sponsored health insurance coverage. The family threshold applies to an employee only if such individual and at least one other beneficiary are enrolled in coverage other than self-only coverage under an employer-sponsored health insurance plan that provides minimum essential coverage (as determined for purposes of the individual responsibility requirements) and under which the benefits provided do not vary based on whether the covered individual is the employee or other beneficiary.

For all employees covered by a multiemployer plan, the family threshold applies regardless of whether the individual maintains individual or family coverage under the plan. For purposes of the provision, a multiemployer plan is an employee health benefit plan to which more than one employer is required to contribute, which is maintained pursuant to one or more collective bargaining agreements between one or more employee organizations and more than one employer.

Amount of applicable premium

Under the provision, the aggregate value of all employer-sponsored health insurance coverage, including any supplementary health insurance coverage not excluded from the value of employer-sponsored health insurance, is generally calculated in the same manner as the applicable premiums for the taxable year for the employee determined under the rules for COBRA continuation coverage, but without regard to the excise tax. If the plan provides for the same COBRA continuation coverage premium for both individual coverage and family coverage, the plan is required to calculate separate individual and family premiums for this purpose. In determining the coverage value for retirees, employers may elect to treat pre-65 retirees together with post-65 retirees.

Value of coverage in the form of Health FSA reimbursements

In the case of a Health FSA from which reimbursements are limited to the amount of the salary reduction, the value of employer-sponsored health insurance coverage is equal to the dollar amount of the aggregate salary reduction contributions for the year. To the extent that the Health FSA provides for employer contributions in excess of the amount of the employee's salary reduction, the value of the coverage generally is determined in the same manner as the applicable premium for COBRA continuation coverage. If the plan provides for the same COBRA continuation coverage premium for both individual coverage and family coverage, the plan is required to calculate separate individual and family premiums for this purpose.

Amount subject to the excise tax and reporting requirement

The amount subject to the excise tax on high cost employer-sponsored health insurance coverage for each employee is the sum of the aggregate premiums for health insurance coverage, the amount of any salary reduction contributions to a Health FSA for the taxable year, and the dollar amount of employer contributions to an HSA or an Archer MSA, minus the dollar amount of the threshold. The aggregate premiums for health insurance coverage include all employer-sponsored health insurance coverage including coverage for any supplementary health insurance coverage. The applicable premium for health coverage provided through an HRA is also included in this aggregate amount.

Under a separate rule,[138] an employer is required to disclose the aggregate premiums for health insurance coverage for each employee on his or her annual Form W-2.

Under the provision, the excise tax is allocated pro rata among the insurers, with each insurer responsible for payment of the excise tax on an amount equal to the amount subject to the total excise tax multiplied by a fraction, the numerator of which is the amount of employer-sponsored health insurance coverage provided by that insurer to the employee and the denominator of which is the aggregate value of all employer-sponsored health insurance coverage provided to the employee. In the case of a self-insured group health plan, a Health

[138] See the explanation of section 9002 of the Senate amendment, "Inclusion of Cost of Employer Sponsored Health Coverage on W-2."

FSA or an HRA, the excise tax is allocated to the plan administrator. If an employer contributes to an HSA or an Archer MSA, the employer is responsible for payment of the excise tax, as the insurer. The employer is responsible for calculating the amount subject to the excise tax allocable to each insurer and plan administrator and for reporting these amounts to each insurer, plan administrator and the Secretary, in such form and at such time as the Secretary may prescribe. Each insurer and plan administrator is then responsible for calculating, reporting and paying the excise tax to the IRS on such forms and at such time as the Secretary may prescribe.

For example, if in 2018 an employee elects family coverage under a fully-insured health care policy covering major medical and dental with a value of $31,000, the health cost adjustment percentage for that year is 100 percent, and the age and gender adjusted excess premium amount for the employee is $600, the amount subject to the excise tax is $2,900 ($31,000 less the threshold of $28,100 ($27,500 multiplied by 100 percent and increased by $600)). The employer reports $2,900 as taxable to the insurer, which calculates and remits the excise tax to the IRS.

Alternatively, if in 2018 an employee elects family coverage under a fully-insured major medical policy with a value of $28,500 and contributes $2,500 to a Health FSA, the employee has an aggregate health insurance coverage value of $31,000. If the health cost adjustment percentage for that year is 100 percent and the age and gender adjusted excess premium amount for the employee is $600, the amount subject to the excise tax is $2,900 ($31,000 less the threshold of $28,100 ($27,500 multiplied by 100 percent and increased by $600)). The employer reports $2,666 ($2,900 x $28,500/$31,000) as taxable to the major medical insurer which then calculates and remits the excise tax to the IRS. If the employer uses a third-party administrator for the Health FSA, the employer reports $234 ($2,900 x $2,500/$31,000) to the administrator and the administrator calculates and remits the excise tax to the IRS. If the employer is acting as the plan administrator of the Health FSA, the employer is responsible for calculating and remitting the excise tax on the $234 to the IRS.

Penalty for underreporting liability for tax to insurers

If the employer reports to insurers, plan administrators and the IRS a lower amount of insurance cost subject to the excise tax than required, the employer is subject to a penalty equal to the sum of any additional excise tax that each such insurer and administrator would have owed if the employer had reported correctly and interest attributable to that additional excise tax as determined under Code section 6621 from the date that the tax was otherwise due to the date paid by the employer. This may occur, for example, if the employer undervalues the aggregate premium and thereby lowers the amount subject to the excise tax for all insurers and plan administrators (including the employer, when acting as plan administrator of a self-insured plan).

The penalty will not apply if it is established to the satisfaction of the Secretary that the employer neither knew, nor exercising reasonable diligence would have known, that the failure existed. In addition, no penalty will be imposed on any failure corrected within the 30-day period beginning on the first date that the employer knew, or exercising reasonable diligence, would have known, that the failure existed, so long as the failure is due to reasonable cause and not to willful neglect. All or part of the penalty may be waived by the Secretary in the case of any failure due to reasonable cause and not to willful neglect, to the extent that the payment of the penalty would be excessive or otherwise inequitable relative to the failure involved.

The penalty is in addition to the amount of excise tax owed, which may not be waived.

Increased thresholds for certain retirees and individuals in high-risk professions

The threshold amounts are increased for an individual who has attained age of 55 who is non-Medicare eligible and receiving employer-sponsored retiree health coverage or who is covered by a plan sponsored by an employer the majority of whose employees covered by the plan are engaged in a high risk profession or employed to repair or install electrical and telecommunications lines. For these individuals, the threshold amount in 2018 is increased by (1) $1,650 for individual coverage or $3,450 for family coverage and (2) the age and gender adjusted excess premium amount (as defined above). In 2019, the additional $1,650 and $3,450 amounts are indexed to the CPI-U, plus one percentage point, rounded to the nearest $50. In 2020 and thereafter, the additional threshold amounts are indexed to the CPI-U, rounded to the nearest $50.

For purposes of this rule, employees considered to be engaged in a high risk profession are law enforcement officers, employees who engage in fire protection activities, individuals who provide out-of-hospital emergency medical care (including emergency medical technicians, paramedics, and first-responders), individuals whose primary work is longshore work, and individuals engaged in the construction, mining, agriculture (not including food processing), forestry, and fishing industries. A retiree with at least 20 years of employment in a high risk profession is also eligible for the increased threshold.

Under this provision, an individual's threshold cannot be increased by more than $1,650 for individual coverage or $3,450 for family coverage (indexed as described above) and the age and gender adjusted excess premium amount, even if the individual would qualify for an increased threshold both on account of his or her status as a retiree over age 55 and as a participant in a plan that covers employees in a high risk profession.

Deductibility of excise tax

Under the provision, the amount of the excise tax imposed is not deductible for Federal income tax purposes.

Regulatory authority

The Secretary is directed to prescribe such regulations as may be necessary to carry out the provision.

Effective Date

The provision is effective for taxable years beginning after December 31, 2017.

B. Inclusion of Cost of Employer-Sponsored Health Coverage on W-2 (sec. 9002 of the Senate amendment and sec. 6051 of the Code)

Present Law

In many cases, an employer pays for all or a portion of its employees' health insurance coverage as an employee benefit. This benefit often includes premiums for major medical, dental, and other supplementary health insurance coverage. Under present law, the value of employer-provided health coverage is not required to be reported to the IRS or any other Federal agency. The value of the employer contribution to health coverage is excludible from an employee's income.[139]

Under current law, every employer is required to furnish each employee and the Federal government with a statement of compensation information, including wages, paid by the employer to the employee, and the taxes withheld from such wages during the calendar year. The statement, made on the Form W-2, must be provided to each employee by January 31 of the succeeding year. There is no requirement that the employer report the total value of employer-sponsored health insurance coverage on the Form W-2,[140] although some employers voluntarily report the amount of salary reduction under a cafeteria plan resulting in tax-free employee benefits in box 14.

Explanation of Provision

Under the provision, an employer is required to disclose on each employee's annual Form W-2 the value of the employee's health insurance coverage sponsored by the employer. If an employee enrolls in employer-sponsored health insurance coverage under multiple plans, the employer must disclose the aggregate value of all such health coverage (excluding the value of a health flexible spending arrangement). For example, if an employee enrolls in employer-sponsored health insurance coverage under a major medical plan, a dental plan, and a vision plan, the employer is required to report the total value of the combination of all of these health related insurance policies. For this purpose, employers generally use the same value for all similarly situated employees receiving the same category of coverage (such as single or family health insurance coverage).

To determine the value of employer-sponsored health insurance coverage, the employer calculates the applicable premiums for the taxable year for the employee under the rules for COBRA continuation coverage under section 4980B(f)(4) (and accompanying Treasury regulations), including the special rule for self-insured plans. The value that the employer is required to report is the portion of the aggregate premium. If the plan provides for the same COBRA continuation coverage premium for both individual coverage and family coverage, the plan would be required to calculate separate individual and family premiums for this purpose.

---

[139] Sec. 106.

[140] Any portion of employer sponsored coverage that is paid for by the employee with after-tax contributions is included as wages on the W-2 Form.

Effective Date

The provision is effective for taxable years beginning after December 31, 2010.

C. Distributions for Medicine Qualified Only if for Prescribed Drug or Insulin (sec. 9003 of the Senate amendment and secs. 105, 106, 220, and 223 of the Code)

Present Law

Individual deduction for medical expenses

Expenses for medical care, not compensated for by insurance or otherwise, are deductible by an individual under the rules relating to itemized deductions to the extent the expenses exceed 7.5 percent of adjusted gross income ("AGI").[141] Medical care generally is defined broadly as amounts paid for diagnoses, cure, mitigation, treatment or prevention of disease, or for the purpose of affecting any structure of the body.[142] However, any amount paid during a taxable year for medicine or drugs is explicitly deductible as a medical expense only if the medicine or drug is a prescribed drug or is insulin.[143] Thus, any amount paid for medicine available without a prescription ("over-the-counter medicine") is not deductible as a medical expense, including any medicine recommended by a physician.[144]

Exclusion for employer-provided health care

The Code generally provides that employees are not taxed on (that is, may exclude from gross income) the value of employer-provided health coverage under an accident or health plan.[145] In addition, any reimbursements under an accident or health plan for medical care expenses for employees, their spouses, and their dependents generally are excluded from gross income.[146] An employer may agree to reimburse expenses for medical care of its employees (and their spouses and dependents), not covered by a health insurance plan, through a flexible spending arrangement ("FSA") which allows reimbursement not in excess of a specified dollar amount. Such dollar amount is either elected by an employee under a cafeteria plan ("Health FSA") or otherwise specified by the employer under an HRA. Reimbursements under these arrangements are also excludible from gross income as employer-provided health coverage. The general definition of medical care without the explicit limitation on medicine applies for purposes of the exclusion for employer-provided health coverage and medical care.[147] Thus, under an HRA or under a Health FSA, amounts paid for prescription and over-the-counter

---

[141] Sec. 213(a).

[142] Sec. 213(d). There are certain limitations on the general definition including a rule that cosmetic surgery or similar procedures are generally not medical care.

[143] Sec. 213(b).

[144] Rev. Rul. 2003-58, 2003-1 CB 959.

[145] Sec 106.

[146] Sec. 105(b).

[147] Sec. 105(b) provides that reimbursements for medical care within the meaning of section 213(d) pursuant to employer-provided health coverage are excludible from gross income. The definition of medical care in section 213(d) does not include the prescription drug limitation in section 213(b).

medicine are treated as medical expenses, and reimbursements for such amounts are excludible from gross income.

Medical savings arrangements

Present law provides that individuals with a high deductible health plan (and generally no other health plan) purchased either through the individual market or through an employer may establish and make tax-deductible contributions to a health savings account ("HSA").[148] Subject to certain limitations,[149] contributions made to an HSA by an employer, including contributions made through a cafeteria plan through salary reduction, are excluded from income (and from wages for payroll tax purposes). Contributions made by individuals are deductible for income tax purposes, regardless of whether the individuals itemize. Distributions from an HSA that are used for qualified medical expenses are excludible from gross income.[150] The general definition of medical care without the explicit limitation on medicine also applies for purposes of this exclusion.[151] Similar rules apply for another type of medical savings arrangement called an Archer MSA.[152] Thus, a distribution from a HSA or an Archer MSA used to purchase over-the-counter medicine also is excludible as an amount used for qualified medical expenses.

Explanation of Provision

Under the provision, with respect to medicines, the definition of medical expense for purposes of employer-provided health coverage (including HRAs and Health FSAs), HSAs, and Archer MSAs, is conformed to the definition for purposes of the itemized deduction for medical expenses, except that prescribed drug is determined without regard to whither the drug is available without a prescription. Thus, under the provision, the cost of over-the-counter medicines may not be reimbursed with excludible income through a Health FSA, HRA, HSA, or Archer MSA, unless the medicine is prescribed by a physician.

Effective Date

The provision is effective for expenses incurred after December 31, 2010.

---

[148] Sec. 223.

[149] For 2009, the maximum aggregate annual contribution that can be made to an HSA is $3,000 in the case of self-only coverage and $5,950 in the case of family coverage ($3,050 and $6,150 for 2010). The annual contribution limits are increased for individuals who have attained age 55 by the end of the taxable year (referred to as "catch-up contributions"). In the case of policyholders and covered spouses who are age 55 or older, the HSA annual contribution limit is greater than the otherwise applicable limit by $1,000 in 2009 and thereafter. Contributions, including catch-up contributions, cannot be made once an individual is enrolled in Medicare.

[150] Sec. 223(f).

[151] Sec. 223(d)(2).

[152] Sec. 220.

D. Increase in Additional Tax on Distributions from HSAs Not Used for Medical Expenses (sec. 9004 of the bill and sec. 220 and 223 of the Code)

Present Law

Health savings account

Present law provides that individuals with a high deductible health plan (and generally no other health plan) may establish and make tax-deductible contributions to a health savings account ("HSA").[153] An HSA is a tax-exempt account held by a trustee or custodian for the benefit of the individual. An HSA is subject to a condition that the individual is covered under a high deductible health plan (purchased either through the individual market or through an employer). The decision to create and fund an HSA is made on an individual-by-individual basis and does not require any action on the part of the employer.

Subject to certain limitations, contributions made to an HSA by an employer, including contributions made through a cafeteria plan through salary reduction, are excluded from income (and from wages for payroll tax purposes). Contributions made by individuals are deductible for income tax purposes, regardless of whether the individuals itemize their deductions on their tax return (rather than claiming the standard deduction). Income from investments made in HSAs is not taxable and the overall income is not taxable upon disbursement for medical expenses.

For 2010, the maximum aggregate annual contribution that can be made to an HSA is $3,050 in the case of self-only coverage and $6,150 in the case of family coverage. The annual contribution limits are increased for individuals who have attained age 55 by the end of the taxable year (referred to as "catch-up contributions"). In the case of policyholders and covered spouses who are age 55 or older, the HSA annual contribution limit is greater than the otherwise applicable limit by $1,000 in 2010 and thereafter. Contributions, including catch-up contributions, cannot be made once an individual is enrolled in Medicare.

A high deductible health plan is a health plan that has an annual deductible that is at least $1,200 for self-only coverage or $2,400 for family coverage for 2010 and that limits the sum of the annual deductible and other payments that the individual must make with respect to covered benefits to no more than $5,950 in the case of self-only coverage and $11,900 in the case of family coverage for 2010.

---

[153] An individual with other coverage in addition to a high deductible health plan is still eligible for an HSA if such other coverage is "permitted insurance" or "permitted coverage." Permitted insurance is: (1) insurance if substantially all of the coverage provided under such insurance relates to (a) liabilities incurred under worker's compensation law, (b) tort liabilities, (c) liabilities relating to ownership or use of property (e.g., auto insurance), or (d) such other similar liabilities as the Secretary may prescribe by regulations; (2) insurance for a specified disease or illness; and (3) insurance that provides a fixed payment for hospitalization. Permitted coverage is coverage (whether provided through insurance or otherwise) for accidents, disability, dental care, vision care, or long-term care. With respect to coverage for years beginning after December 31, 2006, certain coverage under a Health FSA is disregarded in determining eligibility for an HSA.

Distributions from an HSA that are used for qualified medical expenses are excludible from gross income. Distributions from an HSA that are not used for qualified medical expenses are includible in gross income. An additional 10 percent tax is added for all HSA disbursements not made for qualified medical expenses. The additional 10-percent tax does not apply, however, if the distribution is made after death, disability, or attainment of age of Medicare eligibility (currently, age 65). Unlike reimbursements from a flexible spending arrangement or health reimbursement arrangement, distributions from an HSA are not required to be substantiated by the employer or a third party for the distributions to be excludible from income.

As in the case of individual retirement arrangements,[154] the individual is the beneficial owner of his or her HSA, and thus the individual is required to maintain books and records with respect to the expense and claim the exclusion for a distribution from the HSA on their tax return. The determination of whether the distribution is for a qualified medical expense is subject to individual self-reporting and IRS enforcement.

Archer medical savings account

An Archer MSA is also a tax-exempt trust or custodial account to which tax-deductible contributions may be made by individuals with a high deductible health plan.[155] Archer MSAs provide tax benefits similar to, but generally not as favorable as, those provided by HSAs for individuals covered by high deductible health plans. The main differences include: (1) only self-employed individuals and employees of small employers are eligible to have an Archer MSA; (2) for Archer MSA purposes, a high deductible health plan is a health plan with (a) an annual deductible for 2010 of at least $2,000 and no more than $3,000 in the case of self-only coverage and at least $4,050 and no more than $6,050 in the case of family coverage and (b) maximum out-of pocket expenses for 2010 of no more than $4,050 in the case of self-only coverage and no more than $7,400 in the case of family coverage; and (3) the additional tax on distributions not used for medical expenses is 15 percent rather than 10 percent. After 2007, no new contributions can be made to Archer MSAs except by or on behalf of individuals who previously had made Archer MSA contributions and employees who are employed by a participating employer.

---

[154] Sec. 408.

[155] Sec. 220.

Explanation of Provision

The additional tax on distributions from an HSA or an Archer MSA that are not used for qualified medical expenses is increased to 20 percent of the disbursed amount.

Effective Date

The change is effective for disbursements made during tax years starting after December 31, 2010.

E. Limitation on Health Flexible Spending Arrangements Under Cafeteria Plans (sec. 9005[156] of the Senate amendment and sec. 125 of the Code)

Present law

Exclusion from income for employer-provided health coverage

The Code generally provides that the value of employer-provided health coverage under an accident or health plan is excludible from gross income.[157] In addition, any reimbursements under an accident or health plan for medical care expenses for employees, their spouses, and their dependents generally are excluded from gross income.[158] The exclusion applies both to health coverage in the case in which an employer absorbs the cost of employees' medical expenses not covered by insurance (i.e., a self-insured plan) as well as in the case in which the employer purchases health insurance coverage for its employees. There is no limit on the amount of employer-provided health coverage that is excludable. A similar rule excludes employer-provided health insurance coverage from the employees' wages for payroll tax purposes.[159]

Employers may also provide health coverage in the form of an agreement to reimburse medical expenses of their employees (and their spouses and dependents), not reimbursed by a health insurance plan, through flexible spending arrangements which allow reimbursement for medical care not in excess of a specified dollar amount (either elected by an employee under a cafeteria plan or otherwise specified by the employer). Health coverage provided in the form of one of these arrangements is also excludible from gross income as employer-provided health coverage under an accident or health plan.[160]

Qualified benefits

Qualified benefits under a cafeteria plan are generally employer-provided benefits that are not includable in gross income under an express provision of the Code. Examples of qualified benefits include employer-provided health coverage, group term life insurance coverage not in excess of $50,000, and benefits under a dependent care assistance program. In order to be

---

[156] Section 9005 of the Senate amendment, as amended by section 10902, is further amended by section 1403 of the Reconciliation bill.

[157] Sec. 106. Health coverage provided to active members of the uniformed services, military retirees, and their dependents are excludable under section 134. That section provides an exclusion for "qualified military benefits," defined as benefits received by reason of status or service as a member of the uniformed services and which were excludable from gross income on September 9, 1986, under any provision of law, regulation, or administrative practice then in effect.

[158] Sec. 105(b).

[159] Secs. 3121(a)(2), and 3306(a)(2). See also section 3231(e)(1) for a similar rule with respect to compensation for purposes of Railroad Retirement Tax.

[160] Sec. 106.

excludable, any qualified benefit elected under a cafeteria plan must independently satisfy any requirements under the Code section that provides the exclusion. However, some employer-provided benefits that are not includable in gross income under an express provision of the Code are explicitly not allowed in a cafeteria plan. These benefits are generally referred to as nonqualified benefits. Examples of nonqualified benefits include scholarships;[161] employer-provided meals and lodging;[162] educational assistance;[163] and fringe benefits.[164] A plan offering any nonqualified benefit is not a cafeteria plan.[165]

Flexible spending arrangement under a cafeteria plan

A flexible spending arrangement for medical expenses under a cafeteria plan ("Health FSA") is health coverage in the form of an unfunded arrangement under which employees are given the option to reduce their current cash compensation and instead have the amount of the salary reduction contributions made available for use in reimbursing the employee for his or her medical expenses.[166] Health FSAs are subject to the general requirements for cafeteria plans, including a requirement that amounts remaining under a Health FSA at the end of a plan year must be forfeited by the employee (referred to as the "use-it-or-lose-it rule").[167] A Health FSA is permitted to allow a grace period not to exceed two and one-half months immediately following the end of the plan year during which unused amounts may be used.[168] A Health FSA can also include employer flex-credits which are non-elective employer contributions that the employer makes for every employee eligible to participate in the employer's cafeteria plan, to be used only for one or more tax excludible qualified benefits (but not as cash or a taxable benefit).[169]

A flexible spending arrangement including a Health FSA (under a cafeteria plan) is generally distinguishable from other employer-provided health coverage by the relationship between the value of the coverage for a year and the maximum amount of reimbursement reasonably available during the same period. A flexible spending arrangement for health coverage generally is defined as a benefit program which provides employees with coverage under which specific incurred medical care expenses may be reimbursed (subject to

---

[161] Sec. 117.

[162] Sec. 119.

[163] Sec.127.

[164] Sec. 132.

[165] Proposed Treas. Reg. sec. 1.125-1(q). Long-term care services, contributions to Archer Medical Savings Accounts, group term life insurance for an employee's spouse, child or dependent, and elective deferrals to section 403(b) plans are also nonqualified benefits.

[166] Sec. 125 and proposed Treas. Reg. sec. 1.125-5.

[167] Sec. 125(d)(2) and proposed Treas. Reg. sec. 1.125-5(c).

[168] Notice 2005-42, 2005-1 C.B. 1204 and proposed Treas. Reg. sec. 1.125-1(e).

[169] Proposed Treas. Reg. sec. 1-125-5(b).

reimbursement maximums and other conditions) and the maximum amount of reimbursement reasonably available is less than 500 percent of the value of such coverage.[170]

Health reimbursement arrangement

Rather than offering a Health FSA through a cafeteria plan, an employer may specify a dollar amount that is available for medical expense reimbursement. These arrangements are commonly called HRAs. Some of the rules applicable to HRAs and Health FSAs are similar (e.g., the amounts in the arrangements can only be used to reimburse medical expenses and not for other purposes), but the rules are not identical. In particular, HRAs cannot be funded on a salary reduction basis and the use-it-or-lose-it rule does not apply. Thus, amounts remaining at the end of the year may be carried forward to be used to reimburse medical expenses in following years.[171]

Explanation of Provision

Under the provision, in order for a Health FSA to be a qualified benefit under a cafeteria plan, the maximum amount available for reimbursement of incurred medical expenses of an employee, the employee's dependents, and any other eligible beneficiaries with respect to the employee, under the Health FSA for a plan year (or other 12-month coverage period) must not exceed $2500.[172] The $2,500 limitation is indexed to CPI-U, with any increase that is not a multiple of $50 rounded to the next lowest multiple of $50 for years beginning after December 31, 2013.

A cafeteria plan that does not include this limitation on the maximum amount available for reimbursement under any FSA is not a cafeteria plan within the meaning of section 125. Thus, when an employee is given the option under a cafeteria plan maintained by an employer to reduce his or her current cash compensation and instead have the amount of the salary reduction be made available for use in reimbursing the employee for his or her medical expenses under a Health FSA, the amount of the reduction in cash compensation pursuant to a salary reduction election must be limited to $2,500 for a plan year.

It is intended that regulations would require all cafeteria plans of an employer to be aggregated for purposes of applying this limit. The employer for this purpose is determined after applying the employer aggregation rules in section 414(b), (c), (m), and (o).[173] In the event of a

---

[170] Sec. 106(c)(2) and proposed Treas. Reg. sec. 1.125-5(a).

[171] Guidance with respect to HRAs, including the interaction of FSAs and HRAs in the case of an individual covered under both, is provided in Notice 2002-45, 2002-2 C.B. 93.

[172] The provision does not change the present law treatment as described in proposed Treas. Reg. sec. 1.125-5 for dependent care flexible spending arrangements or adoption assistance flexible spending arrangements.

[173] Section 414(b) provides that, for specified employee benefit purposes, all employees of all corporations which are members of a controlled group of corporations are treated as employed by a single employer. There is a similar rule in section 414(c) under which all employees of trades or businesses (whether or not incorporated) which are under common control are treated under regulations as employed by a single employer, and, in section 414(m),

plan year or coverage period that is less than 12 months, it is intended that the limit be required to be prorated.

The provision does not limit the amount permitted to be available for reimbursement under employer-provided health coverage offered through an HRA, including a flexible spending arrangement within the meaning of section 106(c)(2), that is not part of a cafeteria plan.

Effective Date

The provision is effective for taxable year beginning after December 31, 2012.

under which employees of an affiliated service group (as defined in that section) are treated as employed by a single employer. Section 414(o) authorizes the Treasury to issue regulations to prevent avoidance of the requirements under section 414(m). Section 125(g)(4) applies this rule to cafeteria plans.

F. Additional Requirements for Charitable Hospitals (sec. 9007[174] of the Senate amendment and secs. 501(c) and 6033 and new sec. 4959 of the Code)

Present Law

Tax exemption

Charitable organizations, i.e., organizations described in section 501(c)(3), generally are exempt from Federal income tax, are eligible to receive tax deductible contributions,[175] have access to tax-exempt financing through State and local governments (described in more detail below),[176] and generally are exempt from State and local taxes. A charitable organization must operate primarily in pursuit of one or more tax-exempt purposes constituting the basis of its tax exemption.[177] The Code specifies such purposes as religious, charitable, scientific, educational, literary, testing for public safety, to foster international amateur sports competition, or for the prevention of cruelty to children or animals. In general, an organization is organized and operated for charitable purposes if it provides relief for the poor and distressed or the underprivileged.[178]

The Code does not provide a per se exemption for hospitals. Rather, a hospital qualifies for exemption if it is organized and operated for a charitable purpose and otherwise meets the requirements of section 501(c)(3).[179] The promotion of health has been recognized by the IRS as a charitable purpose that is beneficial to the community as a whole.[180] It includes not only the establishment or maintenance of charitable hospitals, but clinics, homes for the aged, and other providers of health care.

Since 1969, the IRS has applied a "community benefit" standard for determining whether a hospital is charitable.[181] According to Revenue Ruling 69-545, community benefit can include,

---

[174] Section 9007 of the Senate amendment is amended by section 10903 of the Senate amendment.

[175] Sec. 170.

[176] Sec. 145.

[177] Treas. Reg. sec. 1.501(c)(3)-1(c)(1).

[178] Treas. Reg. sec. 1.501(c)(3)-1(d)(2).

[179] Although nonprofit hospitals generally are recognized as tax-exempt by virtue of being "charitable" organizations, some might qualify for exemption as educational or scientific organizations because they are organized and operated primarily for medical education and research purposes.

[180] Rev. Rul. 69-545, 1969-2 C.B. 117; see also Restatement (Second) of Trusts secs. 368, 372 (1959); see Bruce R. Hopkins, *The Law of Tax-Exempt Organizations*, sec. 6.3 (8th ed. 2003) (discussing various forms of health-care providers that may qualify for exemption under section 501(c)(3)).

[181] Rev. Rul. 69-545, 1969-2 C.B. 117. From 1956 until 1969, the IRS applied a "financial ability" standard, requiring that a charitable hospital be "operated to the extent of its financial ability for those not able to

for example: maintaining an emergency room open to all persons regardless of ability to pay; having an independent board of trustees composed of representatives of the community; operating with an open medical staff policy, with privileges available to all qualifying physicians; providing charity care; and utilizing surplus funds to improve the quality of patient care, expand facilities, and advance medical training, education and research. Beginning in 2009, hospitals generally are required to submit information on community benefit on their annual information returns filed with the IRS.[182] Present law does not include sanctions short of revocation of tax-exempt status for hospitals that fail to satisfy the community benefit standard.

Although section 501(c)(3) hospitals generally are exempt from Federal tax on their net income, such organizations are subject to the unrelated business income tax on income derived from a trade or business regularly carried on by the organization that is not substantially related to the performance of the organization's tax-exempt functions.[183] In general, interest, rents, royalties, and annuities are excluded from the unrelated business income of tax-exempt organizations.[184]

Charitable contributions

In general, a deduction is permitted for charitable contributions, including charitable contributions to tax-exempt hospitals, subject to certain limitations that depend on the type of taxpayer, the property contributed, and the donee organization. The amount of deduction generally equals the fair market value of the contributed property on the date of the contribution. Charitable deductions are provided for income, estate, and gift tax purposes.[185]

Tax-exempt financing

In addition to issuing tax-exempt bonds for government operations and services, State and local governments may issue tax-exempt bonds to finance the activities of charitable organizations described in section 501(c)(3). Because interest income on tax-exempt bonds is excluded from gross income, investors generally are willing to accept a lower pre-tax rate of return on such bonds than they might otherwise accept on a taxable investment. This, in turn, lowers the cost of capital for the users of such financing. Both capital expenditures and limited working capital expenditures of charitable organizations described in section 501(c)(3) generally may be financed with tax-exempt bonds. Private, nonprofit hospitals frequently are the beneficiaries of this type of financing.

---

pay for the services rendered and not exclusively for those who are able and expected to pay." Rev. Rul. 56-185, 1956-1 C.B. 202.

[182] IRS Form 990, Schedule H.

[183] Secs. 511-514.

[184] Sec. 512(b).

[185] Secs. 170, 2055, and 2522, respectively.

Bonds issued by State and local governments may be classified as either governmental bonds or private activity bonds. Governmental bonds are bonds the proceeds of which are primarily used to finance governmental functions or which are repaid with governmental funds. Private activity bonds are bonds in which the State or local government serves as a conduit providing financing to nongovernmental persons (e.g., private businesses or individuals). For these purposes, the term "nongovernmental person" generally includes the Federal government and all other individuals and entities other than States or local governments, including section 501(c)(3) organizations. The exclusion from income for interest on State and local bonds does not apply to private activity bonds, unless the bonds are issued for certain permitted purposes ("qualified private activity bonds") and other Code requirements are met.

Reporting and disclosure requirements

Exempt organizations are required to file an annual information return, stating specifically the items of gross income, receipts, disbursements, and such other information as the Secretary may prescribe.[186] Section 501(c)(3) organizations that are classified as public charities must file Form 990 (Return of Organization Exempt From Income Tax),[187] including Schedule A, which requests information specific to section 501(c)(3) organizations. Additionally, an organization that operates at least one facility that is, or is required to be, licensed, registered, or similarly recognized by a state s a hospital must complete Schedule H (Form 990), which requests information regarding charity care, community benefits, bad debt expense, and certain management company and joint venture arrangements of a hospital.

An organization described in section 501(c) or (d) generally is also required to make available for public inspection for a period of three years a copy of its annual information return (Form 990) and exemption application materials.[188] This requirement is satisfied if the organization has made the annual return and exemption application widely available (e.g., by posting such information on its website).[189]

---

[186] Sec. 6033(a). An organization that has not received a determination of its tax-exempt status, but that claims tax-exempt status under section 501(a), is subject to the same annual reporting requirements and exceptions as organizations that have received a tax-exemption determination.

[187] Social welfare organizations, labor organizations, agricultural organizations, horticultural organizations, and business leagues are subject to the generally applicable Form 990, Form 990-EZ, and Form 990-T annual filing requirements.

[188] Sec. 6104(d).

[189] Sec. 6104(d)(4); Treas. Reg. sec. 301.6104(d)-2(b).

Explanation of Provision

Additional requirements for section 501(c)(3) hospitals[190]

In general

The provision establishes new requirements applicable to section 501(c)(3) hospitals. The new requirements are in addition to, and not in lieu of, the requirements otherwise applicable to an organization described in section 501(c)(3). The requirements generally apply to any section 501(c)(3) organization that operates at least one hospital facility. For purposes of the provision, a hospital facility generally includes: (1) any facility that is, or is required to be, licensed, registered, or similarly recognized by a State as a hospital; and (2) any other facility or organization the Secretary of the Treasury (the "Secretary"), in consultation with the Secretary of HHS and after public comment, determines has the provision of hospital care as its principal purpose. To qualify for tax exemption under section 501(c)(3), an organization subject to the provision is required to comply with the following requirements with respect to each hospital facility operated by such organization.

Community health needs assessment

Each hospital facility is required to conduct a community health needs assessment at least once every three taxable years and adopt an implementation strategy to meet the community needs identified through such assessment. The assessment may be based on current information collected by a public health agency or non-profit organizations and may be conducted together with one or more other organizations, including related organizations. The assessment process must take into account input from persons who represent the broad interests of the community served by the hospital facility, including those with special knowledge or expertise of public health issues. The hospital must disclose in its annual information report to the IRS (i.e., Form 990 and related schedules) how it is addressing the needs identified in the assessment and, if all identified needs are not addressed, the reasons why (e.g., lack of financial or human resources). Each hospital facility is required to make the assessment widely available. Failure to complete a community health needs assessment in any applicable three-year period results in a penalty on the organization of up to $50,000. For example, if a facility does not complete a community health needs assessment in taxable years one, two or three, it is subject to the penalty in year three. If it then fails to complete a community health needs assessment in year four, it is subject to another penalty in year four (for failing to satisfy the requirement during the three-year period beginning with taxable year two and ending with taxable year four). An organization that fails to disclose how it is meeting needs identified in the assessment is subject to existing incomplete return penalties.[191]

---

190 No inference is intended regarding whether an organization satisfies the present law community benefit standard.

191 Sec. 6652.

Financial assistance policy

Each hospital facility is required to adopt, implement, and widely publicize a written financial assistance policy. The financial assistance policy must indicate the eligibility criteria for financial assistance and whether such assistance includes free or discounted care. For those eligible for discounted care, the policy must indicate the basis for calculating the amounts that will be billed to such patients. The policy must also indicate how to apply for such assistance. If a hospital does not have a separate billing and collections policy, the financial assistance policy must also indicate what actions the hospital may take in the event of non-response or non-payment, including collections action and reporting to credit rating agencies. Each hospital facility also is required to adopt and implement a policy to provide emergency medical treatment to individuals. The policy must prevent discrimination in the provision of emergency medical treatment, including denial of service, against those eligible for financial assistance under the facility's financial assistance policy or those eligible for government assistance.

Limitation on charges

Each hospital facility is permitted to bill for emergency or other medically necessary care provided to individuals who qualify for financial assistance under the facility's financial assistance policy no more than the amounts generally billed to individuals who have insurance covering such care. A hospital facility may not use gross charges (i.e., "chargemaster" rates) when billing individuals who qualify for financial assistance. It is intended that amounts billed to those who qualify for financial assistance may be based on either the best, or an average of the three best, negotiated commercial rates, or Medicare rates.

Collection processes

Under the provision, a hospital facility (or its affiliates) may not undertake extraordinary collection actions (even if otherwise permitted by law) against an individual without first making reasonable efforts to determine whether the individual is eligible for assistance under the hospital's financial assistance policy. Such extraordinary collection actions include lawsuits, liens on residences, arrests, body attachments, or other similar collection processes. The Secretary is directed to issue guidance concerning what constitutes reasonable efforts to determine eligibility. It is intended that for this purpose, "reasonable efforts" includes notification by the hospital of its financial assistance policy upon admission and in written and oral communications with the patient regarding the patient's bill, including invoices and telephone calls, before collection action or reporting to credit rating agencies is initiated.

Reporting and disclosure requirements

The provision includes new reporting and disclosure requirements. Under the provision, the Secretary or the Secretary's delegate is required to review information about a hospital's community benefit activities (currently reported on Form 990, Schedule H) at least once every three years. The provision also requires each organization to which the provision applies to file with its annual information return (i.e., Form 990) a copy of its audited financial statements (or, in the case of an organization the financial statements of which are included in a consolidated financial statement with other organizations, such consolidated financial statements).

The provision requires the Secretary, in consultation with the Secretary of HHS, to submit annually a report to Congress with information regarding the levels of charity care, bad debt expenses, unreimbursed costs of means-tested government programs, and unreimbursed costs of non-means tested government programs incurred by private tax-exempt, taxable, and governmental hospitals, as well as the costs incurred by private tax-exempt hospitals for community benefit activities. In addition, the Secretary, in consultation with the Secretary of HHS, must conduct a study of the trends in these amounts, and submit a report on such study to Congress not later than five years from date of enactment.

Effective Date

Except as provided below, the provision is effective for taxable years beginning after the date of enactment. The community health needs assessment requirement is effective for taxable years beginning after the date which is two years after the date of enactment.[192] The excise tax on failures to satisfy the community health needs assessment requirement is effective for failures occurring after the date of enactment.

[192] For example, assume the date of enactment is April 1, 2010. A calendar year taxpayer would test whether it meets the community health needs assessment requirement in the taxable year ending December 31, 2013. To avoid the penalty, the taxpayer must have satisfied the community health needs assessment requirements in 2011, 2012, or 2013.

G. Imposition of Annual Fee on Branded Prescription Pharmaceutical Manufacturers and Importers (sec. 9008[193] of the Senate amendment)

Present Law

There are two Medicare trust funds under present law, the Hospital Insurance ("HI") fund and the Supplementary Medical Insurance ("SMI") fund.[194] The HI trust fund is primarily funded through payroll tax on covered earnings. Employers and employees each pay 1.45 percent of wages, while self-employed workers pay 2.9 percent of a portion of their net earnings from self-employment. Other HI trust fund revenue sources include a portion of the Federal income taxes paid on Social Security benefits, and interest paid on the U.S. Treasury securities held in the HI trust fund. For the SMI trust fund, transfers from the general fund of the Treasury represent the largest source of revenue, but additional revenues include monthly premiums paid by beneficiaries, and interest paid on the U.S. Treasury securities held in the SMI trust fund.

Present law does not impose a fee creditable to the Medicare trust funds on companies that manufacture or import prescription drugs for sale in the United States.

Explanation of Provision

The provision imposes a fee on each covered entity engaged in the business of manufacturing or importing branded prescription drugs for sale to any specified government program or pursuant to coverage under any such program for each calendar year beginning after 2010. Fees collected under the provision are credited to the Medicare Part B trust fund.

The aggregate annual fee for all covered entities is the applicable amount. The applicable amount is $2.5 billion for calendar year 2011, $2.8 billion for calendar years 2012 and 2013, $3 billion for calendar years 2014 through 2016, $4 billion for calendar year 2017, $4.1 billion for calendar year 2018, and $2.8 billion for calendar year 2019 and thereafter. The aggregate fee is apportioned among the covered entities each year based on such entity's relative share of branded prescription drug sales taken into account during the previous calendar year. The Secretary of the Treasury will establish an annual payment date that will be no later than September 30 of each calendar year.

The Secretary of the Treasury will calculate the amount of each covered entity's fee for each calendar year by determining the relative market share for each covered entity. A covered entity's relative market share for a calendar year is the covered entity's branded prescription drug sales taken into account during the preceding calendar year as a percentage of the aggregate branded prescription drug sales of all covered entities taken into account during the preceding calendar year. The branded prescription drug sales taken into account during any calendar year

---

[193] Section 9008 of the Senate amendment is amended by section 1404 of the Reconciliation bill.

[194] See 2009 Annual Report of the Boards of Trustees of the Federal Hospital Insurance and Federal Supplementary Medical Insurance Trust Funds, available at http://www.cms.hhs.gov/ReportsTrustFunds/downloads/tr2009.pdf.

with respect to any covered entity is: (1) zero percent of sales not more than $5 million, (2) 10 percent of sales over $5 million but not more than $125 million, (3) 40 percent of sales over $125 million but not more than $225 million, (4) 75 percent of sales over $225 million but not more than $400 million, and (5) 100 percent of sales over $400 million.

For purposes of the provision, a covered entity is any manufacturer or importer with gross receipts from branded prescription drug sales. All persons treated as a single employer under section 52(a) or (b) or under section 414(m) or 414(o) will be treated as a single covered entity for purposes of the provision. In applying the single employer rules under 52(a) and (b), foreign corporations will not be excluded. If more than one person is liable for payment of the fee imposed by this provision, all such persons are jointly and severally liable for payment of such fee. It is anticipated that the Secretary may require each covered entity to identify each member of the group that is treated as a single covered entity under the provision.

Under the provision, branded prescription drug sales are sales of branded prescriptions drugs made to any specified government program or pursuant to coverage under any such program. The term branded prescription drugs includes any drug which is subject to section 503(b) of the Federal Food, Drug, and Cosmetic Act and for which an application was submitted under section 505(b) of such Act, and any biological product for which an application was submitted under section 351(a) of such Act. Branded prescription drug sales, as defined under the provision, does not include sales of any drug or biological product with respect to which an orphan drug tax credit was allowed for any taxable year under section 45C. The exception for orphan drug sales does not apply to any drug or biological product after such drug or biological product is approved by the Food and Drug Administration for marketing for any indication other than the rare disease or condition with respect to which the section 45C credit was allowed.

Specified government programs under the provision include: (1) the Medicare Part D program under part D of title XVIII of the Social Security Act; (2) the Medicare Part B program under part B of title XVIII of the Social Security Act; (3) the Medicaid program under title XIX of the Social Security Act; (4) any program under which branded prescription drugs are procured by the Department of Veterans Affairs; (5) any program under which branded prescription drugs are procured by the Department of Defense; or (6) the TRICARE retail pharmacy program under section 1074g of title 10, United States Code.

The Secretary of HHS, the Secretary of Veterans Affairs, and the Secretary of Defense will report to the Secretary of the Treasury, at a time and in such a manner as the Secretary of the Treasury prescribes, the total branded prescription drug sales for each covered entity with respect to each specified government program under such Secretary's jurisdiction. The provision includes specific information to be included in the reports by the respective Secretaries for each specified government program.

The fees imposed under the provision are treated as excise taxes with respect to which only civil actions for refunds under the provisions of subtitle F will apply. Thus, the fees may be assessed and collected using the procedures in subtitle F without regard to the restrictions on assessment in section 6213.

The Secretary of the Treasury has authority to publish guidance as necessary to carry out the purposes of this provision. It is anticipated that the Secretary of the Treasury will publish guidance related to the determination of the fee under this section. For example, the Secretary may publish initial determinations, allow a notice and comment period, and then provide notice and demand for payment of the fee. It is also anticipated that the Secretary of the Treasury will provide guidance as to the determination of the fee in situations involving mergers, acquisitions, business divisions, bankruptcy, or any other situations where guidance is necessary to account for sales taken into account for determining the fee for any calendar year.

The fees imposed under the provision are not deductible for U.S. income tax purposes.

Effective Date

The provision is effective for calendar years beginning after December 31, 2010.

H. Imposition of Annual Fee on Medical Device Manufacturers and Importers (sec. 9009[195] of the Senate amendment)

Repeal

The provision imposing an annual fee on manufactures and importers of medical devices is repealed.

Effective Date

The repeal is effective as of the date of enactment of the Senate amendment.

[195] Section 9009 of the Senate amendment is repealed by section 1405(d) of the Reconciliation bill.

I. Imposition of Annual Fee on Health Insurance Providers (sec. 9010[196] of the Senate amendment)

Present Law

Present law provides special rules for determining the taxable income of insurance companies (subchapter L of the Code). Separate sets of rules apply to life insurance companies and to property and casualty insurance companies. Insurance companies are subject to Federal income tax at regular corporate income tax rates.

An insurance company that provides health insurance is subject to Federal income tax as either a life insurance company or as a property insurance company, depending on its mix of lines of business and on the resulting portion of its reserves that are treated as life insurance reserves. For Federal income tax purposes, an insurance company is treated as a life insurance company if the sum of its (1) life insurance reserves and (2) unearned premiums and unpaid losses on noncancellable life, accident or health contracts not included in life insurance reserves, comprise more than 50 percent of its total reserves.[197]

Some insurance providers may be exempt from Federal income tax under section 501(a) if specific requirements are satisfied. Section 501(c)(8), for example, describes certain fraternal beneficiary societies, orders, or associations operating under the lodge system or for the exclusive benefit of their members that provide for the payment of life, sick, accident, or other benefits to the members or their dependents. Section 501(c)(9) describes certain voluntary employees' beneficiary associations that provide for the payment of life, sick, accident, or other benefits to the members of the association or their dependents or designated beneficiaries. Section 501(c)(12)(A) describes certain benevolent life insurance associations of a purely local character. Section 501(c)(15) describes certain small non-life insurance companies with annual gross receipts of no more than $600,000 ($150,000 in the case of a mutual insurance company). Section 501(c)(26) describes certain membership organizations established to provide health insurance to certain high-risk individuals. Section 501(c)(27) describes certain organizations established to provide workmen's compensation insurance.

An excise tax applies to premiums paid to foreign insurers and reinsurers covering U.S. risks.[198] The excise tax is imposed on a gross basis at the rate of one percent on reinsurance and life insurance premiums, and at the rate of four percent on property and casualty insurance premiums. The excise tax does not apply to premiums that are effectively connected with the conduct of a U.S. trade or business or that are exempted from the excise tax under an applicable income tax treaty. The excise tax paid by one party cannot be credited if, for example, the risk is reinsured with a second party in a transaction that is also subject to the excise tax.

---

[196] Section 9010 of the Senate amendment, as amended by section 10905, is further amended by section 1406 of the Reconciliation bill.

[197] Sec. 816(a).

[198] Secs. 4371-4374.

IRS authority to assess and collect taxes is generally provided in subtitle F of the Code (secs. 6001 -7874), relating to procedure and administration. That subtitle establishes the rules governing both how taxpayers are required to report information to the IRS and to pay their taxes, as well as their rights. It also establishes the duties and authority of the IRS to enforce the Federal tax law, and sets forth rules relating to judicial proceedings involving Federal tax.

Explanation of Provision

Under the provision, an annual fee applies to any covered entity engaged in the business of providing health insurance with respect to United States health risks. The fee applies for calendar years beginning after 2013. The aggregate annual fee for all covered entities is the applicable amount. The applicable amount is $8 billion for calendar year 2014, $11.3 billion for calendar years 2015 and 2016, $13.9 billion for calendar year 2017, and $14.3 billion for calendar year 2018. For calendar years after 2018, the applicable amount is indexed to the rate of premium growth.

The annual payment date for a calendar year is determined by the Secretary of the Treasury, but in no event may be later than September 30 of that year.

Under the provision, the aggregate annual fee is apportioned among the providers based on a ratio designed to reflect relative market share of U.S. health insurance business. For each covered entity, the fee for a calendar year is an amount that bears the same ratio to the applicable amount as (1) the covered entity's net premiums written during the preceding calendar year with respect to health insurance for any United States health risk, bears to (2) the aggregate net written premiums of all covered entities during such preceding calendar year with respect to such health insurance.

The provision requires the Secretary of the Treasury to calculate the amount of each covered entity's fee for the calendar year, determining the covered entity's net written premiums for the preceding calendar year with respect to health insurance for any United States health risk on the basis of reports submitted by the covered entity and through the use of any other source of information available to the Treasury Department. It is intended that the Treasury Department be able to rely on published aggregate annual statement data to the extent necessary, and may use annual statement data and filed annual statements that are publicly available to verify or supplement the reports submitted by covered entities.

Net written premiums is intended to mean premiums written, including reinsurance premiums written, reduced by reinsurance ceded, and reduced by ceding commissions. Net written premiums do not include amounts arising under arrangements that are not treated as insurance (i.e., in the absence of sufficient risk shifting and risk distribution for the arrangement to constitute insurance).[199]

The amount of net premiums written that are taken into account for purposes of determining a covered entity's market share is subject to dollar thresholds. A covered entity's

---

[199] See *Helvering v. Le Gierse*, 312 U.S. 531 (1941).

net premiums written during the calendar year that are not more $25 million are not taken into account for this purpose. With respect to a covered entity's net premiums written during the calendar year that are more than $25 million but not more than $50 million, 50 percent are taken into account, and 100 percent of net premiums written in excess of $50 million are taken into account.

After application of the above dollar thresholds, a special rule provides an exclusion, for purposes of determining an otherwise covered entity's market share, of 50 percent of net premiums written that are attributable to the exempt activities[200] of a health insurance organization that is exempt from Federal income tax[201] by reason of being described in section 501(c)(3) (generally, a public charity), section 501(c)(4) (generally, a social welfare organization), section 501(c)(26) (generally, a high-risk health insurance pool), or section 501(c)(29) (a consumer operated and oriented plan ("CO-OP") health insurance issuer).

A covered entity generally is an entity that provides health insurance with respect to United States health risks during the calendar year in which the fee under this section is due. Thus for example, an insurance company subject to tax under part I or II of subchapter L, an organization exempt from tax under section 501(a), a foreign insurer that provides health insurance with respect to United States health risks, or an insurer that provides health insurance with respect to United States health risks under Medicare Advantage, Medicare Part D, or Medicaid, is a covered entity under the provision except as provided in specific exceptions.

Specific exceptions are provided to the definition of a covered entity. A covered entity does not include an employer to the extent that the employer self-insures the health risks of its employees. For example, a manufacturer that enters into a self-insurance arrangement with respect to the health risks of its employees is not treated as a covered entity. As a further example, an insurer that sells health insurance and that also enters into a self-insurance arrangement with respect to the health risks of its own employees is treated as a covered entity with respect to its health insurance business, but is not treated as a covered entity to the extent of the self-insurance of its own employees' health risks.

A covered entity does not include any governmental entity. For this purpose, it is intended that a governmental entity includes a county organized health system entity that is an independent public agency organized as a nonprofit under State law and that contracts with a State to administer State Medicaid benefits through local care providers or HMOs.

A covered entity does not include an entity that (1) qualifies as nonprofit under applicable State law, (2) meets the private inurement and limitation on lobbying provisions described in section 501(c)(3), and (3) receives more than 80 percent of its gross revenue from government

---

[200] The exempt activities for this purpose are activities other than activities of an unrelated trade or business defined in section 513 of the Code.

[201] Section 501(m) of the Code provides that an organization described in section 501(c)(3) or (4) is exempt from Federal income tax only if no substantial part of its activities consists of providing commercial-type insurance. Thus, an organization otherwise described in section 501(c)(3) or (4) that is taxable (under the Federal income tax rules) by reason of section 501(m) is not eligible for the 50-percent exclusion under the insurance fee.

programs that target low-income, elderly, or disabled populations (including Medicare, Medicaid, the State Children's Health Insurance Plan ("SCHIP"), and dual-eligible plans).

A covered entity does not include an organization that qualifies as a VEBA under section 501(c)(9) that is established by an entity other than the employer (i.e., a union) for the purpose of providing health care benefits. This exclusion does not apply to multi-employer welfare arrangements ("MEWAs").

For purposes of the provision, all persons treated as a single employer under section 52(a) or (b) or section 414(m) or (o) are treated as a single covered entity (or as a single employer, for purposes of the rule relating to employers that self-insure the health risks of employees), and otherwise applicable exclusion of foreign corporations under those rules is disregarded. However, the exceptions to the definition of a covered entity are applied on a separate entity basis, not taking into account this rule. If more than one person is liable for payment of the fee by reason of being treated as a single covered entity, all such persons are jointly and severally liable for payment of the fee.

A United States heath risk means the health risk of an individual who is a U.S. citizen, is a U.S. resident within the meaning of section 7701(b)(1)(A) (whether or not located in the United States), or is located in the United States, with respect to the period that the individual is located there. In general, it is intended that risks in the following lines of business reported on the annual statement as prescribed by the National Association of Insurance Commissioners and as filed with the insurance commissioners of the States in which insurers are licensed to do business constitute health risks for this purpose: comprehensive (hospital and medical), vision, dental, Federal Employees Health Benefit plan, title XVIII Medicare, title XIX Medicaid, and other health.

For purposes of the provision, health insurance does not include coverage only for accident, or disability income insurance, or a combination thereof. Health insurance does not include coverage only for a specified disease or illness, nor does health insurance include hospital indemnity or other fixed indemnity insurance. Health insurance does not include any insurance for long-term care or any Medicare supplemental health insurance (as defined in section 1882(g)(1) of the Social Security Act).

For purposes of procedure and administration under the rules of Subtitle F of the Code, the fee under this provision is treated as an excise tax with respect to which only civil actions for refund under Subtitle F apply. The Secretary of the Treasury may redetermine the amount of a covered entity's fee under the provision for any calendar year for which the statute of limitations remains open.

For purposes of section 275, relating to the nondeductibility of specified taxes, the fee is considered to be a nondeductible tax described in section 275(a)(6).

A reporting rule applies under the provision. A covered entity is required to report to the Secretary of the Treasury the amount of its net premiums written during any calendar year with respect to health insurance for any United States health risk.

A penalty applies for failure to report, unless it is shown that the failure is due to reasonable cause. The amount of the penalty is $10,000 plus the lesser of (1) $1,000 per day while the failure continues, or (2) the amount of the fee imposed for which the report was required. The penalty is treated as a penalty for purposes of subtitle F of the Code, must be paid on notice and demand by the Treasury Department and in the same manner as tax, and with respect to which only civil actions for refund under procedures of subtitle F. The reported information is not treated as taxpayer information under section 6103.

An accuracy-related penalty applies in the case of any understatement of a covered entity's net premiums written. For this purpose, an understatement is the difference between the amount of net premiums written as reported on the return filed by the covered entity and the amount of net premiums written that should have been reported on the return. The penalty is equal to the amount of the fee that should have been paid in the absence of an understatement over the amount of the fee determined based on the understatement. The accuracy-related penalty is subject to the provisions of subtitle F of the Code that apply to assessable penalties imposed under Chapter 68.

The provision provides authority for the Secretary of the Treasury to publish guidance necessary to carry out the purposes of the provision and to prescribe regulations necessary or appropriate to prevent avoidance of the purposes of the provision, including inappropriate actions taken to qualify as an exempt entity under the provision.

Effective Date

The annual fee is required to be paid in each calendar year beginning after December 31, 2013. The fee under the provision is determined with respect to net premiums written after December 31, 2012, with respect to health insurance for any United States health risk.

J. Study and Report of Effect on Veterans Health Care (sec. 9011 of the Senate amendment)

Present Law

No provision.

Explanation of Provision

The provision requires the Secretary of Veterans Affairs to conduct a study on the effect (if any) of the fees assessed on manufacturers and importers of branded prescription drugs, manufacturers and importers of medical devices, and health insurance providers on (1) the cost of medical care provided to veterans and (2) veterans' access to branded prescription drugs and medical devices.

The Secretary of Veterans Affairs will report the results of the study to the Committee on Ways and Means of the House of Representatives and to the Committee on Finance of the Senate no later than December 31, 2012.

Effective Date

The provision is effective on the date of enactment.

K. Repeal Business Deduction for Federal Subsidies for Certain Retiree Prescription Drug Plans (sec. 9012[202] of the Senate amendment and sec. 139A of the Code)

Present Law

In general

Sponsors[203] of qualified retiree prescription drug plans are eligible for subsidy payments from the Secretary of HHS with respect to a portion of each qualified covered retiree's gross covered prescription drug costs ("qualified retiree prescription drug plan subsidy").[204] A qualified retiree prescription drug plan is employment-based retiree health coverage[205] that has an actuarial value at least as great as the Medicare Part D standard plan for the risk pool and that meets certain other disclosure and recordkeeping requirements.[206] These qualified retiree prescription drug plan subsidies are excludable from the plan sponsor's gross income for the purposes of regular income tax and alternative minimum tax (including the adjustment for adjusted current earnings).[207]

Subsidy amounts

For each qualifying covered retiree enrolled for a coverage year in a qualified retiree prescription drug plan, the qualified retiree prescription drug plan subsidy is equal to 28 percent of the portion of the allowable retiree costs paid by the plan sponsor on behalf of the retiree that exceed the cost threshold but do not exceed the cost limit. A "qualifying covered retiree" is an individual who is eligible for Medicare but not enrolled in either a Medicare Part D prescription

---

[202] Section 9012 of the Senate amendment is amended by section 1407 of the Reconciliation bill.

[203] The identity of the plan sponsor is determined in accordance with section 16(B) of ERISA, except that for cases where a plan is maintained jointly by one employer and an employee organization, and the employer is the primary source of financing, the employer is the plan sponsor.

[204] Sec. 1860D-22 of the Social Security Act (SSA), 42 USC Sec. 1395w-132.

[205] Employment-based retiree health coverage is health insurance coverage or other coverage of health care costs (whether provided by voluntary insurance coverage or pursuant to statutory or contractual obligation) for Medicare Part D eligible individuals (their spouses and dependents) under group health plans based on their status as retired participants in such plans. For purposes of the subsidy, group health plans generally include employee welfare benefit plans (as defined in section 607(1) of ERISA) that provide medical care (as defined in section 213(d)), Federal and State governmental plans, collectively bargained plans, and church plans.

[206] In addition to meeting the actuarial value standard, the plan sponsor must also maintain and provide the Secretary of HHS access to records that meet the Secretary of HHS's requirements for purposes of audits and other oversight activities necessary to ensure the adequacy of prescription drug coverage and the accuracy of payments made to eligible individuals under the plan. In addition, the plan sponsor must disclose to the Secretary of HHS whether the plan meets the actuarial equivalence requirement and if it does not, must disclose to retirees the limitations of their ability to enroll in Medicare Part D and that non-creditable coverage enrollment is subject to penalties such as fees for late enrollment. 42 U.S.C. 1395w-132(a)(2).

[207] Sec. 139A.

drug plan or a Medicare Advantage-Prescription Drug plan, but who is covered under a qualified retiree prescription drug plan. In general, allowable retiree costs are, with respect to prescription drug costs under a qualified retiree prescription drug plan, the part of the actual costs paid by the plan sponsor on behalf of a qualifying covered retiree under the plan.[208] Both the threshold and limit are indexed to the percentage increase in Medicare per capita prescription drug costs; the cost threshold was $250 in 2006 ($310 in 2010) and the cost limit was $5,000 in 2006 ($6,300 in 2010).[209]

Expenses relating to tax-exempt income

In general, no deduction is allowed under any provision of the Code for any expense or amount which would otherwise be allowable as a deduction if such expense or amount is allocable to a class or classes of exempt income.[210] Thus, expenses or amount paid or incurred with respect to the subsidies excluded from income under section 139A would generally not be deductible. However, a provision under section 139A specifies that the exclusion of the qualified retiree prescription drug plan subsidy from income is not taken into account in determining whether any deduction is allowable with respect to covered retiree prescription drug expenses that are taken into account in determining the subsidy payment. Therefore, under present law, a taxpayer may claim a business deduction for covered retiree prescription drug expenses incurred notwithstanding that the taxpayer excludes from income qualified retiree prescription drug plan subsidies allocable to such expenses.

Explanation of Provision

The provision eliminates the rule that the exclusion for subsidy payments is not taken into account for purposes of determining whether a deduction is allowable with respect to retiree prescription drug expenses. Thus, under the provision, the amount otherwise allowable as a deduction for retiree prescription drug expenses is reduced by the amount of the excludable subsidy payments received.

For example, assume a company receives a subsidy of $28 with respect to eligible drug expenses of $100. The $28 is excludable from income under section 139A, and the amount otherwise allowable as a deduction is reduced by the $28. Thus, if the company otherwise meets the requirements of section 162 with respect to its eligible drug expenses, it would be entitled to an ordinary business expense deduction of $72.

Effective Date

The provision is effective for taxable years beginning after December 31, 2012.

---

[208] For purposes of calculating allowable retiree costs, actual costs paid are net of discounts, chargebacks, and average percentage rebates, and exclude administrative costs.

[209] http://www.cms.hhs.gov/MedicareAdvtgSpecRateStats/Downloads/Announcement2010.pdf. Retrieved on March 19, 2010.

[210] Sec. 265(a) and Treas. Reg. sec. 1.265-1(a).

L. Modify the Itemized Deduction for Medical Expenses (sec. 9013 of the Senate amendment and sec. 213 of the Code)

Present Law

Regular income tax.

For regular income tax purposes, individuals are allowed an itemized deduction for unreimbursed medical expenses, but only to the extent that such expenses exceed 7.5 percent of AGI.[211]

This deduction is available both to insured and uninsured individuals; thus, for example, an individual with employer-provided health insurance (or certain other forms of tax-subsidized health benefits) may also claim the itemized deduction for the individual's medical expenses not covered by that insurance if the 7.5 percent AGI threshold is met. The medical deduction encompasses health insurance premiums to the extent they have not been excluded from taxable income through the employer exclusion or self-insured deduction.

Alternative minimum tax.

For purposes of the alternative minimum tax ("AMT"), medical expenses are deductible only to the extent that they exceed 10 percent of AGI.

Explanation of Provision

This provision increases the threshold for the itemized deduction for unreimbursed medical expenses from 7.5 percent of AGI to 10 percent of AGI for regular income tax purposes. However, for the years 2013, 2014, 2015 and 2016, if either the taxpayer or the taxpayer's spouse turns 65 before the end of the taxable year, the increased threshold does not apply and the threshold remains at 7.5 percent of AGI. The provision does not change the AMT treatment of the itemized deduction for medical expenses.

Effective Date

The provision is effective for taxable years beginning after December 31, 2012.

---

[211] Sec. 213.

M. Limitation on Deduction for Remuneration Paid by Health Insurance Providers (sec. 9014 of the Senate amendment and sec. 162 of the Code)

Present Law

An employer generally may deduct reasonable compensation for personal services as an ordinary and necessary business expense. Section 162(m) provides explicit limitations on the deductibility of compensation expenses in the case of corporate employers.

Section 162(m)

In general

The otherwise allowable deduction for compensation paid or accrued with respect to a covered employee of a publicly held corporation[212] is limited to no more than $1 million per year.[213] The deduction limitation applies when the deduction would otherwise be taken. Thus, for example, in the case of compensation resulting from a transfer of property in connection with the performance of services, such compensation is taken into account in applying the deduction limitation for the year for which the compensation is deductible under section 83 (i.e., generally the year in which the employee's right to the property is no longer subject to a substantial risk of forfeiture).

Covered employees

Section 162(m) defines a covered employee as (1) the chief executive officer of the corporation (or an individual acting in such capacity) as of the close of the taxable year and (2) the four most highly compensated officers for the taxable year (other than the chief executive officer). Treasury regulations under section 162(m) provide that whether an employee is the chief executive officer or among the four most highly compensated officers should be determined pursuant to the executive compensation disclosure rules promulgated under the Securities Exchange Act of 1934 ("Exchange Act").

In 2006, the Securities and Exchange Commission amended certain rules relating to executive compensation, including which executive officers' compensation must be disclosed under the Exchange Act. Under the new rules, such officers consist of (1) the principal executive officer (or an individual acting in such capacity), (2) the principal financial officer (or an individual acting in such capacity), and (3) the three most highly compensated executive officers, other than the principal executive officer or financial officer. In response to the Securities and

---

[212] A corporation is treated as publicly held if it has a class of common equity securities that is required to be registered under section 12 of the Securities Exchange Act of 1934.

[213] Sec. 162(m). This deduction limitation applies for purposes of the regular income tax and the alternative minimum tax.

Exchange Commission's new disclosure rules, the IRS issued updated guidance on identifying which employees are covered by section 162(m).[214]

Remuneration subject to the limit

Unless specifically excluded, the deduction limitation applies to all remuneration for services, including cash and the cash value of all remuneration (including benefits) paid in a medium other than cash. If an individual is a covered employee for a taxable year, the deduction limitation applies to all compensation not explicitly excluded from the deduction limitation, regardless of whether the compensation is for services as a covered employee and regardless of when the compensation was earned. The $1 million cap is reduced by excess parachute payments (as defined in sec. 280G, discussed below) that are not deductible by the corporation.

Certain types of compensation are not subject to the deduction limit and are not taken into account in determining whether other compensation exceeds $1 million. The following types of compensation are not taken into account: (1) remuneration payable on a commission basis; (2) remuneration payable solely on account of the attainment of one or more performance goals if certain outside director and shareholder approval requirements are met ("performance-based compensation"); (3) payments to a tax-qualified retirement plan (including salary reduction contributions); (4) amounts that are excludable from the executive's gross income (such as employer-provided health benefits and miscellaneous fringe benefits[215]); and (5) any remuneration payable under a written binding contract which was in effect on February 17, 1993.

Remuneration does not include compensation for which a deduction is allowable after a covered employee ceases to be a covered employee. Thus, the deduction limitation often does not apply to deferred compensation that is otherwise subject to the deduction limitation (e.g., is not performance-based compensation) because the payment of compensation is deferred until after termination of employment.

Executive compensation of employers participating in the Troubled Assets Relief Program

In general

Under section 162(m)(5), the deduction limit is reduced to $500,000 in the case of otherwise deductible compensation of a covered executive for any applicable taxable year of an applicable employer.

An applicable employer means any employer from which one or more troubled assets are acquired under the "troubled assets relief program" ("TARP") established by the Emergency Stabilization Act of 2008[216] ("EESA") if the aggregate amount of the assets so acquired for all

[214] Notice 2007-49, 2007-25 I.R.B. 1429.

[215] Sec. 132.

[216] Pub. L. No. 110-343.

taxable years (including assets acquired through a direct purchase by the Treasury Department, within the meaning of section 113(c) of Title I of EESA) exceeds $300,000,000. However, such term does not include any employer from which troubled assets are acquired by the Treasury Department solely through direct purchases (within the meaning of section 113(c) of Title I of EESA). For example, if a firm sells $250,000,000 in assets through an auction system managed by the Treasury Department, and $100,000,000 to the Treasury Department in direct purchases, then the firm is an applicable employer. Conversely, if all $350,000,000 in sales take the form of direct purchases, then the firm would not be an applicable employer.

Unlike section 162(m), an applicable employer under this provision is not limited to publicly held corporations (or even limited to corporations). For example, an applicable employer could be a partnership if the partnership is an employer from which a troubled asset is acquired. The aggregation rules of section 414(b) and (c) apply in determining whether an employer is an applicable employer. However, these rules are applied disregarding the rules for brother-sister controlled groups and combined groups in sections 1563(a)(2) and (3). Thus, this aggregation rule only applies to parent-subsidiary controlled groups. A similar controlled group rule applies for trades and businesses under common control.

The result of this aggregation rule is that all corporations in the same controlled group are treated as a single employer for purposes of identifying the covered executives of that employer and all compensation from all members of the controlled group are taken into account for purposes of applying the $500,000 deduction limit. Further, all sales of assets under the TARP from all members of the controlled group are considered in determining whether such sales exceed $300,000,000.

An applicable taxable year with respect to an applicable employer means the first taxable year which includes any portion of the period during which the authorities for the TARP established under EESA are in effect (the "authorities period") if the aggregate amount of troubled assets acquired from the employer under that authority during the taxable year (when added to the aggregate amount so acquired for all preceding taxable years) exceeds $300,000,000, and includes any subsequent taxable year which includes any portion of the authorities period.

A special rule applies in the case of compensation that relates to services that a covered executive performs during an applicable taxable year but that is not deductible until a later year ("deferred deduction executive remuneration"), such as nonqualified deferred compensation. Under the special rule, the unused portion (if any) of the $500,000 limit for the applicable tax year is carried forward until the year in which the compensation is otherwise deductible, and the remaining unused limit is then applied to the compensation.

For example, assume a covered executive is paid $400,000 in cash salary by an applicable employer in 2008 (assuming 2008 is an applicable taxable year) and the covered executive earns $100,000 in nonqualified deferred compensation (along with the right to future earnings credits) payable in 2020. Assume further that the $100,000 has grown to $300,000 in 2020. The full $400,000 in cash salary is deductible under the $500,000 limit in 2008. In 2020, the applicable employer's deduction with respect to the $300,000 will be limited to $100,000 (the lesser of the $300,000 in deductible compensation before considering the special limitation, and $500,000 less $400,000, which represents the unused portion of the $500,000 limit from 2008).

Deferred deduction executive remuneration that is properly deductible in an applicable taxable year (before application of the limitation under the provision) but is attributable to services performed in a prior applicable taxable year is subject to the special rule described above and is not double-counted. For example, assume the same facts as above, except that the nonqualified deferred compensation is deferred until 2009 and that 2009 is an applicable taxable year. The employer's deduction for the nonqualified deferred compensation for 2009 would be limited to $100,000 (as in the example above). The limit that would apply under the provision for executive remuneration that is in a form other than deferred deduction executive remuneration and that is otherwise deductible for 2009 is $500,000. For example, if the covered executive is paid $500,000 in cash compensation for 2009, all $500,000 of that cash compensation would be deductible in 2009 under the provision.

Covered executive

The term covered executive means any individual who is the chief executive officer or the chief financial officer of an applicable employer, or an individual acting in that capacity, at any time during a portion of the taxable year that includes the authorities period. It also includes any employee who is one of the three highest compensated officers of the applicable employer for the applicable taxable year (other than the chief executive officer or the chief financial officer and only taking into account employees employed during any portion of the taxable year that includes the authorities period).[217]

Executive remuneration

The provision generally incorporates the present law definition of applicable employee remuneration. However, the present law exceptions for remuneration payable on commission and performance-based compensation do not apply for purposes of the $500,000 limit. In addition, the $500,000 limit only applies to executive remuneration which is attributable to services performed by a covered executive during an applicable taxable year. For example, assume the same facts as in the example above, except that the covered executive also receives in 2008 a payment of $300,000 in nonqualified deferred compensation that was attributable to services performed in 2006. Such payment is not treated as executive remuneration for purposes of the $500,000 limit.

---

[217] The determination of the three highest compensated officers is made on the basis of the shareholder disclosure rules for compensation under the Exchange Act, except to the extent that the shareholder disclosure rules are inconsistent with the provision. Such shareholder disclosure rules are applied without regard to whether those rules actually apply to the employer under the Exchange Act. If an employee is a covered executive with respect to an applicable employer for any applicable taxable year, the employee will be treated as a covered executive for all subsequent applicable taxable years (and will be treated as a covered executive for purposes of any subsequent taxable year for purposes of the special rule for deferred deduction executive remuneration).

Taxation of insurance companies

Present law provides special rules for determining the taxable income of insurance companies (subchapter L of the Code). Separate sets of rules apply to life insurance companies and to property and casualty insurance companies. Insurance companies are subject to Federal income tax at regular corporate income tax rates. An insurance company generally may deduct compensation paid in the course of its trade or business.

Explanation of Provision

Under the provision, no deduction is allowed for remuneration which is attributable to services performed by an applicable individual for a covered health insurance provider during an applicable taxable year to the extent that such remuneration exceeds $500,000. As under section 162(m)(5) for remuneration from TARP participants, the exceptions for performance based remuneration, commissions, or remuneration under existing binding contracts do not apply. This $500,000 deduction limitation applies without regard to whether such remuneration is paid during the taxable year or a subsequent taxable year. In applying this rule, rules similar to those in section 162(m)(5)(A)(ii) apply. Thus in the case of remuneration that relates to services that an applicable individual performs during a taxable year but that is not deductible until a later year, such as nonqualified deferred compensation, the unused portion (if any) of the $500,000 limit for the year is carried forward until the year in which the compensation is otherwise deductible, and the remaining unused limit is then applied to the compensation.

In determining whether the remuneration of an applicable individual for a year exceeds $500,000, all remuneration from all members of any controlled group of corporations (within the meaning of section 414(b)), other businesses under common control (within the meaning of section 414(c)), or affiliated service group (within the meaning of sections 414(m) and (o)) are aggregated.

Covered health insurance provider and applicable taxable year

An insurance provider is a covered health insurance provider if at least 25 percent of the insurance provider's gross premium income from health business is derived from health insurance plans that meet the minimum creditable coverage requirements in the bill ("covered health insurance provider"). A taxable year is an applicable taxable year for an insurance provider if an insurance provider is a covered insurance provider for any portion of the taxable year. Employers with self-insured plans are excluded from the definition of covered health insurance provider.

Applicable individual

Applicable individuals include all officers, employees, directors, and other workers or service providers (such as consultants) performing services for or on behalf of a covered health insurance provider. Thus, in contrast to the general rules under section 162(m) and the special rules executive compensation of employers participating in the TARP program, the limitation on the deductibility of remuneration from a covered health insurance provided is not limited to a small group of officers and covered executives but generally applies to remuneration of all employees and service providers. If an individual is an applicable individual with respect to a covered health insurance provider for any taxable year, the individual is treated as an applicable individual for all subsequent taxable years (and is treated as an applicable individual for purposes of any subsequent taxable year for purposes of the special rule for deferred remuneration).

Effective Date

The provision is effective for remuneration paid in taxable years beginning after 2012 with respect to services performed after 2009.

N. Additional Hospital Insurance Tax on High Income Taxpayers (sec. 9015[218] of the Senate amendment and new secs. 3101 and 1401 of the Code)

Present Law

Federal Insurance Contributions Act tax

The Federal Insurance Contributions Act imposes tax on employers based on the amount of wages paid to an employee during the year. The tax imposed is composed of two parts: (1) the old age, survivors, and disability insurance ("OASDI") tax equal to 6.2 percent of covered wages up to the taxable wage base ($106,800 in 2010); and (2) the HI tax amount equal to 1.45 percent of covered wages. Generally, covered wages means all remuneration for employment, including the cash value of all remuneration (including benefits) paid in any medium other than cash. Certain exceptions from covered wages are also provided. In addition to the tax on employers, each employee is subject to FICA taxes equal to the amount of tax imposed on the employer.

The employee portion of the FICA tax generally must be withheld and remitted to the Federal government by the employer.[219] The employer generally is liable for the amount of this tax whether or not the employer withholds the amount from the employee's wages.[220] In the event that the employer fails to withhold from an employee, the employee generally is not liable to the IRS for the amount of the tax. However, if the employer pays its liability for the amount of the tax not withheld, the employer generally has a right to collect that amount from the employee. Further, if the employer deducts and pays the tax the employer is indemnified against the claims and demands of any person for the amount of any payment of the tax made by the employer.[221]

Self-Employment Contributions Act tax

As a parallel to FICA taxes, the Self-Employment Contributions Act ("SECA") imposes taxes on the net income from self employment of self employed individuals. The rate of the OASDI portion of SECA taxes is equal to the combined employee and employer OASDI FICA tax rates and applies to self employment income up to the FICA taxable wage base. Similarly, the rate of the HI portion is the same as the combined employer and employee HI rates and there is no cap on the amount of self employment income to which the rate applies.[222]

---

[218] Section 9015 of the Senate bill is amended by section 10906 of the Senate bill.

[219] Sec. 3102(a).

[220] Sec. 3102(b).

[221] *Ibid.*

[222] For purposes of computing net earnings from self employment, taxpayers are permitted a deduction equal to the product of the taxpayer's earnings (determined without regard to this deduction) and one-half of the sum of the rates for OASDI (12.4 percent) and HI (2.9 percent), i.e., 7.65 percent of net earnings. This deduction reflects

For purposes of computing net earnings from self employment, taxpayers are permitted a deduction equal to the product of the taxpayer's earnings (determined without regard to this deduction) and one-half of the sum of the rates for OASDI (12.4 percent) and HI (2.9 percent), i.e., 7.65 percent of net earnings. This deduction reflects the fact that the FICA rates apply to an employee's wages, which do not include FICA taxes paid by the employer, whereas the self-employed individual's net earnings are economically equivalent to an employee's wages plus the employer share of FICA taxes.

Explanation of Provision

Additional HI tax on employee portion of HI tax

Calculation of additional tax

The employee portion of the HI tax is increased by an additional tax of 0.9 percent on wages[223] received in excess of the threshold amount. However, unlike the general 1.45 percent HI tax on wages, this additional tax is on the combined wages of the employee and the employee's spouse, in the case of a joint return. The threshold amount is $250,000 in the case of a joint return or surviving spouse, $125,000 in the case of a married individual filing a separate return, and $200,000 in any other case.

Liability for the additional HI tax on wages

As under present law, the employer is required to withhold the additional HI tax on wages but is liable for the tax if the employer fails to withhold the amount of the tax from wages, or collect the tax from the employee if the employer fails to withhold. However, in determining the employer's requirement to withhold and liability for the tax, only wages that the employee receives from the employer in excess of $200,000 for a year are taken into account and the employer must disregard the amount of wages received by the employee's spouse. Thus, the employer is only required to withhold on wages in excess of $200,000 for the year, even though the tax may apply to a portion of the employee's wages at or below $200,000, if the employee's spouse also has wages for the year, they are filing a joint return, and their total combined wages for the year exceed $250,000.

For example, if a taxpayer's spouse has wages in excess of $250,000 and the taxpayer has wages of $100,000, the employer of the taxpayer is not required to withhold any portion of the additional tax, even though the combined wages of the taxpayer and the taxpayer's spouse are over the $250,000 threshold. In this instance, the employer of the taxpayer's spouse is obligated to withhold the additional 0.9-percent HI tax with respect to the $50,000 above the threshold with respect to the wages of $250,000 for the taxpayer's spouse.

---

the fact that the FICA rates apply to an employee's wages, which do not include FICA taxes paid by the employer, whereas the self-employed individual's net earnings are economically equivalent to an employee's wages plus the employer share of FICA taxes.

[223] Sec. 3121(a).

In contrast to the employee portion of the general HI tax of 1.45 percent of wages for which the employee generally has no direct liability to the IRS to pay the tax, the employee is also liable for this additional 0.9-percent HI tax to the extent the tax is not withheld by the employer. The amount of this tax not withheld by an employer must also be taken into account in determining a taxpayer's liability for estimated tax.

Additional HI for self-employed individuals

This same additional HI tax applies to the HI portion of SECA tax on self-employment income in excess of the threshold amount. Thus, an additional tax of 0.9 percent is imposed on every self-employed individual on self-employment income[224] in excess of the threshold amount.

As in the case of the additional HI tax on wages, the threshold amount for the additional SECA HI tax is $250,000 in the case of a joint return or surviving spouse, $125,000 in the case of a married individual filing a separate return, and $200,000 in any other case. The threshold amount is reduced (but not below zero) by the amount of wages taken into account in determining the FICA tax with respect to the taxpayer. No deduction is allowed under section 164(f) for the additional SECA tax, and the deduction under 1402(a)(12) is determined without regard to the additional SECA tax rate.

Effective Date

The provision applies to remuneration received and taxable years beginning after December 31, 2012.

[224] Sec. 1402(b).

O. Modification of Section 833 Treatment of Certain Health Organizations (sec. 9010 of the Senate amendment and sec. 833 of the Code)

Present Law

A property and casualty insurance company is subject to tax on its taxable income, generally defined as its gross income less allowable deductions (sec. 832). For this purpose, gross income includes underwriting income and investment income, as well as other items. Underwriting income is the premiums earned on insurance contracts during the year, less losses incurred and expenses incurred. The amount of losses incurred is determined by taking into account the discounted unpaid losses. Premiums earned during the year is determined taking into account a 20-percent reduction in the otherwise allowable deduction, intended to represent the allocable portion of expenses incurred in generating the unearned premiums (sec. 832(b)(4)(B)).

Present law provides that an organization described in sections 501(c)(3) and (4) of the Code is exempt from tax only if no substantial part of its activities consists of providing commercial-type insurance (sec. 501(m)). When this rule was enacted in 1986,[225] special rules were provided under section 833 for Blue Cross and Blue Shield organizations providing health insurance that (1) were in existence on August 16, 1986; (2) were determined at any time to be tax-exempt under a determination that had not been revoked; and (3) were tax-exempt for the last taxable year beginning before January 1, 1987 (when the present-law rule became effective), provided that no material change occurred in the structure or operations of the organizations after August 16, 1986, and before the close of 1986 or any subsequent taxable year. Any other organization is eligible for section 833 treatment if it meets six requirements set forth in section 833(c): (1) substantially all of its activities involve providing health insurance; (2) at least 10 percent of its health insurance is provided to individuals and small groups (not taking into account Medicare supplemental coverage); (3) it provides continuous full-year open enrollment for individuals and small groups; (4) for individuals, it provides full coverage of pre-existing conditions of high-risk individuals and coverage without regard to age, income, or employment of individuals under age 65; (5) at least 35 percent of its premiums are community rated; and (6) no part of its net earnings inures to the benefit of any private shareholder or individual.

Section 833 provides a deduction with respect to health business of such organizations. The deduction is equal to 25 percent of the sum of (1) claims incurred, and liabilities incurred under cost-plus contracts, for the taxable year, and (2) expenses incurred in connection with administration, adjustment, or settlement of claims or in connection with administration of cost-plus contracts during the taxable year, to the extent this sum exceeds the adjusted surplus at the beginning of the taxable year. Only health-related items are taken into account.

---

[225] See H. Rep. 99-426, Tax Reform Act of 1985, (December 7, 1985) at 664. The Committee stated, "[T]he availability of tax-exempt status under [then-]present law has allowed some large insurance entities to compete directly with commercial insurance companies. For example, the Blue Cross/Blue Shield organizations historically have been treated as tax-exempt organizations described in sections 501(c)(3) or (4). This group of organizations is now among the largest health care insurers in the United States." See also Joint Committee on Taxation, General Explanation of the Tax Reform Act of 1986, JCS-10-87 (May 4, 1987) at 583-592.

Section 833 provides an exception for such an organization from the application of the 20-percent reduction in the deduction for increases in unearned premiums that applies generally to property and casualty companies.

Section 833 provides that such an organization is taxable as a stock property and casualty insurer under the Federal income tax rules applicable to property and casualty insurers.

Explanation of Provision

The provision limits eligibility for the rules of section 833 to those organizations meeting a medical loss ratio standard of 85 percent for the taxable year. Thus, under the provision, an organization that does not meet the 85-percent standard is not allowed the 25-percent deduction and the exception from the 20-percent reduction in the unearned premium reserve deduction under section 833.

For this purpose, an organization's medical loss ratio is determined as the percentage of total premium revenue expended on reimbursement for clinical services that are provided to enrollees under the organization's policies during the taxable year, as reported under section 2718 of the PHSA.

It is intended that the medical loss ratio under this provision be determined on an organization-by-organization basis, not on an affiliated or other group basis, and that Treasury Department guidance be promulgated promptly to carry out the purposes of the provision.

Effective Date

The provision is effective for taxable years beginning after December 31, 2009.

P. Excise Tax on Indoor Tanning Services (sec. 9017[226] of the Senate amendment and new sec. 5000B of the Code)

Present Law

There is no tax on indoor tanning services under present law.

Explanation of Provision

In general

The provision imposes a tax on each individual on whom indoor tanning services are performed. The tax is equal to 10 percent of the amount paid for indoor tanning services.

For purposes of the provision, indoor tanning services are services employing any electronic product designed to induce skin tanning and which incorporate one or more ultraviolet lamps and intended for the irradiation of an individual by ultraviolet radiation, with wavelengths in air between 200 and 400 nanometers. Indoor tanning services do not include any phototherapy service performed by a licensed medical professional.

Payment of tax

The tax is paid by the individual on whom the indoor tanning services are performed. The tax is collected by each person receiving a payment for tanning services on which a tax is imposed. If the tax is not paid by the person receiving the indoor tanning services at the time the payment for the service is received, the person performing the procedure pays the tax.

Payment of the tax is remitted quarterly to the Secretary by the person collecting the tax. The Secretary is given discretion over the manner of the payment.

Effective Date

The provision applies to services performed on or after July 1, 2010.

---

[226] Section 9017 of the Senate amendment, as amended by section 10907.

Q. Exclusion of Health Benefits Provided by Indian Tribal Governments (sec. 9021 of the Senate amendment and new sec. 139D of the Code)

Present Law

Present law generally provides that gross income includes all income from whatever source derived.[227] Exclusions from income are provided, however, for certain health care benefits.

Exclusion from income for employer-provided health coverage

Employees generally are not taxed on (that is, may "exclude" from gross income) the value of employer-provided health coverage under an accident or health plan.[228] In addition, any reimbursements under an accident or health plan for medical care expenses for employees, their spouses, and their dependents generally are excluded from gross income.[229] As with cash or other compensation, the amount paid by employers for employer-provided health coverage is a deductible business expense. Unlike other forms of compensation, however, if an employer contributes to a plan providing health coverage for employees (and the employees' spouses and dependents), the value of the coverage and all benefits (including reimbursements) in the form of medical care under the plan are excludable from the employees' income for income tax purposes.[230] The exclusion applies both to health coverage in the case in which an employer absorbs the cost of employees' medical expenses not covered by insurance (i.e., a self-insured plan) as well as in the case in which the employer purchases health insurance coverage for its employees. There is no limit on the amount of employer-provided health coverage that is excludable.

In addition, employees participating in a cafeteria plan may be able to pay the portion of premiums for health insurance coverage not otherwise paid for by their employers on a pre-tax basis through salary reduction.[231] Such salary reduction contributions are treated as employer contributions and thus also are excluded from gross income.

---

[227] Sec. 61.

[228] Sec 106.

[229] Sec. 105(b).

[230] Secs. 104, 105, 106, 125. A similar rule excludes employer provided health insurance coverage and reimbursements for medical expenses from the employees' wages for payroll tax purposes under sections 3121(a)(2), and 3306(a)(2). Health coverage provided to active members of the uniformed services, military retirees, and their dependents are excludable under section 134. That section provides an exclusion for "qualified military benefits," defined as benefits received by reason of status or service as a member of the uniformed services and which were excludable from gross income on September 9, 1986, under any provision of law, regulation, or administrative practice then in effect.

[231] Sec. 125.

Employers may agree to reimburse medical expenses of their employees (and their spouses and dependents), not covered by a health insurance plan, through flexible spending arrangements which allow reimbursement not in excess of a specified dollar amount (either elected by an employee under a cafeteria plan or otherwise specified by the employer). Reimbursements under these arrangements are also excludible from gross income as employer-provided health coverage.

The general welfare exclusion

Under the general welfare exclusion doctrine, certain payments made to individuals are excluded from gross income. The exclusion has been interpreted to cover payments by governmental units under legislatively provided social benefit programs for the promotion of the general welfare.[232]

The general welfare exclusion generally applies if the payments: (1) are made from a governmental fund, (2) are for the promotion of general welfare (on the basis of the need of the recipient), and (3) do not represent compensation for services.[233] A representative of the IRS recently expressed the view that the general welfare exclusion does not apply to persons with significant income or assets, and that any such extension would represent a departure from well-established administrative practice.[234] The representative further expressed the view that

---

[232] See, e.g., Rev. Rul. 78-170, 1978-1 C.B. 24 (government payments to assist low-income persons with utility costs are not income); Rev. Rul. 76-395, 1976-2 C.B. 16, 17 (government grants to assist low-income city inhabitants to refurbish homes are not income); Rev. Rul. 76-144, 1976-1 C.B. 17 (government grants to persons eligible for relief under the Disaster Relief Act of 1974 are not income); Rev. Rul. 74-153, 1974-1 C.B. 20 (government payments to assist adoptive parents with support and maintenance of adoptive children are not income); Rev. Rul. 74-205, 1974-1 C.B. 20 (replacement housing payments received by individuals under the Housing and Urban Development Act of 1968 are not includible in gross income); Gen. Couns. Mem. 34506 (May 26, 1971) (federal mortgage assistance payments excluded from income under general welfare exception); Rev. Rul. 57-102, 1957-1 C.B. 26 (government benefits paid to blind persons are not income). The courts have also acknowledged the existence of this doctrine. See, e.g., *Bailey v. Commissioner*, 88 T.C. 1293, 1299-1301 (1987) (new building façade paid for by urban renewal agency on taxpayer's property under facade grant program not considered payments under general welfare doctrine because awarded without regard to any need of the recipients); *Graff v. Commissioner*, 74 TC 743, 753-754 (1980) (court acknowledged that rental subsidies under Housing Act were excludable under general welfare doctrine but found that payments at issue made by HUD on taxpayer landlord's behalf were taxable income to him), *affd. per curiam* 673 F.2d 784 (5th Cir. 1982).

[233] See Rev. Rul. 98-19, 1998-1 C.B. 840 (excluding relocation payments made by local governments to those whose homes were damaged by floods). Recent guidance as to whether the need of the recipient (taken into account under the second requirement of the general welfare exclusion) must be based solely on financial means or whether the need can be based on a variety of other considerations including health, educational background, or employment status, has been mixed. Chief Couns. Adv. 200021036 (May 25, 2000) (excluding state adoption assistant payments made to individuals adopting special needs children without regard to financial means of parents; the children were considered to be the recipients); Priv. Ltr. Rul. 200632005 (April 13, 2006) (excluding payments made by Tribe to members based on multiple factors of need pursuant to housing assistance program); Chief Couns. Adv. 200648027 (Jul 25, 2006) (excluding subsidy payments based on financial need of recipient made by state to certain participants in state health insurance program to reduce cost of health insurance premiums).

[234] Testimony of Sarah H. Ingram, Commissioner, Tax Exempt and Government Entities, Internal Revenue Service, before the Senate Committee on Indian Affairs, *Oversight Hearing to Examine the Federal Tax Treatment of Health Care Benefits Provided by Tribal Governments to Their Citizens*, September 17, 2009.

application of the general welfare exclusion to an Indian tribal government providing coverage or benefits to tribal members is dependent upon the structure and administration of the particular program.[235]

Explanation of Provision

The provision allows an exclusion from gross income for the value of specified Indian tribe health care benefits. The exclusion applies to the value of: (1) health services or benefits provided or purchased by the Indian Health Service ("IHS"), either directly or indirectly, through a grant to or a contract or compact with an Indian tribe or tribal organization or through programs of third parties funded by the IHS;[236] (2) medical care (in the form of provided or purchased medical care services, accident or health insurance or an arrangement having the same effect, or amounts paid directly or indirectly, to reimburse the member for expenses incurred for medical care) provided by an Indian tribe or tribal organization to a member of an Indian tribe, including the member's spouse or dependents;[237] (3) accident or health plan coverage (or an arrangement having the same effect) provided by an Indian tribe or tribal organization for medical care to a member of an Indian tribe, including the member's spouse or dependents; and (4) any other medical care provided by an Indian tribe or tribal organization that supplements, replaces, or substitutes for the programs and services provided by the Federal government to Indian tribes or Indians.

This provision does not apply to any amount which is deducted or excluded from gross income under another provision of the Code.

No change made by the provision is intended to create an inference with respect to the exclusion from gross income of benefits provided prior to the date of enactment. Additionally, no inference is intended with respect to the tax treatment of other benefits provided by an Indian tribe or tribal organization not covered by this provision.

---

[235] *Ibid.*

[236] The term "Indian tribe" means any Indian tribe, band, nation, pueblo, or other organized group or community, including any Alaska Native village, or regional or village corporation, as defined by, or established pursuant to, the Alaska Native Claims Settlement Act (43 U.S.C. 1601 et. seq.), which is recognized as eligible for the special programs and services provided by the United States to Indians because of their status as Indians. The term "tribal organization" has the same meaning as such term in section 4(l) of the Indian Self-Determination and Education Assistance Act (25 U.S.C. 450b(1)).

[237] The terms "accident or health insurance" and "accident or health plan" have the same meaning as when used in section 105. The term "medical care" is the same as the definition under section 213. For purposes of the provision, dependents are determined under section 152, but without regard to subsections (b)(1), (b)(2), and (d)(1)(B). Section 152(b)(1) generally provides that if an individual is a dependent of another taxpayer during a taxable year such individual is treated as having no dependents for such taxable year. Section 152(b)(2) provides that a married individual filing a joint return with his or her spouse is not treated as a dependent of a taxpayer. Section 152(d)(1)(B) provides that a "qualifying relative" (i.e., a relative that qualifies as a dependent) does not include a person whose gross income for the calendar year in which the taxable year begins equals or exceeds the exempt amount (as defined under section 151).

Effective Date

The provision applies to benefits and coverage provided after the date of enactment.

R. Require Information Reporting on Payments to Corporations (sec. 9006 of the Senate amendment and sec. 6041 of the Code)[238]

Present Law

Present law imposes a variety of information reporting requirements on participants in certain transactions.[239] These requirements are intended to assist taxpayers in preparing their income tax returns and to help the IRS determine whether such returns are correct and complete.

The primary provision governing information reporting by payors requires an information return by every person engaged in a trade or business who makes payments aggregating $600 or more in any taxable year to a single payee in the course of that payor's trade or business.[240] Payments subject to reporting include fixed or determinable income or compensation, but do not include payments for goods or certain enumerated types of payments that are subject to other specific reporting requirements.[241] The payor is required to provide the recipient of the payment with an annual statement showing the aggregate payments made and contact information for the payor.[242] The regulations generally except from reporting, payments to corporations, exempt organizations, governmental entities, international organizations, or retirement plans.[243] However, the following types of payments to corporations must be reported: Medical and healthcare payments;[244] fish purchases for cash;[245] attorney's fees;[246] gross proceeds paid to an

---

[238] This description is based upon the discussion at page 334 in S. Report 111-89, final Committee Report of the Senate Finance Committee on "America's Healthy Future Act of 2009," published October 21, 2009.

[239] Secs. 6031 through 6060.

[240] Sec. 6041(a). The information return is generally submitted electronically as a Form-1099 or Form-1096, although certain payments to beneficiaries or employees may require use of Forms W-3 or W-2, respectively. Treas. Reg. sec. 1.6041-1(a)(2).

[241] Sec. 6041(a) requires reporting as to "other fixed or determinable gains, profits, and income (other than payments to which section 6042(a)(1), 6044(a)(1), 6047(c), 6049(a) or 6050N(a) applies and other than payments with respect to which a statement is required under authority of section 6042(a), 6044(a)(2) or 6045)[.]" These excepted payments include most interest, royalties, and dividends.

[242] Sec. 6041(d).

[243] Treas. Reg. sec. 1.6041-3(p). Certain for-profit health provider corporations are not covered by this general exception, including those organizations providing billing services for such companies.

[244] Sec. 6050T.

[245] Sec. 6050R.

[246] Sec. 6045(f)(1) and (2); Treas. Reg. secs. 1.6041-1(d)(2) and 1.6045-5(d)(5).

attorney;[247] substitute payments in lieu of dividends or tax-exempt interest;[248] and payments by a Federal executive agency for services.[249]

Failure to comply with the information reporting requirements results in penalties, which may include a penalty for failure to file the information return,[250] and a penalty for failure to furnish payee statements[251] or failure to comply with other various reporting requirements.[252]

Detailed rules are provided for the reporting of various types of investment income, including interest, dividends, and gross proceeds from brokered transactions (such as a sale of stock).[253] In general, the requirement to file Form 1099 applies with respect to amounts paid to U.S. persons and is linked to the backup withholding rules of section 3406. Thus, a payor of interest, dividends or gross proceeds generally must request that a U.S. payee (other than certain exempt recipients) furnish a Form W-9 providing that person's name and taxpayer identification number.[254] That information is then used to complete the Form 1099.

Explanation of Provision

Under the provision, a business is required to file an information return for all payments aggregating $600 or more in a calendar year to a single payee (other than a payee that is a tax-exempt corporation), notwithstanding any regulation promulgated under section 6041 prior to the date of enactment. The payments to be reported include gross proceeds paid in consideration for property or services. However, the provision does not override specific provisions elsewhere in the Code that except certain payments from reporting, such as securities or broker transactions as defined under section 6045(a) and the regulations thereunder.

---

[247] *Ibid.*

[248] Sec. 6045(d).

[249] Sec. 6041(d)(3).

[250] Sec. 6721. The penalty for the failure to file an information return generally is $50 for each return for which such failure occurs. The total penalty imposed on a person for all failures during a calendar year cannot exceed $250,000. Additionally, special rules apply to reduce the per-failure and maximum penalty where the failure is corrected within a specified period.

[251] Sec. 6722. The penalty for failure to provide a correct payee statement is $50 for each statement with respect to which such failure occurs, with the total penalty for a calendar year not to exceed $100,000. Special rules apply that increase the per-statement and total penalties where there is intentional disregard of the requirement to furnish a payee statement.

[252] Sec. 6723. The penalty for failure to timely comply with a specified information reporting requirement is $50 per failure, not to exceed $100,000 for a calendar year.

[253] Secs. 6042 (dividends), 6045 (broker reporting) and 6049 (interest) and the Treasury regulations thereunder.

[254] See Treas. Reg. sec. 31.3406(h)-3.

Effective Date

The provision is effective for payments made after December 31, 2011.

S. Establishment of SIMPLE Cafeteria Plans for Small Businesses (sec. 9022 of the Senate amendment and sec. 125 of the Code)

Present Law

Definition of a cafeteria plan

If an employee receives a qualified benefit (as defined below) based on the employee's election between the qualified benefit and a taxable benefit under a cafeteria plan, the qualified benefit generally is not includable in gross income.[255] However, if a plan offering an employee an election between taxable benefits (including cash) and nontaxable qualified benefits does not meet the requirements for being a cafeteria plan, the election between taxable and nontaxable benefits results in gross income to the employee, regardless of what benefit is elected and when the election is made.[256] A cafeteria plan is a separate written plan under which all participants are employees, and participants are permitted to choose among at least one permitted taxable benefit (for example, current cash compensation) and at least one qualified benefit. Finally, a cafeteria plan must not provide for deferral of compensation, except as specifically permitted in sections 125(d)(2)(B), (C), or (D).

Qualified benefits

Qualified benefits under a cafeteria plan are generally employer-provided benefits that are not includable in gross income under an express provision of the Code. Examples of qualified benefits include employer-provided health insurance coverage, group term life insurance coverage not in excess of $50,000, and benefits under a dependent care assistance program. In order to be excludable, any qualified benefit elected under a cafeteria plan must independently satisfy any requirements under the Code section that provides the exclusion. However, some employer-provided benefits that are not includable in gross income under an express provision of the Code are explicitly not allowed in a cafeteria plan. These benefits are generally referred to as nonqualified benefits. Examples of nonqualified benefits include scholarships;[257] employer-provided meals and lodging;[258] educational assistance;[259] and fringe benefits.[260] A plan offering any nonqualified benefit is not a cafeteria plan.[261]

---

[255] Sec. 125(a).

[256] Proposed Treas. Reg. sec. 1.125-1(b).

[257] Sec. 117.

[258] Sec. 119.

[259] Sec.127.

[260] Sec. 132.

[261] Proposed Treas. Reg. sec. 1.125-1(q). Long-term care services, contributions to Archer Medical Savings Accounts, group term life insurance for an employee's spouse, child or dependent, and elective deferrals to section 403(b) plans are also nonqualified benefits.

Employer contributions through salary reduction

Employees electing a qualified benefit through salary reduction are electing to forego salary and instead to receive a benefit that is excludible from gross income because it is provided by employer contributions. Section 125 provides that the employee is treated as receiving the qualified benefit from the employer in lieu of the taxable benefit. For example, active employees participating in a cafeteria plan may be able to pay their share of premiums for employer-provided health insurance on a pre-tax basis through salary reduction.[262]

Nondiscrimination requirements

Cafeteria plans and certain qualified benefits (including group term life insurance, self-insured medical reimbursement plans, and dependent care assistance programs) are subject to nondiscrimination requirements to prevent discrimination in favor of highly compensated individuals generally as to eligibility for benefits and as to actual contributions and benefits provided. There are also rules to prevent the provision of disproportionate benefits to key employees (within the meaning of section 416(i)) through a cafeteria plan.[263] Although the basic purpose of each of the nondiscrimination rules is the same, the specific rules for satisfying the relevant nondiscrimination requirements, including the definition of highly compensated individual,[264] vary for cafeteria plans generally and for each qualified benefit. An employer maintaining a cafeteria plan in which any highly compensated individual participates must make sure that both the cafeteria plan and each qualified benefit satisfies the relevant nondiscrimination requirements, as a failure to satisfy the nondiscrimination rules generally results in a loss of the tax exclusion by the highly compensated individuals.

---

[262] Sec. 125.

[263] A key employee generally is an employee who, at any time during the year is (1) a five-percent owner of the employer, or (2) a one-percent owner with compensation of more than $150,000 (not indexed for inflation), or (3) an officer with compensation more than $160,000 (for 2010). A special rule limits the number of officers treated as key employees. If the employer is a corporation, a five-percent owner is a person who owns more than five percent of the outstanding stock or stock possessing more than five percent of the total combined voting power of all stock. If the employer is not a corporation, a five-percent owner is a person who owns more than five percent of the capital or profits interest. A one-percent owner is determined by substituting one percent for five percent in the preceding definitions. For purposes of determining employee ownership in the employer, certain attribution rules apply.

[264] For cafeteria plan purposes, a "highly compensated individual" is (1) an officer, (2) a five-percent shareholder, (3) an individual who is highly compensated, or (4) the spouse or dependent of any of the preceding categories. A "highly compensated participant" is a participant who falls in any of those categories. "Highly compensated" is not defined for this purpose. Under section 105(h), a self-insured medical expense reimbursement plan must not discriminate in favor of a "highly compensated individual," defined as (1) one of the five highest paid officers, (2) a 10-percent shareholder, or (3) an individual among the highest paid 25 percent of all employees. Under section 129 for a dependent care assistance program, eligibility for benefits, and the benefits and contributions provided, generally must not discriminate in favor of highly compensated employees within the meaning of section 414(q).

Explanation of Provision

Under the provision, an eligible small employer is provided with a safe harbor from the nondiscrimination requirements for cafeteria plans as well as from the nondiscrimination requirements for specified qualified benefits offered under a cafeteria plan, including group term life insurance, benefits under a self insured medical expense reimbursement plan, and benefits under a dependent care assistance program. Under the safe harbor, a cafeteria plan and the specified qualified benefits are treated as meeting the specified nondiscrimination rules if the cafeteria plan satisfies minimum eligibility and participation requirements and minimum contribution requirements.

Eligibility requirement

The eligibility requirement is met only if all employees (other than excludable employees) are eligible to participate, and each employee eligible to participate is able to elect any benefit available under the plan (subject to the terms and conditions applicable to all participants). However, a cafeteria plan will not fail to satisfy this eligibility requirement merely because the plan excludes employees who (1) have not attained the age of 21 (or a younger age provided in the plan) before the close of a plan year, (2) have fewer than 1,000 hours of service for the preceding plan year, (3) have not completed one year of service with the employer as of any day during the plan year, (4) are covered under an agreement that the Secretary of Labor finds to be a collective bargaining agreement if there is evidence that the benefits covered under the cafeteria plan were the subject of good faith bargaining between employee representatives and the employer, or (5) are described in section 410(b)(3)(C) (relating to nonresident aliens working outside the United States). An employer may have a shorter age and service requirement but only if such shorter service or younger age applies to all employees.

Minimum contribution requirement

The minimum contribution requirement is met if the employer provides a minimum contribution for each nonhighly compensated employee (employee who is not a highly compensated employee[265] or a key employee (within the meaning of section 416(i))) in addition to any salary reduction contributions made by the employee. The minimum must be available for application toward the cost of any qualified benefit (other than a taxable benefit) offered under the plan. The minimum contribution is permitted to be calculated under either the nonelective contribution method or the matching contribution method, but the same method must be used for calculating the minimum contribution for all nonhighly compensated employees. The minimum contribution under the nonelective contribution method is an amount equal to a uniform percentage (not less than two percent) of each eligible employee's compensation for the plan year, determined without regard to whether the employees makes any salary reduction

[265] Section 414(q) generally defines a highly compensated employee as an employee (1) who was a five-percent owner during the year or the preceding year, or (2) who had compensation of $110,000 (for 2010) or more for the preceding year. An employer may elect to limit the employees treated as highly compensated employees based upon their compensation in the preceding year to the highest paid 20 percent of employees in the preceding year. Five-percent owner is defined by cross-reference to the definition of key employee in section 416(i).

contribution under the cafeteria plan. The minimum matching contribution is the lesser of 100 percent of the amount of the salary reduction contribution elected to be made by the employee for the plan year or (2) six percent of the employee's compensation for the plan year. Compensation for purposes of this minimum contribution requirement is compensation with the meaning of section 414(s).

A simple cafeteria plan is permitted to provide for the matching contributions in addition to the minimum required but only if matching contributions with respect to salary reduction contributions for any highly compensated employee or key employee are not made at a greater rate than the matching contributions for any nonhighly compensated employee. Nothing in this provision prohibits an employer from providing qualified benefits under the plan in addition to the required contributions.

Eligible employer

An eligible small employer under the provision is, with respect to any year, an employer who employed an average of 100 or fewer employees on business days during either of the two preceding years. For purposes of the provision, a year may only be taken into account if the employer was in existence throughout the year. If an employer was not in existence throughout the preceding year, the determination is based on the average number of employees that it is reasonably expected such employer will employ on business days in the current year. If an employer was an eligible employer for any year and maintained a simple cafeteria plan for its employees for such year, then, for each subsequent year during which the employer continues, without interruption, to maintain the cafeteria plan, the employer is deemed to be an eligible small employer until the employer employs an average of 200 or more employees on business days during any year preceding any such subsequent year.

The determination of whether an employer is an eligible small employer is determined by applying the controlled group rules of sections 52(a) and (b) under which all members of the controlled group are treated as a single employer. In addition, the definition of employee includes leased employees within the meaning of sections 414(n) and (o).[266]

Effective Date

The provision is effective for taxable years beginning after December 31, 2010.

---

[266] Section 52(b) provides that, for specified purposes, all employees of all corporations which are members of a controlled group of corporations are treated as employed by a single employer. However, section 52(b) provides certain modifications to the control group rules including substituting 50 percent ownership for 80 percent ownership as the measure of control. There is a similar rule in section 52(c) under which all employees of trades or businesses (whether or not incorporated) which are under common control are treated under regulations as employed by a single employer. Section 414(n) provides rules for specified purposes when leased employees are treated as employed by the service recipient and section 414(o) authorizes the Treasury to issue regulations to prevent avoidance of the requirements of section 414(n).

T. Investment Credit for Qualifying Therapeutic Discovery Projects (sec. 9023 of the Senate amendment and new sec. 48D of the Code)

Present Law

Present law provides for a research credit equal to 20 percent (14 percent in the case of the alternative simplified credit) of the amount by which the taxpayer's qualified research expenses for a taxable year exceed its base amount for that year.[267] Thus, the research credit is generally available with respect to incremental increases in qualified research.

A 20-percent research tax credit is also available with respect to the excess of (1) 100 percent of corporate cash expenses (including grants or contributions) paid for basic research conducted by universities (and certain nonprofit scientific research organizations) over (2) the sum of (a) the greater of two minimum basic research floors plus (b) an amount reflecting any decrease in nonresearch giving to universities by the corporation as compared to such giving during a fixed-base period, as adjusted for inflation. This separate credit computation is commonly referred to as the "university basic research credit."[268]

Finally, a research credit is available for a taxpayer's expenditures on research undertaken by an energy research consortium. This separate credit computation is commonly referred to as the "energy research credit." Unlike the other research credits, the energy research credit applies to all qualified expenditures, not just those in excess of a base amount.

The research credit, including the university basic research credit and the energy research credit, expired for amounts paid or incurred after December 31, 2009.[269]

Qualified research expenses eligible for the research tax credit consist of: (1) in-house expenses of the taxpayer for wages and supplies attributable to qualified research; (2) certain time-sharing costs for computer use in qualified research; and (3) 65 percent of amounts paid or incurred by the taxpayer to certain other persons for qualified research conducted on the taxpayer's behalf (so-called contract research expenses).[270] Notwithstanding the limitation for contract research expenses, qualified research expenses include 100 percent of amounts paid or incurred by the taxpayer to an eligible small business, university, or Federal laboratory for qualified energy research.

---

[267] Sec. 41.

[268] Sec. 41(e).

[269] Sec. 41(h).

[270] Under a special rule, 75 percent of amounts paid to a research consortium for qualified research are treated as qualified research expenses eligible for the research credit (rather than 65 percent under the general rule of section 41(b)(3) governing contract research expenses) if (1) such research consortium is a tax-exempt organization that is described in section 501(c)(3) (other than a private foundation) or section 501(c)(6) and is organized and operated primarily to conduct scientific research, and (2) such qualified research is conducted by the consortium on behalf of the taxpayer and one or more persons not related to the taxpayer. Sec. 41(b)(3)(C).

Present law also provides a 50-percent credit[271] for expenses related to human clinical testing of drugs for the treatment of certain rare diseases and conditions, generally those that afflict less than 200,000 persons in the United States. Qualifying expenses are those paid or incurred by the taxpayer after the date on which the drug is designated as a potential treatment for a rare disease or disorder by the Food and Drug Administration ("FDA") in accordance with section 526 of the Federal Food, Drug, and Cosmetic Act.

Present law does not provide a credit specifically designed to encourage investment in new therapies relating to diseases.

Explanation of Provision

In general

The provision establishes a 50 percent nonrefundable investment tax credit for qualified investments in qualifying therapeutic discovery projects. The provision allocates $1 billion during the two-year period 2009 through 2010 for the program. The Secretary, in consultation with the Secretary of HHS, will award certifications for qualified investments. The credit is available only to companies having 250 or fewer employees.[272]

A "qualifying therapeutic discovery project" is a project which is designed to develop a product, process, or therapy to diagnose, treat, or prevent diseases and afflictions by: (1) conducting pre-clinical activities, clinical trials, clinical studies, and research protocols, or (2) by developing technology or products designed to diagnose diseases and conditions, including molecular and companion drugs and diagnostics, or to further the delivery or administration of therapeutics.

The qualified investment for any taxable year is the aggregate amount of the costs paid or incurred in such year for expenses necessary for and directly related to the conduct of a qualifying therapeutic discovery project. The qualified investment for any taxable year with respect to any qualifying therapeutic discovery project does not include any cost for: (1) remuneration for an employee described in section 162(m)(3), (2) interest expense, (3) facility maintenance expenses, (4) a service cost identified under Treas. Reg. Sec. 1.263A-1(e)(4), or (5) any other expenditure as determined by the Secretary as appropriate to carry out the purposes of the provision.

Companies must apply to the Secretary to obtain certification for qualifying investments.[273] The Secretary, in determining qualifying projects, will consider only those

---

[271] Sec. 45C.

[272] The number of employees is determined taking into account all businesses of the taxpayer at the time it submits an application, and is determined taking into account the rules for determining a single employer under section 52(a) or (b) or section 414(m) or (o).

[273] The Secretary must take action to approve or deny an application within 30 days of the submission of such application.

projects that show reasonable potential to: (1) result in new therapies to treat areas of unmet medical need or to prevent, detect, or treat chronic or acute disease and conditions, (2) reduce long-term health care costs in the United States, or (3) significantly advance the goal of curing cancer within a 30-year period. Additionally, the Secretary will take into consideration which projects would have the greatest potential to: (1) create and sustain (directly or indirectly) high quality, high paying jobs in the United States, and (2) advance the United States' competitiveness in the fields of life, biological, and medical sciences.

Qualified therapeutic discovery project expenditures do not qualify for the research credit, orphan drug credit, or bonus depreciation.[274] If a credit is allowed for an expenditure related to property subject to depreciation, the basis of the property is reduced by the amount of the credit. Additionally, expenditures taken into account in determining the credit are nondeductible to the extent of the credit claimed that is attributable to such expenditures.

Election to receive grant in lieu of tax credit

Taxpayers may elect to receive credits that have been allocated to them in the form of Treasury grants equal to 50 percent of the qualifying investment. Any such grant is not includible in the taxpayer's gross income.

In making grants under this section, the Secretary of the Treasury is to apply rules similar to the rules of section 50. In applying such rules, if an investment ceases to be a qualified investment, the Secretary of the Treasury shall provide for the recapture of the appropriate percentage of the grant amount in such manner as the Secretary of the Treasury determines appropriate. The Secretary of the Treasury shall not make any grant under this section to: (1) any Federal, State, or local government (or any political subdivision, agency, or instrumentality thereof),(2) any organization described in section 501(c) and exempt from tax under section 501(a), (3) any entity referred to in paragraph (4) of section 54(j), or (4) any partnership or other pass-thru entity any partner (or other holder of an equity or profits interest) of which is described in paragraph (1), (2) or (3).

Effective Date

The provision applies to expenditures paid or incurred after December 31, 2008, in taxable years beginning after December 31, 2008.

[274] Any expenses for the taxable year that are qualified research expenses under section 41(b) are taken into account in determining base period research expenses for purposes of computing the research credit under section 41 for subsequent taxable years.

TITLE X – STRENGTHENING QUALITY, AFFORDABLE HEALTH CARE FOR ALL AMERICANS

A. Study of Geographic Variation in Application of FPL (sec. 10105 of the Senate amendment)

Present Law

No provision.

Explanation of Provision

The Secretary of HHS is instructed to conduct a study on the feasibility and implication of adjusting the application of the FPL under the provisions enacted in the bill for different geographical areas so as to reflect disparities in the cost of living among different areas in the United States, including the territories. If the Secretary deems such an adjustment feasible, then the study should include a methodology for implementing the adjustment. The Secretary is required to report the results of the study to Congress no later than January 1, 2013. The provision requires that special attention be paid to the impact of disparities between the poverty levels and the cost of living in the territories and the impact of this disparity on the expansion of health coverage in the territories. The territories are the Commonwealth of Puerto Rico, the U.S. Virgin Islands, Guam, the Commonwealth of the Northern Mariana Islands and any other territory or possession of the United States.

Effective Date

The provision is effective on date of enactment.

B. Free Choice Vouchers
(sec. 10108 of the Senate amendment and sec. 139D of the Code)

Present Law

No provision.

Explanation of Provision

Provision of vouchers

Employers offering minimum essential coverage through an eligible employer-sponsored plan and paying a portion of that coverage must provide qualified employees with a voucher whose value can be applied to purchase of a health plan through the Exchange. Qualified employees are employees whose required contribution for employer sponsored minimum essential coverage exceeds eight percent, but does not exceed 9.5 percent of the employee's household income for the taxable year and the employee's total household income does not exceed 400 percent of the poverty line for the family. In addition, the employee must not participate in the employer's health plan.

The value of the voucher is equal to the dollar value of the employer contribution to the employer offered health plan. If multiple plans are offered by the employer, the value of the voucher is the dollar amount that would be paid if the employee chose the plan for which the employer would pay the largest percentage of the premium cost.[275] The value of the voucher is for self-only coverage unless the individual purchases family coverage in the Exchange. Under the provision, for purposes of calculating the dollar value of the employer contribution, the premium for any health plan is determined under the rules of section 2204 of PHSA, except that the amount is adjusted for age and category of enrollment in accordance with regulations established by the Secretary.

In the case of years after 2014, the eight percent and the 9.5 percent are indexed to the excess of premium growth over income growth for the preceding calendar year.

Use of vouchers

Vouchers can be used in the Exchange towards the monthly premium of any qualified health plan in the Exchange. The value of the voucher to the extent it is used for the purchase of a health plan is not includable in gross income. If the value of the voucher exceeds the premium

---

[275] For example, if an employer offering the same plans for $200 and $300 offers a flat $180 contribution for all plans, a contribution of 90 percent for the $200 plan and a contribution of 60 percent for the $300 plan, and the value of the voucher would equal the value of the contribution to the $200 since it received a 90 percent contribution, a value of $180. However, if the firm offers a $150 contribution to the $200 plan (75 percent) and a $200 contribution to the $300 plan (67 percent), the value of the voucher is based on the plan receiving the greater percentage paid by the employer and would be $150. If a firm offers health plans with monthly premiums of $200 and $300 and provides a payment of 60 percent of any plan purchased, the value of the voucher will be 60 percent the higher premium plan, in this case, 60 percent of $300 or $180.

of the health plan chosen by the employee, the employee is paid the excess value of the voucher. The excess amount received by the employee is includible in the employee's gross income.

If an individual receives a voucher the individual is disqualified from receiving any tax credit or cost sharing credit for the purchase of a plan in the Exchange. Similarly, if any employee receives a free choice voucher, the employer is not be assessed a shared responsibility payment on behalf of that employee.[276]

Definition of terms

The terms used for this provision have the same meaning as any term used in the provision for the requirement to maintain minimum essential coverage (section 1501 of the Senate amendment and new section 5000A). Thus for example, the terms "household income," "poverty line," "required contribution," and "eligible employer-sponsored plan" have the same meaning for both provisions. Thus, the required contribution includes the amount of any salary reduction contribution.

Effective Date

The provision is effective after December 31, 2013.

---

[276] Section 1513 of the Senate amendment and new section 4980H.

C. Exclusion for Assistance Provided to Participants in State Student Loan Repayment Programs for Certain Health Professionals (sec. 10908 of the Senate amendment and sec. 108(f)(4) of the Code)

Present Law

Gross income generally includes the discharge of indebtedness of the taxpayer. Under an exception to this general rule, gross income does not include any amount from the forgiveness (in whole or in part) of certain student loans, provided that the forgiveness is contingent on the student's working for a certain period of time in certain professions for any of a broad class of employers.

Student loans eligible for this special rule must be made to an individual to assist the individual in attending an educational institution that normally maintains a regular faculty and curriculum and normally has a regularly enrolled body of students in attendance at the place where its education activities are regularly carried on. Loan proceeds may be used not only for tuition and required fees, but also to cover room and board expenses. The loan must be made by (1) the United States (or an instrumentality or agency thereof), (2) a State (or any political subdivision thereof), (3) certain tax-exempt public benefit corporations that control a State, county, or municipal hospital and whose employees have been deemed to be public employees under State law, or (4) an educational organization that originally received the funds from which the loan was made from the United States, a State, or a tax-exempt public benefit corporation.

In addition, an individual's gross income does not include amounts from the forgiveness of loans made by educational organizations (and certain tax-exempt organizations in the case of refinancing loans) out of private, nongovernmental funds if the proceeds of such loans are used to pay costs of attendance at an educational institution or to refinance any outstanding student loans (not just loans made by educational organizations) and the student is not employed by the lender organization. In the case of such loans made or refinanced by educational organizations (or refinancing loans made by certain tax-exempt organizations), cancellation of the student loan must be contingent upon the student working in an occupation or area with unmet needs and such work must be performed for, or under the direction of, a tax-exempt charitable organization or a governmental entity.

Finally, an individual's gross income does not include any loan repayment amount received under the National Health Service Corps loan repayment program or certain State loan repayment programs.

Explanation of Provision

The provision modifies the gross income exclusion for amounts received under the National Health Service Corps loan repayment program or certain State loan repayment programs to include any amount received by an individual under any State loan repayment or loan forgiveness program that is intended to provide for the increased availability of health care services in underserved or health professional shortage areas (as determined by the State).

Effective Date

The provision is effective for amounts received by an individual in taxable years beginning after December 31, 2008.

D. Expansion of Adoption Credit and the Exclusion from Gross Income for Employer-Provided Adoption Assistance (sec. 10909 of the Senate amendment and secs. 23 and 137 of the Code)

Present Law

Tax credit

Non-special needs adoptions

Generally a nonrefundable tax credit is allowed for qualified adoption expenses paid or incurred by a taxpayer subject to the maximum credit. The maximum credit is $12,170 per eligible child for taxable years beginning in 2010. An eligible child is an individual who: (1) has not attained age 18; or (2) is physically or mentally incapable of caring for himself or herself. The maximum credit is applied per child rather than per year. Therefore, while qualified adoption expenses may be incurred in one or more taxable years, the tax credit per adoption of an eligible child may not exceed the maximum credit.

Special needs adoptions

In the case of a special needs adoption finalized during a taxable year, the taxpayer may claim as an adoption credit the amount of the maximum credit minus the aggregate qualified adoption expenses with respect to that adoption for all prior taxable years. A special needs child is an eligible child who is a citizen or resident of the United States whom a State has determined: (1) cannot or should not be returned to the home of the birth parents; and (2) has a specific factor or condition (such as the child's ethnic background, age, or membership in a minority or sibling group, or the presence of factors such as medical conditions, or physical, mental, or emotional handicaps) because of which the child cannot be placed with adoptive parents without adoption assistance.

Qualified adoption expenses

Qualified adoption expenses are reasonable and necessary adoption fees, court costs, attorneys fees, and other expenses that are: (1) directly related to, and the principal purpose of which is for, the legal adoption of an eligible child by the taxpayer; (2) not incurred in violation of State or Federal law, or in carrying out any surrogate parenting arrangement; (3) not for the adoption of the child of the taxpayer's spouse; and (4) not reimbursed (e.g., by an employer).

Phase-out for higher-income individuals

The adoption credit is phased out ratably for taxpayers with modified adjusted gross income between $182,520 and $222,520 for taxable years beginning in 2010. Under present law, modified adjusted gross income is the sum of the taxpayer's adjusted gross income plus amounts excluded from income under sections 911, 931, and 933 (relating to the exclusion of income of U.S. citizens or residents living abroad; residents of Guam, American Samoa, and the Northern Mariana Islands; and residents of Puerto Rico, respectively).

EGTRRA sunset[277]

For taxable years after 2010, the adoption credit will be reduced to a maximum credit of $6,000 for special needs adoptions and no tax credit for non-special needs adoptions. Also, the credit phase-out range will revert to the pre-EGTRRA levels (i.e., a ratable phase-out between modified adjusted gross income between $75,000 and $115,000). Finally, the adoption credit will be allowed only to the extent the individual's regular income tax liability exceeds the individual's tentative minimum tax, determined without regard to the minimum foreign tax credit.

Exclusion for employer-provided adoption assistance

An exclusion from the gross income of an employee is allowed for qualified adoption expenses paid or reimbursed by an employer under an adoption assistance program. For 2010, the maximum exclusion is $12,170. Also for 2010, the exclusion is phased out ratably for taxpayers with modified adjusted gross income between $182,520 and $222,520. Modified adjusted gross income is the sum of the taxpayer's adjusted gross income plus amounts excluded from income under Code sections 911, 931, and 933 (relating to the exclusion of income of U.S. citizens or residents living abroad; residents of Guam, American Samoa, and the Northern Mariana Islands; and residents of Puerto Rico, respectively). For purposes of this exclusion, modified adjusted gross income also includes all employer payments and reimbursements for adoption expenses whether or not they are taxable to the employee.

Adoption expenses paid or reimbursed by the employer under an adoption assistance program are not eligible for the adoption credit. A taxpayer may be eligible for the adoption credit (with respect to qualified adoption expenses he or she incurs) and also for the exclusion (with respect to different qualified adoption expenses paid or reimbursed by his or her employer).

Because of the EGTRRA sunset, the exclusion for employer-provided adoption assistance does not apply to amounts paid or incurred after December 31, 2010.

Explanation of Provision

Tax credit

For 2010, the maximum credit is increased to $13,170 per eligible child (a $1,000 increase). This increase applies to both non-special needs adoptions and special needs adoptions. Also, the adoption credit is made refundable.

The new dollar limit and phase-out of the adoption credit are adjusted for inflation in taxable years beginning after December 31, 2010.

[277] "EGTRRA" refers to the Economic Growth and Tax Relief Reconciliation Act of 2001.

The EGTRRA sunset is delayed for one year (i.e., the sunset becomes effective for taxable years beginning after December 31, 2011).

Adoption assistance program

The maximum exclusion is increased to $13,170 per eligible child (a $1,000 increase).

The new dollar limit and income limitations of the employer-provided adoption assistance exclusion are adjusted for inflation in taxable years beginning after December 31, 2010.

The EGTRRA sunset is delayed for one year (i.e., the sunset becomes effective for taxable years beginning after December 31, 2011).

Effective Date

The provisions generally are effective for taxable years beginning after December 31, 2009.

HEALTH CARE AND EDUCATION RECONCILIATION ACT OF 2010

A. Adult Dependents
(sec. 1004 of the Reconciliation bill and secs. 105, 162, 401, and 501 of the Code)

Present Law

Definition of dependent for exclusion for employer-provided health coverage

The Code generally provides that employees are not taxed on (that is, may "exclude" from gross income) the value of employer-provided health coverage under an accident or health plan.[278] This exclusion applies to coverage for personal injuries or sickness for employees (including retirees), their spouses and their dependents.[279] In addition, any reimbursements under an accident or health plan for medical care expenses for employees (including retirees), their spouses, and their dependents (as defined in section 152) generally are excluded from gross income.[280] Section 152 defines a dependent as a qualifying child or qualifying relative.

Under section 152(c), a child generally is a qualifying child of a taxpayer if the child satisfies each of five tests for the taxable year: (1) the child has the same principal place of abode as the taxpayer for more than one-half of the taxable year; (2) the child has a specified relationship to the taxpayer; (3) the child has not yet attained a specified age; (4) the child has not provided over one-half of their own support for the calendar year in which the taxable year of the taxpayer begins; and (5) the qualifying child has not filed a joint return (other than for a claim of refund) with their spouse for the taxable year beginning in the calendar year in which the taxable year of the taxpayer begins. A tie-breaking rule applies if more than one taxpayer claims a child as a qualifying child. The specified relationship is that the child is the taxpayer's son, daughter, stepson, stepdaughter, brother, sister, stepbrother, stepsister, or a descendant of any such individual. With respect to the specified age, a child must be under age 19 (or under age 24 in the case of a full-time student). However, no age limit applies with respect to individuals who are totally and permanently disabled within the meaning of section 22(e)(3) at any time during the calendar year. Other rules may apply.

Under section 152(d), a qualifying relative means an individual that satisfies four tests for the taxable year: (1) the individual bears a specified relationship to the taxpayer; (2) the individual's gross income for the calendar year in which such taxable year begins is less than the exemption amount under section 151(d); (3) the taxpayer provides more than one-half the individual's support for the calendar year in which the taxable year begins; and (4) the individual is not a qualifying child of the taxpayer or any other taxpayer for any taxable year beginning in the calendar year in which such taxable year begins. The specified relationship test for qualifying relative is satisfied if that individual is the taxpayer's: (1) child or descendant of a child; (2) brother, sister, stepbrother or stepsister; (3) father, mother or ancestor of either; (4)

---

[278] Sec 106.

[279] Treas. Reg. sec. 1.106-1.

[280] Sec. 105(b).

stepfather or stepmother; (5) niece or nephew; (6) aunt or uncle; (7) in-law; or (8) certain other individuals, who for the taxable year of the taxpayer, have the same principal place of abode as the taxpayer and are members of the taxpayer's household.[281]

Employers may agree to reimburse medical expenses of their employees (and their spouses and dependents), not covered by a health insurance plan, through flexible spending arrangements which allow reimbursement not in excess of a specified dollar amount (either elected by an employee under a cafeteria plan or otherwise specified by the employer). Reimbursements under these arrangements are also excludible from gross income as employer-provided health coverage. The same definition of dependents applies for purposes of flexible spending arrangements.

Deduction for health insurance premiums of self-employed individuals

Under present law, self-employed individuals may deduct the cost of health insurance for themselves and their spouses and dependents. The deduction is not available for any month in which the self-employed individual is eligible to participate in an employer-subsidized health plan. Moreover, the deduction may not exceed the individual's self-employment income. The deduction applies only to the cost of insurance (i.e., it does not apply to out-of-pocket expenses that are not reimbursed by insurance). The deduction does not apply for self-employment tax purposes. For purposes of the deduction, a more than two percent shareholder-employee of an S corporation is treated the same as a self-employed individual. Thus, the exclusion for employer-provided health care coverage does not apply to such individuals, but they are entitled to the deduction for health insurance costs as if they were self-employed.

Voluntary Employees' Beneficiary Associations

A VEBA is a tax-exempt entity that is a part of a plan for providing life, sick or accident benefits to its members or their dependents or designated beneficiaries.[282] No part of the net earnings of the association inures (other than through the payment of life, sick, accident or other benefits) to the benefit of any private shareholder or individual. A VEBA may be funded with employer contributions or employee contributions or a combination of employer contributions and employee contributions. The same definition of dependent applies for purposes of receipt of medical benefits through a VEBA.

Qualified plans providing retiree health benefits

A qualified pension or annuity plan can establish and maintain a separate account to provide for the payment of sickness, accident, hospitalization, and medical expenses for retired employees, their spouses and their dependents ("401(h) account"). An employer's contributions to a 401(h) account must be reasonable and ascertainable, and retiree health benefits must be

---

[281] Generally, same-sex partners do not qualify as dependents under section 152. In addition, same-sex partners are not recognized as spouses for purposes of the Code. Defense of Marriage Act, Pub. L. No. 104-199.

[282] Secs. 419(e) and 501(c)(9).

subordinate to the retirement benefits provided by the plan. In addition, it must be impossible, at any time prior to the satisfaction of all retiree health liabilities under the plan, for any part of the corpus or income of the 401(h) account to be (within the taxable year or thereafter) used for, or diverted to, any purpose other than providing retiree health benefits and, upon satisfaction of all retiree health liabilities, the plan must provide that any amount remaining in the 401(h) account be returned to the employer.

Explanation of Provision

The provision amends sections 105(b) to extend the general exclusion for reimbursements for medical care expenses under an employer-provided accident or health plan to any child of an employee who has not attained age 27 as of the end of the taxable year. This change is also intended to apply to the exclusion for employer- proved coverage under an accident or health plan for injuries or sickness for such a child. A parallel change is made for VEBAs and 401(h) accounts.

The provision similarly amends section 162(l) to permit self-employed individuals to take a deduction for any child of the taxpayer who has not attained age 27 as of the end of the taxable year.

For purposes of the provision, "child" means an individual who is a son, daughter, stepson, stepdaughter or eligible foster child of the taxpayer.[283] An eligible foster child means an individual who is placed with the taxpayer by an authorized placement agency or by judgment, decree, or other order of any court of competent jurisdiction.

Effective Date

The provision is effective as of the date of enactment.

[283] Sec. 152(f)(1). Under section 152(f)(1), a legally adopted child of the taxpayer or an individual who is lawfully placed with the taxpayer for legal adoption by the taxpayer is treated as a child of the taxpayer by blood.

B. Unearned Income Medicare Contribution (sec. 1402 of the Reconciliation bill and new sec. 1411 of the Code)

Present Law

Social security benefits and certain Medicare benefits are financed primarily by payroll taxes on covered wages. FICA imposes tax on employers based on the amount of wages paid to an employee during the year. The tax imposed is composed of two parts: (1) the OASDI tax equal to 6.2 percent of covered wages up to the taxable wage base ($106,800 in 2010); and (2) the Medicare hospital insurance ("HI") tax amount equal to 1.45 percent of covered wages. In addition to the tax on employers, each employee is subject to FICA taxes equal to the amount of tax imposed on the employer. The employee level tax generally must be withheld and remitted to the Federal government by the employer.

As a parallel to FICA taxes, SECA imposes taxes on the net income from self employment of self employed individuals. The rate of the OASDI portion of SECA taxes is equal to the combined employee and employer OASDI FICA tax rates and applies to self employment income up to the FICA taxable wage base. Similarly, the rate of the HI portion is the same as the combined employer and employee HI rates and there is no cap on the amount of self employment income to which the rate applies.[284]

Explanation of Provision

In general

In the case of an individual, estate, or trust an unearned income Medicare contribution tax is imposed.

In the case of an individual, the tax is the 3.8 percent of the lesser of net investment income or the excess of modified adjusted gross income over the threshold amount.

The threshold amount is $250,000 in the case of a joint return or surviving spouse, $125,000 in the case of a married individual filing a separate return, and $200,000 in any other case.

Modified adjusted gross income is adjusted gross income increased by the amount excluded from income as foreign earned income under section 911(a)(1) (net of the deductions and exclusions disallowed with respect to the foreign earned income).

---

[284] For purposes of computing net earnings from self employment, taxpayers are permitted a deduction equal to the product of the taxpayer's earnings (determined without regard to this deduction) and one-half of the sum of the rates for OASDI (12.4 percent) and HI (2.9 percent), i.e., 7.65 percent of net earnings. This deduction reflects the fact that the FICA rates apply to an employee's wages, which do not include FICA taxes paid by the employer, whereas the self-employed individual's net earnings are economically equivalent to an employee's wages plus the employer share of FICA taxes.

In the case of an estate or trust, the tax is 3.8 percent of the lesser of undistributed net investment income or the excess of adjusted gross income (as defined in section 67(e)) over the dollar amount at which the highest income tax bracket applicable to an estate or trust begins.

The tax does not apply to a non-resident alien or to a trust all the unexpired interests in which are devoted to charitable purposes. The tax also does not apply to a trust that is exempt from tax under section 501 or a charitable remainder trust exempt from tax under section 664.

The tax is subject to the individual estimated tax provisions. The tax is not deductible in computing any tax imposed by subtitle A of the Internal Revenue Code (relating to income taxes).

Net investment income

Net investment income is investment income reduced by the deductions properly allocable to such income.

Investment income is the sum of (i) gross income from interest, dividends, annuities, royalties, and rents (other than income derived from any trade or business to which the tax does not apply), (ii) other gross income derived from any business to which the tax applies, and (iii) net gain (to the extent taken into account in computing taxable income) attributable to the disposition of property other than property held in a trade or business to which the tax does not apply.[285]

In the case of a trade or business, the tax applies if the trade or business is a passive activity with respect to the taxpayer or the trade or business consists of trading financial instruments or commodities (as defined in section 475(e)(2)). The tax does not apply to other trades or businesses conducted by a sole proprietor, partnership, or S corporation.

In the case of the disposition of a partnership interest or stock in an S corporation, gain or loss is taken into account only to the extent gain or loss would be taken into account by the partner or shareholder if the entity had sold all its properties for fair market value immediately before the disposition. Thus, only net gain or loss attributable to property held by the entity which is not property attributable to an active trade or business is taken into account.[286]

Income, gain, or loss on working capital is not treated as derived from a trade or business. Investment income does not include distributions from a qualified retirement plan or amounts subject to SECA tax.

---

[285] Gross income does not include items, such as interest on tax-exempt bonds, veterans' benefits, and excluded gain from the sale of a principal residence, which are excluded from gross income under the income tax.

[286] For this purpose, a business of trading financial instruments or commodities is not treated as an active trade or business.

Effective Date

The provision applies to taxable years beginning after December 31, 2012.

C. Excise Tax on Medical Device Manufacturers[287]
(sec. 1405 of the Reconciliation bill and new sec. 4191 of the Code)

Present Law

Chapter 32 imposes excise taxes on sales by manufacturers of certain products. Terms and procedures related to the imposition, payment, and reporting of these excise taxes are included in various provisions within the Code.

Certain sales are exempt from the excise tax imposed on manufacturers. Exempt sales include sales (1) for use by the purchaser for further manufacture, or for resale to a second purchaser in further manufacture, (2) for export or for resale to a second purchaser for export, (3) for use by the purchaser as supplies for vessels or aircraft, (4) to a State or local government for the exclusive use of a State or local government, (5) to a nonprofit educational organization for its exclusive use, or (6) to a qualified blood collector organization for such organization's exclusive use in the collection, storage, or transportation of blood.[288] If an article is sold free of tax for resale to a second purchaser for further manufacture or for export, the exemption will not apply unless, within the six-month period beginning on the date of sale by the manufacturer, the manufacturer receives proof that the article has been exported or resold for the use in further manufacturing.[289] In general, the exemptions will not apply unless the manufacturer, the first purchaser, and the second purchaser are registered with the Secretary of the Treasury.

The lease of an article is generally considered to be a sale of such article.[290] Special rules apply for the imposition of tax to each lease payment. Rules are also imposed that treat the use of articles subject to tax by manufacturers, producers, or importers of such articles, as sales for the purpose of imposition of certain excise taxes.[291]

There are also rules for determining the price of an article on which excise tax is imposed.[292] These rules provide for: (1) the inclusion of containers, packaging, and certain transportation charges in the price, (2) determining a constructive sales price if an article is sold for less than the fair market price, and (3) determining the tax due in the case of partial payments or installment sales.

---

[287] The excise tax on medical devices as imposed by this provision replaces the annual fee on medical device manufacturers and importers under section 9009 of the Senate amendment.

[288] Sec. 4221(a).

[289] Sec. 4221(b).

[290] Sec. 4217(a).

[291] Sec. 4218.

[292] Sec. 4216.

A credit or refund is generally allowed for overpayments of manufacturers excise taxes.[293] Overpayments may occur when tax-paid articles are sold for export and for certain specified uses and resales, when there are price adjustments, and where tax paid articles are subject to further manufacture. Generally, no credit or refund of any overpayment of tax is allowed or made unless the person who paid the tax establishes one of four prerequisites: (1) the tax was not included in the price of the article or otherwise collected from the person who purchased the article; (2) the tax was repaid to the ultimate purchaser of the article; (3) for overpayments due to specified uses and resales, the tax has been repaid to the ultimate vendor or the person has obtained the written consent of such ultimate vendor; or (4) the person has filed with the Secretary of the Treasury the written consent of the ultimate purchaser of the article to the allowance of the credit or making of the refund.[294]

Explanation of Provision

Under the provision, a tax equal to 2.3 percent of the sale price is imposed on the sale of any taxable medical device by the manufacturer, producer, or importer of such device. A taxable medical device is any device, defined in section 201(h) of the Federal Food, Drug, and Cosmetic Act,[295] intended for humans. The excise tax does not apply to eyeglasses, contact lenses, hearing aids, and any other medical device determined by the Secretary to be of a type that is generally purchased by the general public at retail for individual use. The Secretary may determine that a specific medical device is exempt under the provision if the device is generally sold at retail establishments (including over the internet) to individuals for their personal use. The exemption for such items is not limited by device class as defined in section 513 of the Federal Food, Drug, and Cosmetic Act. For example, items purchased by the general public at retail for individual use could include Class I items such as certain bandages and tipped applicators, Class II items such as certain pregnancy test kits and diabetes testing supplies, and Class III items such as certain denture adhesives and snake bite kits. Such items would only be exempt if they are generally designed and sold for individual use. It is anticipated that the Secretary will publish a list of medical device classifications[296] that are of a type generally purchased by the general public at retail for individual use.

The present law manufacturers excise tax exemptions for further manufacture and for export apply to tax imposed under this provision; however exemptions for use as supplies for

---

293 Sec. 6416.

294 Sec. 6416(a).

295 21 U.S.C. 321. Section 201(h) defines device as an instrument, apparatus, implement, machine, contrivance, implant, in vitro reagent, or other similar or related article, including any component, part, or accessory, which is (1) recognized in the official National Formulary, or the United States Pharmacopeia, or any supplement to them, (2) intended for use in the diagnosis of disease or other conditions, or in the cure, mitigation, treatment, or prevention of disease, in man or other animals, or (3) intended to affect the structure or any function of the body of man or other animals, and which does not achieve its primary intended purposes through chemical action within or on the body of man or other animals and which is not dependent upon being metabolized for the achievement of its primary intended purposes.

296 Medical device classifications are found in Title 21 of the Code of Federal Regulations, Parts 862-892.

vessels or aircraft, and for sales to State or local governments, nonprofit educational organizations, and qualified blood collector organizations are not applicable.

The provision repeals section 9009 of the Senate amendment (relating to an annual fee on medical device manufacturers and importers).

Effective Date

The provision applies to sales after December 31, 2012.

The repeal of section 9009 of the Senate amendment is effective on the date of enactment of the Senate amendment.

D. Elimination of Unintended Application of Cellulosic Biofuel Producer Credit (sec. 1408 of the Reconciliation bill and sec. 40 of the Code)

Present Law

The "cellulosic biofuel producer credit" is a nonrefundable income tax credit for each gallon of qualified cellulosic fuel production of the producer for the taxable year. The amount of the credit is generally $1.01 per gallon.[297]

"Qualified cellulosic biofuel production" is any cellulosic biofuel which is produced by the taxpayer and which is: (1) sold by the taxpayer to another person (a) for use by such other person in the production of a qualified cellulosic biofuel mixture in such person's trade or business (other than casual off-farm production), (b) for use by such other person as a fuel in a trade or business, or (c) who sells such cellusic biofuel at retail to another person and places such cellulosic biofuel in the fuel tank of such other person; or (2) used by the producer for any purpose described in (1)(a), (b), or (c).

"Cellulosic biofuel" means any liquid fuel that (1) is produced in the United States and used as fuel in the United States, (2) is derived from any lignocellulosic or hemicellulosic matter that is available on a renewable or recurring basis, and (3) meets the registration requirements for fuels and fuel additives established by the Environmental Protection Agency ("EPA") under section 211 of the Clean Air Act. The cellulosic biofuel producer credit cannot be claimed unless the taxpayer is registered by the IRS as a producer of cellulosic biofuel.

Cellulosic biofuel eligible for the section 40 credit is precluded from qualifying as biodiesel, renewable diesel, or alternative fuel for purposes of the applicable income tax credit, excise tax credit, or payment provisions relating to those fuels.[298]

Because it is a credit under section 40(a), the cellulosic biofuel producer credit is part of the general business credits in section 38. However, the credit can only be carried forward three taxable years after the termination of the credit. The credit is also allowable against the alternative minimum tax. Under section 87, the credit is included in gross income. The cellulosic biofuel producer credit terminates on December 31, 2012.

The kraft process for making paper produces a byproduct called black liquor, which has been used for decades by paper manufacturers as a fuel in the papermaking process. Black liquor is composed of water, lignin and the spent chemicals used to break down the wood. The amount of the biomass in black liquor varies. The portion of the black liquor that is not consumed as a fuel source for the paper mills is recycled back into the papermaking process.

---

[297] In the case of cellulosic biofuel that is alcohol, the $1.01 credit amount is reduced by the credit amount of the alcohol mixture credit, and for ethanol, the credit amount for small ethanol producers, as in effect at the time the cellulosic biofuel fuel is produced.

[298] See secs. 40A(d)(1), 40A(f)(3), and 6426(h).

Black liquor has ash content (mineral and other inorganic matter) significantly above that of other fuels.

In an informal Chief Counsel Advice ("CCA"), the IRS has concluded that black liquor is a liquid fuel from biomass and may qualify for the cellulosic biofuel producer credit, as well as the refundable alternative fuel mixture credit.[299] A taxpayer cannot claim both the alternative fuel mixture credit and the cellulosic biofuel producer credit. The alternative fuel credits and payment provisions expired December 31, 2009.

Explanation of Provision

The provision modifies the cellulosic biofuel producer credit to exclude fuels with significant water, sediment, or ash content, such as black liquor. Consequently, credits will cease to be available for these fuels. Specifically, the provision excludes from the definition of cellulosic biofuel any fuels that (1) are more than four percent (determined by weight) water and sediment in any combination, or (2) have an ash content of more than one percent (determined by weight). Water content (including both free water and water in solution with dissolved solids) is determined by distillation, using for example ASTM method D95 or a similar method suitable to the specific fuel being tested. Sediment consists of solid particles that are dispersed in the liquid fuel and is determined by centrifuge or extraction using, for example, ASTM method D1796 or D473 or similar method that reports sediment content in weight percent. Ash is the residue remaining after combustion of the sample using a specified method, such as ASTM D3174 or a similar method suitable for the fuel being tested.

Effective Date

The provision is effective for fuels sold or used on or after January 1, 2010.

[299] IRS C.C.A. 200941011, 2009 W.L. 3239569 (June 30, 2009). The Code provides for a tax credit of 50 cents for each gallon of alternative fuel used to produce an alternative fuel mixture that is used or sold for use as a fuel. (sec. 6426(e)). Under Notice 2006-92, an alternative fuel mixture is a mixture of alternative fuel and a taxable fuel (such as diesel) that contains at least 0.1 percent taxable fuel. Liquid fuel derived from biomass is an alternative fuel (sec. 6426(d)(2)(G)). Diesel fuel has been added to black liquor to qualify for the alternative mixture credit and the mixture is burned in a recovery boiler as fuel. Persons that have an alternative fuel mixture credit amount in excess of their taxable fuel excise tax liability may make a claim for payment from the Treasury in the amount of the excess.

E. Codification of Economic Substance Doctrine and Imposition of Penalties (sec. 1409 of the Reconciliation bill and secs. 7701, 6662, 6662A, 6664 and 6676 of the Code)

Present Law

In general

The Code provides detailed rules specifying the computation of taxable income, including the amount, timing, source, and character of items of income, gain, loss, and deduction. These rules permit both taxpayers and the government to compute taxable income with reasonable accuracy and predictability. Taxpayers generally may plan their transactions in reliance on these rules to determine the Federal income tax consequences arising from the transactions.

In addition to the statutory provisions, courts have developed several doctrines that can be applied to deny the tax benefits of a tax-motivated transaction, notwithstanding that the transaction may satisfy the literal requirements of a specific tax provision. These common-law doctrines are not entirely distinguishable, and their application to a given set of facts is often blurred by the courts, the IRS, and litigants. Although these doctrines serve an important role in the administration of the tax system, they can be seen as at odds with an objective, "rule-based" system of taxation.

One common-law doctrine applied over the years is the "economic substance" doctrine. In general, this doctrine denies tax benefits arising from transactions that do not result in a meaningful change to the taxpayer's economic position other than a purported reduction in Federal income tax.[300]

Economic substance doctrine

Courts generally deny claimed tax benefits if the transaction that gives rise to those benefits lacks economic substance independent of U.S. Federal income tax considerations –

---

[300] *See, e.g., ACM Partnership v. Commissioner*, 157 F.3d 231 (3d Cir. 1998), *aff'g* 73 T.C.M. (CCH) 2189 (1997), *cert. denied* 526 U.S. 1017 (1999); *Klamath Strategic Investment Fund, LLC v. United States,* 472 F. Supp. 2d 885 (E.D. Texas 2007), *aff'd* 568 F.3d 537 (5th Cir. 2009); *Coltec Industries, Inc. v. United States,* 454 F.3d 1340 (Fed. Cir. 2006), *vacating and remanding* 62 Fed. Cl. 716 (2004) (slip opinion at 123-124, 128); *cert. denied,* 127 S. Ct. 1261 (Mem.) (2007).

Closely related doctrines also applied by the courts (sometimes interchangeable with the economic substance doctrine) include the "sham transaction doctrine" and the "business purpose doctrine." *See, e.g., Knetsch v. United States*, 364 U.S. 361 (1960) (denying interest deductions on a "sham transaction" that lacked "commercial economic substance"). Certain "substance over form" cases involving tax-indifferent parties, in which courts have found that the substance of the transaction did not comport with the form asserted by the taxpayer, have also involved examination of whether the change in economic position that occurred, if any, was consistent with the form asserted, and whether the claimed business purpose supported the particular tax benefits that were claimed. *See, e.g., TIFD III-E, Inc. v. United States*, 459 F.3d 220 (2d Cir. 2006); *BB&T Corporation v. United States*, 2007-1 USTC P 50,130 (M.D.N.C. 2007), *aff'd* 523 F.3d 461 (4th Cir. 2008). Although the Second Circuit found for the government in *TIFD III-E, Inc.*, on remand to consider issues under section 704(e), the District Court found for the taxpayer. See, *TIFD III-E Inc. v. United States*, No. 3:01-cv-01839, 2009 WL 3208650 (D. Conn. Oct. 23, 2009).

notwithstanding that the purported activity actually occurred. The Tax Court has described the doctrine as follows:

> The tax law . . . requires that the intended transactions have economic substance separate and distinct from economic benefit achieved solely by tax reduction. The doctrine of economic substance becomes applicable, and a judicial remedy is warranted, where a taxpayer seeks to claim tax benefits, unintended by Congress, by means of transactions that serve no economic purpose other than tax savings.[301]

Business purpose doctrine

A common law doctrine that often is considered together with the economic substance doctrine is the business purpose doctrine. The business purpose doctrine involves an inquiry into the subjective motives of the taxpayer – that is, whether the taxpayer intended the transaction to serve some useful non-tax purpose. In making this determination, some courts have bifurcated a transaction in which activities with non-tax objectives have been combined with unrelated activities having only tax-avoidance objectives, in order to disallow the tax benefits of the overall transaction.[302]

Application by the courts

Elements of the doctrine

There is a lack of uniformity regarding the proper application of the economic substance doctrine.[303] Some courts apply a conjunctive test that requires a taxpayer to establish the presence of both economic substance (i.e., the objective component) and business purpose (i.e., the subjective component) in order for the transaction to survive judicial scrutiny.[304] A narrower approach used by some courts is to conclude that either a business purpose or economic substance is sufficient to respect the transaction.[305] A third approach regards economic

---

[301] *ACM Partnership v. Commissioner*, 73 T.C.M. at 2215.

[302] See, *ACM Partnership v. Commissioner*, 157 F.3d at 256 n.48.

[303] "The casebooks are glutted with [economic substance] tests. Many such tests proliferate because they give the comforting illusion of consistency and precision. They often obscure rather than clarify." *Collins v. Commissioner*, 857 F.2d 1383, 1386 (9th Cir. 1988).

[304] See, e.g., *Pasternak v. Commissioner*, 990 F.2d 893, 898 (6th Cir. 1993) ("The threshold question is whether the transaction has economic substance. If the answer is yes, the question becomes whether the taxpayer was motivated by profit to participate in the transaction."). *See also, Klamath Strategic Investment Fund v. United States*, 568 F. 3d 537, (5th Cir. 2009) (even if taxpayers may have had a profit motive, a transaction was disregarded where it did not in fact have any realistic possibility of profit and funding was never at risk).

[305] See, e.g., *Rice's Toyota World v. Commissioner*, 752 F.2d 89, 91-92 (4th Cir. 1985) ("To treat a transaction as a sham, the court must find that the taxpayer was motivated by no business purposes other than obtaining tax benefits in entering the transaction, and, second, that the transaction has no economic substance because no reasonable possibility of a profit exists."); *IES Industries v. United States,* 253 F.3d 350, 358 (8th Cir. 2001) ("In determining whether a transaction is a sham for tax purposes [under the Eighth Circuit test], a transaction will be characterized as a sham if it is not motivated by any economic purpose outside of tax considerations (the

substance and business purpose as "simply more precise factors to consider" in determining whether a transaction has any practical economic effects other than the creation of tax benefits.[306]

One decision by the Court of Federal Claims questioned the continuing viability of the doctrine. That court also stated that "the use of the 'economic substance' doctrine to trump 'mere compliance with the Code' would violate the separation of powers" though that court also found that the particular transaction at issue in the case did not lack economic substance. The Court of Appeals for the Federal Circuit ("Federal Circuit Court") overruled the Court of Federal Claims decision, reiterating the viability of the economic substance doctrine and concluding that the transaction in question violated that doctrine.[307] The Federal Circuit Court stated that "[w]hile the doctrine may well also apply if the taxpayer's sole subjective motivation is tax avoidance even if the transaction has economic substance, [footnote omitted], a lack of economic substance is sufficient to disqualify the transaction without proof that the taxpayer's sole motive is tax avoidance."[308]

Nontax economic benefits

There also is a lack of uniformity regarding the type of non-tax economic benefit a taxpayer must establish in order to demonstrate that a transaction has economic substance. Some courts have denied tax benefits on the grounds that a stated business benefit of a particular structure was not in fact obtained by that structure.[309] Several courts have denied tax benefits on

---

business purpose test), and if it is without economic substance because no real potential for profit exists (the economic substance test)."). As noted earlier, the economic substance doctrine and the sham transaction doctrine are similar and sometimes are applied interchangeably. For a more detailed discussion of the sham transaction doctrine, see, e.g., Joint Committee on Taxation, *Study of Present-Law Penalty and Interest Provisions as Required by Section 3801 of the Internal Revenue Service Restructuring and Reform Act of 1998 (including Provisions Relating to Corporate Tax Shelters)* (JCS-3-99) at 182.

[306] See, e.g., *ACM Partnership v. Commissioner*, 157 F.3d at 247; *James v. Commissioner*, 899 F.2d 905, 908 (10th Cir. 1995); *Sacks v. Commissioner*, 69 F.3d 982, 985 (9th Cir. 1995) ("Instead, the consideration of business purpose and economic substance are simply more precise factors to consider . . . We have repeatedly and carefully noted that this formulation cannot be used as a 'rigid two-step analysis'.")

[307] *Coltec Industries, Inc. v. United States*, 62 Fed. Cl. 716 (2004) (slip opinion at 123-124, 128); *vacated and remanded,* 454 F.3d 1340 (Fed. Cir. 2006), *cert. denied,* 127 S. Ct. 1261 (Mem.) (2007).

[308] The Federal Circuit Court stated that "when the taxpayer claims a deduction, it is the taxpayer who bears the burden of proving that the transaction has economic substance." The Federal Circuit Court quoted a decision of its predecessor court, stating that "*Gregory v. Helvering* requires that a taxpayer carry an unusually heavy burden when he attempts to demonstrate that Congress intended to give favorable tax treatment to the kind of transaction that would never occur absent the motive of tax avoidance." The Court also stated that "while the taxpayer's subjective motivation may be pertinent to the existence of a tax avoidance purpose, all courts have looked to the objective reality of a transaction in assessing its economic substance." *Coltec Industries, Inc. v. United States*, 454 F.3d at 1355, 1356.

[309] See, e.g., *Coltec Industries v. United States,* 454 F.3d 1340 (Fed. Cir. 2006). The court analyzed the transfer to a subsidiary of a note purporting to provide high stock basis in exchange for a purported assumption of liabilities, and held these transactions unnecessary to accomplish any business purpose of using a subsidiary to

the grounds that the subject transactions lacked profit potential.[310] In addition, some courts have applied the economic substance doctrine to disallow tax benefits in transactions in which a taxpayer was exposed to risk and the transaction had a profit potential, but the court concluded that the economic risks and profit potential were insignificant when compared to the tax benefits.[311] Under this analysis, the taxpayer's profit potential must be more than nominal. Conversely, other courts view the application of the economic substance doctrine as requiring an objective determination of whether a "reasonable possibility of profit" from the transaction existed apart from the tax benefits.[312] In these cases, in assessing whether a reasonable possibility of profit exists, it may be sufficient if there is a nominal amount of pre-tax profit as measured against expected tax benefits.

Financial accounting benefits

In determining whether a taxpayer had a valid business purpose for entering into a transaction, at least two courts have concluded that financial accounting benefits arising from tax savings do not qualify as a non-tax business purpose.[313] However, based on court decisions that recognize the importance of financial accounting treatment, taxpayers have asserted that financial accounting benefits arising from tax savings can satisfy the business purpose test.[314]

---

manage asbestos liabilities. The court also held that the purported business purpose of adding a barrier to veil-piercing claims by third parties was not accomplished by the transaction. 454 F.3d at 1358-1360 (Fed. Cir. 2006).

[310] See, e.g., *Knetsch*, 364 U.S. at 361; *Goldstein v. Commissioner*, 364 F.2d 734 (2d Cir. 1966) (holding that an unprofitable, leveraged acquisition of Treasury bills, and accompanying prepaid interest deduction, lacked economic substance).

[311] See, e.g., *Goldstein v. Commissioner*, 364 F.2d at 739-40 (disallowing deduction even though taxpayer had a possibility of small gain or loss by owning Treasury bills); *Sheldon v. Commissioner*, 94 T.C. 738, 768 (1990) (stating that "potential for gain . . . is infinitesimally nominal and vastly insignificant when considered in comparison with the claimed deductions").

[312] See, e.g., *Rice's Toyota World v. Commissioner,* 752 F. 2d 89, 94 (4th Cir. 1985) (the economic substance inquiry requires an objective determination of whether a reasonable possibility of profit from the transaction existed apart from tax benefits); *Compaq Computer Corp. v. Commissioner*, 277 F.3d 778, 781 (5th Cir. 2001) (applied the same test, citing *Rice's Toyota World*); *IES Industries v. United States*, 253 F.3d 350, 354 (8th Cir. 2001); *Wells Fargo & Company v. United States*, No. 06-628T, 2010 WL 94544, at *57-58 (Fed. Cl. Jan. 8, 2010).

[313] See *American Electric Power, Inc. v. United States*, 136 F. Supp. 2d 762, 791-92 (S.D. Ohio 2001), *aff'd*, 326 F.3d.737 (6th Cir. 2003) and *Wells Fargo & Company v. United States*, No. 06-628T, 2010 WL 94544, at *59 (Fed. Cl. Jan. 8, 2010).

[314] See, e.g., Joint Committee on Taxation, *Report of Investigation of Enron Corporation and Related Entities Regarding Federal Tax and Compensation Issues, and Policy Recommendations* (JSC-3-03) February, 2003 ("Enron Report"), Volume III at C-93, 289. Enron Corporation relied on Frank Lyon Co. v. United States, 435 U.S. 561, 577-78 (1978), and Newman v. Commissioner, 902 F.2d 159, 163 (2d Cir. 1990), to argue that financial accounting benefits arising from tax savings constitute a good business purpose.

Tax-indifferent parties

A number of cases have involved transactions structured to allocate income for Federal tax purposes to a tax-indifferent party, with a corresponding deduction, or favorable basis result, to a taxable person. The income allocated to the tax-indifferent party for tax purposes was structured to exceed any actual economic income to be received by the tax indifferent party from the transaction. Courts have sometimes concluded that this particular type of transaction did not satisfy the economic substance doctrine.[315] In other cases, courts have indicated that the substance of a transaction did not support the form of income allocations asserted by the taxpayer and have questioned whether asserted business purpose or other standards were met.[316]

Penalty regime

General accuracy-related penalty

An accuracy-related penalty under section 6662 applies to the portion of any underpayment that is attributable to (1) negligence, (2) any substantial understatement of income tax, (3) any substantial valuation misstatement, (4) any substantial overstatement of pension liabilities, or (5) any substantial estate or gift tax valuation understatement. If the correct income tax liability exceeds that reported by the taxpayer by the greater of 10 percent of the correct tax or $5,000 (or, in the case of corporations, by the lesser of (a) 10 percent of the correct tax (or $10,000 if greater) or (b) $10 million), then a substantial understatement exists and a penalty may be imposed equal to 20 percent of the underpayment of tax attributable to the understatement.[317] The section 6662 penalty is increased to 40 percent in the case of gross valuation misstatements as defined in section 6662(h). Except in the case of tax shelters,[318] the amount of any understatement is reduced by any portion attributable to an item if (1) the treatment of the item is supported by substantial authority, or (2) facts relevant to the tax treatment of the item were adequately disclosed and there was a reasonable basis for its tax treatment. The Treasury Secretary may prescribe a list of positions which the Secretary believes do not meet the requirements for substantial authority under this provision.

The section 6662 penalty generally is abated (even with respect to tax shelters) in cases in which the taxpayer can demonstrate that there was "reasonable cause" for the underpayment and

---

[315] See, e.g., *ACM Partnership v. Commissioner,* 157 F.3d 231 (3d Cir. 1998), *aff'g* 73 T.C.M. (CCH) 2189 (1997), *cert. denied* 526 U.S. 1017 (1999).

[316] See, e.g., *TIFD III-E, Inc. v. United States,* 459 F.3d 220 (2d Cir. 2006). Although the Second Circuit found for the government in *TIFD III-E, Inc.*, on remand to consider issues under section 704(e), the District Court found for the taxpayer. See, *TIFD III-E Inc. v. United States*, No. 3:01-cv-01839, 2009 WL 3208650 (Oct. 23, 2009).

[317] Sec. 6662.

[318] A tax shelter is defined for this purpose as a partnership or other entity, an investment plan or arrangement, or any other plan or arrangement if a significant purpose of such partnership, other entity, plan, or arrangement is the avoidance or evasion of Federal income tax. Sec. 6662(d)(2)(C).

that the taxpayer acted in good faith.[319] The relevant regulations for a tax shelter provide that reasonable cause exists where the taxpayer "reasonably relies in good faith on an opinion based on a professional tax advisor's analysis of the pertinent facts and authorities [that] . . . unambiguously concludes that there is a greater than 50-percent likelihood that the tax treatment of the item will be upheld if challenged" by the IRS.[320] For transactions other than tax shelters, the relevant regulations provide a facts and circumstances test, the most important factor generally being the extent of the taxpayer's effort to assess the proper tax liability. If a taxpayer relies on an opinion, reliance is not reasonable if the taxpayer knows or should have known that the advisor lacked knowledge in the relevant aspects of Federal tax law, or if the taxpayer fails to disclose a fact that it knows or should have known is relevant. Certain additional requirements apply with respect to the advice.[321]

<u>Listed transactions and reportable avoidance transactions</u>

<u>In general</u>

A separate accuracy-related penalty under section 6662A applies to any "listed transaction" and to any other "reportable transaction" that is not a listed transaction, if a significant purpose of such transaction is the avoidance or evasion of Federal income tax[322] (hereinafter referred to as a "reportable avoidance transaction"). The penalty rate and defenses available to avoid the penalty vary depending on whether the transaction was adequately disclosed.

Both listed transactions and other reportable transactions are allowed to be described by the Treasury department under section 6011 as transactions that must be reported, and section 6707A(c) imposes a penalty for failure adequately to report such transactions under section 6011. A reportable transaction is defined as one that the Treasury Secretary determines is required to be disclosed because it is determined to have a potential for tax avoidance or evasion.[323] A listed transaction is defined as a reportable transaction which is the same as, or substantially similar to,

---

[319] Sec. 6664(c).

[320] Treas. Reg. sec. 1.6662-4(g)(4)(i)(B); Treas. Reg. sec. 1.6664-4(c).

[321] See Treas. Reg. Sec. 1.6664-4(c). In addition to the requirements applicable to taxpayers under the regulations, advisors may be subject to potential penalties under section 6694 (applicable to return preparers), and to monetary penalties and other sanctions under Circular 230 (which provides rules governing persons practicing before the IRS). Under Circular 230, if a transaction is a "covered transaction" (a term that includes listed transactions and certain non-listed reportable transactions) a "more likely than not" confidence level is required for written tax advice that may be relied upon by a taxpayer for the purpose of avoiding penalties, and certain other standards must also be met. Treasury Dept. Circular 230 (Rev. 4-2008) Sec. 10.35. For other tax advice, Circular 230 generally requires a lower "realistic possibility" confidence level or a "non-frivolous" confidence level coupled with advising the client of any opportunity to avoid the accuracy related penalty under section 6662 by adequate disclosure. Treasury Dept. Circular 230 (Rev. 4-2008) Sec. 10.34.

[322] Sec. 6662A(b)(2).

[323] Sec. 6707A(c)(1).

a transaction specifically identified by the Secretary as a tax avoidance transaction for purposes of the reporting disclosure requirements.[324]

Disclosed transactions

In general, a 20-percent accuracy-related penalty is imposed on any understatement attributable to an adequately disclosed listed transaction or reportable avoidance transaction.[325] The only exception to the penalty is if the taxpayer satisfies a more stringent reasonable cause and good faith exception (hereinafter referred to as the "strengthened reasonable cause exception"), which is described below. The strengthened reasonable cause exception is available only if the relevant facts affecting the tax treatment were adequately disclosed, there is or was substantial authority for the claimed tax treatment, and the taxpayer reasonably believed that the claimed tax treatment was more likely than not the proper treatment. A "reasonable belief" must be based on the facts and law as they exist at the time that the return in question is filed, and not take into account the possibility that a return would not be audited. Moreover, reliance on professional advice may support a "reasonable belief" only in certain circumstances.[326]

Undisclosed transactions

If the taxpayer does not adequately disclose the transaction, the strengthened reasonable cause exception is not available (i.e., a strict liability penalty generally applies), and the taxpayer is subject to an increased penalty equal to 30 percent of the understatement.[327] However, a taxpayer will be treated as having adequately disclosed a transaction for this purpose if the IRS Commissioner has separately rescinded the separate penalty under section 6707A for failure to disclose a reportable transaction.[328] The IRS Commissioner is authorized to do this only if the failure does not relate to a listed transaction and only if rescinding the penalty would promote compliance and effective tax administration.[329]

A public entity that is required to pay a penalty for an undisclosed listed or reportable transaction must disclose the imposition of the penalty in reports to the SEC for such periods as the Secretary specifies. The disclosure to the SEC applies without regard to whether the taxpayer determines the amount of the penalty to be material to the reports in which the penalty must appear, and any failure to disclose such penalty in the reports is treated as a failure to disclose a listed transaction. A taxpayer must disclose a penalty in reports to the SEC once the

---

[324] Sec. 6707A(c)(2).

[325] Sec. 6662A(a).

[326] Section 6664(d)(3)(B) does not allow a reasonable belief to be based on a "disqualified opinion" or on an opinion from a "disqualified tax advisor."

[327] Sec. 6662A(c).

[328] Sec. 6664(d).

[329] Sec. 6707A(d).

taxpayer has exhausted its administrative and judicial remedies with respect to the penalty (or if earlier, when paid).[330]

Determination of the understatement amount

The penalty is applied to the amount of any understatement attributable to the listed or reportable avoidance transaction without regard to other items on the tax return. For purposes of this provision, the amount of the understatement is determined as the sum of: (1) the product of the highest corporate or individual tax rate (as appropriate) and the increase in taxable income resulting from the difference between the taxpayer's treatment of the item and the proper treatment of the item (without regard to other items on the tax return);[331] and (2) the amount of any decrease in the aggregate amount of credits which results from a difference between the taxpayer's treatment of an item and the proper tax treatment of such item.

Except as provided in regulations, a taxpayer's treatment of an item will not take into account any amendment or supplement to a return if the amendment or supplement is filed after the earlier of when the taxpayer is first contacted regarding an examination of the return or such other date as specified by the Secretary.[332]

Strengthened reasonable cause exception

A penalty is not imposed under section 6662A with respect to any portion of an understatement if it is shown that there was reasonable cause for such portion and the taxpayer acted in good faith. Such a showing requires: (1) adequate disclosure of the facts affecting the transaction in accordance with the regulations under section 6011;[333] (2) that there is or was substantial authority for such treatment; and (3) that the taxpayer reasonably believed that such treatment was more likely than not the proper treatment. For this purpose, a taxpayer will be treated as having a reasonable belief with respect to the tax treatment of an item only if such belief: (1) is based on the facts and law that exist at the time the tax return (that includes the item) is filed; and (2) relates solely to the taxpayer's chances of success on the merits and does not take into account the possibility that (a) a return will not be audited, (b) the treatment will not be raised on audit, or (c) the treatment will be resolved through settlement if raised.[334]

A taxpayer may (but is not required to) rely on an opinion of a tax advisor in establishing its reasonable belief with respect to the tax treatment of the item. However, a taxpayer may not

---

[330] Sec. 6707A(e).

[331] For this purpose, any reduction in the excess of deductions allowed for the taxable year over gross income for such year, and any reduction in the amount of capital losses which would (without regard to section 1211) be allowed for such year, will be treated as an increase in taxable income. Sec. 6662A(b).

[332] Sec. 6662A(e)(3).

[333] See the previous discussion regarding the penalty for failing to disclose a reportable transaction.

[334] Sec. 6664(d).

rely on an opinion of a tax advisor for this purpose if the opinion (1) is provided by a "disqualified tax advisor" or (2) is a "disqualified opinion."

Disqualified tax advisor

A disqualified tax advisor is any advisor who: (1) is a material advisor[335] and who participates in the organization, management, promotion, or sale of the transaction or is related (within the meaning of section 267(b) or 707(b)(1)) to any person who so participates; (2) is compensated directly or indirectly[336] by a material advisor with respect to the transaction; (3) has a fee arrangement with respect to the transaction that is contingent on all or part of the intended tax benefits from the transaction being sustained; or (4) as determined under regulations prescribed by the Secretary, has a disqualifying financial interest with respect to the transaction.

A material advisor is considered as participating in the "organization" of a transaction if the advisor performs acts relating to the development of the transaction. This may include, for example, preparing documents: (1) establishing a structure used in connection with the transaction (such as a partnership agreement); (2) describing the transaction (such as an offering memorandum or other statement describing the transaction); or (3) relating to the registration of the transaction with any Federal, state, or local government body.[337] Participation in the "management" of a transaction means involvement in the decision-making process regarding any business activity with respect to the transaction. Participation in the "promotion or sale" of a transaction means involvement in the marketing or solicitation of the transaction to others. Thus, an advisor who provides information about the transaction to a potential participant is involved in the promotion or sale of a transaction, as is any advisor who recommends the transaction to a potential participant.

Disqualified opinion

An opinion may not be relied upon if the opinion: (1) is based on unreasonable factual or legal assumptions (including assumptions as to future events); (2) unreasonably relies upon representations, statements, finding or agreements of the taxpayer or any other person; (3) does

---

[335] The term "material advisor" means any person who provides any material aid, assistance, or advice with respect to organizing, managing, promoting, selling, implementing, or carrying out any reportable transaction, and who derives gross income in excess of $50,000 in the case of a reportable transaction substantially all of the tax benefits from which are provided to natural persons ($250,000 in any other case). Sec. 6111(b)(1).

[336] This situation could arise, for example, when an advisor has an arrangement or understanding (oral or written) with an organizer, manager, or promoter of a reportable transaction that such party will recommend or refer potential participants to the advisor for an opinion regarding the tax treatment of the transaction.

[337] An advisor should not be treated as participating in the organization of a transaction if the advisor's only involvement with respect to the organization of the transaction is the rendering of an opinion regarding the tax consequences of such transaction. However, such an advisor may be a "disqualified tax advisor" with respect to the transaction if the advisor participates in the management, promotion, or sale of the transaction (or if the advisor is compensated by a material advisor, has a fee arrangement that is contingent on the tax benefits of the transaction, or as determined by the Secretary, has a continuing financial interest with respect to the transaction). See Notice 2005-12, 2005-1 C.B. 494 regarding disqualified compensation arrangements.

not identify and consider all relevant facts; or (4) fails to meet any other requirement prescribed by the Secretary.

Coordination with other penalties

Any understatement upon which a penalty is imposed under section 6662A is not subject to the accuracy related penalty for underpayments under section 6662.[338] However, that understatement is included for purposes of determining whether any understatement (as defined in sec. 6662(d)(2)) is a substantial understatement under section 6662(d)(1).[339] Thus, in the case of an understatement (as defined in sec. 6662(d)(2)), the amount of the understatement (determined without regard to section 6662A(e)(1)(A)) is increased by the aggregate amount of reportable transaction understatements for purposes of determining whether the understatement is a substantial understatement. The section 6662(a) penalty applies only to the excess of the amount of the substantial understatement (if any) after section 6662A(e)(1)(A) is applied over the aggregate amount of reportable transaction understatements.[340] Accordingly, every understatement is penalized, but only under one penalty provision.

The penalty imposed under section 6662A does not apply to any portion of an understatement to which a fraud penalty applies under section 6663 or to which the 40-percent penalty for gross valuation misstatements under section 6662(h) applies.[341]

Erroneous claim for refund or credit

If a claim for refund or credit with respect to income tax (other than a claim relating to the earned income tax credit) is made for an excessive amount, unless it is shown that the claim for such excessive amount has a reasonable basis, the person making such claim is subject to a penalty in an amount equal to 20 percent of the excessive amount.[342]

The term "excessive amount" means the amount by which the amount of the claim for refund for any taxable year exceeds the amount of such claim allowable for the taxable year.

This penalty does not apply to any portion of the excessive amount of a claim for refund or credit which is subject to a penalty imposed under the accuracy related or fraud penalty provisions (including the general accuracy related penalty, or the penalty with respect to listed and reportable transactions, described above).

---

[338] Sec. 6662(b) (flush language). In addition, section 6662(b) provides that section 6662 does not apply to any portion of an underpayment on which a fraud penalty is imposed under section 6663.

[339] Sec. 6662A(e)(1).

[340] Sec. 6662(d)(2)(A) (flush language)

[341] Sec. 6662A(e)(2).

[342] Sec. 6676.

Explanation of Provision

The provision clarifies and enhances the application of the economic substance doctrine. Under the provision, new section 7701(o) provides that in the case of any transaction[343] to which the economic substance doctrine is relevant, such transaction is treated as having economic substance only if (1) the transaction changes in a meaningful way (apart from Federal income tax effects) the taxpayer's economic position, and (2) the taxpayer has a substantial purpose (apart from Federal income tax effects) for entering into such transaction. The provision provides a uniform definition of economic substance, but does not alter the flexibility of the courts in other respects.

The determination of whether the economic substance doctrine is relevant to a transaction is made in the same manner as if the provision had never been enacted. Thus, the provision does not change present law standards in determining when to utilize an economic substance analysis.[344]

The provision is not intended to alter the tax treatment of certain basic business transactions that, under longstanding judicial and administrative practice are respected, merely because the choice between meaningful economic alternatives is largely or entirely based on comparative tax advantages. Among[345] these basic transactions are (1) the choice between capitalizing a business enterprise with debt or equity;[346] (2) a U.S. person's choice between utilizing a foreign corporation or a domestic corporation to make a foreign investment;[347] (3) the choice to enter a transaction or series of transactions that constitute a corporate organization or reorganization under subchapter C;[348] and (4) the choice to utilize a related-party entity in a

---

[343] The term "transaction" includes a series of transactions.

[344] If the realization of the tax benefits of a transaction is consistent with the Congressional purpose or plan that the tax benefits were designed by Congress to effectuate, it is not intended that such tax benefits be disallowed. See, e.g., Treas. Reg. sec. 1.269-2, stating that characteristic of circumstances in which an amount otherwise constituting a deduction, credit, or other allowance is not available are those in which the effect of the deduction, credit, or other allowance would be to distort the liability of the particular taxpayer when the essential nature of the transaction or situation is examined in the light of the basic purpose or plan which the deduction, credit, or other allowance was designed by the Congress to effectuate. Thus, for example, it is not intended that a tax credit (e.g., section 42 (low-income housing credit), section 45 (production tax credit), section 45D (new markets tax credit), section 47 (rehabilitation credit), section 48 (energy credit), etc.) be disallowed in a transaction pursuant to which, in form and substance, a taxpayer makes the type of investment or undertakes the type of activity that the credit was intended to encourage.

[345] The examples are illustrative and not exclusive.

[346] See, e.g., *John Kelley Co. v. Commissioner,* 326 U.S. 521 (1946) (respecting debt characterization in one case and not in the other, based on all the facts and circumstances).

[347] See, e.g., *Sam Siegel v. Commissioner,* 45. T.C. 566 (1966), *acq.* 1966-2 C.B. 3. But see *Commissioner v. Bollinger,* 485 U.S. 340 (1988) (agency principles applied to title-holding corporation under the facts and circumstances).

[348] See, e.g., *Rev. Proc. 2010-3 2010-1 I.R.B. 110, Secs. 3.01(38), (39),(40,) and (42)* (IRS will not rule on certain matters relating to incorporations or reorganizations unless there is a "significant issue"); *compare Gregory v. Helvering.* 293 U.S. 465 (1935).

transaction, provided that the arm's length standard of section 482 and other applicable concepts are satisfied.[349] Leasing transactions, like all other types of transactions, will continue to be analyzed in light of all the facts and circumstances.[350] As under present law, whether a particular transaction meets the requirements for specific treatment under any of these provisions is a question of facts and circumstances. Also, the fact that a transaction meets the requirements for specific treatment under any provision of the Code is not determinative of whether a transaction or series of transactions of which it is a part has economic substance.[351]

The provision does not alter the court's ability to aggregate, disaggregate, or otherwise recharacterize a transaction when applying the doctrine. For example, the provision reiterates the present-law ability of the courts to bifurcate a transaction in which independent activities with non-tax objectives are combined with an unrelated item having only tax-avoidance objectives in order to disallow those tax-motivated benefits.[352]

Conjunctive analysis

The provision clarifies that the economic substance doctrine involves a conjunctive analysis – there must be an inquiry regarding the objective effects of the transaction on the taxpayer's economic position as well as an inquiry regarding the taxpayer's subjective motives for engaging in the transaction. Under the provision, a transaction must satisfy both tests, i.e.,

---

[349] See, e.g., *National Carbide v. Commissioner,* 336 U.S. 422 (1949), *Moline Properties v. Commissioner,* 319 U.S. 435 (1943); *compare, e.g. Aiken Industries, Inc. v. Commissioner*, 56 T.C. 925 (1971), *acq*., 1972-2 C.B. 1; *Commissioner v. Bollinger,* 485 U.S. 340 (1988); see also sec. 7701(l).

[350] See, e.g., *Frank Lyon Co. v. Commissioner*, 435 U.S. 561 (1978); *Hilton v. Commissioner*, 74 T.C. 305, *aff'd*, 671 F. 2d 316 (9th Cir. 1982), *cert. denied*, 459 U.S. 907 (1982); *Coltec Industries v. United States,* 454 F.3d 1340 (Fed. Cir. 2006), *cert. denied,* 127 S. Ct. 1261 (Mem) (2007); *BB&T Corporation v. United States*, 2007-1 USTC P 50,130 (M.D.N.C. 2007), *aff'd,* 523 F.3d 461 (4th Cir. 2008); *Wells Fargo & Company v. United States*, No. 06-628T, 2010 WL 94544, at *60 (Fed. Cl. Jan. 8, 2010) (distinguishing leasing case *Consolidated Edison Company of New York*, No. 06-305T, 2009 WL 3418533 (Fed. Cl. Oct. 21, 2009) by observing that "considerations of economic substance are factually specific to the transaction involved").

[351] As examples of cases in which courts have found that a transaction does not meet the requirements for the treatment claimed by the taxpayer under the Code, or does not have economic substance, see e.g., *BB&T Corporation v. United States*, 2007-1 USTC P 50,130 (M.D.N.C. 2007) *aff'd*, 523 F.3d 461 (4th Cir. 2008); *Tribune Company and Subsidiaries v. Commissioner*, 125 T.C. 110 (2005); *H.J. Heinz Company and Subsidiaries v. United States,* 76 Fed. Cl. 570 (2007); *Coltec Industries, Inc. v. United States*, 454 F.3d 1340 (Fed. Cir. 2006), *cert. denied* 127 S. Ct. 1261 (Mem.) (2007); *Long Term Capital Holdings LP v. United States,* 330 F. Supp. 2d 122 (D. Conn. 2004), *aff'd,* 150 Fed. Appx. 40 (2d Cir. 2005); *Klamath Strategic Investment Fund, LLC v. United States,* 472 F. Supp. 2d 885 (E.D. Texas 2007); *aff'd*, 568 F. 3d 537 (5th Cir. 2009); *Santa Monica Pictures LLC v. Commissioner,* 89 T.C.M. 1157 (2005).

[352] See, e.g., *Coltec Industries, Inc. v. United States*, 454 F.3d 1340 (Fed. Cir. 2006), *cert. denied* 127 S. Ct. 1261 (Mem.) (2007) ("the first asserted business purpose focuses on the wrong transaction--the creation of Garrison as a separate subsidiary to manage asbestos liabilities. . . . [W]e must focus on the transaction that gave the taxpayer a high basis in the stock and thus gave rise to the alleged benefit upon sale…") 454 F.3d 1340, 1358 (Fed. Cir. 2006). See also *ACM Partnership v. Commissioner*, 157 F.3d at 256 n.48; *Minnesota Tea Co. v. Helvering*, 302 U.S. 609, 613 (1938) ("A given result at the end of a straight path is not made a different result because reached by following a devious path.").

the transaction must change in a meaningful way (apart from Federal income tax effects) the taxpayer's economic position and the taxpayer must have a substantial non-Federal-income-tax purpose for entering into such transaction, in order for a transaction to be treated as having economic substance. This clarification eliminates the disparity that exists among the Federal circuit courts regarding the application of the doctrine, and modifies its application in those circuits in which either a change in economic position or a non-tax business purpose (without having both) is sufficient to satisfy the economic substance doctrine.[353]

Non-Federal-income-tax business purpose

Under the provision, a taxpayer's non-Federal-income-tax purpose[354] for entering into a transaction (the second prong in the analysis) must be "substantial." For purposes of this analysis, any State or local income tax effect which is related to a Federal income tax effect is treated in the same manner as a Federal income tax effect. Also, a purpose of achieving a favorable accounting treatment for financial reporting purposes is not taken into account as a non-Federal-income-tax purpose if the origin of the financial accounting benefit is a reduction of Federal income tax.[355]

Profit potential

Under the provision, a taxpayer may rely on factors other than profit potential to demonstrate that a transaction results in a meaningful change in the taxpayer's economic position or that the taxpayer has a substantial non-Federal-income-tax purpose for entering into such

---

[353] The provision defines "economic substance doctrine" as the common law doctrine under which tax benefits under subtitle A with respect to a transaction are not allowable if the transaction does not have economic substance or lacks a business purpose. Thus, the definition includes any doctrine that denies tax benefits for lack of economic substance, for lack of business purpose, or for lack of both.

[354] See, e.g., Treas. Reg. sec. 1.269-2(b) (stating that a distortion of tax liability indicating the principal purpose of tax evasion or avoidance might be evidenced by the fact that "the transaction was not undertaken for reasons germane to the conduct of the business of the taxpayer"). Similarly, in *ACM Partnership v. Commissioner*, 73 T.C.M. (CCH) 2189 (1997), the court stated:

> Key to [the determination of whether a transaction has economic substance] is that the transaction must be rationally related to a useful nontax purpose that is plausible in light of the taxpayer's conduct and useful in light of the taxpayer's economic situation and intentions. Both the utility of the stated purpose and the rationality of the means chosen to effectuate it must be evaluated in accordance with commercial practices in the relevant industry. A rational relationship between purpose and means ordinarily will not be found unless there was a reasonable expectation that the nontax benefits would be at least commensurate with the transaction costs. [citations omitted]

[355] Claiming that a financial accounting benefit constitutes a substantial non-tax purpose fails to consider the origin of the accounting benefit (i.e., reduction of taxes) and significantly diminishes the purpose for having a substantial non-tax purpose requirement. *See, e.g., American Electric Power, Inc. v. United States*, 136 F. Supp. 2d 762, 791-92 (S.D. Ohio 2001) ("AEP's intended use of the cash flows generated by the [corporate-owned life insurance] plan is irrelevant to the subjective prong of the economic substance analysis. If a legitimate business purpose for the use of the tax savings 'were sufficient to breathe substance into a transaction whose only purpose was to reduce taxes, [then] every sham tax-shelter device might succeed,'") (citing *Winn-Dixie v. Commissioner*, 113 T.C. 254, 287 (1999)); *aff'd,* 326 F3d 737 (6th Cir. 2003).

transaction. The provision does not require or establish a minimum return that will satisfy the profit potential test. However, if a taxpayer relies on a profit potential, the present value of the reasonably expected pre-tax profit must be substantial in relation to the present value of the expected net tax benefits that would be allowed if the transaction were respected.[356] Fees and other transaction expenses are taken into account as expenses in determining pre-tax profit. In addition, the Secretary is to issue regulations requiring foreign taxes to be treated as expenses in determining pre-tax profit in appropriate cases.[357]

Personal transactions of individuals

In the case of an individual, the provision applies only to transactions entered into in connection with a trade or business or an activity engaged in for the production of income.

Other rules

No inference is intended as to the proper application of the economic substance doctrine under present law. The provision is not intended to alter or supplant any other rule of law, including any common-law doctrine or provision of the Code or regulations or other guidance thereunder; and it is intended the provision be construed as being additive to any such other rule of law.

As with other provisions in the Code, the Secretary has general authority to prescribe rules and regulations necessary for the enforcement of the provision.[358]

Penalty for underpayments and understatements attributable to transactions lacking economic substance

The provision imposes a new strict liability penalty under section 6662 for an underpayment attributable to any disallowance of claimed tax benefits by reason of a transaction lacking economic substance, as defined in new section 7701(o), or failing to meet the requirements of any similar rule of law.[359] The penalty rate is 20 percent (increased to 40 percent if the taxpayer does not adequately disclose the relevant facts affecting the tax treatment in the return or a statement attached to the return). An amended return or supplement to a return

---

[356] See, e.g., *Rice's Toyota World* v. *Commissioner,* 752 F.2d at 94 (the economic substance inquiry requires an objective determination of whether a reasonable possibility of profit from the transaction existed apart from tax benefits); *Compaq Computer Corp.* v. *Commissioner,* 277 F.3d at 781 (applied the same test, *citing Rice's Toyota World*); *IES Industries* v. *United States,* 253 F.3d at 354 (the application of the objective economic substance test involves determining whether there was a "reasonable possibility of profit . . . apart from tax benefits.").

[357] There is no intention to restrict the ability of the courts to consider the appropriate treatment of foreign taxes in particular cases, as under present law.

[358] Sec. 7805(a).

[359] It is intended that the penalty would apply to a transaction the tax benefits of which are disallowed as a result of the application of the similar factors and analysis that is required under the provision for an economic substance analysis, even if a different term is used to describe the doctrine.

is not taken into account if filed after the taxpayer has been contacted for audit or such other date as is specified by the Secretary. No exceptions (including the reasonable cause rules) to the penalty are available. Thus, under the provision, outside opinions or in-house analysis would not protect a taxpayer from imposition of a penalty if it is determined that the transaction lacks economic substance or fails to meet the requirements of any similar rule of law. Similarly, a claim for refund or credit that is excessive under section 6676 due to a claim that is lacking in economic substance or failing to meet the requirements of any similar rule of law is subject to the 20 percent penalty under that section, and the reasonable basis exception is not available.

The penalty does not apply to any portion of an underpayment on which a fraud penalty is imposed.[360] The new 40-percent penalty for nondisclosed transactions is added to the penalties to which section 6662A will not also apply.[361]

As described above, under the provision, the reasonable cause and good faith exception of present law section 6664(c)(1) does not apply to any portion of an underpayment which is attributable to a transaction lacking economic substance, as defined in section 7701(o), or failing to meet the requirements of any similar rule of law. Likewise, the reasonable cause and good faith exception of present law section 6664(d)(1) does not apply to any portion of a reportable transaction understatement which is attributable to a transaction lacking economic substance, as defined in section 7701(o), or failing to meet the requirements of any similar rule of law.

Effective Date

The provision applies to transactions entered into after the date of enactment and to underpayments, understatements, and refunds and credits attributable to transactions entered into after the date of enactment.

---

[360] As under present law, the penalties under section 6662 (including the new penalty) do not apply to any portion of an underpayment on which a fraud penalty is imposed.

[361] As revised by the provision, new section 6662A(e)(2)(b) provides that section 6662A will not apply to any portion of an understatement due to gross valuation misstatement under section 6662(h) or nondisclosed noneconomic substance transactions under new section 6662(i).

F. Time for Payment of Corporate Estimated Taxes (sec. 1410 of the Reconciliation bill and sec. 6655 of the Code)

Present Law

In general, corporations are required to make quarterly estimated tax payments of their income tax liability.[362] For a corporation whose taxable year is a calendar year, these estimated tax payments must be made by April 15, June 15, September 15, and December 15. In the case of a corporation with assets of at least $1 billion (determined as of the end of the preceding taxable year), payments due in July, August, or September, 2014, are increased to 157.75 percent of the payment otherwise due and the next required payment is reduced accordingly.[363]

Explanation of Provision

The provision increases the required payment of estimated tax otherwise due in July, August, or September, 2014, by 15.75 percentage points.

Effective Date

The provision is effective on the date of enactment of the bill.

---

[362] Sec. 6655.

[363] The Hiring Incentives to Restore Employment ("HIRE") Act, Sec.561; Pub. L. No. 111-124, Sec. 4; Pub. L. No. 111-92, Sec. 18; Pub. L. No. 111-42, Sec. 202(b)(1).